QuickBooks 2015

the missing manual®

The book that should have been in the box®

Bonnie Biafore

Beijing | Cambridge | Farnham | Köln | Sebastopol | Tokyo

QuickBooks 2015: The Missing Manual

by Bonnie Biafore

Published by O'Reilly Media, Inc.,
1005 Gravenstein Highway North, Sebastopol, CA 95472.

O'Reilly books may be purchased for educational, business, or sales promotional use. Online editions are also available for most titles (*https://www.safaribooksonline.com*). For more information, contact our corporate/institutional sales department: (800) 998-9938 or *corporate@oreilly.com*.

October 2014: First Edition.

Revision History for the First Edition:

2014-10-10 First release

See *http://www.oreilly.com/catalog/errata.csp?isbn=0636920032700* for release details.

ISBN-13: 978-1-4919-4713-5

[LSI]

Contents

Part Five: Appendixes

NOTE Appendixes C–G are available from this book's Missing CD page at *www.missingmanuals.com/cds*. (To learn about the Missing CD page, turn to page xxvii.)

The Missing Credits

ABOUT THE AUTHOR

Bonnie Biafore has always been fascinated with math in its practical and more esoteric forms. As an engineer and project manager, she's thorough and steadfastly attentive to detail but redeems herself by using her sick sense of humor to transform these sleep-inducing subjects into entertaining reading. She writes about accounting and project management. Her books *NAIC Stock Selection Handbook* and *Successful Project Management* won major awards from the Society of Technical Communication and APEX Awards for Publication Excellence (but the raves she receives from readers mean much more to her).

Bonnie is also the author of O'Reilly's *Microsoft Project 2013: The Missing Manual, Personal Finance: The Missing Manual,* and *Online Investing Hacks.* She has recorded numerous courses on QuickBooks, project management, Microsoft Project, and other software for Lynda.com. As a consultant, she manages projects for clients, provides training, and wins accolades for her ability to herd cats.

When not chained to her computer, she hikes and cycles in the mountains near her home in Colorado, walks her dogs, takes aerial dance classes, and cooks gourmet meals. She has also published a novel, *Fresh Squeezed,* featuring hit men, stupid criminals, and much political incorrectness. You can learn more at Bonnie's website, *www.bonniebiafore.com,* or email her at *bonnie.biafore@gmail.com.*

ABOUT THE CREATIVE TEAM

Dawn Schanafelt (editor) is assistant editor for the Missing Manual series. When not working, she plays soccer, beads, and causes trouble (though not simultaneously). Email: *dawn@oreilly.com.*

Kara Ebrahim (production editor) lives, works, and plays in Cambridge, MA. She loves graphic design and all things outdoors. Email: *kebrahim@oreilly.com.*

Michael Cobb (tech reviewer) is an information designer with Real World Training and enjoys jamming the blues on guitar, drinking way too much coffee, and sharing life with his gorgeous wife and rambunctious son. Email: *michael_cobb@realworldtraining.com.*

Julie Van Keuren (proofreader) quit her newspaper job in 2006 to move to Montana and live the freelancing dream. She and her husband, M.H. (who is living the novel-writing dream), have two sons, Dexter and Michael. Email: *little_media@yahoo.com.*

Ron Strauss (indexer) specializes in the indexing of information technology publications of all kinds. Ron is also an accomplished classical violist and lives in Northern California with his wife and fellow indexer, Annie, and his miniature pinscher, Kanga. Email: *rstrauss@mchsi.com*.

ACKNOWLEDGEMENTS

No O'Reilly book that I author can go to print without me acknowledging the awesome team at O'Reilly. Dawn Schanafelt is editor extraordinaire. She can spot potential points of confusion in my writing from a mile away and usually comes up with a wonderfully clear alternative. If she's stumped, she asks for clarification in a way that even a diva (oh, I so hope I haven't become one) wouldn't mind. She stays on top of details so they're taken care of before anyone even thinks to ask. She keeps me company via email as we both work weekend after weekend to complete this book.

My thanks also go to Kara Ebrahim and the rest of the O'Reilly folks for shepherding my book through the production process. There's nothing like curling up in a comfy chair with a glass of wine and a great book index. My thanks to Ron Strauss for making this book's index special. I am grateful for the eagle eye of proofreader Julie Van Keuren for wrangling punctuation, capitalization, and ungainly sentences into submission. Michael Cobb was my technical go-to guy. He made sure my explanations make sense, my instructions are accurate, and answered the questions I couldn't.

THE MISSING MANUAL SERIES

Missing Manuals are witty, superbly written guides to computer products that don't come with printed manuals (which is just about all of them). Each book features a handcrafted index and cross-references to specific pages (not just chapters). Recent and upcoming titles include:

Access 2013: The Missing Manual by Matthew MacDonald

Adobe Edge Animate: The Missing Manual by Chris Grover

Buying a Home: The Missing Manual by Nancy Conner

Creating a Website: The Missing Manual, Third Edition by Matthew MacDonald

CSS3: The Missing Manual, Third Edition by David Sawyer McFarland

Dreamweaver CS6: The Missing Manual by David Sawyer McFarland

Dreamweaver CC: The Missing Manual by David Sawyer McFarland and Chris Grover

Excel 2013: The Missing Manual by Matthew MacDonald

FileMaker Pro 13: The Missing Manual by Susan Prosser and Stuart Gripman

Flash CS6: The Missing Manual by Chris Grover

Galaxy Tab: The Missing Manual by Preston Gralla

Galaxy S5: The Missing Manual by Preston Gralla

Google+: The Missing Manual by Kevin Purdy

HTML5: The Missing Manual, Second Edition by Matthew MacDonald

iMovie: The Missing Manual by David Pogue and Aaron Miller

iPad: The Missing Manual, Sixth Edition by J.D. Biersdorfer

iPhone: The Missing Manual, Seventh Edition by David Pogue

iPhone App Development: The Missing Manual by Craig Hockenberry

iPhoto: The Missing Manual by David Pogue and Lesa Snider

iPod: The Missing Manual, Eleventh Edition by J.D. Biersdorfer and David Pogue

iWork: The Missing Manual by Jessica Thornsby and Josh Clark

JavaScript & jQuery: The Missing Manual, Second Edition by David Sawyer McFarland

Kindle Fire HD: The Missing Manual by Peter Meyers

Microsoft Project 2013: The Missing Manual by Bonnie Biafore

Motorola Xoom: The Missing Manual by Preston Gralla

NOOK HD: The Missing Manual by Preston Gralla

Office 2011 for Macintosh: The Missing Manual by Chris Grover

Office 2013: The Missing Manual by Nancy Conner and Matthew MacDonald

OS X Mavericks: The Missing Manual by David Pogue

Personal Investing: The Missing Manual by Bonnie Biafore

Photoshop CS6: The Missing Manual by Lesa Snider

Photoshop CC: The Missing Manual, Second Edition by Lesa Snider

Photoshop Elements 13: The Missing Manual by Barbara Brundage

PHP & MySQL: The Missing Manual, Second Edition by Brett McLaughlin

Switching to the Mac: The Missing Manual, Mavericks Edition by David Pogue

Windows 7: The Missing Manual by David Pogue

Windows 8: The Missing Manual by David Pogue

WordPress: The Missing Manual, Second Edition by Matthew MacDonald

Your Body: The Missing Manual by Matthew MacDonald

Your Brain: The Missing Manual by Matthew MacDonald

Your Money: The Missing Manual by J.D. Roth

For a full list of all Missing Manuals in print, go to *www.missingmanuals.com/library.html.*

Introduction

Thousands of small companies and nonprofit organizations turn to QuickBooks to keep their finances on track. And over the years, Intuit has introduced various editions of the program to satisfy the needs of different types of companies. Back when milk was simply milk, you either used QuickBooks or you didn't. But now, when you can choose milk from soybeans, nuts, rice, *and* cows—with five different levels of fat—it's no surprise that QuickBooks comes in a variety of editions (which, in some cases, are dramatically different from their siblings), as well as six industry-specific editions. From the smallest of sole proprietorships to burgeoning enterprises, one of these editions is likely to meet your organization's needs *and* budget.

QuickBooks isn't hard to learn. Many of the features that you're familiar with from other programs work the same way in QuickBooks—windows, dialog boxes, drop-down lists, and keyboard shortcuts, to name a few. And with each new version, Intuit has added enhancements and features to make your workflow smoother and faster. The challenge is knowing what to do according to accounting rules, and how to do it in QuickBooks. This book teaches you how to use QuickBooks *and* explains the accounting concepts behind what you're doing.

What's New in QuickBooks 2015

Despite the fluctuating size of the tax code, accounting and bookkeeping practices don't change much each year. The changes in QuickBooks 2015 are mostly small tweaks and subtle improvements, but some of them might be just what you've been waiting for:

- **Insights tab in the Home window.** In previous versions of QuickBooks, the Home window contained, well, the Home Page, which shows bookkeeping workflow and helps you access the QuickBooks features you use most often. In QuickBooks 2015, the Home window has *two* tabs at its top left. As you might expect, the Home Page tab displays the Home Page you're familiar with. When you click the new Insights tab (page 44), you see a dashboard that highlights your company's financial status and activity. Initially, the tab's top panel displays a colorful Profit & Loss graph: green bars represent your monthly income, blue bars indicate your monthly expenses, and a black line graphs your profit by month. But that's not all! You can click the arrows on either side of this panel to view other high-level graphs, such as a comparison between the current year and the previous year, top customers by sales, and trends in income and expenses.

  The bottom half of the Insights tab displays more details about your income and expenses. On the left, the Income section is like a mini Income Tracker (described next, and covered in detail on page 338); it lets you quickly scan totals for unpaid invoices, overdue invoices, and customer payments received in the past 30 days. And the Expenses list and pie chart on the right help you identify where you spend the most money.

- **Income Tracker upgrades.** Income Tracker (page 338) boasts a couple of helpful enhancements. In addition to colored boxes for estimates, open invoices (that is, invoiced income that isn't due yet), overdue invoices, and recent customer payments, Income Tracker now also displays a box for unbilled time and expenses. In QuickBooks 2015, you can specify the unbilled categories you want to see by clicking the Settings icon at the window's top right (it looks like a gear), and then clicking the checkboxes to turn unbilled categories on or off.

- **Updated Reminders window.** The Reminders window (page 483) has a new look. On the left side of the window, you now see to-dos and transactions that are due as of today, so you know what's on deck for your workday. The list on the window's right shows to-dos and transactions that are coming up soon. If a category is collapsed, click the flippy triangle next to its heading to show each reminder in that section. To collapse a category, click the flippy triangle to hide its individual reminders.

- **Pinned notes.** QuickBooks' various centers have a new twist: You can now select a note associated with a vendor, customer, or employee and "pin" it so it appears at the center's top right when you select that name in the center's name list (page 481). For example, say you create a note about an issue a customer has with an order. You can pin that note in the Customer Center so that, whenever you select that customer in the Customer Center, the note is easy to spot.

- **New report formatting.** QuickBooks' reports sport new formatting that makes them much easier to read (page 583). The rows for top-level categories are shaded gray, lower-level category rows are shaded beige, and rows with totals are shaded light gray.

- **Updated online payments.** If you install QuickBooks 2015 when it's first released (this version of the program is called R1 and usually comes out in September), you won't see online payment links and settings. Big changes for online payments were still in the works when this book was written. To learn about these new features, download Appendix E from this book's Missing CD page at *www.missingmanuals.com/cds.*

When QuickBooks May Not Be the Answer

When you run a business (or a nonprofit), you track company finances for two reasons: to keep your business running smoothly and to generate the reports required by the IRS, SEC, and anyone else you have to answer to. QuickBooks helps you perform basic financial tasks, track your financial situation, and manage your business to make it even better. But before you read any further, here are a few things you *shouldn't* try to do with QuickBooks:

- **Work with more than 14,500 unique inventory items or 14,500 contact names.** QuickBooks Pro and Premier company files can hold up to 14,500 inventory items and a combined total of up to 14,500 customer, vendor, employee, and other (Other Names List) names. (In the QuickBooks Enterprise Solutions edition of the program, the number of names is virtually unlimited.)
- **Track personal finances.** Even if you're a company of one, keeping your personal finances separate from your business finances is a good move, particularly when it comes to tax reporting. In addition to opening a separate checking account for your business, you should also track your personal finances somewhere else (like in Quicken). If you do decide to use QuickBooks, at least create a separate company file for your personal financial info.
- **Track the performance of stocks and bonds.** QuickBooks isn't meant to keep track of the capital gains and dividends you earn from investments such as stocks and bonds. Of course, companies invest in things like equipment and office buildings, and you should track investments such as these in QuickBooks. However, in QuickBooks, they show up as *assets* of your company (page 57).
- **Manage specialized details about customer relationships.** Lots of information goes into keeping customers happy. With QuickBooks, you can stay on top of customer activities with features like to-dos, notes, reminders, and memorized transactions. You can also keep track of leads before they turn into customers. But if you need to track details for thousands of members or customers, items sold on consignment, project progress, or tasks related to managing projects, a customer-management program or a program like Microsoft Excel or Access might be a better solution.

NOTE Some third-party customer-management programs integrate with QuickBooks (page 94).

Choosing the Right Edition

QuickBooks comes in a gamut of editions, offering options for organizations at both ends of the small-business spectrum. QuickBooks Pro handles the basic needs of most businesses, whereas Enterprise Solutions (the most robust and powerful edition of QuickBooks) boasts enhanced features and speed for the biggest of small businesses. On the other hand, the online editions of QuickBooks offer features that are available anytime you're online.

WARNING QuickBooks for Mac and QuickBooks Online both differ *significantly* from the Windows version of the program, so this book isn't meant to be a guide to the Mac version or QuickBooks Online. Likewise, features vary in the desktop editions for different countries; this book covers the U.S. version.

This book focuses on QuickBooks Pro because its balance of features and price makes it the most popular edition. Throughout this book, you'll find notes about features offered in the Premier edition, which is one step up from Pro. (Whether you're willing to pay for these additional features is up to you.) Here's an overview of what each edition can do:

- **QuickBooks Online Simple Start** is a low-cost online option for small businesses with very simple accounting needs and only one person running QuickBooks at a time. It's easy to set up and use, but it doesn't offer features like entering bills, managing inventory, tracking time, or sharing your company file with your accountant, and you can download transactions from only one bank (or credit card) account.
- **QuickBooks Online Essentials** allows up to three people to run QuickBooks at a time and lets you connect to as many bank or credit card accounts as you want. As its name suggests, it offers essential features like automated invoicing, entering bills, and controlling what users can access.
- **QuickBooks Online Plus** has most of the features of QuickBooks Pro, but you access the program via the Web instead of running it on your PC.

NOTE These online editions let you use QuickBooks anywhere, on any computer, tablet, or smartphone, so they're ideal for someone who's always on the go. They're subscription-based, so you pay a monthly fee to use them. Although a year's subscription adds up to more than what you'd typically pay to buy a license for QuickBooks Pro, with a subscription, your software is always up to date—you don't have to upgrade it or convert your company files to the new versions you install.

- **QuickBooks Pro** is the workhorse desktop edition. It lets up to three people work on a company file at a time and includes features for tasks such as invoicing; entering and paying bills; job costing; creating estimates; saving and distributing reports and forms as email attachments; creating budgets; projecting cash flow; tracking mileage; customizing forms; customizing prices with price levels; printing shipping labels; and integrating with Word, Excel, and hundreds of other programs. QuickBooks Pro's name lists—customers, vendors, employees, and so on—can include up to a combined total of 14,500 entries. Other lists, like the chart of accounts, can have up to 10,000 entries each.

NOTE QuickBooks Pro Plus is a subscription product that costs a little more than the one-time license fee you pay for QuickBooks Pro, but QuickBooks Pro Plus offers mobile access, unlimited phone support, online backups, and always-up-to-date software. Similarly, QuickBooks Premier Plus is the premier version of the subscription product.

- **QuickBooks Premier** is another multi-user edition (up to five simultaneous users). It can handle inventory items assembled from other items and components, generate purchase orders from sales orders and estimates, apply price levels to individual items, export report templates, produce budgets and forecasts, and work with different units of measure for items. Plus, it offers enhanced invoicing for time and expenses, and includes a few extra features like reversing journal entries. When you purchase QuickBooks Premier, you can choose from six different industry-specific flavors (see the next section). Like the Pro edition, Premier can handle a combined total of up to 14,500 name list entries.
- **Enterprise Solutions** is the edition for midsized operations. It's faster, bigger, and more robust than its siblings. Up to 30 people can access a company file at the same time, and this simultaneous access is at least twice as fast as in the Pro or Premier edition. The program's database can handle more than 100,000 names in its Customer, Vendor, Employee, and Other Names lists. It can track inventory in multiple warehouses or stores and produce combined reports for those companies and locations. And because more people can use your company file at once, this edition has features such as an enhanced audit trail, more options for assigning or limiting user permissions, and the ability to delegate administrative functions to the other people using the program. And if you subscribe to Intuit's Advanced Inventory service, you can value inventory by using first in/first out (FIFO) valuation.

TIP You don't have to pay list price for QuickBooks. Your local office supply store, Amazon, and any number of other retail outlets usually offer the program at a discount. (If you buy QuickBooks from Intuit, you pay full price, but you also have 60 days to return the program for a full refund.) In addition, accountants can resell QuickBooks to clients, so it's worth asking yours about purchase and upgrade pricing. QuickBooks ProAdvisors (you can find a local one by going to *http://proadvisor.intuit.com/find-a-proadvisor/search.jsp*) can get you up to a 40 percent discount on QuickBooks Pro or Premier, *and* you'll have 60 days to return the program for a refund.

The QuickBooks Premier Choices

If you work in one of the industries covered by QuickBooks Premier, you can get additional features unique to your industry. (When you install QuickBooks Premier, you choose the industry version you want to run. If your business is in an industry other than one of the five options, choose General Business.) Some people swear that these customizations are worth every penny, while others say the additional features don't warrant the Premier price. On the QuickBooks website (*http://quickbooks.intuit.com/premier*), you can tour the Premier features to decide for yourself. Or you can purchase QuickBooks Accountant, which can run *any* QuickBooks edition, from QuickBooks Pro to the gamut of Premier's industry-specific versions.

NOTE QuickBooks' Accountant edition is designed to help professional accountants and bookkeepers deliver services to their clients. It lets you run any QuickBooks edition (Pro or any of the Premier versions). It also lets you review your clients' data and easily correct mistakes you find, transfer an accountant's copy to your client, design financial statements and other documents, process payroll for clients, reconcile clients' bank accounts, calculate depreciation, prepare clients' tax returns, and work on two company files at a time.

Here are the industries that have their own Premier editions:

- The **General Business** edition has Premier goodies like per-item price levels, sales orders, and so on. It also has sales and expense forecasting, the Inventory Center, more built-in reports than QuickBooks Pro, and a business plan feature.
- The **Contractor** edition includes features near and dear to construction contractors' hearts: job-cost and other contractor-specific reports, the ability to set different billing rates by employee, and tools for managing change orders.
- **Manufacturing & Wholesale** is targeted at companies that manufacture products. Its chart of accounts and menus are customized for manufacturing and wholesale operations. You can use it to manage inventory assembled from components and to track customer return merchandise authorizations (RMAs) and damaged goods.
- If you run a nonprofit organization, you know that several things work differently in the nonprofit world, as the box on page xxi details. The **Nonprofit** edition of QuickBooks includes features such as a chart of accounts customized for nonprofits, forms and letters targeted to donors and pledges, info about using the program for nonprofits, and the ability to generate Statement of Functional Expenses 990 forms.
- The **Professional Services** edition (not to be confused with QuickBooks Pro) is designed for companies that deliver services to their clients. Unique features include project-costing reports, templates for proposals and invoices, billing rates that you can customize by client or employee, and professional service-specific reports and help.
- The **Retail** edition is customized for retail businesses. It includes specialized menus, reports, forms, and help, as well as a custom chart of accounts. Intuit offers companion products that you can integrate with this edition to support all aspects of your retail operation. For example, QuickBooks' Point of Sale product tracks sales, customers, and inventory as you ring up purchases, and it shoots that information over to your QuickBooks company file.

FREQUENTLY ASKED QUESTION

Nonprofit Dilemma

I'm doing the books for a tiny nonprofit corporation. I'd really like to avoid spending any of our hard-raised funds on a special edition of QuickBooks. Can't I just use QuickBooks Pro?

You may be tempted to save some money by using QuickBooks Pro instead of the more expensive QuickBooks Nonprofit edition, and you can—if you're willing to live with some limitations. As long as funding comes primarily from unrestricted sources, the Pro edition will work reasonably well. You'll have to accept using the term "customer" when you mean donor or member, or the term "job" for grants you receive. Throughout this book, you'll find Notes and Tips about tracking nonprofit finances with QuickBooks Pro or Premier (the General Business edition—not the Nonprofit edition).

However, if you receive restricted funds or track funds by program, if you use QuickBooks Pro, you'll have to manually post them to equity accounts and allocate them to accounts in your chart of accounts, since the program doesn't automatically perform these staples of nonprofit accounting. Likewise, QuickBooks Pro doesn't generate all the reports you need to satisfy your grant providers or the government, although you can export reports (page 688) and then modify them in a spreadsheet program. In that case, QuickBooks Premier Nonprofit might be a real timesaver.

Accounting Basics: The Important Stuff

QuickBooks helps people who don't have a degree in accounting handle most accounting tasks. However, you'll be more productive *and* have more accurate books if you understand the following concepts and terms:

- **Double-entry accounting** is the standard method for tracking where your money comes from and where it goes. Following the old saw that money doesn't grow on trees, money always comes from somewhere when you use double-entry accounting. For example, as shown in Table I-1, when you sell something to a customer, the money on your invoice comes in as income and goes into your Accounts Receivable account. Then, when you deposit the payment, the money comes out of the Accounts Receivable account and goes into your checking account. (See Chapter 16 for more about double-entry accounting and journal entries.)

NOTE Each side of a double-entry transaction is either a debit or a credit. As you can see in Table I-1, when you sell products or services, you credit your income account (since your income increases when you sell something), but debit the Accounts Receivable account (because selling something also increases how much customers owe you). You'll see examples throughout the book of how transactions translate to account debits and credits.

TABLE I-1 *Following the money through accounts*

TRANSACTION	ACCOUNT	DEBIT	CREDIT
Sell products or services	Accounts Receivable	$1,000	
Sell products or services	Service Income		$1,000
Receive payment	Checking Account	$1,000	
Receive payment	Accounts Receivable		$1,000
Pay for expense	Office Supplies	$500	
Pay for expense	Checking Account		$500

- **Chart of accounts**. In bookkeeping, an *account* is a place to store money, just like your real-world checking account is a place to store your ready cash. The difference is that you need an account for *each* kind of income, expense, asset, and liability you have. (See Chapter 3 to learn about all the different types of accounts you might use.) The *chart of accounts* is simply a list of all the accounts you use to keep track of your company's money.

- **Cash vs. accrual accounting**. Cash and accrual are the two different ways companies can document how much they make and spend. Cash accounting is the choice of many small businesses because it's easy: You don't show income until you've received a payment (regardless of when that happens), and you don't show expenses until you've paid your bills.

  The accrual method, on the other hand, follows something known as the *matching principle*, which matches revenue with the corresponding expenses. This approach keeps income and expenses linked to the period in which they happened, no matter when cash comes in or goes out. The advantage of this method is that it provides a better picture of profitability because income and its corresponding expenses appear in the same period. With accrual accounting, you recognize income as soon as you record an invoice, even if you'll receive payment during the next fiscal year. For example, if you pay employees in January for work they did in December, those wages are part of the previous fiscal year.

- **Financial reports**. You need three reports to evaluate the health of your company (they're described in detail in Chapter 17):

  - The *income statement*, which QuickBooks calls a *Profit & Loss* report (page 445), shows how much income you've brought in and how much you've spent over a period of time. This QuickBooks report gets its name from the difference between income and expenses, which results in your profit (or loss) for that period.

  - The *balance sheet* (page 451) is a snapshot of how much you own and how much you owe. Assets are things you own that have value, such as buildings, equipment, and brand names. Liabilities are the money you owe to others (like money you borrowed to buy one of your assets, say). The difference between your assets and liabilities is the *equity* in the company—like the equity you have in your house when the house is worth more than you owe on the mortgage.

- The *statement of cash flows* (page 454) tells you how much hard cash you have. You might think that a profit and loss report would tell you that, but noncash transactions—such as depreciation—prevent it from doing so. The statement of cash flows doesn't include noncash transactions; it shows only the money generated or spent operating the company, investing in the company, or financing.

UP TO SPEED

Learning More about Accounting

If you need to learn a lot about QuickBooks and a little something about accounting, you're holding the right book. But if bookkeeping and accounting are unfamiliar territory, some background training may help you use QuickBooks better and more easily (without calling your accountant for help five times a day).

Real World Training offers "Mastering Accounting Basics for QuickBooks," an Intuit-endorsed product that teaches basic accounting concepts using QuickBooks in its examples. It's available online on demand or on CD or DVD. Check it out at *http://tinyurl.com/rwaccounting.*

Alternatively, the Accounting & Business School of the Rockies offers an online accounting and bookkeeping course. The course presents real-life accounting situations, so you'll learn to solve common small-business accounting problems, and it includes hands-on exercises to help you master the material. It doesn't take long to complete, so you'll be up and accounting in no time. To contact the school, visit *www.absrschool.com* or call 1-303-755-6885.

About This Book

QuickBooks Help provides a healthy dose of accounting background and troubleshooting tips. If you don't find the answer you need in the program's "Have a Question?" window (page 746), the Intuit Community—which lets you ask your peers and experts for answers (page 747)—or by searching with keywords, where do you turn next?

This book provides lots of real-world examples, and you can search for topics in its index. In addition, with this book, you can mark your place, underline key points, jot notes in the margin, or read about QuickBooks while sitting in the sun—stuff that's hard to do when reading on a screen.

This book applies to the U.S. *Windows* version of QuickBooks Pro and Premier. (Because the Mac version of the program differs significantly from the Windows one, this book won't be of much help if you have QuickBooks for Mac. For the same reason, this book doesn't cover QuickBooks Online. Versions for other countries differ from the U.S. version, too, primarily in how you work with payroll and taxes.)

In these pages, you'll find step-by-step instructions for using every QuickBooks Pro feature, including progress invoicing (page 284), making journal entries (page 426), writing off losses (page 387), handling customer refunds (page 288), and so on. If you're just starting out with QuickBooks, read the first few chapters as you set up your company file. After that, go ahead and jump from topic to topic depending on the bookkeeping task at hand. As mentioned earlier, you'll also learn about some of the extra bells and whistles in the QuickBooks Premier edition. (All the features in QuickBooks Pro—and in this book—are also in Premier.) To keep you productive, this book evaluates features to help you figure out which ones are most useful and when to use them.

NOTE Although each version of QuickBooks introduces new features and enhancements, you can still use this book if you're using an earlier version. Of course, the older your version of the program, the more discrepancies you'll run across.

QuickBooks 2015: The Missing Manual is designed to accommodate readers at every technical level. The primary discussions are written for people with beginner or intermediate QuickBooks skills. If you're using QuickBooks for the first time, read the boxes titled "Up to Speed," which provide the introductory info you need to understand the current topic. On the other hand, people with advanced skills should watch for similar boxes labeled "Power Users' Clinic," which include tips, tricks, and shortcuts for more experienced QuickBooks wranglers.

About the Outline

This book is divided into five parts, each containing several chapters:

- **Part One: Setting Up QuickBooks** explains how to set up QuickBooks based on your organization's needs. These chapters cover creating a company file and setting up accounts, customers, jobs, vendors, invoice items, and other lists.
- **Part Two: Bookkeeping** follows the money from the moment you rack up time and expenses for your customers and add charges to a customer's invoice to the tasks you have to perform at the end of the year to satisfy the IRS and other interested parties. These chapters describe how to track time and expenses, pay for things you buy, bill customers, manage the money that customers owe you, pay for expenses, manage your bank accounts, and perform other bookkeeping tasks.
- **Part Three: Managing Your Business** delves into the features that can help you make your company a success—or even more successful than it already is. These chapters explain how to keep track of the financial tasks you need to perform, manage QuickBooks files, keep your inventory at just the right level, work with sales tax, build budgets, and use QuickBooks reports to evaluate every aspect of your enterprise.

- **Part Four: QuickBooks Power** helps you take your copy of the program to the next level. You'll learn how to save time and prevent errors by downloading transactions; boost your productivity by setting the program's preferences to match the way you like to work and integrating QuickBooks with other programs; customize the program's components to look the way you want; and—most important—set up QuickBooks so your financial data is secure.
- **Part Five: Appendixes** provides a guide to installing and upgrading QuickBooks and a reference to helpful resources.

NOTE You can find five bonus appendixes online at this book's Missing CD page at *www.missingmanuals.com/cds*: Appendix C: Keyboard Shortcuts, Appendix D: Working with Intuit QuickBooks Payroll Services, Appendix E: Using Intuit e-Invoicing, Appendix F: Tracking Time with the Standalone QuickBooks Pro Timer, and Appendix G: Advanced Form Customization.

The Very Basics

To use this book (and QuickBooks), you need to know a few basics. This book assumes that you're familiar with the following terms and concepts:

- **Clicking**. This book includes instructions that require you to use your computer's mouse or trackpad. To *click* means to point your cursor (the arrow pointer) at something on the screen and then—without moving the cursor—press and release the left button on the mouse (or laptop trackpad). To *right-click* means the same thing, but you press the *right* mouse button instead. (Clicking usually selects an onscreen element or presses an onscreen button, whereas right-clicking typically reveals a *shortcut menu*, which lists some common tasks specific to whatever you right-clicked.) To *double-click* means to click the left button twice in rapid succession, without moving the pointer. And to *drag* means to move the cursor while holding down the left mouse button the entire time.

  When you're told to *Shift-click* something, you click while pressing the Shift key. Related procedures, like *Ctrl-clicking*, work the same way—just click while pressing the specified key.
- **Menus**. The *menus* are the words at the top of your screen: File, Edit, and so on. Click one to make a list of commands appear, as though they're written on a window shade you've just pulled down. Some people click to open a menu and then release the mouse button; after reading the menu choices, they click the option they want. Other people like to press the mouse button continuously as they click the menu title and drag down the list to the desired command; only then do they release the mouse button. Both methods work, so use whichever you prefer.
- **Keyboard shortcuts**. Nothing is faster than keeping your fingers on your keyboard to enter data, choose names, trigger commands, and so on—without losing

time by grabbing your mouse, carefully positioning it, and then choosing a command or list entry. That's why many experienced QuickBooks fans use keyboard shortcuts to accomplish most tasks. In this book, when you read an instruction like "Press Ctrl+A to open the Chart of Accounts window," start by pressing the Ctrl key; while it's down, type the letter A; and then release both keys.

About→These→Arrows

Throughout this book, and throughout the Missing Manual series, you'll find sentences like this one: "Choose Lists→Customer & Vendor Profile Lists→Customer Type List." That's shorthand for a much longer instruction that directs you to navigate three nested menus in sequence, like this: "At the top of your screen, click the Lists menu. On the Lists menu, point to the Customer & Vendor Profile Lists menu item. On the submenu that appears, choose Customer Type List." Figure I-1 shows the menus this sequence opens.

Similarly, this arrow shorthand also simplifies the instructions for opening nested folders, such as Program Files→QuickBooks→Export Files.

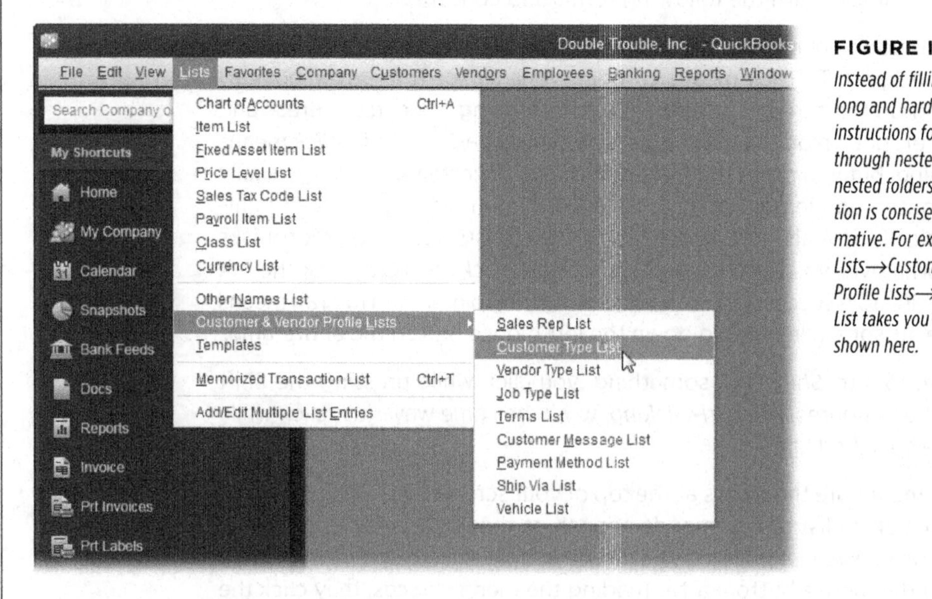

FIGURE I-1

Instead of filling pages with long and hard-to-follow instructions for navigating through nested menus and nested folders, the arrow notation is concise and just as informative. For example, choosing Lists→Customer & Vendor Profile Lists→Customer Type List takes you to the menu item shown here.

About the Online Resources

As the owner of a Missing Manual, you've got more than just a book to read. Online, you'll find tips, articles, and additional content that helps you stay current with QuickBooks changes that occur after this book is published. You can also communicate with the Missing Manual team and tell us what you love (or hate) about the book. Head over to *www.missingmanuals.com*, or go directly to one of the following sections.

Missing CD

This book doesn't have a CD pasted inside the back cover, but you're not missing out on anything. Go to *www.missingmanuals.com/cds* and click the "Missing CD-ROM" link for this book to download five additional appendixes. If Intuit releases significant QuickBooks enhancements or new features after this book goes to print, you'll also be able to download files with the full scoop on those new offerings. And so you don't wear down your fingers typing long web addresses, the Missing CD page offers a list of clickable links to the websites mentioned in this book.

Registration

If you register this book at oreilly.com, you'll be eligible for special offers—like discounts on future editions of *QuickBooks: The Missing Manual*. Registering takes only a few clicks. To get started, type *http://oreilly.com/register* into your browser to hop directly to the Registration page.

Feedback

Got questions? Need more information? Fancy yourself a book reviewer? On our Feedback page, you can get expert answers to questions that come to you while reading, and you can share your thoughts on this book. To have your say, go to *www.missingmanuals.com/feedback*.

Errata

In an effort to keep this book as up to date and accurate as possible, each time we print more copies, we'll make any confirmed corrections you've suggested. We also note such changes on the book's website, so you can mark important corrections into your own copy of the book, if you like. Go to *http://tinyurl.com/QB15errata* to report an error or view existing corrections.

Safari® Books Online

Safari® Books Online (*http://safaribooksonline.com*) is an on-demand digital library that lets you easily search over 7,500 technology and creative reference books and videos to find the answers you need quickly.

With a subscription, you can read any page and watch any video from our library online. Read books on your cellphone and mobile devices. Access new titles before they are available for print, and get exclusive access to manuscripts in development and post feedback for the authors. Copy and paste code samples, organize your favorites, download chapters, bookmark key sections, create notes, print out pages, and benefit from tons of other time-saving features.

PART 1

Setting Up QuickBooks

CHAPTER

1

Creating a Company File

A *company file* is where you store your company's financial records in QuickBooks, so it's the first thing you need to work on in the program. You can create a company file from scratch or convert records that you previously kept in a different small-business accounting program, Quicken, or even another edition of QuickBooks like QuickBooks for Mac.

If you're new to bookkeeping, another approach is to use a file that *someone else* created. For example, if you've worked with an accountant to set up your company, she might provide you with a QuickBooks company file already configured for your business so you can hit the ground running.

This chapter starts by explaining how to launch your copy of QuickBooks. Then, if you need to create your company file yourself, you'll learn how to use the QuickBooks Setup dialog box or the EasyStep Interview to get started (and find out which other chapters explain how to finish the job). If you're converting your records from another program, this chapter provides some hints for making the transition as smooth as possible. Finally, you'll learn how to open a company file, update one to a new version of QuickBooks, and modify basic company information.

Opening QuickBooks

Here are the easiest ways to open QuickBooks:

- **Desktop icon**. Double-click the desktop shortcut that QuickBooks created during installation.

- **Windows taskbar**. The fastest way to open QuickBooks is to click its icon on the Windows taskbar, shown in Figure 1-1—but first you have to put it there. To do that in Windows 7 and Windows 8.1, right-click the QuickBooks desktop icon and then, on the shortcut menu that appears, choose "Pin to Taskbar." If you're still using Windows 8 (not 8.*1*), pinning the QuickBooks desktop icon to the taskbar takes a few more steps: Point the cursor at the screen's upper-right corner to display the Charms menu, click the Search icon (the magnifying glass), type *quickbooks* in the Search box, and then press Enter. When you see the QuickBooks icon, right-click it, and then choose "Pin to Taskbar."

FIGURE 1-1

Windows' taskbar keeps your favorite icons near at hand. The taskbar is easy to reach, because program windows don't hide it the way they do desktop shortcuts. You can rename desktop icons, as was done here. To do that, right-click the icon, and then choose Rename on the shortcut menu. Type the label you want to use, and then press Enter.

- **Start menu**. You can also launch QuickBooks from the Start menu. In Windows 7, click Start→QuickBooks Pro 2015 (or QuickBooks Premier 2015). If QuickBooks isn't already listed in the Start menu, choose Start→All Programs→QuickBooks→QuickBooks Pro 2015 (or QuickBooks Premier 2015). In Windows 8, point the cursor at the screen's upper-right corner to display the Charms menu, click Start, and then click the QuickBooks icon on the screen's right. And in Windows 8.1, you can right-click the QuickBooks desktop icon and choose "Pin to Start."

The first time you launch QuickBooks, you're greeted by the QuickBooks Setup dialog box, whose sole purpose is to help you create a company file in one way or another. The rest of this chapter explains how to create a company file, and then how to open company files you create. After that, you'll be ready to dive into bookkeeping.

Before You Create a Company File

If you've just started a business and want to inaugurate your books with QuickBooks, your prep work will be a snap. If, on the other hand, you have existing records for your business, you have a few small tasks to complete before you jump into QuickBooks' setup. Whether your books are paper ledgers or electronic files in another program, gather your company information *before* you open QuickBooks. That way, you can hunker down in front of your computer and crank out a company file in record time. This section explains what you need to create a company file in QuickBooks.

Choosing a Start Date

To keep your entire financial history at your fingertips, you need to put every transaction and speck of financial information in your QuickBooks company file. But you have better things to do than enter years' worth of checks, invoices, and deposits, so the comprehensive approach is practical only if you just recently started your company.

The more realistic approach is to enter your financial data into QuickBooks starting as of a specific date and, from then on, add all *new* transactions to QuickBooks. The date you choose is called the *start date*. (The start date isn't something that you enter in a field in QuickBooks; it's simply the earliest transaction date in your company file.) You should choose it carefully. Here are your start date options and the ramifications of each one:

- **The last day of the previous fiscal year**. The best choice is to fill in your records for the entire current fiscal year. To do that, use the last day of your company's *previous* fiscal year as the company file's start date. That way, the account balances on your start date are like the ending balances on a bank statement, and you're ready to start bookkeeping fresh on the first day of the fiscal year.

  Yes, you have to enter checks, credit card charges, invoices, payments, and other transactions that have happened since the beginning of your fiscal year (see the box on page 6), but that won't take as much time as you think. And you'll regain those hours when tax time rolls around, as you nimbly generate the reports you need to complete your tax returns.

  If more than half of your fiscal year has already passed, the best approach is to be patient and postpone your QuickBooks setup until the *next* fiscal year. (Intuit releases new versions of QuickBooks in October or November each year for just that reason.) But waiting isn't always feasible. In cases like that, go with the next option in this list.

TIP For practice, you can start entering transactions that occur after the closing date of your bank statement from the month *before* you begin entering transactions in QuickBooks. For example, if you plan to start tracking your business finances in QuickBooks starting January 1, grab the bank statement whose closing date is before that (December 15, say). In QuickBooks, record all the transactions that occurred between that statement's opening and closing dates—November 16 through December 15, in this example. Then you can practice reconciling that statement with your QuickBooks records (page 389).

- **The last day of the previous fiscal period**. The next best start date is the last day of the previous fiscal quarter (or fiscal month, at the very least). Since your company file won't contain a full year's worth of detail if you go this route, you might have to switch between QuickBooks and your old filing cabinets to prepare your tax returns and look up financial information.

POWER USERS' CLINIC

Entering History in the Right Order

If you enter transactions from the beginning of your fiscal year, it's important to add them in the right order so the information you need is available when you need it. Here's the order to use:

1. **Add purchase transactions, such as purchase orders, bills, bill payments, checks, credit card charges, and so on.** By entering these transactions first, you'll have inventory information and reimbursable expenses ready to go when you start entering invoices and other sales transactions.
2. **If you charge customers for hours worked or pay employees by the hour, then enter timesheet information next.** By doing so, you can create invoices or generate paychecks for hours worked.
3. **Enter sales transactions, such as sales receipts, invoices, and credit memos.** You need these transactions in place before you can record customer payments or process sales tax.
4. **Record customer payments and other deposits.**
5. **Record sales tax payments for the goods and services you sold.**
6. **If you use QuickBooks for payroll, add payroll transactions.**
7. **Enter other bank transactions, such as transfers and bank fees.**

Account Balances and Transactions

Unless you begin using QuickBooks when you start your business, to get things rolling, you need to know your account balances as of your selected start date. For example, if your checking account has $342 at the end of the year, that value goes into QuickBooks during setup. You also need every transaction that's happened since the start date you chose—expenses you've incurred, sales you've made, payroll and tax transactions, and so on—to establish your asset, liability, equity, income, and expense accounts. So dig that information out of your existing accounting system (or shoebox). (If you don't want to record individual transactions, the box on page 8 tells you how to quickly enter your account totals as of a specific date.)

Here are the balances and transactions you need and where you can find them in your records:

- **Cash balances**. For each bank account you use in your business (checking, savings, money market, and so on), find the bank statements with statement dates as close to—but *earlier* than—the start date of your QuickBooks company file. Hop onto your bank's website to identify the transactions that haven't yet cleared; you'll need them to enter transactions, unless you download transactions from your bank (page 617). If you have petty cash lying around, count it and use that number to set up your petty cash account (page 215).

TIP For Subchapter C corporations, Subchapter S corporations, and partnerships, the balance sheet that you included with your previous year's tax return is a great starting point for account balances. Your tax return also shows your federal tax ID number, which you'll need, too.

- **Customer balances**. If customers owe you money, pull the paper copy of every *unpaid* invoice or statement out of your filing cabinet (or find the electronic versions you saved on your computer) so you can give QuickBooks what it needs to calculate your Accounts Receivable balance. If you didn't keep copies, you can ask your customers for copies of the invoices they haven't paid or simply create invoices in QuickBooks to match the payments you receive.
- **Vendor balances**. If your company thinks handing out cash before you have to is more painful than data entry, then find the bills you haven't yet paid and get ready to enter them in QuickBooks so you can generate your Accounts Payable balance. (Or, to reduce the number of transactions you have to enter, simply pay those outstanding bills and then record the bill payments in QuickBooks.)
- **Asset values**. When you own assets such as buildings or equipment, their value depreciates over time. If you included a balance sheet with the tax return you filed for your company, you can find asset values and accumulated depreciation on your most recent tax return (yet another reason to start using QuickBooks at the beginning of your fiscal year). If you haven't filed a tax return for your company yet, an asset's value is typically the price you paid for it.
- **Liability balances**. Find the current balances you owe on any business loans or mortgages.
- **Inventory**. If you stock products that you sell and track them as inventory, you need to know how many items you had in stock as of the start date, how much you paid for them, and what you expect to sell them for.
- **Payroll**. Payroll services are a great value for the money, which you'll grow to appreciate as you collect the info you need for payroll (including salaries and wages, tax deductions, benefits, pensions, 401(k) deductions, and other stray payroll deductions you might have). You also need to know who receives withholdings, such as tax agencies or the company handling your 401(k) plan. Oh, yeah—and you also need payroll details for each employee. Chapter 15 explains the payroll options available inside and outside of QuickBooks.

TIP If you have outstanding payroll withholdings such as employee payroll taxes, then send in the payments *before* you start recording transactions in QuickBooks so you don't have to enter those open transactions in your company file.

WORKAROUND WORKSHOP

Summarizing Midyear Account Balances

If you need to switch to QuickBooks in the middle of a fiscal year but don't want to trudge through transaction data entry, don't despair. A single journal entry can bring your income and expense account totals up to date. Although you won't have the details you get from individual transactions, your account balances will be accurate and ready for tasks like creating financial reports and filing taxes.

First, you need to know your income and expense accounts' totals. To get those numbers, generate an income statement from your previous accounting system. (Run a cash-basis or accrual-basis report, depending on which method you use. See page xxii to learn about cash versus accrual accounting.)

To record those year-to-date income and expense numbers in QuickBooks, create a journal entry (page 426). Fill in the Date field with the last day of the historical period, such as 6/30/15, to record financial results for the first half of the calendar year. In the journal entry's table, add a line for each income and expense account, as shown in Figure 1-2. Finally, enter values for income accounts in the Credit column and values for expense accounts in the Debit column.

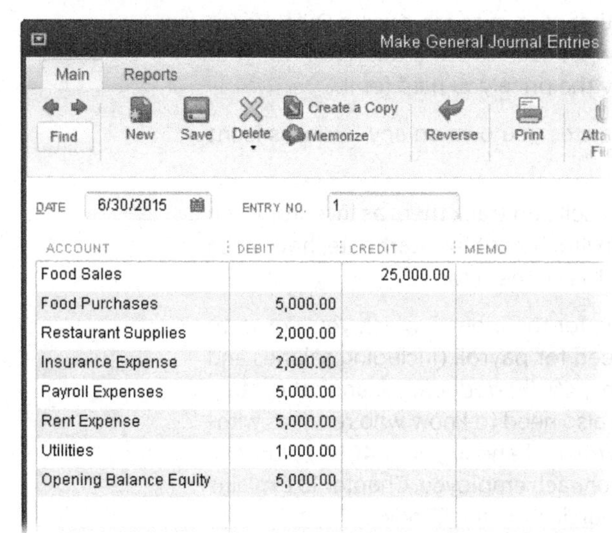

FIGURE 1-2

A journal entry that records income and expense totals is a compromise you can make when you must start using QuickBooks midyear. Each row in the journal entry's table allocates funds to an income or expense account. Enter an income account total in the Credit cell. Enter an expense account total in the Debit cell.

If total expense is less than total income, assign the leftover amount in the debit column to the Opening Balance Equity account. (That remaining amount is profit, which becomes your equity in the company, as described on page 454.)

Creating a Company File

Keeping books requires accuracy, attention to detail, and persistence—hence the customary image of spectacled accountants scanning row after row of numbers. QuickBooks can help you keep your books without ruining your eyesight—as long as you start your company file with good information. If you want to practice with QuickBooks, you can experiment with a sample file, as the box below explains.

GEM IN THE ROUGH

Experimenting with a Sample File

You don't have to use your *real* company file to test out QuickBooks features you've never used. The program comes with a couple of sample files: one for a basic product-based business and one for a basic service-based business. And if you have QuickBooks Premier, you can experiment with several other sample files for more specialized pursuits like contracting, consulting, manufacturing, and so on.

To experiment with QuickBooks features before you put them into production, in the No Company Open window, click "Open a sample file," and then choose the one you want. (To display the No Company Open window, you have to close any open company files by choosing File→Close Company [or File→Close Company/Logoff if there's more than one user set up for the file]. If the QuickBooks Setup dialog box is open, close it, too.)

Don't try to use one of these sample files as your actual company file. They come with accounts, customers, vendors, and transactions (such as checks, invoices, and purchase orders). Besides, QuickBooks sets "today's" date in these files to 12/15/2019, which makes transactions later than you or your vendors would like (although you can edit the values in date boxes).

QuickBooks makes it easy to create a company file from scratch. (The box on page 10 tells you how to find someone who can help you create one.) You can opt for a short and sweet process, which asks you for the bare minimum of info before it creates your file. Or you can use a wizard that guides you through the process with a series of questions that takes about 15 minutes to answer. The questions cover the basics of creating and customizing a company file to fit your business. QuickBooks needs to know some company information, the industry you're in, and the features you want to use. The program then sets your preferences and creates a few accounts (like basic income and expense accounts and your checking account). The box on page 21 lists additional setup tasks you need to perform to flesh out your company file—and where in this book to learn more about those tasks.

Options for Creating a Company File

You can create a company file in several ways, and the QuickBooks Setup dialog box—which opens automatically the very first time you start QuickBooks—is your ticket to all of them. If you don't see this dialog box, choose File→New Company (or click "Create a new company" in the No Company Open window). The dialog box takes up most of the screen, so you can stay focused on creating your company file.

UP TO SPEED

Getting Help Creating a New Company File

The proud owners of brand-new businesses face a dilemma: They have more important things to do than muddle through setting up company files in QuickBooks, but money is usually as short as free time. If you don't know much about bookkeeping or accounting, a few hours of an accountant's time is a worthwhile investment when you're getting started in QuickBooks. You'll not only save untold hours, but you'll also know that your books are set up properly. Accountants well versed in QuickBooks can create a flawless company file without breaking a sweat.

If you plan to do without an accountant but you want some help setting up your company file, you can choose Help→Find A Local QuickBooks Expert. By answering a few questions on the Local QuickBooks Expert website (*http://tinyurl.com/find-qbadvisor*), you can locate someone in your area who can help you get started.

The three basic approaches to creating a company file are covered by the QuickBooks Setup dialog box's three buttons:

- **Express Start**. This button is in pole position because it's the best option if this is your first time creating a company file. If you go this route, QuickBooks holds your hand and asks for a few bits of info at a time before moving to each new screen. If you stop filling in information before QuickBooks creates your company file, the program *won't* save any of the values you entered. So make sure you have at least 15 minutes to complete the first set of steps. Instructions for Express Start begin on page 11.
- **Advanced Setup**. If you've been around the QuickBooks block before, choose this option to launch the EasyStep Interview window, which asks for more information on each screen than Express Start does. If you need help during the process, you can always click the "Get answers" link at the top right of the window. You can also use Advanced Setup to go back and modify info you entered previously, whether you entered it using Express Start or the EasyStep Interview. (The instructions for the EasyStep Interview begin on page 14. If you're unsure what to put in any of the fields you're supposed to fill in, they're described in the Express Start section, because you fill in much of the same information regardless of which approach you use.)
- **Other Options**. This button covers the rest of the bases. You can use it to open an existing company file or convert existing records that are in Quicken or another accounting program (page 23) for use in QuickBooks.

NOTE If you use QuickBooks Accountant edition, you can create a company file from an existing file by choosing File→"New Company from Existing Company File."

Whether you use Express Start or the EasyStep Interview, you tell QuickBooks the basic 411 about your company, such as its name and tax ID. (If any of the fields confuse you, try clicking the "Need help? Give us a call" button in the QuickBooks Setup dialog box or the "Get answers" link in the upper-right corner of the EasyStep Interview window.) The next section has the full scoop on the information you need to provide.

Using Express Start

As its name implies, Express Start gets you going as quickly as possible by asking for the minimum amount of info (you can fill in the details later). To use it, choose File→New Company and then, in the QuickBooks Setup dialog box, click Express Start. The "Tell us about your business" screen appears, and you can start entering info. The following sections explain what the program needs to know to create your company file.

COMPANY INFORMATION

On the "Tell us about your business" screen, shown in Figure 1-3, you need to cough up only three answers, but these responses are the foundation of many of the preferences that QuickBooks sets:

- **Company Name**. Type the name you want to appear on invoices, reports, and other forms. (QuickBooks also uses the name you type here to name your company file.) Later on, you can specify your company's legal name (page 28).
- **Industry**. Start typing your industry in this box (as shown in Figure 1-3) and see if QuickBooks finds a match. If not, click "Help me choose" to the right of this field to see all your options. If you don't see an obvious choice in the Industry list, then scroll to the bottom and choose either General Product-based Business or General Service-based Business.

  Choose your industry carefully. QuickBooks adjusts its preferences and chart of accounts based on your choice to match how your business operates. For example, the program creates income and expense accounts for your type of business and automatically turns on features like sales tax and inventory if your industry typically uses them. If QuickBooks makes assumptions you don't like, you can alter your preferences (Chapter 25) and accounts (page 56) later.
- **Company Type**. The tax form you use depends on the type of business entity you have. This drop-down list contains the most common types, from sole proprietorships and partnerships to corporations and nonprofits. When you select a type, QuickBooks assigns the corresponding tax form to your company file. After you finish creating your company file, you can see the tax form the program selected by choosing Company→My Company, which brings up the dialog box shown in Figure 1-9 (page 27). The Income Tax Form Used box at the bottom of that dialog box lists the tax form for your company type.

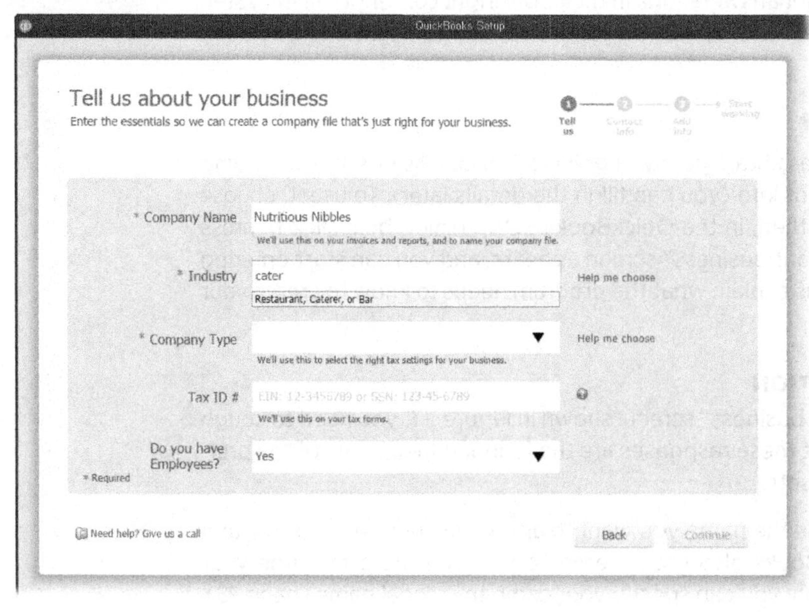

FIGURE 1-3

QuickBooks' list of industries is robust, so chances are good you'll find one that's close to what your company does. You can start typing an industry, and the program displays options that match what you've typed so far, such as cater *to display the industry "Restaurant, Caterer, or Bar" shown here. Or you can click the "Help me choose" link to see all the industries the program offers.*

- **Tax ID #**. This box is for the federal tax ID number you use when you file taxes. You don't *have* to enter it now, but you'll need it come tax time. You'll use a federal Employer Identification Number (EIN) if your company is a corporation or partnership, you have employees, or fit a few other criteria (go to *www.irs.gov* to see if you need an EIN). Otherwise, your tax ID is your Social Security number or Individual Tax Identification Number (ITIN).
- **Do you have employees?** The choice you make in this box doesn't affect the settings in your company file. If this field is set to Yes (as it is initially) or to "No, but I might in the future," then Intuit will tempt you with payroll service offers. If you don't have employees or don't want to receive those offers, choose No in the drop-down list.

When you finish filling out this screen, click Continue.

BUSINESS CONTACT INFORMATION

Next, you can enter your basic contact info. If you're itching to start printing and emailing invoices, bills, and other forms, fill in the following fields:

- **Legal Name**. This is the name you use on contracts and other legal documents. Your company name and legal name are usually the same unless you use a DBA (doing business as) company name. If you own a corporation, the legal name is what appears on your Certificate of Incorporation.

- **Contact info**. Enter your mailing address, telephone number, email address, and website address, if you have one. The Zip and Phone fields are the only ones that are required.

Click Preview Your Settings to see which features QuickBooks selected for you based on the industry and company type you provided (Figure 1-4). The Preview Your Company Settings dialog box lets you fine-tune the accounts QuickBooks selected and choose a different place to store your company file. Here's what you can do on each tab of this dialog box:

- **Features Selected**. This tab is purely informational. You can't modify the settings listed here, but you can change the program's preferences later (Chapter 25) to suit your needs.
- **Chart of Accounts**. This tab lists accounts typically used in your industry. The accounts that QuickBooks chose have checkmarks next to their names. You can include or exclude accounts in your chart of accounts by turning their checkmarks on or off.

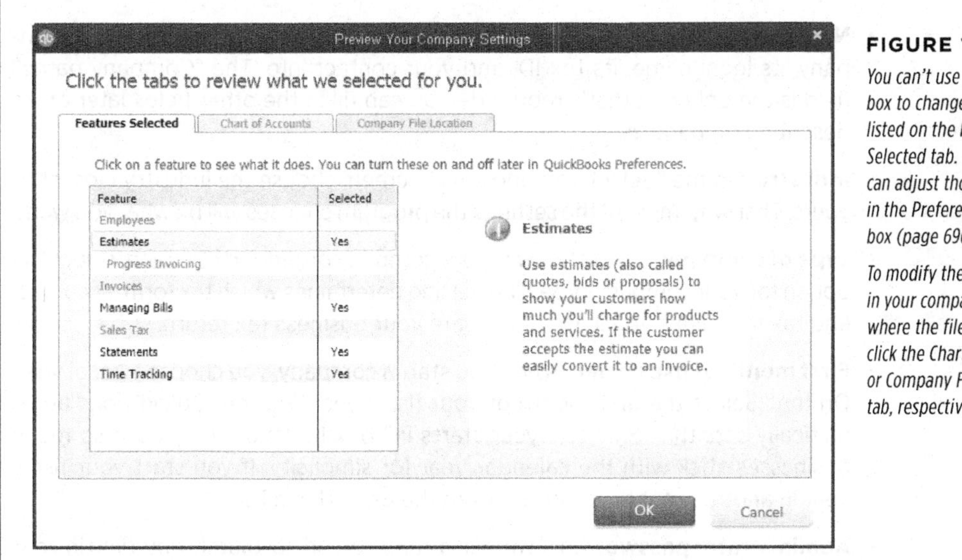

FIGURE 1-4

You can't use this dialog box to change the features listed on the Features Selected tab. However, you can adjust those settings in the Preferences dialog box (page 696).

To modify the accounts in your company file or where the file is stored, click the Chart of Accounts or Company File Location tab, respectively.

- **Company File Location**. This tab shows where on your computer the program plans to save your company file. To choose a different spot, click Change Location, and then select the folder you want. If the folder doesn't exist, in the "Browse for Folder" dialog box, click Make New Folder, type the folder's name, and then press Enter. To close the "Browse for Folder" dialog box, click OK.

When you've made the changes you want to your company settings, in the Preview Your Company Settings dialog box, click OK to return to the main QuickBooks Setup dialog box.

■ CREATING YOUR COMPANY FILE

Once everything is the way you want it, in the main QuickBooks Setup dialog box, click Create Company File. A Working message box appears to show QuickBooks' progress in creating your file. You know it's finished when the "You've got a company file! Now add your info" screen appears.

If you have time, you can now add your customers, vendors, and employees; the products and services you sell; and your bank accounts. To learn how, jump to page 19.

Using the EasyStep Interview

The EasyStep Interview also guides you through the setup process, but it gives you more control over setting up your company file than Express Start does. For example, you can provide more info about your company up front and choose which features to turn on.

To access the EasyStep Interview, choose File→New Company and then, in the QuickBooks Setup dialog box, click Advanced Setup. The "Enter your company information" screen appears. As you enter the following info, click Next to proceed to each new screen:

- **Name and contact info**. The first screen wants to know the name of your company, its legal name, its tax ID, and your contact info. The "Company name" field is the only one that's required—you can fill in the other fields later on as described on page 26.
- **Industry**. On the "Select your industry" screen, choose the industry closest to yours. That way, most of the settings the program chooses will be what you want.
- **Type of company**. On the "How is your company organized?" screen, select the option for your company type. This setting determines which tax form, accounts, and tax form lines you'll use to prepare your business tax return.
- **First month of fiscal year**. When you start a company, you choose a fiscal year. On the "Select the first month of your fiscal year" screen, QuickBooks automatically sets the "My fiscal year starts in" box to January because so many businesses stick with the calendar year for simplicity. If you start your fiscal year in another month, choose it from the drop-down list.
- **Administrator password**. The administrator can do absolutely *anything* in your company file: set up other users, log in as other users, and access any area of the company file. Although QuickBooks lets you click Next and skip right past the "Set up your administrator password" screen, this is no time for shortcuts, as the box on page 15 explains. Type the password you want to use in both the "Administrator password" and "Retype password" boxes, and then keep the password in a safe but memorable place. (Page 718 explains how to change the administrator name and password.)

UP TO SPEED

Safe Login Practices

Don't even *think* about having everyone who works with a company file share one login. You don't want everyone to have access to payroll data, and you wouldn't know which person to fire if you found any less-than-legal transactions in the file. Even if you run a small business from home, an administrator password prevents the chimney sweep from swiping your business credit card number. Chapter 28 has much more about keeping your QuickBooks files secure, but here are some password basics:

- Choose a password that's at least eight characters long and is a combination of letters and numbers.
- Passwords are case sensitive, so make sure that Caps Lock isn't turned on by mistake.
- *Type* the password in both the "Administrator password" and "Retype password" boxes. If you copy and paste the password from one box to the other, you could copy a typo and not be able to open the company file you just created.

If you forget the administrator login and password or lose the piece of paper they're written on, you won't be able to open your company file without some fancy footwork, so keep a record of them someplace safe. If you've tried everything and your administrator password is *still* missing in action, see page 720 to learn how to reset it.

CREATING YOUR COMPANY FILE

After you set the administrator password and click Next, the "Create your company file" screen appears. (If you're new to QuickBooks, click the "Where should I save my company file?" link, which opens a Help Article dialog box that explains the pros and cons of storing company files in different places.)

When you're ready to create the file, on the "Create your company file" screen, click Next to wrap up the creation process by specifying the filename and location. QuickBooks opens the "Filename for New Company" dialog box, which is really just a Save As dialog box. Navigate to the folder where you want to store your company file. QuickBooks automatically sets the "File name" box to the company name you entered, and the "Save as type" box to "QuickBooks Files (*.QBW, *.QBA)." Here are some guidelines for naming and saving your company file:

- If you want to call the file something other than the company name you entered earlier in the interview, simply type a new name in the "File name" box. For example, you may want one that's shorter or that better identifies the company's records within.
- Consider storing your company file in a folder with the rest of your company data so that it gets backed up along with everything else. For example, if you're the only person who uses QuickBooks, you could create a Company Files folder inside your Documents folder. See page 742 for more about choosing a location for company files.

When you click Save in the "Filename for New Company" dialog box, QuickBooks may take a minute or so to create the new file. In the meantime, a message box with a progress bar appears. When the company file is ready, the "Customizing QuickBooks for your business" screen appears. Click Next to dig in.

TIP At this point, the progress bar in the left margin of the EasyStep Interview window is depressingly short because you still have to do the bulk of the company file setup. If you need a break before continuing, click Leave at the bottom of the window. The next time you open that company file, the EasyStep Interview continues where you left off.

CUSTOMIZING YOUR COMPANY FILE

Click Next on the "Customizing QuickBooks for your business screen" to see a series of EasyStep Interview screens that ask questions about your business to help QuickBooks decide which features to turn on, what to include on your Home Page, and so on. The interview displays "(recommended for your business)" next to the options that are typical for a company in your industry, as shown in Figure 1-5.

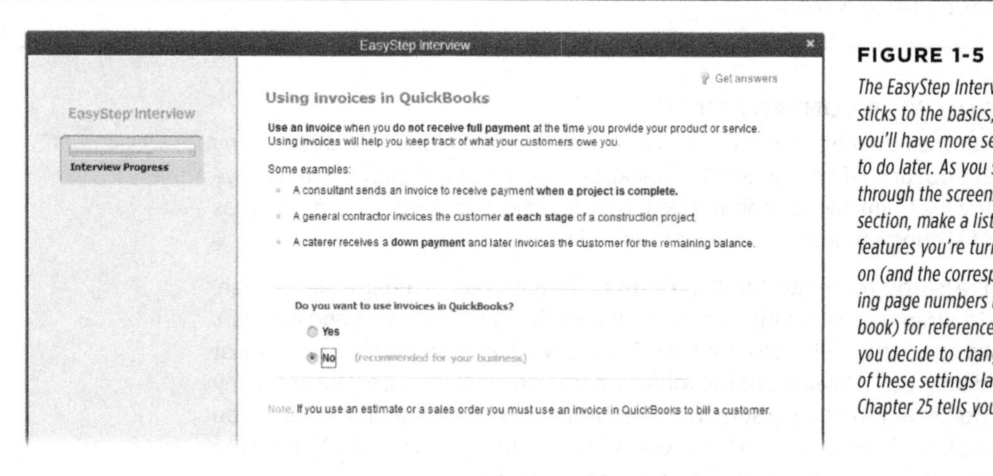

FIGURE 1-5

The EasyStep Interview sticks to the basics, so you'll have more setup to do later. As you step through the screens in this section, make a list of the features you're turning on (and the corresponding page numbers in this book) for reference. If you decide to change any of these settings later, Chapter 25 tells you how.

Here are some guidelines for answering the questions on the various screens:

- The **What do you sell?** screen is where you tell QuickBooks whether you offer services, products, or both. When you choose one of these options, the program figures out which types of income accounts you need. If you select "Products only" or "Both services and products," another screen later in the interview asks whether you want to track inventory.
- The **Do you charge sales tax?** screen has only two options: Yes and No. If you're one of the unfortunate souls who has to navigate the rocky shoals of sales tax, select Yes. If you don't charge sales tax, select No. For detailed instructions on dealing with sales tax in QuickBooks, see Chapter 21.

- On the **Do you want to create estimates in QuickBooks?** screen, choose Yes or No to turn the estimate feature on or off. If you prepare quotes, bids, or estimates for your customers and want to do so in QuickBooks (page 278), select Yes.

NOTE If you use QuickBooks Premier, the "Tracking customer orders in QuickBooks" screen appears, asking whether you want to use sales orders to track backorders (page 261) or other orders that you plan to fill at a later date. QuickBooks Pro doesn't include sales orders.

- The **Using statements in QuickBooks** screen is where you tell the program whether you generate statements to send to customers (page 295). For example, your wine-of-the-month club might send monthly statements to its members. Or if you're a consultant, you could send invoices for work performed and then send a statement that summarizes the fees, payments, and outstanding balance.
- The **Using invoices in QuickBooks** screen appears only if you chose No on the "Do you want to create estimates in QuickBooks?" screen. (If you chose Yes on that screen, QuickBooks automatically turns on the invoicing feature.) Select Yes to tell the program that you want to use invoices, which you probably do because invoices are the most flexible sales forms (page 222). If you answer No (if, for example, you own a restaurant), QuickBooks jumps to the "Managing bills you owe" screen.
- If you answer Yes on the "Using invoices in QuickBooks" screen, the **Using progress invoicing** screen asks whether you invoice customers based on the percentage you've completed on a job. See page 284 to learn why (and how) you might use this feature.
- The **Managing bills you owe** screen asks whether you plan to write checks to pay bills immediately (select No) or enter bills in QuickBooks and then pay them later (select Yes). You can read about bill preferences on page 638 and payment preferences on page 657.

TIP Entering bills in QuickBooks (page 186) requires more steps than simply writing checks *without* entering the bills in QuickBooks, but there's a benefit to the extra effort: The program can remind you when bills are due or qualify for timely payment discounts, and it can keep track of the total you owe.

- The **Tracking inventory in QuickBooks** screen is where you tell the program whether you keep track of the products you have in stock. This screen provides a few examples of when to track or bypass inventory, and page 99 has info about how to decide whether tracking inventory makes sense for your business.
- **Tracking time in QuickBooks** is ideal if you bill by the hour or pay people based on the number of hours they work. In that case, select Yes on this screen to track the hours people work and create invoices for their time. Chapter 8 explains how to set up time tracking.

- The **Do you have employees?** screen is where you specify whether you want to use QuickBooks' payroll and 1099 features. If you do, select Yes and turn on the appropriate checkbox(es). If you use non-Intuit services to run payroll or to generate contractors' 1099s, select No.

When you click Next on the "Do you have employees?" screen, you see the "Using accounts in QuickBooks" screen, and the progress bar indicates that you're almost done with the interview. Click Next to set these final options:

- The **Select a date to start tracking your finances** screen summarizes what you learned about start dates on page 5. To start at the beginning of this fiscal year (which QuickBooks can figure out using the current calendar year and the starting month you select), choose the "Beginning of this fiscal year: 01/01/15" option. (The year you see listed depends on the current calendar year.) If you've decided to start on a different date, select the "Use today's date or the first day of the quarter or month" option instead. You can then type or choose any date you want in the box, such as the last day of the previous fiscal period.
- The **Review income and expense accounts** screen (Figure 1-6) lists the accounts typically used by companies in your industry.

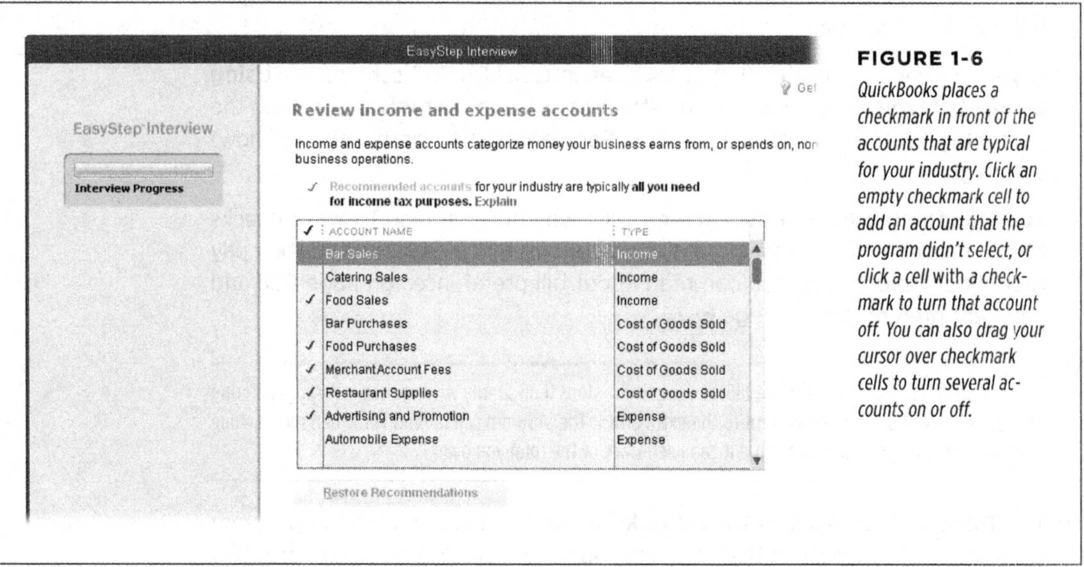

FIGURE 1-6

QuickBooks places a checkmark in front of the accounts that are typical for your industry. Click an empty checkmark cell to add an account that the program didn't select, or click a cell with a checkmark to turn that account off. You can also drag your cursor over checkmark cells to turn several accounts on or off.

When you click Next, you see a bright orange—but premature—"Congratulations!" You still have a few more steps to complete before you can open your company file. Click "Go to Setup," and then read the next section.

Beginning to Use QuickBooks

After you create your company file with Express Start or the EasyStep Interview, you'll see the "You've got a company file!" screen, which is where you perform the additional steps you have to complete, such as adding people you do business with, items you sell, and bank accounts.

If you want to dive into your work without QuickBooks' help on these steps, click Start Working at the window's bottom right and jump to page 20. If you want step-by-step guidance through these processes, click the Add buttons in these sections (if your lists already contain people and items, you'll see Add More buttons instead):

- **Add the people you do business with**. Adding these folks is a snap. Click the first Add button, and then you can import names from your email program (Outlook, Yahoo, or Gmail), paste data from an Excel workbook, or enter info manually. If you select one of the import options and then click Continue, you'll see a table with the names from your email program, as shown in Figure 1-7.

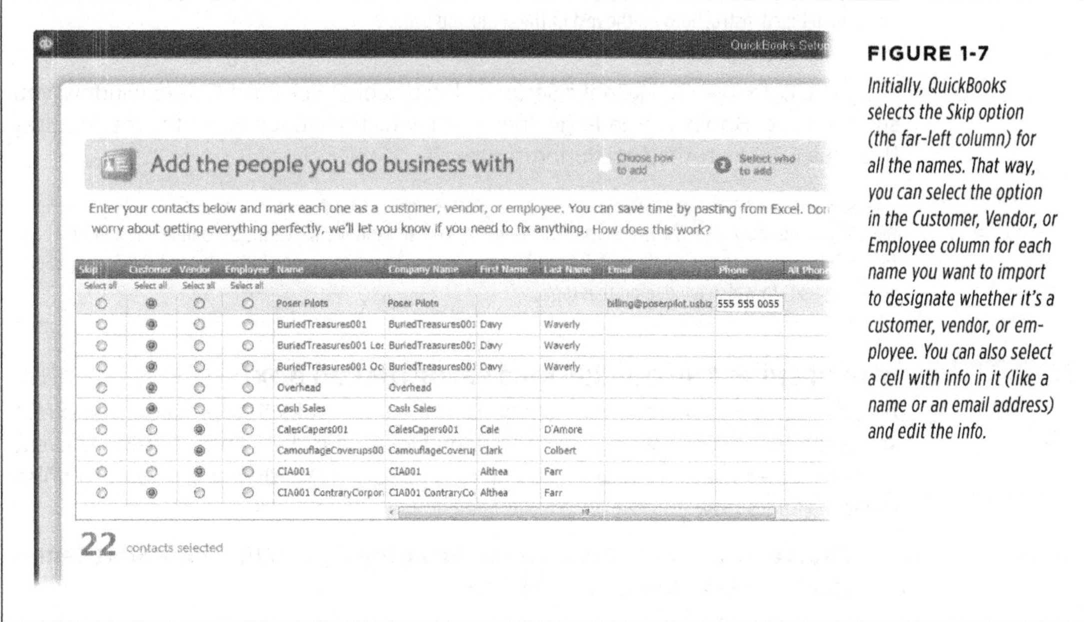

FIGURE 1-7

Initially, QuickBooks selects the Skip option (the far-left column) for all the names. That way, you can select the option in the Customer, Vendor, or Employee column for each name you want to import to designate whether it's a customer, vendor, or employee. You can also select a cell with info in it (like a name or an email address) and edit the info.

- **Add the products and services you sell**. When you click the Add (or Add More) button in this section, you first choose either the Service or "Non-inventory part" option, because you fill in different fields for each type of item. Select the Service option to set up services you sell or the "Non-inventory part" option to create products you sell (see page 517 to learn about products you keep in inventory), and then click Continue. Fill in the names, description, and prices, and then click Continue again to save your items.

- **Add your bank accounts**. For bank accounts, you fill in the account name, account number, opening balance, and opening balance date.

TIP If you're in the middle of entering names, products and services, or bank accounts and want to get back to the "You've got a company file!" screen, click Cancel.

START WORKING

Whether you finish or skip these additional steps, click Start Working to open the Quick Start Center window. In this window, you can click icons and links to open the corresponding features. For example, click Create Invoices to open the Create Invoices window. To reopen the QuickBooks Setup dialog box, click "Return to Add Info" at the window's top right.

TIP If you'd rather perform these tasks later or want more control over setup, click the Close button (the X at the top-right corner of the Quick Start Center window). The box on page 21 tells you where to turn in this book for more detailed instructions on the rest of the setup you need.

After you close the QuickBooks Setup dialog box or Quick Start Center window, you see the QuickBooks Home Page (page 35), which includes icons for the features that QuickBooks turned on during setup.

NOTE You may also see the QuickBooks Learning Center window, which includes links to tutorials (page 750). (You can open this window anytime by choosing Help→Learning Center Tutorials.) In the window, click a link (blue text) to watch a video on that topic.

REOPENING THE QUICKBOOKS SETUP DIALOG BOX

As you learned in the previous sections, the QuickBooks Setup dialog box offers shortcuts for adding info to your company file. If your data-entry session was cut short by other pressing tasks, you can jump back to this dialog box later to finish the job. Here's how:

1. **Choose Help→Quick Start Center. At the top right of the Quick Start Center window, click "Return to Add Info."**

   The QuickBooks Setup dialog box opens to the "You've got a company file!" screen.

2. **Click the Add button for the type of info you want to enter, and then jump back to the instructions on page 19.**

When you're done, click the Close button (the X) at the top right of the QuickBooks Setup dialog box to close it and get to work.

FREQUENTLY ASKED QUESTION

What's Next?

Now that I've created my company file, what do I do next?

Whether you used Express Start or the EasyStep Interview, quite a bit of the setup process is complete—but you aren't quite done. If you need guidance for the rest, look no further than the book in your hands. Here are the ways you can flesh out your company file:

- **Set up your users and passwords:** See page 722.
- **Review and/or change the preferences that QuickBooks set:** See Chapter 25.
- **Set up or edit the accounts in your chart of accounts:** If you haven't set up all your accounts yet, you can create them now. See page 56.
- **Create a journal entry to specify accounts' opening balances:** See the box on page 429 to learn how. And see page 434 to learn how to record your initial contribution of cash or assets to your company.
- **Create items for the products and services you sell:** See Chapter 5.
- **Set up sales tax:** See Chapter 21.
- **Set up your 1099 tracking:** See page 468.
- **Sign up for Intuit QuickBooks Payroll Service:** See online Appendix D..

Converting from Another Program to QuickBooks

If you launched your small business from your basement and kept your records with Quicken Home & Business, your accountant has probably recommended that you make the leap to QuickBooks. Or maybe you used another accounting program like Peachtree or Small Business Accounting and have decided to move to QuickBooks. Or perhaps you're switching from QuickBooks for Mac to QuickBooks for Windows. Whatever your situation, this section tells you how to prep your file for a smooth conversion and bring it over into QuickBooks for Windows.

Converting from Quicken Home & Business

Quicken doesn't report your business performance in the way that most accountants want to see, nor does it store your business transactions the way QuickBooks does. Bottom line: You have to prep your Quicken file before you convert it to QuickBooks.

CLEANING UP YOUR QUICKEN FILE

To make the conversion proceed as smoothly as possible, some cleanup of your Quicken file is in order. For example, record overdue scheduled transactions and send online payments before you convert your Quicken file. Also, in Quicken, delete accounts you no longer need, because once they're in QuickBooks, you can't delete them if they contain any transactions. And make sure that customer names are consistent and unique.

QuickBooks doesn't support repeating online payments, so you also have to tell Quicken to delete any repeating online payments you've set up. In addition, you need complete reports of your past payrolls because Quicken payroll transactions don't convert to QuickBooks.

Intuit publishes a detailed guide to help you prepare for a Quicken conversion. Go to *http://tinyurl.com/pu6vntq* and follow the instructions there.

CONVERTING YOUR QUICKEN FILE

When your Quicken file is ready for conversion to QuickBooks, you have two options in QuickBooks:

- **Choose File→New Company.** In the QuickBooks Setup dialog box, click Other Options, and then choose Convert Quicken Data.
- **Choose File→Utilities→Convert→From Quicken.**

NOTE If you cleaned up your Quicken file but you run into conversion problems in QuickBooks, check the QuickBooks company file for errors by choosing File→Utilities→Verify Data, as described on page 507. Another potential solution is to remove transactions prior to the current fiscal year in Quicken before converting the file. If nothing you try works *and* you're willing to send your Quicken file to Intuit, contact QuickBooks technical support by choosing Help→Support. A browser window opens to the Intuit QuickBooks Support page. In the horizontal navigation bar, click Contact Us. QuickBooks may agree to convert the file for you (for a fee).

FINE-TUNING YOUR CONVERTED QUICKEN DATA

Now that your Quicken data is resting comfortably in a QuickBooks file, you might think you're ready to start using QuickBooks. However, there are some *post*-conversion steps you should take to get your newly minted company file into shape:

- **Enter your company information in QuickBooks.** Info like your company's legal name and address, federal Employer Identification Number, and business type don't come over with your Quicken data. See page 26 to learn how to add them to your company file.
- **Set up your bank feeds in QuickBooks.** Page 610 tells you how to get your QuickBooks bank accounts and your real-world bank accounts talking.
- **Change Quicken names to QuickBooks customers, vendors, and employees.** When you convert from Quicken to QuickBooks, QuickBooks adds all the converted names to its Other Names List. See page 148 to learn how to move these names to other lists.

TIP If your Quicken data file has tons of names, an easy way to convert them is to export them to a spreadsheet and then import them using QuickBooks' Add/Edit Multiple List Entries feature (page 124).

- **Set up Accounts Payable in QuickBooks.** If your Quicken file contained unpaid bills, simply write checks (page 202) to pay them in QuickBooks. Once your vendor balances are zero, you're ready to enter new bills in QuickBooks. When you record your first bill, the program automatically adds a new account called Accounts Payable to your chart of accounts.

Converting from QuickBooks for Mac

Moving a file from QuickBooks for Mac to QuickBooks for Windows is mainly about getting the file into a QuickBooks for Windows format. To do that, simply create a backup of the file in QuickBooks for Mac, and then restore that backup (page 501) in QuickBooks for Windows.

Converting from a Non-Intuit Program

To convert files created in other accounting programs, like Peachtree or Small Business Accounting, you have to download a conversion tool from the Intuit website. In QuickBooks, choose File→Utilities→Convert, and then choose the program you want to convert from. In the browser window that opens, scroll down to the "Are you ready to convert your data?" section, click the "Convert from Peachtree, Microsoft SBA, & Microsoft Office Accounting" link, and then click the Download button that appears. In the File Download dialog box that opens, click Save to download *QuickBooksConversionToolSetup.exe* to your computer.

Opening an Existing Company File

After you've opened a company file in one QuickBooks session, the next time you launch the program, it automatically opens that same company file. If you keep the books for only one company, you might never have to manually open a QuickBooks company file again.

But if you're an irrepressible entrepreneur or a bookkeeper who works on several companies' books, you can open another company file in QuickBooks anytime, and the program automatically closes the previous one. Because QuickBooks stores data in a database, you don't have to save a company file before you close it. (And if you use QuickBooks Accountant edition, you can have *two* company files open at the same time, as the Tip below explains.) The following sections describe the different ways to open a company file.

TIP With QuickBooks Accountant and QuickBooks Enterprise, you can have two company files open at the same time, although the second file that you open has some restrictions. (To learn about these restrictions, search QuickBooks Help for "second company.") To open a second company file, choose File→Open Second Company, and your computer launches a new instance of QuickBooks. In the new window, double-click the name of the file you want to open. The second company file opens with the text "(Secondary)" after the company name in the QuickBooks window's title bar. (In the first QuickBooks window, the text "(Primary)" appears after the company name.)

Opening a Recently Opened Company File

If you work on more than one company file, you may frequently switch between them. The easiest way to open a recent file is to choose File→Open Previous Company, and then choose the file you want to open, as shown in Figure 1-8. If the Open Previous Company submenu doesn't list the file you want, follow the steps in the next section instead.

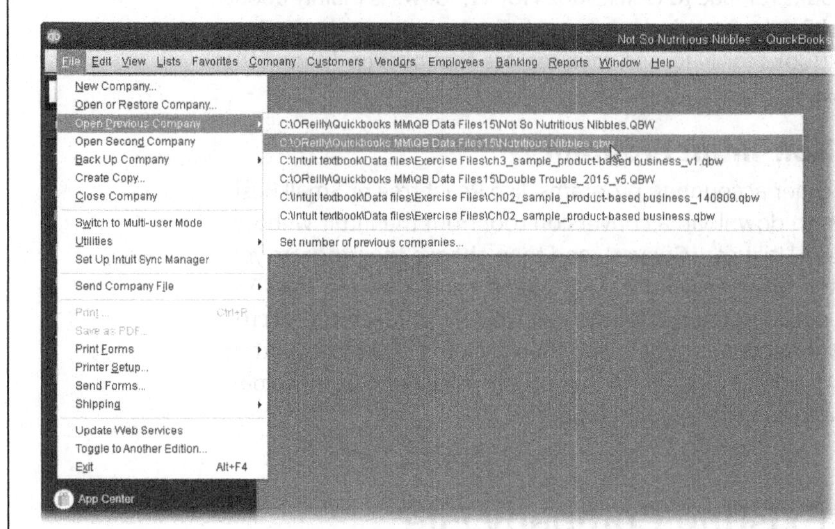

FIGURE 1-8

To open a company file you've worked on recently, click it in the Open Previous Company submenu.

If the No Company Open window (not shown here) is visible, you can open a recent file by double-clicking its filename in that window's list. (Opening a sample file is the only task the No Company Open window performs that you can't also perform via the File menu.)

Opening Any Company File

Sometimes, a company file you want to open falls off the recent-file list. (The box on page 25 explains how to tell QuickBooks how many files to include on the File→Open Previous Company submenu.) Say your bookkeeping business is booming and you work on dozens of company files every month. Or maybe you want to update a file from a previous version of QuickBooks (see the box on page 26). Here's how to open *any* company file, no matter how long it's been since you last used it:

1. **Choose File→"Open or Restore Company."**

   If the No Company Open window is visible, you can click "Open or restore an existing company" instead.

2. **In the "Open or Restore Company" dialog box, select the "Open a company file" option, and then click Next.**

   QuickBooks closes your current company file and then opens the "Open a Company" dialog box.

3. **Navigate to the folder with the company file you want and double-click the file's name.**

   You can also click the filename and then click Open.

4. **If the QuickBooks Login window appears (which it will if you've assigned a password to the Administrator user account or set up multiple users), type your user name and password.**

   If the Administrator is the only user, the Password box is the only one that appears. But if you have more than one user for the company file, both the User Name and Password boxes appear.

5. **Click OK.**

   QuickBooks opens the company file, and you're ready to keep the books.

NOTE Backup files are the answer to the adrenaline rush you get when you do something dumb with your company file, when your hard drive crashes, or when a plume of smoke wafts up from your computer. To learn how to create or restore backup files, see page 495 or page 501, respectively.

ORGANIZATION STATION

Fast Access to Several Companies

If you work on several sets of company books at the same time, choosing File→Open Previous Company is the quickest way to hop between company files.

Out of the box, QuickBooks lists up to 20 companies on this submenu (it lists them starting with the most recent). If you work with fewer companies, the submenu may have company files that you'd rather forget. You can change the number of companies QuickBooks lists on this submenu to match the number of companies you work with. With a clever workaround, you can also clear out old entries that you don't want to see.

Here's how to change the number of companies on the Open Previous Company submenu:

1. Make sure you have a company file open, and then choose File→Open Previous Company→"Set number of previous companies."
2. In the "Set Number of Previous Companies" dialog box, type the maximum number of companies you want to see on the submenu, and then click OK.
3. To clear old entries off the menu, change the number of entries to 1, and then click OK. After you do so, QuickBooks lists only the most recent company file, clearing all the others off the list.
4. If you want to see more than one company, reset the number of entries again, this time to a higher number. Now, when you open another company file, it will appear on the list.

Opening a Portable Company File

A *portable file* is a special type of file that makes QuickBooks company files compact so you can email them more easily. These files take up less space because they don't contain other files related to your company file, like letters, templates, logos, and images. A portable file also doesn't contain a transaction log (.tlg file), which Intuit Technical Support can use to restore transactions if your file is damaged in some way.

Opening a portable file is similar to opening a regular company file:

1. **Choose File→"Open or Restore Company."**

   The "Open or Restore Company" dialog box opens.

2. **Select the "Restore a portable file" option, and then click Next.**

   The Open Portable Company File dialog box appears. QuickBooks automatically sets the "Files of type" box to "QuickBooks Portable Company Files (*.QBM)."

3. **Navigate to the folder with the portable file and double-click its filename.**

   QuickBooks opens the file.

FREQUENTLY ASKED QUESTION

Updating a QuickBooks File

How do I update a company file to the newest version of QuickBooks?

If you've used a previous version of QuickBooks, your company file is set up to work with that version. When you upgrade to QuickBooks 2015, the program has to make some changes to your company file.

Once you update a company file, your coworkers won't be able to open it until you install QuickBooks 2015 on their computers. So to prevent work disruptions, plan to upgrade all copies of QuickBooks and the company file during downtime.

Fortunately, updating a company file is easy: All you have to do is open it in the new version of QuickBooks and follow the onscreen instructions. Here are the steps:

1. **In your new version of QuickBooks, choose File→"Open or Restore Company."**
2. **In the "Open or Restore Company" dialog box, select the "Open a company file" option, and then click Next.**
3. **In the "Open a Company" dialog box, double-click the company file you want to update.** If you see the User Name and Password box, enter your user name and password.
4. **In the "Update Company File for New Version" dialog box, turn on the "I understand that my company file will be updated to this new version of QuickBooks" checkbox, and then click Update Now.**
5. **Click OK to create a backup before you upgrade.** Follow the steps to create a backup copy of your company file (page 495).
6. **When the Update Company message box appears, click Yes to start the update.** Keep in mind that this process could take a while if your company file is large or if you're updating from several QuickBooks versions back.

Modifying Company Info

When you use Express Start or the EasyStep Interview, QuickBooks gets the basic facts about your company in small chunks spread over several screens. But after you create your company file, you can easily view and edit any of this information. Here's how:

1. **Choose Company→My Company or click the My Company entry in the icon bar (page 30).**

   The My Company window opens. As shown in Figure 1-9 (background), info about your copy of QuickBooks appears on the window's left and your company info appears on the right. Apps, services, and subscriptions that you've signed up for (like accepting credit cards, payroll, and so on) appear below your company info. Other products that Intuit would like to sell you appear at the bottom of the window.

2. **To edit your company info, click the edit icon at the window's top right (it looks like a pencil).**

   The Company Information dialog box opens with your company information grouped into several categories (see Figure 1-9, foreground).

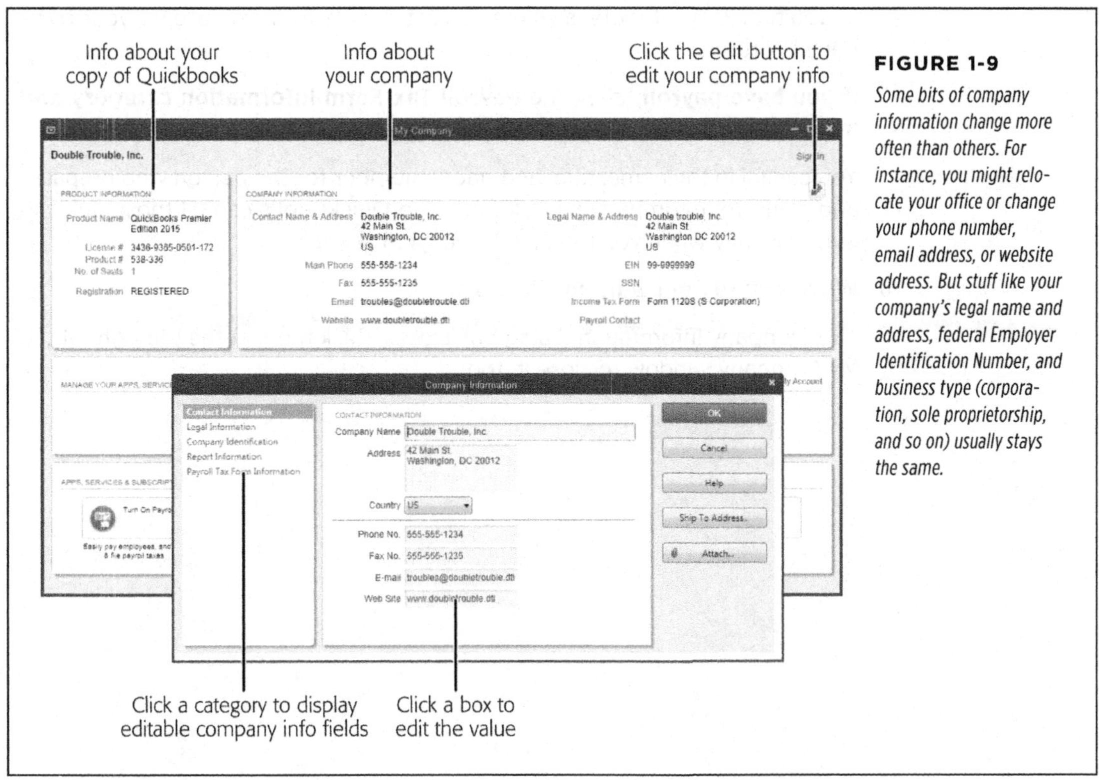
Info about your copy of Quickbooks
Info about your company
Click the edit button to edit your company info
Click a category to display editable company info fields
Click a box to edit the value

FIGURE 1-9

Some bits of company information change more often than others. For instance, you might relocate your office or change your phone number, email address, or website address. But stuff like your company's legal name and address, federal Employer Identification Number, and business type (corporation, sole proprietorship, and so on) usually stays the same.

3. **To edit your company's contact info, in the Company Information dialog box, click the Contact Information category on the left, and then make the changes you want.**

   This category includes fields for your company address, phone number, email address, and website.

4. **To change your company's legal name and address, click the Legal Information category.**

   Remember, your company's legal name and address are the ones you use on federal and state tax forms.

5. **To edit the tax identification number you use, click the Company Identification category.**

   This category includes the federal Employee Identification Number (EIN) and Social Security Number (SSN) fields. Fill in (or edit) the one that you use for your company.

6. **To specify info for reports you generate, click the Report Information category.**

   You can specify the starting month for both your fiscal year and your tax year. In addition, this category is where you set the tax form you use for your company tax return.

7. **If you have payroll, click the Payroll Tax Form Information category and make the changes you want.**

   You can fill in the name, title, and phone number for the person who prepares and signs your company payroll forms, so QuickBooks can fill those fields in automatically when you use an Intuit payroll service.

8. **When you're done editing, click OK.**

   The Company Information dialog box closes. Click the X at the top right of the My Company window to close it, too.

CHAPTER

2

Getting Around in QuickBooks

You have more than enough to do running your business, so you don't want bookkeeping to take any more time than necessary. QuickBooks' icon bar (which comes in two flavors: left and top) offers shortcuts to your favorite features. Each version of the icon bar has its pros and cons, so you have to decide which one you prefer (or you can hide them). This chapter shows you how to access QuickBooks' features from both the menu bar and icon bars.

During a rousing bookkeeping session, you might end up with several QuickBooks windows open at the same time. In this chapter, you learn how to work with all the windows you open. For example, if you prefer to focus on one task, you can tell QuickBooks to display only one window at a time.

Another way to get your accounting done quickly and efficiently is by accessing features via the QuickBooks Home Page. This page not only provides a visual roadmap of the bookkeeping tasks you perform regularly, but it also gives you quick access to tasks and information related to vendors, customers, and employees, along with the features and overall financial info you use most often. Click an icon, and the corresponding window or dialog box appears, such as Chart of Accounts, Item List, Write Checks, or everyone's favorite—Make Deposits.

This chapter explains how to use the workflow icons on the Home Page, as well as the Vendor, Customer, and Employees Centers that open when you click the corresponding buttons in the Home Page's panels. (The Inventory Center, which is available in QuickBooks Premier and Enterprise, is described on page 538.) You'll also see how to review your company's finances in the Company Snapshot window and the Home window's new Insights tab.

Menus and the Icon Bar

The menu bar at the very top of the QuickBooks window (Figure 2-1) is a convenient way to launch different activities. It's handy because it's always visible and serves up every feature the program has to offer.

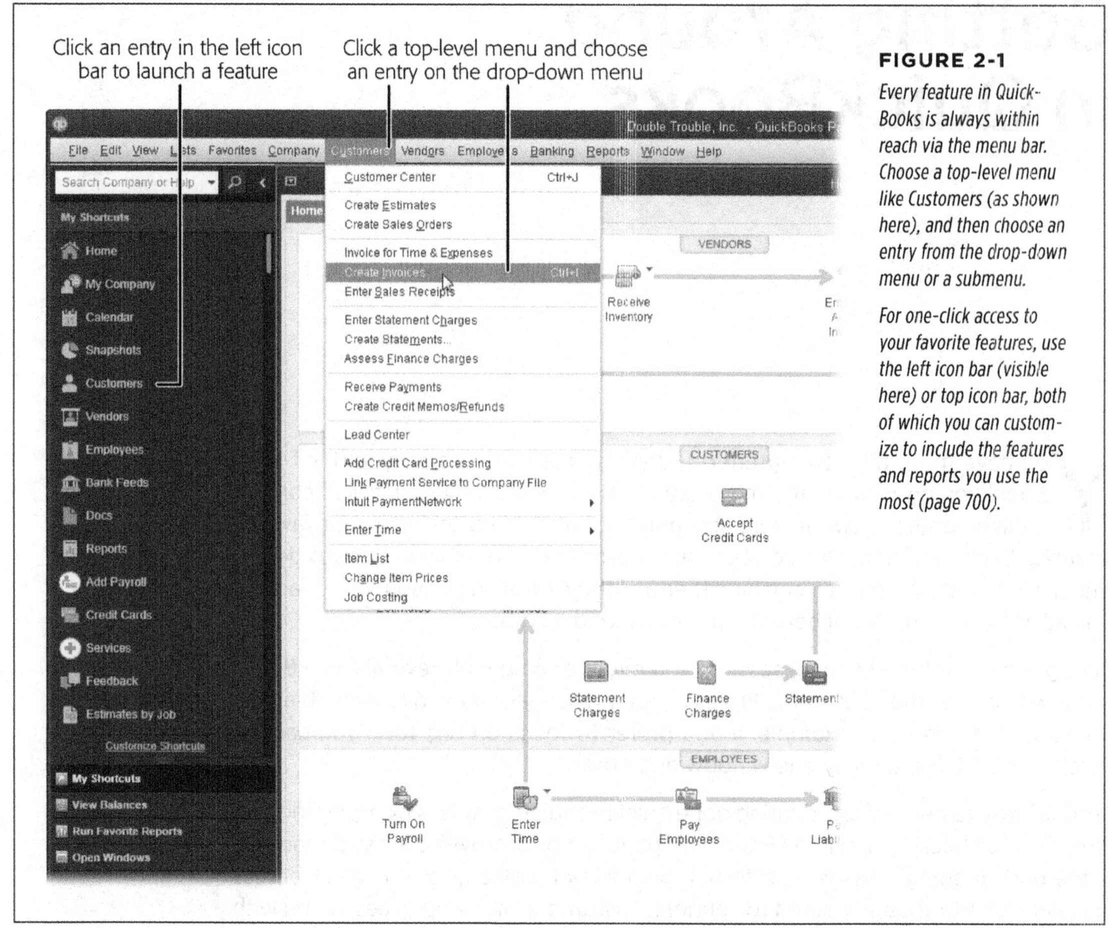

FIGURE 2-1

Every feature in QuickBooks is always within reach via the menu bar. Choose a top-level menu like Customers (as shown here), and then choose an entry from the drop-down menu or a submenu.

For one-click access to your favorite features, use the left icon bar (visible here) or top icon bar, both of which you can customize to include the features and reports you use the most (page 700).

You can use the View menu to choose between two versions of the icon bar: top and left. The top icon bar (View→Top Icon Bar) has been around for years. If you haven't graduated to a large, widescreen monitor, this icon bar is both convenient and space-saving. (If you *really* need more space, you can hide the icon bar by choosing View→Hide Icon Bar.) It sits just below the menu bar and displays your favorite features as icons with brief identifying labels. Click an icon, such as Home, Calendar, or Bill, and the corresponding feature launches.

The left icon bar (View→Left Icon Bar), shown in Figure 2-2, appears the first time you launch QuickBooks 2015. The categories in the middle section of this icon bar determine what's displayed in its top section. Here's what the entries in the middle section of the left icon bar do:

- **My Shortcuts**. This category, which appears at the top of the left icon bar whenever you launch QuickBooks, is a great way to keep your favorite features within easy reach. Out of the box, this category includes features that most people use frequently. But you can add other features *you* use all the time and get rid of shortcuts you *don't* use simply by right-clicking anywhere within the My Shortcuts section (except on the My Shortcuts heading), and then clicking Customize Shortcuts.

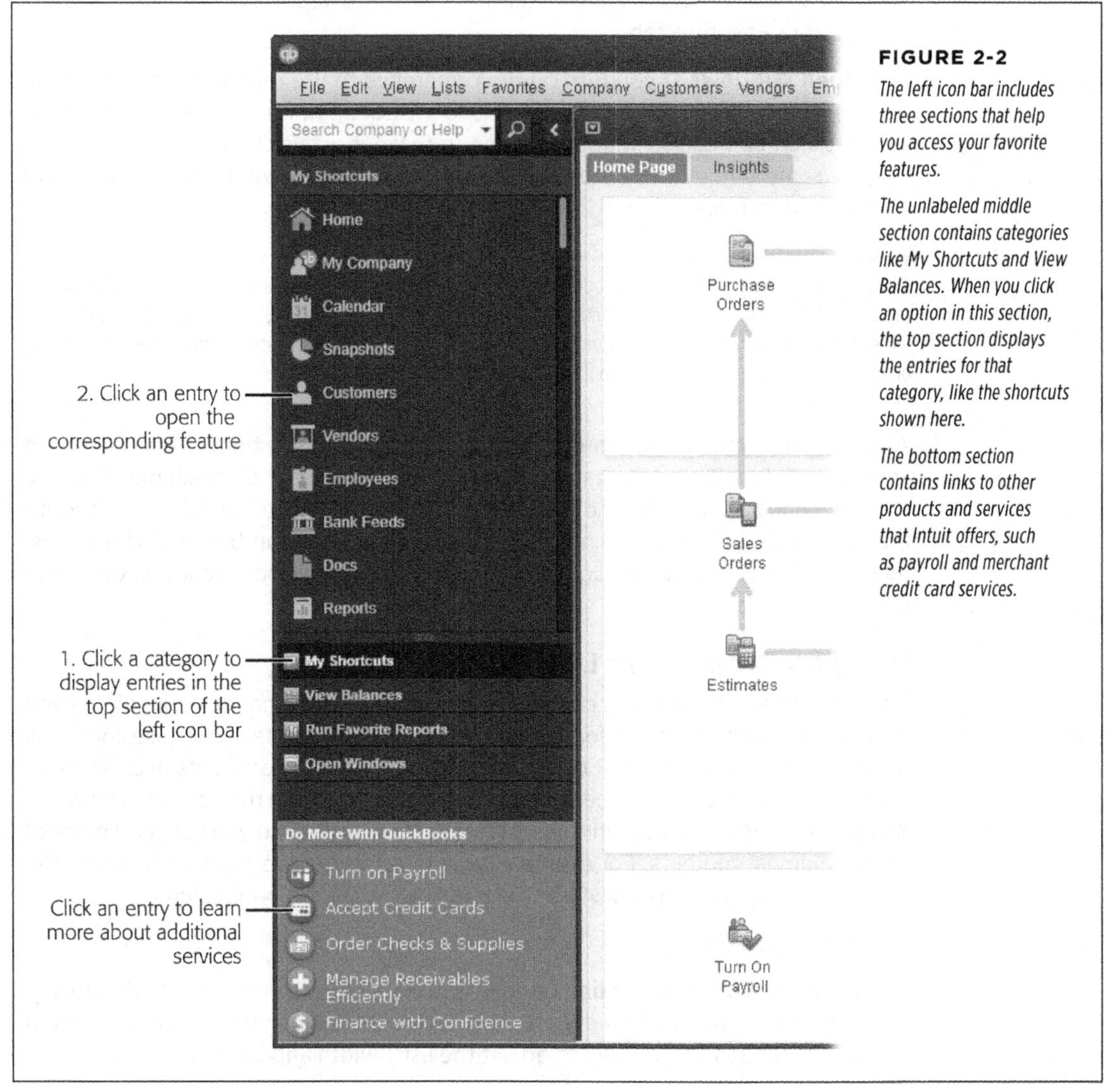

FIGURE 2-2

The left icon bar includes three sections that help you access your favorite features.

The unlabeled middle section contains categories like My Shortcuts and View Balances. When you click an option in this section, the top section displays the entries for that category, like the shortcuts shown here.

The bottom section contains links to other products and services that Intuit offers, such as payroll and merchant credit card services.

NOTE The shortcuts in the My Shortcuts list are the same ones you see as icons if you display the top icon bar.

- **View Balances**. When you use the left icon bar, the Home Page doesn't display account balances on its right side as it does when you use the top icon bar. To see your account balances at the top of the left icon bar, click this category. (Page 699 explains how to customize which account balances you see.)
- **Run Favorite Reports**. Clicking this category lists the reports that you've flagged as your favorites (page 579). The reports you see are the same ones that appear when you choose Reports→Favorite Reports or display the Report Center's Favorites tab.
- **Open Windows**. If you turn on the preference to use multiple windows (page 643), you can click this category to see a list of open windows at the top of the left icon bar. Click a window's name to make it active. This category displays the same windows you see if you choose View→Open Window List when using the top icon bar.

TIP The left icon bar takes up a couple of inches on the left side of the main QuickBooks window, so it's more useful if you have a widescreen monitor. With older and smaller monitors, you'll have trouble fitting the left icon bar and your transaction windows onscreen at the same time. In that case, the menu bar, top icon bar, and Home Page (which you'll learn about in a sec) are ready to assist you.

After shortcut menus (which you display by right-clicking things) and keyboard shortcuts (which you can read about in online Appendix C, available at *www.missingmanuals.com/cds*), the icon bar is the fastest way to launch your favorite features. As page 700 explains, you can customize the icon bar to add features, memorized reports, and windows you open often—and remove features you don't use.

Resizing Drop-Down Lists and Columns

Throughout QuickBooks, you can resize drop-down lists to change their heights and widths. This comes in handy, for example, when you want to see your customers' full names in a Customer:Job List drop-down list or view more accounts in an account drop-down list so you don't have to scroll as much to locate the account you want. You can also resize columns in transaction windows' tables so you can read more of those columns' contents. For example, you might widen the Memo column on the Enter Bills window's Expenses tab while narrowing the Amount column.

Here's what you do:

- **To resize a drop-down list**, open it, and then put your cursor over the dots in the list's lower-right corner (circled in Figure 2-3). When the cursor changes to a two-headed arrow, drag to adjust the list's width and height.

- **To change the widths of columns in a table**, place your cursor over the vertical dots between two column headings (also circled in Figure 2-3), and then drag left or right to shrink or widen the column to the left.

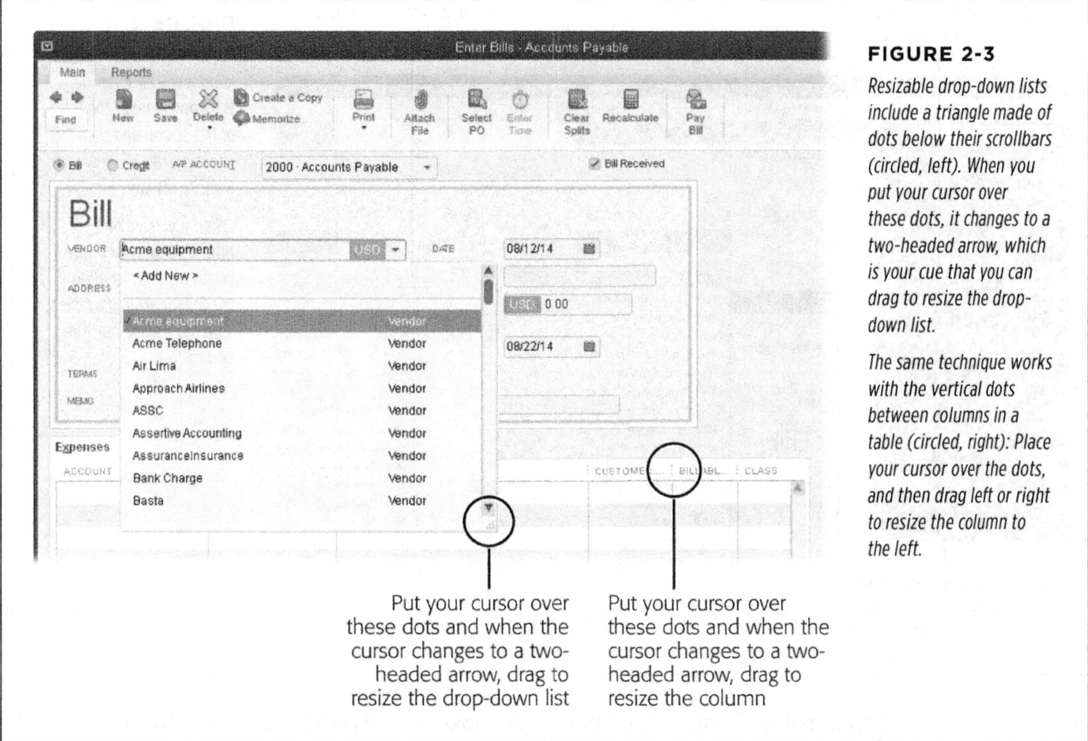
Enter Bills - Accounts Payable
Put your cursor over these dots and when the cursor changes to a two-headed arrow, drag to resize the drop-down list
Put your cursor over these dots and when the cursor changes to a two-headed arrow, drag to resize the column

FIGURE 2-3

Resizable drop-down lists include a triangle made of dots below their scrollbars (circled, left). When you put your cursor over these dots, it changes to a two-headed arrow, which is your cue that you can drag to resize the drop-down list.

The same technique works with the vertical dots between columns in a table (circled, right): Place your cursor over the dots, and then drag left or right to resize the column to the left.

Switching among Open Windows

If you tend to work on one bookkeeping task for hours on end, you can set QuickBooks up to display one full-size window at a time by choosing View→One Window. That way, when you open additional windows, they get stacked on top of one another so you see only the last one you opened.

If you go with the one-window approach, you have several ways to choose the window you want to see:

- In the middle section of the left icon bar, click Open Windows as shown in Figure 2-4. Then, in the top section of the left icon bar, click the name of the window you want.
- If you use the top icon bar, you can see a list of open windows by choosing View→Open Window List. Then, in the list, simply click the name of the window you want to work with.

- On the menu bar, choose Window, and then choose the name of the one you want to see.

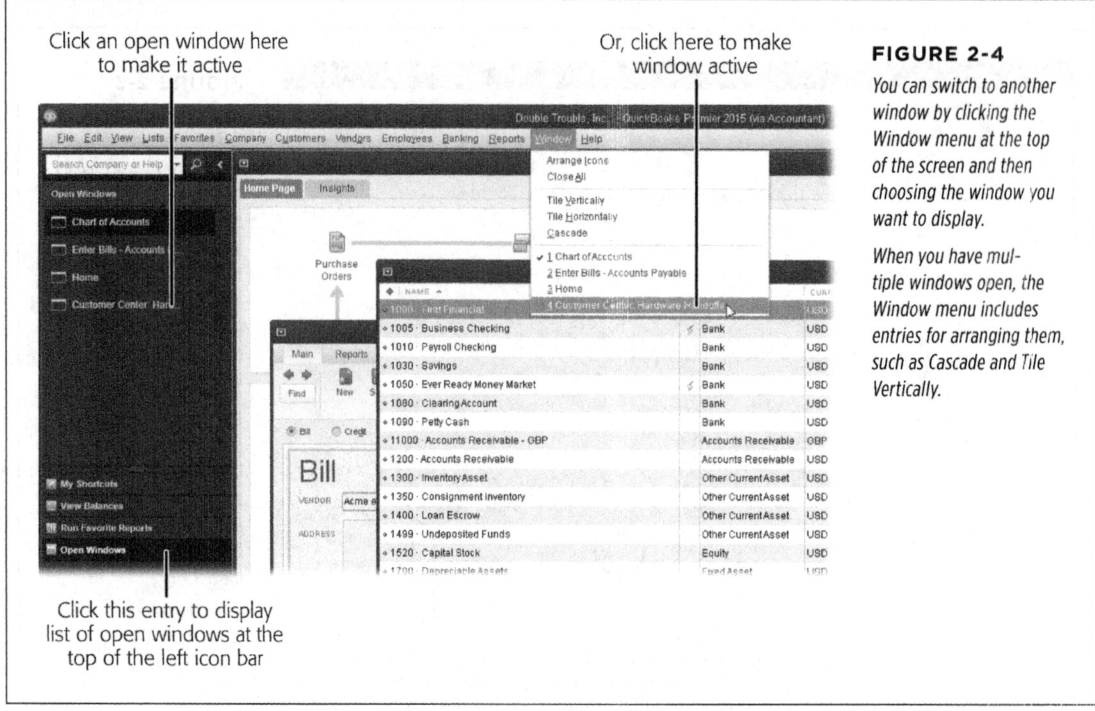
Click an open window here to make it active
Or, click here to make window active
Click this entry to display list of open windows at the top of the left icon bar

FIGURE 2-4

You can switch to another window by clicking the Window menu at the top of the screen and then choosing the window you want to display.

When you have multiple windows open, the Window menu includes entries for arranging them, such as Cascade and Tile Vertically.

If, on the other hand, you flit between bookkeeping tasks like a honeybee in an alfalfa field, you probably want to display several windows at a time. QuickBooks can do that: just choose View→Multiple Windows.

Like windows in other programs, simply click a window to bring it to the front, or use the buttons in its upper right to minimize, maximize, or close it. You can reposition windows by dragging their title bars or resize them by dragging their edges and corners. If the window you want is hidden behind other windows, choose the one you want in the Open Windows List or from the Window menu on the menu bar.

Supermax View

When you want to see as much information as possible in a transaction window, such as Create Invoices, Supermax view, shown in Figure 2-5, is just the ticket. To switch a transaction window to Supermax mode, at the window's top right, click the four-headed arrow.

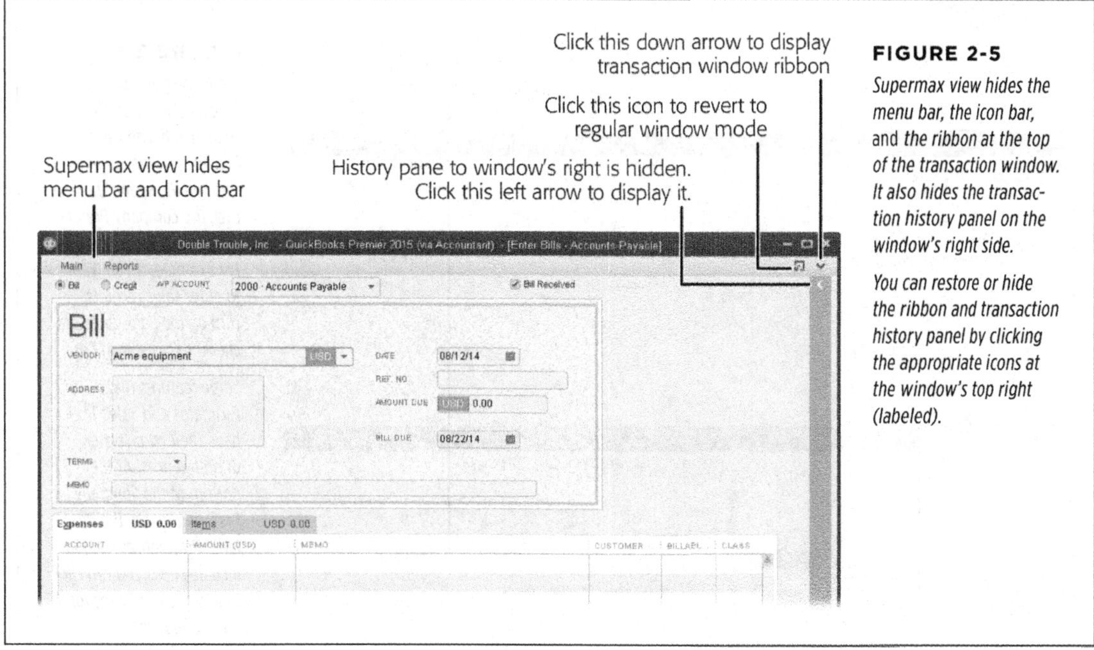
Click this down arrow to display transaction window ribbon
Click this icon to revert to regular window mode
Supermax view hides menu bar and icon bar
History pane to window's right is hidden. Click this left arrow to display it.
Bill

FIGURE 2-5

Supermax view hides the menu bar, the icon bar, and the ribbon at the top of the transaction window. It also hides the transaction history panel on the window's right side.

You can restore or hide the ribbon and transaction history panel by clicking the appropriate icons at the window's top right (labeled).

This view does several things so you can see more of the data-entry lines:

- Hides the QuickBooks menu bar and (if you use it) the icon bar.
- Minimizes the *ribbon* (which is similar to the ribbons in Microsoft programs) at the top of the transaction window.
- Fills the entire QuickBooks window with the transaction window you Supermaxed.
- Hides the transaction history panel on the window's right side.

To revert to regular window mode, click the icon that looks like a square with an arrow pointing to its lower left (labeled in Figure 2-5). When you revert to regular window mode, the menu bar, icon bar, and feature panel at the top of the transaction window all reappear.

The Home Page

The QuickBooks Home Page (Figure 2-6, background) is a slick way to work through your company's bookkeeping tasks in the right order. (If it isn't visible, display it by choosing Company→Home Page or clicking Home in the left icon bar's My Shortcuts section.) This section explains how to use the Home Page to best advantage.

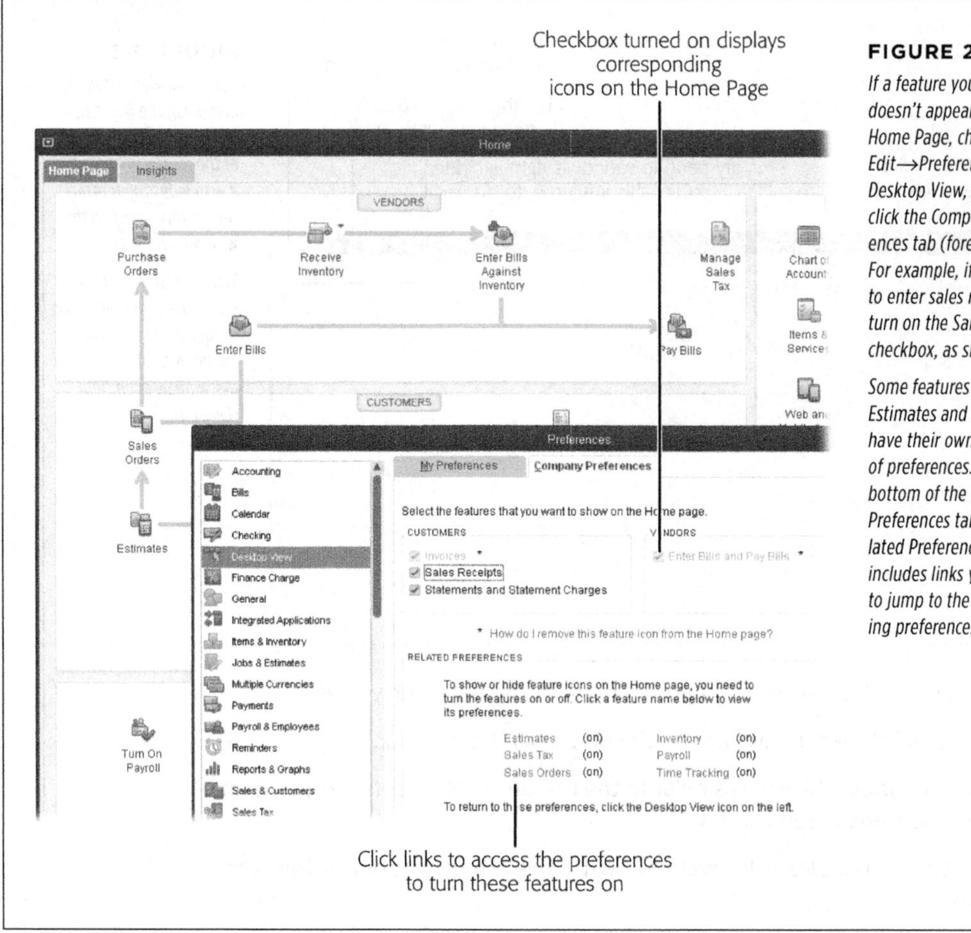
Checkbox turned on displays corresponding icons on the Home Page
Click links to access the preferences to turn these features on

FIGURE 2-6

If a feature you use doesn't appear on the Home Page, choose Edit→Preferences→Desktop View, and then click the Company Preferences tab (foreground). For example, if you want to enter sales receipts, turn on the Sales Receipts checkbox, as shown here.

Some features (like Estimates and Sales Tax) have their own section of preferences. At the bottom of the Company Preferences tab, the Related Preferences section includes links you can click to jump to the corresponding preferences.

The settings you chose when you created your company file determine what initially appears on the Home Page. Depending on your choices, you'll see several *panels*—Vendors, Customers, Employees, Company, and Banking—that each contain various icons. For example, if you told QuickBooks that you invoice customers and send statements, the Customers panel includes icons for invoicing and preparing statements. Or if you run a one-person shop with no employees, you won't see the Employees panel.

NOTE In Figure 2-6, the Invoices and "Enter Bills and Pay Bills" checkboxes are grayed out. That's because QuickBooks turns on some settings automatically based on other settings you chose. For example, if you turn on the estimates feature (as in Figure 2-6), the program automatically turns on invoices, because you can convert estimates you create into invoices.

The Home Page also has icons for other important features, like the Chart of Accounts icon in the Company panel, which opens the Chart of Accounts window, and the Check Register icon in the Banking panel, which opens an account register window for the bank account you select.

TIP The Home Page appears each time you log into a company file. If you prefer to keep the Home Page hidden, choose Edit→Preferences→Desktop View, click the My Preferences tab, and then turn off the "Show Home page when opening a company file" checkbox. After that, when you want to see the Home Page, simply choose Company→Home Page.

Vendors, customers, and employees each have their own panel on the Home Page, and the various arrows show how bookkeeping tasks fit together so you can follow your money from start to finish. The bookkeeping tasks for each group are laid out like breadcrumbs you can follow. However, each company is different, so you don't *have* to use every icon you see. This section outlines the tasks you can perform from each panel and where to find detailed instructions elsewhere in this book.

Vendors

Whether you purchase products and services to run your company or to sell to your customers, the Home Page's Vendors panel steps you through purchasing and paying for those goods and services; these steps are described in detail in Chapter 9.

The Vendor Center (Figure 2-7) is the best place to create, edit, and view what's going on with your vendors and vendor-related transactions. To open it, click the Vendors button at the top of the Home Page's Vendors panel or choose Vendors→Vendor Center. Here's what you can do there:

- **Create a new vendor**. In the Vendor Center toolbar at the top of the window, click New Vendor→New Vendor and the New Vendor window opens so you can create a new vendor record, as described on page 84. If you click New Vendor→Add Multiple Vendors instead, QuickBooks lets you create *several* vendors in one window (page 127).
- **Find a vendor**. If you have a bazillion vendors, you can shorten the vendor list that you see in the Vendors tab on the window's left side. The tab's unlabeled drop-down list is initially set to Active Vendors. If you want to see active and inactive vendors alike, click the field and choose All Vendors instead. If you'd rather see only the vendors you owe money to, choose "Vendors with Open Balances." Choose Custom Filter to specify exactly the criteria you want.

  To do a quick search of vendor records, type part of a vendor's name in the Vendors tab's *second* unlabeled box, and then click the Find button, which has a magnifying glass on it. (The Find button then changes to an X, which you can click to clear the value in the Find box and redisplay the full list.)
- **Review a vendor's record**. When you select a vendor on the Vendors tab, basic info about that vendor appears at the window's top right, as shown in Figure 2-7.

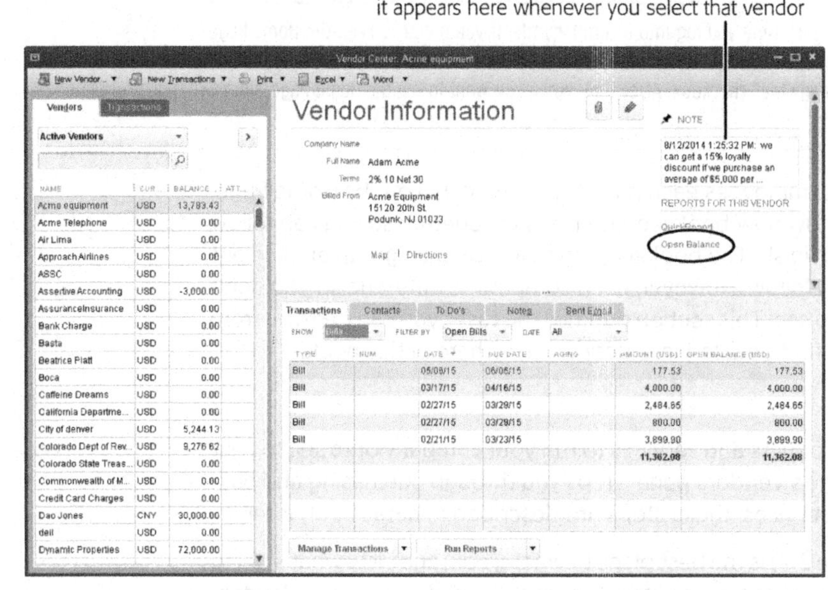
In QuickBooks, you can pin a vendor note so it appears here whenever you select that vendor
Vendor Information

FIGURE 2-7

The Vendor Center puts all vendor-related tasks in a single window. When you choose a vendor in the list on the left, the Vendor Information pane on the right displays info about that vendor. Click the Open Balance link (circled) to see the transactions that contribute to your balance with that vendor. You can even click the Map or Directions link to find out how to get to your vendor. And new in QuickBooks 2015, you can pin a note (page 481) you created in a vendor's record so it appears at the Vendor Information pane's top right, as shown here.

- **Edit an existing vendor's record**. To change a vendor's record, on the Vendors tab, right-click the vendor's name, and then choose Edit Vendor; or, on the right side of the Vendor Center, click the Edit button (its icon looks like a pencil tip). Either way, the Edit Vendor window opens with the same fields you filled in when you created the vendor's record (page 84).
- **Attach an electronic document to a vendor record**. Page 314 explains how to add attachments to a vendor's record.
- **Create transactions for a vendor**. In the Vendor Center toolbar, click New Transactions to display a drop-down menu of vendor-related features like Enter Bills, Pay Bills, and Receive Items. (These do the same thing as the icons in the Home Page's Vendors panel.) If you need to review and record several transactions for the same vendor, this drop-down menu is a real timesaver. After you select the vendor in the Vendors tab and then choose an entry on this drop-down menu, the corresponding transaction window opens with that vendor already selected.
- **Review and manage transactions, contacts, to-dos, notes, and emails for a vendor**. When the Vendors tab is displayed, the bottom-right part of the Vendor Center displays tabs for transactions, contacts, to-dos, notes, and sent email.

When you select a vendor in the Vendors tab, the Transactions tab at the bottom right of the Vendor Center lists that vendor's transactions. By filtering these transactions, you can find out which purchase orders are still open, whether any bills are overdue, and what payments you've made. To see a specific kind of transaction, in the Show drop-down list, choose a type, like Bills or Bill Payments. The Filter By drop-down list lets you restrict the transactions in the table by their status, such as Open Bills or Overdue Bills. To track down transactions within a specific date range, choose an option from the Date drop-down list. (The options in this menu are the same as the ones available in report windows; see page 591.)

TIP To view a transaction in its corresponding window, double-click it in the Transactions tab's table.

Click the Contacts, To Do's, Notes, or Sent Email tab to create, edit, or view contacts, to-dos, notes, or sent email for the selected vendor.

- **Review transactions for *all* vendors**. When you click the Transactions tab on the left side of the window (*not* the bottom right) and then click a type of transaction, such as Bills or Bill Payments, you'll see transactions of that type for all vendors on the right side of the window. You can filter these transactions by status (such as open or overdue), by date, and, if you use multiple currencies, by currency.
- **Print or export vendor information**. When you click the Vendors tab on the left side of the window, you can easily print, copy, import, or export vendor info. In the Vendor Center toolbar, click Print to print vendor lists, vendor info, or vendor transactions. Click Excel to paste, import, or export vendor info and transactions (page 133). If you click the Transactions tab on the left side of the window instead, you can print or export *transactions*.
- **Prepare vendor letters**. When the Vendors tab on the left side of the window is selected, click Word in the Vendor Center toolbar to create letters to vendors (page 672).

Customers

The Home Page's Customers panel has icons for creating customer-oriented features like invoices, statements, sales receipts, and so on. (Chapter 10 describes how to work with invoices, estimates, sales orders, refunds, and customer credits. Chapter 11 covers creating statement charges and statements. And Chapter 13 explains how to receive payments and create sales receipts for cash sales.) Click the Customers button at the top of the panel (or choose Customers→Customer Center) to open the Customer Center (Figure 2-8), where you can perform the following tasks:

- **Create a new customer or job**. In the Customer Center toolbar at the top of the window, click New Customer & Job. In the drop-down menu, choose New Customer to create a new customer record (page 70), or choose Add Multiple Customer:Jobs to add *several* customers.

- **Add a job to an existing customer.** Select the customer in the Customers & Jobs tab on the left side of the Customer Center, and then click New Customer & Job→Add Job (page 81).
- **Find a customer**. You can filter the list in the Customers & Jobs tab to show active customers, only customers who owe you money (customers with open balances), and so on, simply by choosing an option in the tab's unlabeled drop-down list (it's initially set to Active Customers). Choose Custom Filter to specify criteria for the customers you want to see. To search for a specific customer, type part of the customer's name in the tab's second unlabeled box, and then click the Find button (it has a magnifying glass on it). The Find button then changes to an X, which you can click to clear the value in the Find box and redisplay the complete list.
- **Review a customer or job record**. When you select a customer or job in the Customers & Jobs tab, the right side of the center displays the basic 411 about that customer or job. In the Customer Information (or Job Information) section, shown in Figure 2-8, you can get directions to its location, look at key information like the customer's or job's open balance, attach electronic documents to the record, or run reports about the customer or job.

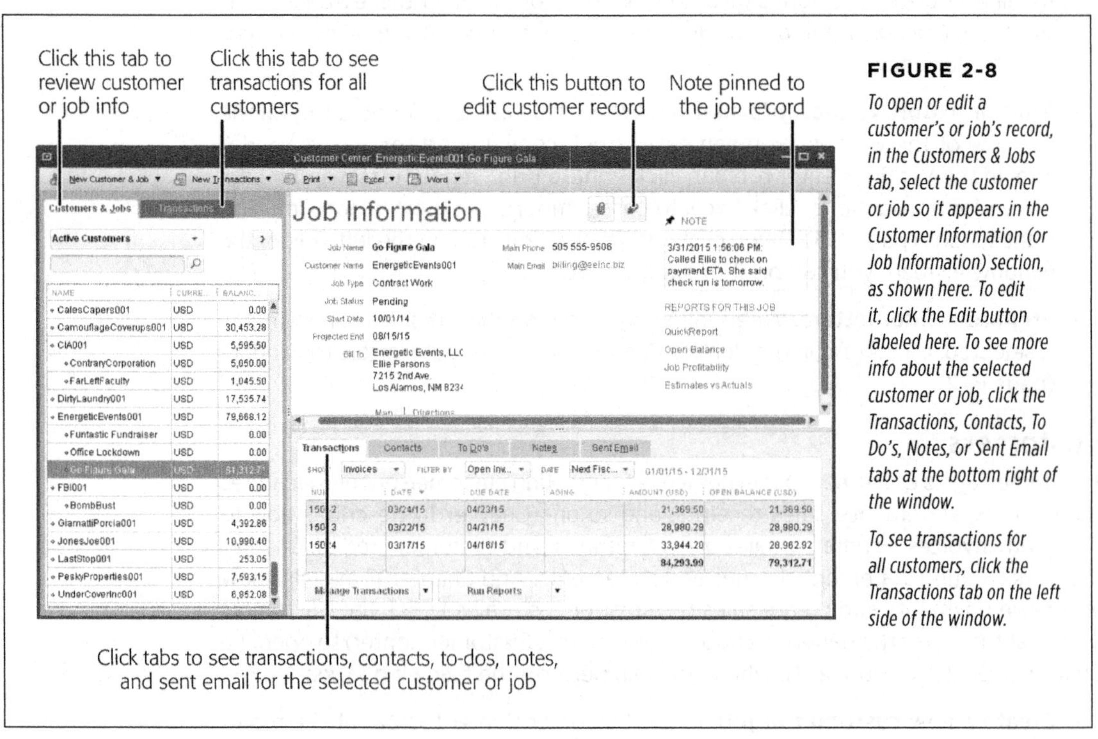
Click this tab to review customer or job info
Click this tab to see transactions for all customers
Click this button to edit customer record
Note pinned to the job record
Job Information
Click tabs to see transactions, contacts, to-dos, notes, and sent email for the selected customer or job

FIGURE 2-8

To open or edit a customer's or job's record, in the Customers & Jobs tab, select the customer or job so it appears in the Customer Information (or Job Information) section, as shown here. To edit it, click the Edit button labeled here. To see more info about the selected customer or job, click the Transactions, Contacts, To Do's, Notes, or Sent Email tabs at the bottom right of the window.

To see transactions for all customers, click the Transactions tab on the left side of the window.

- **Review a customer's or job's status**. Suppose you want to look at a bar graph of sales you've made to a customer by time period, review the items that customer buys the most, and then scan a customer's recent invoices and payments. First, select the customer in the Customers & Jobs tab. Then, on the right side of the Customer Center, click the Customer Snapshot link to open the Company Snapshot window (page 43) to the Customer tab.
- **Edit a customer or job**. To open the Edit Customer or Edit Job window, in the Customers & Jobs tab, right-click a customer's or job's name, and then choose Edit Customer or Edit Job, respectively. Or select a customer or job, and then click the Edit button labeled in Figure 2-8.
- **Attach an electronic document to a customer's or job's record**. You can add attachments to a customer's or job's record or scan images of them into QuickBooks, as described on page 314.
- **Create transactions for a customer or job**. If you're reviewing a customer's or job's transactions and realize you forgot to record an invoice or other transaction, you can easily create transactions right from the Customer Center window. Select the customer or job on the Customers & Jobs tab and then, in the window's toolbar, click New Transactions and choose a transaction type from the drop-down menu, such as Estimates, Invoices, or Receive Payments. The items in this menu are the same as the icons in the Home Page's Customers panel and open the corresponding window to record that type of transaction.
- **Review and manage transactions, contacts, to-dos, notes, and emails for a customer or job**. When the Customers & Jobs tab is displayed on the left side of the window, the bottom right of the Customer Center includes tabs for transactions, contacts, to-dos, notes, and sent emails. If you click the Transactions tab at the bottom right of the window, you'll see a table with the transactions for the customer or job you selected in the Customers & Jobs tab. You can filter these transactions by type (estimates or invoices, for example), status, and date. Double-click a transaction in the list to open a window with details about it. Click the Contacts, To Do's, Notes, or Sent Email tabs to create, edit, or view contacts, to-dos, notes, or emails for the selected customer.
- **Review transactions for *all* customers**. When you click the Transactions tab on the left side of the window and then click a type of transaction (such as Estimate, Invoices, or Received Payments), the right side of the window displays transactions of that type for all customers. Depending on the type you choose, you can filter these transactions by status (such as open or overdue), payment method, date, and—if you use multiple currencies—currency.
- **Print or export customer information**. When you click the Customers & Jobs tab on the left side of the window, you can print, copy, import, or export customer info. In the center's toolbar, click Print to print customer information (page 158) or click Excel to import or export customer and job info (page 133). If you click the Transactions tab on the left side of the window instead, you can print or export customer *transactions*.

- **Prepare customer letters**. In the Customer Center toolbar, click Word to create letters to customers (page 672).

Employees

The Home Page's Employees panel has only a few icons. The devilish details arise when you click one of these icons to enter time, set up paychecks, or pay payroll tax liabilities. The Employee Center works the same way as the Vendor and Customer centers you just learned about. To open it, click the Employees button at the top of the panel on the Home Page or choose Employees→Employee Center.

In the Employee Center, you can create new records for employees, update info for existing employees, and view transactions like paychecks. On the Employees tab on the left side of the center, you can filter the list to view active employees, released employees (ones who no longer work for you), or all employees. See Chapter 8 to learn how to record the time that employees work. And online Appendix D (available at *www.missingmanuals.com/cds*) covers the process of paying employees and other payroll expenses.

Company Features

The Company panel is on the right side of the Home Page. The two icons in this panel that you'll probably click most often are Chart of Accounts and Items & Services, which open the Chart of Accounts (page 56) and Item List (page 106) windows, respectively. Click Calendar to review transactions and to-dos in the Calendar window (page 486).

If you track inventory, click the Inventory Activities icon and then choose a feature, such as Adjust Quantity/Value On Hand, which lets you change the quantity and value of your inventory (page 542). If you use QuickBooks Premier or Enterprise, click Inventory Center to open a window similar to the Customer Center except that it focuses on the status of—and transactions involving—your inventory items (page 538). If you're interested in other apps and services that Intuit has to offer, click the "Web and Mobile Apps" icon, and a browser window opens to Intuit's App Center.

Banking

The Home Page's Banking panel is a one-stop shop for banking tasks. Whether you visit this panel frequently or rarely depends on how you like to record transactions. For example, you can click the Write Checks icon to open the Write Checks window (page 202) or simply press Ctrl+W to do the same thing. (Or, if you like to record checks in a check register window, you might prefer to click the Check Register icon instead.) Similarly, clicking the Enter Credit Card Charges icon opens the Enter Credit Card Charges window (page 213), though you can also record credit card charges directly in a credit card account's register (page 374).

Clicking the Record Deposits icon opens the "Payments to Deposit" window so you can record bank deposits (page 368). The Reconcile icon opens the Begin Reconciliation dialog box so you can reconcile your QuickBooks records to your bank statement (page 389). And the Print Checks icon opens the "Select Checks to

Print" dialog box so you can choose the ones you want to print and send them to a printer loaded with blank checks.

NOTE If you use the left icon bar (View→Left Icon Bar), you can see account balances by clicking View Balances in the icon bar's middle section. (See page 30 for more about the icon bar.)

If you use the top icon bar (View→Top Icon Bar), the top-right part of the Home Page shows account balances. Below those is a "Do More with QuickBooks" section that includes a few links to additional services that Intuit offers. You also see a Backup Status section that tells you when your last backup ran and includes info about the Intuit Data Protect backup service (page 497). If any of these sections are collapsed, click the section's down arrow to expand it. Click a section's up arrow to collapse it.

The Company Snapshot

The Company Snapshot window (Figure 2-9) is a dashboard that shows important aspects of your company's financial state, like account balances, income breakdown (by top-level income accounts), customers who owe you money, best-selling items, and reminders. To open this window, choose Company→Company Snapshot or click the Snapshots icon in either icon bar. You can choose from 12 different views (page 705) to see the information you care most about.

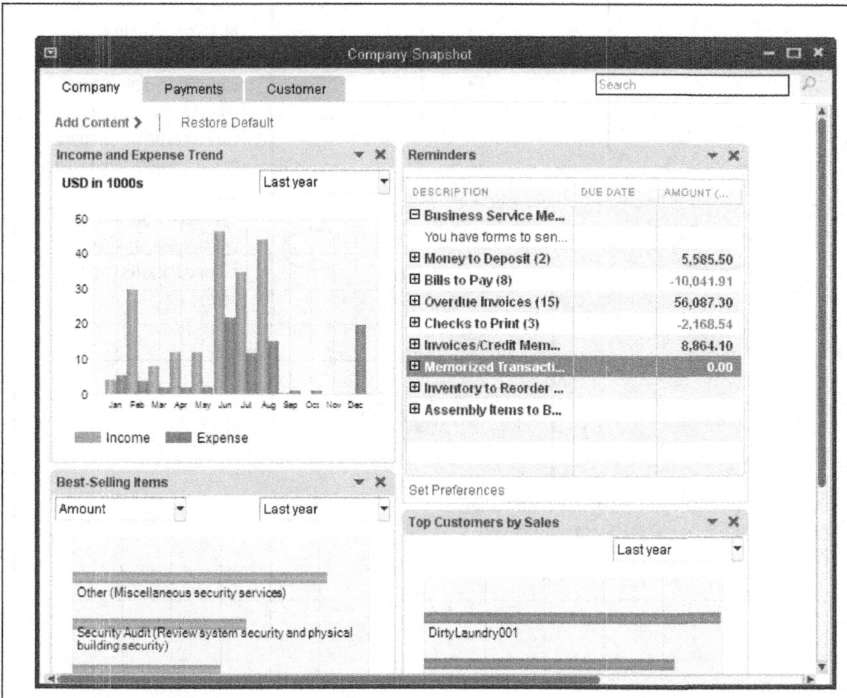

FIGURE 2-9

Not only can you quickly scan your company's financial status in this window, but you can also double-click entries here to dig into the details.

You can even add or remove items from this window or drag items to rearrange them, as described on page 706.

The Insights Tab

In QuickBooks 2015, the Home window has two tabs at its top left. Clicking the Home Page tab displays the Home Page described on page 35. If you click the new Insights tab, you'll see a dashboard that provides a 50,000-foot view of your company's financial status (Figure 2-10). You can change date ranges and click various parts of the dashboard to get a closer look:

- **Graphs**. Initially, the tab's top panel displays a Profit & Loss graph in which monthly income is represented by green bars above the horizontal axis and monthly expenses appear in blue below the axis. The black line hopping from month to month is your monthly profit. To change the graph's date range, choose the range you want from the drop-down list at the graph's top left. To view other graphs, click the left and right arrows on either side of the top panel.

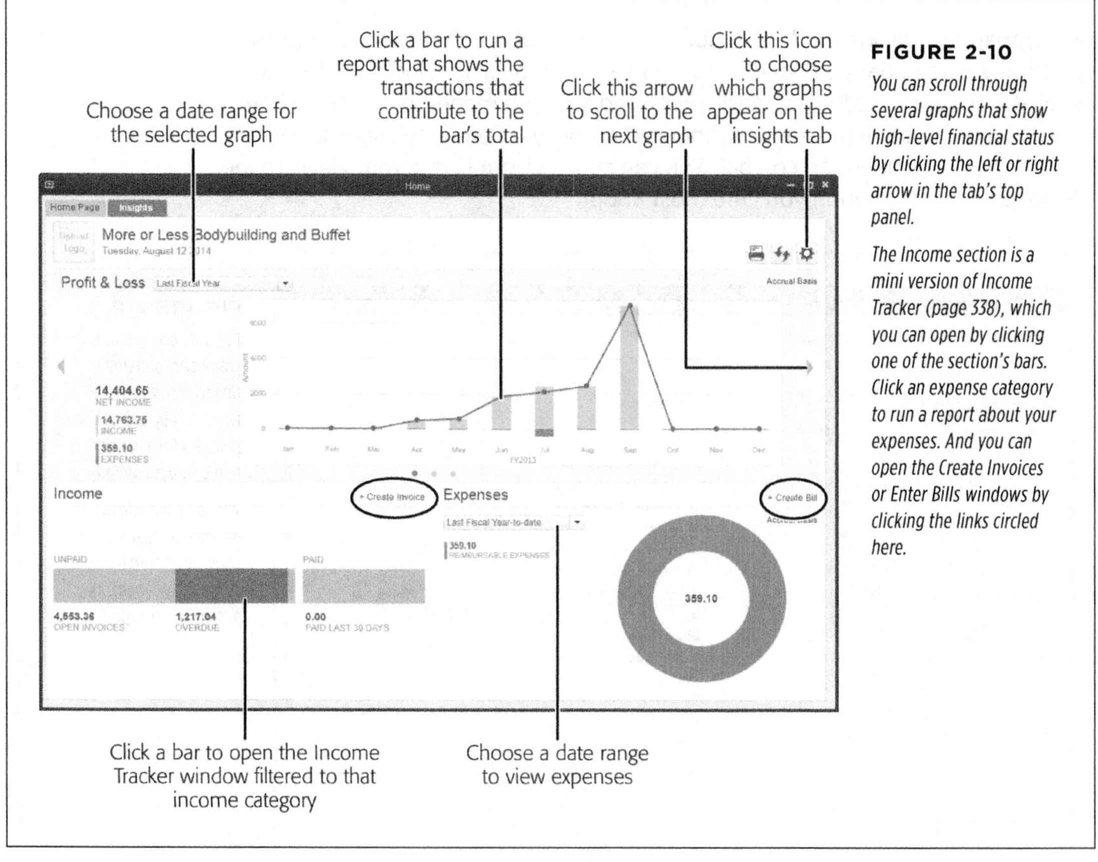
Choose a date range for the selected graph
Click a bar to run a report that shows the transactions that contribute to the bar's total
Click this arrow to scroll to the next graph
Click this icon to choose which graphs appear on the insights tab
Home
Home Page
Insights
More or Less Bodybuilding and Buffet
Profit & Loss
Last Fiscal Year
Accrual Basis
14,404.65
NET INCOME
14,763.75
INCOME
359.10
EXPENSES
Income
+ Create Invoice
Expenses
+ Create Bill
Last Fiscal Year-to-date
359.10
UNPAID
PAID
4,553.36
OPEN INVOICES
1,217.04
OVERDUE
0.00
PAID LAST 30 DAYS
Click a bar to open the Income Tracker window filtered to that income category
Choose a date range to view expenses

FIGURE 2-10

You can scroll through several graphs that show high-level financial status by clicking the left or right arrow in the tab's top panel.

The Income section is a mini version of Income Tracker (page 338), which you can open by clicking one of the section's bars. Click an expense category to run a report about your expenses. And you can open the Create Invoices or Enter Bills windows by clicking the links circled here.

TIP To choose which graphs appear in the top panel, click the Customize icon (it looks like a gear) at the tab's top right. In the "What do you want to see?" drop-down menu, turn view checkboxes on or off to show or hide them, respectively. For example, the other graphs you can choose are Previous Year Income Comparison, "Top Customers by Sales," and "Income and Expense Trend."

- **Income**. This section at the tab's bottom left looks like the bars in the Income Tracker window—and for good reason. After you scan the open and overdue invoice totals, you can click one of these bars to open Income Tracker, already filtered to show the income category you clicked. For example, if you click the red Overdue bar, Income Tracker opens and lists your customers' overdue invoices.
- **Expenses**. The Expenses section in the tab's bottom right shows where you spend the most money. Choose a date range in the drop-down list to display expenses for that period. To view the transactions that contribute to expense totals, click an expense category in the Expenses list or click the corresponding section of the pie chart.

CHAPTER

3

Setting Up a Chart of Accounts

If you've just started running a business and keeping your company's books, all this talk of accounts, credits, and debits might have you flummoxed. Accounting is a cross between mathematics and the mystical arts; its goal is to record and report the financial performance of an organization. The end result of bookkeeping and accounting is a set of financial statements (page 443), but the starting point is the chart of accounts.

In accounting, an *account* is more than a real-world account you have at a financial institution; it's like a bucket for holding money used for a specific purpose. When you earn money, you document those earnings in an income account, just as you might toss the change from a day's take at the lemonade stand into the jar on your desk. When you buy supplies for your business, that expense shows up in an expense account that works a lot like the shoebox you throw receipts into. If you buy a building, its value ends up in an asset account. And if you borrow money to buy that building, the mortgage owed shows up in a liability account.

Accounts come in a variety of types to reflect whether you've earned or spent money, whether you own something or owe money to someone else, as well as a few other financial situations. Your *chart of accounts* is a list of all the accounts you use to track money in your business.

Neophytes and experienced business folks alike will be relieved to know that you don't have to build a chart of accounts from scratch in QuickBooks. This chapter explains how to get a ready-made chart of accounts for your business and what to do with it once you've got it. If you want to add or modify accounts in your chart of accounts, you'll learn how to do that, too.

NOTE Industry-specific Premier editions of QuickBooks include a chart of accounts, an Item List, Payroll items, and preferences already tuned to your industry (such as construction, manufacturing, nonprofit, professional services, or retail). The industry-specific editions also have features unique to each industry, like the Contractor edition's enhanced job costing. These features may save you time during setup and in your day-to-day bookkeeping, but you have to decide whether you want to spend a few hundred dollars more than the QuickBooks Pro price tag to get them.

Acquiring a Chart of Accounts

When you create a new QuickBooks company file and choose an industry (page 11), the program automatically sets up the chart of accounts with accounts that are typical for that industry. For example, if you choose a product-oriented industry, you'll see an income account for product or parts income, while a service-oriented business gets an income account for service or labor income. If your company is like many small businesses, the chart of accounts that QuickBooks creates includes everything you need.

However, if you want to customize your chart of accounts to mirror your company's needs, the easiest—although probably not the cheapest—way to get a chart of accounts is from your accountant. Accountants understand the accounting guidelines set by the Financial Accounting Standards Board (FASB—pronounced "faz bee"), a private-sector organization that sets standards with the SEC's blessing. When your accountant builds a QuickBooks chart of accounts for you, you can be reasonably sure that it includes all the accounts you need to track your business and that those accounts conform to accounting standards. If you're a business owner and want a specific account or want to see your business financials in a particular way, ask your accountant what type of accounts to use and how to set them up.

NOTE Don't worry—getting an accountant to build a chart of accounts for you probably won't bust your budget, since the accountant won't start from scratch. Many financial professionals maintain spreadsheets of accounts and build a chart of accounts by importing a customized account list into QuickBooks. Or they may keep QuickBooks company files around to use as templates for new ones.

If you don't want to pay an accountant to create a chart of accounts for you, how about finding one built by experts and available at no charge? A quick search on the Web for "QuickBooks chart of accounts" returns links to sites with predefined charts of accounts. For example, in the not-for-profit world, the National Center for Charitable Statistics website includes downloadable QuickBooks files that contain the Unified Chart of Accounts for nonprofits (known as the UCOA); see *http://nccs.urban.org/projects/ucoa.cfm*. You can download a QuickBooks backup file of a nonprofit company file, complete with a chart of accounts (see page 501 to learn how to restore a backup file), an .iif file that you can import into QuickBooks, or a backup file for the Mac version of QuickBooks.

NOTE If you have an Excel spreadsheet with your company account information, you can import that info directly into your company file. Page 133 has the full story on importing from Excel.

If you run a restaurant, you can go to *www.rrgconsulting.com/restaurant_coa.htm* and download a free .iif file with a restaurant-oriented chart of accounts that you can import into QuickBooks, as explained in the next section.

Importing a Chart of Accounts

If you download an .iif file with a chart of accounts, you can import that file into a QuickBooks company file. Because you're importing a chart of accounts, you want to create your company file with basic info about your company and as few accounts as possible in the chart of accounts list. Here's how you create a QuickBooks company file with bare-bones information and then import a chart of accounts from an .iif file:

1. **Choose File→New Company and then, in the QuickBooks Setup dialog box that appears, click Express Start.**

   If you see a screen that asks for your email address and password, enter the email address and password for your Intuit account, and then click Continue.

2. **On the "Tell us about your business" screen, enter your company's name, type, and tax ID. In the Industry box, enter *Other/None*, and then click Continue.**

3. **On the "Enter your business contact information" screen, do just that.**

   See Chapter 1 for details. If you click Preview Your Settings and then click the Chart of Accounts tab, you see that the accounts list is empty, which is what you want. Click OK to close the preview window.

4. **After you finish filling in your contact info, click Create Company File.**

   QuickBooks creates your company file and then displays the "You've got a company file! Now add your info" screen in the QuickBooks Setup dialog box.

5. **To close the QuickBooks Setup dialog box, click Start Working, and then click the X at the top right of the Quick Start Center window that appears.**

   You can also close the QuickBooks Setup dialog box by clicking the X at the window's upper right.

6. **Choose File→Utilities→Import→IIF Files.**

   QuickBooks opens the Import dialog box to the folder where you stored your company file and sets the "Files of type" box to "IIF Files (*.IIF)."

7. **Navigate to the folder that contains the .iif file you want to import, select the file, and then click Open.**

   A message box appears that shows how the import is progressing. If all goes well, QuickBooks then displays a message box that tells you that it imported the data successfully; click OK.

If QuickBooks runs into problems with the data in the .iif file, it tells you that it didn't import the data successfully. In that case, you have to open the .iif file in a text editor or Excel and correct the account info. (You can see what information QuickBooks expects by *exporting* an account list, as described on page 685.)

To admire your new chart of accounts, in the QuickBooks Home Page's Company panel, click Chart of Accounts (or press Ctrl+A). Now that your chart of accounts is in place, you can add more accounts, hide accounts you don't need, merge accounts, or edit the accounts on the list. The rest of this chapter explains how to do all these things.

Planning the Chart of Accounts

A chart of accounts is a tool for tracking your company's finances at a relatively high level—it helps you produce financial statements and prepare your business tax returns. When setting up your chart of accounts, bear in mind that it will be easier to work with if you keep the number of accounts to a minimum. (The published income statements of even ginormous global corporations typically fit on a single page.) This section helps you figure out which accounts you need and provides guidelines for naming and numbering them.

Do You Need Another Account?

QuickBooks offers several features—including items, jobs, and classes—that can provide details about your company's performance without you having to add additional accounts. So before you create an account, think about whether another feature can track the information you want instead. Here's a brief description of what each feature does and when to use it:

- **Accounts**. When you create transactions in QuickBooks, the program allocates money to accounts in your chart of accounts. Then, when you run a Profit & Loss report (page 448), you see financial results by account. So create a new account if you want to see a particular pool of money broken out in your financial reports. For example, add an income account for services you're offering in addition to your product sales.

NOTE *Subaccounts* (page 58) are an option if you want to break one category into several smaller pieces, such as divvying up travel expenses into airfare, lodging, transportation, and meals.

- **Items**. In QuickBooks, items track details about what you buy and sell. For example, you might create dozens of items for each specific service you provide, such as cutting down trees, cutting logs, chipping wood, splitting wood, and hauling trash. However, each of those items can be assigned to the same services income account. Chapter 5 provides the full story on items.

- **Jobs**. If you work on different projects for the same customer, you can create separate jobs for each project (page 81). That way, you can assign invoices to specific jobs and track income by job. You can also track job expenses by making items, time, or other expenses billable to specific jobs.
- **Classes**. If your business is broken into segments—such as regions, business units, or partners in a partnership—you can turn to classes (page 140). You can assign a class to each transaction, such as an invoice or bill, which lets you track income and expenses across accounts, customers, vendors, and more. For example, if you create a class for each business unit in your company, you can assign the appropriate class to each transaction you record. Then a Profit & Loss by Class report (page 451) will produce an income statement for each business unit.

Naming and Numbering Accounts

Account names and numbers make it easy for accountants, bookkeepers, and company employees to find the accounts they need. In addition, with standardized naming and numbering, you can compare your company's financial performance with others in your industry. This section suggests some rules to follow as you set up naming and numbering conventions.

If you accept the accounts that QuickBooks recommends when you set up your company file, then they already have assigned names and numbers, as shown in Figure 3-1. You might think this lets you off the hook. But by taking the time to learn standard account numbers and names, you'll find working with accounts more logical and understand more of what your accountant and bookkeeper say.

ORGANIZING ACCOUNT NUMBERS

Account numbers are initially turned off when you create a new company file in QuickBooks (page 54 explains how to display them), and you don't have to use them. However, account numbers make it easier for your bookkeeper or accountant to work with your financial records. This section explains the typical numbering convention that financial folks use.

Companies reserve ranges of numbers for different types of accounts, so they can identify the *type* of account by its number alone. Business models vary, so you'll find account numbers carved up in different ways depending on the industry. Think about your personal finances: You spend money on lots of different things, but your income derives from a precious few sources. Businesses and nonprofits are no different. So you might find income accounts numbered from 4000 to 4999 and expense accounts using numbers anywhere from 5000 through 9999 (see Table 3-1).

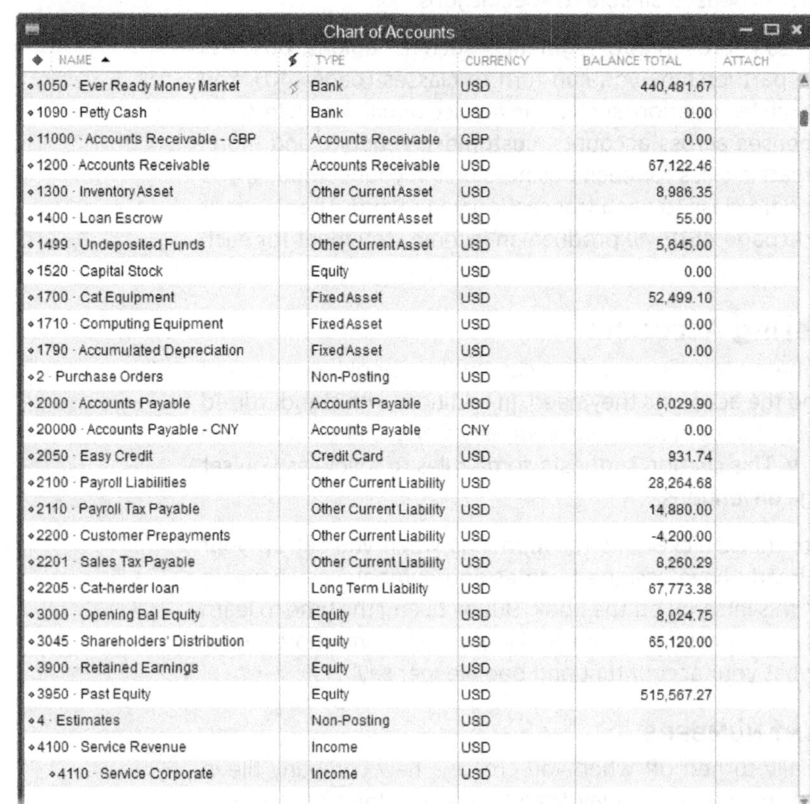

FIGURE 3-1

Accounts that QuickBooks adds to your chart of accounts during setup come with assigned names and numbers, as you can see here.

To open the Chart of Accounts window, press Ctrl+A. If you don't see account numbers in this window, page 54 tells you how to display them.

TABLE 3-1 *Typical ranges for account numbers*

RANGE	ACCOUNT TYPE
1000–1999	Assets
2000–2999	Liabilities
3000–3999	Equity
4000–4999	Income
5000–5999	Cost of goods sold, cost of sales, job costs, or general expenses
6000–7999	Expenses, overhead costs, or other income
8000–9999	Expenses or other expenses

NOTE Most businesses use the same account-numbering scheme up until the number 4999. After that, things can differ because some companies require more income accounts, but in most businesses, expense accounts are the most numerous.

Account numbering conventions don't just carve number ranges up for account types. If you read annual reports as a hobby, you know that companies further compartmentalize their finances. For example, assets and liabilities get split into *current* and *long-term* categories. (Current means something that's expected to happen within the next 12 months, such as a loan that's due in 3 months; long-term is anything beyond 12 months.) Typically, companies show assets and liabilities progressing from the shortest to the longest term, and the asset and liability account numbers follow suit. Here's one way to allocate account numbers for current and progressively longer-term assets:

- **1000–1099**. Immediately available cash, such as a checking account, savings account, or petty cash.
- **1100–1499**. Assets you can convert into cash within a few months to a year, including Accounts Receivable, inventory assets, and other current assets.
- **1500–1799**. Long-term assets, such as land, buildings, furniture, and other fixed assets.
- **1800–1999**. Other assets.

Companies also break expenses down into smaller categories. For example, many companies keep an eye on whether their sales team is doing its job by tracking sales expenses separately and monitoring the ratio of sales to sales expenses. Sales expenses often appear in the 5000–5999 range. QuickBooks reinforces this standard by automatically creating a Cost of Goods Sold account numbered 5001. (You can create as many Cost of Goods Sold accounts as you need to track expenses that relate directly to your income, such as the cost of purchasing products you sell, as well as what you pay your salespeople.) Other companies assign overhead expenses to accounts in the 7000–7999 range, so they can assign a portion of those expenses to each job performed.

TIP When you add new accounts to your chart of accounts, increment the account number by 5 or 10 to leave room in the numbering scheme for similar accounts you might need in the future. For example, if your checking account number is 1000, assign 1010 or 1020 to your new savings account rather than 1001.

In QuickBooks, an account number can be up to seven digits long, but the program sorts numbers beginning with the leftmost digit. So if you want to categorize in excruciating detail, slice your number ranges into sets of 10,000. For example, assets range from 10000 to 19999; income accounts span 40000 to 49999, and so on.

NOTE Because QuickBooks sorts accounts by number, beginning with the leftmost digit, account 4100020 appears before account 4101.

VIEWING ACCOUNT NUMBERS

If you want to see or hide account numbers in QuickBooks, here's how to turn them on or off:

1. **Choose Edit→Preferences→Accounting, and then in the Preferences dialog box, click the Company Preferences tab.**

   You have to be a QuickBooks administrator (page 718) to open this tab.

2. **Turn on the "Use account numbers" checkbox to show account numbers.**

   To hide them, turn *off* this checkbox.

3. **Click OK to close the Preferences dialog box.**

With this setting turned on, account numbers appear in the Chart of Accounts window, account drop-down lists, and account fields. In addition, the Add New Account and Edit Account windows display the Number box so you can add or modify an account's number.

NOTE Turning off the "Use account numbers" checkbox doesn't remove account numbers you've already added; it simply hides them in the spots mentioned above. You can see them again by turning the checkbox back on. However, you can't *add* account numbers to any accounts you create while the checkbox is turned off. If you create an account anyway, you can then edit it (page 63) to add an account number *after* you turn on the "Use account numbers" checkbox.

CHOOSING GOOD ACCOUNT NAMES

Account names should be meaningful, both to you and your accountant (or bookkeeper). In addition, your accounts should be unique in name and function because you don't need two accounts for the same type of income, expense, or financial bucket. For example, if you consider advertising and marketing two distinctly different activities, then create an account for each. But if advertising and marketing blur in your mind, then create one account with a name like "Marketing & Advertising."

NOTE Because accounts represent high-level categories, stick to names that summarize the income or expense, such as Service Income and Product Income. Accounts and names like Tom's Consulting, Dick's Consulting, and Harry's Consulting are too specific—and might cause confusion if Rosie takes over Harry's work.

QuickBooks does its part to enforce unique account names. Say you try to create a new expense account named Postage, but an account by that name already exists. QuickBooks displays the message "This name is already in use. Please use another name." What QuickBooks *can't* do is ensure that each account represents a unique category of money. Without a naming standard, you could end up with multiple accounts with unique names, each representing the same category, as shown by the following names for accounts used to track postage:

Expense-postage

Postage

Postage and delivery

Shipping

If you haven't used QuickBooks before, here are some rules you can apply to help make your account names consistent:

- **Word order**. If you include the account type in the name, then append it to the *end* of the name. You'll spot "Postage Expense" more easily than "Expense Postage."
- **Consistent punctuation**. Choose "and" or "&" for accounts that cover more than one item, like "Dues and Subscriptions." And decide whether to include apostrophes, as in "Owners Draw" or "Owner's Draw."
- **Spaces**. Decide whether to include spaces for readability or to eliminate them for brevity; for example, "Dues & Subscriptions" vs. "Dues&Subscriptions."
- **Abbreviation**. If you abbreviate words in account names, then choose a standard abbreviation length. If you go with four-letter abbreviations, for example, "Postage" would become "Post." For a three-letter abbreviation, you might use "Pst."

WARNING QuickBooks won't enforce your naming standards. So after you set the rules for account names, write them down so you don't forget them. A consistent written standard encourages everyone (yourself included) to trust and follow the naming rules. Also, urge everyone to display inactive accounts (page 63) and scan the chart of accounts for synonyms to see if such an account already exists *before* creating a new one. These rules are easier to enforce if you limit the number of people who can create and edit accounts (page 725).

Creating Accounts and Subaccounts

As the box on page 57 explains, different types of accounts represent dramatically different financial animals. The good news is that every type of account in QuickBooks shares most of the same fields, so you need to learn only one account-creation procedure.

If you look closely at the chart of accounts list in Figure 3-1, you'll notice that accounts fall into two main categories: those with balances and those without. If you're *really* on your toes, you might also notice that accounts with balances are the ones that appear on the Balance Sheet report. (Accounts without balances appear on the Profit & Loss report.) To learn more about financial statements and the accounts they reference, see Chapter 23.

Creating an Account

After you've had your business for a while, you won't add new accounts very often. However, you might need one if you start up a new line of income, take on a mortgage for your new office building, or want a new expense account for the subcontractors you hire to manage your workload.

Creating accounts in QuickBooks is simple. Before you can create an account, you have to open the Chart of Accounts window. Here are a few ways to do that:

- Press Ctrl+A (which you can do from anywhere in the program).
- At the top right of the Home Page, in the Company panel, click Chart of Accounts.
- In the menu bar, choose Lists→Chart of Accounts.

The Chart of Accounts window works much like other list windows. For example, you can sort the account list by different columns or drag accounts in the list to different locations. (See page 158 to learn how to sort and rearrange lists.)

TIP You can create accounts on the fly by choosing <Add New> in any Account drop-down list. Suppose you create a new Service item (in the Item List window, press Ctrl+N) and want a new income account to track revenue for that service. In the New Item dialog box, scroll to the top of the Account drop-down list and then choose <Add New>. In the Add New Account window that appears, fill in the various fields, and then click Save & Close. Back in the New Item dialog box, QuickBooks displays the new account in the Account field, and you can finish creating your item.

Once you've opened the Chart of Accounts window, here's how to create an account:

1. **Press Ctrl+N to open the Add New Account window.**

   Alternatively, on the menu bar at the bottom of the Chart of Accounts window, click Account→New. Or right-click anywhere in the Chart of Accounts window, and then choose New from the shortcut menu. No matter which method you use, QuickBooks opens the Add New Account window shown in Figure 3-2.

2. **Select the type of account you want to create, such as Bank for a bank account, and then click Continue.**

   The Add New Account window lists the most common kinds of accounts. If you don't see the type you want—Cost of Goods Sold, for example—select the Other Account Types option, and then choose from the drop-down menu visible in Figure 3-2.

UP TO SPEED

Making Sense of Account Types

QuickBooks' account types are standard ones used in finance. Here's a quick introduction to the different types and what they represent:

- **Bank**. Accounts that you hold at a financial institution, such as a checking, savings, money market, or petty cash account.
- **Accounts Receivable**. The money that your customers owe you, like outstanding invoices and goods purchased on credit.
- **Other Current Asset**. Things you own that you'll use or convert to cash within 12 months, such as prepaid expenses.
- **Fixed Asset**. Things your company owns that decrease in value over time (depreciate), like equipment that wears out or becomes obsolete.
- **Other Asset**. If you won't convert an asset to cash in the next 12 months and it isn't a depreciable asset, then it's—you guessed it—an other asset. A long-term note receivable is one example.
- **Accounts Payable**. This is a special type of current liability account (money you owe in the next 12 months) that represents what you owe to vendors.
- **Credit Card**. Just what it sounds like: a credit card account.
- **Other Current Liability**. Money you owe in the next 12 months, such as sales tax and short-term loans.
- **Long Term Liability**. Money you owe *after* the next 12 months, like mortgage payments you'll pay over several years.
- **Equity**. The owners' equity in your company, including the original capital invested in the company and retained earnings. (Money that owners withdraw from the company also shows up in an equity account but reduces the value of the account.)
- **Income**. The revenue you generate through your main business functions, like sales or consulting services.
- **Cost of Goods Sold**. The cost of products and materials that you originally held in inventory but then sold. You can also use this type of account to track other expenses related to sales, such as commissions and what you pay subcontractors to do work for your customers.
- **Expense**. The money you spend to run your company.
- **Other Income**. Money you receive from sources other than business operations, such as interest income.
- **Other Expense**. Money you pay out for things other than business operations, like interest.
- **Non-posting Account**. QuickBooks creates non-posting accounts automatically when you use features such as estimates and purchase orders. For example, when you create an estimate (page 278), you don't want that money to appear on your financial reports, so QuickBooks stores those values in non-posting accounts.

3. **In the Number box in the upper right of the Add New Account window (Figure 3-3), type the account number you want to use in the chart of accounts. (If you don't see the Number box, flip to page 54 to learn how to display it.)**

   If you keep the Chart of Accounts window in view while creating accounts, you can review the account numbers for similar types of accounts. That way, you can give the new account a number that's 5 or 10 higher than an existing account number, so that the new one snuggles in with its compatriots in the chart of accounts.

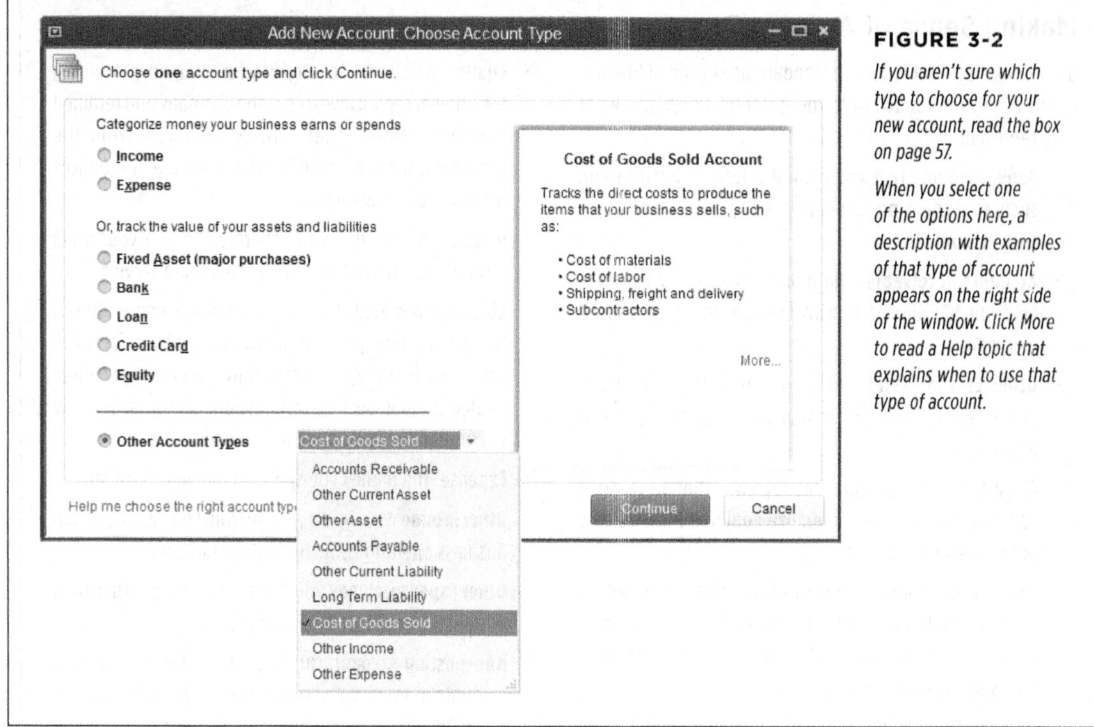

FIGURE 3-2

If you aren't sure which type to choose for your new account, read the box on page 57.

When you select one of the options here, a description with examples of that type of account appears on the right side of the window. Click More to read a Help topic that explains when to use that type of account.

4. **In the Account Name box, type a name for the account.**

   See page 54 for tips on standardizing account names.

NOTE If you create an account and don't see one of the fields mentioned here, it simply doesn't apply to that account type.

5. **If you want the account to be a subaccount, then turn on the "Subaccount of" checkbox. Then, in the drop-down list, choose the account that you want to act as the parent.**

   As the box on page 60 explains, subaccounts are a good way to track your finances in more detail. In the chart of accounts, subaccounts are indented below their parent accounts to make the hierarchy easy to see, as shown at the bottom of Figure 3-1.

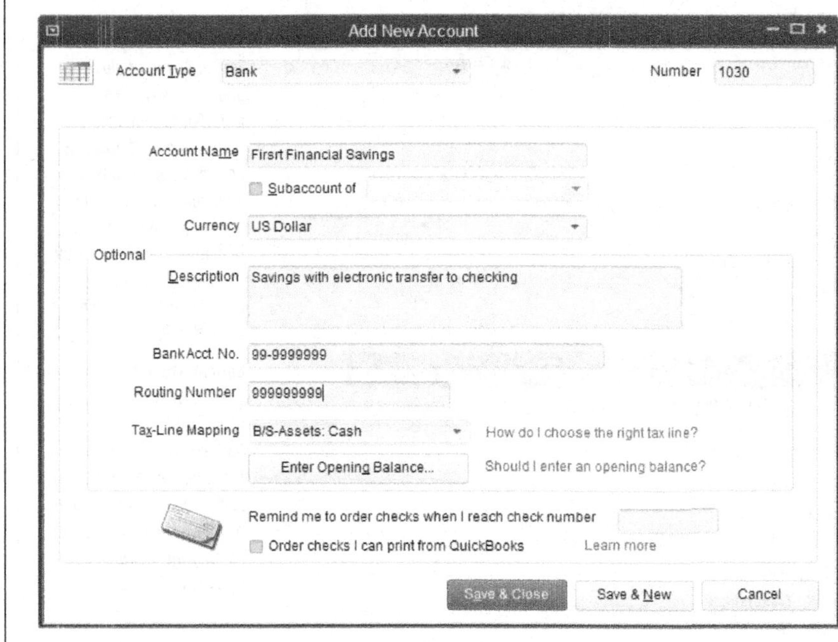

FIGURE 3-3

The Bank account type includes every account field except Note, as well as a few fields that you won't find in any other account type, such as Bank Acct. No. and Routing Number. If you want QuickBooks to remind you to order checks, in the "Remind me to order checks when I reach check number" field, type the check number you want to use as a trigger. And if you want the program to open a browser window to an Intuit site where you can order supplies, turn on "Order checks I can print from QuickBooks." If you get checks from somewhere else, just reorder checks the way you normally do.

TIP When you use subaccounts, QuickBooks displays both the parent account's name and the subaccount's name in the Account fields throughout the program, which often makes it impossible to tell which account a transaction uses, as you can see in Figure 3-4 (top). If you want to see only the lowest-level subaccount in Account fields, head to the Accounting section of the Preferences dialog box, click the Company Preferences tab, and then turn on the "Show lowest subaccount only" checkbox (see page 636).

6. **If you've turned on QuickBooks' multiple currency preference, the Currency box appears below the "Subaccount of" checkbox. If the currency for the account is different from the one listed there, choose the correct currency in the drop-down list.**

   If you do business in more than one currency, see page 656 to learn how to set up multiple currencies in QuickBooks.

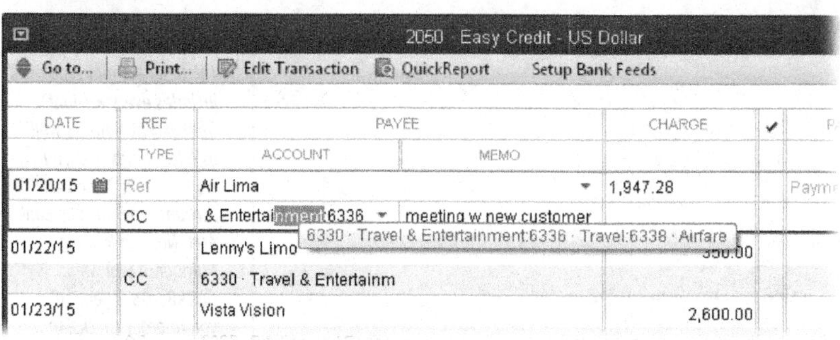

FIGURE 3-4

Top: In Account fields and drop-down lists, QuickBooks combines the names of parent accounts and their subaccounts into one long name, as you can see in this travel example. In many instances, only the top-level account is visible unless you scroll within the Account field.

Bottom: When you turn on the "Show lowest subaccount only" preference, the Account field shows the subaccount number and name instead, which is exactly what you need to identify the assigned account (in this case, Airfare).

UP TO SPEED

Adding Detail with Subaccounts

Say your company's travel expenses are sky-high and you want to start tracking what you spend on different types of travel, such as airfare, lodging, and limousine services. Subaccounts make it easy to track details like these. Subaccounts are nothing more than partitions within higher-level accounts (called *parent* accounts).

When you post transactions to subaccounts only (not their parent account), your reports show the subtotals for the subaccounts *and* a grand total for the parent account, such as the Travel account (number 6336, say) and its subaccounts Airfare (6338), Lodging (6340), and Transportation (6342), for example.

Subaccounts also come in handy for assigning similar expenses to different lines on tax forms. For example, the IRS doesn't treat all travel expenses the same: You can deduct only half of your meal and entertainment expenses, while other travel expenses are fully deductible. For this reason, you might create "Meals and Entertainment" as a separate subaccount within the Travel account.

7. **To add a description of the account, fill in the Description box.**

   For instance, you can define whether a bank account is linked to another account or give examples of the types of expenses that apply to a particular expense account. The Description field can hold up to 200 characters, which should be more than enough.

8. **If you see a field for an account number—such as Bank Acct. No., Credit Card Acct. No., or simply Account No.—type in the number for your real-world account at your financial institution (checking account, savings account, loan, and so on).**

   If the account type you chose in step 2 doesn't include a field for an account number, you see the Note field instead, which you can use to store any additional information you want to document about the account.

9. **For a bank account, in the Routing Number box, type your bank's routing number.**

   This is the nine-digit number in funny-looking font at the bottom of your checks.

10. **To associate the account with a tax form and a specific line on that form, in the Tax-Line Mapping drop-down list, choose the entry for the appropriate tax form and tax line.**

    If you haven't specified the tax form that your company files with the IRS, the Tax-Line Mapping field is set to <Unassigned>. See page 11 to learn how to choose a tax form for your company.

    If QuickBooks hasn't assigned a tax line for you, you can scan the entries in the drop-down list for a likely match. If you don't find an entry that seems right or if QuickBooks tells you the one you chose isn't compatible with the account type, your best bet is to call your accountant or the IRS. You can also get a hint of an appropriate tax line for the account you're creating by examining one of QuickBooks' sample files (page 9).

    To remove a tax line from an account, in the drop-down list, choose <Unassigned>.

NOTE Below the Tax-Line Mapping field, you may see the Enter Opening Balance button. It's easy to figure out the opening balance for a brand-new account—it's zero—so you can ignore this button. If you're setting up QuickBooks with accounts that existed prior to your QuickBooks start date, those accounts *do* have opening balances. Even so, clicking the Enter Opening Balance button isn't the best way to specify an opening balance for an account you're adding to your company file. The box on page 62 explains how to specify opening balances for all your accounts in just a few steps.

11. **Click the Save & New button to save the current account and create another one.**

    To save the account you just created and close the Add New Account window, click Save & Close instead. Click Cancel to discard the account-in-progress and close the Add New Account window.

12. **If the Set Up Bank Feed dialog box appears, click Yes if you want to set up a bank account for online services.**

    When you click Yes, QuickBooks' windows close while you go through the setup process. (See Chapter 24 to learn about online services and QuickBooks.)

    If you want to set up Bank Feeds later—or never—click No.

FREQUENTLY ASKED QUESTION

Doing Opening Balances Right

When I add an account to my company file, can I just click the Enter Opening Balance button and type the balance I want to start with in the Opening Balance field? That seems the most logical place for it.

You *can*, but your accountant may not be too happy about it. Filling in the Opening Balance field from the Add New Account window (or in the Edit Account window, for that matter) automatically adds that balance to the Opening Bal Equity account, which accountants consider sloppy bookkeeping. Instead, they usually recommend creating a journal entry from your trial balance for most of your accounts. (To see what an opening balance journal entry looks like, head to page 429.)

The three exceptions are your Accounts Receivable (AR), Accounts Payable (AP), and bank accounts. Because QuickBooks requires customer names and vendor names in journal entries that contain AR and AP accounts, you're better off creating invoices and bills to define your AR and AP opening balances. With bank accounts, you can enter your previous reconciled balance in the journal entry and then bring the account up to date by recording all the transactions since your last reconciliation. If you work with an accountant, ask her how she'd like you to enter opening balances—or better yet, have her do it for you.

Whoa! What's a journal entry? What's a trial balance?

Here's the deal: *Journal entries* (page 426) are mechanisms for moving money between accounts—on paper, that is. A *trial balance* (page 442) is a report (from your accountant or your old accounting system) that lists all your accounts with their balances in either the Debit or Credit column. In the days of paper-based ledgers, bean counters totaled the Debit and Credit columns. If the totals weren't equal, the accountant had to track down the arithmetic error. Happily, QuickBooks' digital brain does the math for you, without errors. But it's up to you to set up the opening-balance journal entry properly in the first place.

If you look at the trial balance on the first day of your fiscal year, it's quite simple—it includes balances only for your balance sheet accounts, not income and expense accounts. You can use these values to fill in a journal entry to assign all your accounts' opening balances: First, set the journal entry's date to the last day of the previous fiscal year; that way, you can start fresh for your current fiscal year. Next, for each account *except* your AR and AP accounts, add a line in the journal entry with the account name and the balance from your trial-balance report in either the Debit or Credit column. Finally, create invoices and bills to define the opening balances for your AR and AP accounts.

Working with Accounts

From time to time, you might need to modify your accounts to, for example, change an account's name or description. If you no longer need an account, you can hide it to keep your chart of accounts list tidy. On the other hand, if you created an account by mistake, you can delete it. And merging accounts comes in handy if you find several accounts that represent the same thing. This section describes how to make all these changes to accounts.

Modifying Accounts

If you stick to your account numbering and naming conventions, you'll have few reasons to edit accounts. But just in case, the Edit Account window lets you tweak an account's name and description, adjust its number to make room for new accounts, and change its level in the chart of accounts hierarchy.

You're not likely to change an account's type unless you chose the wrong one when you created the account. If you do need to change the account type, back up your QuickBooks file first (see page 495) in case the change has effects that you didn't anticipate. Also, note that QuickBooks has several restrictions on changing account types. You can't change an account's type if:

- It has subaccounts.
- It's an Accounts Receivable or Accounts Payable account. (You also can't change other types of accounts *to* AR or AP accounts.)
- QuickBooks automatically created the account, like Undeposited Funds.

To modify an account, in the Chart of Accounts window, select the account you want to edit, and then press Ctrl+E or click Account→Edit Account. In the Edit Account window that appears, make your changes, and then click Save & Close.

Hiding Accounts

If you create an account by mistake, you can delete it (you'll learn how in a sec). However, because QuickBooks drops your financial transactions into account buckets and you don't want to throw away historical information, you'll usually want to *hide* accounts that you don't use anymore instead of deleting them.

Records of past transactions are important, whether you want to review the amount of business you've received from a customer or the IRS is asking unsettling questions. When you hide an account in QuickBooks, the account continues to hold your historical transactions, but it doesn't appear in account lists, so you can't choose it by mistake with a misplaced click. For example, you wouldn't delete your Nutrition Service income account just because you've discontinued your nutrition-consulting service to focus on selling your new book, *The See Food Diet*. The income you earned from that service in the past needs to stay in your records.

Hiding and reactivating accounts (Figure 3-5) can also come in handy if QuickBooks created a chart of accounts for you based on the industry you chose during setup (page 11). If the chart of accounts it created includes accounts you don't think you need, simply hide those accounts for the time being. That way, if you find yourself saying, "Gosh, I wish I had an account for the accumulated depreciation of vehicles," the solution might be as simple as reactivating a hidden account.

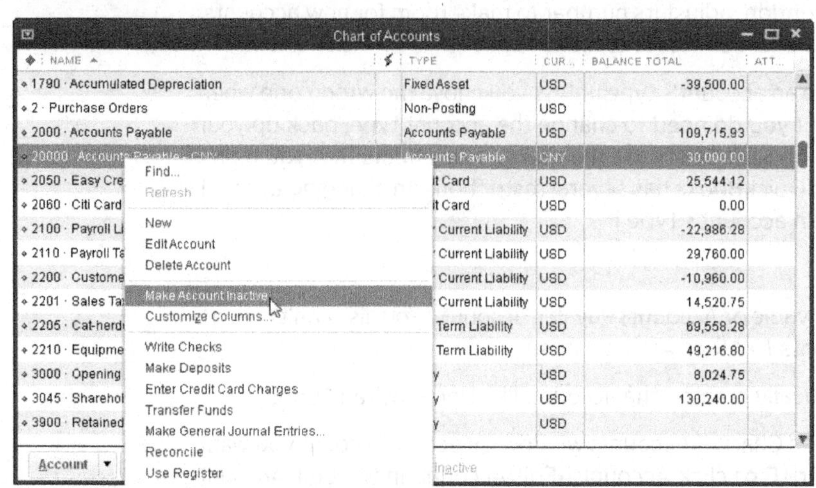

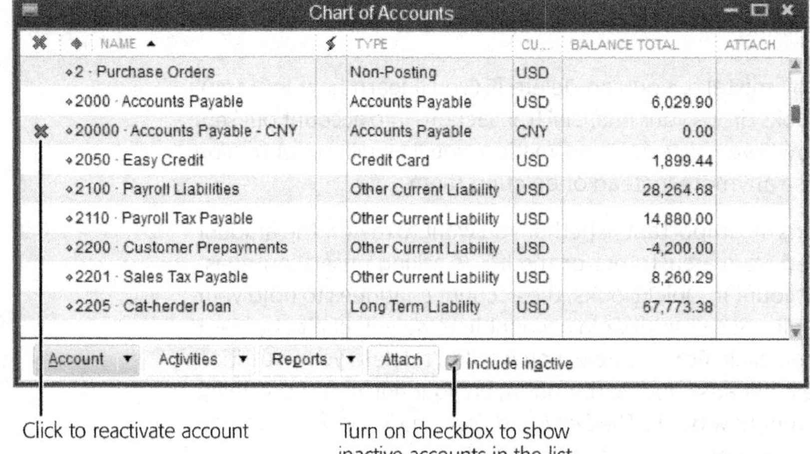
Click to reactivate account
Turn on checkbox to show inactive accounts in the list

FIGURE 3-5

Top: To hide an account, in the Chart of Accounts window, right-click the account and choose Make Account Inactive from this shortcut menu. The account and any subaccounts that belong to it disappear from the list.

Bottom: To reactivate a hidden account, first display all your accounts by turning on the "Include inactive" checkbox at the bottom of the Chart of Accounts window. When you do that, QuickBooks adds a column with an X as its heading and displays an X in that column for every hidden account in the list. To un-hide an account, click the X next to its name.

If the account has subaccounts, QuickBooks displays the Activate Group dialog box; there, click Yes to reactivate the account and all its subaccounts.

Deleting Accounts

You can delete an account *only if* nothing in QuickBooks references it in any way. An account with references is a red flag that deleting it might not be the right choice. If you try to delete such an account, QuickBooks displays a message box telling you it can't delete the account and recommends making it inactive instead. If that isn't enough to deter you, the sheer tedium of removing references to an account should nudge you toward hiding the account instead. If you *insist* on deleting an account, here are the conditions that prevent you from doing so and what you have to do to remove these constraints:

- **An item uses the account**. If you create any items that use the account as an income account, expense account, cost of goods sold account, or inventory asset account, you can't delete it. You have to edit the items to use other accounts first, as described on page 118.
- **The account has subaccounts**. You have to delete all subaccounts before you can delete the parent account.
- **Payroll uses the account**. You can't delete an account if your payroll setup uses it.
- **A transaction references the account**. If you created even one transaction that uses the account, either edit that transaction to use a different account or hide the account if you want to keep the transaction the way it is.
- **The account has a balance**. An account balance comes from either an opening balance transaction or other transactions that reference the account. You remove an account balance by reassigning all the transactions to another account.

To delete or reassign transactions, in the Chart of Accounts window, double-click the account's name. For accounts with balances, QuickBooks opens a register window where you can select a transaction and then edit it or press Ctrl+D to delete it. For accounts without balances, QuickBooks opens an Account QuickReport window. To edit or delete a transaction that appears in this report, double-click the transaction. QuickBooks then opens a window related to that transaction (for instance, the Write Checks window appears if the transaction is a check). Edit the transaction to use a different account, or right-click anywhere in that window and choose Delete Check or the corresponding delete command for the type of transaction.

After you've deleted all references to the account, in the Chart of Accounts window, select the account you want to delete, and then press Ctrl+D or choose Account→Delete Account. QuickBooks asks you to confirm that you want to delete the account; click OK.

Merging Accounts

Suppose you find multiple accounts with the same purpose—Postage and Mail Expense, say—lurking in your chart of accounts. No problem! You can merge the accounts into one and then remind everyone who creates accounts in QuickBooks about your naming conventions. (If you haven't gotten around to setting up naming conventions, see page 54 for some guidelines.)

TIP Before you merge accounts, see what your accountant thinks. There's no going back once you've merged two accounts—they're combined for good. And QuickBooks' audit trail (page 437) doesn't keep track of this kind of change.

QuickBooks sweeps all the transactions from the account you merge into the account you keep, so you can merge accounts only if they're the same type. (As an experienced manager, you can imagine the havoc that merging income and expense accounts would cause in your financial statements.) In addition, accounts must be at the same level in the chart of accounts; in other words, they both have to be parent accounts or subaccounts. To move an account to another level, in the Chart of Accounts window, position your cursor over the small diamond to the left of the account's name. When the cursor turns into a four-headed arrow, drag to the left or right so that the account is indented the same amount as the other account.

NOTE If you find two accounts with similar names but different types, those accounts might not represent the same thing. For instance, an expense account named Telephone Ex. probably contains your monthly telephone service costs, while an asset account named Telephone Eq. might represent the money you invested in a big telephone switch that your mega-corporation owns. In this situation, the accounts are different types and should be separate, although more meaningful names and descriptions would help differentiate them.

Here's how to eliminate an extraneous account:

1. **Switch to single-user mode, as described on page 489.**

   You have to be in single-user mode to merge accounts. Be nice to your fellow QuickBooks users by making these changes outside of working hours. If you *have* to merge accounts during the workday, remember to tell your coworkers they can log into the program after you've switched the company file back to multi-user mode.

2. **Press Ctrl+A to open the Chart of Accounts window. Then, in the chart of accounts list, click the name of the account you want to *eliminate* and then press Ctrl+E.**

   The Edit Account window opens.

3. **In the Edit Account window, change the account number and name to match the values for the account you want to *keep*.**

   As long as you get the letters and numbers right, QuickBooks takes care of matching uppercase and lowercase for you.

   If you don't remember the number and name of the account you're keeping, drag the Chart of Accounts window and the Edit Account window so you can see both at the same time. (If QuickBooks won't let you do that, you might have the One Window preference turned on; see page 643 to learn how to change your settings to display multiple windows.)

4. **In the Edit Account window, click Save & Close, read the message informing you that the name is in use and asking whether you want to merge the accounts, and then click Yes.**

   In the chart of accounts list, the account you renamed disappears, and any transactions for that account are now associated with the account you kept.

CHAPTER

4

Setting Up Customers, Jobs, and Vendors

You may be fond of strutting around your sales department proclaiming, "Nothing happens until somebody sells something!" As it turns out, you can quote that tired adage in your accounting department, too. Whether you sell products or services, the first sale to a new customer often initiates a flurry of activity, including creating a new *customer* in QuickBooks, assigning a *job* for the work, and the ultimate goal of all this effort—*invoicing* your customer (sending a bill for what you sold that states how much the customer owes) to collect some income.

The people who buy what you sell have plenty of nicknames: customers, clients, consumers, patrons, patients, purchasers, donors, members, shoppers, and so on. QuickBooks throws out the thesaurus and applies one moniker to every person or organization that buys from you: customer. In QuickBooks, a *customer* is a record of information about your real-life customer. The program takes the data you enter about customers and uses it to fill in invoices and other sales forms with your customers' names, addresses, payment terms, and other info.

Real-world customers are essential to your success, but do you need customers in your QuickBooks company file? Even if you run a primarily cash business, creating customers in QuickBooks could still be a good idea. For example, setting up QuickBooks records for the repeat customers at your store saves you time by automatically filling in their information on each new sales receipt.

If your business revolves around projects, you can create a job in QuickBooks for each project you do for a customer. To QuickBooks, a *job* is a record of a real-life project that you agreed (or perhaps begged) to perform for a customer—remodeling a kitchen, designing an ad campaign, or whatever. Suppose you're a plumber and you regularly do work for a general contractor. You could create several jobs, one for each place you plumb: Smith house, Jones house, and Winfrey house. In QuickBooks, you can then track income and expenses by job and gauge each one's profitability. However, if your company doesn't take on jobs, you don't have to create them in QuickBooks. For example, retail stores sell products, not projects. If you don't need jobs, you can simply create your customers in QuickBooks and then move on to invoicing them or creating sales receipts for their purchases.

Even before you start receiving payments from customers, you're going to do business with vendors and pay *them* for their services and products. The telephone company, your accountant, and the subcontractor who installs Venetian plaster in your spec houses are all *vendors*. The information QuickBooks needs about vendors isn't all that different from what you specify for customers.

This chapter guides you through creating and managing customers, jobs, and vendors in QuickBooks. It also helps you decide how to apply the program's customer, job, and vendor fields to your business.

ALTERNATE REALITY

Tracking Donors for Nonprofits

For nonprofit organizations, any individual or organization that sends money is a *donor*, but the term "donor" doesn't appear in most QuickBooks editions. The Premier Nonprofit edition of the program mentions donors, pledges, and other nonprofit terms, but QuickBooks Pro and other Premier editions focus single-mindedly on customers, so you may have to get used to thinking "donor" whenever you see "customer" in QuickBooks.

Likewise, a job in QuickBooks is the equivalent of a contract or grant. If you need to report on a grant or contract, add a separate job for it to the customer (er, donor) who donated the funds.

Entering members or individual donors as separate customers can max out QuickBooks' customer name limit or make the program run slowly. The Enterprise Solutions edition of QuickBooks can handle a larger number of customers, but most nonprofits would choke at that edition's price tag. To solve this dilemma, create customers in QuickBooks to represent generic pools, such as donors and members. For example, create a customer called Unrestricted and then post all unrestricted donations to that customer. Then keep the details of your donor and member names in a separate donor database, spreadsheet, or program designed specifically for nonprofits.

Creating Customers in QuickBooks

Alas, you first have to persuade customers to work with your company. But once you've cleared *that* hurdle, creating those customers in QuickBooks is easy. (The box above describes how to use QuickBooks customer records to set up donors for nonprofits, and the box on page 71 provides some hints on keeping customers straight in QuickBooks.) The program offers several methods for creating customer records:

- **QuickBooks Setup**. When you're getting started with the program, you can use the QuickBooks Setup dialog box to quickly import piles of customer information (as well as vendor and employee info) from your email program or by copying and pasting data from Excel, as described on page 19. You can return to the QuickBooks Setup dialog box at any time (page 20) to add more records.
- **One at a time**. The New Customer window lets you create one customer at a time, although you can create several records in a row without closing the window. The next section (page 70) describes how to create customers with this window and explains what each customer field represents.

TIP If you don't add customers very often, you can create a customer record when you create that customer's first invoice or sales receipt: In the invoice's or sales receipt's Customer:Job box, type the customer's name, and then press Tab to move to the next field. When you do that, the Customer:Job Not Found dialog box appears. To add the new customer to the Customer:Job List without filling in any other info, click Quick Add. Alternatively, click Set Up to open the New Customer dialog box, where you can fill in as many fields as you want. If you typed a nonexistent customer name by mistake, click Cancel.

- **Copying data**. You can also create customers in batches. With the Add/Edit Multiple List Entries feature (page 124), you can paste data from Excel or copy values from customer to customer.
- **Importing data**. This method is ideal when you have scads of customer records to set up. After you create a map between QuickBooks' fields and fields in another program, you can transfer your customer info as described on page 133.

The Customer Center (Figure 4-1) is a one-stop shop for customers and jobs: creating, modifying, and viewing their records, and creating transactions for them. QuickBooks gives you four easy ways to open the Customer Center window:

- From anywhere in the program, press Ctrl+J.
- On the QuickBooks Home Page, at the top of the Customers panel, click Customers.
- On the QuickBooks menu bar, choose Customers→Customer Center.
- In the icon bar, click Customers.

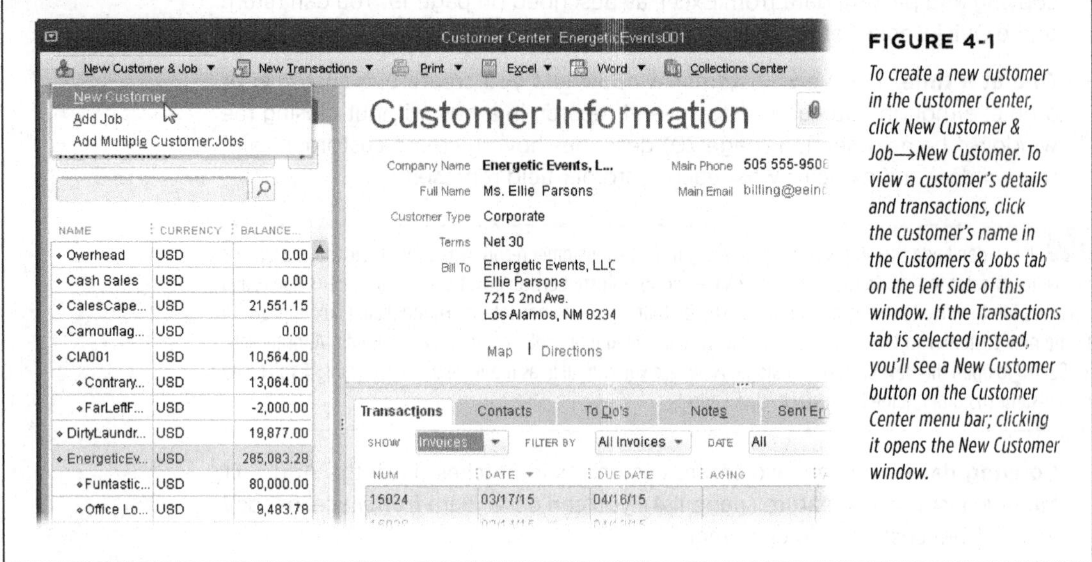

FIGURE 4-1

To create a new customer in the Customer Center, click New Customer & Job→New Customer. To view a customer's details and transactions, click the customer's name in the Customers & Jobs tab on the left side of this window. If the Transactions tab is selected instead, you'll see a New Customer button on the Customer Center menu bar; clicking it opens the New Customer window.

Creating a New Customer

Here's the short and sweet method of creating one customer in QuickBooks:

1. **In the Customer Center toolbar, click New Customer & Job→New Customer, or press Ctrl+N.**

   The New Customer window opens (Figure 4-2).

2. **In the Customer Name field, type a unique name or code for this customer, following the naming convention you've chosen (see the box on page 71).**

   This is the only field you *have* to fill in—the rest are optional.

3. **To save that customer's record and close the New Customer window, click OK.**

   To discard what you entered and close the window, click Cancel instead.

WORD TO THE WISE

Making Customers Easy to Identify

In QuickBooks, the Customer Name and Vendor Name fields don't show the names that appear on invoices or bills. Instead, they display a code that uniquely identifies each customer or vendor so you can tell them apart.

If you own a small company, you're not likely to mistakenly create multiple records for the same customer or vendor. Your Customer and Vendor lists are short, so you can probably remember all the people and companies on them. Even so, it's a good idea to define a standard for names.

Consistent naming can help you avoid having multiple records for the same customer or vendor by preventing you from creating slightly different values in the Customer Name or Vendor Name field. For example, you could end up with three customer records in QuickBooks all representing the same real-world customer, such as Cales's Capers, Cales Capers, and CalesCapers. The same holds true for vendors.

QuickBooks doesn't enforce naming conventions. So after you define rules that work for your business, you have to be disciplined and apply those rules each time you create a new customer or vendor. (You're free to use alphanumeric characters and punctuation in names.) Here are a few of the more common naming conventions:

- **The first few letters of the customer's or vendor's company name, followed by a unique numeric identifier.** This standard is easy to apply and differentiates customers or vendors as long as their names don't all begin with the same words. For example, if the companies you do business with aren't imaginative, your names could end up as Wine001, Wine002, and Wine003. But if the companies are Zinfandels To Go, Merlot Mania, and Cabernet Cabinet, this system works nicely.
- **For individuals, the person's last name followed by a comma, his first name, and then a numeric ID to make the name unique.** Although unusual names such as Zaphod Beeblebrox render a numeric ID unnecessary, using this standard ensures that *all* names are unique.
- **The actual company name with any punctuation and spaces omitted.** Removing spaces and punctuation from company names helps eliminate multiple versions of the same name. If you choose this convention, using capital letters at the beginning of each word (called *camel caps*) makes the names more readable. For instance, Icantbelieveitsyogurt is a headache waiting to happen, but ICantBelieveItsYogurt looks more like its spaced and punctuated counterpart.
- **A unique alphanumeric code.** Customer:Job drop-down menus and reports sort entries by the values in the Customer Name field of customer records. (Vendor drop-down menus and reports sort by the Vendor Name field.) Codes like X123Y4JQ use only a few characters to produce unique identifiers, but they're also so cryptic that they make it difficult to pick out the name you want in drop-down lists, or to sort reports in a meaningful way. Stick with using part of the company name (at the beginning of the name, since names appear alphabetically) unless you have hundreds or thousands of customers or vendors.

TIP If you buy from and sell to the same company or individual, you probably already know that you can't use the same name in the Customer, Vendor, Employee, and Other Names lists. If a customer is also a vendor, you need *two* records for that company or individual—and they have to have different names. The solution? Add text to the Customer Name and Vendor Name fields to identify which list the record belongs to, such as "Tek Turner (Cust)" in the customer record's Customer Name field and "Tek Turner (Vend)" in the vendor record's Vendor Name field. Fortunately, QuickBooks doesn't care if the *other* fields in the customer and vendor records contain the same info.

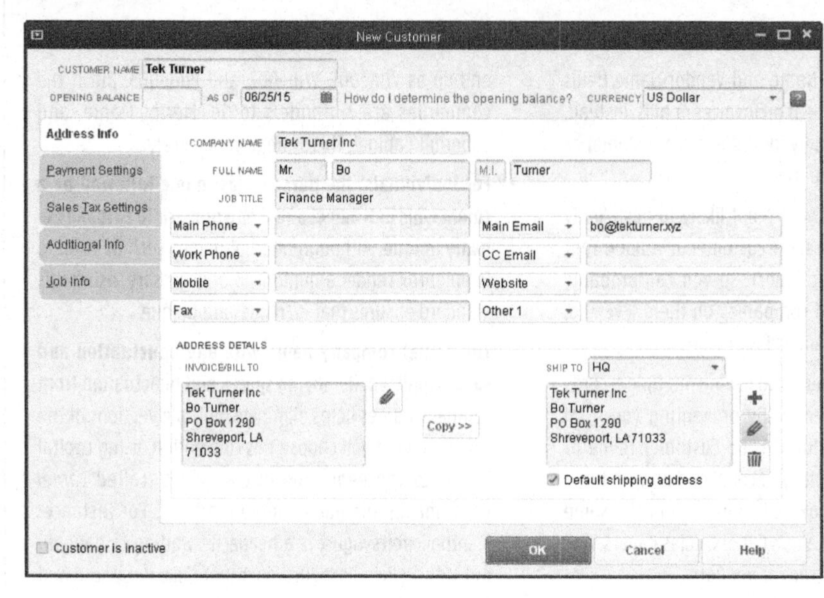

FIGURE 4-2

Although the Opening Balance box beckons from below the Customer Name field here, it's better to leave it blank. The box on page 74 explains the best way to define a customer's opening balance, and the following sections explain what's on each of this window's tabs (Address Info, Payment Settings, and so on).

The box on page 73 tells you how to prevent your QuickBooks Customer:Job List from growing out of control.

The New Customer (and Edit Customer) windows group info onto several tabs so it's easier to find the fields you want to fill in. The contact and address info is all on the first tab, Address Info. All the fields related to payments are on the Payment Settings tab. The Sales Tax Settings tab contains fields for sales tax, so you can skip it entirely if you don't sell taxable goods. The Additional Info tab holds a few miscellaneous fields like customer type, sales rep, and any custom fields you've created. You'll learn about the Job Info tab on page 83. The next several sections step you through each tab and the fields on each one.

NOTE If you've turned on QuickBooks' multiple currency option (page 656), a Currency box appears at the top right of the New Customer window, as shown in Figure 4-2. QuickBooks automatically fills in this box with your home currency, so you usually don't have to change this value. But if the customer pays in a foreign currency, choose it in the Currency drop-down list. (QuickBooks creates a separate Accounts Receivable account for each currency you use.)

TROUBLESHOOTING MOMENT

How Many Names?

If you're a big fish in the small-business pond, you might bump up against limitations on the number of names you can add to your QuickBooks company file. In QuickBooks Pro and Premier editions, the maximum number of names you can have in the Customer, Vendor, Employee, and Other Names lists combined is 14,500. Here are a few techniques you can use to avoid maxing out your name lists:

- **Conserve names**. Be frugal with names by creating one customer or vendor to represent many individual sales or purchases. For example, you can aggregate all your cash sales under a single customer named Cash Sales. Or you can combine all your meal expenses by using a single vendor named Meals. Just keep in mind that, by doing so, you can't produce reports by individual names. However, you can store a customer's name in the Bill To field in sales forms or in the Memo field in a bill, check, or credit card charge.
- **Keep an eye on how many names you have**. Press F2 anytime to call up the Product Information window so you can view the number of entries you have in each list. They appear in the List Information box on the right side of the window.
- **Upgrade**. If there's no getting around your company's gluttony for names, QuickBooks Enterprise Solutions lets you add more than 100,000 names, although Intuit warns you that the program might not run as quickly as the number of names increases.

ENTERING CONTACT INFORMATION

If you plan to bill your customers, ship products to them, or call them to make them feel appreciated, address and contact information is important. You record this info on the New Customer window's Address Info tab. Here's a guide to what you enter on this tab:

- **Company Name**. Unlike the Customer Name field, where you enter whatever name or code you want to use to identify this customer, this field is where you enter the customer's name as you want it to appear on invoices and other forms you create. QuickBooks automatically copies what you type here into the Invoice/Bill To box below.
- **Full Name**. To address invoices, letters, and other company communications, enter the primary contact's salutation or title, first name, middle initial, and last name in the appropriate fields here. QuickBooks automatically copies what you type in these fields into the Invoice/Bill To fields. You can also fill in the Job Title box with this person's title.

NOTE After you create a customer, you can add additional contacts for that customer in the Customer Center. Page 79 tells you how.

FREQUENTLY ASKED QUESTION

Opening Act

Should I add an opening balance for new customers?

Since the Opening Balance field is always visible at the top of the New Customer window (Figure 4-2), you might think you should fill it in. But you're actually better off skipping it.

Entering an opening balance as of a specific date is a shortcut that eliminates having to create the invoices that generate the customer's current balance. But that shortcut comes at a price: If customers haven't paid, then you might have a hard time collecting the money they owe you, especially if you can't tell them what services and products you delivered, how much they cost, the invoice numbers, and when the invoices were due. And when your customers *do* pay, you can't accept those payments against specific invoices to track your Accounts Receivable. In addition, QuickBooks creates a new account in your chart of accounts called Uncategorized Income and creates an invoice that increases (debits) your Accounts Receivable account and increases (credits) your Uncategorized Income account by the amount of the opening balance you enter.

The best way to record a customer's balance is to create QuickBooks invoices for the invoices the customer hasn't paid yet (called "open invoices"). That way, you'll have complete documentation of those sales, the corresponding balance in your Accounts Receivable account, and credits to the correct income accounts. Also, you can then apply the payments that come in to settle those invoices. See Chapter 10 to learn all about invoicing.

TIP The Address Info tab has additional fields for contact information, including four phone numbers, two email addresses, the company's website, and a field labeled "Other 1." If you look closely, you'll notice that the labels for these eight fields have down arrows on them, so you can set these fields to any of 24 contact-related fields, such as Home Phone, LinkedIn, Facebook, Twitter, URL 1, and Skype ID.

- **Invoice/Bill To**. QuickBooks uses the address you enter in this box on invoices. To edit this address, click the Edit button to its right (it has a pencil icon on it). Then, in the Edit Address Information dialog box, fill in the street address, city, state, country, and postal code, or paste that info from another program. QuickBooks automatically turns on the "Show this window again when address is incomplete or unclear" checkbox, which tells the program to notify you when you forget a field like City or when the address is ambiguous. For example, say you fill in the Invoice/Bill To box with "Santa Claus, North Pole." If you then click Copy>> to use that address as a shipping address, QuickBooks opens the Edit Address Information dialog box so you can flesh out the address with a street, city, and arctic postal code.

TIP You can quickly enter addresses and contact info for all your customers by importing data from another program (page 133) or by using QuickBooks' Add/Edit Multiple List Entries feature (page 124).

- **Ship To**. If you don't ship products to this customer, you can skip this field. If the billing and shipping addresses are the same, click Copy>> to replicate the contents of the Invoice/Bill To field in the Ship To field. (The greater-than symbols on the button indicate the direction that QuickBooks copies the address—left to right.) Otherwise, click the + button to this field's right, and then fill in the Add Shipping Address Information dialog box.

TIP You can define more than one ship-to address for a single customer, which is perfect if that customer has multiple locations. To add another ship-to address, click the + button to the field's right, and then fill in the Add Shipping Address Information dialog box. Once you've added shipping addresses, you can choose the one you want from the Ship To drop-down list. When the shipping address you use most often is visible, turn on the "Default shipping address" checkbox below the Ship To field to tell QuickBooks to pick that address automatically. Click the Edit button (the pencil icon to the field's right) or the Delete button (the trash can icon) to modify or remove a shipping address, respectively.

ENTERING PAYMENT INFORMATION

The Payment Settings tab (Figure 4-3) is the place to indicate how the customer pays and how much credit you're willing to extend.

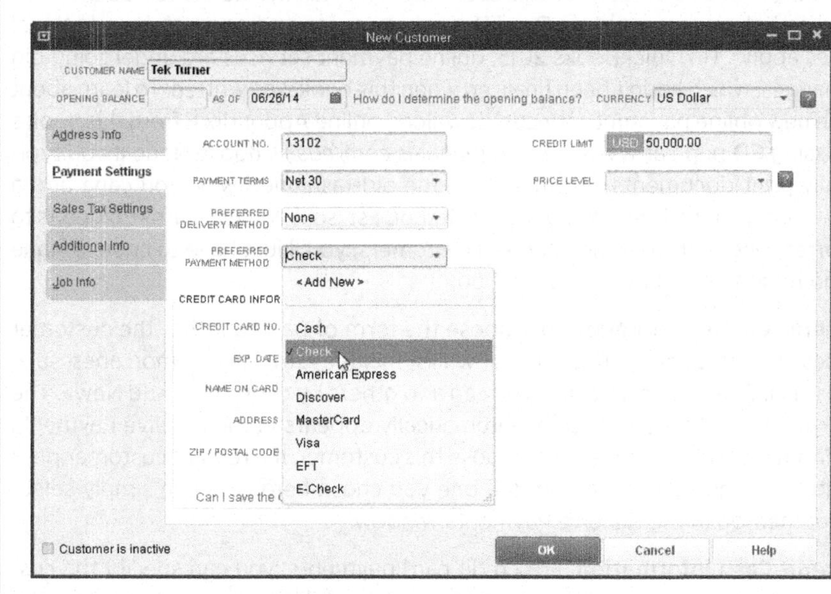

FIGURE 4-3

Several of the fields on this tab use QuickBooks' lists. To jump directly to the list entry you want, in any text box with a drop-down list, type the first few characters of the entry. QuickBooks selects the first entry that matches what you've typed and continues to reselect the best match as you continue typing. You can also scroll to the entry in the list and click to select it. If the entry you want doesn't exist, click <Add New> to create it.

You can use the following fields to specify the customer's payment info:

- **Account No.** Account numbers are optional in QuickBooks. Large accounting programs often assign unique account numbers to customers, which reduces the time it takes to locate a customer's record. In QuickBooks, the Customer Name field works like an identifier, so you're best off reserving the Account No. field for an account number generated by one of your other business systems.

- **Payment Terms**. What you select here represents the payment terms the customer has agreed to. The entries in this drop-down list come from the Terms List (page 150), which QuickBooks uses for both payment terms for your customers *and* the ones you accept from your vendors. Out of the box, this list includes several of the most common payment terms, such as "Due on receipt" and Net 30, but you can choose <Add New> at the top of this list to define additional payment terms. If you leave this field blank in a customer's record, you have to choose the payment terms every time you create an invoice for that customer.

NOTE QuickBooks' payment terms are more than just labels. If you use terms like "1% 10 Net 30" and the customer pays within 10 days, the program is smart enough to calculate a 1 percent discount on the customer's balance.

- **Preferred Delivery Method**. Choose E-mail, Mail, or None to identify the method that your customer prefers for receiving information. If you choose E-mail, QuickBooks automatically turns on the E-mail checkbox when you create forms (such as invoices) for this customer. The Mail method is for QuickBooks Billing Solutions, an add-on QuickBooks service for mailing invoices (additional fees apply). (In QuickBooks 2015, online payment services are undergoing big changes, which hadn't been finalized when this book was written. To learn about the new online payment services, download online Appendix E from this book's Missing CD page at *www.missing manuals.com/cds.*) Choose None if you typically print documents and mail them the old-fashioned way. You can't add a new entry to the Preferred Delivery Method list, so if you use carrier pigeons to correspond with your incarcerated customers, you'll just have to choose None and remember that delivery method.
- **Preferred Payment Method**. Choose the form of payment that the customer uses most frequently. This drop-down list includes several common ones, such as Cash, Check, and Visa, but you can add others by choosing <Add New>. The payment method you specify automatically appears in the Receive Payments window (page 345) when you choose this customer. If a regular customer pays with a method different from the one you chose here, you can simply select that method in the Receive Payments window.
- **Credit Card Information**. For credit card payments, you can specify the customer's card number, the name on the card, the billing address, the Zip/postal code, and the expiration date. (You can enter only one credit card number for each customer.)

NOTE If you store customer credit card numbers in QuickBooks, turn on the Customer Credit Card Protection feature (choose Company→Customer Credit Card Protection, and then click Enable Protection). That way, the program helps you comply with credit card industry security requirements (page 721). For example, any user who views complete credit card information has to create a complex password. In addition, QuickBooks doesn't let you store the card's security code (the three-digit number on the back of the card) because doing so violates your merchant account agreement and PCI (Payment Card Industry) standards.

- **Credit Limit**. This is where you can specify the amount of credit that you're willing to extend to the customer. If you do, then QuickBooks warns you when an order or invoice exceeds this customer's credit limit, but that's as far as it goes—it's up to you to reject the order or to ship your products COD. If you don't plan to enforce the credit limits you assign, then don't bother entering a value in this field.
- **Price Level**. More often than not, customers pay different prices for the same product. Just think about the labyrinth of pricing options for seats on airplanes, for instance. In QuickBooks, price levels represent discounts or markups that you apply to transactions. For example, you might have one price level called Top20, which applies a 20 percent discount for your best customers, and another price level called AuntMabel that extends a 50 percent discount to your Aunt Mabel because she fronted you the money to start your business. (Page 144 explains how to define price levels.) Once you create a price level, you can tell QuickBooks to apply it to every transaction for a customer by choosing it in this box.

NOTE In QuickBooks 2015, Intuit e-Invoicing is the new and improved online payment subscription service. It replaces the Online Payment service available in previous versions of QuickBooks. If you want to email invoices to customers and receive payments electronically, head to Appendix E (available from this book's Missing CD page at *www.missing manuals.com/cds*) for the full scoop on Intuit e-Invoicing.

SPECIFYING SALES TAX INFORMATION

The Sales Tax Settings tab appears whether or not you turn on QuickBooks' Sales Tax preference (page 664). However, if sales tax isn't turned on, the fields on this tab are grayed out. If the customer pays sales tax, choose Tax in the Tax Code drop-down list. Then, in the Tax Item drop-down list, choose the option that specifies the tax rate the customer pays. (Chapter 21 tells the whole story of setting up, charging, and remitting sales tax.)

SPECIFYING ADDITIONAL CUSTOMER INFORMATION

The New Customer window's Additional Info tab serves up a few fields that let you categorize your customers. Here are the fields and some ways to use them:

- **Customer Type**. You might want to classify customers so you can send customized communications to each type or determine which types are the most profitable. (Turn to page 87 to learn how to set up customer and job types and different ways to use them.) Once you've set up customer types, you can categorize a customer by choosing from this drop-down list, which displays the entries from your Customer Type List, such as government, health insurance, or private pay, if you run a healthcare company.
- **Rep**. Choosing a name in this field links a customer to a sales representative, which is helpful if you want to track sales reps' results. But reps don't have to be *sales* representatives: One of the best ways to provide good customer service is to assign a customer service rep to each customer. When you choose <Add

New> here to create a new Rep entry (page 147), you can select existing names from the Employee List, Vendor List, or Other Names List, or add a new name to one of those lists to use as a rep.

- **Custom Fields**. QuickBooks offers 15 custom fields, which you can use to store important info that QuickBooks doesn't include fields for out of the box. Because custom fields don't use drop-down lists, you have to type your entries and take care to enter values consistently. The box below has more about custom fields.

GEM IN THE ROUGH

Defining Custom Fields for Lists

QuickBooks' customer, vendor, employee, and item records include lots of fields you can fill in, but those fields may not cover *all* the information you need. For example, you might want to note which branch office supports a customer. Or for employees, you could track whether they participate in your company's community service program.

QuickBooks' answer to this issue is custom fields. After you create a custom field and apply it to a list, QuickBooks adds the custom field's label and a text box to the Additional Info tab (Figure 4-4, background). You have to type your entries in custom field boxes each time; there's no drop-down list or a way to compare it with text you entered in other records. So it's up to you to make sure that your data entry is correct and consistent.

To set up a custom field, follow these steps:

1. **In the appropriate New or Edit window (New Customer or Edit Vendor, for example), click the Additional Info tab.**
2. **Click the Define Fields button.** The "Set up Custom Fields for Names" dialog box (Figure 4-4, foreground) opens.
3. **In one of the 15 Label cells, type a name for the field.**
4. **If you're associating a custom field with a customer, vendor, or employee record, click the cell for the appropriate list (Cust, Vend, or Empl) and QuickBooks puts a checkmark there.** For example, if the Region custom field applies to both the Customer:Job List and the Vendor List, you'd want checkmarks in both the Cust and Vend columns. You can associate up to seven custom fields with the Customer:Job List, Vendor List, or Employee List. To create a custom field or assign one to an item, in the New Item or Edit Item window, click Custom Fields. The Item List can have up to five custom fields associated with it.
5. **Click OK.** QuickBooks adds your custom field to the appropriate Additional Info tab(s).

NOTE The New Customer window also includes a Job Info tab, which (not surprisingly) has fields for job-related information. If a customer hires you to do more than one job, skip the Job Info tab, since you'll create separate jobs to track that info, as described on page 81. On the other hand, if you don't track jobs, you could use this tab's Job Status field to store the overall status of your work for the customer, although a contact-management or project-management program is probably more useful.

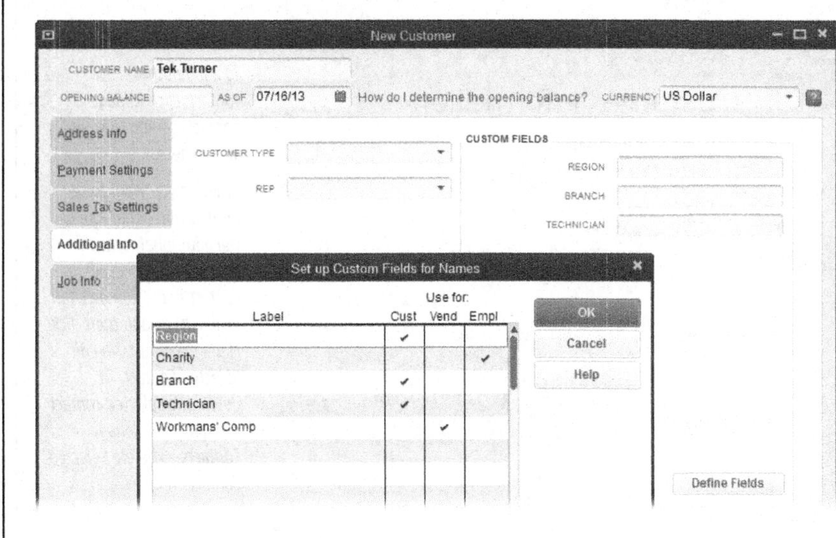

FIGURE 4-4

The "Set up Custom Fields for Names" dialog box (which opens when you click Define Fields in a New or Edit window for customers, vendors, or employees) lets you create up to 15 custom fields. To associate a custom field with a customer, vendor, or employee, click the corresponding cell in the field's row in the table. You can associate a custom field with one or more types of names; for example, with both customers and employees.

Adding More Customer Contacts

When you create a customer, you can specify information about one contact (typically the primary contact) on the New Customer window's Address Info tab (page 73). After you finish creating the customer's record, you can then add more contacts to it. For example, you might add contacts for the person who handles day-to-day billing questions, the employee who resolves shipping issues, and the person to contact if you need to escalate a problem. You can also edit or delete contacts as the people you deal with change offices or transfer to new jobs.

When you select a customer in the Customer Center's Customers & Jobs list, you see contact info for that customer on the right side of the window. To add more contacts to the customer's record, click the Contacts tab in the window's lower-right pane (Figure 4-5). To add a new contact, click Manage Contacts at the bottom of the pane, and then choose Add New to open the Contacts window. Then fill in the boxes, such as Job Title, First Name, Last Name, and so on. After you finish filling them in, click "Save and New" to add another contact or "Save and Close" to close the window.

NOTE The fields in the Contacts dialog box are a subset of those on the New Customer window's Address Info tab. They include Job Title and Name fields, as well as five other fields that are initially set to Work Phone, Work Fax, Mobile, Main Email, and Additional Email. However, if you contact the person via Skype or LinkedIn, click the field label and then choose the appropriate type of contact info from the drop-down list to switch the customer field associated with that box.

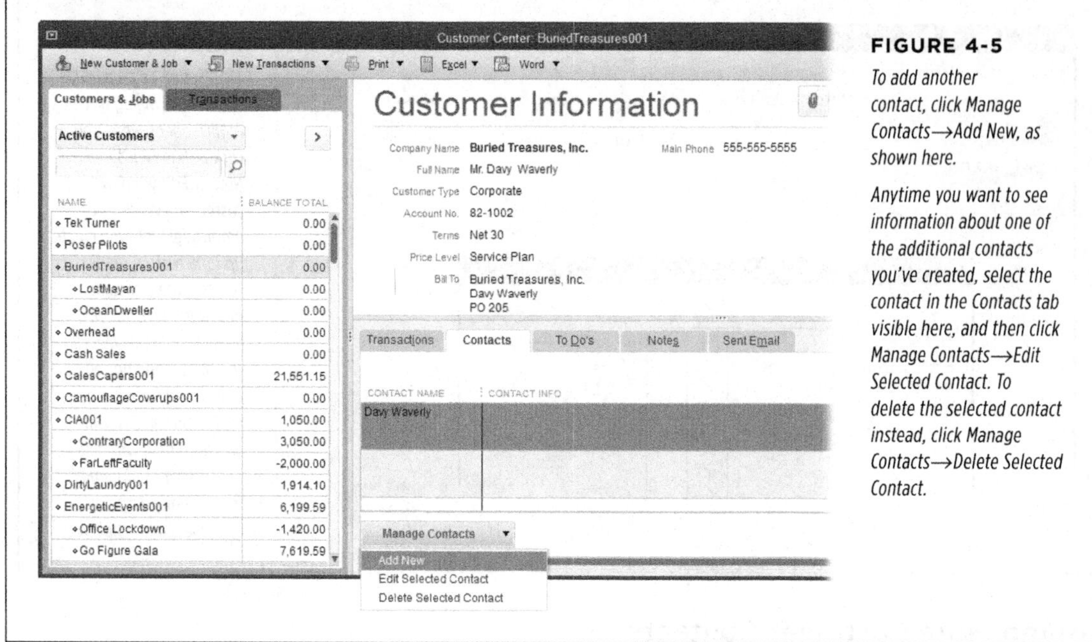

FIGURE 4-5

To add another contact, click Manage Contacts→Add New, as shown here.

Anytime you want to see information about one of the additional contacts you've created, select the contact in the Contacts tab visible here, and then click Manage Contacts→Edit Selected Contact. To delete the selected contact instead, click Manage Contacts→Delete Selected Contact.

Creating Jobs in QuickBooks

Project-based work means that your current effort for a customer has a beginning and an end (even if it sometimes *feels* like the project will last forever). Whether you build custom homes or custom home entertainment systems, you can use QuickBooks' job-tracking features to analyze financial performance by project (known as *job costing*).

Suppose you want to know whether you're making more money on the mansion you're building or on the bungalow remodel, and the percentage of profit you made on each project. As long as you create jobs for each project you want to track, QuickBooks can calculate these financial measures.

NOTE If you sell products and don't give a hoot about job tracking, you can simply invoice customers for the products you sell without ever creating a job in QuickBooks.

In QuickBooks, jobs cling to customers like baby possums to their mothers. A QuickBooks job *always* belongs to a customer. In fact, if you try to create a job before you create a customer, you'll see a message box telling you to create a customer first. Both the New Customer and Edit Customer windows include tabs for customer info *and* job info. So when you create a customer, in effect, you create one job automatically, but you can add as many as you need. This section explains how.

Creating a New Job

Because jobs belong to customers, you have to create a customer (page 70) before you can create any of that customer's jobs. Once the customer exists, follow these steps to add a job to the customer's record:

1. **In the Customer Center's Customers & Jobs tab, right-click the customer you want to create a job for, and then choose Add Job from the shortcut menu.**

   You can also select the customer in the Customers & Jobs tab and then, in the Customer Center toolbar, choose New Customer & Job→Add Job. Either way, the New Job window opens.

2. **In the Job Name box, type a name for the job.**

   This name will appear on invoices and other customer documents. You can type up to 41 characters in this box. The best names are short but easily recognizable to both you *and* the customer.

   QuickBooks fills in most of the remaining job fields with the information you entered for the customer associated with this job. The only time you have to edit the fields on the Address Info, Payment Settings, and Additional Info tabs is when the information on these tabs is different for this job. For example, if materials for the job go to a different shipping address than the customer's, type the address in the fields on the Address Info tab.

3. **If you want to add info about the job type, dates, or status, click the Job Info tab and enter values in the appropriate fields.**

   If you add job types (page 89), you can analyze jobs with similar characteristics, no matter which customer hired you to do the work. Filling in the Job Status field lets you see what's going on by scanning the Customer Center, as shown in Figure 4-6. If you want to see whether you're going to finish the work on schedule, you can document your estimated and actual dates for the job in the Date fields; see the box on page 83 for more about these fields.

NOTE To change the values you can choose in the Job Status field, modify the status text in QuickBooks' preferences (see page 655).

4. **After you've filled in the job fields, click OK to save the job and close the New Job window.**

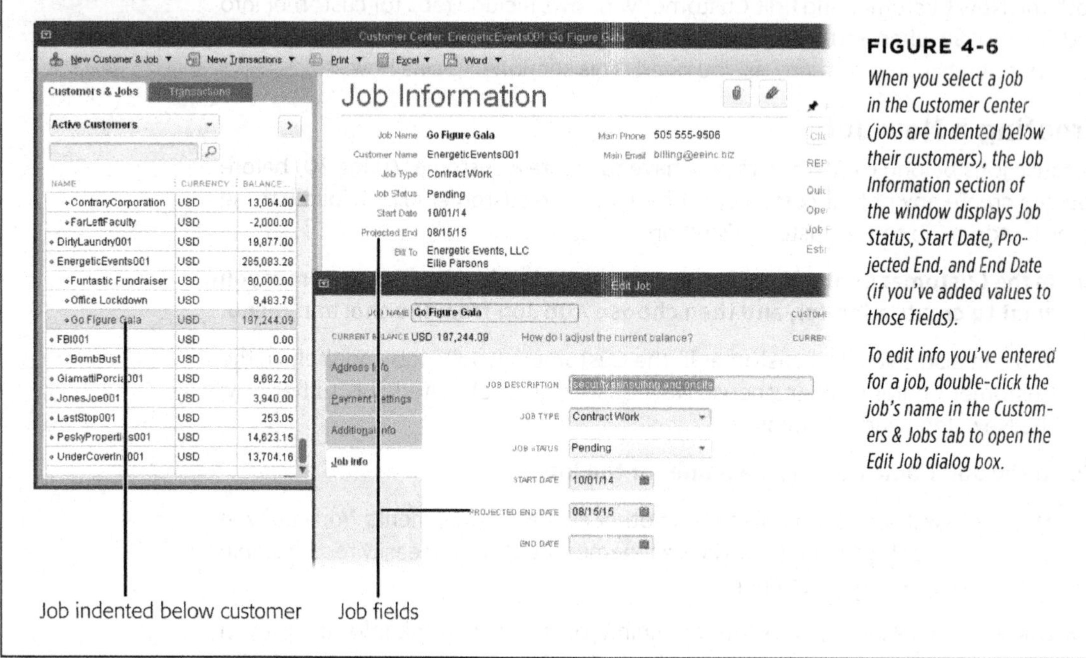

FIGURE 4-6

When you select a job in the Customer Center (jobs are indented below their customers), the Job Information section of the window displays Job Status, Start Date, Projected End, and End Date (if you've added values to those fields).

To edit info you've entered for a job, double-click the job's name in the Customers & Jobs tab to open the Edit Job dialog box.

TIP You can create a new job for a customer right in the Create Invoices window or the Enter Sales Receipts window. To do so, in either window's Customer:Job box, type the name of the existing customer, type a colon, and then type the name of the job. When you press Tab or click in another field, the Customer:Job Not Found message box opens. To simply add the new job to the Customer:Job List, click Quick Add. To open the New Job window so you can enter detailed job info, click Set Up instead. Or click Cancel to close the message box without creating a new job. (This shortcut works only if you haven't filled in the Job Info tab of the customer's record. If the customer's Job Info tab already has data in it, then you'll have to create the job using the New Job window.)

Setting Up Vendors

The methods for creating vendor records are similar to those for creating customers:

- **QuickBooks Setup**. You can use the QuickBooks Setup dialog box to quickly import vendor information from your email program or by copying and pasting data from Excel, as described on page 133.

UP TO SPEED

Specifying Job Information

The fields on the New Job (and Edit Job) window's Job Info tab are optional—you can invoice a customer for a job even if every one is blank. However, both the Job Status and Job Type fields can help you analyze your business performance, past and future. You don't even have to use the terms that QuickBooks provides in the Job Status drop-down list; you can customize the list by adjusting the Jobs and Estimates preferences described on page 655.

Here's a guide to the Job Info tab's fields and how you can put them to use:

- **Job Description**. Here's where you can type a detailed description to remind you about the work in case the job's name doesn't ring any bells.
- **Job Type**. If you categorize your jobs, choose the job type (page 89) from this drop-down menu.
- **Job Status**. This field can indicate trends in your business. If several jobs are set to Pending status, for example, a resource crunch might be in your future.
- **Start Date**. Set this field to your projected or actual start date.
- **Projected End**. If you've estimated when you'll complete the job, select that date here.
- **End Date**. When you complete the job, set this field to the date you actually finished up. By comparing the actual end date with your projection, you can improve future estimates or change how you work in order to finish jobs on time.

- **One at a time**. The New Vendor window lets you create one vendor at a time, although you can create several records in a row without closing the window. Page 84 describes how to create vendors with this window and explains what each field represents.
- **Copying data**. You can also create multiple vendor records with the Add/Edit Multiple List Entries feature (page 124), which lets you paste data from Excel or copy values from vendor to vendor.

TIP You can create a vendor record when you create that vendor's first bill (page 186). Simply choose <Add New> in the Enter Bills window's Vendor drop-down list.

- **Importing data**. This method is another fast way to create oodles of vendor records. After you create a map between QuickBooks' fields and the fields in another program, you can transfer all your vendor info, as described on page 133.

The Vendor Center makes it a breeze to create, edit, and review vendors. It lists the details of your vendors and their transactions in one easy-to-use dashboard. To open the Vendor Center window, choose Vendors→Vendor Center or, in the Vendors panel of the QuickBooks Home Page, click Vendors.

Creating a Vendor

You create a new vendor from the Vendor Center window by pressing Ctrl+N or, in the Vendor Center menu bar, by clicking New Vendor→New Vendor. Either way, the New Vendor window opens.

Many of the fields in this window should be familiar from creating customers in QuickBooks. For example, the Vendor Name field corresponds to the Customer Name field, which you might remember is actually more of a code than a name. Use the same sort of naming convention for vendors that you use for customers (see the box on page 71). And, as with customer records, you're better off leaving the Opening Balance field blank and building your current vendor balance by entering the invoices or bills they send.

The following sections explain how to fill out the rest of the fields in a vendor record.

ADDRESS INFO

If you print checks and envelopes to pay your bills, you'll need address and contact information for your vendors. The New Vendor window's Address Info tab has fields for the vendor's address and contact info, which are almost identical to customer address and contact fields, so see page 70 if you need help filling them in.

PAYMENT SETTINGS

The fields related to payments reside on the Payment Settings tab. Here are the fields and how you fill them in:

- **Account No**. When you create customers, you can assign account numbers to them; when it's *your* turn to be a customer, your vendors return the favor and assign an account number to your company. If you fill in this box with the account number that the vendor gave you, QuickBooks prints it in the memo field of checks you print. Even if you don't print checks, keeping your account number in QuickBooks is handy if a question arises about one of your payments.
- **Payment Terms**. Choose the payment terms that the vendor extended to your company. The entries in this drop-down list come from the Terms List (page 150), so they're the same as for customers.
- **Print Name On Check As**. QuickBooks automatically fills in this box with whatever you enter in the vendor's Company Name field on the Address Info tab. When you print checks, QuickBooks fills in the payee field with the contents of this box, so to print a different name, simply edit what's in this box. For example, say you hire subcontractors and fill in the Company Name field with last names followed by first names. You can then fill in this box with first name followed by last name so the payee on a check appears the way people's names are usually written.
- **Credit Limit**. If the vendor has set a credit limit for your company (like $30,000 from a building supply store), type that value in this box. That way, QuickBooks

warns you when you create a purchase order that pushes your credit balance above this limit.

- **Billing Rate Level**. If you use the Contractor, Professional Services, or Accountant edition of QuickBooks, this is another list that lets you set up custom billing rates for employees and vendors. Billing rates let you price the *services* you sell the same way a Price Level helps you adjust the prices of products you sell. Say you have three carpenters: a newbie, an old-timer, and a finish carpenter. You can set up a Billing Rate Level for each one based on experience. Then, when you create an invoice for your carpenters' billable time, QuickBooks automatically applies the correct rate to each carpenter's hours.

TAX SETTINGS

QuickBooks keeps the two sales tax-related fields on the Tax Settings tab. Here's what they do:

- **Vendor ID**. You have to put the vendor's Employer Identification Number (EIN) or Social Security number in this field *only if* you plan to create a 1099 for this vendor.
- **Vendor eligible for 1099**. Turn on this checkbox if you're going to create a 1099 for this vendor (page 468).

NOTE When you hire subcontractors to do work for you, you have them fill out a W-9 form, which tells you the subcontractor's Taxpayer Identification Number. Then, at the end of the year, you fill out a 1099 tax form that indicates how much you paid them, which they use to prepare their tax returns. See page 468 to learn how QuickBooks can help with 1099s.

ACCOUNT SETTINGS

When you write checks, record credit card charges, or enter bills for a vendor, you have to indicate the expense account to which you want to assign the payment. The Account Settings tab of the New Vendor (and Edit Vendor) window lets you tell QuickBooks which accounts you typically use. But there's an easier approach to filling in expense accounts than selecting accounts on this tab: telling QuickBooks to automatically recall your previous transactions. That way, when you record a bill, check, or credit card charge for a vendor, the program creates a new transaction using the total amount and the accounts you chose on the previous transaction. Page 650 explains how to set the "Automatically recall last transaction for this name" preference.

ADDITIONAL INFO

This tab is rather sparse—it contains only two fields:

- **Vendor Type**. If you classify vendors or generate reports based on their types, choose an entry in this drop-down list or choose <Add New> to create a new type in the Vendor Type List (page 149). For example, if you assign a Tax type to all the tax agencies you remit taxes to, you can easily prepare a report of your tax liabilities and payments.

- **Custom Fields**. If you want to track vendor information that isn't handled by the fields that QuickBooks provides, you can add up to seven custom fields here (see the box on page 78). Say your subcontractors are supposed to have current certificates for workers' comp insurance, and you could be in big trouble if you hire one whose certificate has expired. If you create a custom field to hold the expiration date for each subcontractor's certificate, you can generate a report of these dates.

Working with Customers, Jobs, and Vendors

After you create customer, job, and vendor records, you might have to come back to add more data or change what's already there. For example, you can add contact info as you gather it over time. Or you may decide to categorize customers, jobs, and vendors, which is handy for slicing and dicing your financial performance to analyze income, expenses, profitability, and so on.

Because customers, jobs, and vendors come and go, eventually your Customer:Job List and Vendor List will become cluttered with people and organizations you no longer do business with. Hiding these obsolete names keeps your lists focused. Of course, if you create records by mistake, you can delete them. You can also merge records to, for example, combine the records of two companies that merged in real life. This section explains how to perform all these modifications.

Modifying Customer, Job, and Vendor Information

You can edit customer, job, and vendor records at any time after you create them. For example, you might change address and contact info, increase a credit limit, or shorten payment terms.

QuickBooks gives you a few ways to open the edit windows for these records (Edit Customer, Edit Job, and Edit Vendor). Here are your options:

- **Edit a customer or job**. In the Customer Center (choose Customers→Customer Center), on the Customers & Jobs tab, double-click the customer or job you want to tweak. Alternatively, right-click the customer or job, and then choose Edit Customer:Job from the shortcut menu. You can also select the customer or job you want to edit, and then press Ctrl+E or, on the right side of the Customer Center, click the Edit button (its icon looks like a pencil).

- **Edit a vendor**. In the Vendor Center (choose Vendors→Vendor Center), on the Vendors tab, double-click the vendor you want to modify. You can also right-click the vendor and then choose Edit Vendor from the shortcut menu. Another method is to select the vendor in the list and then press Ctrl+E or, on the right side of the Vendor Center, click the Edit button (its icon looks like a pencil).

NOTE If you want to modify *multiple* customer, job, or vendor records at once, see page 127.

When you edit these records, you can make changes to all the fields except Current Balance. QuickBooks calculates that value from the opening balance (if you provide one) and any unpaid invoices for that customer or job (or unpaid bills for a vendor). Once you create a customer, job, or vendor record, QuickBooks modifies its current balance when you create transactions like invoices (page 226), credit memos (page 288), bills (page 186), journal entries (page 426), or payment discounts (page 352).

You can't change the currency assigned to a customer, job, or vendor if you've recorded any transactions for them. So if the company moves from Florida to France and starts using euros, you'll need to close its current balance by receiving payments for outstanding customer or job invoices, or by paying a vendor's bills. Then you create a *new* customer, job, or vendor record in QuickBooks and assign the new currency to it. After the new record is ready to go, you can make the old record inactive (page 90).

WARNING Unless you've revamped your naming standard (page 71), don't edit the value in a record's name field (Customer Name, Job Name, or Vendor Name). Why? Because doing so can mess up things like customized reports you've created that are filtered by a specific name; such reports aren't smart enough to automatically use the new name. So if you do modify a Customer Name, Job Name, or Vendor Name field, make sure to modify any customizations to use the new name.

Categorizing Customers, Jobs, and Vendors

If you want to report and analyze your financial performance to see where your business comes from and what you spend your money on, categorizing your QuickBooks customers, jobs, and vendors is the way to go. For example, customer and job types can help you produce a report of kitchen remodel jobs that you're working on for residential customers. With that report, you can order catered dinners to treat those clients to customer service they'll brag about to their friends. If you run a construction company, knowing that your commercial customers cause fewer headaches *and* that doing work for them is more profitable than residential jobs is a strong motivator to focus future marketing efforts on commercial work. Similarly, you might categorize vendors to track what you spend with companies versus individual contractors or to classify vendors by geographic location. (Page 140 explains other ways to analyze your business.)

You can add and assign customer, job, and vendor *types* anytime. If you don't have time to add types now, come back to this section when you're ready to learn how.

UNDERSTANDING CUSTOMER, JOB, AND VENDOR TYPES

Business owners often like to look at the performance of different segments of their businesses. Say your building-supply company has expanded over the years to include sales to homeowners, and you want to know how much you sell to homeowners versus professional contractors. In that case, you can make this comparison by using customer types to designate each customer as a homeowner or a contractor, and then total sales by Customer Type, as shown in Figure 4-7. Job types and vendor types work similarly. For example, job types could help you evaluate the profitability of new construction, remodeling, and maintenance work. As you'll learn on page 77, categorizing a customer, job, or vendor is as easy as choosing from the Customer Type, Job Type, or Vendor Type lists.

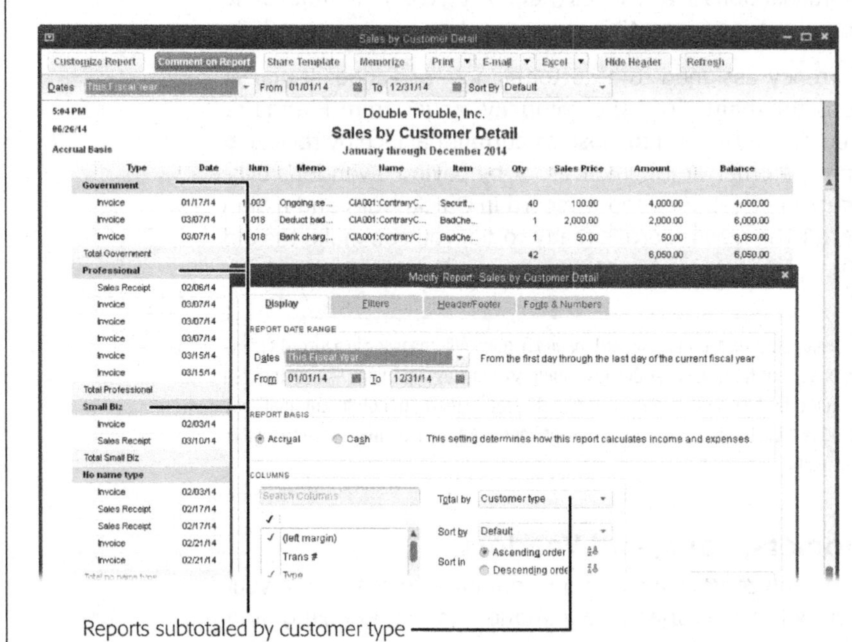

FIGURE 4-7

The Sales by Customer Detail report initially totals income by customer. To subtotal income by customer type (in this example, government, professional, small biz, and so on), click Customize Report in the report window's button bar. On the Display tab of the dialog box that appears, choose "Customer type" in the "Total by" drop-down list (circled), and then click OK.

Types are yours to mold into whatever categories help you analyze your business. A healthcare provider might classify customers by their insurance, because reimbursement levels depend on whether a patient has Medicare, uses major medical insurance, or pays privately. A clothing maker might classify customers as custom, retail, or wholesale, because the markup percentages are different for each. And a training company could categorize customers by how they learned about the company's services. This flexibility applies to job and vendor types, too.

NOTE The Class Tracking feature is a powerful way to categorize results. Classes are particularly potent because of their ability to cross income, expense, account, customer, job, *and* vendor boundaries (which types can't do). To see whether classes can help you analyze your business, turn to page 140.

If you create a company file by using an industry-specific edition of QuickBooks or you select an industry when creating your company file (page 11), QuickBooks fills in the Customer Type, Job Type, and Vendor Type lists with a few types that are typical for your industry. If your business sense is eccentric, you can delete QuickBooks' suggestions and replace them with your own entries. For example, if you're a landscaper, you might include customer types such as Green Thumb, Means Well, and Lethal, so you can decide whether orchids, cacti, or Astroturf are most appropriate.

TIP A common mistake is creating customer types that don't relate to customer characteristics. (The same holds true for job types and vendor types.) For example, if you provide several kinds of services—like financial forecasting, investment advice, and fortunetelling—your customers might hire you to perform any or all of those services. So if you classify your customers by the services you offer, you'll wonder which customer type to choose when someone hires you for two different services. Instead, go with customer types that describe the customer in some way, like Corporate, Individual, and Government.

Here are some suggestions for using customer, job, and vendor types and other QuickBooks features to analyze your business in different ways:

- **Customer business type**. Use customer types to classify your customers by their business sector, such as Corporate, Government, and Small Business.
- **Nonprofit "customers."** For nonprofit organizations, customer types such as Member, Individual, Corporation, Foundation, and Government Agency can help you target fundraising efforts.
- **Job type**. Jobs are optional in QuickBooks, so job types matter only if you track your work by the job. If your sole source of income is selling chocolates in your store, jobs and job types don't matter—your relationship with your customers is one long run of selling and delivering products. But for project-based businesses, job types add another level of filtering to the reports you produce. If you're a writer, then you can use job types to track the kinds of documents you produce (Manual, White Paper, and Marketing Propaganda, for instance) and filter the Job Profitability Report by job type to see which forms of writing are most lucrative. (Page 597 describes how to filter reports.)
- **Vendor type**. Use vendor types to categorize vendors in different ways, such as by industry, location, or type of company.
- **Location or region**. If your company spans multiple regions, offices, or business units, classes can help track business performance. See page 140 for info.
- **Services**. To track how much of your business comes from each type of service you offer, set up separate income accounts or subaccounts in your chart of accounts, as outlined on page 50.
- **Products**. To track product sales, create one or more income accounts or subaccounts in your chart of accounts.

TIP Create income accounts for broad categories of income, such as services and products. Don't create separate accounts for each service or product you sell; instead, you can use items to track sales for each service and product, as described in Chapter 5.

- **Expenses**. To track expenses, create one or more expense accounts or subaccounts in your chart of accounts.
- **Marketing**. To identify your income based on how customers learned about your services, enter this info in a custom field (page 78). That way, you can create a report that shows the revenue you've earned from different marketing efforts—and figure out which ones are worth the money.

CREATING A VENDOR, CUSTOMER, OR JOB TYPE

You can create these types when you set up your QuickBooks company file or at any time after setup. See page 148 to learn how to create customer, job, and vendor types and subtypes. Here's how to see the different type *lists*:

- **Customer types:** Choose Lists→Customer & Vendor Profile Lists→Customer Type List.
- **Job types:** Choose Lists→Customer & Vendor Profile Lists→Job Type List.
- **Vendor types:** Choose Lists→Customer & Vendor Profile Lists→Vendor Type List.

Hiding Records

Hiding customers, jobs, and vendors isn't about barricading them in a conference room when the competition shows up to talk to you. Because QuickBooks lets you delete these records only in very limited circumstances, hiding them helps keep your lists manageable and your financial history intact.

Although your work with a customer, job, or vendor might be over, you still have to keep records about your past relationship. But old records can clutter up your QuickBooks lists, making it difficult to select the people and companies you still work with. The solution is to *hide* old records, which also removes those names from all the lists that appear in transaction windows so you can't select them by mistake. Hiding old records is better than deleting them because QuickBooks retains the historical transactions for those customers, jobs, and vendors so you can reactivate them if you renew the relationship.

To hide a customer or job, in the Customer Center's Customers & Jobs tab, right-click the customer or job and then, from the shortcut menu, choose Make Customer:Job Inactive. The customer and any associated jobs disappear from the list. Figure 4-8 shows you how to *unhide* (reactivate) customers.

To hide a vendor, in the Vendor Center's Vendors tab, right-click the vendor and then, from the shortcut menu, choose Make Vendor Inactive.

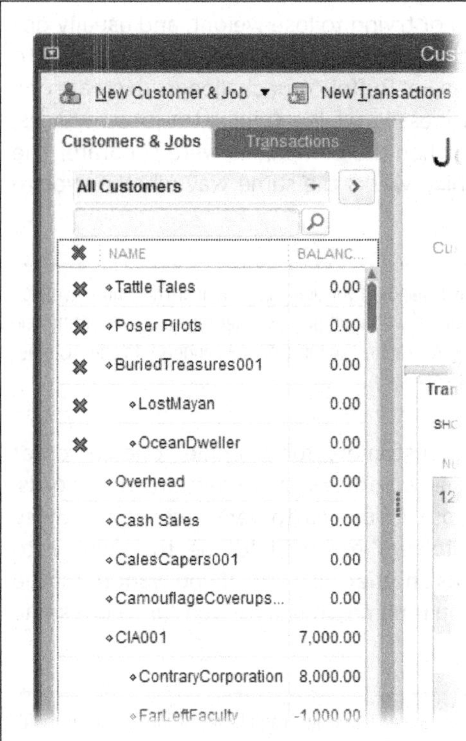

FIGURE 4-8

To make hidden customers visible again and reactivate their records, in the drop-down list at the top of the Customers & Jobs tab, choose All Customers, as shown here.

When you do that, QuickBooks displays an X to the left of every inactive customer in the list. Simply click that X to restore the customer to active duty.

Deleting Records

You can delete customers, jobs, or vendors only if there's no activity for them in your QuickBooks file. If you try to delete a record that has even one transaction associated with it, QuickBooks tells you that you can't delete that record. In that case, you can still hide the customer, job, or vendor, as described in the previous section.

If you created a customer, job, or vendor by mistake and the record has no transactions associated with it, here's how to delete it:

1. **In the Customer Center, on the Customers & Jobs tab (or in the Vendor Center, on the Vendors tab), select the customer, job, or vendor you want to delete.**
2. **Press Ctrl+D (or choose Edit→Delete Customer:Job or Edit→Delete Vendor.)**

   If the customer, job, or vendor has no transactions, QuickBooks asks you to confirm that you want to delete the record; click OK. If you see a message stating that you *can't* delete it, read the previous section (page 90) to learn how to hide the record instead.

Merging Records

Suppose you remodeled buildings for two companies run by brothers: Morey's City Diner and Les' Exercise Studio. Morey and Les conclude that their businesses have a lot of synergy—people are either eating or trying to lose weight, and usually doing both. To smooth out their cash flow, they decide to merge their companies into More or Less Body Building and All You Can Eat Buffet. Your challenge: to create one customer in QuickBooks from the two businesses, while retaining the jobs, invoices, and other transactions that you created when the companies were separate. The solution: QuickBooks' merge feature, which works the same way whether you're merging customers, jobs, or vendors.

TIP Here's another instance when merging can come in handy: If you don't use a standard naming convention (page 71 offers several easy conventions), you could end up with multiple customer records representing one real-life customer, such as Les' Exercise Studio and LesEx. You can merge these doppelgangers into one customer just as you can merge two truly separate companies into one.

When you merge records in QuickBooks (customers, for example), one customer retains the entire transaction history for the two original customers. In other words, you don't so much merge two customers as turn one customer's records into those of another. If you want to merge two customers' records into one, the secret is to rename one customer to the same name as another. Likewise, if you want to merge two jobs' or vendors' records into one, you rename one job or vendor to the same name as another.

NOTE There's a catch to renaming customers: The customer you rename can't have any jobs associated with it. So if there are jobs associated with the customer you want to rename, you have to move all those jobs to the customer you intend to keep *before* you start the merge. Your best bet: Subsume the customer with fewer jobs so you don't have to move very many. (If you don't use jobs, then subsume whichever customer you want.)

To merge customer, job, or vendor records with a minimum of frustrated outbursts, follow these steps:

1. **If you work in multi-user mode, switch to single-user mode for the duration of the merging process.**

   See page 489 to learn how to switch to single-user mode and then back to multi-user again after the merge is complete.

2. **Open the Customer Center or Vendor Center.**

   To open the Customer Center, in the Home Page's Customers panel, click Customers. To open the Vendor Center, in the Home Page's Vendors panel, click Vendors.

3. **If you're going to subsume a customer that has jobs associated with it, on the Customers & Jobs tab, position your cursor over the diamond to the left**

of the job you want to reassign. If you're merging jobs or vendors instead, jump to step 6.

Jobs are indented beneath the customer to which they belong.

4. **When your cursor changes to a four-headed arrow, drag the job under the customer you plan to keep.**

   As you drag, the cursor changes to a horizontal line between two arrowheads, as shown in Figure 4-9, left.

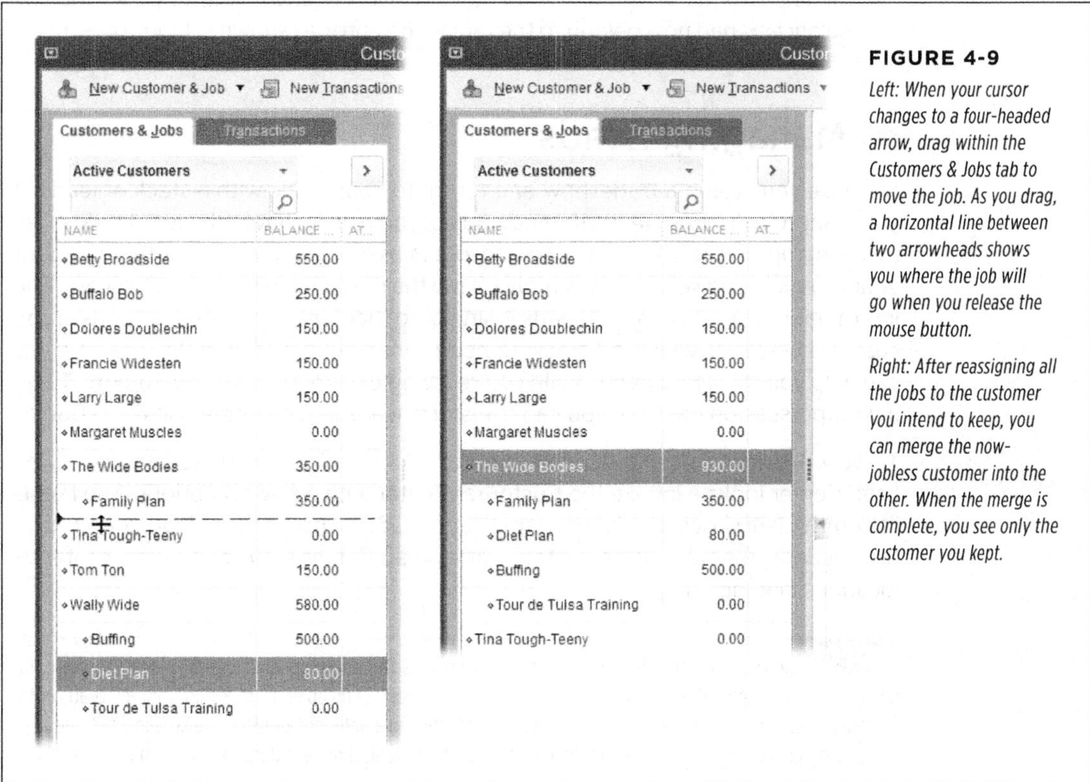

FIGURE 4-9

Left: When your cursor changes to a four-headed arrow, drag within the Customers & Jobs tab to move the job. As you drag, a horizontal line between two arrowheads shows you where the job will go when you release the mouse button.

Right: After reassigning all the jobs to the customer you intend to keep, you can merge the now-jobless customer into the other. When the merge is complete, you see only the customer you kept.

5. **Repeat steps 3 and 4 for each job that belongs to the customer you're going to subsume.**

   If the customer has hundreds of jobs, moving them is tedious at best—but move them you must.

6. **For a customer or job, on the Customers & Jobs tab, double-click the name of the customer or job you want to subsume. For a vendor, on the Vendors tab, double-click the name of the vendor you want to subsume.**

   You can also edit a record by selecting its name on the Customers & Jobs or Vendors tab and then, on the right side of the Customer or Vendor Center, clicking the Edit button (the pencil icon). Depending on the type of record you selected, the Edit Customer, Edit Job, or Edit Vendor dialog box opens.

7. **In the edit dialog box, edit the Customer Name, Job Name, or Vendor Name field to match the name of the record you intend to keep, and then click OK.**

   QuickBooks displays a message letting you know that the name is in use and asking if you want to merge the records.

8. **Click Yes to complete the merge.**

   In the Customer or Vendor Center, the record you renamed disappears and any balances it had now belong to the remaining entry, as shown in Figure 4-9, right.

Managing Leads

Suppose you attend a tradeshow and return to your office with a stack of leads. If you want to turn those leads into new sales, you usually have a host of to-dos, like following up on the questions that prospects asked, sending out more info about your products and services, or simply taking the next step in your sales process. The information you collect about leads is similar to that for customers, but leads aren't customers—yet. If your lead-tracking needs are simple, QuickBooks' Lead Center can help you track prospects while you're trying to turn them into customers. Then, if your persuasion pays off, you can transform leads into customers in QuickBooks.

To work with leads, open the Lead Center by choosing Customers→Lead Center. The Lead Center looks a lot like the Customer Center with a few exceptions. The Leads list on the left shows the leads' names and status. And because leads don't have transactions, the tabs at the bottom of the Lead Center focus on to-dos, contacts, locations, and notes.

NOTE The Lead Center's features aren't as powerful as the ones you find in market-leading customer relationship management (CRM) programs. For example, you can't send an email to a lead from the Lead Center or create an estimate for a lead. But if your leads are scribbled in a notebook or listed in a spreadsheet, the Lead Center can help you organize them—and because it's built into QuickBooks, it doesn't cost extra.

If you need more sophisticated lead-tracking tools, skip the Lead Center and check out CRM programs that integrate with QuickBooks. You can find a few dozen listed at the Intuit marketplace (*http://tinyurl.com/7xntgpe*). QuickBooks also integrates with Salesforce, a major CRM provider. You can learn about this program in the Lead Center window by clicking the "Learn about Salesforce" button to the right of the Lead Information heading.

Here are some of the actions you can perform with leads:

- **Create a new lead**. In the Lead Center toolbar, click New Lead. In the Add Lead dialog box, name the lead. The Status field lets you classify leads as Hot, Warm, or Cold, so you know which ones to focus on first. The Company tab contains fields for info such as company name, telephone number, email address, website, and main address. (You can add other addresses if the company has several locations.) The Contacts tab lets you add contact info for people in the company. The first contact you enter is designated the Primary Contact, but you can add other contacts by clicking the Add Another Contact button.

NOTE After you create a lead, you can add more contacts or locations to it by double-clicking it on the left side of the Lead Center to open the Edit Lead dialog box.

- **View leads**. Like the Customer Center, the Lead Center lists your leads on the left side of the window. The list shows the leads' names and status. You can filter the list by choosing an entry from the drop-down menu above the lead list. For example, choose Active Leads to see all the leads you're working on, or choose Hot to filter the list for all your most promising leads.
- **Search leads**. If your sales team is prolific, your lead list could be quite long. You can search for specific leads by typing part of the lead's name in the unlabeled text box above the lead list and then clicking the magnifying glass icon. QuickBooks filters the list to show all the leads that contain the text you typed.
- **Edit a lead**. After you create a lead, you can view its information and edit it. Simply double-click the lead in the list on the left side of the Lead Center.
- **Create a to-do**. To add a to-do for a lead, select the lead in the Lead Center's list. Next, click the To Do's tab at the bottom right of the Lead Center, and then click To Do at the bottom of the tab. (See page 478 to learn how to create different types of to-dos.) The To Do's tab shows info about that lead's to-dos, including the type of to-do, its priority, when it's due, and whether it's complete.
- **Add notes**. To add notes about a lead, first select the lead in the Lead Center's list. Next, click the Notes tab at the bottom right of the Lead Center, and then click Add Notes. In the "Note For [customer]" dialog box, type the information you want to record. For example, you might specify the particular products or services that lead is interested in or her budget. When you add a note, QuickBooks automatically records the date you wrote it. To filter the notes by date, choose a time period in the Notes tab's Date drop-down list.
- **Convert a lead to a customer**. Leads are stored in a separate list from your customers. When you turn a lead into a customer in real life, you can easily do the same in QuickBooks. Simply right-click the lead in the Lead Center's list and choose "Convert to a Customer" in the shortcut menu (or click the "Convert this Lead to a Customer" button in the Lead Center's upper right). QuickBooks asks you to confirm this action, because you can't *undo* it. When you click OK, the lead disappears from the Active Leads list. You can see the leads you've converted to customers by choosing Converted Leads from the drop-down list at the top left of the Lead Center. Although you can still view converted leads in the Lead Center, you can no longer edit them there. They now appear as customers in the Customer Center, and you can edit them there as you do other customers (page 86).

- **Import leads**. To import information about several leads, in the Lead Center toolbar, click Import Multiple Leads. The Import Leads dialog box that appears lets you type values into a table, but you can also copy and paste information from an Excel spreadsheet like you do in the Add/Edit Multiple List Entries window (page 124).

CHAPTER

5

Setting Up Items

Whether you build houses, sell gardening tools, or tell fortunes on the Internet, you'll probably use *items* in QuickBooks to represent the products and services you sell. But to QuickBooks, things like subtotals, discounts, and sales tax are items, too. In fact, *nothing* appears in the body of a QuickBooks sales form (such as an invoice) unless it's an item.

Put another way, to create invoices (which you'll learn how to do in Chapter 10), sales receipts, and other sales forms in QuickBooks, you need customers *and* items. (You can also use items to fill in the bills and other purchase forms you record.) So, now that you've got your chart of accounts, customers, jobs, and vendors set up in QuickBooks, it's time to dive into items.

This chapter begins by helping you decide whether your business is one of the few that doesn't need items at all. But if your organization is like most and uses business forms like invoices, sales receipts, and so on, the rest of the chapter will teach you how to create, name, edit, and manage the items you add to forms. You'll then learn how to use items in invoices and other forms in the remaining chapters of this book.

What Items Do

For your day-to-day work with QuickBooks, items save time and increase consistency on sales and purchase forms. Here's the deal: Items form the link between what you sell (and buy) and the income, expense, and other types of accounts in your chart of accounts. When you create an item, you describe what the item is, how much you pay for it, how much you sell it for, and the accounts to which you post the corresponding income, expense, cost of goods sold, and asset value. You also create items for other stuff you add to sales forms, like discounts, shipping charges, and subtotals.

For example, say you charge $75 an hour for the bookkeeping service you provide, and you want that income to show up in your Financial Services income account. In that case, you'd create an item for bookkeeping and associate it with your income account. That way, when you add the item to a sales form, QuickBooks automatically multiplies the price per hour by the number of hours to calculate the full charge, and then posts the income to your Financial Services account.

Items make it easy to look at your company's finances from different perspectives. You can set up your chart of accounts based on the accounts you want to show on your financial statements (page 443), which are usually summarized to include only what your bankers or other interested parties need to know. Items also let you track income and expenses to the level of detail you want. For example, you might set up two income accounts: one for services and one for products. However, you can create items for *every* type of service and product you sell.

When it's time to analyze how your business is doing, items shine. QuickBooks has built-in item-based reports that show the dollar value of sales by item or the number of inventory units you've sold. (To learn how to use inventory reports, see page 534. Other item-based reports are described throughout this book.) You can work out which accounts to assign items to on your own or with the help of your accountant (a good idea if you're new to bookkeeping), and then specify those accounts in your items, as shown in Figure 5-1. QuickBooks remembers these assignments from then on.

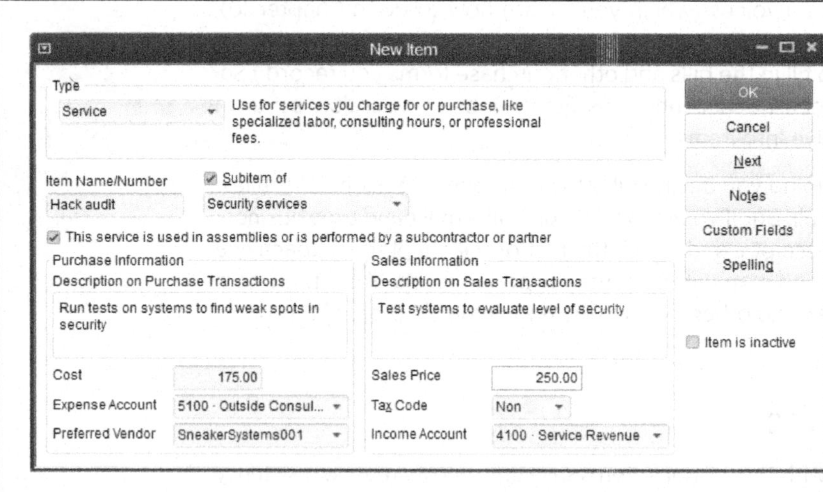

FIGURE 5-1

If you had to enter item details each time you added an entry to an invoice, you'd be bound to make mistakes. But by setting up an item using this window, you can make sure you use the same information on sales and purchase forms each time you sell or buy that item. (When the inevitable exception to the rule arises, you can edit the item info that QuickBooks fills in on the sales form.)

When You Don't Need Items

Without items, you can't create any type of sales form in QuickBooks, including invoices, statements, sales receipts, credit memos, and estimates. But if you don't *use* sales forms, you don't need items. Not many organizations operate without these forms, but here are a few examples of ones that do:

- Old Stuff Antiques sells junk—er, antiques—on consignment. Kate, the owner, doesn't pay for the pieces; she just displays them in her store. When she sells a consignment item, she writes paper sales receipts. She deposits the money customers hand over into her checking account and writes checks to sellers for their cut of the proceeds.
- Tony owns a tattoo parlor specializing in gang insignias. He doesn't care how many tattoos he creates and—for safety's sake—he doesn't want to know his customers' names. All Tony does is deposit the cash he receives upon completing each masterpiece.
- Dominic keeps the books for his charity for iceberg-less penguins. The charity accepts donations of money and fish, and it doesn't sell any products or perform services to earn additional income. He deposits the monetary donations into the charity's checking account and enters each deposit in QuickBooks. He keeps track of the donors' contributions and his frozen fish inventory in a spreadsheet.

Should You Track Inventory with Items?

If your business is based solely on selling services, you can skip this section. But if you sell products, keep reading to understand your options.

You can handle products in two ways: by stocking and tracking inventory or by buying products only when work for your customers requires them. The approach you use affects the types of items you create in QuickBooks.

If you buy products specifically for customers, you need items, but you don't have to track the quantity on hand. In this case, you create *Non-inventory Part items*, which you'll learn about shortly. For example, caterers prepare meals for various types of events, so they usually purchase the materials and food they need for a specific job and charge the customer for those goods. Because caterers don't keep food in stock, they don't have to track inventory and can therefore use Non-inventory Part items.

On the other hand, grocery stores sell the same kinds of food products over and over. These businesses purchase goods and store them in their stores, selling them to their customers each day. These goods can be set up as *Inventory Part items* (page 519) in QuickBooks. When you use the program's inventory feature, QuickBooks keeps track of how many products you have on hand, increasing the number as you purchase them and decreasing the number when you sell them to customers.

So, before you start working with items in QuickBooks, you actually have *two* inventory decisions to make: First, should you track inventory? And second, should you track inventory *in QuickBooks*? Read on to learn how to make these decisions.

Because tracking inventory requires more effort than buying only the materials you need, use the following guidelines to determine whether your business should track inventory:

- **Track inventory if you keep products in stock to resell to customers**. If your company stocks faux pony placemats to resell to customers, those placemats are inventory. By tracking inventory, you know how many units you have on hand, how much they're worth, and how much money you made on the placemats you've sold.

  On the other hand, the faux pony mousepads you keep in the storage closet for your employees are business supplies. Most companies don't bother tracking inventory for supplies like these, which they consume in the course of running their business.

- **Track inventory if you want to know when to reorder products so you don't run out**. If you sell the same items over and over, keeping your shelves stocked means more sales (because the products are ready to ship out as soon as an order comes in). QuickBooks can remind you when it's time to reorder a product.

- **Don't track inventory if you purchase products specifically for jobs or customers**. If you special-order products for customers or buy products for specific jobs, you don't need to track inventory. After you deliver the special order or complete the job, your customer has taken and paid for the products, and you simply have to account for the income and expenses you incurred.

- **Don't track inventory if you rent equipment to customers**. If you receive income from renting or leasing assets you own, then you can show the value of the for-rent products as an asset in QuickBooks and the rental income as a Service item (page 108), so you don't need Inventory Part items.

Your business model might dictate that you track inventory. However, QuickBooks' inventory-tracking feature has some limitations. For example, it lets you store only 14,500 items, max. How can you tell whether QuickBooks' inventory fits the bill? If you answer yes to any of the following questions, then QuickBooks *isn't* the program to use to handle the products you sell:

- **Do you sell products that are unique?** In the business world, tracking inventory is meant for businesses that sell commodity products, such as electronic equipment, and stock numerous units of each product. If you sell unique items, such as fine art or compromising Polaroid photos, you'd eventually hit QuickBooks' 14,500 item limit. For such items, consider using a spreadsheet to track the products you have on hand.

TIP Here's one way to handle unique products using QuickBooks: When you sell your unique handicrafts, record the sales in QuickBooks using generic Non-inventory Part items. For example, use an item called Oil Painting on the sales receipts for the artwork you sell and put more specific information about the painting in the sales receipt's Description field.

- **Do you manufacture the products you sell out of raw materials?** QuickBooks' inventory can't follow materials as they wend through a manufacturing process or track inventory in various stages of completion.

NOTE QuickBooks Premier and Enterprise editions can track inventory for products that require *some* assembly. For instance, if you create Wines from Around the World gift baskets using the wine bottles in your store, you can build an Inventory Assembly item (page 522) out of wine and basket Inventory Part items. The box on page 524 explains another way to track assembled inventory.

- **Do you value your inventory using a method other than average cost?** QuickBooks Pro and Premier calculate inventory value by average cost. If you want to use other methods—like last in/first out (LIFO) or first in/first out (FIFO)—you can export inventory data to a spreadsheet program and then calculate inventory cost there (page 688). Or you can upgrade to QuickBooks Enterprise and subscribe to Intuit's Advanced Inventory add-on service (which costs extra).
- **Do you use a point-of-sale system to track inventory?** Point-of-sale inventory systems often blow QuickBooks' inventory tracking out of the water. If you forgo QuickBooks' inventory feature, then you can periodically update your QuickBooks file with the value of your inventory from the point-of-sale system.

NOTE If you like the point-of-sale idea but don't have a system yet, consider Intuit's QuickBooks Point of Sale, an integrated, add-on product for retail operations that tracks store sales, customer info, and inventory. Head to *http://pointofsale.intuit.com* for details.

You don't have to use QuickBooks' inventory feature if you don't want to. For example, if you perform light manufacturing, you can track the value of your manufactured inventory in a database or other program. You can then periodically add journal entries (page 426) to QuickBooks to show the value of in-progress and completed inventory.

If you *do* opt to use QuickBooks to track inventory, Chapter 20 shows you how, from first step to last.

TIP The answer to your inventory dilemma could be an add-on program that tracks inventory *and* keeps QuickBooks informed. One of the best is FishBowl Inventory (*www.fishbowlinventory.com*).

Planning Your Items

Setting up items in QuickBooks is a lot like shopping at a grocery store. If you need only a few things, you can shop without a list. Similarly, if you're going to use just a few QuickBooks items, you don't need to write them down before you start creating them. But if you use dozens or even hundreds of items, planning your Item List can save you lots of frustration.

NOTE If you jumped straight to this section, now is the time to go back and read page 99, which helps you decide whether to use items that represent services, inventory, or non-inventory products.

By deciding how to name and organize your items *before* you create them in QuickBooks, you won't waste time editing and reworking existing items to fit your new naming scheme. Read on to learn what you should consider before creating items.

Generic or Specific?

Conservation can be as important with QuickBooks' items as it is for the environment. QuickBooks Pro and Premier can hold no more than 14,500 items, which is a problem if you sell unique products, such as antiques, or products that change frequently, such as current clothing styles for teenagers. Once you use an item in a transaction, you can't delete that item, so you could end up with lots of items you no longer use. By planning how specific your items will be, you can keep your Item List lean.

For instance, a generic item such as Top can represent a girl's black Goth T-shirt one season and a white, poplin button-down shirt the next. Generic items have their limitations, though, so use them only if necessary. For example, you can't track inventory properly when you use generic items. QuickBooks might show that you have 100 tops in stock, but that doesn't help when your customers are clamoring for white button-downs and you have 100 black Goth T-shirts. In addition, the information you store with a generic item won't match the specifics of each product you sell. So, when you add generic items to an invoice or a sales form, you'll have to edit a few fields, such as Description or Price, as shown in Figure 5-2.

Naming Items

Brevity and recognizability are equally desirable characteristics in item names. Short names are easier to type and manage, but they can be unintelligible. Longer names take more effort to type and manage but are easier to decipher. Decide ahead of time which kind of name you prefer, and then stick with it as you create items.

QuickBooks encourages brevity because it limits item names to 31 characters (including spaces). If you sell only a handful of services, you can name your items the same things you call them. For instance, for a tree service company, names like Cut, Limb, Trim, Chip, and Haul work just fine. But if your Item List runs into the hundreds or thousands, some planning is in order. Here are factors to consider when naming items:

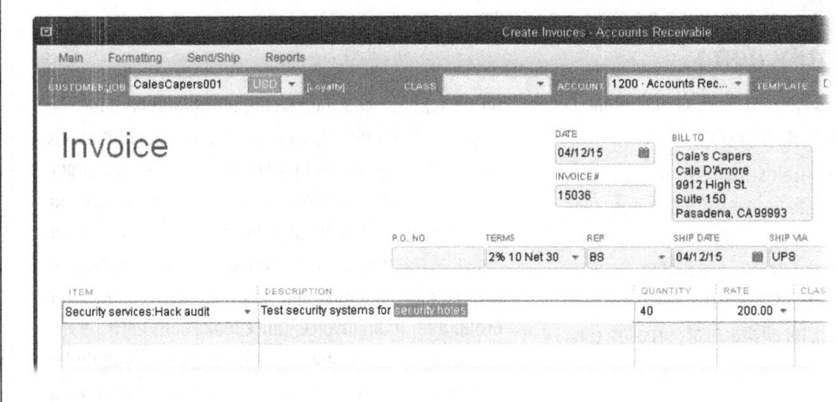

FIGURE 5-2

QuickBooks automatically fills in fields like Description and Price (or Rate, as shown here) with values you've saved in item records. But you can edit those fields once you add an item to an invoice or bill, whether you use generic or specific items to describe what you sell. Just click a field in a form, select the text you want to change, and then type the new value.

- **Aliases**. Create a pseudonym to represent the item. For a carpet company, "Install standard" could represent the installation along with vacuuming and hauling waste, while "Install deluxe" could include the standard installation *plus* moving and replacing furniture. You can include the details in the item's description.
- **Sort order**. In the Item List window (Lists→Item List), QuickBooks sorts items first by type and then in alphabetical order by name. So if you want your items to appear in some logical order in drop-down lists (like an invoice item table), pay attention to the order of characteristics in your item names. For example, if you created "Deluxe install" and "Standard install" Service items, other Service items beginning with the intervening letters of the alphabet would separate them in drop-down lists. By naming your installation items "Install deluxe" and "Install standard" instead, they'll show up in your Item List one after the other.
- **Abbreviations**. If you have to compress a great deal of information into an item name, you'll have to abbreviate. For example, suppose you want to convey all the things you do when you install a carpet, including installing tack strips, padding, and carpet; trimming carpet; vacuuming; and hauling waste. That's more than the 31 characters you have to work with. Poetic won't describe it, but something like "inst trim vac haul" says it all in very few characters. The box on page 104 suggests two other ways to identify complicated items.

POWER USERS' CLINIC

Other Ways to Identify Items

If you want to keep item names lean but still include detailed information, look to these two item features:

- **Descriptions**. Items have fields for both names and descriptions. When you create an invoice, you choose the item's name from a drop-down list, but the invoice that the customer sees shows the item's description. So you can keep your item names brief by putting the details in the Description field, which, for all practical purposes, can hold an unlimited amount of text.
- **Group**. Instead of creating one item that represents several phases of a job, you can create separate items for each phase and then create a *Group item* (page 114) to include those phases on an invoice. For instance, create one item for installing tack strips, padding, and carpet, and then create additional items for vacuuming, hauling, and moving and replacing furniture. Then create a Group item that contains all the individual Service items included in a carpet-installation job. That way, when you add that Group item to an invoice, QuickBooks adds each Service item to a line on the invoice. A Group item isn't limited to just Service items, though. It can include other types of items, such as Non-inventory Part, Inventory Part, and Other Charge items.

NOTE Construction companies in particular can avoid long hours of item data entry by using third-party estimating programs. Construction-estimating programs usually include thousands of entries for standard construction services and products. If you build an estimate with a program that integrates with QuickBooks, you can import that estimate into QuickBooks and then sit back and watch as it automatically adds all the items in the estimate to your Item List. To find such QuickBooks-integrated programs, go to *http://marketplace.intuit.com*. On the menu bar, click Find Software→Find Solutions by Industry. Then, on the By Industry tab, choose Construction/Contractors.

Subitems

If you keep all your personal papers in one big stack, you probably have a hard time finding everything from birth certificates to tax forms to bills and receipts. If you've got one big list of items in QuickBooks, you're in no better shape. To locate items more easily, consider designing a hierarchy of higher-level items (*parents*) and one or more levels of subitems, as shown in Figure 5-3. The box on page 105 explains how to make sure you have items for every purpose.

For example, a landscaping business might create top-level items for trees, shrubbery, cacti, and flower bulbs. Within the top-level tree item, the landscaper might create subitems for several species: maple, oak, elm, sycamore, and dogwood. You can create up to five levels of subitems to represent categories such as size (seedling, established, and mature, say).

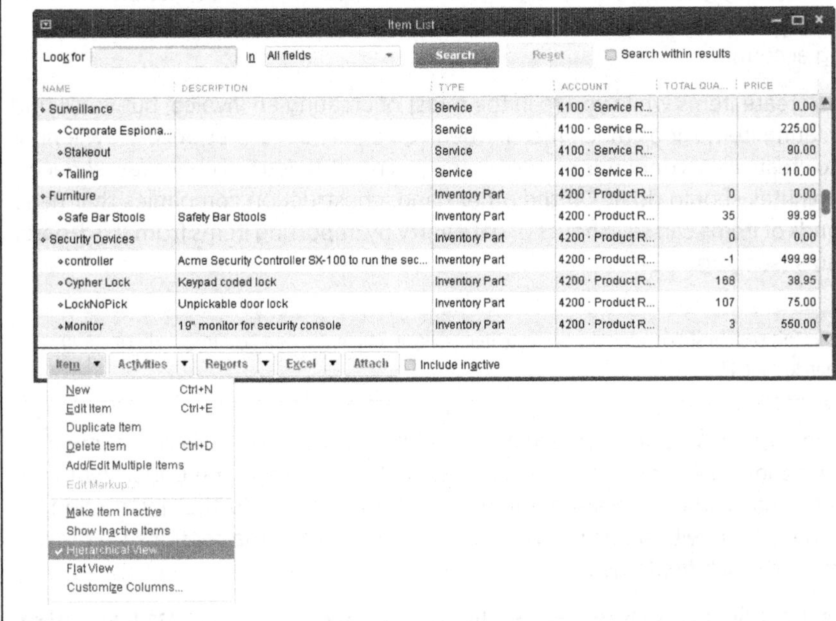

FIGURE 5-3

The Item List window's Hierarchical View (shown here) indents subitems, making it easy to differentiate the items you use to categorize the list from the items you actually sell. To check which view you're seeing, click the Item button at the bottom of the window to display the menu shown here.

If you work with long lists of subitems, the parent item might end up off the screen. To keep the hierarchy of items visible at all times, choose Flat View, wherein QuickBooks uses colons to separate the names of each level of item and subitem.

WORD TO THE WISE

Catchall Subitems

When you develop a hierarchy of parent items and subitems, eventually someone in your company will run across a service or product that doesn't fit any of the existing subitems. If you assign a transaction to a parent item that has subitems, then QuickBooks automatically creates a subitem called "Other" as a catch basin. For example, if you have a parent item called Security Services, you'd get a subitem called Security Services-Other.

Catchall items can act as holding pens while you figure out which specific subitem you should use. They're also an easy way to look for transactions that should be reassigned to a different subitem. For instance, you can create a transaction by using the Security Services-Other item, and then change the item in the transaction later (page 293) when you've identified (or created) the correct subitem.

Creating Items

The best time to create items is *after* you've created your accounts but *before* you start purchasing goods from vendors or invoicing customers. Each item links to an account in your chart of accounts, so creating items goes quicker if you can choose existing accounts.

You can create items while you're in the midst of creating an invoice, but you'll find that creating items goes much faster when you create several at once. How long it takes to create items depends on how many you need. If you sell only a few services, a few minutes should do it. On the other hand, construction companies that need thousands of items can save hours of data entry by importing items from third-party programs (see page 681).

NOTE This section shows you how to create items one at a time. To learn how to quickly create *multiple* items, jump to page 124.

Each item type has its own assortment of fields, but the overall process of creating an item is the same for every type. With the following procedure under your belt, you'll find that you can create many of your items without further instruction. (If you *do* need help with fields for a specific item type, read the sections that follow to learn what each field does.)

1. **On the QuickBooks Home Page, click Items & Services (or choose Lists→Item List) to open the Item List window.**

   When you first display the Item List, QuickBooks sorts the entries in it by type. The sort order for the item types isn't alphabetical—it's the order that types appear in the Type drop-down list, as shown in Figure 5-4. You can change the Item List's sort order by clicking a column heading.

2. **Press Ctrl+N or click Item→New.**

   QuickBooks opens the New Item window and selects Service in the Type drop-down list. (You'll learn about the various item types starting on page 108.)

3. **To create a Service item, just press Tab to proceed with naming the item. To create any *other* type of item, choose it in the Type drop-down list.**

   Some item types won't appear in the list if you haven't turned on the corresponding feature. For example, the Inventory Item type doesn't appear unless you've turned on inventory tracking.

4. **In the Item Name/Number box, type a unique identifier for the item.**

   For example, if you opt for long and meaningful names, you might type *Install carpet and vacuum*. For a short name, you might type *Inst Carpt*. See page 102 for guidelines on naming items.

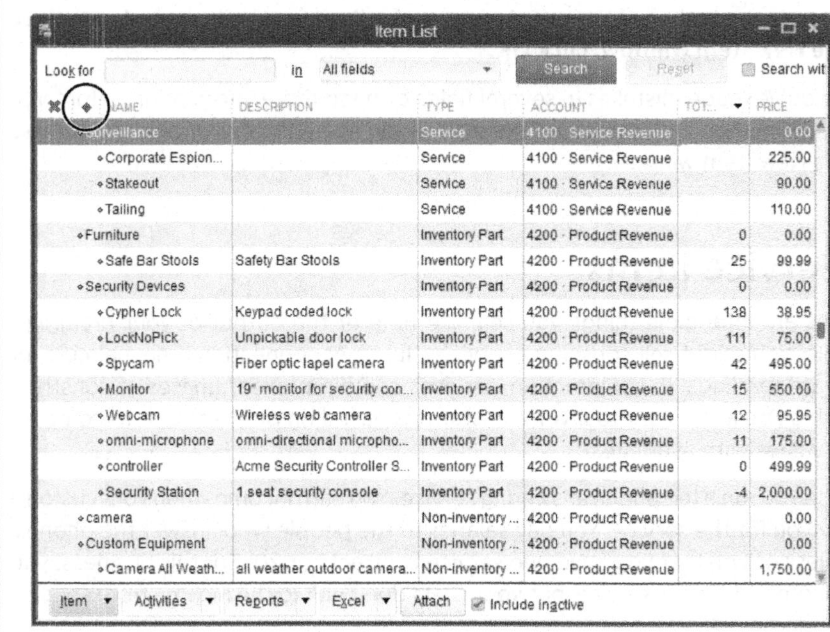

FIGURE 5-4

QuickBooks lists items by type and then in alphabetical order within each type.

You can change the list's sort order by clicking a column heading. If you click the heading again, QuickBooks toggles the list between ascending and descending order.

To return the list to being sorted by type, click the diamond to the left of the column headings (circled), which appears anytime the list is sorted by a column other than Type.

5. **To make this item a subitem, turn on the "Subitem of" checkbox, and then choose the item that you want to act as the parent.**

   If the parent item already exists, simply choose it from the "Subitem of" drop-down list. To create the parent *while* creating the subitem, choose <Add New> at the top of the "Subitem of" list, and then jump back to step 3 to begin the parent-creation process.

NOTE Subitems and parents have to be the same type, and you can't create subitems for Subtotal, Group, or Payment items.

6. **Complete the other fields as described in the following sections for the type of item you're creating.**

   QuickBooks will use the info you enter to fill in these fields on sales and purchase forms. For example, it uses the sales price you enter here on invoices when you sell some units. If the sales price changes each time, simply leave the item's sales price field (which is labeled Rate, Price, or Sales Price depending on the type of item and the item's settings) set to zero. That way, QuickBooks doesn't fill in a price, so you can type one in each time you sell the item. (Even if you set a value for an item, you can overwrite it whenever you use that item on a sales form.)

NOTE You have to assign an account to every item, whether it's a parent item or not.

7. **If you have additional items to create, click Next to save the current item and start another. If you want to save the item you just created and close the New Item window, click OK.**

   If you've made mistakes in several fields or need more information before you can complete an item, click Cancel to throw away the current item and close the New Item window.

Service Items

Services are intangible things you sell, like time or the output of your brain. For example, you might sell consulting services, Internet connection time, haircuts, or tarot card readings. In construction, services could represent phases of construction, which makes it easy to invoice customers based on progress and to compare actual values with estimates.

Suppose you run a telephone answering service. You earn income when your customers pay you for the service. You pay salaries to the people who answer the phones, regardless of whether you have two service contracts or 20. For this business, you earn income with your service, but your costs don't link to the income from specific customers or jobs.

On the other hand, in some companies, such as law practices, the partners get paid based on the hours they bill, so the partners' compensation is an expense associated directly with the firm's income. Services that you farm out to subcontractors work similarly. If you offer a 900 number for gardening advice, you might have a group of freelancers who field the calls and whom you pay only for their time on the phone. In these scenarios, you still earn income for the service you sell, but you also have to pay the law-practice partners or the subcontractors who do the work. The partners' or subcontractors' cost relates to the income for that service.

The mighty Service item single-handedly manages *all* types of services, whether you charge by the hour or by the service, with associated expenses or without. Conveniently, QuickBooks displays different fields depending on whether a service has costs associated with income. This section describes the fields you fill in when creating Service items.

Service Items Without Associated Costs

Here's how the fields in the New Item window work when you're creating a Service item that *doesn't* include purchasing services from someone else (that is, when you leave the "This service is used in assemblies or is performed by a subcontractor or partner" checkbox turned *off*, as shown in Figure 5-5):

- **Description**. Type a detailed explanation of the service in this box. This text appears on invoices and sales forms, so use terms that your customers will understand.

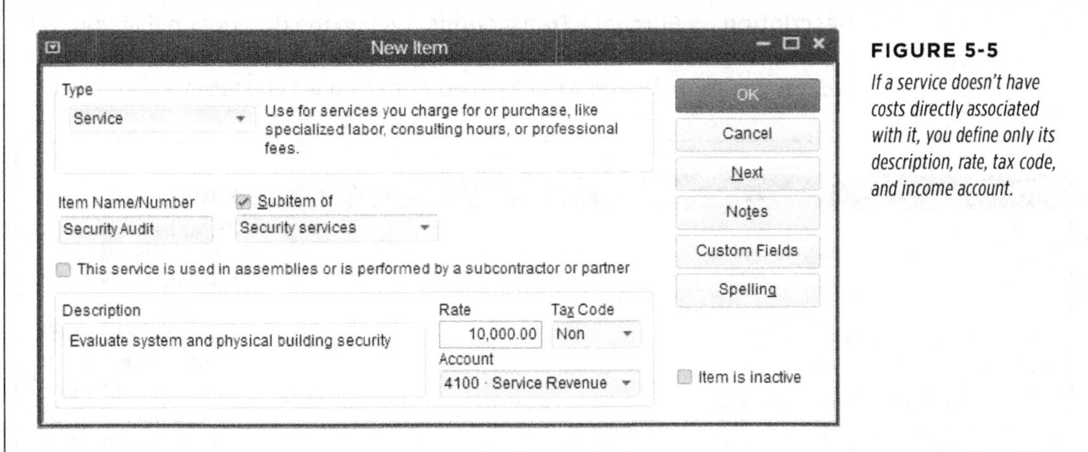

FIGURE 5-5

If a service doesn't have costs directly associated with it, you define only its description, rate, tax code, and income account.

- **Rate**. Type how much you charge customers for the service. You can enter a flat fee or a charge per unit of time. For example, you might charge $9.95 per call, charge by the minute, or charge $200 for unlimited calls each month. When you add the item to an invoice, QuickBooks multiplies the quantity by the sales price to calculate the total charge.

  If the item's cost varies, leave the Rate set to 0; you can then enter the price when you create an invoice or other sales form. If the rate is often the same, fill in the most common rate. Then, when you add the item to an invoice, you can modify the rate if you want to use a different amount. For services that carry a flat fee, use a quantity of *1* on your invoices.

NOTE QuickBooks multiplies the rates by the quantities you add to sales forms. Be sure to define the rate in the same units (by hours or days, for example) so that QuickBooks calculates your income and expenses correctly.

- **Tax Code**. Most Service items are nontaxable, so you'll choose *Non* here more often than not. (This field appears only if you've turned on the sales tax feature, as described on page 547.)
- **Account**. Choose the income account to which you want to post the income for this service, whether it's a catchall income account for all your services or one you created specifically for this type of service.

Service Items with Associated Costs

If you sell services that have associated costs, such as when you hire someone else to perform those services, you have to set up the Service item to include those costs.

The key to displaying the fields you need to fill in is the "This service is used in assemblies or is performed by a subcontractor or partner" checkbox, which is turned on in Figure 5-6. In addition to the basics like Item Name/Number and "Subitem of," here are the fields you fill in when an item *does* have associated costs:

- **Description on Purchase Transactions**. Type in the description that you want to appear on the purchase orders you issue to subcontractors or vendors and the bills you record in QuickBooks to go with the ones you receive from vendors.

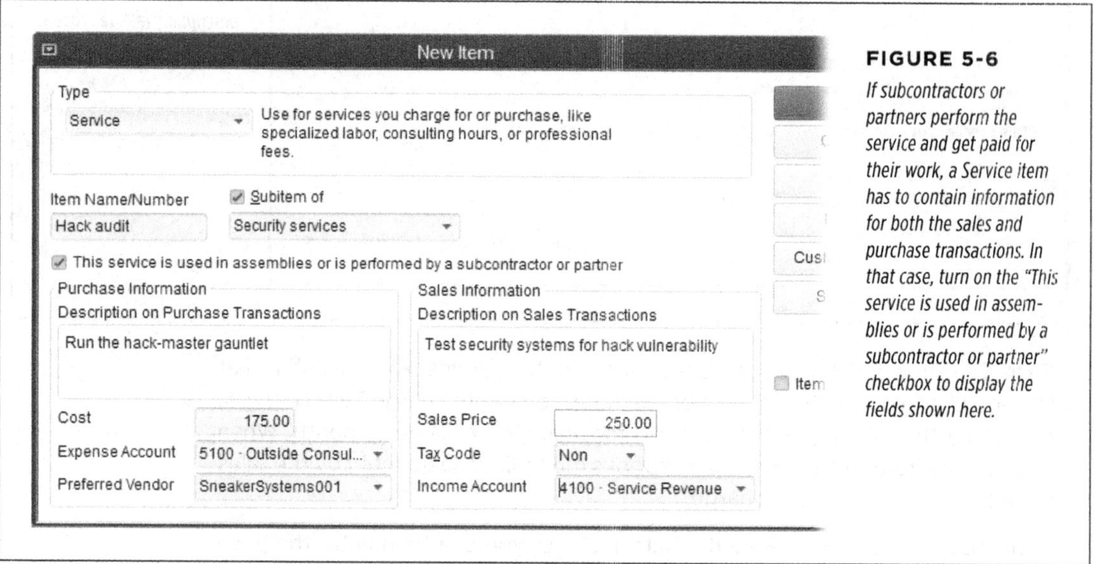

FIGURE 5-6

If subcontractors or partners perform the service and get paid for their work, a Service item has to contain information for both the sales and purchase transactions. In that case, turn on the "This service is used in assemblies or is performed by a subcontractor or partner" checkbox to display the fields shown here.

- **Cost**. Enter what you pay for the service, which can be an hourly rate or a flat fee. For example, if a subcontractor performs the service and receives $175 for each hour of work, type *175* in this field. If the cost varies, leave this field set to 0; you can enter the actual cost when you create a purchase order.
- **Expense Account**. Choose the account where you want to post what you pay for the service. If a subcontractor does the work, choose a Cost of Goods Sold account or an expense account for subcontractor or outside consultants' fees. If a partner or owner performs the work, choose a Cost of Goods Sold account or an expense account for service-related costs.
- **Preferred Vendor**. If you almost always use the same vendor for a service, choose that vendor in this drop-down list. That way, if you don't select a vendor when you create a purchase order, QuickBooks selects that vendor when you add this Service item. However, if you purchase the item from several vendors, leave this field blank.
- **Description on Sales Transactions**. This field appears on sales forms like invoices and sales receipts. QuickBooks automatically copies the text from the Description on *Purchase* Transactions box into this field, but if your vendors

use technical jargon that your customers wouldn't recognize, you can change the text in this box to something more meaningful.

- **Sales Price**. Type in how much you charge customers for the service, as you would in the Rate field for a Service item that you *don't* purchase from someone else (page 109).
- **Tax Code**. Most Service items are nontaxable, so you'll choose *Non* here most of the time. (This field appears only if you've turned on QuickBooks' sales tax feature, as described on page 547.)
- **Income Account**. Choose the income account to which you want to post the income for this service, whether it's a catchall income account for all services or one you created specifically for this type of service.

Product Items

Products you sell to customers fall into three categories: ones you keep in inventory, ones you special order, and ones you assemble. QuickBooks can handle inventory as long as your company passes the tests on page 100. Likewise, products you purchase specifically for customers or jobs are no problem. But to handle products you assemble like gift baskets or gizmos made from widgets, you'll need QuickBooks Premier or Enterprise edition (which include Inventory Assembly items [page 522]).

This section describes the three types of product items that QuickBooks offers and shows you how to fill in the New Item window's fields for Non-inventory Part items. See Chapter 20 for the full scoop on creating inventory-related items.

Choose one of these three QuickBooks item types for the products you sell:

- **Non-inventory Part**. If you purchase products specifically for a job or customer and don't track how many products you have on hand, use Non-inventory Part items. Unlike Inventory Part items, this type has at most two account fields: one for income you receive when you sell the part, and another for the expense of purchasing the part in the first place.
- **Inventory Part**. Use this type for products you purchase and keep in stock for resale. Retailers and wholesalers are the obvious examples of inventory-based businesses, but other types of companies like building contractors may track inventory, too. With Inventory Part items, you can track how many you have, how much they're worth, and when you should reorder.

NOTE You can create Inventory Part items only if you turn on QuickBooks' inventory feature as described on page 519.

- **Inventory Assembly**. This item type (available only in QuickBooks Premier and Enterprise editions) is perfect when you sell products built from your inventory items. For example, say you stock wine bottles and related products like corkscrews and glasses, and you assemble them into gift baskets. With an Inventory Assembly item, you can track the number of gift baskets you have on hand, as well as the individual inventory items that go into them. You can also assign a different price to the gift basket than the total of the individual products.

Non-Inventory Part Fields

You'll need Non-inventory Part items if you use purchase orders to buy supplies or other products that you don't track as inventory. For example, suppose you're a general contractor and you buy materials for a job. When you use Non-inventory Part items, QuickBooks posts the cost of those products to an expense account and the income from selling them to an income account. You don't have to bother with an inventory asset account because you transfer ownership of these products to the customer almost immediately. (See page 192 to learn how to charge your customer for these reimbursable expenses.)

The good news is that Non-inventory Part items use all the same fields as Service items (page 108), although there are a few subtle differences you need to know. Take the following disparities into account when you create Non-inventory Part items:

- **This item is used in assemblies or is purchased for a specific customer:job**. This checkbox goes by a different name than the one for Service items, but its effect is the same. Turn it on when you want to use different values on purchase and sales transactions for items you resell. When this checkbox is on, QuickBooks displays Purchase Information and Sales Information sections, like the ones shown in Figure 5-6 (page 110). For Non-inventory Part items, choose income and expense accounts you set up specifically for products.

  If the Non-inventory Part item is for office supplies (or other items you don't resell) that you want to place on a purchase order, then leave this checkbox off because you won't have sales values. Read on to find out what happens when you turn off this checkbox.

- **Account**. If you don't resell this product, leave the "This item is used in assemblies or is purchased for a specific customer:job" checkbox turned off, and you'll see only one Account field. QuickBooks considers the account in this field the expense account for the purchase.
- **Tax Code**. This field works exactly the same way as it does for a Service item. Choose Non if the products are nontaxable (like groceries), and Tax if they're taxable. (This field appears only if you've turned on QuickBooks' sales tax feature, as described on page 547.)

TIP Many companies don't bother with purchase orders—forms that record what you order from a vendor—when buying office supplies. But if you want to track whether you receive the supplies you bought, you can create purchase orders for them (page 523). Then use Non-inventory Part items for supplies you add to purchase orders but don't track as inventory. (Purchase orders are non-posting transactions [page 57], so they don't affect the balances in your accounts.)

Other Types of Items

If a line on a sales form isn't a service *or* a product, read this section to figure out the type of item you need. (Chapter 21 covers setting up Sales Tax items.)

Other Charge

The Other Charge item type is aptly named because you use it for any charge that isn't quite a service or a product, like shipping charges, finance charges, or bounced-check charges. Other Charge items can be percentages or fixed amounts. For example, you could set up shipping charges that are the actual cost of shipping, or calculate shipping as a percentage of the product cost.

If customers hold back a percentage of what they owe until you complete their jobs satisfactorily, create an Other Charge item for the *retainer* (the portion of your fee that the customer doesn't initially pay). Then, when you create the invoice, enter a negative percentage so QuickBooks deducts the retainer from the invoice total. When your customer approves the job, create another invoice, this time using another Other Charge item named Retention, to charge the customer for the amount she withheld.

TIP Progress invoices (page 284) are another way to invoice customers for a portion of a job. They're ideal if you invoice the customer based on the percentage of the job you've completed or on the parts of the job that are complete.

Other Charge items can be linked to expenses—or not. Here are your options:

- **A charge linked to expenses**. For Other Charge items, the checkbox for hiding or showing both purchase and sales fields is labeled "This item is used in assemblies or is a reimbursable charge." Turn on this checkbox when you want to set the Cost field to what you pay and the Sales Price field to what you charge your customers. You'll see the same sets of fields for purchases and sales as you do for Service and Non-inventory Part items.
- **A charge without associated expenses**. You can create charges that *don't* link directly to expenses by leaving the "This is used in assemblies or is a reimbursable charge" checkbox turned off. You can then create a percentage-based charge, which is useful for calculating shipping based on the value of the products being shipped. With the checkbox turned off, instead of the Cost and Sales Price fields, you see the "Amount or %" field. If you want to create a charge for a specific amount (like the value for a country club's one-time initiation fee), type a whole or decimal number in this field, as shown in Figure 5-7. To create a percentage-based charge, type a number followed by "%," such as *10%*, in this field instead.

NOTE When you add a percentage-based Other Charge item to an invoice, such as shipping, QuickBooks applies the percentage to the previous line in the invoice. So if you want to apply the Other Charge percentage to *several* items, then add a Subtotal item (explained next) to the invoice on the line above the Other Charge item.

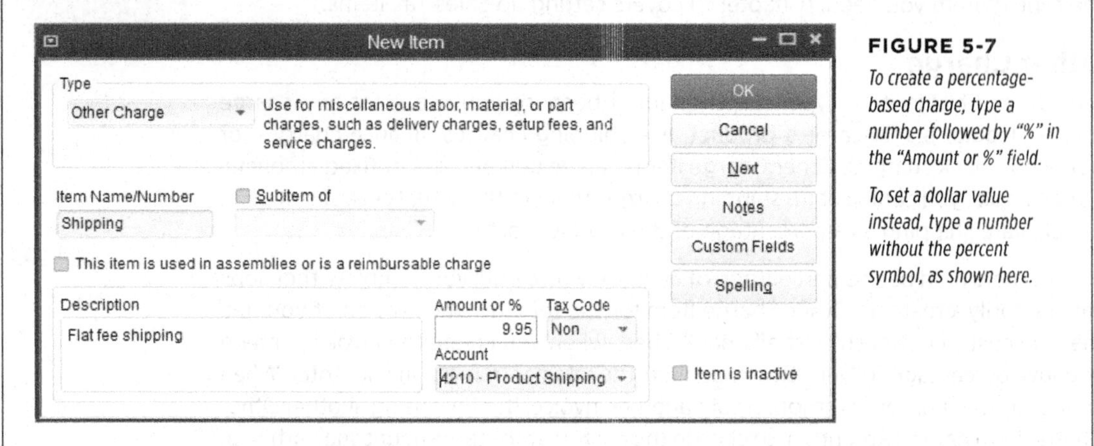

FIGURE 5-7

To create a percentage-based charge, type a number followed by "%" in the "Amount or %" field.

To set a dollar value instead, type a number without the percent symbol, as shown here.

Subtotal

You'll need a Subtotal item if you discount only some of the items on a form or calculate shipping based on the value of the order. You need to create only *one* Subtotal item in QuickBooks, because a Subtotal item does just one thing: totals all the amounts of the preceding lines up to the last subtotal or the beginning of the invoice. That means you can add more than one subtotal to an invoice. For example, you can use one Subtotal item to add up the services you sell before applying a preferred-customer discount, and a second Subtotal item for product sales when you have to calculate shipping.

Because you can't change a Subtotal item's behavior, Subtotal items have just two fields: Item Name/Number and Description. You can type any name and description you wish in these fields, but in practically every case, Subtotal says it all.

Group

Group items are great timesavers, and they're *indispensable* if you tend to forget things. As the name implies, a Group item represents several related items you often buy or sell together. Create a Group item that contains items that always appear together, such as each service you provide for a landscaping job. That way, when you add the Landscaping Group item to an invoice, QuickBooks automatically adds the Service items for the various phases, such as Excavation, Grading, Planting, and Cleanup. You can also use a Group item to show or hide the underlying items, which is useful when you create fixed-price invoices (page 240) and don't want the customer to see the underlying details.

Here's how you fill in the New Item window's fields for a Group item:

- **Group Name/Number**. Type a name for the group that gives a sense of the individual items within it, such as Security Package.
- **Description**. Type the description that you want to appear on sales forms.
- **Print items in group**. To show all the underlying items on your invoices, turn on this checkbox. Figure 5-8 shows an invoice that prints all the items in a group (top) and what an invoice looks like when you leave this checkbox turned off (bottom).

P.O. No.	Terms	Project

Quantity	Description	Rate	Amount
4	Review system security and physical building security	200.00	800.00
8	Install custom-designed security system	150.00	1,200.00
1	1 seat security console	2,000.00	2,000.00T
4	Wireless web camera	95.95	383.80T
5	Wireless web camera	95.95	479.75T
	Full package for security including audit, install, basic equipment		4,863.55

P.O. No.	Terms	Project

Quantity	Description	Rate	Amount
	Full package for security including audit, install, basic equipment		4,863.55

FIGURE 5-8

Top: If you turn on the "Print items in group" checkbox when you create a Group item (Security Package, in this example) and then add it to an invoice, QuickBooks lists the individual items it contains.

Bottom: If you leave the "Print items in group" checkbox turned off, you'll see the individual items in the Create Invoices window, but the invoice you print to send to the customer will list only the Group item itself, along with the total price for all the items in the group.

- **Item**. To add an item to a group, click a blank cell in the Item column, shown in Figure 5-9, and then choose the item you want. You can also create a new item by choosing <Add New> from the drop-down list.
- **Qty**. Group items can include different quantities of items, just like a box of notecards usually includes a few more envelopes than cards. For each item in the group, type how many you typically sell as part of that group. If the quantity of each item varies, type *0* in the Qty cells. You can then specify the quantities on your invoices after you add the Group item.

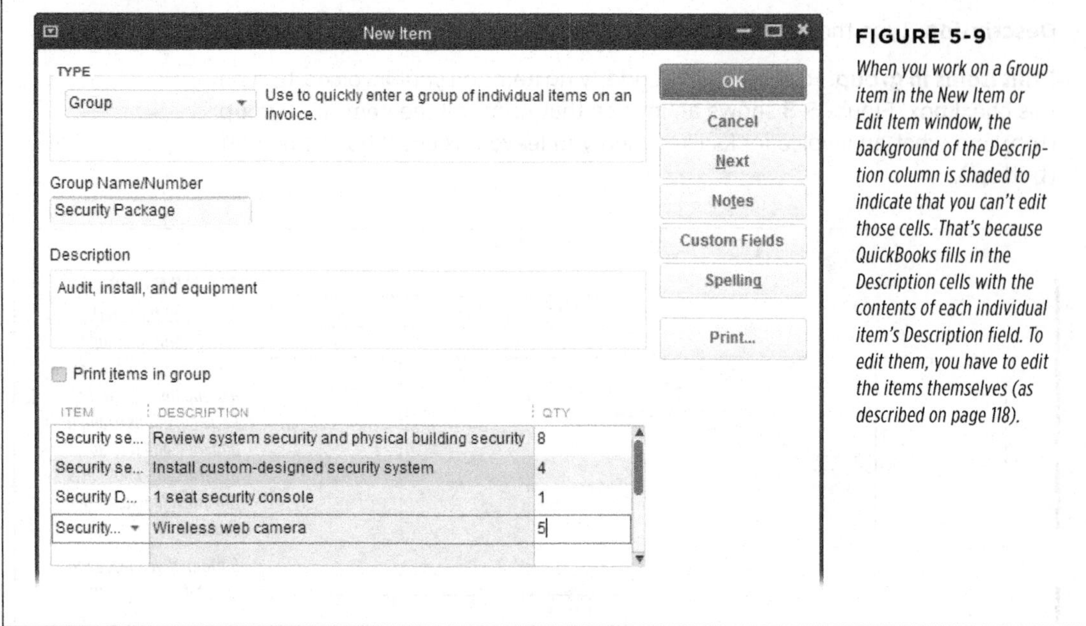

FIGURE 5-9

When you work on a Group item in the New Item or Edit Item window, the background of the Description column is shaded to indicate that you can't edit those cells. That's because QuickBooks fills in the Description cells with the contents of each individual item's Description field. To edit them, you have to edit the items themselves (as described on page 118).

Discount

As you know, a discount is an amount you deduct from the standard price you charge, such as a volume discount, customer-loyalty discount, or sale discount. QuickBooks' Discount item calculates deductions like these. Discount items deduct either a dollar amount or a percentage for discounts you apply at the time of sale. By using both Subtotal and Discount items, you can apply discounts to some or all of the charges on a sales form.

NOTE Early payment discounts don't appear on sales forms because you won't know that a customer pays early until long after that form is complete. So instead, you apply early payment discounts in the Receive Payments window, described on page 352.

The New Item window's fields for a Discount item are similar to those of an Other Charge item with a few small differences:

- **Amount or %**. To deduct a dollar amount, type a positive number (whole or decimal) in this field. To deduct a percentage, type a whole or decimal number followed by "%," like *5.5%*.
- **Account**. Choose the account to which you want to post the discounts you apply. You can post discounts to either an income or expense account. When you post

discounts to an income account, they appear as negative income, so your gross profit reflects what you actually earned after deducting them. Posting discounts to an expense account, on the other hand, makes your income look better than it actually is, but the discounts increase the amount in your expense account, so your net profit is the same no matter which approach you use.

- **Tax Code**. Most of the time, you choose a taxable code in this field (which appears only if you have the program's sales tax features turned on) so that QuickBooks applies the discount *before* it calculates sales tax. For instance, if customers buy products on sale, they pay sales tax on the *sale* price, not the original price. If you choose a nontaxable code in this field, QuickBooks applies the discount *after* it calculates sales tax. You'll rarely want to do this, though, because it means you'll collect less sales tax from customers than you have to send to the tax agencies.

Payment

When customers send you payments, you can record them in QuickBooks using the Receive Payments feature (page 345). But if you're in the middle of creating invoices when the checks arrive, you can avoid that task by recording those payments right in your invoices by adding a Payment item. As Figure 5-10 explains, Payment items do more than just reduce the amount owed on the invoice.

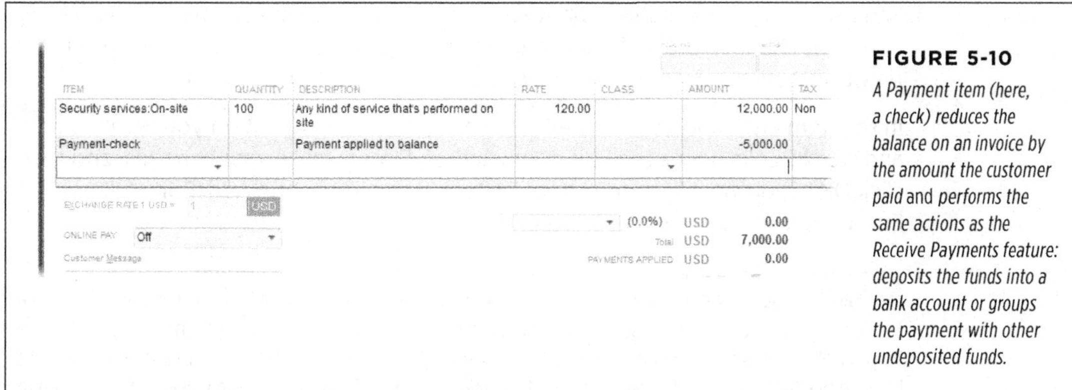

FIGURE 5-10

A Payment item (here, a check) reduces the balance on an invoice by the amount the customer paid and performs the same actions as the Receive Payments feature: deposits the funds into a bank account or groups the payment with other undeposited funds.

In the New Item window, after you fill in the Type, Item Name/Number, and Description fields, the remaining Payment item fields are unlike those for other items. These unique fields tell QuickBooks the method of payment that the customer used and whether you deposit the funds in a specific bank account or group them with other undeposited funds. Here are the details:

- **Payment Method**. Choose a method such as cash, check, or a brand of credit card. That way, when you choose Banking→Make Deposits (page 368) to make a deposit and the "Payments to Deposit" window opens, you can filter pending deposits by payment method.

- **Group with other undeposited funds**. Choose this option if you want to add the payment to other payments you've received. For example, choose this option if you save up the checks customers send so you can make one trip to deposit them all in your bank. That way, when you add this Payment item to a sales form, QuickBooks adds the payment to the list of undeposited funds. To actually complete the deposit of all your payments, choose Banking→Make Deposits (page 368).
- **Deposit To**. If payments flow into an account without any action on your part, such as credit card or electronic payments, choose this option, and then choose the appropriate bank account in the drop-down list.

Working with Items

Item info changes from time to time: Prices increase or decrease, descriptions change, or you decide to use different accounts. You can make changes like this anytime. In addition, you can hide items so only the ones you currently sell appear in item drop-down lists. And if you created an item by mistake, you can delete it to remove it permanently. This section explains how to perform all these tasks.

Modifying Items

You can change information about an item even if you've already used it in transactions. The changes you make don't affect *existing* transactions, but when you create *new* transactions using that item, QuickBooks uses the updated info.

In the Item List window (Lists→Item List), double-click the item you want to edit, and QuickBooks opens the Edit Item window. Simply make your changes, and then click OK. If you want to modify several items at once, use the Add/Edit Multiple List Entries feature (page 124 in Chapter 6) instead.

NOTE If you change an account associated with an item (like the income account to which sales post), the Account Change dialog box appears when you save the edited item. This dialog box tells you that all future transactions for that item will use the new account. If you also want to change the account on all *existing* transactions that use the item, consult with your accountant to make sure that change is OK before you click Yes. Click No to keep the old account on existing transactions that use the item.

Be particularly attentive if you decide to change an item's Type field. You can change only Non-inventory Part and Other Charge items to other item types, and you can change them only into certain other item types: Service, Inventory Part, Inventory Assembly (available only in QuickBooks Premier and Enterprise), Non-inventory Part, or Other Charge. For example, you can't change a Non-inventory Part item *back* once you change it to an Inventory Part item. To prevent type-change disasters, back up your QuickBooks file (see page 495) before switching item types.

TIP The inventory you keep in stock is an asset of your company, but Non-inventory Parts show up simply as expenses. So if you change a Non-inventory Part item to an Inventory Part item, be sure to choose a date in the "As of" field that's *after* the date of the last transaction that uses the item in its non-inventory guise.

Hiding Items

Hiding items and deleting them are two totally different actions, although the visible result is the same: QuickBooks doesn't display the items in the Item List window or in item drop-down lists, which prevents you from selecting them accidentally and keeps your Item List more concise. But unlike deleting (which you'll learn about in a sec), hiding is *reversible*: You can switch items back to active status if you start selling them again. Suppose you hid the item for bell-bottom hip-huggers in 1974. Decades later, now that '70s fashions have become cool again, you can reactivate that item and use it on sales forms. (Of course, you'll probably want to edit the cost and sales price to reflect today's economy.)

If you've sold an item in the past, then the *only* way to remove it from the Item List is to hide it—QuickBooks won't let you delete items that have transactions associated with them.

Here's a guide to hiding and reactivating items:

- **Hide an item**. In the Item List, right-click the item and choose Make Item Inactive from the shortcut menu. The item disappears from the list.
- **View all items, active or inactive**. At the bottom of the Item List window, turn on the "Include inactive" checkbox. (This checkbox is grayed out when all your items are active.) QuickBooks then displays a column with an X as its heading and shows an X in that column for every inactive item in the list.
- **Reactivate a hidden item**. First, turn on the "Include inactive" checkbox to display all items. Then click the X next to the name of the item you want to reactivate. When you click the X next to a *parent* item, QuickBooks opens the Activate Group dialog box. If you want to reactivate all the subitems as well as the parent, click Yes; to reactivate only the parent item, click No.

Deleting Items

The only time you'll delete an item is when you create it by mistake and want to eliminate it permanently. You can delete an item only if it doesn't have any transactions associated with it.

If you erroneously create an item and catch your mistake immediately, deleting the offender is no sweat. Open the List Item window (Lists→Item List), and then use one of these methods:

- Select the item, and then press Ctrl+D.
- Right-click the item, and then choose Delete Item from the shortcut menu.

- Select the item, and then head to the main QuickBooks menu bar and choose Edit→Delete Item.
- At the bottom of the Item List window, click Item→Delete Item.

TIP If you delete an item, you have only one shot at undoing the deletion: You can restore the deleted item by immediately choosing Edit→Undo. If you do anything else in QuickBooks after deleting an item, that item is gone for good—unless you recreate it from scratch.

If you try to delete an item that's used in even *one* transaction, QuickBooks warns you that you can't delete it. Say you created an item by mistake and then compounded the problem by inadvertently adding the item to an invoice. When you realize your error and try to delete the item, QuickBooks refuses to oblige. Fortunately, it's pretty easy to run a report to find the transactions that contain that item, and then replace it with another item:

1. **Open the Item List window (Lists→Item List), and then right-click the item and choose "QuickReport: [item name]" from the shortcut menu.**

   QuickBooks opens the Item QuickReport window. Depending on how your report preferences are set, the Modify Report dialog box might open as well.

2. **If the Modify Report dialog box appears, then on the Display tab, choose All at the top of the Dates drop-down list, and then click OK.**

   If the Modify Report dialog box *doesn't* appear, in the Item QuickReport window, choose All in the Dates drop-down list.

3. **In the report window, double-click the transaction, and then edit the transaction to remove the erroneous item.**

   QuickBooks opens the dialog box or window that corresponds to the type of transaction you double-clicked. For example, if you double-click an invoice, QuickBooks opens the Create Invoices window and displays the invoice you chose. In the Create Invoices window's Item column, click the cell containing the item you want to delete, click the down arrow in that cell, and then choose the replacement item from the Item drop-down list.

4. **To save the transaction with the revised item, click Save & Close.**

   The transaction window closes.

5. **In the button bar at the top of the report window, click Refresh to update the report with the change you just made.**

   You'll know that you've successfully eliminated the item from all sales transactions when the Item QuickReport window shows no transactions.

6. **To close the report window, click the X at its upper right.**

   QuickBooks takes you back to the Item List window.

7. **In the Item List window, select the item you want to delete, and then press Ctrl+D. In the Delete Item message box that appears, click OK to confirm that you want to get rid of the item.**

   The item disappears from your Item List for good, and you're ready to get back to work.

CHAPTER

6

Data Entry Shortcuts for Lists

If you frequently add or edit more than one customer, vendor, or item at a time, working in a New or Edit window (like New Customer or Edit Item) isn't only tedious, but it also takes up time you should spend on more important tasks, like selling, managing cash flow, or finding out who has the incriminating pictures from the last company party.

When you set up your company file, the QuickBooks Setup dialog box helps you bring information in from an email program or Excel (page 19), and you can use that same window anytime you want to add more customers or vendors. Another option is the Add/Edit Multiple List Entries feature, which you can use to paste data from Excel into QuickBooks when you're creating customers, vendors, or items. Or, to edit existing records, you can filter or search the list in that window to show just the customers, vendors, or items you want to update, and then paste in Excel data, type in values, or copy values between records. This chapter shows you how to perform all these tasks.

Then again, you might store info about customers, vendors, and items in other programs such as a database or word-processing program where you create mailing labels. If your other programs can create *Excel-compatible files* or *delimited text files*, you can avoid data-entry grunt work by transferring data to or from QuickBooks. (Delimited text files are simply files that separate each piece of data with a comma, space, tab, or other character.) In both types of files, the same kind of info appears in the same position in each line or row, so QuickBooks (and other programs) can pull the information into the right places. When you want to transfer a *ton* of data from another program into QuickBooks, importing is the way to go. By mapping QuickBooks' fields to the fields in the other program, you can quickly transfer hundreds or even thousands of records. In this chapter, you'll learn about the keywords

QuickBooks uses to put your data into the correct fields and how to get your import file set up to work with QuickBooks. The chapter wraps up by explaining the steps for importing data into your company file. (Chapter 26 provides the full story on importing and exporting data.)

Adding and Editing Multiple Records

The Add/Edit Multiple List Entries feature is a great tool for adding or updating values in the Customer, Vendor, and Item lists. If you have data in an Excel spreadsheet, you can paste it directly into a table in the Add/Edit Multiple List Entries window. The window's features for copying or duplicating values between records come in handy when you need to make changes like updating the billing address for a customer who sends you job after job. (Typing values into the window's cells works, too.) And you can customize the window's table to show only the customers, vendors, or items you want to edit and the fields you want to modify.

This feature goes by different names depending on where you find it in QuickBooks. Choose it in any of these locations to open the Add/Edit Multiple List Entries window:

- **In the Lists menu, choose Add/Edit Multiple List Entries.** When you go this route, QuickBooks sets the window's List box to Customers.
- **In the Customer Center toolbar, click New Customer & Job→Add Multiple Customer:Jobs or Excel→Paste from Excel.** QuickBooks sets the List box to Customers.
- **In the Vendor Center toolbar, click New Vendor→Add Multiple Vendors or Excel→Paste from Excel.** QuickBooks sets the List box to Vendors.
- **At the bottom of the Item List window (page 107), click Item→Add/Edit Multiple Items or Excel→Paste from Excel.** QuickBooks sets the List box to Service Items.

Selecting a List to Work With

As mentioned above, if you open the Add/Edit Multiple List Entries window from the Customer Center, Vendor Center, or Item List window, QuickBooks automatically selects the appropriate list in the List drop-down menu at the window's top left. You can switch lists by choosing Customers, Vendors, Service Items, Inventory Parts, or Non-inventory Parts from this drop-down menu.

TIP If you set up jobs for customers, the Add/Edit Multiple List Entries window's table includes rows for both customers and jobs. The Name column contains the customer's name for a customer row and the job's name for a job row. Usually, you can spot job rows by looking at the Company Name field, since all jobs for that customer will have the customer's Company Name value listed here.

Customizing the Table's Columns

To paste data from Excel in a jiffy, take a minute to get the columns in the Add/Edit Multiple List Entries window's table in the same order as the columns in your Excel spreadsheet. (Or, if you're an Excel whiz, you may prefer to rearrange the columns in your spreadsheet.) You can customize the table in QuickBooks by clicking Customize Columns in the window's upper right to open the Customize Columns dialog box shown in Figure 6-1.

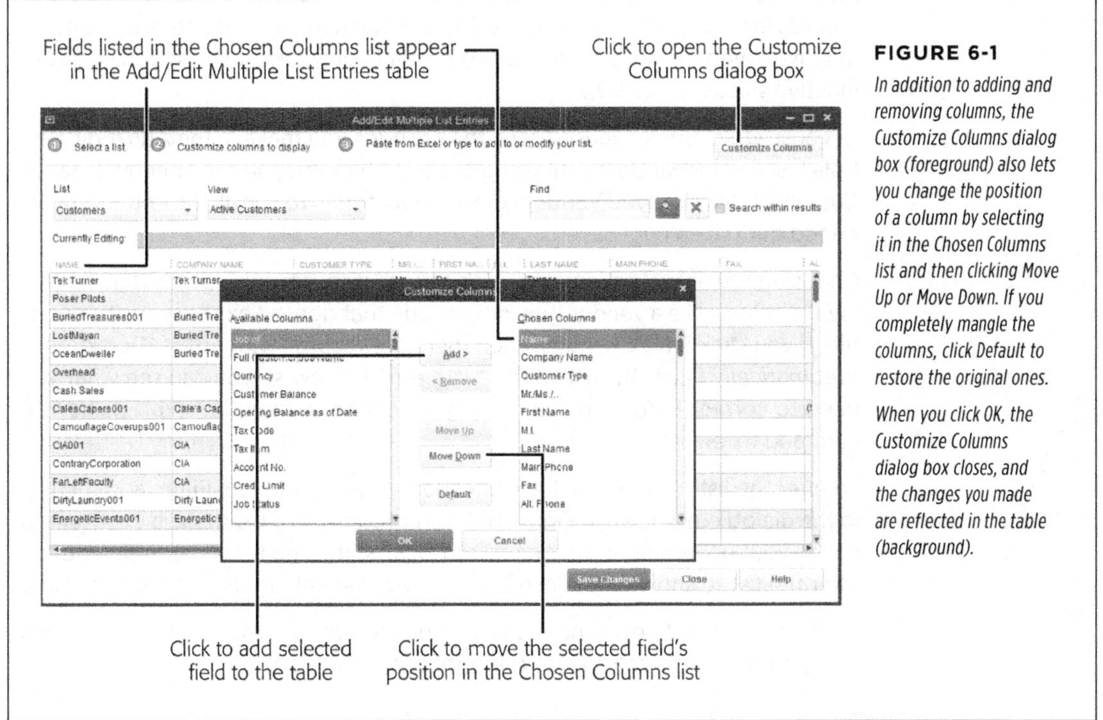
Fields listed in the Chosen Columns list appear in the Add/Edit Multiple List Entries table
Click to open the Customize Columns dialog box
Click to add selected field to the table
Click to move the selected field's position in the Chosen Columns list

FIGURE 6-1

In addition to adding and removing columns, the Customize Columns dialog box (foreground) also lets you change the position of a column by selecting it in the Chosen Columns list and then clicking Move Up or Move Down. If you completely mangle the columns, click Default to restore the original ones.

When you click OK, the Customize Columns dialog box closes, and the changes you made are reflected in the table (background).

Here are the table customizations you can make:

- **Add a column.** Select the field you want in the Available Columns list, and then click Add. The field jumps over to the Chosen Columns list.
- **Remove a column.** Select a field in the Chosen Columns list, and then click Remove. The field moves back over to the Available Columns list. You can't remove required fields like Name; QuickBooks grays out the Remove button if you select a required field in the Chosen Columns list.
- **Reorder columns.** In the Chosen Columns list, select the field you want to move to a different position in the table, and then click Move Up or Move Down to move the field up or down in the list. Moving a field up in the list positions the field farther to the left in the table; moving it down in the list pushes the field's column farther to the right in the table.

Displaying the Records You Want

In addition to customizing the columns in the Add/Edit Multiple List Entries window's table, you can also control which records the table displays. For example, editing entries is easier if you filter the list to display only the ones you want to edit. Here are some ways to control what you see in the table:

- **Filter the entries.** The View drop-down menu includes several choices for filtering the list. Choose the Active entry (Active Customers, Active Vendors, Active Service Items, and so on) if you want to make changes to only active records in your company file. Choosing the Inactive entry (Inactive Customers, Inactive Inventory Items, and so on) displays only records that you've set to inactive status (page 90).

  Because QuickBooks doesn't save the changes you make in the Add/Edit Multiple List Entries window until you click Save Changes, you can filter by Unsaved Customers (or Unsaved Vendors or Unsaved Items) to see all the entries you've edited but haven't yet saved.

  Choosing the entry that ends in "with errors" displays only entries that contain invalid values, like a vendor type or tax code that doesn't exist in your company file. If you click Save Changes when there are records with errors, QuickBooks *automatically* filters the list to the "with errors" view so you can see what you need to correct before you can save your changes. Page 132 explains how to spot and fix errors.

  To filter the list to your exact specifications, choose Custom Filter, and then fill in the dialog box shown in Figure 6-2 (foreground). For example, if you want to divide your government customers into local, state, and federal groups, you can filter the list to show only records with "Government" in their customer fields.

  To clear a custom filter or the search criteria you typed in the Find box (explained next), simply click the red X to the right of the Find box.

NOTE QuickBooks is quite literal in its searches, so the entries you see in your search results exactly match what you specified in your custom filter or typed in the Find box. For example, if you type *New York*, QuickBooks displays customer records that contain that exact phrase, but not ones that use the abbreviation NY. Or if you type *(555)* to look for the 555 area code, records that don't have parentheses around the area code won't show up.

- **Find entries.** Typing a word, value, or phrase in the window's Find box is similar to applying a custom filter to the list, except that QuickBooks searches *all* fields. For example, if you type *555* in the Find box and then click the Search button (which has a magnifying glass on it), QuickBooks displays records that contain 555 anywhere, whether it's in the company name, telephone number, address, or account number field.

FIGURE 6-2

In the Custom Filter dialog box, you can type a word, value, or phrase to look for, and specify the fields you want QuickBooks to search.

For example, type cia *in the For field and set the "in" drop-down list to "All common fields" to find customers with "cia" in fields like Name, Company Name, and so on.*

After you search for one value, you can search for something else within the results from the *first* search. For example, you could do an initial search for customers with "Texas" in their addresses, and then search within those results to zero in on customers in Dallas. To do so, type the second search value in the Find box, turn on the "Search within results" checkbox, and then press Enter or click the Search button (the magnifying glass).

- **Sort the list entries**. To sort the entries in the table, click the column heading for the field you want to sort by, and QuickBooks sorts the records in ascending order (from A to Z or from low to high numbers). Click again to sort in descending order. When the table is sorted by the values in a given column, a small triangle appears to the right of that column's heading. The triangle points up when the column is sorted in ascending order and down when the values are sorted in descending order.

Adding or Editing List Entries

Whether you want to add new entries or edit existing ones, the Add/Edit Multiple List Entries window offers several handy options. You can type in values or use features like Copy Down to copy values between records. If your data is in an Excel spreadsheet, pasting the info from Excel into the table is a breeze. (When you want to add a *new* record, you first have to click the first empty row at the bottom of the list.) This section explains how to enter data directly in the table or paste it from Excel.

ENTERING DATA DIRECTLY IN THE TABLE

For an edit here and a new entry there, the Add/Edit Multiple List Entries table helps take the tedium out of data entry. Here are the various ways to enter values in records:

- **Type values in cells.** This method is straightforward: Click a cell and make your changes. When you click a cell that already contains data, the program automatically selects the cell's contents so you can start typing to replace the existing value. You can also use common editing techniques like dragging to select text or clicking to position your cursor in the text.

- **Copy and paste data within the table.** You can also copy and paste data from one cell in the table to another. For example, if a customer with several jobs has relocated its main office, you can copy values from Bill To cells and paste them into the cells for the customer's jobs. When you copy and paste data within the table, you can copy only one cell at a time. Right-click the cell you want to copy and then choose Copy on the shortcut menu. Then right-click the cell into which you want to paste the data and choose Paste on the shortcut menu. Keyboard shortcuts work, too: Press Ctrl+C to copy a cell and Ctrl+V to paste the copied data. If you want to move the data from the original cell to a new home, use Ctrl+X to *cut* the data rather than copy it.

TIP If you want to copy *several* cells in the Add/Edit Multiple List Entries table, it's quicker to make the changes in an Excel spreadsheet and then paste the data from Excel into the Add/Edit Multiple List Entries table (page 129).

- **Duplicate a row.** To create a new record that has many of the same values as an existing record, right-click a cell in the existing row, and then choose Duplicate Row from the shortcut menu. The new record appears in the row below the original and contains all the same values as the original record, except that the value in the first field begins with "DUP" to differentiate it from the original. First, edit the Name cell to reflect the new name. Then edit the cells in the row that have different values.

- **Copy values down a column.** You can quickly fill in several cells in a column by using the Copy Down feature. Because this feature copies data into *all* cells below the one you select, it's important to filter the list (page 126) to show only the records you want to change. Then right-click the cell you want to copy down the column and choose Copy Down from the shortcut menu. QuickBooks copies the value in the selected cell to all the cells below it in the column, overwriting any existing data. For example, if you want to change the contact name for all the jobs for a particular customer, filter the list to show just the records for that customer (in the Find box, type the customer's name, and then click the magnifying glass icon). Next, type the new contact into the first Contact cell. Then right-click that cell and choose Copy Down.

- **Insert a row.** If you want to insert a blank line in the table (to create a new job for a customer, for example), right-click the row that's currently where you want the blank line, and then choose Insert Line from the shortcut menu (or press Ctrl+Insert).

- **Delete a row.** If you created a record by mistake, you can get rid of it by right-clicking anywhere in its row and then choosing Delete Line. (This command is grayed out if the entry is used in a transaction or other record, because you can't delete a record if it's referenced somewhere else in your company file.)
- **Clear a column.** To clear all the values in a column, right-click in the column, and then choose Clear Column from the shortcut menu. If you chose this command by mistake, you can undo the deletion by clicking the window's Close button and then, in the Unsaved [list name] message box, clicking No.

COPYING AND PASTING VALUES FROM EXCEL

If you're a fan of copying and pasting (and who isn't?), you can copy data from an Excel spreadsheet (a single cell, a range of cells, one or more rows, or one or more columns) and paste it into the Add/Edit Multiple List Entries table. The only requirement is that the rows and columns in the table and in the spreadsheet have to contain the same information in the same order. You can rearrange the rows and columns either in the Add/Edit Multiple List Entries window (page 125) or in Excel, whichever you prefer.

If you want to copy and paste customers and jobs (or items with subitems), you first have to create the top-level entries, as shown in Figure 6-3. That's because jobs you paste include the name of the customer in their Company Name fields (for items, the parent item's name appears in the "Subitem of" field). Once the parent entries exist, you can use the Add/Edit Multiple List Entries window again to paste jobs (or subitems).

NOTE To prevent errors when you copy and paste data, make sure the values you reference—such as accounts, tax codes, and so on—already exist in your company file.

Here's how to get started with entering data via the Add/Edit Multiple List Entries window, using items as an example:

1. **On the QuickBooks Home Page, in the Company panel, click Items & Services.**

   The Item List window opens.

2. **Right-click the Item List window, and then choose Add/Edit Multiple Items from the shortcut menu. (Alternatively, at the bottom of the window, click Item→Add/Edit Multiple Items.)**

   The Add/Edit Multiple List Entries window opens with the List box set to Service Items or the type of item you selected the last time you used this window. The table initially displays the active items for the type selected in the List box (Figure 6-4), which makes sense because you typically want to add or edit items that you're currently using. To filter the list to show specific kinds of items, in the View drop-down menu, choose the kind you want.

Add/Edit Multiple

1 Select a list. 2 Customize columns to display. 3 Paste from Excel or type to add to or modify

List: Service Items — View: Active Service Items — Find

Currently Editing: Security services

ITEM NAME	SUBITEM OF	SALES PRICE	INCOME ACCOUNT
Security services		0.00	4100 · Service Revenue
Background Check	Security services	175.00	4100 · Service Revenue
Develop requirements	Security services	150.00	4100 · Service Revenue
Hack audit	Security services	250.00	4100 · Service Revenue
On-site	Security services	120.00	4100 · Service Revenue
Other	Security services	90.00	4100 · Service Revenue
Security Audit	Security services	200.00	4100 · Service Revenue
Security Install	Security services	150.00	4100 · Service Revenue
Security planning	Security services	150.00	4100 · Service Revenue
Security Retainer	Security services	100.00	4100 · Service Revenue
Service No Doc		0.00	4101 · Service Revenue No Doc
Dirty Tricks	Service No Doc	210.00	4101 · Service Revenue No Doc
Rabble Rousing	Service No Doc	90.00	4101 · Service Revenue No Doc
Surveillance		0.00	4100 · Service Revenue

Add higher-level items first.

Subitems refer to the parent in the Subitem of the field.

FIGURE 6-3

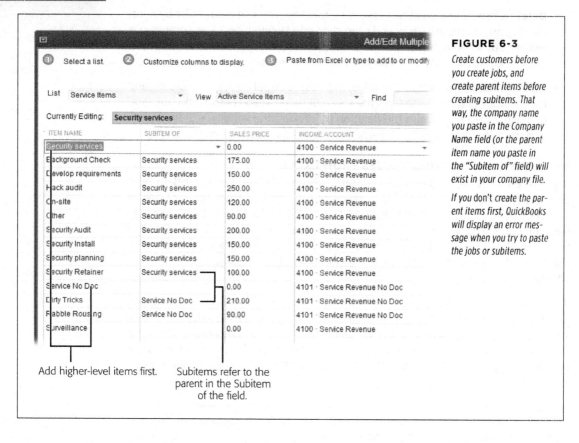

Create customers before you create jobs, and create parent items before creating subitems. That way, the company name you paste in the Company Name field (or the parent item name you paste in the "Subitem of" field) will exist in your company file.

If you don't create the parent items first, QuickBooks will display an error message when you try to paste the jobs or subitems.

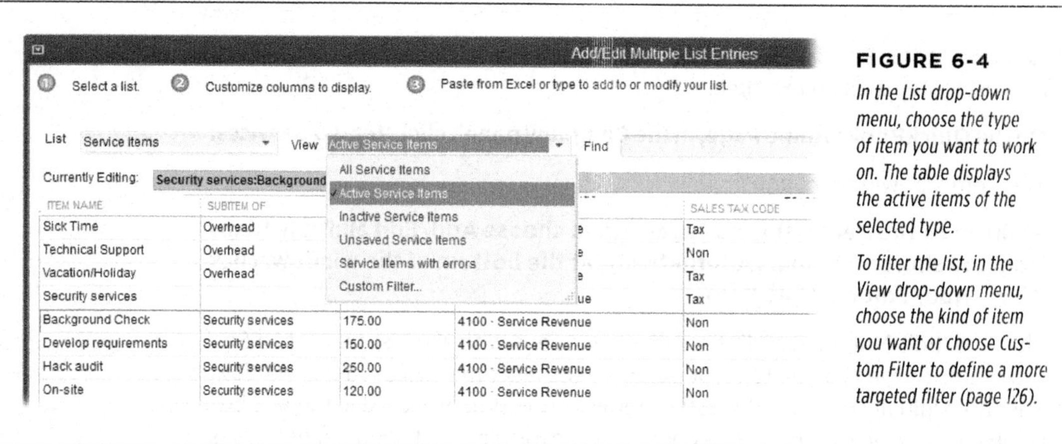

FIGURE 6-4

In the List drop-down menu, choose the type of item you want to work on. The table displays the active items of the selected type.

To filter the list, in the View drop-down menu, choose the kind of item you want or choose Custom Filter to define a more targeted filter (page 126).

3. **If you want to work with a different type of item, in the List drop-down menu, choose Customers, Vendors, Service Items, Inventory Parts, or Non-inventory Parts.**

   The columns in the table vary depending on the list you select and the preferences you've turned on. For example, for Service items, the table includes columns for Item Name, Subitem of, Sales Price, Income Account, and—if you've turned on the sales tax preference (page 547)—Sales Tax Code. If you've turned on the preference for inventory (page 653) and choose Inventory Parts, you see a COGS Account column, among others. If you choose the Customers or Vendors list, the table initially displays contact info and a few other fields. (See page 125 to learn how to customize the columns that appear in the table.)

4. **Switch to Excel and copy the data you want from your spreadsheet.**

   As explained earlier, the order of the columns in the Add/Edit Multiple List Entries window's table and your Excel spreadsheet have to match or you'll see errors when you paste the data (which you'll do in the next step). To fix that, reorder the columns in either Excel or QuickBooks (page 125). When the programs' columns match, in Excel, select the information you want to paste into QuickBooks, and then press Ctrl+C to copy it.

5. **Back in the Add/Edit Multiple List Entries window, click the first blank Item Name cell (or Name cell, if you're pasting customer or vendor info), and then press Ctrl+V (or choose Edit→Paste in the main QuickBooks menu bar).**

   When you paste Excel data into existing records in the Add/Edit Multiple List Entries window, QuickBooks overwrites the existing values in the cells. To paste Excel data into *new* records, be sure to select the first empty row in the window's table before pasting the data.

   QuickBooks pastes the copied data into the selected cell and then continues pasting into the cells below and to the right of the selected cell. Cells that contain data with errors, such as invalid values or list entries that don't exist in QuickBooks, appear in red text. See page 132 to learn how to correct these errors.

TIP If you want to paste parent items and subitems into the Add/Edit Multiple List Entries window's table, paste the top-level items first, and then click Save Changes. Then follow with a separate paste pass for each subsequent level of your Item List. (For customers with jobs, paste the customers first, and then paste their jobs on a second pass.) That way, the parent items you need will already exist so the subitems will paste in without errors.

Saving Changes

After you've completed the additions and modifications you want in the Add/Edit Multiple List Entries window, click Save Changes to save your work. QuickBooks saves all the entries that have no errors and tells you how many records it saved.

Correcting Errors

If you try to save changes and QuickBooks finds any errors, like a value that doesn't exist in the Terms list or a job that belongs to a customer who doesn't exist in QuickBooks, it filters the entries in the Add/Edit Multiple List Entries window's table to just those with errors and displays the incorrect values in red text. Point your cursor at a cell to see a hint about the error. For example, if you typed a letter in a price field, QuickBooks tells you that the field contains an invalid character. If the problem is a list entry that doesn't exist, the "[list name] Not Found" dialog box opens (where "[list name]" is a list such as Terms) and tells you the value isn't in the list. In the dialog box, click Set Up to add the entry to the list. Fix any other errors, and then click Save Changes again.

TIP If you don't know what's causing the error, select the incorrect value and delete it by pressing Delete or Backspace. Then, when you figure out what the value *should* be, you can edit that record in the Add/Edit Multiple List Entries window or the corresponding Edit dialog box.

Importing Customer, Vendor, and Item Information

If you have hundreds of records to stuff into QuickBooks, even copying and pasting can be tedious. But if you can produce a delimited text file or a spreadsheet of customer or vendor info in the program where you currently store it (page 691), then you can match up your source data with QuickBooks' fields and import all your records in one fell swoop.

Delimited files and spreadsheets compartmentalize data by separating each piece of info with a comma or a tab, or by cubbyholing them into columns and rows in a spreadsheet file. These files aren't necessarily ready to import into QuickBooks, though. Headings in a delimited file or spreadsheet might identify the field names in the program that originally held the information, but QuickBooks has no way of knowing the correlation between those fields and its own.

But don't worry: QuickBooks helps you import your Excel data for customers, vendors, and items. There's a data-import wizard right in the program. You can use its pre-formatted Excel templates to import data from your Excel spreadsheet. (If you don't need any handholding, head to page 691 in Chapter 26 for the full scoop on importing data into QuickBooks.)

TIP Always back up your company file *before* you import data in case you run into problems. That way, you can restore your pre-import file and try again. Page 495 dishes out the details on creating a backup file.

Importing with the Excel Import Wizard Templates

QuickBooks' Excel import wizard is easy to get to *and* easy to use. The pre-formatted spreadsheets that come with it contain a small subset of the fields associated with each list you can import. For example, the customer template includes columns for basic contact info and an account number. If the fields you want to import *are* in the wizard's Excel templates, you can't beat this wizard for ease of use. (The wizard's Advanced Import button helps you import info from other Excel spreadsheets. The next section shows you how to put that button to use.)

NOTE To use the Excel Import Wizard templates or to import data from your own Excel workbook, you need to have Excel installed on your computer.

Here's how to use the Excel import wizard and its built-in spreadsheets:

1. **In QuickBooks, choose File→Utilities→Import→Excel Files.**

   The "Add Your Excel Data to QuickBooks" wizard opens. (If you see the Add/ Edit Multiple List Entries dialog box, click No to proceed to the wizard. If you don't want to see this message again, turn on the "Do not display this message in the future" checkbox.)

2. **Click the button for the type of data you want to import: Customers, Vendors, or Products I Sell.**

   You see a message warning that you can't undo the import and recommending that you back up your company file first. If you want to create a backup, click No, create the backup, and then begin with step 1 again. If you're ready to import data, click Yes to close the message box.

   QuickBooks opens an Excel template for the type of data you're importing, as shown in Figure 6-5.

3. **Copy your data into the template.**

   Open the Excel spreadsheet whose info you want to get into QuickBooks, select the data you want to copy, and then press Ctrl+C. Next, switch to the Excel template QuickBooks created, click the cell where you want to begin pasting your data (Excel pastes from the top-left cell down and to the right), and then press Ctrl+V. (If you need help, click the template's Show Detailed Instructions button.)

4. **After you've copied all the data from your spreadsheet into the Excel template and none of the template's cells are yellow, choose File→Save to save the template.**

   Then close the spreadsheet you copied data from.

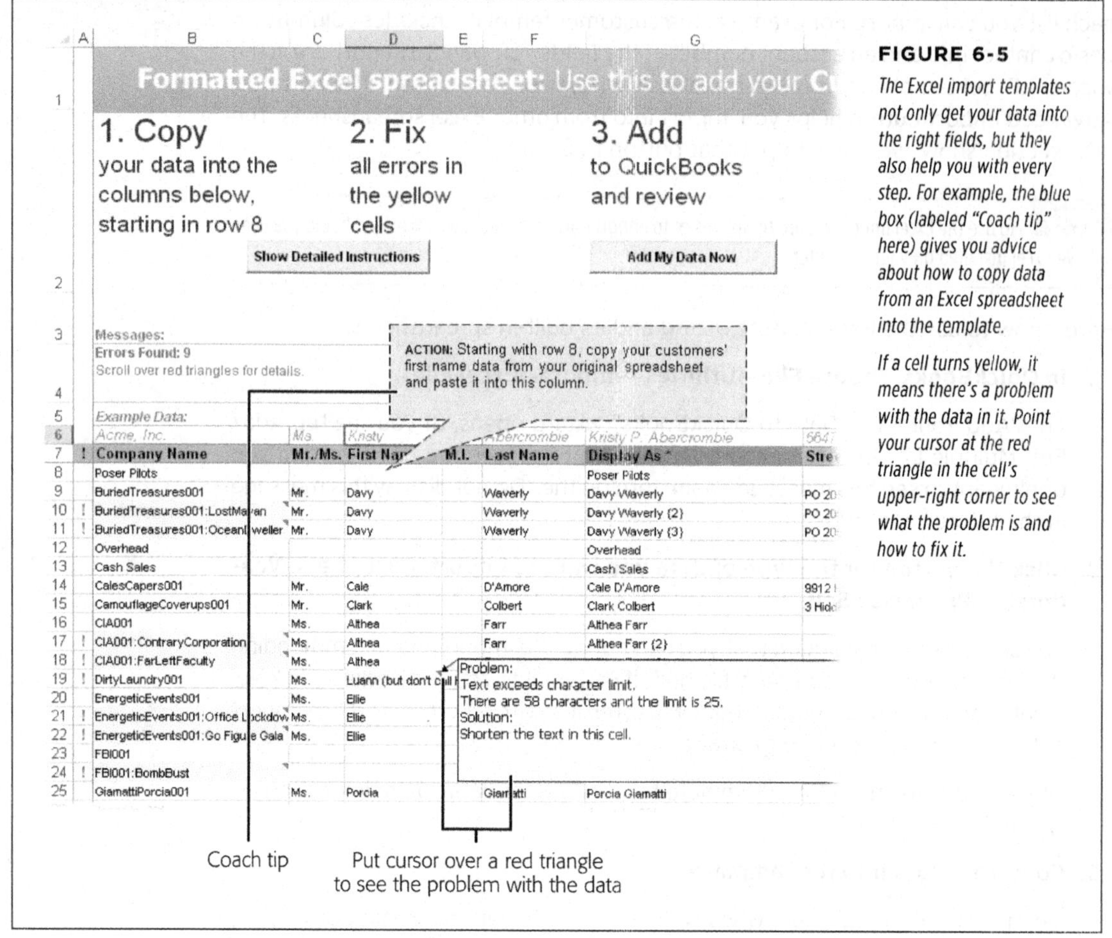

FIGURE 6-5

The Excel import templates not only get your data into the right fields, but they also help you with every step. For example, the blue box (labeled "Coach tip" here) gives you advice about how to copy data from an Excel spreadsheet into the template.

If a cell turns yellow, it means there's a problem with the data in it. Point your cursor at the red triangle in the cell's upper-right corner to see what the problem is and how to fix it.

5. **In QuickBooks' Excel template, click Add My Data Now.**

   The "Add Your Excel Data to QuickBooks" wizard shows the progress it's making importing the data. When it's done, it places green checkmarks to the left of all three steps and shows how many records it imported. You can click the button that says "View [type of imported info]" to see the list you imported, or click Close and view your lists as you usually do. For example, to see your Customer:Job List, click Customers→Customer Center.

Importing Data from Your Own Excel File

You don't have to use the data-import wizard's spreadsheets. If your data is already sitting in a spreadsheet, the wizard's Advanced Import button helps you map your spreadsheet's columns to QuickBooks' fields and then import your data. Here's how it works:

1. **In QuickBooks, choose File→Utilities→Import→Excel Files. In the "Add Your Excel Data to QuickBooks" wizard, click the Advanced Import button.**

   The "Import a file" dialog box opens.

TIP What if you don't have data in an Excel spreadsheet? There's no need to set up your own file. The "QuickBooks Import Excel and CSV toolkit" (*http://tinyurl.com/7chnkqn*) includes a sample Excel spreadsheet with four worksheets. Each worksheet comes with columns that correspond to the fields associated with the Customer, Vendor, Item, and Account Lists. Follow the instructions on the web page to download the toolkit to your computer.

2. **In the "Import a file" dialog box, on the "Set up Import" tab, click Browse, and then select the Excel file you want to import.**

   QuickBooks then populates the "Choose a sheet in this Excel workbook" drop-down list with the names of the worksheets in the workbook you selected.

3. **Use the "Choose a sheet in this Excel workbook" drop-down list to pick the worksheet you want to import.**

   QuickBooks automatically turns on the "This data file has header rows" checkbox, which is perfect when the first row of the Excel workbook contains text labels for the columns.

4. **In the "Choose a mapping" drop-down list, choose <Add New>.**

   The Mappings dialog box (Figure 6-6) opens.

5. **In the "Mapping name" box, type a name for the set of correspondences between fields and columns you're about to create. In the "Import type" drop-down list, choose the kind of data you're importing.**

   You can choose Customer, Vendor, Item, or Account to import data into any of those lists.

6. **For each QuickBooks field listed in the left column, in the Import Data column, choose the corresponding Excel header or column name, as shown in Figure 6-6.**

   The QuickBooks column lists every field associated with the list you selected in the "Import type" drop-down list. If you don't want to import data into a QuickBooks field, leave the corresponding cell in the Import Data column blank.

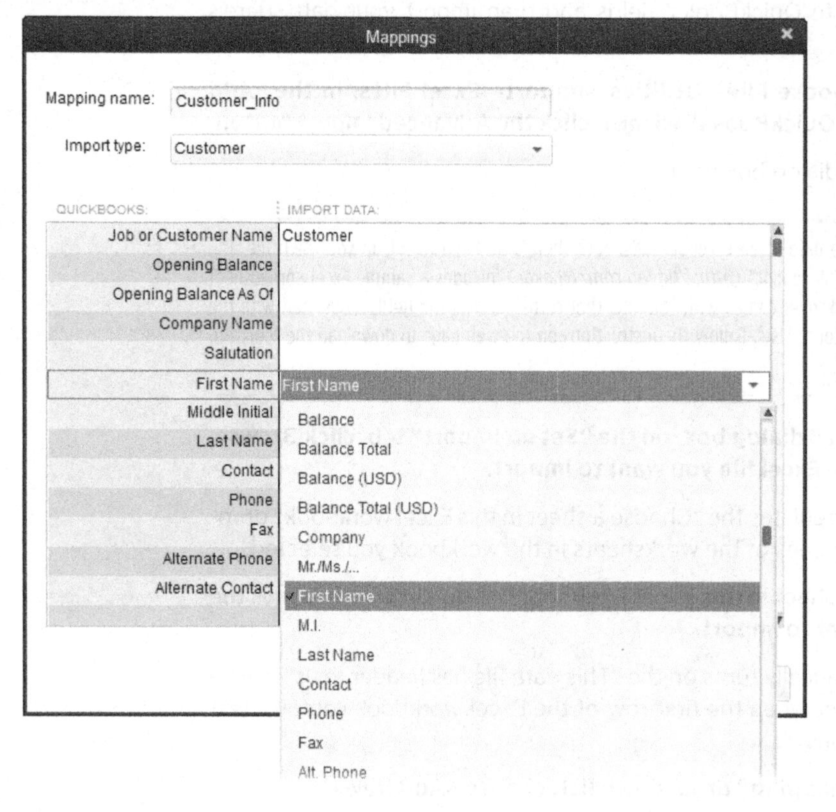

FIGURE 6-6

If you kept the "This data file has header rows" checkbox turned on in step 3, then the drop-down lists that appear when you click a cell in the Import Data column show the column headings from your Excel spreadsheet.

If your spreadsheet doesn't contain header rows, then the drop-down list will display entries like Column A, Column B, and so on.

7. **After you've mapped all the columns you want to import to QuickBooks fields, click Save.**

   The Mappings dialog box closes and QuickBooks takes you back to the "Import a file" dialog box.

8. **To tell QuickBooks how to handle duplicate records and errors, click the "Import a file" dialog box's Preferences tab, and then choose the settings you want.**

   Out of the box, QuickBooks selects the "Prompt me and let me decide" option in the tab's Duplicate Handling section, which puts *you* in charge of deciding what to do. If the records in your company file are up to date, you can choose the "Keep existing data and discard import data" option to keep the records in QuickBooks when the same record exists in your company file and the Excel spreadsheet. Or you can tell the program to replace your existing data in QuickBooks with or without blank fields.

Similarly, in the tab's Error Handling section, QuickBooks selects the option that imports all records but leaves fields with errors blank. If you prefer, you can tell the program to skip records with errors.

9. **To review the data you're about to import, click Preview. In the Preview dialog box, in the "In data preview show" drop-down list, choose "only errors" to see rows of data that contain errors.**

   When you select an entry with an error, the "Details for" table shows the values you're trying to import and what the problem is so you can correct it. You can also select options to skip importing rows with errors or import records and leave error fields blank.

10. **Click OK to close the Preview dialog box.**

    Or, if you want to start the import without jumping back to the "Import a file" dialog box first, simply click Import in the Preview dialog box and then click Yes to complete the import.

11. **Back in the "Import a file" dialog box, click Import, and then click Yes to complete the import.**

    A message box tells you how many records QuickBooks imported and the number of records with errors or warnings. Click OK to close the message box and the "Import a file" dialog box.

That's it! Go ahead and open the list with the data you imported and admire your handiwork. (For example, click Customers on the Home Page to open the Customer Center.)

CHAPTER

7

Setting Up Other QuickBooks Lists

Open any QuickBooks window, dialog box, or form, and you're bound to bump into at least one drop-down list. These lists make it easy to fill in transactions and forms. Creating an invoice? If you pick the customer and job from the Customer:Job drop-down list, QuickBooks fills in the customer's address, payment terms, and other fields for you. Selecting payment terms from the Terms List tells the program how to calculate an invoice's due date. If you choose an entry in the Price Level List, QuickBooks calculates the discount or markup you extend to your customers for the goods they buy. Even the products and services you sell to customers come from the Item List, which you learned about in Chapter 5.

In this chapter, you'll discover what many of these lists can do for you and learn whether it makes sense for you to set them up for your business. Because some lists have their own unique fields (such as the Price Level Type for a Price Level entry), you'll also find out what the various fields are for and how to fill them in. If you already know which lists and list entries you want, you can skip to page 154 to master the techniques that work for most lists, such as adding and tweaking entries, hiding entries, and so on. Once you know how to work with one QuickBooks list, the doors to almost every other list open, too.

NOTE A few lists—such as the Customer, Vendor, and Employee lists—behave a little differently from the ones described in this chapter. Here are the other chapters that provide instructions for working with the QuickBooks lists that aren't covered here:

- The **chart of accounts**, which is a list of your bookkeeping accounts, is explained in Chapter 3.
- The **Customer:Job List**, which includes entries for both customers and their jobs, is the topic of Chapter 4.
- The **Vendor List** is also described in Chapter 4.
- The **Item List** helps you fill in bills, invoices, and other transaction forms with services and products you sell; it's covered in Chapter 5.
- Although the **Sales Tax Code List** appears on the Lists menu, sales tax codes are inextricably linked to how you handle sales tax. The details of setting up this list are described in Chapter 21 on page 550.
- Chapter 12 shows you how to have QuickBooks memorize transactions and store them in the **Memorized Transaction List** so you can reuse them.
- If you turn on QuickBooks' payroll feature, the Lists menu includes the **Payroll Item List**, which covers the deposits and deductions on your payroll. Payroll items are quite specialized, and you use them only if you use one of Intuit's payroll services. To learn about QuickBooks payroll services and the Payroll Item List, see online Appendix D, which you can download from this book's Missing CD page at *www.missing manuals.com/cds.*

Categorizing with Classes

Classes are the only solution if you want to classify income and expenses by categories that span multiple accounts in your chart of accounts; multiple customers, jobs, and vendors; or even multiple time periods. Classes help you track financial results by categories such as business unit, location, partner, or magazine issue.

Suppose you have business units that all sell to the same customers and rack up the same types of expenses, and you want to track the profitability of each unit. Your income accounts show sales by products and services, even if each region sells all those items. Customer types won't help if some large customers buy products from several regions. The same goes if a job requires a smorgasbord of what you sell. The solution? Creating classes that represent business units in QuickBooks' Class List. Classes also come in handy for tracking the allocation of functional expenses that nonprofit organizations have to show on financial statements.

When you turn on QuickBooks' class-tracking feature, every transaction includes a Class field. Unlike the Customer Type, Job Type, and Vendor Type fields—which you assign when you create a customer, job, or vendor—a transaction's Class field starts out blank. For each invoice, sales receipt, bill, and so on, simply choose the class related to the income or expense. That way, you can produce a report broken down by class (page 451).

TIP Before you decide to use classes, use QuickBooks without them for a few weeks or months. If it turns out that you can generate all the reports you need *without* classes, don't burden yourself with another field to fill in. But if you work without classes and then decide to use them after all, you can go back and edit past transactions to assign classes to them, or just start using classes at the beginning of a new fiscal period. For more help deciding whether to use classes, see the box below.

UP TO SPEED

Do You Need Classes?

Not every company needs classes, so don't feel that you *have* to use them. You can call on several other QuickBooks features to help keep track of your business. Each tracking feature has its advantages, so how do you decide which one(s) to use to evaluate your performance? Here's a brief description of each feature and the best use for it:

- **Accounts**. You can use accounts to segregate income and expenses in several ways. For instance, keep income from services separate from your product sales by creating two different income accounts. Accounts are the fastest way to see performance because QuickBooks' built-in Profit & Loss reports (page 448) automatically display results by account.
- **Customer, job, and vendor types (page 87)**. To analyze income by wholesale, retail, online, and other types of customers, classify your customers by type. That way, you can filter the reports you generate to show results for a specific kind of customer. However, types are more limited in scope than accounts—for example, customer types apply only to customers. Likewise, job types and vendor types help you categorize only by job and vendor, respectively.
- **Classes**. Classes cut across accounts, income, expenses, customers, jobs, vendors, and even time, because you assign a class to an individual transaction, such as a check, bill, or invoice. So classes are perfect for categories that span accounts, customers, vendors, and types. Suppose the partners in your company help customers implement technology and tighten their security. You've decided to use separate income accounts to track technology sales and security sales, and to use customer types to track work for the government versus the private sector. You also want to track income and expenses by partner, but each partner works on all types of service for all types of customers. Happily, you can create classes to track partners' sales and expenses, regardless of which service they deliver or the type of customer. A "Profit & Loss by Class" report (page 451) will then tell you how each partner is performing.

Here's another example of putting classes to work: tracking profitability for a monthly publication or event. Start by creating classes for each month. Then assign income and expense transactions to the class that corresponds to the publication month, such as May. That way, you can track ad income or printing expenses for the May issue, even if the transactions occur in March, April, or July.

If you choose to work with classes, be sure to follow these guidelines to get the most out of them:

- **Pick one use for classes**. You can assign just one class to each transaction, and QuickBooks has only one list of classes, so every class should represent the same type of classification. However, if you want to use classes for two different purposes—business units and office branches, say—you can create top-level classes for each business unit and *subclasses* for office branches within each top-level class.

- **Use classes consistently**. Make sure to use classes on *every* transaction that relates to your classification method. For example, if you classify income and expenses by partner, assign a class to every invoice and expense that's related to a partner's work; otherwise, your class-based reports won't be accurate. But if expenses are overhead and don't relate to the work partners do, create a class for overhead and assign that class to all overhead transactions. That way, you can run a report like Profit & Loss Unclassified to look for transactions where you forgot to assign a class.
- **Create a catchall class**. Set up a class like Other so that you can still classify transactions even if they don't fit into any of the specific classes you've defined.

Turning on Class Tracking

Before you can start assigning classes, you have to turn on QuickBooks' class-tracking feature. To see whether classes are turned on, in the main QuickBooks menu bar, click Lists. If you don't see a Class List item in the menu, then the class-tracking feature is turned off. Here's how to turn it on:

1. **Choose Edit→Preferences→Accounting, and then click the Company Preferences tab.**

   To turn class tracking on, you need to be a QuickBooks administrator, because classes affect everyone in your organization who uses the program. (If you aren't a QuickBooks administrator, you'll have to persuade someone who is to turn on classes.)

2. **Turn on the "Use class tracking for transactions" checkbox.**

   When you do that, QuickBooks automatically turns on the "Prompt to assign classes" checkbox. With this checkbox turned on, if you try to save a transaction without an entry in the Class field, QuickBooks gives you a chance to add the class (or save the transaction without one). Turn this checkbox off if you don't want to be reminded to assign classes.

3. **Click OK to close the Preferences window.**

The Class List entry now appears on the Lists menu.

Setting Up Classes

Once you've turned on class tracking, here's how you create classes:

1. **In the main QuickBooks menu bar, choose Lists→Class List.**

   The Class List window opens.

2. **In the Class List window, press Ctrl+N or click Class→New.**

   The New Class window opens.

3. **In the Class Name box, type a name for the class.**

   If you want to create a class that's a subclass of a parent (to set up subclasses for each region within a business unit, say), turn on the "Subclass of" checkbox. Then, in the drop-down list, choose the parent class you want. (Obviously, you can create subclasses only once you've created at least one regular class.)

4. **Click Next to create another class, or click OK to close the New Class window.**

If you realize you need another class while you're working on a transaction, you can create an entry by choosing <Add New> in the Class drop-down list shown in Figure 7-1.

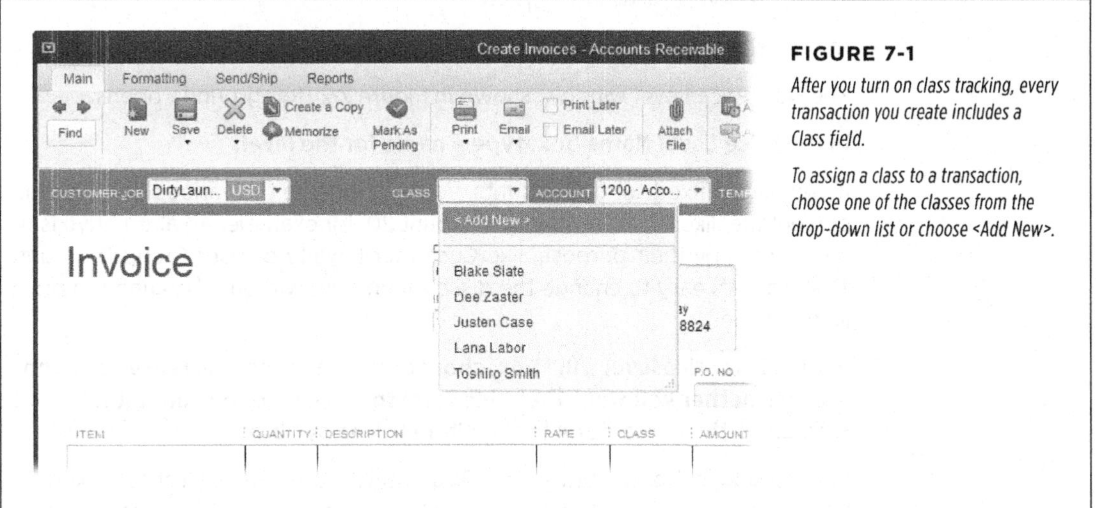

FIGURE 7-1

After you turn on class tracking, every transaction you create includes a Class field.

To assign a class to a transaction, choose one of the classes from the drop-down list or choose <Add New>.

Price Levels

Whether you give your favorite customers price breaks or increase other customers' charges because they keep asking for "just one more thing," you can apply discounts and markups when you create invoices. But remembering who gets discounts and how big is tough when you have a lot of customers, and it's bad form to mark up a favorite customer's prices by mistake.

Say hello to QuickBooks' Price Level List. When you define price levels and assign them to customers, QuickBooks takes care of adjusting the prices on every invoice you create. You can also apply a price level to specific lines on invoices to mark up or discount individual items. For example, suppose you create a price level that represents a 15 percent discount. If you apply that price level to a customer, the sales forms you create for that customer automatically discount prices by 15 percent. And if you apply that price level to a product on a customer's invoice, the product's price gets reduced by 15 percent.

Creating a Price Level

To create a price level, do the following:

1. **Make sure the Price Level preference is turned on (you have to be a QuickBooks administrator to turn it on).**

   If QuickBooks' Price Level preference is turned off, you won't see the Price Level List item in the Lists menu. In that case, choose Edit→Preferences→Sales & Customers, and then click the Company Preferences tab. Select the Enable Price Levels radio button, and then click OK.

2. **Choose Lists→Price Level List.**

   The Price Level List window opens.

3. **In the Price Level List window, press Ctrl+N or click Price Level→New.**

   The New Price Level window, shown in Figure 7-2 (foreground), opens.

4. **In the Price Level Name box, type a name for the level.**

   If you have a fixed set of discounts, you might name the various levels by the percentage, like Discount 10 and Discount 20, for example. An alternative is to name them by their purpose, like Customer Loyalty or User Group Discount. That way, it's easy to change the discount amount without changing the price level's name.

5. **In the "This price level will" box, choose "increase" or "decrease" depending on whether you want the price level to mark up or discount items, and then enter the percentage in the "item prices by" box.**

   In QuickBooks Pro, the Price Level Type box is automatically set to "Fixed %" because you can create price levels that increase or decrease prices only by a fixed percentage, as described in Figure 7-2. See the box on page 145 to learn about the Per Item price level available in QuickBooks Premier and Enterprise.

6. **For percentage price levels, in the "Round up to nearest" drop-down list, choose the type of rounding you want to apply.**

   The "Round up to nearest" setting is handy if the percentages you apply result in fractions of pennies or amounts too small to bother with. It lets you round discounts to pennies, nickels, dimes, quarters, half-dollars, and even whole dollars (if you *really* hate making change). The box on page 146 explains other, fancier kinds of rounding you can apply.

7. **Click OK to close the New Price Level window.**

   To create another price level, repeat steps 3–7.

NOTE You can't create price levels on the fly while you're creating an invoice. The easiest solution to a missing price level is to adjust the price on the invoice manually. Then, after the invoice is done, add the price level to your Price Level List.

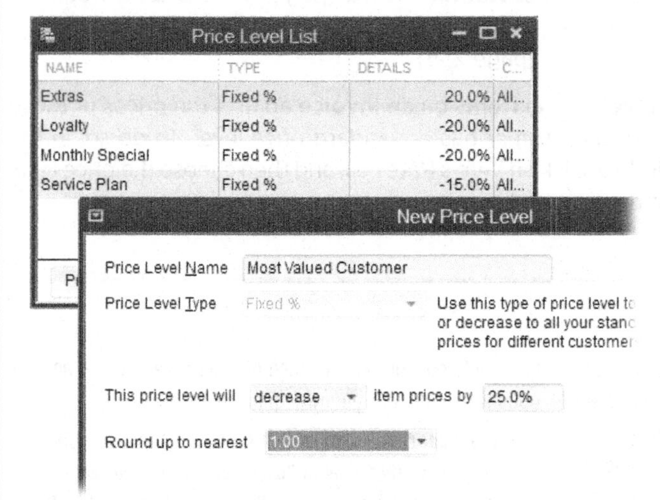

FIGURE 7-2

Think of fixed-percentage price levels as standard discounts or markups. For example, you can create a price level called Most Valued Customer to discount prices by 25 percent. Then assign that price level in the customer record (page 77) of every big spender you work with.

(Although price levels' names don't appear on your customer invoices, it's still a good idea to choose names that are meaningful without being rude.)

POWER USERS' CLINIC

Per-Item Price Levels

In QuickBooks Premier and Enterprise, you can create price levels that apply to individual items in your Item List. To do that, in the New Price Level window's Price Level Type drop-down list, choose Per Item. The window then displays a table containing all the items in your Item List.

In the Custom Price column, type the price for an item at that price level. For example, suppose you sell calendars to retail stores for $5 each. The Standard Price column would show 5.00 for the calendar item. If you're creating a price level for nonprofit organizations, you could type *3.50* in the item's Custom Price cell so that a nonprofit would pay only $3.50 for a calendar.

If you want to apply percentages to several items in the table displayed in the New Price Level window, there's a shortcut for calculating custom prices:

1. Turn on the checkboxes for all the items that use the same percentage increase or decrease.
2. In the "Adjust price of marked items to be" box, type the percentage. In the drop-down list next to it, choose "lower" or "higher." And in the "than its" drop-down list, choose an entry to tell QuickBooks to calculate the price level based on the standard price, the cost, or the current custom price.
3. Click the Adjust button, and QuickBooks fills in the Custom Price cells for the marked items with the new, custom prices.
4. To apply different percentages to another set of items, clear any checkmarks and then repeat steps 1–3.

If you work with more than one currency and turn on the multiple currency preference (page 656), you can create price levels for individual items to set their prices in different currencies. Here's how: In the New Price Level window, choose the currency in the Currency drop-down list. Then, in the Custom Price cell, type the price for the item in the foreign currency. After that, when you add the item to a sales form, simply choose the currency price level in that form's Rate drop-down list, and QuickBooks recalculates the price.

Applying Price Levels

You can apply price levels in two ways:

- **Applying a price level to a customer record** (page 77) tells QuickBooks to automatically adjust all the prices on every new invoice for that customer by that price level's percentage (page 235).
- **Applying a price level to line items on an invoice** adjusts the prices of those items whether or not a customer has a standard price level. To do so, in the Create Invoices window, click an item's Rate cell, and then choose the price level you want from the drop-down list.

POWER USERS' CLINIC

Rounding Price Level Values

When you use percentages to calculate markups and discounts, the resulting values may not be what you want. The basic choices in the New Price Level window's "Round up to nearest" drop-down list take care of the most common rounding—to the nearest penny, dime, quarter, dollar, and so on. But other entries on the list let you give QuickBooks more complex rounding instructions.

The seven entries that include the word "minus" help you position prices at magic marketing points like $29.99 or $1.95. For example, the ".10 minus .01" entry ensures that the price always ends in 9. With this setting, if the discounted price comes out to $8.74, QuickBooks rounds up to the nearest 10 cents ($8.80) and then subtracts 1 cent, so the rounded value is $8.79.

If you like to undercut your competitors with unusual price points, in the "Round up to nearest" drop-down menu, choose "user defined." QuickBooks then displays several boxes and options for defining your own rounding:

- **The "nearest" drop-down menu**. In the unlabeled drop-down menu below "user defined," you can choose "to nearest," "up to nearest," or "down to nearest." "To nearest" rounds in whichever direction is closest (for example, rounding from 1.73 to 1.70 or from 1.77 to 1.80).
- **The first $ box**. Type the value you want to round to, like .01, .25, or 1.00.
- **Plus or Minus and the second $ box**. Select the Plus or Minus radio button depending on whether you want to add or subtract money after you've rounded the value. Then, in the second $ box, type the amount you want to add or subtract from the rounded value. (If you don't want to use this feature, just leave the second $ box set to 0.)

Customer and Vendor Profile Lists

Filling in fields goes much faster when you can choose info from drop-down lists instead of typing values. The lists that appear on the Customer & Vendor Profile Lists submenu (to see it, choose Lists→Customer & Vendor Profile Lists) pop up regularly, whether you're creating an invoice, paying a bill, or generating a report. For example, when you create an invoice, QuickBooks fills in the Payment Terms field with the terms you assigned to the customer's record (page 76), but you can choose different terms from the drop-down list to urge your customer to pay more quickly.

For many of these lists, creating entries involves nothing more than typing the entry's name and specifying whether that entry is a subentry of another. This section describes how to add entries to each list and how to put these lists to work for you.

Sales Rep List

The Sales Rep List is perfect when you want to assign people as points of contact for your customers. The people you add to this list can be sales reps you pay on commission or employees who are dedicated contacts for customers. For example, if you assign people as sales reps to your customers (page 77) and add the appropriate rep to your sales transactions, you can then generate reports by sales rep (page 597). But first you have to add the names of your sales reps and contacts to the Sales Rep List.

NOTE If you'd like an add-on program to help you calculate commissions, go to *http://workplace.intuit.com/appcenter.* In the "Search for apps" box, type *sales commission*, and then press Enter.

To add a name to the Sales Rep List:

1. **Choose Lists→Customer & Vendor Profile Lists→Sales Rep List; in the Sales Rep List window that opens, press Ctrl+N or click Sales Rep→New.**

   The New Sales Rep window opens.

2. **In the Sales Rep Name drop-down list, choose a name; in the Sales Rep Initials box, type the person's initials.**

   The Sales Rep Name list displays names from the Employee List, the Vendor List, and the Other Names List (page 148). QuickBooks automatically fills in the Sales Rep Type field with Employee, Vendor, or Other Name, depending on which list the name came from or, if you just added the name, the type you assigned when you added that person. (The box on page 148 gives hints about when to use the Other Names List.)

   If the name you want doesn't exist, choose <Add New> at the top of the list. In the Select Name Type dialog box that appears, select Vendor, Employee, or Other, and then click OK. Then, in the New Name window that opens, fill in the Name box and any other fields you want.

3. **Click Next to add another sales rep, or click OK to close the New Sales Rep window.**

   If you select a name and realize that it's misspelled, you can edit it right from the New Sales Rep window: Click Edit Name, and QuickBooks opens the Edit Employee, Edit Vendor, or Edit Name dialog box so you can change the name.

GEM IN THE ROUGH

When to Use the Other Names List

If you have more than a few names on your Other Names List, you're probably not getting the most out of QuickBooks. In fact, unless you're a sole proprietor or several partners share ownership of your company, you can run QuickBooks without *any* names on the Other Names List.

The entries in the Other Names List show up in the drop-down menus for a few types of transactions, such as checks and credit card charges (page 202). But they don't appear for other types of transactions, like invoices, purchase orders, and sales receipts.

So what are Other Names good for? People who aren't customers, vendors, or employees—for example, *your* name as sole proprietor or the names of company partners. That way, when you write partners' distribution checks, you can choose their names from the Other Names List.

To create an entry on the Other Names List:

1. Choose Lists→Other Names List.
2. When the Other Names List window opens, press Ctrl+N.
3. Fill in the fields in the New Name dialog box, which are similar to the ones in the New Customer dialog box (page 70).
4. Click OK.

The Other Names List can also serve as a holding tank. If you aren't sure which list to put someone on, you can temporarily add that person to the Other Names List. Then, when you figure out which list she should be on, you can move her. Because QuickBooks needs to close all open windows to move people between lists, it's best to save this task for a lull in your workday. When you're ready, open the Other Names List window and click Activities→Change Other Name Types. In the Change Name Types dialog box that appears, find the person's name, and then click the cell in the appropriate column (Customer, Vendor, or Employee) to assign that type. Click OK to complete the makeover.

If you realize that you created two entries for the same person in the Other Names List, you can merge one into the other. Merging entries in the Other Names List is similar to merging customers (page 92). The alternative is to make one of the two entries inactive, as described on page 90, and then use the other entry for all future transactions.

Customer Type List

Customer types help you analyze your income and expenses by customer category (page 87). For example, a healthcare provider might create Government and Private customer types to see how much a change in government reimbursement might hurt revenue.

You first create customer types in the Customer Type List and then assign one of those types in each customer's record. Creating all your customer types up front is fast—as long as you already know what entries you want to create:

1. **Choose Lists→Customer & Vendor Profile Lists→Customer Type List; when the Customer Type List window opens, press Ctrl+N.**

   The New Customer Type window opens (Figure 7-3).

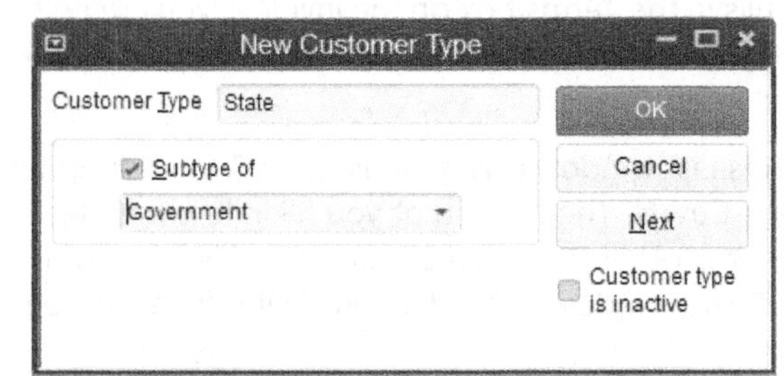

FIGURE 7-3

The only thing you have to fill in here is the Customer Type field.

If this type represents a portion of a larger customer category, turn on the "Subtype of" checkbox, and then choose the parent type. For example, if you have a Government customer type, you might create subtypes like Federal, State, County, and so on.

2. **Enter a name in the Customer Type field.**

   If the new type is a subtype of another, turn on the "Subtype of" checkbox, and then choose the parent type from the drop-down list.

3. **Click OK if you're done, or click Next to create another type.**

You can also create entries as you work: If you're creating or modifying a customer in the New Customer or Edit Customer window, click the Additional Info tab. In the Customer Type drop-down list, choose <Add New> to open the New Customer Type window so you can create a new customer type, as shown in Figure 7-3.

Vendor Type List

Vendor types work similarly to customer types—you can filter reports or subtotal expenses by different types of vendors. For example, if you create a Contractor vendor type, you could generate a report showing how much you spend on subcontractors you hire.

You create Vendor Type entries the way you create Customer Type entries: Choose Lists→Customer & Vendor Profile Lists→Vendor Type List, and then press Ctrl+N to open the New Vendor Type window.

TIP To create a new vendor type while you're creating a vendor, in the New Vendor dialog box, click the Additional Info tab and then, in the Vendor Type drop-down list, choose <Add New> to open the New Vendor Type window.

Job Type List

Job types also follow the customer-type lead. You can use job types to classify the projects you perform for customers, as described on page 87. For instance, you can filter a Profit & Loss report to show how profitable your spec-house projects are compared with your remodeling contracts. You create Job Type entries the way you create Customer Type entries: Open the Job Type List window by choosing Lists→Customer & Vendor Profile Lists→Job Type List, and then press Ctrl+N.

Terms List

The Terms List includes both the payment terms you require of your customers and the payment terms your vendors ask of you. If you assign terms in a customer's record, then QuickBooks automatically fills in the Terms box on the invoices you create for that customer. Likewise, filling in terms in a vendor record means that QuickBooks fills in the Terms box on bills you enter.

To add a new term, open the Terms List window (Lists→Customer & Vendor Profile Lists→Terms List), and then press Ctrl+N. The fields that you fill in to create terms (Figure 7-4) are different from those in other Customer & Vendor Profile lists. The following sections explain the New Terms window's Standard and Date Driven options.

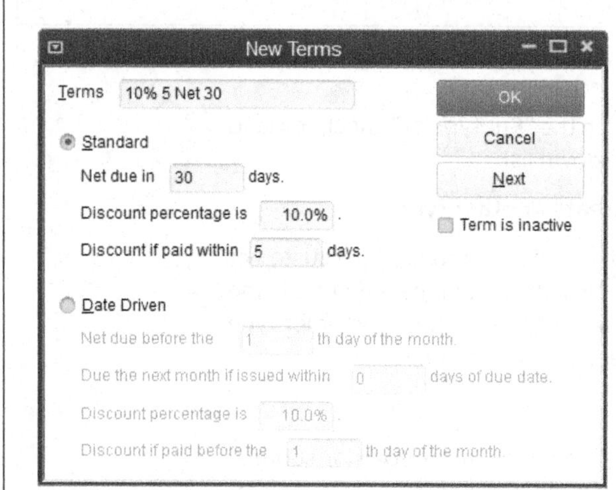

FIGURE 7-4

Because payment terms apply to both vendors and customers, consider using generic names that say something about the terms themselves.

For example, the "10% 5 Net 30" entry shown here is an enticement for early payments because it means that the amount is due 30 days from the invoice date, but you can deduct 10 percent from your bill if you pay within 5 days.

SETTING UP TERMS USING ELAPSED TIME

The New Terms window's Standard option is ideal when the payment due date is a specific number of days after the invoice date (or the date you receive a bill from a vendor). If you send invoices whenever you complete a sale, choose the Standard option.

Here's what the Standard option's fields do:

- **Net due in _ days**. Type the maximum number of days after the bill or invoice date that you or a customer can pay. For example, if you type *30*, customers have up to 30 days to pay an invoice or you have up to 30 days to pay a bill. If you charge penalties for late payments, QuickBooks uses the value in this field to figure out when customer payments are late so you can assess finance charges (page 359).
- **Discount percentage is**. If you or your vendor offer a discount for early payments, type the discount percentage in this box.

- **Discount if paid within _ days**. Type the number of days after the bill or invoice date within which you or a customer has to pay to receive the early payment discount.

NOTE When your terms reduce a customer's bill for early payments, QuickBooks deducts these discounts in the Receive Payments window (page 352), where the program can determine whether the customer paid early. If a *vendor* offers discounts for early payments, you can take advantage of those in the Pay Bills window (page 195).

SETTING UP DATE-DRIVEN TERMS

The Date Driven option sets up terms for payments that are due on a specific date, regardless of the date on the invoice. This option is handy if you or your vendors send invoices on a schedule—say, on the last day of the month. For example, home mortgages often assess a late fee if payments arrive after the 15th of the month.

Here's what the New Terms window's Date Driven options do:

- **Net due before the _ th day of the month**. Type the day that the payment is due. For example, if a payment is due before the 15th of the month, no matter what date appears on your statement, type *15* in this box.
- **Due the next month if issued within _ days of due date**. Your customers might get annoyed if you require payment by the 15th of the month and send out your invoices on the 14th. They would have no way of paying on time—unless they camped out in your billing department.

  You can type a number of days in this box to automatically push the due date to the following month when you issue invoices too close to the due date. Suppose payments are due on the 15th of each month and you type *5* in this box. In that case, for invoices you create between August 10 and August 15, QuickBooks automatically changes the due date to September 15.
- **Discount percentage is**. If you or your vendors extend a discount for early payments, type the discount percentage in this box.
- **Discount if paid before the _ th day of the month**. Type the day of the month before which you or a customer has to pay to receive the early payment discount.

Customer Message List

When you create an invoice, you can add a short message to it, such as "If you like the service we deliver, tell your friends. If you don't like our service, tell us." To save time and prevent embarrassing typos, add your stock messages to the Customer Message List (Lists→Customer & Vendor Profile Lists→Customer Message List).

In the Customer Message List window, press Ctrl+N to open the New Customer Message dialog box. This dialog box has only one field—Message—which can hold up to 101 characters (including spaces).

TIP Don't use the Customer Message List for notes that change with every invoice (like one that specifies the date range that an invoice covers) because you'll fill the list with unique messages and won't be able to add any more. If you want to include unique information, do so in the cover letter (or email) that accompanies your invoice.

Payment Method List

Categorizing payments by the method the customer uses can be handy. For instance, when you select Banking→Make Deposits (page 368), you can choose to process all the payments you've received via a specific payment method—deposit all the checks and cash you received into your checking account, say, but deposit the payments you receive via credit cards to a dedicated merchant account.

You categorize payments by using the entries on the Payment Method List. QuickBooks starts the list for you with entries for cash, check, credit cards (such as American Express and Visa), and electronic payments. To add another payment method—for payments through PayPal, for example—choose Lists→Customer & Vendor Profile Lists→Payment Method List, and then press Ctrl+N. In the New Payment Method dialog box, type a name for the method, and then choose a type. For PayPal, choose Other in the Payment Type drop-down list. The list of types also includes options like Debit Card, Gift Card, and E-Check.

Ship Via List

When your invoices include the shipping method that you use, your customers know whether to watch for the mailman or the UPS truck. QuickBooks creates several shipping methods for you: DHL, Federal Express, UPS, and US Mail. If you use another method, like a bike messenger in New York City or your own delivery truck, simply create additional entries in the Ship Via List window (Lists→Customer & Vendor Profile Lists→Ship Via List) by pressing Ctrl+N. In the Shipping Method field (the only field in the New Ship Method dialog box), type a name for the method, and then click OK.

TIP If you use one shipping method most of the time, you can have QuickBooks fill in the Shipping Method field on invoices with that entry automatically. See page 663 to learn about the Usual Shipping Method preference and the Usual Free on Board location.

Vehicle List

If you want to track mileage (page 175) on the vehicles you use for your business, create entries for your cars and trucks in the Vehicle List (Lists→Customer & Vendor Profile Lists→Vehicle List). Press Ctrl+N and then use the Vehicle box to name the vehicle: *Ford Prefect 1982 Red*, for example. The Description field holds up to 256 characters, so you can use it to store the VIN, license plate, and even the insurance policy number.

TIP If you want to charge your customers for mileage, see page 178.

Fixed Asset Items

Assets that you can't convert to cash quickly—such as backhoes, buildings, and supercomputers—are called *fixed assets*. If you track information about your fixed assets in another program or have only a few fixed assets, there's no reason to bother with QuickBooks' Fixed Asset Item List. As you can see in Figure 7-5 QuickBooks can track info such as when you bought the item and how much you paid. But in QuickBooks Pro, *you* have to calculate depreciation (see the box on page 435) for each asset at the end of the year and create journal entries to adjust the values in your asset accounts.

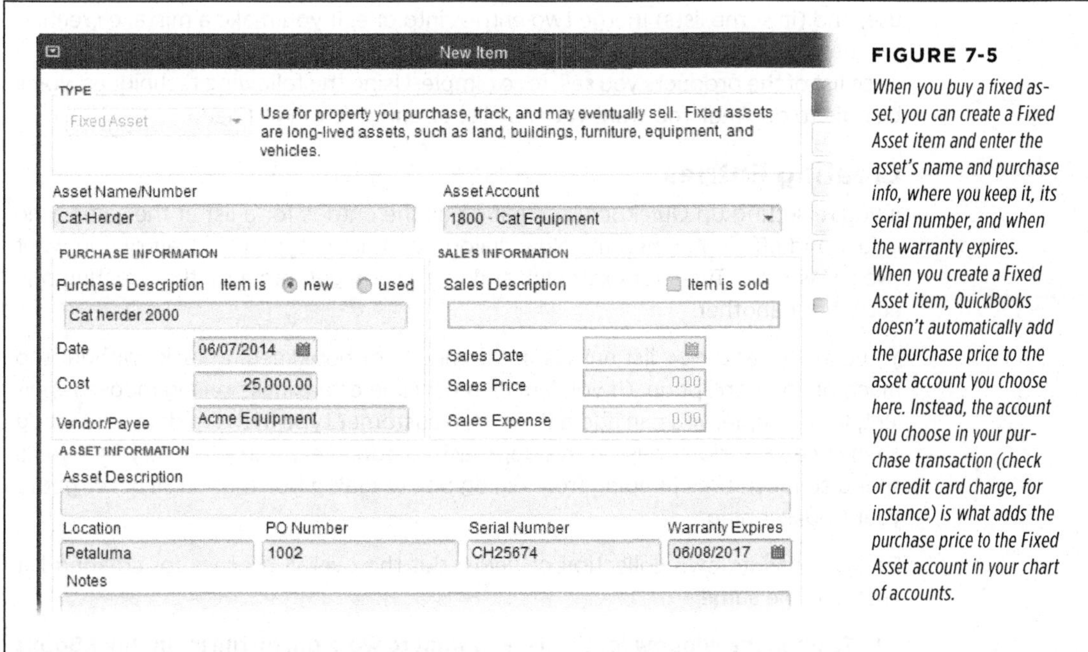

FIGURE 7-5

When you buy a fixed asset, you can create a Fixed Asset item and enter the asset's name and purchase info, where you keep it, its serial number, and when the warranty expires. When you create a Fixed Asset item, QuickBooks doesn't automatically add the purchase price to the asset account you choose here. Instead, the account you choose in your purchase transaction (check or credit card charge, for instance) is what adds the purchase price to the Fixed Asset account in your chart of accounts.

NOTE QuickBooks Premier Accountant edition and QuickBooks Enterprise edition include the Fixed Asset Manager, which figures out the depreciation on your assets and posts depreciation to an account in your QuickBooks company file. If you have an accountant prepare your depreciation schedule, then go with the number your accountant gives you. The depreciation that QuickBooks calculates may be close to, but different from, the number your accountant calculates.

When you sell an asset, open the Edit Item dialog box (choose Lists→Fixed Asset Item List, select the asset you sold, and then press Ctrl+E) and turn on the "Item is sold" checkbox. When you do that, the sales fields come to life so you can specify when you sold the asset, how much you got for it, and any costs associated with the sale.

If you decide to track the details about your fixed assets outside QuickBooks, you still need to include the *value* of those assets in your financial reports. Simply create Fixed Asset accounts for each fixed asset (page 57) to hold those values. Then, each year, add a journal entry to record the amount of depreciation for your fixed assets (page 433).

Managing Lists

Every list in QuickBooks responds to the same set of commands. As your business changes, you can add new entries, edit existing ones, hide entries that you no longer use, and (in some lists) merge two entries into one. If you make a mistake creating an entry, you can delete it. You can also print your QuickBooks lists to produce a price list of the products you sell, for example. Using the following techniques, you'll be able to do what you want with any list or entry you might need.

Creating Entries

If you're setting up QuickBooks, creating all the entries for a list at the same time is fast and efficient. Open the New dialog box for the type of list entry you want (New Customer Type, for example), and you'll soon get into a rhythm creating one entry after another.

You can also add new list entries in the middle of bookkeeping tasks without too much of an interruption. (If you launch a new line of business selling moose repellent, for example, you can add a Burly Men customer type in the middle of creating an invoice.) But don't rely on this approach to add every entry to every list—you'll spend so much time jumping from dialog box to dialog box that you'll never get to your bookkeeping.

Each list has its own collection of fields, but the overall process for creating list entries is the same:

1. **To open the window for the list you want to work on, on the main QuickBooks menu bar, click Lists, and then select the list you want on the submenu.**

   For example, to open the Class List window, choose Lists→Class List.

   Several lists are tucked away one level deeper on the Lists menu. For lists that include characteristics of your customers or vendors, such as Vendor Type or Terms, choose Lists→Customer & Vendor Profile Lists, and *then* choose the list you want, as shown in Figure 7-6.

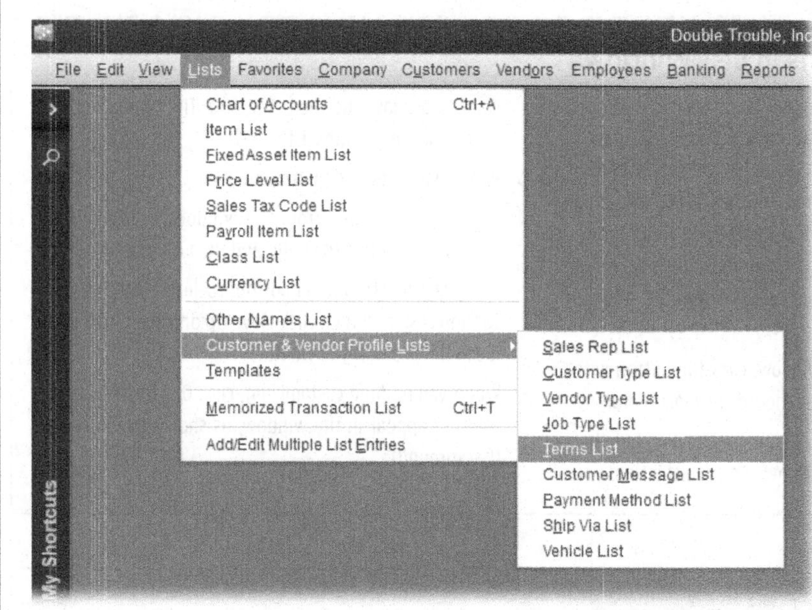

FIGURE 7-6

To boost your productivity, take note of the keyboard shortcuts for lists you're likely to access most often. For example, Ctrl+A opens the Chart of Accounts window. (Online Appendix C lists lots of other handy keyboard shortcuts.)

In addition, when you see an underlined letter in a menu entry, you can type that letter to launch that feature. For example, when the Lists menu is open, press C to open the Class List window.

2. **To create a new entry, press Ctrl+N; right-click the list window and choose New on the shortcut menu that appears; or, at the bottom of the window, click the button with the list's name on it, and then choose New.**

   For instance, to create an entry in the Class List, make sure that the Class List window is active, and then press Ctrl+N. Or, at the bottom of the window, click Class→New. Either way, QuickBooks opens the New Class window.

3. **After you've completed one entry, simply click Next to save the current entry and begin another. To save the entry you just created and close the dialog box, click OK.**

   To toss an entry that you botched, click Cancel to throw it away and close the dialog box.

NOTE Unlike all the other New windows for lists, the New Price Level window doesn't include a Next button.

Editing Entries

To modify a list entry, open the window for that list. Then select the entry you want to edit and press Ctrl+E or double-click the entry. (You can customize the columns that appear in list windows so it's easier to see values associated with list entries;

the box below tells you how.) When the Edit dialog box opens, make the changes you want, and then click OK.

POWER USERS' CLINIC

Customizing Columns in List Windows

Some list entries don't come with many fields, such as the items in the Ship Via List, so all you need to see in that list window is the names of the shipping methods you've created. But other lists, such as Terms, store a plethora of information, including discounts and days of the month associated with the terms. Fortunately, you can customize the columns that appear in list windows so you can see list entries' values without editing the entries. Here's how:

1. At the bottom of the list window, click the button with the list's name on it, and then choose Customize Columns.
2. In the "Customize Columns - [list name]" dialog box that appears, in the Available Columns list, select a field you want to display, and then click Add. The column moves to the Chosen Columns list.
3. Repeat step 2 to add more columns.
4. To remove a column from the window, in the Chosen Columns list, select the field, and then click Remove.
5. To move a field to another position, select it in the Chosen Columns list, and then click Move Up or Move Down until it's in the position you want.
6. When you're done customizing, click OK. The fields you selected appear in the window, as shown in Figure 7-7 (background).

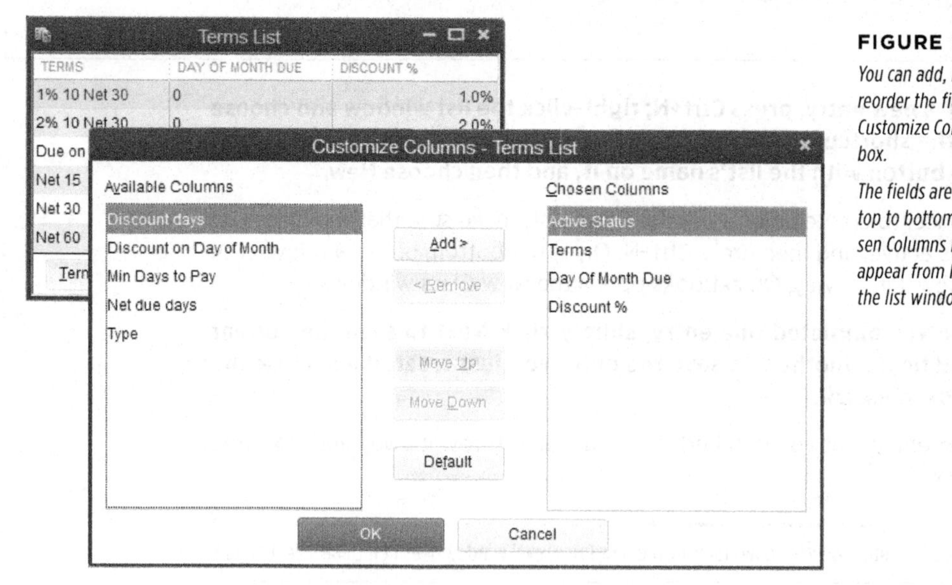

FIGURE 7-7

You can add, remove, and reorder the fields in the Customize Columns dialog box.

The fields are listed from top to bottom in the Chosen Columns list, but they appear from left to right in the list window.

Hiding Entries

Deleting entries is only for discarding entries that you create by mistake. If you've already used list entries in transactions, hide the entries you don't use anymore so your historical records are complete. For example, you wouldn't delete the "Net 30" payment term just because you're lucky enough to have only Net 15 clients right now; you may still extend Net 30 terms to some clients in the future.

Hiding list entries that you no longer use does two things:

- **Keeps your records intact**. Your previous transactions still use the entries you've hidden, so your historical records don't change.
- **Declutters your lists**. When you create new transactions, the hidden entries don't appear in drop-down lists, so you can't choose them by mistake.

The methods for hiding and reactivating list entries are exactly the same regardless of which list you're working on:

- **To hide an entry**: In the list's window, right-click the entry and choose "Make [list name] Inactive" from the shortcut menu, where [list name] is the list you're editing, such as Class or Sales Rep. The entry disappears from the list.
- **To view all the entries in a list**: At the bottom of the list window, turn on the "Include inactive" checkbox so you can see both active and hidden entries. QuickBooks adds a column with an X as its heading and displays an X in that column for every inactive entry in the list. (If no entries are inactive, the "Include inactive" checkbox is grayed out.)
- **To reactivate an entry**: First, display all the entries as described above, and then click the X next to the entry you want to reactivate. If the entry has subentries, then in the Activate Group dialog box that appears, click Yes to reactivate the entry *and* all its subentries.

Deleting Entries

You can delete a list entry only if nothing in your QuickBooks company file references it in any way. To delete a list entry, open the appropriate list window, select the entry you want to delete, and then press Ctrl+D or, in the main QuickBooks menu bar, choose Edit→"Delete [list name]." As long as the entry isn't used in any records or transactions, QuickBooks asks you to confirm that you want to delete the entry; click Yes.

If you realize immediately that you *didn't* want to delete the entry, press Ctrl+Z to undo the delete. But if you've already performed any other action in QuickBooks, you can't undo the deletion. The only way to get the list entry back is to recreate it.

Finding List Entries in Transactions

If QuickBooks won't let you delete a list entry because a transaction is still using it, don't worry—it's easy to find transactions that use a specific list entry. Here's how:

1. **Open the list that contains the entry you want to find and, in the list window, right-click the entry and choose Find on the shortcut menu.**

   The Find dialog box opens already set up to search for transactions that use the list entry you selected.

2. **Click Find.**

   The table at the bottom of the Find dialog box displays all the transactions that use that entry.

3. **To modify the list entry a transaction uses, select the transaction in the table, and then click Go To.**

   QuickBooks opens the window or dialog box that corresponds to the type of transaction. If you're trying to eliminate references to a list entry so you can delete it, choose a different list entry, and then save the transaction.

Sorting Lists

QuickBooks sorts lists alphabetically by name, which is usually what you want. The only reason to sort a list another way is if you're having trouble finding the entry you want to edit. For example, if you want to find equipment you bought within the last few years, you could sort the Fixed Asset List by purchase date to find the machines that you're still depreciating. Figure 7-8 shows you how to change the sort order.

NOTE Sorting in a list window doesn't change the order in which entries appear in drop-down lists, unless you *manually* sort a list by dragging the diamond icons to the left of list items' names.

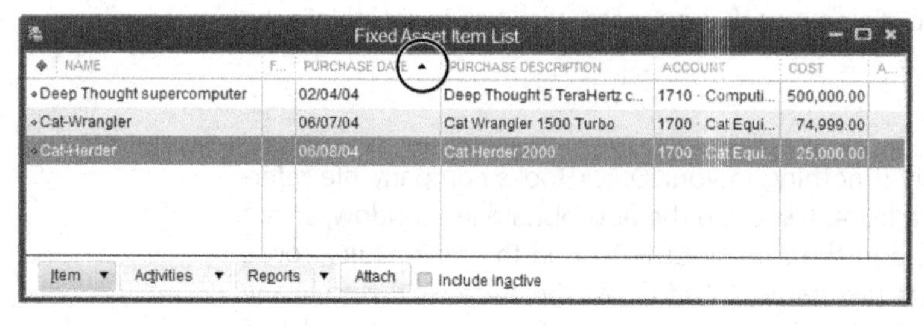

FIGURE 7-8

To sort a list by a column, click the column's heading, such as Purchase Date. The first time you click the heading, QuickBooks sorts the list in ascending order, and the small black triangle in the heading (circled) points up, as shown here. To toggle between ascending and descending order, click the heading again, and the triangle points down.

NOTE As mentioned above, QuickBooks initially sorts lists by their Name columns. If you sort a list by a different column, you see a gray diamond to the left of the column heading that it used to sort the list initially. For example, if you sort the Fixed Asset Item List by Purchase Date, a gray diamond appears to the left of the Name heading, as shown in Figure 7-8. To return the list to the order that QuickBooks originally used, click this diamond.

Printing Lists

After you spend all that time building lists in QuickBooks, you'll be happy to know that it's much easier to get information about those lists *out* of the program than it was to put it in. For instance, suppose you want to print a price list of all your inventory items. QuickBooks makes short work of printing lists or turning them into files that you can use in other programs.

BLASTING OUT A QUICK LIST

Here's the fastest way to produce a list, albeit one that doesn't give you any control over the report's appearance:

1. **At the bottom left of a list window, click the button labeled with the list's name—like Price Level, for example—and then, in the drop-down menu, choose Print List (or press Ctrl+P).**

   QuickBooks might display a message box telling you to try list reports if you want to customize or format your reports; that method is covered in the next section. For now, in the message box, click OK. The Print Lists dialog box opens.

NOTE To print Customer, Vendor, or Employee lists, in the Customer Center, Vendor Center, or Employee Center toolbar, click Print. On the Print submenu, choose an entry, such as Customer & Job List, to print a list of customers and jobs with their open balances. Choosing Print→Customer & Job Information prints information about the selected customer or job. And Choosing Print→Customer & Job Transaction List prints a report of the selected customer's or job's transactions.

2. **To print the list, select the Printer option, and then choose a printer in the drop-down list. To output the list to a file, choose the File option instead, and then select the format you want.**

   If you go with the Printer option, you can specify print settings, as you can in many other programs. Choose landscape or portrait orientation, the pages to print, and the number of copies.

   If you choose File, you can create ASCII text files, comma-delimited files, or tab-delimited files (page 685).

3. **Click Print.**

   QuickBooks prints the report or creates the type of file you selected.

CUSTOMIZING A PRINTED LIST

If the Print List feature described above scatters fields over the page or produces a comma-delimited file that doesn't play well with your email program, you'll be happy to know that QuickBooks might offer a report closer to what you have in mind. For example, an Item Price List is only two clicks away.

To access the reports that come with QuickBooks, in the program's main menu bar, go to Reports→List, and then choose the report you want. If these reports fall short, you can modify them to change the fields and records they include, and format them in a variety of ways. Chapter 23 has the whole story on customizing reports.

PART 2

Bookkeeping

CHAPTER 16:
Making Journal Entries

CHAPTER 17:
Performing Year-End Tasks

CHAPTER

8

Tracking Time and Mileage

When customers pay for your services, they're really buying your knowledge of how to get the job done the best and fastest possible way. That's why an inexperienced carpenter charges $15 an hour, whereas a master woodworker who hammers faster and straighter than a nail gun charges $80 an hour. When it comes right down to it, time is money, so you want to keep track of both with equal accuracy. Product-based companies track time, too. For example, companies that want to increase productivity often start by tracking the time that employees work and what they work on.

There are hordes of off-the-shelf and homegrown time-tracking programs out there, but if your time-tracking needs are fairly simple, you can record time directly in QuickBooks or use its companion program, QuickBooks Pro Timer, which you can provide to each person whose work hours you want to track. The advantage of tracking time in QuickBooks is that the hours you record are ready to attach to an invoice (see page 253) or use in payroll (see online Appendix D). In this chapter, you'll learn how to record time in QuickBooks itself. Appendix F (available from this book's Missing CD page at *www.missingmanuals.com/cds*) explains the ins and outs of the standalone Timer program.

NOTE If your time-tracking needs outpace QuickBooks' time-tracking features, Intuit's marketplace (*http://marketplace.intuit.com*) lists about 50 time-tracking solutions that integrate with QuickBooks. Click Search By Business Need, and then click Time Tracking. You can then specify features you're looking for by turning on the checkboxes that appear, such as online access or the ability to track time against projects. Intuit's App Center (*http://appcenter.intuit.com*) also lists a few time-tracking solutions. Type *time tracking* in the Search box, and then click the Search button (it looks like a magnifying glass). To search further afield, type keywords like *QuickBooks time tracking* into your favorite Internet search engine.

Mileage is another commodity that many companies track—or should. Whether your business hinges on driving or merely requires the occasional jaunt, the IRS lets you deduct vehicle mileage, as long as you can *document* the miles you deduct. And you might charge customers for the miles driven in conjunction with the work you do for them. As you'll learn in this chapter, QuickBooks can help you track the mileage of company vehicles; you can then use that info for tax deductions or to charge customers.

Setting Up Time Tracking

For many businesses, *approximations* of time worked are fine. For example, employees who work on only one or two tasks each day can review the past week and log their hours in a weekly timesheet. But for people with deliciously high hourly rates, you want to capture every minute spent on an activity.

QuickBooks can help you track time whether you take a conscientious approach or a more cavalier one. You can choose from two different ways of recording time within QuickBooks:

- **Enter time data in QuickBooks**. You can enter time for individual activities or fill in a weekly timesheet. In the Time/Enter Single Activity dialog box, you can type in the number of hours for a single activity. The dialog box also includes a stopwatch, so you can have it track the time you spend working on a task.
- **Use QuickBooks Pro Timer's stopwatch**. This program, which comes on the QuickBooks CD, lets you time activities as you work so you can track your time to the second—as long as you remember to start and stop the Timer at the right moments. (If you forget to turn the Timer on or off, you can edit time entries to correct them.) The best thing about Timer is that you can use it to record time even when QuickBooks isn't running. Moreover, you can give a copy of Timer to all your employees and subcontractors so they can send you time data to import into QuickBooks.

NOTE If you download QuickBooks and want the Timer program, head online to *http://support.quickbooks.intuit.com/support/Articles/HOW13261* to learn how to get it without a DVD.

No matter which technique you use to capture time, the setup is the same: You tell QuickBooks that you want to track time and then set up the people who need to track their time (employees and outside contractors alike). You use the customers and items you've set up in QuickBooks to identify the billable time you work. If you want to track nonbillable time, you need a few more entries in QuickBooks, which you'll learn about in the following sections.

Turning on Time Tracking

If you told QuickBooks that you want to track time when you created your company file (page 17), the time-tracking preferences and features should be ready to go. To see whether time tracking is turned on, choose Edit→Preferences→Time & Expenses (you may have to scroll down to see this category), and then click the Company Preferences tab shown in Figure 8-1 (only a QuickBooks administrator can turn time tracking on or off). If the Yes radio button below "Do you track time?" isn't selected, click it. (If your company file is in multi-user mode, QuickBooks tells you that you have to switch to single-user mode [page 489] first.)

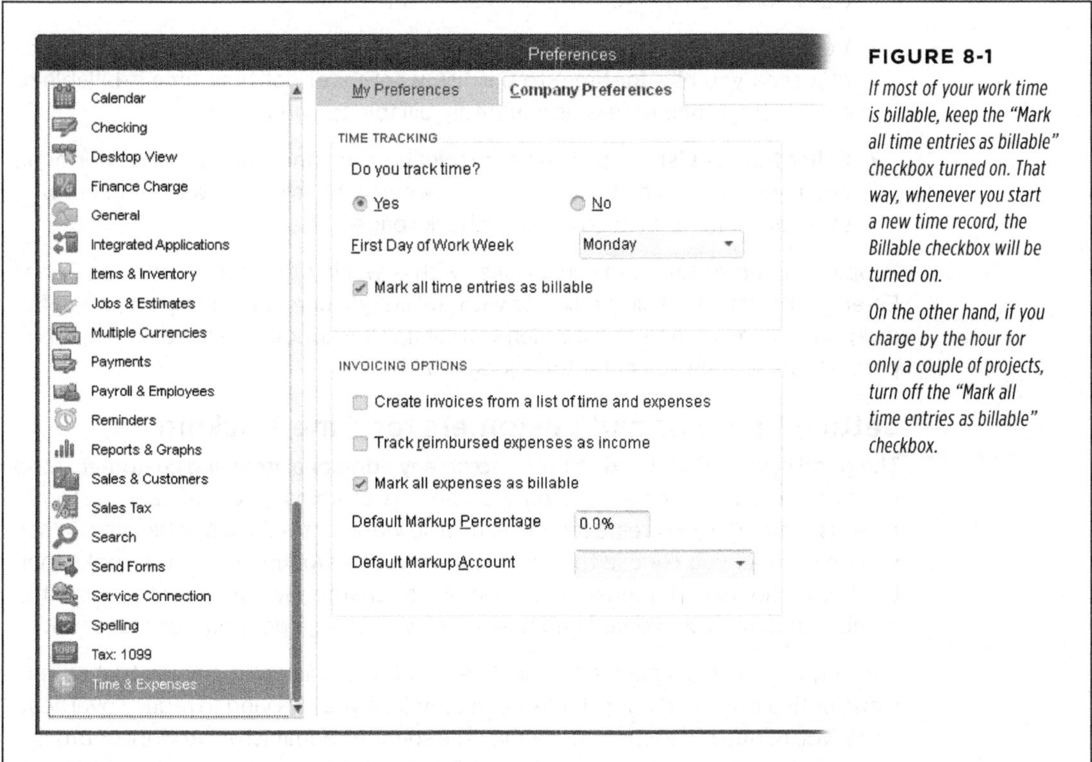

FIGURE 8-1

If most of your work time is billable, keep the "Mark all time entries as billable" checkbox turned on. That way, whenever you start a new time record, the Billable checkbox will be turned on.

On the other hand, if you charge by the hour for only a couple of projects, turn off the "Mark all time entries as billable" checkbox.

QuickBooks automatically sets the "First Day of Work Week" box to Monday to match the Monday-through-Friday workweek of so many businesses. For round-the-clock services, self-employed people, and workaholics, choose whichever day feels most like the beginning of the week. For example, many companies on a seven-day workweek start the week on Sunday. If you use QuickBooks to generate hours for payroll, you should set the program's workweek to end on the same day as your pay periods. For instance, if your payroll cutoff dates are on Fridays, in the "First Day of Work Week" drop-down list, choose Saturday so that QuickBooks' workweek ends on Friday, just like your payroll.

TIP To learn about time-related invoicing options, see page 252.

Setting Up the People Who Track Time

You can't enter or import people's time into QuickBooks unless their names appear in one of your name lists (the Employee List, Vendor List, or Other Names List). If someone whose time you want to track isn't on one of those lists yet, here's how you decide which list to use:

- **Employee List**. Use this list for your employees whether you pay them using QuickBooks' payroll features or in some other way.
- **Vendor List**. Add subcontractors and outside consultants (people or companies that send you bills for time) to this list, whether or not their time is billable to customers. (Their time is undoubtedly billable to *you*.)
- **Other Names List**. By process of elimination, anyone who isn't a vendor or an employee belongs on this list, such as owners who take a draw or partners who take distributions instead of a paycheck (page 419).

People who enter time in QuickBooks (with a weekly timesheet or in the Time/Enter Single Activity dialog box, not with the standalone Timer program) need the program's permission to do so. When you set up QuickBooks users, you can set their permissions so they can enter time (page 727).

Setting Up Items and Customers for Time Tracking

The good news is that you don't have to do any additional item and customer setup to be able to bill time to your customers. The Service items (page 108) and customer records (page 70) you create for invoicing also work for tracking billable time. When you enter time, you choose the Service item you're working on. QuickBooks then totals your hours and figures out how much to charge the customer based on the number of hours you worked and how much you charge per hour for that service.

The only reason you'd need additional items is if you track *all* the hours that people work, both billable and nonbillable. For example, if you're trying to reduce overhead costs, you might add items to track the time spent on administrative work or providing customer service, as shown in Figure 8-2. (Page 106 explains how to add items.) The level of detail you track in QuickBooks for nonbillable activities is up to you.

Here's how you fill in the New Item dialog box's fields when you create items to track time that you *don't* bill to a customer:

- **Type**. Use the Service item type (page 108) because that's the only one QuickBooks' time-tracking feature recognizes.
- **Rate**. This is where you enter how much you charge for the service. Because no money changes hands for nonbillable time, leave this field set to 0.

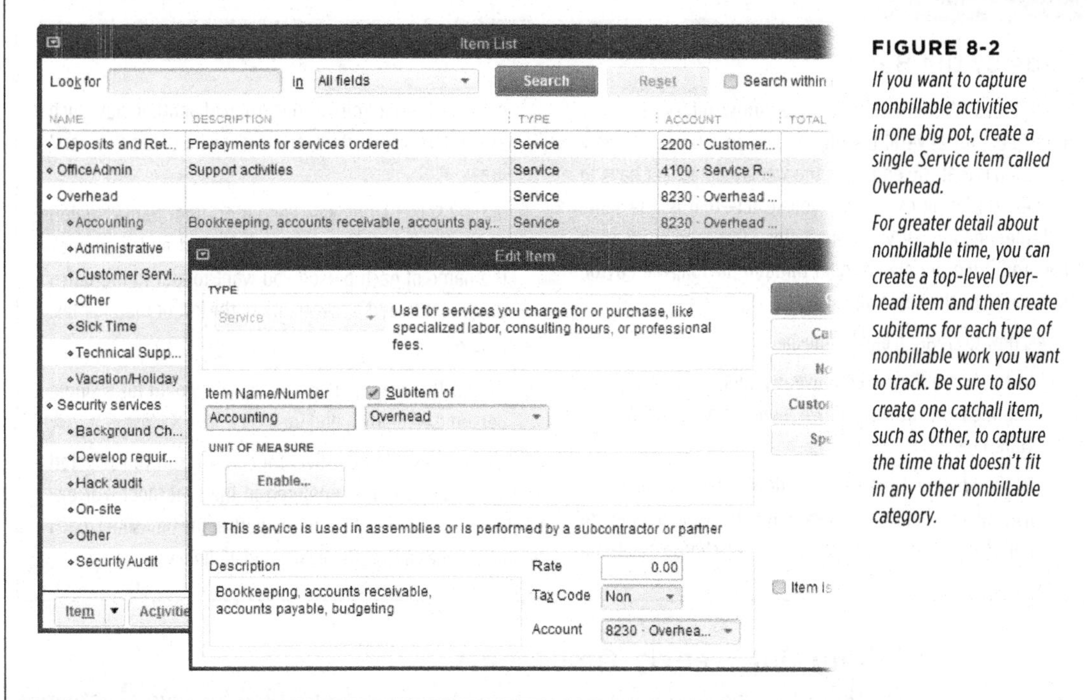

FIGURE 8-2

If you want to capture nonbillable activities in one big pot, create a single Service item called Overhead.

For greater detail about nonbillable time, you can create a top-level Overhead item and then create subitems for each type of nonbillable work you want to track. Be sure to also create one catchall item, such as Other, to capture the time that doesn't fit in any other nonbillable category.

- **Account**. You can't create an item without assigning it to an account, so create an expense account (page 56) and call it something like Nonbillable Work or Overhead Time. If you number accounts, assign the account a number that places it near the end of your Expense type accounts (like 8230).
- **This service is used in assemblies or is performed by a subcontractor or partner**. If a subcontractor performs nonbillable work for you, turn on this checkbox. That way, you can assign the subcontractor's costs to an expense account and use time tracking to make sure the subcontractor's bills are correct. For nonbillable items performed by owners and partners, leave this checkbox turned off.

Entering Time in QuickBooks

QuickBooks lets you enter and view time for a single activity or for whole weeks. If you record time after the fact, a weekly timesheet is the fastest way to enter time (and you can enter weekly timesheets for more than one person at once). If you already have one timesheet filled out, you can copy it to speed up your data entry, as the box on page 171 explains.

To time work as you perform it, the Time/Enter Single Activity dialog box (explained starting on page 171) is the way to go.

GEM IN THE ROUGH

Time by the Batch

QuickBooks' Weekly Timesheet window lets you create timesheets for several people at the same time. The only limitation is that the entries in the weekly timesheet have to be identical for all the people you select—that is, the same customer and job, Service item, notes, class, and hours each day. And if the people are paid through payroll, the Payroll item has to be the same, too.

Here's how to create a batch timesheet:

1. In the Home Page's Employees panel, click Enter Time and then, on the drop-down menu, choose Use Weekly Timesheet.
2. In the Weekly Timesheet window's Name drop-down list, choose "Multiple names (Payroll)" if the people are paid through your payroll service, or choose "Multiple names (Non-Payroll)" if they're paid another way, such as vendors, contractors, or owners who take an owners' draw.
3. In the "Select Employee, Vendor or Other Name" dialog box, keep the Manual option selected and then click the name of each person you want to add to the batch timesheet to add a checkmark to the left of their names.
4. Click OK.
5. Fill out the weekly timesheet as you would for a single person (see below), and then click Save & Close.

QuickBooks creates a timesheet for each person you selected with the information you entered in the timesheet. For example, if you recorded 40 hours of work in the timesheet, each person now has a timesheet showing 40 hours.

Filling Out Weekly Timesheets

QuickBooks' weekly timesheet is the fastest way to enter time for several activities or work that spans several days. Here's what you do:

1. **In the Home Page's Employees panel, click Enter Time and then, on the drop-down menu, choose Use Weekly Timesheet.**

   QuickBooks opens the Weekly Timesheet window.

NOTE Even though you can track time for people *other* than employees (like contractors), you access QuickBooks' time tracking feature from the Employees menu or the Employees panel on the Home Page.

2. **In the Name drop-down list, choose the person who performed the work.**

   Because time tracking is rarely limited to only the people with permission to use QuickBooks, you can enter time for yourself or anyone else. After you choose a name, the program displays a timesheet for the current week and shows any time already entered for that week, as shown in Figure 8-3. (See the box above to learn how to create a batch of timesheets in one fell swoop.)

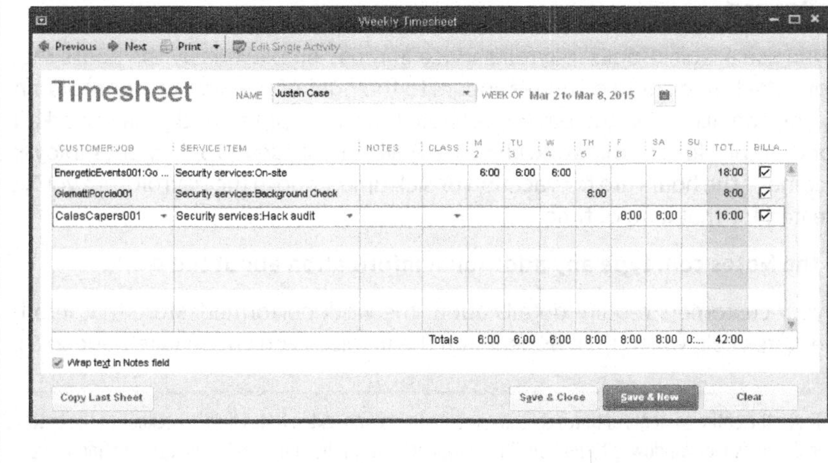

FIGURE 8-3

The weekly timesheet doesn't provide much room to display customer names, job names, or more than a few letters of the Service item for the task performed. To see the full contents of a cell, click the cell's down arrow, and QuickBooks highlights the selected item in the drop-down list. If the cell doesn't have a down arrow, position your cursor over the cell to display a popup tooltip. You can also drag a corner of the window to resize it or click the Maximize icon (the rectangle) near the top right of the window to enlarge it.

3. **To enter time for a different week, in the window's toolbar, click Previous or Next until the week you want appears.**

   To choose a week that's quite a ways in the past, click the calendar icon to the right of the timesheet's date range. In the Set Date dialog box that appears, click the arrows to the left or right of the month heading to move to a past or future month. Click any date during the week to choose that workweek. For example, choosing 6 in the March 2015 calendar switches the timesheet to the week beginning March 2, 2015.

TIP If an earlier timesheet has entries with customers and items that apply to the current timesheet, you can copy the earlier timesheet as described in the box on page 171.

4. **In the first blank Customer:Job cell (the first column of the timesheet table), choose the customer or job associated with the work that was performed, if applicable.**

   If the work is billable, choose the customer or job that pays for it. If the time isn't billable, you can leave this cell blank or choose the customer you created to track nonbillable time. Depending on whether you prefer to keep your hands on the keyboard or the mouse, you can then move to the Service Item cell by clicking it or by pressing the Tab key.

5. **In the Service Item cell, choose the item that represents the work the person performed.**

   If you use a QuickBooks' payroll service and pay employees by the hours they work, the Payroll Item column appears to the right of the Service Item column, so you can also fill in the payroll-related item that applies to the time worked. For example, for billable work, choose a Payroll item such as Salary or Employee Income. If the hours are for vacation or sick time, choose the Payroll item you've created for that kind of time.

6. **In the Notes cell, type any additional information about the work.**

   If your customers require details about the work performed, store that info in the Notes cell, which then appears on the invoices you create (see page 255).

TIP To see the entire contents of Notes cells, make sure the "Wrap text in Notes field" checkbox at the bottom of the Weekly Timesheet window is turned on. That way, each row in the Timesheet table takes up more space, but you won't have to position your cursor over every Notes cell to see what it contains.

7. **If you use classes to track income and expenses (page 140), in the Class column, choose one for the work.**

   This column appears only if you've turned on QuickBooks' class preference. If you track profit by partner, for example, choose the class for the partner who handles that customer. If you use classes to track office branches, choose the class for the branch where the person works.

8. **To enter time for a day during the week, click the cell for that day or press the Tab key until you reach the right cell.**

   You can enter time in several ways. If you know the number of hours, type them as a decimal or as hours and minutes. For example, for seven and a half hours, type either *7.5* or *7:30*. QuickBooks displays the hours in the timesheet based on the time format preference you set (page 651). If you know the starting and ending time, QuickBooks can calculate the hours for you. For example, if you type *9-5* in a cell, the program transforms it into eight hours when you move to a different cell (by pressing Tab or clicking another cell).

   As you enter time for each day of the week, the Total *column* on the right side of the table shows the total hours for each activity. The numbers in the Totals *row* below the table show the total hours for each day and for the entire week.

NOTE Each row in a weekly timesheet represents one Service item, one customer or job, and one note. So if you perform the same type of work for two different customers, you have to enter that time in two separate rows. You also have to create another row if you want to record a different note for the same customer and the same Service item. You might do this if, for example, you did web-development work for a customer but want to differentiate the work you did on its online-store web page and on its marketing web pages.

9. **If the time is for overhead or you aren't billing the customer for the work and the checkmark in the "Billable?" column is turned on, click it to turn it off. Conversely, if the checkmark is turned off and the time is billable, click the checkbox to turn it on.**

   If you've turned on the "Mark all time entries as billable" preference (page 669), QuickBooks automatically puts a checkmark in the "Billable?" column. If this preference is turned off, the "Billable?" checkbox is blank unless you click it.

TIP Adding billable time to customer invoices is easy; it's described in detail on page 252.

10. **To save the timesheet, click Save & Close or Save & New.**

    If you're entering time for a number of people, click Save & New to save the current timesheet and open a new, blank one. Clicking Save & Close saves the timesheet and closes the Weekly Timesheet window.

UP TO SPEED

Copying Timesheets

People often work on the same tasks from week to week. QuickBooks can reduce tedium and mistakes—and save you time—by copying entries from a person's previous timesheet. Here's how:

1. In the Weekly Timesheet window's Name field, choose the person's name.
2. Display the weekly timesheet you want to copy information *into* by clicking Previous or Next, or clicking the calendar icon.
3. At the bottom of the dialog box, click the Copy Last Sheet button. If the timesheet that's currently displayed is empty, QuickBooks fills in all the rows with the entries from the person's last timesheet, including the customer, Service item, class, notes, and hours. If the current timesheet already has values, QuickBooks asks whether you want to replace the entries. Click Yes to *replace* the entries with the ones from the last timesheet you opened. Click No to *append* the entries from the last timesheet as additional rows in this week's timesheet. To keep the currently displayed timesheet just the way it is, click Cancel.

Entering Time for One Activity

Entering time in the Weekly Timesheet window is quick, but the width of the columns makes it hard to see which customer and Service item you're tracking. If you prefer readability to speed, the Time/Enter Single Activity dialog box is a better choice. It even includes a stopwatch you can use to time your work.

TIP One drawback to the Time/Enter Single Activity dialog box is that you have to fill in *every* field for every activity. If you grow tired of this form of time entry, then in the dialog box's toolbar, click Timesheet to switch to the Weekly Timesheet window. The weekly timesheet that appears is for the person you selected in the Time/Enter Single Activity dialog box and the week that includes the selected day.

Here's how to enter time for one activity at a time:

1. **In the Home Page's Employees panel, click Enter Time and then, on the drop-down menu, choose Time/Enter Single Activity.**

   The Time/Enter Single Activity dialog box opens to today's date.

2. **If you want to record time for a different day, then in the Date field, click the calendar icon and choose the date when the work took place.**

   When you first open the Time/Enter Single Activity dialog box, QuickBooks selects all the text in the Date box. You can replace that date by simply typing a new one, like *3/6/15*.

3. **In the Name drop-down list—which includes vendors, employees, and names from the Other Names List—select the person who performed the work.**

   Employees and other names are near the end of the list.

NOTE When you first open the Time/Enter Single Activity dialog box, it includes the Payroll Item field. If you select an employee who's paid based on her time (see online Appendix D on this book's Missing CD page at *www.missingmanuals.com*), then use this field to select the Payroll item to which the time applies so that the time data generates the values on the person's paycheck. If you choose the name of a person who *isn't* paid based on her time, then the Payroll Item field disappears.

4. **In the Customer:Job drop-down list, choose a customer or job.**

   If someone performs work for a real customer or job, choose that customer or job whether or not you bill the time. To track overhead time, you can create a customer (page 70) called something like Overhead.

5. **If the time is billable and the "Billable?" checkbox in the upper-right corner of the window is turned off, click it to turn it on. For nonbillable time, make sure the "Billable?" checkbox is turned off.**

   If you've turned on the "Mark all time entries as billable" preference (page 669), QuickBooks puts a checkmark in the "Billable?" checkbox automatically. If that preference is turned off, the "Billable?" checkbox is blank unless you click it.

6. **In the Service Item drop-down list, choose the item that represents the work performed.**

   Choose the appropriate item, whether it's one you use to invoice customers or a nonbillable item you created to track overhead activities. When you're done, press the Tab key to move to the Duration box (or just click it).

7. **In the Duration box, enter the hours worked.**

   If you pressed Tab to move to the Duration box, QuickBooks automatically selects the contents of the box, so you can simply type the hours worked. If you *clicked* the Duration box instead, drag to select its contents.

   Enter hours as a decimal or as hours and minutes, such as *5.5* or *5:30*. Or, if you know the starting and ending times, type the range to have QuickBooks calculate the hours. For example, if you type *11-5*, the program converts it to *6:00* when you tab or click away from the Duration box.

   If you work in QuickBooks most of the time, you can also use the Time/Enter Single Activity dialog box to time your work, as shown in Figure 8-4.

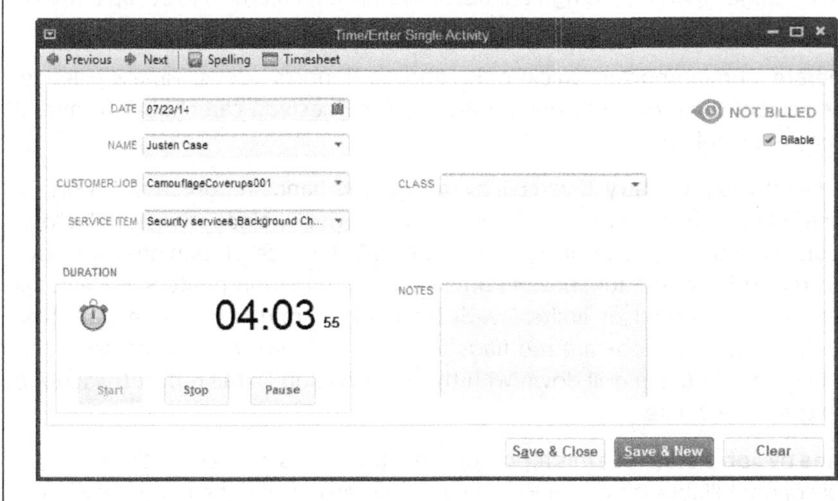

FIGURE 8-4

To time your current activity, the Date field has to be set to today, since you can't run a stopwatch for work performed on a different day. To start timing, click the Start button, which is grayed out here. You'll see the seconds that are passing to the right of the Duration box (where it says "55" here) to show that QuickBooks is timing your work. To pause the stopwatch, click Pause; click Start to start timing again. When you finish the task, click Stop. As long as the stopwatch isn't timing, you can edit the time by typing the time you want.

NOTE If you click Previous at the top of the Time/Enter Single Activity dialog box to display another single activity for today and then click Start, the stopwatch feature starts adding additional time to what you've already recorded.

8. **If you track classes, in the Class field, choose the appropriate one. (This field appears only if classes are turned on.) To add notes about the activity, type them in the Notes box.**

   These notes appear in the Notes column of the Weekly Timesheet window and, for billable work, appear on invoices you generate from time worked.

9. **To save the transaction, click Save & New or Save & Close.**

   When you click Save & New, the saved activity represents time for only one day. To record time for another day's work (even if it's for the same worker, customer, and Service item), you have to create a new activity.

Running Time Reports

Customers don't like being charged for too many hours, and workers are quick to complain if they're paid for too few. So before you use time records either for billing customers or feeding your payroll records, it's a good idea to generate reports to make sure your time data is correct. (Online Appendix D—available from this book's Missing CD page at *www.missingmanuals.com/cds*—explains how to set up employees in QuickBooks so their reported time links to your QuickBooks payroll service.)

To generate a time report in QuickBooks, choose Reports→Jobs, Time & Mileage, and then select the report you want. Here are the ones you can choose from and what they're useful for:

- **Time by Job Summary**. If you bill by the job, this handy report shows hours by customer or job, summarized by Service items, which helps you review the total hours worked on a job during a given period. Because of its high-level view, this report is perfect for spotting time charged to inappropriate Service items or hours that exceed job limits. Overly high or low hours—or Service items that don't belong on a job—are red flags for data-entry errors. If hours seem too high or low, you can drill down with the Time by Job Detail report (described next) to investigate.
- **Time by Job Detail**. Use this report to verify that hours were correctly set as billable or nonbillable. It's grouped first by customer/job, and then by Service item, but each time entry shows the date the hours were worked, who performed the work, and whether the work is billable (the billing status is listed as Unbilled for billable hours not yet invoiced, Billed for invoiced billable hours, or Not Billable).
- **Time by Name**. This report shows the hours people have worked on each customer or job, as shown in Figure 8-5. QuickBooks initially sets the report's date range to This Fiscal Year-to-date, but if you want to check timesheets for accuracy, you can change it to Last Week, This Week, or whatever time period you want. If a person reports too many or too few hours for a period, use the Weekly Timesheet window (page 168) to look for signs of inaccurate or missing time reports.
- **Time by Item**. This report groups hours by Service item and then by customer or job. You can use this report to analyze how your billable and nonbillable time is spent, either to cut unproductive activities or to determine staffing needs.

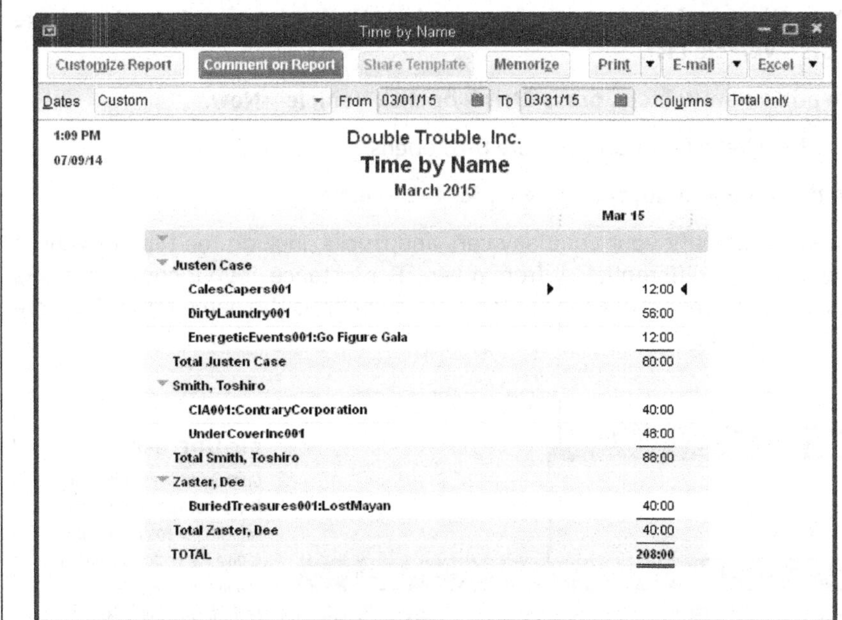

FIGURE 8-5

The Time by Name report summarizes the hours someone works for each customer or job.

To see the dates and times of the work, put your cursor over an hourly total. When the magnifying glass icon appears (not shown here), double-click the time to open a "Time by Name Detail" report.

Tracking Mileage

If you charge customers for mileage, keeping track of the billable miles you drive helps you get all the reimbursements you're due. But *all* business-related mileage is tax-deductible, so tracking nonbillable business mileage is important, too. Customers and the IRS alike want records of the miles you drive, and QuickBooks can help you produce that documentation.

NOTE QuickBooks' mileage-tracking feature is intended for tracking the miles you drive using company vehicles (and, if you run your own company, the business miles you drive using your own car), not other vehicle expenses, such as fuel or tolls. Likewise, you don't use QuickBooks to record miles driven by employees, vendors, or subcontractors, which instead go straight to an expense account. For example, if a vendor bills you for mileage, when you enter the bill in QuickBooks (page 186), you assign that charge to an expense account you've created for such things, such as Travel-Mileage. Or when you write a check to reimburse an employee for mileage driven, you assign that reimbursement to the expense account for mileage.

Adding a Vehicle

To track mileage for a company vehicle, you first have to add the vehicle to QuickBooks' Vehicle List. Here's how:

1. **Open the Vehicle List window by choosing Lists→Customer & Vendor Profile Lists→Vehicle List.**

2. **To add a new vehicle, press Ctrl+N or click Vehicle→New.**

   The New Vehicle window (Figure 8-6) opens.

3. **In the Vehicle field, type a name for the vehicle.**

   To easily identify your company cars and trucks, include the type of vehicle and a way to differentiate it from others. For instance, if your company's cars are all white Jeeps, use the license plate number as the name rather than the make and color.

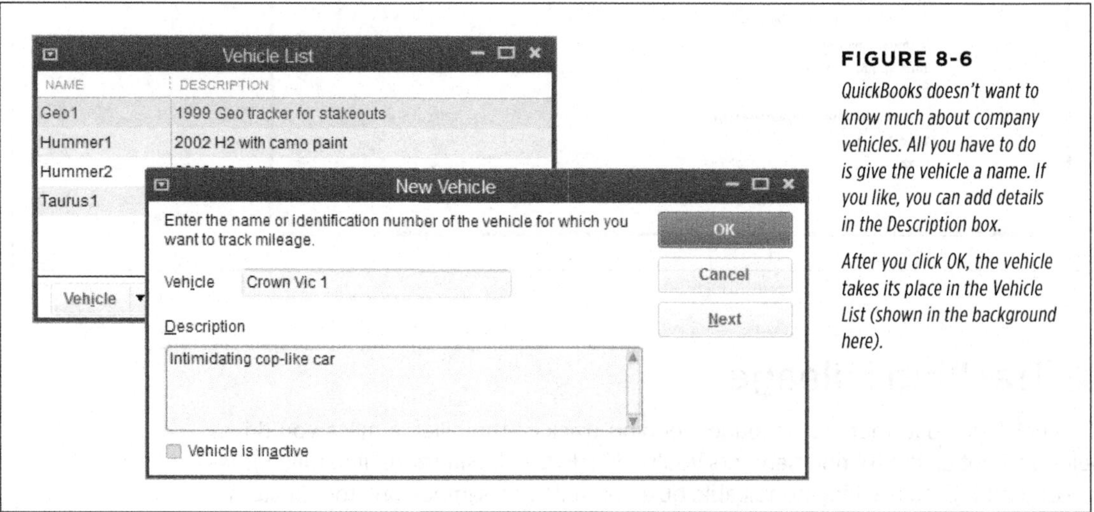

FIGURE 8-6

QuickBooks doesn't want to know much about company vehicles. All you have to do is give the vehicle a name. If you like, you can add details in the Description box.

After you click OK, the vehicle takes its place in the Vehicle List (shown in the background here).

4. **In the Description box, type additional info such as the year, make, model, license plate number, or vehicle identification number (VIN).**

   To change this information later, in the Vehicle List window, double-click the vehicle's name and then, in the Edit Vehicle dialog box, edit the name or description.

5. **Click OK.**

That's it. The name and description appear in the Vehicle List window.

Setting the Mileage Rate

For tax purposes, you can deduct mileage expenses based on a standard rate or by tracking the actual costs of operating and maintaining your vehicles. Using a standard mileage rate is convenient—simply multiply the miles you drove by this rate to calculate your vehicle deduction. The box on page 178 explains how you charge customers for mileage if your mileage charge differs from the IRS standard rate. (You don't have to set a mileage rate to *record* the miles you drive, but you'll need a rate in place before you run your tax reports.)

TIP If you own an expensive car with expensive maintenance needs, actual costs might provide a larger deduction than the IRS's standard rate. (You can deduct either the standard-rate amount *or* your actual costs, not both.) But to deduct what you spend on gas, tires, repairs, insurance, and so on, you have to keep track of these expenses. As usual, the tax rules for deducting operating and maintenance costs are, well, taxing. So before you choose this approach, ask your accountant or the IRS if you can deduct actual costs and whether it's the best approach.

QuickBooks stores multiple mileage rates along with their effective dates, because standard mileage rates usually change at the beginning of each calendar year. Here's how to set a mileage rate:

1. **Choose Company→Enter Vehicle Mileage.**

   The Enter Vehicle Mileage window opens.

2. **In the window's toolbar, click Mileage Rates.**

   QuickBooks opens the Mileage Rates window shown in Figure 8-7.

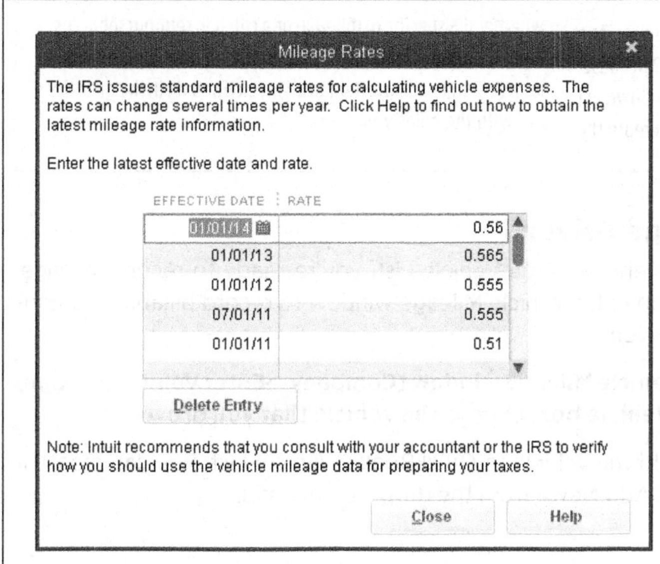

FIGURE 8-7

QuickBooks displays the most recent standard mileage rate at the top of this table and lists older rates below it.

3. **To add a new rate, click the first blank Effective Date cell at the bottom of the list, and then choose the date that the new mileage rate becomes effective, such as 1/1/2015.**

   You can either type the date or click the calendar icon.

4. **In the Rate cell, type the rate in dollars, such as *.56* for 56 cents.**

   The mileage rate is 56 cents per mile beginning January 1, 2014, as documented on the IRS website, *www.irs.gov.* If you're reading this after 2014, be sure to check that site to see whether this rate has changed.

5. **Click Close.**

   When it's time to prepare your tax return, you can run the Mileage by Vehicle Summary report to see the miles driven for each company vehicle and the resulting mileage deduction. To calculate your deduction, QuickBooks multiplies the recorded miles by the mileage rate that was in effect when they were driven.

FREQUENTLY ASKED QUESTION

Mileage Rates and Invoice Items

What if the IRS's rate is different from the rate I charge customers for mileage?

The rates you enter in the Mileage Rates window (page 177) are the standard rates set by the IRS for tax purposes. The IRS doesn't care one whit what you charge your customers for miles, so you can charge them whatever you want. And you don't have to record mileage driven to do that.

For the reimbursable miles that you drive, you need to create a Service or Other Charge item in your Item List. (Why? Because, in the Enter Vehicle Mileage window, the Item drop-down list includes only these two types of items.) When you create the item, you can assign it the rate that you charge customers per mile or, if you charge variable mileage rates, leave the rate at zero.

For an Other Charge item, the "Amount or %" box is the place to enter the mileage rate, as shown in Figure 8-8. (For a Service item, use the Rate box instead.) In the Account box, choose the income or expense account you use for reimbursable mileage, whether it's specific to mileage or a catchall reimbursable cost account. Then you can either record mileage driven using this item or simply add the item to an invoice and fill in the quantity cell with the miles you drove.

Recording Mileage Driven

Once you've added a vehicle to the Vehicle List, you're ready to record mileage. Here's how you fill in the Enter Vehicle Mileage window to record billable and non-billable miles you've driven:

1. **Open the Enter Vehicle Mileage window (Company→Enter Vehicle Mileage) and then, in the Vehicle box, choose the vehicle that you drove.**

   If you forgot to add the vehicle to QuickBooks' Vehicle List, you can create it now by choosing <Add New> from the drop-down menu.

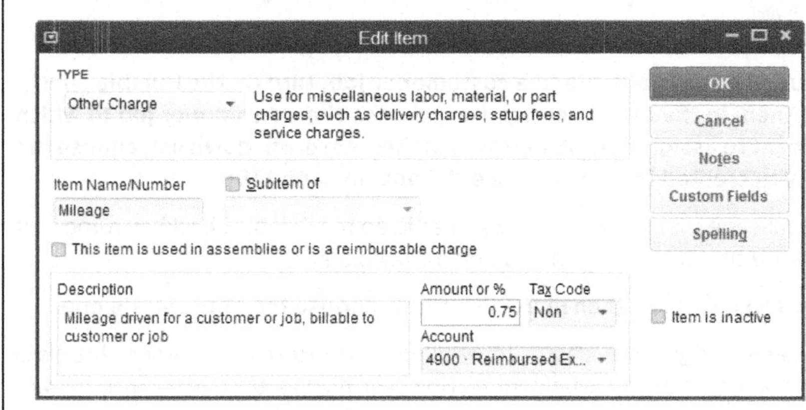

FIGURE 8-8

When you create an item for mileage, you can enter whatever rate per mile you want.

Then, when you add mileage to an invoice, QuickBooks multiplies the number of billable miles driven by the rate you set for that mileage item.

2. **In the Trip Start Date and Trip End Date boxes, choose when you started and completed the trip.**

   If you're recording mileage for one day of onsite work, choose the same day in both boxes. On the other hand, if you used a company car to drive to another city for several days, the Trip Start Date is the day you headed out of town and the Trip End Date is the day you returned.

3. **In the Odometer Start and Odometer End boxes, type what the vehicle's mileage was before you began driving and what it was when you returned, as shown in Figure 8-9. Or just type how far you drove into the Total Miles box.**

   If you fill in the Odometer boxes, QuickBooks automatically calculates the miles you drove and plops that number in the Total Miles box.

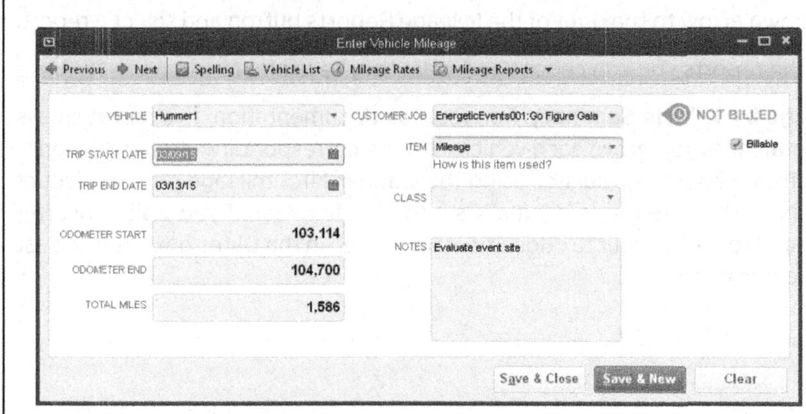

FIGURE 8-9

If you usually forget to check your starting mileage, you can ignore the Odometer Start and Odometer End boxes entirely. Instead, in the Total Miles box, type the mileage you drove, such as 1,586 for a 1,586-mile trip for your customer. You can type the mileage with or without commas (1,586 or 1586).

NOTE The drawback to filling in the Enter Vehicle Mileage dialog box's Total Miles field is that your mileage record doesn't include the odometer readings that the IRS wants to see. But if *every* mile you drive is for business, you can prove your deduction by showing the IRS an odometer reading at the beginning of the year and one at the end of the year.

4. **If your mileage is billable to a customer or job, turn on the Billable checkbox. Then, in the Customer:Job box, choose the customer or job to which you want to assign the mileage and, in the Item drop-down list, choose the item you created for mileage (see the box on page 178).**

   If the mileage *isn't* billable to a customer, keep the Billable checkbox turned off and leave the Customer:Job and Item boxes blank.

5. **If you track classes, then in the Class box, choose the appropriate one.**

   For example, if you use classes to track branch performance, choose the class for the branch the vehicle belongs to. However, if you track partner income with classes and the mileage is nonbillable, you don't need to assign a class (or you can choose a class you set up for overhead).

6. **To document the reason for the mileage, type details in the Notes box. Then, to save the mileage and close the dialog box, click Save & Close.**

   If you want to enter additional mileage for other customers and jobs, click Save & New instead.

Generating Mileage Reports

Mileage reports come in handy when you prepare your taxes or if your customers question their mileage charges. These reports are simple, mainly because you don't track that much mileage information in QuickBooks. You can generate mileage reports by choosing Reports→Jobs, Time & Mileage, and then selecting a report. Or, if you have the Enter Vehicle Mileage window open, in the window's toolbar, click the down arrow to the right of the Mileage Reports button and select a report.

Here are the reports you can choose and what they're useful for:

- **Mileage by Vehicle Summary**. For your tax documentation, this report shows the total miles you drove each vehicle and the corresponding mileage expense (which QuickBooks calculates using the standard IRS mileage rate in effect at the time). The date range is initially set to This Tax Year. If you wait until after January 1 to gather your tax documentation, then in the Dates box, choose Last Tax Year instead.

- **Mileage by Vehicle Detail**. This report shows each trip that contributed to a vehicle's mileage. For each one, it includes the trip's end date, miles driven, mileage rate, and mileage expense. If you have questions about your deductions, double-click an entry to open the Enter Vehicle Mileage window for that transaction.
- **Mileage by Job Summary**. If you charge customers for mileage, run this report to see both total miles driven and the billable mileage by customer and job. QuickBooks uses the rate you set in the Service or Other Charge item to calculate the billable amount.
- **Mileage by Job Detail**. If a customer has a question about mileage you charged, this report is the quickest way to find those charges. The report groups mileage by customer or job but lists each trip in its own line. The report shows each trip's end date, miles driven, billing status, mileage rate, and billable amount, so you can answer almost any mileage-related question a customer might have.

CHAPTER

9

Paying for Expenses

Although most small business owners sift through the daily mail looking for envelopes containing payments, they usually find more containing *bills*. One frustrating aspect of running a business is that you often have to pay for the items you sell before you can invoice your customers for the goods.

If you want your financial records to be right, you have to tell QuickBooks about the expenses you've incurred. And, if you want your vendors to leave you alone, you have to pay the bills they send. Paying for expenses can take several forms, and QuickBooks is up to the challenge.

This chapter explains your choices for paying bills (now or later) and describes how to enter bills and record your bill payments. If you pay right away, you'll learn the QuickBooks procedures for writing checks, using a debit or credit card, and paying with cash, among other options. If you enter bills in QuickBooks for payment later, you'll learn how to handle the recurring ones, such as rent, as well as reimbursable expenses and inventory. QuickBooks is happy to help you through every step of the process: entering bills you receive if you want to pay later, setting up bill payments, and even printing checks you can mail to vendors.

When to Pay Expenses

When it comes to handling expenses, you can pay now or pay later; QuickBooks has features for both options. (You can choose to *not* pay bills, but QuickBooks can't help you with collection agencies or represent your company in bankruptcy court.) Here are the pros and cons of each approach:

- **Pay now**. If bills arrive about as infrequently as meteor showers, why not pay each one immediately so you're sure they're paid on time? In QuickBooks, paying right away means writing a check, entering a debit card transaction, entering a credit card charge, making an online payment, or using money from petty cash—all of which are described in this chapter. When you pay immediately, you don't have to enter a bill in QuickBooks; you can simply record the expense-payment transaction.

NOTE When you're out of the office and pay for something by charging it to a credit card or writing a check by hand, simply enter that transaction in QuickBooks without entering a corresponding bill. (See page 214 for info on recording payments made with debit cards, PayPal, and so on.)

- **Pay later**. If bills arrive as steadily as orders at the local coffee shop, you'll probably want to set aside time to pay them all at once when it won't interfere with delivering services or selling products. What's more, most companies don't pay bills until just before they're due—unless there's a good reason to (like an early payment discount). Setting up vendor bills for later payment is known as *using Accounts Payable* because you store the unpaid expenses in an Accounts Payable account.

  In QuickBooks, entering bills for later payment delivers all the advantages of convenience and good cash management. You can tell the program when you want to pay bills—for instance, to take advantage of an early payment discount or the grace period that a vendor allows. Then you can go about your business without distraction, knowing that QuickBooks will notify you when bills are on deck for payment.

Once you decide whether you're going to pay bills now or later, use that method consistently. Otherwise, you could pay for something twice by entering a bill in QuickBooks and then, a few days later, writing a paper check for the same expense. To prevent duplicate payments, always enter bills you receive in the mail (or email) as bills in QuickBooks and pay them by using the Pay Bills feature (page 194). The Enter Bills window (Figure 9-1) includes a list of recent transactions, which you can use to look for payments you've already made.

Entering Bills

At first glance, entering bills in QuickBooks and then paying them later might *seem* like more work than just writing checks. But as you'll learn in this chapter, there are several advantages to entering bills in QuickBooks, and the program makes it incredibly easy to pay them.

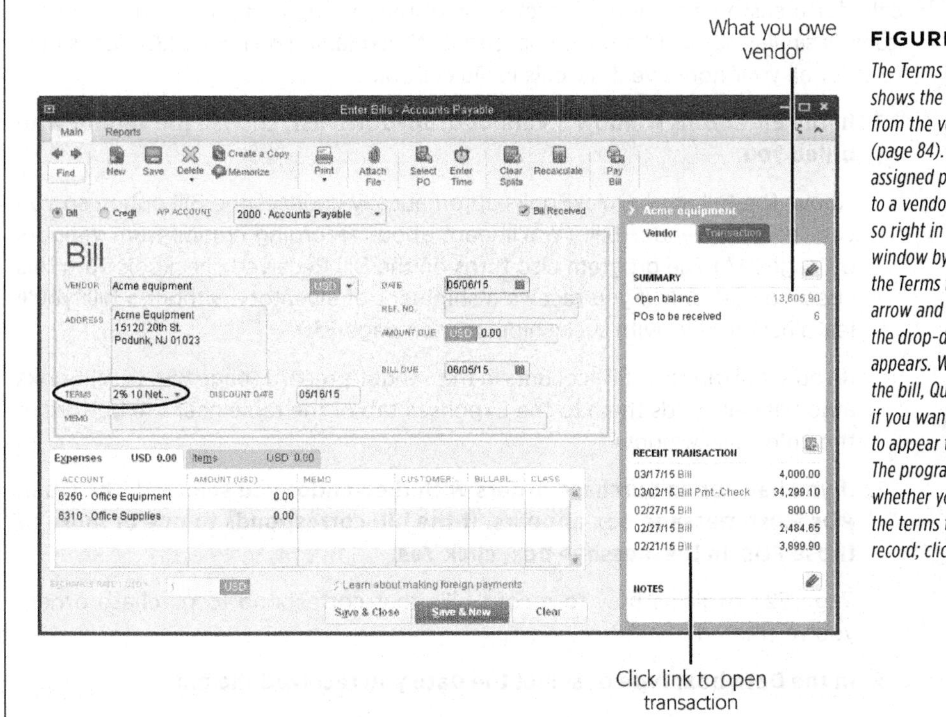

FIGURE 9-1

The Terms field (circled) shows the payment terms from the vendor's record (page 84). If you haven't assigned payment terms to a vendor, you can do so right in the Enter Bills window by simply clicking the Terms field's down arrow and choosing from the drop-down list that appears. When you save the bill, QuickBooks asks if you want the new terms to appear the next time. The program is asking whether you want to save the terms to the vendor's record; click Yes.

To get started, open the Enter Bills window using any of the following methods:

- On the Home Page, in the Vendors panel, click Enter Bills.
- Choose Vendors→Enter Bills.
- In the Vendor Center window's icon bar, click New Transactions→Enter Bills.

TIP Many of your bills are due at the same time every month, and some are even the same *amount* every month, such as your office rent. Bills like these are perfect candidates for QuickBooks' memorized transaction feature, which memorizes bills so you can reuse them. With a memorized transaction, you can tell QuickBooks to remind you when a bill is due or even record it automatically without any action on your part. You can even create a group of bills so that you can process all the bills due on the same day of the month with just a click or two. See page 321 for the full scoop on these handy timesavers.

The fields in the Enter Bills window are similar to the ones on invoices you create. In fact, if your vendors use QuickBooks, the bills you receive are just another company's QuickBooks invoices (see Chapter 10) or statements (see Chapter 11).

Entering Bills for Services and Non-Inventory Items

This section explains how to enter bills for services you've hired someone to perform and non-inventory items you've purchased, such as products you purchase specifically for a customer or job. (The process of purchasing and paying for *inventory* items is similar but a tad more complicated; it's explained on page 518.) Here's how to enter all your non-inventory bills in QuickBooks:

1. **In the Enter Bills window's Vendor drop-down list, choose the vendor who billed you.**

   Above the Bill area, QuickBooks automatically chooses the Bill option so you can record a vendor bill. (You'll learn about recording credits from vendors on page 217.) The program also turns on the Bill Received checkbox. Turn this checkbox off *only if* you receive a shipment of inventory without a bill; you'll learn how to deal with such shipments on page 530.

   If you set up any pre-fill accounts in the vendor's record (page 85), QuickBooks automatically adds them to the Expenses tab of the table near the bottom of the Enter Bills window.

2. **If you have open purchase orders with the vendor you selected, the Open POs Exist message box appears. If the bill corresponds to one or more of those POs, in the message box, click Yes.**

   Page 527 explains how to record bills that correspond to purchase orders you've created.

3. **In the Date box, type or select the date you received the bill.**

   If you specified payment terms in the vendor's record (page 84), QuickBooks uses the date you enter in the Date box to figure out when the bill is due and fills in the Bill Due field, as shown in Figure 9-1. For example, if the bill date is 5/6/2015 and the vendor's payment terms are Net 30, the bill is due 30 days after the bill date—6/5/2015.

   If the date that QuickBooks fills in doesn't match the due date on the bill you received, then in the Bill Due field, enter the date printed on the vendor's bill—it's the one to go by.

TIP The Vendor tab on the right side of the Enter Bills window summarizes the vendor's info and your recent transactions with that vendor. The Summary section shows your balance (the total amount you owe the vendor) and open purchase orders with that vendor. If you see any info you want to change, like the terms or address, click the Edit button (its icon looks like a pencil) to open the vendor's record in the Edit Vendor dialog box. The Vendor tab's Recent Transactions section lists bills, bill payments, credits, and other transactions, which is a great way to catch that you have a credit available or have already paid the bill you're about to enter. To open one of these recent transactions in its corresponding window, click a link, like the "Bill" link labeled in Figure 9-1.

4. **In the Ref. No. box, type the vendor's invoice number, the statement date, or another identifying feature of the bill you're paying.**

   The Ref. No. box accepts any alphanumeric character, not just numbers, so you can type in things like "1242," "Invoice 1242," or "Statement 3/31/2015."

   If you want to include additional notes about the bill, type them in the Memo box.

5. **In the Amount Due box, type the total from the bill.**

   The only time you'd type a different amount is when you take a discount that the vendor forgot to apply or deduct a portion of the bill because the goods were defective.

   In the lower half of the Enter Bills window, QuickBooks initially displays the Expenses tab, which is where you enter information about expenses such as utility bills, office supply bills, and attorney's fees. If you assign only one pre-fill account (page 85) to this vendor, QuickBooks automatically fills in the first cell in the table's Amount column with the Amount Due value.

NOTE The section "Entering Bills in Foreign Currencies" on page 188 tells you what to do when you receive a bill from a vendor who uses a different currency.

---

6. **In the first cell of the Expenses tab's Account column, choose the expense account from your chart of accounts that corresponds to the first expense on the bill.**

   When you click a cell in the Account column, a down arrow appears. Clicking the arrow displays a drop-down list of *every* account in your chart of accounts, but QuickBooks automatically displays the expense account section of the list. To choose a different expense account—the one for your legal fees, say—scroll in the drop-down list and click the one you want.

7. **If the bill covers several types of expenses (such as airfare, lodging, and your travel agent's fees), in the first Amount cell, type the amount that belongs to the expense account in that row.**

   If you assign more than one pre-fill account to a vendor, QuickBooks subtracts the amount you typed in the first row from the total amount due and puts the remaining amount in the second row. Bottom line: You have to type the amounts in each row's Amount cell.

8. **If an expense relates to a job, in the Customer:Job column, choose the customer or job.**

   If you fill in the Customer:Job cell, QuickBooks puts a checkmark in the "Billable?" column. If you don't want to charge the customer for the expense, click the checkmark to remove it.

TIP If you're recording reimbursable expenses, which will eventually appear on a customer's invoice (page 252), be sure to type a meaningful description in each Memo cell in the table. QuickBooks uses the text in this cell as the description of the expense on your invoice. If there's no Memo text, your invoice includes charges without descriptions, which are bound to generate a call from the customer.

9. **If you're tracking classes, choose the appropriate class for the expense.**

   The Expenses tab's Class column appears only if you use QuickBooks classes (page 140).

10. **If the bill you're entering includes different types of expenses, repeat steps 6–9 to add a row for each type, as shown in Figure 9-2.**

    As soon as you finish one row in the table, QuickBooks fills in the Amount cell in the next row with the amount that's still unallocated. For the first through the next-to-last row, you have to edit the amount that the program fills in to match your expense. The amount QuickBooks enters in the last row should be correct if you haven't made any typos.

    If the multiple accounts and amounts are hopelessly mangled, at the top of the Enter Bills window, click Clear Splits to clear the table so you can start over.

11. **To add an item to a bill—such as a Service, Non-inventory Part, or Other Charge item—click the Items tab. In the first cell of the Item column, choose the item you want to add, and then fill in the other cells in the row, as you did on the Expenses tab.**

    The program fills in the Description and Cost cells with the values from the item's record. If you want, you can type a different description and enter a new cost.

12. **Click Save & Close to save the bill and close the window.**

    Or, if you have other bills to enter, click Save & New to save that bill and display a new, blank one.

Entering Bills in Foreign Currencies

Before you can enter bills with values in foreign currencies, you have to turn on QuickBooks' multiple currencies preference by choosing Edit→Preferences→Multiple Currencies, clicking the Company Preferences tab, and then selecting the "Yes, I use more than one currency" option (see page 656 for details). After that, you can assign a currency to each vendor. In the New Vendor or Edit Vendor window (page 84), below and to the right of the Vendor Name box, choose the currency that the vendor uses.

Once you do that, the Enter Bills window displays the vendor's currency in several places. It appears in the window's title bar and to the right of the vendor's name, as shown in Figure 9-3. The Amount Due box also shows the foreign currency to the left of the amount, with the corresponding value in your home currency below it. And the Expenses and Items tabs both show the foreign currency to indicate that the values you enter are in that currency.

Here's how to fill out a bill a vendor submitted in a foreign currency:

1. **Download the most recent exchange rates for the currencies you use.**

   See page 461 to learn how to enter or download currencies and exchange rates into the Currency List.

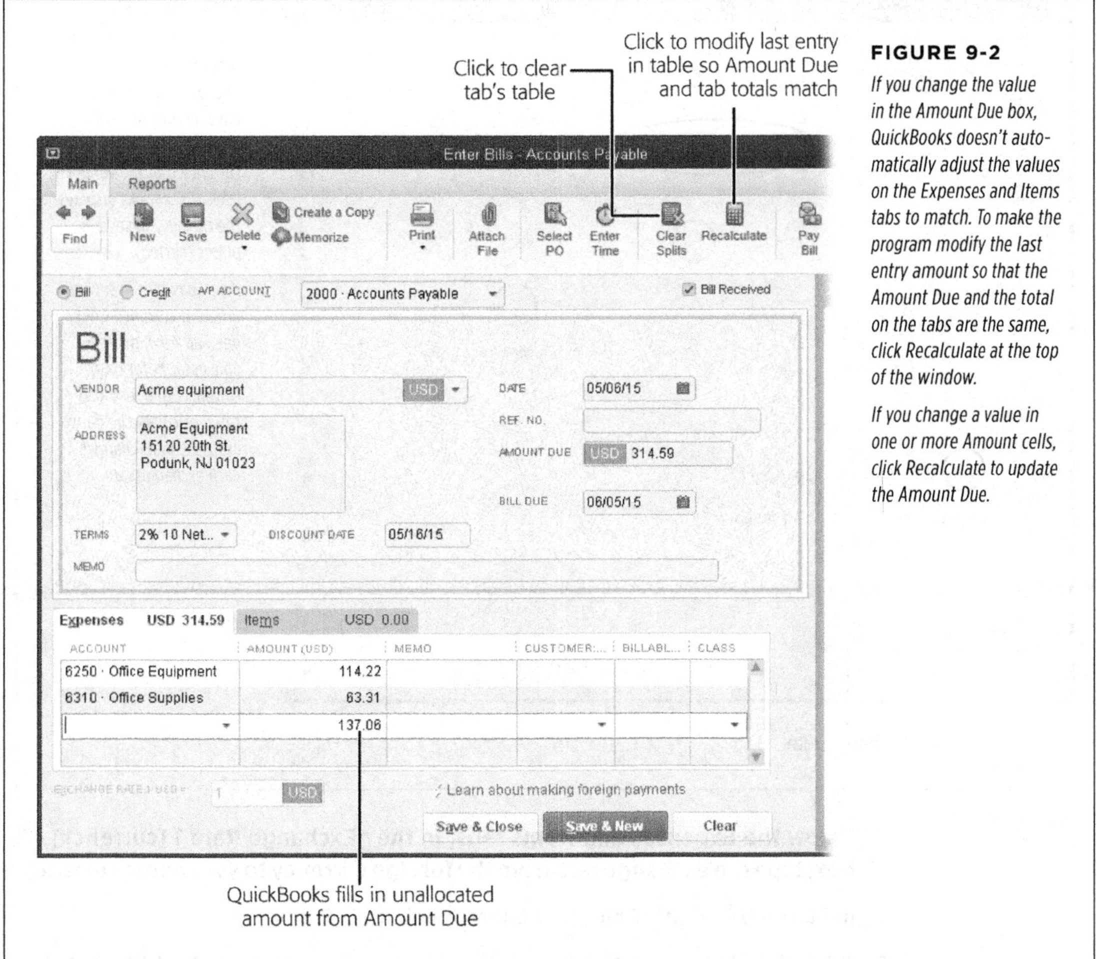

FIGURE 9-2

If you change the value in the Amount Due box, QuickBooks doesn't automatically adjust the values on the Expenses and Items tabs to match. To make the program modify the last entry amount so that the Amount Due and the total on the tabs are the same, click Recalculate at the top of the window.

If you change a value in one or more Amount cells, click Recalculate to update the Amount Due.

2. **In the Enter Bills window's A/P Account box, choose the Accounts Payable account that corresponds to the foreign currency.**

   When you assign a currency to a vendor in the New Vendor or Edit Vendor window, QuickBooks automatically creates a separate Accounts Payable account for that currency.

3. **In the Amount Due box, type the bill's value in the foreign currency.**
4. **On the Expenses and Items tabs' Amount cells, type the amounts in the foreign currency.**

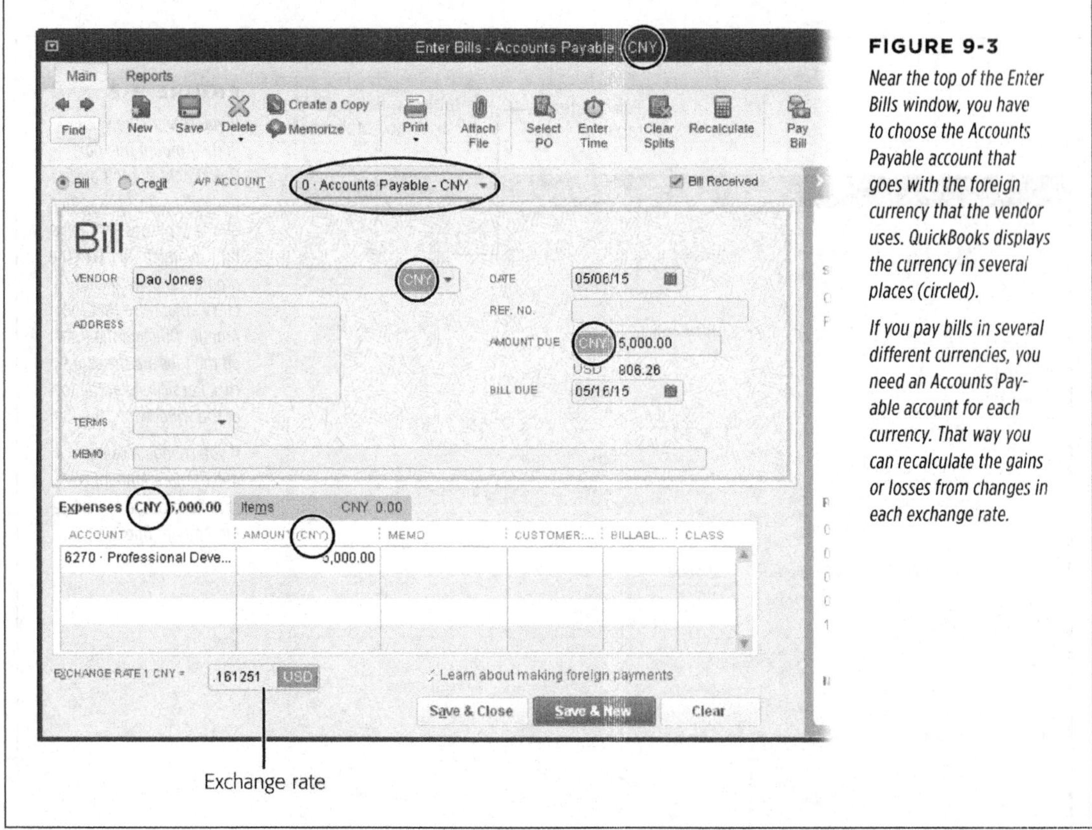

FIGURE 9-3

Near the top of the Enter Bills window, you have to choose the Accounts Payable account that goes with the foreign currency that the vendor uses. QuickBooks displays the currency in several places (circled).

If you pay bills in several different currencies, you need an Accounts Payable account for each currency. That way you can recalculate the gains or losses from changes in each exchange rate.

5. **Below the Expenses and Items tabs, in the "Exchange Rate 1 [currency] =" box, type the exchange rate from the foreign currency to your home currency.**

   In Figure 9-3, that's Chinese yuan renminbi to U.S. dollars.

6. **Click Recalculate at the top of the window to calculate the bill's total in your home currency.**

   QuickBooks recalculates the total based on the value in the Exchange Rate field.

7. **Click Save & Close to save the bill.**

   Click Clear to clear all the fields and start over.

TIP You can't change a vendor's currency after you've recorded your first transaction for that vendor. To switch to a different currency, you have to create a new vendor record that uses the new currency. The alternative is to calculate the bill's values in your home currency based on the going exchange rate, and then enter the bill in QuickBooks with those converted values.

Recording a Deposit to a Vendor

Suppose a vendor requires you to pay a deposit before it will deliver a service or product. In QuickBooks, you can record the deposit payment so it shows up as a credit to that vendor. Then, when the bill arrives, you can apply that credit to the bill. Here's what you do:

1. **Write a check (page 202), enter a credit card charge (page 213), or use another payment method (page 214) to pay the deposit. Choose the vendor's name in the "Pay to the Order of," "Purchased From," or other corresponding name field, depending on the transaction you're recording.**

   If you have an open purchase order for items from that vendor, QuickBooks displays a message box about it; click No because it's too early to use the purchase order—you aren't purchasing the items yet.

2. **In the Write Checks or Enter Credit Card Charges window, click the Expenses tab; in the first Account cell, choose your Accounts Payable account.**

   Choosing this account creates a credit for you with that vendor.

3. **In the first Amount cell, enter the amount of the deposit.**

   When you click away from this Amount cell, the transaction amount listed in the top half of the window changes to the deposit amount you just entered.

4. **In the Memo field, type a note to remind yourself that this transaction is for a vendor deposit.**

   That way, when it's time to record the final bill, it'll be easy to find this transaction.

5. **Click Save & Close (or Save & New) to save the payment transaction.**

   You don't have to do anything else until the final bill arrives.

6. **When you receive the bill, enter it in QuickBooks as you would any other bill.**

   Fill in the Account fields with the expense accounts for the products or services you received (page 187) or, on the Items tab, fill in the Item fields with the items you're putting a deposit on.

7. **Apply the vendor credit to the bill as described on page 197.**

   The credit reduces the balance due.

8. **Save the bill.**

That's it! When it's time to pay the bill, simply pay it using the new, lower balance (page 194).

TIP You can also use this technique to edit a check or credit card charge so you can apply it to a bill that you forgot you'd already entered. Simply edit the check or credit card charge and change the account to Accounts Payable. Then use the credit to pay all or a portion of the bill.

Handling Reimbursable Expenses

Reimbursable expenses are costs you incur that a customer subsequently pays. Products you purchase specifically for a customer or a subcontractor you hire to work on a customer's job are costs you pass on to the customer. For example, travel costs are a common type of reimbursable expense, and you've probably seen telephone and photocopy charges on your attorney's statements.

There are two ways to track reimbursable expenses, and QuickBooks can handle them both:

- **As income**. With this method, QuickBooks posts the expenses on a bill you record to the expense account you specify. When you invoice your customer, QuickBooks posts the reimbursement as income in a separate income account. Your income is higher this way, but it's offset by higher expenses. This approach is popular because it lets you compare income from reimbursable expenses with the reimbursable expenses themselves to make sure they match. The box on page 193 describes the income accounts you need for tracking reimbursable expenses this way.
- **As expenses**. Tracking reimbursements as expenses doesn't change the way QuickBooks handles bills—expenses still post to the expense accounts you specify. But, when your customer pays you for the reimbursable expenses, QuickBooks posts those reimbursements right back to the expense account, so the expense account balance looks as if you never incurred the expense in the first place. Because you use the same expense account to record both the expense and the reimbursement, you don't have to do any special setup in QuickBooks.

Setting Up Reimbursements as Income

If you want to track reimbursable expenses as income, choose Edit→Preferences→Time & Expenses. Then, on the Company Preferences tab, turn on the "Track reimbursed expenses as income" checkbox. With this preference turned on, whenever you create or edit an *expense* account (in the Add New Account or Edit Account window), QuickBooks adds a "Track reimbursed expenses in Income Acct." checkbox and drop-down list to the bottom of the window, as shown in Figure 9-4.

WORKAROUND WORKSHOP

Accounts for Reimbursable Expenses

QuickBooks won't let you assign the same income account to more than one reimbursable expense account, so you have to create a separate income account (see Chapter 3) for each type of reimbursable expense.

To keep your chart of accounts neat, create a top-level income account called something like Reimbursed Expenses. Then create an income subaccount for each *type* of reimbursable expense. When you're done, your income accounts will look something like this:

- 4100 Service Revenue
- 4200 Product Revenue
- 4900 Reimbursed Expenses - Income

Subaccounts for account 4900:

- 4910 Reimbursed Telephone
- 4920 Reimbursed Postage
- 4930 Reimbursed Photocopies
- 4940 Reimbursed Travel

An alternative approach is to create Other Charge items for each type of reimbursable expense. By doing so, you can assign those items to a single income account, and you can see the details of each reimbursable category by running a Sales By Item report (page 459).

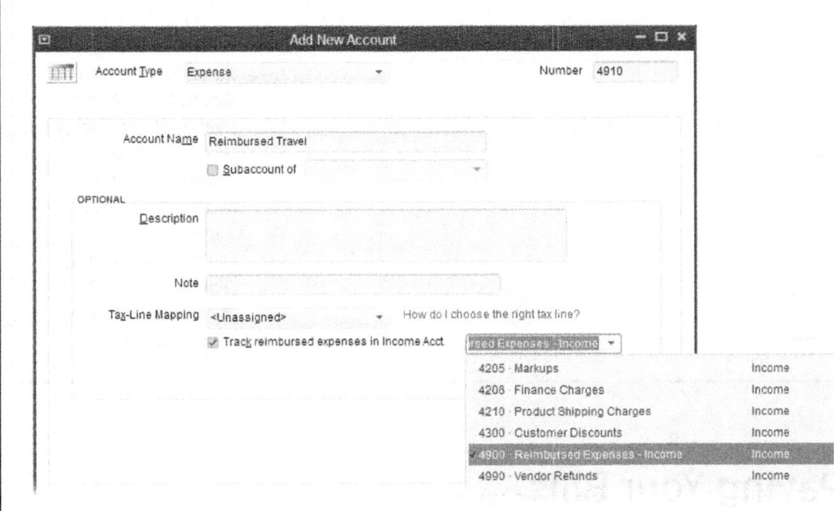

FIGURE 9-4

To track a reimbursable expense as income, in the Add New Account or Edit Account window, turn on the "Track reimbursed expenses in Income Acct." checkbox and then, in the drop-down list, choose the income account to use. If you've already created your expense accounts, you'll have to edit each one that's reimbursable (travel, telephone, equipment rental, and so on) and add the income account as shown here.

Once you've assigned an income account to all your reimbursable expenses, here's what happens as you progress from paying bills to invoicing customers:

1. **When you assign an expense or item on a bill as reimbursable to a customer, QuickBooks posts the money to the expense account you specified.**

2. **When you create an invoice for that customer, the program reminds you that you have reimbursable expenses or items.**

3. **When you add the reimbursable expenses or items to the customer's invoice, they post to the income account you specified for that type of expense or item. (See the box on page 193 to learn more about creating income accounts for reimbursable expenses.)**

Recording Reimbursable Expenses

As you enter bills (page 186) or make payments with checks or credit cards, you add designated expenses as reimbursable, as shown in Figure 9-5. When you choose a customer or job in the Customer:Job column, QuickBooks automatically adds a checkmark to the "Billable?" cell. Be sure to type a note in the Memo cell to identify the expense, because QuickBooks uses the text in that cell as the description of the reimbursable expense on your invoice.

TIP Sometimes you want to track expenses associated with a customer or job, but you don't want to display all those individual expenses on invoices, like when you have a fixed-price contract. In that situation, click the "Billable?" cell for that expense to remove the checkmark.

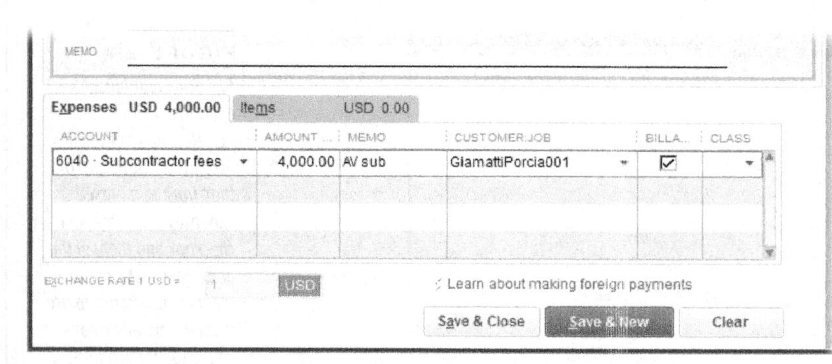

FIGURE 9-5

The tables in the Enter Bills, Write Checks, and Enter Credit Card Charges windows all include columns to designate reimbursable expenses and the customers or jobs to which they apply. (You can click Splits in an account register to access these columns.)

Paying Your Bills

Entering bills in QuickBooks isn't the same as *paying* bills. The bills you enter in your company file are a record of what you owe and when, but they do nothing to send money to your vendors. Pay Bills is the QuickBooks feature that actually pushes your money out the door. It lets you select the bills you want to pay; specify how much to pay on each one; and choose the payment method, account, and date. If you have credits or early payment discounts, you can include those, too. This section covers all the details.

TIP If you want to evaluate all your unpaid bills before you pay them, the Unpaid Bills Detail report displays the bills due up to the current date, grouped by vendor. To run it, choose Reports→Vendors & Payables→Unpaid Bills Detail or, at the top left of the Enter Bills window, click the Reports tab and then click the Unpaid Bills Detail icon. The window's Reports tab offers several other vendor-related reports like Open Purchase Order Detail and Purchases By Vendor Detail.

Selecting Bills to Pay

You begin the payment process by choosing the bills you want to pay. Here are the steps:

1. **Choose Vendors→Pay Bills (or click the Pay Bills icon on the Home Page).**

   QuickBooks opens the Pay Bills window and displays the bills due on or before the date in the window's aptly named "Due on or before" box. As Figure 9-6 shows, you can change which bills are displayed, view bill details, or apply credits and discounts.

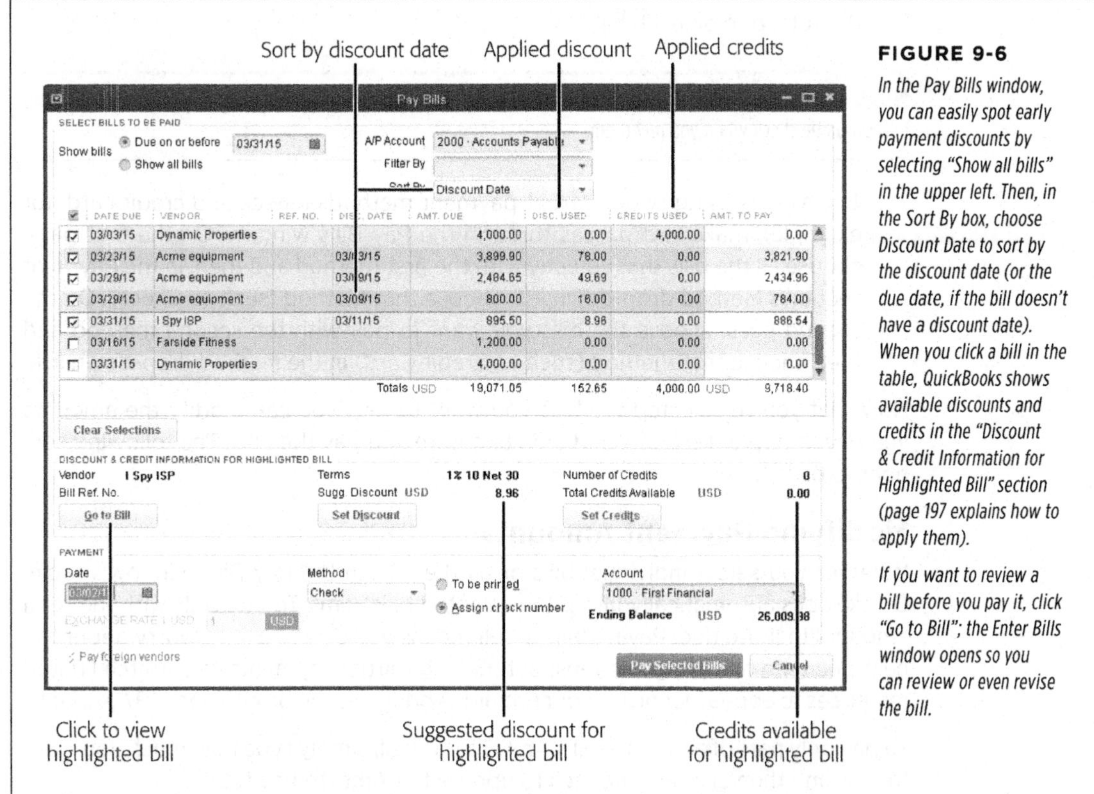

FIGURE 9-6

In the Pay Bills window, you can easily spot early payment discounts by selecting "Show all bills" in the upper left. Then, in the Sort By box, choose Discount Date to sort by the discount date (or the due date, if the bill doesn't have a discount date). When you click a bill in the table, QuickBooks shows available discounts and credits in the "Discount & Credit Information for Highlighted Bill" section (page 197 explains how to apply them).

If you want to review a bill before you pay it, click "Go to Bill"; the Enter Bills window opens so you can review or even revise the bill.

   If you've turned on multiple currencies (page 656) and receive bills in different currencies, in the A/P Account drop-down list at the top of the window, choose the corresponding Accounts Payable account for the currency in which you have to pay bills.

The window then displays the bills you've entered in that currency. (The bill amounts appear in the foreign currency.) Below the table, you see the total amount you have to pay in the foreign currency and your home currency.

NOTE If you pay bills in more than one currency, you have to make a separate pass through the Pay Bills window for each one. If you don't use multiple currencies, the Pay Bills window doesn't include the A/P Account or Exchange Rate fields.

2. **Select the bills you want to pay by clicking their checkboxes in the first column of the window's table.**

   Clicking the Select All Bills button below the table makes QuickBooks select *all* the bills displayed in the window's table. (The button's label changes to Clear Selections when at least one bill is selected.) Whether you select all the bills or just a few, QuickBooks fills in the Amt. To Pay cells for the selected bills with the total due on each bill.

NOTE If you select more than one bill from the same vendor, QuickBooks automatically combines those bills onto one check when you pay them.

   To pay bills using two different payment methods (check and credit card, for example), make two passes through the Pay Bills window. On the first pass, choose all the bills that you pay with the first method and then, in the Payment section's Method drop-down list, choose that method (such as Check). On the second pass, choose the bills you want to pay with the second method and then choose that method (such as Credit Card) in the Method drop-down list.

Now that you've selected the bills you want to pay, you can modify the amounts you pay or apply discounts and credits before you pay the bills. The following sections explain how.

Modifying Payment Amounts

Whether you select individual bills or all the bills in the Pay Bills window's table, QuickBooks automatically fills in the selected bills' Amt. To Pay cells with the total amounts that are due. Paying bills in full means you don't have to worry about the next due date or paying late fees, but making partial payments can stretch limited resources to appease more of your unpaid vendors, as the box on page 197 explains.

To pay only part of a bill, in a bill's Amt. To Pay cell, simply type how much you want to pay, and then click another cell to update the Amt. To Pay total.

TIP If you keep your cash in an interest-bearing account until you need it, you'll want to know how much money you need to transfer to your checking account to pay the bills. In the Pay Bills window, the number at the bottom of the Amt. Due column is the total of all the bills displayed, and the number at the bottom of the Amt. To Pay column is the total of all the bills you've selected. The two totals may differ if you've set up QuickBooks to automatically apply credits and discounts (see below), because any available credits and discounts reduce how much you owe.

UP TO SPEED

When Cash Is Tight

If your cash accounts are dwindling, you may face some tough decisions about whom to pay and when. To help keep your business afloat until the hard times pass, here are a few strategies to consider:

- Pay the vendors whose products or services are essential to your business.
- Pay government obligations (taxes and payroll withholdings) first. In the Pay Bills window's Sort By box, choose Vendor to make it easy to spot all your government bills.
- Make partial payments to all your vendors rather than full payments to some and no payments to others.
- If you want to pay small bills in full, in the Sort By box, choose Amount Due to sort your outstanding bills by dollar value.

Applying Discounts and Credits to Payments

Most companies like to use their discounts and credits as soon as possible. By far the easiest way to deal with discounts and credits you receive from vendors is to let QuickBooks handle them automatically.

Here's how to delegate applying early payment discounts and available credits to QuickBooks:

1. **Choose Edit→Preferences→Bills, and then click the Company Preferences tab.**

   Because these settings are on the Company Preferences tab, you have to be a QuickBooks administrator to change them. The settings you choose here apply to every person who logs into your company file.

2. **To make QuickBooks apply available credits automatically, turn on the "Automatically use credits" checkbox.**

   With this setting turned on, QuickBooks automatically applies vendor credits to the corresponding vendor's bills to reduce the amount you have to pay. If you'd rather choose when to apply credits, leave this checkbox turned off.

3. **Turn on the "Automatically use discounts" checkbox and, in the Default Discount Account box, choose the account you use to track vendor discounts.**

If you haven't set up an account for vendor discounts, in the Default Discount Account drop-down list, choose <Add New>, and then create a new account (page 56) called something like Vendor Discounts.

NOTE Whether you create an income account or an expense account for vendor discounts is neither an accounting rule nor a QuickBooks requirement, but a matter of how you view vendor discounts. If you think of them as expenses you've saved by paying early, create an expense account. If you view them as money you've made, create an income account instead. Either way, discounts you receive from vendors are different from discounts you extend to your customers. So, in the Default Discount Account box, choose an account specifically for *vendor* discounts, not your customer discount account.

As you'd expect, turning on these checkboxes tells QuickBooks to apply early payment discounts and available credits to bills without further instructions from you. The program uses your payment terms to figure out the early payment discounts you've earned, and it applies them and all available credits to their corresponding bills. Whether these checkboxes are on or off, you can still control the discounts and credits QuickBooks applies to your bills, as you'll learn shortly. For example, you might want to delay a large credit until the following year in order to increase your expenses in the current year and thereby decrease this year's taxable income.

APPLYING DISCOUNTS MANUALLY

If you want to apply discounts by hand or change a discount that QuickBooks added, here's what to do:

1. **On the Home Page, click the Pay Bills icon or choose Vendors→Pay Bills.**
2. **In the Pay Bills window's table, turn on the checkmark cell (in the first column) for the bill whose discount you want to edit.**

   In the window's "Discount & Credit Information for Highlighted Bill" section, QuickBooks shows the discount and credits that are available for the selected bill. More importantly, the program activates the Set Discount and Set Credits buttons so you can click them to apply discounts and credits. (If the bill's checkmark cell is turned off, QuickBooks shows the suggested discount and available credits, but the Set Discount and Set Credits buttons are dimmed.)

TIP When you're applying discounts manually, look for dates in the Disc. Date column that are in the *future*. Those bills qualify for early payment discounts.

3. **To apply or modify a discount to the selected bill, click Set Discount.**

   QuickBooks opens the "Discount and Credits" dialog box to the Discount tab (Figure 9-7). If you've turned on multiple currencies, the currency you set for the vendor appears to the left of the Suggested Discount label and in the "Amount of Discount" box.

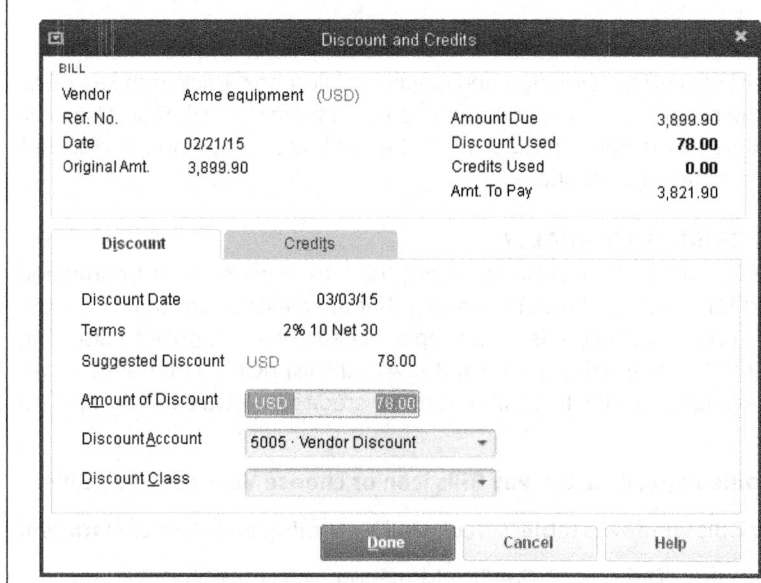

FIGURE 9-7

In the "Discount and Credits" dialog box, QuickBooks automatically selects the Discount tab and displays your payment terms, the discount date, and the amount of discount you deserve.

If the suggested discount is worth an early separation from your money, click Done to deduct the discount from your bill. Otherwise, click Cancel.

If you also want to work on credits (page 200), then when you're done modifying the discount, click the Credits tab.

4. **In the "Amount of Discount" box, QuickBooks fills in the suggested discount. To apply a different discount, type the new value.**

   Many companies try to save money by taking early payment discounts when they haven't actually paid early. Some companies apply discounts regardless of what their payment terms are, and many vendors honor these undeserved discounts in the name of goodwill.

5. **In the Discount Account drop-down list, choose the account you use to track vendor discounts.**

   If you use an income account, discounts increase the balance of the income account. If you use an expense account, discounts reduce how much you spend on expenses.

TIP If you want to track discounts on inventory separately from other discounts you receive, create a cost of goods sold account specifically for inventory discounts. For example, if QuickBooks created account 5000 for Cost of Goods Sold, you can create two subaccounts: 5005 for Cost of Inventory Sold and 5010 for Inventory Discounts. In your financial reports, the two subaccounts show your original cost and the discounts you receive. Account 5000 adds the two subaccounts together to show your net cost of goods sold.

6. **If you track classes, choose a class for the discount.**

   Typically, you'll choose the same class for the discount that you used for the original expense.

7. **Click Done.**

   QuickBooks closes the "Discount and Credits" dialog box. Back in the Pay Bills window, the program adds the discount you entered in the bill's Disc. Used cell and recalculates the value in the Amt. To Pay cell by subtracting the discount amount from the amount due.

APPLYING CREDITS MANUALLY

When you select a bill in the Pay Bills window, the "Discount & Credit Information for Highlighted Bill" section shows the credits that are available for that bill. If the "Discount and Credits" dialog box is already open because you've applied a discount, just click the Credits tab and then perform step 4 of the list below. Otherwise, here's how to apply available credits to a bill or remove credits that QuickBooks applied for you:

1. **On the Home Page, click the Pay Bills icon or choose Vendors→Pay Bills.**

2. **In the Pay Bills window's table, select a bill by turning on its checkmark cell.**

   In the window's "Discount & Credit Information for Highlighted Bill" section, QuickBooks shows the credits available for that vendor, if any, and activates the Set Credits button.

3. **To apply a credit to the selected bill, click Set Credits.**

   QuickBooks opens the "Discount and Credits" dialog box and displays the Credits tab, shown in Figure 9-8. Credits that are already applied to the bill have checkmarks next to them.

4. **Turn on the checkmark cell for each credit you want to apply. If you want to use a credit later, turn *off* its checkmark cell. Then click Done.**

   QuickBooks closes the dialog box and applies the credits.

Setting the Payment Method and Account

After you've selected the bills you want to pay and applied any discounts and credits, you still have to tell QuickBooks how and when you want to pay those bills. These payment settings at the very bottom of the Pay Bills window are the last ones you have to adjust before paying your vendors:

- **Date**. QuickBooks fills in the current date automatically. To predate or postdate your payments, choose a different date here. (Page 650 explains how to get QuickBooks to date checks using the day you print them.)

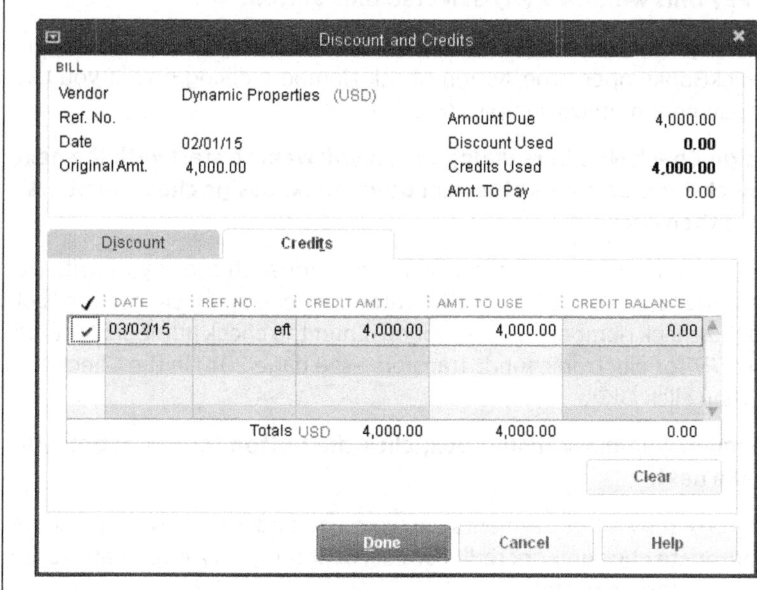

FIGURE 9-8

On the "Discount and Credits" dialog box's Credits tab, click a credit's checkmark cell to toggle between applying the credit and removing it from the bill.

When you click Done here, QuickBooks updates the Pay Bills window's Credits Used value to show the amount of credit applied to the bill, and the Amt. To Pay value to reflect the amount you have to pay based on applied discounts and credits.

- **Method**. In this drop-down list, choose how you want to pay the bills: Check, Credit Card, or (if you subscribe to QuickBooks' online bill-payment service) Online Bank Pmt. (If you pay bills using your bank's online bill-payment service, electronic payment via the vendor's website, or another non-QuickBooks bill-payment service, choose Check.) If you pick Check, you have one other choice to make here:
  - If you print your checks from QuickBooks, choose the **To be printed** option, and the program automatically adds the bills you selected to its queue of checks to be printed. (You'll learn about printing these checks on page 211.)
  - If you write checks by hand, choose the **Assign check number** option. That way, you can assign check numbers when you click the Pay Selected Bills button (explained in a moment).
- **Account**. If you specified a default account for the Pay Bills window to use (page 640), QuickBooks automatically selects that account here. To use a different one, in this drop-down list, choose the account you use to pay bills, such as a checking or credit card account.

Paying Selected Bills

When you're done setting up bills to pay, it's time to pay them. Here are the steps:

1. **Click the Pay Bills window's Pay Selected Bills button.**

   If you write paper checks for your bills and chose the "Assign check number" option, QuickBooks opens the Assign Check Numbers dialog box. If you use any *other* payment method, jump to step 3.

2. **In the Assign Check Numbers dialog box, if you want to start with the next unused check number, choose the "Let QuickBooks assign check numbers" option, and then click OK.**

   If you instead want to specify the check numbers for each check you write (to match the paper checks you've already written, for example), choose the "Let me assign the check numbers below" option. Enter the check numbers (or type a code like *EFT* for electronic funds transfers—see page 204) in the Check No. cells, and then click OK.

3. **In the Payment Summary dialog box, click the button for the action you want to take next.**

   This dialog box shows the payments you've made and adds those payments to the appropriate checking or credit card account register. All you have to do is click the appropriate button:

   - If you write paper checks, click Done. Then write the checks and mail them, as described in the next section.
   - If you chose the "To be printed" option to print checks from QuickBooks, click Print Checks and see page 211 for details. Or, if you aren't ready to print checks just yet, click Done.
   - To create another batch of bill payments (for example, to pay bills using another method), click Pay More Bills.

NOTE The next time you open the Enter Bills window, you'll see a PAID stamp on bills you've paid.

Writing Checks Without Entering Bills

You might enter bills in QuickBooks for the majority of your vendor transactions so you can keep track of early payment discounts or when bills are due. But you're still likely to write a quick check from time to time to pay for an expense immediately. For example, when the person who plows your parking lot knocks on the door and asks for payment, he won't want to wait while you step through the bill-entering and bill-paying process in QuickBooks—he just wants his $100. And if you write only a couple of checks a month, there's nothing wrong with writing checks to pay vendors without entering a bill in QuickBooks.

When you're new to QuickBooks and want some guidance, use the Write Checks window to make sure you enter all the required info. Once you're more experienced, you can record checks directly in QuickBooks' checking account register. This section describes how to do both.

Using the Write Checks Window

The Write Checks window is like a trimmed-down version of the Enter Bills window. Because you're paying immediately, there's no need for fields such as Bill Due or Terms. For a payment without a bill, you have to provide information about the expenses or items you're paying for, which is why the Write Checks window includes the Expenses and Items tabs. QuickBooks fills in a few fields for you, and the rest are like the ones you've met already in the Enter Bills window (page 186).

NOTE Don't use the Write Checks (or Enter Bills) window to write checks to pay sales tax, payroll, payroll taxes, or other payroll liabilities. Instead, see page 555 to learn how to pay sales tax, and Chapter 15 for info about payroll transactions.

To write a check in the Write Checks window, follow these steps:

1. **Open the Write Checks window by pressing Ctrl+W, choosing Banking→Write Checks, or clicking the Write Checks icon in the Home Page's Banking section.**

   As you can see in Figure 9-9, QuickBooks tries to flatten the learning curve by making the upper part of the window look like a paper check. If you use multiple currencies, QuickBooks lists the currency for your checking account in the Bank Account box, the currency for the vendor on the right side of the "Pay to the Order of" box, and the currency for the check to the left of the check amount.

   If you set up bank account preferences (page 640), such as which bank account to use when you open the Write Checks window, QuickBooks automatically chooses that account for you.

2. **If you want to print the check, at the top of the window, make sure the Print Later checkbox is turned on, and then skip to step 4.**

   When this checkbox is on, the words "To Print" appear to the right of the No. label, and QuickBooks adds the check to a print queue. When you print the checks in the queue (page 211), QuickBooks replaces "To Print" with check numbers.

NOTE If you don't use multiple currencies, the Pay Online checkbox appears below the Print Later checkbox. Turn on the Pay Online checkbox to send this payment electronically (page 615).

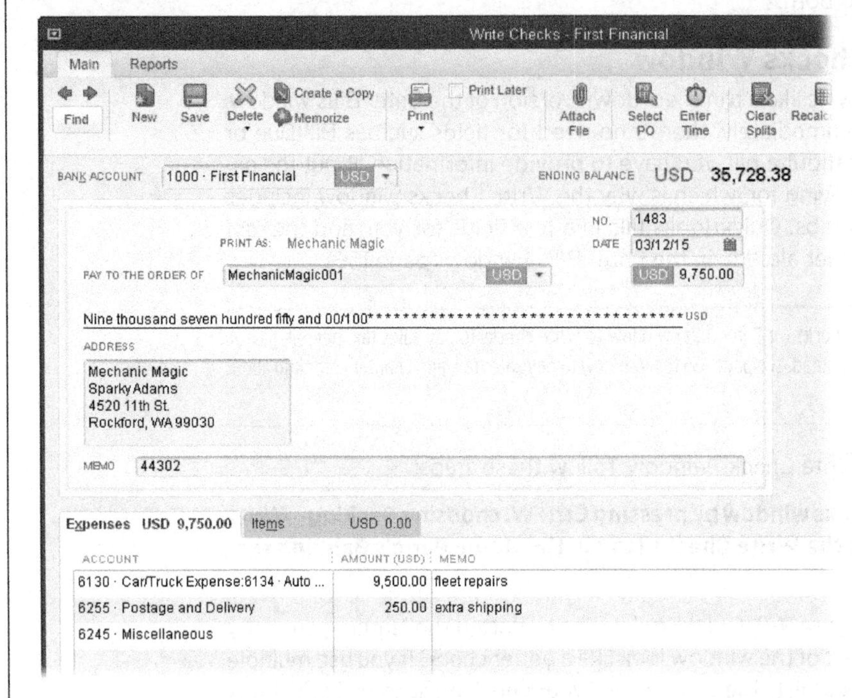

FIGURE 9-9

Choosing a name in the "Pay to the Order of" field fills in the Address box, which is perfect for printing checks for mailing in window envelopes. Even though the company name appears in the "Pay to the Order of" field, QuickBooks also displays the company name in the Address box to show you what it prints on checks.

If you include account numbers in your vendor records, QuickBooks adds the account number to the Memo field.

3. **If you're writing checks by hand, turn off the Print Later checkbox and make sure the number in the No. box is correct.**

   When you turn off the Print Later checkbox, QuickBooks automatically fills in the No. box with the next check number for the selected bank account. If the number it fills in doesn't match the check you're writing by hand, type in the number from your paper check. If you type a check number that's already been used, QuickBooks warns you about the duplicate number when you try to save the check. In the warning message box, click Cancel, and then, in the Write Checks window, edit the value in the No. field.

TIP If you suspect that there's more than one check number awry, open the checking account register (page 374) to review multiple checks at once. To renumber a check in the register window, double-click the check transaction's Number cell, type the new number, and then press Enter to save the change. As long as you keep editing check numbers until all the duplicates are gone, it's OK to save a duplicate check number.

4. **In the "Pay to the Order of" drop-down list, choose whom you want to pay.**

   This list includes customers, vendors, employees, and names from the Other Names List. If you entered the vendor's name in the "Print on Check as" box when you set up the vendor, you'll see "Print As: [name]" above the "Pay to the Order of" field.

5. **Add entries to the Expenses and Items tabs for the things the check is paying for, just like you do when you enter a bill (page 187).**

   QuickBooks calculates the check amount as you add entries on these tabs. If you fill in the check amount and *then* start adding expenses and items, you'll know that the check total and the posted amounts match when no unallocated dollars remain. If you mangle the entries on either tab, you can start over by clicking the Clear Splits button at the top of the window.

6. **Click Save & Close to record the check.**

   To write another check, click Save & New. To throw away any values in the window and start over, click Clear.

Adding Checks to an Account Register

In QuickBooks, entering checks in a bank account register is fast, easy, and—for keyboard aficionados—addictive. By combining typing and keyboard shortcuts, such as tabbing from cell to cell, you can make short work of entering checks. Here's how to create checks in a register window:

1. **Press Ctrl+A to open the Chart of Accounts window, and then double-click your bank account.**

   You can also open the register by clicking Check Register in the Home Page's Banking section; next, in the Use Register dialog box, select the checking account, and then click OK. Either way, QuickBooks opens the account register window and positions the cursor in the Date cell of the first blank transaction.

2. **To adjust the check's date by a few days, press the plus key (+) or minus key (–) until the date is what you want.**

   See Appendix C (available from this book's Missing CD page at *www.missingmanuals.com/cds*) for more date-related keyboard shortcuts.

3. **Press Tab to move to the Number cell.**

   QuickBooks automatically fills in the next check number for that bank account. If the number doesn't match the paper check you want to write, press + or – until the number is correct or simply type the new number. (Pages 214–216 explain how to fill in the Number cell if you make a payment with a debit card, ATM card, electronic transaction, or other method.)

4. **Press Tab to move to the Payee cell, and then start typing the name of the payee.**

   QuickBooks scans the lists of names in your company file and selects the first one that matches all the letters you've typed so far. As soon as it selects the one you want, press Tab to move to the Payment cell.

5. **In the Payment cell, type the amount of the check.**

   If you previously recorded a check for that vendor, QuickBooks fills in this cell with the amount from the previous check. To use a different amount, simply type the new value.

6. **Click the Account cell.**

   If the payee is a vendor with more than one pre-fill account assigned to it (page 85), QuickBooks adds "-split-" to the Account cell. In that case, click Splits below the table to open the Splits panel (see Figure 9-10) so you can enter amounts for the accounts. You can also use the Splits panel if your check covers more than one type of expense and you want to allocate the payment among several accounts. For each allocation, specify the account, amount, memo, customer, and class (if you track classes), and then click Close.

7. **If the check applies to only one expense account, in the Account drop-down list, choose the appropriate account.**

   You can also choose an account by typing the account's number or the first few letters of its name. As you type, QuickBooks selects the first account that matches what you've typed. When the selected account is correct, press Tab to move to the Memo cell.

8. **To add a description of the check, in the Memo cell, type your notes.**

9. **When you've filled in all the fields you need, click Record to save the check.**

   To add more checks to the register, lather, rinse, repeat.

Producing Checks

When you choose Check in the Pay Bills window's Method field, your checking account register shows check transactions, but you still have to generate physical checks to send to your vendors. For companies that produce lots of checks, printing them in QuickBooks can prevent carpal tunnel syndrome. But for a sole proprietorship that generates only a few checks each month, writing them by hand is easy enough. As this section explains, QuickBooks accepts either approach with equal aplomb.

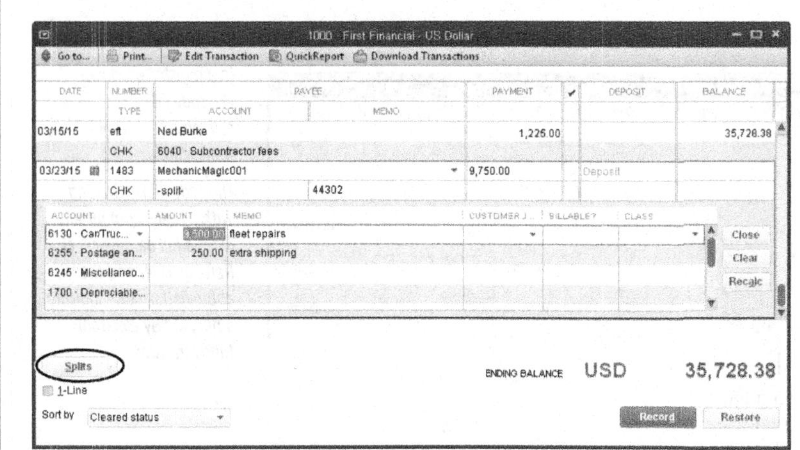

FIGURE 9-10

To allocate a check to multiple accounts or to specify a customer, job, or class in the check register, click the Splits button (circled) to open the panel shown here so you can assign them. If you modify the value in the Payment cell or any values in the Amount cells, click Recalc to change the check payment amount to the total of the splits.

Writing Checks by Hand

Handwriting checks doesn't require any work in QuickBooks, but you still have to keep your company file in sync with your paper checks. Whether you're writing checks for bills you've paid in QuickBooks or scratching out a spur-of-the-moment check to pay for the pizza you had delivered, you want to make sure that the check numbers in your bank account register match your paper checks.

If you've already recorded your check transactions in QuickBooks by paying bills (page 194) or entering a check transaction in your checking account register window for an immediate payment (page 205), synchronizing check numbers is as easy as writing the paper checks in the same order as you entered them in QuickBooks. First, open the checking account register window. You've got a few ways to do this: You can press Ctrl+A to open the Chart of Accounts window and then either double-click the checking account's row or right-click it and choose Use Register. Alternatively, in the Home Page's Banking panel, click Check Register; next, in the Use Register dialog box, select your checking account and then click OK.

Once the register window is open, you can use the bill payments and check transactions to guide your paper check writing, as shown in Figure 9-11.

NOTE If the next check number in QuickBooks isn't the one on your next paper check, figure out why they don't match. The answer might be as simple as a voided check that you forgot to enter in QuickBooks or a check you wrote earlier that was out of sequence. But if someone is walking off with blank checks, you need to take action.

Until you find the reason for the mismatched check number, editing the check numbers that QuickBooks assigns in the checking account register is the easiest way to get checks into the mail. In the register window, simply double-click an incorrect check number, and then type the number that's on your paper check.

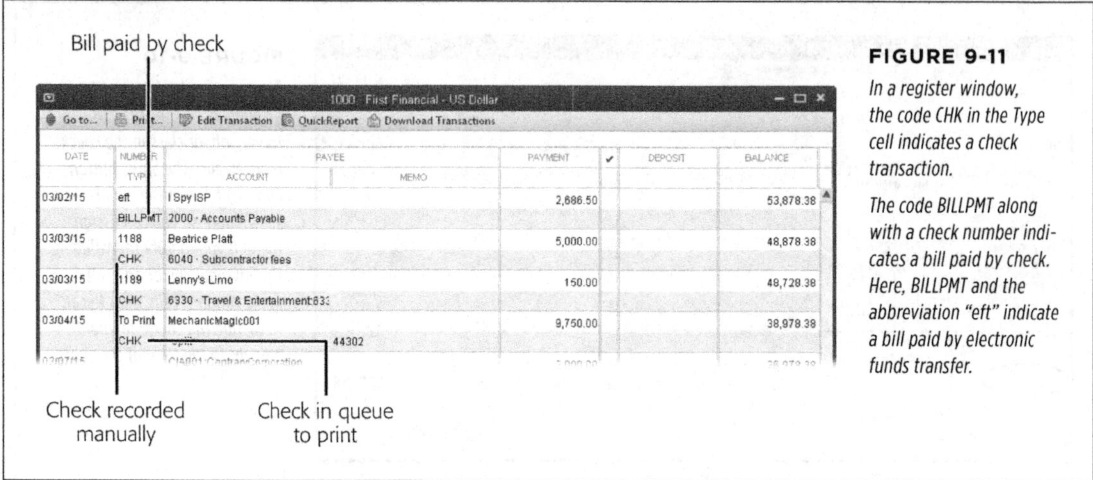

FIGURE 9-11

In a register window, the code CHK in the Type cell indicates a check transaction.

The code BILLPMT along with a check number indicates a bill paid by check. Here, BILLPMT and the abbreviation "eft" indicate a bill paid by electronic funds transfer.

Setting Up QuickBooks to Print Checks

If you have scads of checks to generate, printing on preprinted computer checks is well worth the small amount of setup you have to do. And if you dedicate a printer to check printing and keep it stocked with checks, setup is truly a one-time event.

TIP Lock up your preprinted checks and any printer stocked with them. Otherwise, you might discover checks missing, which can lead to money disappearing from your bank account.

The first step is telling QuickBooks which printer to print to and the type of checks you use. (The program remembers these settings, so you need to go through this process just once.) After you've specified your check-printing settings, QuickBooks fills them in automatically in the Print dialog box, though you can always change those options before you print.

Here's how you set QuickBooks up to print checks:

1. **Open the "Printer setup" dialog box by choosing File→Printer Setup.**

   The dialog box's Form Name drop-down list includes all the forms you can print in QuickBooks, so you can choose different print settings for each one.

2. **In the Form Name drop-down list, select Check/PayCheck.**

   When you select this option, the Check Style section appears in the bottom of the dialog box; step 4 describes what to choose there.

3. **In the "Printer name" drop-down list, choose the printer you want to use.**

   If you choose a printer brand that QuickBooks recognizes (there are only a few it doesn't), the program automatically fills in the "Printer type" box. If you use a very old or very odd printer, you'll have to manually choose the type of printer. "Page-oriented (Single sheets)" refers to printers that feed one sheet at a time. Choose Continuous (Perforated Edge) if the printer feeds a roll of paper.

NOTE If you print to checks on continuous-feed paper, properly aligning the paper in the printer is critical. You can save time and a lot of wasted checks by aligning the paper *before* you print batches of checks, as described on page 310.

4. **In the Check Style section, choose the option that represents the type of check you purchased. (The box on page 210 explains where you can buy checks.)**

   The "Printer setup" dialog box displays examples of each check style it can deal with, making it easy to choose the right one, as shown in Figure 9-12. Voucher checks print one to a page, so they're by far the easiest to use. However, if you use standard or wallet checks to save paper, see the box on page 212 to learn how to tell QuickBooks how you want it to handle partial pages of checks.

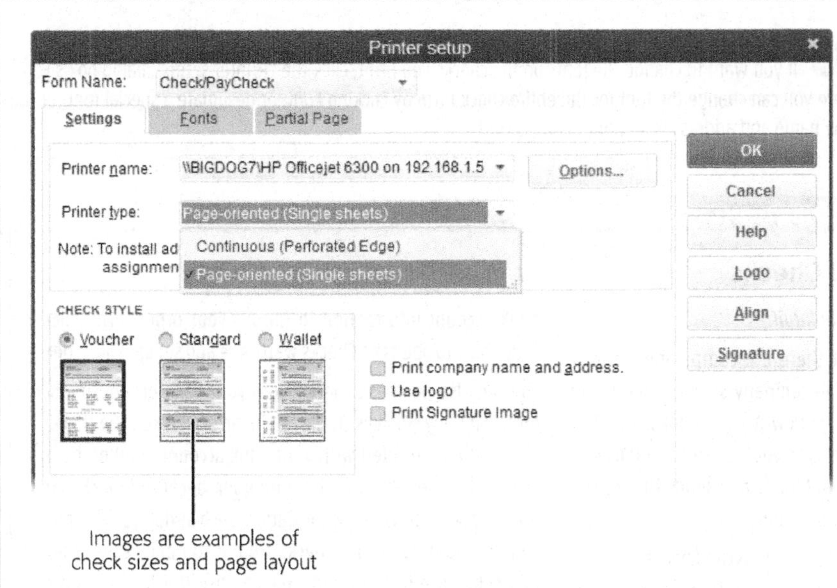

FIGURE 9-12

The Voucher option represents one-page forms that include both a check and a detachable stub for payroll or check info. The Standard option sets QuickBooks up to print checks that fit in a #10 business envelope; they typically come three to a page. Wallet checks are narrower than standard business checks and have a perforation on the left for tearing off the check, leaving a stub containing check information that you can file.

5. **If the company you buy checks from wants too much money to print your company info and logo on the checks, turn on the "Print company name and address" and "Use logo" checkboxes.**

   Turning on the "Print company name and address" checkbox tells QuickBooks to print the company name and address you filled in when you created your company file (page 11). If you turn on the "Use logo" checkbox, the program opens the Logo dialog box. Click File and, in the Open Logo File dialog box, select the file containing your logo, and then click Open. (QuickBooks can handle BMP, GIF, JPEG, PNG, and TIFF formats.) Back in the Logo dialog box, click OK.

   If your company info and logo are preprinted on your checks, leave these checkboxes turned off.

6. **If you have an image of your signature saved on your computer, you can print it on your checks by turning on the Print Signature Image checkbox.**

   When you turn on this checkbox, QuickBooks opens the Signature dialog box. Click File and then, in the Open Logo File dialog box, locate and double-click the file containing your signature. (One way to create a graphic file of your signature is by signing a piece of paper and then scanning it.)

7. **Click OK to save your check-printing settings.**

The next section tells you how to actually print checks.

NOTE If you want to change the fonts on the checks you print, click the "Printer setup" dialog box's Fonts tab. There you can change the font for the entire check form by clicking Font, or designate a special font for the company name and address by clicking Address Font.

FREQUENTLY ASKED QUESTION

Buying Preprinted Checks

Do I have to order checks from Intuit?

The short answer is no, but there are compelling reasons to go with Intuit's checks. The company sells competitively priced preprinted checks that work with QuickBooks. Also, the program keeps track of the checks you've used and tells you when to order more. It then automatically sends the correct bank account number with your order.

To order Intuit checks, at the top of the Write Checks window, click Order Checks. If you haven't ordered from Intuit before, select the "I'm ordering from Intuit for the first time" option. QuickBooks turns on the checkbox to use your company and bank account information to fill out your order form. Click Order Now to open the Checks web page and set up your order.

You can also purchase checks from your bank or a business-form company (such as Clarke American or Deluxe). The checks have to be preprinted with your bank account number, bank routing number, and the check number, because QuickBooks prints only the payment information, such as date, payee, and amount. So if you order checks from a company other than Intuit, be sure to tell them that you use QuickBooks, since the checks need to have fields positioned to match where QuickBooks prints data.

Printing Checks

In the Pay Bills window's Method section, choosing the "To be printed" option tells QuickBooks to add the checks you've selected for payment to a print queue when you click the Pay Selected Bills button. You can also tell QuickBooks to add a check to a print queue by turning on the Print Later checkbox at the top of the Write Checks window.

After you confirm that your preprinted checks are in the printer and that the checks are aligned properly, you can print queued-up checks by following these steps:

1. **If you're at the end of the Pay Bills process and the Payment Summary dialog box is open, click Print Checks. Otherwise, choose File→Print Forms→Checks.**

   QuickBooks opens the "Select Checks to Print" dialog box and selects all the unprinted checks, as shown in Figure 9-13.

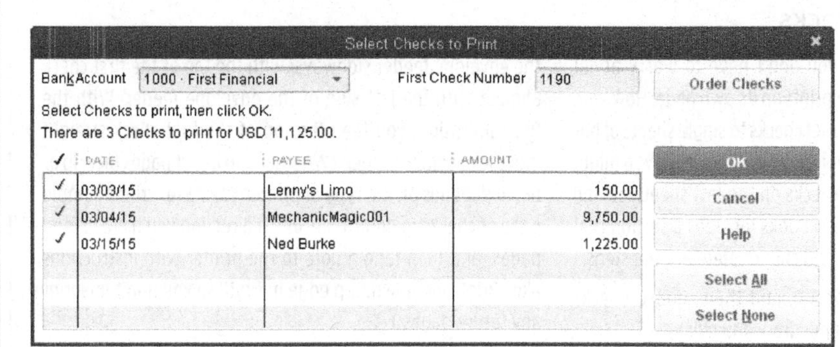

FIGURE 9-13

The first time you print checks, QuickBooks sets the First Check Number box to 1. If necessary, change this number to match the one on the first check loaded in your printer.

2. **If you don't want to print a particular check that's listed, turn off its checkbox. When only the checks you want to print are selected, click OK.**

   QuickBooks opens the Print Checks dialog box, which looks much like the "Printer setup" dialog box for checks (Figure 9-12).

3. **If you're printing standard or wallet checks and the first page of checks in your printer is a partial page, in the "Number of checks on first page" box, type how many checks there are.**

   You won't see this box if you're printing to voucher checks because they print one to a page. But for standard or wallet checks, this box lets you use leftover checks from previous print runs (assuming you have a page-oriented printer). Type the number of leftover checks on the partial page, and then insert that page into your printer's envelope feeder. After QuickBooks prints checks to that page, it will begin feeding full sheets of checks from the paper tray. See the box on page 212 for the full scoop on telling QuickBooks how you want it to handle partial pages of checks.

4. **Click Print.**

   Because of the problems that can happen during printing (paper jams, low toner, or an unfortunate coffee spill), QuickBooks opens the "Print Checks – Confirmation" dialog box after it prints checks.

5. **If there was a problem, in the "Print Checks – Confirmation" dialog box, click the Reprint cell for each check that didn't print correctly.**

   If the whole batch is a loss, click Select All.

6. **Click OK to reprint the misprinted checks.**

   In addition to printing the checks, QuickBooks also removes the words "To Print" from those checks in your checking account register, replacing them with the check numbers it used.

GEM IN THE ROUGH

Using Leftover Checks

If you use voucher checks, you don't have to worry about leftovers, because each check prints on its own page. However, when you print standard or wallet checks to single sheets of paper (which usually have three checks on each sheet), you might print only one or two of the checks on the last sheet, leaving a leftover or two. Happily, QuickBooks includes a setting that lets you print on those orphaned checks. Here are the steps:

1. Choose File→Printer Setup, and then choose Check/PayCheck in the Form Name drop-down list.
2. Click the Partial Page tab.
3. Choose the option (Side, Center, or Portrait) that corresponds to how your printer feeds envelopes, and then click OK to save the setting.

The Side and Portrait options are the most common methods. If you select Side, you insert the partial page of checks into the envelope feeder sideways, with the top of the first check aligned with the left side of the envelope feeder. With the Portrait option, you feed the top of the first check straight into the envelope feeder. (Whether you insert pages face up or down depends on the type of printer you have. Print a sample page of checks to determine which direction you have to feed pages, and then tape a note to the printer with instructions like "Print side down, top edge in first" so you don't misprint any future pages.)

Before you start printing, feed the page with orphaned checks into your printer's envelope feeder. That way, QuickBooks prints to those orphaned checks before printing to the full pages of checks in the paper tray.

Paying Using Other Payment Methods

These days, you can choose from a plethora of payment methods besides checks, such as credit cards, debit cards, online services like PayPal, electronic transactions, and even cold cash. Fortunately, recording these transactions in QuickBooks is a lot like recording checks. This section describes the other payment methods you can use and how they differ from writing checks.

Paying with Credit Cards

When you make credit card purchases, the easiest way to record those charges in your company file is by signing up for online banking with your financial institution (page 610), setting up bank feeds (page 611), and then downloading the transactions (page 617). But you can also enter credit charges manually.

TIP Regardless of whether you download charges, entering charges manually is a great way to catch erroneous or fraudulent charges that appear on your statement. For example, after entering your charges manually, you can download the charges from your credit card company. If you see additional charges that don't match the ones you entered, either you forgot a charge or there's an error in your account.

Recording credit card charges is almost the same as writing checks except that, instead of the Write Checks window, you use the Enter Credit Card Charges window, shown in Figure 9-14. Behind the scenes, QuickBooks adds the credit card charge to your credit card account, which is a current liability account. That means the balance in the account increases because you owe more money. (When you write a check out of your checking account, the account's balance decreases because you have less money in that *asset* account.)

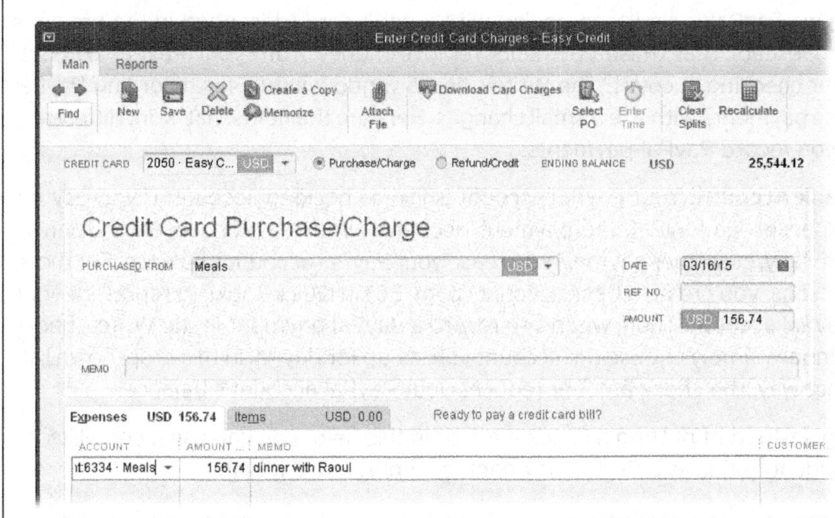

FIGURE 9-14

Unless you want your Vendor List awash with every pizza parlor, gas station, and parking lot you patronize, consider creating generic vendors such as Meals, Gas, and Parking. If you want to track specific vendors, type their names in the Memo field here. You can leave the Ref. No. field blank or enter your receipt number there. Allocating a charge to multiple accounts or to a customer works the same as for bills (page 187).

To open the Enter Credit Card Charges window, choose Banking→Enter Credit Card Charges or, in the Home Page's Banking section, click Enter Credit Card Charges. You can also enter charges directly in the credit card account register, just as you do with checks.

NOTE To enter a refund for a credit card charge, near the top of the Enter Credit Card Charges window, choose the Refund/Credit option, and then fill in the window's fields with info about the refund you received.

Paying with a Debit Card

Paying with a debit card is like writing a check, because the transaction removes money from your checking account. For that reason, you use the Write Checks window to record debit card transactions. In fact, you can also use the Write Checks window to record electronic funds transfers. The only difference between these transactions and regular checks is what you enter in the window's No. field.

Instead of putting a check number in this field, you can use a code to identify the type of payment. For example, enter *DB* for a debit card or *EFT* for electronic transactions like an online bill payment you make with your bank's bill-pay service or directly through a vendor's website. If you have several debit cards for your bank account, you may want to include the last four digits of the card number after the code so you can tell your transactions from your partner's transactions.

Debit card transactions are different from credit card charges, which is why you don't use the Enter Credit Card Charges window to record them. Debit card charges reduce the balance in your checking account, which is a current asset account (page 57), whereas credit card charges increase the balance in your credit card account, which is a current liability account (page 57).

Paying with PayPal

Paying via PayPal is similar to paying with a debit card (described in the previous section), except that these payments remove money from your PayPal account, not your checking account. The Write Checks window works for recording PayPal expense payments with a few small changes. Here are the fields that work differently when you record PayPal payments:

- **Bank Account**. Your PayPal account is like a checking account: If you pay for expenses via PayPal, the payment decreases your PayPal account's balance. Similarly, customer payments increase your PayPal account's balance. For those reasons, you create a bank account (page 56) in QuickBooks to represent your PayPal account. Then, when you record a PayPal payment in the Write Checks window, simply choose the account you set up for PayPal in this drop-down list. That way, the check amount reduces your PayPal account's balance.
- **No**. Instead of putting a check number in this field, you can use a code like *PP* to identify this as a PayPal payment, or simply leave it blank.

TIP PayPal's idiosyncrasies can make tracking transactions difficult. For example, PayPal transactions might show up as pending for a few days before they clear. And PayPal reports don't present the info you need to reconcile your account in the most helpful format. If your PayPal account sees a lot of action—both in terms of payments you make as well as customer deposits—a third-party program that downloads PayPal transactions into QuickBooks may be the answer. One of the most popular is SimplePort (*www.simpleport.net*).

Paying with Cash

Dashing out to buy an extension cord so you can present a pitch to a potential client? Chances are you'll grab money from the petty cash drawer at your office. *Petty cash* is the common term for money spent on small purchases, typically less than $20.

Many companies keep a cash drawer at the office and dole out dollars for small, company-related purchases that employees make. But for the small business owner with a bank card, getting petty cash is as easy as withdrawing money from an ATM. Either way, petty cash is still company money, and that means you have to keep track of it and how it's spent. The following sections explain how to do that.

RECORDING ATM WITHDRAWALS AND DEPOSITS TO PETTY CASH

Before you can pay for something with petty cash, you need to put some money into your petty cash drawer. In QuickBooks, adding money to your petty cash account mirrors the real-world transaction: You either write a check made out to Cash (or the trustworthy employee who's cashing the check), or you withdraw money from an ATM. To write a check to withdraw cash for your petty cash account, simply use the Write Checks window (choose Banking→Write Checks) to record the transaction. If you withdraw cash from an ATM, use the Transfer Funds window (choose Banking→Transfer Funds) instead.

You don't have to use the Write Checks or Transfer Funds windows to record petty cash transactions. If you're OK with creating transactions in an account register window, here are the steps for replenishing your petty cash with a check:

1. **In the Chart of Accounts window (press Ctrl+A to open it), double-click your checking account to open its register window.**

   QuickBooks selects the date in the first blank transaction. Depending on the date preference you choose (page 650), the program fills in either the current date or the last date you entered in a transaction. If you added money to petty cash on a different day, choose the correct date.

2. **If you're withdrawing money from an ATM, in the Number cell, either type *ATM* or clear the value that's there.**

   If you're writing a check to get petty cash and QuickBooks fills in the Number cell with the correct check number, continue to the Payee cell. Otherwise, type the correct check number in the cell.

3. **Whether you're writing a check or withdrawing money from an ATM, in the Payee cell, type a name such as *Cash* or *Petty Cash*.**

   If you made a check out to one of your employees, in the Payee cell's drop-down list, choose that person's name.

4. **In the Payment cell, type the amount that you're moving from the checking account to petty cash.**

If you track classes in QuickBooks, this is one time to *ignore* the Class cell. You assign classes only when you record purchases made with petty cash (as explained in the next section).

5. **In the Account cell, choose your petty cash account.**

   If you don't already have a petty cash account in your chart of accounts, create the account now by choosing <Add New>, and then be sure to choose the Bank account type. That way, your petty cash account appears at the top of your balance sheet with your other savings and checking accounts.

6. **Click Record to save the transaction.**

That's it!

TIP If you make a withdrawal from an ATM to get petty cash, use QuickBooks' Transfer Money feature (page 386) to record the transaction. In the Transfer Funds From box, choose your bank account; in the Transfer Funds To box, choose your petty cash account.

RECORDING PURCHASES MADE WITH PETTY CASH

As long as company cash sits in a petty cash drawer or your wallet, the petty cash account in QuickBooks keeps track of it. But when you spend some of the petty cash in your wallet or an employee brings in a sales receipt for purchases, you have to record what was bought. (The box on page 217 explains how to track petty cash if an employee wants cash *before* he's made a purchase.)

The petty cash account's register is as good a place as any to record these purchases. In the Chart of Accounts window, double-click the petty cash account to open its register window. Then, in a blank transaction, follow these guidelines to record your petty cash expenditures:

- **Number**. Although petty cash expenditures don't use check numbers, QuickBooks automatically puts the next check number in this cell. The easiest thing to do is ignore the number and move on to the Payee cell.
- **Payee**. You don't have to enter anything here, and for many petty cash transactions, entering a Payee would just clog your list of names, so leave this cell blank.
- **Memo**. Type the vendor's name or details of the purchase here.
- **Payment**. Enter the amount that was spent.
- **Account**. Choose an account like Office Supplies to track the expense.

TIP To distribute the petty cash spent to several accounts, click Splits. In the table that appears, specify the account, amount, customer or job, class, and a memo for each split (page 207).

When you're done, click Record.

WORKAROUND WORKSHOP

Petty Cash Advances

Good management practices warn against dishing out petty cash without a receipt. But suppose an employee asks for cash in advance to purchase a new lava lamp for the conference room? There's no receipt, but you really want the lava lamp to impress the CEO of a tie-dye company.

The solution in the real world is to write a paper IOU and place it in the petty cash drawer until the employee coughs up a receipt. In QuickBooks, record the advance as if the purchase were already complete. For example, create the transaction in the petty cash account register using entries like these:

- In the Payee cell, type the name of the vendor you're purchasing from.
- In the Amount cell, type the amount of money you advanced to the employee.
- In the Account cell, choose the account that corresponds to the expense, such as Office Supplies.
- In the Memo cell, type a note about the employee who received the advance, the IOU in the petty cash drawer, and what the advance is for.

When the employee comes back with a receipt, you can update the transaction's Memo cell to show that the IOU has been repaid. If the employee brings change back, create a deposit to put that money back in the petty cash account using the same payee and account as the original withdrawal transaction.

Recording Vendor Refunds and Credits

Say you ordered 30 dozen lightweight polypropylene tank tops for your summer Death Valley marathon, but your vendor mistakenly silk-screened the logo on long-sleeved cotton T-shirts heavy enough to survive a nuclear blast. If you raise a ruckus, the vendor may issue you a refund check or a credit. Either way, it's easy to record the money you get back in QuickBooks.

Here's how to deposit a vendor's refund check or credit card refund:

1. **Choose Banking→Make Deposits or, in the Home Page's Banking panel, click Record Deposits.**

2. **If the "Payments to Deposit" window appears, turn on the checkmark cell for each payment you want to deposit along with the refund check, and then click OK to open the Make Deposits window.**

   The "Payments to Deposit" window opens only if you have other deposits to make.

3. **In the Make Deposits window's Deposit To drop-down list, choose the bank account where you're going to deposit the refund.**

   If you selected other deposits in the "Payments to Deposit" window in the previous step, they appear in the Make Deposit window's table.

4. **In the first blank Received From cell, choose the vendor who issued the refund check.**

   If the check isn't from a vendor, you can choose a customer, employee, or other name instead.

5. **In the From Account cell, choose the account associated with the refund.**

   For a refund for shirts you purchased, you might choose a cost of goods sold account that you use for products you buy specifically for customers. If the refund is for office supplies, choose the expense account for office supplies.

6. **Fill in the other fields, and then click Save & Close.**

   Enter a note about the refund (in the Memo cell), the check number (if you received a refund check), the payment method (to indicate whether you received a refund check or a credit card refund), and the amount of the refund.

If the vendor insists on issuing you a credit with its company instead of a refund check, here's how to record that credit in QuickBooks:

1. **Choose Vendors→Enter Bills or, in the Home Page's Vendors panel, click Enter Bills.**

   QuickBooks opens the Enter Bills window as if you're going to enter a bill.

2. **Just below the window's ribbon, choose the Credit option.**

   QuickBooks changes the window's giant heading to "Credit" and the Amount Due label to Credit Amount. The other fields stay the same.

3. **On the Expenses and Items tabs, fill in the cells with the items for which you received credit.**

   Enter positive numbers just as you did when you entered the original bill. QuickBooks takes care of posting the credit amounts to your accounts. Your inventory account decreases due to the inventory items you returned, your cost of goods sold account decreases due to the non-inventory items you returned, and your expense accounts' balances decrease due to expense credits. The total credit amount also reduces the balance in your Accounts Payable account.

4. **Click Save & Close.**

   That's all there is to it. See page 200 to learn how to *apply* a credit.

Running Expense-Related Reports

QuickBooks' Vendors & Payables reports tell you how much you owe each vendor and when the payments are due. The reports in the program's Purchases category, on the other hand, focus on how much you've bought from each vendor you work with. In addition, QuickBooks' new Insights tab is a great way to examine your expenses. This section tells you how to put several expense-related reports to work.

A/P Aging and Vendor Balance Reports

If your company is flush with cash and you pay bills as soon as they appear in the Pay Bills window, your A/P Aging reports and Vendor Balance reports will contain mostly zeroes. If you want an overview of how much you owe each vendor and how much is overdue, use one of the following reports listed under Reports→Vendors & Payables:

- **A/P Aging Summary**. This report shows all the vendors you owe money to and how old your balances are for each one. Double-click a value to see a report of the transactions that produced the amount owed.
- **A/P Aging Detail**. Run this report to see each unpaid bill sorted by its billing date and grouped into bills that are current, 1 to 30 days overdue, 31 to 60 days overdue, 61 to 90 days overdue, and more than 90 days late.
- **Vendor Balance Detail**. This report shows your bills and payments grouped by vendor.

TIP You can also see the details of a vendor's balance in the Vendor Center: Select the vendor on the Vendor's tab and then, on the right side of the window, click the Open Balance link.

- **Unpaid Bills Detail**. If you want to evaluate all your unpaid bills before you pay them, this report is helpful because it displays the bills due up to the current date, grouped by vendor. To include bills due in the *future*, in the report window's Dates box, choose All. If you want to inspect a bill more closely, double-click anywhere in its row, and the Enter Bills window opens with the bill's details. (You can also run this report from the Enter Bills window: Click the Reports tab at the top of the window, and then click the Unpaid Bills Detail button.)

Reports about Purchases

Purchasing reports (Reports→Purchases) tell you how much you've spent by vendor or item. And if you create purchase orders for items you buy, you can review all your open purchase orders. Here are a few of the purchasing reports you can use:

- **Purchases by Vendor Summary**. This report shows how much you've spent with each vendor during a given time period. For example, this report can help you figure out whether you should ask for better terms due to the volume of business you do with a vendor, or perhaps if you should line up additional vendors in case one goes out of business. Double-click a vendor's row in the report to run the Purchases by Vendor Detail report, which shows every transaction for that vendor.
- **Purchases by Item Summary**. This report shows the quantity and value of your purchases by item.
- **Open Purchase Orders**. As you'd expect, this report shows you all the purchase orders you've created that haven't been fulfilled yet. If stock is getting low, double-click a purchase order in this report to open it in the Create Purchase

Orders window, and then call the vendor to get an update on the estimated delivery date.

The Insights Tab

New in QuickBooks 2015, the Insights tab (located at the top of the Home Page) provides an overview of your income and expenses. (Page 44 provides the full story on this handy new dashboard.) The Expenses graph at the bottom right of the tab initially displays your top five categories of expenses. To change the date range, click the down arrow in the date range box, and then choose the period you want, such as Last Fiscal Year. You can also click the graph to run a report that shows all your expense-related transactions grouped by account.

CHAPTER

10

Invoicing

Telling your customers how much they owe you and how soon they need to pay is an important step in bookkeeping. After all, if money isn't flowing into your organization from outside sources, eventually you'll close up shop and close your QuickBooks company file for the last time.

Although businesses use several different sales forms to bill customers, the *invoice* is the most popular, and, unsurprisingly, customer billing is often called *invoicing*. This chapter begins by explaining the differences between invoices, statements, and sales receipts—each of which is a way of billing customers in QuickBooks—and when each is most appropriate.

After that, you'll learn how to fill in invoice forms in QuickBooks, whether you're invoicing for services, products, or both. If you send invoices for the same items to many of your customers (and don't use the program's multiple currencies feature), QuickBooks' batch invoice feature can help: You select the customers, add the items you want on the invoices, and the program creates all the invoices for you. If you track billable hours and reimbursable expenses with QuickBooks, you can also have the program chuck those charges into the invoices you create.

Finally, you'll find out how to handle a few special billing situations, like creating invoices when products you sell are on backorder and how to handle products you sell on consignment. You'll also learn how to create estimates for jobs and then use them to generate invoices as you perform the work. And, since you occasionally have to give money back to customers, you'll learn how to assign a credit to a customer's account, which you can then deduct from an existing invoice, refund by cutting a refund check, or apply to the customer's next invoice.

NOTE Chapter 11 continues the invoicing lesson by teaching you how to produce statements that show your customers' account status. It also explains how to create sales receipts when customers pay you right away. And Chapter 12 explains how to get any kind of sales form into your customers' hands, along with a few other timesaving techniques, like finding transactions and memorizing them for reuse.

Choosing the Right Type of Form

In QuickBooks, you can choose from three different sales forms to document what you sell, and each form has strengths and limitations. Invoices can handle any billing task you can think of, so they're the best choice if you have any doubts about which one to use. Table 10-1 summarizes what each sales form can do. The sections that follow explain the forms' capabilities in detail and give guidance on when to choose each one.

TABLE 10-1 *What each QuickBooks sales form can do*

ACTION	SALES RECEIPT	STATEMENT	INVOICE
Track customer payments and balances		X	X
Accept payments in advance	X	X	X
Accumulate some charges before sending sales form	X	X	X
Collect payment in full at time of sale	X	X	X
Create summary sales transaction	X	X	X
Apply sales tax	X		X
Apply percentage discounts	X		X
Use Group items to add charges to form	X		X
Add long descriptions for items	X		X
Subtotal items	X		X
Include customer message	X		X
Include custom fields	X		X

NOTE QuickBooks Premier and Enterprise editions include one more type of sales form: the sales order. In those editions, when you create a sales order for the products that a customer wants to buy, you can create an invoice for the items that are in stock and keep track of out-of-stock items that you'll need to send to your customer when a new shipment arrives (see page 260).

Sales Receipts

The sales receipt is the simplest sales form that QuickBooks offers, and it's also the shortest path between making a sale and having money in the bank (at least in QuickBooks). But this form is suitable *only if* your customers pay the full amount at the time of the sale—for example, in a retail store, restaurant, or beauty salon. However, you can also accumulate charges for time (page 167) and billable expenses (page 194), and then add them to a sales receipt. But for products you sell, sales receipts handle only payment in full.

When you create and save a sales receipt in QuickBooks, the program immediately posts the money you receive to the Undeposited Funds account or to the bank account you choose. As you'll learn in this chapter and the next, invoices and statements take several steps to move from billing to bank deposits, so ease of depositing is one advantage of sales receipts over those other sales forms.

Sales receipts can handle sales tax, discounts, and subtotals—or any other item in your Item List. But when you operate a cash business, creating a sales receipt in QuickBooks for each newspaper and pack of gum your newsstand sells is *not* good use of your time. Instead, consider creating a sales receipt that summarizes a day's or a week's sales (page 362), using a customer named Cash Sales that you create specifically for that purpose.

Statements

Suppose you're a lawyer and you spend 15 minutes here and 15 minutes there working on a client's legal problem over the course of a month. Each time you do so, that's another charge to the client's account. In QuickBooks, each of those charges is called a *statement charge*. You can enter them individually (page 296) or, if you track time in QuickBooks, you can add your time to an invoice just as easily, as described on page 253.

Businesses often turn to statements when they charge the same amount each month, such as a fixed monthly fee for Internet service or full-time work as a contract programmer. Although statements work for these fixed fees, you can also use memorized invoices (page 322) and QuickBooks' batch invoice feature (page 243) to do the same thing just as easily.

Where statements really shine is in summarizing a customer's account. Behind the scenes, a statement adds up all the transactions that affect the customer's open balance over a period of time, which includes statement charges, payments, and invoices. The statement shows the customer's previous balance, any payments that the customer has made, any invoices that she hasn't paid, and any new charges on the account. From all that information, QuickBooks calculates the total and displays it on the statement, so you know how much money is outstanding and whether it's overdue.

Invoices

If statements or sales receipts don't work for your situation, don't be afraid to use invoices. They accept any item you've created in your Item List (see Chapter 5) *and* they track what customers owe you.

Besides offering all the features listed in Table 10-1, an invoice is also the only type of QuickBooks sales form you can generate from an estimate (page 282). If you're a general contractor and prepare a detailed estimate of the services and products for a job, you'll save a huge chunk of time by turning that estimate into an invoice for billing. And if you have to refund some of your customer's money, you can also turn an invoice into a credit memo (page 288).

Sales Forms and Accounts

An invoice or other sales form is the first step in the flow of money through your company, so now is a good time to look at how QuickBooks posts income and expenses from your invoices to the accounts in your chart of accounts. Suppose your invoice has the entries shown in Figure 10-1. Table 10-2 shows how the amounts on that invoice post to accounts in your chart of accounts.

NOTE The lines on the invoice in Figure 10-1 don't show *all* the movements between accounts listed in Table 10-2. Behind the scenes, QuickBooks transfers money to your cost of goods sold and inventory accounts.

TABLE 10-2 *Debits and credits have to balance*

ACCOUNT	DEBIT	CREDIT
Accounts Receivable	4,822.23	
Services Revenue		5,000.00
Product Revenue		499.75
Sales Discounts	750.00	
Sales Tax Payable		37.48
Shipping Income		35.00
Cost of Goods Sold	249.78	
Inventory		249.78
Total	**5,822.01**	**5,822.01**

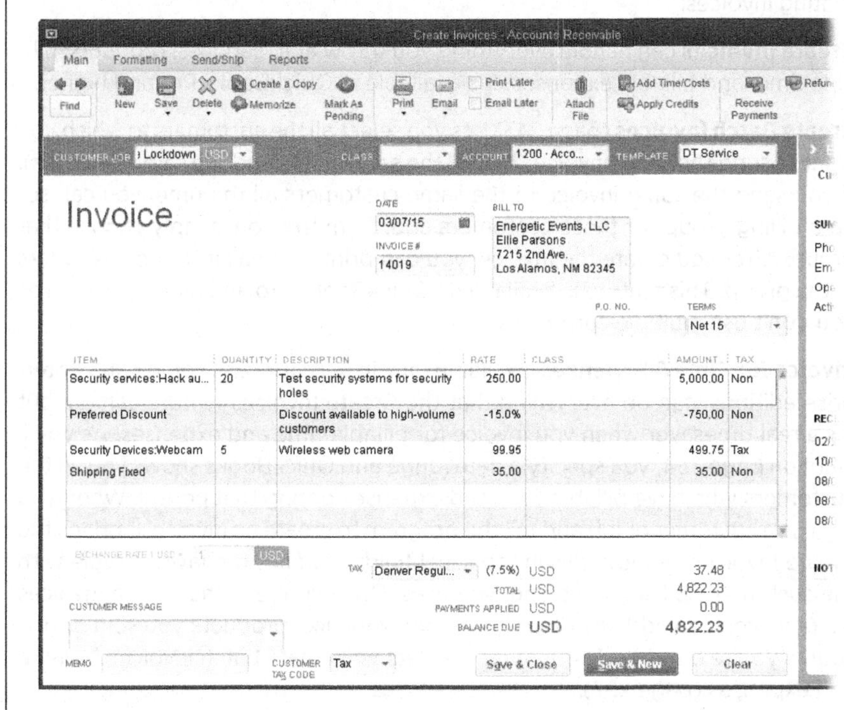

FIGURE 10-1

If you're still getting used to double-entry accounting, balancing the debit and credit amounts for an invoice is a brainteaser.

For example, the items for services and products on the invoice shown here turn up as credits in your income accounts, as in Table 10-2. The discount reduces your income, so it's a debit to the Sales Discounts income account. Although the debits and credits appear in different accounts, the total debit must equal the total credit.

Here's why the amounts post the way they do:

- You sold $5,000 of services and $499.75 of products, which is income. The income values appear as credits to your Services Revenue and Product Revenue accounts to increase your income because you sold something. In this example, the discount is in an income account, so the discount is in the Debit column to *reduce* your income.
- The $37.48 of sales tax you collect is a credit to the Sales Tax Payable account.
- The shipping charge ($35.00) is a credit in your shipping income account to show what you charged for shipping.
- All those credits need to balance against a debit. Because your customer owes you money, the amount owed ($4,822.23) belongs in the Accounts Receivable account, indicated by the debit.
- You also sold some products from inventory. You credit the Inventory account with the cost of the products, $249.78, which decreases the Inventory account's balance. You offset that credit with a debit for the same amount to the Cost of Goods Sold account, which is an income statement account.

Creating Invoices

Depending on which edition of QuickBooks you use, you have up to three features for creating invoices:

- **Create Invoices** can handle everything you throw at it: services, products, billable time, and billable expenses. It's available in QuickBooks Pro and higher.
- **Create Batch Invoices** (page 243) lets you select all the customers to which you want to send the same invoice (that is, the same items and the same amounts). If you send the same invoice to the same customers all the time, you can set up a billing group for those customers and, from then on, simply choose that group. After you create the invoice, you can print or email it to the customers in the group. This feature is available in QuickBooks Pro and higher, as long as you don't use multiple currencies.
- **Invoice for Time & Expenses**, available only in QuickBooks Premier and Enterprise editions, can do everything that the Create Invoices feature can do, but it's a real timesaver when you invoice for billable time and expenses. As you'll learn on page 254, you specify a date range and QuickBooks shows you all the customers who have billable time and expenses during that period. When you choose a customer or job and tell the program to create an invoice, it opens the Create Invoices window, fills in the usual fields, *and* fills the invoice table with the customer's billable time and expenses. Once you're in the Create Invoices window, you can add any other items you want, like products you sold or discounts you're offering. This feature also lets you create batch invoices for time and expenses (page 257).

Invoices tell your customers everything they need to know about what they purchased and what they owe you. If you created customers and jobs with settings such as payment terms, tax item, and sales rep (page 70), as soon as you choose a customer and job in the Create Invoices window's Customer:Job field, QuickBooks fills in many of the fields for you.

Some invoice fields are more influential than others, but they all come in handy at some point. To understand the purpose of the fields on an invoice more easily, you can break the form up into three basic parts (see Figure 10-2). Because the invoices you create for product sales include a few more fields than the ones for services only, the following sections of this chapter use a *product* invoice to explain how to fill in each field you might run into on the invoices you create. These sections also tell you what to do if the information that QuickBooks fills in for you is incorrect.

NOTE If you charge customers based on the progress you've made on a project, invoices are a *little* more complicated, but you'll learn how to handle this situation on page 284.

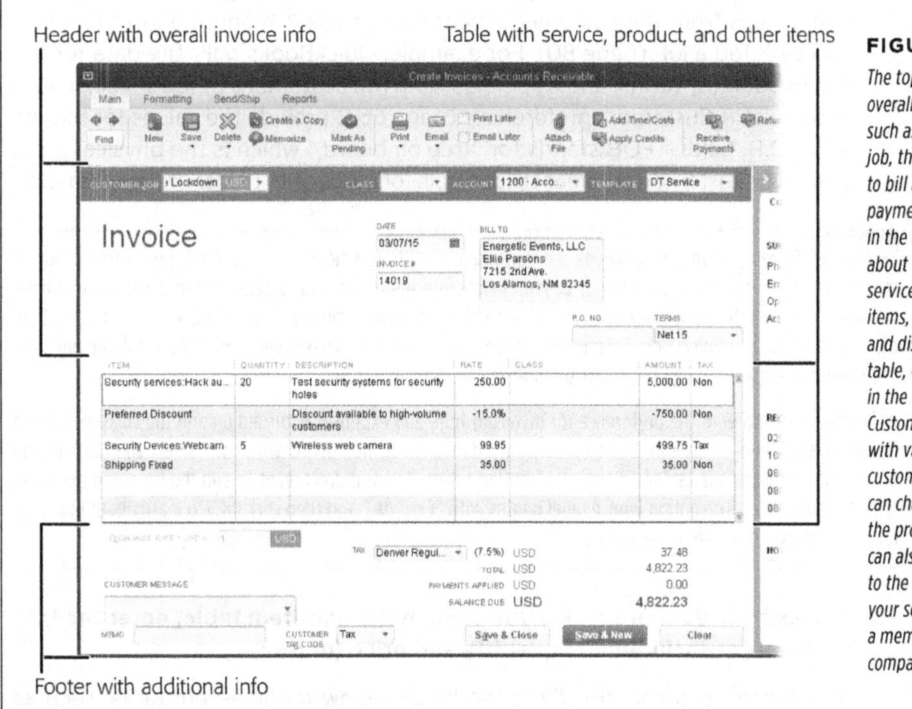

FIGURE 10-2

The top of the invoice has overall sale information, such as the customer and job, the invoice date, who to bill and ship to, and the payment terms. The table in the middle has info about the products and services sold, and other items, such as subtotals and discounts. Below the table, QuickBooks fills in the Tax field and the Customer Tax Code field with values from the customer's record, but you can change any values that the program fills in. You can also add a message to the customer, choose your send method, or type a memo to store in your company file.

Creating an Invoice

In the sections that follow, you'll find details about filling in all the fields on an invoice. (The box on page 229 describes some of the ways nonprofit invoicing differs from for-profit invoicing.) For now, here's the basic procedure for creating and saving one or more invoices by using the Create Invoices feature:

1. **Press Ctrl+I; in the Home Page's Customers panel, click the Create Invoices icon; or, in the Customer Center toolbar, choose New Transactions→Invoices.**

   If you use QuickBooks Pro or if the preference for invoicing time and expenses isn't turned on, then clicking the Home Page's Create Invoices icon opens the Create Invoices window immediately.

   If you use QuickBooks Premier or Enterprise and you've turned on the preference to invoice for time and expenses (page 669), then the Home Page displays the Invoices icon instead of the *Create* Invoices icon. Clicking Invoices displays a shortcut menu with two entries: "Invoice for Time & Expenses" and Create Invoices. Choose Create Invoices to create a regular invoice. Page 254 explains how to use the shortcut menu's other entry to invoice for billable time and expenses.

2. **In the Create Invoices window's Customer:Job box, choose the customer or job associated with the invoice.**

   When you pick a customer or job, QuickBooks fills in many of the invoice fields with values from the customer's record (see page 70) and the job's record if you selected a job (page 80). For example, QuickBooks pulls the data for the Bill To address, Terms, and Rep fields from the customer's or job's record. And your Sales & Customers preferences (page 663) provide the values for the Via and F.O.B. fields. (FOB stands for "free on board," which is the physical point where the customer becomes responsible for damage to or loss of the shipment.)

NOTE Depending on the QuickBooks edition you use and transactions you've entered, a few other windows may open when you choose a customer or job. If the customer or job you selected has an available estimate, the Available Estimates dialog box opens so you can fill in the invoice simply by selecting an estimate, and then clicking OK. If you use QuickBooks Premier and there's an outstanding sales order (page 261), the Available Sales Order window appears so you can select the one you want to invoice.

In QuickBooks Premier, if the preference for invoicing time and expenses is turned on and the customer or job has associated time or expenses, the Billable Time/Costs dialog box opens with the "Select the outstanding billable time and costs to add to this invoice" option selected. If you don't want to add the time and expenses to this invoice, select the option whose label begins with "Exclude," and then click OK. (To learn about invoicing for time and expenses, see page 252.)

3. **For each product or service you sold, in the line-item table, enter the info for the item, including its quantity and price (or rate).**

   If you want, you can also fill in the boxes below the line-item table, such as Customer Message and Memo. You'll rarely need to change the sales tax rate associated with the customer, but you can if necessary.

4. **Maintain your professional image by checking for spelling errors before you send the invoice.**

   To run QuickBooks' spell-checker, at the top of the Create Invoices window, click the Formatting tab, and then click Spelling. (If you checked spelling when you created your customers and invoice items, then the main source of spelling errors will be any edits you've made to item descriptions.) If the spell-checker doesn't work the way you want, then change your Spelling preferences (page 668).

5. **To save the invoice you just created and close the Create Invoices window, click Save & Close.**

   If you're unhappy with the choices you made in the current invoice, click Clear to start over with a fresh, blank invoice. If you have additional invoices to create, click Save & New to save the current invoice and begin another.

NOTE If you create or modify an invoice and then click the Print icon in the Create Invoices window's Main tab, QuickBooks saves the invoice before printing it, which helps prevent financial hanky-panky.

ALTERNATE REALITIES

Invoicing for Nonprofits

For nonprofits, invoices can record the pledges, donations, grants, or other contributions you've been promised.

Invoicing for nonprofits differs from the for-profit world's approach. First of all, many nonprofits don't send invoices to donors. Nonprofits might send reminders to donors who haven't sent in the pledged donations, but they don't add finance charges to late payments.

Moreover, because some donors ask for specific types of reports, nonprofits often use several Accounts Receivable accounts to track money coming from grants, dues, pledges, and other sources. When you have multiple Accounts Receivable accounts, the Create Invoices window includes an Account field so you can choose the appropriate Accounts Receivable account (just like when you work with multiple currencies, as described in the Note on page 233). For example, when you create an invoice for pledges, you'd choose the Pledges Receivable account.

To compensate for this additional field, QuickBooks includes a handy feature when you use multiple Accounts Receivable accounts: It remembers the last invoice number used for each AR account in your QuickBooks chart of accounts, so you can create unique invoice numbering schemes for each of them. For example, if you create an invoice for the Pledges Receivable account and set the Invoice # field to "PL-100," QuickBooks automatically assigns invoice number "PL-101" to the next invoice you create for that account.

Filling in Invoice Header Fields

If you fill in all the fields in your customer and job records (see Chapter 4), QuickBooks takes care of filling in most of the fields in the header section of invoices. Here's what the header fields do and where QuickBooks gets the values it fills in automatically.

CHOOSING THE CUSTOMER OR JOB

The selection you make in the Customer:Job field (shown in Figure 10-3) is your most important choice on any invoice. In addition to billing the correct customer for your work, QuickBooks uses the settings from the customer's or job's record to fill in many of the invoice's fields.

NOTE If you've turned on the preference for multiple currencies, the last column in the Customer:Job drop-down list shows the customer's currency (as shown in Figure 10-3).

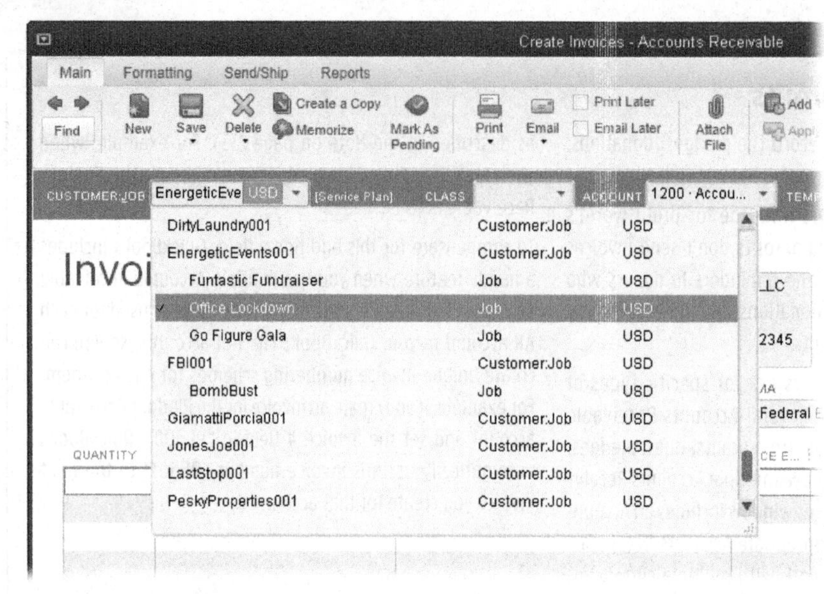

FIGURE 10-3

If you work on different jobs for a customer, click the name of the job, which is indented under the customer's name. If your work for a customer doesn't relate to jobs, just click the customer's name.

The column to the right of the customer and job names provides another way to differentiate customers and jobs: It displays "Customer:Job" for a customer entry, and "Job" for a job entry.

Once you select a customer or job, the panel on the right side of the Create Invoices window shows a summary of the customer's account and recent transactions (Figure 10-4). The Customer tab displays the customer's open balance and the credit limit you've set for that customer so you can see whether the new invoice exceeds that limit. You can also review recent transactions to check whether payments have come in before you send an invoice for finance charges. Any notes that you've entered for the customer appear at the bottom of the panel. Click the > at the panel's top left to expand or collapse it.

NOTE The right-hand panel's Transaction tab shows information about the transaction that's currently displayed in the Create Invoices window. The tab's Summary section shows who created and edited the transaction and when. If there are related transactions, such as a payment or credit memo, they appear in the Related Transactions section.

CHOOSING AN INVOICE TEMPLATE

The option you choose in the Template drop-down list near the top of the Create Invoices window determines which fields appear on your invoices and how they're laid out. For example, you might use two templates: one for printing on your company letterhead and one for invoices you send electronically. Choosing a template *before* doing anything else is the best way to prevent printing the wrong invoice on expensive stationery.

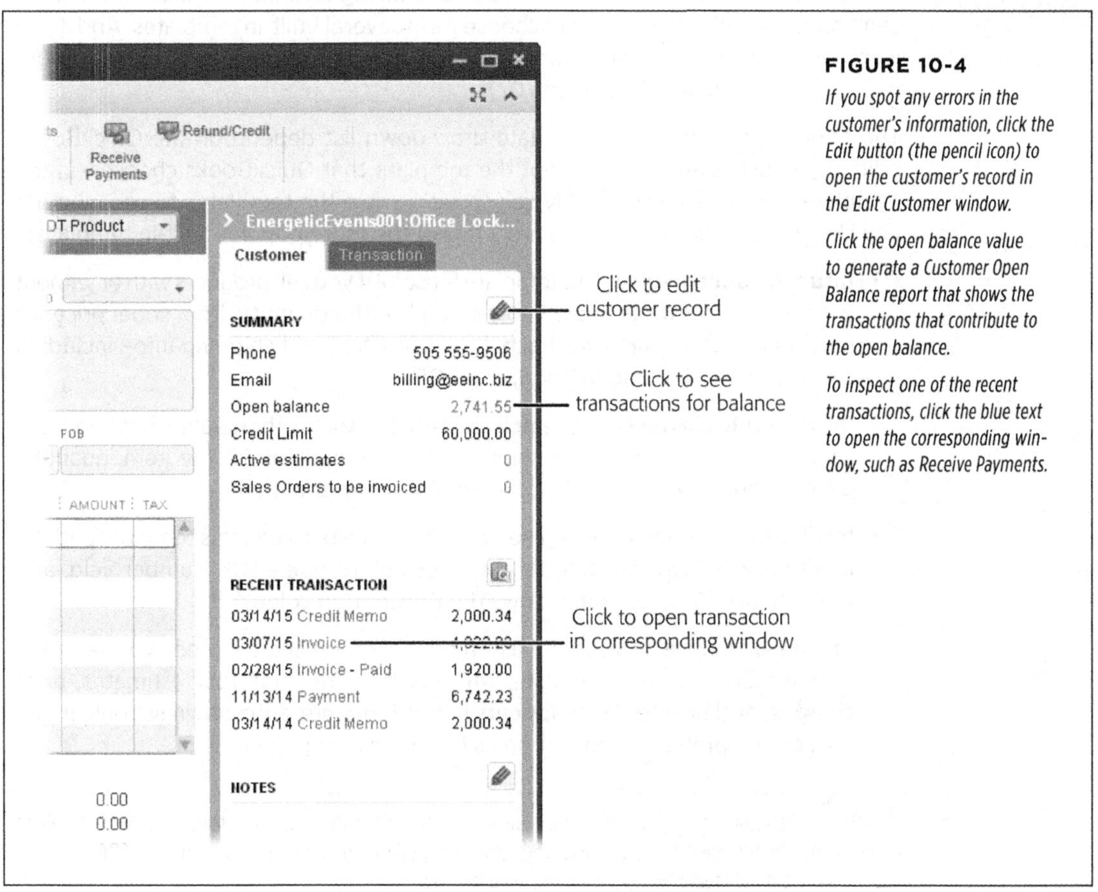

FIGURE 10-4

If you spot any errors in the customer's information, click the Edit button (the pencil icon) to open the customer's record in the Edit Customer window.

Click the open balance value to generate a Customer Open Balance report that shows the transactions that contribute to the open balance.

To inspect one of the recent transactions, click the blue text to open the corresponding window, such as Receive Payments.

QuickBooks remembers which template you chose when you created your last invoice. So if you use only one invoice template, choose it on your first invoice, and the program chooses it for you from then on. But if you switch among invoices, be sure to select the correct template for the invoice you're creating.

NOTE Templates aren't linked to customers. If you pick a template when you create an invoice for one customer, QuickBooks chooses that same template for your next invoice, regardless of which customer it's for.

You can switch templates anytime. When you choose a template, the Create Invoices window displays the appropriate fields and layout. If you've already filled in an invoice, changing the template doesn't throw out the data you entered; QuickBooks simply displays it in the new template. However, QuickBooks won't display settings like your company logo, fonts, and other formatting until you print or preview the invoice (page 308).

Many small companies are perfectly happy with the invoice templates that QuickBooks provides. When you create your first invoice, you might not even think about the layout of the fields. But if you run across a billing task that the current template can't handle, don't panic: You can choose from several built-in templates. And if you want your invoices to reflect your company's style and image, you can create your own custom templates (see page 707).

The options you see in the Template drop-down list depend on the QuickBooks edition you use. Before you accept the template that QuickBooks chooses, in the Template drop-down list, quickly select and review the templates to see whether you like any of them better. Here are a few of the more popular built-in templates:

- **Intuit Product Invoice**. This template is useful if you sell products with or without services. It's set up to show information like the quantity, item code, price for each item, total charge for each item, sales tax, and shipping info—including the ship date, shipping method, and FOB.
- **Intuit Service Invoice**. This template doesn't bother with shipping fields because services are performed, not shipped. It includes fields for the item, quantity, description, rate, amount, tax, and purchase order number.
- **Intuit Professional Invoice**. The only difference between this template and the Intuit Service Invoice is that this one doesn't include a P.O. Number field, and the quantity (Qty) column follows the Description column.
- **Progress Invoice**. If you bill customers based on the progress you've made on their jobs, use this template, which has columns for your estimates, prior charges, and new totals. It appears in the Template drop-down list only if you turn on the preference for progress invoicing (see page 655).

NOTE The Intuit Packing Slip template is included in the Template drop-down list even though it isn't an invoice template. It's listed there because, when you ship products to customers, you can print an invoice *and* packing slip from the Create Invoices window (see page 312).

- **Fixed Fee Invoice**. This template drops the quantity and rate fields, since the invoice shows only the total charge. It includes fields for the date, item, description, tax, and purchase order number.
- **Time & Expense Invoice**. If you bill customers by the hour, this template is the one to use. It includes columns for hours and an hourly rate, and it calculates the resulting total. (The Attorney's Invoice template is identical to this one except in name.)

THE OTHER HEADER FIELDS

As Figure 10-5 shows, QuickBooks can fill in most of the remaining header fields for you. Although the following fields don't appear on every invoice template, here's how to fill in any empty fields or change the ones that QuickBooks didn't complete the way you want:

- **Class**. If you turned on the class-tracking feature (page 140) to categorize your income and expenses in different ways, choose a class for the invoice. If you skip this box and have the class reminder preference turned on, QuickBooks tells you that the box is empty when you try to save the invoice. Although you *can* save the invoice without a class (if classes don't apply to the transaction, say), it's important to assign classes to every class-related transaction if you want your class-based reports to be accurate. For example, if you use classes to track income by partner and save an invoice without a class, the partner who delivered the services on the invoice might complain about the size of her paycheck.

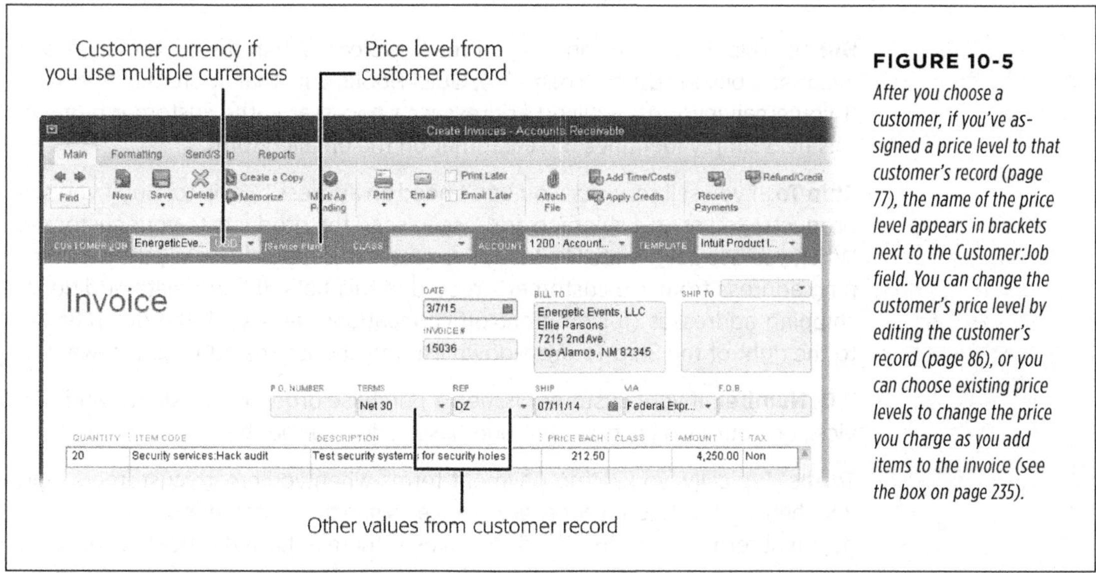

FIGURE 10-5

After you choose a customer, if you've assigned a price level to that customer's record (page 77), the name of the price level appears in brackets next to the Customer:Job field. You can change the customer's price level by editing the customer's record (page 86), or you can choose existing price levels to change the price you charge as you add items to the invoice (see the box on page 235).

NOTE If you work with multiple currencies, then at the top of the Create Invoices window, the Account box appears and shows the Accounts Receivable (AR) account for the invoice's income. QuickBooks creates an additional Accounts Receivable account (page 57) for a currency, such as Account Receivable-EUR, when you assign that currency to the first new customer that uses it and then save the customer record.

- **Date**. Out of the box, QuickBooks fills in the current date here, which is fine if you create invoices when you make sales. But service businesses often send invoices on a schedule—the last day of the month is a popular choice. If you want to get a head start on your invoices, you can change your QuickBooks preferences so the program uses the same date for every subsequent invoice (until you change the date), making your end-of-month invoicing a tiny bit easier. Page 650 tells you how to do that.

- **Invoice #**. When you create your first invoice, type the number that you want to start with. For example, if you'd rather not reveal that this is your first invoice, type a number such as 245. Then, each time you create a new invoice, QuickBooks increases the number in this field by one: 246, 247, and so on.

TIP Press the plus (+) or minus (–) key to increase or decrease the invoice number by one. When you save the current invoice, QuickBooks considers its invoice number the starting point for subsequent numbers.

If your last invoice was a mistake, the best thing to do is to void it (page 294). If you delete it instead, you'll end up with a gap in your invoice numbers. For example, when you delete invoice number 203, QuickBooks has already set the next invoice number to 204. So, if you notice the gap, in the Invoice # box, type the number you want to use to get QuickBooks back on track, and void incorrect invoices from now on.

- **Bill To**. This field is essential if you mail invoices. When the customer record includes a billing address (page 74), QuickBooks puts that address in this field. If you email invoices, a billing address isn't necessary—the customer name in this field simply identifies the customer on the emailed form.
- **Ship To**. If you sell services, you don't need an address to ship to. But if you sell products, you need a shipping address to send the products to your customer. When you use a template like Intuit Product Invoice, QuickBooks puts the shipping address from the customer's record in this field. If you create additional shipping addresses (for different office locations, say), click the down arrow to the right of the Ship To drop-down list and choose the address you want.
- **P.O. Number**. If your customer issued a purchase order for the goods and services on your invoice, type that purchase order number here.
- **Terms**. Typically, you set up payment terms when you create customers, and you then use those terms for every invoice. When the customer's record includes payment terms (page 76), QuickBooks uses them to fill in this field. However, if you decide to change the terms—perhaps due to the customer's failing financial strength—choose a different term here, such as "Due on receipt."

NOTE If QuickBooks fills in fields with incorrect values, make the corrections on the invoice. When you save the invoice, QuickBooks asks if you'd like the new values to appear the next time, as shown in Figure 10-6.

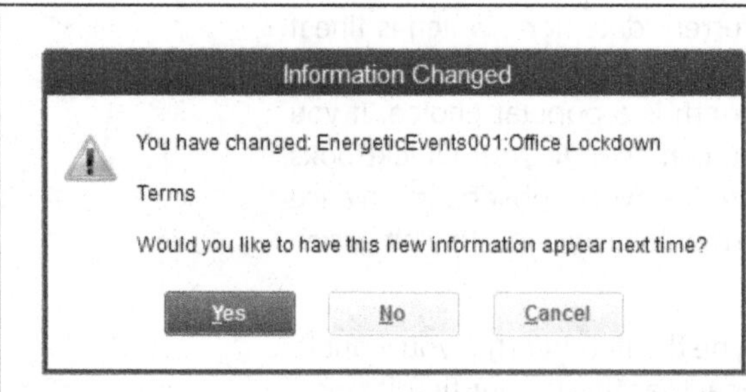

FIGURE 10-6

If you click Yes here, QuickBooks changes the corresponding fields in the customer and job records.

If you click No, it changes the values only on this particular invoice.

- **Rep**. If you assigned a sales rep in the customer's record (page 77), QuickBooks fills in this field for you. If the sales rep changes from invoice to invoice (for instance, when the rep is the person who takes a phone order) and you left the Rep field blank in the customer's record, choose the right person here. Leave the field blank if the transaction doesn't have a sales rep.
- **Ship**. QuickBooks fills in the current date here. If you plan to ship on a different date (when the products arrive from your warehouse, for example), type or choose the correct date.
- **Via**. If you specified a value in the Usual Shipping Method preference (page 663), QuickBooks enters that value here. To choose a different shipping method for this invoice—for instance, when your customer needs the order right away—click this field and select the one you want. (Some templates label this field "Ship Via.")
- **F.O.B**. This stands for "free on board" and signifies the physical point at which the customer becomes responsible for the shipment. That means that if the shipment becomes lost or damaged beyond the FOB point, it's the customer's problem. If you set the Usual FOB preference (page 663), QuickBooks enters that location here. To choose a different FOB for this order, type the location you want.

NOTE Unlike many of the other fields in the invoice header area, the F.O.B. box doesn't include a drop-down list. QuickBooks doesn't keep a list of FOB locations because most companies pick one FOB point and stick with it.

FREQUENTLY ASKED QUESTION

Mysterious Price Changes

One of my Service items costs $150 per hour. But when I created a customer invoice for that item, the Price Each came up as $120. What's going on?

Before you rush to correct that Service item's price, look near the top of the Create Invoices window, to the right of the Customer:Job field. If you see text in square brackets, such as "[Loyalty]," you'll know that you set up your customer with a price level (page 77). Instead of a mistake, this price adjustment on your invoice is actually a clever and convenient feature.

Price levels are percentage increases or decreases that you can apply to the prices you charge. For example, you can set up price levels to give discounts to your high-volume customers or mark up prices for customers known for their frequent use of your customer-service line. To use price levels, you have to turn on the Price Level preference (page 663).

If you assign a price level to a customer, QuickBooks automatically applies that price-level percentage to every item you add to invoices for that customer. The only indication that QuickBooks has applied the price level is the price level's name to the right of the Customer:Job field (and the items' altered prices).

You can also apply price levels to individual items on an invoice. For example, suppose you offer a 20 percent discount on a different item each month. When an item is the monthly special, you can apply the Monthly Special price level to just that item, as shown in Figure 10-7.

When you use price levels, your customers don't see that the price increases or decreases, which means they could take your discounts for granted. So if you want to emphasize the discounts you apply, use a Discount item instead to visibly reduce prices on your invoices (see page 241).

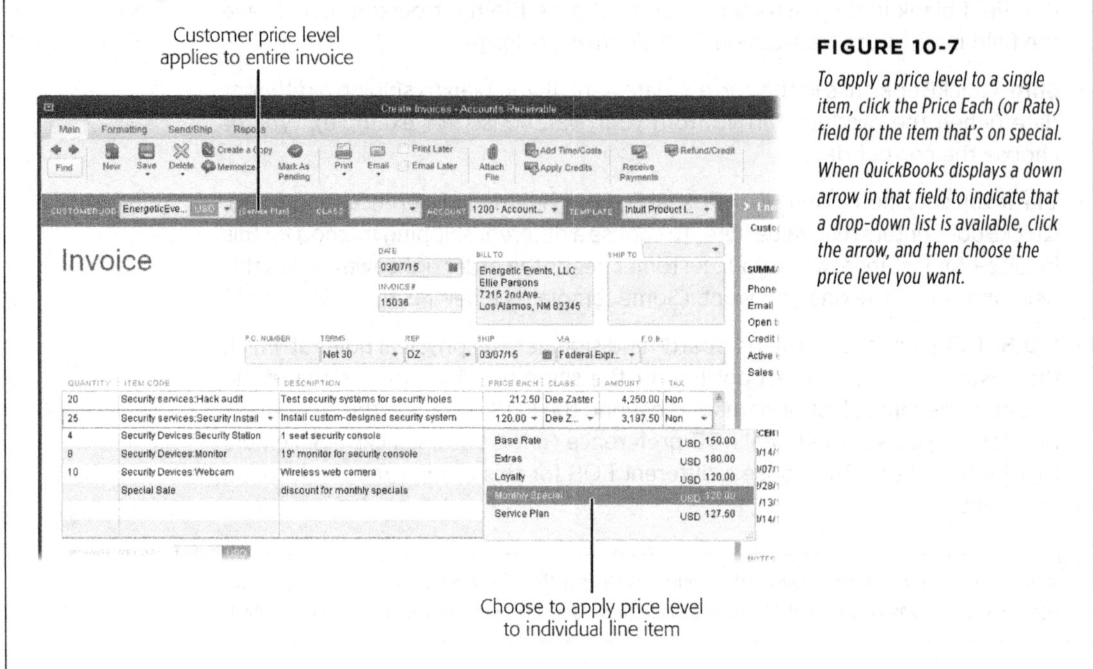
Customer price level applies to entire invoice
Choose to apply price level to individual line item

FIGURE 10-7

To apply a price level to a single item, click the Price Each (or Rate) field for the item that's on special. When QuickBooks displays a down arrow in that field to indicate that a drop-down list is available, click the arrow, and then choose the price level you want.

Entering Invoice Line Items

If you dutifully studied Chapter 5, you know about the different types of items you can add to invoices. This section describes how to fill in a line in the Create Invoices window's line-item table to charge your customers for the things they buy. (The box on page 238 explains a shortcut for speeding up this process.)

The order in which you add items to an invoice is important. For example, when you add a Subtotal item, QuickBooks subtotals all the preceding items up to the previous Subtotal item (if there is one). The program does nothing to check that you add items in the correct order—you can add a Subtotal item as the first line item, even though that does nothing for your invoice. See page 239 for the full scoop on adding Subtotal, Discount, and Other Charge items in the right order.

NOTE If multiple currencies are turned on and you have customers set up to use foreign currencies, when you create an invoice for one of those customers, QuickBooks automatically applies the exchange rate you entered for that currency to item prices and service rates. (See the box on page 461 to learn how to download exchange rates and obtain exchange rates for certain dates.) To use a specific exchange rate in an invoice, fill in the "Exchange Rate 1 [currency] =" box with the exchange rate *before* you add items to the invoice. (If you forgot to change the exchange rate before adding items, delete the lines in the invoice, adjust the exchange rate, and then add the items again.)

The order of columns in the line-item table varies from template to template. This section lists the columns in the order they appear on the Intuit Product Invoice template (shown in Figure 10-8):

- **Quantity**. For products, type a quantity. For services you sell by the hour (or other units of time), type the number of time units. (See page 255 to learn how to select hours from a timesheet.) If you sell services at a flat rate, you can leave this cell blank and simply fill in the Amount cell.

NOTE If you type a quantity for a product that exceeds the number you have on hand, QuickBooks Pro simply warns you that you don't have enough. QuickBooks Premier displays the same warning *and* tells you how many you have on hand, how many are on sales orders (page 260), and the total available.

  Quantity doesn't apply if the item is a discount, subtotal, or sales tax. So if you choose one of these items after entering a quantity, QuickBooks removes the value in the Quantity cell.

- **Item Code**. Click this cell and then choose an item from the drop-down list (see Chapter 5 for details on items). Depending on the info you entered when you created this item (page 106), QuickBooks may fill in the Description and Price Each (or Rate) cells for you.

- **Description**. If you set up inventory items with standard descriptions, QuickBooks automatically puts them in this cell. But you can edit a description to, for example, add details—like changing the generic description "Security service" to the more specific "Nightly rounds every two hours."

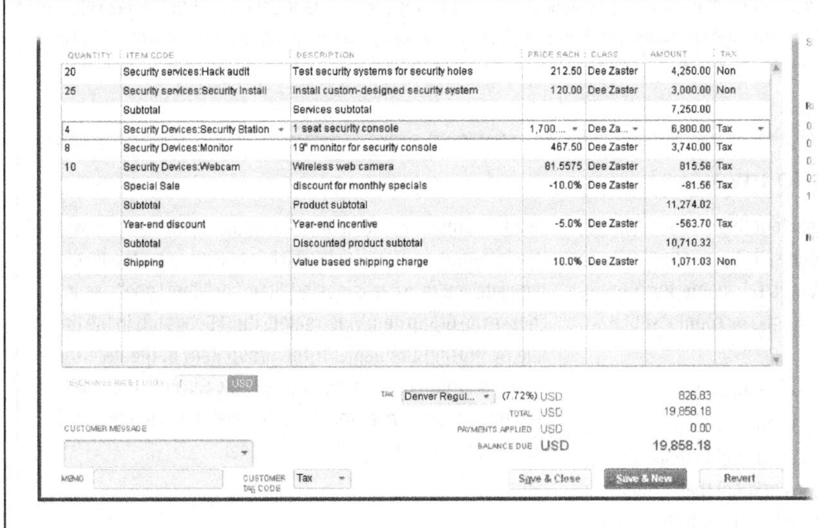

FIGURE 10-8

In the Intuit Product Invoice template, the Quantity column comes first. After you choose an item, make sure to check the value in the Amount cell. If the number looks too large or small, the quantity you entered might not match the item's units. For example, if you charge for developing training materials by the hour but charge for teaching a training class by the day, the quantity for developing training materials has to be in hours and the quantity for teaching in days.

- **Price Each (or Rate)**. Depending on the type of item you're adding to the invoice, QuickBooks goes to the item's record and grabs the value in the Sales Price field or Rate field and puts it here. For example, an Inventory Part item's price always comes from the Sales Price field, whereas Service items use the Rate field (unless a partner or subcontractor performs the work, in which case they use the Sales Price field).
- **Class**. If you turned on classes (page 140), you can pick a class for this item here.
- **Amount**. QuickBooks calculates the value in this cell by multiplying the quantity by the number in the Price Each (or Rate) field. But nothing stops you from simply typing a value in this field, which is exactly what you want for a fixed-fee contract. (For the full story on invoicing for fixed-fee contracts, see the box on page 240.)
- **Tax**. If you turned on the sales tax preference (page 664), QuickBooks displays this cell and fills it in with the taxable status you specified in the item's record, and fills in the Tax box *below* the table with the Sales Tax item you set in the customer's record. (The tax rate for the Sales Tax item you select appears in the Create Invoices window's footer to the right of the Tax box.) With the taxable status of your customers (page 77) and the items you sell (page 109) in place, QuickBooks can automatically handle sales tax on your invoices. For example, when an item is taxable *and* the customer is liable for paying sales tax, the program calculates the total sales tax by adding up all the taxable items on your invoice and multiplying that number by the tax rate in the Tax box below the table; it then displays this value below the table (see Figure 10-8).

TIP If you notice that an item's taxable status isn't correct, don't change the value in the Tax cell. You're better off correcting the customer's or item's tax status so QuickBooks can calculate tax correctly in the future.

POWER USERS' CLINIC

Adding Group Items to Invoices

If the same items frequently appear together on your invoices, you can add all those items in one step by creating a Group item (page 114). Any type of item is fair game for a Group item, so you can include Service items, discounts, subtotals, and other charges.

For example, customers who buy your deluxe vinyl sofa covers also tend to purchase the dirt-magnet front hall runner and the faux-marble garage floor liner. So you could create a Group item (perhaps called the Neat Freak Package) that includes the items for the sofa cover, runner, and liner, with the quantity you typically sell of each item.

To add a Group item to an invoice, in the Create Invoices window's item drop-down list (which, depending on the invoice template you're using, is labeled "Item" or "Item Code"), simply choose the Group item you created. QuickBooks fills in the first line by putting the name of the Group item in the item cell. Then the program adds additional lines (including quantity, description, and price) for the individual items in the group, such as the sofa cover, runner, and liner.

MODIFYING LINE ITEMS

Sometimes you forget to add line items you need. For example, say you've added several services and inventory items to your invoice and then realize that you need Subtotal items following the last service and last inventory items so you can apply a shipping charge to only the inventory items. Or if your customer changes his mind, you can insert or delete a line item. You can also copy and paste line items.

Here's how to modify lines in the line-item table:

- **Insert a line**. Right-click the line above which you want to add a line, and then choose Insert Line from the shortcut menu, as shown in Figure 10-9. If you prefer keyboard shortcuts, press Ctrl+Insert instead.
- **Delete a line**. Right-click the line you want to get rid of and choose Delete Line from the shortcut menu, or press Ctrl+Delete.
- **Copy a line**. Right-click the line you want to copy, and then choose Copy Line from the shortcut menu. Why might you do this? Suppose you filled in a line for a taxable product below the Subtotal item you added for taxable items. Instead of recreating the line item in the right location, it might be quicker to copy this line, and then paste it where it *should* go. Then be sure to delete the original line.
- **Paste a line**. Right-click the line above which you want to paste the copied line and choose Paste Line from the shortcut menu.

QuickBooks adjusts the invoice's lines accordingly.

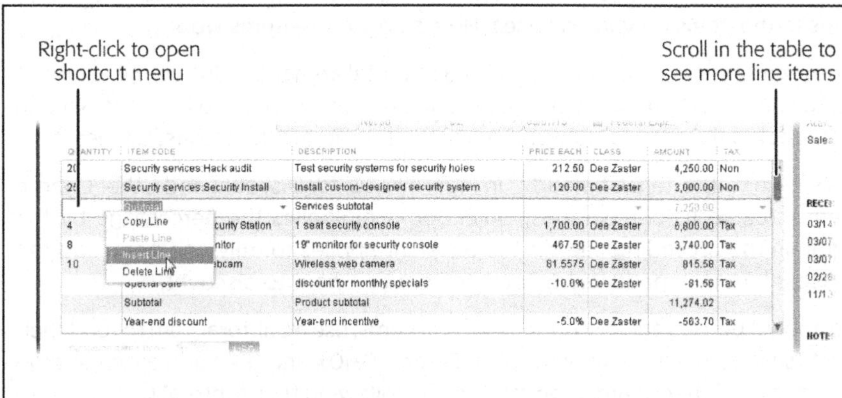
Right-click to open shortcut menu
Scroll in the table to see more line items
Copy Line
Paste Line
Insert Line
Delete Line

FIGURE 10-9

As you add items to the table, QuickBooks adds blank lines (and new pages, if needed) to your invoice. The number of items visible depends on the size of the Create Invoices window. You can also move the scroll bar up or down, or resize the window by maximizing it or dragging a corner of it.

Applying Subtotals, Discounts, and Percentage Charges

When you add Services, Inventory Parts, and Non-inventory Parts (see Chapter 5) to an invoice's line-item table, they don't affect their neighbors in any way. However, when you offer percentage discounts on what you sell or include Other Charge items that calculate shipping as a percentage of price, the order in which you add items becomes crucial. And if you want to apply a percentage calculation like a discount or a shipping fee to several items, you'll need one or more Subtotal items to make the calculation work.

GEM IN THE ROUGH

Invoicing Fixed-Price Contracts

Fixed-price contracts are risky because you have to swallow any cost overruns beyond the fixed price you charge. But if you've sharpened your skills on similar projects in the past and can estimate your costs with reasonable accuracy, fixed-price contracts can provide opportunities for better-than-average profit.

Once you and your customer agree on the fixed price, that amount is all that matters to the customer. Even if *you* track the costs of performing a job, your customer never sees those numbers. In QuickBooks, you can invoice fixed-price contracts in two different ways:

- **Group item**. If you use the same set of services and products for multiple jobs, create a Group item that includes each service and product you deliver and set up the Group item to hide the details of the underlying services and products (page 114). Then add the Group item to your invoice and change the price of the Group item to your fixed price.
- **Service item**. If every fixed-price job is different, create a Service item (page 108) called something like Fixed Fee and leave its Rate field set to 0.00. When you add that item to an invoice, fill in its Rate field with the full amount of the fixed-price contract. Then, when you reach a milestone that warrants a payment, create a progress invoice: In the Quantity column, type the decimal that equates to the percentage completed (such as *.25* for 25 percent), and QuickBooks calculates the payment by multiplying the quantity by the fixed-price amount.

You first learned about Subtotal, Discount, and Other Charge items in Chapter 5. Figure 10-10 shows how to combine them to calculate percentage discounts and add markups to the items on your invoices. Here's how these items work:

- The item labeled "1" in Figure 10-10 is a Subtotal item that adds up the values of all the items up to the *previous* Subtotal item. For example, to keep the Service items out of the product subtotal, add a Subtotal item after the last Service item.
- As shown by the item labeled "2" in Figure 10-10, for Discount and Other Charge items created as percentages, QuickBooks multiplies the percentage by the total on the preceding line. (If the discount applies to only one item, add the Discount item immediately below the item you want to discount.)
- To apply a percentage discount to *several* items, use a Subtotal item to total their cost (such as the item labeled "3" in Figure 10-10), and then add a percentage Discount or Other Charge item on the line following that subtotal (like the item labeled "4" in Figure 10-10).

Here are the steps for arranging Subtotal, Discount, and Other Charge items to calculate percentages on invoice items:

1. **If you want to discount several items on an invoice, enter all those items one after the other.**

   Even though the Balance Due field below the line-item table shows the total of all items, to apply a discount to all of them, you'll need to add a Subtotal item to the line-item table.

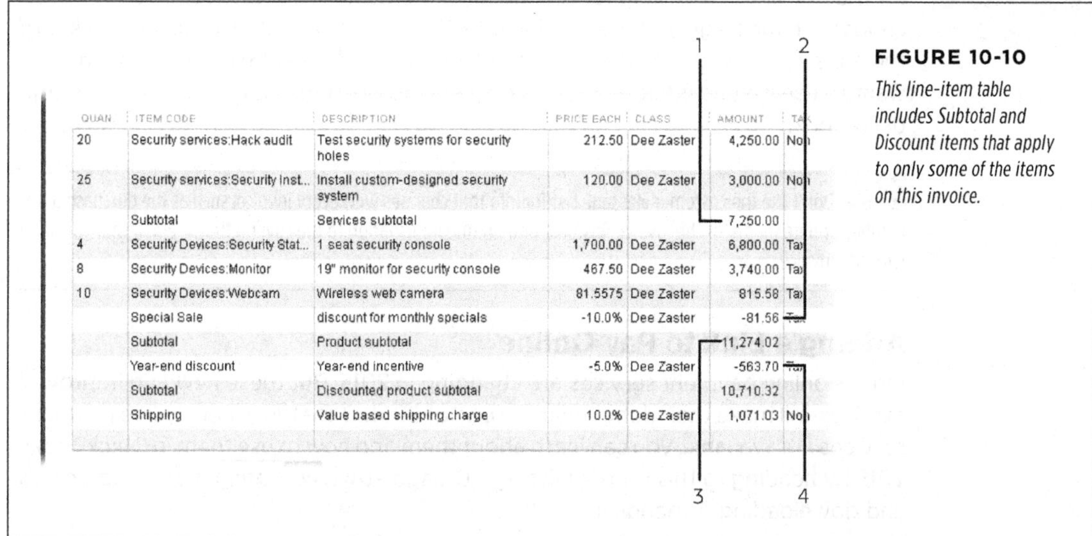

QUAN	ITEM CODE	DESCRIPTION	PRICE EACH	CLASS	AMOUNT	TA
20	Security services:Hack audit	Test security systems for security holes	212.50	Dee Zaster	4,250.00	No
25	Security services:Security Inst...	Install custom-designed security system	120.00	Dee Zaster	3,000.00	No
	Subtotal	Services subtotal			7,250.00	
4	Security Devices:Security Stat...	1 seat security console	1,700.00	Dee Zaster	6,800.00	Ta
8	Security Devices:Monitor	19" monitor for security console	467.50	Dee Zaster	3,740.00	Ta
10	Security Devices:Webcam	Wireless web camera	81.5575	Dee Zaster	815.58	Ta
	Special Sale	discount for monthly specials	-10.0%	Dee Zaster	-81.56	
	Subtotal	Product subtotal			11,274.02	
	Year-end discount	Year-end incentive	-5.0%	Dee Zaster	-563.70	
	Subtotal	Discounted product subtotal			10,710.32	
	Shipping	Value based shipping charge	10.0%	Dee Zaster	1,071.03	No

FIGURE 10-10

This line-item table includes Subtotal and Discount items that apply to only some of the items on this invoice.

2. **Add a Subtotal item after the last item you want to discount, like the Product Subtotal item labeled "3" in Figure 10-10.**

   The Subtotal item adds up all the preceding line items up to the previous Subtotal. For example, in Figure 10-10, the Services Subtotal item (labeled "1") is a subtotal of all the Service items on the invoice. The Product Subtotal item (labeled "3") adds up all items between the Services Subtotal and the Product Subtotal items.

3. **To apply a percentage discount or charge to the subtotal, add a Discount or Other Charge item (labeled "4" in Figure 10-10) to the line immediately below the Subtotal item you added in step 2.**

   If you've already added other items to the invoice, right-click the line immediately below the Subtotal item, and then choose Insert Line from the shortcut menu. That inserts the percentage discount or charge item on the line below the Subtotal item.

4. **If you have additional items that you don't want to include in the discount or charge, add those below the Discount or Other Charge item.**

NOTE These steps also work for Other Charge items that you set up as percentages, such as shipping, as shown at the bottom of Figure 10-10.

Adding a Message to the Customer

Your invoices can include messages to your customers—for instance, thanking them for their business or asking for feedback. In the Customer Message drop-down list, choose the message you want to include. The messages in this drop-down list are the ones you've added to the Customer Message List (page 151). If the message you want to use isn't listed, then click <Add New> to open the New Customer Message dialog box.

TIP Don't use the Customer Message List for info that changes with every invoice, such as the purchase order number or date range for the invoice. Instead, add unique information to the cover letter or email that you send with the invoice.

Adding a Link to Pay Online

Intuit's online payment services are changing in 2015. But these new and improved services will make their debut near the end of 2014. Once these new online payment services are available, you can learn about them and how to use them in QuickBooks 2015 by heading to this book's Missing CD page at *www.missing manuals.com/cds* and downloading Appendix E.

Choosing How to Send the Invoice

On the Create Invoices window's Main tab (if it's not selected, click it in the window's upper-left corner), you'll find two checkboxes that simplify sending invoices to customers: Print Later and Email Later. But these checkboxes don't tell the whole story—you actually have *five* options for sending invoices:

- **Print now**. If you create only the occasional invoice and send it as soon as it's complete, turn off both checkboxes. Then, on the Create Invoices window's Main tab, click Print and follow the instructions on page 313.
- **Print later**. If you want to add the invoice to a queue to print later, turn on the Print Later checkbox. That way you can print all the invoices in the queue, as described on page 313.
- **Email now**. In the Create Invoices window's Main tab, click the Email button (it looks like an envelope) and follow the instructions for emailing invoices on page 319.
- **Email later**. If you want to add the invoice to a queue to email later, turn on the Email Later checkbox. You can then send all the invoices in the queue, as described on page 319.

TIP See page 665 if you want to set a preference that automatically turns on the Email Later checkbox if the customer's Preferred Delivery Method is email. Page 665 also explains how QuickBooks works with email programs.

- **Print *and* email later**. Turn on both checkboxes if you want to email invoices to get the ball rolling and then follow up with paper copies.

If you're sending an invoice for products you've sold, you also have to ship those products to your customer. See the box below to learn a convenient and money-saving way to ship products.

Adding a Memo to Yourself

The Create Invoices window includes a Memo box, which works just like Memo boxes throughout QuickBooks. You can use it to remind yourself about something special on the invoice or to summarize the transaction. For example, if the invoice is the first one for a new customer, you can note that in the Memo box. The memo won't print on the invoices you send to your customers. However, it *does* appear on your sales reports and customer statements, so be careful what you type here.

UP TO SPEED

Shipping Products

If you sell products, making regular runs to the FedEx or UPS office gets old quickly. But sitting quietly within QuickBooks is a free service that could change the way you ship packages.

The program's Shipping Manager feature lets you sign up for shipping services and start sending out packages right away. You can print FedEx, UPS, and U.S. Postal Service shipping labels; schedule pickups; and even track package progress right in QuickBooks. Shipping Manager fills in shipping labels with customer addresses from your QuickBooks invoices, sales receipts, or customer records. All you pay are the FedEx, UPS, or postal service charges on your shipment.

Here's where you can find Shipping Manager:

- If you're creating an invoice for products you plan to ship, at the top of the Create Invoices or Sales Receipt window, click the Send/Ship tab, and then click the button for the shipping method you want to use. In the drop-down menu that appears, choose what you want to do, such as ship a package, schedule a pickup, or track a package that's already on its way.
- Choose File→Shipping, and then choose Ship FedEx Package, Ship UPS Package, or Ship USPS Package.

The first time you choose a shipping action, such as Ship FedEx Package, a setup wizard steps you through creating an account for that shipping company.

NOTE The Open Invoices report (Reports→Customers & Receivables→Open Invoices) is handy when you want to see all the invoices for which you haven't yet received payment. It lists all the invoices for each customer and job, when they're due, and their open balances. If the invoices are overdue, the Aging column shows just how late they are. Income Tracker (page 338) is another way to check up on upcoming or overdue income.

Creating Batch Invoices

If you send invoices with the same items and the same quantities to many of your customers, QuickBooks can save you lots of time. Instead of creating individual invoices for each customer, you can set up a single *batch invoice* and send it to as many customers as you want. And you can speed things up even more by creating a billing group that includes all the customers that receive the invoice, so you don't have to re-select them each time you send a batch invoice.

NOTE You can't use the batch invoice feature if you have multiple currencies turned on (page 656). That's why, when that preference is turned on, the Create Batch Invoices option doesn't appear in the Customers menu.

Before You Create Your First Batch Invoice

Batch invoices use the payment terms, sales tax rates, and send methods you specify for each customer, so be sure to fill in these fields in customers' records before you create your first batch invoice. These fields are on the Payment Settings, Sales Tax Settings, and Additional Info tabs of the Create Customer and Edit Customer windows; they're explained on page 75, page 77, and page 77, respectively. The easiest way to find and fill in any missing values is with the Add/Edit Multiple List Entries window (page 127).

Setting Up a Batch Invoice

Here's how to create a batch invoice for several customers:

1. **Choose Customers→Create Batch Invoices.**

   The Batch Invoice window opens (Figure 10-11).

NOTE If this is your first time using Create Batch Invoices, the "Is your customer info set up correctly?" message box appears, reminding you that you need to fill in terms, sales tax, and send method settings for your batch invoice customers. Click OK to close it and open the Batch Invoice window. If you need to fill in information for your customers, close the Batch Invoice window and choose Lists→Add/Edit Multiple List Entries to open the Add/Edit Multiple List Entries window to complete your customers' records.

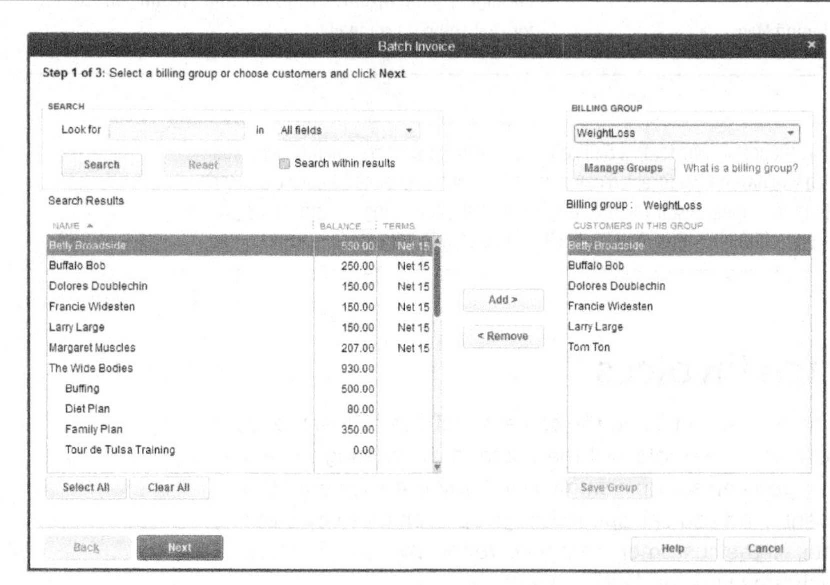

FIGURE 10-11

You can rename or delete the billing groups you create by clicking Manage Groups.

To select a different billing group, choose it from the Billing Group drop-down list. If you modify the customers in the list, click Save Group to update the billing group with the current set of customer names.

2. **To add individual customers, select them in the Batch Invoice window's Search Results list, and then click Add to add them to the Customers In This Group box on the window's right side. To add a group of customers, choose an existing group from the Billing Group drop-down list.**

   If you select individual customers, you can choose adjacent names by clicking the first customer's name and then Shift-clicking the last customer's name. You can also Ctrl-click each customer name you want to select.

   If you choose a billing group, the name of the group appears above the Customers In This Group box, and the individual names appear in the box itself, as shown in Figure 10-11. (The box on page 246 explains how to create billing groups.)

NOTE If you add individual customers *and* a billing group to the Customers In This Group list, when you click away from the list, a Batch Invoice message box asks if you want to save the changes to the billing group. Click Yes to add the individual customers to this billing group and use the full list for the batch invoice. Click No to use the list of customers for this batch invoice while leaving the saved billing group as it is. Or click Cancel to return to the Batch Invoice window to make additional changes.

---

3. **After you add the appropriate customers to the Customers In This Group list, click Next.**

   On the "Step 2 of 3" screen that appears, QuickBooks automatically puts today's date in the Date box and displays a table for the next step in the process: adding items to the invoice.

4. **To use a different date, choose it in the Date box.**

   You can also choose a different invoice template from the Template drop-down list.

5. **In the line-item table (Figure 10-12), fill in the items you want to add to the invoice just as you do for a regular invoice (page 226).**

   You can add any item from your Item List to a batch invoice.

6. **After you fill in the items for the invoice, click Next.**

   The "Step 3 of 3" screen lists the customers who will receive the invoice, including their terms, send methods, tax info, and other information. If you notice any errors or omissions, click Back to correct them.

7. **When everything looks good, click Create Invoices.**

   QuickBooks creates invoices for the selected customers. The Batch Invoice Summary dialog box appears and shows how many invoices are set up to print and how many to email, based on the customers' preferred delivery methods. (The dialog box mentions the customer's Preferred Send Method, but the field in the customer record is actually labeled "Preferred Delivery Method.") If the Preferred Delivery Method for any of the customers is set to None, the dialog box's "unmarked" entry shows how many invoices aren't marked to be mailed or emailed; you can send them later by choosing File→Send Forms or File→Print Forms (page 312).

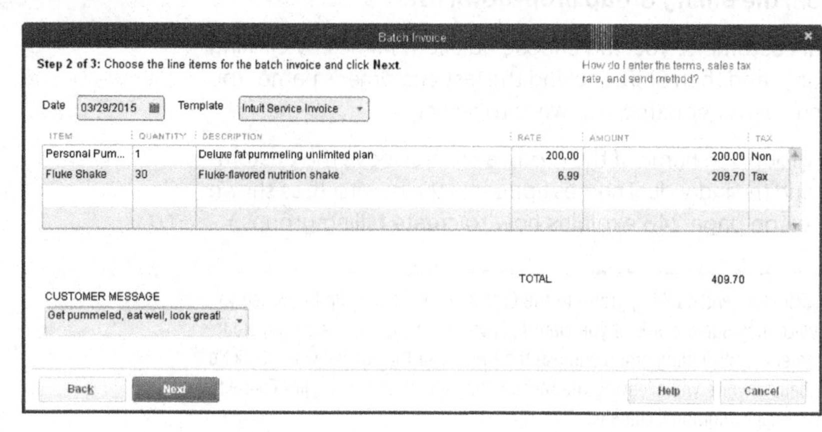

FIGURE 10-12

Fill in the items for the batch invoice as you do the line items in the Create Invoices window. (The exact fields you see in the table depend on the invoice template you're using.)

TIP You can view or change each customer's delivery method in the Customer Center. Simply right-click the customer's name and choose Edit. Then click the Payment Settings tab to see the customer's current delivery-method setting.

8. **Click Print to print the invoices marked to print; click Email to send the invoices marked to be emailed.**

   If you want to print or email the invoices later, click Close. Then you can print or email them by choosing File→Print Forms→Invoices or File→Send Forms.

UP TO SPEED

Creating a Billing Group

Billing groups make it easy to select all the customers who receive the same batch invoice. Once you set up a billing group, you can select it in the Batch Invoice window, and QuickBooks automatically adds all the customers in it to the Customers In This Group box in one fell swoop.

Here's how to create a billing group:

1. In the Batch Invoice window (Customers→Create Batch Invoices), before you select customer names, in the Billing Group drop-down list, choose <Add New>.
2. In the Group Name dialog box, type a name of the group (such as *WeightLoss* for all the customers on your monthly diet plan, for example), and then click Save.
3. In the Batch Invoice window's Search Results list, Ctrl-click all the customers you want to add to the group, and then click Add to copy their names to the Customers In This Group box.
4. Below the Customers In This Group box, click the Save Group button.

QuickBooks saves your new billing group so you can use it again simply by selecting it in the Batch Invoice window.

Deposits, Down Payments, and Retainers

Deposits, down payments, and retainers are all *prepayments*: money that customers give you that you haven't actually earned yet. For example, a customer might give you a down payment to reserve a spot in your busy schedule. Receiving money for something you didn't do feels good, but don't make the mistake of considering that money yours. Until you perform services or deliver products to earn that money, the down payment is more like a loan from the customer than income. Prepayments belong to your customers until you earn them, and they require a bit more care than payments you receive for completed work and delivered products. This section explains how to manage the intricacies of customer prepayments.

Setting Up QuickBooks for Prepayments

If you accept prepayments of any kind, you need an account in your chart of accounts to keep that money separate from your income. You also need an item that you can add to your invoices to deduct prepayments from what your customers owe:

- **Prepayment account**. Because unearned money from a customer is like a loan, create an Other Current Liability account in your chart of accounts (see page 57) to hold prepayments. Call it something like Customer Prepayments.

- **Prepayment item**. Create a Prepayment item in your Item List, as shown in Figure 10-13.

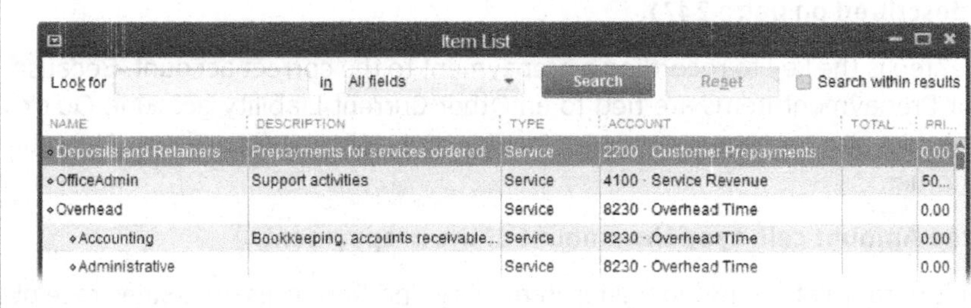

FIGURE 10-13

Whether you accept deposits or retainers for services or products, create a Service item for these prepayments. When you create this item, assign it to the prepayment account you created.

Recording Prepayments

When a customer hands you a check for a deposit or a down payment, the first thing you should do is wait until she's out of earshot to yell, "Yippee!" The second thing is to record the prepayment in QuickBooks. You haven't done any work yet, so there's no invoice to apply the payment to. Fortunately, a sales receipt can not only record a prepayment in QuickBooks: when you print it, it also acts as a receipt for your customer. Here's how to create one:

1. **Make sure the Sales Receipts preference is turned on.**

   If you don't see a Create Sales Receipts icon in the Home Page's Customers panel or an Enter Sales Receipts entry in the Customers menu, choose

Edit→Preferences→Desktop View, and then click the Company Preferences tab. Turn on the Sales Receipts checkbox, and then click OK.

2. **On the Home Page, click the Create Sales Receipts icon (or choose Customers→Enter Sales Receipts).**

   QuickBooks opens the Enter Sales Receipts window to a blank receipt.

3. **In the Customer:Job box, choose the customer or job from which you received the prepayment.**

   QuickBooks fills in some of the fields, such as the customer's address in the Sold To box, with information from the customer's record.

4. **Fill in the other header boxes as you would for a regular sales receipt (see page 362).**

   If you use classes, in the Class box, choose a class to track the prepayment. If you have a customized template just for prepayments (page 707), in the Template drop-down list, select that template. In the Date box, choose the date that you received the prepayment. In the Payment Method box, pick the method the customer used to pay you. If the customer paid by check, in the Check No. box, type the check number for reference.

5. **As shown in Figure 10-14, in the window's table, click the first Item cell and use its drop-down list to choose the Prepayment item you set up (for example, a Service item called something like "Deposits and Retainers," as described on page 247).**

   This step is the key to recording a prepayment to the correct account. Because your Prepayment items are tied to an Other Current Liability account, QuickBooks doesn't post the payment as income, but rather as money owed to your customer.

6. **In the Amount cell, type the amount of the prepayment.**

   Don't bother with entering values in the Qty and Rate cells—the sales receipt simply records the total that the customer gave you. You'll add the details for services and products later when you create invoices.

7. **Complete the sales receipt as you would any other payment form.**

   For example, add a message to the customer, if you like. At the top of the Enter Sales Receipt window, click Email or Print to provide the customer with a receipt. If you turned off the preference to use the Undeposited Funds account (page 657), you'll see a Deposit To box. In this box, choose Undeposited Funds if you plan to hold the payment and deposit it with others; if you're going to race to the bank as soon as you record the transaction, choose your bank account instead. (If you turn on the preference to use the Undeposited Funds account, QuickBooks automatically deposits payments to the Undeposited Funds account, so the Deposit To box *doesn't* appear in the Enter Sales Receipt window.)

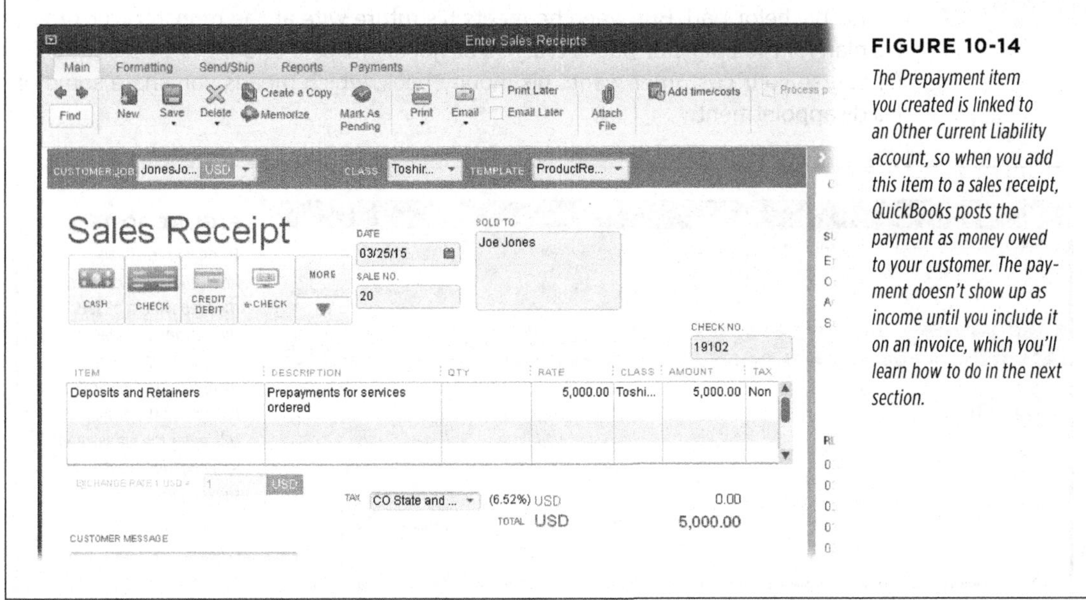

FIGURE 10-14

The Prepayment item you created is linked to an Other Current Liability account, so when you add this item to a sales receipt, QuickBooks posts the payment as money owed to your customer. The payment doesn't show up as income until you include it on an invoice, which you'll learn how to do in the next section.

8. **Click Save & Close.**

   QuickBooks posts the payment to your prepayment account and closes the Enter Sales Receipts window.

Applying a Deposit, Down Payment, or Retainer

When you finally start to deliver stuff to customers who've paid up front, you invoice them as usual. But the invoice you create needs one additional line item that deducts the customer's prepayment from the invoice balance.

Create the invoice as you normally would with items for the services, products, charges, and discounts (page 226). After you've added all *those* items, add the item for the prepayment and fill in the Amount cell with a *negative* number to deduct the prepayment from the invoice amount, as shown in Figure 10-15. Once you apply the prepayment to an invoice in this way, QuickBooks transfers the money from your prepayment account to reduce the customer's Accounts Receivable balance.

NOTE If the charges on the invoice are less than the amount of the customer's deposit, deduct only as much of the deposit as you need; you can apply the rest of it to the next invoice.

Refunding Prepayments

Deposits and down payments don't guarantee that your customers will follow through with their projects or orders. For example, say a customer makes a deposit on decor for his bachelor pad. But when he meets his future wife at the monster truck rally, his plan for the bachelor pad is crushed as flat as the cars under the trucks' wheels. Of course your customer wants his money back, which means you share some of his disappointment.

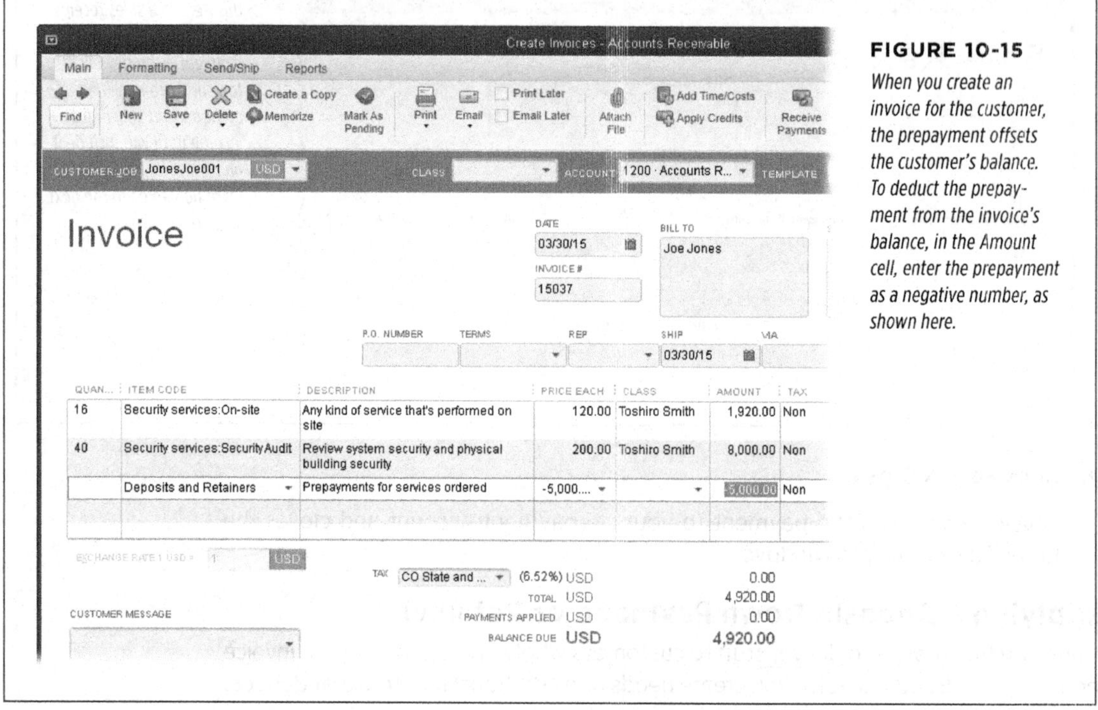

FIGURE 10-15

When you create an invoice for the customer, the prepayment offsets the customer's balance. To deduct the prepayment from the invoice's balance, in the Amount cell, enter the prepayment as a negative number, as shown here.

Your first step is to determine how much money the customer gets back. For example, if a customer cancels an order before you've purchased the products, you might refund the entire deposit. However, if the leopard-print wallpaper has already arrived, you might keep part of the deposit as a restocking fee.

After you decide how much of the deposit you're going to keep, you have to do two things: move the portion of the deposit that you're *keeping* from the prepayment account to an income account, and then refund the rest of the deposit. Here's how to do both:

1. **Create an invoice for the customer or job by choosing Customers→Create Invoices, and then, in the Customer:Job box, choosing the customer.**

   You create an invoice to turn the deposit you're keeping into income.

2. **In the first Item cell, choose an item related to the canceled job or order.**

   For example, if you're keeping a deposit for a product you ordered, choose the item for that product. If the deposit was for services you planned to perform, choose the appropriate Service item instead.

3. **In the item's Amount cell, type the amount of the deposit that you're keeping.**

   Because these items are connected to income accounts (see Chapter 5), this first line in the invoice is where you assign the amount of the deposit that you're keeping to the correct income account for the products or services you sold.

4. **In the table's second line, add the Prepayment item and fill in the amount of the deposit you're keeping as a negative amount, as shown in Figure 10-16.**

   This item removes the amount of the deposit you're keeping from your liability account so you no longer owe the customer that money.

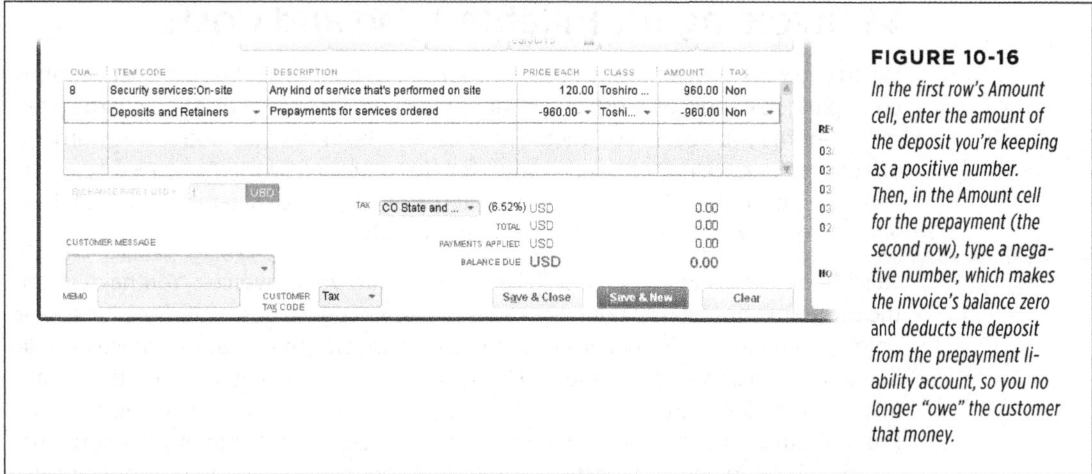

FIGURE 10-16

In the first row's Amount cell, enter the amount of the deposit you're keeping as a positive number. Then, in the Amount cell for the prepayment (the second row), type a negative number, which makes the invoice's balance zero and deducts the deposit from the prepayment liability account, so you no longer "owe" the customer that money.

5. **Click Save & Close.**

   QuickBooks removes the deposit you're keeping from the prepayment liability account and posts that money to the income account associated with the item you selected in step 2. If you're keeping the whole deposit, you're done. But if you aren't keeping the entire amount, you have to refund the rest to the customer, so continue on to the next step.

6. **To refund the rest of the deposit, create a credit memo for the remainder (page 288).**

   In the Create Credit Memos/Refunds window's table, add the Prepayment item you used in the invoice. In the Amount cell, type the amount that you're refunding.

7. **Click Save & Close.**

   QuickBooks removes the remaining deposit amount from your prepayment liability account. Because the credit memo has a credit balance, QuickBooks opens the Available Credit dialog box.

8. **In the Available Credit dialog box, choose the "Give a refund" option, and then click OK.**

   QuickBooks opens the Issue a Refund dialog box and fills in the customer or job, the account from which the refund is issued, and the refund amount. If you want to refund the deposit from a different account, choose a different refund payment method or account.

9. **Click OK to create the refund.**

All that's left for you to do is mail the refund check.

Invoicing for Billable Time and Costs

When you work on a time-and-materials contract, you charge the customer for labor costs plus job expenses. Cost-plus contracts are similar except that you charge a fee on top of the job costs. Contracts like these are both low risk and low reward—in effect, you're earning an hourly wage for the time you work. For these types of contracts, it's critical that you capture all the expenses associated with the job or you'll lose some of the profit that the contract offers.

QuickBooks helps you get those billable items into your invoices. You have to tell the program about every hour worked and every expense you incur for a customer or job. But once you do that, it's easy to build an invoice that captures these billable items. You can add billable time and costs to an invoice when it's open in the Create Invoices window. And, when you open the Create Invoices window in QuickBooks Pro or Premier and choose a customer or job, the program reminds you about outstanding billable time and costs. QuickBooks Premier also has a feature specifically for creating invoices for billable time and costs. The following sections tell you how to perform all these tasks.

Setting Up Invoicing for Time and Costs

In some industries, like consulting and law, invoicing for time and expenses is the norm. But before you can pop your billable time and expenses into QuickBooks invoices, you first need to record them as billable items and assign them to the correct customer or job. Here are the billable items you can add to invoices and the chapters that tell you about them:

- **Billable time**. Chapter 8 (page 169) describes how to track billable time and assign hours to a customer or job.
- **Mileage**. Chapter 8 (page 180) describes how to track mileage and assign billable mileage to a customer or job.

- **Purchases and expenses related to a customer or job.** Reimbursable expenses include products you purchase specifically for a job, services performed by a subcontractor, and other expenses such as shipping and postage. Chapter 9 describes how to make items and expenses reimbursable to a customer or job (page 192) as you enter bills, checks, or credit card charges in QuickBooks.

Adding Billable Time and Costs to Invoices

If you use QuickBooks Pro or Premier, you can add billable time and costs directly in the Create Invoices window. Here's how:

1. **Press Ctrl+I or choose Customers→Create Invoices to open the Create Invoices window.**
2. **In the Customer:Job drop-down list, choose the customer or job you want to invoice.**

   If the customer or job has outstanding billable time or expenses, the Billable Time/Costs dialog box opens and automatically selects the "Select the outstanding billable time and costs to add to this invoice?" option, as shown in Figure 10-17 (foreground).

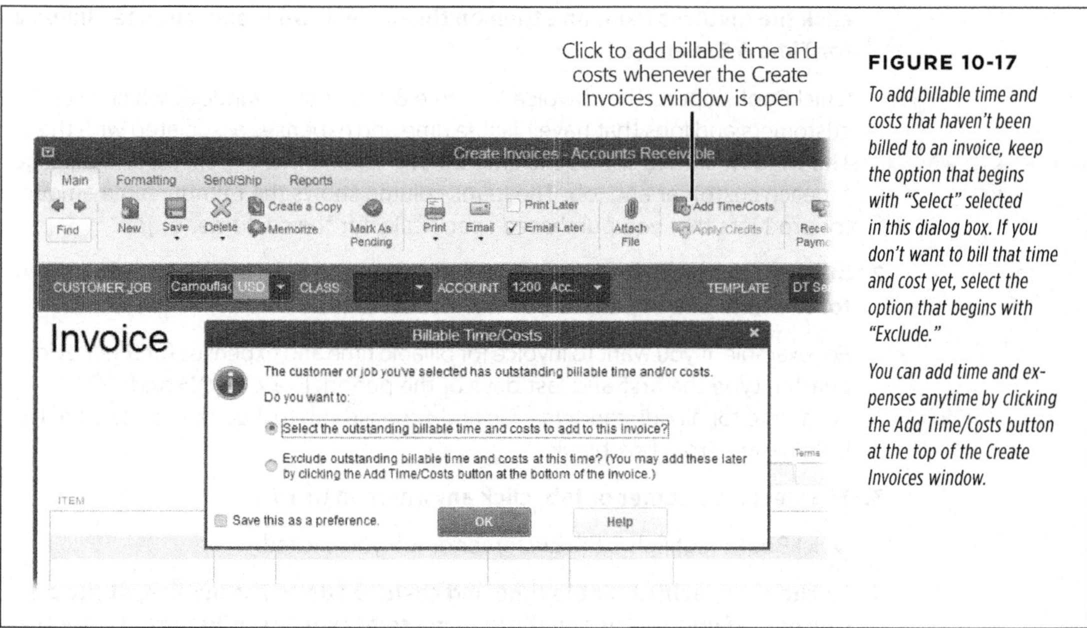

FIGURE 10-17

To add billable time and costs that haven't been billed to an invoice, keep the option that begins with "Select" selected in this dialog box. If you don't want to bill that time and cost yet, select the option that begins with "Exclude."

You can add time and expenses anytime by clicking the Add Time/Costs button at the top of the Create Invoices window.

3. **In the Billable Time/Costs dialog box, click OK.**

   The "Choose Billable Time and Costs" dialog box opens.

NOTE You can open the "Choose Billable Time and Costs" dialog box anytime the Create Invoices window is open by clicking the Add Time/Costs button on the window's Main tab.

4. **Select the time and costs you want to add to the invoice by following the instructions that begin on page 255.**

Using Invoice for Time & Expenses

If you use QuickBooks Premier or Enterprise, the program has a special "Invoice for Time & Expenses" feature for adding billable items to invoices. If you turn on this feature, it shows you every customer with billable time and expenses waiting to be invoiced and how much there is of each type, so it's easy to see all your outstanding billable hours and reimbursable expenses.

To turn on this feature, choose Edit→Preferences→Time & Expenses. On the Company Preferences tab, turn on the "Create invoices from a list of time and expenses" checkbox. (Leave this checkbox turned off if invoicing for time and expenses is the exception rather than the rule. If you leave it off, you can still add time and other costs to an invoice in the Create Invoices window, as described in the previous section.)

Here's how to use the "Invoice for Time & Expenses" feature to create an invoice for billable time and expenses (see page 243 to learn how to create a *batch* of billable invoices):

1. **Choose Customers→"Invoice for Time & Expenses" or, on the Home Page, click the Invoices icon, and then on the drop-down menu, choose "Invoice for Time & Expenses."**

   QuickBooks opens the "Invoice for Time & Expenses" window, which lists the customers and jobs that have billable time and expenses associated with them. The window's table shows the amount of billable time, expenses, and mileage for each customer and job. The Items column shows the reimbursable amount for products that you purchased specifically for the customer or job.

2. **In the Date Range From and To boxes, type the starting and ending dates for the time and expenses you want to invoice.**

   For example, if you want to invoice for billable time and expenses for the previous quarter, type the first and last days of the period, like *1/1/2015* and *3/31/2015*. To invoice for all outstanding time and expenses up to a certain date, leave the Date Range From box blank.

3. **To select a customer or job, click anywhere in its row.**

   QuickBooks highlights the customer or job you clicked.

4. **To choose specific billable time and costs to add to the invoice, at the bottom of the window, turn on the "Let me select specific billable costs for this Customer:Job" checkbox.**

   This checkbox is active only when one customer or job is selected. If you select more than one customer or job (see page 243 to learn how to create a batch of time and expenses invoices), this checkbox is grayed out. If you leave this checkbox turned off, the program adds *all* billable time and costs to the invoice.

5. **Click Create Invoice.**

   If you turned on the "Let me select specific billable costs for this Customer:Job" checkbox, QuickBooks opens the "Choose Billable Time and Costs" dialog box shown in Figure 10-18, which includes tabs for time, expenses, mileage, and items (products). (This dialog box is the same one you see if you click Add Time/Costs in the Create Invoices window. Proceed to page 255 to learn how to add specific billable time and costs to an invoice.)

   If you left the "Let me select specific billable costs for this Customer:Job" checkbox turned off, the Create Invoices window opens with your invoice already filled out. All you have to do is save it by clicking Save & Close.

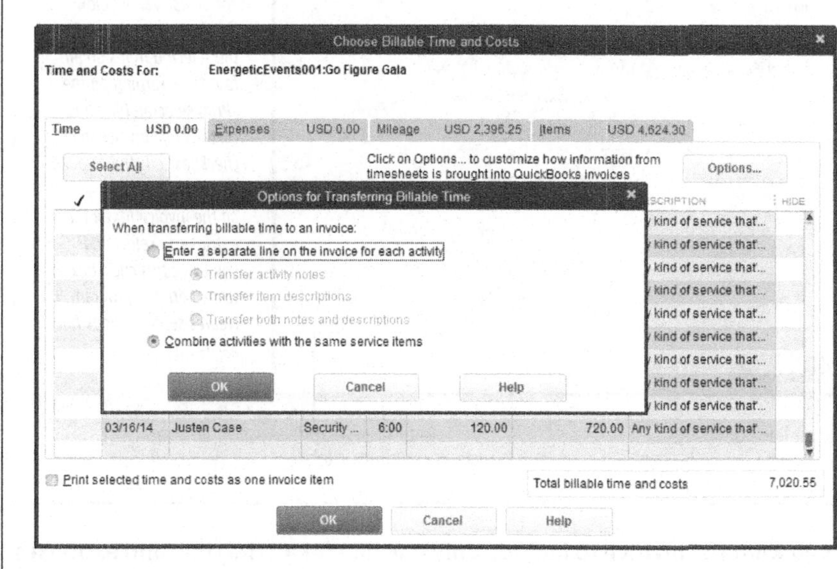

FIGURE 10-18

On the "Choose Billable Time and Costs" dialog box's Time tab (background), click the Options button to tell QuickBooks how to handle different activities. In the "Options for Transferring Billable Time" dialog box (foreground), the program automatically selects the setting that displays the total hours for each Service item. Choose the other setting if you want QuickBooks to add a separate line for each activity (to show the hours worked each day, for instance); with each activity on its own line, you can transfer activity descriptions, notes, or both to the invoice.

Selecting Billable Time and Costs

Regardless of how you open the "Choose Billable Time and Costs" dialog box (Figure 10-18), the steps for selecting the billable time and costs to add to an invoice are the same. Here's what you do:

1. **In the "Choose Billable Time and Costs" dialog box, to select all the entries on the Time tab, click the Select All button.**

   QuickBooks adds a checkmark in the first column for every activity and shows the total value of the entries you've selected on that tab. As you select billable costs on other tabs, each tab shows the total value of the entries you selected, as shown in Figure 10-19. The "Total billable time and costs" value below the table is the total of *all* the selected items on all four tabs.

To select or deselect a single row, click its checkmark cell to toggle it on or off.

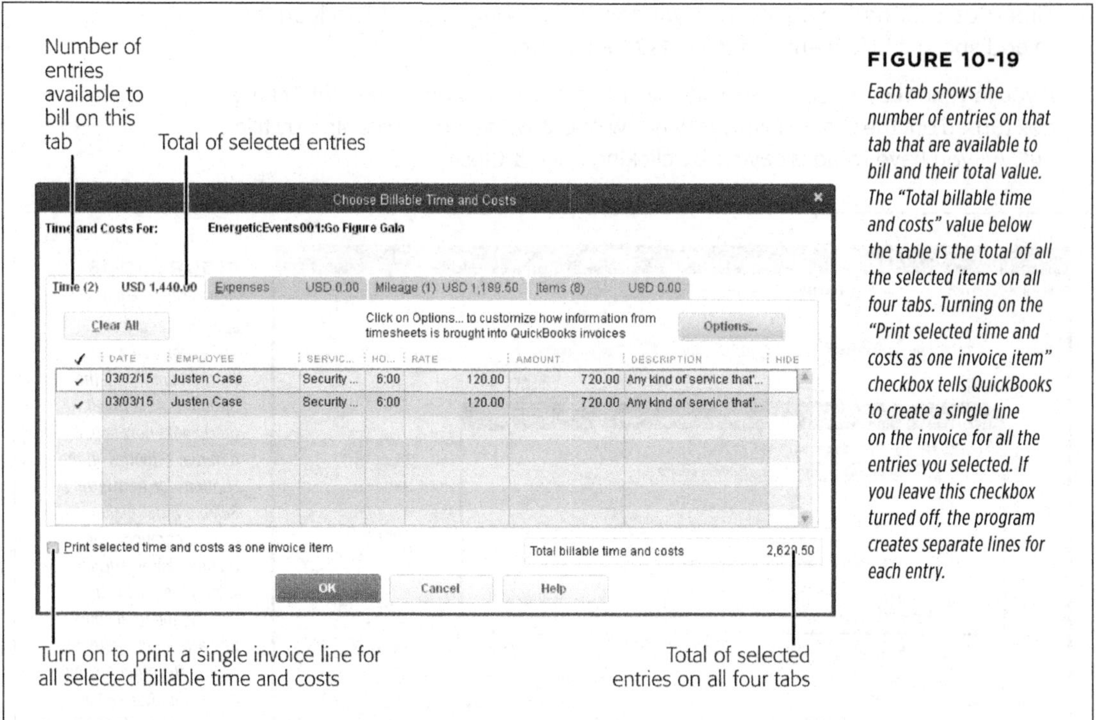

FIGURE 10-19

Each tab shows the number of entries on that tab that are available to bill and their total value. The "Total billable time and costs" value below the table is the total of all the selected items on all four tabs. Turning on the "Print selected time and costs as one invoice item" checkbox tells QuickBooks to create a single line on the invoice for all the entries you selected. If you leave this checkbox turned off, the program creates separate lines for each entry.

2. **If you want the invoice to include only one line for all the time and expenses you've selected, turn on the "Print selected time and costs as one invoice item" checkbox below the table.**

   After you create the invoice in step 6 of this list, in the Create Invoices window, you'll see separate entries for billable items so you can verify that the invoice is correct. However, with this checkbox turned on, the printed invoice will include only one line, labeled Total Reimbursable Expenses.

NOTE If you've created the invoice with one line for time and costs, it takes several steps to recreate it showing individual costs. To change an invoice back to a line-by-line listing, in the Create Invoices window, delete the Total Reimbursable Expenses line item. Then click Add Time/Costs on the window's Main tab to open the "Choose Billable Time and Costs" dialog box and reselect all the entries you want. Finally, turn off the "Print selected time and costs as one invoice item" checkbox, and then click OK.

3. **Click the Expenses tab, and then click the checkmark cell for each expense (like meals, airfare, and other costs) you want to add to the invoice.**

   If you mark up expenses, such as phone calls and postage, the Expenses tab lets you track your markups. In the "Markup Amount or %" box, type the markup's dollar value or percentage. Then choose the income account for the markup. (The box on page 258 tells you how to apply different markups to different expenses.)

   To have QuickBooks calculate sales tax, turn on the "Selected expenses are taxable" checkbox. (If the customer is tax exempt, QuickBooks doesn't add sales tax even if you turn on this checkbox.)

NOTE On the Expenses tab, the Memo column displays what you typed in the Memo field of the original vendor bill, check, or credit card charge. QuickBooks uses the entries in this column as the description on the invoice. (You can't edit the Memo text in this dialog box. So, if you didn't enter a Memo in the original expense transaction, you'll have to type the description for each expense after QuickBooks adds it to the invoice in step 6.)

4. **Click the Mileage tab and select any mileage you want to add to the invoice.**

   Click Options to tell QuickBooks whether to show one line for mileage or a separate line for each trip, like you did on the Time tab (Figure 10-18).

5. **On the Items tab, select the products you bought specifically for this customer or job that you want to add to this invoice.**

   Click an item's checkmark cell to add it to the invoice.

6. **When you've selected all the billable items you want to add, click OK.**

   QuickBooks closes the "Choose Billable Time and Costs" dialog box and adds all the items you selected to the invoice, as shown in Figure 10-20. If it looks good, click Save & Close. If not, edit the invoice to include what you want or click Clear to start from scratch.

Creating a Batch of Time and Expenses Invoices

If you have QuickBooks Premier or Enterprise and your company is set to use a *single* currency (page 656), you can create time and expenses invoices for more than one customer or job. Here are the steps:

1. **Choose Customers→"Invoice for Time & Expenses" or, on the Home Page, click the Invoices icon and then, on the drop-down menu, choose "Invoice for Time & Expenses."**

   The "Invoice for Time & Expenses" window shows all the customers with outstanding billable time and expenses and includes a checkmark column on the left side of the table.

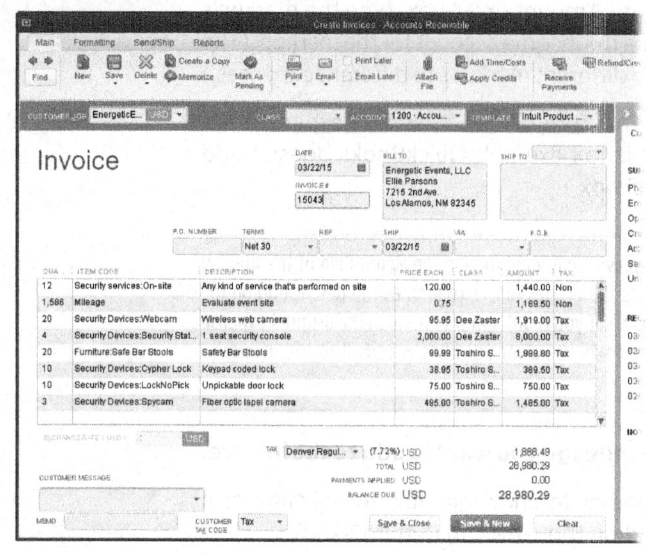

FIGURE 10-20

You can edit the item descriptions in the Create Invoices window. If you didn't type memos in the original expense transactions, you have to type the descriptions for billable expenses directly into the Description fields here.

Because the invoice is open in the Create Invoices window, you can also add additional line items to it before you save it.

WORKAROUND WORKSHOP

Adding Different Markups to Billable Expenses

The Expenses tab of the "Choose Billable Time and Costs" dialog box has only one "Markup Amount or %" box, which might seem like a problem if you add different markups to some of your billable expenses. But there's nothing stopping you from adding these expenses to your invoice in more than one batch with a different markup amount or percentage for each batch. Here's how:

1. In the "Choose Billable Time and Costs" dialog box, click the Expenses tab.
2. In the "Markup Amount or %" box, type the markup for the first batch of expenses.
3. Turn on the checkmark cell for each expense that you want to apply that markup to.
4. Click OK to add the selected expenses to the invoice.
5. On the Create Invoices window's Main tab, click Add Time/Costs.
6. In the "Choose Billable Time and Costs" dialog box, click the Expenses tab.
7. Change the value in the "Markup Amount or %" box to the next markup value, turn on the checkmark cell for the expenses that use this markup, and then click OK to close the dialog box.
8. Repeat steps 5–7 for each additional markup.

This technique works just as well when some of the expenses are taxable and others aren't. Simply choose the taxable items, turn on the "Selected expenses are taxable" checkbox, and then add the taxable expenses to the invoice. Next, reopen the "Choose Billable Time and Costs" dialog box, choose the nontaxable items, turn off the "Selected expenses are taxable" checkbox, and then add the nontaxable expenses to the invoice.

2. **In the Date Range From and To boxes, select the date range you want.**
3. **To select several customers or jobs, click the checkmark cells for the ones you want, or click Select All.**

   When a customer or job is selected, a checkmark appears in the checkmark column, as shown in Figure 10-21.

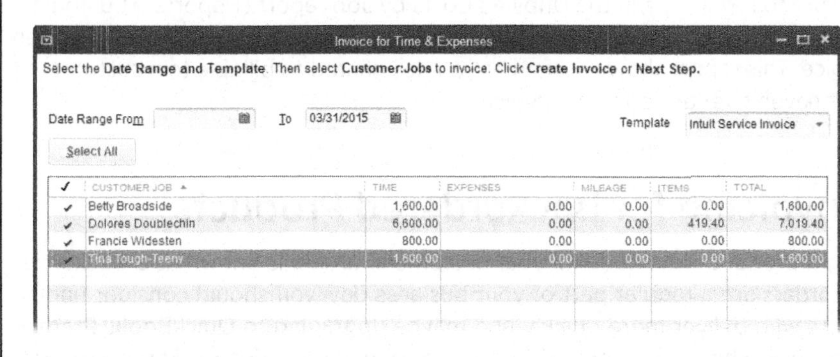

FIGURE 10-21

As long as you use QuickBooks Premier or Enterprise and don't use multiple currencies, you can select more than one customer here using the checkmark column. You can click individual checkmark cells or drag over the cells to toggle them on or off.

4. **Click Next Step.**

   The "Batch Invoice for Time & Expenses" dialog box opens. Its table lists the customers and jobs you selected.

5. **To specify the options for the invoices, click Edit Options below the table. Choose the settings you want, and then click OK.**

   Like the "Options for Transferring Billable Time" dialog box shown in Figure 10-18, the "Options for Transferring Billables" dialog box has options for showing time for each activity on separate invoice lines or showing the total hours for each Service item. If each activity is on its own line, you can transfer descriptions, notes, or both to the invoice. You can also specify a markup percentage and account for expenses.

6. **Back in the "Batch Invoice for Time & Expenses" dialog box, if you want to look at the details for a customer or job, click Review Billables.**

   In the "Review Billable Time and Costs" dialog box, click the down arrow to the right of the "Time and Costs For" box, and then choose a customer or job. The dialog box's table shows the billable info for that customer or job. When you're done reviewing this info, click OK to close the dialog box.

7. **Click Create Invoices.**

   QuickBooks creates the invoices for the selected customers. The Time & Expenses Summary dialog box appears and shows how many invoices are set up to print and how many to email, based on your customers' preferred delivery methods (page 76). Click Print to print the invoices marked to print; click Email to send the invoices marked to be emailed. To print or email the invoices later, click Close. You can then print or email them by choosing File→Print Forms→Invoices or File→Send Forms.

Checking for Unbilled Costs

Most Customers & Receivables reports focus on charges you've already invoiced. Forgetting to invoice customers for reimbursable costs takes a bite out of your profits. So be sure to regularly run the Unbilled Costs by Job report (Reports→Customers & Receivables→Unbilled Costs by Job) to look for expenses that you've forgotten to invoice. This report shows costs that you designated as billable to a customer or job but haven't yet added to an invoice.

Invoicing for Backordered Products

Placing a product order to fulfill your customers' orders is known as a *backorder*. If backorders are a regular part of your business day, you should consider finding suppliers who deliver more quickly and maybe upgrading to QuickBooks Premier or Enterprise, which have a built-in sales order form for tracking backordered items. If you have QuickBooks Pro, you can handle backorders using pending invoices.

When you tell customers that a product is out of stock, they might ask you to handle the backorders in different ways. Here are the most common requests for backorders:

- **Remove the backordered items from the order**. Customers in a hurry may ask you to fill the order with only the products you have in stock. If they can't find the backordered products anywhere else, they can call in a new order.
- **Ship all items at once**. If convenience is more important than speed, you can hold the customer's order until the backordered products arrive, and then ship the whole order at once.
- **Ship backordered items when they arrive**. Many customers request that you process their orders for the products you *do* have in stock, and then send the backordered products when you receive them.

If your customer wants you to remove backordered items from an order, then you can remove the backordered items from the invoice, send it to the customer immediately, and ship the rest of the order. But when customers ask you to hold all or part of their orders until backordered products arrive, they usually expect you to invoice them for backordered products only when you ship them. If that's the case, you don't want the income appearing in your account balances until the order ships. This section describes two ways to handle this situation.

TIP If you need help remembering how customers want you to handle their backorders, store backorder preferences in a custom field in customer records (page 78). An alternative approach is to add a note in the Customer Center (select the customer, and then click the Notes tab). When you choose a customer in the Create Invoices window, the Notes section on the right side displays notes you've added to the customer's record (see Figure 10-22).

Using Pending Invoices for Backorders

If you don't have QuickBooks Premier or Enterprise, a pending invoice is the way to track backorders. In QuickBooks, setting an invoice's status to Pending places it in a holding pattern with no income or expenses posting to your accounts. Such invoices are easy to spot in the Create Invoices window—they sport a "Pending" stamp.

To set an invoice to pending status, follow these steps:

1. **Press Ctrl+I to open the Create Invoices window.**

   Fill in the invoice fields as usual (page 226).

2. **On the Create Invoices window's Main tab, click Mark As Pending (or right-click the Create Invoices window, and then choose Mark Invoice As Pending from the shortcut menu).**

   QuickBooks adds a "Pending/non-posting" stamp to the invoice, as shown in the background of Figure 10-22.

3. **Click Save & Close.**

   The invoice is ready for action, but none of its values post to any accounts.

4. **When the backordered products arrive, open the invoice in the Create Invoices window (choose Reports→Sales→Pending Sales, and then double-click the invoice to open it). In the window's Main tab, click Mark As Final (see Figure 10-22), and then click Save & Close.**

   QuickBooks posts the invoice's values to the appropriate income and expense accounts.

Using Sales Orders for Backorders

QuickBooks Premier and Enterprise include a sales order form that's perfect for backorders. The Create Sales Orders window looks like the Create Invoices window except that the item table includes an Ordered column, which holds the number of items the customer ordered but that you haven't yet invoiced. In effect, it's a record of how much stock you need to have on hand to fill the order.

TIP To see all your sales orders at once, choose Reports→Sales, and then select either Open Sales Orders by Customer or Open Sales Orders by Item.

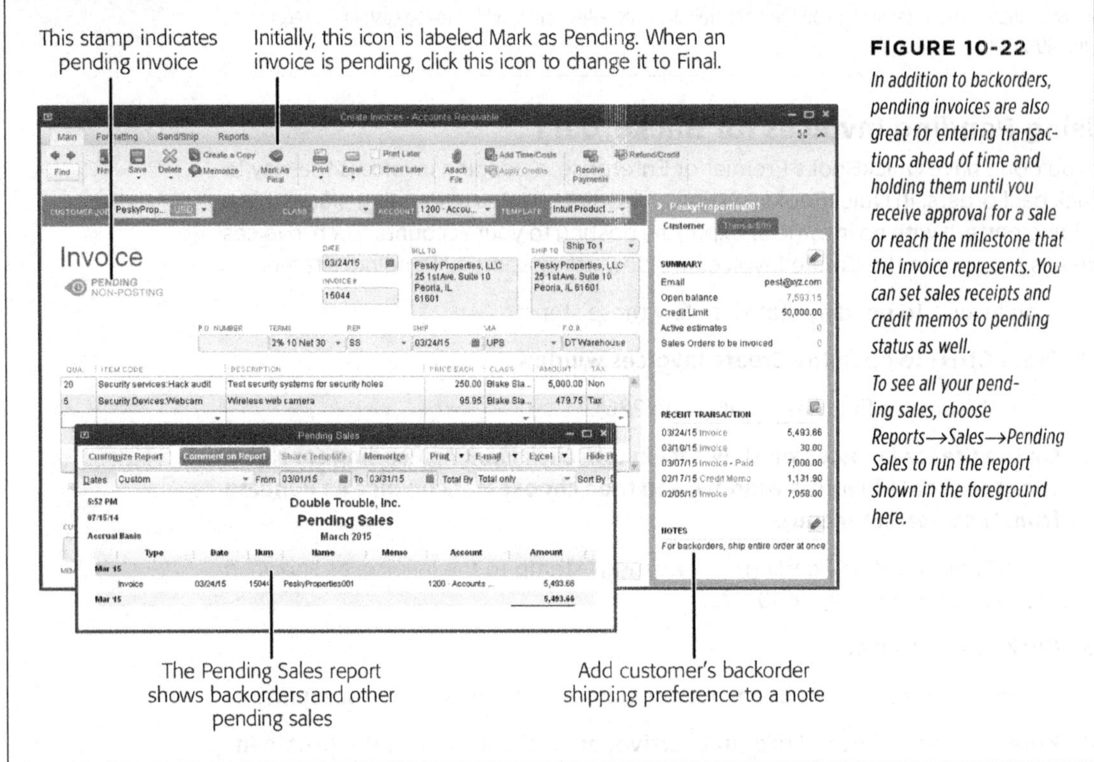

This stamp indicates pending invoice
Initially, this icon is labeled Mark as Pending. When an invoice is pending, click this icon to change it to Final.
The Pending Sales report shows backorders and other pending sales
Add customer's backorder shipping preference to a note

FIGURE 10-22

In addition to backorders, pending invoices are also great for entering transactions ahead of time and holding them until you receive approval for a sale or reach the milestone that the invoice represents. You can set sales receipts and credit memos to pending status as well.

To see all your pending sales, choose Reports→Sales→Pending Sales to run the report shown in the foreground here.

If you try to add more items to an *invoice* than you have in stock, you'll see an error message warning of the shortfall. QuickBooks Pro simply warns you that you don't have enough. But in QuickBooks Premier and Enterprise, the message box tells you how many you have on hand, how many are on other sales orders, and the remaining quantity available, as shown in Figure 10-23. (For example, if you have two items on hand and two on other sales orders, the quantity available is 0.) When you see this message, click OK to close the message box, and then click Clear to cancel the invoice.

If you already know that your inventory is woefully low or nonexistent (and you use QuickBooks Premier or Enterprise), simply create a sales order for the customer's order. Then you can create a partial invoice for the items you *do* have in stock and use the sales order to track the backordered items. Since QuickBooks keeps a running balance of backordered items based on your sales orders, you can easily create a purchase order to restock the products you need. (See Chapter 20 to learn more about managing inventory.) Here's how to create a sales order for backordered items:

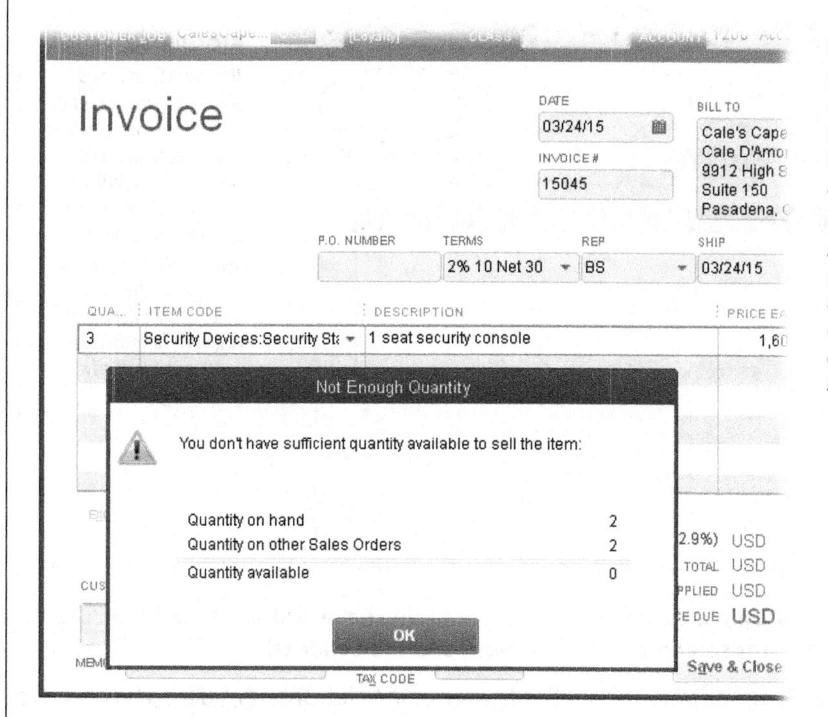

FIGURE 10-23

When you select an item and quantity that exceeds the number you have available, the Not Enough Quantity message box appears; click OK to close it.

To create a sales order instead of an invoice, in the Create Invoices window, click Clear, and then close the window. Then Choose Customers→Create Sales Orders or, on the Home Page, click the Sales Orders icon.

1. **Make sure the preference for using sales orders is turned on.**

   Choose Edit→Preferences→Sales & Customers, and then click the Company Preferences tab. In the Sales Orders section, make sure the Enable Sales Orders checkbox is on.

2. **On the Home Page, click Sales Orders or choose Customers→Create Sales Orders.**

   The Create Sales Orders window opens.

3. **Fill in the sales order's fields as you would the fields in an invoice (page 226).**

   The only difference is that the column where you record the quantity of items you're ordering is labeled "Ordered" instead of "Quantity."

4. **If some of the items the customer ordered are in stock, on the Create Sales Orders window's Main tab, click Create Invoice.**

   The aptly named Create Invoice Based On Sales Order(s) dialog box opens (Figure 10-24).

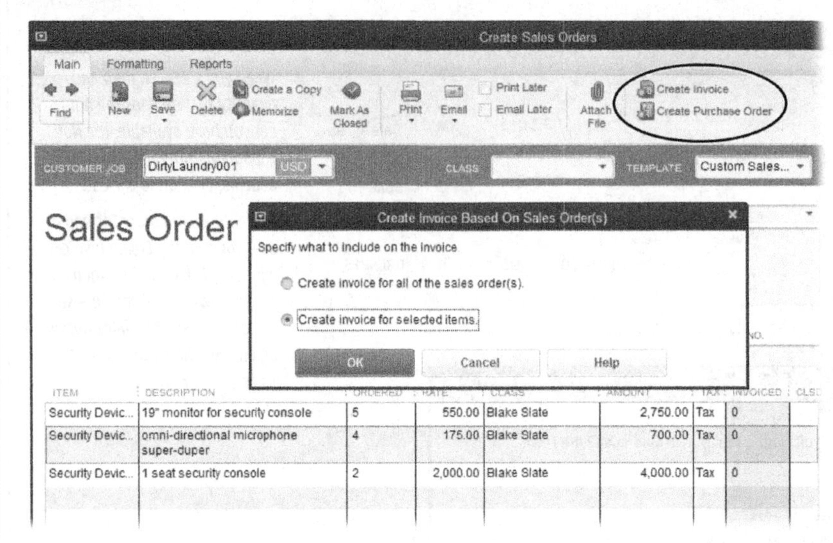

FIGURE 10-24

The Create Sales Orders window's Main tab has two buttons for creating transactions associated with sales orders (circled). Click Create Invoice to create a customer invoice for the items you have on hand to ship. Click Create Purchase Order to order items that customers have purchased but that you don't have on hand to ship.

5. **To create a *partial* invoice for the items you have in stock, select the "Create invoice for selected items" option, and then click OK.**

   The "Specify Invoice Quantities for Items on Sales Order(s)" dialog box (Figure 10-25) appears. Turn on the "Show quantity available instead of quantity on hand" checkbox to see how many items are *really* available to ship and invoice. (Quantity available is the quantity that's physically on hand minus the quantity that's already committed on other sales orders or already used in Inventory Assembly items.)

6. **Click OK to create the invoice for the in-stock items.**

   QuickBooks opens the Create Invoices window and fills in the invoice. You might see a message telling you that the invoice has at least one zero amount item (the one that's backordered) and instructions for preventing QuickBooks from printing those items on the invoice. Click OK to close the message box, and then click Save & Close.

7. **To order the backordered item(s), open the Create Sales Orders window again (see step 2) and, on the Main tab, click the left-pointing arrow (this is the Previous button) until you see the sales order on which you based the invoice.**

   It's a good idea to place an order for the backordered items while it's still fresh in your mind. The quantity of backordered items appears in the window's Ordered column.

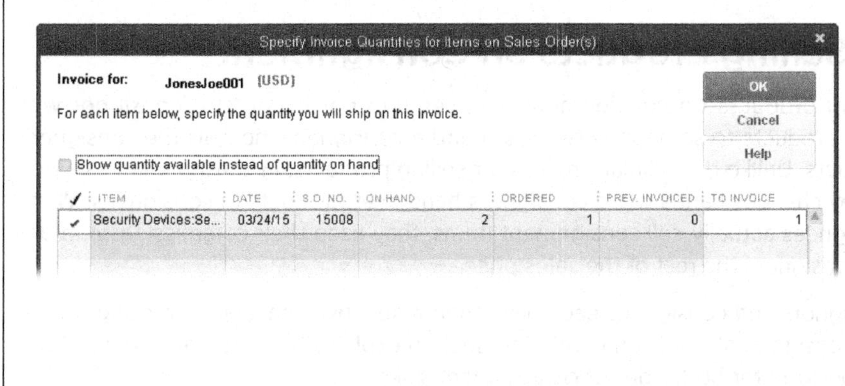

FIGURE 10-25

This dialog box lists each item on the sales order and shows how many you have in stock. QuickBooks automatically fills in the To Invoice column with the number of items on hand because you usually invoice for only the products you can ship, but you can edit the quantity if you want to invoice the customer for the full order.

8. **On the window's Main tab, click Create Purchase Order, circled in Figure 10-24).**

   The "Create Purchase Order Based on the Sales Transaction" dialog box opens.

9. **Select the "Create purchase order for selected items" option, and then click OK.**

   The "Specify Purchase Order Quantities for Items on the Sales Transaction" dialog box opens. If you specified preferred vendors in your item records (page 521), QuickBooks automatically fills in the Preferred Vendor cells. It also fills in the Qty cells with how many items you have to order to fulfill the backorder. If you want to order some spare inventory, edit the values in the Qty cells.

10. **Click the checkmark cell for each item you want to order from one vendor.**

    If you purchase the items from multiple vendors, you'll have to create separate purchase orders for each vendor.

11. **Click OK.**

    The Create Purchase Orders window appears, filled in with the items you're ordering. QuickBooks automatically puts the preferred vendor's name in the Vendor box, if you specified one in the item's record. If the Vendor box is blank or you want to use a different vendor, choose the one you want from the drop-down list.

12. **When the purchase order is filled out the way you want, click Save & Close, and then send it to the vendor (see page 308 to learn how to print forms or page 318 to learn how to email them).**

After you receive the items you ordered, return to step 4 to create a final invoice from the sales order.

Selling Products on Consignment

Selling products on consignment involves two participants: a *consignor* who gives products to someone else to sell and a *consignee* who sells the consigner's products. Unlike the regular process for selling products, in consignment sales, no money changes hands when consignors hand over products to consignees. When consignees actually *sell* consignment items, they keep their commissions and pay the consignors the rest of the sales price.

Consignors and consignees each have their respective challenges tracking money and consignment items on hand. This section explains the setup and transactions you perform for both sides of consignment sales.

Consigning Products to Someone Else to Sell

As a consignor, you need to keep track of the products you give to someone else to sell, as well as how much money you should receive when the consignee sells some of your items. In QuickBooks, sales orders are the way to track consignment goods that are sitting in someone else's store or warehouse—so you need QuickBooks Premier or Enterprise (remember, QuickBooks Pro doesn't include sales orders). This section describes the setup you need to perform as a consignor and the transactions you record to track your consignment items until they're sold and you receive your money.

Here are the accounts and items you need to track products you give to others on consignment:

- **An Other Current Asset account to track the value of your consignment inventory.** You create this account so you can differentiate your consignment inventory from inventory you have in your *own* warehouse or store. Follow the steps on page 56 to open the Add New Account window. There, in the Other Account Types drop-down list, choose Other Current Asset, and then click Continue. In the Account Name box, type a name, such as *Inventory on Consignment*. (See page 57 to learn how to fill in the other fields.) Finally, click Save & Close.
- **A parent item for your inventory that's on consignment.** Create a new Inventory Part item (page 519). In the Item Name/Number box, type something like *Consignment Items*. In the Income Account box, choose an income account, such as Product Revenue (or you can create an income account specifically for consignment sales). In the Asset Account box, choose the Other Current Asset account you created in the previous bullet point, and then click OK to save the item.
- **Subitems for each type of consignment item you give to consignees.** The easiest way to create consignment subitems is to duplicate your regular inventory items and tweak the duplicates. To do that, in the Item List window

(Lists→Item List), right-click the inventory item you're going to consign, and then choose Duplicate Item on the shortcut menu. QuickBooks opens the New Item window and fills in the fields with the values from the original item. (The program adds "DUP" to the beginning of the item's name.) In the Item Name/Number box, delete "DUP" and append the word "Consignment" to the end of the name. Next, turn on the Subitem Of checkbox and, in the drop-down list below it, choose the parent item you created in the previous bullet point. Change the Asset Account field to the consignment inventory account you created in the first bullet point. If necessary, change the Income Account to the account you want to use for consignment income. And if the price the consignee pays is different than your regular price, edit the value in the Sales Price box. When everything looks good, click OK to save the new consignment inventory subitem.

Now your Item List includes a separate parent item for consignment inventory with the consignment subitems indented beneath it.

WHEN YOU DELIVER PRODUCTS TO CONSIGNEES

When you send products to consignees, your records need to reflect that some of your inventory is in others' warehouses. To do that, you first record an inventory adjustment to switch some of your *regular* inventory on hand to *consignment* inventory on hand. Then you create sales orders to record the products you've given to each consignee.

Here's how you record an inventory adjustment to reclassify the inventory you give to a consignee as consignment inventory:

1. **Choose Vendors→Inventory Activities→Adjust Quantity/Value on Hand.**

   The Adjust Quantity/Value on Hand dialog box opens. Leave the Adjustment Type box set to Quantity. Because you're changing regular inventory items to consignment items, the total value of your inventory doesn't change, so you *don't* need to change this setting to Total Value.

2. **In the Adjustment Account box, choose an expense account (such as Supplies or Materials) or an Other Expense account.**

   The adjustment value is zero, so you can choose any expense account you want. It's a good idea to select an account related to product expenses.

3. **In the table, fill in the first Item cell with the *regular* inventory item, and then, in the next row's Item cell, choose the corresponding *consignment* inventory item, as shown in Figure 10-26.**

4. **In the regular item's Qty Difference cell, type a negative number. In the consignment item's Qty Difference cell, type a positive number.**

   Typing a negative number for the regular item reduces your regular inventory item's quantity on hand. The consignment item's positive number adds that quantity of items to your consignment inventory on hand.

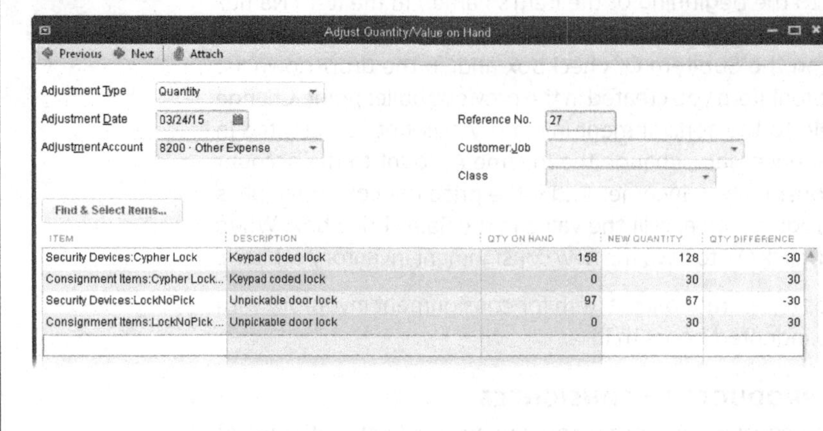

FIGURE 10-26

Typing a negative number in a regular inventory item's Qty Difference cell reduces the number of regular inventory items on hand, so you have fewer to sell directly to your customers. A positive number in a consignment inventory item's Qty Difference cell increases the number of consignment inventory items on hand—at your consignees' locations.

5. **Click OK to save the adjustment.**

Now you can look at the Item List window's Total Quantity column to see the number of regular and consignment inventory items you have.

You also need to tell QuickBooks how many items you give to each consignee. That's where a sales order comes into play. Here's how to record a sales order for consignment items you send out:

1. **In QuickBooks Premier or Enterprise, on the Home Page, click Sales Orders. In the Sales Orders window, choose the person or company who is selling goods on consignment for you.**

   You have to set up your consignees as *customers* (page 70) so they appear in the Sales Orders window's Name drop-down list.

2. **In the Date box, choose the date that you sent (or will send) goods to the consignee.**

3. **Fill in each line of the table (page 236) with the items and quantities that you're sending to the consignee.**

   That way, when the consignee sells some of the products, you can create an invoice for him directly from the sales order. Doing this also puts the consignment inventory in your consignment-inventory asset account.

4. **When you're done, click Save & Close.**

This sales order actually does double duty. It not only provides a record of the consignment items the "customer" (a.k.a. consignee) has on hand; if you use Inventory

Part items for your consigned goods as described on page 266, it also moves the value of the consignment inventory into your consignment-inventory asset account.

WHEN CONSIGNEES SELL YOUR STUFF

If your consignees sell some of your consignment items, you can give a quick whoop of joy before you create an invoice for what the consignee owes you. In fact, you can whoop a second time, because you can easily create an invoice from the sales order you created in the previous section. Here are the steps for creating an invoice from a consignment sales order:

1. **On the Home Page, click Customers. In the Customer Center, click the Customers & Jobs tab, and then select the consignee who sold some of your consignment goods.**

   Information and transactions for that customer appear on the window's right.

2. **In the pane at the Customer Center's bottom right, click the Transactions tab. In the tab's Show drop-down list, choose Sales Orders.**

   QuickBooks displays the sales orders for that customer. If the Transactions tab is rife with sales orders, in the Filter By drop-down list, choose Open Sales Orders. In the Date drop-down list, you can choose a date range, such as This Fiscal Quarter.

3. **Double-click the sales order associated with the sold consignment items.**

   The sales order opens in the Create Sales Order window.

4. **At the top of the window, click Create Invoice. In the Create Invoice Based on Sales Order(s) dialog box, select the "Create invoice for selected items" option, and then click OK.**

   The Specify Items and Quantities for Invoice dialog box opens. All the items from the sales order appear in the table.

5. **In the To Invoice cell for each consignment item, type the number of items the consignee sold, and then click OK.**

   The Create Invoices window opens with a new invoice already filled in with the consignee's info, as well as the items and quantities sold (see Figure 10-27).

6. **In the Create Invoices window, click Save & Close.**

   QuickBooks jumps into action behind the scenes: it reduces the number of consignment inventory items on hand, on sales orders, and available. It also reduces the balance in your consignment inventory asset account and moves that money into your Accounts Receivable account to show what your consignee owes you. To see the number of consignment items sold by each consignee, you can run the Sales by Customer Detail report (see page 593).

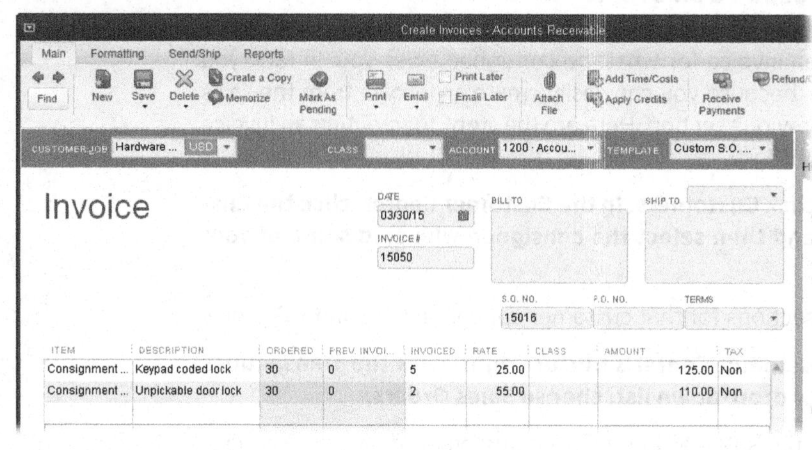

FIGURE 10-27

The invoice you create for consignment sales does more than just record the amount the consignee owes you. It also reduces the balance of your consignment inventory asset account and increases the Accounts Receivable balance for the consignee.

Selling Consignment Goods Received from Someone Else

As a consignee, you have to track the consignment goods you have on hand. And when you sell consignment items, you have to track your earnings as well as what you owe the consignors. To wrap up the process, you need to pay consignors their share of the revenue.

You don't pay anything up front for goods you sell on consignment. When you sell these items, you keep a percentage of the sales revenue as a commission and pay the consignor the rest. You need to keep track of how many consignment items you receive, how many you've sold, and how many you still have on hand. This section guides you through setting up QuickBooks so you can sell vendors' products on consignment and through creating the transactions you record to handle consignment sales from start to finish.

Here are the accounts and items you need to track products you sell as a consignee:

- **An Other Current Liability account to track what you owe the consignor.** This account will track how much you owe the consignor for consignment items you sell. (See page 56 for info on creating accounts.) Name the account something like Consignment Sales - Liability.
- **An Income account to track your sales commission.** This account tracks how much you make from selling consignment items. Name it something like Consignment Commission.
- **A Service item for deducting your commission from what you owe the consignor**. Create a Service item (page 108) called something like Commission Deduction. In the New Item dialog box's Description field, type a description,

such as "Reduce liability for commission earned on sale." In the Rate field, type a *negative* percentage that represents your commission on a consignment sale. For example, if you take 30 percent of the sales price, type *-30%* in the box. In the Account box, choose the Other Current Liability account you created to track what you owe the consignor. That way, when you record the sale, QuickBooks deducts your commission from what you owe the consignor.

- **A Service item for your commission income**. This Service item gets your income into the right place in your chart of accounts. Name this item something like Commission Income. In the New Item dialog box's Description field, type a more thorough description, such as "Commission on consignment sale." In the Rate field, type your commission percentage as a *positive* number, such as 30%. In the Account drop-down list, choose the income account you created to track your consignment income (Consignment Commission, in this example).
- **A parent Inventory Part item for your consignment inventory.** You'll use this Inventory Part item to track all the consignment goods you sell. Call it something like Consignment Goods - Held. Link this item to the basic COGS account that QuickBooks creates when you create your first inventory item (page 519). In the New Item dialog box's Income Account box, choose the Other Current Liability account you created to track what you owe the consignor (Consignment Sales - Liability, in this example). In the Asset Account box, choose the asset account you use to track inventory.
- **Subitems for each category of consignment item you sell.** Create Inventory Part subitems for each *type* of consignment item you receive from consignors (see Figure 10-28), not for each individual consignment item. For example, say you sell miniature cameras on consignment. Create one subitem to track them and name it something descriptive like "Camera Tiny - Consigned." Be sure to turn on the "Subitem of" checkbox and, in the drop-down list below it, choose the Consignment Goods - Held parent item. Leave the Cost field set to 0.00, since you don't pay anything for a consignment item up front. In the Sales Price field, enter the price you sell the product for. In the Asset Account box, choose your inventory asset account.

To track items by consignor, set up a custom field called Consignor, and link it to the Item List. (See page 78 to learn how to set up custom fields for lists.) Then, in the Consignor field, for each Inventory Part subitem you create for consignment items, type the consignor's name.

NOTE If you sell scads of *unique* consignment items, creating an Inventory Part item for each one would fill up your Item List with one-off entries. Instead, create a single Non-inventory Part item and call it something like Consignment Items. In the New Item dialog box, turn on the "This item is used in assemblies or is purchased for a specific customer:job" checkbox. Keep both the Cost and Sale Price fields set to 0.00. In the Expense Account drop-down list, choose the asset account you created to track your consignment inventory (Inventory Asset, in this example). And in the Income Account drop-down list, choose the income account you use to track your consignment income (Consignment Commission, in this example).

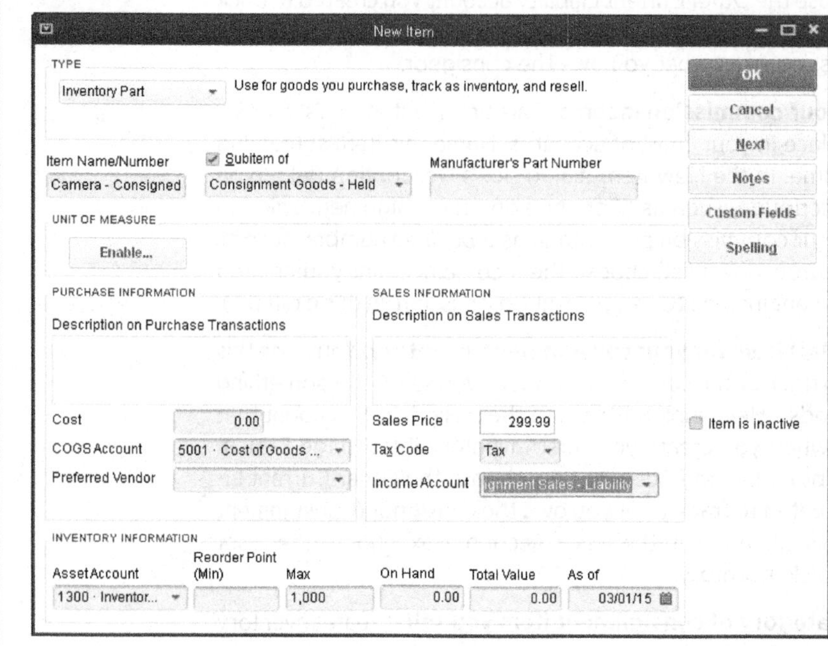

FIGURE 10-28

This inventory item helps you track how many consignment items you have on hand.

Because the Cost is 0.00, these items don't affect the balance in your COGS and inventory asset account. By using the Consignment Sales - Liability account as the Income account, you'll be able to see how much you owe consignors for consignment products you sell.

- **A Group item for each consignment subitem you created per the previous bullet point**. There's a lot to keep track of when you sell consignment goods. This Group item (see Figure 10-29) moves consignment money to the right accounts and tracks how many you have on hand. When creating this Group item in the New Item dialog box, you add the consigned item to the first line in the Item table and set the Qty cell to *1*. That way, when you sell an item, QuickBooks takes care of reducing the number of this item that you have on hand. The second line in the Item table is the Service item for your commission (Consignment Commission, in this example). And the third item is the Service item you use to deduct your commission from what you owe the consignor (Commission Deduction, in this example). By adding these two lines to the group, when you sell an item, QuickBooks adds your commission to your commission income account and the remainder of the money to the Other Current Liability account that tracks what you owe the consignor. Keep the "Print items in group" checkbox turned off so the Group item is the only thing customers see on invoices and sales receipts.

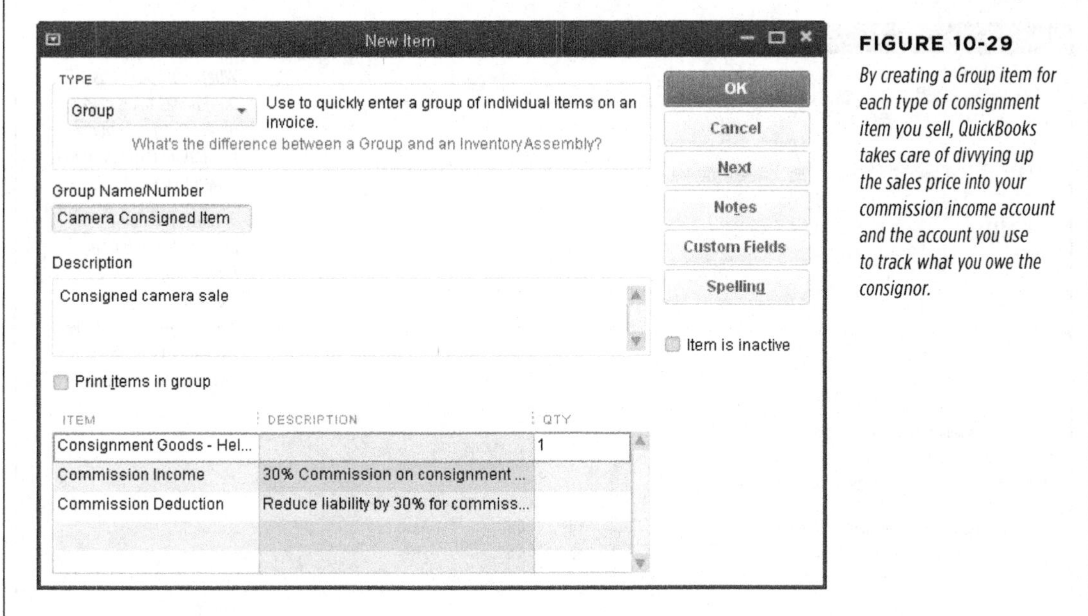

FIGURE 10-29

By creating a Group item for each type of consignment item you sell, QuickBooks takes care of divvying up the sales price into your commission income account and the account you use to track what you owe the consignor.

ADDING CONSIGNMENT ITEMS TO YOUR INVENTORY

When you receive consignment goods from a consignor, you need to update your records to show how many consignment items you have on hand. The easiest way to do that is to create a bill for those items. Here are the steps:

1. **Create a bill for the items you receive on consignment.**

   On the Home Page, click Enter Bills. In the Enter Bills window's Vendor field, choose the vendor who consigned items to you. In the Date field, choose the date you received the items.

2. **In the Amount Due field, type *0*.**

   Because you don't pay the vendor for consigned goods until they're sold, you create a bill for $0.

3. **On the window's Items tab, fill in the lines with the consignment items and quantities you received, as shown in Figure 10-30.**

   In the first Item cell, select the Inventory Part item you created for the consigned item, not the Group item. Fill in that row's Qty cell with the number of items you received. (Because you set up the inventory item with $0 cost, the cost on the bill is 0.00.)

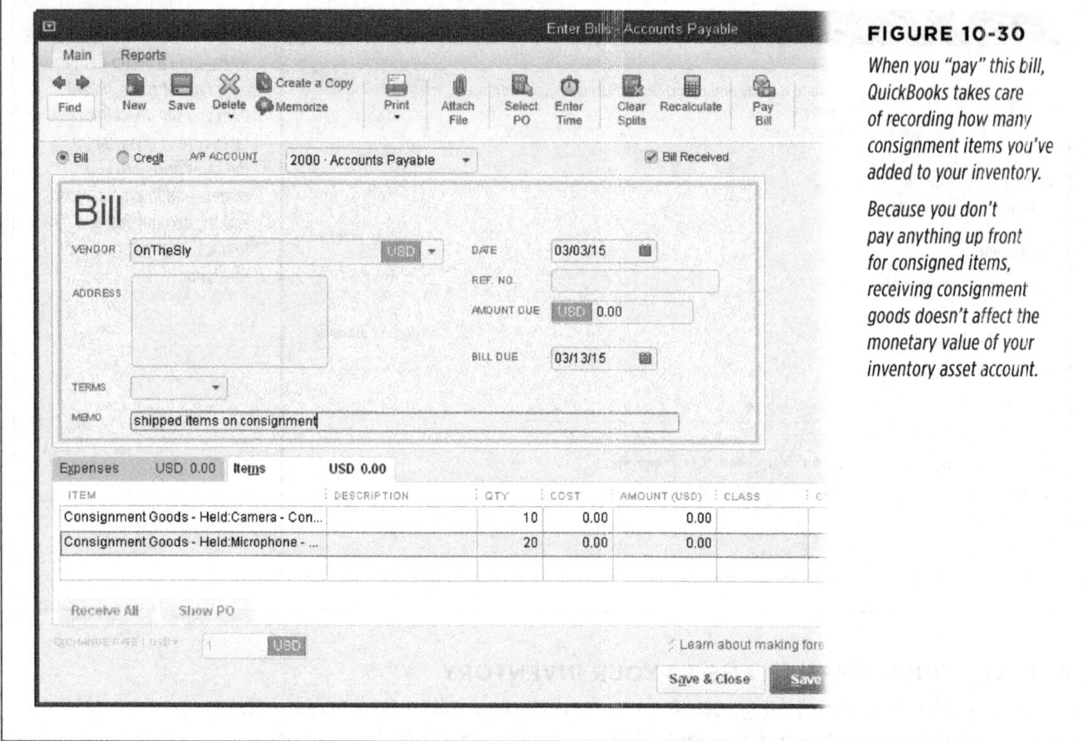

FIGURE 10-30

When you "pay" this bill, QuickBooks takes care of recording how many consignment items you've added to your inventory.

Because you don't pay anything up front for consigned items, receiving consignment goods doesn't affect the monetary value of your inventory asset account.

4. **At the top of the Enter Bills window, click Pay Bill. In the message box that asks whether you want to record your changes, click Yes.**

   If a Bill Already Paid message box appears, click OK to close it.

5. **Click Save & Close.**

To confirm that the consigned items are now in inventory, open the Item List window (on the Home Page, click Items & Services). Scroll down to the Inventory Part items you created for consigned items and check the value in the Total Quantity cells.

RECORDING CONSIGNMENT SALES

When you sell consignment goods, you record the customer invoice *almost* as you do any other invoice. The consignment Group items you add to the invoice are the key to tracking your consignment inventory and following the consignment money trail. However, you need to add the Consignor custom field to your invoice template so you can identify which consignor you need to pay for the sold goods.

Here are the steps to adding the Consignor custom field to your invoice template:

1. **Choose Lists→Templates.**

   The Templates window opens.

2. **Click the template you want to use as a basis for your consignment template (for example, a custom invoice template you set up for your company), and then, at the bottom of the Templates window, click Templates→Duplicate.**

   The Select Template dialog box appears.

3. **In the Select Template Type dialog box, select the Invoice option, and then click OK.**

   The copy appears in the Templates list with the words "Copy of" at the beginning of its name.

4. **Right-click the new template and choose Edit Template from the shortcut menu.**

   To rename the template, in the Basic Customization dialog box, click Manage Templates. In the Template Name field on the dialog box's right, type a new name, such as *Consignment Sales*, and then click OK.

5. **At the bottom of the Basic Customization dialog box, click Additional Customization. In the additional Customization dialog box that appears, click the Columns tab.**

   The Columns tab includes fields that appear in the item table.

6. **Below the Screen heading, turn on the Consignor checkbox (you'll see this checkbox only if you created a Consignor custom field and associated it with the Item List, as described on page 271).**

   That way, the Consignor field will appear in the item table when you're filling out the invoice onscreen, but it won't appear on the invoice that the customer receives.

7. **Click OK to close the Additional Customization dialog box, and then click OK again to close the Basic Customization dialog box.**

Your custom template for consignment sales is now ready to use. Here's how you record a consignment sale:

1. **Create an invoice for the sale by choosing Customers→Create Invoices.**

   Fill in the Customer:Job, Class, Date, and other header fields the way you do for a regular invoice. In the Template field, choose the custom template you just created (the one you made by following the steps in the numbered list above).

2. **In the first item cell, choose the Group item you created for the consignment item you sold. In the Quantity cell, fill in the number that you sold (see Figure 10-31).**

QuickBooks automatically adds the Group item's underlying line items to the invoice. (Remember, these lines won't appear on the printed invoice, because you turned off the "Print items in group" checkbox when you created the Group item [page 272].) When you change the Quantity cell on the Group item's line, QuickBooks automatically changes the quantities on the other lines. (To see what the invoice or sales receipt looks like, at the top of the transaction window, click Print→Preview.)

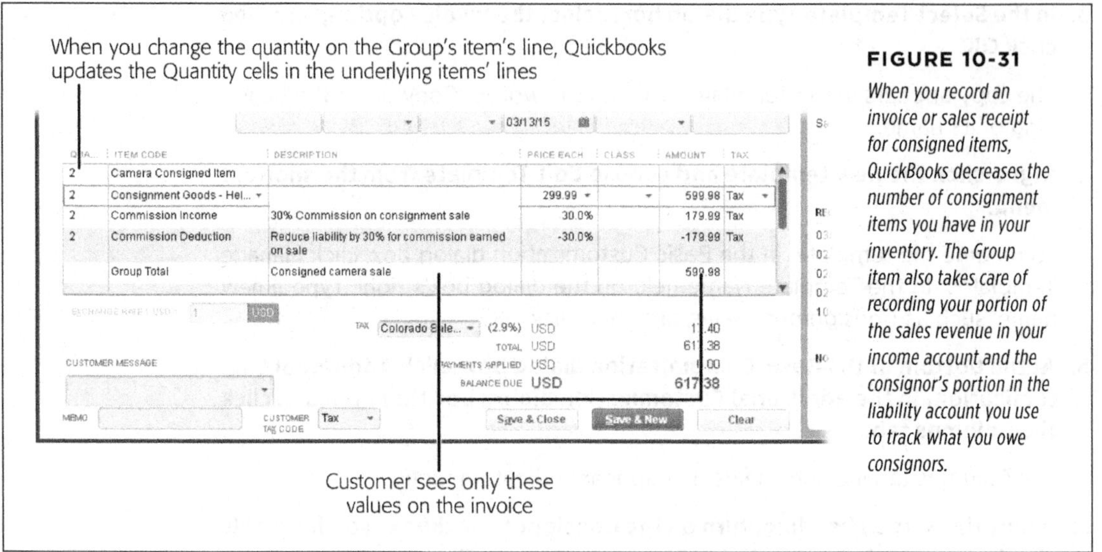
When you change the quantity on the Group's item's line, Quickbooks updates the Quantity cells in the underlying items' lines
Customer sees only these values on the invoice

FIGURE 10-31

When you record an invoice or sales receipt for consigned items, QuickBooks decreases the number of consignment items you have in your inventory. The Group item also takes care of recording your portion of the sales revenue in your income account and the consignor's portion in the liability account you use to track what you owe consignors.

3. **In each line below the Group item, click the Consignor cell and type the name of the consignor.**

   In the next section, you'll learn how to use this field to create a report that shows what you owe each consignor.

4. **Repeat steps 2 and 3 for each type of consignment item you sold. When you're done, click Save & Close.**

   When you save the invoice, QuickBooks does several things behind the scenes. It decreases the quantity on hand for the consignment items you sold and posts the income to the Consignment Sales - Liability account (which tracks what you owe consignors). It also deducts your commission from that account and puts the money in your Commission Income account.

PAYING CONSIGNORS

The last step in the consignment process is paying consignors their portion of the sales revenue. You can use the Consignor custom field to create a report that shows you how much you owe each consignor. Then all you have to do is write a check.

Here's how to customize a report to show consignor liabilities:

1. **Choose Reports→Custom Reports→Transaction Detail. In the Dates drop-down list, choose the period you want to pay consignors for, such as Last Month.**

   The Modify Report window opens automatically when you create a custom report.

2. **In the Modify Report window, in the Display tab's Columns list, click the Consignor entry (you may have to scroll down to see it).**

   Doing this makes the Consigner field appear as a column in the report.

3. **Click the Filters tab and, in the Filter list on the left, choose Item. In the Item drop-down list that appears, choose "Multiple items." In the Select Item dialog box that appears, click the Commission Deduction item and each consignment Inventory Part item you sell, and then click OK.**

   This filter limits the report to transactions related to your consignment items.

4. **Back on the Modify Report dialog box's Filters tab, in the Filter list on the left, choose Account. Then, in the Account drop-down list, choose the Other Current Liability account you set up to track what you owe consignors (Consignment Sales – Liability, in this example).**

5. **In the Filter list on the left, click Consignor, and then type the name of the consignor you want to pay. Click OK to run the report.**

   The total at the bottom of the report's Amount column is what you owe the consignor.

TIP To memorize this custom report so you can run it in the future, press Ctrl+M. In the Memorize Report dialog box, in the Name box, type a name for the report, such as Consignment Payments, and then click OK. To run the memorized report, choose Reports→Memorized Reports→[name of report].

Now you can use that amount to write a check to the consignor. Here's how:

1. **On the Home Page, click Write Checks.**

   The Write Checks window opens.

2. **In the "Pay to the Order of" box, choose the vendor who is your consignor.**

   To provide more information about the sale, type details in the Memo field.

3. **On the Expenses tab near the bottom of the window, in the first Account cell, choose the Consignment Sales - Liability account.**

4. **If you want to print the check, turn o n the Print Later checkbox. If you hand-write checks, simply click Save & Close.**

The check reduces your liability to the consignor. To confirm that you've paid the consignor what you owe, on the Home Page, click Vendors. In the Vendor Center window, on the Vendors tab, the Balance for the vendor should be zero.

Estimating Jobs

Many customers ask for an estimate before hiring you. If you're good with numbers, you might total up the costs in your head and scribble the estimate on a napkin. But creating estimates in QuickBooks not only generates a more professional-looking estimate; it also feeds numbers into the invoices you create as you perform work for customers. When you create an estimate in QuickBooks, you add the items you'll sell or deliver and set the markup on those items.

NOTE The estimate feature needs to be turned on before you can create estimates in QuickBooks. Choose Edit→Preferences→Jobs & Estimates, and then click the Company Preferences tab. In the "Do You Create Estimates?" section, make sure that Yes is selected, and then click OK.

QuickBooks estimates make short work of pricing time and materials for small jobs. But QuickBooks estimating isn't for every business. Particularly if you work in construction, where a major project might require hundreds or even *thousands* of items, you definitely don't want to enter all the data you'd need to build the Item List for your project. That's why most construction firms turn to third-party estimating programs that come with databases of the services and products you need. Many of these programs integrate with QuickBooks, which means you can import an estimate you created in another program (see Chapter 26) and use it to produce your invoices.

NOTE The totals on estimates don't post to accounts in your chart of accounts. After all, an estimate doesn't mean that your customer has committed to going ahead with the job. Estimates show the *potential* value of a job without showing up in your financial reports. When the preference for estimates is turned on (page 655), QuickBooks automatically creates a *non-posting* account called Estimates, where it stores estimate values. (If you use account numbers [page 635], its number is 4.)

Creating an Estimate

If you've mastered QuickBooks' invoices, you'll feel right at home with the fields that appear in a QuickBooks estimate. Figure 10-32 shows the Create Estimates window.

Here's how to create an estimate and handle the small differences between invoices and estimates:

1. **On the Home Page, click the Estimates icon, or choose Customers→Create Estimates.**

   QuickBooks opens the Create Estimates window. Depending on which edition of QuickBooks you have, the program may choose a different estimate template from the one shown in Figure 10-32. If you've created your own estimate template (page 707), choose it from the Template drop-down list (QuickBooks automatically uses your custom template from then on).

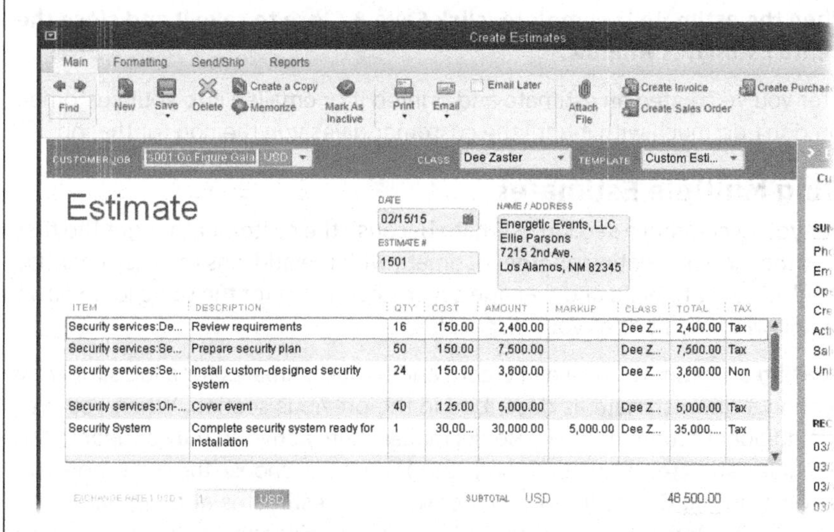

FIGURE 10-32

QuickBooks automatically makes the estimates you create active, which means you can experiment with several and then build your invoices from the one your customer approves.

To make an estimate inactive, on the Create Estimates window's Main tab, click Mark As Inactive.

2. **As you would for an invoice, build your estimate by adding items to the line-item table (page 236).**

   In a blank line in the table, in the Item drop-down list, choose the item that you want to add to the estimate. When you fill in the quantity, QuickBooks uses the cost and sales price from the item's record to fill in the Cost, Amount, and Total cells.

   The markup percentage that QuickBooks fills in is based on how much you pay for the item and the sales price you charge. If you want to apply a different markup percentage, click the item's Markup cell, and then either type the percentage you want to use or choose a price level (page 235) from the drop-down list. From then on, the markup is visible only while you work on the estimate. When you print the estimate or email it to your customer, only the Cost and Total columns appear in the form.

NOTE The calculated value in an item's Total cell isn't set in stone. If you change the Total value, QuickBooks recalculates the markup percentage for you. Likewise, if you change the percentage in the Markup cell, QuickBooks recalculates the value in the Total cell.

3. **To email the estimate to your customer later, on the window's Main tab, turn on the Email Later checkbox.**

   QuickBooks queues up the estimate so you can email it later (page 318). For reasons unknown, you can't queue up an estimate to *print* later. If you want to print an estimate, in the Create Estimates window's Main tab, click Print, and then choose Estimate on the drop-down menu. Alternatively, you can choose Print→Save As PDF, and then print the PDF later.

4. **When the estimate is complete, click Save & Close to save it and close the Create Estimates window.**

   After you've created an estimate and printed it or emailed it to your customer, you don't do much with it until the customer gives you the nod for the job.

Creating Multiple Estimates

Whether you're creating a second estimate because the customer thought the first price was too high or creating another estimate with the add-ons the customer has requested, it's easy to build and manage several estimates for the same job. You've got the following methods at your disposal:

- **Creating an estimate**. You can create additional estimates for a job simply by creating a new estimate as described in the previous section. When you create additional estimates, QuickBooks makes them active so they appear in the Available Estimates dialog box (page 283) when you choose the corresponding customer in the Create Invoices window. Active estimates also appear in the Estimates by Job report (Reports→Jobs, Time & Mileage→Estimates by Job) shown in Figure 10-33.

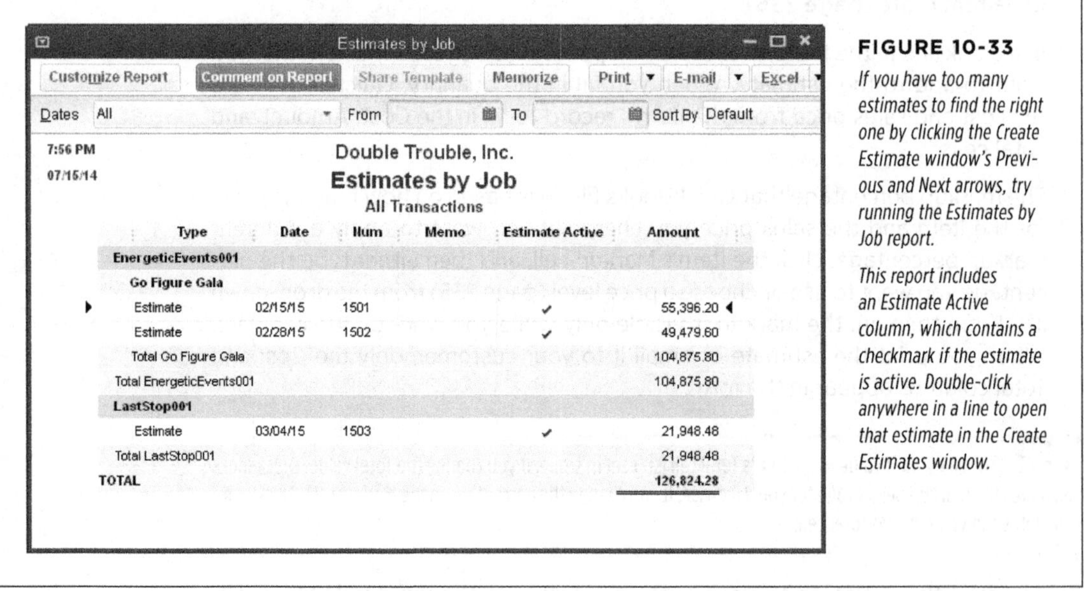

Type	Date	Num	Memo	Estimate Active	Amount
EnergeticEvents001					
Go Figure Gala					
Estimate	02/15/15	1501		✓	55,396.20
Estimate	02/28/15	1502		✓	49,479.60
Total Go Figure Gala					104,875.80
Total EnergeticEvents001					104,875.80
LastStop001					
Estimate	03/04/15	1503		✓	21,948.48
Total LastStop001					21,948.48
TOTAL					126,824.28

FIGURE 10-33

If you have too many estimates to find the right one by clicking the Create Estimate window's Previous and Next arrows, try running the Estimates by Job report.

This report includes an Estimate Active column, which contains a checkmark if the estimate is active. Double-click anywhere in a line to open that estimate in the Create Estimates window.

- **Duplicating an estimate**. If you want to play what-if games with an existing estimate, you can duplicate it and then make your adjustments. In the Create Estimates window, display the estimate you want to copy and then, on the Main tab, click "Create a Copy" or right-click the estimate and choose Duplicate Estimate from the shortcut menu. Either way, QuickBooks pulls everything from the existing estimate onto a new one and assigns it the next estimate number in sequence. After you make the changes you want, click Save & Close or Save & New. (The box on page 282 tells you how to create boilerplate estimates, which is faster if you intend to duplicate an estimate frequently.)

- **Finding an estimate**. When you know the estimate you want exists, you can search for it based on the customer or job, when you created it, its number, or the amount. On the Create Estimates window's Main tab, click Find or right-click in the window and then choose Find Estimates from the shortcut menu. In the Find Estimates dialog box that appears, fill in what you know about the estimate, and then click Find. If you click Advanced, QuickBooks opens the full-blown Find window so you can set more specific criteria (page 333).

- **Making an estimate inactive**. When you create several estimates for the same work, eventually you and your customer will pick one to run with. Once you've picked an estimate, make the others inactive. To do that, display an estimate in the Create Estimates window and then, on the Main tab, click Mark As Inactive. Then click Save & New to save the estimate while keeping the Create Estimates window open. If you want to make another estimate inactive, on the Main tab, click the left arrow (Previous) or the right arrow (Next) until the estimate in question appears, and then repeat these steps.

  QuickBooks won't display inactive estimates in the Available Estimates dialog box (page 283), but you still have a record of them, which you can see by clicking the Next or Previous arrow on the Create Estimates window's Main tab, or by running the Estimates by Job report.

- **Deleting an estimate**. Deleting an estimate isn't the no-no that deleting an invoice is. (The only risk is that you'll realize you wanted to keep the estimate as soon as you delete it.) In the Create Estimates window, display the estimate you want to axe and then, on the Main tab, click Delete. Alternatively, right-click the estimate in the Create Estimates window and then choose Delete Estimate from the shortcut menu. In the Delete Transaction dialog box, click OK to get rid of the estimate.

NOTE To protect profit margins from being nibbled away by small changes, many businesses keep track of every change that a customer requests (called *change orders*). The Contractor and Accountant editions of QuickBooks let you track change orders on estimates.

POWER USERS' CLINIC

Building Boilerplate Estimates

Suppose you've put a lot of thought into the typical tasks you perform and the materials you need for different types of jobs. Creating boilerplate estimates that take into account your performance on similar, completed jobs helps you quickly produce estimates for new jobs. Your new customer will be impressed by your speedy response, and you'll be confident that you haven't forgotten anything.

To create a boilerplate estimate, build an estimate with all the information you reuse, and then have QuickBooks memorize it. Here's how:

1. In the Create Estimates window, fill in all the fields and line items you want in the boilerplate estimate. If you want to capture the items you use but not the quantities, in the line-item table, leave the quantity (Qty) cells blank.
2. To memorize the estimate, press Ctrl+M or right-click the estimate and then choose Memorize Estimate from the shortcut menu. You can also click Memorize on the Create Estimates window's Main tab.
3. QuickBooks tells you that it will remove the Customer:Job so you can use the memorized estimate for any customer. Click OK to dismiss the message.
4. In the Memorize Transaction dialog box, type a name for the estimate, such as *Dinner Dance* for a boilerplate estimate for a fancy soiree. And because you'll use this estimate only when you get a similar job, choose the Do Not Remind Me option.
5. Click OK to add the estimate to your Memorized Transaction List.

That's all there is to it. To use your boilerplate estimate to bid on a similar job, press Ctrl+T to open the Memorized Transaction List window (or choose Lists→Memorized Transaction List). Double-click the memorized estimate to open the Create Estimates window with the memorized estimate's information displayed; QuickBooks fills in the current date and the next estimate number in the sequence. In the Customer:Job box, choose the new customer. Make any other changes you want, and then click Save & Close.

Creating an Invoice from an Estimate

Whether you create one estimate for a job or several, you can generate invoices from your estimates. In fact, if you open the Create Invoices window and choose a customer or job for which estimates exist, QuickBooks displays the Available Estimates dialog box, which lists all the active estimates for that customer or job.

NOTE This section explains how to turn an *entire* estimate into an invoice. See page 284 to learn how to use estimates to generate progress invoices when you reach milestones on large projects.

To use an estimate to create an invoice, do the following:

1. **Press Ctrl+I to open the Create Invoices window and then, in the Customer:Job drop-down list, choose the customer or job you want to invoice.**

   If one or more estimates exist for that customer or job, the Available Estimates dialog box opens, listing the active estimates for that customer or job, as shown in Figure 10-34.

NOTE You don't *have* to use your estimate to create an invoice if, say, you want to invoice for your actual time and materials. In that situation, click Cancel. The Available Estimates dialog box closes, and you can fill in the Create Invoices window's line-item table.

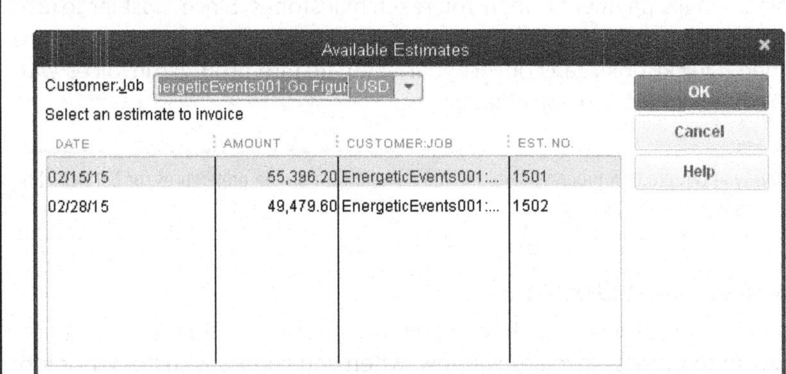

FIGURE 10-34

To keep your customer happy, be sure to choose the estimate that she accepted. The Available Estimates dialog box shows the date, amount, and estimate number. Usually, Amount is the field you use to choose the agreed-upon estimate.

2. **In the Available Estimates dialog box, click anywhere in the row for the estimate you want, and then click OK.**

   The Create Progress Invoice Based On Estimate dialog box appears with the "Create invoice for the entire estimate (100%)" option selected.

3. **Click OK.**

   QuickBooks opens the Create Invoices window and fills in the information from the estimate.

4. **Make any changes you want and then click Save & Close.**

   You're done!

Comparing Estimates to Actuals

Customers who write you blank checks are rare, so most jobs require estimates of what the work will cost. When you finish a job that you estimated, take some time to run the Job Estimates vs. Actuals Summary report (it's on the Reports→Jobs, Time & Mileage submenu) to see how you did compared with your estimate. Do this a few times, and the accuracy of your estimates should improve dramatically.

If you invoice jobs based on the progress you've made (as described in the next section), run the Job Progress Invoices vs. Estimates report instead (it's on the Reports→Jobs, Time & Mileage submenu *if* you have the progress invoicing preference [page 655] turned on). It compares your estimate with actual performance through your most recent progress invoice.

Creating Progress Invoices

When you work on jobs and projects that take more than a few days, you probably don't want to wait until a job is completely finished to charge for some of your work. *Progress invoices* include charges based on your estimate *and* the progress you've made on the job. These invoices are common for jobs that are broken into phases or when customers make payments when you reach milestones. Since most large jobs start with an estimate, you won't have to start from scratch when it's time to invoice your customer—QuickBooks can convert your estimate into progress invoices with only a few additional pieces of information.

NOTE Before you can produce progress invoices, you have to turn on the preferences for both creating estimates and progress invoicing (page 655).

Progress Invoicing Options

Progress invoices are still invoices; they just happen to link to estimates you've created for a job. In the Create Invoices window, when you choose a customer or job, QuickBooks checks to see if an estimate exists. If there's at least one estimate for that customer or job, QuickBooks opens the Available Estimates dialog box so you can choose an estimate to invoice against.

To get started creating a progress invoice, select an estimate in the Available Estimates dialog box, and then click OK; QuickBooks opens the Create Progress Invoice Based On Estimate dialog box (Figure 10-35). When you create your *first* progress invoice for a job, this dialog box lets you choose to invoice the entire estimate or only a portion. Here are your options and when you might use them:

- **Create invoice for the entire estimate (100%)**. This option is perfect if you prepared an estimate to get approval before starting a job and you completed the job in a short period of time. QuickBooks takes care of the grunt work of transferring all the services, products, and other items from the estimate to the invoice.

NOTE You can edit the invoice amounts that come from an estimate, which is handy if your actual costs were higher than your estimate, for instance. However, the contract you signed determines whether your customer will actually *pay* the revised amounts!

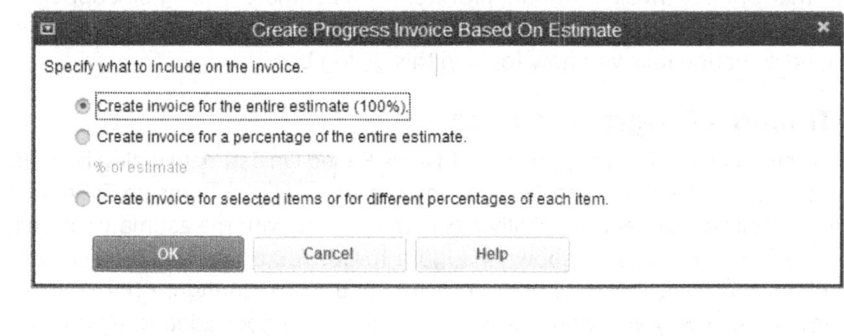

FIGURE 10-35

The "Create invoice for the entire estimate (100%)" option is available only the first time you create a progress invoice for an estimated job. After that, you have to invoice based on a percentage of the entire estimate, by picking individual items, or for the remaining amounts on the estimate (that last option isn't shown here).

- **Create an invoice for the remaining amounts of the estimate**. For every progress invoice *after* the first one for a job, you'll see *this* option instead of "Create invoice for the entire estimate (100%)." Pick this option when you're ready to create your last invoice for the job. Its sole purpose is to save you the hassle of calculating the percentages that you haven't yet billed.

- **Create invoice for a percentage of the entire estimate**. Choose this option if you negotiated a contract that pays a percentage when you reach a milestone, such as 15 percent when the house's foundation is complete. (Of course, you and the customer have to *agree* that a milestone is complete; QuickBooks can't help you with that.) This option is also handy if your contract specifies a number of installment payments. In the "% of estimate" box, type the percentage you've completed.

  Don't use this option if you include inventory on the estimate, because the invoice you create might contain fractional quantities of inventory items. For example, if you estimate 10 inventory items and then create a progress invoice for 33 percent of the job, the invoice will include 3.33 inventory items. You can avoid this by using the selected items option (described next) instead.

TIP Suppose your contract includes a clause that covers cost overruns, and the job ended up costing 20 percent more than your estimate. You might wonder how you can charge for that extra 20 percent. The hidden solution is that the "% of estimate" box doesn't limit you to 100 percent. So in this example, you'd type *120* percent for the last invoice to reflect the costs that exceeded the estimate.

- **Create invoice for selected items or for different percentages of each item**. This option is the most flexible and a must if you bill customers only for the work that's actually complete. For example, if you're building an office complex, one building might be complete while another is still in the framing phase. When you select this option, you can choose the services and products to include on the invoice and specify different percentages for each one. When you click OK, the "Specify Invoice Amounts for Items on Estimate" dialog box appears, initially showing your estimated amounts and any previously invoiced amounts. The next section tells you how to fill in this dialog box.

Fine-Tuning a Progress Invoice

When you click OK in the Create Progress Invoice Based On Estimate dialog box (or, if you chose items to invoice, the "Specify Invoice Amounts for Items on Estimate" dialog box), QuickBooks automatically fills in the invoice with the estimate's items, percentages, and amounts, as shown in Figure 10-36. You don't have to stick with the numbers that QuickBooks comes up with—you can reconfigure the charges on the invoice any way you want. However, it's always a good idea to review the customer's contract and get approval before you make any increases or additions not covered by the contract.

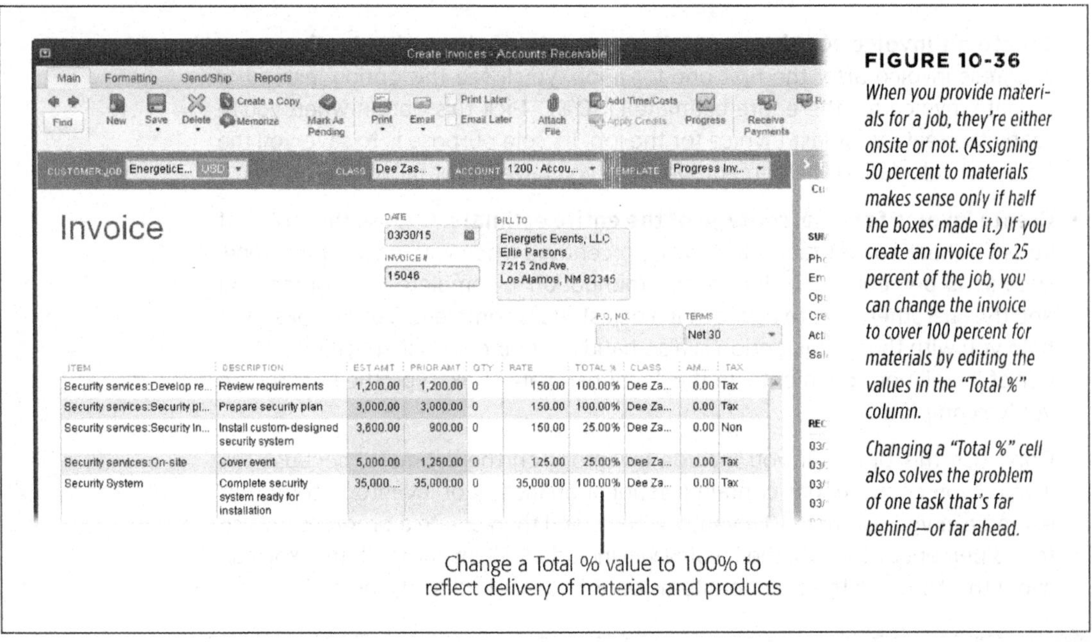
Create Invoices - Accounts Receivable
Invoice
Change a Total % value to 100% to reflect delivery of materials and products

FIGURE 10-36

When you provide materials for a job, they're either onsite or not. (Assigning 50 percent to materials makes sense only if half the boxes made it.) If you create an invoice for 25 percent of the job, you can change the invoice to cover 100 percent for materials by editing the values in the "Total %" column.

Changing a "Total %" cell also solves the problem of one task that's far behind—or far ahead.

You can modify line items directly in a QuickBooks invoice, but that approach doesn't create a record of your changes. If you want to keep a record of the changes you make between the estimate and the progress invoice, follow these steps instead:

1. **Open the progress invoice in the Create Invoices window.**

   Press Ctrl+I, and then click the window's left arrow (Previous) button until the progress invoice you want appears. You can also open an invoice from the Customer Center: On the center's Customers & Jobs tab, select the customer you want. Then, on the Transactions tab in the center's lower right, in the Show drop-down list, click Invoices. Finally, double-click the invoice you want to open.

2. **On the Create Invoices window's Main tab, click Progress.**

   The "Specify Invoice Amounts for Items on Estimate" dialog box shown in Figure 10-37 opens.

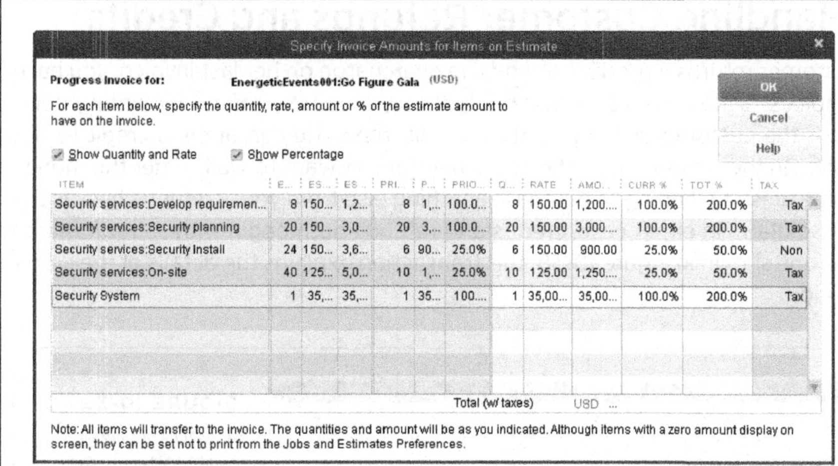

FIGURE 10-37

You can change only the cells in columns with a white background.

The columns with a gray background simply show the values from the estimate and previous progress invoices.

3. **Before you begin changing values, make sure that the correct columns are visible by turning on the "Show Quantity and Rate" and/or Show Percentage checkbox.**

   For example, if you're invoicing based on overall progress, turn on the Show Percentage checkbox. That way, you can invoice for the percentage of the work that's done, such as 40%. If you want to invoice for the materials you've used and the hours people have worked, turn on the "Show Quantity and Rate" checkbox. QuickBooks remembers which checkbox(es) you turn on and turns the same one(s) on the next time you open this dialog box.

4. **To change a value on the progress invoice, click the cell you want to change.**

   Changing a rate is a rare occurrence. However, it might happen if, say, you have a contract that bumps your consulting rate by 10 percent for the next calendar year. Then, if the job runs into the next calendar year, you can increase the rate for the hours worked in January.

   When you change a value in the table, QuickBooks recalculates the other columns. For example, if you type a percentage in a "Curr %" (current percentage) cell, QuickBooks calculates the amount to invoice by multiplying your estimated amount by the current percentage. The "Tot %" column shows the sum of previously invoiced amounts and the current amount.

5. **To apply your changes, click OK.**

   QuickBooks closes the "Specify Invoice Amounts for Items on Estimate" dialog box and takes you back to the modified progress invoice.

6. **Save the progress invoice by clicking Save & New or Save & Close.**

Handling Customer Refunds and Credits

If a customer returns a product or finds an overcharge on her last invoice, you have two choices: Issue a credit against her balance, or issue a refund by writing her a check. If the customer is happy with a credit, then you can apply a credit to her account. On the other hand, if the customer doesn't want to wait to get the money she's due or isn't planning to purchase anything else from you, a refund check is the logical solution. In either case, credits and refunds both begin with a *credit memo* like the one shown in Figure 10-38; this transaction explains the details of the credit or refund.

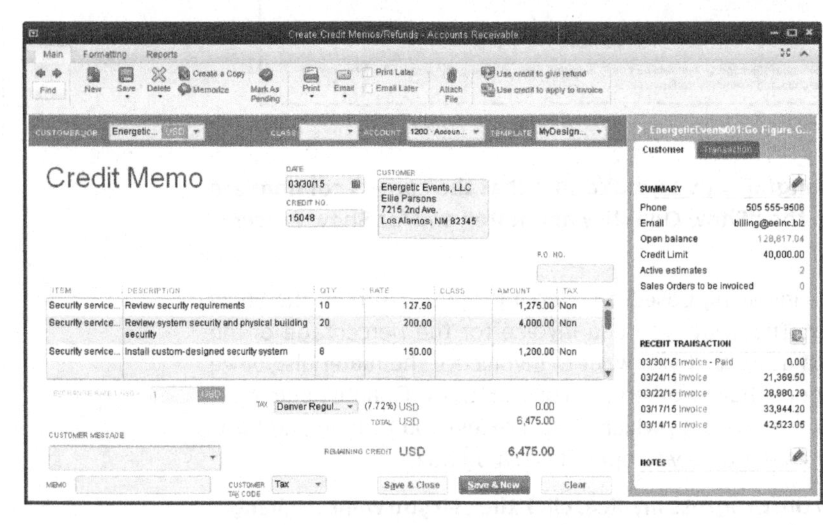

FIGURE 10-38

A credit memo looks a lot like an invoice, except that the items you add represent money flowing from you to the customer instead of the other way around. Don't enter negative numbers—QuickBooks takes care of calculating the money due based on the value of the items.

The right side of the Create Credit Memos/ Refunds window displays a summary of the customer or job and recent transactions.

Creating a Credit Memo from an Invoice

Here's how to transform an invoice into a credit memo to refund a customer's money:

1. **Open the invoice in the Create Invoices window.**

   The easiest way to find and open the invoice is by clicking Find on the Create Invoices window's Main tab. In the Find box, type the customer's name or the invoice number, and then click Find. When you see the correct invoice in the Find box, click it, and then click Go To.

2. **On the right side of the Create Invoices window's Main tab, click the Refund/ Credit button.**

   QuickBooks opens the Create Credit Memos/Refunds window (Figure 10-38) and copies the information from the invoice into the credit memo.

3. **If necessary, edit the credit memo.**

   For example, if you want to refund only a *portion* of the invoice, you can edit values or delete lines from the credit memo. Simply right-click a line in the line-item table and choose Delete Line on the shortcut menu.

4. **If you want to print or email the credit memo, turn on the Print Later or Email Later checkbox.**

5. **When you're done, click Save & Close.**

   The Available Credit dialog box appears with three options for handling the credit, as shown in Figure 10-39.

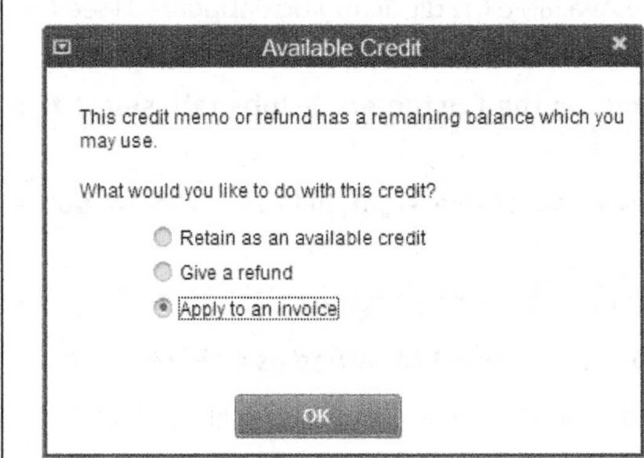

FIGURE 10-39

When you save a credit memo with available credit, QuickBooks displays this dialog box.

To keep the credit around and apply it later (page 292)—to the next invoice you create for the customer, for example—choose "Retain as an available credit." If you choose "Give a refund," QuickBooks opens the Issue a Refund window so you can write the refund check.

Don't choose "Apply to an invoice" unless that customer has an open invoice you can apply the refund to.

Creating Credit Memos

You can also create a credit memo from scratch to, for example, write off bad debt for all of a customer's open invoices. Here's how:

1. **In the Home Page's Customers panel, click Refunds & Credits, or choose Customers→Create Credit Memos/Refunds.**

   The Create Credit Memos/Refunds window opens. If you stay on top of your invoice numbers, you'll notice that QuickBooks automatically uses the next invoice number as the credit memo's number.

2. **As you would for an invoice, choose a Customer:Job.**

   Choose a class if you use classes, and, if necessary, choose the credit memo template you want to use.

3. **In the line-item table, add a line for each item you want to credit.**

   Be sure to include *all* the charges you want to refund, including shipping and taxes.

TIP If you want to include a message to the customer, choose it in the Customer Message box.

4. **If you want to print or email the credit memo, turn on the Print Later or Email Later checkbox.**
5. **When you're done, click Save & Close.**

When you save a credit memo with an available credit balance, the Available Credit dialog box appears with three options for handling the credit, as explained in Figure 10-39.

Creating Refund Checks

If your customer is dreadfully disgruntled, you'll probably want to write a refund check. If you didn't do that when the Available Credit dialog box appeared (see the previous section), here's how to do it now:

1. **Open the Customer Center and, on the Customers & Jobs tab, select the customer.**
2. **On the Transactions tab in the window's lower right, in the Show drop-down list, choose Credit Memos.**

   The list of open credit memos for that customer appears.

3. **Double-click the credit memo that you want to refund as a check.**

   The Create Credit Memos/Refunds window opens to that credit memo.

4. **In the window's Main tab, click the "Use credit to give refund" button.**

   QuickBooks opens the Issue a Refund window and fills in all the information you need to create the refund.

5. **In the Issue a Refund window, make sure the settings are correct.**

   In the window's "Issue this refund via" box, QuickBooks chooses Check and selects the checking account you set in your checking preferences (page 640). If the red-faced customer is staring at you from across the counter, choose Cash instead, and then click OK.

   If the Issue a Refund window's "To be printed" checkbox is turned on (which it is automatically), QuickBooks adds the check to the queue of checks waiting to be printed. Click OK to close the Issue a Refund window, and then click Save & Close in the Create Credit Memos/Refunds window. Then, to print the refund check right away, choose File→Print Forms→Checks. In the Select Checks to Print dialog box, make sure that the checkmark cell for the refund check is turned on, and then click OK. (See page 211 for the full story on printing queued-up checks.)

NOTE You can also refund money via credit card or other methods, such as E-Check and EFT, depending on the payment services you've signed up for.

Applying Credits to Existing Invoices

If a customer has an unpaid invoice or statement, you can apply a credit to it and reduce the amount that the customer owes. Here's how:

1. **Open the invoice in the Create Invoices window.**

   In the Customer Center (Customers→Customer Center), on the Customers & Jobs tab, select the customer. Next, on the Transactions tab in the window's lower right, in the Show drop-down list, choose Invoices. Then, in the Filter By box, choose Open Invoices. When you see the correct invoice in the table, click it to open it in the Create Invoices window.

2. **At the top of the Create Invoices window, click Apply Credits.**

   The Apply Credits dialog box shown in Figure 10-40 opens.

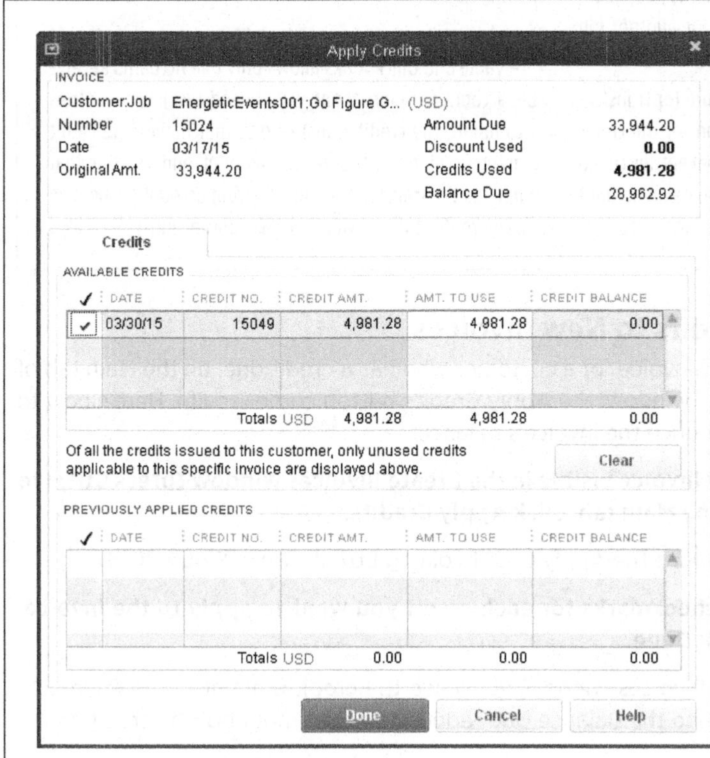

FIGURE 10-40

When you turn on the checkmark cells next to credits listed in the Available Credits table, the Credits Used value near the top of the dialog box shows the total amount of credit you're applying, and the Balance Due number shows how much is still due on the invoice.

If the original invoice's balance is less than the available credit, QuickBooks applies only enough of the credit to set the invoice's balance to zero. You can apply the remaining credit to another invoice by repeating the steps in this section.

3. **To apply one of the customer's credits, in the Available Credits table, turn on the checkmark cell for that credit.**

   If the customer has only one credit, QuickBooks turns on its checkmark cell automatically. If you don't see the credit you expect, it might apply to a different job or to the customer only. In that case, click Cancel and start again with step 1. The box below explains how to transfer a credit for one job to another job.

4. **In the Apply Credits dialog box, click Done.**

   QuickBooks takes you back to the Create Invoices window, which shows the credit amount in the Payments Applied field and the Balance Due reduced by the amount of the credit.

5. **Click Save & Close.**

That's all there is to it.

WORKAROUND WORKSHOP

Applying a Credit for One Job to a Different Job

If you work on several jobs for the same customer, the customer might ask you to apply a credit from one job to another. For example, perhaps the job with the credit is already complete and the customer wants to use that credit for another job that's still in progress.

QuickBooks doesn't have a ready-made feature for transferring credits between jobs. If you want to transfer the credit *and* satisfy your accountant, a couple of journal entries (page 432) will do the trick, but first you have to create an account to hold these credit transfers. In your chart of accounts, create an Other Expense account (page 57) and call it something like Credit Memo Transfers, Credit Memo Swap Account, or Clearing Account.

Because you're moving money into and out of Accounts Receivable and QuickBooks allows only one Accounts Receivable account per journal entry, you need *two* journal entries to complete the credit transfer: one that moves the credit from the first job into the clearing account, and a second that completes the transfer from the clearing account to the new job. Figure 10-41 shows what the two journal entries look like.

Applying Credits to New Invoices

If you create a new invoice for a customer who has a credit due, on the Main tab of the Create Invoices window, the Apply Credits button comes to life. Here's how to apply a credit to reduce the invoice's balance:

1. **With the new invoice visible in the Create Invoices window (press Ctrl+I to open it), on the Main tab, click Apply Credits.**

   QuickBooks opens the Apply Credits dialog box shown in Figure 10-41.

2. **Turn on the checkmarks for each credit you want to apply to the invoice, and then click Done.**

   In the Create Invoices window, you'll see the credit amount in the Payments Applied field and the Balance Due reduced by the amount of the credit.

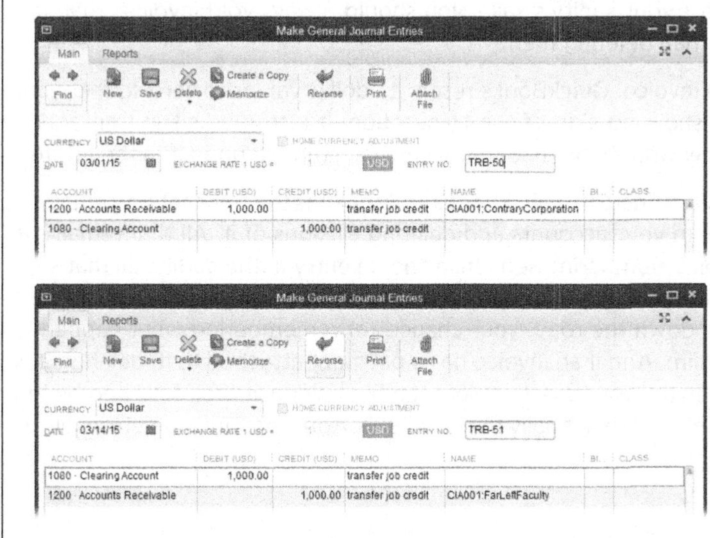

FIGURE 10-41

Top: The first journal entry transfers the amount of the credit memo from the first job into the clearing account; you have to choose the customer and job in the Name cell. (Typing a note in the Memo cell can help you follow the money trail later.)

Bottom: The second journal entry transfers the amount of the credit memo from the clearing account to the second job.

Modifying Invoices

You can make changes to invoices as you work on them or after you've saved them to, for example, add or remove items a customer requests. And if a customer decides to cancel an entire order, you can void an invoice, which zeroes out its total. You can even delete an invoice, although this maneuver makes sense only if you created the invoice by mistake. This section describes how to perform all these invoice-related tasks.

Editing Invoices

While you're in the process of creating an invoice or a sales receipt, you can jump to any field and change its value, delete lines, or insert new ones.

Even after you've saved an invoice, editing it is easy: Anytime an invoice is visible in the Create Invoices window, you can click any field and make whatever change you want. If you've already printed the invoice, turn on the Print Later checkbox so you don't forget to *reprint* the form with the changes you made.

TIP If you've already received a payment against an invoice, *don't* edit that invoice; doing so can disrupt the connections between payment, invoice, and accounts to the point that you'll never straighten it out. If you undercharged the customer, simply create a new invoice with the missing charges on it. If you charged the customer for something she didn't buy, issue a credit memo or refund (see page 288).

Voiding and Deleting Invoices

Sometimes, you want to eliminate an invoice—for instance, when you create one by mistake and want to remove its values from your accounts. QuickBooks provides two options, but for your sanity's sake, you should *always* void invoices that you don't want rather than deleting them.

When you void an invoice, QuickBooks resets its dollar values to zero so that your account balances show no sign of the transaction. It also marks the transaction as void so you know what happened to it when you stumble upon it in the future.

If you delete an invoice instead, QuickBooks *truly* deletes the transaction, removing its dollar values from your accounts and deleting all signs of it. All that remains is a hole in your invoice-numbering sequence and an entry in the audit trail that says you deleted the transaction (page 437). If your accountant or the IRS looks at your books a few years down the road, your chances of remembering what happened to the invoice are slim. And if an invoice has a payment attached to it, deleting it is even *more* problematic: You have to delete the bank deposit first, followed by the customer's payment, and then finally the invoice. Bottom line: Don't delete invoices; void them instead.

To void an invoice:

1. **Open the Create Invoices window, and then, on the Main tab, click Find.**
2. **In the Find Invoices dialog box, fill in the invoice number, customer name, or date, and then click Find. In the Find dialog box that appears, double-click the invoice you want to void.**

   The invoice appears in the Create Invoices window.
3. **Right-click in the Create Invoices window, and then choose Void Invoice from the shortcut menu. Alternatively, on the Create Invoices window's Main tab, choose Delete→Void.**

   All the values in the form change to zero, and QuickBooks adds "VOID" to the Memo field. To remind yourself why you voided this transaction, type the reason after "VOID."
4. **Click Save & Close.**

NOTE If you open the Accounts Receivable register's window, you might get nervous when you see the word "Paid" in the Amt Paid column of a voided transaction. Don't worry: Notice that the amount paid is zero, and that the word "Void" is in the Description field. The word "Paid" in the Amt Paid column is just QuickBooks' way of telling you the invoice is no longer open.

CHAPTER

11

Producing Statements

Statements are the perfect solution for businesses that charge individuals for time and other services in bits and pieces, such as law offices, cellphone service providers, and astrology advisors. Statements can summarize the charges racked up during the statement period (usually a month). They're also great for showing payments and outstanding balances, the way your cable bill shows the charges for your monthly service, the pay-per-view movies you ordered, your last payment, and your current balance. So even if you invoice your customers, you can send statements to show them their previous balances, payments received, new charges, and overdue invoices. (To learn about what statements *don't* do, see page 222.)

However, business-to-business invoicing is another story. Most accounting departments process only vendor invoices and credit memos for payments, so statements end up in the wastebasket. So if you do business only with other businesses, you're better off turning *off* QuickBooks' statements feature (the Note on page 296 explains where to find the preference to do that).

In this chapter, you'll find out how to produce statements, whether you accumulate charges over time or simply summarize your customers' account statuses.

Generating Statements

Think of a statement as a report of all the charges and payments during the statement period that you can send to your customer. The dates you choose for the statement determine its previous balance and the charges and customer payments it includes. Businesses typically send statements out once a month, but you can generate them for any time period you want.

NOTE To work with statements and statement charges, make sure the statements preference is turned on. Choose Edit→Preferences→Desktop View, and then click the Company Preferences tab. Make sure the "Statements and Statement Charges" checkbox is turned on, and then click OK.

In QuickBooks, creating statements is a simple process:

1. **If you want to charge your customers directly on statements, in the Accounts Receivable account register, enter statement charges (explained in a moment) for the services or other items you delivered to your customers.**

   If you use statements simply to show invoices, payments, and the resulting balance, you can skip this step.

2. **Generate statements for your customers.**

The following pages explain how to complete both these steps.

Creating Statement Charges

Statement charges are charges for services and items you deliver to your customers that you add directly to the Accounts Receivable account. They look like the line items you see on invoices, except for a few small but important omissions. When you select an item for a statement charge, you won't see any Sales Tax, percentage discount, Subtotal, or Group items in the Item drop-down list because QuickBooks doesn't let you use those features in statements. When you generate statements (explained in the next section), QuickBooks automatically grabs any payments that have been made, so you don't see Payment items in the Item drop-down list, either.

Here are the types of items that you can use to create statement charges:

- Service items
- Inventory Part items
- Inventory Assembly items (if you use QuickBooks Premier or Enterprise)
- Non-inventory Part items
- Other Charge items

TIP Statement charges don't handle sales tax. For that reason, you should use an *invoice* to bill for taxable items so QuickBooks can calculate the sales tax for you. Then, if you generate statements, QuickBooks scoops up that invoice and pops it into the appropriate statement.

Unlike invoice line items, you create statement charges directly in the Accounts Receivable register for the customer or job that racked up the charges, as shown in Figure 11-1. A statement charge has fields much like those for a line item in an invoice, although they're scrunched into two lines in the Accounts Receivable register. If you track your time and billable expenses in QuickBooks, you can use the Time/Costs feature to add billable time and expenses to the customer's Accounts Receivable register without going through the steps to create statement charges. This section explains how to add statement charges directly to the Accounts Receivable register and how to use the Time/Costs feature.

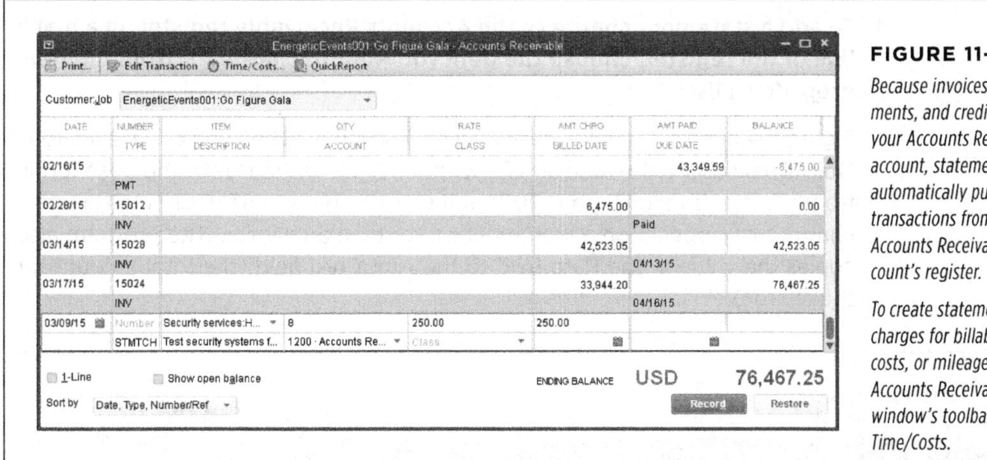

FIGURE 11-1

Because invoices, payments, and credits post to your Accounts Receivable account, statements automatically pull those transactions from your Accounts Receivable account's register.

To create statement charges for billable time, costs, or mileage, in the Accounts Receivable window's toolbar, click Time/Costs.

You enter statement charges in a customer's Accounts Receivable register (which is where QuickBooks stores the customer's invoices, credits, and payments), so the total in the register represents the customer's balance. Here's how to create a statement charge:

1. **Choose Customers→Enter Statement Charges or, in the Home Page's Customers panel, click the Statement Charges icon.**

   The Accounts Receivable register window opens.

2. **In the Customer:Job drop-down list, choose the customer or job to whom you want to assign the statement charge.**

   The Accounts Receivable register window then shows only Accounts Receivable for the customer or job you chose.

NOTE If you set up the customer or job to use a foreign currency, you can't record statement charges for that customer or job directly in the Accounts Receivable register. Instead, choose Company→Make General Journal Entry, and then record the charge as a journal entry. (You can also open the Make General Journal Entries window by clicking Edit Transaction in the Accounts Receivable window's toolbar.)

3. **If you track billable time, costs, or mileage, create statement charges for those items by clicking Time/Costs in the Accounts Receivable window's toolbar.**

   The "Choose Billable Time and Costs" dialog box that opens is the same one you see when you add billable time and costs to an invoice (page 255). Select the time and expenses you want to add, and then click OK. QuickBooks adds the selected items to the Accounts Receivable register and sets their Type to STMTCHG to indicate that the charges will appear on a statement instead of an invoice.

4. **To add a statement charge to the Accounts Receivable register, in a blank line of the register, choose the item you want to charge for from the Item drop-down list.**

   Figure 11-2 shows the fields for a blank transaction. When you choose an item, QuickBooks fills in the Rate and Description fields with the rate and description from the item's record (page 109) and sets the Type to STMTCHG to denote a charge that appears on a statement rather than an invoice. The program also copies the value in the Rate field to the Amt Chrg field (the total amount for the charge).

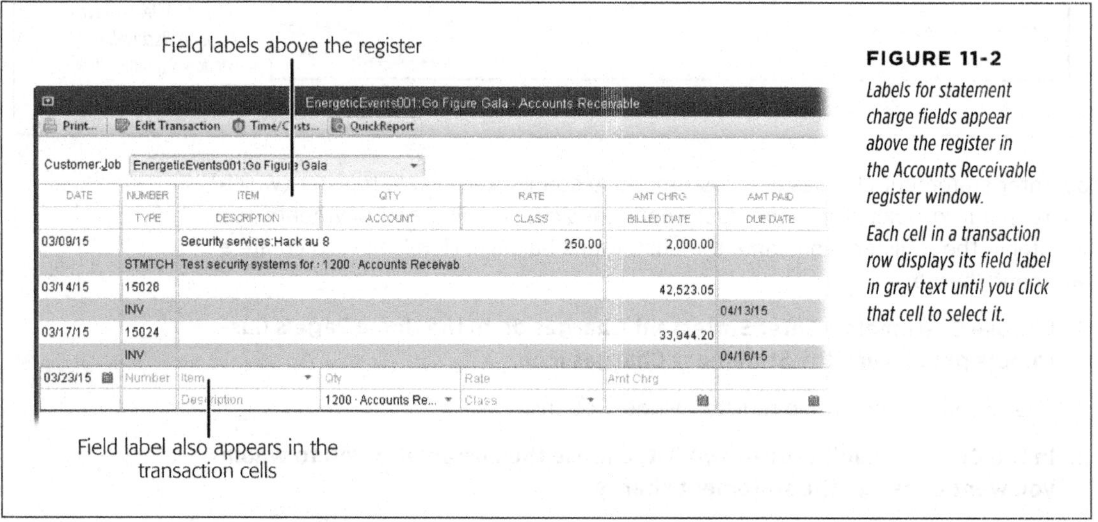

FIGURE 11-2

Labels for statement charge fields appear above the register in the Accounts Receivable register window.

Each cell in a transaction row displays its field label in gray text until you click that cell to select it.

5. **Press Tab to move to the Qty field, and then type a quantity for the item. (If you don't use a quantity and rate, then type the amount you want to charge in the Amt Chrg field instead.)**

   If you enter a quantity (based on the units for the item as described in the Note on page 109), then when you move to another field (by pressing Tab or clicking the field), QuickBooks updates the total amount in the Amt Chrg field by multiplying the rate by the quantity.

6. **If you want to change the rate, press Tab to move to the Rate field, and then type the correct value.**

   When you edit the value in the Rate field, QuickBooks recalculates the amount in the Amt Chrg field.

7. **If you want to revise the charge's description (which will appear on the statement you create), edit the Description field.**

   QuickBooks automatically fills in this field with the first paragraph of the Description field (labeled "Description on Sales Transaction" if the service is performed by a subcontractor or partner) from the item's record, but you can see only a smidgeon of it. To see the whole thing, put your cursor over the Description field, and QuickBooks displays the field's full contents in a tooltip just below the field.

8. **If you use classes (page 140), in the Class field, choose the one you want.**

   You can skip the Class field if it doesn't apply to this statement charge. If you set the preference to make QuickBooks prompt you about classes (page 636), then when you try to save the statement charge, QuickBooks asks if you want to save it without a class. Click Save Anyway to omit the class, or click Cancel to return to the transaction and add one.

9. **To control which statement the charge appears on, in the Billed Date field, choose a date for the charge.**

   QuickBooks uses the value in this field to determine which statement includes the charge. When you add a statement charge that you want to save for a future statement, be sure to choose a billed date within the correct time period. For example, if a membership fee comes due in April, choose a billed date that falls in April. That way, the statement charge won't show up until you generate the customer's April statement. On the other hand, if you forgot a charge from the previous month, set its billed date to a day in the current month so the charge appears on this month's statement.

10. **If you plan to assess finance charges for late payments, then in the Due Date field, choose the day when payment is due.**

    QuickBooks uses this date along with your preferences for finance charges (page 646) to calculate any late charges the customer owes you. (The due date is based on the terms you apply to the customer [page 76].) But late-charge calculations don't happen until you generate statements.

11. **To save the statement charge, click the Record button.**

TIP If you charge the same amount every month, memorize the first statement charge: With the statement charge filled in and selected in the register, either press Ctrl+M or right-click the statement charge and choose Memorize Stmt Charge on the shortcut menu. In the Memorize Transaction dialog box, set its recurrence schedule to the same day each month and choose the option to record the transaction automatically (page 324), and then click OK. QuickBooks then takes care of entering your statement charges for you, so all you have to do is generate customer statements once a month.

Generating Customer Statements

QuickBooks is smart, but it can't read your mind. The statements it generates include only the statement charges and other transactions you've entered. So before you produce monthly statements, double-check that you've entered all payments, credits, and refunds that your customers are due, and all new statement charges for the period.

To begin creating statements, choose Customers→Create Statements or, in the Home Page's Customers panel, click the Statements icon. As Figure 11-3 shows, everything about the statements you generate appears in the Create Statements window, including the date range for the statements, the customers you want to send statements to, the template you're using, printing options, and finance charges. The sections that follow explain your options and the best ways to apply them.

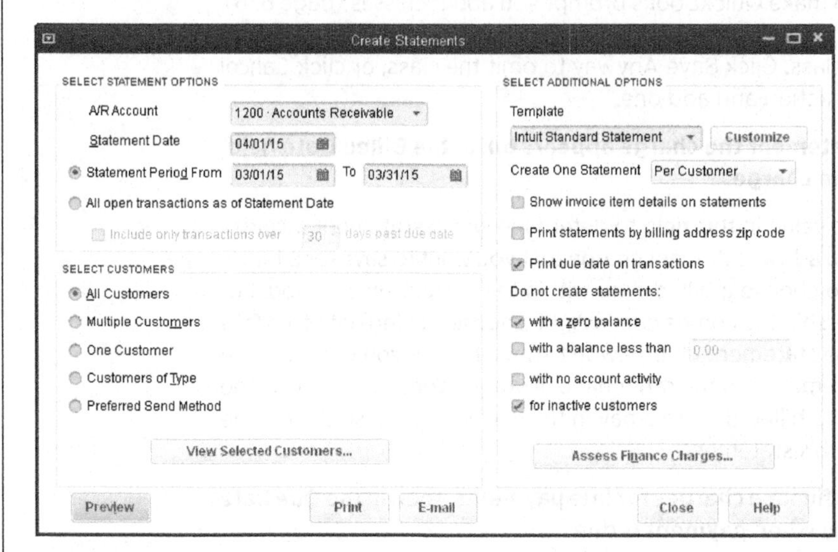

FIGURE 11-3

The options in the Select Customers section let you create statements for a subset of your customers, which comes in handy if you send statements to some customers by email and to some by U.S. mail, for example. In that case, you'd create two sets: one for email and the other for paper. You can also create a statement for a single customer if you made a mistake and want a corrected version. Or you can generate statements only for customers with balances.

NOTE If you've turned on the multiple currency preference (page 656), the Create Statement window displays the A/R Account box at its top left (it's visible in Figure 11-3). Use it to choose the correct Accounts Receivable account for the currency that applies to the statements you want to create. Repeat the statement-generation steps for each currency you use.

CHOOSING THE DATE RANGE

Statements typically cover a set time period, like a month. But the statement's date doesn't have to be during that period. For example, you might wait until the day *after* the period ends to generate the statement so you're sure to capture every transaction. In the Create Statements window's Select Statement Options section, you can adjust the following settings:

- **Statement Date**. In this field, type the date that you want to appear on the statement. In Figure 11-3, for example, the statement date is the day after the last day of the statement period.
- **Statement Period From _ To _**. Select this option to create statements for a period of time. For example, if you produce monthly statements, in the From box, choose the first day of the month, and in the To box, choose the last day of the month. Or you can choose dates to generate statements for a quarter or other date range.
- **All open transactions as of Statement Date**. Choosing this option adds *every* unpaid statement charge to the statement, regardless of when the charge happened. This option is particularly helpful when you want to generate a list of all overdue charges so you can send a reminder to woefully tardy customers. To filter the list of open transactions to only those overdue by a certain number of days, turn on the "Include only transactions over _ days past due date" checkbox, and then type the number of days late.

SELECTING CUSTOMERS

In the Create Statements window's Select Customers section, QuickBooks initially selects the All Customers option because most companies send statements to every customer. But you can choose another option to limit the list of recipients. (The next time you open the Create Statements window, QuickBooks remembers the option you chose and selects it automatically.) Here are your other options and the reasons you might choose each one:

- **Multiple Customers**. To specify the exact set of customers to whom you want to send statements (customers who received statements with errors on them, say), choose this option. After you do that, click the Choose button that appears to its right. In the Print Statements dialog box that opens, QuickBooks automatically selects the Manual option, so you can select each customer or job that you want to send a statement to (click individual customers or jobs in the dialog box's list or drag over adjacent customers to select them and display checkmarks next to their names). The Automatic option isn't really automatic—you have to type a customer's name *exactly* as it appears in the Customer Name field in the customer's record to select that single customer. So it's much easier to select the Manual option and then scroll to the name you want.
- **One Customer**. To create a corrected statement for a single customer, choose this option. In the field that appears, click the down arrow, and then choose the customer or job.
- **Customers of Type**. If you categorize customers by type and process their statements differently, choose this option. For example, you might spread your billing work out by sending statements to your corporate customers at the end of the month and to individuals on the 15th. In the drop-down list that appears, choose a customer type.

- **Preferred Send Method**. If you print some statements and email others, you'll have to create statements in two batches. Choose this option and, in the drop-down list that appears, pick one of the send methods. For example, choose E-mail here, and then click the E-mail button at the bottom of the window to send statements to the customers who prefer to receive bills that way. (Page 318 explains how to email forms.)

TIP If you loathe stuffing envelopes and licking stamps, offer your customers a discount for receiving their statements (or invoices and credit memos) via email. They're likely to say yes, and you can then send them statements from QuickBooks in the blink of an eye.

- **View Selected Customers**. Before you generate statements by clicking Print or E-mail, click this button to make sure you've chosen the correct customers.

SETTING ADDITIONAL OPTIONS

In the Create Statements window's Template box, QuickBooks automatically selects Intuit Standard Statement, but you can choose your own customized template instead (page 707). You can also control what QuickBooks adds to statements and which statements it should skip:

- **Create One Statement**. In this drop-down list, choosing Per Customer can save some trees because it makes QuickBooks generate one statement for each customer, no matter how many jobs you do for them. (On the statements, charges are grouped by job.) If each job has its own mailing address, you can create separate statements for each job instead by choosing Per Job here.
- **Show invoice item details on statements**. If you send statements only to find yourself answering customers' questions about what line items represent, turn on this checkbox to include invoice details on statements. That way, your customers can see all the info about the invoices on the statement, which could lead to faster payments. Say you run a landscaping company and mow lawns once a week. By turning on this checkbox, you don't have to send weekly invoices; instead, you can send a monthly statement that includes the individual invoice details.
- **Print statements by billing address zip code**. Turn on this checkbox if you have a bulk-mail permit, which requires that you mail by Zip code.
- **Print due date on transactions**. QuickBooks automatically turns on this checkbox because you'll typically want to show the due date for each entry on your statements.
- **Do not create statements**. Printing unnecessary statements is a waste of time and paper. QuickBooks includes several settings that you can choose to skip certain statements. For example, you can turn on the "with a zero balance" checkbox to skip statements for customers who don't owe you anything. (Leave this checkbox off if you want to send a statement to show that the customer's last payment arrived and that its balance due is zero.)

You might also decide to skip customers unless their balance exceeds your typical cost of processing a statement. With the cost of a first-class stamp and letterhead, envelope, and a label, you might skip statements unless the balance is at least $5 or so. Turn on the "with a balance less than" checkbox and, in the box to its right, type a dollar value.

You can also skip customers with no activity during the statement period—no charges, no payments, no transactions whatsoever—by turning on the "with no account activity" checkbox.

QuickBooks automatically turns on the "for inactive customers" checkbox because there's no reason to send statements to customers who aren't actively doing business with you.

- **Assess Finance Charges**. Not surprisingly, you have to turn on QuickBooks' finance charge feature before you can assess finance charges (see page 646). Once you've done that, you can click this button to add finance charges to your statements. In the Assess Finance Charges dialog box, you have the opportunity to turn off the checkmarks for individual customers. For example, if a squirrel ate your customer's last statement, you can turn off the checkmark in that customer's entry to tell QuickBooks not to penalize her with a finance charge. (You can also assess finance charges *before* you start the statement process by clicking the Finance Charges icon on the Home Page.)

Previewing Statements

Before you print statements on expensive letterhead or email them to your customers, it's a good idea to preview them to make sure you've chosen the right customers and that the statements are correct. Here's how to preview statements before you print or email them:

1. **In the Create Statements window, click Preview.**

   QuickBooks opens the Print Preview window (Figure 11-4), which works like its counterparts in other programs.

2. **Click "Prev page" or "Next page" to view the other statements in this batch.**

   If you left your reading glasses at home, click Zoom In to get a closer look. (The button's label changes to "Zoom Out" so you can click it to return to a bird's-eye view.)

3. **To return to the Create Statements window and print or email your statements, click Close.**

   The Print Preview window includes a Print button, but it's not the best way to print statements. Clicking it begins printing your statements *immediately,* so you don't have a chance to set your print options, like which printer to use or the number of copies. To adjust those settings as described on page 308, click Close, and then click Print in the Create Statements window instead.

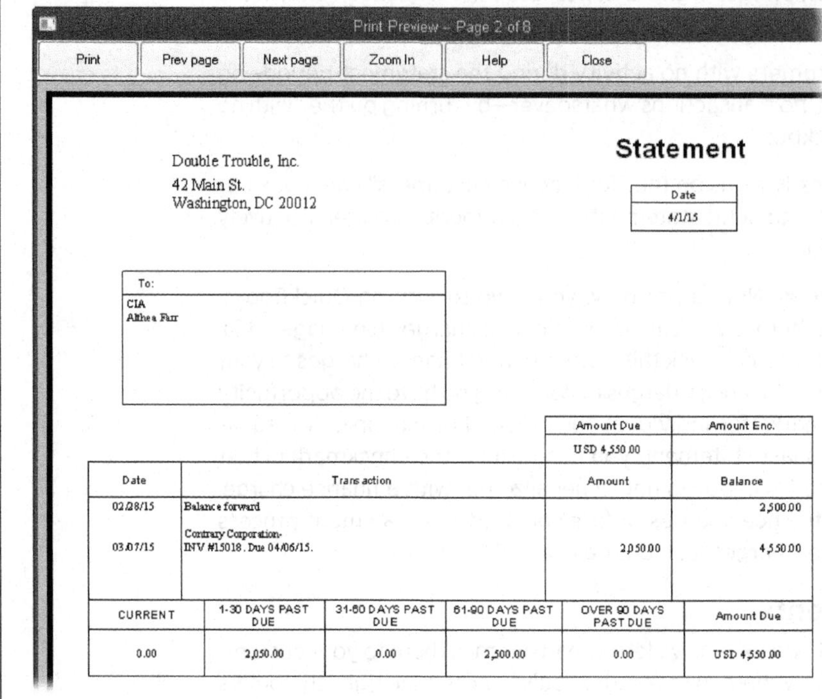

Double Trouble, Inc.
42 Main St.
Washington, DC 20012

Statement

Date
4/1/15

To:
CIA Althea Farr

Amount Due	Amount Enc.
USD 4,550.00	

Date	Transaction	Amount	Balance
02/28/15	Balance forward		2,500.00
03/07/15	Contrary Corporation- INV #15018. Due 04/06/15.	2,050.00	4,550.00

CURRENT	1-30 DAYS PAST DUE	31-60 DAYS PAST DUE	61-90 DAYS PAST DUE	OVER 90 DAYS PAST DUE	Amount Due
0.00	2,050.00	0.00	2,500.00	0.00	USD 4,550.00

FIGURE 11-4

If you generate statements for a given time period, the first line in the body of a statement is "Balance forward," which is the amount due prior to this statement's opening date.

The value in the Amount Due field is the total amount the customer owes you, which is the sum of the "Balance forward" value plus all the transactions for that customer or job that happened during the statement's date range, including payments.

At the bottom of the statement, the Amount Due figure is carved up into how much is current and how much is past due.

Generating Statements

When you're sure the statements are correct, in the Create Statements window, click Print or E-mail to generate your statements. This section describes how to do both.

EMAILING STATEMENTS

To email statements directly from QuickBooks, in the Create Statements window, click E-mail. If you use Microsoft Outlook, QuickBooks creates email messages in Outlook and automatically fills in the customers' email addresses. The messages contain the standard message you've set up for statements (page 665).

If you set up QuickBooks to use a web-based email service instead (page 665), the Send Forms dialog box opens, showing the statements you're about to email. There you can select additional statements, turn off statements you don't want to send, and click a statement to preview its content. Click Send Now to dispatch them to your customers.

PRINTING STATEMENTS

Here's how to print statements:

1. **In the Create Statements window, click Print.**

   QuickBooks opens the Print Statement(s) dialog box.

2. **Choose the printer you want to use.**

   For example, if you have a printer loaded with preprinted forms, select it in the "Printer name" drop-down list. (See page 309 to learn how to designate a printer so QuickBooks uses it every time you print statements.)

3. **Select one of the "Print on" options.**

   If you select "Intuit Preprinted forms," QuickBooks doesn't print the name of the form or the lines around fields, because they're already on the preprinted page. The "Blank paper" option tells the program to print the statements exactly the way you see them in the Print Preview window. The Letterhead option shrinks the form to leave a 2-inch band at the top of the page for your company logo.

TIP If your letterhead is laid out in an unusual way (your logo runs down the left side of the page, for instance), create a custom statement template (page 707) that leaves room for your letterhead elements, and then choose the "Blank paper" option.

4. **In the "Number of copies" box, type the number of copies of each statement you want to print.**

   For example, if you want one copy for the customer and one for your files, type *2*.

5. **Click Print.**

CHAPTER

12

Transaction Timesavers

QuickBooks can zip you through the two basic ways of producing and distributing invoices and other forms: on paper and electronically. Within those two camps, you can choose to produce and send forms as soon as you complete them *or* place them in a queue to process in batches. For sporadic forms, it's easier to print or email them as you go. But when you generate dozens or even hundreds of sales orders, invoices, statements, or checks, printing and emailing batches is a much better use of your time.

If you have workhorse transactions that you enter again and again, QuickBooks can memorize them and then fill in most, if not all, of the fields in future transactions for you. For transactions that happen on a regular schedule—like monthly customer invoices or vendor bills—the program can remind you when it's time to record them, or even add the transactions without any help from you. You can also memorize transactions that you use occasionally, such as estimates, and call on them only when you need them.

Once you've created lots of transactions, you'll need a way to locate them. QuickBooks' search features can help you track down financial info, which you can appreciate if you've ever hunted frantically for a transaction. Whether you want to correct a billing problem on a customer's invoice, check whether you paid a vendor's bill, or look for the item you want to add to an estimate, QuickBooks gives you several ways to search. You can look for different types of transactions within various date ranges in the Customer, Vendor, and Employee centers—and the Inventory Center, if you use QuickBooks Premier or Enterprise. The Item List window sports a few search boxes for finding the items you want. Form windows, such as Create Invoices, have a Find button on their Main tabs so you can quickly find transactions of the corresponding type. You can use the program's Search feature to search throughout your company file or QuickBooks. And the full-blown Find feature is perfect for surgical searches.

This chapter explains all your options.

NOTE QuickBooks' Attachments feature lets you attach files to records, such as customers and vendors, and to transactions, such as invoices. See the box on page 314 for more info.

Printing Forms

Before you can start printing, you have some setup to do. But once QuickBooks' print settings are in place and there's paper in your printer, you can print forms with just a click or two.

If you want to apply special settings to certain types of forms, then for each one, QuickBooks needs to know the printer you want to use, the paper you print to (like preprinted forms or letterhead), and a few other details. (The program remembers these settings, so you have to go through this process only once for each type of form.) From then on, QuickBooks fills in the Print dialog box's settings automatically when you choose a type of form to print, although you can change the settings before you print.

With these prep tasks behind you, you're ready to print. You can either print a form right away or add it to a queue to print in batches. This section explains how to accomplish all these printing tasks.

TIP To make sure you don't forget to process forms, you can create reminders (page 483) for invoices, credit memos, sales receipts, and—if you use QuickBooks Premier or Enterprise—sales orders that are queued up to print.

Setting Print Options

For the forms you print using basic settings—such as printing to your workhorse printer on blank paper using portrait orientation—you don't have to bother specifying print options. But if you print invoices on multipart forms, paychecks on preprinted check forms, statements on letterhead, and reports on plain paper, you can assign a different printer and settings to the forms with special printing needs. Keep each printer stocked with the right type of paper, and you can print your documents with barely a glance at the print options. If you set up print settings in QuickBooks before you print, the program will fill in those settings for you automatically when you choose a type of form. (However, print dialog boxes still appear, so you can change any print options before committing your documents to paper.)

TIP Many of the options in the "Printer setup" dialog box are the same as options you can set within your operating system, as Figure 12-1 shows. However, QuickBooks keeps the options you choose in its "Printer setup" dialog box separate from your operating system settings. So, for example, if you use Windows' printer options to set your most popular printer to use portrait orientation, you can set that same printer to use landscape orientation in QuickBooks.

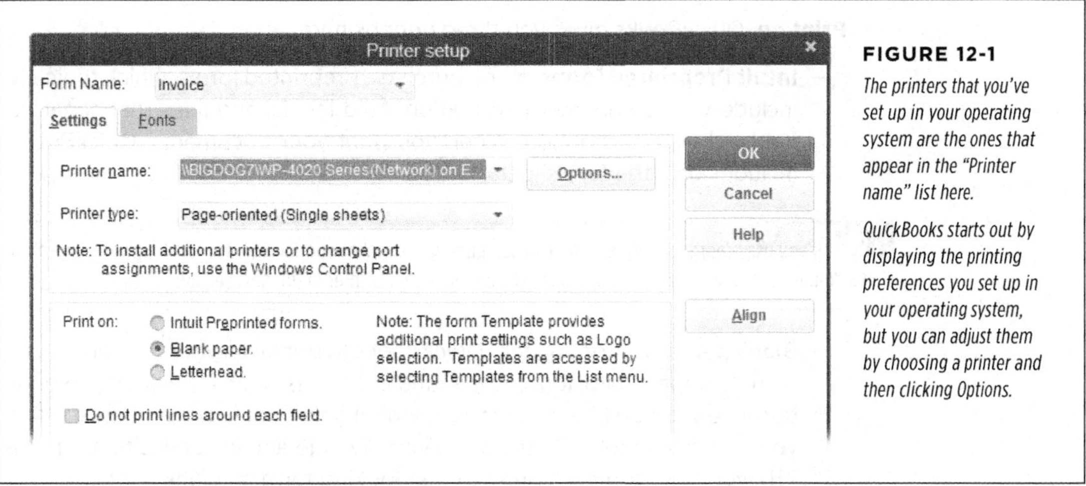

FIGURE 12-1

The printers that you've set up in your operating system are the ones that appear in the "Printer name" list here.

QuickBooks starts out by displaying the printing preferences you set up in your operating system, but you can adjust them by choosing a printer and then clicking Options.

To assign and set up printers for forms in QuickBooks, choose File→Printer Setup. Then adjust the following settings:

- **Form Name**. As you learned earlier, in QuickBooks, each form has its own print settings, so you're free to print invoices on letterhead, timesheets in landscape orientation, and checks to a printer filled with preprinted checks. Use this drop-down list to choose the form you want to set up for printing.
- **Printer name**. Choose a printer here to designate it as the standard for the form you selected above. Whenever you print that type of form, QuickBooks will automatically select this printer, but you can always choose a different printer—for instance, when you switch between printing paper documents and creating Adobe PDF files that you can email.
- **Options**. If you want to adjust the properties for the printer you chose, click this button. In the dialog box that appears, depending on the type of printer, you can change things like the document's orientation, page order, pages per sheet, print quality, paper tray, color, and so on.

NOTE The rest of the settings in this list appear for *most* of the forms in the Form Name drop-down list, but not all of them. For example, you don't see the "Printer type" setting for reports (to learn about print settings for reports, see page 586).

- **Printer type**. When you choose a printer name, QuickBooks fills in this box with its best guess of the type (it usually guesses right). If it guesses wrong, simply choose the correct type in this drop-down list. If the printer feeds individual pages through, such as letterhead or blank paper, choose "Page-oriented (Single sheets)." If it feeds continuous sheets of paper with perforations on the edges, such as the green-striped paper so popular in the past, choose "Continuous (Perforated Edge)."
- **Print on**. QuickBooks gives you three options here:
  - **Intuit Preprinted forms**. If you purchase preprinted forms, which typically include your company's information, field labels, and lines that separate fields, choose this option. When you print your documents, QuickBooks includes only the forms' data.

TIP If you use preprinted forms, a small misalignment can make your documents look sloppy and unprofessional. You'll learn how to align documents to the paper in your printer in the next section.

  - **Blank paper**. This option tells QuickBooks to print *everything* in your document: company info, logo, labels, and data. This is the easiest way to print because you don't have to worry about aligning the paper and the form. If you set up a template with your company logo and attractive fonts (page 711), you can produce a professional-looking form on blank paper.
  - **Letterhead**. When you print to letterhead that already includes your company's address and other information, you don't need to print that info on your documents. Choose this option to tell QuickBooks to skip printing your company information.

TIP The Letterhead option tells QuickBooks to start printing the form 2 inches from the top of the paper. If your letterhead has your logo and company information somewhere *other* than the top of the page, don't use this option. Instead, create a custom template for your form (page 707) to leave room for the logo. Then, when you print, select the "Blank paper" option.

- **Do not print lines around each field**. Turning on this checkbox is a matter of personal preference. Lines around each field make it clear which information belongs to which label, but you might consider those lines unnecessary. If your template separates fields to your satisfaction, turn off this checkbox to print only the labels and data, not borders around each field. (Because preprinted forms include borders, QuickBooks automatically turns on this checkbox if you choose the "Intuit Preprinted forms" option.)

Aligning Forms and Paper

If you've ever gotten lost in an office-supply store, you understand why printing includes so many options. You can print on different types of paper using different types of printers, and making the two line up properly can be a delicate process.

And besides invoices and other forms, you might also print ancillary documents like mailing labels and packing slips.

To save some trees and your sanity, make sure the paper in your printer is aligned properly *before* you print, especially if you use fancy letterhead or preprinted forms. (When you use preprinted forms or continuous-feed paper with perforations for page breaks, the alignment of the paper is crucial: If it's not lined up properly, your data won't appear next to the correct labels or an invoice might print over a page break.) It's a good idea to print a sample to check the alignment of your forms and paper every time you print, but it's particularly important if you're printing a big batch of forms. If the sample's alignment is off, here's how to save time, paper, and your mental health:

1. **Choose File→Printer Setup.**

   The "Printer setup" dialog box opens.

NOTE You can also align forms just before you print a batch: Choose File→Print Forms, and then choose the type of form you want to align, such as Invoices. In the "Select [forms] to Print" dialog box, select the ones you want to print, and then click OK to open the "Print [forms]" dialog box, such as Print Invoices if you're printing invoices. In that dialog box, click Align.

2. **From the Form Name drop-down list, choose the type of form you want to align, and then click Align.**

   If you have more than one template to choose from, QuickBooks opens the Align Printer dialog box. Choose the template you want to use to align your paper, and then click OK.

   If you have only one template, the program goes straight to a different dialog box; exactly which one depends on the type of paper that's selected in the "Printer setup" dialog box's "Printer type" list:

   — If the Continuous (Perforated Edge) option is selected, you'll perform both steps 3 and 4.

   — If the Page-oriented (Single sheets) option is selected, the Fine Alignment dialog box appears and you can skip to step 4.

3. **If the Printer type is Continuous (Perforated Edge), the "Use 'Coarse' for Big Vertical Adjustments" dialog box opens. Position the paper so the print head is just below a page break, click Coarse, and then click OK to print a sample form.**

   After you print a sample form, don't adjust the paper in your printer (QuickBooks warns you several times not to). The form that prints includes text indicating a pointer line. When the Coarse Alignment dialog box appears on your screen, in the Pointer Line Position box, type the number of the line preprinted in the paper's margin where the pointer line text printed. QuickBooks uses that number to align the form and the paper. Click OK to print another sample. When the alignment is correct, click Close. You can then perform a fine alignment, if necessary, by clicking Fine Align.

4. **In the Fine Alignment dialog box's Vertical and Horizontal boxes (Figure 12-2), type numbers to represent the hundredths of an inch to move the form to line it up with the paper.**

   After you tweak the alignment, click Print Sample to check the printed form's appearance. When the form is aligned, click OK—and keep your mitts off the paper in the printer.

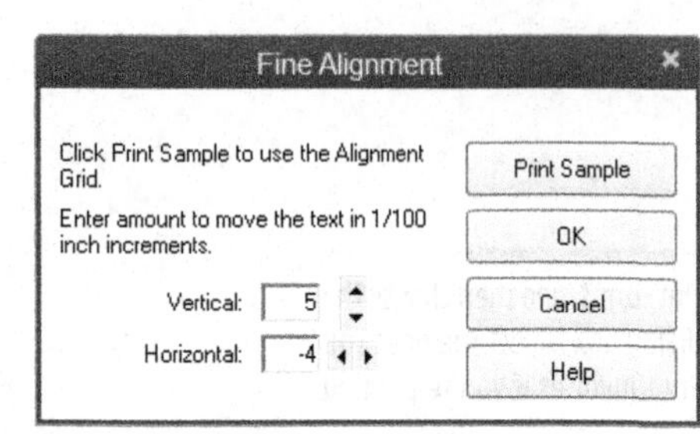

FIGURE 12-2

Typing a positive number in the Vertical box moves the form toward the top of the page. A positive number in the Horizontal box moves the form to the right on the page.

Negative vertical and horizontal numbers move the form down and to the left, respectively.

Choosing a Print Method

At the top of each QuickBooks form's window are the same basic printing options; Figure 12-3 shows the Create Invoices window as an example. Here's a guide to your choices for printing documents:

- **Preview a form before printing**. On the form window's Main tab, click Print, and then choose Preview from the drop-down menu.
- **Print one form**. If you want to print the current form, on the form window's Main tab, click Print, and then choose the type of form from the drop-down menu (in Figure 12-3, that's Invoice).
- **Printing in batches**. If you turn on the Print Later checkbox at the top of the form window, QuickBooks adds the current form to a queue that you can print as a batch. To print the batch of forms, at the top of the form window, click Print, and then choose Batch from the drop-down menu.
- **Print special forms**. If you want to print a packing slip, shipping label, or envelope to go with the form you're printing, at the top of the form window, click Print, and then choose Packing Slip, Shipping Label, or Envelope from the drop-down menu. If you choose Envelope, you have to specify the size and whether you want to include the return address (you don't if your envelopes already have your return address on them). You can even print a delivery barcode for addresses in the United States.

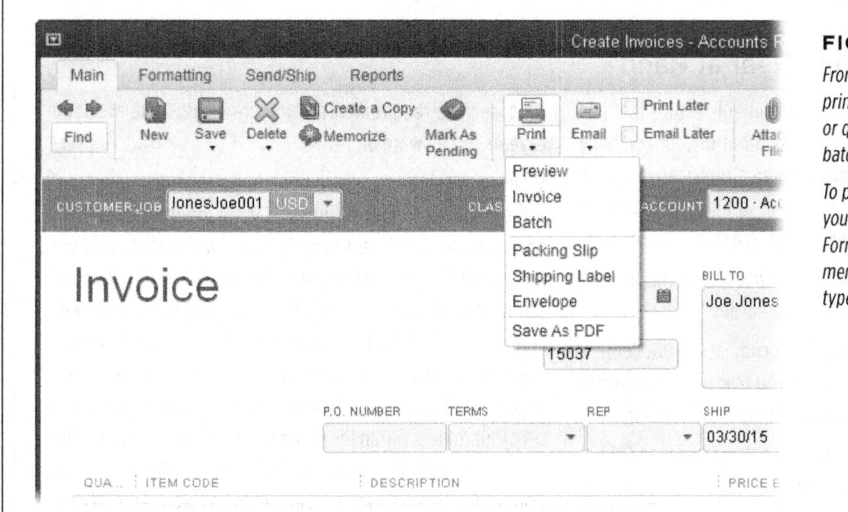

FIGURE 12-3

From a form's window, you can print one document at a time or queue them up to print in batches.

To process batches of documents, you can choose File→Print Forms from the main QuickBooks menu bar and then choose the type of form you want to print.

Printing One Form

When you display a form in its corresponding window, you can print it right away. To preview the form before you print it, on the window's Main tab, click Print→Preview. The Print Preview window opens and shows you what the form will look like when you print it. Click Close to close the Print Preview window and return to the form's window.

To print the current form, click Print, and then choose the form type (Invoice, in this example). QuickBooks displays the Print One Invoice dialog box, where you can choose the printer and paper. (You can also preview the form by clicking Preview in this dialog box.)

NOTE To prevent embezzling, QuickBooks automatically saves forms when you print them. That way, if you change a form after you print it, the audit trail shows a record of the change.

Printing in Batches

If the Print Later checkbox is turned on when you save a form, QuickBooks adds that form to a print queue. After you've checked that your printer contains the correct paper and that the paper is aligned properly, you can print all the forms in the queue in just a few steps:

GEM IN THE ROUGH

Keeping Related Info Near at Hand

QuickBooks offers a helpful file-attachment feature that lets you attach files to records and transactions in your company file. For example, you can attach an electronic copy of a job contract to a customer record, a photo of an item you sell to the item's record, or a scanned receipt to a credit card charge.

QuickBooks gives you several different ways to use this feature, depending on where you are in the program:

- In the *Doc Center* (Company→Documents→Doc Center), you can attach documents that you scan in with a scanner or drag over from Outlook or folders on your computer.
- In the Customer Center, Vendor Center, Employee Center, or Inventory Center, select the name or item you want to attach a file to, and then click the Attach button at the window's upper right (the button has a paper-clip icon on it).
- In a transaction window like Create Invoices, display the transaction you want to attach something to, and then click the Attach File button on the window's Main tab.

When you click either the Attach or Attach File button, the Attachments window appears. At the top of the window, click the Computer, Scanner, or Doc Center button to tell QuickBooks where the file you want to attach is coming from. Or simply drag the file onto the area labeled "Drop document from Outlook, your desktop, or folders here."

Attaching documents to records and transactions keeps reference info within easy reach. Whenever you open a record or transaction in QuickBooks that has files attached to it, you can see those files by clicking the Attach or Attach File button. However, if you want to attach files that *change* from time to time, such as requirements or job drawings, there are some caveats to be aware of.

When you create an attachment in QuickBooks, you *aren't* attaching the original document. (Some programs, like Word and Excel, let you insert hyperlinks to files so that clicking a link opens the original file regardless of where it's located, but QuickBooks doesn't work that way.) Instead, QuickBooks creates a *copy* of the file and attaches the copy. So if you edit the original document, you won't see those changes in the attached document. QuickBooks puts the copies it creates in a set of subfolders within the folder that holds your company file. For example, say your company file is stored in *My Documents\Data_Files*. If you attach a document to an invoice, QuickBooks stores a copy of the file in the folder *My Documents\Data_Files\Attach\[company file name]\Txn\[ID]*, where "ID" identifies the transaction. If you attach a document to a customer's record, the copy ends up in *My Documents\Data_Files\Attach\[company file name]\List\Name\[ID]*, where "ID" is a code that represents the customer.

QuickBooks is particular about where a company file's Attach folder is located. If you move it, your attached files for that company file won't show up in the Doc Center. If files go missing in the Doc Center, make sure the Attach folder is in the same folder that holds the corresponding company file. Then, in QuickBooks, choose Company→Documents→Repair Attached Document Links.

Fortunately, you don't have to navigate to the Attach folders to find your file attachments. You can simply manage your attached files in the Doc Center.

1. **Choose File→Print Forms, and then choose the type of form you want to print. (Or, on the Main tab of the form's window—like Create Invoices, for example—click Print→Batch.)**

   Either way, QuickBooks opens the "Select [forms] to Print" dialog box with all your unprinted forms selected, as shown in Figure 12-4. You can turn checkmarks on or off one at a time or by dragging down the checkmark column. You can also select or deselect all the forms by clicking Select All or Select None.

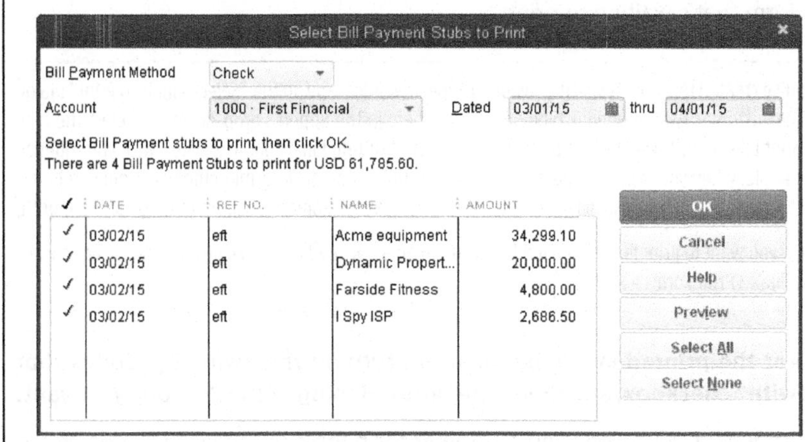

FIGURE 12-4

To remove any form from the batch, click its checkmark to turn it off. After you pay a bill, you can print a bill payment receipt: Choose File→Print Forms→Bill Payment Stubs to see the bill payment receipts that are ready to print.

2. **If you want to print labels for the selected forms, click Print Labels.**

   The next section dishes out the details on printing labels. After you print the labels, you're back in the "Select [forms] to Print" dialog box, so you can print the forms that go with them.

3. **Click OK to print the selected forms. In the "Print [forms]" dialog box that appears, click Print.**

   Because problems can occur during printing (paper jams, low toner, or smears), QuickBooks opens the "Print [forms] - Confirmation" dialog box after it prints the forms.

4. **If the forms printed correctly, click OK to close the confirmation dialog box.**

   If a problem occurred, in the "Print [forms] - Confirmation" dialog box, click the Reprint cell for each form that didn't print correctly. If the whole batch is a loss, click Select All. Either way, click OK to reprint the forms you selected.

Printing Mailing and Shipping Labels

QuickBooks can print mailing labels to go with some of the forms you print, such as invoices. The trick is that you have to print the labels *before* you print the forms because, after you print the forms, they disappear from the "Select [forms] to Print" dialog box. Here's how you print labels for your forms:

1. **Choose File→Print Forms, and then choose the type of form for which you want labels.**

   QuickBooks opens the "Select [forms] to Print" dialog box (Figure 12-4) with all your unprinted forms selected.

2. **In the "Select [forms] to Print" dialog box, click Print Labels.**

   QuickBooks opens the "Select Labels to Print" dialog box and automatically chooses the Name option, which prints labels for the names associated with each form that's waiting to print.

TIP If you've created forms for a specific customer type or vendor type, in the "Select Labels to Print" dialog box, choose the Customer Type or Vendor Type option and then, in the option's drop-down list, select the type you want to print labels for. These options are better suited for printing labels *not* associated with your queued forms—for example, when you want to send a letter to your retail customers informing them of product rebates. Or you might use them if you process forms for retail and wholesale customers at different times of the month.

Alternatively, if you want to print labels for a mailing *without* an associated form (like an open-house announcement) choose File→Print Forms→Labels.

3. **To filter the printed labels by location, turn on the "with Zip Codes that start with" checkbox, and then type the beginning of the Zip code you want.**

   For example, if you're offering a seminar for people in the Denver area, you'd type *801* in the box, as shown in Figure 12-5.

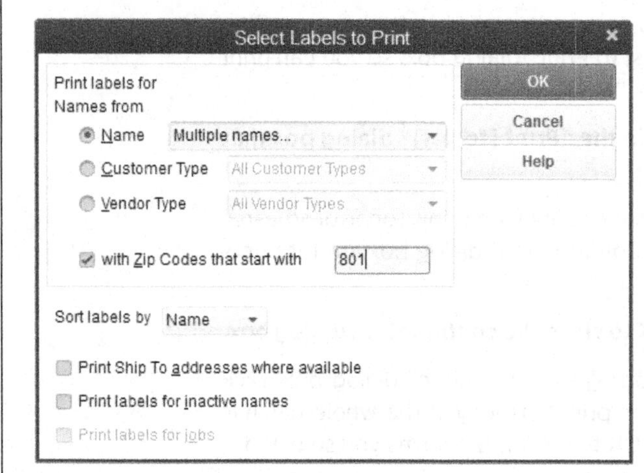

FIGURE 12-5

If you want to print labels for a mailing that has nothing to do with money (like an announcement about your new office location), choose File→Print Forms→Labels.

When you do that, this dialog box opens so you can jump right to selecting the recipients.

4. **In the "Sort labels by" box, choose Name or Zip Code.**

   If you use bulk mail, choose Zip Code so you can bundle your mail by Zip code as your bulk-mail permit requires.

5. **To print *shipping* labels rather than labels that use billing addresses, turn on the "Print Ship To addresses where available" checkbox.**

   The "Print labels for inactive names" checkbox can come in handy from time to time—for instance, if you need to send a letter to past *and* present customers to tell them about a product recall.

When you want to send communications to different addresses for each job, even if the jobs are for the same customer, turn on the "Print labels for jobs" checkbox.

6. **Make sure you've selected the labels you want, and then click OK.**

   QuickBooks opens the Print Labels dialog box.

7. **If you've already chosen the printer and settings for labels in Printer Setup, click Print and you're done.**

   If you want to print to different labels, in the Label Format drop-down list, choose the type of label you're using. (You can find the vendor and label number—like Avery #5262—on the box of labels.) The drop-down list includes popular Avery formats and several other options.

   After you print your labels, QuickBooks closes the Print Labels dialog box, and the "Select [forms] to Print" dialog box reappears so you can click OK to proceed to printing your queued forms as explained on page 308.

Printing Packing Slips

When you ship products to a customer, it's common to include a packing slip that describes what should be in the shipment. In QuickBooks, you have to print each packing slip individually from the Create Invoices window. (The packing-slip template that Intuit provides is basically an invoice without prices.)

Here are the steps for printing the packing slip for an invoice:

1. **If the Create Invoices window is already open, click the left arrow (Previous) in the window's Main tab until you find the invoice you're interested in, or click the Find button, fill in fields that identify the invoice, and then click Find.**

   To find an invoice when the Create Invoices window *isn't* open, on the Home Page, click Customers to open the Customer Center. Next, click the Transactions tab on the window's left, and then choose Invoices in the tab's list of transaction types. Finally, in the table on the right, double-click the invoice you want, and QuickBooks opens it in the Create Invoices window.

2. **In the Create Invoices window, click Print→Packing Slip.**

   QuickBooks sets the window's Template box to the packing slip template and opens the Print Packing Slip dialog box, where you can set print options, if necessary.

3. **Once the settings look good, click Print.**

   QuickBooks closes the Print Packing Slip dialog box and prints the packing slip.

4. **Back in the Create Invoices window, click Save & Close.**

   QuickBooks automatically changes the Template box from the packing slip template back to the invoice template.

TIP If you want QuickBooks to always use a particular packing slip template, change the packing slip template preference as described on page 663.

Emailing Forms

If you've grown tired of paper cuts, then sending invoices and other forms electronically is much more satisfying. But to make your electronic sending as efficient as possible, be sure that all your customer records include email addresses. Otherwise, you'll waste time typing email addresses one after another, and the chance of a typo increases with each address you type.

If you use a popular email program, such as Outlook, QuickBooks automatically uses that program to send forms. When you email a form as described in this section, QuickBooks opens new messages in your email program, which you can edit as you would any email. When you send the emails, they show up in your Sent Items folder or Sent box. You can also tell QuickBooks to use a web-based email service like Gmail. This section explains all your emailing options.

Choosing a Send Method

QuickBooks gives you a couple of ways to email forms: Similar to printing, you can email the current form or add it to a queue to send in batches:

- **Send one form**. To email the current form, at the top of the form window, click the Email button, and then choose the form's name, such as Invoice, as shown in Figure 12-6. If the form has files attached in QuickBooks and you want to attach those files to the email, choose "[form] and Attached Files" instead, such as "Invoice and Attached Files."

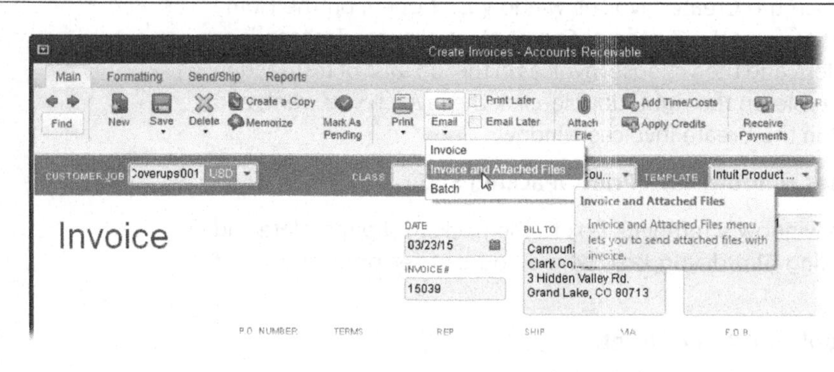

FIGURE 12-6

When you click the Email button, you can choose the form's name (Invoice, in this example) to email the form that's open in the window, or choose Batch to email all the forms in your to-be-emailed queue. Choose "[form] and Attached Files" to email the form and any files attached to it in QuickBooks.

- **Sending in batches**. When you turn on the Email Later checkbox at the top of a form window, QuickBooks adds the current form to the queue of forms that you'll email all at once. You can send them by clicking the window's Email button and then choosing Batch.

Emailing One Form

Here's how to email a form when you're looking at it in its window (these steps use the Create Invoices window as an example, but they work equally well for other sales forms):

1. **In the Create Invoices window (or other form window), click the Email button and then choose Invoice (or the corresponding form name).**

   What happens when you choose Email→Invoice depends on the email program you use. If you use one of several popular email programs, the program opens and creates a new message with the fields from QuickBooks filled in and a PDF file of the form attached to it.

   If you use web-based email (see page 665 to learn how to set it up), the "Send [form]" dialog box opens with the email fields filled in.

NOTE Say you attached files to a form in QuickBooks, as explained in the box on page 314 (like photos to show that the work you're invoicing for is complete, or travel receipts for the reimbursable expenses on an invoice), and you want to attach those files to the email. To email a form *and* its attached files, on the form window's Main tab, click Email→"[form name] and Attached Files" ("Invoice and Attached Files," for example). The email message that QuickBooks creates includes a PDF file of the form *and* any files attached to the transaction in QuickBooks. If you want to attach additional files from your computer to the email, click the paper-clip icon to the right of the Attach box (labeled in Figure 12-7).

2. **Modify the message in any way you want.**

   You can change the email addresses, subject, and email text that QuickBooks automatically adds.

3. **If you use web-based email, click the "Send [form]" dialog box's Send Now button. If you use a desktop email program, click its Send button.**

Emailing in Batches

When you turn on the Email Later checkbox on the Main tabs of the windows for forms you create, QuickBooks adds them to an email queue. You can then send all the forms you've queued up in just a couple of steps:

1. **Choose File→Send Forms or, on the Main tab of the window where you create the forms—such as the Create Invoices window—click Email→Batch.**

   QuickBooks opens the Send Forms dialog box, which lists and selects all your unsent forms.

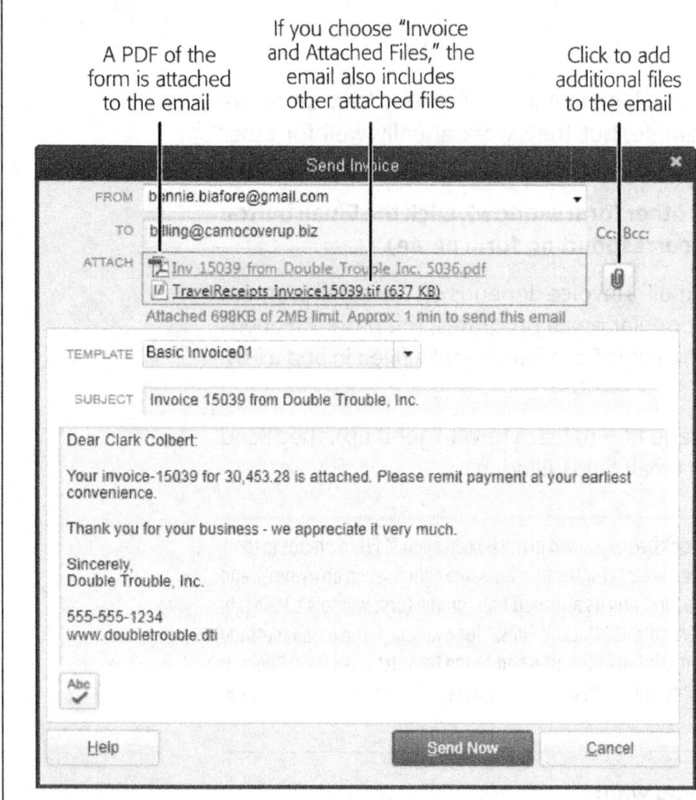

FIGURE 12-7

You send a QuickBooks-generated message just as you would an email you created in your email program. In Outlook, for example, simply click Send. When you email an invoice, QuickBooks attaches it to the email message as an Adobe PDF file.

If you choose Email→"Invoice and Attached Files," the invoice and any files attached to it in QuickBooks show up as attachments in the email message.

2. **If you want to skip some of the forms, click their checkmarks to turn them off.**

   When you select a form in the table on the dialog box's left, a preview of the message appears to the right of the table. If you want to change the message, simply edit it.

NOTE To the left of the Send Now button, the Send Forms window displays QuickBooks' estimate of how long it will take to email the forms you've selected. You won't be able to do any other work in the program until the emails have been sent. So if you're on a tight deadline and don't have time to wait, click Close and then come back later to send the emails.

3. **When you're ready, click Send Now.**

You're email program sends the emails you selected.

Memorizing Transactions

If you enter the same transactions over and over, having QuickBooks memorize them for reuse saves time. The program can then fill in most, if not all, of the fields for you. Once it memorizes a transaction, all you have to do is choose the memorized transaction you want to reuse and make sure that the values in the new transaction are correct before you save it. This section shows you how to memorize transactions and put them to work.

Here are some examples of how you can use memorized transactions to be more productive:

- **Memorizing bills**. You can take some of the sting out of paying bills by memorizing the ones that use the same info each time: bills with the same items or amounts, or bills that are due the same day each month, for example. If a utility bill is always due the same day, you can memorize the bill so QuickBooks fills in the vendor and account and records it on a regular schedule. When you use a memorized transaction like this, all you do is fill in the amount and save the new transaction.

  On the other hand, your office rent bill probably has *all* the same info each month—date, vendor, account, and amount—so you can memorize the bill and even set it up to record itself automatically. Memorized bills also come in handy if you reorder the same products with the same prices from a vendor. (See "Creating Memorized Groups of Transactions" on page 326 to learn how to save even *more* time.)

NOTE Although you can memorize bills, you can't memorize a bill *payment*. The same goes for deposits and invoice payments, because you have to choose the bills or invoices that the payments apply to. However, if you create reminders (page 483) for transactions such as this, then QuickBooks reminds you when the bills or invoices are due to be paid.

- **Memorizing charges and electronic funds transfers (EFTs)**. If you've set up automatic vendor payments, like a monthly health insurance premium charged to your credit card or your telephone bill withdrawn automatically from your checking account, you can memorize those transactions in QuickBooks.
- **Memorizing estimates**. If you've worked on jobs in the past and have a good idea of what they require, you can reuse that hard-won knowledge by memorizing an estimate with the labor hours you spend and the quantities of products and materials you need. The box on page 282 explains how to memorize an estimate to use on similar jobs in the future.

TIP If you reuse transactions only occasionally, you might not want to fill up the Memorized Transaction List with those transactions. Instead, simply duplicate a transaction whenever you need it. For example, display the bill you want to copy in the Enter Bills window, right-click in the window, and choose Duplicate Bill from the shortcut menu. (Alternatively, click "Create a Copy" at the top of the window.) Then simply make any changes you want, like the date and amount, and then click Save & Close.

QuickBooks can also remind you to enter a transaction—such as a recurring client invoice for retainers—or even add the transaction without any help from you. For example, if your company's Internet service costs $259 each month and you pay it with an automatic credit card payment, you can tell QuickBooks to memorize that charge and automatically enter it each month.

Creating a Memorized Transaction

The Memorized Transactions List is an anomaly on the Lists menu because you don't create memorized transactions the way you do entries on other lists. Instead, you tell QuickBooks to memorize *existing* transactions. Here's how:

1. **Open the window for the type of transaction you want to memorize (for example, the Create Invoices window for an invoice, Enter Bills for a bill, or Write Checks for a check).**

   You can memorize many kinds of transactions, including checks, credit card charges, bills, invoices, journal entries, estimates, and so on.

2. **Fill in any fields that remain the same each time you use that transaction. If a value changes, leave its field blank or set to zero.**

   For example, for a bill, add the items you're buying and their prices. If the quantities change from bill to bill, leave the Quantity fields blank or set to zero. Or, for a check, enter the payee and the account to post the expense to. If the amount is the same each time, fill in the amount; if the amount changes, leave the amount field blank. (If an amount field has a value in it, click the field, and then press Backspace to delete the value.) Later, when you use the memorized transaction, QuickBooks fills in all the fields except the ones you left blank, which you fill in with the correct values.

3. **If you want QuickBooks to add the new transactions to your print or email queue, turn on the Print Later or Email Later checkbox.**

   That way, when you save a new transaction that's based on the memorized transaction, the program adds the transaction to the print or email queue.

4. **When the transaction is set up the way you want, press Ctrl+M to open the Memorize Transaction dialog box shown in Figure 12-8, foreground.**

   You can also open this dialog box by right-clicking in a transaction window, such as the Create Invoices window, and then choosing "Memorize [form]" (Memorize Invoice, Memorize Check, or whatever). Or you can click Memorize at the top of the window.

NOTE If you've already memorized a transaction with the same name, the Replace Memorized Transaction message box appears instead. To replace the existing memorized transaction, click Replace. To add a new memorized transaction, click Add; when you do, QuickBooks opens the Memorize Transaction dialog box so you can specify a new name and options for the memorized transaction. If you change your mind about memorizing the transaction, click Cancel.

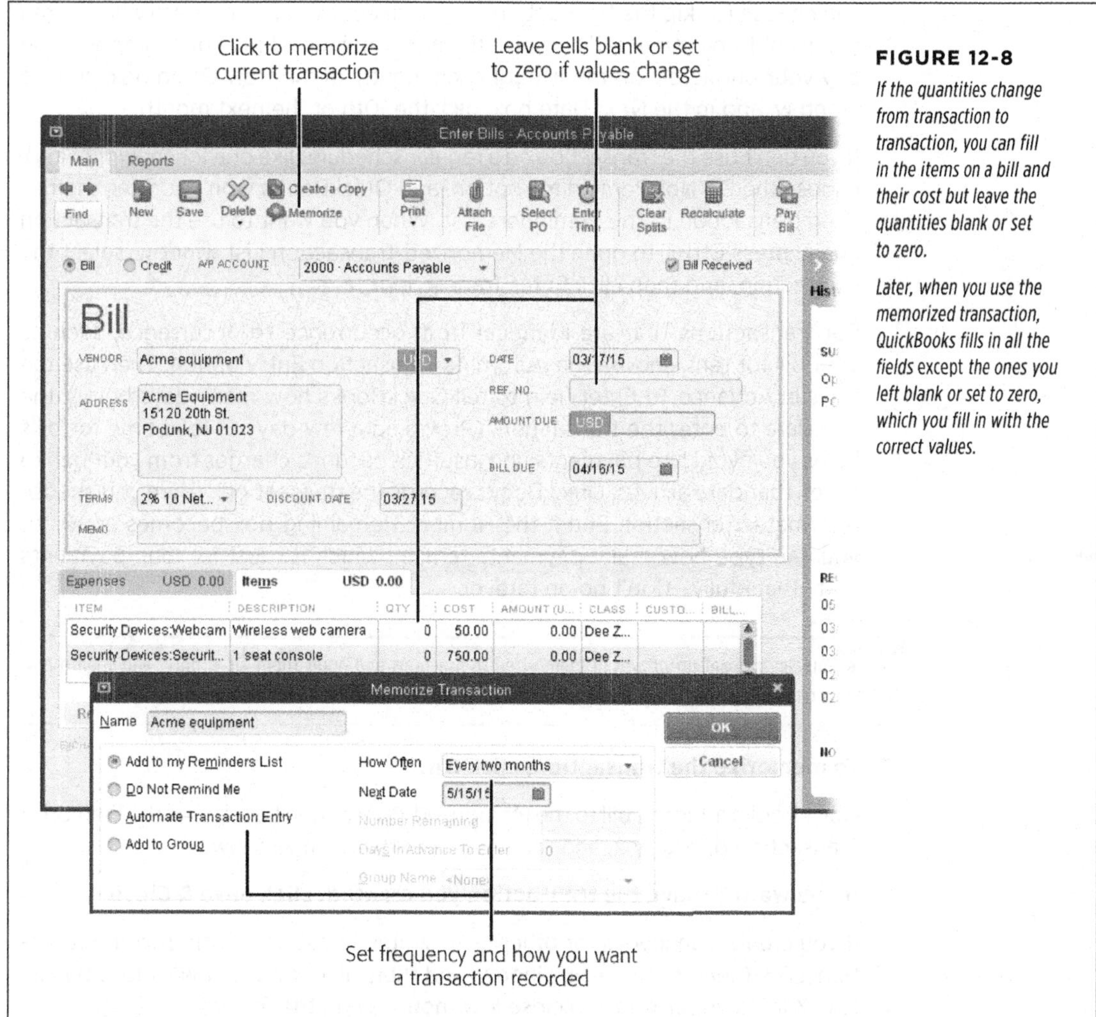

FIGURE 12-8

If the quantities change from transaction to transaction, you can fill in the items on a bill and their cost but leave the quantities blank or set to zero.

Later, when you use the memorized transaction, QuickBooks fills in all the fields except the ones you left blank or set to zero, which you fill in with the correct values.

5. **In the Memorize Transaction dialog box's Name field, type a name that you'll recognize when you see it in the Memorized Transaction List.**

   QuickBooks automatically fills in the Name box with the transaction's Payee name or the name in a transaction, but it's a good idea to enter something more meaningful. You can use names like Monthly Telephone Bill or Health Insurance

Premium for bills you pay, a customer name combined with a sales form's name, or the type of retainer, such as Full-time Programming Contract.

6. **Tell QuickBooks whether you want it to remind you to enter transactions.**

   Choosing the "Add to my Reminders List" option is great for recurring transactions: QuickBooks adds the memorized transaction to the Reminders List (page 483) and prompts you when it's time to enter the next occurrence (though you can choose to skip the transaction). If you select this option, specify how often you want to be reminded and pick the next reminder date. For example, if you pay your phone bill on the 10th of each month, in the How Often box, choose Monthly, and in the Next Date box, pick the 10th of the next month.

   If you don't use the transaction on a regular schedule (like one for snowplowing), choose the Do Not Remind Me option, and QuickBooks won't add the memorized transaction to the Reminders List. When you want to use the transaction again, press Ctrl+T to open the Memorized Transaction List window, select the transaction, and then click Enter Transaction.

   For transactions that are identical from occurrence to occurrence, such as your bill for rent, choose the Automate Transaction Entry option. Then use the Days In Advance To Enter field to tell QuickBooks how many days before the due date to enter the transaction. (Providing a few days of lead time for bills helps you avoid late payments and insufficient-funds charges from your bank.) When that date arrives, QuickBooks records the transaction. When you choose Automate Transaction Entry, the Number Remaining box becomes active so you can type how many payments remain, which is ideal for loan payments that—thankfully—don't go on forever.

TIP You can also set up *groups* of memorized transactions and enter them all at once; you'll learn how starting on page 326.

7. **To memorize the transaction, click OK.**

   QuickBooks adds the bill to the Memorized Transaction List, closes the Memorize Transaction dialog box, and returns you to the form window.

8. **If you want to save the transaction you created, click Save & Close.**

   If you created an invoice or other form simply to set up a memorized transaction, click Clear in the form window, and then click the window's Close button (the X in its upper right) to close it without saving the form.

The next section explains how to *use* memorized transactions.

Using a Memorized Transaction

How you generate a new transaction from one in the Memorized Transaction List depends on whether you've opted for a reminder, no reminder, or total automation. This section describes all three methods.

RECORDING A TRANSACTION WHEN YOU'RE REMINDED

If you create a memorized transaction and tell QuickBooks to remind you (by choosing the "Add to my Reminders List" option) when the scheduled date arrives, the program adds the bill to the Reminders List (page 483). (If the Reminders List displays only the Memorized Transactions Due heading, click it to display the transactions that are scheduled to be recorded.)

Here are the steps for turning a reminder into a transaction:

1. **In the Reminders window, below the Memorized Transactions Due heading, double-click a memorized transaction.**

   The Memorized Transaction List window opens with the transaction selected in the list.

2. **At the bottom of the Memorized Transaction List window, click Enter Transaction.**

   QuickBooks opens it in its corresponding transaction window (like Enter Bills for a memorized bill). The transaction that QuickBooks creates contains only the memorized information.

3. **Make any changes you want, fill in any empty fields, and then click Save & Close.**

   The transaction window closes, and the memorized transaction no longer appears in the Reminders window.

TIP For reminders that are hard to miss, tell QuickBooks to display the Reminders List each time you open the current company file. That way, when you open that company file, the program opens a Start Up box that asks if you want to enter memorized transactions; click Now to add them. (It also opens the Reminders List.) To set this up, choose Edit→Preferences→Reminders and, on the My Preferences tab, turn on the "Show Reminders List when opening a Company file" checkbox.

RECORDING AN OCCASIONAL TRANSACTION

When you memorize a transaction that you use only occasionally or that occurs on an irregular schedule, choosing Do Not Remind Me stores the transaction in the Memorized Transaction List in case you need it. If you memorize a transaction like this, you need a way to create a new transaction based on it. (You'll also use this technique if you set up a memorized transaction on a schedule but want to create one right away.) Here's how to use a memorized transaction at any time:

1. **Choose Lists→Memorized Transaction List or press Ctrl+T.**

   The Memorized Transaction List window opens.

2. **Select the transaction you want, and then click the Enter Transaction button.**

   The corresponding transaction window opens, such as Create Invoices, Write Checks, or Enter Credit Card Charges.

3. **Make any changes you want, and then click Save & Close.**

That's all there is to it!

RECORDING A TRANSACTION AUTOMATICALLY

If you create a memorized transaction and choose the Automate Transaction Entry option, that's exactly what QuickBooks does: When the next scheduled date for the transaction arrives, QuickBooks records a new transaction.

Editing a Memorized Transaction

If you want to change a memorized transaction's recurrence schedule or reminder settings, press Ctrl+T to open the Memorized Transaction List window, select the transaction you want to edit, and then press Ctrl+E (or, at the bottom of the window, click Memorized Transaction→Edit Memorized Transaction). The Schedule Memorized Transaction dialog box appears with settings for reminders and the recurrence schedule (page 324).

If you want to edit the info *within* a memorized transaction, such as the items and services sold, you have to edit the existing transaction and then rememorize it. Here's how:

1. **Press Ctrl+T to open the Memorized Transaction List window. Select the transaction, and then click the Enter Transaction button.**

   QuickBooks opens the corresponding transaction window and creates a new transaction based on the memorized one.

2. **Make the changes you want, and then press Ctrl+M to rememorize it with the changes you've made.**

   The Replace Memorized Transaction message box appears.

3. **Click Replace.**

   The edited transaction takes the place of the previous one in the Memorized Transaction List. (If you want to save both the old *and* new versions, click Add instead.)

Creating Memorized Groups of Transactions

The first day of the month is the nemesis of bill payers everywhere because so many bills are due then. QuickBooks can't ease the pain of watching your money go out the door, but it *can* ease the burden of entering all those bills in your company file. Memorized bills are a start, but why enter individual memorized bills when you can enter several at once?

Fortunately, QuickBooks lets you set up memorized transaction *groups* that act like their individual memorized counterparts—the program can remind you about all the bills due on a specific day or even enter all the recurring transactions automatically. (Memorized groups work equally well for recurring invoices.)

You might wonder how to add a memorized transaction to a group when you open the Memorize Transaction dialog box (page 322) for the very first time; the "Add to Group" option and the Group Name box are visible but grayed out. To add a memorized transaction to a group, you have to first create a *memorized group*. Here's how you do that:

1. **Press Ctrl+T to open the Memorized Transaction List. At the bottom of the window, click Memorized Transaction→New Group.**

   QuickBooks opens the New Memorized Transaction Group dialog box. It's identical to the Memorize Transaction dialog box except that it doesn't include the "Add to Group" option or Group Name box.

2. **Name the group something meaningful like Monthly Bills, and fill in the other fields as you would for a memorized transaction (page 324).**

   Tell QuickBooks how and when you want to be reminded about the bills in this group (if at all).

3. **Click OK to save the group.**

   Now that the group exists, you can add individual transactions to it.

4. **To add an existing memorized transaction to the group, in the Memorized Transaction List window, select the transaction you want to add, and then press Ctrl+E to edit it.**

   The Schedule Memorized Transaction dialog box opens.

5. **Select the "Add to Group" option and then, in the Group Name box, choose the group you just created. When you're done, click OK.**

   When you add a memorized transaction to a group, QuickBooks tucks the transaction underneath the group in the Memorized Transaction List, as shown in Figure 12-9.

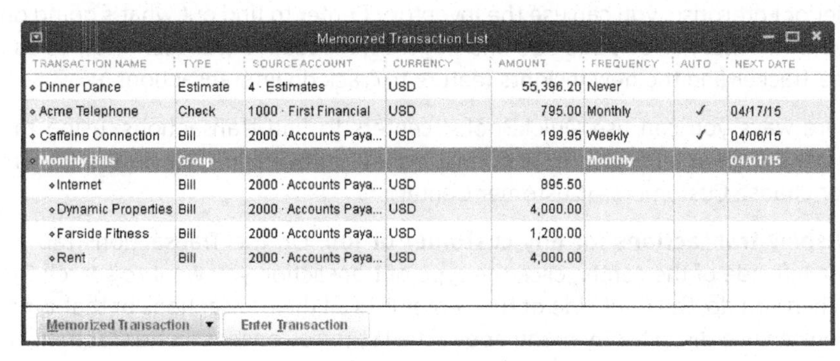

FIGURE 12-9

Memorized transactions take on the schedule and reminder settings of the memorized group you put them in. So if you edit a memorized transaction that belongs to a group, the How Often, Next Date, Number Remaining, and Days In Advance To Enter settings are grayed out.

TIP Create separate memorized groups for bills with consistent amounts and for ones whose amounts vary. That way, you can set up the unvarying memorized group with the Automate Transaction Entry option so QuickBooks simply adds all the bills in that group to your list of bills to be paid without any intervention from you. Then you can set the second memorized group to use the "Add to my Reminders List" option so you can go through each bill and fill in the amount before you record it.

Finding Transactions

When you want to answer a customer's question about what she owes, it's easier if you have the invoice in front of you. The Create Invoices window shows only one invoice at a time, but there are several ways to find a specific invoice out of the hundreds you've sent. Whether you want to find pesky overdue invoices, purchase orders, or paychecks, the Customer, Vendor, and Employee Centers (and the Inventory Center if you use QuickBooks Premier or Enterprise) make it easy to find transactions for a particular customer, vendor, employee, or item. And the Item List window has a few tools for finding specific items.

QuickBooks also offers two additional ways to search. The Search feature scours every inch of QuickBooks and your company file. The Find feature (which you can access most easily by pressing Ctrl+F), on the other hand, is best suited for more precise searches—to find a particular invoice number, transactions related to a specific customer, invoices overdue more than a certain number of days, and so on. This section explains how to use all these features.

Searching with QuickBooks' Centers

The Customer Center is a quick way to answer basic questions about your customers, like "What invoices are unpaid?" and "Does the customer have any credits available?" Likewise, you can track down bills, bill payments, and other vendor-related transactions in the Vendor Center. The Employee Center performs similar tasks for transactions like paychecks and non-payroll transactions. And if you use QuickBooks Premier or Enterprise, you can use the Inventory Center to find out what's going on with your inventory. (See page 338 and page 44, respectively, to learn how to use Income Tracker and the new Insights feature to track down transactions.)

Here are ways you can use QuickBooks' centers to find transactions, using the Customer Center as an example (to open it, on the Home Page, click the Customers icon, or choose Customers→Customer Center):

- **Display transactions for any customer or job**. On the Transactions tab on the left side of the center, click the type of transaction you want to search for. When you do, the right side of the center lists all the transactions of that type. You can use the Filter By menu above the list to see only open transactions or ones within a certain date range.

- **Filter the list of customers**. To narrow the Customer:Job List to those that fit the criteria you want, on the Customers & Jobs tab, click the first unlabeled box (it's usually set to Active Customers). In the drop-down list, choose one of the entries, like Customers with Open Balances, Customers with Overdue Invoices, or Customers with Almost Due Invoices.
- **Find a customer**. If you have trouble finding a customer on the Customers & Jobs tab, in the tab's second unlabeled box, type part of the customer's name and then click the "Find in common fields" button, which has a magnifying glass on it.
- **Review a customer's account**. In the upper-right part of the Customer Center are several links you can click to see various things about a customer's account:
  - **QuickReport** shows all transactions for the customer within the date range you specify.
  - **Open Balance** generates a report of all the Accounts Receivable transactions that contributed to the customer's current balance, like invoices and payments.
  - **Show Estimates** generates a report of any estimates you've created for that customer or job.
  - **Customer Snapshot** opens the Company Snapshot window to the Customer tab, where you can see statistics like the average days the customer takes to pay, total sales this year, and total sales for the same period last year.
- **Display the transactions for a customer**. When you select a customer on the Customers & Jobs tab, the transactions for that customer appear in the Transactions tab in the lower-right part of the Customer Center. To see a specific type of transaction, in the Show drop-down list above the transaction table, choose the transaction type like Invoices or Refunds, as shown in Figure 12-10. QuickBooks initially displays all the transactions of that type, but you can filter them using these techniques:
  - **Filter transactions by status**. In the Transactions tab's Filter By drop-down menu, choose a category like Open Invoices or Overdue Invoices. The choices in this menu vary depending on the transaction type. For example, if you search for refunds, the menu includes All Refunds, Cash/Check Refunds, and Credit Card Refunds options.
  - **Filter transaction by date range**. In the Transactions tab's Date drop-down menu, choose a period. Your choices here are the same as the ones you can choose for reports (page 591).
  - **Open a transaction**. Double-click a transaction in the Transactions tab's table to open the corresponding window to that transaction.

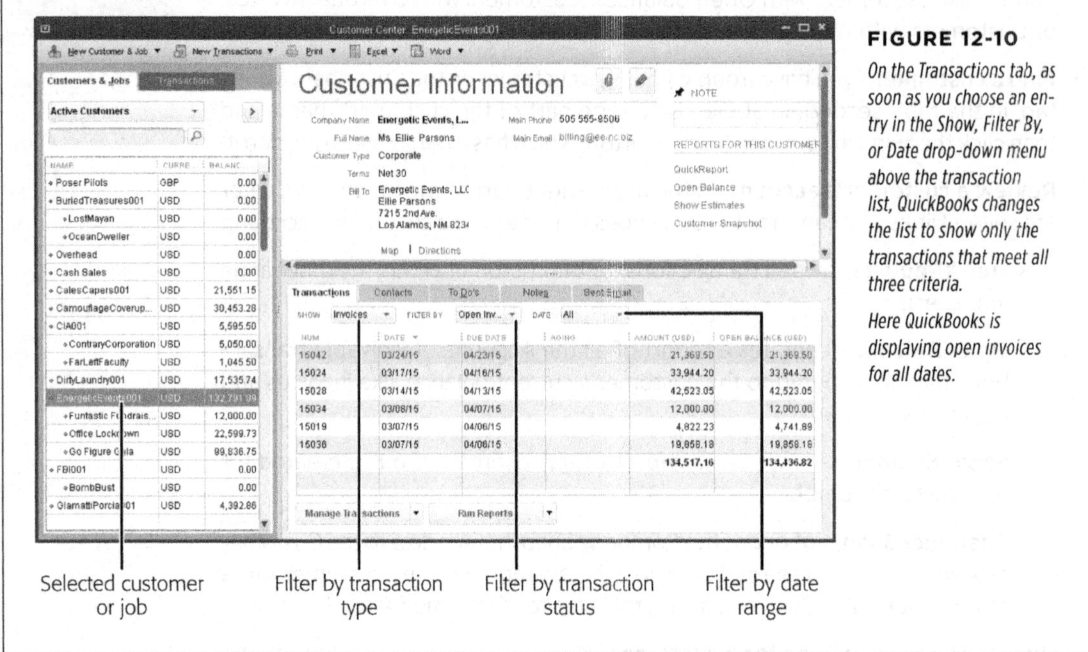

FIGURE 12-10

On the Transactions tab, as soon as you choose an entry in the Show, Filter By, or Date drop-down menu above the transaction list, QuickBooks changes the list to show only the transactions that meet all three criteria.

Here QuickBooks is displaying open invoices for all dates.

Finding Items

The Item List window has its own abbreviated search feature: You type what you're looking for (such as an item name or keyword) and the field you want to search, and then QuickBooks filters the list for matching results. Here's how to search for an item:

1. **Open the Item List window by choosing Lists→Item List or, on the Home Page, clicking Items & Services.**

2. **In the "Look for" box, type the text or value you want to find.**

   If you type more than one word, QuickBooks looks for items that contain the whole phrase you typed. For example, enter *fiber optic* to find all your fiber-optic electronic devices.

3. **In the "in" drop-down list, choose the field you want to search.**

   QuickBooks automatically selects "All fields" here. To narrow your search, choose Item Name/Number, Description (Sales), Purchase Description, Man. Part Number, or another field. You can also choose "Custom fields" to search fields you've created (page 78).

4. **Click Search.**

   The Item List window displays only the items that match your search criteria.

5. **To narrow your search, delete your original search terms, type a new word or phrase in the "Look for" box, turn on the "Search within results" checkbox, and then click Search.**

   If you don't see the "Search within results" checkbox, maximize the Item List window or drag one of its corners to enlarge it. Turning on this checkbox tells QuickBooks to search for the new search term only in the items currently displayed in the list.

   To reset the window's list to display all your items, click Reset (you may need to enlarge the window to see this button).

Using QuickBooks Search

The QuickBooks Search feature can look through your company file or the program's help files, although it automatically searches only your company file. If you want to find something in your company file, simply type in a few key words or values, and it combs through your entire company file for them. For example, type *webcam* and QuickBooks looks for that value in your transactions, Customer:Job List, Vendor List, other name records, items, descriptions, notes, and memos. But if you're trying to find information about a QuickBooks feature, type the feature's name in the Search box, choose Help in the box's drop-down list, and Search tracks down information about it in QuickBooks' Help files.

TIP The Search feature is quick and easy if you want to search by date range or fairly simple filters, such as a specific amount. But if you have really specific search criteria, like invoices that are more than 30 days overdue and more than $10,000, the Find feature (explained on page 332) is a better tool.

Here's how to use Search:

1. **Type the value you want to look for in the Search box, which is at the top of the left icon bar or the right end of the top icon bar (see page 30 for info on the icon bars).**

   As you type in the Search box, the program displays a drop-down list with suggested and recent search terms. For example, if you type "ener" because you're looking for your customer Energetic Events, the drop-down list may display "energetic" and the Customer Name value "energeticevents001." If the term or value you're looking for appears in the drop-down list, click the entry you want to select it.

2. **Click the Search button (which looks like a magnifying glass) or press Enter.**

   The Search window (shown in Figure 12-11) opens. (If you've hidden the icon bar, you can open this window by choosing Edit→Search or pressing F3.)

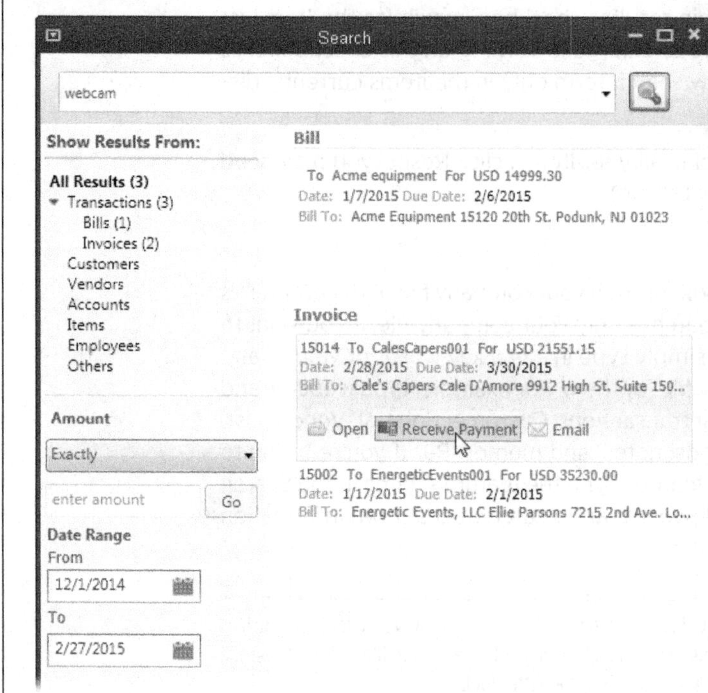

FIGURE 12-11

Below the Search box at the top of this window, you see a summary of the results, such as where QuickBooks found the results.

If you get too many results, you can filter the list by clicking the type of result you want in the Show Results From section, such as Transactions. The results list on the right then displays only that type of result.

3. **To filter the results, below the "Show Results From" heading, click the type of result you want.**

   To see all transactions that matched your criteria, click Transactions. To search for a specific type, click the type, such as Invoices or Bills. You can also choose a date range to specify a period to search. If you're looking for an amount, choose an option to look for values equal to, less than, or greater than the amount.

4. **Put your cursor over a search result.**

   Icons appear below the search result that represent the actions that you can perform, like Open or Receive Payment for an invoice (see Figure 12-11), or Edit for an item in the Item List. Click the icon for the action you want.

Using the Find Feature

QuickBooks' Find feature is ideal for finding transactions that match several criteria. For example, it lets you search for all invoices within a certain date range that include a product you've upgraded, or all the open invoices for work performed by one partner (if you use classes to track that kind of thing). In fact, the Find feature can mine every transaction field except Description (to search descriptions, use the Search feature instead [page 33]).

The Find window has a Simple tab for straightforward searches and an Advanced tab where you can build searches as detailed as you want. QuickBooks remembers which one you used for your last search and displays that tab the next time you open the window.

FINDING MADE SIMPLE

Here's how to use the simple version of the Find feature:

1. **Choose Edit→Find or press Ctrl+F.**

   If you have a form window (like Create Invoices) open, click the Find button at the window's top left to open a smaller version of the Find window's Simple tab. Click Advanced in this simplified dialog box to open the full-blown Find window. If you *don't* have any form windows open, the full Find window opens automatically.

2. **In the Find window, click the Simple tab if it's not already selected.**

   The Transaction Type box at the top of the tab is set to Invoice, and all the other fields are blank.

3. **In the Transaction Type drop-down list, choose a type like Purchase Order or Bill.**

   The search fields are almost identical no matter which transaction type you choose, with a few exceptions, as explained in Figure 12-12. From, To, and Amount fields appear for every type.

4. **Fill in the values you want to search for, and then click the Find button.**

   You can fill in as many or as few fields as you want. When you click Find, any matching transactions appear in the table at the bottom of the window. Double-click a transaction to open it in its corresponding window, like Create Invoices for an invoice.

5. **To clear all the fields and start a new search, click Reset.**

   When you're done, click Close.

ADVANCED FIND METHODS

The Find window's Advanced tab lets you search *any* transaction field. You can even build up a set of filters to locate exactly the transaction you want. Here's how:

1. **Choose Edit→Find (or press Ctrl+F), and then click the Advanced tab. (If a simplified Find dialog box opens, click its Advanced button.)**

   The Advanced tab starts with an almost-clean slate every time you open the Find window—though the right-hand Filter list always starts with Posting Status set to Either.

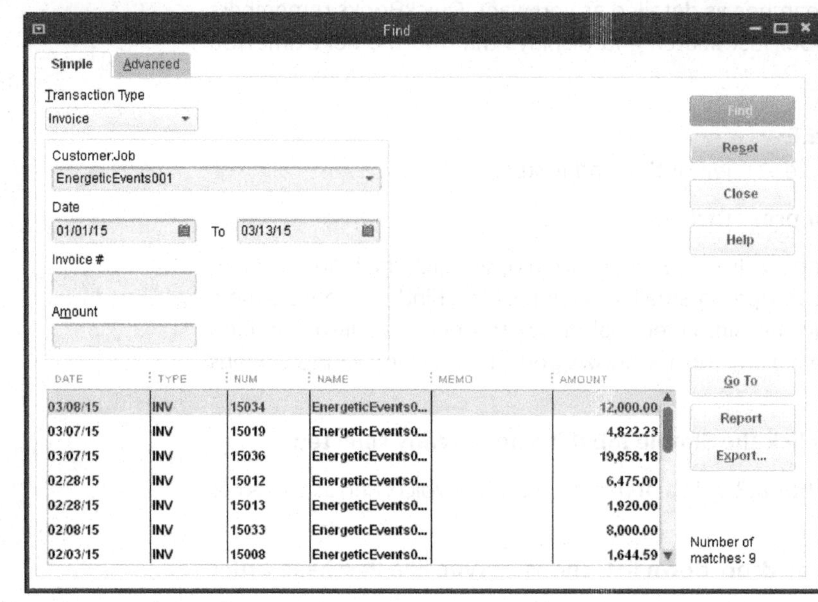

DATE	TYPE	NUM	NAME	MEMO	AMOUNT
03/08/15	INV	15034	EnergeticEvents0...		12,000.00
03/07/15	INV	15019	EnergeticEvents0...		4,822.23
03/07/15	INV	15036	EnergeticEvents0...		19,858.18
02/28/15	INV	15012	EnergeticEvents0...		6,475.00
02/28/15	INV	15013	EnergeticEvents0...		1,920.00
02/08/15	INV	15033	EnergeticEvents0...		8,000.00
02/03/15	INV	15008	EnergeticEvents0...		1,644.59

FIGURE 12-12

In the Find window, the label above the first field after Transaction Type changes to reflect the type you choose. For example, if you select Bill for the transaction type, the next field's label changes to Vendor.

The second-to-last field also varies depending on the transaction type; for example, it's Invoice # for an invoice, Ref. No. for a bill, and P.O. No. for a purchase order.

2. **In the Find window's left-hand Filter list (Figure 12-13), choose the first field you want to search.**

   Fields appear in alphabetical order. If you've turned on multiple currencies, you'll see Currency and Foreign Amount options listed, too.

3. **To the right of the left-hand Filter list, select settings to specify how you want to search the selected field.**

   These settings change depending on the field you select. For example, if you choose TransactionType in the left-hand Filter list, you see only a single drop-down list of QuickBooks transaction types. Choosing Date in the left-hand Filter list displays a drop-down list of time periods, along with From and To boxes to specify dates. And selecting Aging in the left-hand Filters list gives you options to help find late invoices (=, <=, and >=); for instance, you can find invoices that are 30 or more days late by choosing the >= option and typing *30* in the box.

4. **To add another filter to your search, repeat steps 2 and 3.**

   You can add as many filters as you want. The window's Current Choices table lists the fields you're searching and what you're searching for in each one.

5. **Click Find.**

The table at the bottom of the window lists all the matching transactions (or line items within a transaction). The next section explains what you can do with these results.

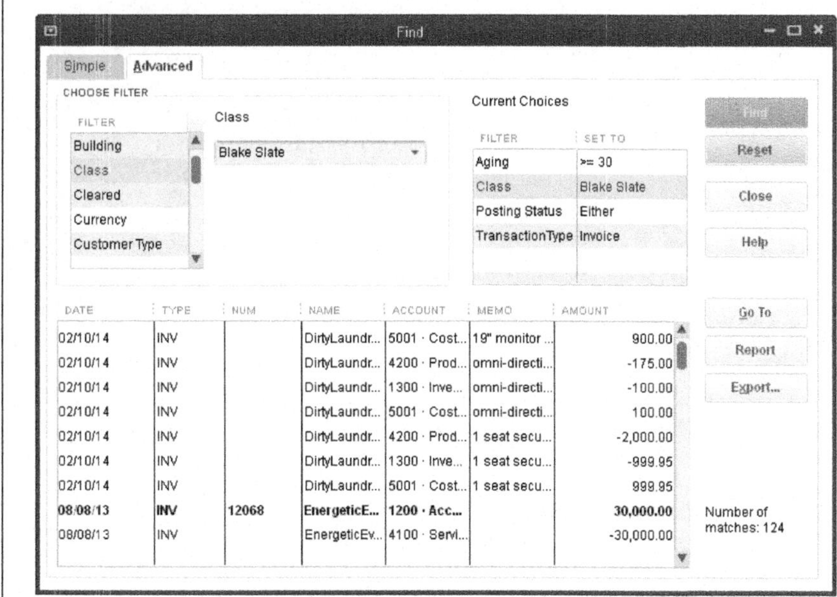

FIGURE 12-13

The filter settings you can choose change depending on the field you select in the left-hand Filter list. For example, if you choose Terms, you can select the terms you want to look for from the drop-down list. Choosing Amount gives you options to find values equal to (=), less than or equal to (<=), or greater than or equal to (>=) the value you fill in. If you select Name, you can specify an individual name, a category of names, or multiple names.

6. **If you get too many or too few results, repeat steps 2 and 3 to add or change filters, and then click Find again.**

   To edit a filter, select the field in the left-hand Filter list and then change its settings. To remove a filter from the Current Choices list, select it in the list and then press Backspace or Delete. To clear *all* the filters, click the Reset button.

7. **When you're done, click Close.**

USING SEARCH RESULTS

After you find what you're looking for, you can inspect your results more closely using the following buttons in the Find window:

- **Go To**. Select one of the results, and then click this button to see the transaction in its corresponding window (like Create Invoices for an invoice) or account register.
- **Report**. This button opens the Find Report window, which includes all the transactions in your search results.
- **Export**. To export your results, click this button. (See page 684 for more on exporting.)

CHAPTER

13

Managing Accounts Receivable

In addition to performing work, invoicing customers, and collecting payments, you also have to keep track of who owes you how much (known as *Accounts Receivable*) and when the money is due. Sure, you can tack on finance charges to light a fire under your customers' accounting departments, but such charges are rarely enough to make up for the time and effort you spend collecting overdue payments. Far more preferable are customers who pay on time without reminders, gentle or otherwise.

Because companies need money to keep things running, you'll have to spend *some* time keeping track of your Accounts Receivable and the payments that come in. In this chapter, you'll learn the ins and outs of tracking what customers owe, receiving payments from them, and dinging them if they don't pay on time. You'll get up to speed on Income Tracker (which Intuit introduced in QuickBooks 2014), a handy dashboard that shows estimates you've created, how much customers owe—both overdue and not—and what's been paid in the past 30 days.

In contrast to invoices, *sales receipts* are the simplest and most immediate sales forms in QuickBooks. When your customers pay in full at the time of the sale—at your retail store, for example—you can create a sales receipt so the customer has a record of the purchase and payment. At the same time, QuickBooks posts the money from the sale into your bank account (in QuickBooks, anyway) or the Undeposited Funds account. (Sales receipts work only when customers pay in full, because that type of sales form can't handle previous customer payments and balances.) In this chapter, you'll learn how to create sales receipts for one sale at a time and to summarize a day's worth of merchandising.

Receivables Aging

You don't have to do anything special to *create* Accounts Receivable—they're the by-product of invoicing your customers. But receivables that are growing long in the tooth are the first signs of potential collection problems. Fortunately, with QuickBooks' Income Tracker, Company Snapshot, Customer Center, and built-in reports, you have four ways to check the state of your Accounts Receivable.

NOTE You can't use Income Tracker if you have multiple currencies turned on (page 656). When that preference is turned on, the Income Tracker entry doesn't appear in the Customers menu. And in QuickBooks Pro and Premier, only users with full access to Sales and Accounts Receivables features (page 726) can use Income Tracker.

Viewing Receivables with Income Tracker

Income Tracker (choose Customers→Income Tracker or click Income Tracker in either icon bar to open it), shown in Figure 13-1, is the best of both worlds: It provides the big picture of your unbilled, outstanding, and paid income *and* lists the transactions that contribute to those high-level numbers. Income Tracker also offers time-saving features for invoicing customers and collecting the money they owe you.

NOTE The new Insights tab (page 44) on the Home Page has an Income section that includes Income Tracker's overview bars for open invoices, overdue invoices, and payments made during the past 30 days. To display the full-blown Income Tracker, simply click any of those bars.

Here's what each part of the Income Tracker window shows you:

- **Estimates**. The blue box at the window's top left shows the total value of estimates you've created. Although the label above the box reads "Unbilled," this value doesn't really represent unbilled income. Estimates are merely potential income. Customers have to *approve* those estimates *and* you have to perform the work or sell the goods before you can turn that money into unbilled income. In addition, you might create multiple estimates for the same customer and job to see which one is the winner.
- **Sales Orders**. You see this light-blue box only if you have QuickBooks Premier or Enterprise; it shows the total value of open sales orders.
- **Time & Expenses**. This dark-blue box is a great way to catch billable time and expenses that you haven't added to invoices yet. It shows the total value of unbilled time and expenses and the number of records that contribute to that total.

TIP In QuickBooks 2015, you can choose whether to hide or display some of Income Tracker's boxes by clicking the Settings icon (the gear) at the window's upper right. To hide estimates or unbilled time and expenses, turn off the Estimates and "Time and Expenses" checkboxes, respectively. (If you use QuickBooks Premier or Enterprise, you can also turn off the Sales Orders box.)

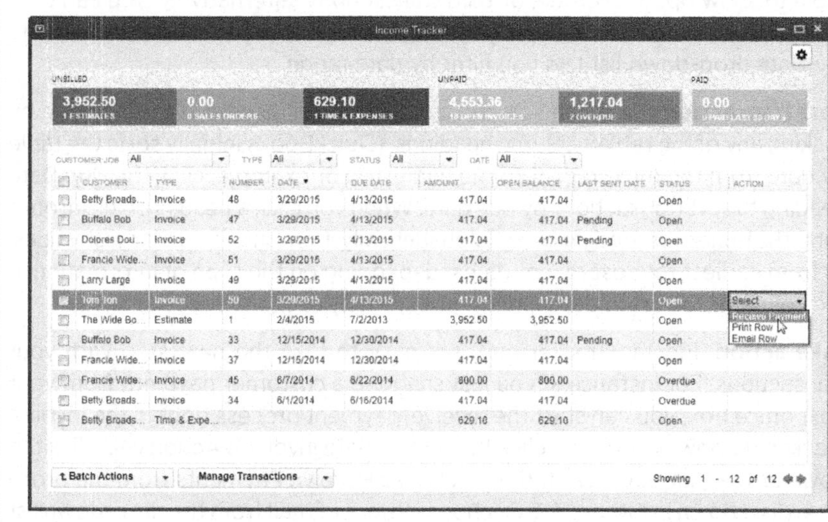

FIGURE 13-1

The panel at the top of the Income Tracker window provides an income overview. The table below it lists the transactions that make up the overall totals.

You can filter the transaction table in different ways: by customer, transaction type, status, or date. You can even process transactions in this window, for example, receiving payment on an open invoice, as shown here.

- **Open Invoices**. The orange box below the Unpaid heading shows the total amount on your open invoices. This is current income that your customers owe—that is, the invoiced income that isn't due yet.
- **Overdue**. The red hue of this box emphasizes the total amount that's overdue from your customers. If that number is larger than you'd like, filter the transaction list (you'll learn how in a sec) to track down the customers you need to nudge into paying.
- **Paid Last 30 Days**. The green box at the window's top right displays how much your customers paid you in the last 30 days. The label at the bottom of the box tells you how many payments are included in that total.
- **The transaction table**. The transactions listed in the Income Tracker window are the ones that contribute to the totals at the top of the window. For example, the number in the orange Open Invoices box is the total of all the open invoices in the table. The number in the red Overdue box is the total of all the table's overdue invoices. The transactions with the word "Paid" in their Status cells make up the total in the green Paid Last 30 Days box. And the estimates in the table contribute to the total in the blue Estimates box.

And here's what you can do in the Income Tracker window:

- **Filter transactions**. Say that business is booming and Income Tracker's table is awash with transactions. You can filter the table to drill down and see, for example, all the overdue invoices for the last quarter. To see transactions for a specific customer, click the down arrow to the Customer:Job box's right, and then, in the drop-down list, choose the customer or job you want. Choose an entry in the Type drop-down list to show only a specific type of transaction, like invoices or received payments. The Status drop-down list lets you filter the table to show open, overdue, or paid transactions (alternatively, you can click one of the colored bars at the top of the window to filter for that status). And the Date drop-down list lets you filter by date range.

- **Sort transactions**. You can sort the transactions in Income Tracker's table by clicking any of the table's column headings. (QuickBooks initially sorts the table by date from the most recent to the earliest.) For example, click the Due Date heading to sort transactions by due date. When you click a heading, QuickBooks sorts the table in ascending order (alphabetically, from smallest to largest values, or from earliest to most recent dates, depending on the type of information in the column). To sort in descending order, simply click the heading again.
- **Take action**. Income Tracker makes it easy to take the next step with your transactions. For instance, if you just snagged a customer payment from your post office box, you can start the receive-payment process right in the Income Tracker window. To do that, click the appropriate invoice's Action cell, click the down arrow that appears, and then choose Receive Payments from the drop-down list shown in Figure 13-1. Or choose Print or Email from the drop-down list to print or email the invoice. For estimates, the Action drop-down list includes additional options like "Convert to Invoice" (page 282) and "Mark as Inactive" (page 281). To open a transaction in its corresponding window, just double-click it or select the transaction in the table, click Manage Transactions at the bottom of the window, and then choose Edit Highlighted Row in the drop-down menu.

NOTE You can also create new transactions from within Income Tracker. Click the Manage Transactions button, and then, beneath the menu's Create New heading, choose the type of transaction you want to create.

- **Print transactions in batches**. You can also print several transactions at a time (invoices, sales receipts, and credit memos or refunds) from the Income Tracker window. For example, suppose you want to print new copies of all the invoices that are overdue to nudge your customers about paying them. To do that, click the red Overdue bar at the top of the window to display the overdue transactions. Next, in the table's first column, turn on the checkboxes for all the transactions you want to print. Then click the down arrow to the right of the Batch Actions button and choose the type of transaction; QuickBooks opens the "Print [forms]" dialog box. (See page 308 to learn how to print forms.)

NOTE Although Income Tracker makes it easy to stay on top of overdue invoices, some folks prefer the Collections Center, which includes an Overdue tab that shows customers with overdue invoices, the number of days overdue, and the customers' phone numbers. You can also send out email reminders by clicking "Select and Send Email" near the top right of the Collections Center window. To open the Collections Center, in the Customer Center's toolbar, click Collections Center. (If you don't see this option, that means you need to turn on this feature. To do that, choose Edit→Preferences→Sales & Customers, and then click the Company Preferences tab. In the Collections Center section, turn on the Enable Collections Center checkbox.)

Getting a High-Level View with the Company Snapshot

Another handy feature is the Company Snapshot window (Figure 13-2), which can show each customer's balance. To open it, choose Company→Company Snapshot, and then click the window's Company tab if it's not already selected. (When you want to see more detail about receivables, turn to QuickBooks' built-in aging reports instead; they're described in the next section.)

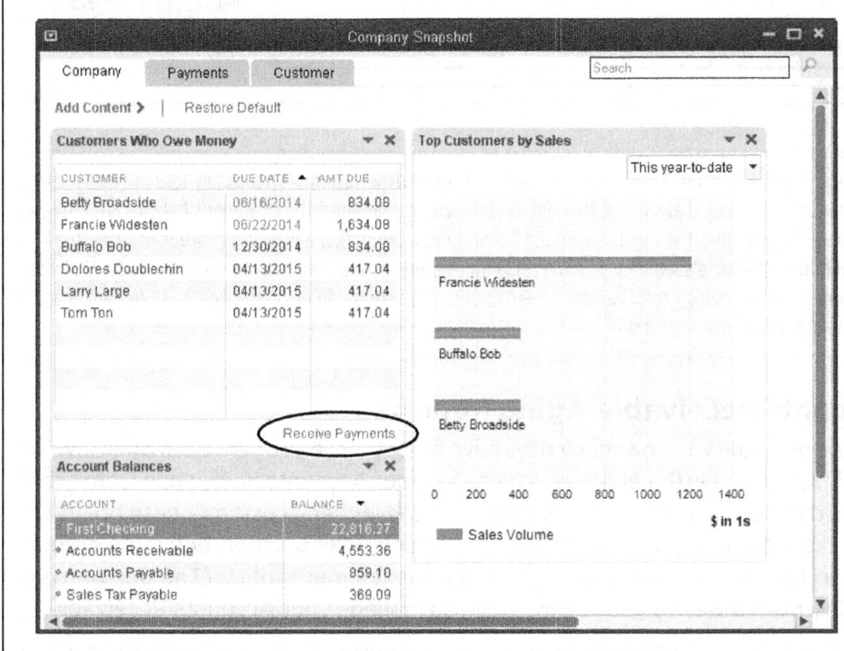

FIGURE 13-2

The Customers Who Owe Money section shows who owes you money, how much they owe, and when it's due. (If you don't see this section, try maximizing the window. If that doesn't work, see page 705 to learn how to display it in the Company Snapshot.) If the due date is in the past, it's displayed in red text.

To record a payment, click the Receive Payments link (circled).

Viewing Receivables Detail in the Customer Center

Yet another way to view your Accounts Receivable is in the Customer Center (choose Customers→Customer Center or, on the Home Page, click Customers). The window's Customers & Jobs tab lists your customers and jobs and the balance owed by each one. If you select a customer or job in the list, you can see the invoices or other sales transactions that generated the open balance on the right side of the window, as shown in Figure 13-3.

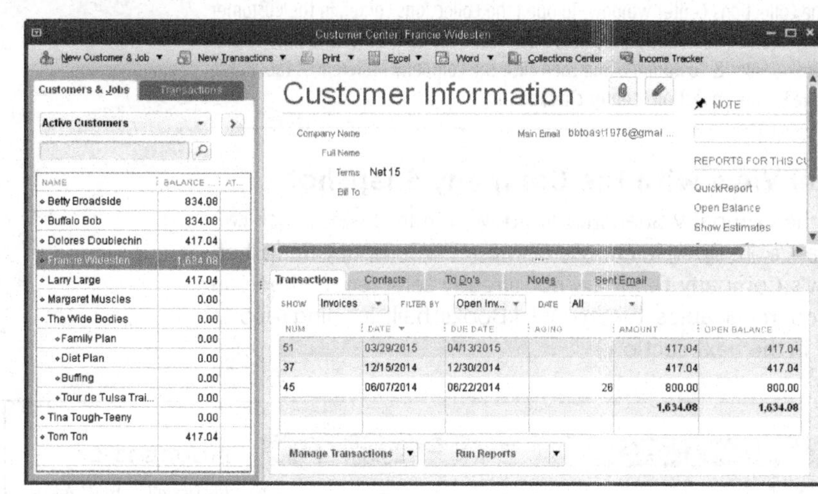

FIGURE 13-3

To see the transactions that make up a customer's balance, select the customer on the Customers & Jobs tab. On the Transactions tab in the lower-right part of the window, in the Show drop-down list, choose Invoices; and in the tab's Filter By drop-down list, choose Open Invoices, as shown here. A value in an invoice's Aging cell indicates the number of days it's past its due date.

NOTE In the Customer Center, if the customer's balance on the Customers & Jobs tab doesn't equal the total in the Transactions table, that's a clue that not all transactions that affect the customer's balance are displayed in the table. For example, if you've tweaked the Transactions table so that it lists only overdue invoices, the total at the bottom of the table's Amount column is only for overdue invoices, whereas the balance on the Customers & Jobs tab is the customer's *total* balance (overdue and not) taking into account invoices, statement charges, credit memos, payments, and so on.

Accounts Receivable Aging Reports

Aging reports tell you how many days have passed since you sent each open invoice, and viewing them is the first step in keeping your Accounts Receivable from growing overly ripe. It's a fact of business life that the longer a customer hasn't paid, the more likely it is that you'll never see that money. Taking action *before* an account lags too far behind limits bad debts and protects your profits. (The box on page 344 describes a way to gauge how well you manage your Accounts Receivable.)

QuickBooks includes two built-in aging reports: A/R Aging Summary and A/R Aging Detail. These reports show how much your customers owe for the current billing period (invoices that are less than 30 days old), as well as unpaid invoices from previous periods (invoices that are between 1 and 30 days late, 31 to 60 days late, 61 to 90 days late, and more than 90 days late). The Accounts Receivable Graph can also show you some useful info. Here's a bit more about each one:

- **A/R Aging Summary**. For a quick look at how much money your customers owe you and how old your receivables are, choose Reports→Customers & Receivables→A/R Aging Summary. To see the transactions that make up a customer's total, put your cursor over a summary value. When the cursor changes to a magnifying glass like the one circled in Figure 13-4, double-click the transaction.

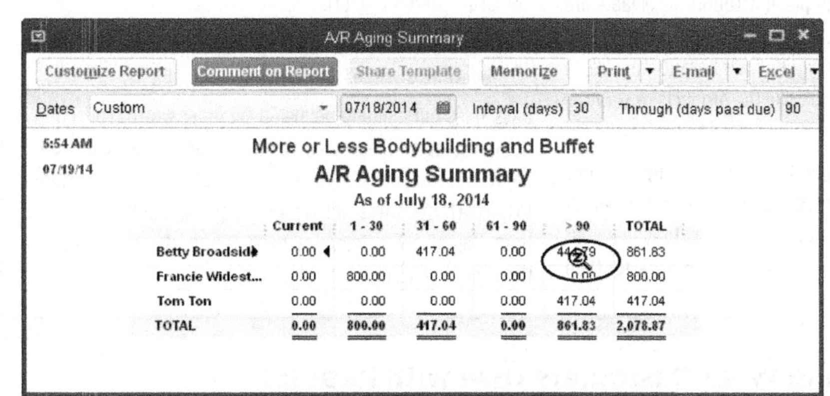

	Current	1 - 30	31 - 60	61 - 90	> 90	TOTAL
Betty Broadside	0.00	0.00	417.04	0.00	444.79	861.83
Francie Widest...	0.00	800.00	0.00	0.00	0.00	800.00
Tom Ton	0.00	0.00	0.00	0.00	417.04	417.04
TOTAL	0.00	800.00	417.04	0.00	861.83	2,078.87

FIGURE 13-4

This report lists customers and jobs and shows the money they owe in each aging period. Ideally, you should see more zero balances as you look at older periods. When you're on a mission to collect overdue accounts, start with the oldest aging period on the right side of the report.

NOTE If you work with more than one currency, the A/R Aging reports and the Accounts Receivable Graph use your home currency for all values. But you can modify the A/R Aging Summary report to see transactions in the currencies in which they were recorded: In the report's window, click Customize Report. On the Display tab of the Modify Report dialog box that appears, below the "Display amounts in" label, select the "The transaction currency" option, and then click OK.

- **A/R Aging Detail**. To see Accounts Receivable transactions for all your customers categorized by age, choose Reports→Customers & Receivables→A/R Aging Detail.
- **Accounts Receivable Graph**. This graph doesn't show as much detail as either of the A/R Aging reports, but its visual nature makes aging problems stand out. To display it, choose Reports→Customers & Receivables→Accounts Receivable Graph. Ideally, you want to see the bars in the graph get smaller or disappear completely as the number of days overdue increases. To see more details for a particular period, double-click a bar in the graph to open a QuickZoom Graph. To see more detail about a customer, double-click the customer's name in the legend or double-click the slice of the pie chart that corresponds to the customer.

POWER USERS' CLINIC

Watching Receivables Trends

In the investment world, financial analysts study trends in Accounts Receivable. For example, if Accounts Receivable are increasing faster than sales, it means that customers aren't paying for everything they bought, either because they're on thin ice financially or they don't like the products or services they've received.

One way to measure how good a job your company does collecting receivables is with *days sales outstanding*, which is the number of days' worth of sales it takes to match your Accounts Receivable. If Accounts Receivable grow faster than sales (meaning customers aren't paying), you'll see this value get larger. Here's the formula:

```
Days sales outstanding =
   Accounts receivable / (Sales/365)
```

Days sales outstanding below 60 (in other words, collecting Accounts Receivable with two months' worth of sales) is good. But if your company is in the retail business, you should aspire to the performance of high-volume giants such as Walmart and Home Depot, who, according to their annual reports, collect their receivables in less than a week.

Seeing What Customers Owe with Reports

Aging reports aren't the only goodies you can generate in QuickBooks. To see all the reports associated with customers and what they owe, choose Reports→Customers & Receivables. Here's an overview of when it makes sense to use these reports:

- **Customer Balance Summary**. This report shows the balances for each job and the customer's total balance. You can find this same total balance information on the Customer Center's Customers & Jobs tab, but unlike that tab, you can easily print this report.

NOTE In QuickBooks 2015, reports have been spiffed up with new fonts and shading to make them easier to read (see page 584).

- **Customer Balance Detail**. This report shows every transaction that makes up customers' balances, so it can get pretty long. It lists every transaction (such as invoices, payments, statement charges, and credit memos) for *every* customer and job in your company file, whether the customer is late or not. To inspect a transaction's details, double-click anywhere in the transaction's row to see it in its corresponding window (Create Invoices for an invoice, for example). If you'd rather see the transactions for just *one* customer, open the Customer Center, select the customer, and then, on the right side of the window, click the Open Balance link.
- **Open Invoices**. This report includes unpaid invoices and statement charges, as well as payments and unapplied credits, so you can see if a payment or unapplied credit closes out a customer's balance. This report is sorted and subtotaled for

each customer and job, so you can find an unpaid invoice quickly. When you find the invoice you want, double-click anywhere in its row to open it.

- **Collections Report**. When you're on a mission to collect the money that's owed to you, this report shows the past-due invoices and statement charges by customer and job, along with the due date and number of days that the transaction is past due. If a customer has questions about a transaction, double-click the transaction's row to view it in detail.

TIP When customers have pushed their credit limits—and your patience—too far, you can easily create collection letters by merging information for overdue customers with mail-merge collection letters in Word. See page 672 for details.

- **Average Days to Pay Summary/Average Days to Pay**. These reports show how long customers take to pay your invoices. The summary report lists each customer and the average days it took it to pay based on all transactions. If you notice customers going far beyond your limits, you might consider increasing your finance charges or looking for new customers.
- **Unbilled Costs by Job**. Another way you might leave money on the table is by forgetting to add reimbursable expenses to invoices. Run this report to see whether there are expenses you haven't billed; if there are, the report lists the type of expense and when you incurred it, among other info. If you spot older expenses that you haven't yet billed, add them to the next invoice (page 252).

Receiving Payments for Invoiced Income

To record a payment, click Receive Payments on the Home Page or choose Customers→Receive Payments. Either way, QuickBooks opens the Receive Payments window, which handles full and partial payments, early payment discounts, credits, and downloaded online payments.

The Receive Payments window works for *most* payments, but you record some types of payments in other places. Here are the windows that can record payments and when to use them:

- **Receive Payments**. When customers send you money to pay their invoices or their statement balances, on the Home Page, click Receive Payments to record the payment as explained below. This window is for full or partial payments that you receive *after* you've made a sale. It lets you apply early payment discounts and credits for returns, as well as downloaded online payments. (See page 370 to find out how to record the deposits for *any* type of payment.)
- **Create Invoices**. As explained in the box on page 350, this window is where you record a partial payment that you receive *before* you prepare an invoice. These payments appear on the next invoice you create and reduce its balance. And if you happen to receive a payment while you're preparing the customer's

next invoice in this window, you can add the payment to the invoice right then. You can also apply available credits in this window.

- **Enter Sales Receipts**. When your customers pay in full at the time of sale (with cash, check, or credit card), record payments in this window (page 362).

To record full or partial payments (with or without discounts or credits) that you receive from customers, follow these steps:

1. **Choose Customers→Receive Payments or, on the Home Page, click Receive Payments. (Alternatively, in the Customer Center, select the customer who sent a payment, and then, in the window's toolbar, choose New Transactions→Receive Payments.)**

   QuickBooks opens the Receive Payments window.

2. **In the Received From box, choose the customer or the job for which you received a payment, as shown in Figure 13-5.**

   If the customer sent a payment that covers more than one job, choose the customer's name rather than a job. QuickBooks then adds the Job column to the Receive Payments window's table and fills in the rows with all the outstanding invoices for all the customer's jobs. When an invoice applies to a specific job, the job's name appears in the table. If the cell in the Job column is blank, the invoice applies directly to the customer, not to a job.

TIP Income Tracker (page 338) can help you record payments more quickly. In the Income Tracker window (Customers→Income Tracker), click the Action cell in the row for the invoice for which you received a payment, and then choose Receive Payment on the drop-down menu. QuickBooks opens a new payment transaction in the Receive Payments window and fills in the Customer:Job box with the customer or job associated with the invoice you selected.

3. **In the Payment Amount box, type the amount of the payment (if the customer uses a foreign currency, type the amount received in the foreign currency).**

   If you select a customer who is set up to use a foreign currency, QuickBooks automatically sets the A/R Account box to the Accounts Receivable account for that currency. For euros, for example, you'll see "Accounts Receivable - EUR."

TIP If you choose a job and don't see the invoice you expect, in the Received From box, choose the customer to see all invoices for that customer *and* its jobs. If the invoice is assigned to the wrong customer or the wrong job, edit the invoice (page 293), and *then* choose the correct job in the Received From box.

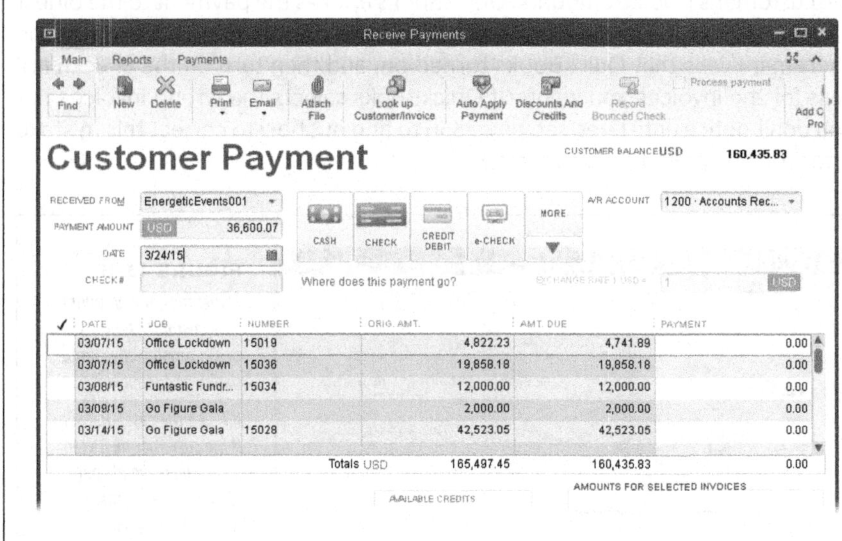

FIGURE 13-5

When you choose a customer or job in the Received From box, the Customer Balance at the window's top right shows the corresponding balance, and QuickBooks fills in the table with every unpaid invoice for that customer or job. If you choose a customer (as shown here), QuickBooks adds the Job column to the table and fills in the rows with the customer's outstanding invoices. The cell in the Job column lists the job's name when an invoice applies to a specific job, and it's blank when the invoice applies to the customer.

TIP You don't have to fill in the Payment Amount box if you've turned on the "Automatically calculate payments" preference (page 657). With this setting turned on, QuickBooks fills in the payment transaction's Payment Amount field with the value of the first invoice you select. As you select (or deselect) additional invoices, the program recalculates the total payment.

If this preference is turned off, you have to fill in the Payment Amount field with the payment amount in order to select invoices in the table. If you leave the Payment Amount field blank and try to select an invoice in the table, QuickBooks warns you that you can't apply an amount greater than the total payment plus any credits the customer has. The advantage to turning this preference off is that a discrepancy between the customer's payment and the selected invoice total is easy to spot—the Underpayment or Overpayment section shown in Figure 13-6 appears, showing the difference between the two values.

4. **If you turned off the "Automatically apply payments" preference (page 657), in the window's table, turn on the checkmark cells (in the first column) for the invoices to which you want to apply the payment, as shown in Figure 13-6.**

   To tell QuickBooks to choose the invoices for you, on the window's Main tab, click Auto Apply Payment. (Once you've selected at least one invoice to pay, this button's label changes to Un-Apply Payment.) The box on page 350 explains how to adjust the amount of the payment that's applied to the invoices you select.

If the "Automatically apply payments" preference is turned on, after you enter the payment amount and either press Tab or click another box, QuickBooks automatically selects an invoice for you. If the payment doesn't match any of the customer's invoice amounts, QuickBooks applies the payment to the oldest invoices first. If the program doesn't select the correct invoices, turn off the checkmark cells that QuickBooks turned on, and then turn on the checkmark cells for the invoices you want. (If QuickBooks selects the wrong invoices but you don't notice until later, see page 356 to find out how to correct this mistake *after* you've applied the payment.)

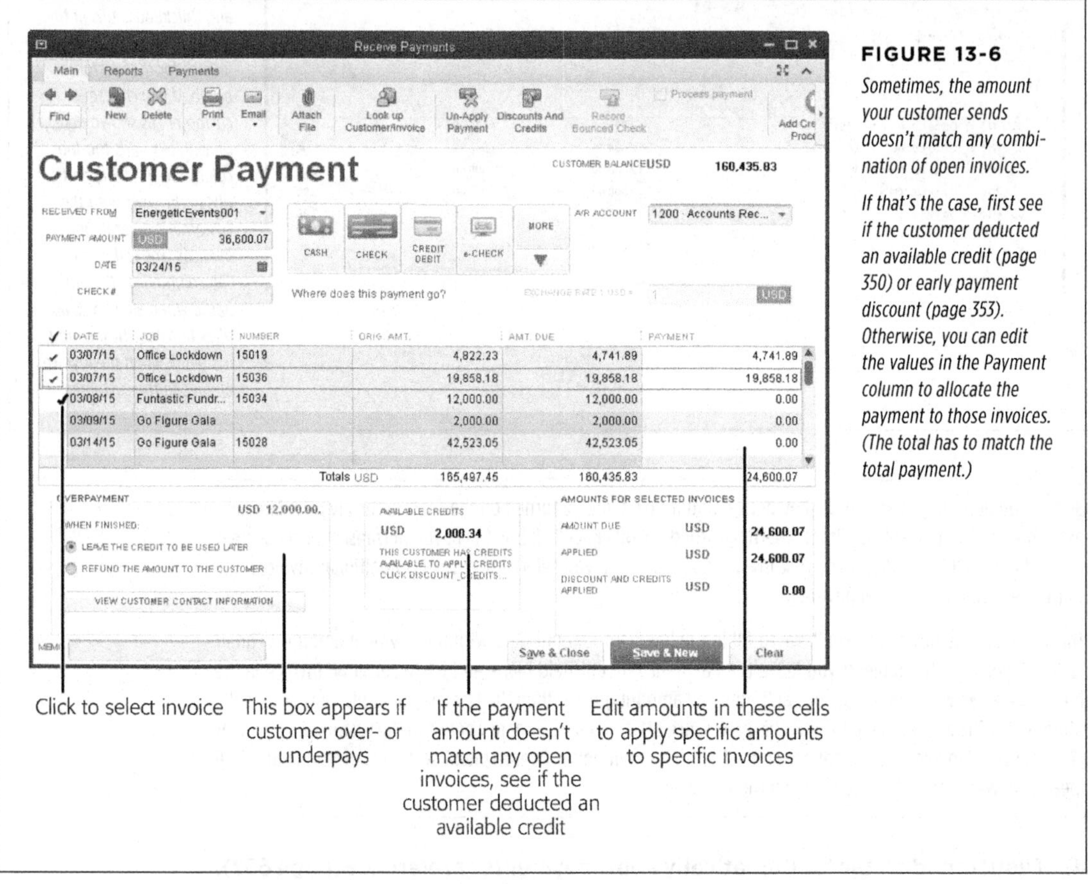

FIGURE 13-6

Sometimes, the amount your customer sends doesn't match any combination of open invoices.

If that's the case, first see if the customer deducted an available credit (page 350) or early payment discount (page 353). Otherwise, you can edit the values in the Payment column to allocate the payment to those invoices. (The total has to match the total payment.)

TIP When you select a customer who is set up to use a foreign currency, the Receive Payments window's "Exchange Rate 1 [currency] =" box comes to life, filled in with the current exchange rate set in QuickBooks. If you want to use a different rate, type it in this box. If the exchange rate you use when you receive the payment is different from the rate you used on the invoice, QuickBooks automatically calculates the gain or loss (page 461) for the transaction.

5. **To the right of the Payment Amount box, click the icon that corresponds to the method the customer used to make the payment.**

   If you click Cash, QuickBooks displays the Reference # box, where you can type a receipt number or other identifier. If you click Check, QuickBooks displays the Check # box instead, so you can type the number from the customer's check. For any type of credit card or EFT, in the Card No. box and Exp. Date boxes, type the card's number and the month and year that it expires. The Reference # box that appears is perfect for storing the credit card transaction number.

6. **If the Deposit To box is visible, choose the account for the deposit, such as your checking account, money market account, or Undeposited Funds account.**

   When you first start using QuickBooks, the program's Use Undeposited Funds preference (page 657) is turned on, which tells QuickBooks to automatically deposit payments into your Undeposited Funds account. When this setting is on, you won't see the Deposit To box, and the program holds payments in that account until you tell it to deposit those payments into a specific bank account.

   If electronic payments land directly in your bank account (for example, payments made with PayPal or a merchant credit card service), you can record those deposits to the appropriate bank account in the Receive Payments window. To do that, turn the Use Undeposited Funds preference off and then, in the Receive Payments window, choose the bank account in the Deposit To box.

TIP To make reconciling your bank statement a bit easier, choose the Deposit To account based on the way your bank statement shows deposits you make. For example, if your bank statement shows only a deposit total regardless of how many checks were in the deposit, put payments in the Undeposited Funds account. If your bank shows every check you deposit, choose your QuickBooks bank account instead so that each payment appears separately. (Page 657 explains how to set your QuickBooks preferences so that the program always chooses Undeposited Funds for payments.)

   If the customer paid too much or too little (or you've selected too few or too many open invoices in the Receive Payments window), you'll see an overpayment or underpayment message like the one in the lower-left part of Figure 13-6. Before you edit values in the Payment column, make sure that you've selected the correct invoices. Then see if the Available Credits value equals the Underpayment value. If it does, your customer reduced the payment by its available credit. See page 350 for details about applying credits.

7. **If you want to print a payment receipt, at the top of the Receive Payments window, click Print→Payment.**

   QuickBooks opens the Print Lists dialog box. If necessary, change the print settings, and then click Print.

8. **To assign the payment to the selected invoices and close the window, click Save & Close.**

   If you want to apply another payment, click Save & New instead.

UP TO SPEED

Different Ways to Apply Payments

Most of the time, customers send payments that bear a clear relationship to their unpaid invoices. For those payments, QuickBooks' preference that automatically selects invoices (page 657) is a real timesaver: You type the payment amount in the Receive Payments window's Payment Amount box, and the program selects the most likely invoice(s) for payment. When a payment matches an invoice amount exactly, this feature works perfectly *almost* every time.

But every once in a while you'll receive a payment that doesn't match up, and you'll have to tell QuickBooks how to apply the payment. For example, if the payment and the customer's available credit (taken together) match an open invoice, you can use the method explained on page 350 to apply them to the invoice. (If you have no idea what the customer had in mind, don't guess—contact the customer and ask how to apply the payment.)

Regardless of the situation, you can adjust the values in the Receive Payments window's Payment column to match your customer's wishes. Here's how to handle some common scenarios:

- **Customer includes the invoice number on the payment.** If QuickBooks selects an invoice other than the one the customer specifies, click the selected invoice's checkmark cell to turn it off. Then turn on the checkmark for the desired invoice to make QuickBooks apply the payment to it and type the amount of the payment in the Payment cell.
- **Payment is less than any outstanding invoices.** In this case, QuickBooks applies the payment to the oldest invoice. Simply click Save & Close to apply the payment as is. Your customers will thank you for helping them avoid (or reduce) your finance charges.
- **Payment is greater than the total of the customer's invoices.** If the payment is larger than all the customer's unpaid invoices, apply the payment to all its open invoices and adjust the Payment cells if necessary. Then create a credit or write a refund check for the amount of the overpayment (page 288).

Applying Credits to Invoices When You Receive Payments

When something goes awry with the services or products you sell, customers won't be bashful about asking for a refund or credit. And customers who buy from you regularly might *prefer* a credit against their next order rather than a refund so that checks aren't flying back and forth in the mail (page 288 tells you how to create a credit).

As you saw on page 291, you can apply a credit to a customer's invoice at any time to reduce the amount that the customer owes. But if a credit is still available when you receive a customer's payment, you can apply the credit *and* the payment at the same time. Here's what you do:

1. **Choose Customers→Receive Payments or, on the Home Page, click Receive Payments.**

   QuickBooks opens the Receive Payments window.

2. **In the Received From drop-down list, choose the customer or job you want. In the Payment Amount box, type the customer's payment amount, and to the right of this box, click the button for the payment method the customer used.**

   If you choose a customer or job with an available credit, the Available Credits section appears below the window's table and shows the amount of credit that's available (this section is visible in Figure 13-6). If you choose a customer, the Available Credits value represents all the credits available for all jobs for that customer. If your customer reduced the payment by the amount of its available credit, you'll also see the Underpayment section at the window's bottom left.

3. **To apply the credit to the invoice you selected, at the top of the Receive Payments window, click Discounts And Credits.**

   QuickBooks opens the "Discount and Credits" dialog box (Figure 13-7).

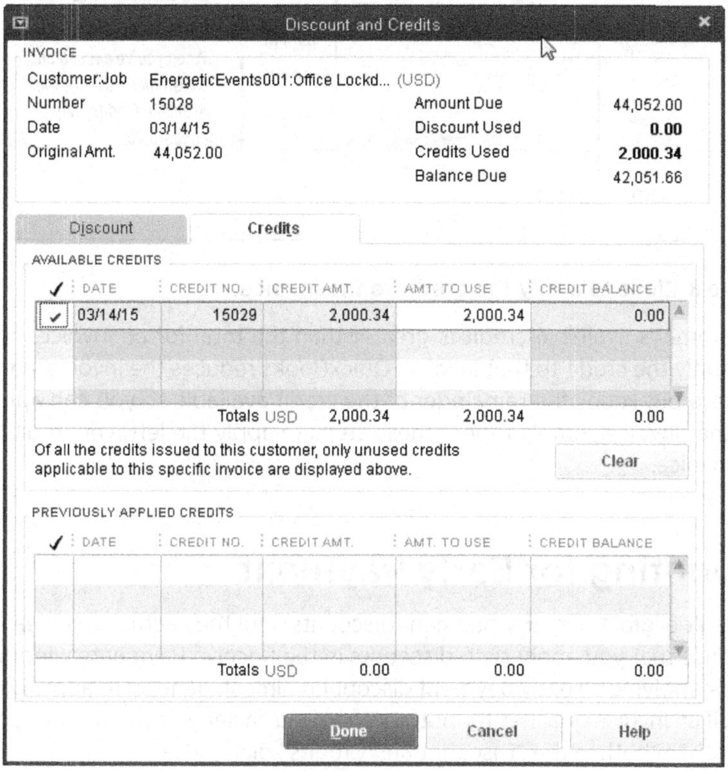

FIGURE 13-7

When you click a credit's checkmark cell in the Available Credits table here, the Credits Used value changes to show the total credit that has been applied to the invoice, and the Balance Due value shows how much is still due on the invoice (if any).

If you applied other credits to the invoice in the past, they appear in the Previously Applied Credits table at the bottom of this dialog box.

4. **If necessary, in the Available Credits table, click the credit's checkmark cell to turn it on.**

   If the customer asked you *not* to apply a credit, turn off that credit's checkmark cell. If the credit doesn't appear in the "Discount and Credits" dialog box, it probably relates to a different job or to the customer only. If you want to apply a credit to a different job or to the customer's account, see the box on page 350.

5. **Click Done.**

   QuickBooks closes the "Discount and Credits" dialog box and returns to the Receive Payments window, where you see the applied credit, as shown in Figure 13-8.

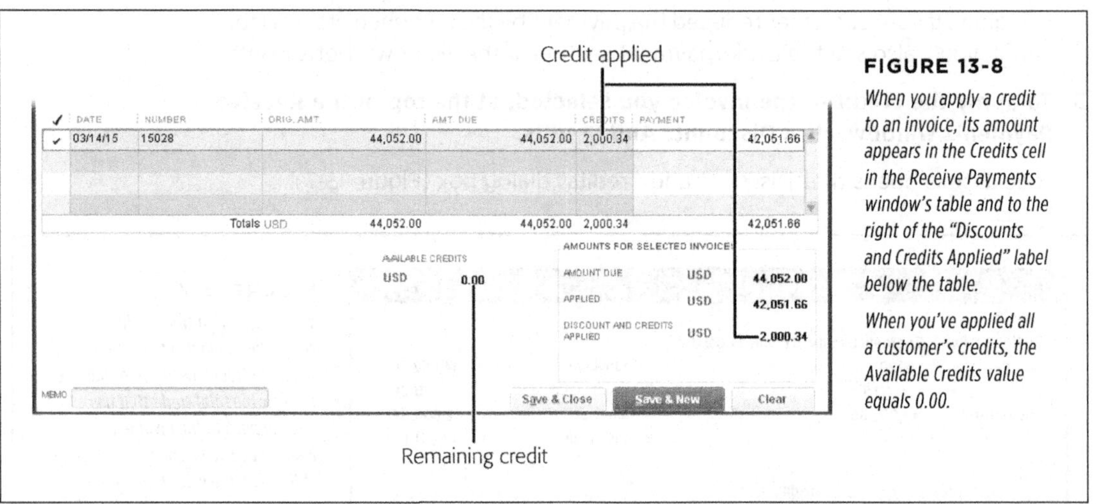

FIGURE 13-8

When you apply a credit to an invoice, its amount appears in the Credits cell in the Receive Payments window's table and to the right of the "Discounts and Credits Applied" label below the table.

When you've applied all a customer's credits, the Available Credits value equals 0.00.

6. **Click Save & Close to apply the credit to the invoice.**

   If the customer's available credit is greater than the total for an invoice, you can still apply the credit to that invoice. QuickBooks reduces the invoice's balance to zero but keeps the remainder of the credit available so you can apply it to another invoice. Simply repeat these steps to apply the leftover credit to another invoice.

Discounting for Early Payment

Customers aren't eligible for early payment discounts until they actually *pay early*, so it makes sense that you apply such discounts in the Receive Payments window. The process for applying an early payment discount is almost identical to applying a credit. In fact, if an invoice qualifies for both a credit *and* an early payment discount, you can apply them both in the "Discount and Credits" dialog box.

NOTE If the discount is for something other than an early payment, such as a product that's on sale, instead of using the technique described in this section, add a Discount item to the invoice when you create it (page 241).

Here's how to apply an early payment discount to a customer:

1. **On the Home Page, click Receive Payments or choose Customers→Receive Payments.**
2. **In the Receive Payments window's Received From drop-down list, choose the customer or job for the payment you received.**

   The window's table then displays all the invoices and/or statements for that customer or job that aren't paid.
3. **In the Payment Amount box, type the payment amount you received from the customer.**

   If the "Automatically apply payments" preference is turned on (page 657), when you click away from this box, QuickBooks applies the payment to the customer or job's open invoices. If QuickBooks doesn't apply the payment to the correct invoices, you can choose the ones you want (page 350). If that preference is turned off, turn on the checkmark cells (in the first column) for the invoices to which you want to apply the payment

   If the customer already deducted the early payment discount, the Receive Payments window shows an underpayment (Figure 13-9).
4. **To apply the early payment discount, at the top of the Receive Payments window, click Discounts And Credits.**

   QuickBooks opens the "Discount and Credits" dialog box. If the Credits tab is visible, click the Discount tab to display the Discount fields shown in Figure 13-10. If the date of the payment is earlier than the Discount Date that's listed, QuickBooks uses the early payment percentage from the customer's payment terms (page 76) to calculate the Suggested Discount. For example, if the customer gets a 2 percent discount for paying early, the suggested discount is 2 percent of the invoice total.

NOTE Customers often deduct their early payment discounts despite sending their payments after the early payment cutoff date. The typical reaction of most business owners is a resigned sigh. Although QuickBooks shows the suggested discount as zero when a customer doesn't actually pay early, you can show your customer goodwill and accept his payment. In the Amount of Discount box, simply type the discount that the customer took.

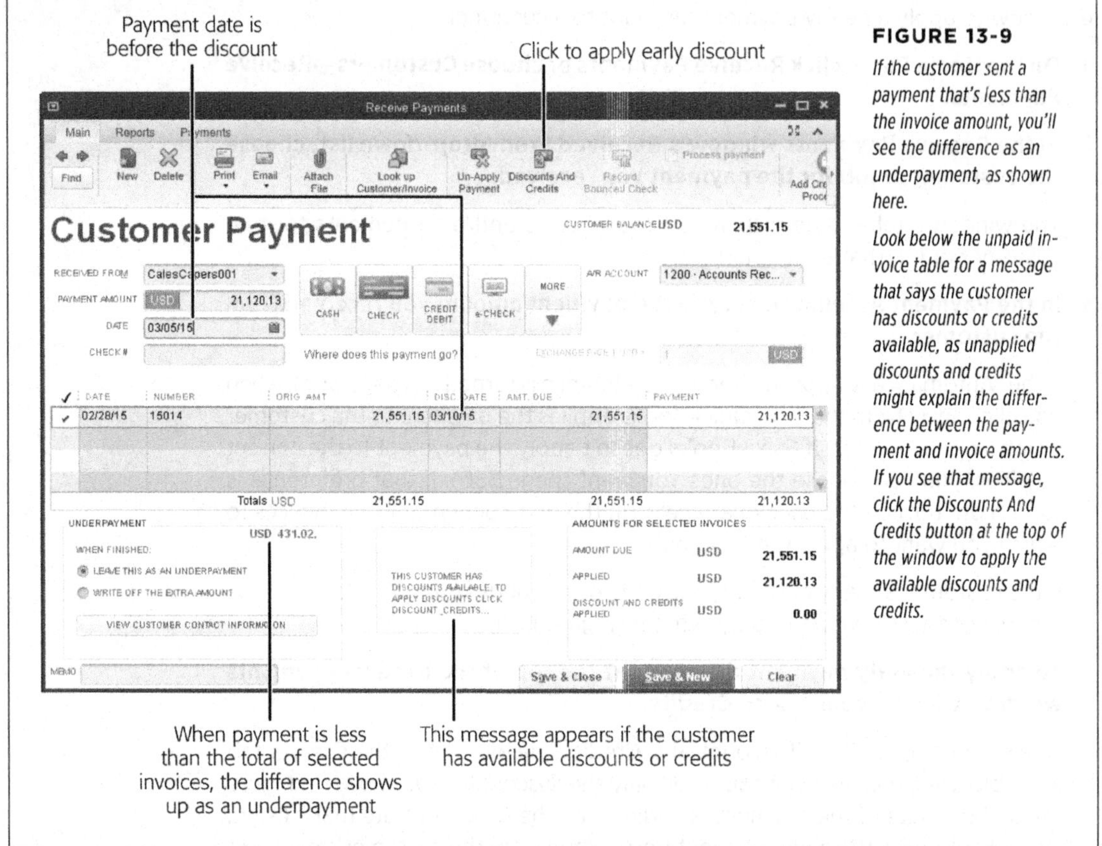
Payment date is before the discount
Click to apply early discount
Receive Payments
Customer Payment
CUSTOMER BALANCE USD 21,551.15
RECEIVED FROM CalesCapers001
PAYMENT AMOUNT USD 21,120.13
DATE 03/05/15
UNDERPAYMENT USD 431.02.
THIS CUSTOMER HAS DISCOUNTS AVAILABLE. TO APPLY DISCOUNTS CLICK DISCOUNT_CREDITS...
When payment is less than the total of selected invoices, the difference shows up as an underpayment
This message appears if the customer has available discounts or credits

FIGURE 13-9

If the customer sent a payment that's less than the invoice amount, you'll see the difference as an underpayment, as shown here.

Look below the unpaid invoice table for a message that says the customer has discounts or credits available, as unapplied discounts and credits might explain the difference between the payment and invoice amounts. If you see that message, click the Discounts And Credits button at the top of the window to apply the available discounts and credits.

5. **In the Discount Account box, choose the income account you've set up to track customer discounts.**

   You might think it makes sense to post customer discounts to one of your income accounts for products or services you sell. But customer discounts tend to fall off your radar when they're buried among your regular income. The best course of action is to keep track of the discounts you give by creating an income account specifically for them, called something imaginative like Customer Discounts.

   If you spot an *expense* account called Discounts, don't use that as your customer discount account, either. An expense account for discounts is meant to track the discounts *you* receive from your vendors.

6. **If you use classes, in the Discount Class box, choose the appropriate one.**

   This class is typically the same one you used for the invoice.

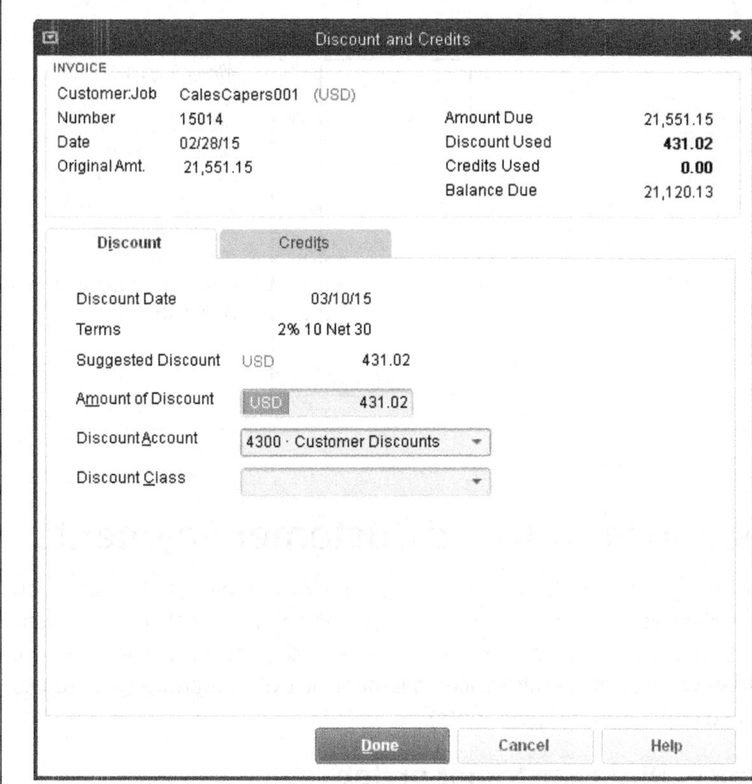

FIGURE 13-10

QuickBooks automatically puts the suggested discount in the Amount of Discount box, but you can type a different amount—if the customer paid only part of the invoice early, for instance.

The Invoice section at the top of the dialog box shows the amount due on the invoice and the balance due after applying the early payment discount you chose. If the customer has already paid the invoice in full, the early payment discount becomes a credit for the next invoice.

7. **Click Done.**

   When QuickBooks closes the "Discount and Credits" dialog box and returns to the Receive Payments window, you'll see the discount in two or three places, as Figure 13-11 shows. The early payment discount appears both in the invoice table's Discount column and below the table next to the "Discount and Credits Applied" label. If the customer paid the invoice in full, the early payment discount also becomes an overpayment (not shown in Figure 13-11).

TIP If a customer overpays, QuickBooks displays two options at the bottom left of the Receive Payments window: "Leave the credit to be used later" and "Refund the amount to the customer." Unless your customer wants a refund, keep "Leave the credit to be used later" selected.

8. **When you're done, click Save & Close.**

You've just recorded the payment with the discount applied.

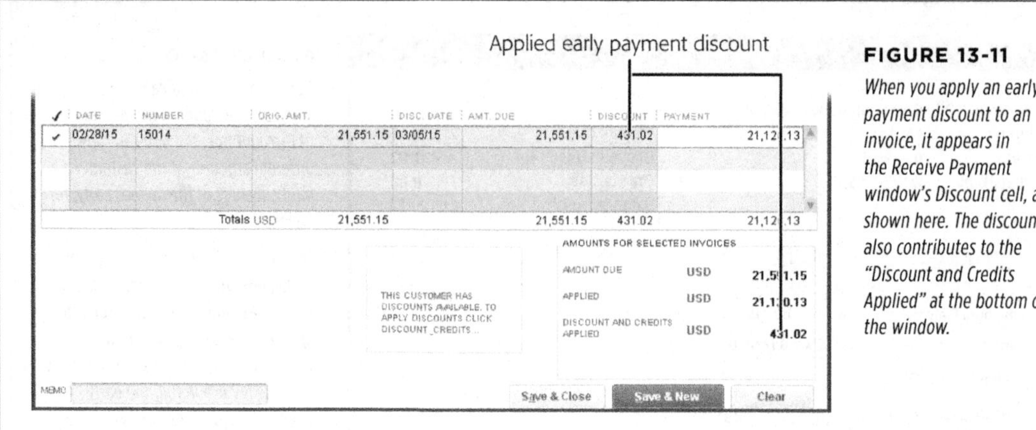

FIGURE 13-11

When you apply an early payment discount to an invoice, it appears in the Receive Payment window's Discount cell, as shown here. The discount also contributes to the "Discount and Credits Applied" at the bottom of the window.

Correcting Misapplied Customer Payments

Say you realize that you've applied a payment to the wrong invoice. The way you correct this mistake depends on whether you applied the payment to a different invoice for the same customer or job, or you applied it to the wrong customer or job. This section shows you how to fix misapplied payments in both situations (regardless of whether you've deposited the payments).

Wrong Invoice, Right Customer or Job

If you simply selected the wrong invoice for a customer or job when you applied a payment, it's easy to set things straight. Here's how:

1. **Choose Customers→Customer Center or, on the Home Page, click Customers. On the Customer Center's Customers & Jobs tab, click the customer or job whose payment you misapplied.**

   The Transactions tab in the Customer Center's lower right displays the transactions for the customer or job you selected.

2. **On the Transactions tab, click the Show box's down arrow, and then choose Received Payments.**

   If you do that but still don't see the payment you're looking for, click the Filter By down arrow and choose All Payment Methods; or click the Date down arrow and choose a different date range.

3. **When you see the payment in question, double-click it.**

   The Receive Payments window opens to the payment you double-clicked.

4. **In the Receive Payments window's unpaid invoice table, you'll see both the wrong invoice and the right one. Turn *off* the checkmark cell for the currently selected invoice; turn *on* the checkmark cell for the correct invoice, and then click Save & Close.**

   QuickBooks applies the payment to the correct invoice.

Wrong Invoice, Wrong Customer

When you apply a payment to the wrong *customer's* invoice, you can't use the steps in the previous section. Here's why: When you open the misapplied payment in the Receive Payments window, the Received From box contains the erroneous customer or job, and the invoices that appear in the window's unpaid invoices table are for that customer. That means there's no way to select the invoice for the correct customer in the Receive Payments window.

To correct this type of misapplied payment, you need to create a new payment for the correct customer and delete the payment you applied to the wrong customer. The good news is that this approach also works if you deposited a payment *without* applying it to an invoice; it even works if you've already reconciled the deposit with your bank account. Here are the steps:

1. **First, create a new payment for the correct customer.**

   To do this, in the Customer Center (Customers→Customer Center), click the Customers & Jobs tab, and then select the customer or job to which the payment *should* be applied. Then, at the top of the window, click New Transactions→Receive Payments and follow the steps on page 346 to record the new payment. Click Save & Close when you're done.

2. **If you already deposited the misapplied payment, on the Home Page, click Record Deposits (or choose Banking→Make Deposits). If you haven't deposited the payment, skip to step 7.**

   If you see the "Payments to Deposit" window, click OK to open the Make Deposits window.

3. **In the Make Deposits window's toolbar, click Previous until you see the deposit you're looking for.**

   If you don't see the deposit, be sure to choose the correct bank account in the window's Deposit To box.

4. **In the window's toolbar, click Payments. In the "Payments to Deposit" window, click the checkmark cell for the payment you created in step 1, and then click OK.**

   The Make Deposits window's table now lists both the old payment and the new payment, as shown in Figure 13-12.

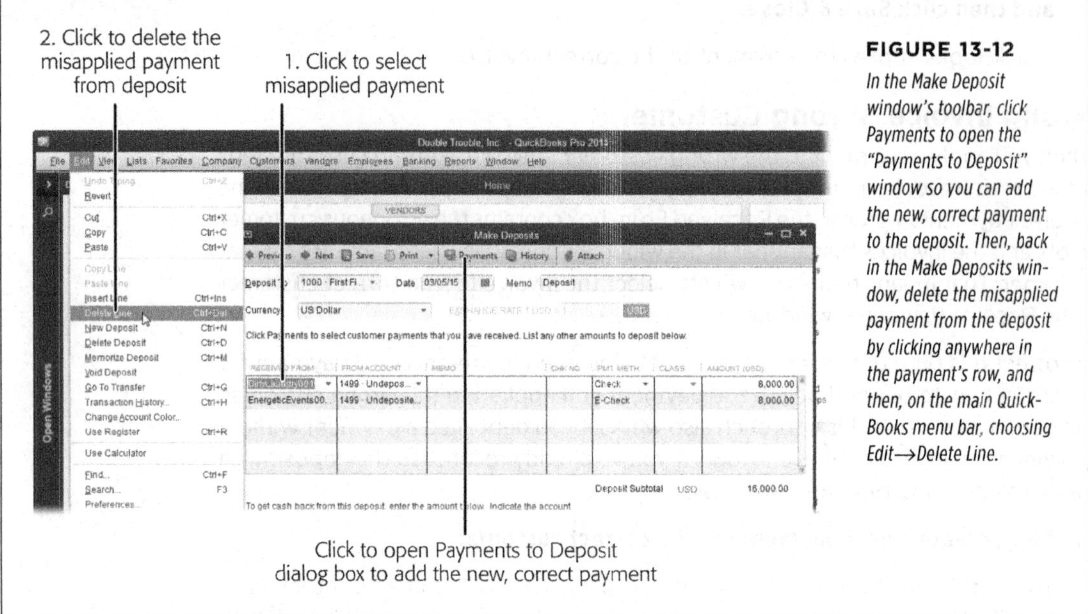
2. Click to delete the misapplied payment from deposit
1. Click to select misapplied payment
Click to open Payments to Deposit dialog box to add the new, correct payment

FIGURE 13-12

In the Make Deposit window's toolbar, click Payments to open the "Payments to Deposit" window so you can add the new, correct payment to the deposit. Then, back in the Make Deposits window, delete the misapplied payment from the deposit by clicking anywhere in the payment's row, and then, on the main QuickBooks menu bar, choosing Edit→Delete Line.

5. **To delete the misapplied payment from the deposit, click anywhere in its row in the payments table, and then, on the main QuickBooks menu bar, choose Edit→Delete Line.**

   The misapplied payment disappears, leaving the correctly applied payment in the table.

6. **Click Save & Close.**

   QuickBooks saves the deposit with the correctly applied payment and closes the Make Deposits windows.

7. **Delete the original, misapplied payment.**

   In the Customer Center, click the Transactions tab on the window's left, and then click Received Payments. Double-click the payment you misapplied to open it in the Receive Payments window. At the top of the Receive Payments window, click Delete, and then, in the message box, click OK.

Because you deleted the original payment, it's a good idea to document what you did. For example, add a note (page 481) to the customer or job to which the deleted payment belonged explaining why you deleted it.

Applying Finance Charges

If you've tried everything but some customers *still* won't pay, you can resort to finance charges. These charges usually don't cover the cost of keeping after the slackers, but QuickBooks at least minimizes the time you spend on this vexing task.

NOTE Typically, only small businesses actually pay finance charges. Corporations usually ignore them, so you may decide to skip finance charges for your corporate clients (you'll just have to reverse the charges later on).

Customers tend to get cranky if you spring finance charges on them without warning, so spend some time up front determining your payment policies: what interest rate you'll charge, what constitutes "late," and so on. Include these terms in the contracts your customers sign and on the sales forms you send. Then, after you configure QuickBooks with your finance-charge settings, a few clicks is all it'll take to add those penalties to customer accounts.

Finance Charge Preferences

Before you apply finance charges, you need to tell QuickBooks how steep your finance charges are, when they kick in, and a few other details. To adjust these settings, choose Edit→Preferences→Finance Charge. Because your finance-charge policies should apply to *all* your customers, these settings are on the Company Preferences tab, which means only a QuickBooks administrator can change them. To learn how to set these preferences, see page 646.

Assessing Finance Charges on Overdue Balances

QuickBooks creates finance-charge invoices for customers tardy enough to warrant late fees, but you don't have to print or send these invoices. Instead, you can assess finance charges just before you print customer statements (page 305) to have QuickBooks include the finance-charge invoices on statements, along with any outstanding invoices and unpaid charges for the customer.

TIP Make sure you apply payments and credits to invoices *before* you assess finance charges. Otherwise, you'll spend most of your time reversing finance charges and working to get back into your customers' good graces.

Here's how to assess finance charges for slow-paying customers:

1. **Choose Customers→Assess Finance Charges or, on the Home Page, click the Finance Charges icon.**

   The Assess Finance Charges window (Figure 13-13) opens.

   If your company file is set up to use multiple currencies, in the A/R Account box, select the account for the currency you want to work with.

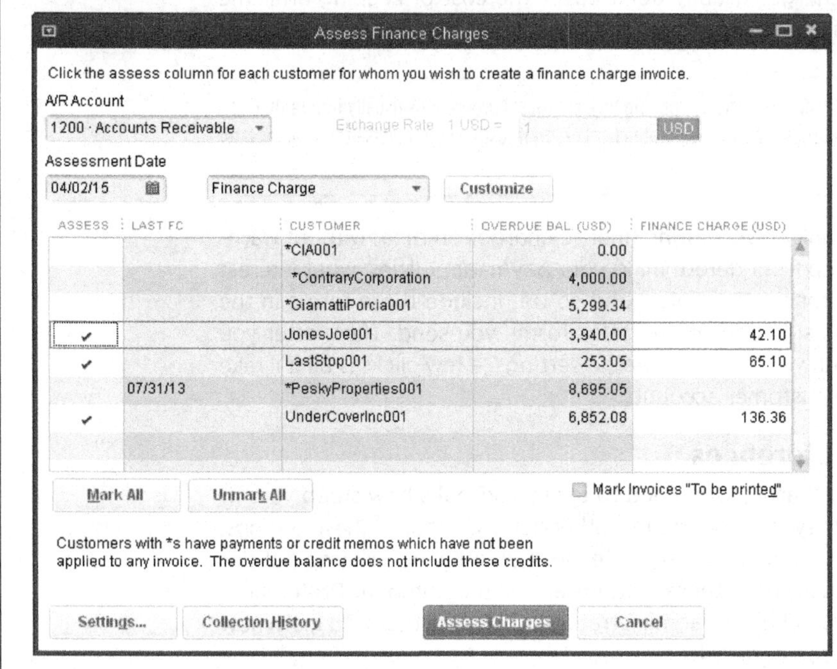

FIGURE 13-13

In this window, if a customer has payments or credits that you haven't yet applied, QuickBooks precedes the customer's name with an asterisk. So if you see any asterisks, click Cancel. After you've applied those payments (page 346) and credits (page 350), you're ready to start back at step 1.

QuickBooks automatically chooses the current date as the date on which you want to assess finance charges and selects all the customers with overdue balances.

2. **If you begin the process of preparing statements a few days before the end of the month, in the Assessment Date box, change the date to the last day of the month.**

   The last day of the month is a popular cutoff date for customer statements. When you change the date in the Assessment Date box and then move to another field, QuickBooks recalculates the finance charges to reflect the charges through that new date.

3. **If you don't want to assess finance charges on one of the customers in the list, in the window's table, click that customer's Assess cell to turn off the checkmark.**

   QuickBooks automatically selects all customers with overdue balances, but you can let some of them slide without penalty. Since there's no way to flag a customer as exempt from finance charges, you have to do this manually. If you reserve finance charges for your most intractable customers, click Unmark All to turn off all the finance charges. Then, in the Assess column, click only the cells for the customers you want to penalize.

To view a customer's invoices, payments, and credits, click the row for that customer, and then click Collection History. QuickBooks displays a Collections Report for that customer that shows every open transaction that's past due.

4. **If you want to change a finance charge amount, click it in the Finance Charge column, and then type the new amount.**

   The only time you might want to do this is when you've created a credit memo (page 288) for a customer but you don't want to apply it to an invoice. As long as the credit memo is out there, it's simpler to forgo the finance charges until you've applied the credit.

5. **If you want to print and send the finance-charge invoices, turn on the "Mark Invoices 'To be printed'" checkbox.**

   If you plan to send customer statements, leave this checkbox turned off. Sending customers statements to remind them of overdue balances is one thing, but sending a statement *and* a finance-charge invoice borders on nagging.

6. **To finalize the finance-charge invoices for the selected customers, click the Assess Charges button.**

   If you turned on the "Mark Invoice 'To be printed'" checkbox, QuickBooks adds the finance-charge invoices to the queue of invoices to be printed. When you print all the queued invoices (page 308), the program prints the finance-charge invoices as well.

Cash Sales

Receiving payment when you deliver a service or product is known as a *cash sale*, even though your customer might pay you with cash, check, or credit card. For example, if you run a thriving massage therapy business, your customers probably pay for their stress relief before they leave your office—and no matter how they pay, QuickBooks considers the transaction a cash sale.

If your customers want records of their payments, you give them sales receipts. In QuickBooks, a sales receipt can do double-duty: It records the cash sale in the program, *and* you can print it as a paper receipt for your customer. (The box on page 363 explains how to record payments you receive through PayPal using QuickBooks sales receipts.)

NOTE Although a cash sale is a simultaneous exchange of money for goods (or services), you don't actually have to create a QuickBooks sales receipt at the time of the sale.

Here are the two most common ways of handling cash sales:

- **Recording individual sales**. If you want to keep track of which customers purchase which products, create a separate sales receipt for each cash sale.

Individual sales receipts track both customers' purchases and the state of your inventory.

NOTE If you keep QuickBooks open on the computer in your store, you can print individual sales receipts for your customers. But keeping QuickBooks running on the store computer could be risky if the wrong people start snooping around in your records. And, unless you're completely proficient with the program's sales receipts, you might find that hand-writing paper sales receipts is faster when your store is swamped. Then, when there's a lull, you can enter individual receipts into your QuickBooks company file.

- **Recording batch sales**. If your shop gets lots of one-time customers, you don't care about tracking who purchases your products, but you still need to know how much inventory you have and how much money you've made. In this situation, you don't have to create a separate sales receipt for each sale. Instead, create one for each business day, which shows how much money you brought in that day and what you sold.

Creating Sales Receipts

Creating sales receipts in QuickBooks is like creating invoices, except for a few small differences. Here's what you do:

1. **Choose Customers→Enter Sales Receipts or, on the Home Page, click Create Sales Receipts.**

NOTE You see the Create Sales Receipt icon only if you've turned on the sales receipt preference (page 697).

   The Enter Sales Receipts window opens.

2. **Click the icon for the method of payment, such as Cash, Check, or Credit Debit. If the customer paid with a check, fill in the Check No. box with the customer's check number.**

   For cash or credit cards, leave the Check No. box blank.

3. **Fill in the item table with the items your customer purchased.**

4. **If you see the Deposit To box, choose an account to tell QuickBooks where to plop the money you made from the sale.**

   The Deposit To box appears only if you've turned off the preference to use the Undeposited Funds account (page 657).

5. **If you want to print the sales receipt now, at the top of the window, click Print→Sales Receipt to have QuickBooks open the Print One Sales Receipt dialog box.**

   To learn more about your printing options, see page 308.

6. **Click Save & Close to save the sales receipt.**

   The Enter Sales Receipts window closes. If you want to record another sales receipt, click Save & New instead to start a new transaction. Click Revert to clear the info you filled in so you can start over.

WARNING Keeping track of customers who make one-time cash purchases can clog your Customer:Job List with unnecessary information. To keep your Customer:Job List lean, create a customer called Cash Sales (page 70).

GEM IN THE ROUGH

Receiving PayPal Payments

If you accept payments via PayPal, those payments are *almost* like cash sales in that they show up in your PayPal account immediately. However, PayPal takes its cut from the money you receive. In QuickBooks, you can create a sales receipt to record a PayPal payment and its fees. But before you can do that, you have to do a bit of setup. Here are the steps:

1. **In QuickBooks, create a bank account (page 56) that represents your PayPal account.** Your PayPal account is similar to a regular bank account because you can deposit payments into it, pay bills with the money in it, and withdraw money from it.
2. **If you don't already have a QuickBooks item for merchant account fees, create an Other Charge item (page 113) for your PayPal fees.** In the New Item window's Account box, choose an expense account for merchant account or bank fees.
3. **For each payment you receive, create a sales receipt (page 362).** In the Enter Sales Receipts window, fill in the boxes as you would for a cash sale, including the items that the customer purchased.
4. **In the next blank line in the Enter Sales Receipts window's item table, add the PayPal fee item you created in step 2.** Fill in the Amount cell with the PayPal fee as a *negative* number, to reduce the net amount you receive.
5. **In the Deposit To box above the sales receipt, choose the bank account you set up for PayPal.** By doing this, the payment is deposited directly in your QuickBooks PayPal account, just like it is in your real-world PayPal account. (If you don't see the Deposit To box, you can record the deposit after you save the sales receipt in the Make Deposits window [page 368].)
6. **Click Save & Close.** The payment increases the balance in your QuickBooks PayPal account and in your real-world PayPal account.

Unless you buy as much as you sell on PayPal, at some point you'll want to transfer money from your PayPal account to your regular bank account. To do this, record a transfer in QuickBooks (page 386), and then hop online, log into your PayPal account, withdraw money from PayPal, and move it to your bank account.

If you sell oodles of stuff via PayPal, recording sales receipts in QuickBooks for each transaction grows old quickly. You can shortcut your data entry with a third-party tool that imports PayPal transactions. One of the most popular products is SimplePort (*www.simpleport.net*). Other programs include WebGility (*www.webgility.com*) and T-HUB (*www.atandra.com*).

Editing Sales Receipts

If you're in the process of creating a sales receipt, you can jump to any field and change its value. You can also insert or delete lines (page 239) in the sales receipt's line-item table as your customer tosses another book on the pile or puts one back on the shelf.

Although you *can* edit sales receipts after you've saved them, you won't do so very often. After all, the sale is complete, and your customer has left with her copy of the receipt. However, you may want to edit the sales receipt after the sale to add more detailed descriptions to items, for example. To do so, in the Enter Sales Receipts window, click the left arrow (Previous) or right arrow (Next) until you see the receipt you want (or click Find, which is described on page 332), and then add the additional info.

Voiding and Deleting Sales Receipts

If you created a sales receipt by mistake and want to remove its values from your accounts, you might think about simply deleting the receipt. However, you should *always* void sales receipts that you don't want rather than deleting them.

If you delete a sales receipt, it's gone for good: QuickBooks removes the dollar values and any sign of the transaction from your accounts. You'll see a hole in your numbering sequence of sales receipts and an entry in the audit trail that says you deleted the transaction (page 437). Voiding a sales receipt, on the other hand, resets the dollar values for the transaction to zero (so your account balances show no sign of the transaction) and marks the transaction as void, so you have a record of it.

Here's how to void a sales receipt:

1. **On the Home Page, click Create Sales Receipts (or choose Customers→Enter Sales Receipts).**

   The Enter Sales Receipts window opens.

2. **Click the left or right arrow until you see the receipt in question, and then right-click the Sales Receipt window and choose Void Sales Receipt on the shortcut menu, as shown in Figure 13-14.**

   All the values in the form change to zero, and QuickBooks adds "VOID:" to the Memo field. To remind yourself why you voided that transaction, type a reason after the colon.

3. **Click Save & Close.**

Memorizing a Batch Sales Transaction

If you want to reduce your paperwork by recording one batch sales receipt for each business day's sales, why not go one step further and *memorize* a batch sales receipt that you can reuse every day? Here's how:

1. **On the Home Page, click Create Sales Receipts or choose Customers→Enter Sales Receipts.**

   QuickBooks opens the Enter Sales Receipts window.

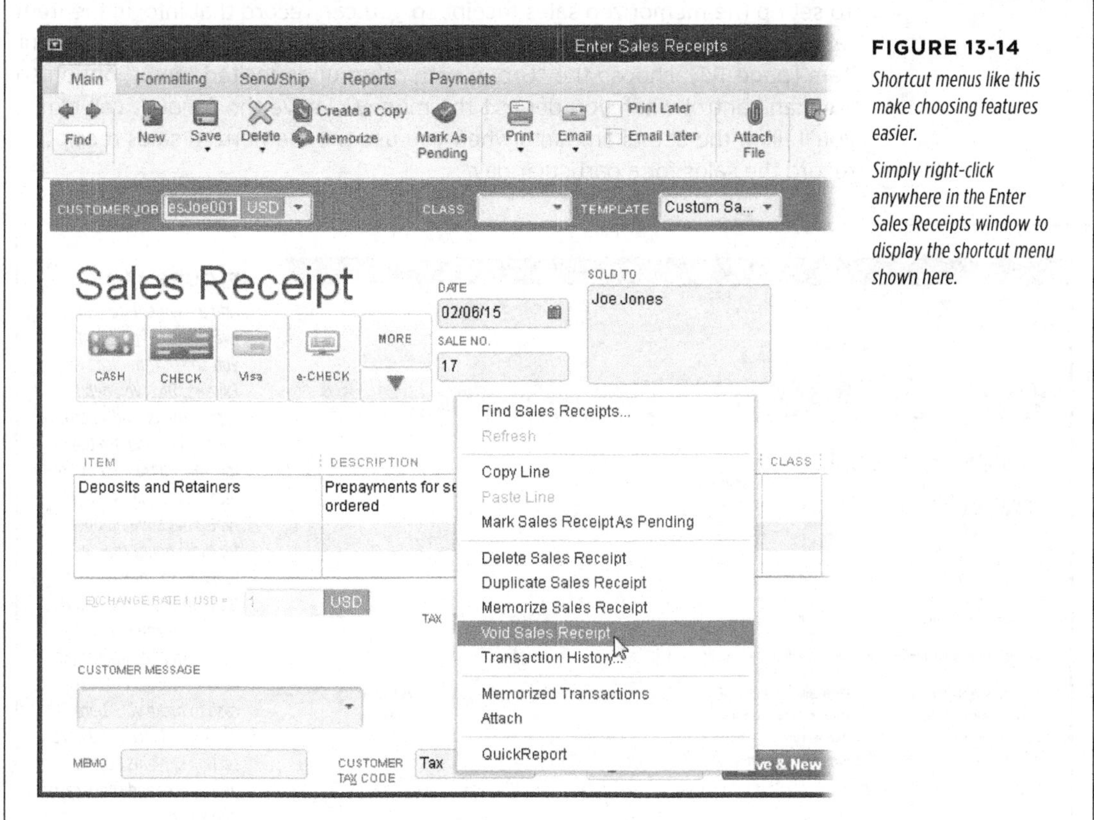

FIGURE 13-14

Shortcut menus like this make choosing features easier.

Simply right-click anywhere in the Enter Sales Receipts window to display the shortcut menu shown here.

2. **In the Customer:Job box, choose the generic customer you created for cash sales.**

   If you haven't set up a cash sale customer yet, in the Customer:Job box, choose <Add New>. In the New Customer dialog box's Customer Name box, type a name like *Cash Sales*. Then click OK to save the customer and use it for the sales receipt.

3. **If you typically sell the same types of items every day, in the table's Item cells, choose those items.**

   Leave the Qty cells blank because those values are almost guaranteed to change each day.

4. **If you want to split your daily sales among different types of payments (like Visa, MasterCard, and so on), add a Payment item for each type of credit card and other form of payment you accept, as shown in Figure 13-15.**

Because sales receipts are meant to handle cash, the total at the bottom of the form represents the bank deposit you make at the end of the day. But it can be helpful to know exactly which forms of payments customers used that day. To set up the memorized sales receipt so you can record that info, in the Item table, choose a Payment item, like Payment-Visa. (When you create a Payment item [page 117], choose the "Group with other undeposited funds" option so you can control when you deposit the money.) Leave the Amount cell blank; you'll fill in the actual amounts when you use the memorized sales receipt to record the sales for a particular day.

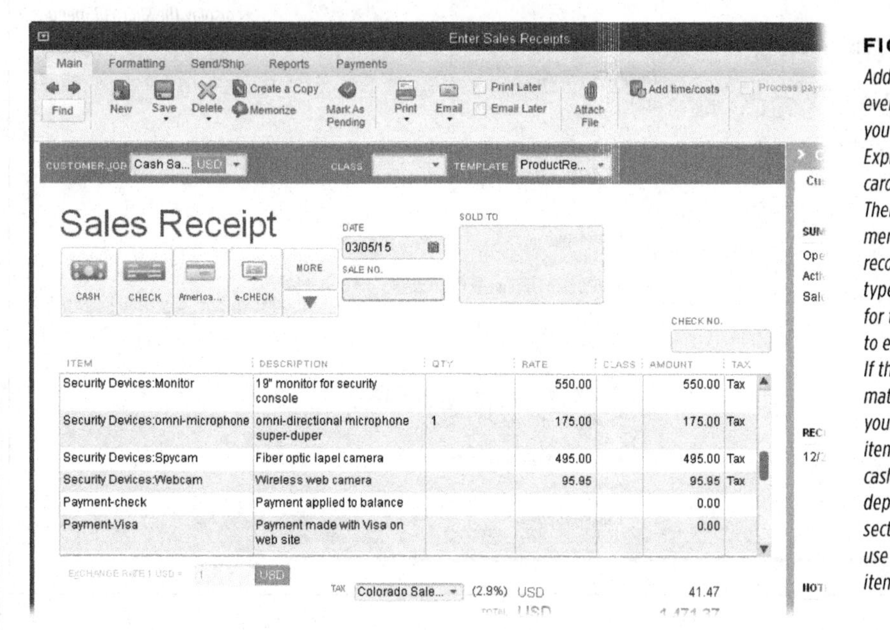

FIGURE 13-15

Add a Payment item for every form of payment you accept (American Express, Discover, debit cards, checks, and so on). Then, when you use the memorized transaction to record batch sales receipts, type a negative number for the amount charged to each type of payment. If the Total value doesn't match the amount of your cash deposit, add an item for excess or short cash to make your bank deposit balance. (The next section explains how to use excess- and short-cash items.)

TIP By splitting a sales receipt among different types of payments, you can make a single deposit to each merchant card account at the end of the day. To do so, choose Banking→Make Deposits. In the "Payments to Deposit" window, choose the payment type in the "View payment method type" drop-down list. Select the deposits for that card, and then click OK to deposit them to the bank or merchant card company. Repeat this process for each type of payment you accept. (This technique works as long as your merchant card company deducts its fees as a single amount, instead of as a fee on every charge transaction.)

5. **When the sales receipt is set up the way you want, press Ctrl+M to open the Memorize Transaction dialog box.**

   In the Name box, type a name for the reusable sales receipt, such as *Day's Cash Sales.*

6. **If you want to use this memorized sales receipt only on the days you have cash sales, choose the Do Not Remind Me option.**

   If you receive cash sales every day, choose the Remind Me option and then, in the How Often box, choose Daily.

7. **To memorize the sales receipt, click OK.**

   QuickBooks closes the Memorize Transaction dialog box and adds the batch sales receipt to the Memorized Transaction List.

8. **If you created the sales receipt simply to memorize it, click Clear, and then close the Enter Sales Receipts window.**

   To use the sales receipt, fill in the values in the table, and then click Save & Close.

Now that you've memorized the batch sales receipt, you can create a new sales receipt for a given day by pressing Ctrl+T to open the Memorized Transaction List window. There, double-click the memorized transaction for your batch sales receipt. QuickBooks opens the Enter Sales Receipts window to a new sales receipt based on the one you memorized. Edit the items in the window's table, their quantities, and the prices to reflect your day's sales, and then click Save & Close.

Reconciling Excess and Short Cash

When you take in paper money and make change, you're bound to make small mistakes. Unless you're lucky enough to have one of those automatic change machines, the money in the cash register at the end of the day rarely matches the sales you record. Over time, the amounts you're short or over tend to balance out, but that's no help when you have to record sales in QuickBooks that don't match your bank deposits.

The solution to this reality of cash sales is one final sales receipt at the end of the day that reconciles your cash register's total with your bank deposit slip. But before you can create this reconciliation receipt, you need to create an account and a couple of items:

- **Over/Under account**. To keep track of your running total for excess and short cash, create an Income account named something like Over/Under. If you use account numbers, give this account a number that makes it appear near the end of your Income accounts. For example, if Uncategorized Income is account number 4999, make the Over/Under account 4998.
- **Over item**. Create an Other Charge item to track the excess cash you collect, and assign it to the Over/Under account. Make sure that you set up this item as nontaxable.
- **Under item**. Create a second Other Charge item to track the amounts that you're short and assign it to the Over/Under account. This item should also be nontaxable.

At the end of each day, compare the income you recorded (run a Profit & Loss report and set the Date box to Today) with the amount of money in your cash register. Then create a sales receipt to make up the difference. Here's how:

- **If you have less cash than you should**, create a sales receipt and, in the first Item cell, add the Under item. In the Amount cell, type the amount that you're short as a *negative* number. When you save this receipt, QuickBooks adjusts your income for the day in your income accounts to match the money in the cash register.
- **If you have too much cash**, create a sales receipt and, in the first Item cell, add the Over item. In the Amount cell, type the excess amount as a positive number. This receipt increases your recorded income to match the money you have on hand.

NOTE If you notice that your cash count at the end of the day is always short, a fluke of probability *could* be at work. But it's more likely that someone is helping herself to the cash in your till.

Making Deposits

Whether customers mail you checks or hand over wads of cash, taking those deposits to the bank isn't enough—you also have to record them in QuickBooks. In the Receive Payments window, if you designate a bank account as the Deposit To account (page 349), there's nothing more to do after you save the payment—QuickBooks records the payment as a deposit to that account. However, if you initially store payments in the Undeposited Funds account, you have to work your way through two dialog boxes: one to record payments you receive, and then one to record the deposits you make in your bank account. (The box on page 369 explains how QuickBooks moves money between accounts as you record these transactions.) This section explains this two-step process. (The box on page 371 explains how to record deposits made with different payment types.)

Choosing Payments to Deposit

If you store payments in the Undeposited Funds account, you end up with a collection of payments ready for deposit that coincide with the paper checks or cash you have to take to the bank (or the credit card payments and electronic funds transfers that show up in your bank account without any action on your part). When you have payments queued up for deposit and choose Banking→Make Deposits (or, in the Home Page's Banking panel, click Record Deposits), QuickBooks opens the "Payments to Deposit" window, where you can choose the payments you want to deposit in several ways, as Figure 13-16 shows.

NOTE If you have other checks to deposit, such as an insurance claim check, you'll have a chance to add those to your deposit in the Make Deposits window as explained in the next section.

UP TO SPEED

Following the Money Trail

If you use QuickBooks' windows to create transactions, the program posts debits and credits to accounts without any action on your part. But in case you're interested in how money weaves its way from account to account, here's what happens from the time you create an invoice to the time you deposit the customer's payment into your bank account.

- **Create Invoices.** When you create an invoice, QuickBooks credits (increases) your income accounts because you've earned income and debits (increases) your Accounts Receivable account because the customer owes you money.
- **Receive Payments.** When you receive payments into the Undeposited Funds account, QuickBooks credits (decreases) the Accounts Receivable account because the customer's balance is now paid off. The program also debits (increases) the Undeposited Funds account because the money is now in that account waiting to be deposited.
- **Make Deposits.** When you deposit the payments queued in the Undeposited Funds account, QuickBooks credits (decreases) the Undeposited Funds account to remove the money from it and debits (increases) your bank account by the amount of the deposit.

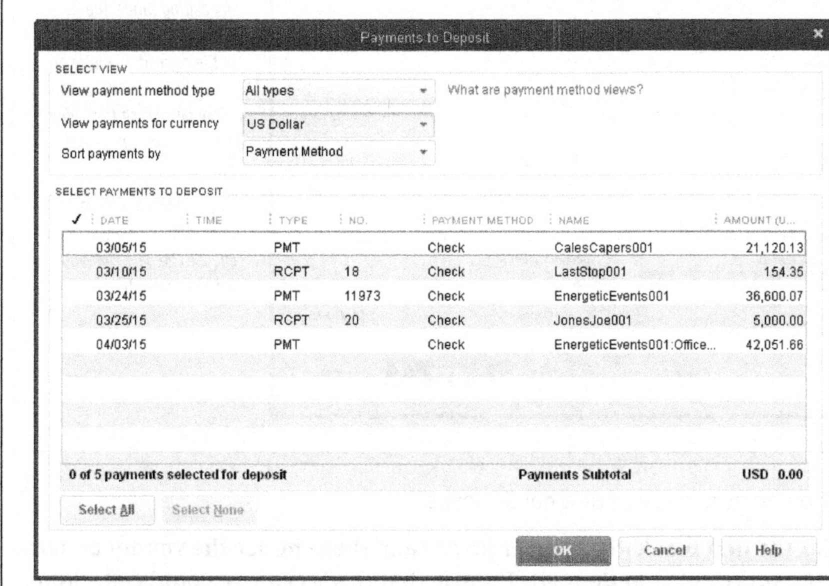

FIGURE 13-16

To filter payments by method, choose one in the "View payment method type" box; QuickBooks then displays only payments of that type.

To record deposits for payments made in a foreign currency, in the "View Payments for currency" drop-down list (which you see only if you have multiple currencies turned on), choose the currency. You enter your bank's exchange rate for the deposit in the Make Deposits window (as explained on page 370).

To choose specific payments to deposit, in the checkmark column, click each one you want to deposit. To select every payment listed, click Select All. When you've selected the payments you want, click OK. QuickBooks closes the "Payments to Deposit" window and opens the Make Deposits window, described next.

Recording Deposits

The Make Deposits window is like an electronic deposit slip, as you can see in Figure 13-17. The payments you chose to deposit in the "Payments to Deposit" window are already filled in. If you have other checks to deposit besides customer payments, they don't automatically show up in this window, but you can add them to the table.

NOTE If you're depositing a payment made in a foreign currency, in the Make Deposit window's "Exchange Rate 1 [currency] =" box, type the exchange rate that your bank used for the transaction (to find it, look at your bank statement or review the transaction on your bank's website). The window's table of deposits then shows the deposit amount in the foreign currency, and the bottom of the window shows the deposit total in both the foreign currency and your home currency.

After you make your foreign-currency deposits, you can see how much you gained or lost due to changes in the exchange rate by choosing Reports→Company & Financial→Realized Gains & Losses. This report shows the payment amounts in your home currency, the exchange rate, and the resulting gain or loss.

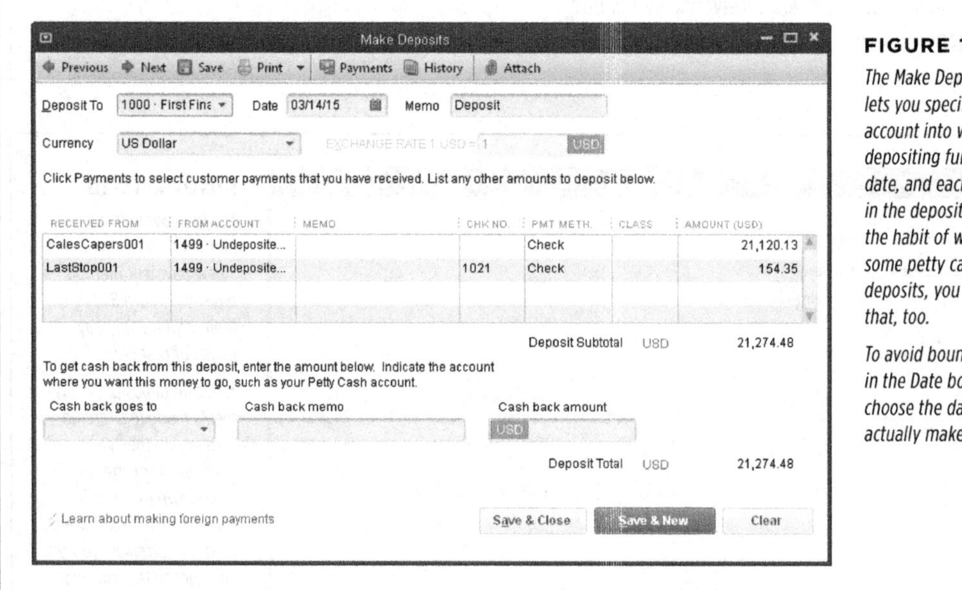

FIGURE 13-17

The Make Deposits window lets you specify the account into which you're depositing funds, the date, and each payment in the deposit. If you're in the habit of withdrawing some petty cash from your deposits, you can record that, too.

To avoid bouncing checks, in the Date box, be sure to choose the date that you actually make the deposit.

Here's how to add these additional deposits:

1. **Click the first blank Received From cell and then choose the vendor or name of the source of your deposit. Then, in that row's From Account cell, choose the account to which you're posting the money.**

   For example, if you're depositing a refund check for some office supplies, choose the expense account for office supplies.

2. **In that same row's Amount cell, fill in the amount of the additional deposit.**

   If you like, fill in the rest of the row's cells. For refunds or checks from other sources, jotting a note in the Memo cell can help you remember why people sent you money. And entering the check number gives your customer or vendor a reference point in case a question arises.

TIP If you want to withdraw some money from your deposit for petty cash (page 215), in the "Cash back goes to" box, choose your petty cash account. (If you own a sole proprietorship, you can choose your owner's draw account here instead.) Then, in the "Cash back amount" box, type the amount you're deducting from the deposit.

3. **Repeat steps 1 and 2 for each additional deposit you want to record.**
4. **When you've filled in all the fields you want, click Save & Close.**

   QuickBooks posts the deposits to your accounts.

UP TO SPEED

Putting Payment Deposit Types to Work

Choosing different types of payments before you get to the Make Deposits window takes extra work, but it's a good idea for several reasons. Here are a few reasons you might make multiple passes through the deposit process:

- **Different deposit types.** Many banks group different types of deposits, such as checks versus electronic transfers. To group your payments in QuickBooks the way your bank groups them on your monthly statements, in the "Payments to Deposit" window's "View payment method type" box, choose a method, and then click Select All to process those payments as a group.
- **Different deposit accounts.** If you deposit some payments in your checking account and others in a merchant account (or PayPal), in the "Payments to Deposit" window, select all the payments you want to deposit into the checking account and then, in the Make Deposits window, select that account in the Deposit To box. Then run through the deposit process a *second* time to deposit other payments to the next account.
- **Reconciling cash deposits.** As you learned earlier in this chapter, the cash-counting process is prone to error, so you're probably used to your bank coming up with a different cash deposit total than you did. Although QuickBooks groups cash and checks as one payment type, process your cash and check payments as two separate deposits. That way, if the bank changes the deposit amount, it's easy to edit your cash deposit.

Depositing Money from Merchant Card Accounts

When you accept payment via credit card, the merchant bank you work with collects your customers' credit card payments and deposits them in your bank account as a lump sum. However, you record your deposits in QuickBooks the way they appear on your bank statement, which might or might not show lump sums. For example, your merchant bank might show payments and merchant bank fees separately, whereas the amount deposited in your checking account is the net amount after the merchant deducts its fees.

Here's how to record deposits of merchant credit card payments and fees into your bank account to match the way they appear on your bank statement:

1. **Choose Banking→Make Deposits or, on the Home Page, click Record Deposits.**

   In the "Payments to Deposit" window's "View payment method type" drop-down list, choose the merchant card whose payments you want to deposit.

2. **In the window's table, select the credit card payments you want to deposit by turning on their checkmark cells, and then click OK.**

   QuickBooks opens the Make Deposits window, which lists the credit card payments in the deposit table. If the Deposit Subtotal amount doesn't match the deposit that appears on your bank statement, the merchant bank probably deducted its fees; you'll record those fees in the next step.

TIP To make merchant card deposits easier to track, ask your merchant card company to charge one lump sum for fees instead of charging for each transaction; it will almost certainly say yes.

3. **In the Make Deposits window's table, in the first blank row's From Account cell, choose the account to which you post merchant card fees (such as Bank Service Charges). Then, in that row's Amount cell, type the merchant card fees as a *negative* number.**

   The Deposit Subtotal amount should equal the deposit that appears on your bank statement.

4. **When you're done, click Save & Close.**

NOTE How soon you can enter your merchant card deposits in QuickBooks depends on how wired your company is. If you use Bank Feeds (Chapter 24), QuickBooks automatically downloads merchant card deposits into your company file. If you have online access to your merchant card account, make the deposit in QuickBooks when you log into your merchant card account online and see the deposit in your transaction listing. If you don't use any online services, enter the deposit in QuickBooks when the merchant card statement arrives in the mail.

CHAPTER

14

Bank Accounts and Credit Cards

You've opened your mail, plucked out the customer payments, and deposited them in your bank account (Chapter 13). In addition to that, you've paid your bills (Chapter 9). Now you can sit back and relax knowing that *most* of the transactions in your bank and credit card accounts are accounted for. What's left?

Some stray transactions might pop up—an insurance-claim check to deposit or handling the aftermath and bank fees for a customer's bounced check, to name a couple. Plus, running a business typically means that money moves between accounts—from interest-bearing accounts to checking accounts, from PayPal or merchant credit card accounts to your checking account, or from your regular checking account to a bank account specifically for payroll. For any financial transaction you perform, QuickBooks has a way to enter it, whether you prefer the guidance of transaction windows or the speed of an account-register window.

Reconciling your accounts to your bank statements is another key process you don't want to skip. You and your bank can both make mistakes, and reconciling your accounts is the way to catch these discrepancies. Once the bane of bookkeepers everywhere, reconciling is practically automatic now that you can let QuickBooks handle the math.

In this chapter, the section on reconciling (page 389) is the only must-read. And if you want to learn the fastest way to enter any type of bank account transaction, don't skip the first section (page 374). You can read about transferring funds, loans, bounced checks, and other financial arcana covered in this chapter as the need arises.

Entering Transactions in an Account Register

QuickBooks includes windows and dialog boxes for making deposits, writing checks, and transferring funds, but you can also record these transactions right in a bank account's register window. Working in a register window has two advantages over other windows and dialog boxes:

- **Speed**. Entering a transaction in a register window is fast, particularly when you use keyboard shortcuts (like pressing Tab to move between fields).
- **Visibility**. *Transaction* windows, such as Write Checks, keep you focused on the transaction at hand; but they take up lots of screen real estate, so it's tough to see more than one of these windows at a time. But in a *register* window, you can look at previous transactions for reference.

Opening a Register Window

Obviously, you have to open a register window before you can enter transactions in it. Luckily, opening these windows couldn't be easier. Here's how to open *any* kind of account's register window:

1. **If the Chart of Accounts window isn't open, press Ctrl+A (or, on the Home Page, click Chart of Accounts) to open it.**

   The window pops open, listing all the accounts in your chart of accounts.

TIP If you use the left icon bar, click View Balances in its middle section and then, in the View Balances section at the top of the icon bar, click the account you want. (If the account you want isn't listed there, see page 699 to learn how to add it.) If you use the top icon bar, you can open a bank account or credit card register by double-clicking the account you want to see in the Account Balances section on the right side of the Home Page.

2. **In the Chart of Accounts window, double-click the account whose register window you want to open (Figure 14-1).**

   This method can open register windows for more than just bank accounts. See the box on page 378 to learn about different ways to handle credit card accounts.

NOTE Income and expense accounts don't have registers in QuickBooks. So when you double-click an income or expense account in the Chart of Accounts window, QuickBooks generates a QuickReport of the transactions for that account. In the report window, you can take a closer look at a transaction by double-clicking it.

Creating a Transaction in an Account Register

The steps for creating a check in your checking account register (page 205) work for deposits and transfers, too, with only a few minor adjustments. Here's how to fill in the cells in a register window to create any kind of bank transaction:

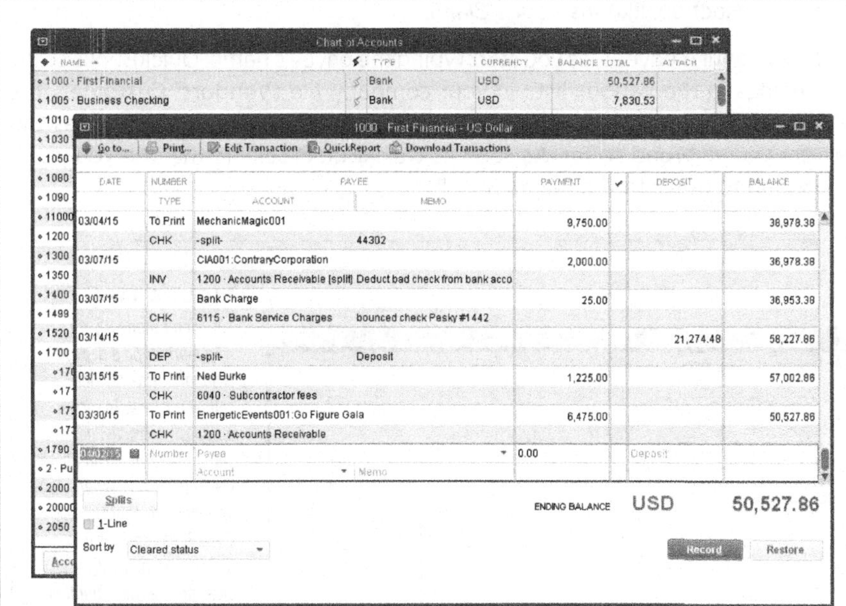

FIGURE 14-1

You can open a register window from the Chart of Accounts window by double-clicking any type of account that has a balance, including checking, savings, money market, and petty cash accounts. In fact, double-clicking opens the register for any account on your balance sheet (Accounts Receivable, Accounts Payable, Credit Card, Asset, Liability, and Equity accounts).

- **Date**. When you first open a bank account's register window, QuickBooks automatically selects the text in the Date field of the first blank transaction. Out of the box, QuickBooks puts the current date in the Date cell, but you can set a preference to have the program fill in the last date you used (page 650). Tweaking the date by a few days is as easy as pressing the + or – key on your keyboard until the date is the one you want. (To become a master of date-related keyboard shortcuts, read the box on page 377.)

- **Number**. For checks, when you jump to the Number cell (by pressing Tab), QuickBooks automatically fills in the next check number for that bank account. If the number doesn't match the paper check you want to write, press + or – until the number is correct. (For some types of accounts, like credit cards and assets, the register window has a Ref field instead of a Number field. You can fill in a reference number for the transaction or leave this field blank.)

  To make an online payment (see Chapter 24), in the Number cell, type *S*, which QuickBooks promptly changes to *Send*. (The program processes online payments only if you've set up an online payment service.) To enter a deposit, you can bypass the Number and Payment cells regardless of what values they contain, as shown in Figure 14-2.

- **Payee**. You don't have to enter a value in this cell. In fact, if it's a payee you only occasionally work with, it's better to *not* type the vendor's or other name in the

Payee cell for deposits, transfers, or petty cash transactions so your Vendors or Customers list doesn't fill up with names you rarely use. Instead, type a generic name like *Deposit* or *Petty Cash*, and then fill in the Memo cell with a description of the transaction, like *Insurance Claim*.

For your regular payees, as you start typing the payee's name, QuickBooks scans the names in the various lists in your company file (Vendors, Customer:Job, Other Names, and so on) and selects the first one it finds that matches the letters you've typed so far. As soon as QuickBooks selects the one you want, press Tab to move to the Payment cell.

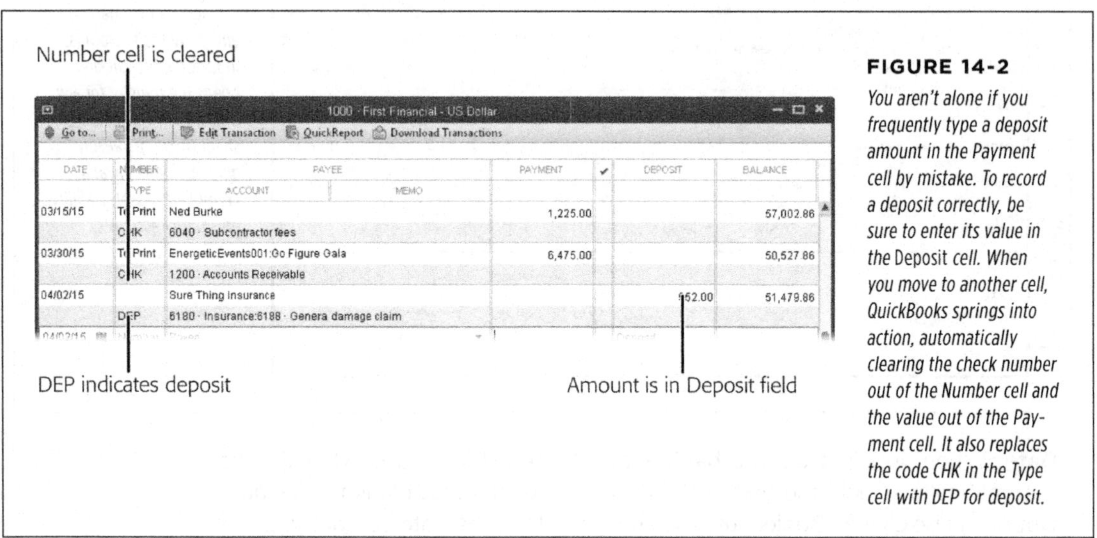

FIGURE 14-2

You aren't alone if you frequently type a deposit amount in the Payment cell by mistake. To record a deposit correctly, be sure to enter its value in the Deposit cell. When you move to another cell, QuickBooks springs into action, automatically clearing the check number out of the Number cell and the value out of the Payment cell. It also replaces the code CHK in the Type cell with DEP for deposit.

NOTE QuickBooks keeps track of handwritten and printed check numbers separately. When you use the register window to create a check, QuickBooks fills in the Number cell by incrementing the last *handwritten* check number. When you choose File→Print Forms→Checks, the program fills in the First Check Number box by incrementing the last *printed* check number.

- **Payment** or **Charge**. For checks you write, fees that the bank deducts from your account, and petty cash withdrawals, type the amount in the Payment cell. In a credit card register, this field is named Charge so you can enter the values of the credit card charges you make.
- **Deposit** or **Payment**. For deposits you make to checking or petty cash, or interest you've earned, type the amount in the Deposit cell. In a credit card register, this field is called Payment, because you make payments *to* a credit card account (the opposite of making payments *from* a checking account).

NOTE In QuickBooks transactions, money either goes out or comes in—there's no in between. So when you enter a value in the Payment cell, QuickBooks clears the Deposit cell's value and vice versa.

POWER USERS' CLINIC

Keyboard Shortcuts for Dates

Pressing the + or – key on your keyboard to increment dates is a great timesaver, but you might also want to add some of the following keyboard shortcuts to your date-selection arsenal. When the cursor is in any Date field, these can help you jump directly to specific dates:

- **Press T (for Today)** to change the date to today.
- **Press M (for Month)** to select the first day of the currently selected month. Pressing M additional times jumps to the first days of previous months.
- **Press H (for montH)** to select the last day of the currently selected month. Pressing H additional times jumps to the last days of future months.
- **Press W (for Week)** to choose the first day of the currently selected week. Pressing W additional times jumps to the first days of previous weeks.
- **Press K (for weeK)** to choose the last day of the currently selected week. Pressing K additional times jumps to the last days of future weeks.
- **Press Y (for Year)** to choose the first day of the currently selected year. Pressing Y additional times jumps to the first days of previous years.
- **Press R (for yeaR)** to choose the last day of the currently selected year. Pressing R additional times jumps to the last days of future years.

You can press these letters multiple times to pick dates further in the past or the future, and combine them with pressing + and – to reach any date you want. But face it: After half a dozen keystrokes, it might be easier to type a numeric date, such as *3/14/15*, or to click the Calendar icon and choose the date.

- **Account**. This cell can play many roles. For instance, when you're creating a check, choose the account for the expense it represents. If you're making a deposit, choose the income or expense account to which you want to post the deposit. (For example, depositing an insurance claim check that pays for equipment repair reduces the balance of the expense account for equipment maintenance and repair.) If you're transferring money to or from another bank account, choose that account instead.
- **Memo**. Filling in this cell can jog your memory no matter what type of transaction you create. Enter the name of the restaurant for a credit card charge, the items you purchased with petty cash, or the bank branch for a deposit (in case your deposit ends up in someone else's account).

TIP Remember your accountant's insistence on an audit trail? If you create a transaction by mistake, don't delete it. Although QuickBooks' audit trail keeps track of deleted transactions, the omission can be confusing to others—or to *you* in the future.

Instead of deleting transactions, *void* them. That way, the payment or deposit amount changes to zero, but the voided transaction still appears in your company file, so you know that it happened. Because the amount is zero, the transaction doesn't affect any account balances or financial reports. Before you void a transaction, type a note in its Memo cell that explains why you're voiding it. Then, in a register window, right-click the transaction and choose the Void option (Void Check, Void Deposit, and so on) on the shortcut menu.

FREQUENTLY ASKED QUESTION

Managing Credit Card Accounts

Are credit cards accounts or vendors?

In QuickBooks, you can set up your credit cards as accounts *or* vendors, depending on how you prefer to record your credit card transactions. Here's the deal:

- **Credit card account**. Tracking credit card charges using an account has several advantages. With a credit card account in QuickBooks, you can enter the charges as they happen (which takes no time at all if you download credit card transactions; page 617 explains how). Then, when you receive your statement, you can reconcile the credit card account as you would a checking account (page 390), so you can see whether your records and your charge card company's match. To prevent credit card charge payee names from filling your Vendor List with entries you don't need, store names in the Memo cell or create general vendors like Parking, Restaurant, and Office Supplies.
- **Credit card vendor**. If you set up a credit card as a vendor, you don't have an account to reconcile when you receive your credit card statement. In addition, the name of every establishment you bless with credit card purchases won't fill up your Vendor List. The drawback to this approach is that you still have to allocate the money you spent to the appropriate accounts, and you can't download that split transaction from your credit card company. With statement in hand, open the Enter Credit Card Charges window (choose Banking→Enter Credit Card Charges) to enter a single transaction allocating the total statement balance to each of the charges you made. (On the window's Expenses and Items tabs, add entries to allocate charges to the appropriate expense accounts or item purchases.) That way, the transaction reconciles your charges to the statement.

Handling Bounced Checks

Bouncing one of your own checks is annoying and embarrassing. It can be expensive, too, since banks charge for each check you bounce (and, often, they craftily pay your larger checks before the smaller ones to rack up as many bounced-check charges as possible). Besides depositing money to cover the shortfall and paying those bank fees, you have to write new checks or tell people to redeposit the checks that bounced.

When someone pays *your* company with a rubber check, it's just as annoying. In addition to the charges your bank might charge for redepositing a bounced check, you have to do a few things to straighten out your records in QuickBooks when a customer's check bounces. The following sections explain how to handle bounced checks, whether you wrote them or your customer did.

Managing Bounced Checks You Wrote

If a bill payment you made overdraws your account, your bank returns the check to whomever you paid. You can handle this financial gaffe in a couple of ways. If your cash shortfall was a temporary problem, the easiest solution is to tell the vendor to redeposit your check. In that case, all you need to do is record your bank's bounced-check fee and enter a new bill for the bounced-check fee that your vendor charges you.

Paying the bill with a new check or by credit card requires a few more steps. Here's what you have to do:

1. **Create a journal entry (page 426) to put the bad check's amount back into your Accounts Payable account *and* your checking account.**

   To do that, in the journal entry's first line, choose your checking account and fill in the Debit cell with the amount of the bounced check, as shown in Figure 14-3 (foreground).

   In the journal entry's second line, choose your Accounts Payable account. (QuickBooks automatically fills in the Credit cell with the bounced check's amount, which is what you want.) In the Name cell, choose the vendor you paid. In the Memo cell, type something like "check bounced" or "NSF check."

   After you record the journal entry, the bad check amount shows up as billed in the Accounts Payable account (Figure 14-3, background) and as a deposit to your checking account.

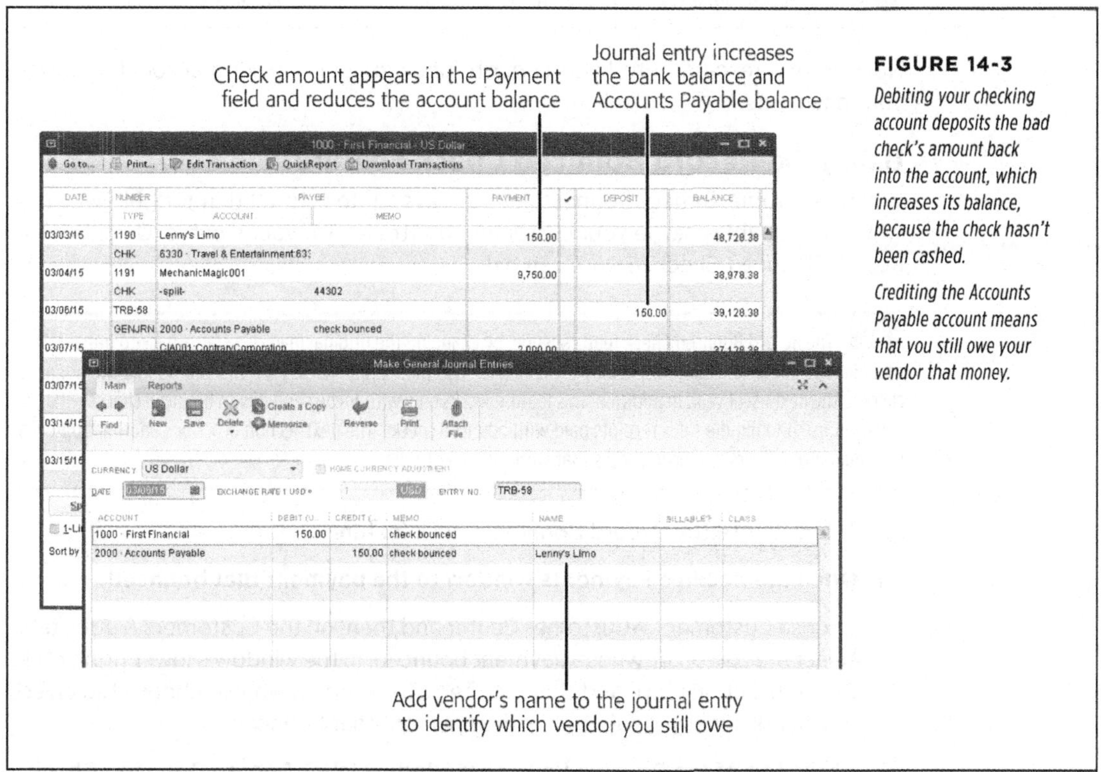
Check amount appears in the Payment field and reduces the account balance
Journal entry increases the bank balance and Accounts Payable balance
Add vendor's name to the journal entry to identify which vendor you still owe

FIGURE 14-3

Debiting your checking account deposits the bad check's amount back into the account, which increases its balance, because the check hasn't been cashed.

Crediting the Accounts Payable account means that you still owe your vendor that money.

2. **Edit the bill payment to switch the bill back to being unpaid.**

   In the Vendor Center (Vendors→Vendor Center), on the Vendors tab, select the vendor you paid with a bad check. In the window's lower right, click the

Transactions tab, and then in the Show drop-down list, choose Bill Payments. In the Transactions tab's table, double-click the payment that bounced; the Bill Payments window opens. In the window's Bills Paid In This Transaction table, turn *off* the Pay cell for the payment you made with a bad check, turn *on* the Pay checkbox for the journal entry, and then click Save & Close.

3. **If the vendor charges you a fee for the bad check, create a bill for that charge.**

   Fill in this bill as you would any other bill (page 186). In the Expenses table, choose an expense account for the fee and enter the amount in the Amount cell.

4. **Finally, pay the original bill and the additional-fee bill using your new payment method.**

   On the Home Page, click Pay Bills. In the Pay Bills window's table, select the original bill (and the additional-fee bill, if you created one). In the Method box, choose how you want to pay the bill, and then click Pay Selected Bills.

NOTE See page 383 to learn how to record the fee that your bank charged you for overdrawing your account.

Now make a resolution to keep enough funds in your checking account to cover your payments.

Using the Record Bounced Check Feature

When a *customer's* check bounces, it takes several steps to set things right—which is why you probably charge your customer an extra fee for your trouble. QuickBooks' Record Bounced Check feature can help.

TIP The Record Bounced Check feature works by changing the original invoice's status back to unpaid. This could lead to some confusion, especially if the invoice was paid in one fiscal year and you handle the bounced check in the next fiscal year. In addition, this feature works only with *invoices* paid with bounced checks—that is, you can't use it to handle sales receipts paid with bounced checks. The next section describes another approach to handling customers' bounced checks that works in *any* situation.

Here's how to use the Record Bounced Check feature:

1. **Open the Receive Payments window to the payment that bounced.**

   Choose Customers→Customer Center and then, on the Customers & Jobs tab, select the customer whose payment bounced. In the window's lower right, click the Transactions tab, and then, in the Show drop-down list, choose Received Payments. Finally, double-click the payment that bounced.

2. **At the top of the Receive Payments window, click Record Bounced Check.**

   The Manage Bounced Check dialog box opens (Figure 14-4).

3. **In the Bank Fee box, type the amount that your bank charged you for the customer's bounced check. In the Expense Account box, choose the account you use for bank service charges.**

   When you complete the Record Bounced Check process, QuickBooks deducts this bank fee from your checking account balance.

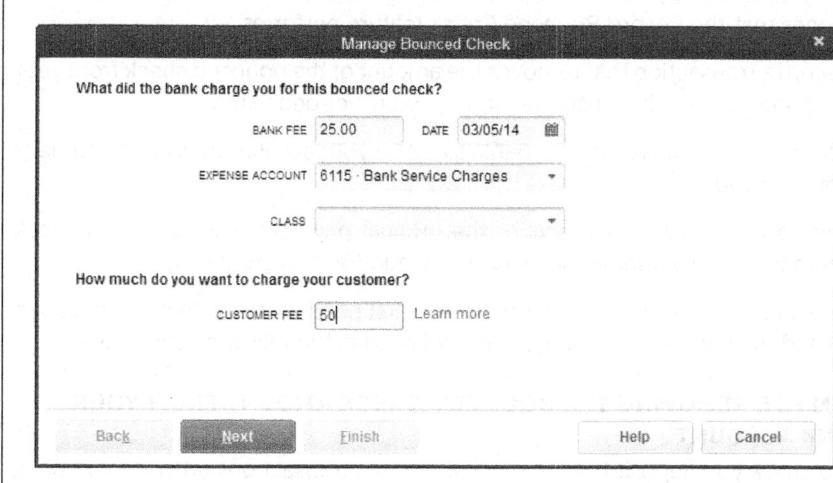

FIGURE 14-4

The amount you enter in the Bank Fee box represents what your bank charged you for depositing the bounced check. QuickBooks creates a transaction that deducts this fee from your checking account balance.

The amount in the Customer Fee box is what you charge your customer for giving you a bad check; it ends up on a new invoice that QuickBooks creates.

4. **In the Customer Fee box, enter the amount you want to charge your customer.**

   For example, if your bank charged you $25 for your customer's bad check and you want to tack on *another* $25 for the inconvenience, enter *50*.

5. **Click Next.**

   The Bounced Check Summary dialog box tells you that QuickBooks will mark the invoice corresponding to the bounced check as unpaid, deduct the bad check amount and bank fees from your bank account, and create a new invoice for the fee you're charging the customer.

6. **To set the bounced-check actions in motion, click Finish.**

   QuickBooks creates a journal entry that deducts the amount of the original invoice from your checking account.

7. **Locate the journal entry QuickBooks created, and then add a note to its Memo field.**

   Choose Company→Make General Journal Entries and then, at the top left of the Make General Journal Entries window, click the Previous button (the left arrow) until you see the bounced check journal entry. Add a note to its Memo field such as "Bounced check 1234 for invoice 19012." That way, you'll know which invoice the bounced check is connected to.

8. **Finally, send the original invoice *and* the new invoice to your customer and hope the *next* check you get from them is good.**

Handling Customers' Bounced Checks on Your Own

As you learned in the previous section, the Record Bounced Check feature doesn't work in all situations. Fortunately, with a bit of setup, you can easily handle customers' bounced checks by re-invoicing your wayward customers. The steps are similar to the ones that the Record Bounced Check feature performs:

- Record a transaction that removes the amount of the bounced check from your checking account, because the money was never deposited.
- Record any charges that your bank levied on your account for your customer's bounced check.
- Invoice the customer to recover the original payment, your bounced-check charges, and any additional charges you add for your trouble.

Before you can re-invoice your customers, you first need to create items for bounced checks and their associated charges, as explained in the following sections.

ITEM FOR REMOVING THE BOUNCED-CHECK AMOUNT FROM YOUR BANK ACCOUNT

When a check you deposit bounces, you'll see two transactions on your next bank statement: the original deposit and a second transaction that removes the deposit amount. You have to create the same transactions in your company file so you don't overestimate your bank balance and write bad checks of your own. And because the customer hasn't really paid you, the amount of the check should go back into your Accounts Receivable account.

To create an item that removes the amount of the bounced check from your bank account, create an Other Charge item. Here's how:

1. **Choose Lists→Item List to open the Item List window, and then press Ctrl+N.**

   The New Item window opens.

2. **In the Type drop-down list, choose Other Charge.**

   The Other Charge item type is perfect for miscellaneous charges that don't fit any other category.

3. **In the Item Name/Number box, type a name for the item, like *BadCheck*. In the Account drop-down list, choose your bank account, and then click OK.**

   The new item appears in the Item List.

ITEMS FOR BOUNCED-CHECK SERVICE CHARGES

Companies typically request reimbursement for bounced-check charges, and many companies tack on *additional* service charges for the inconvenience of processing a bounced check. Depending on how you account for these charges, you'll use one or two Other Charge items:

- **Bounced-check charge reimbursement**. If you want your customer to pay you back for the bounced-check charge that your bank hit you with, you need an Other Charge item that you can add to an invoice, called something like *BadCheck Charge*. (Be sure to choose a nontaxable code for the item so that QuickBooks doesn't calculate sales tax on it.)

  QuickBooks doesn't care whether you post this item to an income account or an expense account, but it's easier to use an income account if you plan to charge customers an extra service charge for bounced checks, as you'll learn shortly. If you post your bank's bounced-check charges to an income account (such as a Service Charge account), then you can use the same item for any *extra* service charge you apply for the hassle of handling bounced checks. Although the customer's reimbursement appears as income, the bank charge you paid is an expense. The effect on your net profit (income minus expenses) is zero.

- **Bounced-check service charge**. Alternatively, you can post bounced-check reimbursements directly to the same expense account you use for bank service charges. With this approach, when you pay your bank's bounced-check charge, it shows up as an expense in your bank service charge account. When the customer pays you back, QuickBooks credits the bank service charge account to reduce your service charge expenses. The effect on net profit is zero.

  When you use this approach, you need an additional item if you ding your customers with your own bounced-check service charges. Create an Other Charge item for the additional service charge. For the item's Account, choose your service-charge income account. Like the bounced-check charge reimbursement item, make this item nontaxable.

Recording Bank Charges

The easiest place to record a bounced-check charge is in the bank account's register window. This technique works for any charge your bank drops on your account, and for service charges and interest your credit card company levies:

1. **Press Ctrl+A to open the Chart of Accounts window; there, double-click your bank account to open its register window.**

   Alternatively, on the Home Page, click Check Register. In the Select Account box's drop-down list, choose your bank account, and then click OK.

2. **In the Date cell for the first blank transaction, choose the date when the bank assessed the charge.**

   QuickBooks automatically fills in the Number cell with the next check number. Be sure to delete that number before saving the transaction to keep your QuickBooks check numbers synchronized with your paper checks.

3. **In the Payee cell, type a generic payee name like *Bank Charge*.**

   Alternatively, you can type the name of your bank or credit card company.

4. **Type the details of the charge in the Memo cell, as shown in Figure 14-5.**

   For a bounced-check charge, include the name of the customer, a note that the check bounced, and the number of the check that bounced.

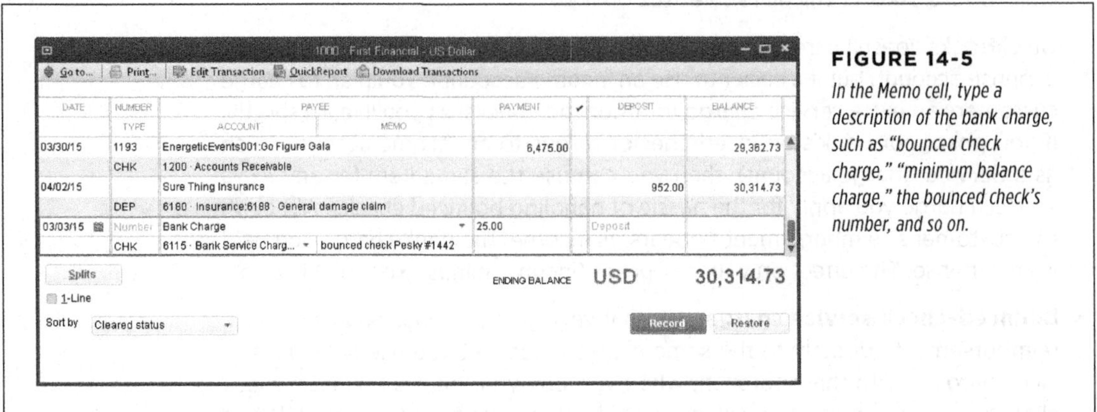

FIGURE 14-5

In the Memo cell, type a description of the bank charge, such as "bounced check charge," "minimum balance charge," the bounced check's number, and so on.

5. **In the Payment cell, type the amount of the charge. In the Account cell, choose the account you use to track bank charges or bounced-check charges.**

   For a bounced-check charge, choose the income or expense account you use for that purpose. (You have to include a bounced-check charge item on a new invoice in order to recoup this cost, as described in the next section.) For other bank service charges, choose the corresponding expense account.

TIP The register window's Customer:Job cell provides a shortcut to invoicing a customer for bounced-check charges: While the transaction is still selected in the register window, click Splits to open the Splits table. The Account, Amount, and Memo fields are already filled in with the values you've provided so far. To make the bank charge billable to the customer who bounced the check, in the Customer:Job cell, choose the customer, and in the "Billable?" cell, turn on the checkbox. You can then add this billable charge to the customer's next invoice (as described in step 5 on page 253).

6. **Click Record.**

   QuickBooks saves the bank charge in your account.

Re-invoicing for Bounced Checks

With the bounced-check items described on page 383, you can update all the necessary account balances just by re-invoicing the customer for the bounced check. Here are the steps:

1. **Press Ctrl+I or, on the Home Page, click the Create Invoices icon (or choose Invoices→Create Invoices if you've set up QuickBooks Permier or Enterprise to invoice for billable time and expenses.**

   The Create Invoices window opens.

2. **In the Customer:Job box, choose the customer who wrote the bad check.**

   You don't have to bother filling in fields like P.O. No. and Ship.

3. **In the item table, add an item for the bounced check (like the BadCheck item in Figure 14-6).**

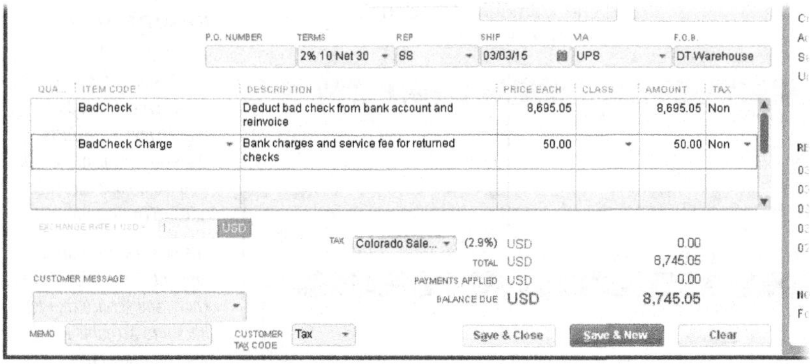

FIGURE 14-6

To re-invoice the customer for the amount of the bad check, in the first Item cell, choose your bounced-check item (BadCheck, in this example). In the Amount cell, type the bounced check's amount. In the second item cell, choose the item you created for bounced-check charges. This item's amount represents what the bank charged you and any additional service fee you charge.

4. **In the Amount cell for the bounced-check item, type the amount of the returned check.**

   Enter the check's full amount.

5. **Add a second item to recoup the bounced-check fees that your bank charged you and any additional service charges you want to include. In the Amount cell for this item, type the amount you're charging.**

   Adding an extra fee can help deter customers from writing bad checks. In Figure 14-6, the BadCheck Charge item covers the bank's $25 charge plus an additional $25 fee your company collects.

   If you recorded the bounced-check charge in your bank account as a billable cost to your customer (see the Tip on page 384), at the top of the Create Invoices window, click Add Time/Costs. In the "Choose Billable Time and Costs" dialog box, click the Expenses tab and select the bank charge, and then click OK to add it to the invoice. Then you can add another line item to add *your* bounced check fee to the invoice.

6. **Click Save & Close to save the invoice.**

   QuickBooks updates the balances of your bank account and Accounts Receivable accounts, as shown in Figure 14-7, which is exactly what you want. Here's why: When you first invoiced the customer, QuickBooks added the invoice amount to your Accounts Receivable balance. The customer's original payment reduced the Accounts Receivable balance, but the bounced check means you have to remove the original payment amount from your records. By re-invoicing the customer, you reestablish the balance as outstanding and add the invoice amount back into Accounts Receivable.

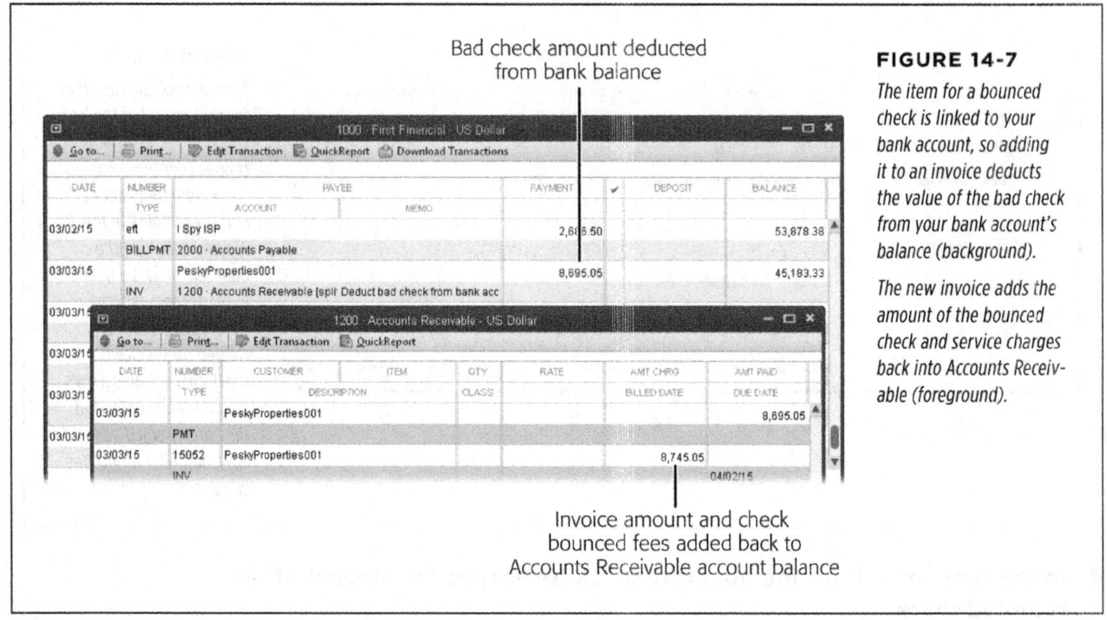
Bad check amount deducted from bank balance
Invoice amount and check bounced fees added back to Accounts Receivable account balance

FIGURE 14-7

The item for a bounced check is linked to your bank account, so adding it to an invoice deducts the value of the bad check from your bank account's balance (background).

The new invoice adds the amount of the bounced check and service charges back into Accounts Receivable (foreground).

7. **When the customer sends you a check for this new invoice, click the Receive Payments icon on the Home Page to apply that check to the new invoice as a payment.**

   QuickBooks reduces the Accounts Receivable balance by the payment amount. (If your customer and the money it owes you are gone for good, see the box on page 387 to learn what to do next.)

Transferring Funds

With the advent of electronic banking services, transferring funds between accounts has become a staple of account maintenance. Companies stash cash in savings and money market accounts to earn interest and then transfer money into checking right before they pay bills.

TROUBLESHOOTING MOMENT

Writing Off Bad Debt

If you try contacting a customer about a payment only to find that his phone is disconnected, his forwarding address has expired, and an eviction notice is stapled to his office door, you probably aren't going to get your money. In accounting, admitting that the money is gone for good is called *writing off bad debt.*

The invoice you create for a customer represents income *only if* the customer pays it. So, to write off bad debt, you have to remove the income for the unpaid invoice from your financial records. You do that by offsetting the income with an equal amount of expense—you guessed it: the bad debt.

Suppose you invoiced a customer for $5,000, which means that $5,000 is sitting in your Accounts Receivable account as an asset, but you now realize that you'll never see the money. Here's how to remove that money from the Accounts Receivable account by means of a bad-debt expense:

1. If you don't have an account for bad debt, create an Other Expense account (page 56) and name it Bad Debt.
2. Create an Other Charge item (page 113) and name it Bad Debt. Point it to the Bad Debt account you created, and be sure to make it nontaxable.
3. Choose Customers→Create Credit Memos/Refunds or, on the Home Page, click the Refunds & Credits icon.
4. In the Create Credit Memos/Refunds window's Customer: Job box, choose the customer.
5. In the first item cell, choose the Bad Debt item. When QuickBooks displays a warning about the item being associated with an expense account, simply click OK.
6. In the Amount cell, type the amount that you're writing off as bad debt, and then click Save & Close to save the credit memo.
7. The Available Credit dialog box opens and asks you what you want to do with the credit. Select the "Apply to an invoice" option, and then click OK.
8. In the "Apply Credit to Invoices" dialog box, turn on the checkmark for the invoice(s) that the customer isn't going to pay, and then click Done.

When you apply the write-off as a credit against an invoice, QuickBooks removes the money from your Accounts Receivable account, so the program no longer thinks your customer owes the money. And it adds the credit amount to the appropriate income account and to the Bad Debt expense account, so your net profit shows no sign of the income. In addition, if you run a Job Profitability Detail report for that customer, the bad debt appears as a negative number in the Actual Revenue column—that is, a cost that reduces the job's profitability.

Funds transfers have nothing to do with income or expenses—they merely move money from one balance sheet account to another. For example, if you keep money in savings until you pay bills, the money moves from your savings account (an asset account in your chart of accounts) to your checking account (another asset account). Your income, expenses, and, for that matter, your total assets, remain the same before and after the transfer.

Transferring funds in QuickBooks is easy, whether you use the Transfer Funds feature or enter the transaction directly in an account register window. The steps for creating a transaction in an account register are explained on page 374. If you create a transfer in a bank account register (a savings account, for example), in the transaction's Account field, choose the bank account to which you're transferring funds (such as checking).

Here's how to use the Transfer Funds Between Accounts window:

1. **Choose Banking→Transfer Funds.**

   QuickBooks opens the Transfer Funds Between Accounts window (Figure 14-8).

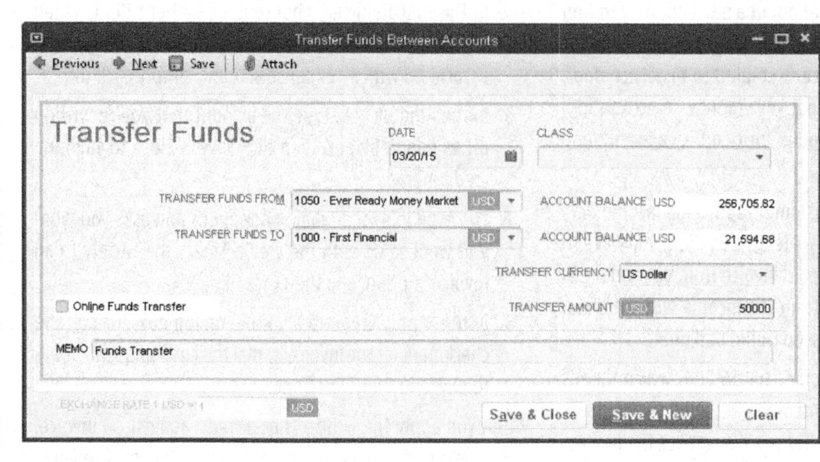

FIGURE 14-8

This window has one advantage over entering transfers in a bank account register: You can't create a payment or deposit by mistake because you can't save it here until you specify both the account that contains the money and the account into which you want to transfer the funds. Also, the Transfer Funds From and Transfer Funds To drop-down menus show only balance sheet accounts (bank, credit card, asset, liability, and equity).

2. **Choose the accounts for the transfer and then, in the Date box, select the date of the transfer. In the Transfer Amount field, type the amount you're transferring.**

   To record the reason for the transfer, in the Memo box, replace "Funds Transfer" (which QuickBooks adds automatically) with your reason.

   If you track classes, the window also includes a Class box. Depending on the preferences you've set, the program might warn you if you leave this box blank. However, transfers usually don't require a class assignment, so you can dismiss the warning or choose a class for overhead, if you created one.

NOTE If the two accounts you select are both set up for online banking at the same financial institution, the Online Funds Transfer checkbox appears in the Transfer Funds Between Accounts window. Turn this checkbox on if you want to send the transfer instructions to your bank through QuickBooks.

3. **Click Save & Close. (If you've got more transfers to make, click Save & New instead.)**

   In the account register windows for both accounts involved in the transfer, QuickBooks identifies the transaction by putting TRANSFR in the Type cell.

You still have to transfer the funds between your real-world bank accounts, of course. If you turned on the Online Funds Transfer checkbox to send the transfer instructions, you have to open the Bank Feeds Center (Banking→Bank Feeds→Bank Feeds Center), and send the instructions from there. See page 617 if you use Bank Feeds in Express mode and page 627 if you use Classic mode.

Reconciling Accounts

Reconciling a bank statement with a paper check register is tedious and error-prone. It's a hassle to check off items on two different paper documents, and the check register and the bank statement never seem to agree—likely due to arithmetic mistakes you've made.

With QuickBooks, you can leave your pencils unsharpened and stow your calculator in a drawer. When all goes well, a few clicks is all it takes to reconcile your account in QuickBooks. Discrepancies crop up less often because the program does the math without making mistakes. But problems still occasionally happen—transactions might be missing or numbers don't match. Fortunately, when your bank statement and QuickBooks account don't agree, the program helps you find the problems.

Preparing for the First Reconciliation

If you didn't set the beginning balance for your QuickBooks account to the beginning balance on your bank statement, you might wonder how you can reconcile the bank account the first time around. The best way to resolve this issue is to enter the transactions that happened between that statement's beginning date and the day you started using QuickBooks. Or you can create a journal entry (page 426) to record the beginning balance. (You'll select these items as part of your first reconciliation, as described on page 392.)

NOTE Alternatively, QuickBooks can align your statement and account the first time you reconcile, as described in the box on page 394. To do so, the program generates a transaction that adjusts your account's opening balance to match the balance on your bank statement. Account opening balances post to your Opening Bal Equity account, so these adjustments affect your balance sheet. If you use this method, let your accountant know that you changed the opening balance so she can address that change (by recording a journal entry to move the money into the correct equity account) while closing your books at the end of the year.

Preparing for Every Reconciliation

QuickBooks lets you create and edit transactions in the middle of a reconciliation, but reconciling your account flows more smoothly when your transactions are up to date. So take a moment *before* you reconcile to make sure that you've entered all the transactions in your account:

- **Bills**. If you paid bills by writing paper checks and forgot to record them in QuickBooks, then on the program's Home Page, click the Pay Bills icon and enter those payments (page 194).

- **Checks**. If you find that checks aren't in your checkbook but you don't see check transactions in QuickBooks, chances are that you wrote a paper check and didn't record it in your company file. Create any missing check transactions in the account register (page 205) or by choosing Banking→Write Checks.
- **Transfers**. Create missing transfers in the appropriate account register (page 374) or by choosing Banking→Transfer Funds.
- **Deposits**. If you forgot to record deposits of customer payments in QuickBooks, on the program's Home Page, click the Record Deposits icon to add them to your bank account (page 368). If a deposit appears on your bank statement but doesn't show up in the "Payments to Deposit" window, you might have forgotten to receive the payment in QuickBooks. For deposits unrelated to customer payments, create the deposit directly in the account's register (page 374).

TIP The easiest way to spot payments you haven't deposited in QuickBooks is to open the "Payments to Deposit" window (Banking→Make Deposits). Any payments that you've received but not deposited in QuickBooks appear in the window's Select Payments To Deposit table.

- **Online transactions**. If you use QuickBooks' Bank Feeds feature to communicate with your bank, download online transactions (page 617).

TIP If you let several months go by without reconciling your account, don't try to reconcile multiple months at once to catch up—doing so makes discrepancies harder to spot, and locating the source of problems will tax your already-overworked brain. Instead, put your bank statements in chronological order, and then walk through the reconciliation process for each statement.

Starting a Reconciliation

Reconciling an account is a two-part process, and QuickBooks has separate windows for each phase. The first phase includes choosing the account you want to reconcile, entering the ending balance from your bank statement, and entering service charges and interest earned during the statement period. Here's how to kick off a reconciliation:

1. **Click the Reconcile icon on the Home Page or choose Banking→Reconcile (or Banking→Reconcile Credit Card if you have a credit card account selected in the Chart of Accounts window).**

   The Begin Reconciliation window appears.

TIP If the bank account's register window is already open, you can start reconciling by right-clicking the register window and choosing Reconcile on the shortcut menu that appears. With this approach, the Begin Reconciliation window opens and automatically selects the active bank account.

2. **In the Begin Reconciliation window's Account drop-down list, choose the account you want to reconcile.**

   The window displays information about the previous reconciliation for this account (if any), as shown in Figure 14-9. The date of the previous reconciliation appears to the right of the Account box (unless you're reconciling this account for the first time). QuickBooks fills in the Statement Date box with a date one month after the previous reconciliation date. If that date doesn't match your bank statement's ending date, replace it with the date from your statement.

   QuickBooks automatically sets the *beginning* balance for this reconciliation to the *ending* balance of the previous reconciliation (unless this is your first reconciliation). If the beginning balance that the program displays doesn't match the beginning balance on your bank statement, you need to correct that discrepancy before you can reconcile your account. Click Cancel and turn to page 396 to learn how to fix the problem.

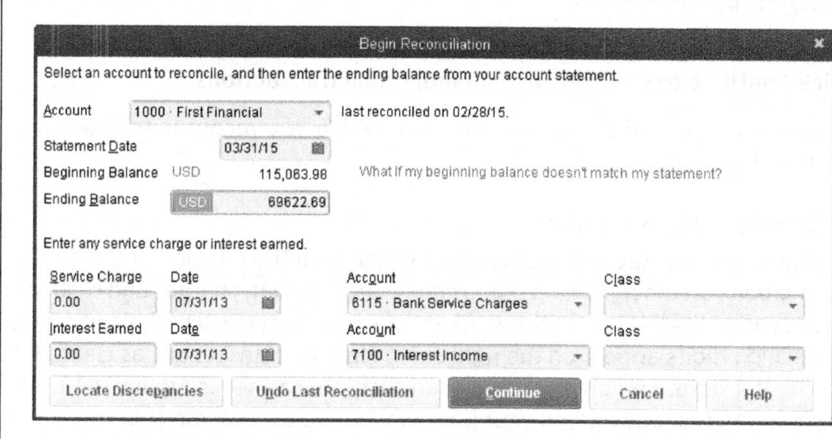

FIGURE 14-9

QuickBooks uses the ending balance from the previous reconciliation to fill in the beginning balance for this reconciliation. If the beginning balance here doesn't match the beginning balance on your bank statement, click Cancel and turn to page 396 to learn how to correct the problem.

3. **In the Ending Balance box, type the ending balance from your bank statement.**

   If you turned on multiple currencies, the account's currency appears to the right of the Beginning Balance and Ending Balance labels. For a foreign-currency account, enter the ending balance in the foreign currency, which is the ending balance that appears on your bank statement.

4. **If your bank levies a service charge on your account, in the Service Charge box, type the charge amount. (If you download transactions from your bank, leave this box blank.)**

   In the Date box to the right of the Service Charge box, choose the date that the charge was assessed if it differs from the statement ending date. In the Account box, choose the account to which you want to post the charge (usually Bank

Service Charges or something similar). QuickBooks then creates a service-charge transaction for you.

TIP If you use Bank Feeds (page 611), chances are you've already downloaded your service-charge and interest transactions. In that case, don't enter them in the Begin Reconciliation window or you'll end up with duplicate transactions.

5. **If you're reconciling an account that pays interest, in the Interest Earned box, type the interest listed on your bank statement.**

   As you did in step 4 for the service charge, specify the date and the account that you use to track interest.

NOTE If you track service fees and interest earned by class, in the Class boxes, choose the appropriate ones. For example, classes might apply if you use them to track performance by region. However, if you use classes to track sales by partner, you don't have to specify a class for interest earned, though you can use a class for overhead if you created one.

6. **Click Continue to start reconciling individual transactions.**

   QuickBooks opens the Reconcile window, where you reconcile transactions, as described next.

Reconciling Transactions

The Reconcile window groups checks and payments on the left side and deposits and other credits on the right side. (For a credit card account, charges and cash advances appear on the left side of the window—since they reduce your balance—and payments and credits appear on the right side.) Marking transactions as cleared is a simple matter of turning on their checkmarks, as you can see in Figure 14-10. For each transaction that appears on your bank statement, turn on the checkmark for the matching QuickBooks transaction. (If you turn on a checkmark by mistake, just click it again to turn it off.)

NOTE QuickBooks initially sorts transactions by date with the earliest transaction listed first. If you want to sort them by another field, click the column heading for that field. For example, click "Chk #" if you're trying to find the check that's preventing you from reconciling successfully. An up arrow next to the heading indicates that the column is sorted in ascending order (smallest to largest values). Click the column heading again to reverse the order (largest to smallest).

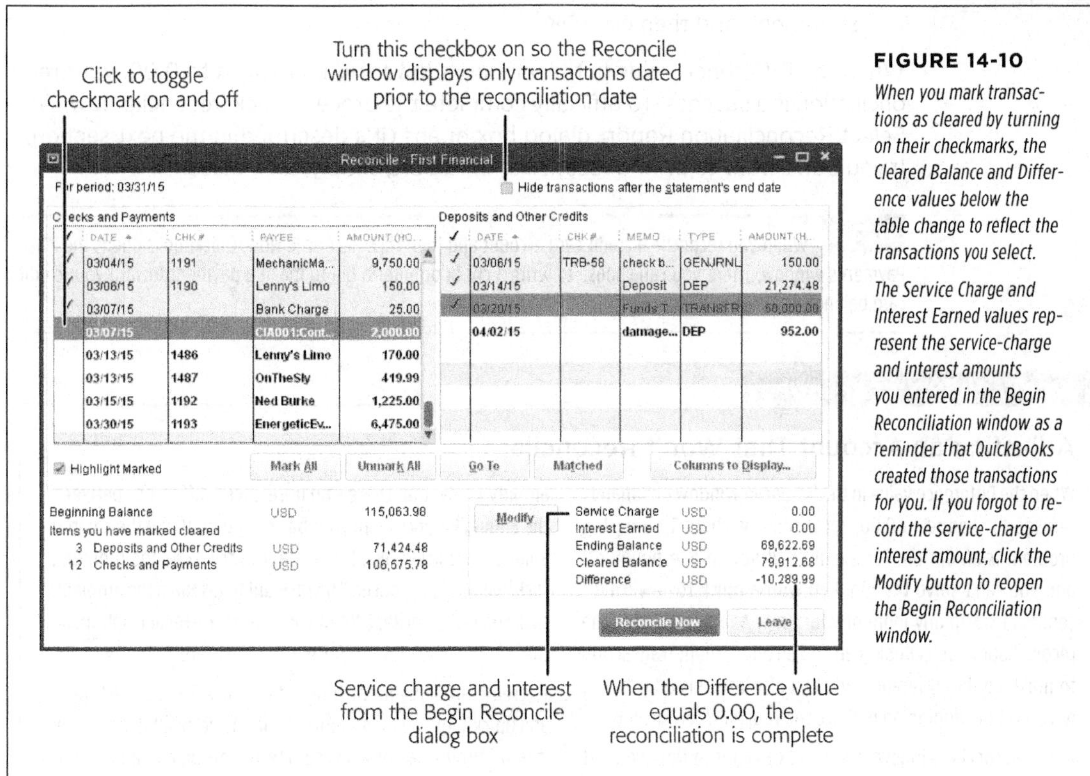

FIGURE 14-10

When you mark transactions as cleared by turning on their checkmarks, the Cleared Balance and Difference values below the table change to reflect the transactions you select.

The Service Charge and Interest Earned values represent the service-charge and interest amounts you entered in the Begin Reconciliation window as a reminder that QuickBooks created those transactions for you. If you forgot to record the service-charge or interest amount, click the Modify button to reopen the Begin Reconciliation window.

TIP Initially, the Reconcile window lists *all* uncleared transactions in the account regardless of when they happened. If transactions after the statement ending date are mixed in, you could select unnecessary transactions by mistake. To filter the list to likely candidates for clearing, turn on the "Hide transactions after the statement's end date" checkbox at the top right of the window. If you don't see transactions that appear on your bank statement, turn this checkbox off; you might have created a transaction with the wrong date.

QuickBooks includes several shortcuts for marking a transaction as cleared:

- **Mark All**. If you usually end up clearing most of the transactions in the list, click Mark All below the table to select all the transactions. Then turn off the checkmarks for the ones that *don't* appear on your bank statement. If you were distracted and selected several transactions by mistake, click Unmark All to start over.
- **Selecting contiguous transactions**. Dragging down the checkmark column selects every transaction you pass. (This approach isn't that helpful if you compare one transaction at a time or if your transactions don't appear in the same order as those on your bank statement.)

- **Online account access**. If you've set up Bank Feeds in QuickBooks, click Matched to automatically clear the transactions that you've already matched from your QuickStatement (see Chapter 24). Enter the ending date from your printed statement, and then click OK.

When the Difference value in the window's lower right changes to 0.00, your reconciliation is a success. To officially complete the process, click Reconcile Now. The Select Reconciliation Report dialog box opens (it's described in the next section). If you don't want to print a reconciliation report, simply click Close.

NOTE When you reconcile a credit card account and then click Reconcile Now, QuickBooks opens the Make Payments window. There you can choose to write a check or enter a bill to make a payment toward your credit card balance.

WORKAROUND WORKSHOP

Adjusting an Account That Won't Reconcile

When the Difference value in the Reconcile window obstinately refuses to change to 0.00, reconciling without finding the problem *is* an option. For example, if you're one penny off and you can't solve the problem with a quick review, that 1 cent isn't worth any more of your time. As you complete the reconciliation, QuickBooks can add an adjustment transaction to make up the difference. You can also use this adjustment to correct the beginning balance for your *first* reconciliation.

In the Reconcile window, if you click Reconcile Now without zeroing the Difference value, QuickBooks opens the Reconcile Adjustment dialog box. The program tells you what you already know: that there's an unresolved difference between the Ending Balance from your bank statement and the Cleared Balance in QuickBooks. If you want to try to fix the problem, click "Return to Reconcile." If you want to research the problem, click Leave Reconcile. (When you restart the reconciliation, all the work you've done so far will still be there.)

To create an adjustment transaction, click Enter Adjustment, and QuickBooks creates a journal entry to zero out the balance. If you stumble across the source of the discrepancy later, you can either void the adjustment journal entry or create a reversing entry (page 431).

Modifying Transactions During Reconciliation

QuickBooks immediately updates the Reconcile window with changes you make in the bank account's register window, so it's easy to complete a reconciliation. Missing transactions? Incorrect amounts? Other discrepancies? No problem. You can jump to the register window and make your changes. Then, when you click back to the Reconcile window, the changes are there.

TIP If you've opened both the bank account's register window and the reconciliation window, click the one you want to work on. If you use the left icon bar, click Open Windows in the bar's middle section to see a list of the open windows at the top of the bar; simply click the name of the one you want to work with. If you use the top icon bar, choose View→Open Window List to display the Open Windows list on the left side of the QuickBooks window; you can then click names there to change the active window or dialog box.

Here's how to make changes while reconciling:

- **Adding transactions**. If a transaction appears on your bank statement but isn't in QuickBooks, switch to the account's register window or the transaction's corresponding window (such as Write Checks) and add the transaction.
- **Deleting transactions**. If you find duplicate transactions, in the account's register window, right-click the transaction and choose the corresponding Delete entry on the shortcut menu (or select the transaction and then press Ctrl+D). When you confirm your decision and QuickBooks deletes the transaction, the transaction also disappears from the Reconcile window.
- **Editing transactions**. If you notice an error in a transaction, in the Reconcile window, double-click the transaction to open its corresponding window (Write Checks for checks, Make Deposits for deposits, and so on). Correct the mistake, and then save the transaction by clicking Record or Save, depending on the window.

Stopping and Restarting a Reconciliation

If your head hurts and you need a break, you don't need to worry about losing the reconciliation work you've already done—QuickBooks saves it for you. Here's how to stop and restart a reconciliation:

1. **In the Reconcile window, click Leave.**

   Although QuickBooks closes the window, it remembers what you've done. If you open the bank account's register window, you'll see asterisks in the checkmark column for transactions that you've marked as cleared, which indicates that your clearing of that transaction is pending.

2. **When you're reenergized, open the account's register window, right-click it, and then choose Reconcile on the shortcut menu.**

   The Begin Reconciliation window opens with the ending balance, service charge, and interest amounts already filled in.

3. **Click Continue.**

   The transactions you marked are, happily, still marked. Pick up where you left off by marking the rest of the transactions that cleared on your bank statement.

Reconciliation Reports

After you click Reconcile Now in the Reconcile window, you might notice a short delay while QuickBooks generates your reconciliation reports. These reports may come in handy as a benchmark when you try to locate discrepancies in a future reconciliation.

When the Select Reconciliation Report dialog box opens, you can display or print reconciliation reports. Choose the Summary option for a report that provides the totals for the checks and payments you made, and for the deposits and credits you received. To save the reports for future reference, click Print. Click Close to close the dialog box without printing or viewing the reports. You can look at them later by choosing Reports→Banking→Previous Reconciliation. (If you use QuickBooks Premier or Enterprise, in the Select Previous Reconciliation Report dialog box, the Statement Ending Date box lists the dates of the previous reconciliations for the account. Click the ending date you want and then click Display to run the report.)

Figure 14-11 shows what a detailed reconciliation report looks like.

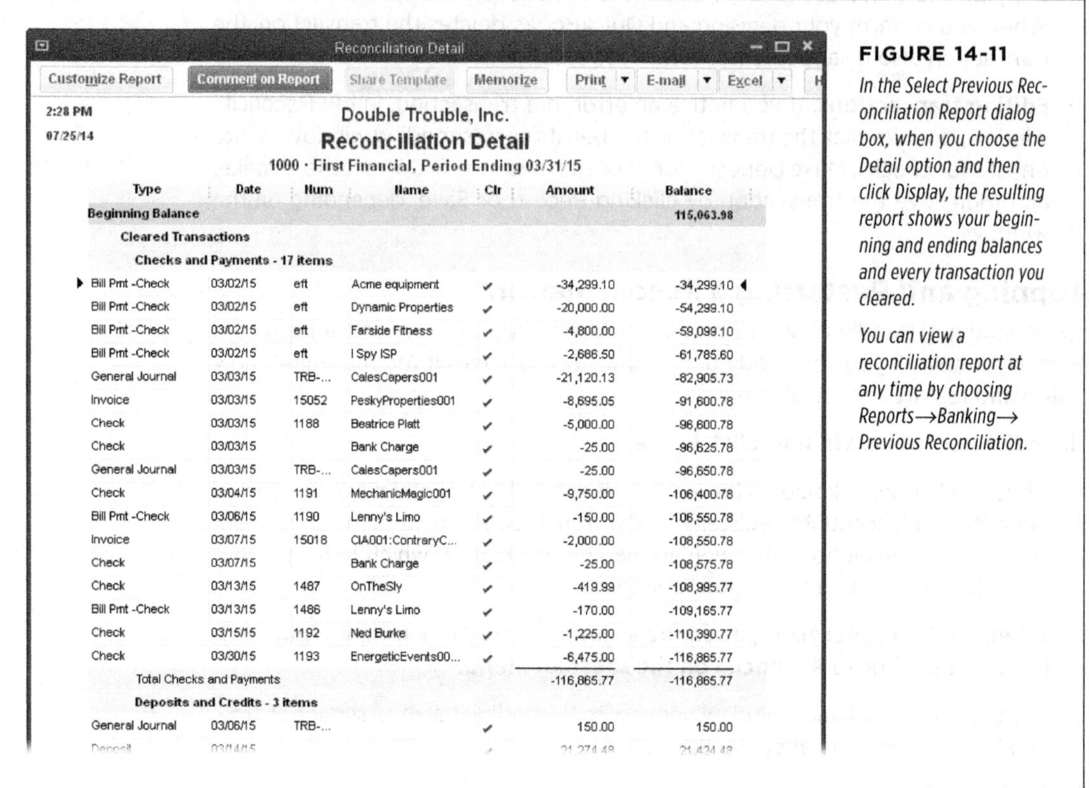

Type	Date	Num	Name	Clr	Amount	Balance
Beginning Balance						115,063.98
Cleared Transactions						
Checks and Payments - 17 items						
Bill Pmt -Check	03/02/15	eft	Acme equipment	✓	-34,299.10	-34,299.10
Bill Pmt -Check	03/02/15	eft	Dynamic Properties	✓	-20,000.00	-54,299.10
Bill Pmt -Check	03/02/15	eft	Farside Fitness	✓	-4,800.00	-59,099.10
Bill Pmt -Check	03/02/15	eft	I Spy ISP	✓	-2,686.50	-61,785.60
General Journal	03/03/15	TRB-...	CalesCapers001	✓	-21,120.13	-82,905.73
Invoice	03/03/15	15052	PeskyProperties001	✓	-8,695.05	-91,600.78
Check	03/03/15	1188	Beatrice Platt	✓	-5,000.00	-96,600.78
Check	03/03/15		Bank Charge	✓	-25.00	-96,625.78
General Journal	03/03/15	TRB-...	CalesCapers001	✓	-25.00	-96,650.78
Check	03/04/15	1191	MechanicMagic001	✓	-9,750.00	-106,400.78
Bill Pmt -Check	03/06/15	1190	Lenny's Limo	✓	-150.00	-106,550.78
Invoice	03/07/15	15018	CIA001:ContraryC...	✓	-2,000.00	-108,550.78
Check	03/07/15		Bank Charge	✓	-25.00	-108,575.78
Check	03/13/15	1487	OnTheSly	✓	-419.99	-108,995.77
Bill Pmt -Check	03/13/15	1486	Lenny's Limo	✓	-170.00	-109,165.77
Check	03/15/15	1192	Ned Burke	✓	-1,225.00	-110,390.77
Check	03/30/15	1193	EnergeticEvents00...	✓	-6,475.00	-116,865.77
Total Checks and Payments					-116,865.77	-116,865.77
Deposits and Credits - 3 items						
General Journal	03/06/15	TRB-...		✓	150.00	150.00

FIGURE 14-11

In the Select Previous Reconciliation Report dialog box, when you choose the Detail option and then click Display, the resulting report shows your beginning and ending balances and every transaction you cleared.

You can view a reconciliation report at any time by choosing Reports→Banking→Previous Reconciliation.

Correcting Discrepancies

If you modify a transaction that you've already reconciled, QuickBooks displays a dialog box warning you that you changed a reconciled transaction and that your change will affect your reconciliation balance. After all, if you cleared a transaction because it appeared on your bank statement, the transaction is complete, and changing it in QuickBooks doesn't change it in your bank account.

While you technically *can* change or delete cleared transactions in QuickBooks, doing so is usually a bad idea. The one situation that usually calls for editing reconciled transactions is when you're trying to correct a reconciliation problem. This section explains what causes discrepancies, how to hunt down transactions that are causing problems, and how to edit transactions to fix discrepancies.

Changing previously cleared transactions is the quickest way to cause mayhem when reconciling accounts. A typical reconciliation problem is when the beginning balance that QuickBooks fills in doesn't match the beginning balance on your bank statement, which is one reason you might be reading this section. Here are some of the most common causes of discrepancies:

- **Changing the cleared status of a reconciled transaction**. In an account register window, you might click a checkmark cell by mistake, which resets the status of that transaction from reconciled (indicated by a checkmark) to cleared (indicated by an asterisk). This change removes that transaction's amount from the Begin Reconciliation window's Beginning Balance when you try to reconcile the account.
- **Editing a reconciled transaction's amount**. Changing a reconciled transaction's amount doesn't change the amount on your bank statement, but it does affect the beginning balance that QuickBooks calculates.
- **Deleting a reconciled transaction**. Suppose you recorded a transaction using the wrong QuickBooks feature, such as writing a check in the Write Checks window to remit your sales tax instead of using the Pay Sales Tax dialog box. Then, to make matters worse, you reconcile that incorrect transaction as part of your bank account reconciliation. If you delete the check so you can pay the sales tax using the *correct* QuickBooks feature, your beginning reconciliation balance won't agree with the one on your bank statement.

  To fix the error, in the bank account register window, delete the transaction that you recorded using the wrong method by right-clicking the transaction and then choosing "Delete [transaction]" from the shortcut menu. (In this example, the transaction is a check to pay sales tax, so you would choose Delete Check, but it could be a check for payroll or another type of transaction.) Then recreate the transaction using the Pay Sales Tax feature. Now your sales tax is paid the right way, but your beginning balance is messed up due to the deleted transaction; see "Re-reconciling corrected transactions" on page 398 to learn how to fix that.

USING THE DISCREPANCY REPORT TO FIND PROBLEM TRANSACTIONS

If your bank statement and QuickBooks records don't agree and you don't know why, the Discrepancy Report can help you find the transactions that are the culprits. This report shows changes that were made to reconciled transactions, so you can restore them to their original states.

To run the Discrepancy Report, in the Begin Reconciliation window, click Locate Discrepancies, and then, in the Locate Discrepancies window, click Discrepancy Report. (You can also choose Reports→Banking→Reconciliation Discrepancy.)

Seeing transactions on the Discrepancy Report is a big step toward correcting reconciliation problems. Here's how to interpret the report's crucial columns:

- **Entered/Last Modified**. This is the date that the transaction was created or modified, which might help you figure out who's changing reconciled transactions.
- **Reconciled Amount**. This column shows the value the transaction had when you reconciled it. If the transaction's amount has been changed, use *this* value to restore the transaction to its original value. For example, –99.95 in this column represents a check or charge for $99.95.
- **Type of Change**. This column indicates what aspect of the transaction was changed. For example, "Amount" means that the transaction's amount changed, "Uncleared" indicates that someone removed the transaction's reconciled checkmark in the account register, and "Deleted" means that the transaction was deleted.

TIP The only way to restore a deleted transaction is to recreate it from scratch. The Discrepancy Report identifies deleted transactions, but it doesn't provide the details you need to recreate them. To see those details, choose Reports→Accountant & Taxes→Voided/Deleted Transactions Detail. This report includes every bit of info about the transaction, so you can recreate it in all its original glory.

- **Effect of Change**. This value indicates how the change affected the beginning balance of your reconciliation. For example, a $99.95 check that was reset added $99.95 to your bank account. When the Beginning Balance is off and the amount in this column matches that discrepancy, you can be sure that restoring these transactions to their original states will fix the problem.

Once you identify a transaction that was edited after it was reconciled, in the Previous Reconciliations Discrepancy Report window, double-click the transaction to open it in its corresponding window (for example, the Write Checks window for a check). If a transaction's status was reset from reconciled to cleared, open the account's register (page 374), find the transaction, and then click its checkmark cell until a checkmark (which represents a reconciled transaction) appears.

TIP If your beginning balance is *still* off after you correct cleared statuses, amounts, and deleted transactions, run the Audit Trail report (page 437) to look for other changes that could throw off your reconciliation (for example, a transaction whose account was changed).

RE-RECONCILING CORRECTED TRANSACTIONS

If you fix changes that were made to reconciled transactions, you then have to *re*-reconcile those transactions. Fortunately, you can perform a surgical reconciliation to accept these transactions. Here are the steps:

1. **Choose Banking→Reconcile and then, in the Begin Reconciliation window's Account drop-down list, choose the bank account you want to re-reconcile (if it isn't already selected).**

2. **Change the date in the Statement Date box to the date on the bank statement that contains the transaction you corrected.**

   For example, if the transaction you corrected was made on February 15, fill in the statement date for your February bank statement.

3. **In the Ending Balance box, fill in the ending balance from the bank statement (the February statement, in this example), and then click Continue.**

   The Reconcile window opens.

4. **In the Reconcile window, find the corrected transactions in the Checks and Payments list and click their checkmark cells to turn on their checkmarks.**

   When you do so, the Difference value changes to 0.00.

5. **Click Reconcile Now to complete this mini-reconciliation.**

   The next time you reconcile the account, the beginning balance will match the beginning balance on your bank statement.

OTHER WAYS TO FIND DISCREPANCIES

Sometimes, your QuickBooks records don't match your bank's records because of subtle errors in transactions or because you've missed something in the current reconciliation. The following techniques can help you spot problems:

- **Search for a transaction equal to the amount of the discrepancy**. Press Ctrl+F to open the Find window. On the Advanced tab, in the Choose Filter list, select Amount. Next, choose the = option and type the amount in the text box, and then click Find to run the search.

  You can also use the Search feature to find a transaction for that amount: Press F3 to open the Search window. In the Amount box, type the amount of the discrepancy, and then click Go. If you use the left icon bar, you can also type the amount of the discrepancy in the Search box at the top of the bar, and then click the Search icon (it looks like a magnifying glass).

NOTE Using Find or Search in this way works only if the discrepancy is caused by *one* transaction that you cleared or uncleared by mistake. If more than one transaction is to blame, the amount you're trying to find is the total of *all* the erroneously cleared transactions, so these methods won't find a matching value.

- **Look for transactions cleared or uncleared by mistake**. Sometimes, the easiest way to find a discrepancy is to start the reconciliation over. In the Reconcile window, click Unmark All to remove the checkmarks from all the transactions. Then begin checking them off as you compare them with your bank statement. Make sure that every transaction on the statement is cleared in the Reconcile window, and that no *additional* transactions are cleared in that window.

- **Look for duplicate transactions**. If you create transactions in QuickBooks *and* download transactions from your bank's website, it's easy to end up with duplicates. And when you clear both of the duplicates, the mistake is hard to spot. If that's the case, you have to scroll through the register window looking for multiple transactions with the same date, payee, and amount.

- **Compare the number of transactions on your bank statement with the number of cleared transactions on the left side of the Reconcile window (Figure 14-12)**. Of course, this technique won't help if you enter transactions in QuickBooks differently than they appear on your bank statement. For example, if you deposit every payment individually but your bank shows one deposit for every business day, then your transaction counts won't match.
- **Look for a deposit entered as a payment or vice versa**. To find an error like this, look for transactions whose amounts are *half* the discrepancy. For example, if a $500 check becomes a $500 deposit by mistake, your reconciliation will be off by $1,000: $500 because a check is missing and another $500 because you have an extra deposit.

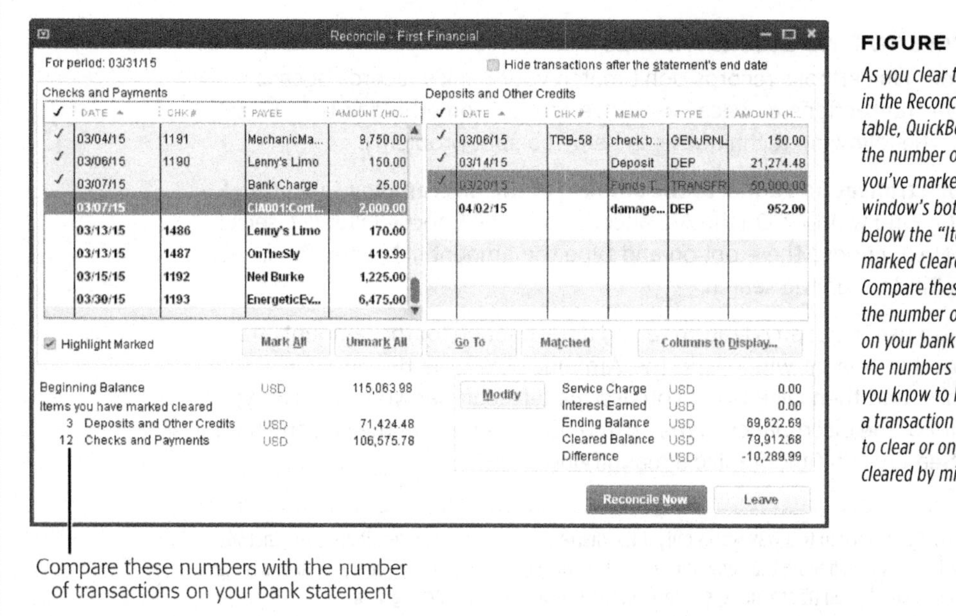
Compare these numbers with the number of transactions on your bank statement

FIGURE 14-12

As you clear transactions in the Reconcile window's table, QuickBooks updates the number of items you've marked at the window's bottom left, below the "Items you have marked cleared" heading. Compare these values with the number of transactions on your bank statement. If the numbers don't agree, you know to look for either a transaction you forgot to clear or one that you cleared by mistake.

- **Look at each cleared transaction for transposed numbers or other differences between your statement and QuickBooks**. It's easy to type *$95.40* when you mean *$59.40*.

NOTE If these techniques don't uncover the problem, your bank might have made a mistake. See page 401 to learn what to do in that case.

Undoing the Last Reconciliation

If you're having problems with this month's reconciliation but suspect that the culprit is hiding in *last* month's reconciliation, you can undo the last reconciliation and start over. When you undo a reconciliation, QuickBooks returns the transactions in it to an uncleared state.

In the Begin Reconciliation window (choose Banking→Reconcile), click Undo Last Reconciliation to open the Undo Previous Reconciliation dialog box. (Although the button's label and the dialog box's title don't match, they both represent the same process.) In the dialog box, click Continue. When the Undo Previous Reconciliation message box appears telling you that the previous reconciliation has been successfully undone, click OK.

QuickBooks unclears all the transactions back to the beginning of the previous reconciliation and returns you to the Begin Reconciliation window. Change the values in the dialog box, and then click Continue to try another reconciliation.

NOTE Although this process makes QuickBooks remove the cleared status from all the transactions included in your last reconciliation, including service charges and interest, the program *doesn't* remove the service charge and interest transactions that it added. So when you restart the reconciliation, don't re-enter the service charges or interest in the Begin Reconciliation window.

When Your Bank Makes a Mistake

Banks do make mistakes: Digits get transposed or amounts are flat wrong. When this happens, you can't ignore the discrepancy. In QuickBooks, add an adjustment transaction (page 394) to make up the difference, and be sure to tell your bank about the mistake. (It's always a good idea to be polite in case the error turns out to be yours.)

When you receive your *next* statement, check that the bank made an adjustment to correct its mistake. You can then delete your adjustment transaction or add a reversing journal entry to remove your adjustment and reconcile as you normally would.

TIP For a reminder to check your next statement, create a To Do Note (choose Company→To Do List, and then click Add To Do).

Managing Loans

Unless your business generates cash at an astonishing rate, you'll probably have to borrow money to purchase big-ticket items that you can't afford to do without, such as a deluxe cat-herding machine.

In real life, the asset you purchase and the loan you assume are intimately linked—you can't get the equipment without borrowing the money. But in QuickBooks, loans and the assets they help purchase aren't connected in any way. You create an asset account to track the purchase price of an asset that you buy. If you take out a loan to pay for that asset, you create a liability account to track the balance of what you owe on the loan. With each payment you make on the loan, you pay off a little bit of the loan's principal as well as a chunk of interest.

NOTE On your company's balance sheet, the value of your assets appears in the Assets section, and the balance you owe on loans shows up in the Liabilities section. The difference between the asset value and the loan balance is your *equity* in the asset. For example, suppose your cat-herding machine is in primo condition and is worth $70,000 on the open market. If you owe $50,000 on the loan, then your company has $20,000 in equity in that machine.

Most loans *amortize* your payoff, which means that each payment represents a different amount of interest and principal. At the beginning of a loan, amortized payments are mostly interest and very little principal; that means the lender gets more of its money up front, but it's also great for your company's tax deductions. By the end of the loan's life cycle, the payments are almost entirely principal.

Making loan payments in which the values change each month would be a nightmare if not for Loan Manager, a separate program that comes with QuickBooks that can exchange info with your company file. Loan Manager calculates your loan's amortization schedule, posts the principal and interest for each payment to the appropriate accounts, and handles escrow payments and fees associated with your loans. This section explains how to use it.

NOTE Loan Manager doesn't handle loans in which the payment covers only the accrued interest (called *interest-only loans*). For loans like these, you have to set up payments yourself (page 408) and allocate payments to principal and interest using the values on your monthly loan statements.

Setting Up a Loan

Regardless of whether you use Loan Manager, you have to create accounts in QuickBooks to keep track of your loan. You probably already know that you need a liability account for the amount of money you owe. You also need accounts for the interest you pay on the loan and escrow payments (such as insurance or property tax) that you make. If you're planning to use Loan Manager to track your loan, make sure you have all of your loan-tracking elements in place *before* you start using it. Here are the things you need:

- **Liability account**. Create a liability account (page 56) to track the money you've borrowed. For mortgages and other loans whose terms are longer than a year, use the Long Term Liability account type. For short-term loans (ones with terms of one year or less), use the Other Current Liability account type.

  When you create the liability account, don't enter an opening balance. The best way to record money you borrow is by recording a deposit (page 370) for the money you borrowed into the account where you deposited the money. (In the From Account cell, choose the liability account for the loan.) You can also record a loan's opening balance with a journal entry (see Chapter 16), which credits the liability account for the loan and debits either the bank account where you deposited the money or the fixed asset account for the asset you purchased.

TIP If you've just started using QuickBooks and have a loan that you've partially paid off, fill in the journal entry with what you owed on the loan statement that's dated just before your QuickBooks company file's start date. Then enter any loan payments you've made since that statement's ending date to get the account to the current balance.

- **Loan interest account**. The interest that you pay on loans is an expense, so create an Expense account (or an Other Expense account, if that's the type of account your company uses for interest paid) called something like Interest Paid. (Loan Manager shows Other Expense accounts in its account drop-down lists, although it lists accounts in alphabetical order, not by type.)
- **Escrow account**. If you make escrow payments for things like property taxes and insurance, create an account to track the escrow you've paid. Because escrow represents money you've paid in advance, use the Current Asset account type.
- **Fees and finance charge expense account**. Chances are you'll pay some sort of fee or finance charge at some point before you pay off the loan. If you don't have an account for finance charges you pay, set up an Expense account for them.
- **The lender in your Vendor List (page 84)**. You also need a vendor record for the institution that lent you the money, so you can use it for the payments you make.

The box below tells you what to do if you forgot to perform any of these steps before starting Loan Manager.

WORKAROUND WORKSHOP

Where Are My Accounts and Vendors?

Loan Manager looks just like any other item in QuickBooks' Banking menu, but it's actually a separate small program. When you start Loan Manager, it gleans information from your company file, such as the liability account you created for the loan and the vendor record you set up for your lender.

If you forgot to create accounts or your lender in QuickBooks before launching Loan Manager, you'll probably jump to your Chart of Accounts window or Vendor List and create them. Although you can create the elements you need by doing that, you *still* won't see them in Loan Manager's drop-down lists because Loan Manager only grabs the info it needs from your company file when you first launch it. To get them to appear, you have to close Loan Manager (and, unfortunately, lose any data you've already entered there), and then create those entries in QuickBooks. After you've created the vendor and all the accounts you need, choose Banking→Loan Manager to restart Loan Manager, which now includes your lender and loan accounts in its drop-down lists.

Adding a Loan to Loan Manager

Loan Manager makes it so easy to track and make payments on amortized loans that it's well worth the steps required to set it up. Before you begin, gather your loan documents like chicks to a mother hen, because Loan Manager wants to know every detail of your loan, as you'll soon see.

BASIC SETUP

Once you've created the necessary accounts and vendor records (see the box on page 403), follow these steps to tell Loan Manager about your loan:

1. **Choose Banking→Loan Manager.**

   QuickBooks opens the Loan Manager window.

2. **In the Loan Manager window, click the "Add a Loan" button.**

   Loan Manager opens the Add Loan dialog box, which has several screens for the details of your loan. They're all described in this section.

3. **In the Account Name drop-down list, choose the liability account you created for the loan.**

   Loan Manager lists only Current Liability and Long Term Liability accounts. Once you choose an account, Loan Manager displays the account's current balance.

NOTE If Loan Manager shows the loan's balance as zero, you aren't off the hook for paying back the loan. Loan Manager grabs this balance from the QuickBooks liability account you created for the loan. The loan balance in Loan Manager is zero if you forgot to set the liability account's opening balance. To correct this, click the Add Loan dialog box's Cancel button, and then close Loan Manager. In QuickBooks, create a deposit or journal entry to set the liability account's opening balance, and then restart Loan Manager and set up the loan.

4. **In the Lender drop-down list, choose the vendor you created for the company you're borrowing money from.**

   If you haven't set up the lender as a vendor in QuickBooks, you have to close Loan Manager. After you create the vendor in QuickBooks, restart Loan Manager, which now includes the lender in its Lender drop-down list.

5. **In the Origination Date box, choose the origination date on your loan documents.**

   Loan Manager uses this date to calculate the number of payments remaining, the interest you owe, and when you'll pay off the loan.

6. **In the Original Amount box, type the total amount you borrowed when you first took out the loan.**

   The Original Amount box is aptly named because it's *always* the amount that you originally borrowed. For new loans, the current balance on the loan and the Original Amount are the same. If you've paid off a portion of a loan, your current balance (shown below the Account Name box in Figure 14-13) is lower than the Original Amount. If the current balance is zero, you forgot to record the money you borrowed in the liability account (page 402).

7. **In the Term boxes, specify the full length of the loan (such as 360 months or 30 years) and then click Next to advance to the screen where you enter payment information (explained next).**

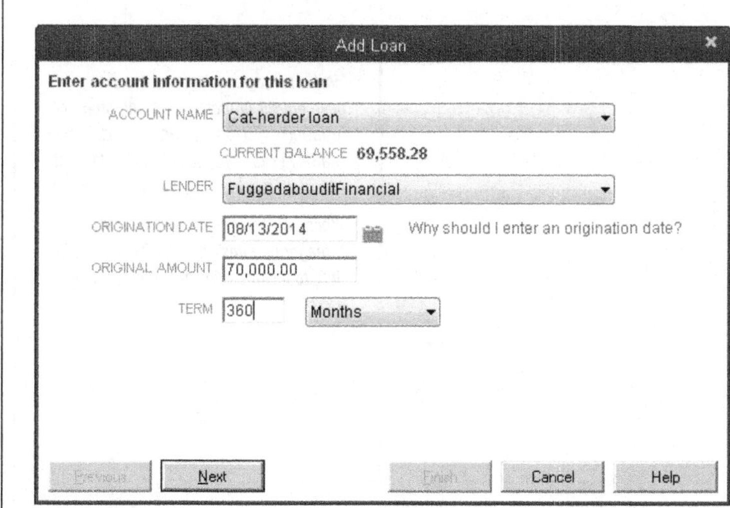

FIGURE 14-13

Loan Manager automatically selects Months in the Term drop-down list. Specifying the number of months for a 30-year loan is a great refresher for your multiplication tables, but you don't want to confuse Loan Manager by making an arithmetic error.

If your loan's term is measured in something other than months, in the Term drop-down list, choose the appropriate period (such as Years). Then you can fill in the Term box with the number of periods shown on your loan documents.

PAYMENT INFORMATION

When you specify a few details about your loan payments, Loan Manager can calculate a payment schedule for you. And to make sure you don't forget a loan payment (and incur outrageous late fees), you can tell Loan Manager to create a QuickBooks reminder for your payments. Here's how:

1. **In the "Due Date of Next Payment" box, choose the next payment date.**

   For a new loan, choose the date of the first payment you'll make. For an existing loan, choose the next payment date, which usually appears on your most recent loan statement.

2. **In the Payment Amount box, type the total amount of your next payment, including principal and interest.**

   Your payment amount is listed on your loan documents. Loan Manager automatically puts 1 in the Next Payment Number box. For loans that you've made payments on already, replace this with the number of the next payment (this, too, should be on your most recent loan statement).

3. **In the Payment Period drop-down list, choose the frequency of your payments.**

   Loans typically require monthly payments, even when their terms are in years, so Loan Manager automatically selects Monthly here. If your loan requires a different payment schedule, select the appropriate time period from this drop-down list.

4. **If your loan includes an escrow payment, choose the Yes option, and then specify the amount of escrow you pay each time and the account to which you want to post the escrow, as shown in Figure 14-14.**

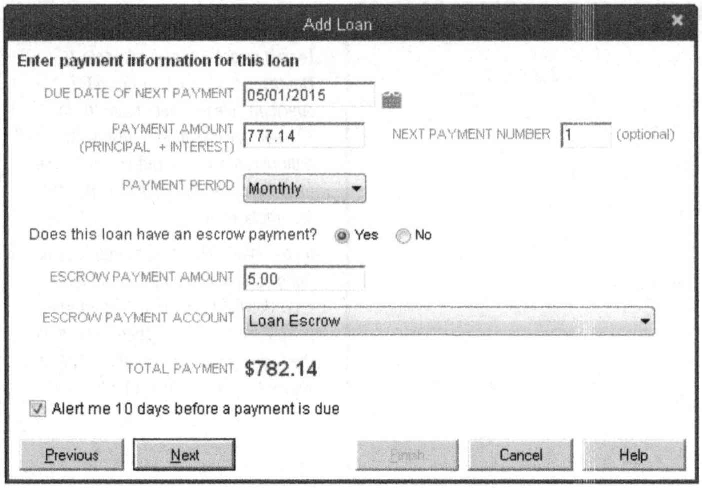

FIGURE 14-14

Most mortgages include an escrow payment for property taxes and property insurance. (Escrow accounts are asset accounts because you're setting aside some money to pay expenses later.)

When you add an escrow payment, Loan Manager updates the Total Payment value here to include principal, interest, and escrow.

5. **If you want a reminder before a loan payment is due, leave the "Alert me 10 days before a payment is due" checkbox turned on.**

   Loan Manager then tells QuickBooks when and how often payments are due, so QuickBooks can create a loan-payment reminder in its Reminders List (page 483). You can't change the number of days before a payment is due for the reminder, but 10 days is usually enough to get your payment in on time.

6. **Click Next to advance to the screen for entering interest rate info (explained next).**

INTEREST RATE INFORMATION

For Loan Manager to calculate your amortization schedule (the amount of principal and interest included with each payment), you have to specify the loan's interest rate. Here's how:

1. **In the Interest Rate box, type the loan's interest rate.**

   Use the rate that appears on your loan documents.

2. **In the Compounding Period box, choose either Monthly or Exact Days, depending on how the lender calculates compounding interest.**

   If the lender calculates the interest on your loan once a month, choose Monthly.

   If the lender calculates interest using the annual interest rate divided over a fixed number of days in a year, choose Exact Days instead. When you do that,

Loan Manager activates the Compute Period box. In the past, many lenders simplified calculations by assuming that a year had 12 months of 30 days each; if your lender uses this method, choose 365/360 as the Compute Period. Today, lenders often use the number of days in a year; in that case, choose the 365/365 Compute Period option instead.

3. **In the Payment Account drop-down list, choose the account from which you make loan payments.**

   Loan Manager includes all your bank accounts in this list.

4. **In the Interest Expense Account drop-down list, choose the account you use to track interest you pay. In the Fees/Charges Expense Account drop-down list, choose the account you use for fees and late charges you pay.**

   Expense accounts and Other Expense accounts are comingled in these lists because they appear in alphabetical order, not sorted by type.

5. **Click Finish.**

   Loan Manager calculates the loan's payment schedule and adds it to its list of loans (Figure 14-15).

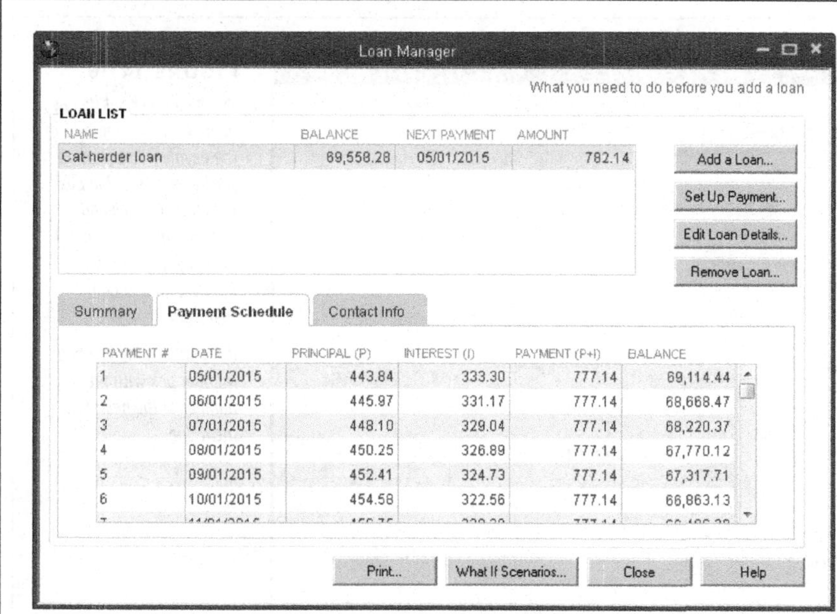

FIGURE 14-15

When you select a loan in the Loan List table here, the tabs at the bottom of the window display information about that loan. Most of the info on the Summary tab is stuff you entered, although Loan Manager calculates the maturity date (the date when you'll pay off the loan). The Payment Schedule tab (shown here) lists every payment and the amount of principal and interest each one represents. The info on the Contact Info tab comes from the lender's vendor record in QuickBooks.

Modifying Loan Terms

Some loan characteristics change from time to time. For example, if you have an adjustable-rate mortgage, the interest rate changes every so often. And your escrow payment changes based on your property taxes and insurance premiums. To make changes like these, in the Loan Manager window (choose Banking→Loan Manager), select the loan, and then click Edit Loan Details.

Loan Manager takes you through the same series of screens you saw when you first added the loan (page 404). If you change the interest rate, the program recalculates your payment schedule. If you make a change in escrow, the program updates your payment to include the new escrow amount.

Setting Up Payments

You can set up a loan-payment check or bill in Loan Manager, which hands off the payment info to QuickBooks so the program can record it in your company file. Although Loan Manager can handle this task one payment at a time, it can't create *recurring* payments to send the payment that's due each month. When you see the QuickBooks reminder for your loan payment, you have to run Loan Manager to generate the payment, like so:

1. **In the Loan Manager window (Banking→Loan Manager), select the loan you want to pay, and then click Set Up Payment.**

   Loan Manager opens the Set Up Payment dialog box and fills in the information for the next payment, as shown in Figure 14-16.

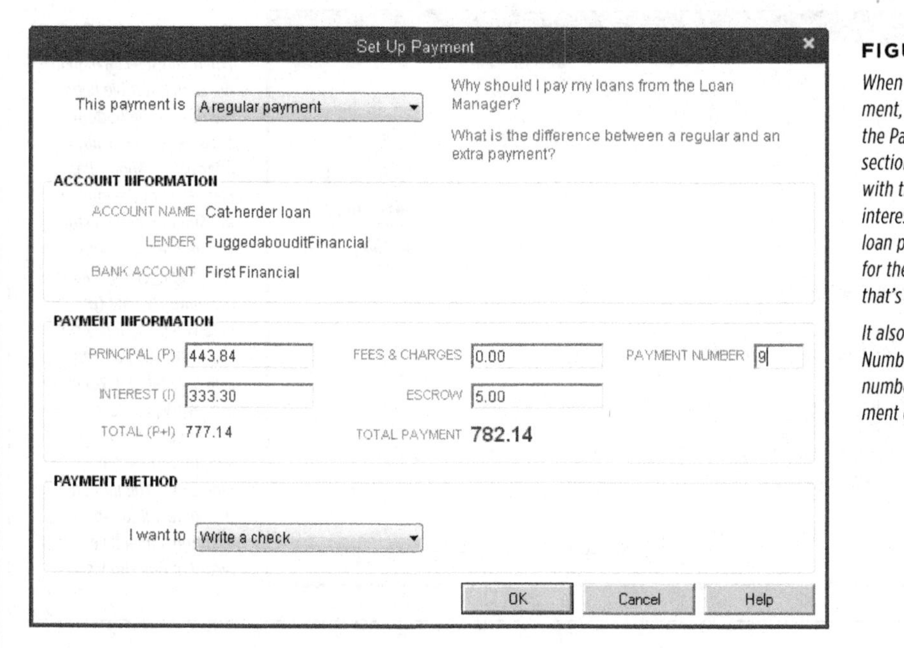

FIGURE 14-16

When you click Set Up Payment, Loan Manager fills in the Payment Information section of this dialog box with the principal and interest amounts from the loan payment schedule for the next payment that's due.

It also fills in the Payment Number box with the number of the next payment due.

NOTE To make an *extra* payment, in the "This payment is" drop-down list, choose "An extra payment." Because extra payments aren't part of the loan's payment schedule, Loan Manager changes the values in the Principal (P), Interest (I), Fees & Charges, and Escrow boxes to zero. If you want to prepay principal on your loan, type the amount that you want to prepay in the Principal (P) box. Or, to pay an annual fee, fill in the Fees & Charges box.

2. **In the "I want to" drop-down list at the bottom of the dialog box, choose "Write a check" or "Enter a bill," and then click OK.**

   Loan Manager opens QuickBooks' Write Checks or Enter Bills window, respectively, and fills in the boxes with the payment information. If you want, you can change the payment date or other values.

3. **In the Write Checks or Enter Bills window, click Save & Close.**

   The window closes and you're back in the Loan Manager window, where the value in the loan's Balance cell has been reduced by the amount of principal that the payment paid off.

If you want to print the payment schedule for your loan, in the Loan Manager window, select it in the Loan List, and then click Print. If you pay off a loan and want to remove it from Loan Manager, select the loan, and then click Remove Loan. (Removing a loan from Loan Manager doesn't delete any loan transactions or loan accounts in QuickBooks.)

NOTE If your loan payments include escrow, each payment deposits the escrow amount into your QuickBooks escrow asset account. When your loan statement shows that the lender paid expenses from escrow—like insurance or property taxes—you can record the corresponding payment in QuickBooks: Open the escrow account's register window (page 374) and, in the first blank transaction row, choose the date and the payee, such as the insurance company or the tax agency. In the Decrease field, type the payment amount (because the payment reduces the balance in the escrow account), and then click Record.

GEM IN THE ROUGH

What-If Scenarios

Because economic conditions and interest rates change, loans aren't necessarily stable. For example, if you have an adjustable-rate loan, you might want to know what your new payment amount is. Or you might want to find out whether it makes sense to refinance an existing loan when interest rates drop. Loan Manager's what-if feature is your dry-erase board for trying out loan changes before you make up your mind. When you click the What If Scenarios button, Loan Manager opens the What If Scenarios dialog box, where you can pick from different scenarios depending on whether you've already created a loan:

- **How much will I pay with a new loan?** You don't have to go through the third degree to see what a loan will cost. Choose this scenario, and then enter the requested info to evaluate the payment amounts, number of payments, total interest, and final balloon payment.
- **Evaluate two new loans**. Type in the details of two loans to see which one is better.
- **What if I change my payment amount?** This scenario is listed only if you've already created a loan in Loan Manager. Paying extra principal can shorten the length of your loan and reduce the total interest you pay. Choose this scenario and then, in the Payment Amount box, type the new amount you plan to pay each month. When you click Calculate, Loan Manager calculates your new maturity date, how much you'll pay overall, and how much you'll pay in interest.
- **What if I change my interest rate?** If you have an adjustable-rate loan set up in Loan Manager, choose this scenario to preview the changes in payment, interest, and balloon payment for a different rate (higher or lower).
- **What if I refinance my loan?** This scenario is listed only if you've already created a loan in Loan Manager. When interest rates drop, companies and individuals alike consider refinancing their debt to save money on interest. With this scenario, you type in a new term, payment, interest rate, and payment date to see whether it's worth refinancing.

The changes you make in the What If Scenarios dialog box don't change your existing loans. And if you switch to a different scenario or close the dialog box, Loan Manager doesn't save the information you've entered. So if you want a record of different scenarios, click Print after you enter the info for each one.

CHAPTER

15

Doing Payroll

When you first start your business, you may be the proud owner of every job title in your company: receptionist, sales rep, technician, bookkeeper, janitor, *and* CEO. But if your company is like most, you'll eventually hire people to help you with all those tasks.

Unless you run an all-volunteer operation, sooner or later, your employees are going to want to get paid. When that time comes, you face the daunting task of dealing with *payroll*, which is the name for all the financial records you have to keep for employees' salaries, wages, bonuses, withholdings, and deductions. If you decide to process payroll in QuickBooks, you should sign up for one of the payroll services that Intuit offers. To keep expenses low, you can choose a bare-bones service that provides only updated tax tables. At the other end of the spectrum, you can opt for Intuit's full-service payroll. Or you can compromise somewhere in the middle.

After you choose a payroll service, your next task is to set up everything QuickBooks needs to calculate payroll amounts. You can walk through each step on your own or use an interview feature built into QuickBooks. (If you opt for Intuit's full-service payroll [page 417], they do some of this setup for you.) Either way, the Payroll Setup interview keeps track of what you've done and what you still have to do.

NOTE Intuit sometimes updates its payroll services between QuickBooks editions. That way, you get the latest tax tables, compliance information, bug fixes, and enhancements right away. So to keep this book's instructions about Intuit payroll services up to date, they're not actually in the book. Instead, you can read them in online Appendix D, which is available from this book's Missing CD page at *www.missing manuals.com/cds*. (Appendix D covers Intuit's *desktop* payroll service, not its online payroll service.)

Another option is to outsource the headaches of payroll to a payroll-service company other than Intuit. If you go that route, then you simply use values from the payroll-service company's reports to create a couple of transactions in QuickBooks for each payroll—to allocate salaries and wages, payroll taxes, and any other payroll expenses to the accounts in your chart of accounts. This chapter explains how to record these payroll transactions.

If you run a sole proprietorship, partnership, or a small Sub-chapter S corporation, you can withdraw money from the company as compensation without fussing over payroll. But to take advantage of retirement savings options like a Simplified Employee Pension (SEP), you have to deal with special rules regarding eligible compensation. For sole proprietors and partners, all you have to do to determine your eligibility for a SEP is calculate your compensation, which is based on company net profits. However, a Subchapter S corporation has to pay you an actual salary for you to be eligible for a SEP plan. In this chapter, you'll learn how to record do-it-yourself payroll transactions, and how to pay yourself *without* payroll.

Getting Started with Payroll

Shortly after you hire employees, you need to write their first paychecks, so setting up payroll can't wait until employees are onboard. If you're already running payroll with a payroll service, you probably have the info you need to set up QuickBooks' payroll features. In that case, skip to page 415 to learn what Intuit's payroll services have to offer. But if you're new to payroll, read on to learn about the tax agency items you need and the payroll decisions you have to make *before* you hire anyone.

What You Need from the Government

Part of the payroll process includes withholding taxes from employees' paychecks and sending that money (along with your company's payroll taxes) to the appropriate government agencies. Before you can do that, you need to get on the government's radar. As you already know, anything tax-related spells paperwork, and payroll is no exception. Here are the IDs, accounts, and forms you need for payroll:

- **Employer Identification Number (EIN)**. If you're a sole proprietor, your Social Security number acts as your business identification number when you fill out your tax return. For any other type of company, you need an EIN. If you don't have one yet, you can apply for one online. Go to *www.irs.gov* and search for "Apply online EIN."
- **An Electronic Federal Tax Payment System (EFTPS) account**. The IRS requires that all federal taxes be paid electronically via EFTPS. (The box on page 413 briefly describes the various payroll-related federal taxes you have to pay.) To sign up for EFTPS, head to *www.eftps.gov/eftps* and click the Enroll button. Sign up using your federal EIN (see the previous bullet point). After the IRS processes your enrollment, it mails you a four-digit PIN. Once you have that, back you go to the EFTPS website to log in again and use the PIN to create a password. That's

it! You're now ready to pay your taxes electronically. When it's time to remit taxes, you log into the EFTPS website, select the tax period and payment date, and fill in the amount. (If you subscribe to Intuit's Enhanced Payroll service, you can use the E-File & Pay feature to log into the EFTPS website. That way, QuickBooks makes the payment and records the transaction. You can also tell QuickBooks to remember your EFTPS login credentials so you don't have to re-enter them each time.)

- **A state payroll account**. Each state is different. To learn about the IDs and forms that each state requires and the agencies that require them, head to *payroll.intuit.com/support/compliance*. You can also call your state's Department of Revenue to find out what you need to do.

Once you have your EIN and payroll tax accounts set up, you're ready to report and pay payroll taxes. Now all you need are some employees.

UP TO SPEED

Federal Taxes, Taxes, and More Taxes

As an employer, you have to handle two types of payroll taxes: the ones that your employees have to pay and those that your company pays. Payroll withholdings get their name because you *withhold* those taxes from your employees' paychecks. But the money you withhold isn't yours to keep: You have to send it to the IRS, the Social Security Administration, and, in some cases, your state. In addition, your company has to pay employer payroll taxes.

Here are the federal taxes you have to deal with:

- **Federal income tax**. You withhold this tax from employees' paychecks each pay period. The withholding amount is based on the info on the W-4 form each employee fills out. How often you remit taxes depends on the amount of withholdings you owe the federal government (the remittance schedule starts monthly and is due the 15th of the following month). You report these taxes on Form 941 (*www.irs.gov/pub/irs-pdf/f941.pdf*), which is due quarterly.
- **Employee portion of Social Security and Medicare**. Employees pay half the tab for these two taxes (6.2% for Social Security and 1.45% for Medicare; high earners pay an additional Medicare tax of 0.9% for wages greater than $200,000). Report Social Security and Medicare withholdings on Form 941 and remit them on the same schedule as your federal income tax.
- **Employer portion of Social Security and Medicare**. As an employer, you pay the other half of the tab for these taxes. (You report and remit them at the same time as the employee portion.)
- **Federal Unemployment (FUTA)**. This unemployment tax is *another* employer expense, so you don't withhold it from your employees' paychecks. This tax is 6 percent of wages up to $7,000 and is due in the quarter your liability reaches $500.00. You report it on Form 940 (*www.irs.gov/pub/irs-pdf/f940.pdf*), which is due in January of each year.

Employee-Related Forms You Need

Hiring employees launches the paperwork journey. Here are the forms prospective employees have to fill out (and keep on file):

- **W-4**. Each employee fills out one of these forms to specify his withholding allowance, such as single, married, and number of dependents. If employees want additional taxes withheld, they can write in the amount. If they want to change their withholdings, they simply fill in a new copy of the form. After you've activated an Intuit Payroll service, you can get a copy of this form in QuickBooks by choosing Employees→Employee Forms. You can also download this form from *www.irs.gov/pub/irs-pdf/fw4.pdf.*

- **I-9 (Employment Eligibility Verification)**. Once you make a job offer to a prospective employee, that person has to fill out this form so you can verify her identity and employment authorization. Although you don't have to submit this form to any agency, you need to keep it on file in case a government representative asks for it. (Not having it may cost you a fine.) Your employee fills in basic info like name, address, Social Security number, birthdate, and so on. The form lists documents that are acceptable forms of identification, such as a driver's license or Social Security card. After you check your employee's document and say "Yup, that's you!" you're done. After you've activated an Intuit Payroll service, you can get a copy of this form in QuickBooks by choosing Employees→Employee Forms. To download this form, head to *www.uscis.gov/files/form/i-9.pdf.*

TIP Don't file an employee's I-9 form in that person's personnel folder. Doing so can lead to legal issues if the employee's personnel file is subpoenaed in an employment lawsuit.

- **State withholding forms**. Many states simply use the withholding allowances from employees' W-4 forms as the state withholding allowance, whereas some require their own forms. If you live in Alaska, Florida, Nevada, South Dakota, Texas, or Washington, you're in luck: You don't have to withhold state income taxes. To learn about state forms, head to *payroll.intuit.com/support/compliance.*

TIP To make sure that you get all the necessary paperwork from employees, create a new-hire packet that contains the W-4, I-9, any state forms, and a copy of your company's policies. That way, you can hand packets to new employees and get all the filled-in forms back before they begin work.

Payroll Decisions You Need to Make

Before you can set up your payroll service, you need to make a few payroll-related decisions:

- **How much?** You need to decide the salary or wages you'll pay for each position, as well as other monetary aspects of positions, like benefits, overtime, commissions, and bonuses. One way to figure out how much to offer workers is to research what other employers in your area are paying and the benefits they offer for similar positions.

- **How often?** Your employees rely on receiving their paychecks on a regular schedule, such as every other week or twice a month. Payroll frequency is up to you. However, once you choose a schedule, you have to stick to it.

GEM IN THE ROUGH

Who Is an Employee?

Some employers think they can avoid the hassle of payroll by paying people as subcontractors instead. No such luck. Strict requirements determine who is and isn't an employee—and you'll pay severe penalties if you're caught trying to beat the system.

The IRS has rules for determining employment status of people providing services to your business. If you answer yes to the following questions, the worker is probably an employee:

- **Behavioral**. Does your company control or have the right to control *what* the worker does and *how* she does her job?
- **Financial**. Do you control the business aspects of the worker's job, such as how the worker is paid and whether his expenses are reimbursed? And do you provide the tools and equipment used on the job?
- **Type of relationship**. Do you have a written contract with the worker? Do you provide her with benefits, such as health insurance, vacation pay, and a pension? Will the relationship continue? Is the work performed a key aspect of your business?

For more info on employees versus independent contractors, head to *www.irs.gov/taxtopics/tc762.html*. If you still aren't sure how to classify someone, ask your accountant or tax advisor. Another option is to fill out form SS-8 (*www.irs.gov/pub/irs-pdf/fss8.pdf*) and submit it to the IRS. The IRS then notifies you whether the person is an employee or an independent contractor.

Keep in mind that a signed contract designating someone as an independent contractor doesn't make it so if the person should be an employee instead. You can't enforce an illegal contract.

- **Pay period end date and paycheck date**. The pay period end date is the day through which you pay people for the hours they work, and the paycheck date is, of course, the day you actually *pay* employees. For example, the paychecks you hand out could pay employees for hours worked through Sunday, but you don't pay your employees for those hours until the following Friday. Make sure to allow enough time between the payroll cutoff date and payday to process payroll. In addition, if you use QuickBooks Direct Deposit (page 417), it takes two days after you submit direct deposit requests for those funds to be available in employees' accounts. If you're using Intuit's Assisted Payroll service in the desktop version of QuickBooks, you have to submit your payroll and direct deposits requests by 5 p.m. two business days before payday (not including federal bank holidays).

Intuit Payroll Services

Payroll involves all sorts of important details, but fortunately *you* don't have to remember them all. Intuit offers several payroll services that handle the nitty-gritty: After you set up your Payroll items and employees, you simply fill out the hours your employees work each pay period, and the payroll service calculates paychecks, withholdings, and your employer payroll tax liability (how much your company owes). After that, all you have to do is get the money to the right places—and payroll services make that easy, too.

Intuit offers three levels of payroll service: a do-it-yourself version, a more helpful option that pitches in with the majority of payroll tasks, and a full-service option that takes care of *everything* except filling in the hours your employees work. You can sign up for either a desktop or online version of any of these service levels. This section describes what each option offers.

With an *online* Intuit payroll service, you don't have to be in the office on payday, and you don't even have to run QuickBooks. These services are available 24/7, and you can access them from anywhere with an Internet connection. You could be on vacation and *still* pay your employees on time by running payroll from your laptop, iPad, iPhone, or Android device. Intuit's online payroll services integrate with QuickBooks, so you can download your payroll info and import it into your QuickBooks company file. (To see the most current features and pricing, head to *http://payroll.intuit.com/payroll_services/online_payroll.jsp.*)

NOTE Time Tracking is an additional service that Intuit Online Payroll offers. Employees can log in and enter their hours, either by clocking in and out or by filling in a timesheet on a password-protected website. In addition, this service sends emails to remind your employees of time reporting deadlines. You then review their hours and either edit or approve them. This feature can keep you compliant with overtime rules, too.

If you use one of Intuit's *desktop* payroll services, you prepare payroll from within QuickBooks, so the data is automatically recorded in your company file.

NOTE Intuit payroll services charge by the month, not for each pay period, as many other services do. You pay the same fee whether you run payroll weekly, every two weeks, or bimonthly.

Here's what each payroll service level offers (though keep in mind that the features listed here could change after this book is published):

- **Basic Payroll** is a do-it-yourself option. You set everything up at the start. Then, for each payroll, you enter hours or payroll amounts, and QuickBooks uses tax tables to calculate payroll taxes and deductions for you. This service then spits out reports with the info you need to fill out the federal and state tax forms you have to file. Your job is to print the paychecks from QuickBooks (or use direct deposit), make tax deposits, and file your payroll tax forms.

TIP Intuit payroll services offer free phone, chat, and email support to help you get set up. So if you have any questions on how to do things, all you have to do is ask.

- **Enhanced Payroll** (the most popular) can handle preparing federal *and* state payroll forms. It provides up-to-date tax forms, fills in most of the tax-form info, and lets you make your tax deposits and file your tax forms electronically from within QuickBooks. This service sends you emails to remind you when payroll, forms, and payroll taxes are due, and to tell you when payroll is direct deposited, taxes have been paid, and tax authorities have accepted your tax forms. In QuickBooks, the Payroll Center reminds you when payroll and payroll taxes are due, and shows the status of direct deposit payments, electronic tax payments, and tax forms that you submitted through QuickBooks. It also archives your tax forms on your desktop as PDFs and displays a table of your most recently archived forms.
- **Full Service Payroll** does it all. If you opt for this service, Intuit sets up payroll *for* you. (If you used another payroll service in the past, it transfers that data into Intuit payroll.) You don't have to make federal and state payroll tax deposits, file required tax reports during the year, or prepare W-2 and W-3 forms at the end of the year—the service handles all these tasks for you. In addition, Intuit guarantees that your payroll and payroll tax deposits and filings will be accurate and on time. Of course, you have to send Intuit the correct data on time in the first place. But if this service then makes a mistake or misses a deadline, Intuit pays the resulting payroll tax penalties.

Recording Transactions from a Payroll Service

Lots of companies use outside payroll services (ADP and Paychex are two popular ones) to avoid the brain strain of figuring out tax deductions and complying with payroll regulations. When you use one of these services, you send it your payroll data. It then writes and distributes your company's payroll checks and sends you reports about the transactions it processed. It even takes care of remitting payroll taxes and other withholdings to the appropriate agencies.

None of these payroll transactions appear in your QuickBooks company file until you add them. Fortunately, you don't have to enter every last detail. You can simply create a journal entry debiting the payroll expense accounts and crediting your bank account (page 426). Or you can create a vendor for payroll and record a split transaction that distributes the money from your checking account into the appropriate expense accounts, as shown in Figure 15-1; here's how:

1. **Create a vendor for your payroll transactions.**

   On the QuickBooks Home Page, click the Vendors button. In the Vendor Center's toolbar, click New Vendor→New Vendor. You don't have to fill in all the fields in the New Vendor window; simply type something like *Payroll Service* in the Vendor Name box, and then click OK.

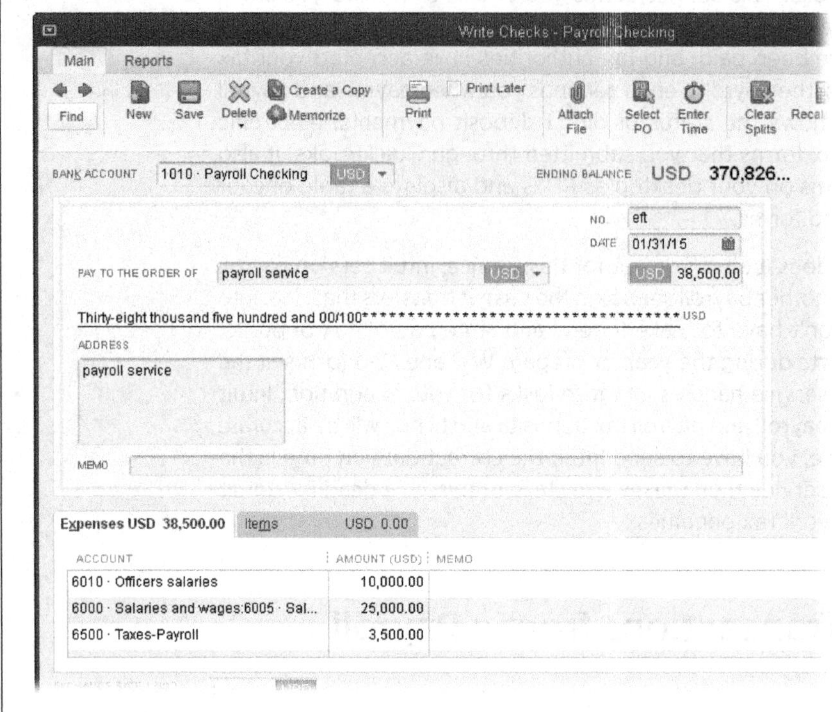

FIGURE 15-1

In most cases, your payroll falls into three categories: Officers salaries represent gross salaries for corporate officers. Salaries, as shown here (sometimes called "Salaries and wages"), represent the gross pay that employees receive on their paychecks. And payroll taxes are the employer payroll taxes that the company pays, such as Social Security and Medicare taxes.

NOTE The example in Figure 15-1 and the instructions in this numbered list apply when your employees are paid using direct deposit, where the money is deposited into their bank accounts electronically. If you *don't* use direct deposit, you also have to record the actual paychecks in QuickBooks (as explained in online Appendix D) in order to reconcile your bank account.

2. **Press Ctrl+W or choose Banking→Write Checks.**

   In the Write Checks window's Bank Account drop-down list, choose the account you use for your payroll.

3. **In the No. field, type *EFT* for "electronic funds transfer."**

   Most payroll services transfer the funds from your bank account electronically.

4. **In the Pay To The Order Of field, type the name of the payroll vendor you just set up.**

5. **If necessary, on the window's Expenses tab, fill in the Account and Amount fields for each payroll expense, as shown in Figure 15-1.**

   If the accounts are already in place but the values differ, simply edit the numbers in the Amount fields.

NOTE To record the payroll service's fee, record a separate transaction in the payroll bank account, using another vendor you create, such as Payroll Service Fees. Assign the transaction to an expense account named something like Payroll Service Fees.

6. **When the transaction is correct, click Save & Close.**

TIP If you turned on the preference to recall the last transaction (page 650), QuickBooks automatically fills in the amounts and accounts the next time you record a transaction for the payroll service.

Paying Yourself

If you own a sole proprietorship, partnership, or Subchapter S corporation (named after Subchapter S of the U.S. tax code), you can take money out of the company for your personal use. These withdrawals go by different names depending on the type of company. For a sole proprietor, the money you withdraw is called *owner's draw*, or simply *draw*. Partners withdraw money and call it *partners' draw*. And if you're a shareholder in a Subchapter S corporation, the money you withdraw is called a *shareholders' distribution*.

If you don't pay yourself a salary, you pay taxes when the company's profits flow through to your personal tax return. However, if you're a Subchapter S shareholder, you can pay yourself using a *combination* of salary and shareholders' distribution. That way, you can contribute to a pension plan, like a SEP, based on your corporate salary.

This section explains how to pay yourself (and other partners and shareholders) no matter which type of business structure you've established.

Taking a Draw

As your company makes money, you can withdraw funds. The easiest way to do this in QuickBooks is to write a check (page 202) made out to you, as shown in Figure 15-2. If you're a sole proprietor and own your own company, choosing the Owner's Contribution/Draw account for the check tells QuickBooks to post the check to show that you've withdrawn equity from your company. You use the same process if you're a partner except that you choose the Partners' Contribution/Draw account instead. The Shareholders' Distribution account shown in Figure 15-2 represents the draw account for shareholders in a Subchapter S corporation.

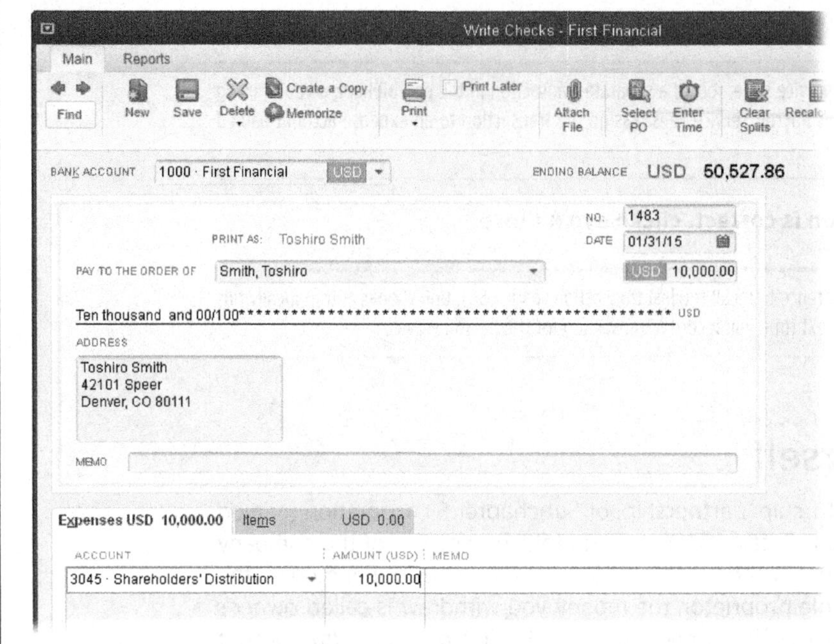

FIGURE 15-2

In the Write Checks window, on the Expenses tab, choose the draw account in the first blank Account cell, as shown here.

When you save the check, QuickBooks debits that equity account, which decreases its balance.

NOTE If you're a sole proprietor, you typically make an initial investment of capital into your business. You record this investment into the Owner's Contribution/Draw equity account as explained on page 434. If your company runs low on cash later on, you can contribute more money and record this addition in the same account.

Reclassifying Shareholders' Distribution to Salary

If shareholders withdraw money from a Subchapter S corporation for personal use, you may want to turn some of that shareholders' distribution into salary so, for example, the partners can qualify to contribute to a retirement account. To prepare payroll in this situation, you have to calculate the applicable payroll withholdings (like federal and state taxes, Social Security, and Medicare) and company payroll taxes. (Alternatively, you can ask your accountant or bookkeeper to calculate them for you.) You also have to record payroll checks (if you issue them) and checks that you send to federal and state tax agencies for withholdings and payroll taxes, as shown in Figure 15-3. And don't forget about preparing and filing federal and state payroll tax returns, including forms W-2 and W-3.

If partners take shareholders' distributions, you can use a journal entry to recategorize some of those dollars as salary. For example, you could assign the money to a salary expense account called Officers Salaries, as shown in Figure 15-4. (You'll learn about the Payroll Tax Payable credit in the next section, and you can read about how to handle the employer portion of payroll tax in online Appendix D, available from this book's Missing CD page at *www.missingmanuals.com*.)

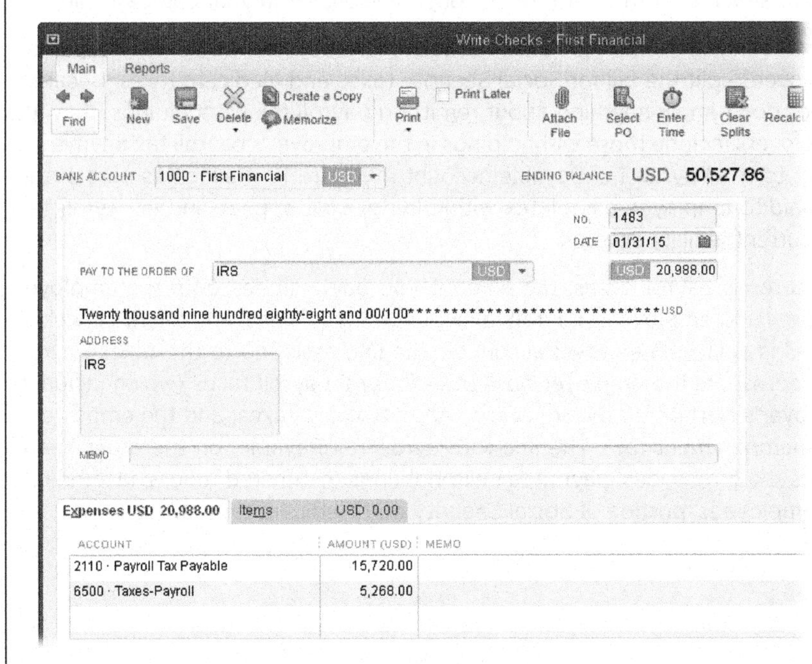

FIGURE 15-3

If you pay shareholders' salaries in a Subchapter S corporation, the payroll taxes you remit to the IRS are split between two different accounts, as shown here: a liability account for the owner's, partners', or shareholders' payroll withholdings (here, that's Payroll Tax Payable) and an expense account for the employer payroll taxes (Taxes-Payroll).

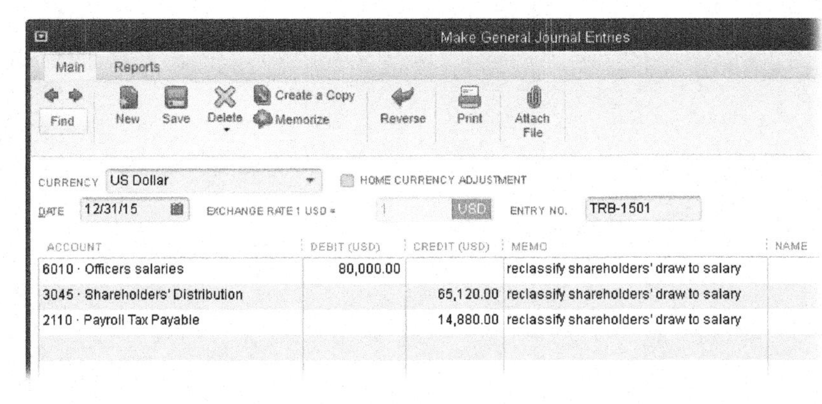

FIGURE 15-4

To recategorize a distribution as salary, you credit the Shareholders' Distribution equity account and debit the salary expense account. The credit to the Shareholder's Distribution equity account increases its balance (which decreased when you took the distribution), whereas the debit to the salary expense account shows your salary as an expense. The Payroll Tax Payable amount represents your employee portion of payroll tax withholdings.

RECLASSIFYING PAYROLL WITHHOLDINGS

After you reclassify shareholders' distributions as salary, you still have to account for your payroll withholdings (such as the federal and state income taxes you pay) and other payroll taxes. When you remit payroll taxes to tax agencies like the IRS, you have to allocate them to the correct payroll accounts in your company file.

The journal entry in Figure 15-4 set your salary to $80,000. However, companies and employees split the bill for Social Security taxes and Medicare taxes. Because employees don't know anything about remitting payroll tax withholdings, they let their employers include those withholdings in the employer's payroll tax payments. The credit to the Payroll Tax Payable account in Figure 15-4 allocates part of the salaries paid to employee payroll tax withholdings so it appears in the Payroll Tax Payable current liability account.

When you remit payroll taxes, the amount you pay includes *both* the employer payroll taxes and employees' payroll tax withholdings. That's why the IRS check in Figure 15-3 is split between two accounts. The line assigned to the Taxes-Payroll account represents the employer portion of federal payroll taxes (which includes the employer's portion of Social Security and Medicare taxes, and the employer's federal unemployment tax). The line for Payroll Tax Payable, on the other hand, represents the employees' payroll tax withholdings (estimated federal income tax and the employees' portion of Social Security and Medicare taxes).

CHAPTER

16

Making Journal Entries

Most of the time, you don't need to know double-entry accounting (page xxi) to use QuickBooks. When you write checks, receive payments, and perform many other tasks in QuickBooks, the program creates transactions that unobtrusively handle the double-entry accounting *for* you. But every once in a while, such transactions can't help, and your only choice is moving money around directly between accounts.

In the accounting world, these direct manipulations are known as *journal entries.* For example, if you posted income to your only income account but have since decided that you need several income accounts to track the money you make, journal entries are the way to reclassify money in that original income account to the new ones.

TIP Although journal entries are the only solution for some tasks in QuickBooks, it's best to use QuickBooks transactions instead whenever possible. By using transactions, your QuickBooks reports will contain all the info you expect, and you'll have the details you need if the IRS starts asking questions.

The steps for creating a journal entry are deceptively easy; it's assigning money to accounts *in the correct way* that's maddeningly difficult for weekend accountants. And, unfortunately, QuickBooks doesn't have any magic looking glass that makes these assignments crystal clear. This chapter gets you started by showing you how to create journal entries, and provides examples of journal entries you're likely to need. However, you'll want to talk to your bookkeeper or accountant about the specific journal entries you need and the accounts to use in them.

NOTE In the accounting world, you'll hear the term "journal entry" and see it abbreviated JE. However, QuickBooks uses the term "*general* journal entry" and the corresponding abbreviation GJE. Don't worry: These terms and abbreviations are interchangeable.

Balancing Debit and Credit Amounts

In double-entry accounting, both sides of any transaction have to balance, as Figure 16-1 shows. When you move money between accounts, you increase the balance in one account and decrease the balance in the other—just as shaking some money out of your piggy bank decreases your savings balance and increases the money in your pocket. These changes in value are called *debits* and *credits*. (Whether the debit and credit increase or decrease the account balance depends on the type of account, as Table 16-1 shows.) If you commit anything about accounting to memory, it should be the definitions of debist and credits, because they're the key to creating successful journal entries, generating accurate financial reports, and understanding what your accountant is talking about.

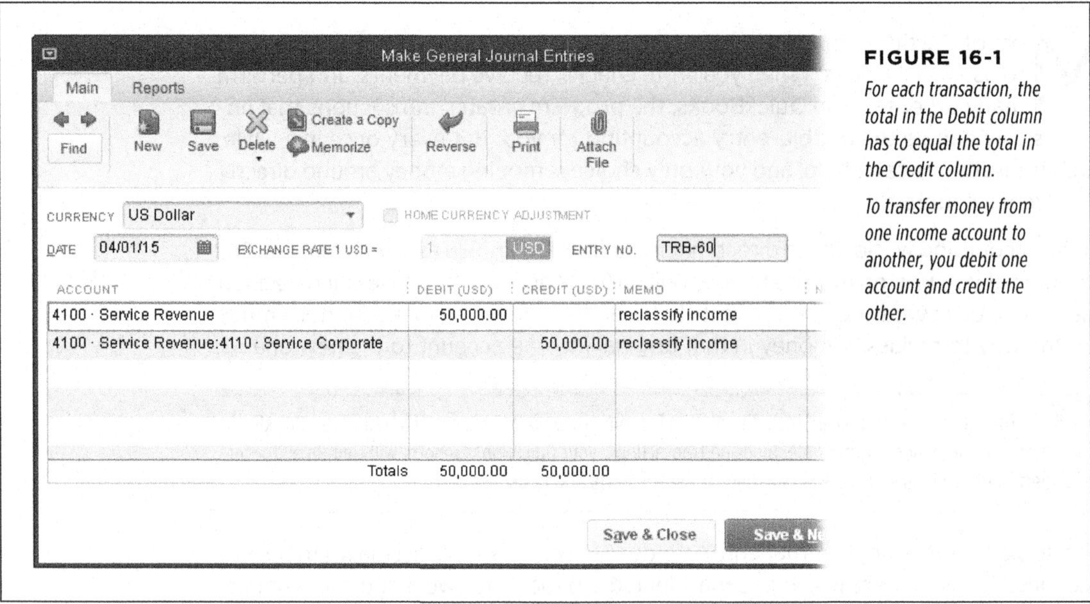

FIGURE 16-1

For each transaction, the total in the Debit column has to equal the total in the Credit column.

To transfer money from one income account to another, you debit one account and credit the other.

Table 16-1 shows what debits and credits do for different types of accounts and can take some of the pain out of creating journal entries. For example, buying a machine is a *debit* to the equipment asset account because it increases the value of the equipment (assets) you own. A loan payment is a *debit* to your loan account because it decreases your loan balance (a liability). And (here's a real mind-bender) a credit card charge is a *credit* to your credit card liability account because purchases on credit increase the amount you owe.

TABLE 16-1 *How debits and credits change the values in accounts*

ACCOUNT TYPE	DEBIT	CREDIT
Asset	Increases balance	Decreases balance
Liability	Decreases balance	Increases balance
Equity	Decreases balance	Increases balance
Income	Decreases balance	Increases balance
Expense	Increases balance	Decreases balance

NOTE One reason that debits and credits are confusing is that the words have the *exact opposite* meanings when your bank uses them. In your personal banking, a debit to your bank account decreases its balance, and a credit to that account increases its balance.

As you'll see in examples in this chapter, you can have more than one debit or credit entry in one journal entry. For example, when you depreciate equipment, you can include a debit for the overall depreciation expense and a separate credit for the depreciation on each piece of equipment.

Some Reasons to Use Journal Entries

Here are a few of the more common reasons that businesses use journal entries:

- **Setting up opening balances in accounts**. You can fill in the opening balance for most of your balance sheet accounts with a single journal entry based on your trial balance from your previous accounting system. The box on page 429 explains how.
- **Reassigning accounts**. As you work with QuickBooks, you might find that the accounts you originally created don't track your business the way you want. For example, suppose you started with one income account for *everything* you sell—services and products alike. But now you want two income accounts: one for income from services and another for income from product sales. To move income from your original account to the correct new account, you debit the income from the original account and credit it to the new account, as described on page 431.
- **Correcting account assignments**. If you assigned an expense to the wrong account, you or your accountant can create a journal entry to reassign the expense to the correct account. If you've developed a reputation for misassigning income and expenses, your accountant might ask you to assign any transactions you're unsure about to an uncategorized income or expense account. That way, when she gets your company file at the end of the year, she can create journal entries to assign those transactions correctly. You can verify that the assignments and account balances are correct by running a Trial Balance report (page 442).

- **Reassigning jobs**. If a customer hires you for several jobs, that customer might ask you to apply a payment, credit, or expense from one job to another. For example, if expenses come after one job is complete, your customer might want to apply them to the job still in progress. QuickBooks doesn't have a feature specifically for transferring money between jobs, but a journal entry does the trick, as page 432 explains.
- **Reassigning classes**. If you use QuickBooks' class feature, journal entries can transfer income or expenses from one class to another. For example, nonprofits often use classes to assign income to programs. If you need to reassign money to a different program, create a journal entry that has debit and credit entries for the same income account but changes the class (see page 428).
- **Depreciating assets**. Each year that you own a depreciable asset, you decrease its value in the appropriate asset account in your chart of accounts. Because no real cash changes hands, you use a journal entry to handle depreciation. As you'll learn on page 433, a journal entry for depreciation debits the depreciation expense account (increasing its value) and credits the asset account (decreasing its value).
- **Recording transactions for a payroll service**. If you use a third-party payroll service like Paychex or ADP, the payroll company sends you reports. You can then use journal entries to get the numbers from those reports into your company file where you need them. For example, you can reclassify some of your owner's draw as salary and make other payroll-related transformations, as page 420 explains.
- **Recording year-end transactions**. The end of the year is a popular time for journal entries, whether your accountant is fixing your more creative transactions or you're creating journal entries for noncash transactions before you prepare your taxes. For example, if you run a small business out of your home, you might want to show a portion of your utility bills as expenses for your home office. When you create a journal entry for this transaction, you debit the office utilities account and credit an equity account for your owner's contributions to the company.

Creating Journal Entries

In essence, every transaction you create in QuickBooks is a journal entry. For example, when you write checks, the program balances the debits and credits behind the scenes. When you want to *explicitly* create journal entries in QuickBooks, you use the Make General Journal Entries window. Here are the basic steps:

1. **Choose Company→Make General Journal Entries.**

   Or, if the Chart of Accounts window is open, right-click anywhere in the window, and then choose Make General Journal Entries on the shortcut menu, or click Activities→Make General Journal Entries.

2. **In the Make General Journal Entries window, choose the date you want associated with this journal entry.**

   If you're creating a journal entry to reassign income or an expense to the correct account, use today's date. However, when you or your accountant make end-of-year journal entries—to add the current year's depreciation, say—it's common to use the last day of the fiscal year instead.

NOTE If you turn on QuickBooks' multiple currency preference (page 656), the Make General Journal Entries window includes boxes for the currency and the exchange rate. If you select an account that uses a foreign currency in a journal-entry line, QuickBooks fills in the exchange rate and asks you to confirm that the rate is correct. If it isn't, open the Currency List (choose Lists→Currency List) and update the exchange rate for that currency.

3. **If you want to change the number that QuickBooks automatically assigned to this journal entry, specify a different number by typing it in the Entry No. box.**

   Entry numbers can contain letters, numbers, *and* punctuation. If you type an entry number value that includes a number, then the *next* time you create a journal entry, QuickBooks fills in the Entry No. box by incrementing the one you typed. For example, suppose your accountant adds several journal entries at the end of the year and uses the numbers ACCT-1, ACCT-2, ACCT-3, and so on. When you begin using the file again, you can type a new value to restart your sequence, such as *TRB-40 or 40TRB*. When you create your next journal entry, QuickBooks automatically fills in the Entry No. box with TRB-41 or 41TRB, respectively.

TIP If you don't want QuickBooks to number journal entries automatically, you can turn off this feature in the program's Accounting preferences (page 636).

4. **In the first Account cell, choose the account you want to debit or credit.**

   Every line of every journal entry has to have an account assigned. So once you enter values in this row, when you click the Account cell in the next row, QuickBooks automatically enters the offsetting balance, as shown in Figure 16-2.

5. **If you want to debit the account you just selected, in the same row of the window's table, type the amount in the Debit cell. To credit the account instead, type the amount in the Credit cell.**

   The first row of your journal entry can be either a debit or a credit. However, most accountants start journal entries with a debit.

6. **Fill in the Memo cell with a brief description of the journal entry's purpose.**

   Entering a memo is a huge help when you go back to review your journal entries. For example, if you're reclassifying an uncategorized expense, type something like "Reclassify expense to correct account." For depreciation, you can include the dates covered by the journal entry.

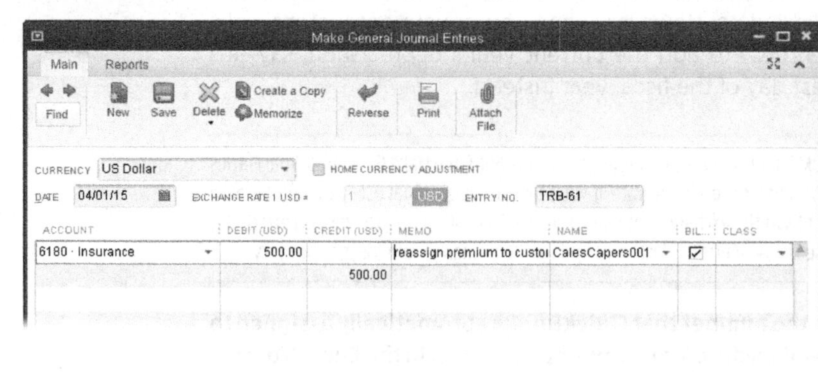

FIGURE 16-2

The Debit column's total has to match the Credit column's total. So if the first line you enter is a debit, QuickBooks helpfully enters the same amount in the second line's Credit column, as shown here. If your first line is a credit, QuickBooks puts the same amount in the second line's Debit column.

NOTE In QuickBooks Premier and Enterprise editions, the "Autofill memo in general journal entry" preference tells the program to fill each subsequent Memo cell with the text from the first one. To adjust this setting, choose Edit→Preferences→Accounting, and then click the My Preferences tab.

7. **If you're debiting or crediting an AR or AP account, choose an option in the Name cell, as explained in the box on page 429.**

   You also fill in this cell if you're creating a journal entry for billable expenses and want to assign the expenses to a customer or job. When you choose a name in this cell, QuickBooks automatically puts a checkmark in the "Billable?" cell, as shown in Figure 16-2, which reassigns some of your existing expenses to be billable to the customer or job. If you don't want to make the value billable to the customer (for example, to assign expenses to a customer's job to reflect its true profitability), then click the checkmark to turn it off.

8. **If you use classes, choose a class for each row to keep your class reports accurate.**

   If you're creating a journal entry to reassign income or expenses to a different class, select the same account on each row but different classes.

9. **Repeat steps 4–8 to fill in the second row of the journal entry.**

   If the offsetting value that QuickBooks adds to the second row is what you want, all you have to do is choose the account for that row, fill in the other cells (if necessary), and then click Save & Close.

   If the second row doesn't balance the Debit and Credit columns, continue adding additional rows until you've added debit and credit amounts that balance.

10. **When the debit and credit columns' totals are the same, click Save & Close to save the journal entry and close the Make General Journal Entries window.**

    If you want to create another journal entry, click Save & New instead.

TIP To display an existing journal entry, at the Make General Journal Entries window's top left, click the left or right arrow to display the previous or next journal entry, respectively. You can also track down a journal entry by clicking the Find button below these arrows. In the Find General Journal Entries window, fill in the fields that identify the journal entry you're looking for—such as the name, date, entry number, or amount—and then click Find.

WORKAROUND WORKSHOP

Creating Opening Balances with Journal Entries

QuickBooks has rules about Accounts Payable (AP) and Accounts Receivable (AR) accounts in journal entries. Each journal entry can have only one AP or AR account, and that account can appear on only one line of the journal entry. And if you add an AP account, you also need to choose a vendor in the Name cell. (For AR accounts, you have to choose a *customer's* name in the Name cell.)

You can get around QuickBooks' AP and AR limitations by setting up the opening balances in all your accounts with a journal entry based on your trial balance (page 442) from your previous accounting system. Simply create the journal entry without the amounts for Accounts Payable and Accounts Receivable, as shown in Figure 16-3.

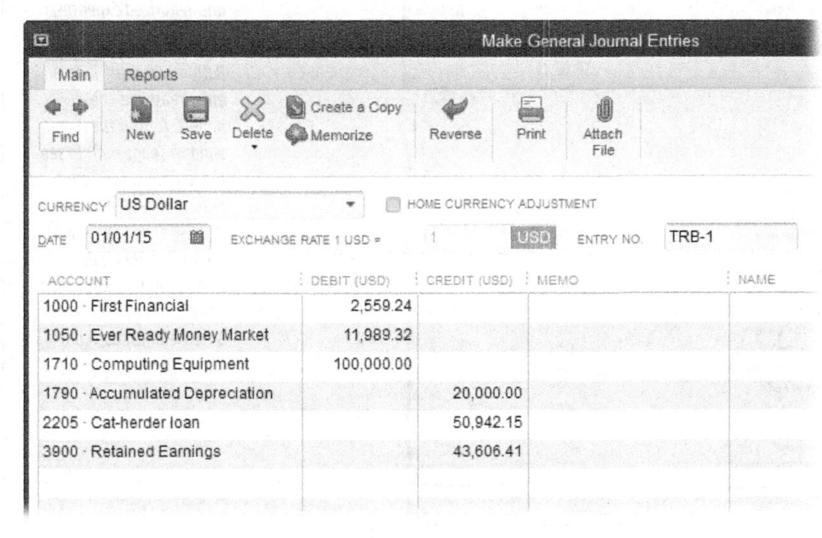

FIGURE 16-3

When you use journal entries to create opening balances, you have to adjust the values in your equity account (like retained earnings) to reflect the omission of AP and AR. Then you can create your open customer invoices and unpaid vendor bills to build the values for Accounts Receivable and Accounts Payable.

When your AP and AR account balances match the values on the trial balance, the equity account will also match its trial balance value.

Checking Journal Entries

If you stare off into space and start mumbling, "Debit entries increase asset accounts" every time you create a journal entry, it's wise to check that the journal entry did what you wanted. Those savvy in the ways of accounting can visualize debits and offsetting credits in their heads, but for novices, thinking about the changes you expect in your profit and loss report or balance sheet is easier.

For example, if you plan to create a journal entry to reassign expenses in the Uncategorized Expenses account to their proper expense-account homes, you'd expect to see the value in the Uncategorized Expenses account drop to zero and the values in the correct expense accounts increase. Figure 16-4 shows how to use a Profit & Loss report (page 445) to check your journal entries.

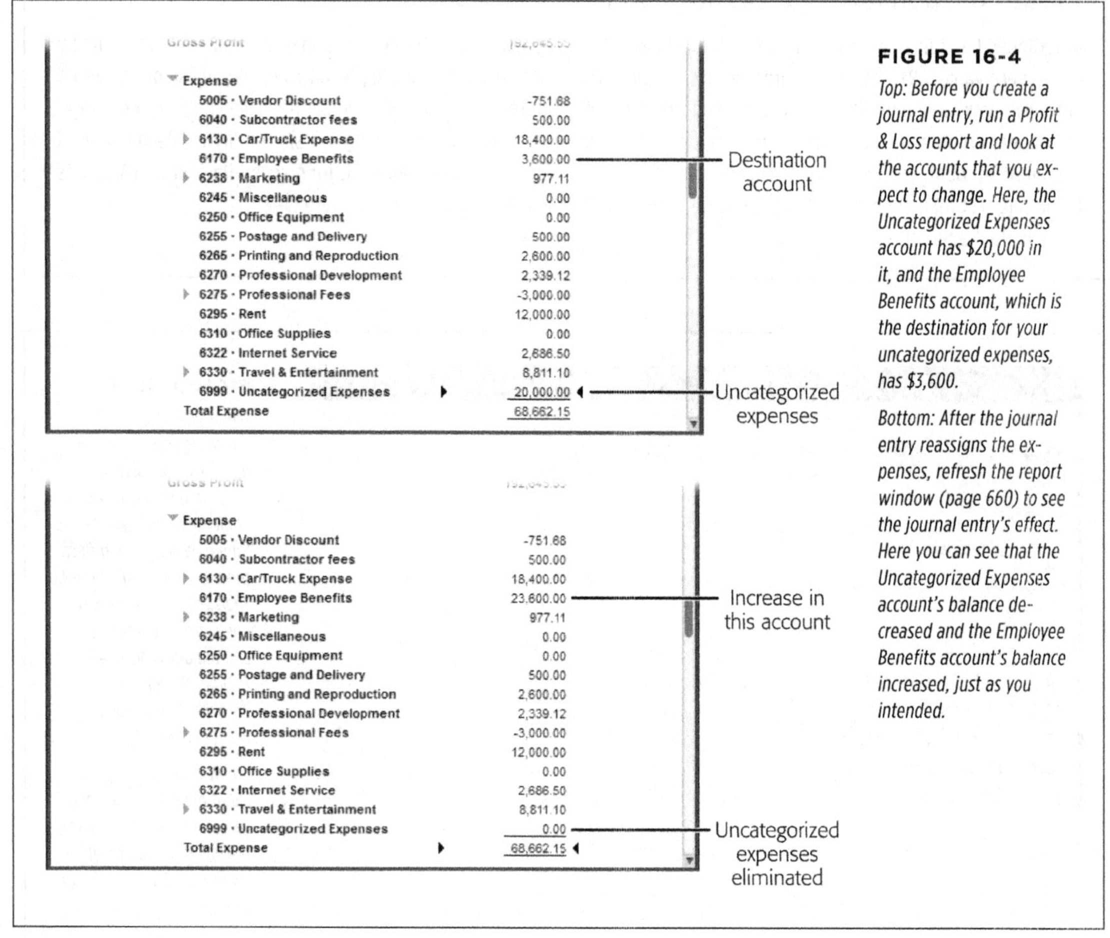

Expense	
5005 · Vendor Discount	-751.68
6040 · Subcontractor fees	500.00
6130 · Car/Truck Expense	18,400.00
6170 · Employee Benefits	3,600.00
6238 · Marketing	977.11
6245 · Miscellaneous	0.00
6250 · Office Equipment	0.00
6255 · Postage and Delivery	500.00
6265 · Printing and Reproduction	2,600.00
6270 · Professional Development	2,339.12
6275 · Professional Fees	-3,000.00
6295 · Rent	12,000.00
6310 · Office Supplies	0.00
6322 · Internet Service	2,686.50
6330 · Travel & Entertainment	8,811.10
6999 · Uncategorized Expenses	20,000.00
Total Expense	68,662.15

Expense	
5005 · Vendor Discount	-751.68
6040 · Subcontractor fees	500.00
6130 · Car/Truck Expense	18,400.00
6170 · Employee Benefits	23,600.00
6238 · Marketing	977.11
6245 · Miscellaneous	0.00
6250 · Office Equipment	0.00
6255 · Postage and Delivery	500.00
6265 · Printing and Reproduction	2,600.00
6270 · Professional Development	2,339.12
6275 · Professional Fees	-3,000.00
6295 · Rent	12,000.00
6310 · Office Supplies	0.00
6322 · Internet Service	2,686.50
6330 · Travel & Entertainment	8,811.10
6999 · Uncategorized Expenses	0.00
Total Expense	68,662.15

FIGURE 16-4

Top: Before you create a journal entry, run a Profit & Loss report and look at the accounts that you expect to change. Here, the Uncategorized Expenses account has $20,000 in it, and the Employee Benefits account, which is the destination for your uncategorized expenses, has $3,600.

Bottom: After the journal entry reassigns the expenses, refresh the report window (page 660) to see the journal entry's effect. Here you can see that the Uncategorized Expenses account's balance decreased and the Employee Benefits account's balance increased, just as you intended.

NOTE Some journal entries affect both Balance Sheet and Profit & Loss reports. For example, as you'll learn on page 433, a depreciation journal entry uses an asset account (which appears only in the Balance Sheet report) and an expense account (which appears only in the Profit & Loss report). In situations like this, you have to review *both* reports to verify your numbers.

Reclassifications and Corrections

As you work with your QuickBooks file, you might realize that you want to use different accounts. For example, as you expand the services you provide, you might switch from one top-level income account to several specific income accounts. Expense accounts are also prone to change—like when you split the Home Office account into separate accounts for utilities, insurance, and repairs, for example.

Any type of account is a candidate for restructuring, as one building grows into a stable of commercial properties, say, or you move from a single mortgage to a bevy of mortgages, notes, and loans. Whatever the situation, journal entries can help you put funds in the proper accounts.

Reclassifying Accounts

Whether you want to shift funds between accounts because you decide to categorize your finances differently or because you simply made a mistake, you're moving money between accounts of the same type. The benefit to this type of journal entry is that you have to think hard about only *one* side of the transaction—as long as you pick the first debit or credit correctly, QuickBooks handles the other side for you.

The debits and credits you choose are the opposite for income and expense accounts. For example, Figure 16-1 shows how to reclassify income, where you debit the original income account to decrease its value and credit the new income accounts to increase their value. Figure 16-5 shows how to reclassify expenses, in which you credit the original expense account to decrease its value and debit the new expense accounts to increase their value.

TIP Accountants sometimes create what are known as *reversing journal entries*, which are journal entries that move money in one direction on one date, and then move the money back to where it came from on another date. Reversing journal entries are common at the end of the year, when you need your books configured one way to prepare your taxes and another way for your day-to-day bookkeeping. To create a reversing journal entry that uses the same accounts—but with opposite assignments for debits and credits—first, in the Make General Journal Entries window, display the journal entry you want to reverse. Then, at the top of the window, click the Reverse icon.

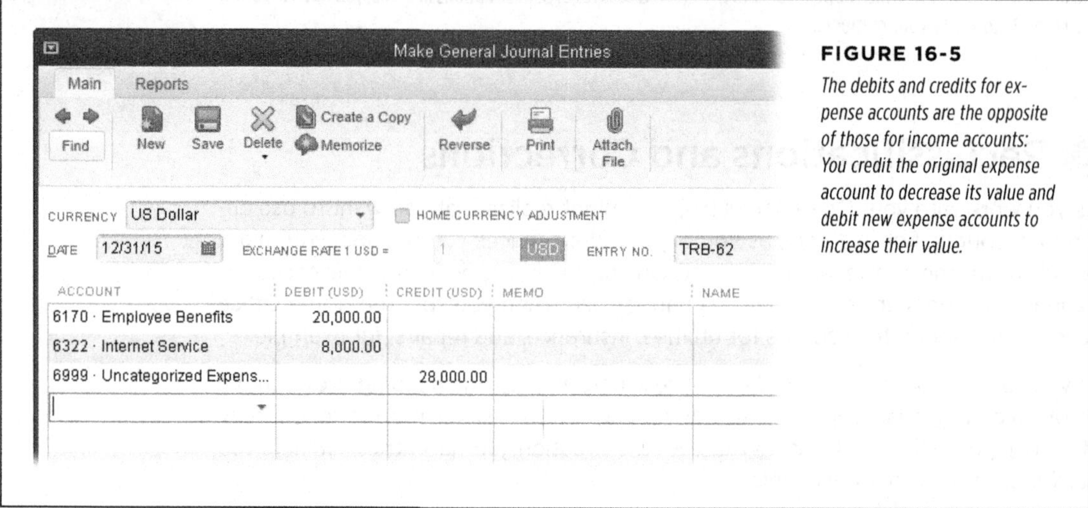

FIGURE 16-5

The debits and credits for expense accounts are the opposite of those for income accounts: You credit the original expense account to decrease its value and debit new expense accounts to increase their value.

Reassigning Jobs

If you need to transfer money between different jobs for the same customer, journal entries are the answer. For example, a customer might ask you to apply a credit from one job to another because the job with the credit is already complete.

When you move money between jobs, you're transferring that money into and out of Accounts Receivable. Because QuickBooks allows only one AR account per journal entry, you need *two* journal entries to transfer the credit completely. (Figure 10-34 on page 283 shows what these journal entries look like.) You also need a special account to hold the credit transfers; an Other Expense account called something like "Clearing Account" will do. After you have the holding account in place, here's how the two journal entries work:

- **Transfer the credit from the first job to the holding account**. In the first journal entry, debit Accounts Receivable for the amount of the credit. (Choose the customer and job in the Name cell.) This half of the journal entry removes the credit from the job's balance. In the second row of the journal entry's table, choose the holding account. The amount is already in the Credit cell, which is where you want it for moving the amount into the holding account.
- **Transfer the money from the holding account to the second job**. In this journal entry, debit the holding account for the money you're moving. Then the AR account receives the amount in its Credit cell. In the Name cell in the AR account row, choose the customer and the second job.

Recording Depreciation with Journal Entries

When you own an asset, such as the Deluxe Cat-o-matic Cat Herder, the machine loses value as it ages and clogs with fur balls. *Depreciation* is an accounting concept, intimately tied to IRS rules, that reduces the value of the machine and lets your financial reports show a more accurate picture of how the money you spend on assets links to the income your company earns. (See the box on page 435 for an example of how depreciation works.)

Typically, you'll calculate depreciation in a spreadsheet so you can also see the asset's current depreciated value and how much more it will depreciate. But depreciation doesn't deal with hard cash, which is why you need to record it with a journal entry. Unlike some journal entries, which can use a wide range of accounts, depreciation journal entries are easy to create because the accounts you can choose are limited. Here's how it works:

- The **debit account** is an expense account, usually called Depreciation Expense. (If you don't have a Depreciation Expense account, see page 55 to learn how to create one.)
- The **credit account** is a fixed asset account called something like Less Accumulated Depreciation. Figure 16-6 (top) shows how to set up your fixed asset accounts for things like machinery, vehicles, and furniture. You create a parent fixed asset account called Depreciable Assets and then create separate fixed asset subaccounts within that account so you can see the total value of all your fixed assets on your balance sheet. The Accumulated Depreciation account (which you also create) appears after the depreciable asset accounts at the same level as the parent Depreciable Assets account, so you can see how much depreciation you've deducted.

TIP If you depreciate the same amount each year, memorize the first depreciation transaction you create (page 321). The following year, when it's time to enter depreciation, press Ctrl+T to open the Memorized Transaction List window, select the depreciation transaction, and then click Enter Transaction.

Another way to copy a journal entry is to open the Make General Journal Entries window and then click the Previous button (the left arrow) until you see the journal entry you want. Then right-click the window and choose Duplicate Journal Entry from the shortcut menu. Make the changes you want, and then click Save & Close.

For a depreciation journal entry, you want to reduce the value of the fixed asset account and add value to the Depreciation Expense account. If you remember that debit entries increase the value of expense accounts, you can figure out that the debit goes with the expense account and the credit goes to the fixed asset account. Figure 16-6 shows how depreciation debits and credits work.

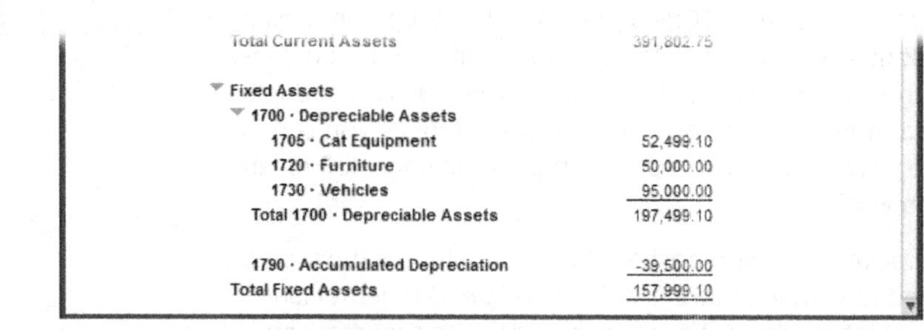

Total Current Assets	391,802.75
Fixed Assets	
1700 · Depreciable Assets	
1705 · Cat Equipment	52,499.10
1720 · Furniture	50,000.00
1730 · Vehicles	95,000.00
Total 1700 · Depreciable Assets	197,499.10
1790 · Accumulated Depreciation	-39,500.00
Total Fixed Assets	157,999.10

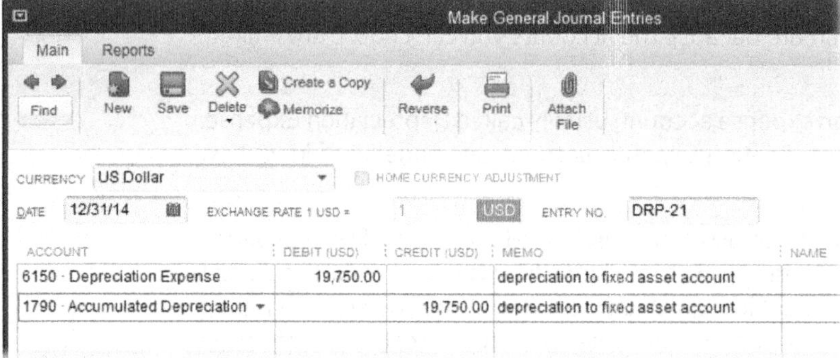

ACCOUNT	DEBIT (USD)	CREDIT (USD)	MEMO	NAME
6150 · Depreciation Expense	19,750.00		depreciation to fixed asset account	
1790 · Accumulated Depreciation		19,750.00	depreciation to fixed asset account	

FIGURE 16-6

Top: A parent fixed asset account called Depreciable Assets acts as a container for all your fixed assets so you can see the total fixed asset value on your balance sheet. The Accumulated Depreciation account follows the parent Depreciable Assets account so you can see the depreciation you've deducted.

Bottom: If you have several assets to depreciate, the commonly accepted approach is to create a spreadsheet showing the depreciation for each asset. In QuickBooks, you simply record a single Depreciation Expense debit for the total of all the depreciation credits, as shown here.

Recording Owner's Contributions

Most attorneys suggest that you contribute some cash to get your company off the ground. However, you might make *noncash* contributions to the company, like your home computer, printer, and other office equipment. Then, as you run your business from your home, you may want to allocate a portion of your mortgage interest, utility bills, homeowners' insurance premiums, home repairs, and other house-related expenses to your company. In both these situations, journal entries are the way to get money into the accounts in your chart of accounts.

TIP If you write a personal check to jump-start your company's checking account balance, simply record a deposit to your business checking account and assign that deposit to your owner's equity account.

UP TO SPEED

How Depreciation Works

When your company depreciates assets, you add dollars here, subtract dollars there—and none of those dollars are real. It sounds like funny money, but depreciation is an accounting concept that presents a more realistic picture of financial performance. To see how it works, here's an example of what happens when a company depreciates a large purchase:

Suppose your company buys a Deep Thought supercomputer for $500,000. You spent $500,000, and you now own an asset worth $500,000. Your company's balance sheet moves that money from your bank account to a fixed asset account, so your total assets remain the same.

The problem arises when you sell the computer, perhaps 10 years later when it would make a fabulous boat anchor. If you don't depreciate the computer, the moment you sell it, its value plummets from $500,000 to your selling price—$1,000, say. This decrease in value shows up as an expense, putting a huge dent in your profits for the 10th year.

Shareholders don't like it when profits change dramatically from year to year—up *or* down. With depreciation, you can spread the cost of a big purchase over several years, which does a better job of matching expenses to the revenue generated by the asset. As a result, shareholders can see how well you use assets to generate income.

Depreciation calculations come in several flavors: straight-line, sum of the years' digits, and double declining balance. Straight-line depreciation is the easiest and most common. To calculate annual straight-line depreciation over the life of the asset, subtract the *salvage* value (how much the asset will be worth when you sell it) from the purchase price, and then divide by the number of years of useful life, like so:

- Purchase price: $500,000
- Expected salvage value after 10 years: $1,000
- Useful life: the 10 years you expect to run the computer
- Annual depreciation: $499,000 divided by 10, which equals $49,900

Every year, you use the computer to make money for your business, and you show $49,900 as an equipment expense associated with that income. On your books, the value of the Deep Thought computer drops by another $49,900 each year, until the balance reaches the $1,000 salvage value at the end of the 10th year. This decrease in value each year keeps your balance sheet (page 451) more accurate and avoids the sudden drop in asset value in year 10.

The other methods—which are more complex—depreciate assets faster in the first few years (called *accelerated depreciation*), making for big tax write-offs in a hurry. Page 433 explains how to record journal entries for depreciation, but your best bet is to ask your accountant how to post depreciation in your QuickBooks accounts.

Recording Initial Noncash Contributions

When you contribute equipment to your company, you've already paid for the equipment, so you want its value to show up in your company file. You can't use the Write Checks window to make that transfer, but a journal entry can record that contribution:

- Credit the owner's equity account (or, if your company is a corporation, the common stock account) with the value of the equipment you're contributing to the company.
- Debit the equipment asset account so its balance shows the value of the equipment that now belongs to the company.

Recording Home-Office Expenses

If you use a home office for your work, the money you spent on home-office expenses is already out the door, but those expenditures are equivalent to personal funds you contribute to your business. If your company is a corporation, you credit your equity account with the amount of these home-office expenses. Here's how you show this contribution in QuickBooks:

- Credit the total home-office expenses to an equity account for your shareholders' distribution or owner's contributions to the company.
- Debit the expense accounts for each type of home-office expense, as shown in Figure 16-7.

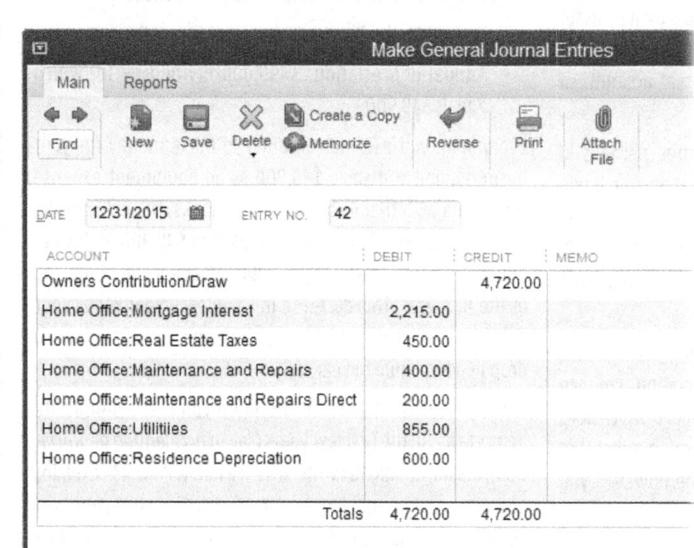

FIGURE 16-7

After you credit the owner's contribution account and debit the home-office expense accounts, your home-office expenses show up in the Profit & Loss report (page 445) and your owner's contribution appears on the Balance Sheet (page 451).

TIP Another way to handle a home office is to charge your company rent for your office space. That way you, as the homeowner, have rental property, so you can depreciate the portion of your home rented to your company. (However, this depreciation complicates things down the road when you sell your home.) If your company is a corporation, it gets to take a tax deduction for rent on its corporate tax return.

CHAPTER

17

Performing Year-End Tasks

As if your typical workday isn't hectic enough, the end of the year brings with it an assortment of additional bookkeeping and accounting tasks. As long as you've kept on top of your bookkeeping during the year, you can delegate most of these year-end tasks to QuickBooks with just a few clicks. (If you shrugged off your data entry during the year, even the mighty QuickBooks can't help.) This chapter describes the tasks you have to perform at the end of each fiscal year (or other fiscal period, for that matter) and how to delegate them to QuickBooks. (The box on page 439 describes a QuickBooks feature that helps you *remember* these various tasks.)

Checking for Problems

If you work with an accountant, you may never run a report from the Reports→Accountant & Taxes submenu unless your accountant asks you to. But if you prepare your own tax returns, running the following reports at the end of each year will help sniff out any problems:

- The **Audit Trail** report (Reports→Accountant & Taxes→Audit Trail) is especially important if several people work on your company file and transactions seem to disappear or change. QuickBooks' audit trail feature is always turned on, keeping track of changes to transactions, who makes them, and when. You can check this permanent record by running the Audit Trail report—shown in Figure 17-1—to watch for things like deleted invoices or modifications to transactions after they've been reconciled. (You have to be the QuickBooks administrator or have permission to generate sensitive financial reports to run this report.)

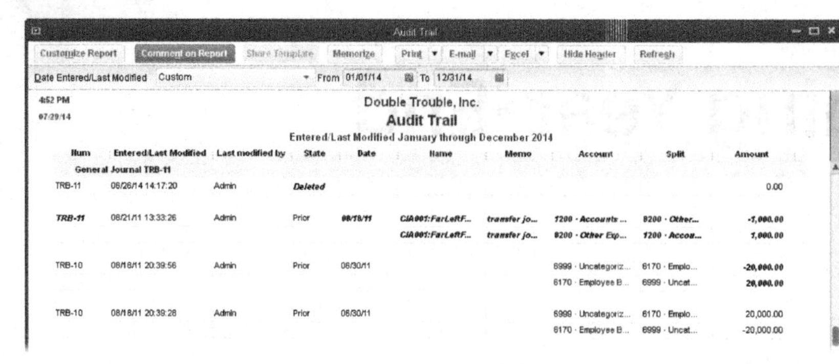

FIGURE 17-1

The Audit Trail report shows every transaction that's been created, changed, or deleted.

To see the details of a transaction, double-click it.

People make mistakes, and this report is also good for spotting inadvertent changes to transactions. QuickBooks initially includes only transactions entered or modified today, but you can choose a different date range to review changes since your last review (in the Audit Trail report's window, choose a date range in the Date Entered/Last Modified drop-down list, or type dates in the From and To boxes).

NOTE QuickBooks' Condense Data utility (page 510) removes the audit trail information for transactions that it deletes. So if you're watching transaction activity, print an Audit Trail report *before* using Condense Data, and (as always), back up your company file regularly.

- The **Voided/Deleted Transactions Summary** and **Voided/Deleted Transactions Detail** reports (which live in the Reports→Accountant & Taxes submenu) focus on transactions that—you guessed it—have been voided or deleted. These reports list who made the changes or deletions and when.

NOTE QuickBooks Accountant edition has a host of features that help accountants and bookkeepers spiff up your books at the end of the year. For example, the Client Data Review tool lists review and cleanup tasks to perform. If your accountant finds any issues, she can add notes about what she plans to do. And if you didn't classify transactions correctly, your accountant can use the Reclassify Transactions features to correct them in a jiffy.

GEM IN THE ROUGH

QuickBooks' Year-End Guide

QuickBooks Help contains a guide to typical year-end tasks, which is especially handy if you aren't familiar with what you have to do to wrap up a year for your business. When you choose Help→Year-End Guide, a special browser window opens displaying the Year-End Guide. It includes a list of activities related to general tax preparation and year-end dealings with subcontractors or employees. You may find some year-end tasks you didn't know you had!

The first time you view the guide, turn on the checkmarks for each activity that pertains to your organization. Since the guide is an HTML document, it works just like a web page: If you need help with the steps for an activity, click its link to open the corresponding QuickBooks Help topic. Click Save Checkmarks to make QuickBooks remember your choices—a handy reminder of your to-do list for the next fiscal year.

Getting Rid of Uncleared Transactions from Closed Periods

You successfully reconciled your bank account (page 389) and your QuickBooks checking account balance matches your bank statement balance. Things are looking good...until you stumble across a few unreconciled transactions (such as checks, bill payments, and deposits) from previous years—years that you've already filed tax returns for and closed in QuickBooks. Good news: there's a way to clean up these old unreconciled transactions *without* messing up your tax returns or your reconciliation.

NOTE You might wonder how unreconciled transactions from closed periods crop up in the first place. The most likely culprit is an adjustment transaction (page 394) that someone used to force a reconciliation to work. For example, perhaps your predecessor couldn't find the unreconciled transactions that you've discovered. To force the account to reconcile, that person clicked Reconcile Now and told QuickBooks to add an adjustment transaction to make QuickBooks' balance match the bank's balance. That adjustment reconciled the account, but it left the real transactions orphaned and unreconciled.

Here's how to look for old, unreconciled transactions:

1. **In the Home Page's Banking panel, click Check Register and then, in the Select Account drop-down list that appears, choose the bank account you want to examine.**

   QuickBooks opens that account's register window.

2. **At the register window's bottom left, in the "Sort by" drop-down list, choose "Cleared status."**

   Sorting by cleared status makes QuickBooks list Reconciled transactions first (they have checkmarks in the checkmark column), followed by cleared transactions (ones you've selected in a reconciliation that's in progress; they're indicated by asterisks in their checkmark cells), and finally uncleared transactions (which have blank checkmark cells).

3. **Scroll up the register window's table to find the first uncleared transaction.**

   Figure 17-2 includes two uncleared transactions dated from a closed period.

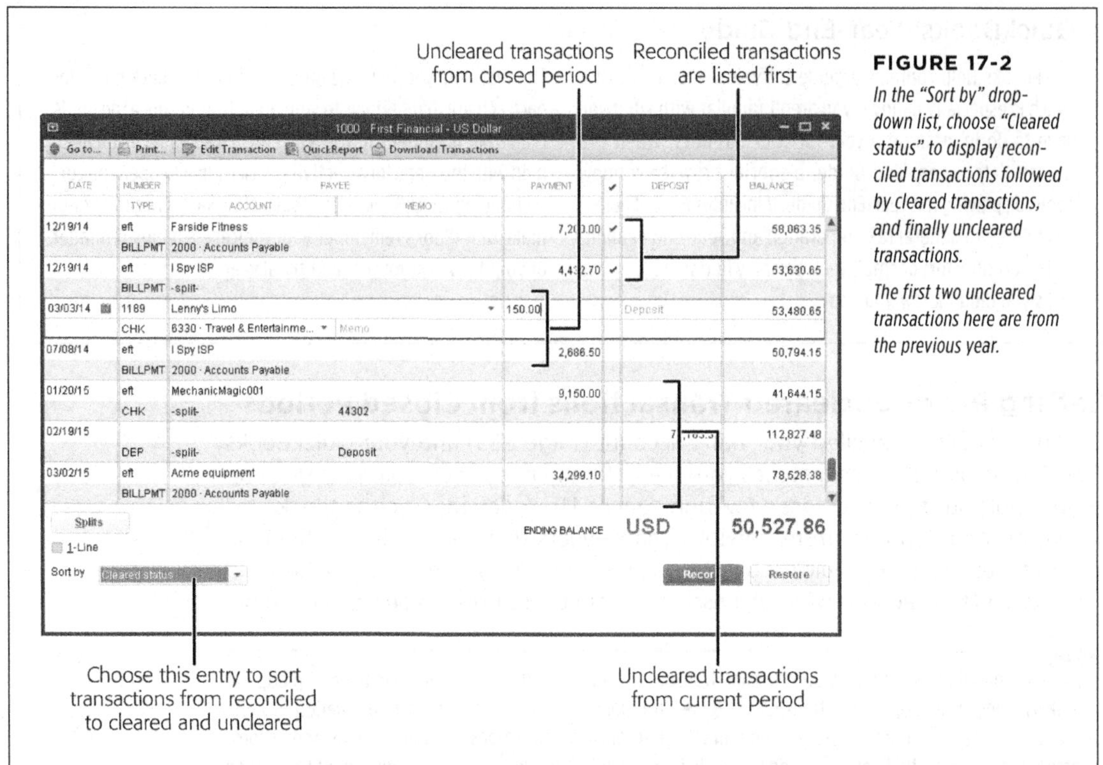

FIGURE 17-2

In the "Sort by" drop-down list, choose "Cleared status" to display reconciled transactions followed by cleared transactions, and finally uncleared transactions.

The first two uncleared transactions here are from the previous year.

Unreconciled transactions from closed periods present a couple of problems. First, they're part of your records that you used to prepare your tax returns: if you void them, you'd have to file an amended tax return. In addition, if you try to reconcile them as is, your next reconciliation won't balance. What you need is an offsetting transaction in the current time period. You can use a journal entry to do that. Here's how:

1. **Choose Company→Make General Journal Entries.**

   The Make General Journal Entries window opens.

2. **In the Date box, choose today's date. If necessary, fill in the Entry No. field with a journal entry number.**

   QuickBooks automatically increments the value in the Entry No. box, but you can type another value if you wish.

3. **In the first Account cell, choose the bank account with the old, unreconciled transaction(s), and then fill in the rest of the fields in that row.**

In the row's Debit cell, fill in the value of the unreconciled transaction (in Figure 17-2, that's $150). Because the unreconciled check in this example decreased the bank balance, you debit the checking account to increase its balance in the current period. In the Memo cell, type a note, such as "To void prior year unreconciled check #1189."

4. **In the second row's Account cell, choose the account used in the unreconciled transaction (in this example, 6342 Transportation).**

   The program automatically fills in the second row's Credit cell with the value you typed in the first row's Debit cell (Figure 17-3). In this example, the original check increased the corresponding expense account's total. This credit decreases the expense account's total in the current time period.

5. **Repeat steps 3 and 4 to void other unreconciled transactions from closed periods.**

   Add pairs of debits and credits for each unreconciled transaction you want to void (you can do this all in the same journal entry).

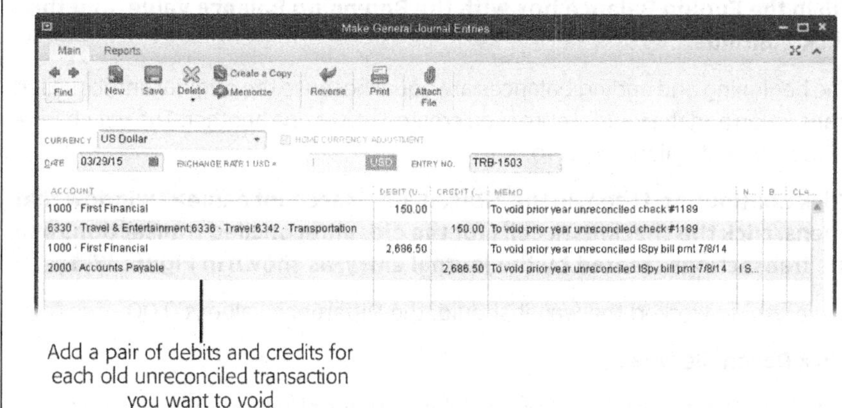
Make General Journal Entries
Add a pair of debits and credits for
each old unreconciled transaction
you want to void

FIGURE 17-3

If you're voiding checks or bill payments, you debit the checking account to increase its balance, and you credit the corresponding expense account to decrease its balance. To void a deposit, you would credit the checking account and debit the account associated with the deposit, such as an income account.

6. **Click Save & Close.**

When you save the journal entry, QuickBooks creates transactions that appear in your bank account register. Now all you have to do is reconcile the old transactions and the journal entry transactions:

1. **In the Home Page's Banking panel, click Reconcile.**

   The Begin Reconciliation window opens.

2. **In the Statement Date box, choose the date from your previous reconciliation (Figure 17-4).**

   For example, if QuickBooks fills in 1/31/15, type *12/31/14* instead.

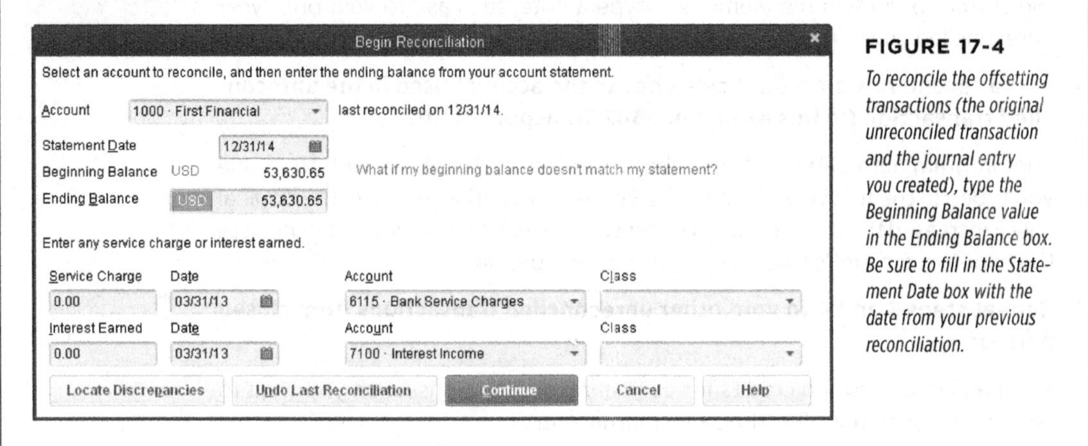

FIGURE 17-4

To reconcile the offsetting transactions (the original unreconciled transaction and the journal entry you created), type the Beginning Balance value in the Ending Balance box. Be sure to fill in the Statement Date box with the date from your previous reconciliation.

3. **Fill in the Ending Balance box with the Beginning Balance value, and then click Continue.**

   The beginning and ending balances are equal because the original unreconciled transaction and the journal entry you created offset one another. The net change to the account balance is zero.

4. **Click Continue and then, in the "Reconcile – <account name>" window that opens, click the checkmark cells for the old, unreconciled transactions and the transactions created by the journal entry, as shown in Figure 17-5.**

   If everything worked the way it should, the Difference value is 0.00.

5. **Click Reconcile Now.**

That's it! The old transactions are reconciled without affecting the values on your filed tax returns. And your QuickBooks bank account balance and reconciliation still match the numbers from your bank statement.

Viewing Your Trial Balance

The *Trial Balance* report is named after the report's original purpose: totaling the balances of every account in the debit and credit columns to see whether the debit and credit totals balanced. If they didn't, the bookkeeper had to track down the mistakes and try again.

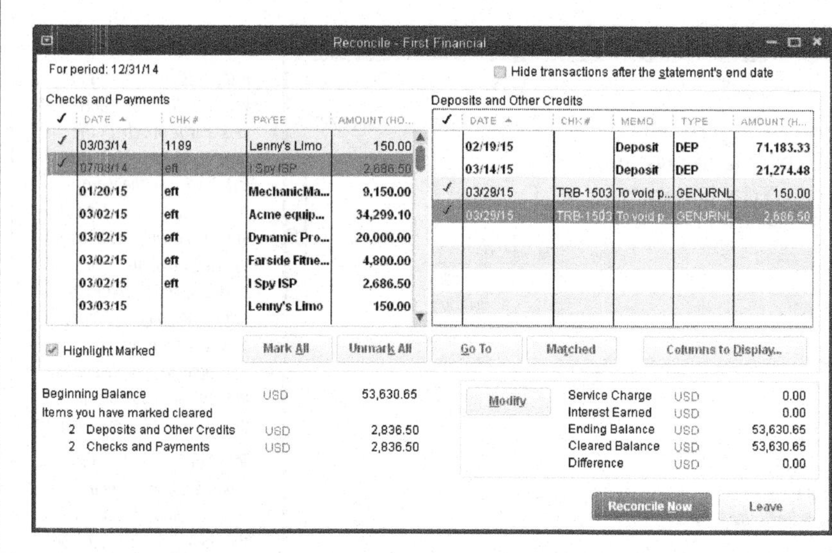

FIGURE 17-5

When you turn on the checkmarks for the old transactions and the off-setting journal entry transactions, the Difference will be 0.00, as shown here.

QuickBooks doesn't make arithmetic mistakes, so you don't need a trial balance to make sure that debits and credits match. Nonetheless, the Trial Balance report is still handy. Accountants like to examine it for errant account assignments before diving into tax preparation or giving financial advice—and for good reason: The Trial Balance report is the only place in QuickBooks where you can see all your accounts *and* their balances in the same place, as shown in Figure 17-6.

To display this report, choose Reports→Accountant & Taxes→Trial Balance, and QuickBooks generates a Trial Balance report for the previous month. The accounts appear in the same order that they're listed in your Chart of Accounts window. If you want to see the trial balance for your entire fiscal year, choose This Fiscal Year in the Dates box.

Generating Financial Reports

When you keep your company's books day after day, all those invoices, checks, and other transactions blur together. But hidden within that maelstrom of figures is important information for you, your accountant, your investors, and the IRS. When consolidated and presented the right way, your books can tell you a lot about what your company does right, does wrong, could do better, and has to pay in taxes.

TIP If you work with more than one currency, the box on page 461 explains how to adjust account balances to reflect currencies' current values based on exchange rates.

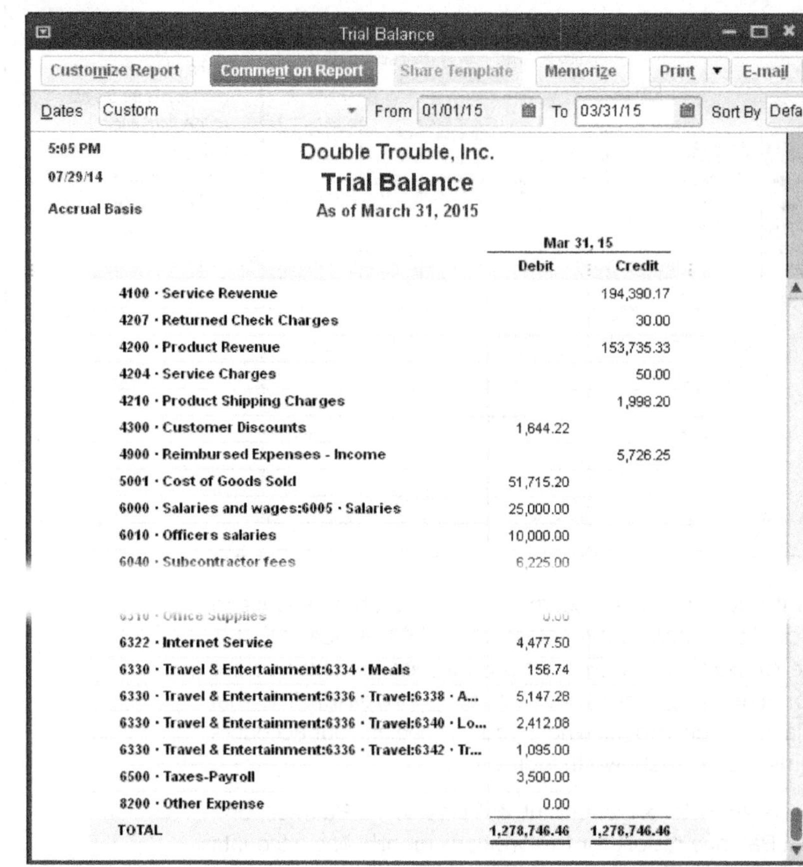

5:05 PM
07/29/14
Accrual Basis

Double Trouble, Inc.
Trial Balance
As of March 31, 2015

	Mar 31, 15	
	Debit	Credit
4100 · Service Revenue		194,390.17
4207 · Returned Check Charges		30.00
4200 · Product Revenue		153,735.33
4204 · Service Charges		50.00
4210 · Product Shipping Charges		1,998.20
4300 · Customer Discounts	1,644.22	
4900 · Reimbursed Expenses - Income		5,726.25
5001 · Cost of Goods Sold	51,715.20	
6000 · Salaries and wages:6005 · Salaries	25,000.00	
6010 · Officers salaries	10,000.00	
6040 · Subcontractor fees	6,225.00	
6310 · Office Supplies	0.00	
6322 · Internet Service	4,477.50	
6330 · Travel & Entertainment:6334 · Meals	156.74	
6330 · Travel & Entertainment:6336 · Travel:6338 · A...	5,147.28	
6330 · Travel & Entertainment:6336 · Travel:6340 · Lo...	2,412.08	
6330 · Travel & Entertainment:6336 · Travel:6342 · Tr...	1,095.00	
6500 · Taxes-Payroll	3,500.00	
8200 · Other Expense	0.00	
TOTAL	1,278,746.46	1,278,746.46

FIGURE 17-6

If the account balances in your Trial Balance report look a little off, check the heading at the report's top left. If you see the words "Accrual Basis" in the heading (as shown here) but you use cash accounting for your business, you've found the culprit (see page 661 to learn how to set this preference). The same goes if the heading says "Cash Basis" but you use accrual accounting.

To set things right, in the report window's menu bar, click Customize Report. In the Modify Report dialog box that appears, on the Display tab, choose the Accrual or Cash option, and then click OK.

Over the years, the Financial Accounting Standards Board (FASB) has nurtured a standard of accounting known as *GAAP* (generally accepted accounting principles). GAAP includes a trio of financial statements that together paint a portrait of company performance: the income statement (also known as the profit and loss report), the balance sheet, and the statement of cash flows.

Generating financial statements in QuickBooks is easy. But unless you understand what these statements *tell* you and you can spot suspect numbers, you may simply end up generating fodder for your paper shredder. If you're new to business, read the next few sections of this chapter, which are about what the income statement, balance sheet, and statement of cash flows show. If you're already an expert in all that, jump to the section on generating these reports (page 448).

NOTE When you close out a year on your company's books, these three special financial reports are a *must.* If you're a business maven and need a bunch of additional reports to manage your business, Chapter 23 has instructions for finding the reports you need and customizing them to your demanding specifications.

The Profit & Loss Report

The Profit & Loss report (Reports→Company & Financial→Profit & Loss Standard) is more like a video than a snapshot. It covers a period of time (a month, a quarter, or a full year, for example) and shows whether your company is making money—or hemorrhaging it.

The money you make selling services or products (called *revenue* or *income*) sits at the top of the Profit & Loss report. Beneath it, your expenses gradually whittle away at that income until you're left with a profit or loss at the bottom. The report shows the progression from sales to the net income your company earned after paying the bills:

- **Income**. The first category in a Profit & Loss report is income, which is simply the revenue your company generates by selling products and services. Regardless of *how* you earn revenue (selling services or products, or even charging fees), the report shows all the income accounts in your chart of accounts and how much you brought into each one (Figure 17-7).

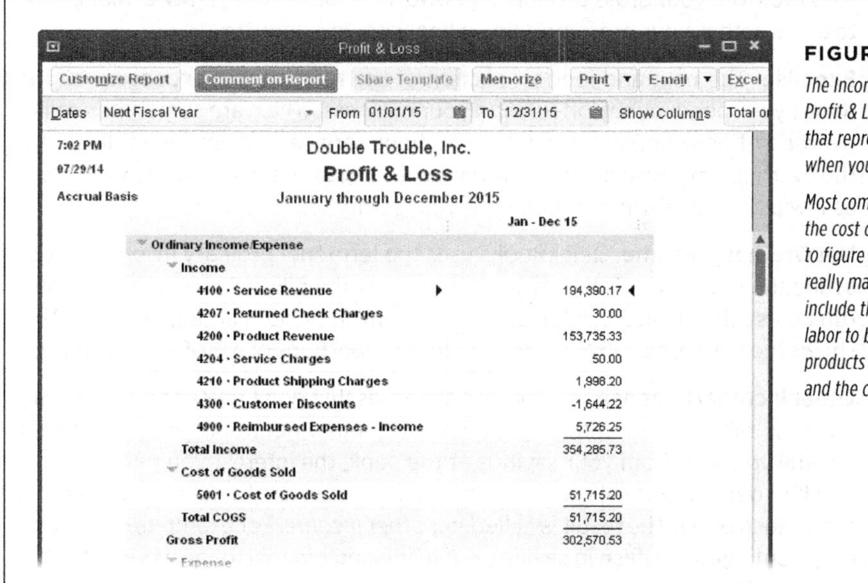

FIGURE 17-7

The Income section at the top of the Profit & Loss report lists the accounts that represent the money you make when you sell to customers.

Most companies have to subtract the cost of goods sold from income to figure out how much profit they really made. Cost of goods sold may include the cost of materials and labor to build products, the cost of products you purchase for resale, and the cost of sales activities.

TIP The Profit & Loss report lists accounts in the order they appear in your company file's chart of accounts. If you want to report your income and expenses in a specific order, you can rearrange the accounts in the Chart of Accounts window (press Ctrl+A to open it). To do that, put your cursor over the diamond to the left of an account's name. When the cursor changes to a four-headed arrow, drag the account to where you want it.

- **Cost of Goods Sold**. Unless you gather rocks from your yard and then sell them as alien amulets, the products you sell carry some initial cost. For example, with products you purchase for resale, the cost of those goods includes the original price you paid for them, the shipping costs you incurred to get them, and so on. The Profit & Loss report's Cost of Goods Sold section adds up the underlying costs associated with your product sales.

NOTE If you don't sell inventory items, you might not have a Cost of Goods Sold section in your report. QuickBooks automatically creates a Cost of Goods Sold account when you create your first inventory item. However, if you want to track other costs associated with selling goods—such as how much you paid for the labor required to build the products you sell, the cost of shipping, the cost of sales, and so on—you can create as many additional Cost of Goods Sold accounts as you want.

- **Gross Profit**. Gross profit is the profit you make after subtracting the cost of goods sold from your total income and before subtracting expenses. For example, if you paid $60,000 to purchase equipment and then sold that equipment for $100,000, your gross profit is $40,000. (The box on page 447 explains how to see whether your gross profit is in line with your industry.)
- **Expense**. The next and longest section of the report is for expenses—all the things you spend money on running your business, which are sometimes called *overhead*. For example, office rent, telephone service, and bank fees all fall into the overhead expense bucket. The name of the game is to keep these expenses as low as possible without hindering your ability to make money.
- **Net Ordinary Income**. QuickBooks uses the term "net ordinary income" to describe the money that's left over after you pay the bills. (You've probably also run across this measure referred to as *net profit* or *net earnings*.) Figure 17-8 shows the Expenses and Net Ordinary Income portions of a Profit & Loss report.
- **Other Income/Expense**. Income and expenses that don't relate to your primary business fall into this category. The most common entrants are the interest income you earn from your savings at the bank, the interest you pay on loans, and bad debt. In this category, income and expense are bundled together and offset each other. The result is called *net other income*. For example, if you have only a smidgeon of cash in savings but a honking big mortgage, your net other income will be a negative number.
- **Net Income**. At long last, you reach the end of the report. *Net income* is the money that's left after subtracting all the costs and expenses you incur. If this number is positive, congratulations—your company made money! If it's negative, your expenses were more than your income, and something's gotta give.

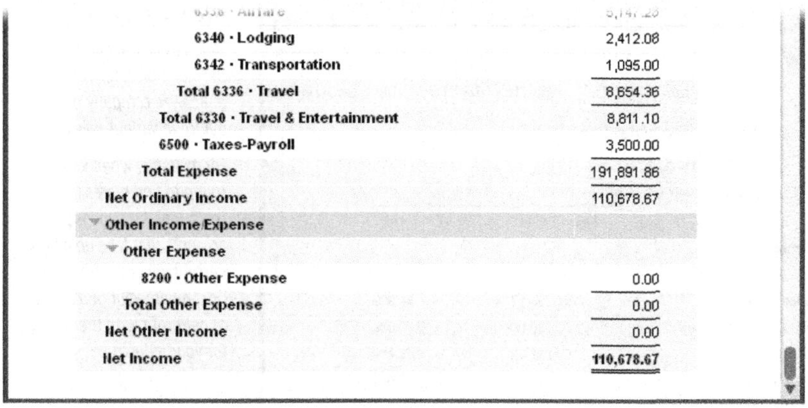

6340 · Lodging	2,412.08
6342 · Transportation	1,095.00
Total 6336 · Travel	8,654.36
Total 6330 · Travel & Entertainment	8,811.10
6500 · Taxes-Payroll	3,500.00
Total Expense	191,891.86
Net Ordinary Income	110,678.67
Other Income/Expense	
Other Expense	
8200 · Other Expense	0.00
Total Other Expense	0.00
Net Other Income	0.00
Net Income	110,678.67

FIGURE 17-8

If your company makes more money than it spends, your net income is a positive number, as shown here.

Profit & Loss reports don't label your result a loss when your company spends more than it makes. Instead, a loss shows up as a negative net income number, whether it's net ordinary, other, or overall net income.

UP TO SPEED

Profit Percentage

There's no question that sales are important. But the *percentage gross profit* you achieve is the real test of whether you're keeping up with your competitors. To see whether your company is in line with what's typical for your industry, compare the ratio of your gross profit to your sales. For example, in construction, gross profit between 40 and 60 percent is typical. (The business reference section of your local library is a great place to find industry statistics, and many libraries offer online access to their reference materials.)

QuickBooks is happy to calculate percentage gross profit for you. Here's what you do:

1. In the Profit & Loss report window's menu bar, click Customize Report.
2. In the Modify Report: Profit & Loss dialog box, click the Display tab (if it isn't already selected).
3. Turn on the "% of Income" checkbox at the dialog box's lower right, and then click OK.

QuickBooks adds a column to the report showing the percentage of income that each row in the report represents. The Gross Profit value in the "% of Income" column, circled in Figure 17-9, is your percentage gross profit.

Percentages also come in handy for comparing job profitability. Because jobs vary in size, it's hard to compare profitability by looking at the raw numbers. For example, one job may produce $50,000 in total income and $10,000 in net income. Another job may also produce $50,000 in total income but only $5,000 in net income. Percentages let you see how profitable customers and jobs truly are. For example, suppose each job's total income represents 10 percent of your total income for the year. The job with $10,000 in net income may represent 15 percent of your total net income, while the other job, at $5,000 net income, is only 7.5 percent.

If you run a "Profit & Loss by Job" report (page 451) and add the "% of Income" column as described above, the Net Income value at the bottom of that column shows the net profit margin for each job. That's the number you want to focus on. When a job's net income percentage is higher than your company's total income percentage, that job is more profitable than average.

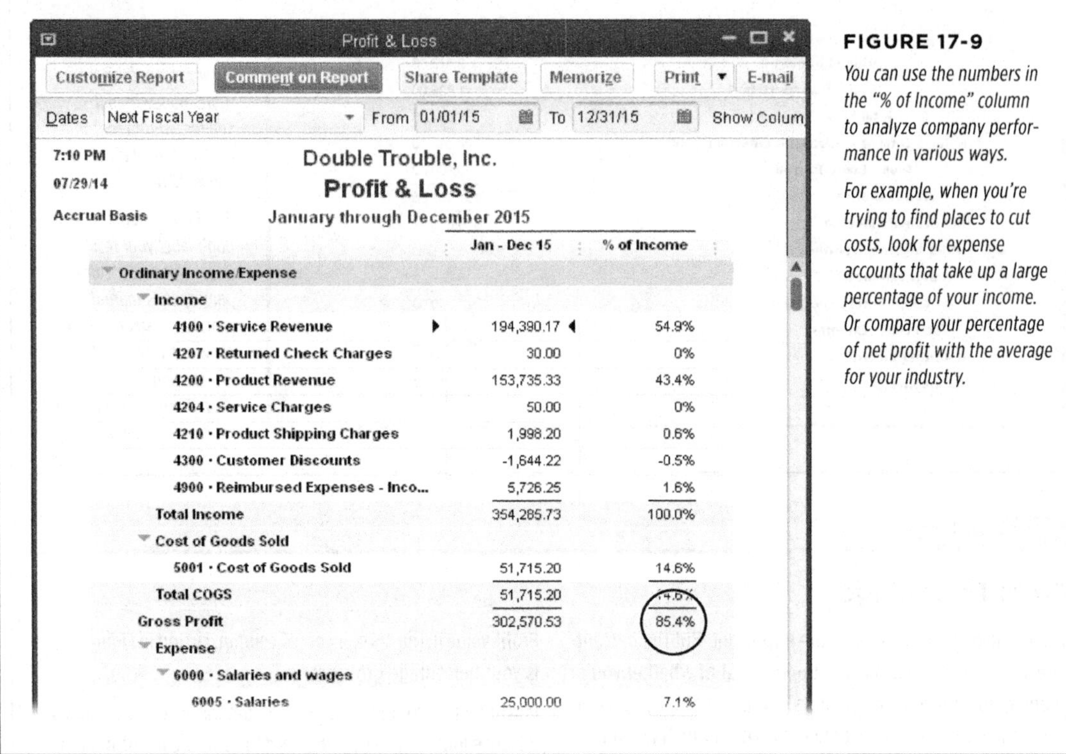

FIGURE 17-9

You can use the numbers in the "% of Income" column to analyze company performance in various ways.

For example, when you're trying to find places to cut costs, look for expense accounts that take up a large percentage of your income. Or compare your percentage of net profit with the average for your industry.

GENERATING A PROFIT & LOSS REPORT

When you choose Reports→Company & Financial, QuickBooks gives you several built-in profit and loss reports to pick from. Choose Profit & Loss Standard to see a month-to-date report. But for many small companies, month-to-date numbers can be rather sparse. Figure 17-10 describes how to change the month-to-date Profit & Loss report that QuickBooks produces into a quarter-to-date or year-to-date report instead. (Page 601 tells you how to save a report after you tweak it to look the way you want.)

NOTE Before you generate your first financial statement, be sure that QuickBooks reports your numbers using your company's accounting basis. The Summary Reports Basis preference (page 661) sets your reports to either accrual or cash accounting. If you choose the Cash option, your Profit & Loss reports show income only after you receive customer payments and show expenses only after you pay bills. With the Accrual option, income appears in Profit & Loss reports as soon as you record an invoice or other type of sale, and expenses show up as soon as you enter bills.

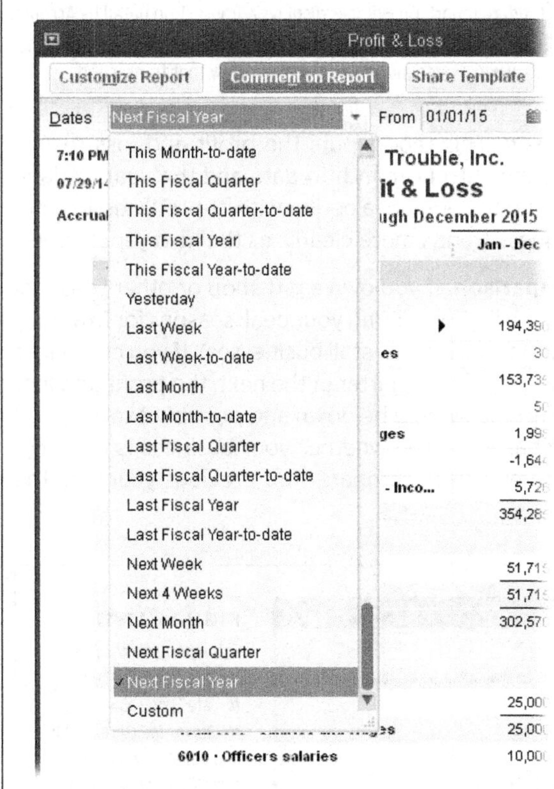

FIGURE 17-10

The Profit & Loss report window's Dates drop-down list includes dozens of commonly used date ranges for the current and previous fiscal year.

If you choose "This Fiscal Year-to-date," for example, the dates in the From and To boxes change to the first day of your fiscal year and today's date, respectively.

To select specific dates, in the report window's From and To boxes, type or choose the dates you want.

OTHER PROFIT & LOSS REPORTS

If the Profit & Loss Standard report described in the previous section isn't what you want, take a few minutes to see if any of QuickBooks' other built-in reports fit the bill. Here's a guide to the other Profit & Loss reports on the Reports→Company & Financial submenu and when you might use them:

- **Profit & Loss Detail**. Only the tiniest of companies—or the most persnickety of bookkeepers—use this report regularly. It's a year-to-date report that includes a separate line for every service and product you sold, every other charge that produced revenue, and every item on every bill you paid. It comes in handy when, for example, you restore a backup copy of your company file and want to look at your previous company file to identify the transactions you have to recreate in the restored backup.

TIP If you spot a questionable number in a report, double-click the number for a closer inspection. (When you put your cursor over a number in a report, it changes to an icon that looks like a Z [for "zoom"] inside a magnifying glass; that's your clue that double-clicking the number will drill down into the details.) For example, if you double-click a number in a Profit & Loss Standard report, QuickBooks displays a Transaction Detail by Account report that lists each transaction that contributed to the total. In a Profit & Loss Detail report, double-clicking a transaction opens the corresponding window (such as Create Invoices) so you can view that transaction.

- **Profit & Loss YTD Comparison**. This report puts the profit and loss results for two periods side by side: the current month to date and the year to date. However, most businesses prefer to compare a period with its predecessor from the previous year to see business trends more clearly, as the next report does.
- **Profit & Loss Prev Year Comparison**. If you own a gift shop or other seasonal business, you know that sales are highest during your peak season (for example, around the holidays for gift shops and many retail businesses). If you compared the last quarter of one year with the first quarter of the next, the profit and loss report would look pretty grim: Sales would be down and possibly exacerbated by returns from holiday purchases. To see whether your business is growing, use this report (shown in Figure 17-11) to compare your previous year with the current year.

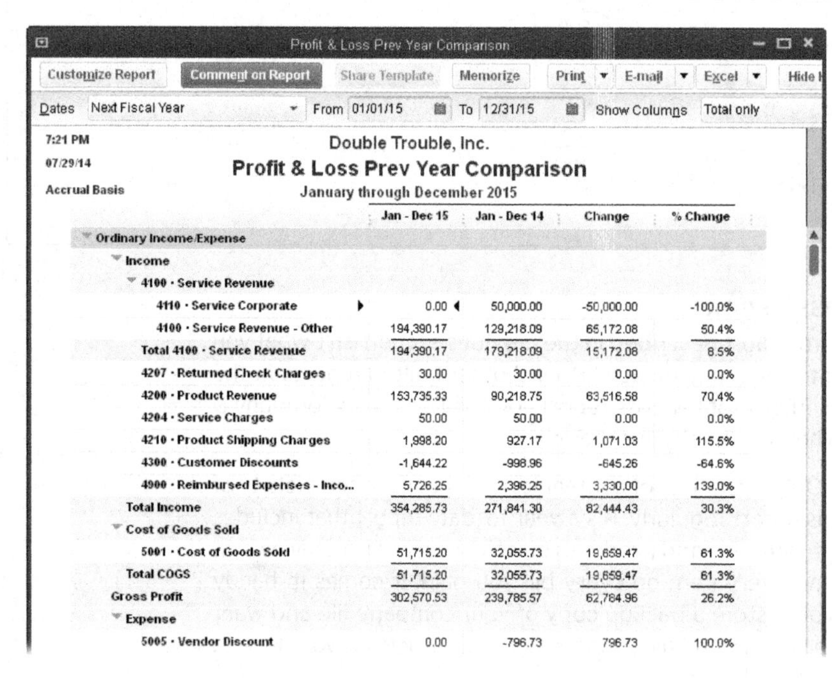

	Jan - Dec 15	Jan - Dec 14	Change	% Change
Ordinary Income/Expense				
Income				
4100 · Service Revenue				
4110 · Service Corporate	0.00	50,000.00	-50,000.00	-100.0%
4100 · Service Revenue - Other	194,390.17	129,218.09	65,172.08	50.4%
Total 4100 · Service Revenue	194,390.17	179,218.09	15,172.08	8.5%
4207 · Returned Check Charges	30.00	30.00	0.00	0.0%
4200 · Product Revenue	153,735.33	90,218.75	63,516.58	70.4%
4204 · Service Charges	50.00	50.00	0.00	0.0%
4210 · Product Shipping Charges	1,998.20	927.17	1,071.03	115.5%
4300 · Customer Discounts	-1,644.22	-998.96	-645.26	-64.6%
4900 · Reimbursed Expenses - Inco...	5,726.25	2,396.25	3,330.00	139.0%
Total Income	354,285.73	271,841.30	82,444.43	30.3%
Cost of Goods Sold				
5001 · Cost of Goods Sold	51,715.20	32,055.73	19,659.47	61.3%
Total COGS	51,715.20	32,055.73	19,659.47	61.3%
Gross Profit	302,570.53	239,785.57	62,784.96	26.2%
Expense				
5005 · Vendor Discount	0.00	-796.73	796.73	100.0%

FIGURE 17-11

This report sets the Dates box to "This Fiscal Year-to-date" and shows your results for the current year in the first column and those from the previous year in the second column. To see where growth is strong or stagnant, add columns that show the change in dollars or percentages (page 589). Right after your fiscal year ends, you can change the Dates box to Last Fiscal Year to compare the year you just finished with the one before it.

- **Profit & Loss by Job**. If you suspect that some of your customers and jobs are less profitable than others—and you want to learn from your mistakes—run this report. It displays each of your customers and jobs in its own column so you can compare how much profit you made from each one. The box on page 447 tells you how to compare apples to apples in this report.
- **Profit & Loss by Class**. If you use classes to track performance for different business units or locations, run this report, which includes a column for each class. (If you'd rather generate a Profit & Loss report that displays only *one* class, modify this report [page 589] to filter for that class.) The last column in this report is Unclassified, which shows all the transactions that don't have a class assignment. The next report can help you find such transactions.
- **Profit & Loss Unclassified**. If you use classes, then before you pretty up and print your class-based Profit & Loss reports, run this one to see the transactions without class assignments. Depending on how you use classes, unclassified transactions might be perfectly acceptable. For example, if you track income by partner, overhead expenses aren't related to individual partners. In that situation, most income accounts should have values, but some expense accounts could have zero balances. However, if you created a class for overhead, then you shouldn't see any transactions in this report. If you do, double-click each transaction to open it in its corresponding window, assign the appropriate class, and then save it.

The Balance Sheet

If a profit and loss report is like a video, a balance sheet is more like a portrait. This report (Reports→Company & Financial→Balance Sheet Standard) shows how much your company owns (assets), how much it owes (liabilities), and the resulting equity in the company at a given point in time. While a profit and loss report tells you whether you're making money, the balance sheet helps you analyze your company's financial strength.

One thing you can count on with a balance sheet is that there's a steady relationship among the total assets, total liabilities, and equity, as you can see in Figure 17-12. Here's the formula that puts the "balance" into balance sheets:

```
Assets - Liabilities = Equity
```

As you buy more or borrow more, the value of your equity changes to make up the difference between the value of your assets and liabilities. Another way to look at this equation is that your asset value equals the sum of your liabilities and equity.

Here's what to look for in each section of a balance sheet:

- **Assets**. Assets are things of value that a company owns, such as equipment, land, product inventory, Accounts Receivable, cash, and even brand names. On a balance sheet, you want to see significantly more money in the Assets section than in the Liabilities section.

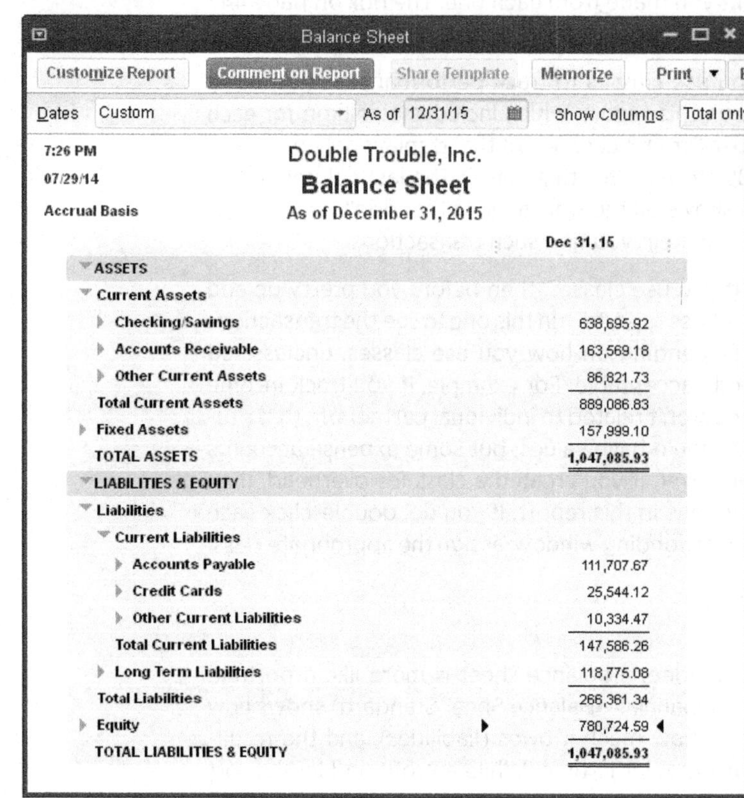

FIGURE 17-12

The key to a good-looking balance sheet is not having too much debt. How much is too much? It depends on the industry you're in, but the acid test is if you closed up shop today and sold all your assets, would you have enough money to pay off your liabilities? If the answer is no, you'll have a hard time finding a bank willing to lend you more money.

NOTE Even with assets, you can have too much of a good thing. Assets aren't corporate collector's items—companies should use assets to make money. A measure called *return on assets* (the ratio of net income to total assets) shows whether a company is using assets effectively to produce income. Return on assets varies from industry to industry, but, typically, less than 5 percent is poor.

- **Liabilities**. Liabilities include Accounts Payable (bills you haven't yet paid), unpaid expenses, loans, mortgages, and even future expenses such as pensions. Debt on its own isn't bad; it's *too much* debt that can drag a company down, particularly when business is slow, since debt payments are due every month whether your business produced revenue or not.
- **Equity**. Equity on a balance sheet is the corporate counterpart of the equity you have in your house. When you buy a house, your initial equity is the down payment you make. But both the decreasing balance on your mortgage and any increase in the value of your house contribute to an increase in your equity.

Equity in a company is the dollar value that remains after you subtract liabilities from assets. (Net income and retained earnings on your balance sheet change when you move into a new fiscal year. The box on page 454 describes what happens behind the scenes.)

GENERATING A BALANCE SHEET REPORT

A balance sheet is a snapshot of accounts on a given date. The various built-in Balance Sheet reports that QuickBooks offers differ in whether they show only account balances or all the transactions that make up those balances. Choose Reports→Company & Financial, and then pick from the following reports:

- **Balance Sheet Standard**. This report includes every asset, liability, and equity account in your chart of accounts except for ones with zero balances, as shown in Figure 17-12. QuickBooks automatically sets the Dates box to "This Fiscal Year-to-date" so the report shows your balance sheet for the current date. If you want to see the balance sheet for the end of a quarter or end of the year instead, in the Dates box, choose This Fiscal Quarter, This Fiscal Year, or Last Fiscal Year.
- **Balance Sheet Detail**. This report shows the transactions in each of your asset, liability, and equity accounts over a period of time. If a number on your Balance Sheet Standard report looks odd, use this report to verify your transactions. Double-click a transaction's value to open the corresponding window, such as Enter Bills.
- **Balance Sheet Summary**. If you want to see the key numbers in your balance sheet without having to scan past the individual accounts in each section, this report shows subtotals for each category of a balance sheet, such as Checking/Savings, Accounts Receivable, Accounts Payable, and so on.
- **Balance Sheet Prev Year Comparison**. If you want to compare your financial strength from year to year, this report has four columns at your service: one each for the current and previous years, one for the dollar-value change, and the fourth for the percentage change.

NOTE When you review your Balance Sheet Prev Year Comparison report, you typically want to see decreasing liabilities. If liabilities have *increased*, then assets should have increased as well, because you don't want to see more debt without more assets to show for the trouble. Equity is the value of your—and your shareholders', if you have them—ownership in the company, so it should increase each year. (If you use QuickBooks to keep the books for your one-person consulting company, the equity may not increase each year if, for example, you don't have many company assets and you withdraw most of the profit you make as your salary.)

- **Balance Sheet by Class**. This report lists your asset, liability, and equity accounts, and includes a column for each class. However, to obtain accurate results from this report, you have to enter transactions in a specific way (for example, using only one class in each transaction, and recording transactions using QuickBooks features like Create Invoices and Receive Payments). To learn more about this report, search QuickBooks Help for "balance sheet by class report."

FREQUENTLY ASKED QUESTION

Net Income and Retained Earnings

I just changed the date on my Balance Sheet report from December 31 of last year to January 1 of this year, and the Net Income and Retained Earnings numbers are different. What's the deal?

At the end of a fiscal year, account balances go through some changes to get your books ready for another year of commerce. For example, at the end of one fiscal year, your income and expense accounts show how much you earned and spent during that year. But come January 1 (or whatever day your fiscal year starts), all those accounts have to be zero so you can start your new fiscal year fresh. QuickBooks makes this happen by adjusting your net income behind the scenes.

Say your net income on the Profit & Loss report is $110,678.67 on December 31, 2015. That number appears at the bottom of the Balance Sheet report as the value of the Net Income account (in the Equity section), as shown in Figure 17-13, top. At the beginning of the new fiscal year, QuickBooks automatically moves the previous year's net income into the Retained Earnings equity account, which resets the Net Income account's value to zero.

Some companies like to keep equity for the current year separate from the equity for all previous years. To do that, you need one additional equity account and one simple journal entry. Create an equity account (page 57) called something like Past Equity with an account number greater than the one you use for Retained Earnings. (For example, if Retained Earnings is 3900, set Past Equity to 3950.) Then, when you close your books at the end of the year, create a journal entry to move the current retained earnings value ($14,043.11 in this example) from the Retained Earnings account to the Past Equity account (Figure 17-13, bottom). That way, when QuickBooks moves the current year's net income into the Retained Earnings equity account, you can see both current and past equity values, as shown in Figure 17-13.

The Statement of Cash Flows

Thanks to noncash accounting anomalies like accrual reporting and depreciation, profit and loss reports don't tell you how much cash you have on hand. Looking at QuickBooks' Statement of Cash Flows report helps you figure out whether your company generates enough cash to keep the doors open. Your balance sheet might look great—$10 million in assets and only $500,000 in liabilities, say—but if a $50,000 payment is due and you have only $3,000 in the bank, you have cash flow problems. (The box on page 458 describes ways to evaluate your cash flow.)

The concept of cash flow is easy to understand. In the words of every film-noir detective, follow the money. Cash flow is nothing more than the real money that flows into and out of your company—not the noncash transactions, such as depreciation, that you see on a profit and loss report. Figure 17-14 shows sources of cash in a sample Statement of Cash Flows.

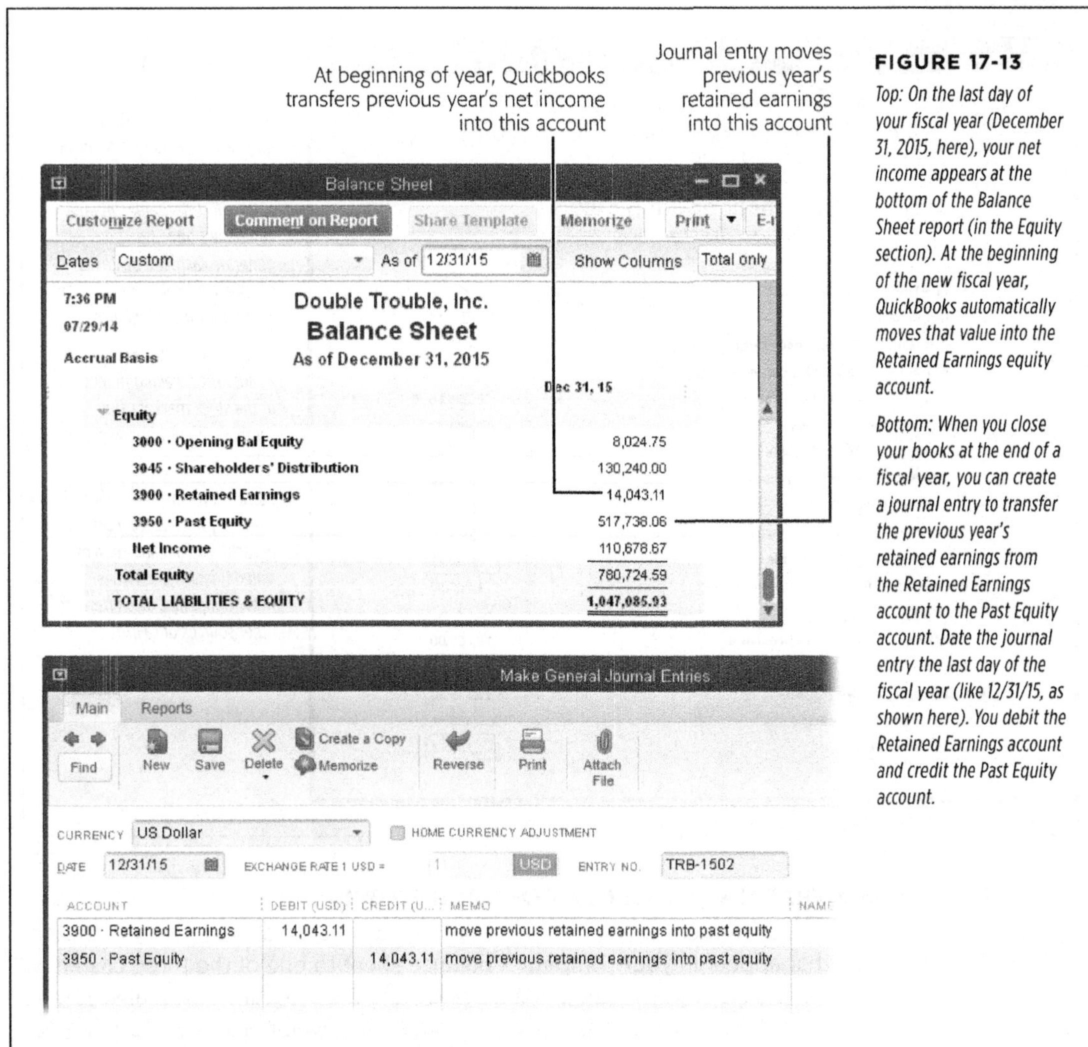

FIGURE 17-13

Top: On the last day of your fiscal year (December 31, 2015, here), your net income appears at the bottom of the Balance Sheet report (in the Equity section). At the beginning of the new fiscal year, QuickBooks automatically moves that value into the Retained Earnings equity account.

Bottom: When you close your books at the end of a fiscal year, you can create a journal entry to transfer the previous year's retained earnings from the Retained Earnings account to the Past Equity account. Date the journal entry the last day of the fiscal year (like 12/31/15, as shown here). You debit the Retained Earnings account and credit the Past Equity account.

WARNING Cash provided by operating activities shows how much money your day-to-day operations produce. When you sell an asset (which is an investing activity), it shows up as a gain or loss on the Profit & Loss report, which *temporarily* increases or reduces your net income. Beware: The effect of investing activities on the Profit & Loss report can hide problems brewing in your operations, which is why you should examine the Statement of Cash Flows report. If your income derives mainly from investing and financing activities instead of operating activities, you've got a problem.

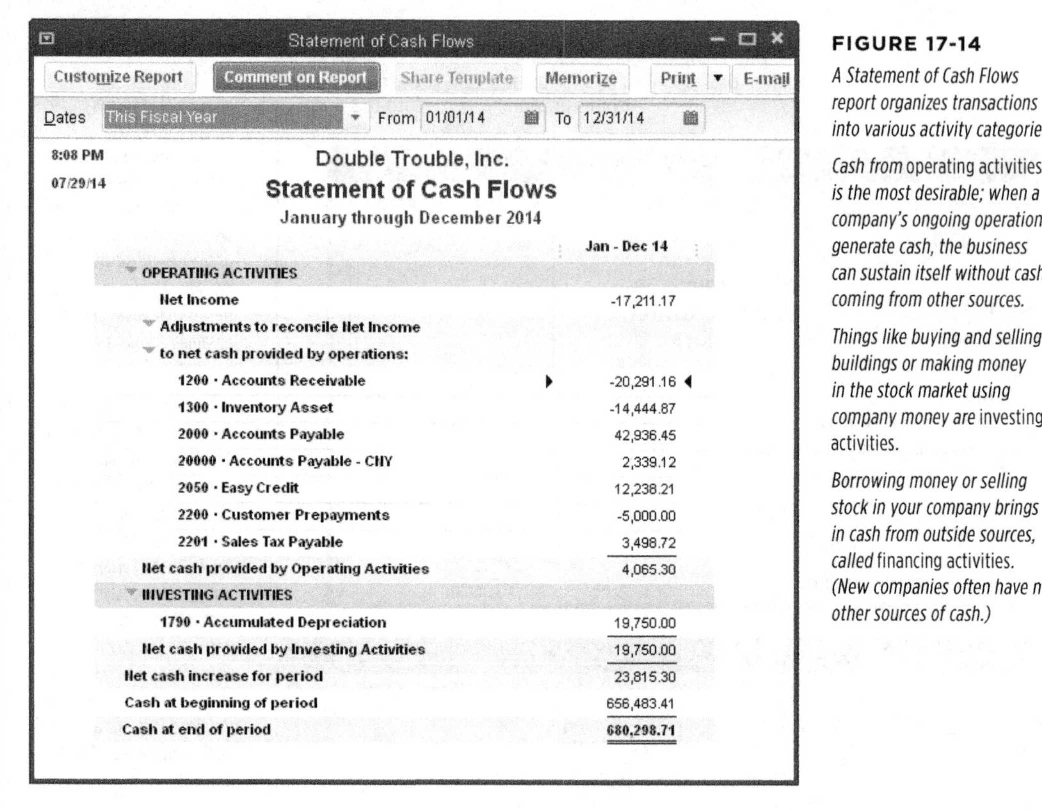

FIGURE 17-14

A Statement of Cash Flows report organizes transactions into various activity categories.

Cash from operating activities *is the most desirable; when a company's ongoing operations generate cash, the business can sustain itself without cash coming from other sources.*

Things like buying and selling buildings or making money in the stock market using company money are investing activities.

Borrowing money or selling stock in your company brings in cash from outside sources, called financing activities. *(New companies often have no other sources of cash.)*

GENERATING A STATEMENT OF CASH FLOWS

To create a Statement of Cash Flows, QuickBooks automatically assigns the accounts that appear in your company's balance sheet to one of the three cash flow categories—operating, investing, or financing—and the program almost always gets those assignments right. For example, Accounts Receivable and Inventory appear as operating accounts, fixed asset accounts show up as investing, and accounts for loans fall under financing. Unless you're a financial expert or your accountant gives you explicit instructions about a change, you're better off leaving QuickBooks' account classifications alone. If you need to reassign accounts for your Statement of Cash Flows report, this section tells you how.

Generating a Statement of Cash Flows is easy because you have only one report to choose from. Simply choose Reports→Company & Financial→Statement of Cash Flows, and QuickBooks creates a report that displays your cash flow for your fiscal year to date. To view the Statement of Cash Flows report for a quarter or a year instead, in the Dates box, choose This Fiscal Quarter or This Fiscal Year.

NOTE The Operating Activities section of the report includes the label "Adjustments to reconcile Net Income to net cash provided by operations." What that means is that QuickBooks calculates the net income at the top of the Statement of Cash Flows report on an *accrual* basis (meaning income appears as of the invoice date, not the day the customer pays). But the Statement of Cash Flows is by nature a cash-based report, so the program has to add and subtract transactions to get net income on a *cash* basis. (See page xxii for more on the difference between cash-based and accrual-based accounting.)

The account assignments for the Statement of Cash Flows report are controlled by a collection of QuickBooks preferences. Here's how to view the account assignments or change them:

1. **In the Statement of Cash Flows report window's toolbar, click the Classify Cash button.**

   The Preferences dialog box opens to the Reports & Graphs section and selects the Company Preferences tab (as long as you have QuickBooks administrator privileges, that is). You can also open this dialog box by choosing Edit→Preferences→Reports & Graphs.

2. **In the Preferences dialog box, click the Classify Cash button.**

   QuickBooks opens the Classify Cash dialog box.

3. **To change the category to which an account belongs (Operating, Investing, or Financing), click the cell in the column for the new category.**

   If you made changes and fear you've mangled the settings beyond repair, click Default to reset the categories to the ones QuickBooks used initially.

4. **When the assignments are the way you want, click OK to close the dialog box.**

   That's it—you've reassigned the accounts.

Other Helpful Financial Reports

Although financial statements are the ones that people like shareholders and the IRS want to see, other financial reports help you, the business owner, keep tabs on how your enterprise is doing. Here are a few QuickBooks reports that can help you evaluate your business's performance:

NOTE Reports that apply to specific bookkeeping and accounting tasks are explained in the chapters about those tasks, such as Accounts Receivable reports in Chapter 13.

POWER USERS' CLINIC

Expert Cash Flow Analysis

Thanks to today's accounting rules, cash isn't always connected to revenues and expenses. And a dollar in sales isn't necessarily a dollar of cash. Here's what financial analysts look for when they evaluate a company's health based on its statement of cash flows:

- A net income value that's close to the amount of cash you earn from operating activities means net income is mostly from business operations and the company can support itself.
- Cash from operations that's growing at the same rate as (or faster than) the growth of net income indicates that the company is maintaining (or even improving) its ability to sustain business.
- Cash that's increasing means the company won't have to resort to financing to keep the business going.
- Negative cash flow is often the sign of a rapidly growing company—without financing, the company grows only as fast as it can generate cash from operations. If a company isn't growing quickly and *still* can't generate cash, then something is wrong.
- If an increase in cash comes primarily from selling assets, the company's future looks grim. Selling assets to raise cash sometimes means the company can't borrow any more because banks don't like what they see. Because assets often produce sales, selling assets means less cash generated in the future—and you can see where that leads.

- **Reviewing income and sales**. If you're introducing enhanced services to keep your best customers—or you're looking for the customers you *want* your competition to steal—use the Income by Customer Summary report (Reports→Company & Financial→Income by Customer Summary). It shows total income for each of your customers; that is, the total dollar amount from all your income and expense accounts associated with each customer. Customers with low income totals might be good targets for more energetic sales pitches. If you find that most of your income comes from only a few customers, you may want to protect your income stream by lining up more customers. (One thing this report *doesn't* show is how profitable your sales to customers are; the box on page 447 explains how to see that.)

TIP If you want to produce a report showing performance over several years to evaluate trends, you can set a report's date range to include the years you want to compare. Then modify the report as explained on page 589 to include a column for each year.

- **Reviewing expenses**. On the expense side, the Expenses by Vendor Summary report (Reports→Company & Financial→Expenses by Vendor Summary) shows how much you spend with each vendor. If you spend tons with certain vendors, maybe it's time to negotiate volume discounts, find additional vendors as back-ups, or set up electronic ordering to speed up deliveries.

TIP The Company Snapshot (page 43) is another tool that helps you evaluate how your business is doing. For example, the Company Snapshot window's Company tab can include graphs such as Prev Year Income Comparison, Income Breakdown, Prev Year Expense Comparison, Expense Breakdown, Income and Expense Trend, and so on.

- **Comparing income and expenses**. The Income & Expense Graph (Reports→Company & Financial→Income & Expense Graph) includes a bar graph that shows income and expenses by month and a pie chart that breaks down either income or expenses (click Income or Expense at the bottom of the report's window to choose which one is displayed). To specify how you want QuickBooks to display your income or expenses, in the window's icon bar, click By Account, By Customer, or By Class. You can't change the time periods for each set of bars on the graph.

- **What you've sold**. Most companies analyze their sales to find ways to improve. Maybe you want to beef up sales to customers who haven't bought from you in a while, turn good customers into great ones, or check how well your stuff is selling. The Sales by Customer Summary report (Reports→Sales→Sales by Customer Summary) is a terse listing of customers and how much you've sold to each one during the timeframe you specify; it initially shows values for this month to date.

  The Sales Graph (Reports→Sales→Sales Graph), on the other hand, presents sales data in a cheery rainbow of colors, and you can quickly switch the graph to show the breakdown of sales by customer, item, or sales rep. The bar graph shows sales by month for the year to date. To change the duration covered by the graph, click Dates and then specify the date range you want. The pie chart shows sales based on the category you choose: In the window's toolbar, click By Item, By Customer, or By Rep.

  The Sales by Item Summary report (Reports→Sales→Sales by Item Summary) shows how much you sell of each item in your Item List, starting with inventory items, followed by Non-inventory Parts, Service items, and finally Other Charge items. This report also includes columns for average cost of goods sold (COGS) and gross margin, which apply only to inventory items you sell.

- **Forecasting cash flow**. Say you're wondering whether you have any invoices due that will cover a big credit card bill that's coming up, or whether income over the next few weeks is enough to meet payroll. At times like that, use the Cash Flow Forecast report (Reports→Company & Financial→Cash Flow Forecast) to see how much cash you should have over the next four weeks, as shown in Figure 17-15. The Beginning Balance row shows the current balance for your Accounts Receivable, Accounts Payable, and bank accounts. The Proj Balance column shows how much money you should have in your bank accounts at the end of each week (or longer if you choose a different option in the Periods drop-down list). If a number in that column starts flirting with zero, you're about to run out of cash. You'll have to speed up some customer payments, transfer cash from another account, or look into a short-term loan.

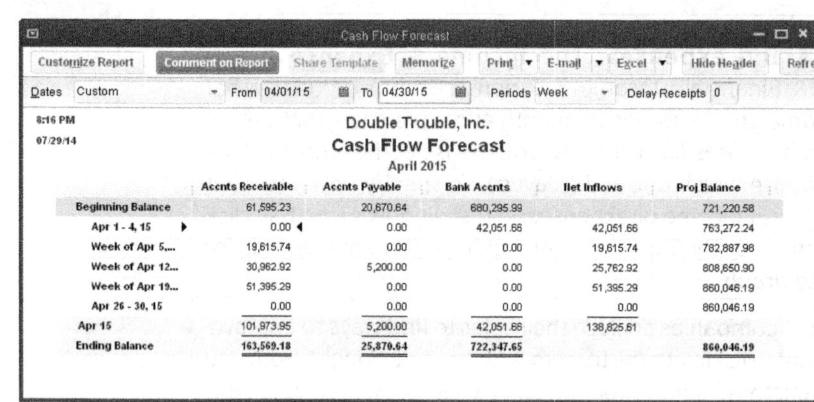

FIGURE 17-15

To view more than four weeks, type the date range you want in the From and To boxes or, in the Dates drop-down list, choose Next Fiscal Quarter or Next Fiscal Year. To change the length of each period in the report, in the Periods drop-down list, choose from Week, Two Weeks, Month, and so on.

Generating Tax Reports

Whether your accountant has the honor of preparing your taxes or you keep that excitement for yourself, you can save accountant's fees and your own sanity by making sure your company file is ready for tax season. The key to a smooth transition from QuickBooks to tax preparation is linking each account in your chart of accounts to the correct tax line and tax form. (The box on page 461 describes another tax-preparation task.)

Reviewing the Income Tax Preparation report (Reports→Accountant & Taxes→Income Tax Preparation) can save you money on accountant's fees *and* prevent IRS penalties (as well as keep more of your hair attached to your scalp). As shown in Figure 17-16, this report lists the accounts in your chart of accounts and the tax lines to which you assigned them. If an account isn't linked to the correct tax line—or worse, not assigned to *any* tax line—the Income Tax Summary report (described in a sec), which lists each line on your tax return with the amount you have to report, won't display the correct values. See page 61 to learn more about choosing tax lines for accounts.

When all the accounts in your chart of accounts are assigned to tax lines, you can generate a report with all the values you need for your company's tax return. Choose Reports→Accountant & Taxes→Income Tax Summary. Because you usually run this report after the fiscal year ends and all the numbers are in, QuickBooks automatically chooses Last Tax Year in the Dates box.

NOTE As one last reminder of unassigned accounts, the last two lines of the Income Tax Summary report are "Tax Line Unassigned (balance sheet)" and "Tax Line Unassigned (income/expense)." To see the transactions that make up either of these unassigned values, double-click the number in the corresponding line.

POWER USERS' CLINIC

Realized Gains and Losses

If you work with more than one currency (page 656), changes in exchange rates can lead to gains or losses on your transactions. Say you send a customer an invoice for €1,000 when the euro-to-dollar exchange rate is 1.459 (that is, 1 euro equals 1.459 dollars). The invoice total in your home currency (dollars, in this example) is $1,459. However, by the time you deposit the customer's payment, the euro-to-dollar exchange rate is 1.325, which means each euro is worth fewer dollars. At that exchange rate, your bank records a deposit of $1,325 in your account, and you've lost $134 on the transaction.

To see how much you've gained or lost on foreign currency transactions, choose Reports→Company & Financial→Realized Gains & Losses. To see *potential* gains or losses based on the latest exchange rate, choose Reports→Company & Financial→Unrealized Gains & Losses. In the Enter Exchange Rates dialog box, type the exchange rates you want to apply. When you click Continue, the Unrealized Gains & Losses report shows gains and losses for the balances in your AR and AP accounts.

To report your financial results accurately, you have to adjust the value of accounts set up in foreign currencies (page 59) based on the exchange rate as of the end date for the report. You can download the most recent exchange rates by choosing Company→Manage Currency→Download Latest Exchange Rates. Or, to find exchange rates for a given date, point your web browser to *www.xe.com/ict*. Then, in QuickBooks, choose Lists→Currency List and edit the currencies to reflect the exchange rates you found online.

To adjust account values, choose Company→Manage Currency→Home Currency Adjustment. In the Home Currency Adjustment window, select the date for the adjustment, and then pick the currency and the exchange rate you want to use. Click Calculate Adjustment, and customers and vendors who use that currency appear in the window's table. Select the ones you want to adjust, and then click Save & Close.

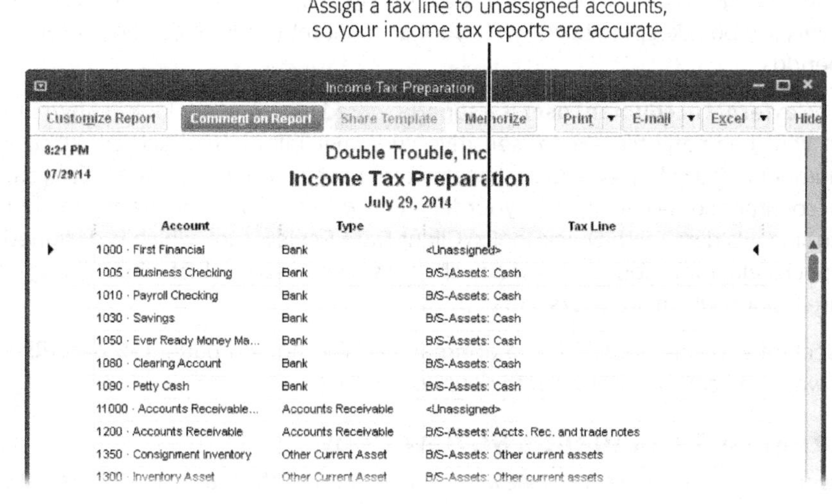

FIGURE 17-16

If you see "<Unassigned>" in the Tax Line column, you need to assign a tax line to that account. (The easiest way to identify the correct tax line is to ask your accountant or tax professional.) To edit an account, press Ctrl+A to display the Chart of Accounts window. Select the account, and then press Ctrl+E to open the Edit Account window. In the Tax Line Mapping drop-down list, choose the tax form and line for that account.

UP TO SPEED

Year-End Journal Entries

Journal entries run rampant at the end of the year. If your accountant makes journal entries for you or gives you instructions, you might be perfectly happy not knowing what these journal entries do. But if you go it alone, you need to know which journal entries to make.

For example, if you purchase fixed assets, you need to create a journal entry to handle depreciation. You might also create journal entries to record home-office expenses as owner's contributions to your company. Chapter 16 covers some of the journal entries you might need and explains how to create them.

If you aren't an accounting expert, don't waste precious time trying to figure out your journal entry needs; the cost of an accountant's or tax professional's services is piddling in comparison.

Sharing a Company File with Your Accountant

If you work with an accountant who uses QuickBooks, there are times when a tug-of-war over your company file is inevitable. You want to perform your day-to-day bookkeeping, but your accountant wants to review your books, correct mistakes you've made, enter journal entries to prepare your books for end-of-quarter or end-of-year reports, and so on. QuickBooks has two ways for you and your accountant to share:

- With an **accountant's review copy**, the two of you can stop squabbling because you each get your own copy of the company file. That way you can work on everyday bookkeeping tasks while your accountant tackles cleaning up earlier periods.
- The **external accountant user** is a superpowered user who can look at anything in your company file *except* sensitive customer information like credit card numbers. You set up an external accountant user in your company file for your accountant so he can log into your file, review every nook and cranny of your company's data (with QuickBooks' Client Data Review tool, which is designed specifically for accountants), make changes, and keep track of which changes are his and which are yours.

This section explains both of these approaches. The box on page 465 describes other ways you can collaborate with your accountant.

Creating an Accountant's Review Copy

The secret to an accountant's review copy is a cutoff date that QuickBooks calls the *dividing date*. Transactions before this date are fair game for your accountant, who can work on the accountant's review copy in the comfort of his own office.

Transactions after that date are under your command in your original company file. When your accountant sends a file with changes back to you, QuickBooks makes short work of merging his changes into your company file.

You have to be in single-user mode to create an accountant's copy. To switch to single-user mode, first make sure that everyone else is logged out of the company file, and then choose File→"Switch to Single-user Mode." After that, creating an accountant's review copy is a lot like creating other kinds of copies of your company file:

TIP If you have a few dozen windows open and laid out just the way you want, there's no need to gnash your teeth as QuickBooks closes all your windows to create the accountant's copy. *Before* you create the accountant's copy, save the current window arrangement so the program can reopen all those windows for you: Simply choose Edit→Preferences→Desktop View. On the My Preferences tab, choose the "Save current desktop" option, and then click OK to close the Preferences dialog box. After you create the accountant's copy, close and then reopen your company file to restore your saved windows.

1. **Choose File→Send Company File→Accountant's Copy→Save File. Then, in the Save Accountant's Copy dialog box (which automatically selects the Accountant's Copy option), click Next.**

   If your accountant needs unrestricted access to the file, select the "Portable or Backup File" option instead and see page 503 to learn how to create those types of files.

2. **On the "Set the dividing date" screen shown in Figure 17-17, choose the date when control over transactions changes hands. Click Next and then, in the message box about closing windows, click OK.**

   Use the Dividing Date drop-down list to choose the date you want as the dividing line between your work and your accountant's work. The upper part of the screen explains what each of you can do before and after the dividing date. (See the box on page 465 for more on accountant copy restrictions.) You can work on transactions *after* the dividing date, but only look at transactions *before* the dividing date. Your accountant, on the other hand, can work on transactions *before* the dividing date, but only look at transactions *after* the dividing date.

3. **In the Save Accountant's Copy dialog box, choose the folder or drive where you want to save the copy.**

   QuickBooks sets the "Save as type" box to "QuickBooks Accountant's Copy Transfer Files (*.QBX)" and automatically names the file using the company file's name followed by "Acct Transfer" and the date and time you created the file. (The extension .qbx stands for QuickBooks Accountant Transfer File.) You're free to edit the filename. Accountant's review copies use the QuickBooks portable file format, so they're usually small enough to email or save to a USB thumb drive. For example, a 20-megabyte company file may shrink to an accountant's review copy that's less than 2 MB.

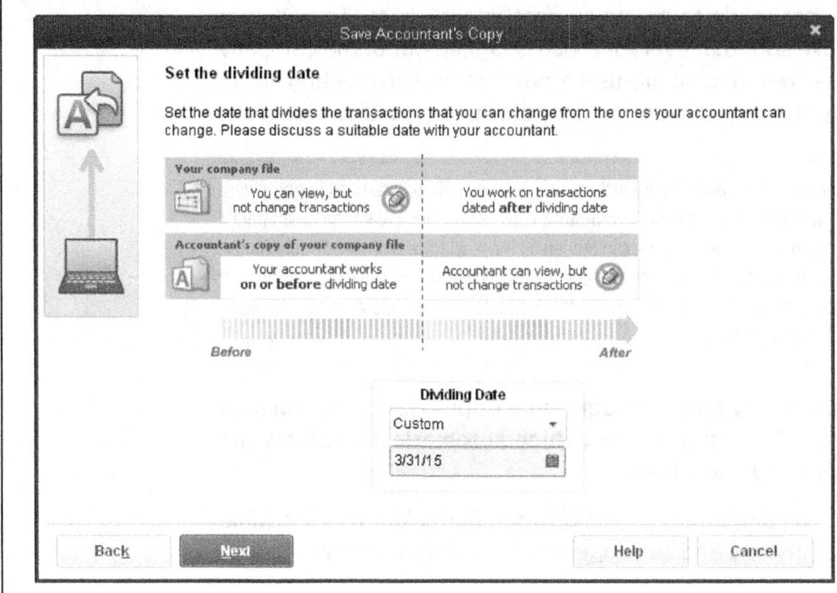

FIGURE 17-17

The dividing date you use is often the end of a fiscal period.

The Dividing Date drop-down list gives you only a few choices: End of Last Month, 2 Weeks Ago, and 4 Weeks Ago. If none of those options is what you want, you can specify a date by choosing Custom and then typing or choosing the date in the box that appears.

4. **To create the accountant's review copy, click Save.**

   Once you create an accountant's copy, QuickBooks reminds you that it exists: In the QuickBooks program window's title bar, you'll see the words "Accountant's Changes Pending" immediately after the company name.

5. **Send the file to your accountant.**

   Email the file to your accountant, or copy it to a CD or a USB thumb drive and send it to him. If you use a password on your company file (an excellent idea, no matter how tiny your company is—see page 723), don't forget to tell your accountant the password for the account you've set up for him.

NOTE If your accountant has access to Intuit's Accountant's Copy File Transfer Service, you can tell QuickBooks to create an accountant's review copy *and* send it to your accountant (choose File→Send Company File→Accountant's Copy→Send to Accountant); the copy goes up on a secure Intuit server, and your accountant gets an email notifying him that the file is waiting there. The only downside to this approach compared with sending the file yourself is that you have to wait until the file is transferred to the Intuit server before you can start working in QuickBooks again.

WORD TO THE WISE

Ways to Work with an Accountant

For most companies, QuickBooks is no substitute for an accountant. As financial professionals, accountants have the inside track on how best to handle your business finances. In addition to (or instead of) giving your accountant a review copy of your company file, here are some other ways you can integrate your accountant's advice into your company file:

- **A backup or portable copy**. You can give your accountant *exclusive* access to your company file by sending her a backup or portable copy (page 503) of it. When she finishes evaluating your books and making the changes she wants, you can either begin using the copy she sends back to you or make adjustments in your company file based on her recommendations. For example, your accountant can send you a document listing the journal entries you have to create to adjust your accounts along with copies of what your income statement and balance sheet should look like. After you create those journal entries, your company file contains all of your transactions and the adjustments she requested. You can confirm that you entered the journal entries correctly by making sure your financial reports match the ones she produced.
- **Working onsite**. An accountant can work on the company file right in your office with a login password from you (the external accountant user feature [page 467] gives your accountant special tools for working with your data). However, accountants are prone to doing things that require the company file to be in single-user mode, which might disrupt your day-to-day bookkeeping process.
- **The paper method**. If your accountant prefers to work with her own accounting system, you'll have to print the lists and reports that she requires. Then, when she gives you a list of changes and journal entries, you'll have to make those changes in your company file.

In addition to these options, QuickBooks Premier and Enterprise editions include a remote-access service, which lets your accountant access your QuickBooks company file over the Internet. Or you can use a remote-access service like those offered at *www.mypc.com* or *www.logmein.com.*

MERGING ACCOUNTANT CHANGES INTO YOUR COMPANY FILE

The company file your accountant sends back to you will have the file extension .qby instead of .qbx to indicate that it's an accountant's review copy import file. (Y follows X in the alphabet. Get it?) If you've imported data (like customer records) into QuickBooks before (page 132), the following steps should be familiar:

1. **If your copy of the company file isn't open, open it and back it up (page 491) before you import your accountant's changes.**
2. **Choose File→Send Company File→Accountant's Copy→Import Accountant's Changes from File. In the Import Accountant's Changes dialog box, navigate to the disk or folder that contains the accountant's file, and then double-click the filename.**

   QuickBooks displays the changes your accountant made, as shown in Figure 17-18. Click the Expand All button to see the entire list. Review the changes to see if any of them conflict with work that you've done while your accountant worked on the copy. Each change comes with an explanation of how to deal with these conflicts.

FREQUENTLY ASKED QUESTION

Bookkeeping During Accountant's Review

Are there any limitations I should know about before I create an accountant's review copy?

QuickBooks locks parts of your company file when an accountant's review copy exists, so both you and your accountant have to live with a few minor restrictions. Fortunately, most of the taboo tasks can wait during the few weeks that your accountant has a copy of your file.

While you and your accountant are working on your respective copies of the company file, you can work on transactions after the dividing date, so your bookkeeping duties are unaffected. You can also add entries to lists or edit the information in list entries, but you *can't* merge or delete list entries until after you import your accountant's changes. Similarly, you can add accounts, but you can't edit, merge, or deactivate accounts. Adding subaccounts is a no-no, too.

With a few restrictions, your accountant can work on transactions dated on or before the dividing date, whether she's adding, editing, voiding, or deleting transactions. However, payroll, non-posting transactions (like estimates), transfers, sales tax payments, and inventory assemblies are completely off limits to her. Because the limitations vary depending on what your accountant is trying to do, QuickBooks highlights fields in an accountant's copy to show the changes she can make that go back to you. (Fields that aren't sent back to you aren't highlighted.)

Your accountant can reconcile periods that end before the dividing date or change the cleared status of these earlier transactions. She can also add accounts to the chart of accounts and add items to some lists. For example, she can add customers, vendors, items, classes, fixed assets, sales tax codes, employees, and other names. Whether she can edit, inactivate, merge, and delete list items depends on the list. However, even if she can't edit them all, your accountant can still *view* all your QuickBooks lists.

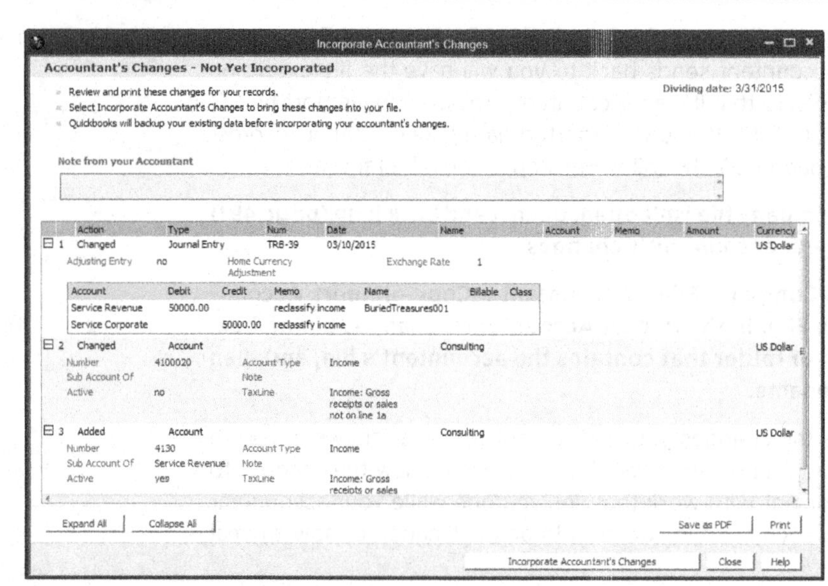

FIGURE 17-18

If you want a record of your accountant's changes, click Print or "Save as PDF."

NOTE If your accountant subscribes to Intuit's file-transfer service, she may tell you that the file she sent you is available on the Web. In that case, choose File→Send Company File→Accountant's Copy→Import Accountant's Changes from Web to retrieve the file.

3. **To make the changes in your company file, click the Incorporate Accountant's Changes button. (If you decide not to import the changes, click Close instead.)**

   QuickBooks backs up your company file and then imports the changes. After you review them, click Close.

CANCELING AN ACCOUNTANT'S REVIEW COPY

From time to time, you might want to get rid of an accountant's review copy without importing any of the changes. For instance, say you created an accountant's review copy by mistake or your accountant had so few changes that she simply told you what tweaks to make. Unlocking your company file so you can get back to performing any type of task requires nothing more than choosing File→Send Company File→Accountant's Copy→Remove Restrictions. The Remove Restrictions dialog box warns you that you won't be able to import changes from the accountant's review copy if you remove restrictions. To show that you know what you're doing, turn on the "Yes, I want to remove the Accountant's Copy restrictions" checkbox, and then click OK. The words "Accountant's Change Pending" disappear from the QuickBooks window's title bar.

Setting Up an External Accountant User

QuickBooks' *external accountant user* feature lets your accountant peruse your bookkeeping data and make changes while protecting your customers' sensitive financial info. When your accountant logs in as this user, she can use the Client Data Review tool to look for problems and clean up any she finds. For example, she can look at the changes you've made to lists like the Chart of Accounts and Item List, scan your company file for payments or credits you haven't applied, and find sales taxes or payroll liabilities you didn't record correctly.

NOTE An external accountant user lets an accountant use the Client Data Review tool from within clients' editions of QuickBooks. When someone logs in as an external accountant user, the Client Data Review item appears in the Company menu in any QuickBooks edition, including Pro and Premier.

Here's how to set up an external accountant user:

1. **Log into your company file as the administrator (page 718).**

   Only an administrator can create an external accountant user (who can perform tasks that even someone with administrator privileges can't, like run the Client Data Review tool).

2. **Choose Company→Set Up Users and Passwords→Set Up Users.**

   After you enter your password, the User List dialog box opens.

3. **Click Add User.**

   The "Set up user password and access" dialog box opens.

4. **In the User Name box, type the name for the external accountant user. In the Password and Confirm Password boxes, type the external accountant user's password, and then click Next.**

   The "Access for user" screen appears.

5. **Select the External Accountant option, and then click Next.**

   Because the external accountant user is so powerful, QuickBooks asks you to confirm that you want to give that level of access to the person. Click Yes.

6. **Click Finish.**

NOTE You can also change an existing user to an exte\rnal accountant user. To do that, log into your company file as an administrator, and then choose Company→Set Up Users and Passwords→Set Up Users. In the User List window that appears, select the person you want to change, and then click Edit User. Change the user's name and password if you want to, and then click Next. On the "Access for user" screen, select the External Accountant option, click Next, click Yes, and then click Finish.

1099s

In QuickBooks, paying independent contractors is no different from paying other vendors: You enter bills from your contractors, and then pay those bills. But at the end of the year, you have to generate 1099s for your independent workers.

If you set up QuickBooks to track 1099 payments (page 668) and designate your contractors as 1099 vendors (page 85), generating 1099s is a piece of cake. But before you push a stack of 1099 forms through your printer, it's a good idea to make sure your records are up to date and accurate; this section explains how to do that.

NOTE If you turn on the preference for QuickBooks payroll, then you can print W-2s for your employees by choosing Employees→Payroll Tax Forms & W-2s→Process Payroll Forms. For the full scoop on Intuit payroll services, download online Appendix D from this book's Missing CD page at *www.missing manuals.com/cds.*

Generating 1099 Reports

To review the amounts you've paid to 1099 vendors, choose Reports→Vendors & Payables, and then select either of the following reports:

- **1099 Summary**. This report includes each vendor you've set up as a 1099 vendor and the total amount you've paid each one. If any amount looks questionable, double-click it to display that vendor's transactions. Although this report lists only the vendors you set up as eligible for 1099 status, as shown in Figure 17-19, you can modify it to make sure you haven't left out any 1099 vendors. To do so, in the first 1099 Options drop-down list, choose "All vendors."

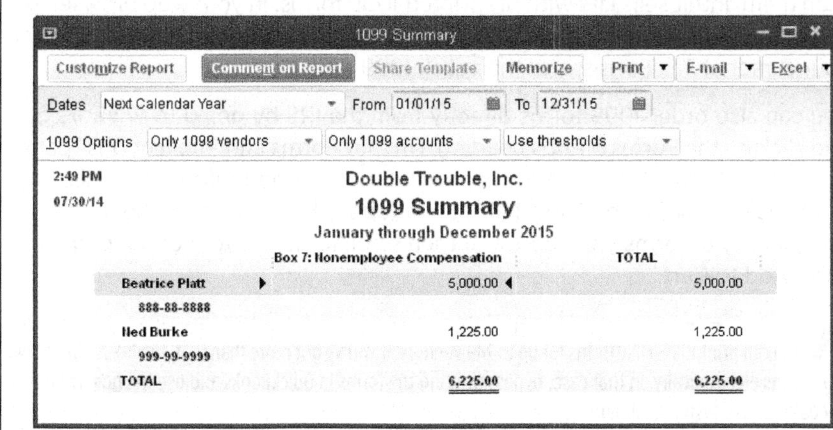

FIGURE 17-19

Regardless of the fiscal year you use for your company, payroll and 1099 tasks run on a calendar year, because your employees and subcontractors pay taxes for each calendar year. That's why the Dates drop-down list for the 1099 Summary report includes calendar-year date ranges.

If the 1099 Summary report is empty, your 1099 account mappings may be missing. In the report window's toolbar, in the middle drop-down list, choose "All allowed accounts," and then click Refresh to see payments you made to 1099 vendors regardless of the account. If your vendors leap into view, you need to map your accounts to 1099 boxes, as described in step 6 on page 471.

NOTE The federal government gives you the tiniest of breaks by setting thresholds for total payments to 1099 vendors. If you pay vendors less than the threshold, you don't have to generate 1099s for them. (For nonemployee compensation, the 2014 threshold is $600.)

In the 1099 Summary report's window, QuickBooks sets the last box in the 1099 Options row to "Use thresholds." This choice filters the vendors in the report to those that exceed the government's threshold (see the preceding Note). If you want to see *all* your 1099 vendors, regardless of what you paid them, choose "Ignore thresholds" here instead.

- **1099 Detail**. If you pay your independent contractors on a regular schedule, this report can pinpoint errors because it shows the transactions that produce vendors' 1099 amounts. If you see a gap in the payment schedule or two transactions in the same month, double-click a transaction amount to open the corresponding window, such as Write Checks.

Printing 1099-MISC Forms

The steps to start printing 1099 forms are simple but, as with any printing task, fraught with niggling details:

1. **Order printable 1099-MISC and 1096 forms or purchase them at your local business supply store.**

   1099-MISC and 1096 forms use special ink so that government agencies can scan them. Intuit sells kits with preprinted 1099 forms. In your web browser, go to *http://intuitmarket.intuit.com*. In that page's horizontal navigation bar, point your cursor at Tax Forms, and then click 1099 Kits.

   You can also order 1099 forms directly from the IRS by going to *www.irs.gov* and clicking the Forms & Pubs heading. On the "Forms and Publications" page, click Order Forms & Pubs, and then click Employer and Information Returns. In the value box for the 1099-MISC form (about halfway down the list), type the quantity of forms you need, and then scroll to the bottom of the page and click "Add to Cart."

NOTE You can print 1099-MISC forms for up to 249 vendors. If you've got more than that, the IRS requires you to file 1099 forms electronically. In that case, bypass printing the forms in QuickBooks and use the government's hopefully easy-to-use system instead.

2. **Load your printer with preprinted 1099-MISC forms.**

   If you use a printer that feeds individual sheets, don't bother placing a Copy 2 form after each Copy 1 form so that you can print multiple copies for each vendor. It's a lot easier to load the Copy 1 sheets and print a set of 1099 forms on those sheets, and then load the Copy 2 forms and print a second set of 1099 forms. You then send the Copy 1 sheets to the 1099 vendors and the Copy 2 sheets to the government in one big batch.

3. **Choose Vendors→Print/E-file 1099s→1099 Wizard. In the QuickBooks 1099 Wizard window that opens, click Get Started.**

   The QuickBooks 1099 wizard helps verify your 1099 information before you print. After you click Get Started, the "Select your 1099 vendors" screen appears.

4. **To transform a vendor into a 1099 vendor, turn on the checkbox in the vendor's Create Form 1099-MISC Column. When you've selected all the 1099 vendors, click Continue.**

   Turn off a vendor's checkbox if you don't need to create a 1099 for him.

5. **On the "Verify your 1099 vendors' information" screen, make any necessary changes to the vendors' tax ID, name, address, and phone number. When the information is correct, click Continue.**

   If required information is missing, the wizard outlines the table cell in red. Simply click the cell and type in the needed info.

6. **On the "Map vendor payment accounts" screen, map the accounts in your chart of accounts to the appropriate box on the 1099 form by clicking the down arrow in the "Apply payments to this 1099 box" cell and then choosing the appropriate 1099 box. When you're done, click Continue.**

   Most payments to 1099 vendors are mapped to Box 7: Nonemployee Compensation, which is why this screen includes a "Report all payments in Box 7" checkbox. To map *all* your 1099 vendors to Box 7, simply turn on this setting.

7. **On the "Review payments for exclusions" screen, click View Included Payments to see payments you made to vendors by credit card, debit card, gift card, or PayPal. If any payments made with those payment types appear in the "Check Payments Included on Forms 1099-MISC" report, double-click the transaction to open the Write Checks window. In the No. field, fill in the payment type, such as Debit, Visa, Giftcard, or PayPal.**

   Ever since the 2011 tax year, the IRS has required you to exclude payments you made by credit card, debit card, gift card, or third-party payment networks such as PayPal from Form 1099-MISC because they're reported by the card issuers and third-party payment networks on Form 1099-K. You can click View Excluded Payments to see which payments QuickBooks has excluded from Form 1099-MISC. If you make a payment in the Write Checks or Pay Bills windows, you can fill in the No. field with the payment type (up to eight characters) so that QuickBooks can automatically exclude that payment from Form 1099-MISC.

8. **When the "Check Payments Included on Forms 1099-MISC" report shows only check payments, click Continue.**

   After you edit transactions, click Refresh in the report window to view an updated report.

9. **On the "Confirm your 1099 entries" screen, review the vendors and their compensation to make sure it's correct, and then click Continue.**

10. **On the "Choose a filing method" screen, click Print 1099s.**

    If you file more than 249 forms, you have to e-file your 1099s. In that case, you can click "Go to Intuit 1099 E-File Service" to use Intuit's e-file service (which costs extra).

11. **In the "Printing 1099-MISC and 1096 Forms" dialog box, click OK.**

    QuickBooks opens the "Select 1099s to Print" dialog box shown in Figure 17-20 and automatically selects every vendor whose pay exceeds the government threshold (page 469).

12. **When the Valid ID and Valid Address columns are replete with the word Yes, click Preview 1099 to see the final forms before you print them.**

    In the Print Preview window, click Zoom In (if necessary) to verify the information. When you've reviewed the forms, click Close.

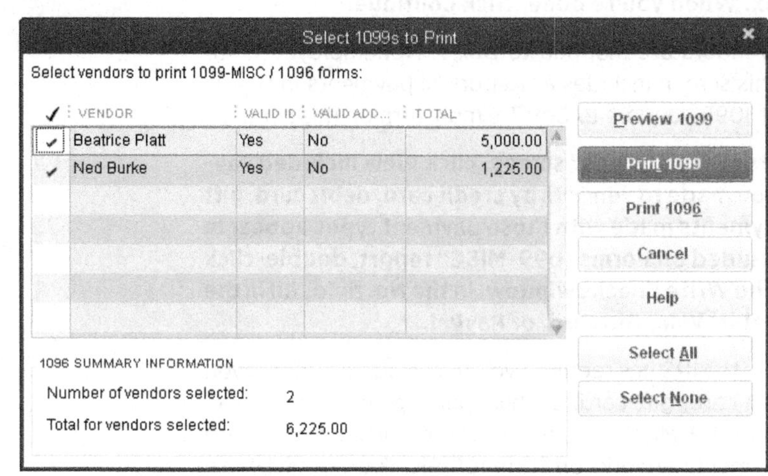

FIGURE 17-20

In addition to columns for the vendors' names and total pay, this table also includes the Valid ID and Valid Address columns. If you tend to create vendors on the fly without bothering to enter pesky details like their tax ID numbers or street addresses, scan these columns for the word "No." If you see it in any cell, click Cancel, and then edit your vendors to add this essential information. Then repeat steps 10 and 11 and verify that all the Valid ID and Valid Address cells say Yes.

13. **Click Print 1099.**

    QuickBooks opens the Print 1099 window. If the preprinted forms are waiting in a printer other than the one that the program chose, in the "Printer name" box, select the printer that holds your preprinted forms.

14. **Click Print.**

TIP Preprinted forms usually include Copy 1 for the vendor and Copy 2 for the government, but you'll also want a copy for your files. Instead of printing a *third* set of 1099s, run one of the printed sets through your copy machine or printer/scanner/copier.

Closing the Books for the Year

A few months after the end of a fiscal year, when tax returns rest under the gimlet-eyed scrutiny of the tax authorities, most companies close their books for the previous fiscal year. Doing so locks the transactions that you've already reported on tax returns or in financial results, because the IRS and shareholders alike don't look kindly on changes to the reports they've received.

QuickBooks, on the other hand, doesn't care whether you close the books in your company file. The closing task is mainly to protect you from the consequences of changing the numbers in previous years (like altering the company file so that it no longer matches what you reported to the IRS). But you're free to keep your books open if you're not worried about editing older transactions by mistake.

If you *do* close your books in QuickBooks, you can still edit transactions prior to the closing date. Unlike other bookkeeping programs in which closed means *closed*, in QuickBooks, folks who know the closing-date password can still change and delete closed transactions to, say, correct an egregious error before you rerun your end-of-year reports.

Closing the books in QuickBooks takes place in the Preferences dialog box. Switch to single-user mode (page 489), and then choose Edit→Preferences→Accounting and click the Company Preferences tab. To close the books as of a specific date, click the Set Date/Password button. Figure 17-21 shows what to do next.

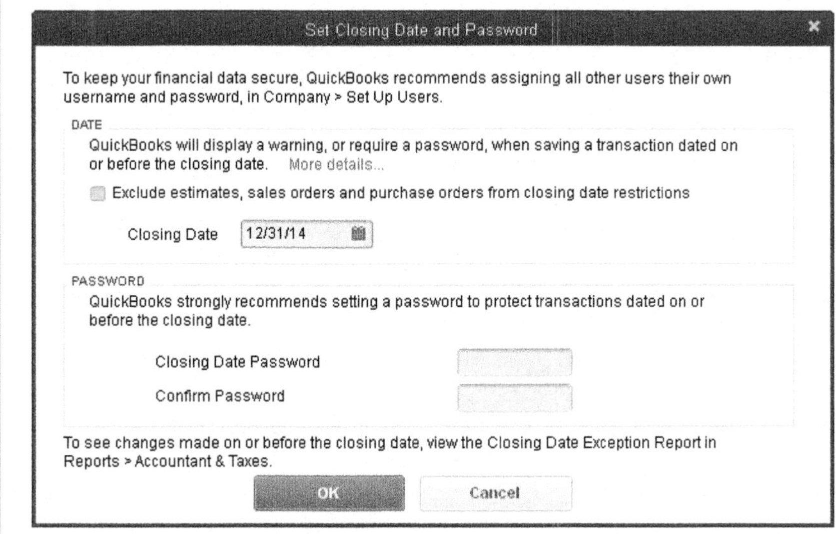

FIGURE 17-21

In the Closing Date box, type or select the last day of the previous fiscal year. If you want to let only authorized people make changes to the closed books, type a password in the Closing Date Password box. Then press Tab and, in the Confirm Password box, type the password a second time.

TIP *Don't* cut and paste the password from the Closing Date Password box to the Confirm Password box. These boxes display dots instead of the actual characters, which means you can't see typos. So if you set a password with a typo in it, you'll be unlikely to stumble on the correct password, and your closed books will remain shut as tight as a clam.

After you've set a password for the closing date, you'll have to enter that password whenever you want to modify transactions prior to that date. For example, if you try to edit a check that you wrote before the closing date, QuickBooks opens a message box with a Password field in it. Type the closing-date password, and then click OK to complete your edit.

TIP After you've completed all your year-end activities in QuickBooks, create a backup of your company file (page 491). With all the data that contributed to your financial reports and tax forms in this backup, it wouldn't be overkill to create *two* copies of it: one to keep close by in your office and one stored safely offsite in case of disaster.

PART 3

Managing Your Business

CHAPTER

18

Keeping Track of Financial Tasks

Attention to detail. Follow-through. These are a couple of the things that keep customers coming back for more. Following through on promises and calling to check that an issue was resolved successfully is good business. But sending reorder brochures after customers have already made purchases can just make them mad. In addition, paying a bill late can result in a whopping late fee. Conversely, you can leave money on the table if you don't take advantage of early payment discounts.

If you use other programs for managing customer relationships and keeping track of what you need to do, you can record these types of details there. But if you tend to work in QuickBooks all day long, the program has several features that can help you stay in customers' and vendors' good graces by tracking what's been going on and what still needs to be done.

QuickBooks' to-dos are preferable to papering the edges of your computer monitor with sticky notes, although you might prefer to keep to-dos in a program that you keep running constantly, like your email or calendar program, so that you see reminders when you need them. This chapter kicks off by explaining how to create and manage to-dos in QuickBooks.

If you collect info about customers, vendors, and employees, QuickBooks' notes feature can keep them close at hand. For instance, you could record one note to document a customer's problem with an order, and then record another note to document how he wants you to apply his credit. And if a note spawns an action item or two, you can create to-dos as you write up your comments. In this chapter, you'll learn how to create and manage notes, and how to create new to-dos at the same time.

Finally, reminders about when to perform bookkeeping tasks can help prevent late fees and keep income rolling in. QuickBooks' reminders prod you into action when it's time to send invoices, pay bills, reorder inventory, and so on. You can even create reminders for QuickBooks to-dos. This chapter shows you how to turn on reminders for the activities you don't want to forget, and how to tell QuickBooks when to remind you. You'll also learn how to use the Calendar window to see when transactions and to-dos are due.

Tracking To-Dos

QuickBooks can help you track business to-dos like phone calls to make, emails to send, meetings and appointments to attend, and tasks to complete. You can create to-dos for customers, leads who aren't yet customers, vendors, employees, or just for yourself. This section shows you how to create and keep track of to-dos.

Creating a To-Do

QuickBooks gives you several ways to open the Add To Do dialog box so you can create to-dos:

- **In the Customer, Vendor, or Employee Center,** select a customer, job, vendor, or employee, and then click the To Do's tab at the bottom of the center's window. Then click Manage To Do's→Create New.
- **In the Lead Center,** select a lead and then, on the To Do's tab at the bottom of the center's window, click the To Do button.
- **In the To Do List window** (which you open by choosing Company→To Do List), click the To Do button at the window's bottom left (shown in Figure 18-1, background).

Once the Add To Do dialog box is open, follow these steps:

1. **In the Type drop-down list, choose the kind of to-do you want to create.**

   To-dos can be calls, faxes, emails, meetings, appointments, or tasks.

2. **In the Priority box, choose High, Medium, or Low.**

   Assigning a priority is a good way to keep track of your most important to-dos. In the To Do List window, you can sort your to-dos by any field, including Priority, as described on page 481.

3. **If the to-do is associated with someone, turn on the With checkbox, and then specify whom it involves.**

   In the drop-down list below the checkbox, choose Lead, Customer, Vendor, or Employee. Then, in the drop-down list below *that*, choose the specific lead, customer, vendor, or employee associated with the to-do, as shown in Figure 18-1 (foreground).

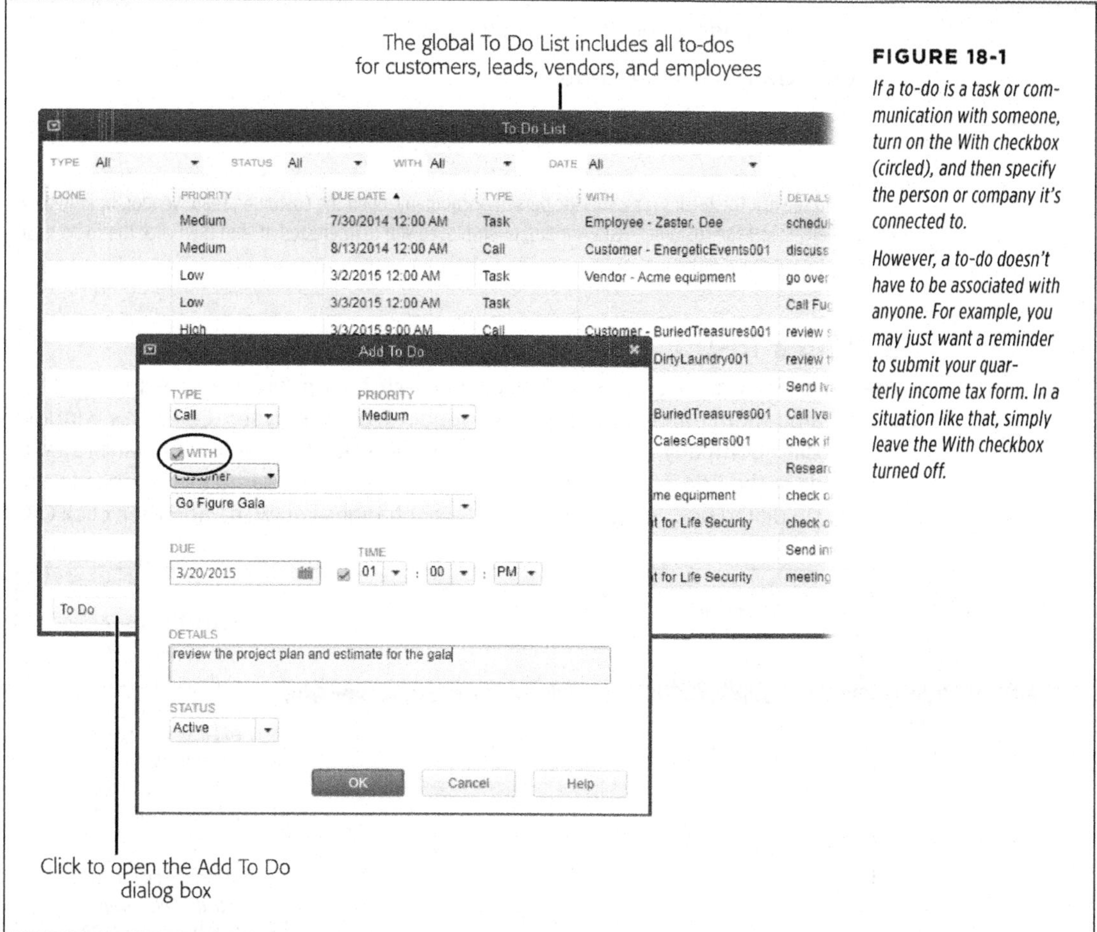
The global To Do List includes all to-dos for customers, leads, vendors, and employees
Click to open the Add To Do dialog box

FIGURE 18-1

If a to-do is a task or communication with someone, turn on the With checkbox (circled), and then specify the person or company it's connected to.

However, a to-do doesn't have to be associated with anyone. For example, you may just want a reminder to submit your quarterly income tax form. In a situation like that, simply leave the With checkbox turned off.

4. **Specify the due date and time.**

   In the Due box, QuickBooks automatically selects today's date, so be sure to choose the date by which you want to complete this to-do. To specify a time, turn on the checkbox to the left of the first Time box, and then set the time. If you want to keep your records complete and record a to-do that you've already finished, choose a date in the past, and then choose Done in the Status box (which you'll learn about in a sec).

5. **In the Details box, type information about the to-do.**

   By filling in the Details box, you can remind yourself what you want to do or delegate the to-do to someone else.

6. **In the Status box, choose Active.**

   Active represents to-dos that aren't complete yet. Later on, you can edit the to-do and change its status to Done when the task is complete, or to Inactive if you no longer need to perform the task.

7. **Click OK to save the to-do.**

   It appears in the To Do List window, which includes all the to-dos you create.

TIP To see just the to-dos for a specific person or company, open the Customer, Lead, Vendor, or Employee center. There, select the customer, lead, vendor, or employee you're interested in, and then click the To Do's tab at the bottom of the window.

Editing a To-Do

The To Do List window (Figure 18-2) is your one-stop shop for editing to-dos, whether you created them for customers, leads, vendors, or employees. Open this window by choosing Company→To Do List. Then double-click the to-do you want to edit. The fields in the Edit To Do dialog box that opens are the same as the ones in the Add To Do dialog box. Simply make whatever changes you want, and then click OK.

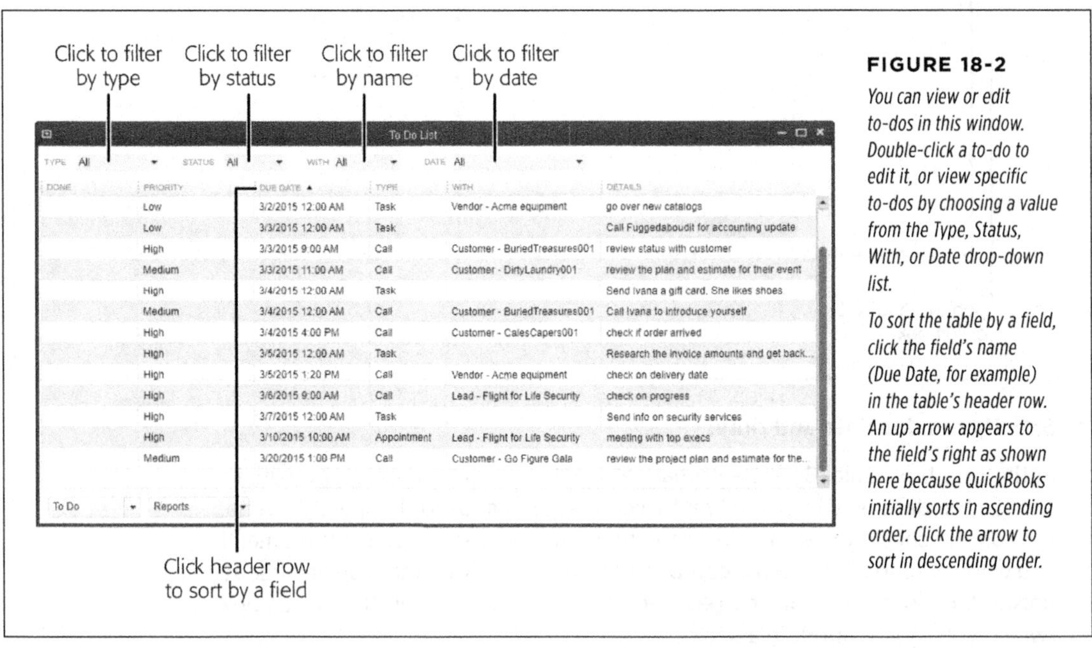
Click to filter by type
Click to filter by status
Click to filter by name
Click to filter by date
To Do List
Click header row to sort by a field

FIGURE 18-2

You can view or edit to-dos in this window. Double-click a to-do to edit it, or view specific to-dos by choosing a value from the Type, Status, With, or Date drop-down list.

To sort the table by a field, click the field's name (Due Date, for example) in the table's header row. An up arrow appears to the field's right as shown here because QuickBooks initially sorts in ascending order. Click the arrow to sort in descending order.

To delete a to-do, first click it in the To Do List window's table. Then, at the bottom of the window, click the down arrow to the To Do button's right, and then choose Delete Selected To Do. Or, in the Customer, Vendor, or Employee center, select a customer, job, vendor, or employee, and then click the To Do's tab at the bottom of the center's window. Select the to-do that you want to delete, and then click Manage To Do's→Delete Selected To Do. (In the Lead Center, select a lead and then, on the To Do's tab at the bottom of the center's window, click the To Do button and choose Delete Selected To Do.)

Viewing To-Dos

The To Do List window (Figure 18-2) shows all the to-dos you've created and lets you filter to-dos in several ways. For example, filtering by date is a great way to see what's on deck for the next few days. Or you can filter by type to see all the calls you need to make. On the other hand, you could filter by name to review what's going on with a customer before you meet with her.

You sort to-dos in the To Do List window by clicking a column heading, such as Priority, or filter the list by choosing entries in the drop-down lists at the top of the window:

- **Filter by type**. Click the Type box and then choose the kind of to-do you want to see, such as calls you need to make. Once you do that, the table displays only to-dos of that type.
- **Filter by status**. To focus on tasks that aren't complete yet, in the Status drop-down list, choose Active.
- **Filter by category of names**. To see to-dos for just leads, customers, vendors, or employees, choose a category in the With drop-down list.
- **Filter by date**. To see to-dos that are due during a specific time period, choose the period in the Date drop-down list.

NOTE To-dos also appear in the QuickBooks Calendar (page 486). And if you want the program to remind you about to-dos, you can set up reminders for them (page 483).

Adding Notes

You can add as many separate notes as you want to customers, leads, vendors, and employees. To view them, simply open the appropriate center (Customer Center, Vendor Center, and so on), select the record you want (customer, job, lead, vendor, or employee), and then click the Notes tab in the lower-right part of the window. All the notes for the selected record appear, as demonstrated with a customer in Figure 18-3 (background).

TIP New in QuickBooks 2015, you can *pin* one of the notes in the Customer Center's Notes tab so that it appears in the Customer Information pane's top right. (You can also pin notes in the Vendor and Employee centers.) When you create your first note for a record, QuickBooks *automatically* pins it. If you create more notes and want to pin a different note, then on the window's Notes tab, click the note's Pinned cell (labeled in Figure 18-3). When you do that, QuickBooks deselects the previous pinned note (if there was one).

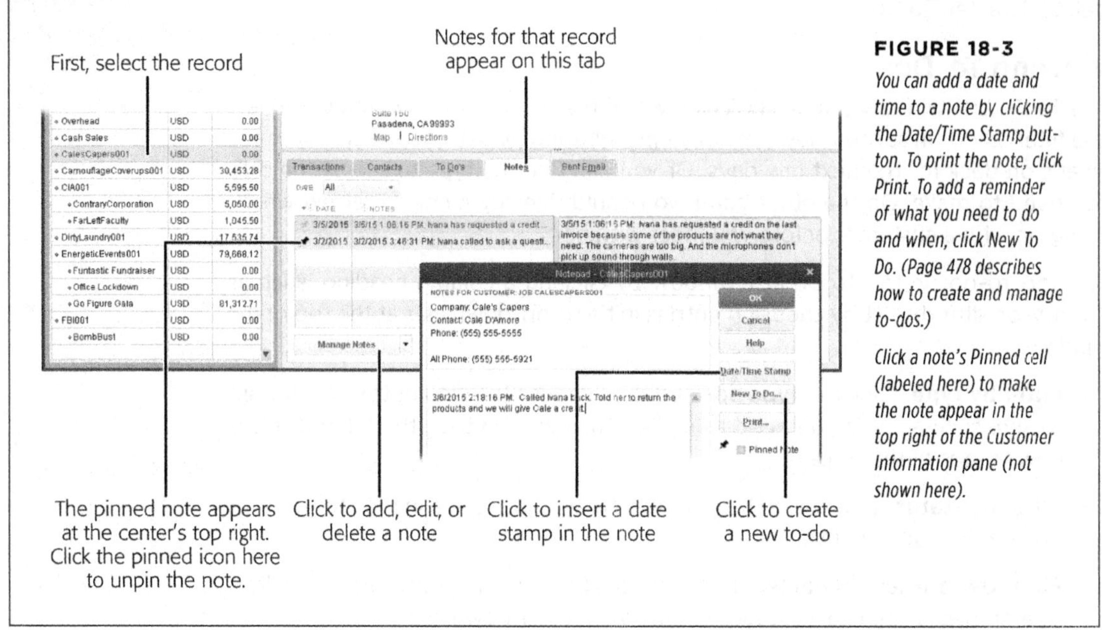

First, select the record
Notes for that record appear on this tab
The pinned note appears at the center's top right. Click the pinned icon here to unpin the note.
Click to add, edit, or delete a note
Click to insert a date stamp in the note
Click to create a new to-do

FIGURE 18-3

You can add a date and time to a note by clicking the Date/Time Stamp button. To print the note, click Print. To add a reminder of what you need to do and when, click New To Do. (Page 478 describes how to create and manage to-dos.)

Click a note's Pinned cell (labeled here) to make the note appear in the top right of the Customer Information pane (not shown here).

On a center's Notes tab, you can add, edit, and delete notes in the same way you work with to-dos (page 478):

- **Add a note**. With a record selected, on the Notes tab, click Manage Notes→Add New. The Notepad dialog box opens with the record's contact information filled in as shown in Figure 18-3 (foreground). To keep track of when conversations happen, click Date/Time Stamp before you start typing. If you're adding a note about something that happened on a day other than today, you have to type in the date.
- **Edit a note**. Select the note you want to edit, and then click Manage Notes→Edit Selected Note.
- **Delete a note**. Select the note you want to delete, and then click Manage Notes→Delete Selected Note.

The Notes tab displays all the notes you've added for the selected record. To limit the notes to a date range, click the Date box and choose the time period you want, such as "This Month-to-date."

Reminders

QuickBooks reminds you when to perform many accounting and business tasks so you can save your brain cells for remembering more important things—like your anniversary. Even if your brain is the size of a small planet, you're likely to rely on QuickBooks' reminders to nudge you when it's time to print checks, print or email invoices, remind your customers to pay overdue invoices, deposit payments, and so on. And when you turn on reminders for to-dos, the program can give you hints about any task that you don't want to forget, whether it's for a customer, vendor, employee, or yourself.

To open the Reminders window, which got a makeover in QuickBooks 2015 and is shown in Figure 18-4, choose Company→Reminders. Alternatively, you can click the "View reminders" icon at the top right of the QuickBooks menu bar; the icon looks like an alarm clock and includes a flag that indicates how many reminders are waiting for you. (See page 659 to learn how to make QuickBooks open the Reminders window every time you open a company file.) You can tell QuickBooks whether you want it to display summaries or individual reminders. A summary displays a heading and the total amount of money for that category. With details, you see each transaction on a separate line.

TIP In the Reminders window, click the flippy triangle to the left of a heading to expand or collapse that section (that is, show or hide its individual reminders). These triangles are labeled in Figure 18-4.

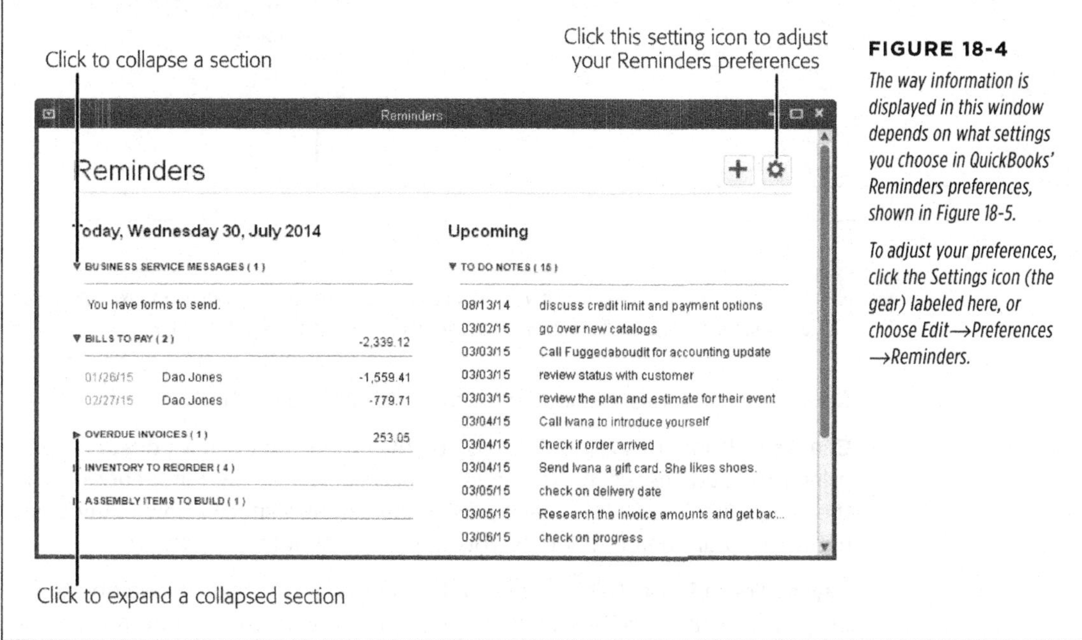

FIGURE 18-4

The way information is displayed in this window depends on what settings you choose in QuickBooks' Reminders preferences, shown in Figure 18-5.

To adjust your preferences, click the Settings icon (the gear) labeled here, or choose Edit→Preferences →Reminders.

Out of the box, QuickBooks automatically sets every kind of reminder to show a summary, but you can tell the program what you want reminders for and when you want to be reminded. To customize your reminders, in the Reminders window, click the Settings icon (it looks like a gear), or choose Edit→Preferences→Reminders, and then click the Company Preferences tab. (Reminders settings apply to everyone who logs into the company file, and you need administrator privileges to change them.)

As shown in Figure 18-5, you can specify the level of detail for each type of reminder and, in some cases, when you want QuickBooks to remind you. The Show Summary options tell QuickBooks to display a single reminder and the total amount of money in the Reminders window, like the Overdue Invoices row in Figure 18-4. The Show List options display each transaction on a separate line instead, as shown below the "Bills to Pay" heading in Figure 18-4; in that example, QuickBooks displays one line with the total amount of bills to pay, followed by a line showing each payment.

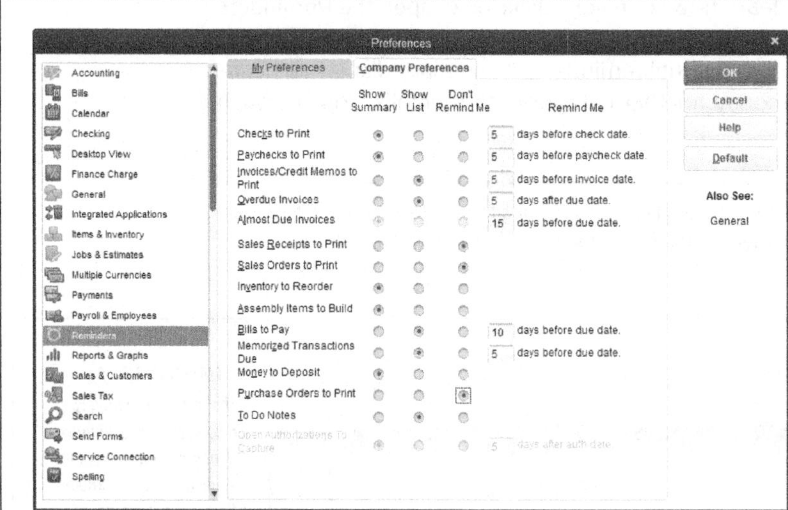

FIGURE 18-5

You can choose how and when QuickBooks reminds you to order inventory, pay bills, and so on. For transactions like bills that require action by a specific date, you can tell QuickBooks how far in advance to remind you.

If you don't want a reminder for a specific type of transaction, choose the Don't Remind Me option.

NOTE You can set up reminders only if you've turned on the corresponding feature. For example, if you don't use QuickBooks inventory, the "Inventory to Reorder" reminder preference is dimmed.

QuickBooks can generate reminders for the following transactions:

- **Checks to Print**. This reminder tells you that you've got checks queued up to print. (You add checks to the queue by turning on the Print Later checkbox in the Write Checks window [page 203].) You can also specify how many days' notice you want before the date you entered to print the checks.
- **Paychecks to Print**. This reminder tells you that paychecks are waiting to be printed. You can specify how many days' notice you want before the payroll date you entered.

- **Invoices/Credit Memos to Print**. To print invoices or credit memos in batches, as described on page 313, in the Create Invoices window, turn on the Print Later checkbox. This reminder notifies you about unprinted invoices or credit memos. You can specify how many days' notice you want before the invoice or credit memo date you entered.
- **Overdue Invoices**. This reminder warns you about invoices that have passed their due dates with no payment from the customer. You can specify how many days overdue an invoice needs to be before QuickBooks reminds you.
- **Almost Due Invoices**. This reminder tells you about invoices that are due soon. QuickBooks automatically selects the Show Summary option for this reminder, and you can't change it. However, you *can* change the number of days before the due date.
- **Sales Receipts to Print**. If you queued up sales receipts to print as a batch (page 313), this is the reminder about printing them. QuickBooks reminds you as soon as you have any sales receipts to print.
- **Sales Orders to Print**. This preference is available only if you use QuickBooks Premier or Enterprise. It reminds you to print sales orders you've queued up.
- **Inventory to Reorder**. When you create Inventory Part items in QuickBooks, you can set a reminder for when you need to reorder inventory (page 521). This reminder warns you when a sales form you create reduces the number of items on hand below your reorder point. (QuickBooks generates a reminder immediately.)
- **Assembly Items to Build**. This preference is available only if you use QuickBooks Premier or Enterprise. It warns you when the quantity of assembled items drops below your build point (page 523).
- **Bills to Pay**. This reminder nudges you about bills you have to pay. (Entering bills is described on page 184.) You can specify how many days' notice you want before the date the bills are due.
- **Memorized Transactions Due**. When you memorize transactions, you can specify a date for the next occurrence (page 324). This reminder tells you about recurring memorized transactions. You can specify how many days' notice you want before the next scheduled occurrence.
- **Money to Deposit**. When you receive payments, you can group them with other undeposited funds so you aren't running to the bank every five minutes as checks pour in. If you want to put your money to work as soon as possible, turn on this checkbox to receive a reminder whenever you have any funds to deposit.
- **Purchase Orders to Print**. This reminder gives you a prod about purchase orders you haven't yet printed.
- **To Do Notes**. To-do items can include dates, as described on page 479. This reminder shows you when to-do items are due.

NOTE The Open Authorizations To Capture setting is grayed out unless you use QuickBooks Enterprise.

Your Financial Calendar

The Calendar window (Figure 18-6) acts as a dashboard that shows when transactions and to-dos were entered or are due. To open it, choose Company→Calendar, or click the Calendar icon on the icon bar or in the Home Page's Company panel.

NOTE Unfortunately, there's no way to exchange the to-dos and transactions on this calendar with an external calendar like Google Calendar or the one in Microsoft Outlook. To see QuickBooks to-dos and transactions on a calendar, you have to launch QuickBooks and open the Calendar window.

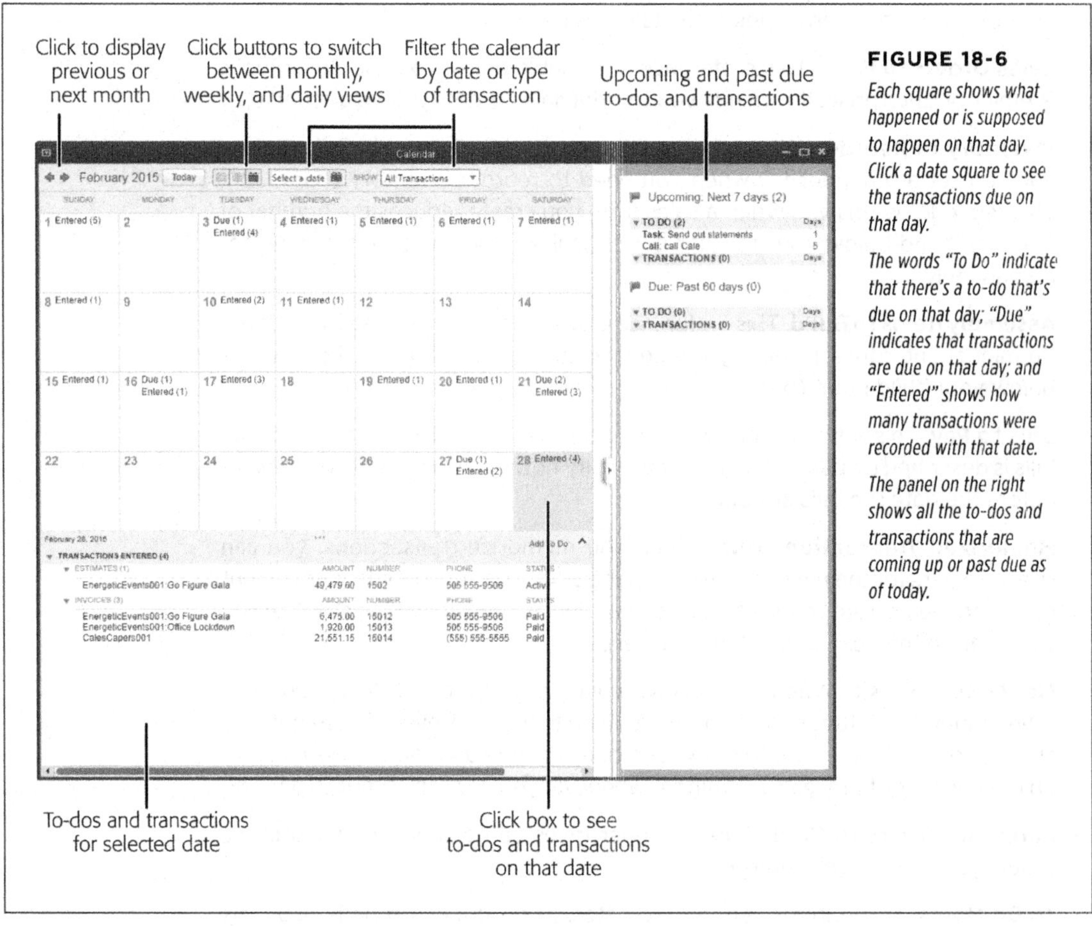
Click to display previous or next month
Click buttons to switch between monthly, weekly, and daily views
Filter the calendar by date or type of transaction
Upcoming and past due to-dos and transactions
To-dos and transactions for selected date
Click box to see to-dos and transactions on that date

FIGURE 18-6

Each square shows what happened or is supposed to happen on that day. Click a date square to see the transactions due on that day.

The words "To Do" indicate that there's a to-do that's due on that day; "Due" indicates that transactions are due on that day; and "Entered" shows how many transactions were recorded with that date.

The panel on the right shows all the to-dos and transactions that are coming up or past due as of today.

NOTE The Calendar window's toolbar includes icons and boxes for controlling your view. Here's what they do from left to right: Click a blue arrow to move to the previous or next time period. Click Today to select the square for today's date. Click the icons to display one day, one week, or one month, from left to right. Use the Show drop-down list to pick the transactions you want to see in the calendar.

Out of the box, the Calendar window has three panes:

- The **calendar** initially displays an entire month. Each square in the calendar summarizes the transactions and to-dos for that day, as shown in Figure 18-6. For example, click a given day, and you see the to-dos and transactions due on that day. Double-click a to-do to open it in the Edit To Do dialog box, or double-click a transaction to open it in its corresponding window (Create Invoices for an invoice, for example).

TIP To see more detail in the calendar, switch to a weekly or even a daily view. At the top of the window, click the *first* button to the right of the Today button to display a single day in the calendar pane. The daily view shows transactions and to-dos for a day, similar to what you see in the bottom pane of the Calendar. Click the *second* button to display a weekly view.

- The **Upcoming and Due pane** on the right lists the to-dos and transactions that are on deck or past due as of today, which is incredibly handy for staying on top of your bookkeeping and business activities. Double-click a to-do to open the Edit To Do dialog box with the details about what you're supposed to do and when. Double-click a transaction to open it in its corresponding window.
- The **activity pane** at the bottom of the window lists the to-dos and transactions that were entered or are due on the date you select in the calendar. The customer's telephone number is listed for invoices, which is handy if you want to call and find out when you can expect a payment. If a day is particularly busy, you can expand this pane by pointing your cursor at the three blue dots at the top of the pane and then dragging.

NOTE To hide the "Upcoming and Due" pane, click the right arrow on its left edge; to restore this pane, click the left arrow on the Calendar pane's right edge. To collapse the activity pane, click the up arrow at its top right; to expand the pane, click the down arrow. If you click the Daily View button at the top of the window (put your cursor over each button to see a tooltip with the button's name), the calendar disappears; to restore the calendar, click the Weekly View or Monthly View button.

CHAPTER

19

Managing QuickBooks Files

When company ledgers were made of paper, you had to be careful not to tear the pages or spill coffee on them. Today's electronic books require their own sort of care. Protecting your QuickBooks files is essential, not only because they tell the financial story of your company, but also because computers are notorious for chewing up data in all sorts of ways.

QuickBooks files have a few advantages over their paper-based relatives. Most importantly, you can easily make copies of them for safekeeping. (QuickBooks can also create a *special* copy of your company file so you and your accountant can both work on it at the end of the year; see page 462 for details.) If several people work on your company file simultaneously, you'll learn when and how to switch from multi-user mode to single-user mode so you can perform the housekeeping tasks that require dedicated access. This chapter focuses on the most important things you can do with your QuickBooks files: back them up and copy them. It also explains why and how to verify, condense, and delete your files, which you'll do less often—if ever.

Switching Between Multi- and Single-User Mode

In QuickBooks, some maintenance tasks require that only one person have access to the company file. So if you told QuickBooks to set up your company file in multi-user mode when you created it, you have to switch to *single-user mode* for the following tasks:

- Merge or delete accounts and items.
- Set up some aspects of your company file, such as finance charges.
- Condense or export data.
- Save an accountant's copy of your company file (although you can open or convert an existing accountant's copy while in multi-user mode).

TIP You can verify data (page 507) while in multi-user mode, although the verification isn't as rigorous as the one performed while in single-user mode. Being in single-user mode can also speed up time-consuming tasks like running humongous reports.

To see which mode your company file is currently in, display QuickBooks' File menu. If you see "Switch to Multi-user Mode" on the menu, you're in single-user mode. If you see "Switch to Single-user Mode" instead, you're in multi-user mode. (The box on page 491 explains how to quickly close a file that's in multi-user mode.)

The good news is that you don't have to remember which tasks demand single-user mode; QuickBooks reminds you to switch modes if you try to perform a single-user-mode task when the company file is chugging away in multi-user mode. Because everyone else has to close the company file before you can switch it to single-user mode, you may find it easiest to wait until no one else is working on the company file (early in the morning or after business hours, say).

Here's how you switch from multi-user mode to single-user mode:

1. **If your single-user task can't wait until off hours, ask everyone else to close the company file you want to work on.**

   They can choose File→Close Company/Logoff or simply exit QuickBooks to close the company file.

2. **When everyone else has closed the company file, open it in QuickBooks by choosing File→Open Previous Company, and then selecting the company file in the submenu.**

   If the company file doesn't appear on the Open Previous File submenu, choose File→"Open or Restore Company" instead. In the "Open or Restore Company" dialog box, select the "Open a company file" option, and then click Next. In the "Open a Company" dialog box that appears, navigate to the folder where you store the file, and then double-click its filename.

3. **Choose File→"Switch to Single-user Mode." In the message box that appears telling you the file is in single-user mode, click OK.**

   QuickBooks closes all open windows before it switches to single-user mode. After you click OK, it reopens the windows from the previously saved desktop (page 644), and you're ready to work solo on the company file.

4. **After you finish your single-user task, switch back to multi-user mode by choosing File→"Switch to Multi-user Mode." When the message box appears telling you the file is in multi-user mode, click OK.**

   You'll see all the windows in QuickBooks close. After you click OK, the previously saved desktop's windows open, and the company file is back in multi-user mode.

Don't forget to tell your colleagues that they can log back into the company file.

POWER USERS' CLINIC

Closing a File in Multi-User Mode—Stat!

Say your IT department is ready to shut down your company's servers for a long-awaited maintenance update. But a couple of your accounting folks went home without logging out of your company file. Shutting down that server while your company file is open is asking for trouble. Fortunately, in QuickBooks 2015, an administrator user can now close a company file even if people are still logged into it.

If you're an administrator user, here's what you do:

1. In your computer's system tray, click the QuickBooks Messenger icon (it looks like a stylized person with a green callout at its top right).
2. In the QuickBooks Messenger window that opens, click the Actions down arrow, and then choose Close Company Files for Users.
3. In the Close Company Files for Users dialog box, select the users whose company files you want to close.
4. If it's truly an emergency, below the "Select users" list, turn on the "Close even if users have unsaved data" checkbox.
5. Click the Close Company File button.

QuickBooks closes the company files that are open and discards any unsaved data *if* you chose that setting.

Backing Up Files

If you already have a backup procedure for *all* your computer files, QuickBooks' Backup feature might seem about as useful as your appendix. Your company-wide backups regularly squirrel your data files away in a safe place, ready to rescue you should disaster strike. Still, QuickBooks' Backup feature complements even the most robust backup plan. And if you run a mom-and-pop business, online backups let you back up all your data without hiring an IT staff. Here are some ways you can put the program's Backup feature to work:

- **Back up one QuickBooks company file**. Before you experiment with a new QuickBooks feature or perform a data-changing task like condensing your company file, you don't want to back up *all* your data—just the company file. That way, if the experiment goes wrong, you can restore the backup and try a different approach. You can also call on QuickBooks Backup when you've worked hard on your company file (pasting hundreds of inventory items into it from Excel, say) and the thought of losing that work makes you queasy. In both of these situations, running a QuickBooks *manual backup* (page 495) creates a backup file immediately.

NOTE QuickBooks backup files aren't merely copies of your company files—they're compressed versions that take up less space (about 20 to 25 percent less, depending on what you store in your company file).

- **Schedule backups of your QuickBooks data**. If you have trouble remembering to back up your work, QuickBooks' scheduled and automatic backups can help. You can set the program to automatically back up a company file after you've opened it a certain number of times. That way, if you mangle your data or it gets corrupted in some way, you can use one of these backups to recover. The program can also create company-file backups automatically according to the schedule you specify—Tuesdays through Saturdays at 2:00 a.m., for example.
- **Back up your data online**. Online backups are a handy alternative to setting up your own backup plan (scheduling regular backups, rotating backup media, storing backups offsite, and so on). You can select which data you want to back up and when. That way, when QuickBooks creates the backups, they're encrypted and stored at secure data centers managed by IT professionals. If you don't have IT staff to back up your data and keep it secure, this method may be worth every penny. See the box on page 497 to learn more.

TIP Don't use QuickBooks portable files as backups. Although these files are smaller and easier to send to others than standard company files, they don't contain all the information that backup files do. For example, unlike backup files, portable files don't contain ancillary files like letters, logos, images, and templates. They also don't contain transaction logs, which Intuit Technical Support can use to help restore transactions if your file is damaged.

Whether you want to set up options for your backups, schedule backups, or run a backup immediately, you start by opening the Create Backup dialog box by choosing File→Backup Company→Create Local Backup.

NOTE What and how often you back up are up to you (or your company's system administrators). It depends on what information you can't afford to lose and how much data you're willing to recreate in case of a disaster. Most companies back up their data every night and also create additional backup copies daily or weekly to store offsite.

If you rely on your company-wide backups, consider testing their reliability at least once a year. Tell the IT folks that you've deleted your QuickBooks company file and see if they can provide you with a recent backup. (Then bring them donuts the next day as a thank-you.)

Choosing Standard Backup Settings

For each company file that you back up, you can choose when, where, and how many backups QuickBooks creates. These standard settings are great timesavers and make for consistent backups. For example, you can tell QuickBooks to ask you about backing up your data after you've closed the company file a specific number of times, or have it automatically append the date and time that you run the backup to the name of the backup file. You simply choose these settings once for each company file, and QuickBooks uses them for every backup of that file—until you change the settings, of course.

Here's how to choose your backup settings:

1. **Choose File→Backup Company→Create Local Backup.**

   The Create Backup dialog box opens with the "Local backup" option selected.

2. **Click Options.**

   The Backup Options dialog box (Figure 19-1) lays out your choices for backing up the current company file.

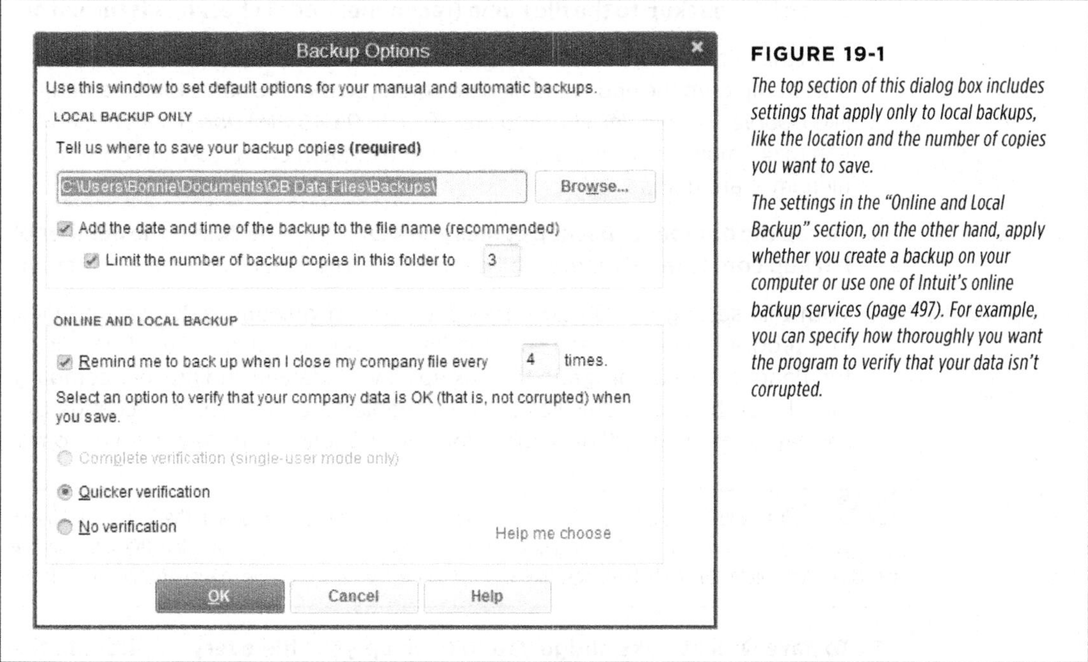

FIGURE 19-1

The top section of this dialog box includes settings that apply only to local backups, like the location and the number of copies you want to save.

The settings in the "Online and Local Backup" section, on the other hand, apply whether you create a backup on your computer or use one of Intuit's online backup services (page 497). For example, you can specify how thoroughly you want the program to verify that your data isn't corrupted.

3. **To the right of the "Tell us where to save your backup copies (required)" box, click Browse. In the "Browse for Folder" dialog box, choose where you want to save the backup file, and then click OK to return to the Backup Options dialog box.**

   To protect your data from both human error and hardware failure, back up your file to a different hard drive than the one where your company file is stored, or to removable media like a CD, DVD, or USB thumb drive. That way, your backup file will be safe if the hard drive that holds your company file crashes. For that reason, if you choose a backup location that's on the drive where you store your company file, when you click OK in the Backup Options dialog box (step 8 below), QuickBooks displays a dialog box with two buttons: Change Location and "Use this location." To play it safe and save the backup in a *different* spot, click Change Location, which returns you to the Backup Options dialog box so you can click Browse again. Or, as long as you run company-wide backups that store your data on another disk or removable media and you're OK with backing up your company file to a hard drive for protection during the day, click "Use this location."

NOTE The "Browse for Folder" dialog box doesn't let you create a new folder. So if you want to save your backups in a folder that doesn't exist yet, click Cancel and create the new folder in Windows Explorer. Then, in the Backup Options dialog box, click Browse.

4. **So that you never overwrite a backup file, make sure the "Add the date and time of the backup to the file name (recommended)" checkbox is turned on.**

   With this setting turned on, when QuickBooks creates the backup file, it tacks a timestamp onto the end of the filename prefix so that the name looks something like *Double Trouble, Inc (Backup Mar 19,2015 08 46 PM).qbb.* That way, unless you make multiple backups within a minute of each other, you can be sure the filenames are unique.

5. **To cap the number of backup copies you save, keep the "Limit the number of backup copies in this folder to" checkbox turned on and choose a number.**

   With this setting on, QuickBooks takes care of deleting older backup files. The program automatically sets the limit to three, which is fine if you use a full-fledged backup program to back up all your data including your company files. If you back up your files to an insatiable hard disk, you can change this setting to save up to 99 backups before QuickBooks starts deleting older ones.

NOTE When you create a backup that hits the limit you set for backup copies in the folder, QuickBooks displays the "Delete Extra Backups?" dialog box, which asks you if you want to keep or delete the oldest backup file. Click "Yes, Delete" to delete the oldest file, or "No, Don't Delete" if you decide to keep the file after all.

6. **To have QuickBooks nudge you to back up your file every so often, in the "Online and local backup" section, make sure the "Remind me to back up when I close my company file every _ times" checkbox is on.**

   That way, when you've closed the company file that number of times (it's set to four unless you change it), QuickBooks displays the Automatic Backup message box. To create a backup of your company file, in the message box, click Yes to display the Create Backup dialog box so you can run a backup. If you decide to bypass this backup opportunity, click No in the message box instead.

7. **Select a verification option.**

   If your company file is in single-user mode, QuickBooks automatically selects "Complete verification (recommended)." For a file in multi-user mode, the program automatically selects "Quicker verification," because complete verification isn't available for multi-user files. Quicker verification, as its name suggests, is speedier than complete verification but risks letting some corrupted data slip through. If you want to make sure that the data you save isn't corrupt, first switch your company file to single-user mode and then, in the Backup Options dialog box, select the "Complete verification (recommended)" option. At the other extreme, for high speed—and higher risk—select "No verification."

8. **When all the settings look good, click OK to close the Backup Options dialog box.**

   If you see a dialog box that includes a Change Location button, see step 3 for help deciding which option to choose.

9. **Back in the Create Backup dialog box, click Finish to run a backup with the settings you chose.**

   Click Cancel to close the dialog box without running a backup.

Backing Up Manually

If you just spent several hours recording tricky transactions in QuickBooks, you definitely want to save that work. To run a backup right away, here's what you do:

1. **To back up your file to removable media like a CD, DVD, or USB thumb drive, put the disc in the drive (or the thumb drive into a USB port).**

   You don't *have* to put the media in until just before you click Save, but you may as well do it now so you don't forget.

2. **Choose File→Backup Company→Create Local Backup.**

   The Create Backup dialog box opens.

3. **To save the file to your computer or removable media, choose "Local backup" (if it isn't already selected), and then click Next.**

   The Create Backup dialog box includes options for backing up your file locally—on your computer or removable media—or online. To create an online backup, select (you guessed it) the "Online backup" option. QuickBooks' online backup service isn't free, but it has its advantages, as the box on page 497 explains.

4. **For a local backup, on the "When do you want to save your backup copy?" screen, choose "Save it now" (if it isn't already selected), and then click Next.**

   The Save Backup Copy dialog box opens to the folder you specified in QuickBooks' backup options (page 492), as Figure 19-2 shows. If you want to save the file somewhere else, browse to the folder.

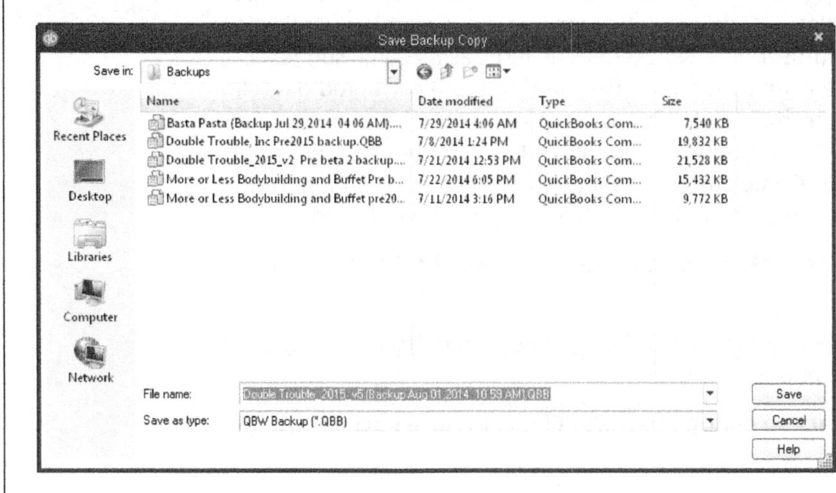

FIGURE 19-2

QuickBooks automatically fills in the "File name" box with the same filename prefix as your company file and adds a timestamp to show when you made the backup—unless you told it not to (see step 4 on page 494). For example, if you're backing up your Double Trouble.qbw *file, the backup file's prefix is something like "Double Trouble (Backup Mar 03,2015 11 38 AM)." The "Save as type" box is automatically set to "QBW Backup (*.qbb)," which is what you want.*

5. **Click Save.**

   The Working message box shows QuickBooks' progress as it verifies your data and creates the backup. When it's done, another message box tells you the backup was successful. Click OK to close the box.

Automated Backups

QuickBooks can back up your data without your help in two different ways:

- **Automatic backup**. This kind of backup runs after you close a company file a specific number of times, which is great for protecting the work you do in a few back-to-back QuickBooks sessions. You simply close the company file at the end of a session and, if this session hits the magic number, QuickBooks asks if you want to create a backup.
- **Scheduled backups**. You can also schedule backups to run at a specific date and time (typically when you aren't around). A scheduled backup for a single company file is ideal when your QuickBooks data is the *only* data on your computer or you want to back up your books more often than your other data. Otherwise, you're better off using your operating system's backup feature (or an online backup service—see the box on page 497) to schedule a backup that captures *all* your data.

This section explains the differences between these options and how you set up each one.

POWER USERS' CLINIC

Backing Up Online

Online backup services cost money, but as long as your Internet connection is relatively fast, they can be a worthwhile investment. You can use one to back up *all* your data—databases, documents, and email—so your backups reside in a data center managed by IT experts who live, eat, and breathe effective backup procedures.

Intuit Data Protect (*http://appcenter.intuit.com/intuitdataprotect*) can back up your entire computer (not just your QuickBooks company files), keeps file versions for up to 45 days, and automatically runs backups in the background every day so they don't interrupt your work—even if files are open. Intuit recommends that you run Intuit Data Protect on only one PC. You can check out the service with a 30-day free trial.

Intuit's backup services aren't the only game in town. If the benefits of backing up online sound good, look at other services before you make your decision. Dropbox (*www.dropbox.com*) is a backup and synchronization service that's perfect for financial professionals on the go. When you store files in a special folder on your computer, Dropbox copies them to your online account. If you hit the road with your laptop, Dropbox synchronizes the files onto your laptop when you go online. You initially get 2 GB of storage for free (and up to 18 GB as you refer other people to the service); 1 TB of storage costs $9.99 a month. SugarSync (*www.sugarsync.com*) is a similar backup and synchronization service, which offers 5 GB of storage free, 60 GB for $7.49 per month, and up to 250 GB for $24.99 per month.

Another option with a different approach is CrashPlan, which lets you back up files to the destination of your choice: another hard disk on your computer, from your laptop to your desktop computer, to a computer in another location, even from a Mac to a PC. CrashPlan compresses your files so backups take no time at all. You can download CrashPlan software at no charge, or purchase its online backup service. See *www.crashplan.com* for pricing details.

SETTING UP AUTOMATIC BACKUPS

Automatic backups require a bit of setup, but once you tell QuickBooks where you want to store the backup files and the number of sessions between backups, they spawn themselves quietly in the background. Here's what you do:

1. **Choose File→Backup Company→Create Local Backup. In the Create Backup dialog box, select the "Local backup" option, and then click Next.**

   The "When do you want to save your backup copy?" screen appears.

2. **Select the "Only schedule future backups" option, and then click Next.**

   QuickBooks displays the settings you can use to define both automatic and scheduled backups (Figure 19-3).

3. **Turn on the "Save backup copy automatically when I close my company file every _ times" checkbox. In the text box, type the number of sessions you want between automatic backups.**

   For example, if you type *5*, QuickBooks creates an automatic backup when you close the company file the fifth time since the last backup.

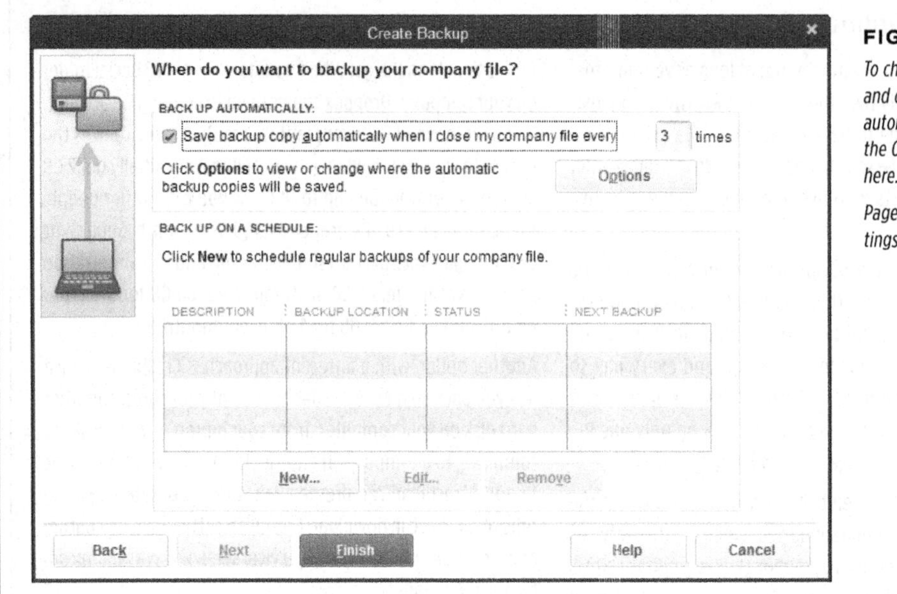

FIGURE 19-3

To change the location and other details of your automatic backups, click the Options button shown here.

Page 492 explains the settings you can choose.

4. **Click Finish.**

   QuickBooks starts counting. After you've completed the number of company-file sessions you specified, the QuickBooks Automatic Backup message box appears, telling you that it's creating the backup.

NOTE The "Remind me to back up when I close my company file every _ times" setting in the Backup Options dialog box (page 494) sounds a lot like the "Save backup copy automatically when I close my company file every _ times" setting for scheduled backups, but they do different things. The former tells QuickBooks to *ask* you if you want to back up your file after you've closed it that many times, whereas the latter tells QuickBooks to create a backup file automatically—*without asking*—after you close the company file that many times.

Here's the file-naming convention that QuickBooks uses for automatic backup files:

ABU_0_[company name] [date stamp] [time stamp].qbb

For example, the first automatic backup file might be *ABU_0_Double Trouble, Inc Mar 13,2015 05 17 PM* (ABU stands for "automatic backup"). When QuickBooks creates the next automatic backup, it renames the file that begins with ABU_0 to start with ABU_1 (*ABU_1_Double Trouble, Inc Mar 13,2015 05 17 PM*, for example), renames the ABU_1 file to start with ABU_2, and so on. With this system, you always know that the automatic backup file that starts with ABU_0 is the most recent.

SCHEDULING BACKUPS FOR A SINGLE COMPANY FILE

Although most companies back up all their computers on a regular schedule, you can set up a scheduled backup for your QuickBooks company file for an extra layer of safety. If you back up all your data every other day, for example, you may want to back up your company file every night, and a QuickBooks scheduled backup is one way to do that. Here's how to schedule backups:

1. **Choose File→Backup Company→Create Local Backup. In the Create Backup dialog box, select the "Local backup" option, and then click Next.**

   The "When do you want to save your backup copy?" screen appears.

2. **Select the "Only schedule future backups" option, and then click Next.**

   To make a backup right away as well as set up the schedule, select the "Save it now and schedule future backups" option instead. Either way, the screen that appears includes a table showing scheduled backups you've already set up (if any), plus each backup's description, location, status, and next occurrence.

3. **To set up a schedule, below the table, click New.**

   QuickBooks opens the Schedule Backup dialog box (Figure 19-4), which includes all the options you need to set up a regularly scheduled backup.

4. **In the Description box, type a meaningful name for the backup, like *Daily* or *Monthly Offsite*.**

   When you finish defining the schedule, this description will appear in the Create Backup dialog box's table. Consider including the backup's frequency and location (such as the network drive or offsite location) in the name.

5. **Click Browse to specify the backup location.**

   QuickBooks opens the "Browse for Folder" dialog box. To choose a folder, hard drive, or other location on your computer, expand the Computer, My Computer, or This PC entry (the name depends on which version of Windows you have), and then choose the location you want. To store the backup on another computer on your network, expand the Network or My Network Places entry instead, and then choose a location. Click OK when you're done.

WARNING If you've set up scheduled backups, don't turn off your computer when you go home, or the backups won't work. And if you back up to a hard drive on another computer, leave that computer running, too.

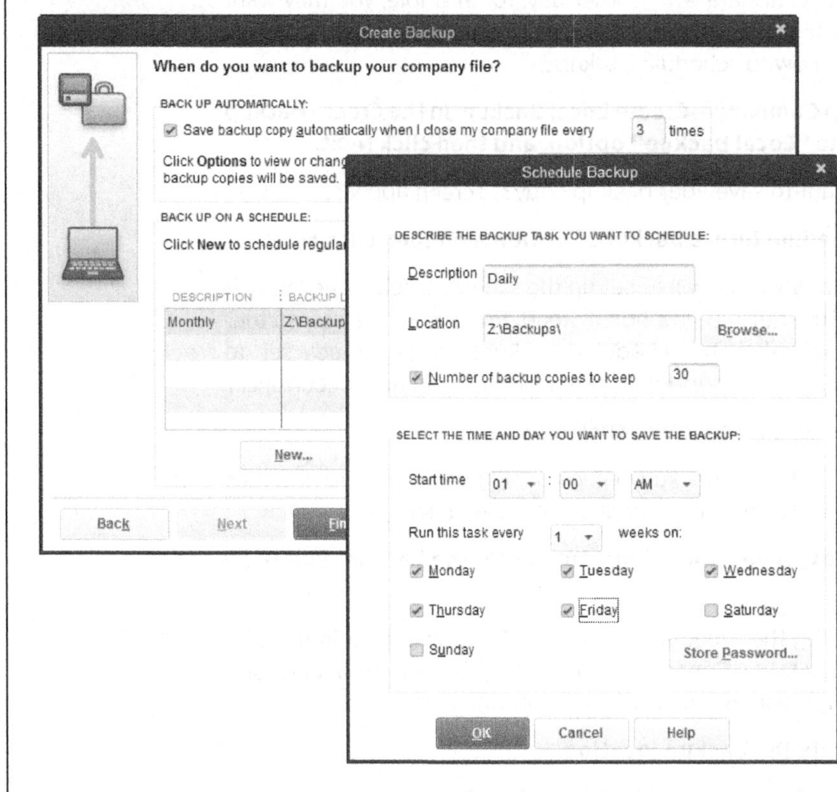

FIGURE 19-4

You won't need more than a few scheduled backups. For instance, you can create one to save your data every weeknight from Monday through Friday, a second to save a weekly backup every Saturday night, and a third to run once a month on Saturday to create a backup DVD that you can store offsite.

6. **If you back up your company file to a hard drive and don't want to overwrite the previous backup each time the scheduled backup runs, turn on the "Number of backup copies to keep" checkbox and, in the box to the right of the label, type the number of previous backups you want QuickBooks to preserve.**

   When you turn on this checkbox, QuickBooks uses the filename *SBU_0_[company name] [date stamp] [time stamp].qbb* (SBU stands for "scheduled backup"). For example, your scheduled backup file might be *SBU_0_Double Trouble, Inc Sep 24,2015 01 00 AM.qbb*. Each time QuickBooks creates a new scheduled backup file, it renames the previous backups to the next number in the list, and then replaces the SBU_0 file with the new backup. For example, if you keep four backups, the SBU_2 backup becomes the SBU_3 file; the SBU_1 file becomes the SBU_2 file; the SBU_0 backup file becomes the SBU_1 file; and the new backup becomes the new SBU_0 file. The most recent backup always starts with "SBU_0."

7. **In the "Start time" boxes, choose when you want the backup to run.**

   These boxes work on a 12-hour clock, so specify the hour, the minute, and AM or PM.

TIP It's easy to confuse midnight and noon on a 12-hour clock (midnight is 12:00 a.m.; noon is 12:00 p.m.). Avoid this gotcha by running your scheduled backups at 11:00 p.m., 1:00 a.m., or later.

---

8. **To set the backup's frequency, in the "Run this task every _ weeks on" box, select the number of weeks you want between backups, and then turn on the checkboxes for each day of the week on which you want the backup to happen.**

   For example, for daily backups, in the "Run this task every _ weeks on" box, choose *1*, and then turn on the checkbox for each weekday.

9. **Click Store Password, and then type your Windows user name and password.**

   QuickBooks needs this info so it can log into the computer to run the backup.

10. **When you're done, click OK.**

    QuickBooks adds this backup to your list of scheduled backups.

Restoring Backups

Having backup files can reduce your adrenaline level in a number of situations:

- You merge two customers by mistake or commit some other major faux pas that you want to undo.
- Your company file won't open, which can happen if it's been damaged by a power outage or a power surge.
- You recently assigned a password to your administrator user (page 718) and can't remember what it is.
- Your hard disk crashes and takes all your data with it.

WARNING These days, hard disk crashes can be deceptively quiet. So if you hear *any* odd sounds emanating from your computer—little chirps or squeaks, for instance—stop what you're doing immediately and take it to a computer repair shop to see if someone can fix it or recover your data. If you shut down your computer and it won't reboot because of a disk crash, a data-recovery company may be able to salvage some of your data, but the price is usually in the thousands of dollars. And if smoke wafts from your computer, don't bother with shutting down—just pull the plug and get that puppy to a repair shop.

Here's how to restore a QuickBooks backup when you need to recover from a mistake or damaged data:

1. **If you backed up your data to removable media, put the disc containing the backup in the appropriate drive.**

   If you backed up your data to another hard drive on your computer or on a network, make sure you have access to that drive.

2. **Choose File→Backup Company→Restore Previous Local Backup and then, on the submenu that appears, choose the backup file you want to restore.**

   If the backup you want isn't listed in the submenu, choose File→"Open or Restore Company" instead. In the "Open or Restore Company" dialog box, shown in Figure 19-5, select the "Restore a backup copy" option, and then click Next. Select "Local backup," and then click Next. Finally, in the Open Backup Copy dialog box, navigate to your backup file and double-click its name.

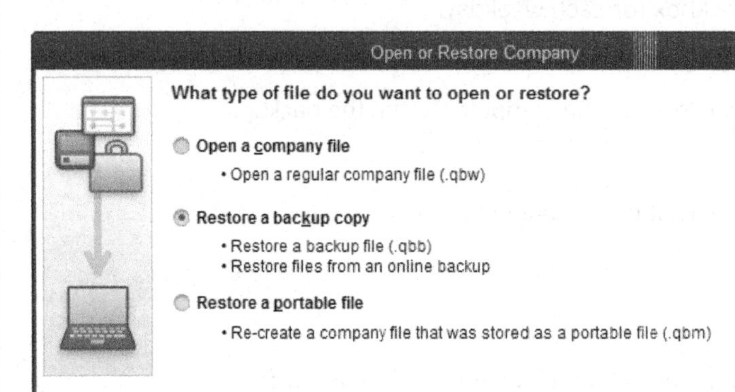

FIGURE 19-5

Similar to when you create backups, you have to tell QuickBooks that you want to restore a backup file and where that file is. From this dialog box, you can open a regular company file, restore a backup, restore a portable file (page 505), or convert an accountant's copy (you'll see this last option only if an accountant's copy of your company file [page 462] exists).

NOTE QuickBooks 2010 and later versions can restore backup files to a format you can use in QuickBooks 2009 or earlier—if, for example, a client is still using QuickBooks 2009 and asks you for a copy of her company file. The box on page 504 tells you why and how to restore a backup for an earlier QuickBooks version.

3. **In the "Open or Restore Company" dialog box, the "Where do you want to restore the file?" screen makes it clear that you need to choose the restore location carefully. Click Next and, in the "Save Company File as" dialog box, choose the folder where you want to restore the file.**

   If you restore the backup to your regular company-file folder, you run the risk of overwriting your existing company file. If that's what you want because your regular file won't open, then fine. Otherwise, to be safe, restore the backup to your desktop. Then, once you know that the restored company file is the one you want, you can move it to the folder where you store your regular company files.

4. **In the "File name" box, type a new name for the file you're about to restore.**

   QuickBooks fills in the "File name" box with the company file's name (minus the timestamp). The safest approach is to modify this name to include a unique identifier, so you don't overwrite your existing company file.

TIP If you give a restored file a different name as a precaution—"Double Trouble Restored," for example—you can trick QuickBooks into renaming the file after you're sure it's the one you want. To do that, create a manual backup of the file (page 495), and then immediately restore it with the company filename you want ("Double Trouble," in this example).

5. **Click Save.**

   If you're restoring a backup of a company file that already exists and didn't use a unique filename in step 4, QuickBooks warns you that you're about to overwrite an existing file. If the original file is corrupt or won't open for some reason, click Yes because that's exactly what you want to do. In the Delete Entire File dialog box that appears, you also have to type *Yes* to confirm that you want to delete the file. (It's better to take these precautions than to overwrite the wrong file and have to dig out yet *another* backup.)

If the restored file has a password, you have to log in, just as you do in a regular company file. When you see a message that says your data has been restored successfully, click OK to open the company file and reenter any transactions that aren't included in the backup.

NOTE If restoring a backup copy from removable media (CD, DVD, or USB thumb drive) doesn't work, try copying the contents of the backup media to your hard drive, and then restoring the backup file from there. If the restore *still* doesn't work, your backup file is probably damaged, so try restoring the next-most-recent backup.

If none of your backups work, Intuit offers a data-recovery service that can extract data from your backup files. The service isn't free, but it might be cheaper than rebuilding your entire company file. To arrange for this service, choose Help→Support, and then, at the top of the page, click Contact Us. On the page that opens, in the Product drop-down list, choose the product you want help with, and then call the phone number listed on the site. If the support person can't resolve the problem with your file, he'll transfer you to the Intuit Data Recovery Services team.

Sending Company Files to Others

QuickBooks company files can grow quite large as you add year after year of financial transactions. Fortunately, QuickBooks can create *portable* company files, a slim format that flies through the email ether and slips effortlessly onto removable media like USB thumb drives and CDs. For example, you can email a portable company file to your accountant before you head out on vacation.

DON'T PANIC

Restoring to an Earlier QuickBooks Version

QuickBooks 2010 and more recent versions use a new and improved method to compress backup files that doesn't work with earlier versions of the program. But when it converts a company file to work with a new version of the program, QuickBooks backs up your file so you can restore it in case you run into trouble. So if you switch back to an earlier version of the program, you can't restore a QuickBooks 2010 or later backup file *directly* in that earlier version. Here's what to do instead:

1. In QuickBooks 2010 or later, choose File→Utilities→Restore Backup For Earlier QuickBooks Version.
2. In the "Select the backup file you want to restore" section of the Restore Your Company File dialog box, click the ellipsis button (...). The Open Backup Copy dialog box appears, displaying the contents of the folder where you last saved backup files.
3. Select the QuickBooks backup file you want to restore, and then click Open.
4. In the "Where do you want to save the restored file?" section of the Restore Your Company File dialog box, click the ellipsis button (...). The "Save Company File as" dialog box appears showing the contents of the backup folder.
5. Navigate to the folder where you want to save the restored file; for example, you might choose the folder you use to store your company files.
6. In the "File name" box, type a unique name for the restored file, such as *CompanyFileRestored_03052015*, and then click Save.
7. Back in the Restore Your Company File dialog box, click OK. A message box appears telling you that the file has been restored and where it is. Click OK to close the message box.

Now you can open the restored file as a regular company file in the earlier version of QuickBooks.

Portable files don't contain all the info that backup files do, such as letters you create in QuickBooks, logos, images, and templates. So if you're handing off your company file for good (for example, when you sell your company to someone else), give the new owner the regular company file or a QuickBooks backup of it. That way, when he copies the company file onto his computer (or restores the backup file), *all* your data will be there.

Because portable files don't contain all your data, they're much smaller than regular company files. For example, a company file that's more than 10 MB in size turns into a portable company file of less than 1 MB. Portable company files have a .qbm file extension, but when you open them, QuickBooks converts them to regular company files with a .qbw file extension.

TIP If you intend to work on the company file at the same time as your accountant and want to merge her changes into your copy, create an accountant's copy (page 462) instead of a portable copy.

And before you transmit a company file electronically—no matter *what* format it's in—be sure you've added a password to it (page 723) so nobody can intercept it and access your financial data. That way, the person you send the file to needs a user name and password to open it (page 25).

Creating a Portable Company File

Creating a portable company file is just a wee bit more complicated than saving a file. (You need to be in single-user mode to create a portable company file, so if you're in multi-user mode, switch to single-user mode as explained on page 489 before getting started.) Here are the steps:

1. **Choose File→Create Copy.**

   The "Save Copy or Backup" dialog box that appears lets you create a backup file, a portable company file, *or* an accountant's copy.

2. **Select the "Portable company file" option, and then click Next.**

   QuickBooks opens the Save Portable Company File dialog box (Figure 19-6). It automatically fills in the "File name" box with the name of your company file, followed by "(Portable)," and sets the "Save as type" box to "QuickBooks Portable Company Files (*.QBM)."

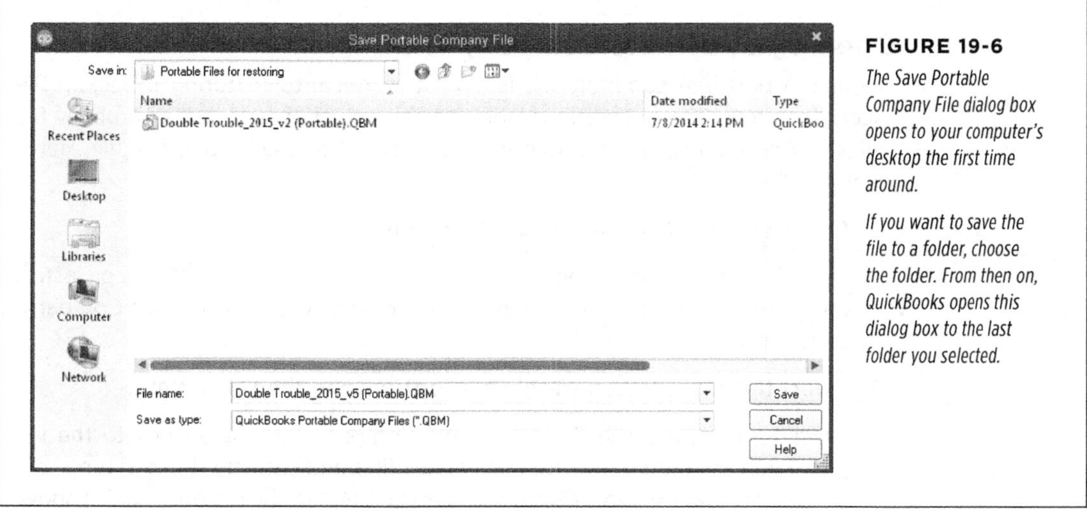

FIGURE 19-6

The Save Portable Company File dialog box opens to your computer's desktop the first time around.

If you want to save the file to a folder, choose the folder. From then on, QuickBooks opens this dialog box to the last folder you selected.

3. **Choose the folder where you want to restore the file.**

   The first time you open the Save Portable Company File dialog box, it selects your computer's desktop. After that, it opens to the last location where you saved a backup file or copy.

4. **If you want to use a different filename, edit the text in the "File name" box, and then click Save.**

   The "Close and reopen" message box tells you that you need to close and reopen your company file to create a portable file.

5. **Click OK to create the file.**

   A message box appears when QuickBooks finishes creating the portable company file. Click OK to reopen your company file. (You can tell that the company file is open when you see its name in the main QuickBooks window's title bar. However, you might have to reopen windows such as the Home Page or the Chart of Accounts window.)

Feel free to view the portable company file in Windows Explorer and admire its sleek size.

TIP If you use a cloud-storage service like Dropbox or Google Drive to share files with your accountant, sending a portable file to him is a breeze: First, choose File→Send Company File→Portable Company File. In the Send Portable Company File dialog box, click Browse, and then, in the Select Shared Folder dialog box, choose the shared folder where you want to create the portable file. Finally, back in the Send Portable Company File dialog box, click Send. In the "Close and reopen" dialog box, click OK. QuickBooks leaps into action, creating a portable file of your company file in the folder you selected.

Opening a Portable Company File

Opening a portable company file is almost identical to restoring a backup file, except for a few different settings labels. When you open a portable company file, QuickBooks essentially converts it into a full-size, bona fide company file. Here's what you do:

1. **Choose File→"Open or Restore Company."**

   Or, if the No Company Open window is visible, you can click "Open or restore an existing company." Either method opens the "Open or Restore Company" dialog box.

2. **Select the "Restore a portable file" option, and then click Next.**

   QuickBooks opens the Open Portable Company File dialog box to the last folder you selected for portable company files and sets the "Files of type" box to "QuickBooks Portable Company Files (*.QBM)" so the dialog box's list shows only portable company files.

3. **Double-click the portable file you want to restore.**

   Alternatively, click its filename and then click Open.

4. **Back in the "Open or Restore Company" dialog box, the "Where do you want to restore the file?" screen makes it clear that you should choose the location carefully. Click Next.**

   If you restore the portable file to your regular company-file folder, you'll overwrite your existing company file. If that's what you want, fine. Otherwise, be sure to choose another folder or to change the filename in the next step.

5. **In the "Save Company File as" dialog box, choose the folder to which you want to restore the file. In the "File name" box, type a new name.**

   The dialog box opens to the folder you last chose for portable files. If you want to replace your company file, choose the folder that holds your everyday company file.

   The safest approach is to modify the filename to include a unique identifier, such as "_restoredportable," so you can easily identify the file you restored. You can then rename the file later (page 503 describes a quick way to do so).

6. **Click Save.**

   If you're restoring a portable file for a company file that already exists, QuickBooks warns you that you're about to overwrite an existing file. If that's what you want, click Yes, and then type *Yes* to confirm that you want to delete the existing file. The Working message box shows the program's progress (restoring a portable file can take several minutes). When the file is ready, the QuickBooks Login dialog box appears or, if the company file doesn't have a password assigned to it, the file opens.

Verifying Your QuickBooks Data

QuickBooks files hiccup now and then. Perhaps you worked through a spectacular thunderstorm and a power spike zapped a bit of your company file, for example. Fortunately, QuickBooks has a feature that can scan your company files and tell you whether they've suffered any damage: the Verify Data utility.

It's a good idea to run this utility every so often, just to make sure your company file is OK. How often you should run it depends on how hard you work your company file, but monthly verifications are in order for most companies. And this utility is indispensable if you notice any of the following symptoms:

- **The file won't open**. Sometimes, memorized transactions become corrupt, which prevents you from opening your company file.
- **Error messages**. If you see a message box telling you that an error has occurred, QuickBooks may have a glitch or your company file might be damaged. Make sure you've installed the latest maintenance release by choosing Help→Update QuickBooks and then clicking Update Now. If you have the latest maintenance release installed and you see the error message box again, then verify your data to correct any data corruption in your company file.
- **Discrepancies on reports**. Your balance sheet doesn't show all your accounts, or transactions show negative values instead of positive ones.

TIP If the totals in your reports don't seem right, first check that the reports' dates are correct and that you're using the right cash or accrual accounting setting (see page 661).

- **Missing transactions and names**. Transactions or names that you're sure you entered don't appear in reports or lists.
- **You can't save transactions**. QuickBooks doesn't save a transaction or shuts down when you try to save a transaction.
- **QuickBooks misbehaves**. It's a good idea to verify your company file if QuickBooks shuts down on its own, your computer crashes, a "Company file in use, please wait" message appears, or you see other strange behavior from QuickBooks or your computer.

Running the Verify Data Utility

Whether you're just giving your company file a checkup or you see signs of problems, the Verify Data utility is easy to use:

1. **Close QuickBooks and then restart it.**

   This makes QuickBooks create a new *QBWIN.log* file, which will contain only the results of the data verification you'll run in step 3. (When you verify data, QuickBooks automatically renames the previous *QBWIN.log* file to *QBWIN.log.old1* so that the *QBWIN.log* file contains information for only the most recent verification. QuickBooks also renames other old files, changing *QBWIN.log.old1* to *QBWIN.log.old2*, and so on.)

NOTE You can verify data in multi-user mode, although no other users will be able to use QuickBooks while it's verifying the company file. In addition, the program can perform a more *thorough* verification when the file is in single-user mode. So you're best off switching to single-user mode (page 489) before running this utility.

2. **To start the utility, choose File→Utilities→Verify Data. (If any windows are open, click OK to give QuickBooks permission to close them.)**

   You can close all QuickBooks windows before you run the utility by choosing Window→Close All.

3. **If you see the message "A data problem prevents QuickBooks from continuing" (Figure 19-7), then your company file has some problems. Continue to the next section to learn how to rebuild your data.**

   If, on the other hand, QuickBooks displays a message saying that it detected no problems with your data, your file isn't necessarily healthy: It could contain a problem that the Verify Data utility doesn't recognize. If you *still* have problems with your company file after verifying it, try rebuilding it as described in the next section.

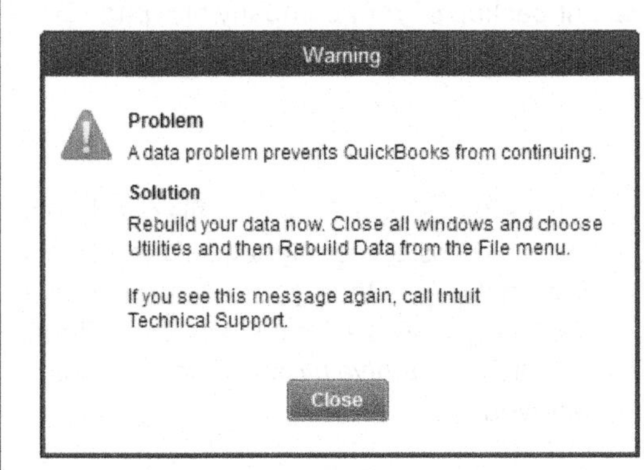

FIGURE 19-7

If you see this message, your company file has suffered some kind of damage.

The Rebuild Data utility (described below) can help fix the problem(s) and get you back to work.

Reviewing Problems

The Verify Data utility writes down any errors it finds in a file named *QBWIN.log*. Before you run the Rebuild Data utility described in the next section (which can help fix the problems QuickBooks found), it's a good idea to take a look at this log file and review your company file's problems. However, you'll need a map to find the log file. Here's how:

1. **Press F2 to open the Product Information dialog box. Then press Ctrl+2 to open the Tech Help dialog box.**

   The Tech Help dialog box includes several tabs for inspecting various aspects of your computer and QuickBooks.

2. **Click the Open File tab. In the "Select a file to open" list, click QBWIN.LOG, and then click the Open File button.**

   The file opens in Notepad, and you can use Notepad's features to move around the file. (If the file doesn't open, launch Notepad, choose File→Open, and then double-click the *QBWIN.log* filename.)

Running the Rebuild Data Utility

If your company file is damaged, QuickBooks' Rebuild Data utility tries to fix it. Intuit recommends that you run the Rebuild Data utility *only* if an Intuit technical support person tells you to. *Always* make a backup of your company file before trying to rebuild it, and take extra care to prevent overwriting your previous backups—those files might be your only salvation if the rebuild doesn't work.

To run the Rebuild Data utility, choose File→Utilities→Rebuild Data. A message box appears telling you that QuickBooks is going to back up your company file and warning you not to overwrite any existing backups. Click OK and make sure to type a unique backup name in the "File name" box before you click Save.

When the utility is done working, close your company file and reopen it; this refreshes the lists in the company file so you can see if the problems are gone. Then run the Verify Data utility once more to see if any damage remains. If this second Verify Data run still shows errors, then restore a recent backup of your company file (page 501).

Condensing Data

As you add transactions and build lists in QuickBooks, your company file gets larger. Although larger company files aren't too big of a hassle, you might be alarmed when your company file reaches hundreds of megabytes. Once you reach that point, backups will take longer and use up more storage space. That's why QuickBooks includes the Condense Data utility, which creates an *archive file* and deletes obsolete list items and transactions prior to the date you choose.

WARNING The Condense Data utility removes the audit trail information for transactions that it deletes. So if you're watching transaction activity, print an Audit Trail report and back up your company file *before* condensing.

When QuickBooks condenses data, it replaces the detailed transactions prior to the date you specify with journal entries that summarize the deleted transactions by month. As a result, some of your financial details are no longer available for running reports, filing taxes, and other accounting activities. Still, there are a couple of compelling reasons to condense data:

- **You no longer refer to old transactions**. If you're a QuickBooks veteran, you probably *don't* need the finer details from eight or more years ago. And if you ever do need details from the past, you can open an archive file (explained in a sec) to run reports.
- **You have obsolete list items**. Cleaning up a company file can remove list items you don't use, like customers you no longer sell to. This option comes in handy if you're nearing the program's limit on the number of names you can store (page xvii).

NOTE If the Condense Data utility isn't the housekeeper you hoped for, you have a couple of options. One is to start a fresh company file. That way, you can export all the lists from your existing company file (page 685) and import them (page 691) into the new one so you start with lists but no transactions. (Set your accounts' opening balances [page 62] to the values for the start date of the new file.) Or you can hand your company file over to a company that provides file-cleanup and repair services, such as "QB or not QB" (*www.qbornotqb.com*).

The Condense Data utility creates an *archive file*, which is a regular company file that contains all your transactions, but it's *read-only*, meaning you can't add data to it or edit it, so you can't inadvertently enter new transactions. If QuickBooks runs into trouble condensing your file, it automatically pulls transaction details from the archive file. An archive copy *isn't* a backup file, which means you can't restore it to replace a corrupt company file. So even if you create an archive copy, you still need to back up your data.

If you decide to condense your company file, here's what you can expect to find afterward, depending on the settings you choose:

- **Journal entries that summarize deleted transactions**. QuickBooks replaces all the deleted transactions that happened during each month with one journal entry. For example, instead of 20 separate invoices for the month of June, you'll see one journal entry with the total income for June for each income account.

NOTE If you see other transactions for the same month, it means that QuickBooks wasn't able to delete those transactions for some reason. For instance, if you tell it not to, QuickBooks won't delete unpaid invoices or other transactions with an open balance, nor will it delete any transactions in the queue to be printed or ones that you haven't reconciled.

- **Inventory adjustments that reflect the average cost of items**. If you tell it to, QuickBooks removes inventory transactions that are complete, such as invoices that have been paid in full. Because inventory transactions use the average cost of inventory items, QuickBooks adds an inventory adjustment to set the average cost of the items as of the condense date. When the program finds an inventory transaction that it can't condense (perhaps because the payment is outstanding), it keeps all the inventory transactions from that date forward.
- **Reports might not include the details you want**. You can still generate summary reports because QuickBooks can incorporate the info in the monthly journal entries the utility creates. Likewise, sales tax reports still include data about your sales tax liabilities. But detailed reports won't include transaction details before the cutoff date you chose for condensing the file. And cash-accounting reports (page xxii) might not be accurate because they need the dates for detailed transactions. Talk with your accountant to see how your cash-basis reports might be affected.
- **You still have payroll info for the current year**. QuickBooks keeps payroll transactions for the current year regardless of the cutoff date you chose for condensing the file.
- **QuickBooks deletes estimates for closed jobs**. If a job has any status other than Closed, QuickBooks keeps the estimates for that job. Or you can tell QuickBooks to remove *all* estimates, sales orders, purchase orders, and pending invoices.
- **QuickBooks retains unbilled expenses, items, time, and mileage**. The program keeps any unbilled charges, unless you tell it to delete those transactions.

Running the Condense Data Utility

If you're ready to condense your company file, first consider *when* to do it. The cleaning process can take several hours for a large company file, and a slow computer or a small amount of memory exacerbates the problem. You might want to condense your file over the weekend so the utility has plenty of time to run before folks come in Monday morning.

Here's how to condense a company file:

1. **If you've created budgets in QuickBooks, export them (page 588) before you condense your data.**

   After you condense your data, you can import them back into your company file (page 570).

2. **Choose File→Utilities→Condense Data.**

   The Condense Data dialog box opens.

3. **Select the "Transactions before a specific date" option.**

   This option deletes old transactions and things like unused accounts and items.

   The "All transactions" option removes transactions but keeps your preferences, lists, and service subscriptions—such as payroll—intact. You won't use this option often, but it comes in handy if, for example, you want to offer your clients a template company file that contains typical list entries but no transactions.

4. **In the "Remove transactions before" box, type or select the ending date for the period you want to condense, and then click Next.**

   If you use an Intuit payroll service (page 415), you can't clean up data for the current year. QuickBooks also won't let you clean up transactions that are newer than the closing date on your company file (page 472). Choosing a date at least two years in the past ensures that you can compare detailed transactions for the current year and the previous year. For example, if it's April 1, 2015, consider using January 1, 2013, or earlier as your cutoff date.

NOTE If there aren't any transactions to condense before the date you picked, you'll see the message "There are no transactions to remove on or before the date you entered. Please verify the Condense process date." Click OK, and then either pick a date closer to today's date or click Cancel, because there aren't any transactions for the utility to condense.

5. **If you see the "How Should Transactions Be Summarized?" screen (you may not), select your preferred method.**

   Your options are to have QuickBooks create one summary journal entry for all the transactions it condenses, create a summary journal entry for each month prior to the date you selected, or not create a summary at all. QuickBooks automatically selects the first option, and you're best off sticking with that so you have a record of your previous transactions without dozens of summary journal entries cluttering your company file.

6. **If you see the "How Should Inventory Be Condensed?" screen, keep the "Summarize inventory transactions (recommended)" option selected and click Next.**

   This removes inventory transactions that QuickBooks can condense and replaces them with inventory adjustments (page 542).

7. **On the "Do You Want To Remove The Following Transactions?" screen, turn *off* the appropriate checkboxes if you want to *keep* transactions that the cleanup process would otherwise condense, and then click Next.**

   Figure 19-8 shows your choices. All the checkboxes are initially turned on. Before you click Next, carefully review your company file to make sure that the settings you choose here won't delete transactions you want to keep. If you want QuickBooks to leave all these transactions alone, click Select None.

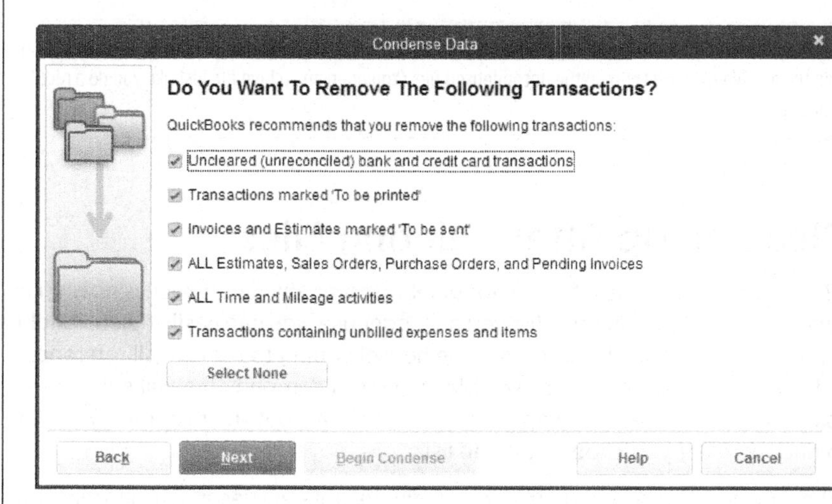

FIGURE 19-8

These checkboxes let you remove transactions that the Condense Data utility would normally leave alone—like transactions marked "To be printed" that you don't need to print. If you have very old, unreconciled transactions, invoices, or estimates marked "To be sent," or transactions with unreimbursed costs, leave the appropriate checkboxes turned on to remove them during the condensing.

8. **On the "Do You Want To Remove Unused List Entries?" screen, turn *off* the appropriate checkboxes if you want QuickBooks to *keep* specific list items, and then click Next.**

   Accounts, customers, jobs, vendors, other names, and invoice items might become orphans when you delete old transactions they're linked to. You can neaten your file by removing these list items, which now have no links to the transactions that still remain. QuickBooks initially turns on all the checkboxes on this screen. But keep in mind that you might work with one of these vendors or customers in the future. In that case, turn off checkboxes to tell the program to keep unused list entries.

9. **On the Begin Condense screen, click Begin Condense.**

   If you're not sure of the options you chose, or if you have any doubts about condensing your file, click Back to return to a previous screen, or click Cancel to exit without condensing.

When you click Begin Condense, QuickBooks first creates an archive file (a QuickBooks company file, not a backup file) in the same folder as your original company file. The archive file's filename has the format *[company name] mm-dd-yyyy Copy.qbw*, where "mm-dd-yyyy" represents the month, day, and year that you created the file.

As QuickBooks proceeds with the condensing process, it scans your data *three* times. You might see message boxes wink on and off in rapid succession; then again, if your file is large, you might not see anything happen for a while. But if your hard disk is working, the condensing process is in progress. When it's finished, QuickBooks displays a message telling you so and shows you where it stored the archive file.

TIP After you condense your company file, run a balance sheet report (page 451) and compare the account balances in the archive file with those in the uncondensed file. (You open an archive file just like you do a regular company file [page 23].)

Cleaning Up After Deleting Files

QuickBooks doesn't include a feature for deleting company files, which is no biggie. If you want to get rid of a practice file you no longer use, you can easily delete it right in Windows. But you'll still have to do some housekeeping to remove all references to that file from QuickBooks. For example, a deleted company file will still appear in QuickBooks' list of previously opened files (page 24), but the program won't be able to find the file if you choose it in the list.

Here's how to delete a company file *and* eliminate stale entries in QuickBooks' list of previously opened files:

1. **In Windows Explorer, navigate to the folder where your QuickBooks company files are stored, and find the file you want to delete.**

   What to look for when searching for your company file depends on how you've set up your folder view. If your folder shows full filenames, look for a file with a .qbw file extension, such as *Double Trouble, Inc.qbw*. If the folder includes a Name column and a Type column, the type you want is QuickBooks Company File.

   Files with .qbx extensions represent accountant's copies (page 462). Files with .qbb file extensions are backup copies of company files. Portable files come with .qbm file extensions. If you delete the company file, go ahead and delete the backups, accountant's copies, and portable files as well if you no longer need them.

2. **Right-click the file and, on the shortcut menu, choose Delete.**

   Windows displays the Delete File message box. Click Yes to move the file to the Recycle Bin. If you have second thoughts, click No to keep the file.

3. **In QuickBooks, choose File→Open Previous Company→"Set number of previous companies."**

   If this menu item is grayed out, it means you don't have a company file open. In that case, in the File→Open Previous Company submenu, choose a file *other* than the one you just deleted. Alternatively, if the No Company Open window is visible, open the company file that you typically work with by double-clicking it. Either way, you should then be able to select the "Set number of previous companies" menu item.

4. **In the "How many companies do you want to list (1 to 20)?" box, type *1*, and then click OK.**

   Now, if you choose File→Open Previous Company, you'll notice that only one company appears—the company file you opened last. The No Company Open window also shows only the company file you opened last.

5. **To reset the number of previously opened companies, with a company file open, choose File→Open Previous Company→"Set number of previous companies" again.**

   In the "How many companies do you want to list (1 to 20)?" box, type the number of companies you'd like to see in the list, and then click OK.

As you open different company files, QuickBooks adds them to the list in the No Company Open window and the Open Previous Company submenu.

CHAPTER

20

Managing Inventory

As you record inventory purchases and sales in QuickBooks, the program keeps track of your inventory, just as the point-of-service system at the grocery store does when a cashier scans items. This chapter begins by explaining how to turn on QuickBooks' inventory features and set up inventory items in your company file so the program can work this magic.

Unless you practice just-in-time inventory management, you need inventory in your warehouse to fill customer orders. If you follow the lead of many companies, you start by creating purchase orders for the inventory you buy so you can verify that you receive what you're supposed to. The next step in the inventory process is receiving the inventory and paying for it. Finally, all that work pays off when you sell products out of inventory to your customers. This chapter shows you how to create purchase orders, receive inventory, and pay for it. Recording inventory sales is just like recording any other sales; QuickBooks handles the extra money transfers between accounts behind the scenes. You'll learn what the program does to track how much inventory you have (and what it's worth) as you record all these transactions.

Good inventory management means more than just updating the number of items that QuickBooks thinks you have on hand. To keep the right number of items in stock, you also need to know how many you've sold and how many are on order. And to make decisions like how much to charge or which vendor to use, you have to evaluate your purchases and how much you pay for your inventory. QuickBooks' inventory reports and Inventory Center help you look at your inventory items and transactions. In this chapter, you'll learn how to make the most of both of these features.

NOTE The Inventory Center is available only in QuickBooks Premier and Enterprise. If you have QuickBooks Pro, you can run inventory reports, but you don't have access to the center.

Another important aspect of inventory is keeping your QuickBooks records in sync with what's sitting on the shelves in your warehouse. Inventory can go missing due to theft or damage, so you might not have as many products in stock as you think you do. QuickBooks can't help with the dusty business of rifling through boxes and counting carafes, coffee mugs, and the occasional centipede. But after the counting is complete, the program *can* help you adjust its records to match the reality in your warehouse. And adjusting inventory is useful for more than just inventory counts. You can also use this process to write off inventory that you have in your warehouse but can't sell because it's dented, dirty, or too darned ugly.

Following the Inventory Money Trail

Inventory Part items are the most complicated type of item because, in accounting, the cost of inventory moves from place to place as you purchase, store, and finally sell your products. Before diving into the details of setting up and recording inventory transactions, it's a good idea to see how inventory works its way through various accounts in your chart of accounts. Table 20-1 and the following steps show the path that inventory-related money takes:

1. You spend money to purchase products to sell in your store. Your checking or credit card account shows the money you pay going out the door.
2. Because the inventory you purchased has value, it represents an asset of your company. Hence, the value of the purchased inventory appears in an inventory asset account in your chart of accounts.
3. When you sell some products, QuickBooks posts the sale to an income account (such as Product Income), and the money your customer owes you shows up in Accounts Receivable.
4. The products leave inventory, so QuickBooks deducts their value from the inventory asset account. The value of the sold goods has to go somewhere, so QuickBooks posts it to a *cost of goods sold account*.

TABLE 20-1 *Following inventory money through accounts*

TRANSACTION	ACCOUNT	DEBIT	CREDIT
Buy inventory	Checking Account		$500
Buy inventory	Inventory Asset	$500	
Sell inventory	Product Income		$1,000
Sell inventory	Accounts Receivable	$1,000	
Sell inventory	Inventory Asset		$500
Sell inventory	Cost of Goods Sold	$500	

In the financial reports you create, your company's gross profit represents your income minus the cost of goods sold (in this example, $1,000 income minus $500 cost of goods sold for $500 gross profit). As soon as you turn on QuickBooks' inventory-tracking preference as explained below, the program adds cost of goods sold and inventory asset accounts to your chart of accounts.

Setting Up Inventory Items

You set the stage for inventory tracking when you turn on QuickBooks' inventory preference and create inventory items in your company file. Inventory item records (which appear in your Item List: Lists→Item List) include purchase costs, sales prices, and accounts, all of which direct the right amount of money into the right income, expense, asset, and cost of goods sold accounts as you buy and sell inventory. This section shows you how to turn on inventory and set up inventory items.

Turning on Inventory

If you want to track inventory in QuickBooks, your first task is turning on the preference for inventory and purchase orders (if you didn't do that when you created your company file). Although the program turns on purchase-order features as part of tracking inventory, you can skip purchase orders if you don't use them in your business.

To turn on inventory in QuickBooks, choose Edit→Preferences→Items & Inventory, and then click the Company Preferences tab. Turn on the "Inventory and purchase orders are active" checkbox, and then click OK. (You need administrator privileges to turn on inventory features because they apply to everyone who logs into your company file.) As soon as you do that, QuickBooks warns you that it needs to close all your open windows. Click OK, and the following changes occur:

- Icons for purchase orders and inventory appear on the Home Page.
- Inventory-related options like Create Purchase Orders and Receive Items appear in the Vendors menu.
- A non-posting account called Purchase Orders appears in your chart of accounts.
- An Other Current Asset account called Inventory Asset appears in your chart of accounts.

Creating Inventory Items

Creating inventory items is similar to creating other types of items: In the Item List window (Lists→Item List), press Ctrl+N, select Inventory Part in the Type drop-down menu, and then fill in the Item Name/Number box with the item's name. (If you want to make the inventory item a subitem of another one, turn on the "Subitem of" checkbox, and then choose the parent item in the drop-down list.) The difference is that you have to fill in more fields than you do for other item types, as you can see in Figure 20-1.

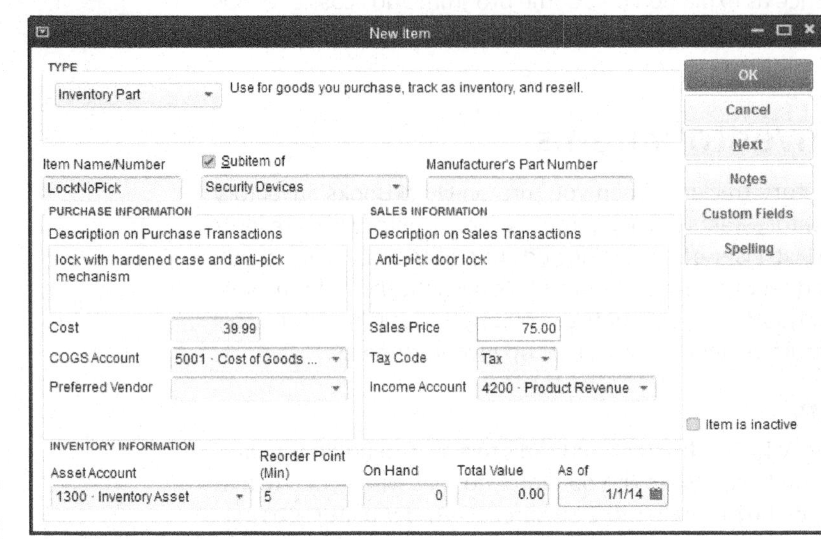

FIGURE 20-1

When you create a new Inventory Part item, QuickBooks displays fields for purchasing and selling that item. The fields in the Purchase Information section show up on purchase orders and bills. The Sales Information section sets the values you see on sales forms, such as invoices and sales receipts. The program simplifies recording your initial inventory by letting you type in the quantity you already have on hand and its value.

NOTE The box on page 522 explains one way to set up inventory items that you assemble from *other* inventory items, such as gift baskets. And the box on page 524 describes another method for tracking large batches of products you assemble.

Here are the fields for an Inventory Part item and how they help you track inventory from initial order to final sale:

- **Manufacturer's Part Number**. If you want your purchase orders to include the manufacturer's part number or unique identifier for the product, enter it here.

NOTE If you use QuickBooks Premier or Enterprise, you'll also see a "Unit of Measure" section, which lets you specify the units the inventory part comes in (bottles, cases, tons, cubic feet, or whatever). When you define units for an inventory part, they appear on invoices, sales forms, and reports. To turn this feature on, in the New Item (or Edit Item) dialog box, click the Enable button, and then choose whether you want to assign one or several units of measure to each item. Once this feature is turned on, the New Item and Edit Item dialog boxes display the U/M box in the "Unit of Measure" section so you can choose the appropriate unit from the drop-down list.

- **Description on Purchase Transactions**. Whatever you type here appears on the purchase orders you issue and bills you pay to buy inventory items. Describe the product in terms that the vendor or manufacturer understands. (As explained in a moment, you can use a different, more customer-friendly description for the invoices that customers see.)

- **Cost**. Enter what you pay for one unit of the product. QuickBooks assumes you sell products in the same units that you buy them. So, for example, if you purchase four cases of merlot but sell wine by the bottle, enter the price you pay *per bottle* in this field.
- **COGS Account**. Choose the account to which you want to post the cost *when you sell the product.* (COGS stands for "cost of goods sold," which is an account for tracking the underlying costs of the things you sell in order to calculate your gross profit, which you can learn about on page 446.)

NOTE If you don't already have a cost of goods sold account in your chart of accounts, QuickBooks creates one as soon as you type the name of your first Inventory Part item in the New Item window.

- **Preferred Vendor**. If you choose a vendor in this drop-down list, QuickBooks selects that vendor when you add this Inventory Part item to a purchase order or bill.
- **Description on Sales Transactions**. QuickBooks automatically copies what you typed in the "Description on Purchase Transactions" field into this box, so it appears on sales forms like invoices, credit memos, and sales receipts. If your customers wouldn't understand that description, type a more customer-friendly one here.
- **Sales Price**. Type in how much you charge for the product, and make sure that the Cost field uses the same units. For example, if you sell a bottle of merlot for $15, type *15* in this field and type the price you pay *per bottle* in the Cost field.
- **Tax Code**. If you turned on the sales tax preference (page 664) in your company file, then when you add an item to an invoice, QuickBooks checks this field to see whether the item is taxable. (QuickBooks comes with two tax codes: *Non* for nontaxable items and *Tax* for taxable items.) Most products are taxable, although groceries are a common exception.
- **Income Account**. This drop-down list includes all the accounts in your chart of accounts. Choose the *income* account you use for the money you receive when you sell one of these products.
- **Asset Account**. Choose the asset account for the value of the inventory you buy. Suppose you buy 100 bottles of merlot, which are each worth the $8 a bottle you paid; QuickBooks posts $800 into your inventory asset account. When you sell a bottle, the program deducts $8 from the inventory asset account and adds that $8 to your COGS account.
- **Reorder Point (Min)**. Type the quantity on hand that would prompt you to order more. When your inventory hits that number, QuickBooks adds a reminder to reorder this product to the Reminders List (page 483). If you use QuickBooks Premier or Enterprise, you'll also see a Max box, where you can enter the maximum quantity you want to have after reordering. For example, if you want 20

on hand, type *20* in the Reorder Point Max box. That way, if you place an order and have nine of the item on hand, the program tells you to reorder 11.

TIP If you can receive products quickly, use a lower reorder point to reduce the money tied up in inventory and prevent write-offs due to obsolete inventory. If products take a while to arrive, set the reorder point higher. Start with your best guess and then edit this field as business conditions change.

- **On Hand**. If you already have some of the product in inventory, type the quantity in this field. From then on, as you record inventory you receive, you can trust QuickBooks to accurately post inventory values in your accounts.
- **Total Value**. If you filled in the On Hand field, then fill in *this* field with the total value of the quantity on hand. QuickBooks increases the value of your inventory asset account accordingly.
- **As of**. The program uses this date for the transaction it creates in your inventory asset account.

NOTE You can enter values for the last three fields listed above *only* when you create a new item, not when you edit an existing one. From then on, QuickBooks calculates how many you have on hand based on the numbers you've received and sold.

POWER USERS' CLINIC

Assembling Products

In the Premier and Enterprise editions of QuickBooks, you can create an Inventory Assembly item that gathers Inventory Part items into a new item that you sell as a whole. As shown in Figure 20-2, the New Item window for an assembled item is similar to the one for an inventory part. The main difference is that you select other Inventory Part items or Inventory Assembly items as the building blocks of your new item.

In the "Bill of Materials" section, you specify the components and the quantity of each, and QuickBooks then calculates the total cost of the *bill of materials*—that is, the list of all the materials that make up the assembled product. In the Sales Price field, type the price you charge for the entire ball of wax, regardless of the cost of the individual pieces.

Purchasing Inventory

Purchasing inventory involves performing three actions in QuickBooks:

- Adding the inventory you purchase to an inventory asset account
- Entering the bill you receive for the inventory you bought
- Paying the bill for the inventory

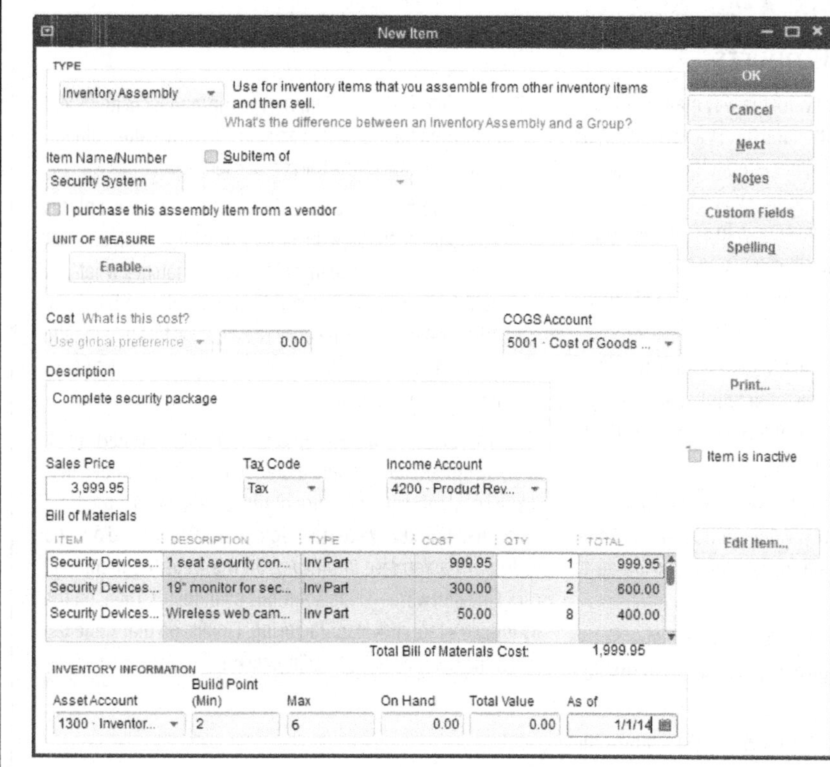

FIGURE 20-2

The New Item (or Edit Item) window for an Inventory Assembly item includes minimum and maximum Build Point fields instead of the Reorder Point field that inventory items have. As you build Inventory Assembly items, QuickBooks keeps track of how many inventory items you use, which can trigger a reorder reminder. Because you build an Inventory Assembly item out of individual components, you fill in the Build Point (Min) field with the minimum number of Inventory Assembly items you want on hand to tell QuickBooks when to remind you to build more. The Max field specifies the maximum number you want on hand.

What's tricky is that you don't know whether the bill or the inventory will arrive first. In many cases, the bill arrives with or after the shipment. But if Samurai Sam requires a deposit before he starts crafting your swords, you can record the deposit payment you make and then apply that payment when the final bill arrives. In the following sections, you'll learn how to use QuickBooks' features to handle any order of bill and inventory arrival.

Creating Purchase Orders

Before you receive inventory and pay the corresponding bills, it's a good idea to make sure that the shipments you receive match what you ordered—not unlike opening a pizza box before you leave the parlor to make sure you didn't get an anchovy-and-garlic pie by mistake. Remembering what you ordered is tougher when products and quantities vary. Most businesses address this problem by creating *purchase orders* for the inventory they buy. That way, when an order arrives, they can compare the shipment with the purchase order to confirm that the items and quantities are correct.

WORKAROUND WORKSHOP

Turning Parts into Products

Inventory Assembly items don't work the way many manufacturers treat assembled items. Manufacturers and distributors often build batches of assembled items, pool the manufacturing costs for the batch, and then assign a value to the resulting batch of products that goes into inventory. To use this approach in QuickBooks, you track the parts you use to build products (Non-inventory Parts) as *assets* instead of Inventory Assembly items. Here's how it works:

1. As you buy ingredients for a batch, assign the costs (via bills and so on) to an asset account specifically for inventory you build (such inventory is often referred to as *WIP* for "work in progress").
2. When the batch is complete, choose Vendors→Inventory Activities→Adjust Quantity/Value on Hand to make an inventory adjustment to add the items you made to inventory.
3. In the "Adjust Quantity/Value on Hand" window, in the Adjustment Type drop-down list, choose "Quantity and Total Value."
4. In the Adjustment Account drop-down list, choose the asset account for your WIP.
5. In the New Quantity column, type the number of items you built from your pool of parts. In the New Value column, type the value of the parts you used.
6. Click Save & Close to save the adjustment, which places the value of the new inventory in your inventory asset account. Because the inventory value matches what you paid for parts, the value adjustment also reduces the WIP asset account's balance to zero, in effect moving the value of your parts from the WIP asset account to your inventory asset account.

You have to know how many units you got out of the parts pool, so this approach works only if you build products in batches. If you constantly manufacture products, you need a program other than QuickBooks to track your inventory. To find one, go to *http://marketplace.intuit.com*. On the website's menu bar, click Find Software→Find Solutions by Industry. Then, on the By Industry tab, click Manufacturing. Finally, on that same tab under the Manufacturing heading, click Inventory Management.

NOTE You can create all the purchase orders you want without altering the balances in your income, expense, and asset accounts; purchase orders don't appear in your Profit & Loss or Balance Sheet reports, either. That's because purchase orders are known as *non-posting* transactions: No money changes hands (or accounts), so there's nothing to post in your chart of accounts. In QuickBooks, the first posting for purchased inventory happens when you receive either the inventory or the bill.

Because purchase orders are typically the first step in purchasing products, the QuickBooks Home Page places the Purchase Orders icon in the pole position in the Vendors panel. Click it to open the Create Purchase Orders window, which is like a mirror image of the Create Invoices window that you use to invoice your customers (page 227). You choose a vendor instead of a customer, and the Ship To address is your company's address, as shown in Figure 20-3.

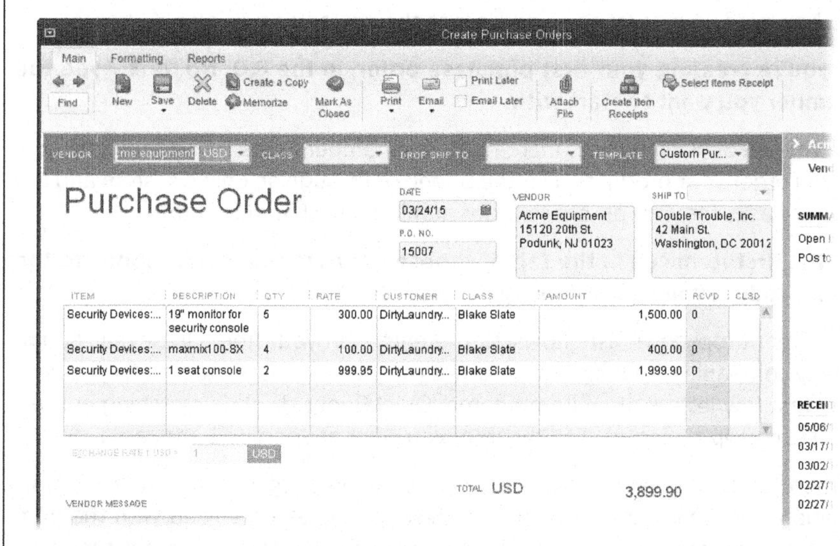

FIGURE 20-3

QuickBooks has one predefined template for purchase orders, although it's called Custom Purchase Order. If you want to customize your purchase order form, at the top of the Create Purchase Orders window, click the Formatting tab, and then click Manage Templates. Page 707 tells the whole story of customizing templates.

Here's how to create a purchase order:

1. **Choose Vendors→Create Purchase Orders or, on the Home Page, click the Purchase Orders icon.**

   In the Create Purchase Orders window that appears, QuickBooks fills in the current date, and there's no reason to change it because purchase orders are merely a paper trail of what you order.

2. **In the Vendor box's drop-down list, choose the vendor you're ordering inventory from.**

   QuickBooks grabs the vendor's name and address from the vendor's record and uses it to fill in the Vendor address box, as shown in Figure 20-3.

NOTE If you use multiple currencies, the vendor's currency appears to the right of the vendor's name. The "Exchange Rate 1 [unit] =" box below the item table becomes active if the vendor is set up to use a currency different from your home currency.

3. **If you use classes to categorize income and expenses (page 636), choose a class for the purchase order.**

   If you use classes and skip the Class box, when you try to save the purchase order, QuickBooks might remind you that you didn't assign a class. If that happens, click Cancel to return to the purchase order so you can choose a class, or click Save Anyway to save the purchase order without a class.

4. **If you're ordering inventory that you want shipped directly to one of your customers, in the Drop Ship To drop-down list, choose that customer (or job).**

   If you select a drop-ship address, QuickBooks changes the address in the Ship To box from your company's address to the customer's or job's address.

5. **If you're creating your first purchase order, in the P.O. No. box, type the number you want to start with.**

   From then on, QuickBooks increments the number in the P.O. No. box by one. If you order your products over the phone or through an online system and the vendor asks for your purchase order number, give him this number.

6. **In the first Item cell in the table, choose the item that corresponds to the first product you're purchasing.**

   The Item drop-down list shows all the entries in your Item List, even though many companies create purchase orders only for inventory items. (As you type the first few letters of an item's name, QuickBooks displays matching entries. You can keep typing or click the item you want as soon as it appears.)

   When you choose an item, QuickBooks fills in other cells in the row with information from that item's record. The Description cell gets filled with the item record's description, which you can keep or edit. The Rate cell grabs the value from the Cost field of the item's record (that's the price *you* pay for the item).

7. **In the Qty cell, type the quantity you want to purchase.**

   Once you do that, QuickBooks fills in the Amount cell with the total purchase price for the item: the quantity multiplied by the rate.

8. **If you're purchasing inventory specifically for a customer or job, choose the customer or job in the Customer cell.**

   The Create Purchase Orders dialog box doesn't include a cell for designating purchases as billable. Don't worry: You'll tell QuickBooks that an item is billable when you create a bill or receive the item into inventory.

9. **Repeat steps 6–8 for each product you're purchasing.**

   You can add, copy, and delete lines in a purchase order. To do so, right-click in the item table, and then choose one of the entries on the shortcut menu:

   - To add a line, choose Insert Line.
   - To copy a line, choose Copy Line; then right-click another table row and choose Paste Line.
   - To delete a line, choose Delete Line.

10. **At the bottom of the Create Purchase Orders dialog box, in the Memo field, type a summary of what you're ordering to help you identify the purchase order.**

    Whatever you type in the Memo field shows up when it's time to apply a purchase order to a bill (which you'll learn about shortly), so you can identify the right purchase order.

11. **If you have additional purchase orders to create, click Save & New to save the current purchase order and start another.**

    To save the one you just created and close the Create Purchase Orders window, click Save & Close instead. Click Clear to throw out your choices or changes on the purchase order.

Receiving Inventory and Bills Simultaneously

For many orders, you'll find the bill tucked into one of the boxes of your shipment like a bonus gift. Although a bill isn't the most welcome of gifts, receiving a bill and inventory simultaneously *is* a bonus because you can record the inventory and accompanying bill in QuickBooks at the same time. Here's how:

1. **Choose Vendors→"Receive Items and Enter Bill" or, on the Home Page, click Receive Inventory, and then choose "Receive Inventory with Bill."**

   Either way, QuickBooks opens the Enter Bills window that you first met on page 184 and automatically turns on the Bill Received checkbox (see Figure 20-4, background) just as it does when you create a regular bill.

2. **In the Vendor drop-down list, choose the vendor who sent the bill.**

   QuickBooks looks for any open purchase orders for that vendor.

3. **If there are any open purchase orders for that vendor and you want to apply the shipment you received to one of them, in the Open POs Exist message box, click Yes. (If the items you received *don't* go with any open purchase orders, click No and skip to step 5.) If you don't see this message box, skip to step 5.**

   When you click Yes, QuickBooks opens the Open Purchase Orders dialog box (Figure 20-4, foreground), which lists purchase order dates, numbers, and memos.

   If the vendor's bill includes the purchase order number, picking the correct one is easy. Or, if you filled in the Memo field when you created the purchase order, that note may help you identify the right one. But if you don't know which one to pick, click Cancel to close the Open Purchase Orders dialog box. Then, to view a report of open purchase orders, head to the right side of the Enter Bills window and take a look at the Vendor tab's Summary section. Click the number to the right of the "POs to be received" label, which is actually a link that opens a Vendor QuickReport containing the open POs for the vendor you selected in step 2. In the report window, double-click a purchase order to view its details.

Once you've identified the correct PO, on the Enter Bills window's Main tab, click Select PO to reopen the Open Purchase Orders dialog box.

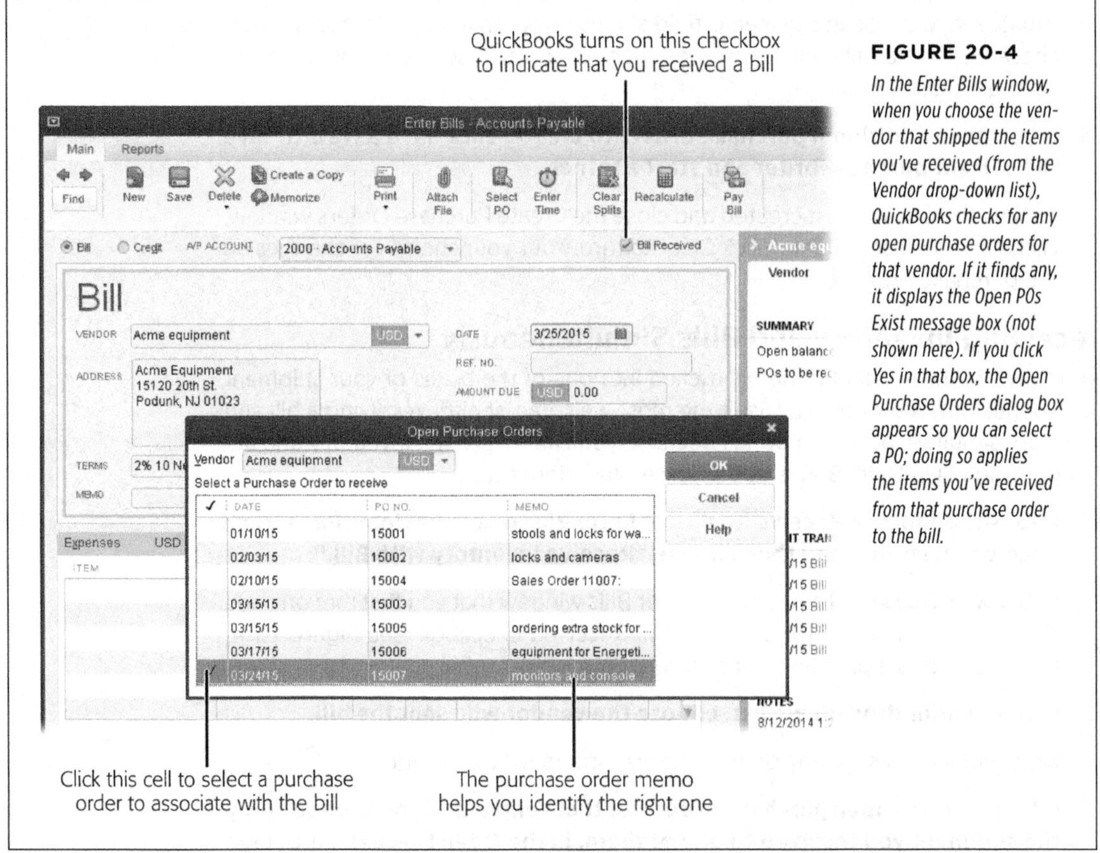
QuickBooks turns on this checkbox to indicate that you received a bill
Click this cell to select a purchase order to associate with the bill
The purchase order memo helps you identify the right one

FIGURE 20-4

In the Enter Bills window, when you choose the vendor that shipped the items you've received (from the Vendor drop-down list), QuickBooks checks for any open purchase orders for that vendor. If it finds any, it displays the Open POs Exist message box (not shown here). If you click Yes in that box, the Open Purchase Orders dialog box appears so you can select a PO; doing so applies the items you've received from that purchase order to the bill.

4. **In the Open Purchase Orders dialog box's table, select the purchase order that goes with the shipment you received by clicking its checkmark cell (the first column), and then click OK.**

   QuickBooks displays a checkmark in the purchase order's checkmark cell. When you click OK, the program closes the Open Purchase Orders dialog box and fills in the bill fields with purchase order info, like the amount and the items ordered, as shown in Figure 20-5. When you work from a purchase order, QuickBooks displays the order's number in the PO No. column in the item table (this column appears only if you choose a purchase order). To open the selected purchase order in the Create Purchase Orders dialog box, click Show PO below the item table.

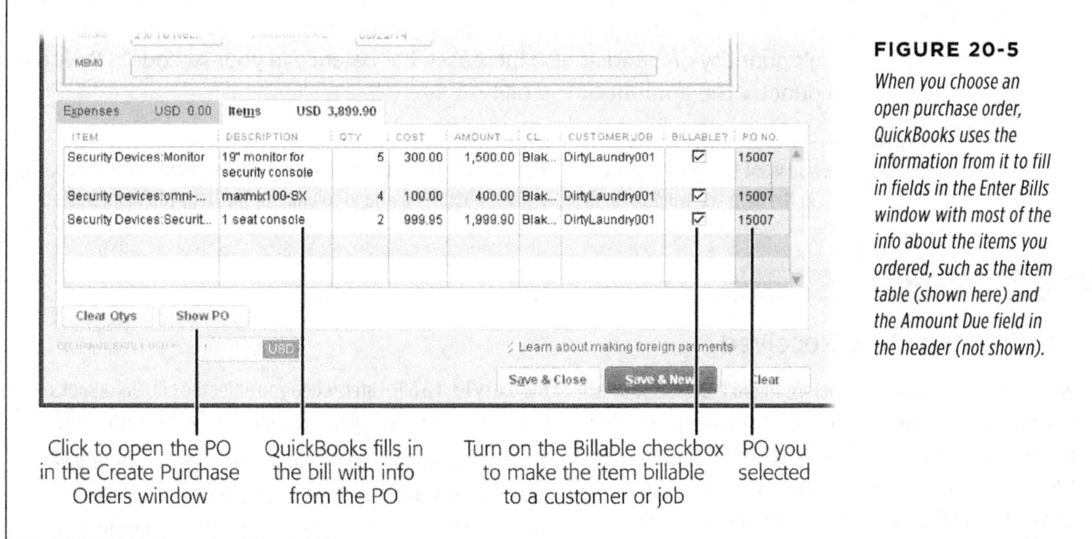
Click to open the PO in the Create Purchase Orders window
QuickBooks fills in the bill with info from the PO
Turn on the Billable checkbox to make the item billable to a customer or job
PO you selected

FIGURE 20-5

When you choose an open purchase order, QuickBooks uses the information from it to fill in fields in the Enter Bills window with most of the info about the items you ordered, such as the item table (shown here) and the Amount Due field in the header (not shown).

TIP It's always a good idea to compare the quantities you received in the shipment with the quantities on your purchase order. If you received fewer items than you ordered, then in the Qty cell for the item, enter the number you *actually* received and adjust the amount due to match what you received.

5. **In the Enter Bills window's Date box, enter the date you received the bill.**

   If you've already defined the payment terms in the vendor's record (page 84), QuickBooks fills in the Terms box and uses those terms to calculate the due date in the Bill Due box. If the bill you received shows different terms or a different due date, update the values in the Bill Due and Terms boxes to match the vendor's bill. (When you save the bill, QuickBooks offers to save the new terms in the vendor's record.)

6. **If you didn't create a purchase order for the shipment you received, fill in the fields as you would for a regular bill.**

   In the Amount Due field, type the amount due from the vendor's bill. You'll also have to fill in the item table manually: For each item you received, in a blank line of the table, specify the item, quantity, customer or job, and class (if you use that feature). QuickBooks fills in the Description and Cost cells by using the values in the item's record, and then calculates the Amount by multiplying the quantity by the item's cost.

7. **Click Save & New or Save & Close.**

   When you save a combination inventory/bill transaction, QuickBooks goes to work behind the scenes. For the inventory you received, the program debits your inventory asset account the amount you paid for the items and updates the item's quantity on hand. It also increases the balance in your Accounts Payable account by the amount of the bill.

TIP If you want to see how many of a particular product you have on hand, on the Home Page, click Items & Services. In the Item List window, look at the Total Quantity On Hand column for the item you're interested in.

TROUBLESHOOTING MOMENT

Posting Inventory Received

When you receive inventory before the bill arrives, your accountant might squawk about how QuickBooks posts inventory to your accounts. In standard accounting practice, only bills show up as credits to the Accounts Payable account. But QuickBooks credits the Accounts Payable account when you receive inventory items without a bill.

When you receive items without a bill, QuickBooks adds an entry for the items to the Accounts Payable register. (To view the register, press Ctrl+A to open the Chart of Accounts window, and then double-click the Accounts Payable account.) The program fills in the Type cell with the text "ITEM RCPT" to indicate that the entry isn't a bill. Later, when you enter the bill, QuickBooks edits the same transaction, replacing "ITEM RCPT" with "BILL."

The result in your company file is correct after you receive the inventory and enter the corresponding bill. However, your accountant might complain about the incomplete audit trail because the transaction changes without some kind of record. If you want to track inventory, bills, and price differences between your purchase orders and the final bills, you can do so *outside* of QuickBooks. Then, once you receive both the inventory and the corresponding bill, you can record the transaction in QuickBooks.

Receiving Inventory Before the Bill

When you receive inventory, you want to record it in QuickBooks so you know that it's available to sell. If you receive inventory without a bill, the best solution is to *pretend* that you received the bill. By creating the bill in QuickBooks, your Accounts Payable stays in sync with what you've purchased. Then, once you receive the bill, you can edit the QuickBooks bill to match it.

Another approach is to record the received inventory in QuickBooks without a bill. (You can do this because the program has separate features for receiving inventory and entering bills when they arrive.) The box above explains how QuickBooks posts amounts to accounts when you receive inventory without a bill. The fields that you specify and the options at your disposal are the same as when you receive inventory *with* a bill (as described in the previous section); they just appear in different windows.

To receive inventory in your company file before the bill arrives:

1. **Choose Vendors→Receive Items or, on the Home Page, click the Receive Inventory icon and then choose "Receive Inventory without Bill."**

QuickBooks opens the Create Item Receipts window, which is a close relative of the Enter Bills window. In fact, other than the window's title, only two things are different, both of which are labeled in Figure 20-6.

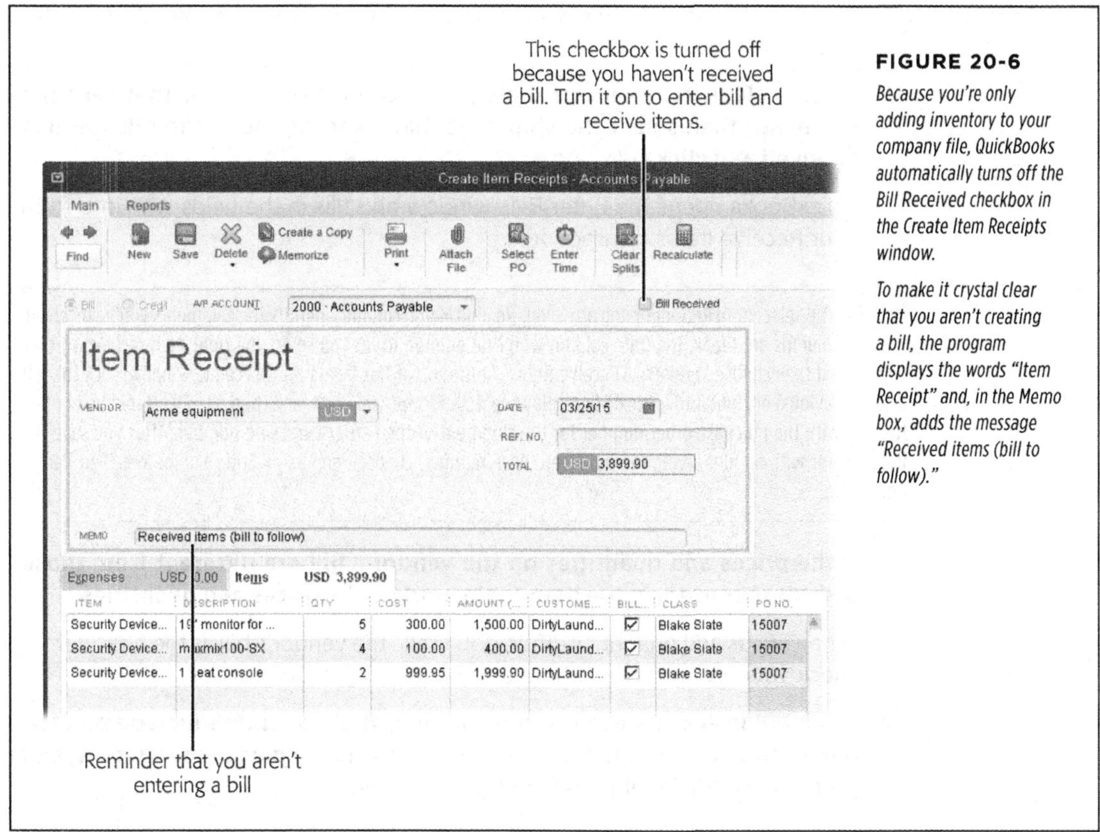

FIGURE 20-6

Because you're only adding inventory to your company file, QuickBooks automatically turns off the Bill Received checkbox in the Create Item Receipts window.

To make it crystal clear that you aren't creating a bill, the program displays the words "Item Receipt" and, in the Memo box, adds the message "Received items (bill to follow)."

TIP If you open the Create Item Receipts window and then realize that you *do* have the bill, there's no need to close the window and choose a different feature. Simply turn on the Bill Received checkbox at the window's top right. When you do, the window changes to the Enter Bills window so you can receive the items *and* create the bill (page 530).

Similar to what happens when you receive inventory and a bill at the same time, the Create Item Receipts window reminds you about open purchase orders that you can select to fill in the items received automatically. The rest of the fields behave like the ones in the Enter Bills window, explained on page 527.

2. **When you've added all the items you received and updated any quantities that differ from those on your purchase order, click Save & Close.**

   QuickBooks records the inventory in your company file, as described in the box on page 530.

Then, when the bill for the items you received finally arrives, here's what you do:

1. **Choose Vendors→"Enter Bill for Received Items," or on the Home Page, click the Enter Bills Against Inventory icon.**

   The box on page 533 tells you how to recover if you choose Vendors→Enter Bills by mistake.

2. **In the Select Item Receipt dialog box, choose the vendor that sent the shipment; then select the shipment that corresponds to the bill you just received and click OK.**

   QuickBooks opens the Enter Bills window and fills in the fields with info from your Receive Items transaction.

TIP The Select Item Receipt dialog box's Ref. No. and Memo columns identify the shipments you've received. If those columns are blank, the Date column won't be enough to let you select the right item receipt, so click Cancel, and then choose Vendors→Receive Items. At the top of the Create Item Receipts window, click the left arrow (Previous) or right arrow (Next) to display the item receipt you want, and then fill in its Memo box or Ref. No. box with the purchase order number for the shipment or the carrier's tracking number. After you save the item receipt with an identifying memo or reference number, choose Vendors→"Enter Bill for Received Items" once more.

3. **If the prices and quantities on the vendor's bill are different from those QuickBooks used, in the item table, update the prices and quantities.**

   When prices and quantities differ, don't take the vendor's bill as the final word—check your record to see where the discrepancy arose.

4. **If the bill includes sales tax and shipping that you didn't include on your purchase order, click the Expenses tab in the lower part of the window, and then fill in additional lines for those charges.**

   If you change anything on the window's Items or Expenses tab, at the top of the Create Item Receipts window, click Recalculate to update the Amount Due field with the new total.

5. **Click Save & Close.**

   You'll see a message box asking if you want to save the changes you made—even if you didn't make any. QuickBooks asks this question because *it* changed the item receipt transaction to a bill in your Accounts Payable account, as the box on page 533 explains. Click Yes to save the changes.

TROUBLESHOOTING MOMENT

Double (Posting) Trouble

When you want to enter a bill for items you received earlier, be extra careful to choose Vendors→"Enter Bill for Received Items" (or click Enter Bills Against Inventory on the Home Page). If you choose Vendors→Enter Bills instead, you'll end up with *two* postings for the same items in your Accounts Payable account. The first posting appears when you receive the items in QuickBooks (the one identified with the ITEM RCPT type); the second posting is for the bill.

If you accidentally create one of these double entries, here's how to correct the problem:

1. In the Chart of Accounts window, double-click the Accounts Payable account.
2. In the Accounts Payable register, select the bill, and then choose Edit→Delete Bill; alternatively, right-click the bill, and then choose Delete Bill on the shortcut menu.
3. Recreate the bill using the "Enter Bill for Received Items" feature (page 532).

Selling Inventory

You don't have to jump through hoops to sell inventory. When you add inventory items to invoices (Chapter 10), sales receipts (Chapter 13), or other sales forms (Chapter 11), QuickBooks deducts the units you sold from each item's Total Quantity On Hand value. The income from the sale posts to an income account, while the cost of the units you sold moves from the inventory asset account to a cost of goods sold account.

When you sell inventory, QuickBooks also compares the new Total Quantity On Hand value with your minimum reorder point (page 521). When the inventory on hand drops below this number, the program reminds you that it's time to order more (page 485). (If you use QuickBooks Premier or Enterprise, the program will tell you how *many* to order based on the item's maximum reorder point.) The box below tells you how to shut off reminders for items you aren't selling at the moment.

TROUBLESHOOTING MOMENT

Managing Seasonal Items

The Item List is home to items for *every* service and product you sell, and it can get really long really fast, especially if you sell different items at different times of the year. For example, if you stock your store with lawn furniture in the spring, you don't want to scroll past dozens of outdoor items or see reminders to reorder them the other nine months of the year.

Fortunately, you can make seasonal items inactive, which temporarily hides them in the Item List and silences their reminders. In the Item List window (Lists→Item List), right-click the item, and then choose Make Item Inactive from the shortcut menu. Page 119 explains how to reactivate items when a new season rolls around.

Running Inventory Reports

Checking the vital signs of your inventory is the best way to keep it healthy. When products are hot, you have to keep them in stock or you'll lose sales. And if products grow cold, you don't want to get stuck holding the bag (or the lime-green luggage).

Most companies keep tabs on inventory trends and compare them with what's going on in sales. For example, when the value of your inventory asset account is increasing faster than sales, sales could be poor because your prices are too high, competition is encroaching on your market, or your spy-cam necklaces simply didn't catch on.

Good inventory management means keeping enough items in stock to meet your sales, but not so many that your inventory grows obsolete before you can sell it. QuickBooks inventory reports aren't fancy, but they tell you most of what you need to know. You can run any of these reports by choosing Reports→Purchases or Reports→Inventory and then picking the one you want. The following sections describe what each report includes.

NOTE QuickBooks inventory reports show only the active inventory items in your Item List. So if you run inventory reports without reactivating all your inventory items (page 119), the values in the reports won't be accurate. By contrast, financial statements such as the Balance Sheet include your *total* inventory value for active and inactive inventory items alike.

Purchases Reports

These reports, not surprisingly, are listed under Reports→Purchases. When you run the Purchases by Vendor Summary report and see high dollar values, you might want to negotiate volume discounts or faster delivery times. This report can also show when you rely too heavily on one vendor—a big risk should that vendor go out of business.

The Purchases by Item Summary report shows how many inventory items you've bought and the total you paid. (This report also comes in handy if you want to use LIFO or FIFO to calculate inventory value, as explained on page 544.) The Purchases by Item Detail report shows each purchase transaction, along with the quantity, cost, and vendor.

If your supplies are dwindling, the Open Purchase Orders report shows when more items are due. (You can also run this report from the Enter Bills window: Click the Reports tab at the top of the window, and then click the Open Purchase Order Detail icon.) The report displays the PO's date, vendor, number, and delivery date. Double-click a purchase order to open the Create Purchase Orders window, which shows the products included in that order.

How Much Is Inventory Worth?

QuickBooks includes two reports that tell you how much your inventory is worth: Inventory Valuation Summary and Inventory Valuation Detail. Here's what each one does.

INVENTORY VALUATION SUMMARY REPORT

The Inventory Valuation Summary report, shown in Figure 20-7, is an overview of the inventory you have on hand, what it's worth as an asset, and what it will be worth when you sell it. (See page 544 to find out what to do if your inventory isn't worth as much as it used to be.)

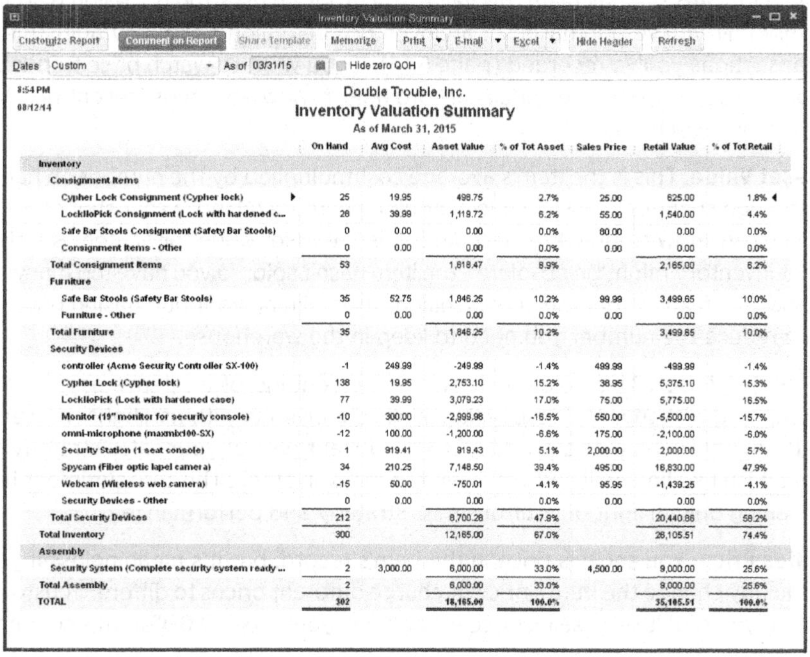

Inventory Valuation Summary

Customize Report | Comment on Report | Share Template | Memorize | Print | E-mail | Excel | Hide Header | Refresh

Dates Custom | As of 03/31/15 | Hide zero QOH

8:54 PM
08/12/14

Double Trouble, Inc.
Inventory Valuation Summary
As of March 31, 2015

	On Hand	Avg Cost	Asset Value	% of Tot Asset	Sales Price	Retail Value	% of Tot Retail
Inventory							
Consignment Items							
Cypher Lock Consignment (Cypher lock)	25	19.95	498.75	2.7%	25.00	625.00	1.8%
LockIloPick Consignment (Lock with hardened c...	28	39.99	1,119.72	6.2%	55.00	1,540.00	4.4%
Safe Bar Stools Consignment (Safety Bar Stools)	0	0.00	0.00	0.0%	80.00	0.00	0.0%
Consignment Items - Other	0	0.00	0.00	0.0%	0.00	0.00	0.0%
Total Consignment Items	53		1,818.47	8.9%		2,165.00	6.2%
Furniture							
Safe Bar Stools (Safety Bar Stools)	35	52.75	1,846.25	10.2%	99.99	3,499.65	10.0%
Furniture - Other	0	0.00	0.00	0.0%	0.00	0.00	0.0%
Total Furniture	35		1,846.25	10.2%		3,499.65	10.0%
Security Devices							
controller (Acme Security Controller SX-100)	-1	249.99	-249.98	-1.4%	499.99	-499.99	-1.4%
Cypher Lock (Cypher lock)	138	19.95	2,753.10	15.2%	38.95	5,375.10	15.3%
LockIloPick (Lock with hardened case)	77	39.99	3,079.23	17.0%	75.00	5,775.00	16.5%
Monitor (19" monitor for security console)	-10	300.00	-2,999.98	-16.5%	550.00	-5,500.00	-15.7%
omni-microphone (maxmix100-SX)	-12	100.00	-1,200.00	-6.6%	175.00	-2,100.00	-6.0%
Security Station (1 seat console)	1	919.41	919.43	5.1%	2,000.00	2,000.00	5.7%
Spycam (Fiber optic lapel camera)	34	210.25	7,148.50	39.4%	495.00	16,830.00	47.9%
Webcam (Wireless web camera)	-15	50.00	-750.01	-4.1%	95.95	-1,439.25	-4.1%
Security Devices - Other	0	0.00	0.00	0.0%	0.00	0.00	0.0%
Total Security Devices	212		8,700.28	47.9%		20,440.86	58.2%
Total Inventory	300		12,165.00	67.0%		26,105.51	74.4%
Assembly							
Security System (Complete security system ready ...	2	3,000.00	6,000.00	33.0%	4,500.00	9,000.00	25.6%
Total Assembly	2		6,000.00	33.0%		9,000.00	25.6%
TOTAL	302		18,165.00	100.0%		35,105.51	100.0%

FIGURE 20-7

Because the report is a snapshot of inventory value, month-to-date, quarter-to-date, and year-to-date ranges all produce the same results. But if you want to see the inventory value as of a different date, in the Dates box, choose the one you want.

To run this report, choose Reports→Inventory→Inventory Valuation Summary or (if you have QuickBooks Premier or Enterprise) at the top right of the Inventory Center (Vendors→Inventory Activities→Inventory Center), click the Inventory Valuation Summary link. QuickBooks initially uses the current month to date as the date range for this report. The first column shows the names of the inventory items from your Item List; subitems appear indented beneath their parent items. Here are the report's other columns and why they are (or aren't) important to inventory health:

- **On Hand**. To calculate this value, QuickBooks subtracts the number of products you sold and adds the number of products you received. The values in this column can help you quickly check for items that are out of or *close* to being out of stock. However, because items sell at different rates, the reorder point reminder (page 521) is a better indication than this column that something is perilously close to selling out.

NOTE When you add an out-of-stock item to an invoice, QuickBooks warns that you don't have inventory, but it doesn't prevent you from invoicing for products you don't have. When the On Hand value is negative, you know it's time to order more—and to ask for express shipping.

- **Avg Cost**. Average cost is the only way QuickBooks Pro and Premier value inventory. (QuickBooks Enterprise can perform "first in/first out" valuation; see page 546.) To calculate this value, the program uses the price you paid for every unit you've purchased of an inventory item along with any adjustment transactions you've recorded (page 544). If you want to watch price trends so you can adjust your sales prices accordingly, review your most recent bills for inventory purchases.
- **Asset Value**. This is the item's average cost multiplied by the number on hand. Although changes in asset value over time are more telling, a snapshot of asset value can show trouble brewing. An excessive asset value for an item is a sign that inventory might be obsolete—the item hasn't sold, so you have too many on hand. If you know that the item *is* selling, streamlining your purchasing process can reduce the number you need to keep in the warehouse.
- **% of Tot Asset**. This column shows the percentage of an item's asset value compared with the total asset value of all your inventory items. Higher percentages might mean that a product is a significant part of your sales strategy or that it isn't selling well and you have too many in stock. This measurement has meaning only in light of your business strategy and performance.
- **Sales Price**. You set this price in the item's record, but it's meaningless if you regularly change the item's price or charge different prices to different customers. If you didn't set a sales price for an item, you'll see "0.00" in this column.
- **Retail Value**. Because an item's retail value is its sales price multiplied by the number on hand, this number is useful only if the value in the Sales Price column is the typical sales price for the item.
- **% of Tot Retail**. This percentage is what portion of your *total* inventory's retail value the item's retail value represents. Different products sell at different profit margins, which you can see when the value in this column differs from the value in the % of Tot Asset column.

INVENTORY VALUATION DETAIL REPORT

This report (Reports→Inventory→Inventory Valuation Detail) lists every transaction that increases or decreases the number of items you have on hand. Although it can grow lengthy, this report can help you figure out where your inventory went (and perhaps jog your memory about inventory transactions that you forgot to record in QuickBooks). As in other reports, you can double-click a transaction to see its details.

Inventory Stock Status

As you might expect, the Inventory Stock Status by Item report (Reports→Inventory →Inventory Stock Status by Item) tells you where your inventory stands today and how it will change based on your outstanding purchase orders. As Figure 20-8 shows, this report is a great way to see which items you need to reorder.

TIP If you want to use a barcode reader to scan your inventory, go to Intuit's marketplace (*http://marketplace.intuit.com*). In either Search Apps Now box, type *barcode* to find third-party barcode readers.

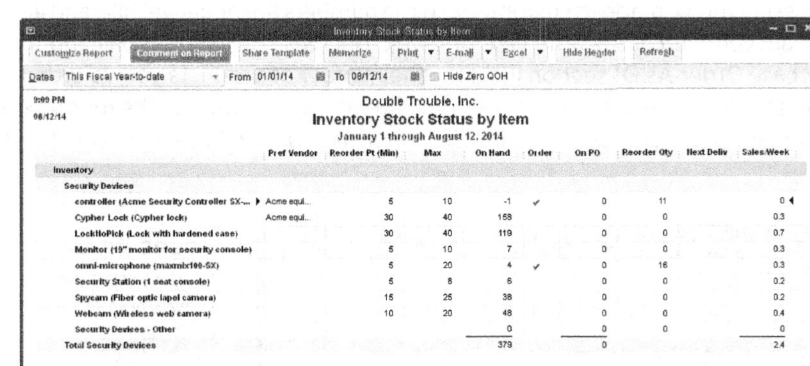

9:09 PM
08/12/14

Double Trouble, Inc.
Inventory Stock Status by Item
January 1 through August 12, 2014

	Pref Vendor	Reorder Pt (Min)	Max	On Hand	Order	On PO	Reorder Qty	Next Deliv	Sales/Week
Inventory									
Security Devices									
controller (Acme Security Controller SX-...	Acme equi...	5	10	-1	✓	0	11		0
Cypher Lock (Cypher lock)	Acme equi...	30	40	158		0	0		0.3
LockNoPick (Lock with hardened case)		30	40	119		0	0		0.7
Monitor (19" monitor for security console)		5	10	7		0	0		0.3
omni-microphone (maxmix100-SX)		5	20	4	✓	0	16		0.3
Security Station (1 seat console)		5	8	6		0	0		0.2
Spycam (Fiber optic lapel camera)		15	25	38		0	0		0.2
Webcam (Wireless web camera)		10	20	48		0	0		0.4
Security Devices - Other				0		0	0		0
Total Security Devices				379		0			2.4

FIGURE 20-8

For every active inventory item, this report shows its minimum reorder point in the Reorder Pt (Min) column (and, if you use QuickBooks Premier or Enterprise, the maximum reorder point in the Max column) and the number you currently have in stock in the On Hand column. However, a checkmark in the Order column is the most obvious sign that you need to reorder.

If you've added an item to a purchase order, the On PO column shows whether the quantity in that shipment is enough to restock your warehouse.

You can also run the Inventory Stock Status by Vendor report to see the same information that's in the Inventory Stock Status by Item report, but grouped and subtotaled by vendor. If you seem to run low on products from a particular vendor, you might want to increase the minimum reorder point for those products to fine-tune your lead time. (If you use QuickBooks Premier or Enterprise, you might raise the minimum reorder point so you can get a new order in time *and* raise the maximum reorder point so the order that comes in lasts awhile.)

NOTE If you upgrade to QuickBooks Premier or Enterprise, the Inventory Stock Status reports also show how many items you've added to sales orders for future delivery.

Viewing One Inventory Item

The Inventory Item QuickReport is a fast yet thorough way to see what's going on with a particular item. To display this report, open the Item List window (Lists→Item List), select the item you want to review, and then press Ctrl+Q or, at the bottom of the window, click Reports→"QuickReport: [item name]." Alternatively, if you use QuickBooks Premier or Enterprise, in the Inventory Center (Vendors→Inventory Activities→Inventory Center), select the item, and then click the QuickReport link in the window's upper right.

This report includes purchase and sales transactions for the item, such as bills and invoices (see Figure 20-9). In the On Hand As Of section, invoice transactions represent the sales you've made to customers, so the numbers are negative; bills and item receipts are your purchases from vendors, which increase the number on hand. The On Purchase Order As Of section includes the number of products you've ordered but haven't yet received. And the Total As Of figure at the bottom of the report tells you how many products you'll have in stock when all your purchase orders are filled.

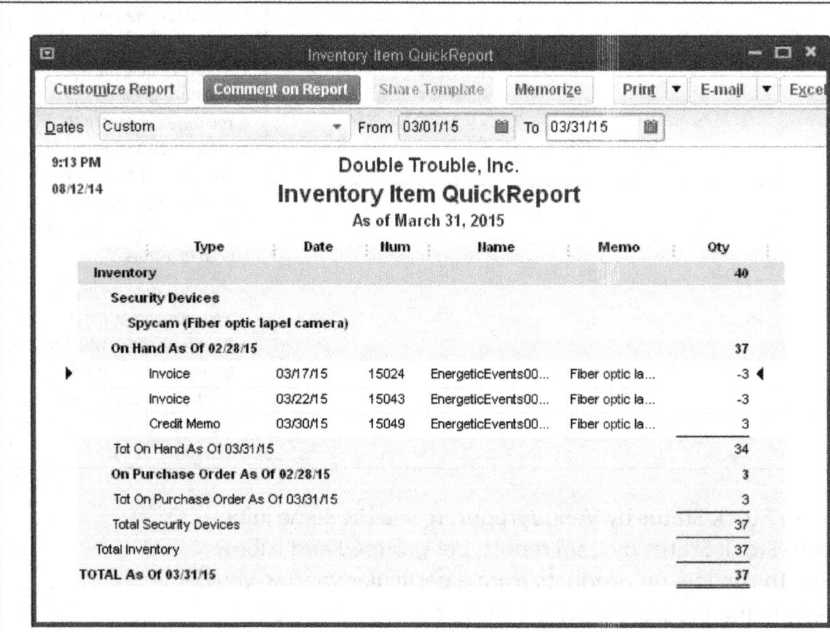

Type	Date	Num	Name	Memo	Qty
Inventory					40
Security Devices					
Spycam (Fiber optic lapel camera)					
On Hand As Of 02/28/15					37
Invoice	03/17/15	15024	EnergeticEvents00...	Fiber optic la...	-3
Invoice	03/22/15	15043	EnergeticEvents00...	Fiber optic la...	-3
Credit Memo	03/30/15	15049	EnergeticEvents00...	Fiber optic la...	3
Tot On Hand As Of 03/31/15					34
On Purchase Order As Of 02/28/15					3
Tot On Purchase Order As Of 03/31/15					3
Total Security Devices					37
Total Inventory					37
TOTAL As Of 03/31/15					37

FIGURE 20-9

This report summarizes how many of an item you have on hand and the number on order.

In the leftmost column, the headings at the beginning of each section show the last day before the date range you select, such as "On Hand As Of 02/28/15" as shown here. Then the report lists the transactions during the report's date range that affect a total, such as invoice and item receipts for the On Hand As Of section. The Tot On Hand As Of and Total As Of labels show the actual as-of date for the report, along with the final total for the inventory item.

Working with the Inventory Center

The Inventory Center (which is available only in QuickBooks Premier and Enterprise) provides information about items you keep in stock. Similar to the Customer Center and Vendor Center, it's a quick way to answer questions like "How many items do I have on hand to sell?" and "What purchase orders and sales orders are open?" To open the Inventory Center (shown in Figure 20-10), choose Vendors→Inventory Activities→Inventory Center. Here's how to use the center to see what's going on with your inventory:

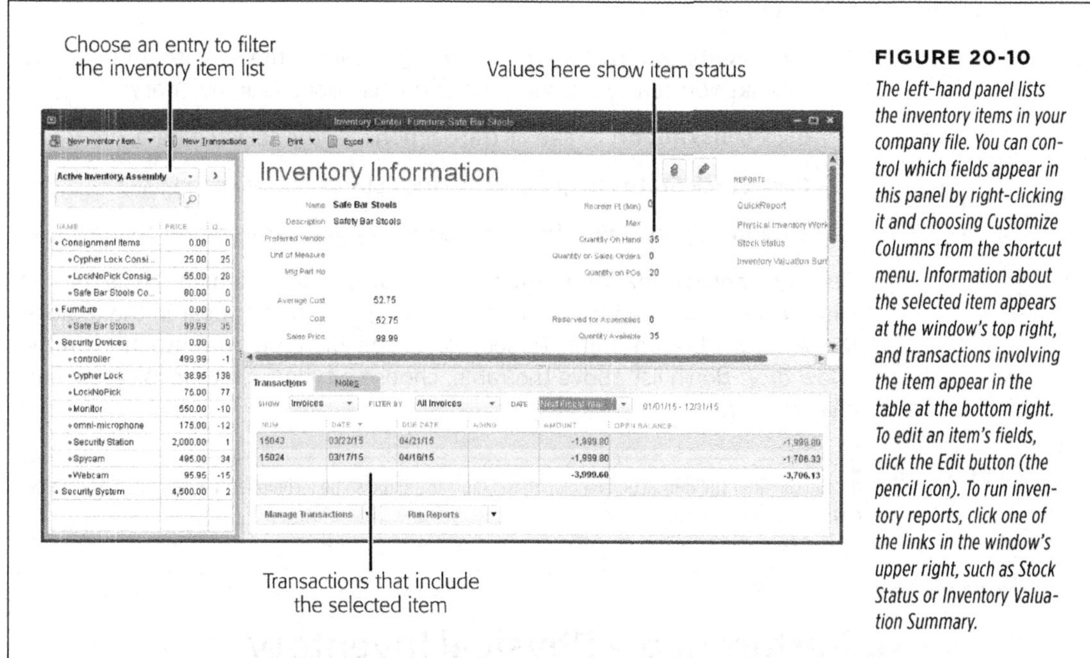
Choose an entry to filter the inventory item list
Values here show item status
Inventory Information
Transactions that include the selected item

FIGURE 20-10

The left-hand panel lists the inventory items in your company file. You can control which fields appear in this panel by right-clicking it and choosing Customize Columns from the shortcut menu. Information about the selected item appears at the window's top right, and transactions involving the item appear in the table at the bottom right. To edit an item's fields, click the Edit button (the pencil icon). To run inventory reports, click one of the links in the window's upper right, such as Stock Status or Inventory Valuation Summary.

- **Display inventory items**. When you first open the Inventory Center, QuickBooks displays your active Inventory Part items (and Inventory Assembly items, if you use them) in the panel on the left. Then, when you click the name of an inventory item in that panel, the Inventory Information section at the window's top right shows info from that item's record.
- **Filter the list of inventory items**. To narrow the list to the items that fit the criteria you want, such as inventory items that are out of stock, in the center's toolbar, click the unlabeled filter box that's located immediately below the New Inventory Item entry (it's labeled in Figure 20-10). In the drop-down list, choose one of the entries, like "QOH < = zero," which is shorthand for "Quantity on hand is less than or equal to zero."
- **Find an inventory item in the list**. If you have scads of inventory items, you can quickly find the one you want with the find box, which is the *second* unlabeled box in the left-hand panel. Simply type part of the item's name, and then press Enter or click the Search button, which has a magnifying glass on it.

- **Change the fields that appear in the center's list**. To display different fields in the list, right-click the panel on the window's left side, and then choose Customize Columns. In the Customize Columns dialog box's Available Columns list, select the fields you want to display, and then click Add to move them to the Chosen Columns list. To remove a column, select it in the Chosen Columns list, and then click the Remove button. When the Chosen Columns list includes the fields you want, click OK.
- **Review inventory status**. In the upper-right part of the Inventory Center are several links you can use to see various things about your inventory:
  - Click **QuickReport** to see all transactions for the selected item.
  - Click **Stock Status** to generate a Stock Status report (page 537).
  - Click **Inventory Valuation Summary** to generate this report (page 535).
- **Display transactions for an item**. When you select an item in the list on the window's left side, the transactions involving that item appear in the table at the window's bottom right. To see only a specific *type* of transaction, in the Show drop-down list above the table, choose a type such as Invoices or Purchase Orders.

TIP You can filter the transactions shown in the table using the same techniques that work in the Customer Center, which are described on page 41.

Performing a Physical Inventory

QuickBooks calculates how many products you have on hand based on your purchases and sales, but it has no way of knowing what's actually happening in your warehouse. Employees may help themselves to products; fire can consume some of your inventory; or a burst pipe could turn your India ink sketches into Rorschach tests. Only a physical count of the items in stock can tell you how many units you *really* have on hand.

QuickBooks does the only thing it can to help you count your inventory: provide the Physical Inventory Worksheet report, which lists each inventory item in your Item List and how many units should be on hand. To see it, choose Reports→Inventory→Physical Inventory Worksheet (or, if you have QuickBooks Premier or Enterprise, click the Physical Inventory Worksheet link in the Inventory Center's upper right). The worksheet's Physical Count column has blank lines so you can write in how many you find, as you can see in Figure 20-11. (The box on page 541 explains how to count inventory while business continues to chug along.)

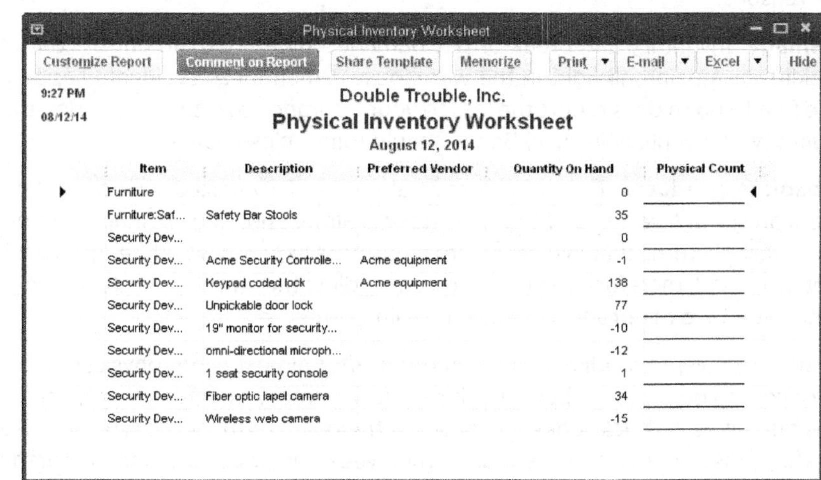

FIGURE 20-11

Your preferred vendor has nothing to do with counting inventory, yet a column with that info appears on this report. To hide that column, click Customize Report in the report window's toolbar. On the Display tab, in the Columns list, click the checkmark to the left of the Preferred Vendor entry (you may have to scroll to see it) to turn it off.

TIP To sort the items in the Physical Inventory Worksheet so they're listed by the warehouse aisles where they're kept, in the Columns list, turn on the Location of Fixed Asset field; next, in the "Sort by" drop-down list, choose Location of Fixed Asset, and then click OK.

TROUBLESHOOTING MOMENT

Freezing Inventory While You Count

It's sheer madness to ship customer orders out and receive inventory shipments while you're trying to count the products you have on hand. QuickBooks doesn't have a feature for freezing inventory while you perform a physical count, but you can follow procedures that do the same thing.

Because physical inventory counts disrupt business operations, most companies schedule them during slow periods and off hours. To keep the disruption to a minimum, print the Physical Inventory Worksheet *just* before you start the count. Then do the following to keep your inventory stable:

- **Sales**. During the count, create invoices in QuickBooks for inventory sales as you would normally. After you save each invoice, edit it to mark it as pending (page 261). When you finish the count, edit the pending invoices again to mark them as final, fill the orders, and then send the invoices.
- **Purchases**. If you receive inventory shipments during the count, don't unpack the boxes or use any of QuickBooks' features for receiving inventory (page 527) until you're done with the count.

Adjusting Inventory in QuickBooks

Your inventory records in QuickBooks may not match your real-world inventory for several reasons:

- **Damage**. Inventory can break or get damaged by a flood, an out-of-control forklift, or a paintball fight in the warehouse. When these accidents happen, the first thing to do is report the loss to your insurance company. Adjusting the quantity of inventory in QuickBooks should follow close behind.
- **Obsolete products**. If you have several cases of oversized, low-resolution webcams, the *true* value of that inventory is almost nothing. Writing them off as unsellable turns that inventory into a business expense, which reduces your net profit and, therefore, the taxes you pay. Adjust the inventory in QuickBooks when you take the products to the recycling center.
- **Theft**. An inventory adjustment is in order after almost every physical inventory count you perform, because the actual inventory quantities rarely match the quantities in QuickBooks. *Shrinkage* is the polite term for the typical cause of these discrepancies. To be blunt, employees, repair people, and passersby attracted by an unlocked door may help themselves to a five-finger discount. And you not only take the hit to your bottom line—you're also stuck adjusting QuickBooks' records to account for the theft.

It's no surprise, then, that QuickBooks has a feature for this multipurpose accounting task. You adjust both the quantity of inventory and its value in the aptly named "Adjust Quantity/Value on Hand" window.

You purchase inventory from vendors, so QuickBooks keeps all inventory features in the same place: the Vendors menu. To open the "Adjust Quantity/Value on Hand" window, choose Vendors→Inventory Activities→"Adjust Quantity/Value on Hand" or, in the Home Page's Company panel, click Inventory Activities→"Adjust Quantity/Value On Hand."

Adjusting Quantities

You need to adjust quantities when you're writing off obsolete inventory or updating your company file to reflect the number of items in stock. When you adjust inventory quantities, QuickBooks fills in or calculates some of the fields for you. Here are guidelines for filling in the remaining fields of the "Adjust Quantity/Value on Hand" window:

- **Adjustment Type**. To adjust inventory items' quantities to match what's in your warehouse or reflect what you're writing off, choose Quantity from this drop-down menu, as shown in Figure 20-12. QuickBooks uses the average cost of each item to calculate the dollar value that the new quantities represent.
- **Adjustment Date**. QuickBooks puts the current date in this box. If you like to keep your journal entries and other bookkeeping adjustments together at the

end of a quarter or year, enter the date when you want to record the adjustment instead.

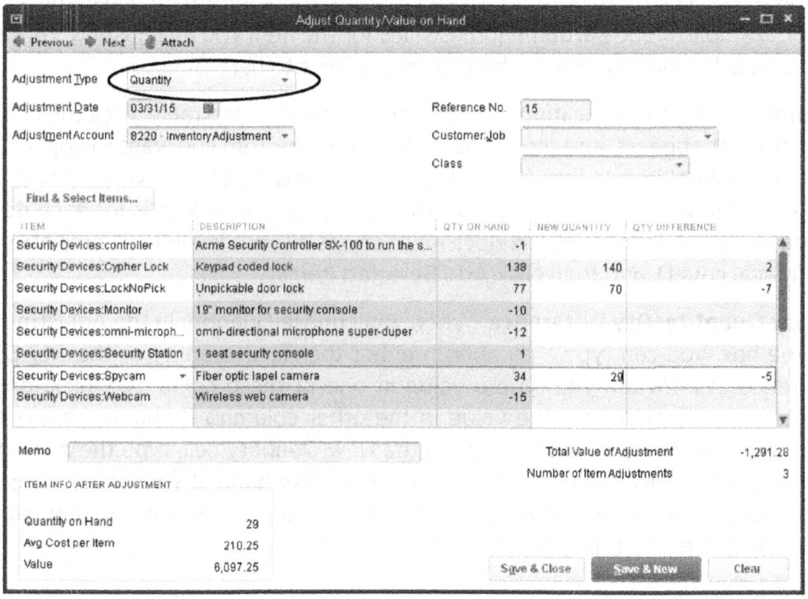

FIGURE 20-12

In this window's table, QuickBooks shades the columns you can't change.

When you choose Quantity in the Adjustment Type box (circled), the Item, New Quantity, and Qty Difference columns are the only ones you can edit.

- **Adjustment Account**. Choose an expense account you created to track the cost of inventory adjustments. For example, if you adjust an item's quantity to match the physical count, choose an expense account such as Inventory Adjustment. If you're writing off obsolete or damaged inventory, choose an expense account such as Unsalable Inventory. (Because you can assign only one account to each inventory adjustment, adjust the quantity once for physical count changes, and then click Save & New to create a *separate* adjustment for write-offs.)

TIP If the expense account you want to use doesn't exist, at the top of the Adjustment Account drop-down list, choose <Add New>, and then fill in the boxes in the Add New Account window. When you click Save & Close, QuickBooks fills in the Adjustment Account box with the account you just created.

- **Reference Number**. You don't *have* to enter reference numbers, but they come in handy when discussing your books with your accountant. If you don't type anything in this box, QuickBooks sets it to 1 and then increments the number here by one each time you adjust inventory.
- **Customer:Job**. If you want to record products you send to a customer or job at no charge—without adding those items to an invoice—choose that customer or job in this drop-down list. QuickBooks then assigns the cost of the adjustment to that customer or job.

TIP A better way to give products to a customer or job is to add them to an invoice with a price of $0.00. That way, your generosity remains on the record lest your customer forgets.

- **Class**. If you use classes to track sales, choose the appropriate one in this box. For example, if one partner handles sales for the item you're adjusting, choose the class for that partner so the expense applies to her.
- **Item**. To adjust a single item, click the first item cell in the table, click the down arrow that appears, and then choose the inventory item you want to adjust. To adjust several items, click the Find & Select Items button above the table. In the Find & Select Items dialog box, turn on the checkmark cells for each item you want to adjust (or click Select All to select *all* your inventory items after a physical count), and then click Add Selected Items.
- **New Quantity/Qty Difference**. When you choose Quantity in the Adjustment Type box, you can type a number in either the New Quantity or the Qty Difference cell. (When you type a value in one of these columns, QuickBooks automatically calculates the value in the other column.) If you're making an adjustment after a physical count, in the New Quantity cell, type the quantity from your physical count worksheet. On the other hand, if you lost two cases of webcams, it's easier to type the number you lost as a negative number (such as *–20*) in the Qty Difference cell.

TIP If you're ready to admit that the pet rock fad isn't coming back, you can write off your entire inventory by putting *0* in an item's New Quantity cell. In the Adjustment Account drop-down list, choose an expense account such as Unsalable Inventory.

- **Memo**. To prevent questions from your accountant, in the Memo cell, type the reason for the adjustment, such as "2015 end-of-year physical count."

After you fill in all the boxes, click Save & Close (or Save & New if you want to create a second adjustment for write-offs, say). If you decreased the quantity on hand, QuickBooks decreases the balance in your inventory asset account (using the average cost per item). To keep double-entry bookkeeping principles intact, the decrease in the inventory asset account also shows up as an *increase* in the expense account you chose. Conversely, if the adjustment increases the quantity or value of your inventory, the inventory asset account's balance increases and the expense account's balance decreases.

Adjusting Quantities and Values

Calculating inventory values by using the items' average cost is convenient—and in QuickBooks Pro and Premier, it's your only option. Using other methods for calculating inventory value, like "first in/first out" (FIFO) and "last in/first out" (LIFO) costing (explained in the box on page 546), quickly turn into a full-time job. But if that's what you want, you can do so manually.

NOTE You can value inventory using FIFO if you upgrade to QuickBooks Enterprise and subscribe to Intuit's Advanced Inventory service (which costs extra).

Because QuickBooks can handle only average cost for inventory, your sole workaround for achieving LIFO or FIFO costing is to adjust dollar values by hand in the "Adjust Quantity/Value on Hand" window (Vendors→Inventory Activities→"Adjust Quantity/Value on Hand"). When you choose Total Value in the window's Adjustment Type box, QuickBooks displays the New Value column. You can then change the asset value of the quantity on hand simply by typing the new value in that column.

You can also change both quantities *and* values to, for example, make the quantity reflect what's in your warehouse and the value reflect the items' poor condition. To do this, in the Adjustment Type box, choose "Quantity and Total Value." QuickBooks then activates the New Quantity, Qty Difference, and New Value columns. To change the number you have, type the value in the New Quantity cell. To adjust an item's value, in the New Value cell for that item, type the dollar value for the quantity on hand.

Mimicking LIFO or FIFO costing takes some effort because you have to review the bills for all your purchases of the inventory item. Here's how to value your inventory using LIFO:

1. **Choose Reports→Purchases→Purchases by Item Detail.**

   QuickBooks generates a report that shows your purchase transactions grouped by inventory item.

2. **For the quantity of the item that you have on hand, add up the prices you paid for your most recent purchases.**

   The Purchases by Item Detail report's Cost Price column shows how much you paid for an item with each purchase. Say you need to know the LIFO value for 10 security stations for your tax return. As shown in Figure 20-13, the first 20 security stations cost $999.95 each, and the last four cost $750.00 each. So the LIFO value for the last 10 security stations would be 4 multiplied by $750.00 and 6 multiplied by $999.95, or $8,999.70.

3. **In the "Adjust Quantity/Value on Hand" window (Vendors→Inventory Activities→"Adjust Quantity/Value on Hand"), type the amount you just calculated into the New Value cell.**

   When you click Save & Close, QuickBooks decreases the balance in your inventory asset account using the value in the New Value cell instead of the average cost per item.

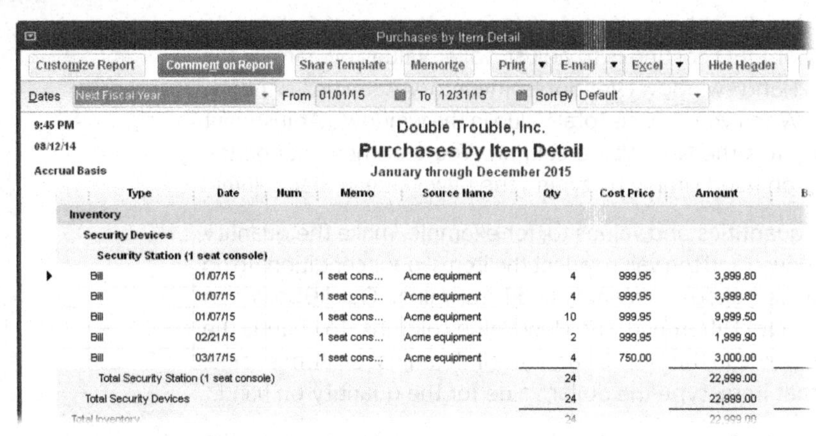

FIGURE 20-13

To value 10 security stations using FIFO, start with the costs for the items purchased first: all 10 security stations at $999.95, or $9,999.50.

UP TO SPEED

FIFO and LIFO Inventory Costing

First in/first out (FIFO) costing means that a company values its inventory as if the first products it receives are the first ones it sells. (Your grocery store always puts the milk closest to its expiration date at the front of the refrigerator, right?)

Last in/first out (LIFO) costing, on the other hand, assumes that the last products in are the first ones sold. This method is like unpacking a moving van: The last valuables you packed are the first ones that come out.

The costing method you use doesn't have to match the order in which you sell products. When you start a business, you can choose whichever costing method you want—but you have to stick with it. For example, when prices are on the rise (as they almost always are), LIFO costing reduces your profit and taxes owed because you're selling the products that cost the most first. However, with the steady decrease in electronics prices, FIFO costing probably produces the least profit. Unless you're sure which method you want to use, you're better off asking your accountant for advice.

Unfortunately, even with the "Adjust Quantity/Value on Hand" window, you can't achieve true LIFO or FIFO costing in QuickBooks Pro or Premier. The program always uses average cost to move money from your inventory asset account to your cost of goods sold account when you add products to an invoice or sales receipt

CHAPTER

21

Working with Sales Tax

Sales tax can be complicated, particularly in states where the number of tax authorities has exploded. You might have to pay sales taxes to several agencies, each with its own rules about when and how much. QuickBooks' sales tax features can't eliminate this drudgery, but they *can* help you pay the right tax authorities the right amounts at the right time—and that's something to be thankful for.

QuickBooks can help you track sales tax based on customers' locations and sales-tax-paying status. The program can also keep track of non-taxable sales. This chapter shows you how to set up the program to handle all these tasks.

Once the sales tax setup is done, QuickBooks takes over and calculates the sales taxes due on invoices and sales receipts you create. However, after you collect sales taxes from your customers, you need to send those funds to the appropriate tax agencies. In this chapter, you'll learn how to remit sales taxes to the right organizations on the schedules they require.

Setting Up Sales Tax

If you have to work with sales tax, the first step is turning on the QuickBooks sales tax preference. Then you set up sales tax codes and items to tell the program about the taxes you need to collect and remit. This section shows you how to get started.

Turning on QuickBooks Sales Tax

When you created your company file, QuickBooks may have turned on sales tax *for* you if the industry you selected typically tracks sales tax. But if you just started selling taxable goods, you have to turn on the program's sales tax features yourself. Here are the steps:

1. **Choose Edit→Preferences→Sales Tax, and then click the Company Preferences tab.**

   Because sales tax applies to your entire company file, you need administrator privileges to change the sales tax setting.

2. **To the right of the "Do you charge sales tax?" label, select the Yes radio button.**

   If you click OK to close the Preferences dialog box, QuickBooks tells you that you need to specify your most common Sales Tax item. Click OK to close the message box, and then proceed to the next step.

3. **In the Preferences dialog box's "Your most common sales tax item" drop-down list, choose the Sales Tax item or Sales Tax Group item (described on page 553) you apply to most of your customers, if one exists, and then skip to step 6.**

   If you're just getting started with sales tax, this drop-down list will contain only the <Add New> entry, because you haven't set up Sales Tax items yet. (If you don't know what Sales Tax items are, jump to page 552 to learn about them and their siblings: sales tax codes. After you do that, proceed to step 4.)

4. **If you need to set up a Sales Tax item, in the Preferences dialog box's "Your most common Sales Tax item" drop-down list, choose <Add New>.**

   The New Item dialog box opens.

5. **In the New Item dialog box, fill in the boxes to create a new Sales Tax item (see page 553 for details), and then click OK.**

   In the Preferences dialog box, QuickBooks fills in the "Your most common Sales Tax item" box with the item you just created.

6. **Click OK to close the Preferences dialog box.**

   At this point, the Updating Sales Tax dialog box may appear. In this dialog box, QuickBooks automatically turns on the "Make all existing customers taxable" and "Make all existing non-inventory and inventory parts taxable" checkboxes. If most of your customers and the products you sell are subject to sales tax, leave these checkboxes turned on and click OK to close the message box. Then click OK in the message box telling you that QuickBooks must close all open windows to change the sales tax preference.

Sales tax is now turned on in your company file, so you can create additional sales tax items and codes, as described on page 552 and page 551, respectively.

TIP The Manage Sales Tax window (choose Vendors→Sales Tax→Manage Sales Tax) guides you through your sales tax tasks from start to finish. For example, click the window's Sales Tax Preferences button to open the Preferences dialog box directly to the Sales Tax category's Company Preferences tab.

Other Sales Tax Preferences

Some of the sales tax preference settings aren't up to you. Tax agencies decide when your sales taxes are due, usually based on how much sales tax you collect. When you receive a notice about your required payment interval from the state or other tax authority, be sure to update your QuickBooks preferences to match. After you set these preferences and then add sales tax to an invoice for the first time, QuickBooks automatically creates a liability account in your chart of accounts called Sales Tax Payable.

In the Preferences dialog box, on the Sales Tax category's Company Preferences tab, QuickBooks provides two sets of payment options to satisfy the tax agencies you're beholden to:

- **When do you owe sales tax?** If your tax agency deems sales taxes due when you add them to customer invoices (known as *accrual basis payment*), choose the "As of invoice date (Accrual Basis)" option. If your tax agency says sales taxes are due when your customers pay them (known as *cash basis payment*), choose the "Upon receipt of payment (Cash Basis)" option instead. When you generate sales tax reports (explained on page 554), QuickBooks uses the setting you chose to calculate the sales taxes you have to remit.
- **When do you pay sales tax?** Tax agencies determine how frequently you have to remit sales taxes based on how much sales tax you collect. If your sales taxes are only a few dollars, you might pay only once a year. But if you collect thousands of dollars of sales tax, you can be sure that the tax agency wants its money more quickly, such as quarterly or monthly. When your tax agency informs you of your remittance frequency, choose Monthly, Quarterly, or Annually here, as appropriate.

Setting Up Sales Tax Features

QuickBooks has two features for dealing with sales tax, *codes* and *items*:

- **Sales tax codes** specify whether an item you sell is taxable—that is, whether QuickBooks calculates sales tax for the item when you add it to a sales form. You also apply these codes to customers to specify whether they must pay sales tax or are exempt.
- **Sales Tax items**, on the other hand, provide the nitty-gritty detail: They let you calculate and organize sales taxes charged by state and local authorities for the items on your invoices and other sales forms.

This section describes both features and how to use them.

TIP If you sell products in a place burdened with multiple sales taxes (state, city, and local, say), you can use a Sales Tax Group item to calculate the total sales tax you have to charge. That way, your sales form shows only the total tax, but QuickBooks keeps track of what you owe to each agency. See the box on page 553 for details.

For most product sales in most areas, you have to keep track of the sales taxes you collect and then send them to the appropriate tax agencies. Labor usually isn't taxable, whereas products usually are. (Groceries are a notable nontaxable exception.) To simplify applying sales tax to the right items or subtotals on your invoices, create separate items for the things you sell that are taxable and the things that are nontaxable. After you assign sales tax codes to your items and customers, QuickBooks takes care of calculating the sales tax that's due, as shown in the Create Invoices window in Figure 21-1.

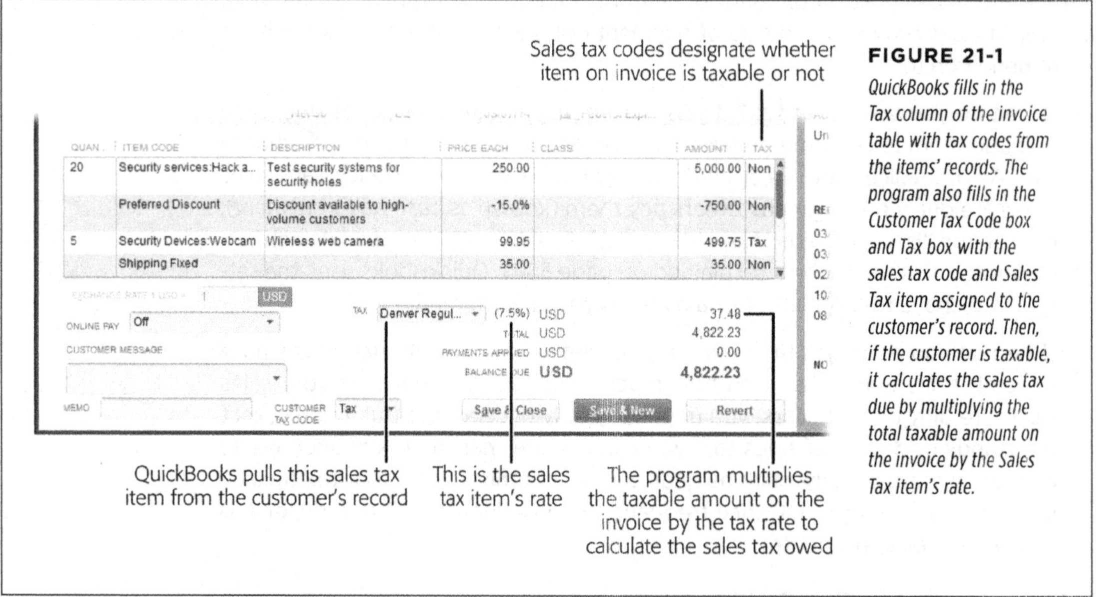
Sales tax codes designate whether item on invoice is taxable or not
QuickBooks pulls this sales tax item from the customer's record
This is the sales tax item's rate
The program multiplies the taxable amount on the invoice by the tax rate to calculate the sales tax owed

FIGURE 21-1

QuickBooks fills in the Tax column of the invoice table with tax codes from the items' records. The program also fills in the Customer Tax Code box and Tax box with the sales tax code and Sales Tax item assigned to the customer's record. Then, if the customer is taxable, it calculates the sales tax due by multiplying the total taxable amount on the invoice by the Sales Tax item's rate.

Sales Tax Codes

Sales tax codes are QuickBooks' way of letting you specify whether to apply sales tax. Out of the box, the program's Sales Tax Code List comes with two self-explanatory options: Tax and Non. If a tax agency requires you to report different types of nontaxable sales, you can add more options, as explained on page 551. You can apply tax codes to customers and to individual items you sell to designate whether sales taxes apply.

■ ASSIGNING TAX CODES TO CUSTOMERS

Nonprofit organizations and government agencies are usually tax-exempt, meaning they don't have to pay sales taxes. To tell QuickBooks whether a customer pays sales tax, open the Edit Customer window (page 41), click the Sales Tax Settings tab, and then choose the appropriate option in the Tax Code field. Here's how QuickBooks interprets a customer's sales tax status:

- **Nontaxable customer**. When you assign Non or another nontaxable sales tax code to customers, QuickBooks doesn't calculate sales tax on *any* items you sell to them. For example, in a sales form, when you choose a non-taxable customer, the program changes all the Tax cells in the form's line-item table to Non, which means that the calculated sales tax is zero regardless of the items' taxable statuses.

- **Taxable customer**. When you assign Tax or any taxable sales tax code to customers, QuickBooks uses items' sales tax codes to determine whether to charge sales tax; it calculates sales tax only on the taxable items on their invoices and other sales forms.

NOTE Customers who buy products for resale usually don't pay sales tax because that would tax the products twice. (Who says tax authorities don't have hearts?) To bypass sales tax for a customer, choose Non (for "nontaxable sales") in the Tax Code drop-down list, and then type the customer's resale number in the Resale No. field. That way, if tax auditors pay you a visit, the resale number tells them where the sales tax burden should fall.

ASSIGNING TAX CODES TO ITEMS

Some items aren't taxable regardless of whether a customer pays sales tax. For example, most services and essential goods like food don't get taxed in most states. If you look carefully at the invoice in Figure 21-1, you'll notice the code "Non" or "Tax" to the right of each amount. QuickBooks applies the sales tax only to items you designate as taxable to calculate the sales taxes on the invoice.

Items include a Tax Code field so you can designate them as taxable or nontaxable. To assign a tax code to an item, in the Create Item or Edit Item window (page 106), choose a code in the Tax Code drop-down list.

NOTE Taxable and nontaxable items can live together peacefully assigned to the same income account. QuickBooks figures out what to do with sales taxes based on the sales tax codes and Sales Tax items you've assigned to customers and the sales tax codes you've assigned to the items you've added to customers' invoices or sales receipts.

CREATING ADDITIONAL SALES TAX CODES

The two built-in sales tax codes, Non and Tax, pretty much cover all possibilities, but you may need to create additional codes to classify nontaxable customers by their *reason* for exemption (nonprofit, government, wholesaler, out-of-state, and so on) to satisfy tax agencies' reporting requirements. If that's the case, here's how to create additional sales tax codes in QuickBooks:

1. **Choose Lists→Sales Tax Code List.**

   QuickBooks opens the Sales Tax Code List window.

2. **To create a new code, press Ctrl+N or, at the bottom of the window, click Sales Tax Code→New.**

   The New Sales Tax Code window opens.

3. **In the Sales Tax Code box, type a one- to three-character code.**

   For example, type *Gov* for government agencies, *Whl* for wholesalers who resell your products, *Npf* for nonprofit customers, and so on.

4. **In the Description box, add some details about the code.**

   Type a description that explains the purpose of the code, like *Government* for Gov.

5. **Select the Taxable or Non-Taxable radio button.**

   Sales tax codes are limited to taxable or nontaxable status.

6. **If you want to add another code, click Next and repeat steps 3–5.**

7. **When you've added all the codes you want, click OK to close the New Sales Tax Code window.**

   The codes you created appear in the Sales Tax Code List window.

As you can see, QuickBooks' sales tax codes don't let you specify a sales tax percentage or note which tax office to send the collected sales taxes to. That's where Sales Tax *items* (described next) come into play.

Sales Tax Items

QuickBooks' built-in sales tax codes are fine for designating taxable status, but you also have to tell QuickBooks the rate and which tax authority levies the tax. If you sell products in more than one tax location, Sales Tax items are the way to deal with varying tax regulations. (Like the IRS, each tax agency wants to receive the taxes it's due.) To track what you owe, create a Sales Tax item for *each* sales tax you must collect.

For example, suppose *both* local and state taxes apply to products you sell in your store. For customers to whom you ship goods in *other* states, sales taxes for those states apply. You can create separate Sales Tax items for the tax that applies to your store and the state sales taxes for each state in which you do business. Or, if you have to collect several sales taxes, QuickBooks has a Sales Tax Group feature (page 553) so you can collect them all regardless of which tax authorities levy them.

Unlike sales tax codes, which can apply to both customers and products, Sales Tax items apply only to customers, which makes sense, since sales tax rates usually depend on the customer's location. If the customer is in the boonies, you might assign the state Sales Tax item because the customer pays only that one tax. But a customer smack in the middle of downtown might have to pay state tax, city tax, *and* a special district tax. Once you assign Sales Tax items to customers (page 72), QuickBooks automatically fills in the Sales Tax item on your invoices and other sales forms to calculate the sales taxes incurred.

To create a Sales Tax item, open the Item List (Lists→Item List), and then press Ctrl+N to open the New Item window (page 106). From the Type drop-down list, choose Sales Tax Item, and then fill in the fields (shown in Figure 21-2) as follows:

- **Sales Tax Name**. Type in a name for the tax. You can use the same identifiers that the tax authority does, or a more meaningful name like Colorado Sales Tax. You can fit up to 31 characters in this field—more than enough to include the four- or five-digit codes that many states use for sales taxes *and* your own description.

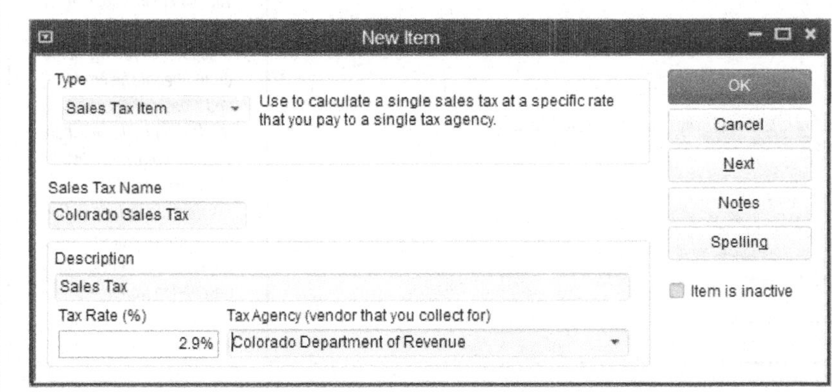

FIGURE 21-2

The "Tax Rate (%)" field sets the tax's percentage. The Tax Agency drop-down list shows the vendors you've set up, so you can choose the agency to which you remit the taxes. If you have to collect multiple sales taxes from a customer, a Sales Tax Group item is the way to go (see the box below).

- **Description**. Type a description of the tax here.
- **Tax Rate (%)**. Type the percentage rate for the tax here. QuickBooks automatically adds the percent sign, so simply type the decimal number—for example, *4.3* for a 4.3 percent tax rate.
- **Tax Agency**. In this drop-down list, choose the tax authority that collects the tax. If you haven't created a vendor record for the tax authority yet, choose <Add New> and create the record now (page 84).

GEM IN THE ROUGH

Sales Tax Groups

A Sales Tax Group item calculates the total tax for multiple Sales Tax items—perfect when you sell goods in an area rife with state, county, city, and local sales taxes. The customer sees only the total tax, but QuickBooks tracks how much you owe to each agency. This type of item works the same way as a Group item (page 114), except that you add Sales Tax items to it instead of Service, Inventory, and Other Charge items.

As shown in Figure 21-3, a Sales Tax Group item applies several Sales Tax items at once. QuickBooks combines the individual tax rates into a total rate for the group, which is what the customer sees on the invoice. For example, businesses in Denver charge a combined sales tax of 7.62 percent, which is made up of a Denver sales tax, the Colorado sales tax, an RTD tax, and special district taxes.

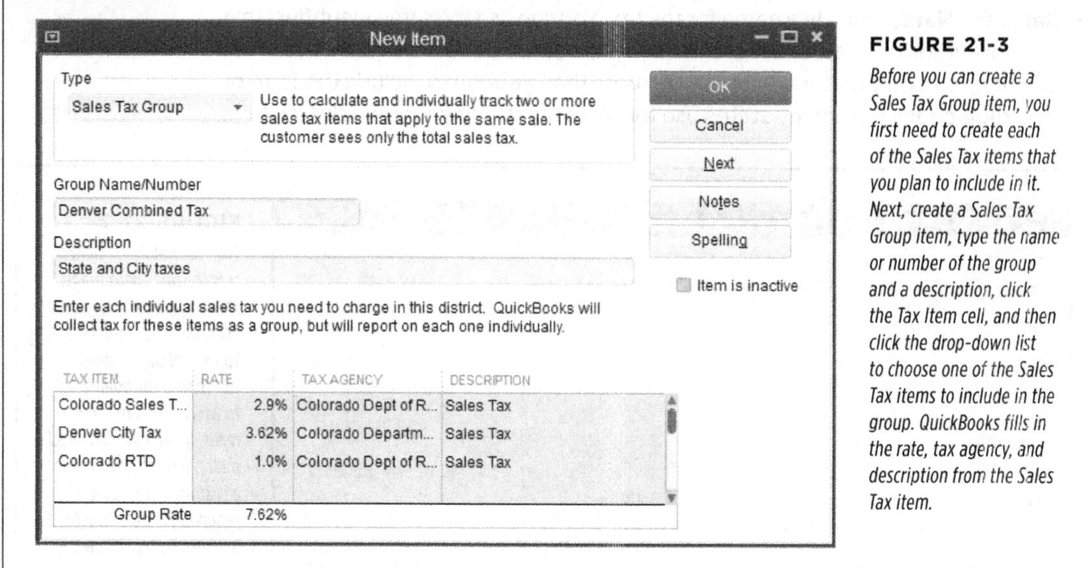

FIGURE 21-3

Before you can create a Sales Tax Group item, you first need to create each of the Sales Tax items that you plan to include in it. Next, create a Sales Tax Group item, type the name or number of the group and a description, click the Tax Item cell, and then click the drop-down list to choose one of the Sales Tax items to include in the group. QuickBooks fills in the rate, tax agency, and description from the Sales Tax item.

Producing Reports of the Sales Tax You Owe

Tax agencies are renowned for their forms. You have to fill out forms to tell the agencies how much sales tax you've collected and how much you're required to remit to them. Fortunately, QuickBooks can take *some* of the sting out of tax paperwork with reports that collate the sales tax info you need to fill out your sales tax return.

Here are the reports you can generate (they're listed under Reports→Vendors & Payables, or you can run them from the Manage Sales Tax window [Vendors→Sales Tax→Manage Sales Tax]):

- **Sales Tax Liability**. This report summarizes the sales taxes you've collected for each tax agency and breaks sales down into non-taxable and taxable. As shown in Figure 21-4, QuickBooks automatically sets the report's dates to match the payment interval you chose when you set your sales tax preferences (page 547).
- **Sales Tax Revenue Summary**. This report shows the dollar values of taxable and non-taxable sales, which is also shown in the Sales Tax Liability report.

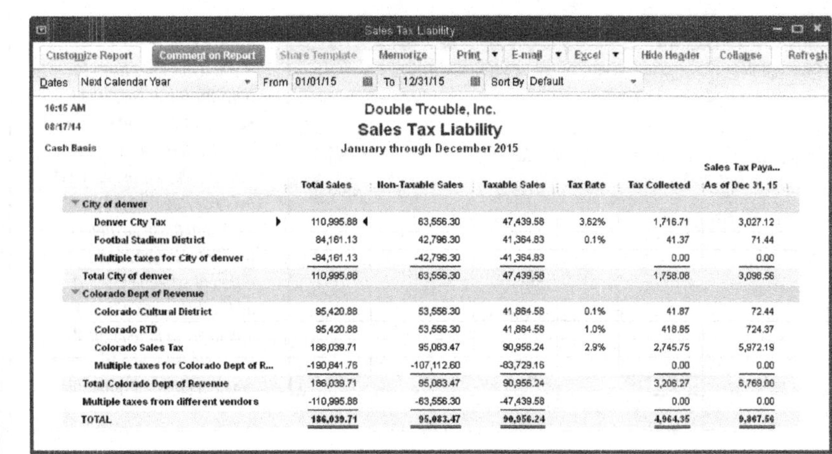

Double Trouble, Inc.

Sales Tax Liability

January through December 2015

	Total Sales	Non-Taxable Sales	Taxable Sales	Tax Rate	Tax Collected	Sales Tax Paya... As of Dec 31, 15
City of denver						
Denver City Tax	110,995.88	63,556.30	47,439.58	3.62%	1,716.71	3,027.12
Footbal Stadium District	84,161.13	42,796.30	41,364.83	0.1%	41.37	71.44
Multiple taxes for City of denver	-84,161.13	-42,796.30	-41,364.83		0.00	0.00
Total City of denver	110,995.88	63,556.30	47,439.58		1,758.08	3,098.56
Colorado Dept of Revenue						
Colorado Cultural District	95,420.88	53,556.30	41,864.58	0.1%	41.87	72.44
Colorado RTD	95,420.88	53,556.30	41,864.58	1.0%	418.85	724.37
Colorado Sales Tax	186,039.71	95,083.47	90,956.24	2.9%	2,745.75	5,972.19
Multiple taxes for Colorado Dept of R...	-190,841.76	-107,112.60	-83,729.16		0.00	0.00
Total Colorado Dept of Revenue	186,039.71	95,083.47	90,956.24		3,206.27	6,769.00
Multiple taxes from different vendors	-110,995.88	-63,556.30	-47,439.58		0.00	0.00
TOTAL	186,039.71	95,083.47	90,956.24		4,964.35	9,867.56

FIGURE 21-4

If you remit sales taxes to several tax agencies, each with its own payment interval, you can rerun this report with a different interval to calculate the sales tax you owe to other agencies. Simply head to the Dates drop-down list and choose another interval, such as Last Calendar Quarter, and then click Refresh.

Paying Sales Tax

You don't pay sales taxes using QuickBooks' Enter Bills or Write Checks windows. Instead, you use the program's aptly named Pay Sales Tax feature. Here's how you keep the tax agencies off your back:

1. **Choose Vendors→Sales Tax→Pay Sales Tax, or, in the Manage Sales Tax window (Vendors→Sales Tax→Manage Sales Tax), click Pay Sales Tax.**

   Either way, QuickBooks opens the Pay Sales Tax dialog box and fills in the amounts you owe for the last collection period (as defined in your Sales Tax preferences [page 548]), as shown in Figure 21-5.

NOTE In some states, you may need to adjust the payments you make to a tax agency; for example, to apply a discount for timely payment, to round sales tax to the nearest dollar, or to include interest and penalties with your payment. In cases like that, click the Adjust button to open the Sales Tax Adjustment dialog box. You can increase or decrease the tax by a dollar value, and you have to specify the account to which you want to post the adjustment (the Sales Tax Payable account, say). If the Entry No. box seems vaguely familiar, that's because this dialog box actually creates a journal entry (page 426) for the adjustment.

2. **If you use more than one checking account, in the Pay From Account drop-down list, choose the account you want to use.**

   QuickBooks automatically selects an account here if you set the "Open the Pay Sales Tax form with _ account" preference (page 640).

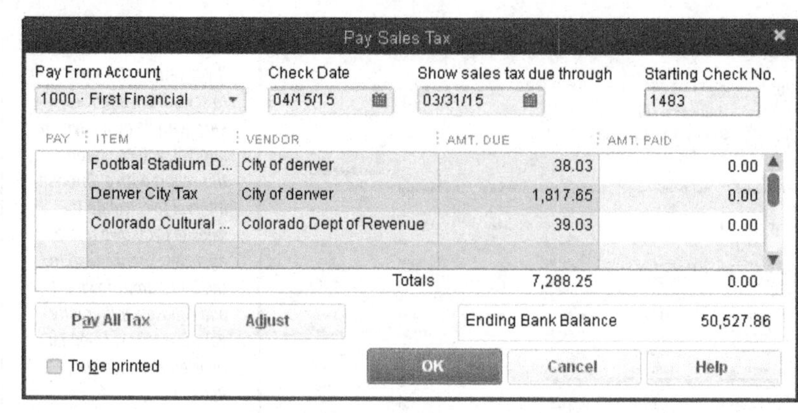

FIGURE 21-5

If you remit sales taxes to only one tax agency or all your sales tax payments are on the same schedule, you can click Pay All Tax to select every payment in the table. But if you make payments to different agencies on different schedules, select all the agencies on the same schedule, and then repeat these steps for agencies that are on a different timetable.

NOTE Make sure the date in the "Show sales tax due through" box is the last day of the current sales tax reporting period. For example, if you pay sales taxes quarterly, choose a date like 3/31/2015.

3. **In the Pay column, click cells to select the payments you want to make.**

   QuickBooks adds a checkmark to indicate that a payment is selected and puts the amount of the remittance in the Amt. Paid cell.

4. **If you want to print the sales tax remittance checks from QuickBooks, make sure the "To be printed" checkbox is turned on, and then click OK.**

   With this checkbox turned on, you'll see the remittance checks the next time you choose File→Print Forms→Checks.

   If you write checks by hand, turn off the "To be printed" checkbox, click OK, and then whip out your checkbook and write those remittance checks.

CHAPTER

22

Budgeting and Planning

As you've no doubt noticed in business and in life, the activities that cost money almost always seem to outnumber those that bring money in. Most companies want to make money and most nonprofits want to do the most with the funds they have, so budgeting and planning are essential business activities.

Like any kind of plan, a budget is an estimate of what's going to happen. Your actual results will never exactly match the numbers you estimate in your budget. (If they do, someone's playing games with your books.) But comparing your actual performance to your budget can tell you that it's time to crack the whip on the sales team, rein in your spending, or both.

Budgeting in QuickBooks is both simple and simplistic. The program handles basic budgets and provides some shortcuts for entering numbers. However, you can't see whether your budget is working as you build it, and playing what-if games with budgets requires some fancy footwork. (The box on page 559 describes one way to create multiple budgets for the same time period.)

The easiest way to handle budgets is to craft them with a spreadsheet program like Excel. You can use all of Excel's commands to massage the numbers and then import your budgetary masterpiece into QuickBooks so you can compare your actual performance with the budget. This chapter explains your budgeting options, teaches you how to import budgets from other programs, and provides an overview of QuickBooks' budget reports.

TIP QuickBooks also includes a Cash Flow Projector (it lives on the Company→Planning & Budgeting submenu). This wizard provides a forecast of cash flow similar to what you can obtain by running a Cash Flow Forecast report (page 459), so it's not covered in this book.

Types of Budgets

To most people, the word "budget" means a profit and loss budget—one that estimates what your income and expenses will be over a period of time. QuickBooks' profit and loss budgets are based on the income and expense accounts in your chart of accounts (see Chapter 3) and typically span your company's fiscal year.

Balance sheet budgets aren't as common, but you can create them in QuickBooks as well. Balance sheets are snapshots of your assets and liabilities, and balance sheet budgets follow the same format by showing the ending balances for your asset, liability, and other balance sheet accounts.

NOTE Most companies plan for major purchases and their accompanying loans outside of the budgeting process. For example, if a company needs an asset to operate, executives usually analyze costs, benefits, payback periods, internal rates of return, and so on before making purchasing decisions. They evaluate cash flow to decide whether to borrow money or use cash generated by operations. But after that, the additional income generated by the asset and the additional interest expense associated with any loans show up in the profit and loss budget.

QuickBooks' profit and loss budgets come in three flavors, each helpful in its own way:

- **Company profit and loss**. The most common type of budget includes all the income and expenses for your entire company. This is the budget that management strives to follow—whether that's to produce the net profit that keeps shareholders happy or to generate the cash needed to run the company. With QuickBooks' Budget vs. Actual report (page 572), you can compare your actual results with your budget.
- **Customer or job budget**. A customer- or job-based profit and loss budget forecasts the income and expenses for a single customer or job. Projects that come with a lot of risk have to offer the potential for lots of profit to be worthwhile. By generating a profit and loss budget for a customer or job, you can make sure that the profitability meets your objectives.
- **Class budget**. If you use classes to track income and expenses, you can create profit and loss budgets for each class. Class budgets work particularly well when you track income and expenses for independent sections of your company: regions, business units, branches, partners, and so on.

Ways to Build Budgets

If you've just started a business, you may have a business plan that includes estimates of your income and expenses. Or you may have run your business for a while without a budget and now want to create a budget using past performance as a starting point. Either way, there's a method for building a budget in QuickBooks. But the easiest approach is to build your budget *outside* QuickBooks and import the results. Here are your options and what each has to offer:

GEM IN THE ROUGH

Budgets vs. Forecasts

If you have QuickBooks Premier or Enterprise, you'll see the Set Up Forecast entry on the Company→Planning & Budgeting submenu. (QuickBooks Pro doesn't include forecasts, so if you use that edition, you have to stick with budgets.) The window that opens when you choose Set Up Forecast is strikingly similar to the Set Up Budgets window (page 560). In fact, other than replacing the word "Budgets" with "Forecast," they're identical. So how do you decide whether to use a budget or a forecast?

In QuickBooks, you can have only one budget for a given period loaded at a time—for example, a 2015 profit and loss budget. A forecast lets you create *another* set of planning numbers for the same timeframe. So you can create a profit and loss budget for 2015 and a separate forecast for the same fiscal year, using the budget to reflect your most likely results and the forecast to show the numbers under more optimistic (or pessimistic) conditions.

QuickBooks has reports that compare your actual performance with budgets and forecasts (Reports→Budgets & Forecasts), so you can use either feature to compare your estimated numbers with your actual performance.

The bottom line: Use budgets unless you want a second set of planning numbers readily available. If you decide to create forecasts instead of—or in addition to—budgets, the instructions in this chapter apply to them, too.

- **From previous year's actual results**. If this is your first budget and you have at least several months' worth of data in QuickBooks, you can use that existing data as a starting point (page 561) and edit only the values that change.
- **From scratch**. This method can be tedious because you have to estimate and fill in *all* the budget numbers (although, as you'll learn on page 564, QuickBooks does offer some data-entry shortcuts). Fortunately, you only have to use this approach for your first budget. The next section explains how.
- **From data in another program**. The best way to build a budget is to create it in a program like Excel and then import it into QuickBooks. Setting up a spreadsheet for your company budget in Excel or some other program offers several advantages. After you set up the Excel file with rows for each account and columns for months and other fields, you can save it as a template for creating future budgets. If you're an Excel wizard, you can use that program's tools to quickly create and fine-tune your budget. You also can copy that file to create what-if scenarios or next year's budget based on the previous year's budget. You can read about building a budget with Excel starting on page 568.

Creating Budgets in QuickBooks

The Set Up Budgets wizard is the place to go for profit and loss budgets; balance sheet budgets; budgets for customers, jobs, and classes; and budgets built from scratch or from previous years' data.

Before you dive into building a budget, you have to perform two setup steps if you want your budgets to work properly:

- **Fiscal year**. QuickBooks uses the first month of your fiscal year as the first month of the budget. To check that you defined your fiscal year correctly, choose Company→My Company or, in the left icon bar, click My Company. In the window that appears, at the top right of the Company Information section, click the Edit button (its icon looks like a pencil). Then, on the left side of the Company Information dialog box, click Report Information and make sure that the month in the Fiscal Year box is correct.
- **Active accounts**. QuickBooks budgets cover only the accounts that are active in your chart of accounts. To activate any accounts you want to budget, press Ctrl+A to open the Chart of Accounts window, and then turn on the "Include inactive" checkbox. (If no accounts are inactive, this checkbox is grayed out.) For any inactive account that you want in your budget, click the X to the left of the account's name to reactivate it.

To start the budget wizard, choose Company→Planning & Budgeting→Set Up Budgets. Depending on whether you already have a budget in QuickBooks, the program displays one of two different wizards. The Create New Budget wizard (Figure 22-1) appears if this is your first budget in this company file. If you already have at least one budget in your company file, QuickBooks opens the Set Up Budgets wizard instead and displays your most recent budget. To create a *new* budget in that wizard, click the Create New Budget button to launch the wizard shown in Figure 22-1.

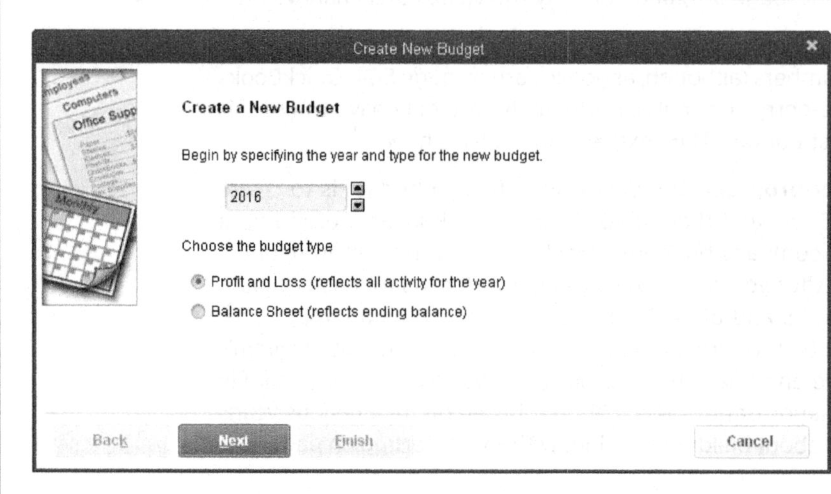

FIGURE 22-1

In the Create New Budget wizard, you first tell QuickBooks about the year and type of budget you want to create.

On the second screen (not shown), you can specify whether the budget works with customers, jobs, or classes. (You'll see the option for creating class budgets only if you've turned on QuickBooks' class feature [page 636].)

The steps for setting up a new budget are the same whether QuickBooks automatically displays the Create New Budget wizard or you click the Create New Budget button in the Set Up Budgets wizard:

1. **On the Create a New Budget screen (Figure 22-1), choose a fiscal year and budget type, and then click Next.**

QuickBooks automatically fills in the next calendar year (perhaps assuming that you're done budgeting for the current year). Click the up and down arrows to the box's right to choose the fiscal year you're budgeting for.

Below the year setting, the program automatically selects the "Profit and Loss (reflects all activity for the year)" option because most budgets cover income and expenses for a year. If you choose this option, continue with the rest of the steps in this list.

If you want to create a balance sheet budget instead, select the "Balance Sheet (reflects ending balance)" option. If you go this route, you don't have to set any additional criteria before you build the budget for your balance sheet accounts, so you don't need to perform the rest of the steps in this list. Simply click Next in the Create New Budget wizard, and QuickBooks displays a screen that tells you to click Finish. When you do, a table containing your balance sheet accounts appears in the Set Up Budgets window, and you can begin typing ending balances, as explained in the "Filling in Budget Values" section on page 564.

2. **On the Additional Profit and Loss Budget Criteria screen, select the flavor of profit and loss budget you want, and then click Next.**

   QuickBooks automatically selects the "No additional criteria" option, which creates the most common type of budget: a profit and loss budget for the entire company. (The next section explains how to create Customer:Job and Class budgets.)

3. **On the "Choose how you want to create a budget" screen, tell QuickBooks how you want to fill in the initial budget data.**

   Keep the "Create budget from scratch" option selected if you want to create a blank budget. If you go this route, jump to page 564 to learn how to enter data in the Set Up Budgets wizard.

   If you have actual data that you want to use as a foundation for your budget, select "Create budget from previous year's actual data" instead. This option transfers the monthly income and expense account totals from the previous year into the budget.

4. **Click Finish.**

   QuickBooks opens the Set Up Budgets window, which includes a monstrous table. The rows represent each active account in your chart of accounts; each column is one month of the fiscal year.

   If you opted to create a budget for a customer, job, or class, the window includes either the Current Customer:Job drop-down list containing all your active customers and jobs (Figure 22-2) or the Class drop-down list containing all your active classes. Before you start entering values for a customer, job, or class budget, choose the customer, job, or class from this list.

   The section on page 564 explains how to fill in the cells in this table.

NOTE If your monitor's resolution is less than 1024 × 768, the Set Up Budgets window also includes the Show Next 6 Months button, because your screen can't display the entire year. In that case, QuickBooks initially displays January through June. Click Show Next 6 Months to display July through December (the button's label changes to Show Prev 6 Months).

Creating Customer:Job or Class Budgets

In QuickBooks, there's no way to store several versions of a fiscal-year budget that covers your *entire* operation. But you *can* create additional budgets for the same fiscal year for different customers and jobs, or for classes.

NOTE Class budgets work the way Customer:Job budgets do. In fact, if you replace every instance of "Customer:Job" in the following tutorial with "Class," you'll have the instructions for creating Class budgets.

Here's how to work with Customer:Job or Class budgets:

1. **Choose Company→Planning & Budgeting→Set Up Budgets as you would for a regular budget. At the Set Up Budgets window's top right, click the Create New Budget button.**

   The Create New Budget window opens. QuickBooks automatically fills in the next calendar year and selects the "Profit and Loss" option. If you want to create a budget for a different year or of a different type, choose the year and/or type.

2. **When the year and budget type are what you want, click Next.**

   The "Additional Project and Loss Budget Criteria" screen appears.

3. **On this screen, select the Customer:Job option or Class option to create a Customer:Job or class budget, respectively, and then click Next.**

   You see the Class option only if you've turned on class tracking (page 636). The rest of this tutorial assumes you're creating a Customer:Job budget, but these instructions work for Class budgets, too.

4. **On the "Choose how you want to create a budget" screen, choose the appropriate option, and then click Finish.**

   QuickBooks adds the Current Customer:Job box to the Set Up Budgets window between the Budget list and the table.

5. **In the Current Customer:Job drop-down list, choose the customer or job that you want to budget, as shown in Figure 22-2.**

   Any budgetary numbers you've previously entered for the customer or job for the selected fiscal year appear in the budget table.

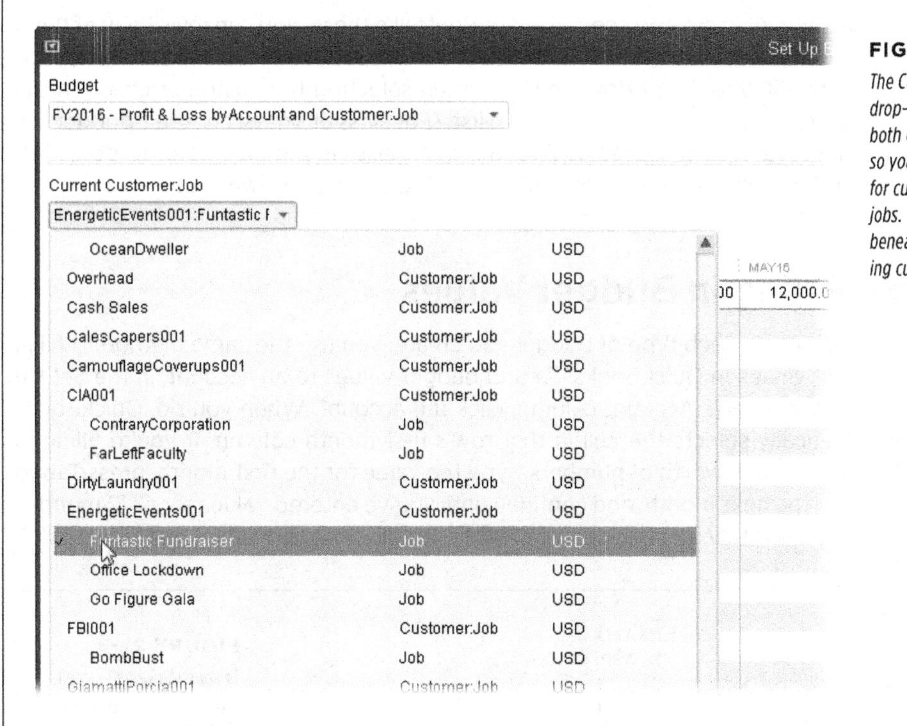

FIGURE 22-2

The Current Customer:Job drop-down list displays both customers and jobs so you can create budgets for customers or specific jobs. (Jobs are indented beneath their corresponding customers.)

6. **In the budget table, fill in values for the Customer:Job budget (see page 564 to learn how).**

   Unlike a budget for your entire operation, Customer:Job budgets may have values for only a few accounts. For example, for a job that includes products, services, and reimbursable expenses, your budget may have values only for income accounts and the expense accounts for reimbursable expenses.

7. **When you're finished entering values, click Save.**

   If you choose another customer or job without clicking Save, QuickBooks asks if you want to record the budget. In the Recording Budget message box, click Yes.

8. **If you want to create a budget for *another* customer, job, or class, in the Set Up Budgets window's Budget drop-down list, choose the fiscal year that you want to budget.**

   For Customer:Job budgets, the Budget drop-down list includes an entry like "FY2016 - Profit & Loss by Account and Customer:Job." (Class budgets show up in the Budget drop-down list looking something like "FY2016 - Profit & Loss by Account and Class.")

9. **In the Current Customer:Job drop-down list, choose the customer, job, or class that you want to create a budget for. Fill in the budget values, and then click Save.**

   After you've created specialized budgets like these, you can revisit any of them by selecting a budget like "FY2016 - Profit & Loss by Account and Customer:Job" in the Budget drop-down list, and then selecting the customer or job in the Current Customer:Job drop-down list. (For class budgets, choose a budget like "FY2016 - Profit & Loss by Account and Class" in the Budget drop-down list, and then choose the class in the Current Class drop-down list.)

Filling in Budget Values

Regardless of which type of budget you create, you use the same method to fill in and edit values in QuickBooks. To add budget values to an account, in the Set Up Budgets window's Account column, click the account. When you do, QuickBooks automatically selects the cell in that row's first month column. If you're filling in the entire year's worth of numbers, type the value for the first month, press Tab to move to the next month, and continue until you've entered values for all 12 months. The Annual Total column displays the total for all months, as shown in Figure 22-3.

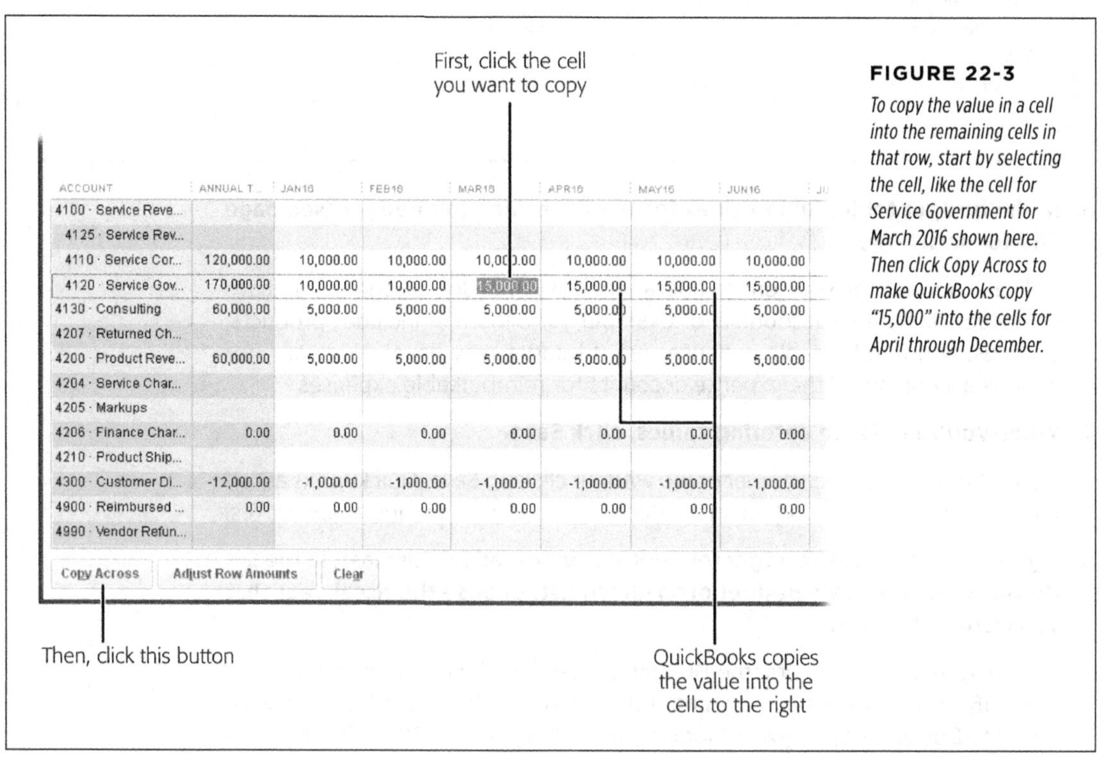
First, click the cell you want to copy
Copy Across
Adjust Row Amounts
Clear
Then, click this button
QuickBooks copies the value into the cells to the right

FIGURE 22-3

To copy the value in a cell into the remaining cells in that row, start by selecting the cell, like the cell for Service Government for March 2016 shown here. Then click Copy Across to make QuickBooks copy "15,000" into the cells for April through December.

Filling in a few budget cells is usually enough to convince you that data entry shortcuts are in order. Luckily, QuickBooks gives you two ways to enter values faster, both described next. And the box below explains what some of the buttons at the bottom of the Set Up Budgets window do.

UP TO SPEED

Managing Budgets

In the Set Up Budgets window, several buttons help you manage the budgeting work you do in QuickBooks. Although you're probably familiar with their functions based on similar buttons in other windows, here's a quick overview:

- **Clear**. Click this button at the window's bottom left to delete *all* the values in a budget—for every account and every month. This is the button to click if you want to start over. (If you click this button by accident, don't worry: QuickBooks displays a confirmation box where you can click No to preserve the numbers you've entered.)
- **Save**. When you've added or updated all the values in a budget, click this button near the window's bottom right to save your work. You can also click Save so you don't lose the work you've done so far. And even if you forget to click this button, if you click OK or choose another budget, QuickBooks asks whether you want to record the one you've been working on, giving you a chance to save.
- **OK**. Clicking this button saves the values you've entered *and* closes the Set Up Budgets window.
- **Cancel**. Clicking this button closes the window *without* saving your work.

Copying Across Columns

Because budgets are estimates, you don't need extraordinarily detailed or precise values. In the Set Up Budgets window, you can copy a number from one cell in a row to all the cells to its right in the same row, as demonstrated in Figure 22-3.

TIP If the account names and budget values are hopelessly truncated and you have screen real estate to spare, enlarge the Set Up Budgets window by dragging a corner or maximizing it. The columns show more of the cell contents as you enlarge the window. To resize a specific column to make it wider or narrower, put your cursor over the three vertical dots to the right of the column's header. When the cursor turns into a two-headed arrow, drag right or left.

This shortcut is fabulous when a monthly expense remains the same throughout the year, like office rent, for example. But it also works if a price changes midyear. For instance, suppose the corporate concierge you've hired to run errands for your employees announces that his rates are going up in May. If your budget contains the old rate in every month, click the cell for May and type the new rate. Then click Copy Across, and QuickBooks lists the new rate for May through December.

TIP If you mistakenly add values to cells that should be blank, Copy Across is the fastest way to empty a row. Clear the first month's cell by selecting its value and then pressing Backspace. Then click Copy Across to have QuickBooks clear all the *other* cells in that row.

Adjust Row Amounts

The Set Up Budgets window's Adjust Row Amounts button lets you increase or decrease monthly values by a specific dollar amount or percentage. Say you created a budget from the previous year's data, but you want to increase all the values in the current year by 10 percent. Or maybe your company is growing quickly and you want to apply some heat to your sales force by increasing the target income each month. In that case, you can tell QuickBooks to compound the increase, so each month's sales target is a little higher than the previous month's value.

Changing all the cells in a row by a fixed dollar amount isn't as useful as you might think, because Copy Across basically does the same thing in most cases. But when you change budget amounts by percentages or compound increases each month, the Adjust Row Amounts feature takes care of the calculations for you. Here's how to adjust row amounts in both of these ways:

1. **Click the row you want to adjust.**

   If you want to start the adjustment in a specific month, click the cell for the starting month.

2. **Click the Adjust Row Amounts button.**

   QuickBooks opens the Adjust Row Amounts dialog box and, in the "Start at" box, automatically selects the option that you chose the last time you opened this dialog box. "1st month" starts adjustments in the first month of the fiscal year. To start with the month you selected instead, choose "Currently selected month" (if you select this option, QuickBooks displays the "Enable compounding" checkbox, which is explained in step 5).

NOTE The Adjust Row Amounts feature is for adjusting *existing* budget values, not for filling in blank cells. For example, if you select the "Increase each remaining monthly amount in this row by this dollar amount or percentage" option and then type *100* in the text box, QuickBooks adds 100 to the values in the month cells. So if the January cell is set to 1,000, it increases to 1,100. However, if the remaining months' cells are zero (0), they increase only to 100.

3. **Select the appropriate option for how the prices change.**

   QuickBooks automatically selects the "Increase each remaining monthly amount in this row by this dollar amount or percentage" option because prices usually go up. But if prices are decreasing, select the option that begins with "Decrease each remaining monthly amount" instead.

4. **In the text box for the option you selected, type the dollar amount or percentage, and then click OK.**

   For example, if the landlord tells you that rent is going up 5 percent, in the box for the Increase option, type *5%*, and QuickBooks increases the value in all the remaining cells by 5 percent. So if your rent was $5,000 a month, the values in all the remaining months change to $5,250.

To add a dollar amount to the remaining cells instead, type that dollar value. For example, to add $250 a month to the Rent cells, in the box for this option, type *250*. Each subsequent cell in the Rent row increases by 250. (Of course, you can do the same thing by typing the new rent amount in the cell for the first month to which it applies and then clicking Copy Across.)

5. **If you chose "Currently selected month" in the "Start at" box in step 2, the "Enable compounding" checkbox appeared; turn it on if you want to adjust each month's value based on the previous month's value.**

   When you compound dollar amounts, QuickBooks adds the dollar amount you specify to the next month's value. For example, if January's value is 5,000 and you change the value by 100, February's value becomes 5,100, March's value increases by another 100 to 5,200, and so on, as shown in Figure 22-4.

   You can also compound by percentage. If you turn on the "Enable compounding" checkbox and then type a percentage in the text box, QuickBooks increases the next month's value by the percentage you specify. If January's value is 5,000 and you increase it by 1 percent, for example, then February's value becomes 5,050, March's value increases another 1 percent to 5,100.50, and so on.

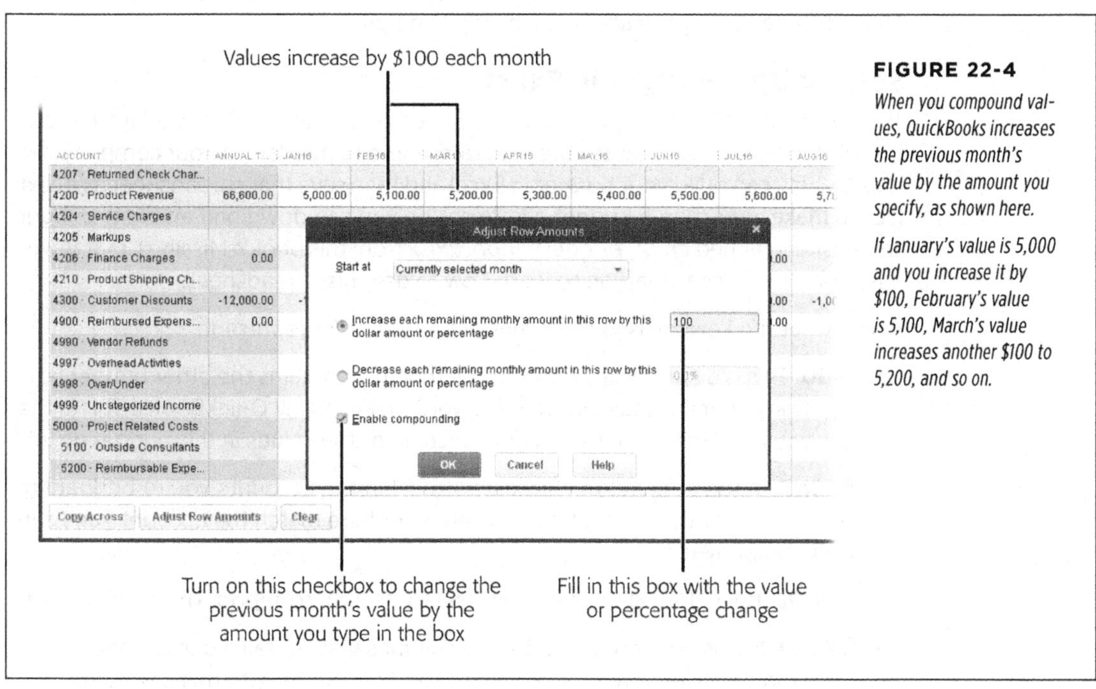

FIGURE 22-4

When you compound values, QuickBooks increases the previous month's value by the amount you specify, as shown here.

If January's value is 5,000 and you increase it by $100, February's value is 5,100, March's value increases another $100 to 5,200, and so on.

Creating and Copying Budgets with Excel

QuickBooks' budget reports can help you plan for the future and evaluate whether your business is going boom or bust. However, the program's tools for building and editing budgets don't compare to what you can do with a program like Excel.

QuickBooks keeps only one budget at a time for the same type of budget and time period—for example, the profit and loss budget for fiscal year 2016—and it doesn't offer a feature for copying a budget. That's where a spreadsheet program comes in handy. You can easily copy a budget spreadsheet, make the changes you want, and then import the final product into QuickBooks. For example, you might create next year's budget from this year's. Or you might experiment with what-if scenarios including a bare-bones budget in case a client with shaky finances disappears and a second happy-dance budget if you snag that big new project.

There are two parts to working on budgets with Excel:

1. **Setting up a budget in an Excel spreadsheet so you can import it into QuickBooks.**
2. **Importing the final budget into your company file.**

The following sections describe each step in detail.

Setting Up a Budget in Excel

To import budgets into QuickBooks, you need to create an IIF file, a QuickBooks text file with keywords that tell the program where to put data in your company file. Happily, you can build your budget in Excel and then save that spreadsheet as a text file. To make importing a budget a little easier, you can download an Excel budget spreadsheet named *ch22_budget_import.xlsx* from this book's Missing CD at *www.missingmanuals/cds*. Read on to learn how to use this spreadsheet.

Here's what the keywords in *ch22_budget_import.xlsx* represent:

- **!BUD**. This is a special keyword for the row that contains the other budget keywords in columns. Basically, this keyword means, "Hey QuickBooks! This is the row you need to look in to find out which fields the values in this budget go in!"
- **ACCNT**. In the cells below this keyword, fill in the accounts you're budgeting. Make sure that the account names you enter here match the account names in your company file.
- **PERIOD**. Keep the cells in this column set to "Month" to import a monthly budget.
- **AMOUNT**. This keyword identifies the columns that contain your budget values. For a monthly, yearlong budget, you need 12 columns with this keyword.
- **STARTDATE**. In the column that contains this keyword, fill in your budget's start date in each row that contains budget values.

- **CLASS**. If you're creating a class budget, fill in the cells below this keyword with the appropriate class.
- **CUSTOMER**. If you're creating a Customer:Job budget, fill in this column with the appropriate customer.
- **BUD**. This keyword goes in the first column's cells below the one that contains the !BUD keyword. Enter BUD in the first cell in every row that contains an account and budget values.

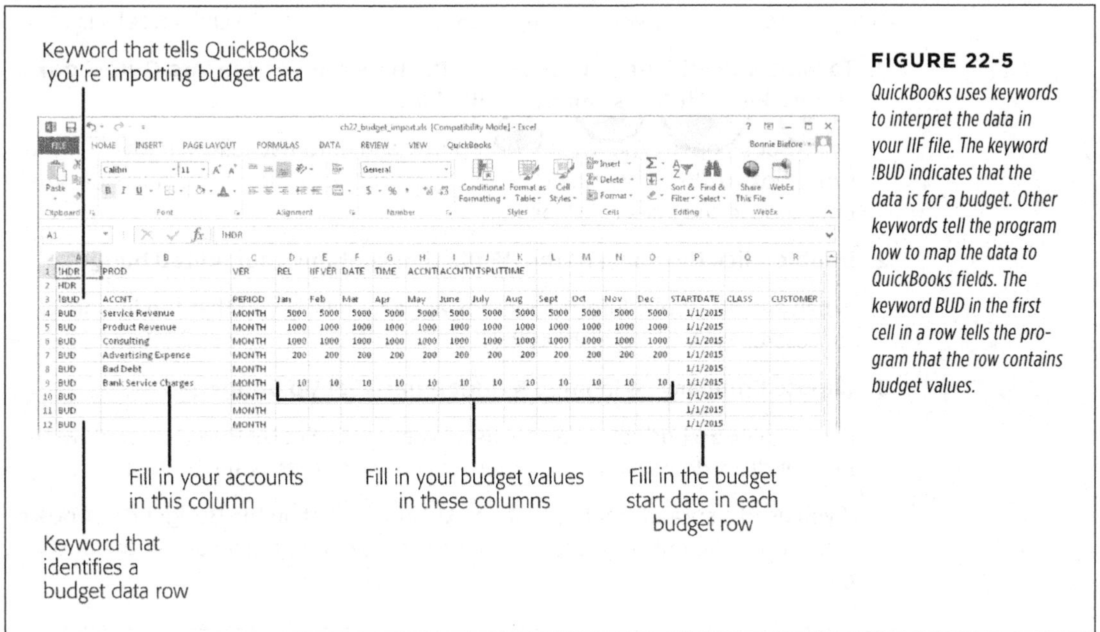
Keyword that tells QuickBooks you're importing budget data
Fill in your accounts in this column
Fill in your budget values in these columns
Fill in the budget start date in each budget row
Keyword that identifies a budget data row

FIGURE 22-5

QuickBooks uses keywords to interpret the data in your IIF file. The keyword !BUD indicates that the data is for a budget. Other keywords tell the program how to map the data to QuickBooks fields. The keyword BUD in the first cell in a row tells the program that the row contains budget values.

After you fill in your budget in Excel, here's how you save it to a format QuickBooks can read:

1. **In Excel, choose File→Save As. In the Save As dialog box's "Save as type" drop-down list, choose "Text (Tab delimited) (*.txt)."**

   Doing so tells Excel to save the spreadsheet as a text file.

2. **In the "File name" box, type a filename such as *full_budget_2016.iif,* and then click Save.**

   The *.iff* part is important, so be sure to include it. Excel warns that you might lose features by saving a text file. Click Yes to continue. Excel saves the file with the filename *full_budget_2016.iif.txt* (or whatever you named it). Don't worry that the file has two suffixes (called *file extensions*) on it—you'll fix that in a sec.

3. **Close the file in Excel.**

4. **In Windows Explorer, open the folder where you saved the text file. Right-click the file and choose Rename on the shortcut menu. Remove the text ".txt" at the end of the filename, and then press Enter to save it.**

   You'll see a warning that the file might become unusable if you change its file name extension. Click Yes.

Now you're ready to import the file into QuickBooks.

Importing a Budget into QuickBooks

After you create or edit your budget in Excel, importing it into QuickBooks is easy:

1. **To import the IIF file you created in the previous section into QuickBooks, choose File→Utilities→Import→IIF Files.**

   QuickBooks opens the Import dialog box and automatically sets the "Files of type" box to "IIF Files (*.IIF)." If you don't see your file, in the "Files of type" box, choose "All Files (*.*)" instead.

2. **Double-click the name of the IIF file that contains your edited budget.**

   When a QuickBooks Information box appears telling you that the import was successful, click OK to dismiss it.

3. **Choose Company→Planning & Budgeting→Set Up Budgets.**

   If you created a budget for a new fiscal year, in the Set Up Budgets window, the Budget drop-down list now contains an entry for that year's budget.

   If you used a spreadsheet to edit an existing budget, in the Budget drop-down list, choose the entry for that budget to see the updated values in the budget table.

NOTE If you're experimenting with several budgets for the same time period, you can import one and then run budget reports to examine it more closely. Just remember to finish by importing the budget you decide to use.

Running Budget Reports

A budget gives you a target to aim for. The Set Up Budgets window lets you type values for income and expense accounts, but it doesn't show you whether your budget results in a net profit or loss. For that, you need a budget report (or your budget set up in a spreadsheet program, as described on page 568). And to compare your business performance with your budget, you need a budget report that shows budget and actual numbers side by side.

QuickBooks provides four types of budget reports: one to review budgets you've created and three to compare your performance with your plan. This section describes the various reports, what they're useful for, and how to create and format them.

NOTE To learn about *all* the options for customizing any QuickBooks report, see Chapter 23. And page 601 explains how to memorize a customized report.

The Budget Overview Report

The Set Up Budgets window shows your accounts and the values you enter for each month, but it doesn't tell you whether your budget produces a profit or loss. The Budget Overview report shows budget numbers for each account and month, too, but it *also* subtotals values if you use top-level accounts and subaccounts in your chart of accounts, as shown in Figure 22-6. To see whether you earn enough income to cover expenses, look at the net income value (income minus expenses) at the bottom of the report for each month and for the entire year.

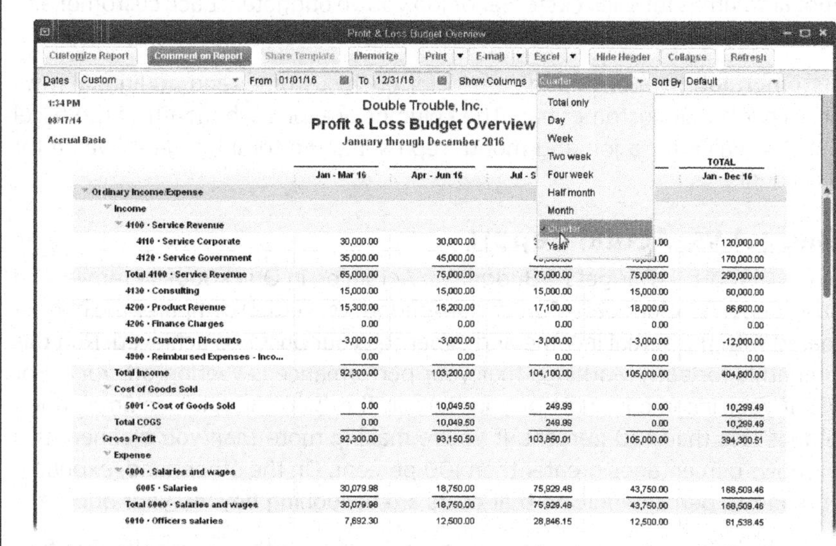

FIGURE 22-6

Although you build budgets month by month, many businesses (particularly ones with shareholders) focus on quarterly performance.

To view your budget by quarter instead of by month, in the Show Columns drop-down list, choose Quarter.

To run this report, choose Reports→Budgets→Budget Overview (or, if you have QuickBooks Premier or Enterprise, Reports→Budgets *& Forecasts*→Budget Overview). In the Budget Report dialog box, first choose the budget you want to view, and then pick a layout (explained in a moment). When you click Finish, QuickBooks opens the Budget Overview report window. (Depending on the report settings you've chosen [page 659], the Modify Report dialog box might appear; if you see that dialog box, simply click Cancel to close it.)

NOTE The Budget Overview report includes only accounts that have budget values.

REPORT LAYOUTS

If you create a report for a profit and loss budget for your entire company, the only layout option in the Budget Report dialog box is Account By Month, in which the first column lists the accounts and each subsequent column shows one month of the fiscal year. You can change the columns to different durations in the Profit & Loss Budget Overview window (Figure 22-6).

On the other hand, if you choose a Customer:Job budget in the Budget Report dialog box and then click Next, the Budget Report dialog box includes these layout options:

- **Account By Month** lists accounts in the first column and months of the fiscal year in the subsequent columns. The values in the monthly columns represent the totals for *all* the Customer:Job budgets you've created.
- **Account By Customer:Job** lists accounts in the first column and includes additional columns for each customer or job you've budgeted. Each customer and job column shows its annual totals.
- **Customer:Job by Month** adds a row for each customer and additional rows for each job that customer has. The columns are for each month of the fiscal year. The value for a job and month represents the total budgeted value for all accounts.

The Budget vs. Actual Report

This report (Reports→Budgets→Budget vs. Actual or, in QuickBooks Premier and Enterprise, Reports→Budgets *& Forecasts*→Budget vs. Actual) compares the budget you created with the actual income and expenses your business achieved. Run this report monthly for early warnings that your performance is veering off track. For example, if your income is short of your target, the "% of Budget" column shows percentages less than 100 percent; if you're making more than you planned, this column shows percentages greater than 100 percent. On the other hand, *expenses* greater than 100 percent indicate that costs are ballooning beyond your budget.

This report includes four columns for each time period in the report: the first four columns show the actual value, budgeted value, and the dollar value and percentage difference between the first two values for the first time period. The next four columns include data related to the second time period, and so on. The column with the heading for a month and year (like "Jan 15" or, for a quarter, "Jan-Mar 15") is your actual performance. The Budget column includes the budgeted values for the same time period. You can also see the difference between the two values for that time period in dollars (in the Over Budget column) and as a percentage (in the "% of Budget" column).

TIP If the numbers in your report don't seem right, the culprit could be the wrong choice of accrual or cash reporting (page xxii explains the difference). In the report window, click Customize Report and then, on the Display tab, click the Accrual or Cash option to match your reporting style. Page 661 explains how to change the reporting preference for accrual or cash reporting.

The Profit & Loss Budget Performance Report

This report (Reports→Budgets→Profit & Loss Budget Performance or, in QuickBooks Premier and Enterprise, Reports→Budgets *& Forecasts*→Profit & Loss Budget Performance) also compares budgeted and actual values but initially shows the actual values for the current month so far with the budgeted values for the entire month in the Budget column. Two additional columns show the actual and budgeted values for the year to date. The rightmost column shows the budget for the entire year.

Use this report to check your performance before the end of each month. Because the budget numbers represent the entire month, you shouldn't expect a perfect match between actual and budgeted values. But if your income or expenses are way off the mark, you can take corrective action.

The Budget vs. Actual Graph

To see a graph comparing your budget to actual performance, choose Reports→Budgets→Budget vs. Actual Graph (or, in QuickBooks Premier and Enterprise, Reports→Budgets *& Forecasts*→Budget vs. Actual Graph). This graph displays the differences between your budgeted and actual values in two ways:

- **The upper bar graph** shows the difference between your actual and budgeted net income for each month. When your actual net income exceeds the budgeted value (meaning you made more money than you planned), the bar is blue and appears above the horizontal axis. If the actual net income is less than budgeted, the bar is red and drops below the horizontal axis.
- **The lower bar graph** sorts accounts, customers, or classes (depending on the report you choose by clicking "P&L by Accounts," "P&L by Accounts and Jobs," or "P&L by Accounts and Classes" in the report window's button bar) that are the furthest from your budgeted values (either above or below). For example, if you click "P&L by Accounts and Jobs," the bars show the customers and jobs that exceeded your budget by the largest amount or fell the furthest short.

If the report window can't display all the bars at the same time, then in the window's button bar, click Next Group to display the bars for the next several accounts.

UP TO SPEED

Memorizing Budget Reports

When you generate budget reports, it takes several clicks to specify the budget and layout you want to see. In addition, after the report window opens, you might click Customize Report to change the date range, the columns that appear, and so on. All in all, getting the budget report you really want might require a dozen or more small customizations.

Rather than reapply all these tweaks each time you generate the report, memorize the customized report so you can regenerate it with just one click. Here's how:

1. **In the report window's button bar, click Memorize.** QuickBooks opens the Memorize Report dialog box.
2. **In the Name box, type a name for the customized report, such as *P&L Budget vs. Actual 2015*.**
3. **If you want to save the report in a special group, turn on the Save in Memorized Report Group checkbox and then, in the drop-down list, choose the group.** For example, you might store budget reports in the Company group. (If you don't save the report to a special group, QuickBooks adds it to the Memorized Report submenu, described in a sec.)
4. **Click OK.**

To run the report, choose Reports→Memorized Reports. If you didn't save the report to a group, choose the report's name on the Memorized Reports submenu. If you *did* save it to a group, in the Memorized Reports submenu, choose the group and then the report's name.

To learn how to add a report to your Favorite Reports, see page 579.

CHAPTER

23

Tracking Finances with Reports and Graphs

QuickBooks comes with loads of built-in reports that show what's going on with your company's finances. But having a dozen report categories with several reports tucked into each one presents a few challenges, particularly if you're new to both business *and* QuickBooks.

The first challenge is knowing what type of report tells you what you need to know. For example, a profit and loss (P&L) report shows how much income and expense you had over a given time period, but a balance sheet tells you how much your company is worth.

The second challenge is finding the report you want within the different report categories. After deciding you want to compare the profit of the items you sell, for example, do you look for the corresponding QuickBooks report in the Customers & Receivables category; Sales category; Inventory category; or Jobs, Time & Mileage category? (If you guessed Jobs, Time & Mileage, you're right.)

The Report Center is a handy way to find the reports you want. But flipping through this book can be even faster, which is why each chapter describes the built-in reports that correspond to the bookkeeping tasks the chapter covers, what they're good for, and where you can find them.

A third challenge—for even the most knowledgeable QuickBooks aficionado—is that the built-in reports might not do exactly what you want. A date range could be off, information that you don't want might be included, or the data could be grouped in ways that don't make sense for your business. After using QuickBooks for a while, most businesses tweak the program's built-in reports. This chapter explains how to customize reports to get what you want. And there's no point in letting that customization go to waste, so you'll also learn how to memorize your customized reports, add them to QuickBooks' menus for fast access, and even exchange particularly handy customized reports between company files.

You'll also learn about new report features in QuickBooks 2015. First, reports have gotten a new look that makes them much easier to read. In addition, you can now add comments to your reports. The following pages have the details.

Finding the Right Reports

If you know what kind of report answers your burning business question, finding that report can be as simple as dragging your mouse through the Reports menu to a likely category, and then, on the category's submenu, clicking the name of the report you want. But if you need help figuring out what a report does and what it looks like, the Report Center could be your new best friend.

To open the Report Center, choose Reports→Report Center or, in the icon bar, click Reports. (Page 702 explains how to add this icon to the icon bar if it isn't visible.) The window that appears includes a clickable list of the same categories and reports as in the Reports menu. But unlike the menu, the Report Center gives you all sorts of hints for finding the right report. It also offers several shortcuts for getting to the right report fast, as you can see in Figure 23-1.

On the left side of the Report Center, you'll initially see built-in report categories. (The categories you see change depending on whether you select the Memorized, Favorites, Recent, or Contributed tab at the top of the window; the categories that these tabs represent are described on page 578.) To see the reports in a category, click the category's name, like Company & Financial, Sales, or Banking.

Reviewing Reports in the Report Center

The Report Center gives you three ways to view the reports in a category:

- **Grid View**, shown in Figure 23-1, is ideal when you need a little help finding the right report. It displays previews of each type of report in the category selected on the left side of the window. To see more reports in that category, scroll down. Date-range info and report-related icons appear below each thumbnail. To display this view, in the Report Center's upper right, click the Grid View icon.
- **List View** is your best bet when you want brief hints about the right reports and want to get to those reports quickly. In this view, you can select a category on the Report Center's left, and the titles of that category's reports and the questions they answer appear in a space-saving list. To use this view, click the List View icon labeled in Figure 23-1.

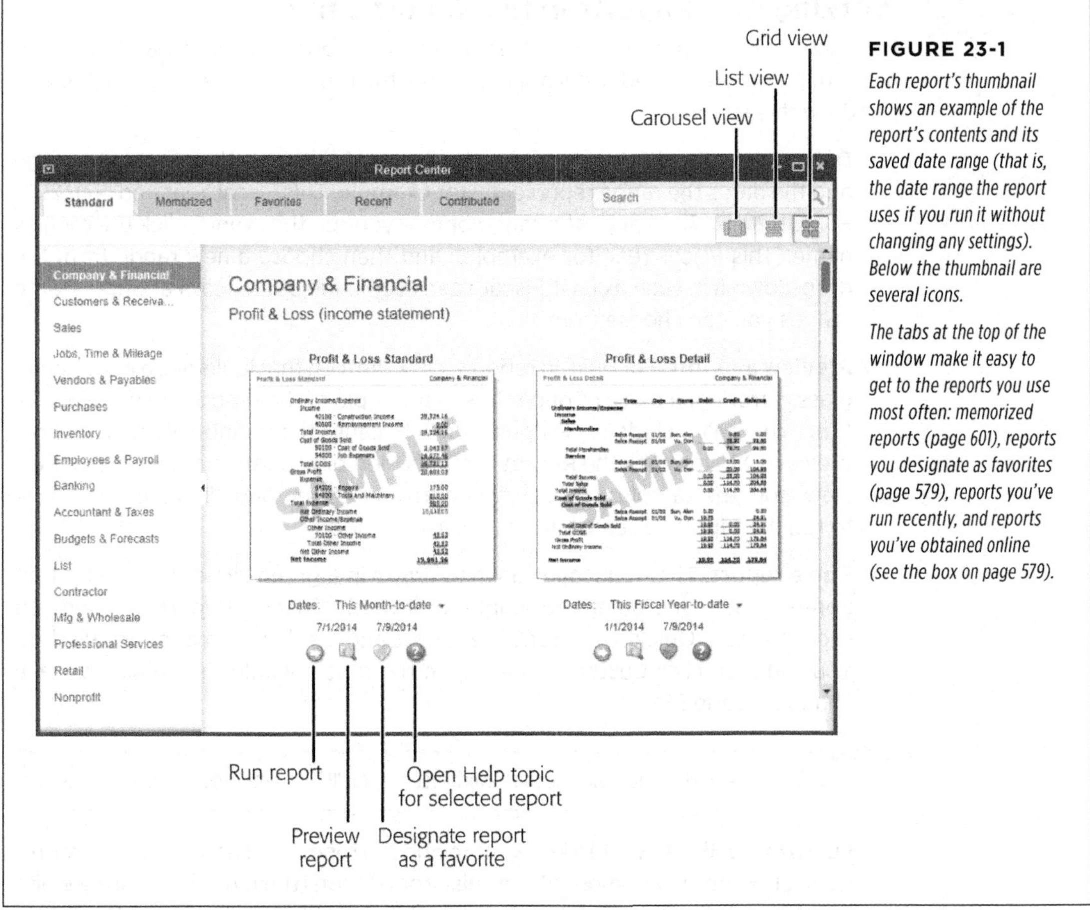

FIGURE 23-1

Each report's thumbnail shows an example of the report's contents and its saved date range (that is, the date range the report uses if you run it without changing any settings). Below the thumbnail are several icons.

The tabs at the top of the window make it easy to get to the reports you use most often: memorized reports (page 601), reports you designate as favorites (page 579), reports you've run recently, and reports you've obtained online (see the box on page 579).

- **Carousel View** displays a sample report (one that doesn't use your company's accounts or data) in the center of the window. In addition to the report's title, the question that it answers appears above the sample, such as "What are my company's total purchases from each vendor?" for the "Purchases by Vendor Summary" report. Below the report, you can change the date range by clicking the down arrow to the right of the current range and choosing a new one. To run the report, double-click its preview or click the Run icon (the white arrow inside a green circle).

  Other reports in the current category wait in the wings to the left and right of the selected report. To access these reports, either click their preview images or use the slider bar at the bottom of the Report Center window to scroll through them until the one you're looking for appears front and center. To use this view, in the upper-right corner of the window, click the Carousel View icon (see Figure 23-1).

Working with Reports in the Report Center

For each report in the Report Center, its saved date range setting and icons for performing report-related tasks appear below the report preview. Here's what you can do with each one:

- **Date range**. QuickBooks displays the name of the report's saved date range and the dates the range represents; for example, This Fiscal Year and "1/1/2015 - 12/31/2015." To change the range before you run the report, click the range's name (This Fiscal Year, for example), and then choose a new range from the drop-down list, such as Last Fiscal Year. (See page 591 to learn about the date ranges you can choose from.)
- **Preview a report**. For built-in reports, click the icon that looks like a magnifying glass in front of a piece of paper to see a sample of the report you've selected. (This icon isn't included in Carousel View because the thumbnails act as report previews.) If you click the Report Center's Memorized tab and then click a Preview icon, the samples just say "Memorized Report" and "Sample"; you have to run the report to see what it looks like.
- **Run a report**. The Run icon is a white arrow in a green circle (the tooltip that appears when you point your cursor at it reads "Display Report.") When you click this icon, QuickBooks runs the report and displays it in a report window. You can then click Customize Report in the report window's toolbar to make changes (page 589).

NOTE The heart icon lets you designate your favorite reports. You'll learn how to do that in the next section.

- **Learn more**. If you want to know more about a report and how you can customize it, click the "Learn more about this report" icon (the blue circle with a white question mark). QuickBooks opens the Help topic for that report, which gives hints about how to use and customize it. If you click this icon for a memorized report, QuickBooks opens the "Work with memorized reports" Help topic instead.

Finding Frequently Used Reports

The Report Center initially displays QuickBooks' built-in reports and the categories to which they belong. However, the center also offers quick access to reports that you run often:

- **Memorized reports**. If you modify reports to suit your needs, you can memorize them (page 601) and run them again and again with all your customized settings in place. In the Report Center, click the Memorized tab to see your memorized report groups (page 602). Select one to display the reports within it.

GEM IN THE ROUGH

Sharing Reports with Others

If you don't see the kind of report you want, you may not have to customize a report yourself. The Report Center's Contributed tab makes it easy to grab reports shared by Intuit and others within the online Intuit Community. When you click this tab, you can filter its list of shared reports by industry and sort it by category. In the View Industry drop-down list, click the industry you want, such as Professional Consulting. Click the Sort By box and choose "Most popular" or "Highly rated" to see the shared reports that others have found helpful. To see recently added reports, choose "Newly shared."

To run a shared report, put your cursor over the one you're interested in to display its icons. (If you're in Carousel View, the icons will already be visible.) Then click its Run icon (the white arrow in a green circle).

If you like, you can rate these shared reports. One of the icons for shared reports is labeled "Rate." When you click it, the "Add a comment and rate this report" dialog box opens. Comments from others appear in the lower half of the dialog box. Type your comments in the upper half and fill in the Name field with your name or nickname. Then click the number of stars you want to give the report; for example, to give it a five-star rating, click the rightmost star. When you're done, click "Add and Close" to post your review and close the dialog box.

You can also return the favor by sharing *your* reports with the community. When you click the Report Center's Memorized tab, each report has a Share icon that looks like two pieces of paper, as shown in Figure 23-2. Click this icon to open the Share Template window. Fill in information about your report, including a title, description, your name, and your email address (in case Intuit has a question about the report), and then click Share.

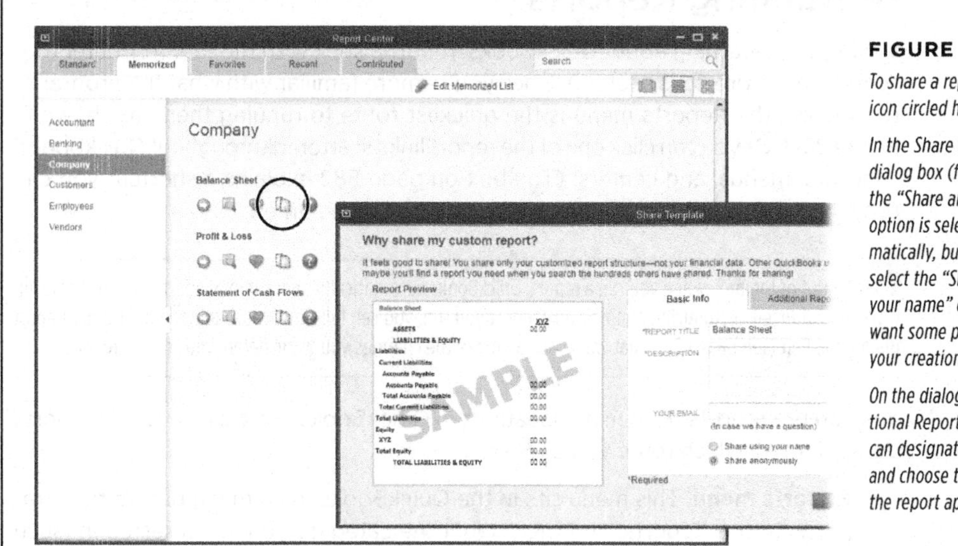

FIGURE 23-2

To share a report, click the icon circled here.

In the Share Template dialog box (foreground), the "Share anonymously" option is selected automatically, but you can select the "Share using your name" option if you want some publicity for your creations.

On the dialog box's Additional Report Info tab, you can designate a category and choose the industries the report applies to.

- **Favorite reports.** QuickBooks lets you indicate your favorite reports so you can get to them in a jiffy. The Report Center's Favorites tab displays all the reports that you designate as favorites. Whenever you select a report in the Report Center, a Fave icon (an orange heart) appears (its tooltip says, "Mark as Favorite"). If the report is one that you run more often than you check email, simply click this icon; QuickBooks adds the report to the Favorites tab and turns the report's heart icon gray to indicate that this is one of your favorites.

- **Recent reports**. You can quickly rerun a report you've used lately by clicking the Recent tab, and then choosing the report you want. For example, if you produced a Sales by Customer report a few days ago and need to run it again, on the left side of the Recent tab, click the "Last 1-7 days" heading, click the report's name, and then click the Display Report icon.
- **Search**. If you don't know which built-in report you want, you can use keywords to narrow down your choices. For example, if you want to see how much equity you have in your company, in the Search box at the Report Center's upper right, type *equity* and then press Enter. A Search Results tab appears with a list of reports that include equity, such as Balance Sheet Standard, Net Worth Graph, and Balance Sheet Prev Year Comparison.

NOTE If you type more than one keyword, your search results are likely to grow longer, not shorter, because QuickBooks looks for reports that contain *any* of the keywords you provide, rather than reports that contain all of them.

Running Reports

While you're learning about QuickBooks' reports, stick with the Report Center (described in the previous section). Once you're more familiar with what the program's reports do, the Reports menu is the quickest route to running them, as shown in Figure 23-3. Or you can click one of the report links scattered throughout QuickBooks' windows, menus, and centers. (The box on page 582 explains a shortcut you can use when you want to run *several* reports at the same time.)

TIP Out of the box, when you run a report, QuickBooks automatically opens it in a report window. However, if you find yourself customizing almost every report you run, you can tell QuickBooks to open the Modify Report dialog box first (see page 659). That way, you can make the changes you want *before* you see the report.

You can run reports from many locations in QuickBooks. Here's how to run reports depending on which route you choose:

- **Reports menu**. This menu sits in the QuickBooks main menu bar. To run a report, choose Reports, and then select the category you're interested in (such as Memorized Reports, Company & Financial, or Vendors & Payables). On the submenu that appears (Figure 23-3), choose the report you want to run. (If *another* submenu appears, drag until you can pick the report you want.)

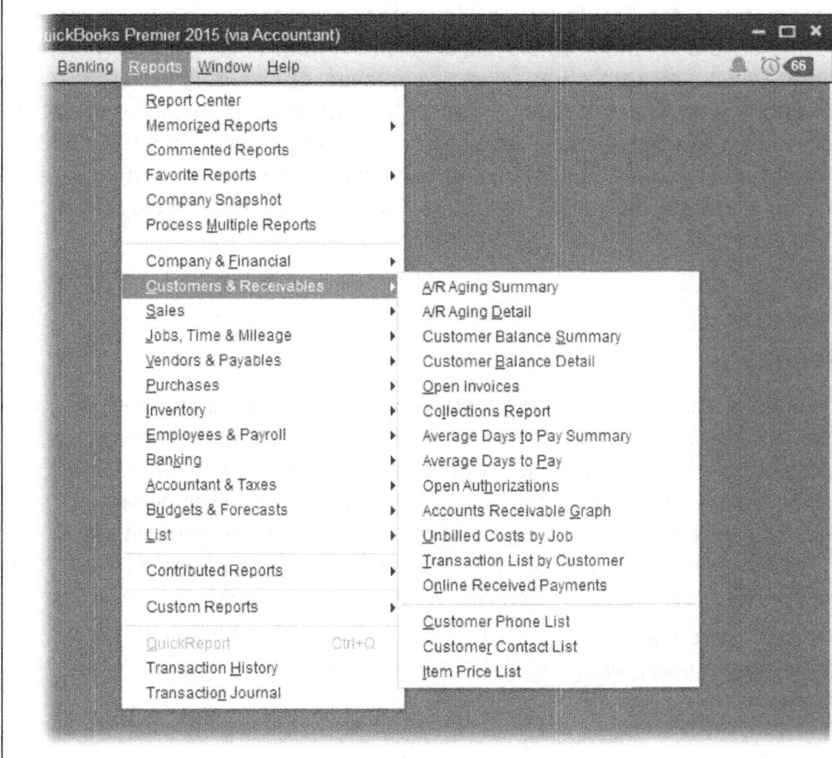

FIGURE 23-3

The Reports menu not only includes built-in QuickBooks reports and reports you memorize; it can also launch the Report Center and the Company Snapshot, and it contains the Process Multiple Reports feature, described in the box on page 582. In QuickBooks 2015, you can also choose Commented Reports to access reports that you or others have added comments to.

- **The Report Center**. Select the report you want to run. If you want to change the date range before you run the report, click the current date range's name and then choose the new one from the drop-down list. To run the report, click the green Run icon.
- **Favorite Reports menu**. This menu is a submenu of the Reports menu. If you add a report to this menu (page 579), you can run it by choosing Reports→Favorite Reports→[report name]. If you use the left icon bar, you can click Run Favorite Reports (in the icon bar's middle section) to list the reports you've designated as your favorites. Then, in the Run Favorite Reports section that appears, click the report you want to run.
- **Icon bar**. You can customize QuickBooks' icon bar (page 700) to include your all-time favorite reports or a category of reports. To run a report from the icon bar, simply click the report's icon.

- **List windows**. In a list window, such as the Chart of Accounts window or Item List window, click the Reports button at the bottom of the window, and then choose the report you want to run on the drop-down list that appears.
- **Customer, Vendor, Employee, and Inventory centers**. To run reports about a specific customer, vendor, employee, or inventory item, open the corresponding center. Select a customer, job, vendor, employee, or inventory item to display info about it on the right side of the center's window. Then click one of the report links, like QuickReport or Open Balance. In a center's toolbar, choose Print or Excel to create a hard copy (as explained in the next section) or export an Excel file (page 588) of a Vendor List, Customer:Job List, Employee List, or Item List report.

GEM IN THE ROUGH

Running Multiple Reports

Perhaps you perform the same tasks every month—calling customers with overdue invoices, checking inventory, and reviewing sales by item, for example—and you need reports to complete each task. Particularly when you print reports, you might sit in front of your computer with nothing but an occasional click to break the monotony, while QuickBooks slowly transforms your data into printed reports one at a time.

But you don't have to do it that way. Tucked away on the Reports menu is the Process Multiple Reports feature, which generates *all* the reports you choose, one after the other. You can stock your printer with paper, make sure the toner cartridge isn't running low, and then use this feature to run dozens of reports while you do something else.

Process Multiple Reports works only with memorized reports, because you don't get the opportunity to customize the reports it runs. So customize each report you run regularly to make sure it includes the correct information and is formatted the way you want, and then memorize each one (page 601).

When you choose Reports→Process Multiple Reports, QuickBooks opens the Process Multiple Reports window. It lists built-in reports along with all your memorized reports in the order they appear on the Memorized Reports submenu. To include a report in the batch you want to run, click its checkmark cell to turn the checkmark on. The Date Range column shows the period covered by the report. To change the range, type the dates you want in the report's From and To cells. When all the reports you want have checkmarks and the correct date range, click Display to make QuickBooks open report windows for each selected report. If you'd rather have hard copies of the reports, click Print instead, and QuickBooks opens the Print Reports dialog box. All you have to do is choose the printer and the number of copies, and then click Print to start pushing reports through the printer.

Another way to run multiple reports is to create a report *group* with all the reports you want to run (see the box on page 604). Call it something like *QuarterlyReports* or *EndofYearReports*. Then you can run the reports by opening the Memorized Reports window (Reports→Memorized Reports→Memorized Reports List). Right-click the report group you want to run, and then choose Process Group on the shortcut menu that appears. The Process Multiple Reports dialog box opens with the Select Memorized Reports From box set to the report group you chose and automatically turns on the checkboxes for all the reports in that group, as shown in Figure 23-4. Simply click Print to make QuickBooks print them all.

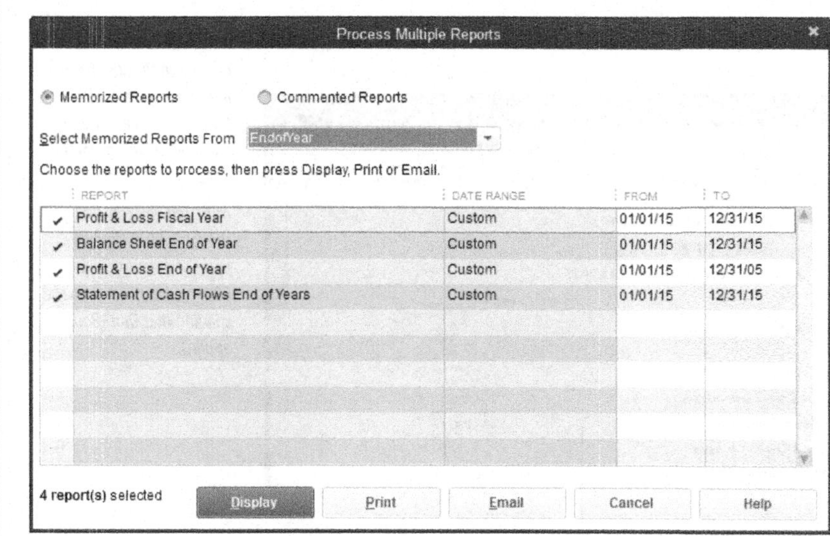

FIGURE 23-4

The Date Range column is grayed out because you can't choose a different date range there. However, the From and To columns' backgrounds are white, which means you can change the starting and ending dates for reports. (If you adjust any dates, the report's Date Range cell changes to read "Custom.") Simply turn on the appropriate checkmarks, and then click Display or Print to run your reports.

NOTE Some features on reports should remain consistent across *every* report your company generates, such as whether you use cash or accrual accounting (page xxii describes the difference between the two methods). A QuickBooks administrator can set company-wide report preferences to ensure that summary reports show financial information correctly and consistently. But even without administrator powers, you can still specify a few settings for the reports and graphs you run. See page 659 to learn how.

It takes QuickBooks time to generate some reports because they pull data from every corner of your company file. If you're hunkering down to a report-running session of epic proportions, here are some tips for speeding things up:

- Wait until everyone else has logged out of the company file.
- If possible, log into QuickBooks from the computer that contains the company file. Otherwise, log into the fastest computer on your network that runs QuickBooks.
- Before running reports, switch the file to single-user mode by choosing File→"Switch to Single-user Mode" (page 489).

In QuickBooks 2015, report formatting received a makeover, as shown in Figure 23-5. Top-level categories are now shaded with a medium gray, lower-level categories are shaded beige, and totals are shaded a lighter gray.

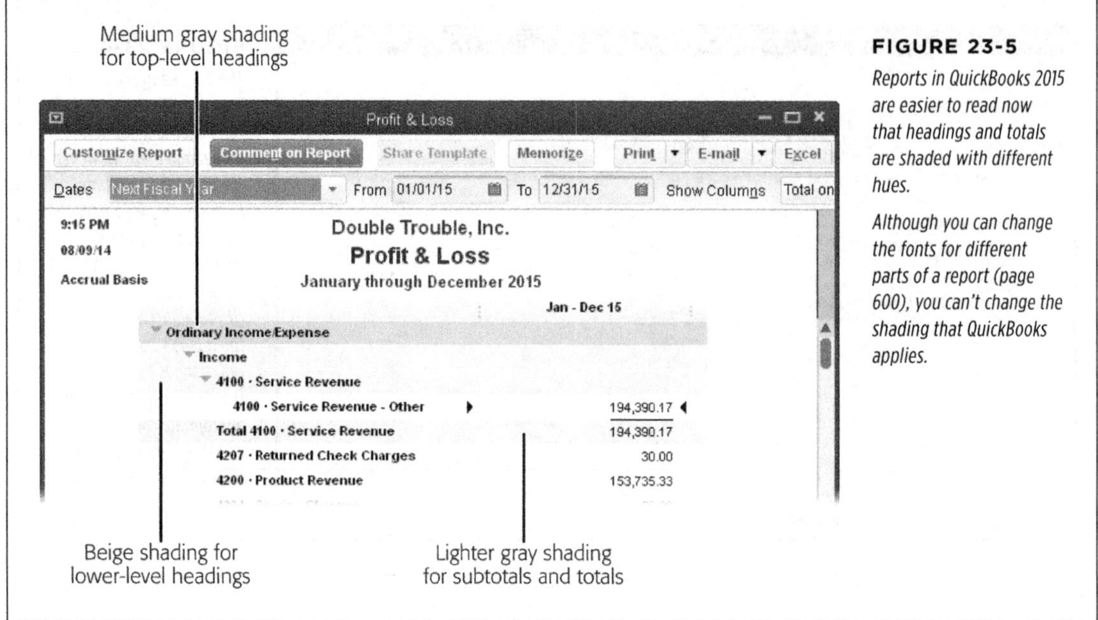

FIGURE 23-5

Reports in QuickBooks 2015 are easier to read now that headings and totals are shaded with different hues.

Although you can change the fonts for different parts of a report (page 600), you can't change the shading that QuickBooks applies.

Adding Comments to Reports

Sometimes, you have information or feedback on reports that you want to share with others. For example, say you're sending your Balance Sheet report to your accountant and you want to tell him that you haven't recorded the fixed assets you purchased this year. Or perhaps you want to know whether the increase in product revenue is likely to continue. New in QuickBooks 2015, you can add comments to any line of a report. Here's how:

1. **Run the report you want, such as Profit & Loss Standard (choose Reports→Company & Financial→Profit & Loss Standard).**

   In the report window's Dates box, choose the date range you want, such as This Fiscal Year.

2. **In the report window's button bar, click "Comment on Report."**

   The "Comment on Report: [report name]" window opens. You'll see small comment boxes to the right of the values in the rightmost column, as shown in Figure 23-6.

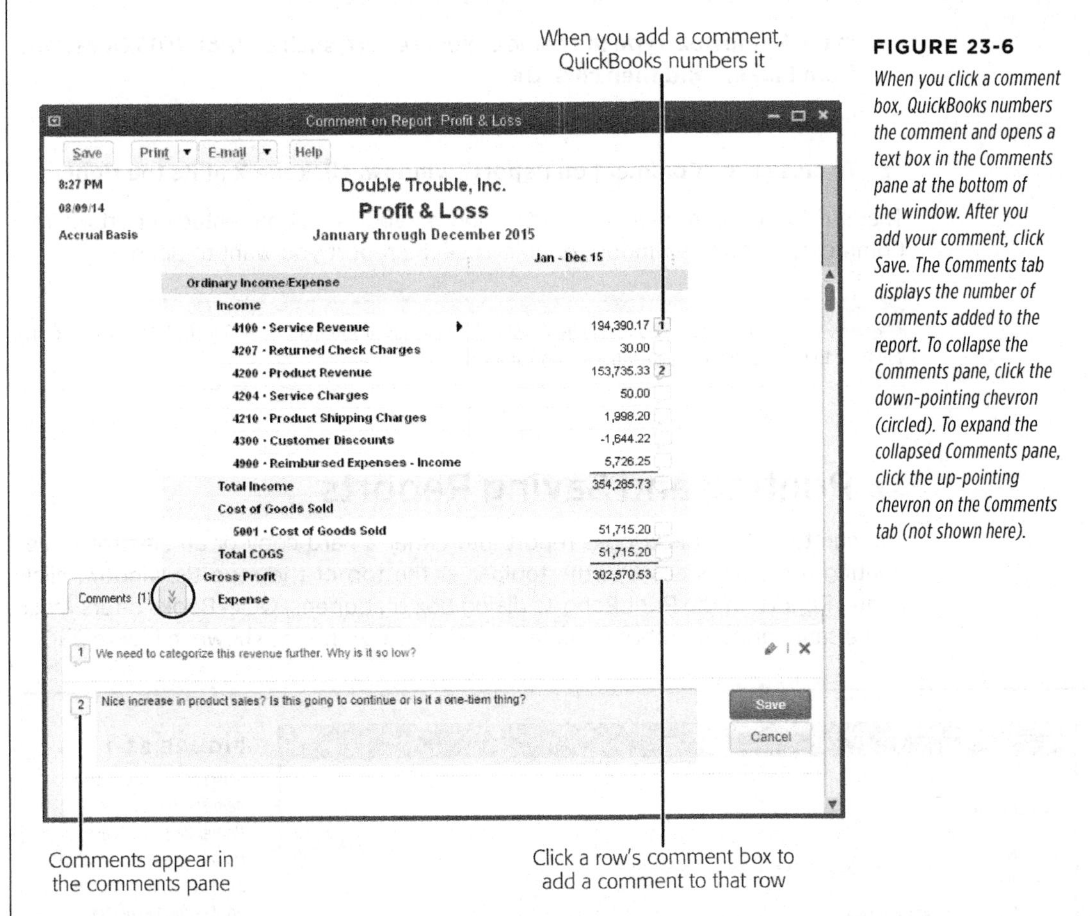

FIGURE 23-6

When you click a comment box, QuickBooks numbers the comment and opens a text box in the Comments pane at the bottom of the window. After you add your comment, click Save. The Comments tab displays the number of comments added to the report. To collapse the Comments pane, click the down-pointing chevron (circled). To expand the collapsed Comments pane, click the up-pointing chevron on the Comments tab (not shown here).

3. **To add a comment to a line of the report, click that line's comment box.**

   QuickBooks adds a number to the comment box to identify the comment and opens the Comments pane at the bottom of the window, as shown in Figure 23-6.

4. **In the Comment pane's text box, type your comment, and then click the pane's Save button.**

   The comment you just added appears in the Comments pane, and the total number of comments in the report appears on the Comments tab.

5. **Repeat steps 3 and 4 to add additional comments to the report.**

   QuickBooks numbers comments in the order that you add them, not in sequence from the top of the report to the bottom.

6. **When you've added all your comments, click the Save button at the window's top left.**

   The Save Your Commented Report dialog box opens.

7. **In the Name box, type the name of your report, such as "P&L 2015 Questions from Blake," and then click OK.**

   In the message box that tells you that the report was saved, click OK.

8. **To close the "Comment on Report" window, click the X at its top right.**

That's it! To view commented reports, choose Reports→Commented Reports. In the Commented Reports window, double-click the report you want to open.

NOTE You can't customize a commented report. For example, if you want to change the report's date range, you have to run the report again and add new comments to it.

Printing and Saving Reports

You can turn any QuickBooks report into either a hard copy or an electronic file. Printing a report is easy: In the toolbar at the top of the report's window, click Print→Report. In the Print Reports dialog box that opens, QuickBooks offers most of the same printing options you find in other programs, as shown in Figure 23-7.

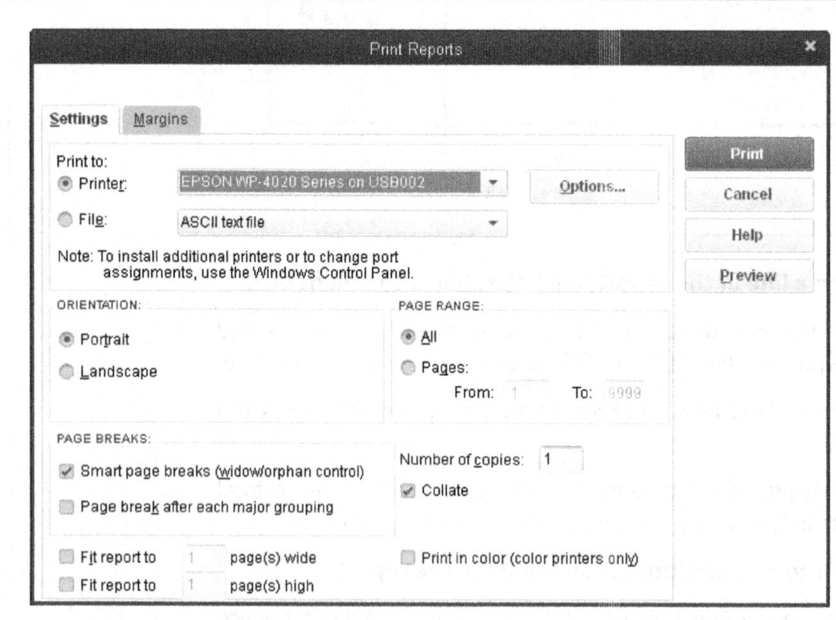

FIGURE 23-7

Select the Printer option here and then, in the Printer drop-down list, choose where you want to send the report. You can print reports in portrait or landscape orientation, and specify the pages you want to print, how many copies, where you want page breaks, and whether to use color. If a report is a bit too wide or too tall to fit on one page, turn on the appropriate "Fit report to" checkboxes, which force the report onto the number of pages you specify.

In the Print Reports dialog box, the Page Breaks section has two checkboxes that control where QuickBooks places page breaks:

- **Smart page breaks (widow/orphan control)**. This checkbox is turned on initially. It tells QuickBooks to insert page breaks in judicious locations to keep associated information on the same page. To stuff as much report as possible onto the fewest pages, turn off this checkbox. When you do, QuickBooks prints to the very last line of a page, even if it means that a single row of a section appears on one page with the rest of the section on another. (The box below describes other ways to squeeze more report onto a page.)
- **Page break after each major grouping**. Turn on this checkbox (which appears only if your report is more than one page long) to add a page break after major sections of the report, like Income and Expenses in a Profit & Loss report. When this checkbox is turned off (as it is initially), the report starts new sections on the same page.

WORKAROUND WORKSHOP

Fitting More Report onto Each Page

When a report is rife with columns, it's hard to fit everything onto a single piece of paper. QuickBooks automatically prints the columns that don't fit on additional pages, but reports that span multiple pages cause paper rustling and lots of grumbling. Try these approaches for keeping your reports to one page:

- Before you click Print, reduce the width of the columns. In the report's window, drag the three vertical dots to the right of a column's heading to the left to make that column narrower, as shown in Figure 23-13, top (page 596).
- To limit the number of pages from left to right, click Print→Report in a report's window and then, in the Print Reports dialog box, turn on the "Fit report to _ page(s) wide" checkbox and, in the text box, type the number of pages wide that you want. To limit the number of pages from top to bottom, turn on the "Fit report to _ page(s) high" checkbox and, in the text box, type the number of pages high.
- In the Print Reports dialog box's Orientation section, choose Landscape. When a report *almost* fits on an 8.5" × 11" sheet of paper, switching to landscape orientation should do the trick. Better yet, if your printer can handle it, use legal-size paper (8.5" × 14").

Saving Reports as Files

If you save a report as a file, you can feed it to other programs to edit it in ways that you can't in QuickBooks. Intuit gives you four ways to transform reports into files. The Print Reports dialog box lets you create three kinds of files: ASCII text files, comma-delimited files, and tab-delimited files. But you can also create comma-delimited files and Excel workbooks by clicking Excel in any report window's button bar. (The comma-delimited files that you create in either place are identical, so you can generate them whichever way you prefer.) You can also save forms and reports as PDF files or create versions to email.

TIP If you plan to import a report into another program, go with a tab- or comma-delimited file, which uses tab characters or commas to separate each value. Many programs can read files in these formats.

Here are the four ways you can create files for reports and the differences among them:

- **Save to file from the Print Reports dialog box**. In a report's window, click Print→Report to open the Print Reports dialog box. Just below the Printer option is the File option, which has a drop-down list that includes "ASCII text file," "Comma delimited file," and "Tab delimited file." After you choose the File option and select a type of file, click Print and QuickBooks opens the Create Disk File dialog box, which is just a File Save As dialog box where you can specify a filename and where to save the file.

NOTE The ASCII text format produces a text file that *looks* like your report, but it uses different fonts and space characters to position values in columns. This type of file isn't suitable for importing into spreadsheets or other programs, but you can use it to store an electronic version of your report.

- **Export to spreadsheet file**. In a report window's button bar, click Excel, and then choose Create New Worksheet or Update Existing Worksheet to open the "Send Report to Excel" dialog box shown in Figure 23-8. There, depending on which option you chose, QuickBooks selects the "Create new worksheet" or "Update an existing worksheet" option. Click Export to open the report in Excel.

  If you select the "Replace an existing worksheet" option, the "Select workbook" box and "Select a sheet" drop-down list appear. After you specify the workbook and worksheet that you want to replace and then click Export, QuickBooks replaces the contents of that worksheet with the report.

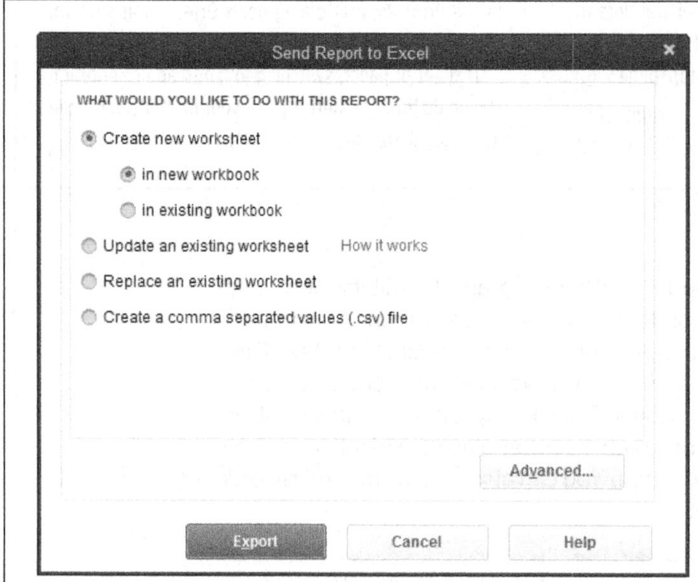

FIGURE 23-8

In a report window's button bar, click Excel→Create New Worksheet or Excel→Update Existing Worksheet to open this dialog box.

If you choose Create New Worksheet, QuickBooks selects the "Create new worksheet" option here, but you can choose whichever option you want. If you select the "Create a comma separated values (.csv) file" option, then when you click Export, the program opens the Create Disk File dialog box, which is described in this section.

TIP QuickBooks is smart about exchanging report information with Excel. When you export a report to an existing worksheet, QuickBooks can update the worksheet while keeping most of the changes you've made to it, such as formulas and formatting.

If you choose the "Create a comma separated values (.csv) file" option and then click Export, QuickBooks opens the Create Disk File dialog box, where you can type a filename and choose where to save the file.

If you want to tell QuickBooks how to set up the Excel spreadsheet, before clicking Export, click Advanced, choose your settings, and then click OK. The Advanced Excel Options dialog box has three sections for setting up a report in Excel. The first section focuses on whether to transfer the fonts, colors, and spacing that you set up in your QuickBooks reports to the Excel workbook. The second section provides checkboxes for turning on Excel features such as AutoFit, which makes columns wide enough to display all the data they contain. And the third section lets you decide whether you want the report's header to appear in the Excel header area (which appears at the top of the printed report) or at the top of the worksheet's grid.

- **Save as a PDF file**. To save a report as a PDF (Acrobat) file, run the report and then, in the report window, choose Print→Save As PDF. In the "Save document as PDF" dialog box, navigate to the folder where you want to save the file, type a filename in the "File name" box, and then click Save.

TIP Choosing Print→Save As PDF also works for saving forms like invoices and sales receipts as PDFs. Just select this option on the corresponding window's Main tab. (When you tell QuickBooks to email a form, it automatically creates a PDF file of the form and attaches it to the email message.)

- **Email an Excel file or PDF file**. To email a report, in the report's window, click E-mail, and then choose "Send report as Excel" or "Send report as PDF."

Customizing Reports

Report windows are teeming with ways to customize reports. Some tools are easy to spot, like the buttons and drop-down lists at the top of the window. But you can also drag and right-click elements in reports to make smaller changes. This section describes all the techniques you can use to make reports display exactly what you want.

Here's where you go to customize a report:

- **Run custom reports from the Reports menu**. If you make it through all of QuickBooks' report categories without finding the report you want, the Reports menu includes two entries for building custom reports from scratch. Choose Reports→Custom Reports and then choose Summary to build a report that displays subtotals by some kinds of categories. For instance, you could customize a summary report to create an income statement for all customers of a particular type. Choosing Reports→Custom Reports→Transaction Detail, on the other hand, lets you customize transaction reports to show exactly the fields you want.

As soon as you choose one of these custom report options, QuickBooks opens both the report window and the Modify Report dialog box—because a custom report needs *some* kind of customization. You can set up the contents and appearance of the report any way you want, as shown in Figure 23-9. For a custom transaction report, the Modify Report dialog box includes a list of fields that you can turn on and off, as well as checkboxes for specifying how you want to sort and total the results.

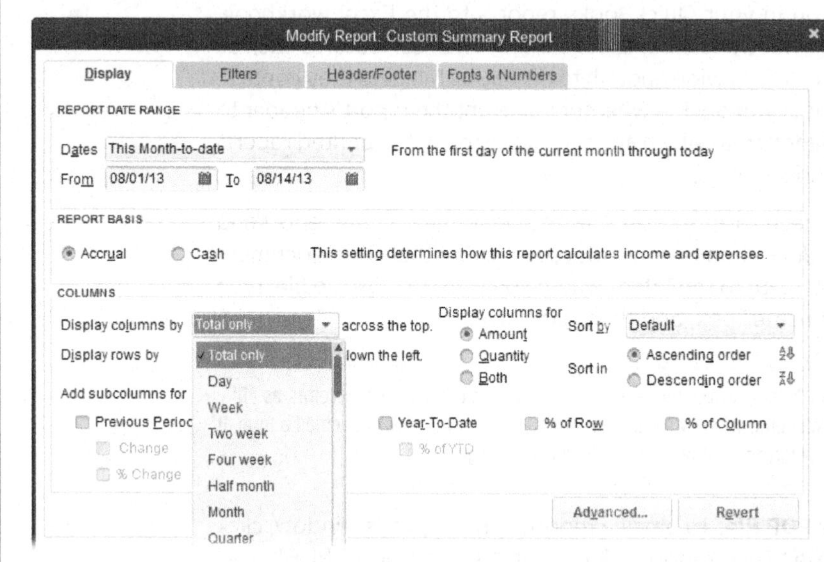

FIGURE 23-9

In addition to date ranges, filters, and other customizations, you can control what appears in a custom report's rows and columns. The "Display columns by" and "Display rows by" drop-down lists include many of the same choices, so you can set up a report to show your data either across or down. (A report that uses the same category for both columns and rows doesn't make any sense, so be sure to choose different entries for columns and rows.)

NOTE The Modify Report dialog box's "Display columns by" drop-down list includes date ranges and the "Total only" option. If you want to customize your report, you can turn on checkboxes for comparing values with previous periods as well as showing dollar and percentage differences, like Budget vs. Actual reports do.

- **Report window button bar**. The bar across the top of a report window includes the Customize Report button, which opens the all-powerful customization tool you just learned about—the Modify Report dialog box. This bar also includes other handy customization buttons like Hide Header and Collapse, discussed in the box on page 590.
- **Report window toolbar**. Below the button bar is a customization toolbar where you can choose the date range, the columns to display, and which column to use for sorting the report's contents.

- **Report window**. Hidden within the report itself are a few customization features. For example, by right-clicking text in a report, you can format its appearance. Dragging the three vertical dots between column headings changes the column width and, for detail reports, you can drag columns to new locations.

FREQUENTLY ASKED QUESTION

Viewing More of a Report

How can I see more of a report on my screen?

If your computer monitor is a closer relative to your mobile phone than to your widescreen TV, you can use a couple of techniques to stuff more of the report onto your screen:

- **Hide Header**. While you're working on a report, you don't need the report's header to tell you which type of report you're viewing, your company's name, or the date range. In the report window's button bar, click Hide Header to hide the report's header and display more content. (The printed report that you send to others still includes the header.) To redisplay the hidden header, in the button bar, click Show Header.
- **Collapse**. If the report window's button bar has a Collapse button, you can click it to get a high-level view of a report that hides subaccounts, the individual jobs for your customers, and subclasses. When you click Collapse, QuickBooks totals the results for the subaccounts, jobs, or subclasses under the main account, customer, or class, respectively. Unlike the Hide Header button, the Collapse button affects your onscreen view *and* the printed report. To redisplay the collapsed entries, click Expand.

Choosing Date Ranges

Different reports call for different date ranges. Financial statements, for example, typically use fiscal periods, such as the last fiscal quarter or the current fiscal year. But many companies manage month by month, so your reports may cover the current month or month to date. Payroll reports span whatever period you use for payroll, whether that's one week, two weeks, or a calendar month. And tax reports depend on the tax periods required by the tax agencies you answer to.

The best place to choose a report's date range depends on how much you intend to modify the report:

- **If the date range is the only thing you want to change**, the report window's toolbar is the way to go. In the Dates drop-down list, choose the range you want, or, in the From and To boxes, pick a starting date and ending date for the report.
- **If you plan to change more than the date**, in the report window, click the Customize Report button. In the Modify Report dialog box that appears, the Report Date Range section includes the same date-setting features as the report window's toolbar, as well as several additional tabs and sections for every other type of customization.

QuickBooks has two dozen preset date ranges that work based on today's date. For example, if it's March 15, 2015, and your company uses the calendar year as its fiscal year, then This Fiscal Year represents January 1 through December 31, 2015, but Today is simply 3/15/2015. And, if none of the program's date ranges do what you want, in the report window's toolbar, you can set specific start and end dates in the From and To boxes.

The preset date ranges are numerous because they mix and match several types of ranges.

- **Durations**. Some preset periods represent durations, such as Week, Month, Fiscal Quarter, Fiscal Year, and Tax Year. At the extremes, you can pick All to encompass *every* date in your company file, or Today, which includes only today.
- **This, Last, and Next**. For each duration, you can choose the current period (such as This Fiscal Quarter), the previous period (Last Fiscal Quarter), or the upcoming period (Next Fiscal Quarter).
- **Full and to-date**. You can also pick between a full period and the period up to today's date. For example, on March 15, "This Month" covers March 1 through March 31, and "This Month-to-date" represents March 1 through March 15.

NOTE QuickBooks includes one additional date-range option: Next 4 Weeks, which many businesses use when checking cash flow.

Selecting Subtotals

Many of QuickBooks' built-in reports calculate subtotals. For instance, Profit & Loss summary reports include subtotals by income, cost of goods sold, expenses, and so on. Sales reports by customer subtotal the sales for all the jobs you do for each customer.

When you run a detail report, such as Sales by Customer Detail, the report shows every relevant transaction, and you can subtotal the results in any way that makes sense for that type of report, as shown in Figure 23-10.

Depending on the report you pick, some choices in the Modify Report dialog box's "Total by" drop-down list are more appropriate than others. For example, you might decide to subtotal a sales report by customer type, rep, or account list to see which types of customer provide the most business, which sales rep makes the most sales, or which income account pulls in the most money. If you choose a "Total by" option that doesn't jibe with the report you've run, the report displays a zero balance and no rows of data.

Customizing Columns

Some reports start with only one column, but they don't have to stay that way. Depending on the type of report, you can change its columns in several ways, like showing columns for each time period or choosing fields to display in separate columns. And if you find that your appetite for columns is larger than your monitor, you can remove, resize, and reorder report columns. This section explains all your options.

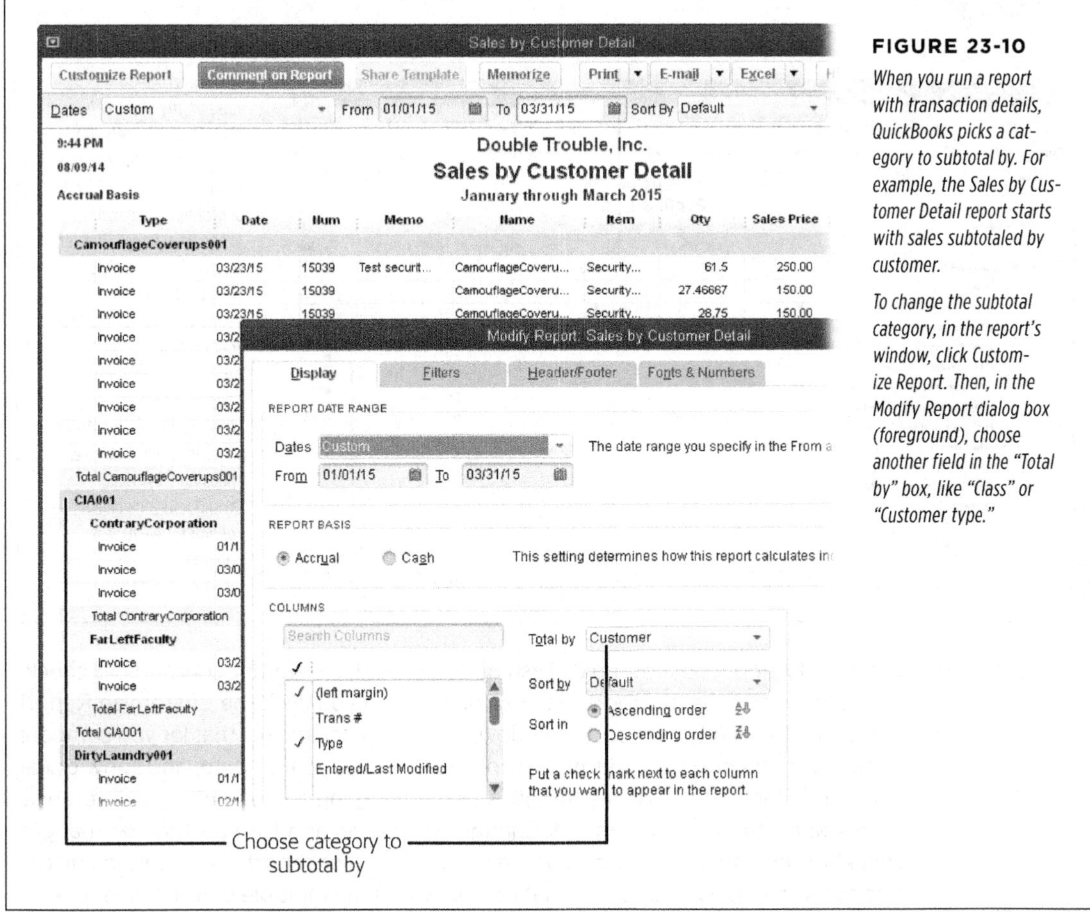

FIGURE 23-10

When you run a report with transaction details, QuickBooks picks a category to subtotal by. For example, the Sales by Customer Detail report starts with sales subtotaled by customer.

To change the subtotal category, in the report's window, click Customize Report. Then, in the Modify Report dialog box (foreground), choose another field in the "Total by" box, like "Class" or "Customer type."

ADDING AND REMOVING COLUMNS IN SUMMARY REPORTS

As you manage your business, you'll want to see results for different date ranges in the reports you generate. For example, during a year, you might create a Profit & Loss report to show your financial status by month, for each fiscal quarter, and for the entire year. If the report window's toolbar includes a Show Columns drop-down list (as it does for summary reports), choosing an entry there is the quickest way to change the categories that columns represent (see Figure 23-11). You can make the same changes in the Modify Report dialog box by using the "Display columns by" drop-down list.

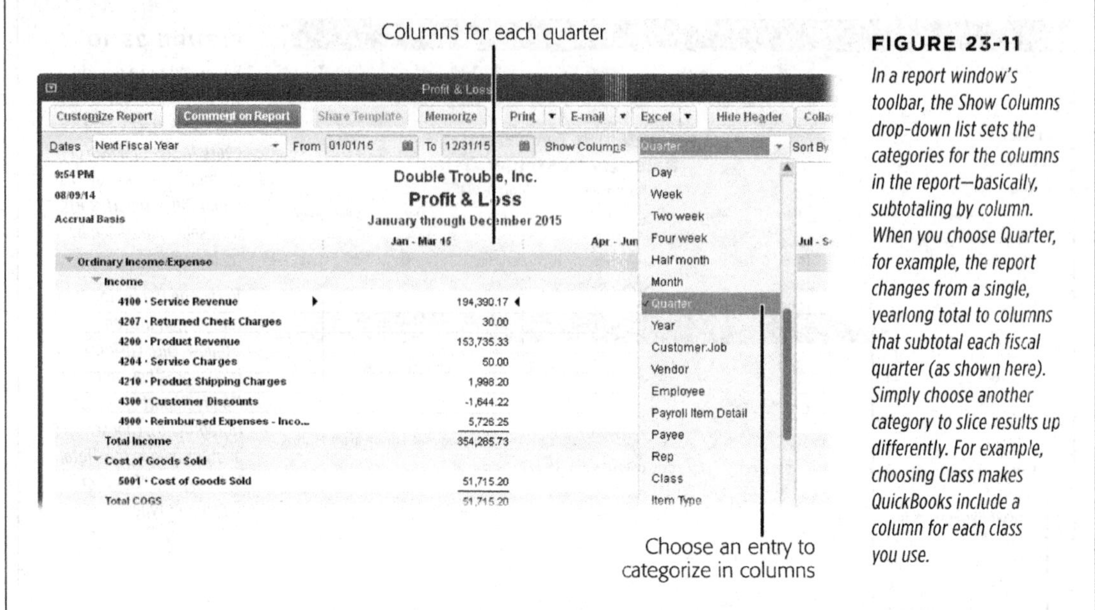
Columns for each quarter
Choose an entry to categorize in columns

FIGURE 23-11

In a report window's toolbar, the Show Columns drop-down list sets the categories for the columns in the report—basically, subtotaling by column. When you choose Quarter, for example, the report changes from a single, yearlong total to columns that subtotal each fiscal quarter (as shown here). Simply choose another category to slice results up differently. For example, choosing Class makes QuickBooks include a column for each class you use.

The Modify Report dialog box's Display tab provides different comparison checkboxes for each type of report. For example, when you click the Customize Report button in a Profit & Loss report's window, you'll see checkboxes that let you compare results with the previous period, previous year, or the year to date, *and* show dollar and percentage comparisons. If you want to focus on the percentage difference, for instance, then turn off the "$ Change" checkbox and turn on the "% Change" checkbox instead. (If you use multiple currencies, your reports can contain currencies other than U.S. dollars. For that reason, when the multiple currency preference is turned on, the "$ Change" checkboxes are simply labeled "Change.")

The Modify Report dialog box for some reports even includes checkboxes such as "% of Column," "% of Row," "% of Income," and "% of Expense." If you generate a profit and loss report by quarter and turn on the "% of Row" checkbox, for example, the report shows each quarter's performance as a percentage of the full year's results.

ADDING OR REMOVING COLUMNS IN DETAIL REPORTS

Reports that show transaction details, such as Profit & Loss Detail or Inventory Valuation Detail, include columns for data fields like Date, Name, Cost, and Memo. To change the columns that appear in a detail report, in the report's window, click Customize Report, and then choose the columns you want to add or remove, as shown in Figure 23-12.

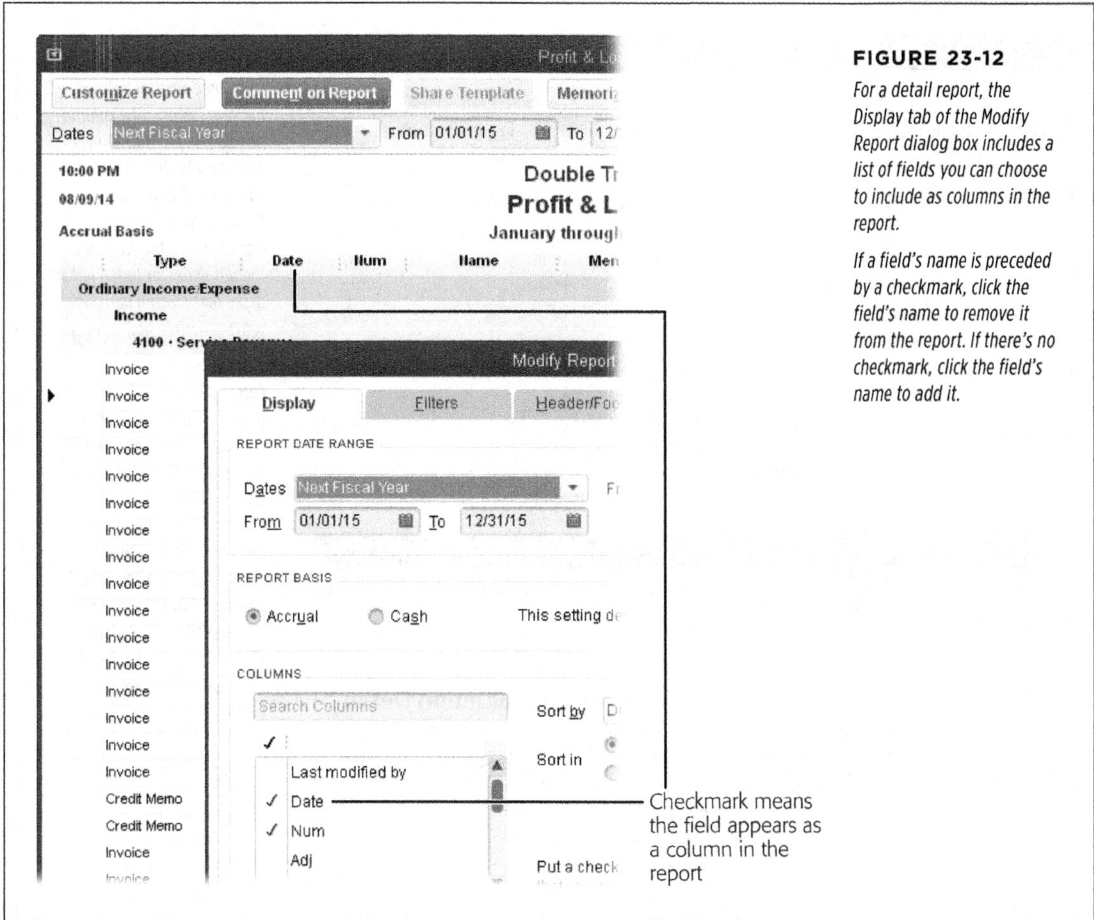

FIGURE 23-12

For a detail report, the Display tab of the Modify Report dialog box includes a list of fields you can choose to include as columns in the report.

If a field's name is preceded by a checkmark, click the field's name to remove it from the report. If there's no checkmark, click the field's name to add it.

RESIZING AND MOVING COLUMNS

Some columns seem to take up more room than they need, while others truncate their contents. Figure 23-13 shows how to resize columns and rearrange the order in which they appear.

NOTE When you resize columns in some reports, like ones with columns for each month, a Resize Columns dialog box asks if you want to set *all* the columns to the same size. Click Yes to resize all the columns, or No to resize only the one.

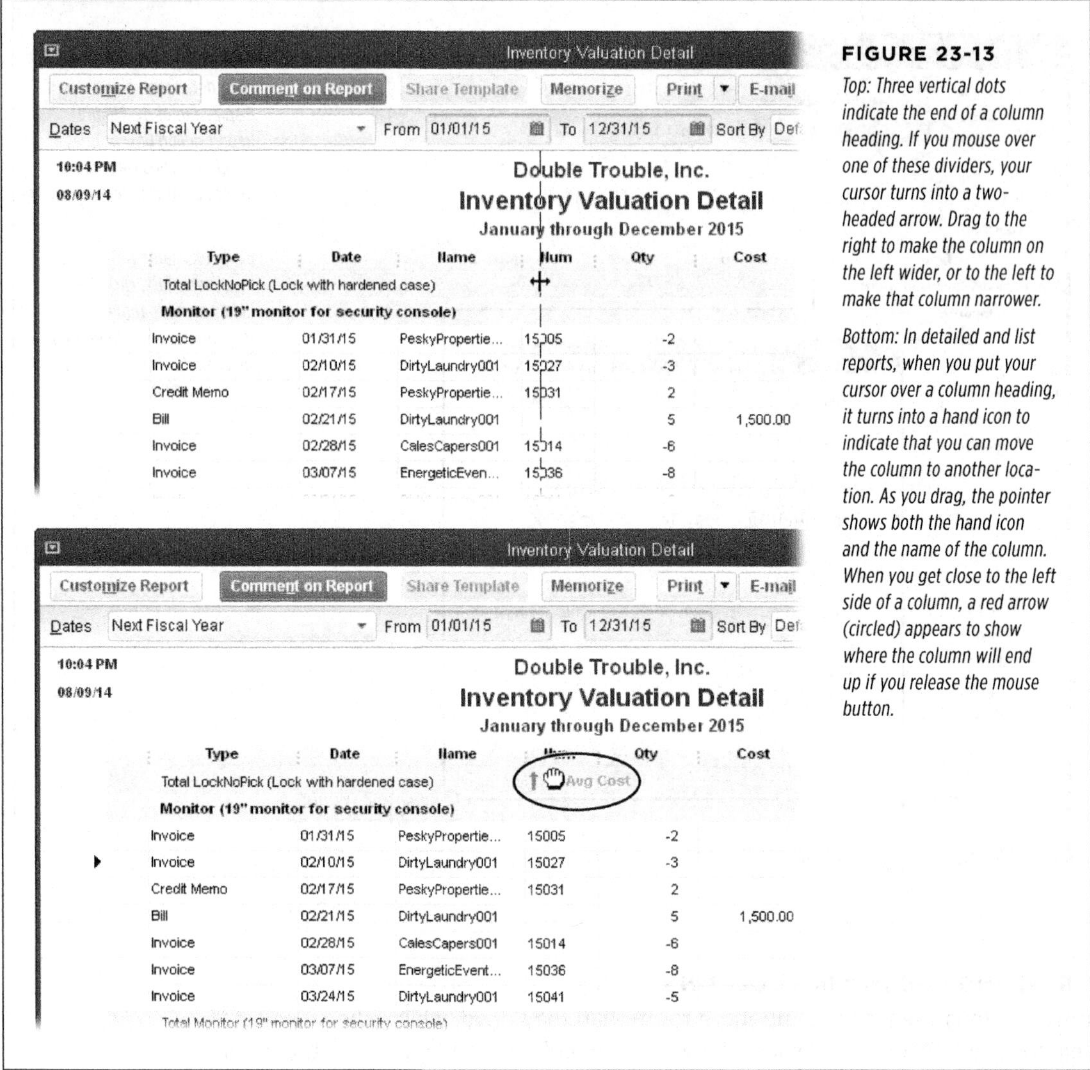

FIGURE 23-13

Top: Three vertical dots indicate the end of a column heading. If you mouse over one of these dividers, your cursor turns into a two-headed arrow. Drag to the right to make the column on the left wider, or to the left to make that column narrower.

Bottom: In detailed and list reports, when you put your cursor over a column heading, it turns into a hand icon to indicate that you can move the column to another location. As you drag, the pointer shows both the hand icon and the name of the column. When you get close to the left side of a column, a red arrow (circled) appears to show where the column will end up if you release the mouse button.

TIP To remove a column from a report, drag the three dots shown in Figure 23-13 to the left past another column's divider.

Sorting Reports

If a report is sortable, you'll see the Sort By box in the report window's toolbar. When you first generate a sortable report, the Sort By box is set to Default, which means different things for different reports. For example, if you create a Sales by Customer Detail report, QuickBooks groups transactions by customer, but it sorts each customer's transactions from earliest to most recent. (QuickBooks sorts reports by only one field at a time.)

In the Sort By drop-down list, choose the column you want to use to sort the report. As soon as you change the Sort By box to something other than Default, the Ascending/Descending button appears to the right of the Sort By box. (It has a blue arrow and the letters A and Z on it; A appears above Z when the sort order is ascending, and Z appears above A when the sort order is descending.) Clicking this button toggles between sorting in ascending and descending order.

The fields you can use to sort depend on the report. For the Sales by Customer Summary report, for example, the Sort By box lets you choose from only two columns: Default and Total. Default sorts the report by customer name in alphabetical order, whereas Total sorts the report by the total sales for each customer, from the smallest to the largest dollar amount. On the other hand, the Sales by Customer Detail report includes several columns of information, and you can sort by any of them.

NOTE The Modify Report dialog box's Display tab also includes a Sort By drop-down list. In this dialog box, select the Ascending or Descending option to change the sort order.

Filtering Reports

Detail reports (the ones that list individual transactions) might show more information than you want. For example, a Purchases by Item Detail report could run page after page, listing your weekly purchases of Turtle Chow. Filtering a report removes transactions that don't meet your criteria, so you can home in on just the Turtle Chow purchases from Myrtle's Turtle Mart.

In QuickBooks, you can apply as many filters as you want at the same time. Each filter adds one test that a transaction has to pass to appear in your report. For example, when you set the date range for a report, what you're really doing is adding a filter that restricts transactions to the ones that happened between the starting and ending dates. Then, if you want to find the sales for only your corporate customers, you can add a filter based on the Customer Type field.

QuickBooks provides dozens of filters, from the most common—such as dates, items, and transaction types—to those you won't apply very often (if ever), such as Workers Comp Codes and FOB (that's "free on board," discussed on page 235).

Built-in reports already have filters, but you can customize a built-in report by adding extra filters or editing or removing the existing ones. Here's how:

1. **In the report's window, click Customize Report and then, in the Modify Report dialog box, click the Filters tab.**

   The left side of the tab lets you choose the field you want to filter by and specify the filter's test. The right side of the tab lists all the filters that are currently applied.

2. **In the left-hand filter list, select the field you want to filter by.**

   Depending on the field you choose, QuickBooks offers different criteria. Figure 23-14 shows one example.

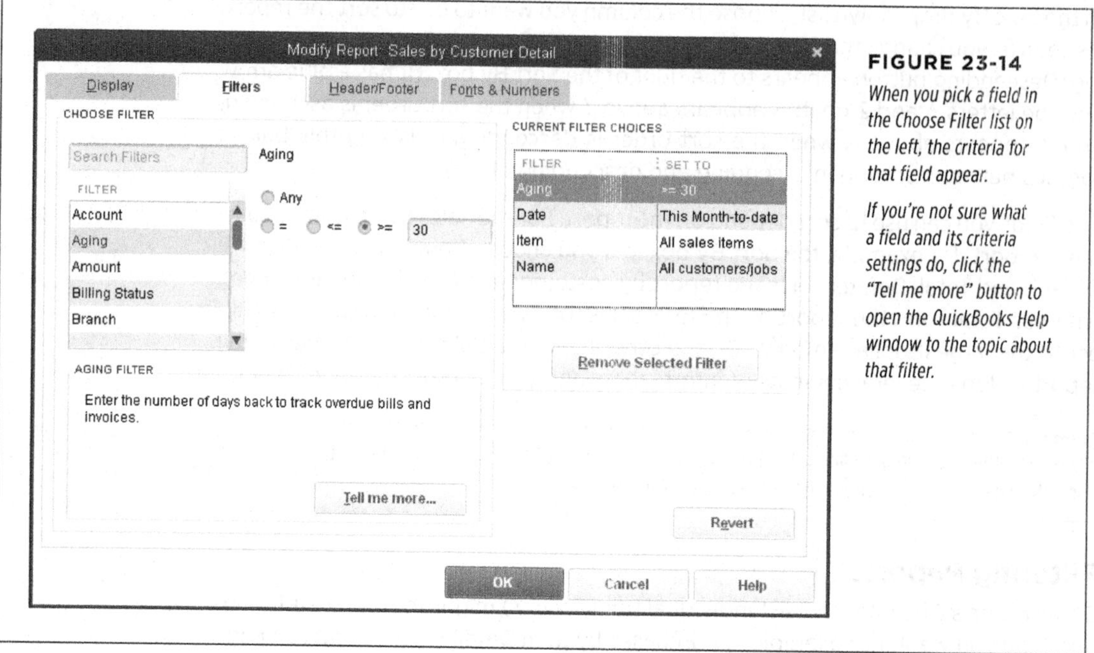

FIGURE 23-14

When you pick a field in the Choose Filter list on the left, the criteria for that field appear.

If you're not sure what a field and its criteria settings do, click the "Tell me more" button to open the QuickBooks Help window to the topic about that filter.

3. **Using the drop-down lists or options that appear, specify the filter criteria you want to apply.**

   For instance, if you filter by account, in the Account drop-down list, you can choose a category such as "All bank accounts"; choose "Multiple accounts" and then click each one you want to include; or click a single account. Whatever option you choose, QuickBooks adds the filter to the right-hand Filter list (in the Current Filter Choices section).

   If you choose a numeric field, you can select a test, like ">=" (greater than or equal to) and then specify the test value. For example, to look for invoices that are late by 30 days or more, choose Aging for the filter, select the ">=" option, and then type *30* in the text box, as shown in Figure 23-14.

4. **To remove a filter, select it in the right-hand Filter list, and then click Remove Selected Filter.**

   QuickBooks removes the filter from the list.

5. **To edit a filter, in the right-hand Filter list, select the filter you want to change. Then, in the Choose Filter section, make the changes you want.**

6. **Click OK to see your report with the new filters applied.**

Report Headers and Footers

You don't have *complete* control over what appears in report headers and footers, but you can choose from several fields common to all of them. For example, fields like Company Name, Report Title, and Date Prepared are options for headers, and Page Number is one option for footers. To change the header and footer contents of the report you're working on, in the Modify Report dialog box, click the Header/Footer tab (Figure 23-15).

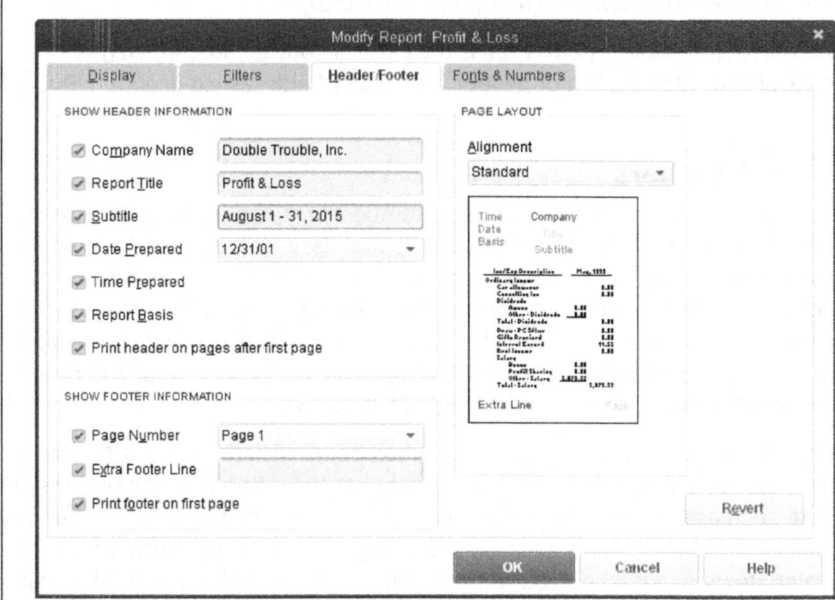

FIGURE 23-15

To realign the header and footer contents, in the Alignment drop-down list, choose Left, Right, Centered, or Standard.

QuickBooks initially chooses Standard, which centers the Company name and title; places the date, time, and report basis (cash or accrual) on the left; and puts the extra footer line (explained below) and page number in the left and right corners of the footer.

NOTE You may notice that, on the Modify Report dialog box's Header/Footer tab, the Date Prepared drop-down list reads something like "12/31/01." Don't worry: That date doesn't mean that QuickBooks gathers data from 2001. The Date Prepared setting simply lets you choose the date *format* that the report uses.

QuickBooks automatically pulls data from your company file to fill in the header and footer text boxes. For example, if you use a built-in Sales by Customer Detail report, the program puts your company's name in the Company Name box. If you have a more eloquent title for the report, type it in the Report Title box.

TIP To set standards for *all* report headers and footers, choose Edit→Preferences→Reports & Graphs and then click the Company Preferences tab. If the "Default formatting for reports" checkbox is turned on, turn it off, and then click the Format button. In the Report Format Preferences dialog box that appears, set the fields you want.

The Header/Footer tab's Show Footer Information section includes an Extra Footer Line box where you can type whatever you want. This text isn't associated with any field in QuickBooks, so it's blank unless you enter something. Whatever you type here appears in the bottom left of the report page.

The last checkbox in both the Show Header Information and Show Footer Information sections controls the pages on which the headers and footers appear. To conserve paper, turn off the "Print header on pages after first page" checkbox so QuickBooks includes the header on the first page only. To omit the page number from the first page, turn off the "Print footer on first page" checkbox.

The right side of the Header/Footer tab is the Page Layout section, which gives you some control over the position of header and footer fields, as explained in Figure 23-15.

Fonts and Numbers

The fonts and formatting you use to display numbers in reports doesn't change the underlying financial message, but an attractive and easy-to-read report can make a good impression. Just like the fields that appear in the header and footer, you can set QuickBooks' preferences to assign the same font and number formats for all your reports (see page 661). On the other hand, changing fonts directly in a report is quick and has the added advantage of letting you see exactly what the report looks like with the new formatting, as Figure 23-16 shows.

If you already have the Modify Report dialog box open, click the Fonts & Numbers tab. The Fonts section on the left side of the tab lists the different text elements in the report, such as Column Labels, Company Name, and Transactions. To change a font, select an element, and then click the Change Font button, which opens the same dialog box you get when you right-click the element in the report (shown in Figure 23-16).

The right side of the Fonts & Numbers tab has options for changing the appearance of numbers. Negative numbers are usually something to pay attention to in the financial world, so accountants use several methods to make them stand out. If you're not sure which style of negative number you like, choose an option and then check out the number in the Example area. You have three style choices:

- **Normally**. This option shows negative numbers preceded by a minus sign: -1200.
- **In Parentheses**. This option puts negative numbers in parentheses without a minus sign: (1200).
- **With a Trailing Minus**. This option places the minus sign after the number: 1200–.

TIP If you use a color printer or display reports on your computer screen, they you can make negative numbers even harder to ignore by turning on the In Bright Red checkbox.

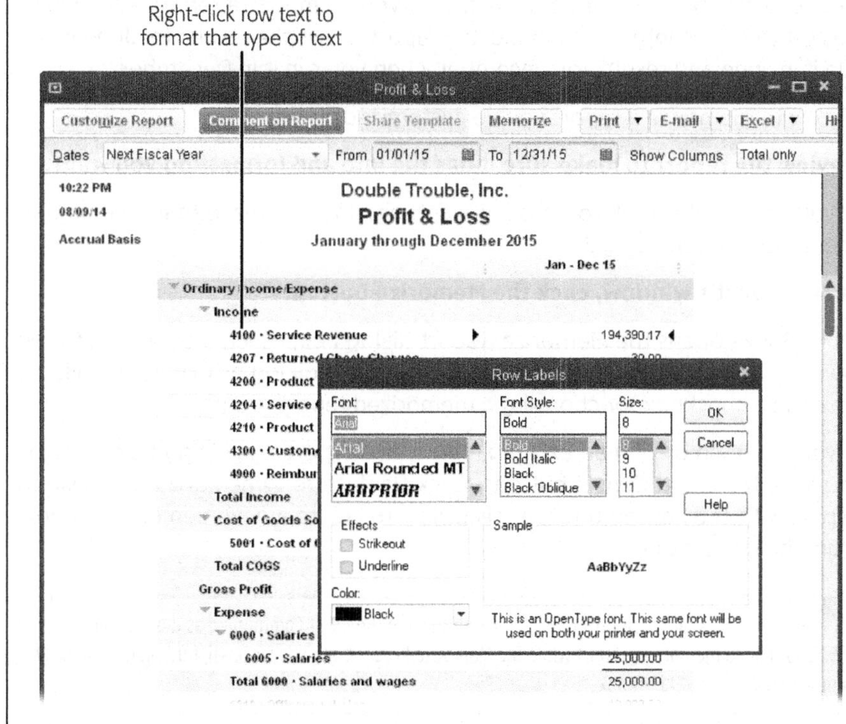

FIGURE 23-16

In a report window, right-click the text you want to format, such as a row label, a column label, or a value. Then change the format in the dialog box that opens (the name of the dialog box depends on which report element you're formatting, but the choices are the same for every element). When you click OK, QuickBooks opens a Changing Font dialog box that asks if you want to change all related fonts. If you click No, it changes the font for only the element you chose. If you click Yes, it changes related elements—often the entire report. If you don't like the format, right-click the text and try something else.

To make big numbers easier to read, in the Show All Numbers section, turn on the Divided By 1000 checkbox. This removes one trio of zeros from numbers in the report—so that $350,000,000 shows up as $350,000, for example—and adds "($ in 1,000's)" to the report's header. And, if a summary report (such as Customer Balance Summary) tends to contain mostly zero values, you can keep it lean by turning on the Except Zero Amounts checkbox. That way, the report omits any rows whose values are zero, such as customers who don't owe you any money. (This checkbox doesn't appear on the Fonts & Numbers tab if you're customizing a transaction-based report, such as Customer Balance Detail.) Turn on the Without Cents checkbox to show only whole dollars.

Memorizing Reports

If you take the time to customize a report so it looks just the way you want, it'd be silly to jump through those same hoops every time you run that report. By memorizing modified reports, you can run them again and again with all your customizations just by choosing Reports→Memorized Reports, and then picking the report's name on the appropriate submenu.

When you memorize a report, QuickBooks remembers your settings—like date range and filter criteria—but not the data itself. So if you memorize a report whose date range is set to This Month, for example, the report shows the results for June when you run it in June and results for December when you run it in December.

Here's how to memorize a report you've customized:

1. **Review the report to make sure it has the info and formatting you want.**

   If you notice later that you missed a setting, you can make that change and memorize the report again.

2. **In the report's window, click the Memorize button.**

   QuickBooks opens the Memorize Report dialog box, which is small and to the point. If you're memorizing a standard report, the dialog box contains a Name box and a checkbox for choosing a memorized report group.

   If you're rememorizing an *existing* memorized report, the dialog box contains Replace, New, and Cancel buttons. Click Replace to rememorize the existing report with the new settings, or click New to create a new memorized report from the current one.

NOTE You can also share memorized reports with others in the Intuit Community, as described in the box on page 579. To share a memorized report while the Memorize Report dialog box is open, turn on the "Share this report template with others" checkbox.

3. **In the Name box, type a name that indicates what the report shows, like *Deadbeat Customers*.**

4. **If you want to save the report in a special group, turn on the Save in Memorized Report Group checkbox, and then choose the appropriate group.**

   QuickBooks comes with several built-in groups like Accountant, Company, and Customers, which appear on the Memorized Reports submenu shown in Figure 23-17. But you can also create your own groups, as the box on page 604 explains.

5. **Click OK to memorize the report.**

   Voilà—you're done. If you're going to use the report over and over, consider adding it to the Favorite Reports menu (page 579) or to the icon bar (page 704) so you can run it by choosing it from the Report→Favorite Reports menu or clicking its icon, respectively.

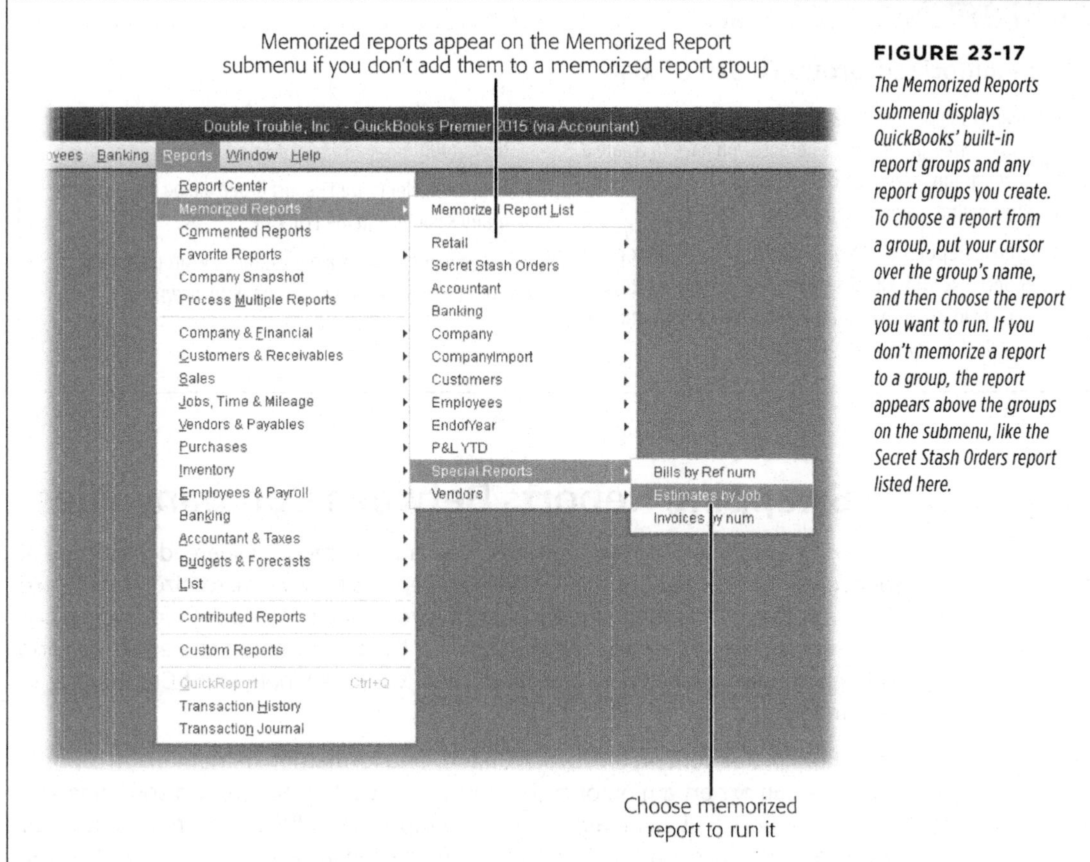

FIGURE 23-17

The Memorized Reports submenu displays QuickBooks' built-in report groups and any report groups you create. To choose a report from a group, put your cursor over the group's name, and then choose the report you want to run. If you don't memorize a report to a group, the report appears above the groups on the submenu, like the Secret Stash Orders report listed here.

TIP The Memorized Report List window comes in handy if you want to edit or delete reports. To display it, choose Reports→Memorized Reports→Memorized Reports List. In the window, select the report you want to work on, and then click Memorized Report at the bottom of the window. From the drop-down menu, choose Edit Memorized Report to change the report's name or the group where it's memorized, or choose Delete Memorized Report to eliminate it from the list.

TROUBLESHOOTING MOMENT

The Memorized Group Doesn't Exist

The Memorize Report dialog box doesn't include a way to create a new memorized group. That's because you have to create a memorized group *before* you can add a report to it. Here's the secret to creating a memorized group:

1. Choose Reports→Memorized Reports→Memorized Report List. QuickBooks opens the Memorized Report List window, which includes memorized groups and the reports they contain.
2. At the bottom of the window, click Memorized Report→New Group.
3. In the New Memorized Report Group dialog box, type the group's name, and then click OK.

Now, when you memorize a report, the new group appears in the Save in Memorized Report Group drop-down list.

Swapping Reports Between Company Files

Suppose you're one of several business owners who meet to share ideas. Some of your colleagues rave about the QuickBooks reports they've customized, and you'd like to use the reports they've created. If they're willing to share their ideas, you can swap reports by trading *report template* files. Or, if you want to share your reports with a broader audience, you can share them with the whole Intuit Community as described in the box on page 579.

Report templates contain the layouts, filters, and formatting of memorized reports. Someone can export a memorized report as a report template, and someone else can then import that template to save the report in a different company file. For example, if your accountant likes to see information in very specific ways, she can give you a report template file so you can produce the reports she wants to see.

Report templates play well between different editions of QuickBooks (Premier, Pro, and Enterprise) and from version to version (2014, 2015, and so on). However, here are a couple of points to keep in mind:

- If you use QuickBooks Pro, you can only import templates that others create. You need QuickBooks Premier or Enterprise Solutions to *export* report templates.
- QuickBooks patches can affect the compatibility between versions, so you might have to install the most recent QuickBooks update if you want to use someone else's report templates. (If there's an update or version incompatibility issue with a report template you try to import, QuickBooks displays a warning to let you know.)

Exporting a Report Template

You can export report templates only if you have QuickBooks Premier or Enterprise Solutions. Whether you export one report or an entire group, QuickBooks stores the report settings in a single file with the file extension .qbr (for "QuickBooks report"). Because report templates are meant to move between QuickBooks company files, all you have to specify are the reports you want to export and the file to which you want to export them. Here's the process:

1. **Choose Reports→Memorized Reports→Memorized Report List.**

   QuickBooks opens the Memorized Report List window.

2. **Select the report or memorized group that you want to export.**

   For example, if your customized reports are all memorized in a group you created named Special Reports, select Special Reports.

NOTE In the Memorized Report List, you can select only a single report or a single group; you can't Ctrl-click or Shift-click to select several individual reports.

3. **Click Memorized Report→Export Template.**

   QuickBooks opens the Specify Filename for Export dialog box, which is nothing more than a Save As dialog box that automatically sets the file type to "QuickBooks Report Files (*.QBR)." The program also puts the report or group's name in the "File name" box. If you want to use a different name (one that includes the date you exported the reports, say), type it in that box.

4. **Navigate to the folder where you want to save the template, and then click Save.**

   QuickBooks saves the settings for the report(s) to the file.

The next section tells you how to *import* a report template.

NOTE QuickBooks won't export memorized reports with filters that reference an account, customer, or other entry specific to your company file, because those filters won't work in a company file that doesn't contain that account, customer, or entry. If you try to export a template for such a report, you see a message box that suggests you look for filter settings that wouldn't work in another company file.

Importing Report Templates

Importing reports from a template file is even easier than exporting report templates. In the Memorized Report List window (Reports→Memorized Reports→Memorized Report List), click Memorized Report→Import Template. QuickBooks opens the Select File to Import dialog box with the "Files of type" box set to "QuickBooks Reports Files (*.QBR)." All you have to do is navigate to the folder that contains the report template file and double-click the filename (or select the filename and then click Open).

When you do that, QuickBooks opens a different dialog box depending on whether you're importing one report or a group:

- **Single report**. QuickBooks opens the Memorize Report dialog box. As you would if you were memorizing a custom report of your own design, in the Name box, type the name you want for the report and, if you wish, choose a memorized report group. Then click OK to save the report template in your company file.
- **Report group**. When you import a report group, QuickBooks opens the Import Memorized Reports Group With Name dialog box and fills in the Name box with the group's name from the original company file, but you can type a different name. When you click OK, the program adds the group to your company file and saves all the imported reports in that group with their original names.

NOTE If you try to import a report or group with the same name as a report or group that's already in your company file, QuickBooks displays a warning and recommends that you change the name of the report or group you're importing. Click OK and then change the imported report or group's name before saving it.

PART

4

QuickBooks Power

CHAPTER

24

Banking Online with QuickBooks

By synchronizing your real-world bank accounts with the bank accounts in QuickBooks, you can download your bank balances and transactions into your QuickBooks company file so you'll always know how much cash you have on hand. (The connection you set up between the two is called *bank feeds* to differentiate it from online banking that you perform by logging into your bank account outside of QuickBooks.) That way, before repaying your aunt the money she lent you to start your business, you can quickly update your QuickBooks accounts, check your balance, and be certain that you aren't giving her a check that will bounce.

Besides managing your cash flow, banking online is much more convenient than the old paper-based methods of yesteryear. For example, you already have a lot of transactions in your QuickBooks account register (from depositing payments you received against invoices or making payments to your vendors) and you can easily match these transactions to the ones you download from the bank so you know how much money you *really* have in your account—and whether someone is helping themselves to your money without permission. Plus you can transfer money between your money market account and your checking account when you find yourself awake at 2 a.m.

Banking online also lets you pay bills without having to print checks, lick stamps, or walk to the mailbox. After you submit payment transactions online, the billing service you use either transfers funds from your bank account to the vendors or generates and mails paper checks. Online billing also lets you set up recurring bills so you can go about your business without worrying about missing a payment.

All this convenience requires some setup. QuickBooks needs to know how to connect to your bank, and your bank needs to know that you want to use its online services. This chapter explains how to apply for online services with your financial institution and set up bank feeds in QuickBooks to perform all these tasks. Once your accounts and bank feeds are set up and online services activated, you'll learn how to download transactions and make online payments. And if you enter transactions in your company file, you'll also learn about matching them with the ones you download—and correcting any discrepancies.

Setting Up Your Accounts for Online Services

Connecting your bank accounts to your accounts in QuickBooks is a lot like running a dating service: You have to prepare each participant for the relationship and then get them together. The services you can subscribe to and the price you pay depend on your financial institution, but they fall into one of these three categories:

- **Banking account access**. This service is usually free. It lets you check transaction status and download transactions into QuickBooks.
- **Credit/charge card access**. You can download credit card transactions as you do checking transactions, as long as you set up your credit card in QuickBooks as a *credit card account* (page 378) and enter individual credit card charges. Setting up a credit card as a *vendor* and entering only the monthly bill payment won't work.
- **Bill payment**. This service usually comes with a fee, but it's often a good deal when you consider the price of stamps and printed checks.

NOTE Although QuickBooks can download transactions in different currencies, the program's online bill payment feature works only with U.S. dollar-based accounts. So if you have a bank account that uses a foreign currency, you have to handle your transactions the old-fashioned way.

Applying for Online Services

The first step in linking QuickBooks to your bank accounts is to apply for online banking services with your financial institution. (If you use more than one bank, you have to apply to each one separately.) Contact your financial institution to find out how to apply.

When your financial institution processes your application and sends you a confirmation and a PIN (personal identification number) or password, check that the information you received, like the account number, is correct. Then you're ready to set up your QuickBooks bank account to talk to your real-world bank account.

NOTE If your bank is behind the times and doesn't offer online bill payment, Intuit is happy to earn more of your business with its add-on bill-pay service. To learn about it, choose Banking→Bank Feeds→Learn About Online Bill Payment. A browser window opens to the Intuit QuickBooks Bill Pay web page.

Activating Online Services for Your QuickBooks Account

When you receive a letter from your bank confirming that your online services are ready to go and you have your customer ID and password (or PIN), all you have to do is set up a bank feed for your corresponding account in QuickBooks to use these online services. The Bank Feed Setup wizard walks you through the steps:

1. **Choose Banking→Bank Feeds→Set Up Bank Feed for an Account.**

   In the message box that opens, click Yes to give QuickBooks permission to close any open windows.

   You can also start online setup in the Add New Account window (page 56). When you create a new account, type the account number and the routing number. Then, when you save the account, the Set Up Bank Feed message box asks if you want to set up online services. Click Yes to set it up now or No to do it later.

   Yet a third option is to head to the Edit Account window (page 63) and then click the Set Up Bank Feeds button at the bottom of the window.

   No matter which of these routes you choose, QuickBooks launches the Bank Feed Setup wizard.

2. **On the "Step 1: Find your bank" screen (Figure 24-1), begin typing the name of your bank. When you see your bank's name in the Matching Results list, click it. Or, if your financial institution is one of the more popular ones, simply click its link in the list on the right side of the dialog box.**

   QuickBooks connects to the Internet to download info about your bank. What you see depends on the type of connection your bank offers. If your bank connects directly to QuickBooks (page 613), the screen that appears asks if you've enrolled in your bank's online services. If you haven't, call the bank's number that's displayed on the screen or click the link to its enrollment site. If your bank doesn't communicate directly with QuickBooks, you'll see the Manually Import Transactions dialog box instead, which explains—you guessed it—how to manually import transactions into your account (page 614).

3. **When you're ready to connect, click Continue.**

   The "Step 2: Connect [your bank's name] to QuickBooks" screen appears.

4. **Fill in the "[bank name] User ID" and "[bank name] Password" boxes, and then click Connect.**

   The User ID is the ID that the bank assigned to you for online services and should be on the confirmation letter it sent you. If you don't have your ID and password, click the X at the dialog box's top right to close it; you can repeat this process after you receive them.

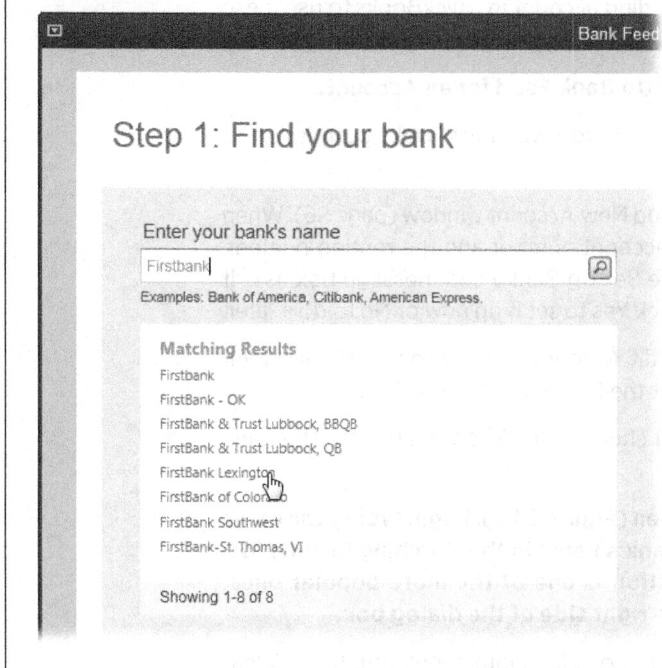

FIGURE 24-1

In the "Enter your bank's name" box, start typing its name. As you type, QuickBooks displays names that match what you've typed so far.

When you see your bank's name in the Matching Results list, click it.

5. **The next screen displays the accounts you have at this financial institution. In the QuickBooks Accounts column, click the down arrow to the right of the "Select existing or create new" box for the account you want to activate and choose an entry.**

   If you already created the bank account in QuickBooks, choose that account in the drop-down list. If you haven't created the account, choose <Create New Account>, fill in the boxes in the Add New Account window that opens, and then click Save & Close.

6. **Click Connect.**

   If your bank account and QuickBooks account connect, the "Success!" page appears and the account's Status cell sports the label "Added."

   If QuickBooks runs into a problem connecting to your bank account—such as a typo in your user name or password—you'll see an error message. In that case, click Back to correct the problem and try again.

7. **On the "Success!" screen, click Close.**

That's it! Your bank account and QuickBooks account are ready to exchange info.

NOTE If you signed up for online banking services with more than one account at the same financial institution, you have to repeat the steps in this section to activate each account at that institution.

Exchanging Data with Your Bank

Your financial institution takes the lead in controlling how QuickBooks can communicate with it. Your bank can set up this pipeline in two ways:

- **Direct connection** uses a secure Internet connection that links directly to your bank's computers. With this type of connection to your financial institution, you can do things like download your bank statements and transactions, transfer funds between accounts, pay bills online, and email your bank (as long as your bank offers those services). If your bank uses a direct connection, you set up your requests for downloads, funds transfers, online bill payments, and emails in QuickBooks *before* you connect.
- **Web Connect** uses a secure connection to your bank's website to download your statement info. With this type of connection, you then have to import the downloaded information into QuickBooks.

NOTE Regardless of the type of connection you have, remember that the online balance you see usually isn't a true picture of your cash balance, because it doesn't show *all* transactions, such as checks you've written that the bank hasn't received.

Regardless of which type of connection you use, connecting to your financial institution begins in the Bank Feeds Center (choose Banking→Bank Feeds→Bank Feeds Center). The first step in the process is exchanging data with your bank; you send any online banking items you've created, like online bill payments or messages you want to send to your financial institution. Once you've exchanged data, QuickBooks tries to match the transactions in your company file with the ones you've downloaded. If it can't match some of the transactions, you step in and tell it what to do. The rest of this chapter explains the whole process.

QuickBooks' Online Banking Modes

The Bank Feeds Center offers two modes to satisfy everyone's tastes. Express mode has so many nifty features, it's the hands-down winner. Classic mode (known as Register mode in earlier versions of QuickBooks) is still around and comes in handy in a few situations. Here's what each one does:

- **Express mode**. The best feature of this mode—which is covered in detail beginning on page 617—is that you can match downloaded transactions to *any* transaction in your company file without leaving the Bank Feeds Center. For example, you can match a downloaded deposit to an open invoice or a paid invoice where the money is sitting in the Undeposited Funds account (page

657), or simply add the downloaded transaction to QuickBooks. You can also add multiple unmatched transactions to your register or delete downloaded items that you've already taken care of in QuickBooks.

In this mode, the Bank Feeds Center shows your online bank account's balance next to the one from your QuickBooks account. After you download transactions, a status area summarizes the work the program has done and what's still left to do. For example, you can see how many transactions QuickBooks matched automatically, how many need your review, and how many you added or changed.

NOTE If you use multiple currencies, Express mode displays only payees and accounts based in U.S. dollars. To see *all* payees and accounts, use Classic mode instead.

Express mode also automatically creates *renaming rules* (page 627) to rename the often-inscrutable names that banks give payees. These rules are more flexible than the aliases that Classic mode sets up. For example, if the payee for a downloaded credit card charge shows up as "Conoco #123-63?#^$&*," you can edit a renaming rule so that the Payee field reads, say, "Conoco" or simply "Gas." From then on, QuickBooks replaces "Conoco #123-63?#^$&*" with "Conoco" or "Gas."

TIP Although you can switch between online banking modes, you're more likely to pick one mode and stick with it. To switch modes, choose Banking→Bank Feeds→Change Bank Feeds Mode. QuickBooks opens the Preferences dialog box to the Checking category's Company Preferences tab, so you can choose the Express Mode or Classic Mode option. When you click OK, QuickBooks closes all open windows to switch modes (and doesn't reopen them when it's done).

- **Classic mode**. This mode is your only option if you have accounts in currencies *other* than U.S. dollars. It lets you see your full account register when you're matching transactions, which is helpful if QuickBooks doesn't find a match. You can scroll through the register and correct a discrepancy that prevented the program from matching a QuickBooks transaction to its downloaded sibling. You can also create aliases to rename payees, similar to Express mode's renaming rules. Classic mode is covered starting on page 626.

NOTE Classic mode doesn't recognize renaming rules you've created in Express mode, nor does Express mode recognize the aliases you created in Classic mode.

Downloading Statements with Web Connect

If your bank communicates via Web Connect (page 613), you can download a file of your transactions and import it into QuickBooks. The easiest way to do that is to use your web browser (such as Internet Explorer or Firefox) to log into your financial institution's website directly. On the website, click the button that creates a file of your transactions, which may be labeled something like "Download to QuickBooks."

Then you can import that file into QuickBooks to load the recent transactions into your company file; simply choose Banking→Bank Feeds→Import Web Connect File.

NOTE You can also access your bank's website from within QuickBooks. In the Bank Feeds Center, choose the financial institution to connect to, and then click the Download Transactions button (if you're in Classic mode, its label reads "Send/Receive" instead). A QuickBooks browser window opens and displays your bank's website; use your customer ID and PIN or password to log in.

Creating Online Items for Direct Connections

Banks that use direct connections can do more than those that use Web Connect. Depending on which services your bank provides, you can do some or all of the following tasks online:

- Receive transactions that cleared in your account
- Pay bills
- Exchange messages with your bank
- Transfer funds between accounts

You don't have to take any action to *receive* transactions from your accounts. Every time you open the Bank Feeds window, QuickBooks automatically sets up a request for cleared transactions from your bank accounts. This section describes what you have to do in QuickBooks to set up electronic bill payments, messages you want to send to your bank, and online transfers between accounts.

If you use Express mode, in the Bank Feeds window's "Send items to your bank" section, the Create New button comes with a drop-down list that lets you create online transactions for the online services you've signed up for with your financial institution or Intuit (Figure 24-2). If you use Classic mode, online items appear in the Items To Send section of the Bank Feeds window.

PAYING BILLS ONLINE

Whether you use the bill-paying service that your bank provides or subscribe to QuickBooks Bill Pay, you don't have to use any special dialog boxes or windows to make electronic payments. However, changing the payment method in a transaction works only when the bank account associated with payments is activated for online bill payment. Here's how to turn the three ways you make payments into electronic transactions:

- **Pay Bills**. In the Pay Bills window (page 195), in the Method drop-down list, choose Online Bank Pmt.
- **Write Checks**. In the Write Checks window's Main tab (page 203), turn on the Pay Online checkbox (which appears only if the multiple currency preference is turned *off* [page 656]).

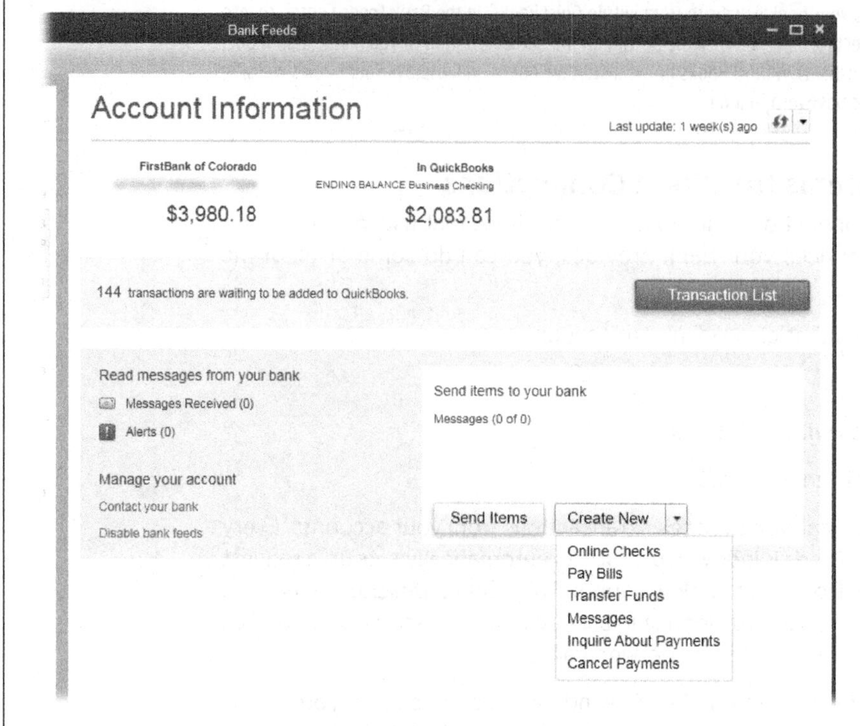

FIGURE 24-2

If you use Express mode and you've signed up for the corresponding online service with your bank or Intuit, you can create online transactions and messages by heading to the Bank Feeds window's "Send items to your bank" section, clicking the Create New button, and then choosing an entry like Online Checks, Pay Bills, and so on. (You can also create online transactions in the corresponding transaction windows, as described in the following sections.)

If you use Classic mode, you create these items in the corresponding transaction windows instead.

- **Account register window**. If you "write" checks by entering transactions in your checking account's register window (page 374), you can turn a transaction into an online payment by typing *Send* in the Number cell.

When you set up a payment as an online transaction, QuickBooks adds the payment to your list of items to send to your bank. Then, when you open the Bank Feeds window, you'll see these payments in the "Send items to your bank" section (or, if you're using Classic mode, the Items To Send section).

When you tell QuickBooks to send transactions (page 617), it sends these electronic payments along with any of your other requests. Once the bill-payment service receives your online payment info, it transfers money from your account to the vendor's account—providing that the vendor accepts electronic payments. Otherwise, the bill-payment service generates a paper check and mails it to the vendor.

SENDING A MESSAGE TO YOUR BANK

If you have an email address for your bank, you can always send messages to it by using your regular email program. (Most bank websites also include a link to send a message to the bank.) But if your bank can send messages through QuickBooks, those messages show up in the program's Bank Feeds window. By sending messages through QuickBooks, you can see all the messages that you've exchanged (until you decide to delete them).

Choose Banking→Bank Feeds→"Create a Message for your Bank," and QuickBooks opens the Bank Feeds Message window. You shouldn't have any trouble figuring out what to do in the window's fields:

- In the "Message to" drop-down list, choose the bank you want to send a message to. QuickBooks automatically timestamps the message with the current date and time and puts your company's name in the From box.
- In the Subject box, type a short but informative blurb.
- If you have more than one account enabled for online services, in the Regarding Account drop-down list, choose the appropriate one.
- In the Message box, type your comment or question.
- If you want to keep a hard copy of the message, click Print before you click OK to send it.

TRANSFERRING FUNDS BETWEEN ACCOUNTS

If you have two accounts at the same financial institution and they're both set up for online banking, you can set up online funds transfers between them in QuickBooks. To get started, choose Banking→Transfer Funds as you would for a non-electronic transfer (page 388). But in the Transfer Funds Between Accounts window, in addition to filling in the fields, be sure to turn on the Online Funds Transfer checkbox. When you save the transaction, QuickBooks adds the transfer as an item to send to your bank.

NOTE Online funds transfers using QuickBooks work only with two bank-feed-enabled accounts at the *same* bank. In other words, you can't transfer funds electronically using QuickBooks if the accounts are at different financial institutions or if you've set up a bank feed for one of the accounts at your bank but not the other.

Banking Online Using Express Mode

Express mode makes it easy to see what's going on with your accounts. You can see online balances, downloaded transactions, and the work you have to do to match them to transactions in your company file. You can do everything you need to do to match downloaded transactions to the ones in QuickBooks without leaving the Bank Feeds window.

Sending and Receiving Transactions

Every time you go online, QuickBooks automatically requests newly cleared transactions from your financial institution. If you've set up items to send to your bank, connecting to it pushes those along, too. Here's what you do to send requests and receive replies in Express mode:

1. **Choose Banking→Bank Feeds→Bank Feeds Center.**

   The Bank Feeds window opens.

2. **If you have bank feeds set up with more than one bank (say, a checking account at one bank and a credit card at another), in the account list on the Bank Feeds window's left, click the one you want to connect to.**

   As Figure 24-3 shows, the window displays your balance according to your financial institution as of the last update and the balance in the corresponding QuickBooks account. The "Last update" label shows how recently you synchronized the QuickBooks account with your online account.

   If you have any items to send to your bank (like messages you've written or online transfers you've created, as described on page 615), they appear in the "Send items to your bank" section. QuickBooks selects all the requests you've set up to send to your bank.

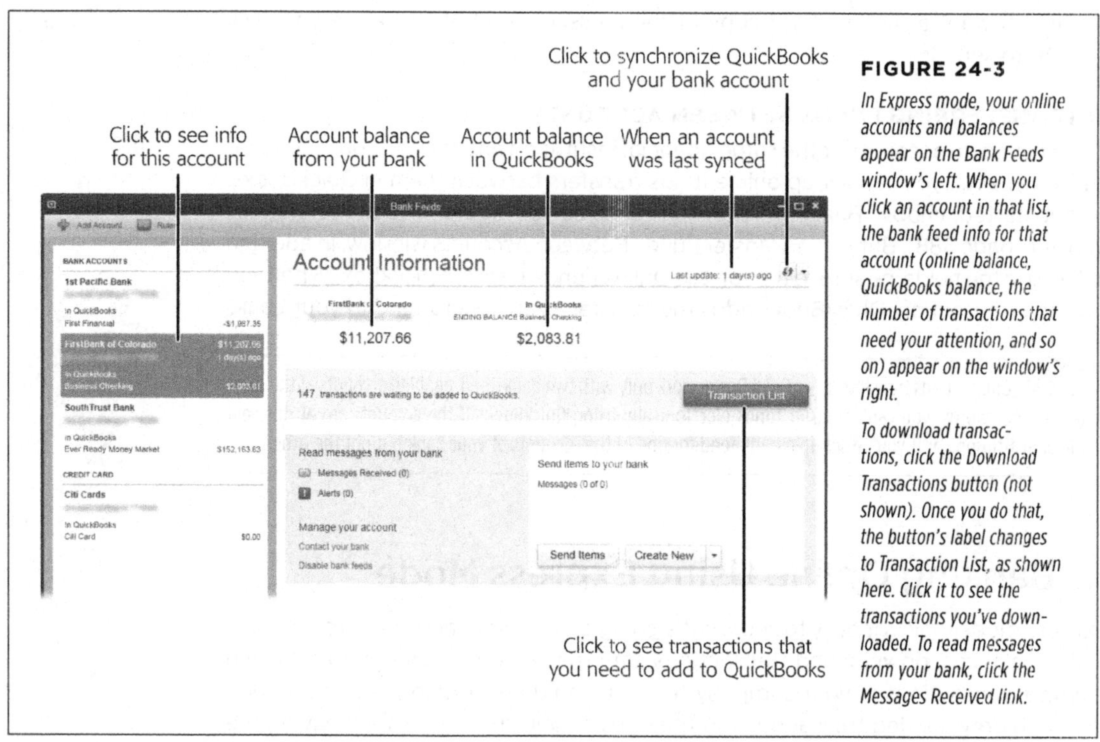

FIGURE 24-3

In Express mode, your online accounts and balances appear on the Bank Feeds window's left. When you click an account in that list, the bank feed info for that account (online balance, QuickBooks balance, the number of transactions that need your attention, and so on) appear on the window's right.

To download transactions, click the Download Transactions button (not shown). Once you do that, the button's label changes to Transaction List, as shown here. Click it to see the transactions you've downloaded. To read messages from your bank, click the Messages Received link.

3. **If you want to edit or delete any items in the "Send items to your bank" section, do that now—*before* you go online. Once you're connected, it's too late.**

   To edit an item like a funds transfer or bill payment you're sending, select the item, and then click Edit. Make your changes, and then click OK. To remove an item like a funds transfer you no longer need, select it and then click Delete.

4. **When the items you want to send are ready, click the Download Transactions button.**

   If you downloaded transactions previously and haven't processed them yet, the button's label reads "Transaction List" instead (as shown in Figure 24-3). If that's the case, you can synchronize the account by clicking the Synchronize button's down arrow (it's at the window's top right and its icon looks like two arrows pointing in opposite directions), and then choosing "Sync this account" or "Sync all for this bank."

   You may briefly see an Update Branding Files message box while QuickBooks and your financial institution talk to each other.

5. **In the "Access to [institution name]" dialog box that appears, type your password or PIN, and then click OK.**

   You enter this info so QuickBooks can communicate with your financial institution. While they're communicating, the word "Updating" appears at the top right of the Bank Feeds window. In addition, the Download Transactions button's label changes to "Downloading." When the two are done talking, the Online Transmission Summary dialog box tells you how many accounts it updated and how many transactions it downloaded.

6. **In the Online Transmission Summary dialog box, click Close.**

   The Account Information section shows the balances of your online accounts and the number of items QuickBooks received, as shown in Figure 24-3.

Matching Transactions

Every time you connect to your financial institution, QuickBooks downloads all the transactions that have cleared since the last time you went online. This section describes how to match downloaded transactions using Express mode.

NOTE The first time you download transactions from an online account, QuickBooks looks at cleared *and* uncleared transactions in your account register. For all subsequent downloads, the program tries to match only transactions that haven't already cleared.

After you send and receive transactions (as described in the previous section), the number of transactions that QuickBooks retrieved appears to the left of the Transaction List button, as shown in Figure 24-3. Here's how you process the items that QuickBooks received:

1. **In the Bank Feeds window, click the Transaction List button.**

   QuickBooks opens the Transactions List window (Figure 24-4) and tries to match the downloaded transactions to the ones you've already entered in the program. After QuickBooks completes its matchmaking, the status bar at the top of the window labeled "Auto" shows how many transactions the program matched on its own. The status bar labeled "Need Your Review" shows how many transactions you have to help it with. In the transaction table, the status of matched transactions is set to Auto, as shown in Figure 24-4, and you don't have to do anything to them; QuickBooks automatically marks them as cleared in the bank account's register (page 374).

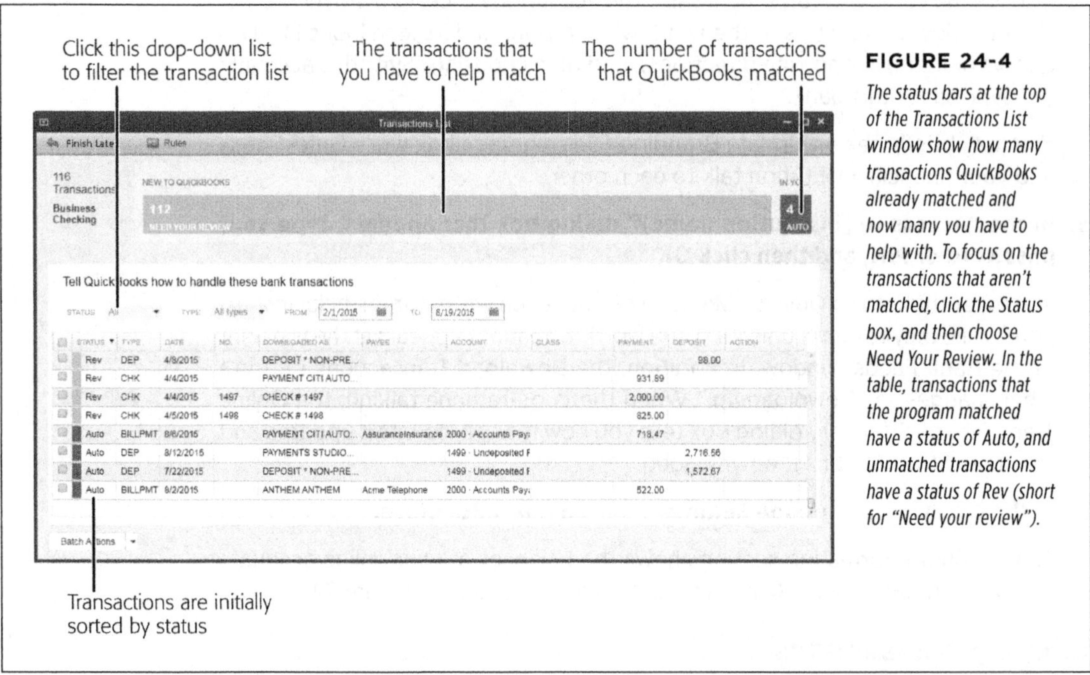
Click this drop-down list to filter the transaction list
The transactions that you have to help match
The number of transactions that QuickBooks matched
Transactions are initially sorted by status

FIGURE 24-4

The status bars at the top of the Transactions List window show how many transactions QuickBooks already matched and how many you have to help with. To focus on the transactions that aren't matched, click the Status box, and then choose Need Your Review. In the table, transactions that the program matched have a status of Auto, and unmatched transactions have a status of Rev (short for "Need your review").

NOTE Depending on what you do with downloaded transactions, you'll see different bars in the status area. For example, if you add info to transactions, the Changed bar appears. And if you create new transactions from ones you download, the Add bar appears.

2. **If you want to filter the transaction list, click the Status button above the transaction table, and then choose Need Your Review to look at the transactions QuickBooks couldn't match. Or click one of the status bars above the transaction table to show only those transactions in the table.**

   Choose "Changed by Rules" instead to see the transactions whose payees QuickBooks renamed using renaming rules (page 627). If you want to make *sure* that QuickBooks matched transactions correctly, choose Auto Matched to see only the transactions that the program matched.

   You can also filter the list by transaction type or date range. For example, to focus on deposits, in the Type drop-down list, choose DEP. To see only transactions that occurred within a specific time frame, choose dates in the From and To boxes.

NOTE For transactions without check numbers, QuickBooks matches a downloaded transaction with the oldest transaction of a matching amount. For example, suppose you withdrew $200 from your checking account twice last month. When you download a $200 withdrawal transaction, QuickBooks automatically matches it with the older of those two transactions.

If QuickBooks matched *every* transaction, your work is done (if you open the account's register [page 374], you'll see a lightning bolt in the Cleared column for every matched transaction). If you're not so lucky, the next section tells you how to handle unmatched transactions.

NOTE When you reconcile an account (page 389), the mark in the Cleared column changes from a lightning bolt to a checkmark for transactions that have been reconciled.

Matching Unmatched Transactions

Unsuccessful attempts to match transactions can happen for several reasons, but the source of the problem is *almost* always a mistake or omission in your QuickBooks account register. If you forgot to record a transaction in QuickBooks before you downloaded transactions, this section tells you how to make everything match up. The box on page 625 describes other problems you might encounter and how to correct them.

MATCHING DEPOSITS

When you use the Receive Payments window to record check or credit card payments you receive, you might place the payment in your Undeposited Funds account and then forget to make the deposit to your bank account using the Make Deposits window (page 370). Or you might forget to receive the payment in your company file in the first place. No worries. As Figure 24-5 shows, QuickBooks can match these deposits to payments in your Undeposited Funds account or even to invoices that are still open.

In the Transactions List window, if a downloaded deposit has a status of Rev, you have to help the program match it to a transaction in your company file. In QuickBooks, there are four ways to handle deposits:

- **Payments in the Undeposited Funds account**. If you used the Receive Payments window to record a customer payment and the money is sitting in the Undeposited Funds account (page 657), click the unmatched deposit's Action cell, click the down arrow that appears, and then choose Add More Details. In the "Transaction Details - Add More Details" dialog box (Figure 24-5, foreground), click the Undeposited Funds tab if it isn't selected. Turn on the checkbox for the received payment that corresponds to the deposit, and then click the Add to QuickBooks button at the bottom of the dialog box. If you look at your bank account register, you'll see that the deposit now has a lightning bolt in its Cleared cell to indicate that it's matched with a transaction downloaded from your bank.

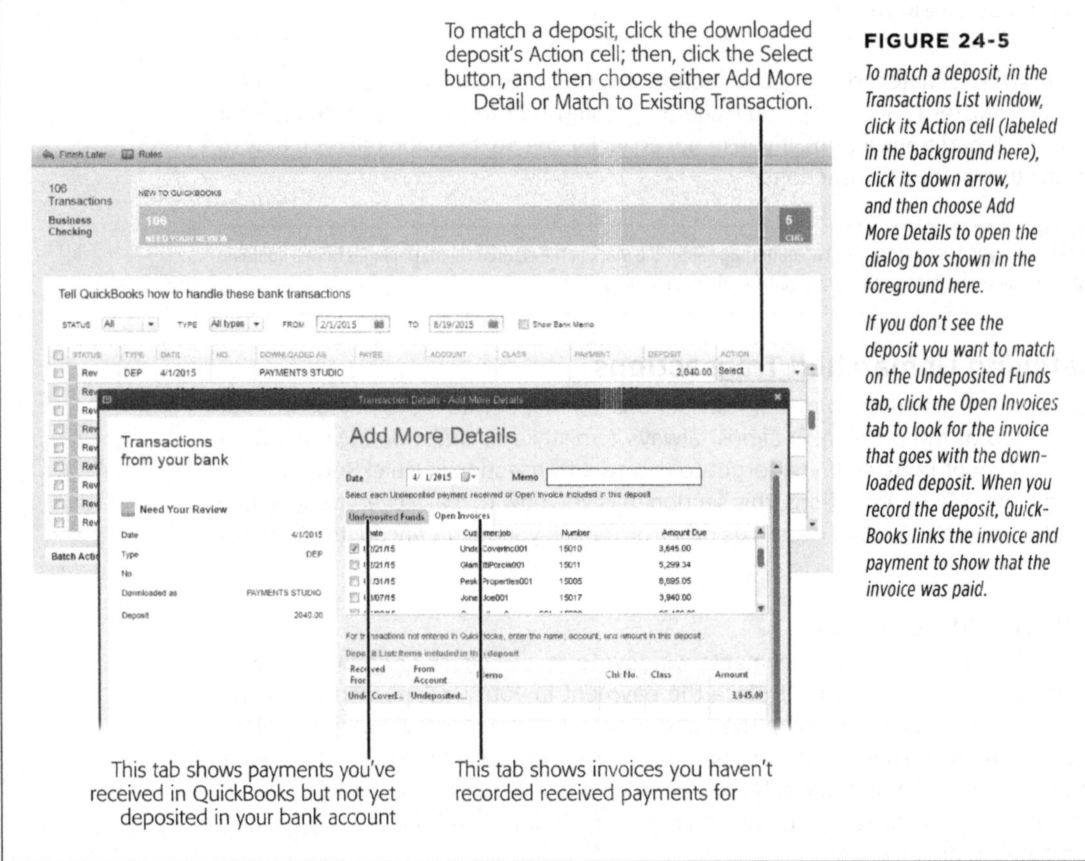
To match a deposit, click the downloaded deposit's Action cell; then, click the Select button, and then choose either Add More Detail or Match to Existing Transaction.
Tell QuickBooks how to handle these bank transactions
Transactions from your bank
Need Your Review
Add More Details
This tab shows payments you've received in QuickBooks but not yet deposited in your bank account
This tab shows invoices you haven't recorded received payments for

FIGURE 24-5

To match a deposit, in the Transactions List window, click its Action cell (labeled in the background here), click its down arrow, and then choose Add More Details to open the dialog box shown in the foreground here.

If you don't see the deposit you want to match on the Undeposited Funds tab, click the Open Invoices tab to look for the invoice that goes with the downloaded deposit. When you record the deposit, QuickBooks links the invoice and payment to show that the invoice was paid.

- **Deposits for open invoices**. If you haven't recorded a received payment in QuickBooks, the money is still tied up in an open invoice, which means it's sitting in the Accounts Receivable account. To match a deposit to an open invoice, in the "Transaction Details – Add More Details" dialog box, click the Open Invoices tab shown in Figure 24-5, foreground, turn on the checkbox for the invoice that corresponds to the deposit, and then click Add to QuickBooks.
- **Existing transactions**. If the deposit transaction is sitting in your account register but QuickBooks didn't match it with the downloaded transaction, click the unmatched deposit's Action cell, click the down arrow that appears, and then choose "Match to Existing Transaction." In the "Transaction Details - Match to Existing Transaction" dialog box's unmatched transaction table, click the transaction that corresponds to the deposit, and then click the Confirm Match button at the bottom of the dialog box.

- **Other deposits**. If you receive some other type of deposit that you haven't recorded in any way in QuickBooks (like an insurance claim refund, say), you can record the deposit's info directly in the Transaction List window's table. In the deposit's Payee cell, choose the customer or vendor who sent the money, and in the Account cell, choose the account to which you want to assign the deposit. Then click the deposit's Action cell, click the down arrow that appears, and then choose Quick Add. (If the Rule Creation dialog box appears, click OK to create a renaming rule that renames the downloaded payee to the one you typed in the Payee cell. To skip the renaming rule, turn off its checkbox, and then click OK.) QuickBooks adds the deposit to your account register and, if this is the first item you've added during this session, the Add status bar appears at the top of the Transactions List window. (If you've already added other transactions, the number displayed in the Add status bar increases by 1.)

TIP If your deposit represents several checks from several customers, in the "Transaction Details - Add More Details" dialog box, you can select more than one open invoice or undeposited funds entry, and add more than one item directly in the Deposit List table. Below the Deposit List, the "Difference remaining" value shows the discrepancy between the deposit amount and the items you've selected. When the difference equals 0.00, you're ready to click Add to QuickBooks.

MATCHING CHECKS AND EXPENSES

When there's no sign of a check transaction in QuickBooks that matches the one you downloaded, you may have forgotten to enter the transaction or created a bill but then forgotten to record that you paid it—or someone is stealing from your account.

In the Transactions List window (Figure 24-4), the amount of a check or bill payment appears in the Payment column. A value in the No. column tells you the payment is a check; if there's no value in this column, the payment is a bank charge, bank transaction, or electronic payment.

Here's how to match checks and payments in the Transactions List window:

- **Checks or charges that aren't bill payments**. These payments include any checks you wrote or electronic payments you made without recording a bill in QuickBooks, or bank charges like monthly service fees and bounced-check charges. To record one of these expenses, in the payment's Payee cell, choose the customer or vendor you paid, and in the Account cell, choose the account to which you want to assign the expense. (When you do this, QuickBooks creates a rule that automatically renames future transactions with the same Downloaded As value to the payee name you selected. See the box on page 627 for the scoop on renaming rules.) Then click the payment's Action cell, click the down arrow that appears, and then choose Quick Add. QuickBooks adds the transaction to your account register and, if this is the first item you've added during this session, the Add status bar appears at the top of the Transactions List window. (If you've already added other transactions, the number displayed in the Add status bar increases by 1.)

TIP If you want to add more information about the transaction, like splitting the amount between several accounts or adding a memo, click the payment's Action cell, click the down arrow that appears, and then choose Add More Details. In the "Transaction Details - Add More Details" dialog box (Figure 24-5, foreground), fill in the Memo box or choose additional accounts. Then click the Add to QuickBooks button at the bottom of the dialog box.

- **Bill payments**. For downloaded transactions that correspond to QuickBooks bill payments, you need to link the payment and the bill so that the bill shows up as paid in QuickBooks. If you recorded the bill but not the bill *payment* in QuickBooks (page 194), click the unmatched payment's Action cell, click the down arrow that appears, and then choose "Select Bills to Mark as Paid." In the "Transaction Details - Select Bills to Mark as Paid" dialog box (Figure 24-6), choose the vendor in the Vendor drop-down list. Turn on the checkbox for the bill that corresponds to the payment, and then click the Add to QuickBooks button at the bottom of the dialog box.

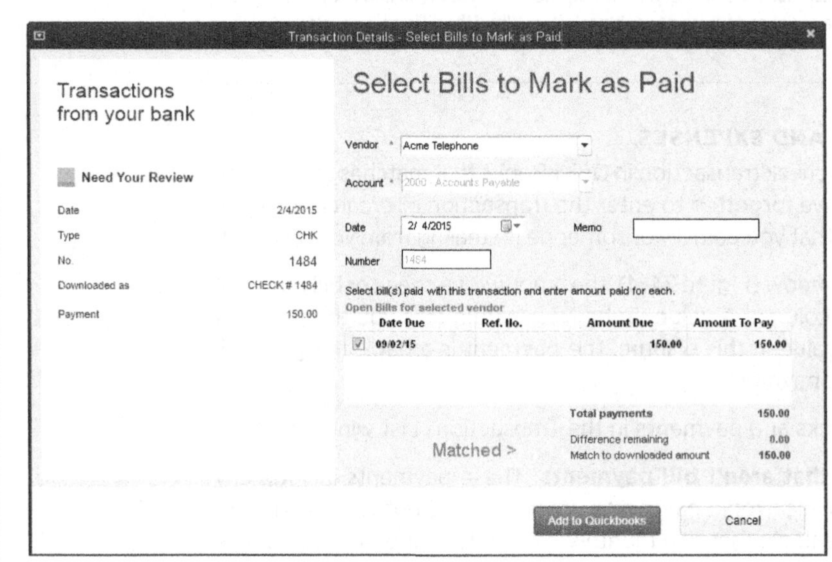

FIGURE 24-6

If you wrote one check to pay several of a vendor's bills, turn on the checkboxes for all the bills that the check covers. As you turn on checkboxes, QuickBooks updates the "Difference remaining" value to show the discrepancy between the downloaded transaction's amount and the total of the bills you selected. When this value equals 0.00, click Add to QuickBooks to save the match.

- **Match an expense manually**. If QuickBooks doesn't match an ATM withdrawal or other expense correctly, you can also match payments to an existing transaction. Click the unmatched payment's Action cell, click the down arrow that appears, and then choose "Match to Existing Transaction." In the "Transaction Details - Match to Existing Transaction" dialog box that appears, the table shows register transactions that haven't yet been matched. For example, if you have two ATM withdrawals, you can pick the one that goes with the downloaded transaction and then click Confirm Match.

TROUBLESHOOTING MOMENT

Why Transactions Don't Match

If you recorded *all* your transactions in QuickBooks but your downloaded transactions refuse to match up with what's in your company file, small discrepancies are probably to blame. For example, with downloaded transactions that include check numbers, QuickBooks first looks for a matching check number and, if it finds one, only then does it look at the amount. So the program considers check transactions matched only if both the check number *and* amount match. If the check already exists in QuickBooks, there are two reasons why the program wouldn't be able to match it:

- **The check number in your register is wrong**. For example, if you handwrote several checks at the same time, you might have entered them in QuickBooks in a different order than the paper checks you wrote out. Open the account's register window (in the Chart of Accounts window, double-click the name of the account), and then find the transaction and edit its check number. QuickBooks might warn you about duplicate check numbers, but go ahead and use the updated number. After you've edited all the check transactions with incorrect numbers, you should be back to unique check numbers.
- **The amounts on the checks don't match**. If the amounts disagree, first look at the account register to see if you typed the amount correctly; if not, fix it.

If transactions from the bank don't include check numbers, QuickBooks scans transactions without check numbers in your account register for matching amounts. If it doesn't find a match, you might have forgotten to record the transaction in the Pay Bills window (page 195), or the check doesn't link to a bill (page 202).

If you're *sure* that a check amount you recorded is correct but the downloaded check amount is different, change the amount in QuickBooks. (Your bank won't go back and edit that transaction.) Then contact your bank and work out the discrepancy. If the bank was at fault, it will issue a separate transaction to correct the error, and you can then download that transaction.

If the amounts for other types of transactions, like ATM withdrawals or debit card purchases, don't match or you haven't recorded the transactions in QuickBooks, then the program can't match them.

Adding Multiple Transactions

If you write only a few checks and receive a few payments each month, matching each one individually isn't too painful. But you have better things to do than match *hundreds* of transactions one by one. Happily, as long as you don't need to match downloaded transactions to open transactions in QuickBooks or do anything fancy like create splits, you can add several transactions at once.

In the Transactions List window, turn on the checkmark cells for the transactions you want to add. Next, click the down arrow to the right of the Batch Actions button, and then choose Add/Approve. You can also fill in details for several transactions and add them all at once. To do this, simply fill in their Payee and Account cells and turn on their checkmark cells. After you do that, click the Batch Actions down arrow, and then choose Add/Approve.

Deleting Downloaded Transactions

Say you've reconciled your credit card account to your statement. You then go online and download transactions only to find that you've downloaded transactions you've *already* reconciled. You don't have to match the downloaded transactions because your account is already matched up with your bank's records, so you want to delete the downloaded transactions. You can do this via the Transactions List window (to open it, in the Bank Feeds window, click Transaction List). Here's how to choose and delete transactions one at a time or as a batch:

- **Delete individual transactions**. To delete a single transaction, click its Action cell, click it again to display the drop-down list shown in Figure 24-7, and then choose Ignore. In the Confirm Delete message box, click Yes to delete the downloaded transaction. If you change your mind and want to keep it, click No instead.
- **Delete several transactions**. This option is perfect if you want to delete all the transactions that you've already reconciled. In the transaction table's first column, click the checkmark cells for each transaction you want to delete. Then, at the window's bottom left, click the down arrow to the right of the Batch Actions button and choose Ignore. In the Confirm Delete message box, click Yes to delete the transactions, or click No to keep them.

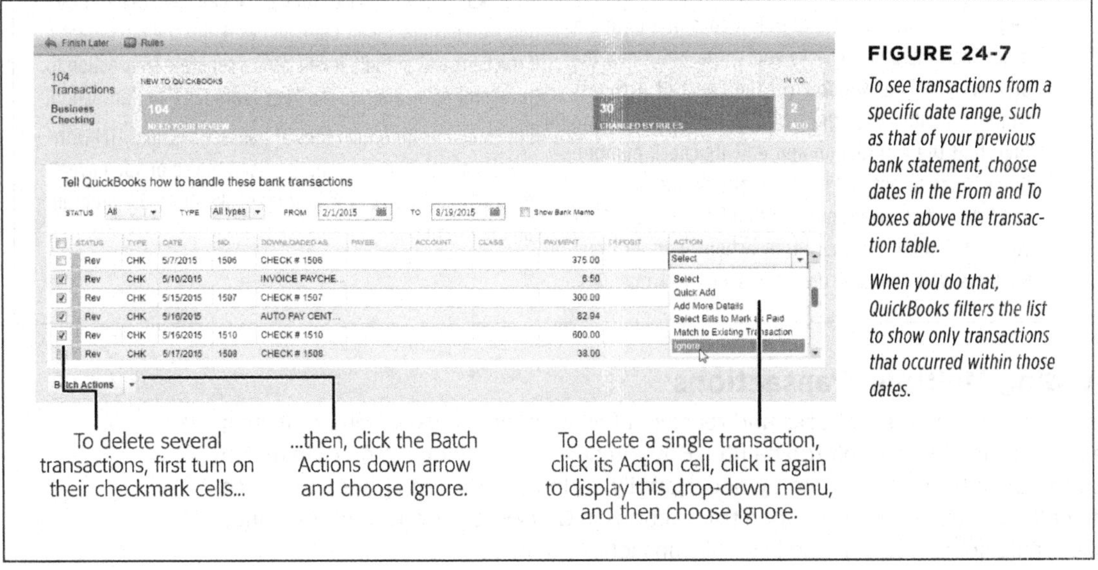

Tell QuickBooks how to handle these bank transactions
Batch Actions
To delete several transactions, first turn on their checkmark cells...
...then, click the Batch Actions down arrow and choose Ignore.
To delete a single transaction, click its Action cell, click it again to display this drop-down menu, and then choose Ignore.

FIGURE 24-7

To see transactions from a specific date range, such as that of your previous bank statement, choose dates in the From and To boxes above the transaction table.

When you do that, QuickBooks filters the list to show only transactions that occurred within those dates.

Banking Online Using Classic Mode

The Bank Feeds Center's Classic mode lets you see your full account register, which makes it easy to find a matching transaction that QuickBooks doesn't recognize. You can edit transactions in the register to, for example, correct a typo that prevented the program from making a match. This section explains how to handle your online banking using Classic mode.

GEM IN THE ROUGH

Renaming Downloaded Payees

One drawback to downloading transactions is the crazy payee names that often show up. For example, a gas-station credit card charge downloads with the station's ID number—*Conoco #00092372918027*—or a payment to your favorite office supply store appears as *Internt PMT Have a Great Day 1429AZ#2*. You want payee names that make sense, like *Gasoline*, or that are at least consistent, like *Office Supply Heaven #121*. If you use Express mode, QuickBooks' *renaming rules* let you replace downloaded payee names with something short, sweet, and meaningful.

(If you use Classic mode, QuickBooks' *payee aliasing* feature lets you associate a downloaded payee name with a name in your company file, such as a vendor's or customer's name. However, you can't define tests, as described in the numbered steps below. That means that you can associate only one name with a downloaded payee using payee aliases.)

QuickBooks automatically creates renaming rules whenever you change the payee name for a downloaded transaction, but the renaming rules it creates might not be what you want. For example, suppose you want to rename any payees that include "Conoco" or "Valero," or you want to rename a payee only if its downloaded name is exactly "Acme Equipment." Here's how to edit a renaming rule:

1. At the top left of the Transactions List window, click Rules.
2. In the Action cell for the rule you want to edit, click the down arrow to the right of the Select button, and then choose Edit Rule on the drop-down menu.
3. In the Edit Rules Details dialog box, in the first drop-down list, click the down arrow to the right of the Description label, and then choose the test you want to use, like Starts With or Matches Exactly.
4. In the second box, type the value that appears in all the downloaded payee names for that vendor, such as *Acme Equipment*.
5. In the second drop-down list, choose either Rename or Categorize to change the payee field or the account, respectively.
6. If you chose Rename, then in the Payee Field To drop-down list, choose the payee name you want to use. If you chose Categorize, in the "It in the Following Account" drop-down list, choose an account.
7. Click Save.

To remove an existing renaming rule, click the down arrow to the right of the rule's Select button, and then choose Delete Rule.

QuickBooks learns from the renaming and categorizing you do in the transaction list and creates renaming rules of its own. The rules it creates have names like *_AutoGeneratedRule-1*.

Sending and Receiving Items

Choose Banking→Bank Feeds→Bank Feeds Center to open the Bank Feeds window. In Classic mode, this window is more compact than its Express mode sibling, as you can see in Figure 24-8.

To send requests to your bank, click Send/Receive. In the "Access to [your bank]" dialog box that appears, type your password or PIN, and then click OK. After you send your requests, the Online Transmission Summary dialog box tells you how many transactions QuickBooks downloaded from your bank. Click Close, and the Items Received From Financial Institution box shows the balances of your online accounts and any messages that your bank sent you.

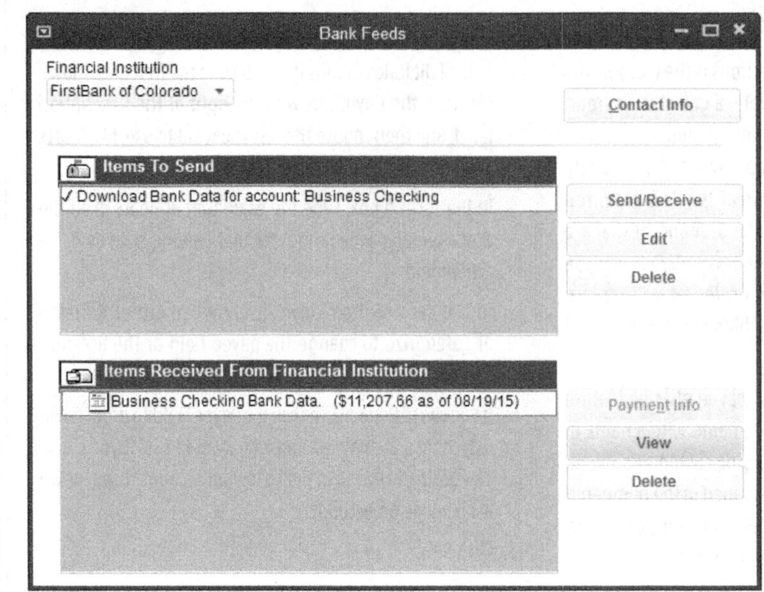

FIGURE 24-8

If you have online services set up with more than one bank (your checking account at one bank and a credit card at another, say), in the Financial Institution drop-down list, choose one to connect to. In the Items To Send box, QuickBooks automatically selects all requests (like downloading your transactions). If you don't want to send an item, click anywhere in its row to uncheck it. Then click Send/Receive to connect to the bank's website and send the selected requests.

Working with Online Items

In the Bank Feeds window (Figure 24-8), you can make changes to items you intend to send *before* you connect to your bank account. And after you receive items from your bank, you can view items or delete them in the same window. Here's how you use the window's various buttons:

- **Edit**. Before you go online in Classic mode, you can edit any items other than a request for a statement, like a funds transfer or bill payment you're sending. Simply select the item and then click Edit. Make the changes you want, and then click OK.

NOTE QuickBooks adds a request for a statement to the Items To Send list every time you open the Bank Feeds window (the request is labeled "Download Bank Data for account: [account name]"—Figure 24-8 shows an example). In this context, a *statement* is simply a list of the transactions that cleared in your account since the last time you retrieved information formatted in a way that QuickBooks can import.

- **Delete**. In Classic mode, the Bank Feeds window includes *two* Delete buttons, one for each of the window's two main boxes. Simply click the button to the right of the appropriate box to delete the items you've selected in it. For example, if you set up a funds transfer between accounts that you no longer need, in the Items To Send box, select the item, and then click the Delete button to its right.

You'll find that your bank is fond of sending you messages about new services or holidays. There's no reason to clutter the Items Received From Financial Institution box with these messages, so simply select them and then click Delete.

- **View**. In the Items Received From Financial Institution box, select an item and then click View to see it in its entirety. When you want to match the transactions in a statement to your QuickBooks bank account transactions, select the statement and then click View; the next section has more details.

Matching Transactions

Every time you connect to your financial institution (by clicking Send/Receive in the Bank Feeds window), QuickBooks requests a statement of all the transactions that have cleared since the last time you went online. After you connect, in the Items Received From Financial Institution box, you'll see an entry for the statement QuickBooks retrieved. To view the downloaded transactions and pull them into your company-file bank account, select this entry and then click View.

When you do, QuickBooks opens the Match Transactions window (Figure 24-9) and tries to match the downloaded transactions to the ones you've already entered in the program. If QuickBooks is able to match transactions, then at the bottom of the Match Transactions window, on the Downloaded Transactions tab, the status for those transactions is set to Matched and you don't have to do anything to them; QuickBooks automatically marks them as cleared in the register. Transactions that the program *can't* match have a status of Unmatched, as shown in Figure 24-9.

NOTE The first time you download transactions from an online account, QuickBooks looks at cleared *and* uncleared transactions in your account register. For all subsequent downloads, the program tries to match only transactions that haven't already cleared.

If QuickBooks matches every transaction, in the account register's Cleared column, you'll see a lightning bolt for every matched transaction and your work is done. If you're not so lucky, here's how to deal with the unmatched items:

- **Unmatched checks**. Select the check that you didn't enter in QuickBooks and then click Add One to Register. In the Add Unmatched Transaction dialog box that opens, you can choose one of three options. The program automatically selects the "Using the register" option. If you keep this option selected and click OK, the Add Unmatched Transaction dialog box closes. If the Name Not Found dialog box opens, click Cancel because you don't want to create a new name record in QuickBooks. In that window's register, you'll see a new transaction with its check number, date, and amount filled in. All you have to do is enter the payee and account, and then click Record.

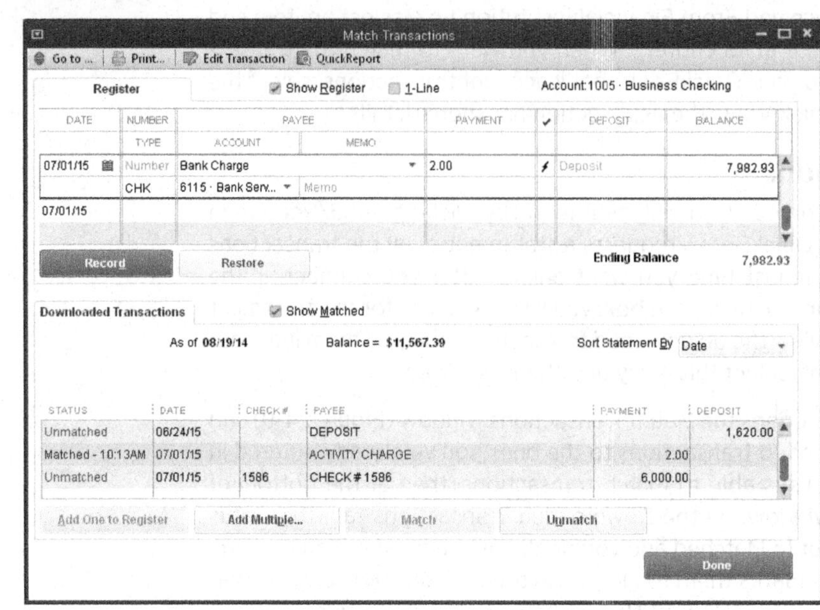

FIGURE 24-9

If you dutifully enter all your transactions before you download your statement, seeing dozens of unmatched transactions might make you nervous. To make QuickBooks compare the downloaded transactions with the ones in your account register, turn on the Show Register checkbox near the top of this window.

If you select the "As a payment made by check, using the Write Checks window" option and then click OK, QuickBooks opens the Write Checks window to a new check transaction and fills in the check number, date, and amount. Fill in the other fields (page 203), and then click Save & Close. If the Name Not Found dialog box opens when you click OK, click Cancel.

If you select the "As a payment for a previously created bill, using the Pay Bills window" option and then click OK, QuickBooks opens the Pay Bills window so you can select and pay the bill that corresponds to this unmatched transaction.

- **Unmatched deposits**. In the list of downloaded transactions, select the deposit, and then click Add One to Register. Similar to the Add Unmatched Transaction dialog box that opens for an unmatched check, the dialog box that opens when you click Add One to Register here contains three options. The program automatically selects the "Using the register" option. If you click OK, the Add Unmatched Transaction dialog box closes and the program adds the new deposit to the Match Transactions window's register with the date and amount filled in. Enter the payee and account, and then click Record.

  If you select the "As a deposit, using the Make Deposits window" option and then click OK, QuickBooks opens the "Payments to Deposit" window. Select the deposit in the list, and then click OK.

If you select the "As a payment on an invoice, using the Receive Payments window" option and then click OK, the Receive Payments window opens so you can apply the deposit to the invoice that corresponds to this unmatched deposit.

- **Bank charges**. For charges including monthly service fees, bounced-check charges, and so on, in the list of downloaded transactions, select the transaction, and then click Add One to Register. In the Add Unmatched Transaction dialog box that opens, leave the "Using the register" option selected and click OK. Back in the Match Transactions window, fill in the transaction's fields, and then click Record.

Adding Multiple Transactions

If you want to add *several* unmatched transactions to the register, in the Match Transactions window, click Add Multiple. The "Add Multiple Transactions to the Register" window opens and lists all the unmatched transactions. As you can see in Figure 24-10, the top half of the window lists transactions that are either ready to go or are missing an account. After you choose accounts for the transactions that don't have them, click Record.

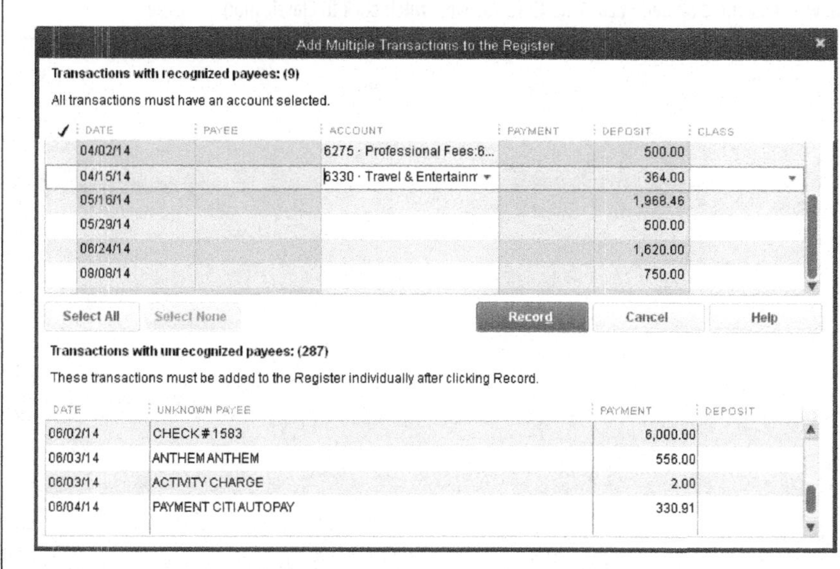

FIGURE 24-10

You can't do anything with the transactions listed at the bottom of this window that have unrecognized payees. To correct those transactions, close this window and, back in the Match Transactions window, select a transaction, and then click Add One to Register. You can then edit the payee name in the register. Repeat this process to fix the other transactions listed in the bottom of the window.

Deleting Downloaded Transactions

Classic mode doesn't give you a way to delete transactions on the Match Transactions window's Downloaded Transactions tab. If you've already reconciled your account and then downloaded the transactions, you might think you have to live with those unmatched transactions forever. But with some fancy footwork, you can get rid of those downloaded orphans. Here's what you do:

1. **At the top of the Match Transactions window, scroll in the register to find the reconciled transaction that pairs with an unmatched transaction.**

   An asterisk in the transaction's cleared cell (the one in the column whose heading is a checkmark) means that transaction is cleared; a checkmark indicates that it's reconciled.

2. **Keep clicking its cleared cell until the cell is blank.**

   As soon as the cleared cell is blank, QuickBooks automatically matches the register transaction and the downloaded transaction. You see a lightning bolt in the cleared cell to indicate the match, and the downloaded transaction disappears from the Downloaded Transactions tab.

3. **Click the cleared cell again until you see a checkmark.**

   The register transaction is back to being reconciled, and the downloaded transaction is gone forever.

TIP If you have *dozens* of transactions that you want to delete and the account doesn't use a foreign currency, switch to Express mode instead (see the Tip on page 614). Then you can delete the transactions in the Transactions List window as described on page 626. After that, you can switch back to Classic mode.

CHAPTER

25

Configuring Preferences to Fit Your Company

An organization's approach to accounting often depends on the type of business it is and its objectives, policies, procedures, and industry. For example, maybe you use inventory tracking and payroll—but maybe you don't. The way you and your accountant like to work also influences your organization's accounting practices. For instance, you might prefer the simplicity of cash accounting to the more intimate pairing of income and expenses that accrual accounting offers (see page xxii).

Enter QuickBooks, which has the Herculean task of satisfying every nuance of business operation and personal proclivity. The program's *preferences* are configurable settings that accommodate different business approaches and personal tastes. During installation, QuickBooks picks the settings likely to work for a majority of organizations. And if you used the QuickBooks Setup feature (page 9) to set up your company file, you might already have most preferences set the way you want.

You can change the program's preferences for each company file to match the way you work, such as whether you create estimates for jobs you go after and how you calculate the amount of inventory that's available. Preferences also let you turn on various QuickBooks features, such as estimates, sales tax, inventory, and payroll. Using QuickBooks for a while can make it clear which preferences you need to change. This chapter presents *all* the program's preferences and helps you determine which settings are appropriate for you and your organization.

NOTE You can toggle most preferences at any time, but you can't turn some preferences off once you turn them on, such as the multiple currencies preference. Before you change *any* preferences, back up your company file. Then feel free to tweak and tinker with your preferences.

Preferences: The Basics

You can't complain that QuickBooks doesn't offer enough preference settings—the program gives you 23 categories of preferences that control the program's behavior. Each category has several settings, so finding the ones that do what you want is the biggest challenge. To view and set preferences, open the Preferences dialog box by choosing Edit→Preferences.

On the left side of the dialog box is a pane that lists each preference category, as shown in Figure 25-1. To display the settings within a category, click the appropriate entry in this pane. QuickBooks highlights the icon you click to indicate that it's selected.

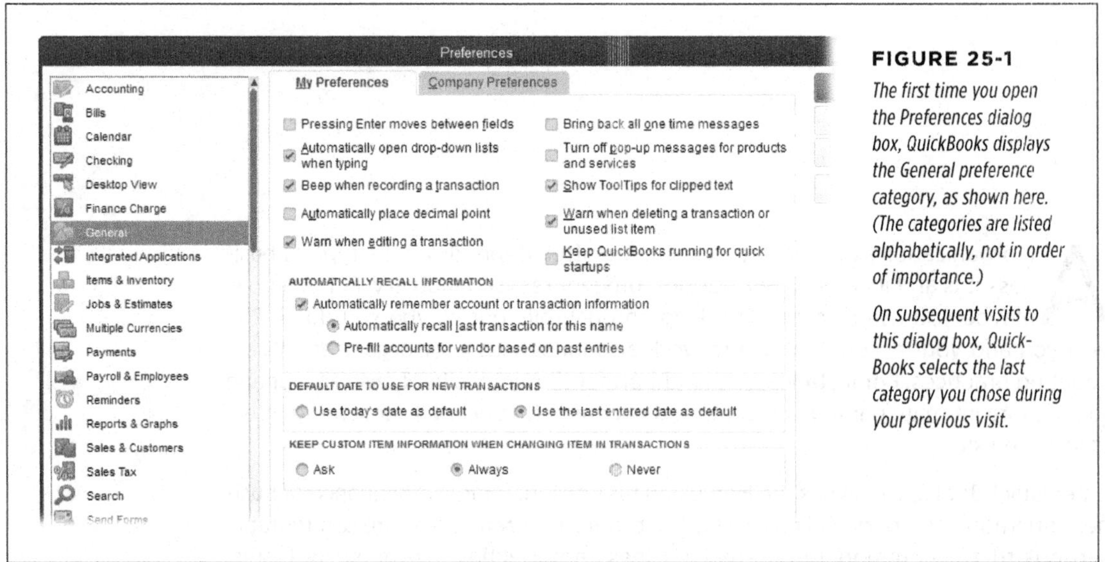

FIGURE 25-1

The first time you open the Preferences dialog box, QuickBooks displays the General preference category, as shown here. (The categories are listed alphabetically, not in order of importance.)

On subsequent visits to this dialog box, QuickBooks selects the last category you chose during your previous visit.

TIP On the right side of the Preferences dialog box, the Also See list identifies other preference categories that affect the one you're currently viewing.

To accommodate both company-wide and personal preferences, QuickBooks includes two tabs for each category:

- **My Preferences.** As you might expect, this tab contains options that people who log into QuickBooks can set for their QuickBooks sessions alone. For example, in the Desktop View category, you can choose options to determine whether you see multiple windows and whether QuickBooks saves the desktop when you close the company file—without forcing your tastes on everyone else.
- **Company Preferences.** Some preferences have to remain consistent for everyone in an organization. For example, the IRS won't tolerate some financial

reports produced using cash accounting and others using accrual accounting (see page xxii for the pros and cons of each method). The settings on this tab ensure consistency because they apply to *everyone* who logs into your company file. To make sure company preferences are set properly, only folks who log in as QuickBooks administrators (page 718) can change the settings on this tab.

NOTE If you're puzzled by QuickBooks' habit of opening the Preferences dialog box to a My Preferences tab that has no preferences, rest assured that Intuit has its reasons. Because only QuickBooks administrators can change settings on the Company Preferences tab, QuickBooks displays the My Preferences tab to avoid taunting the majority of people who log into the company file by showing them preferences they can't modify.

When you click OK to close the Preferences dialog box, QuickBooks saves the changes you made in the current category. But what if you're on an energetic mission to reset preferences in several categories? If you change preferences in one category and then click the icon for another category, QuickBooks asks you whether you want to save the changes in the category you're about to leave. Make sure you save what you want by selecting one of the following options:

- Click **Yes** to save the changes in the current category before switching to the category whose icon you clicked.
- Click **No** to discard your changes and move on to the category whose icon you clicked.
- Click **Cancel** to discard your changes and remain in the current category so you can make other choices.

The rest of this chapter explains each category of preferences. They're listed here in alphabetical order, just as they are in the Preferences dialog box. You'll also find preferences mentioned throughout this book where they apply to specific bookkeeping tasks.

Accounting

These preferences control key accounting practices, such as requiring that accounts be assigned to transactions and closing the books at the end of a fiscal year. Accounting practices stay the same throughout a company, so the preferences in this category all reside on the Company Preferences tab. Here's what they do:

NOTE In QuickBooks Premier and Enterprise, the My Preferences tab has one preference: the "Autofill memo in general journal entry" checkbox. Leave this setting turned on if you want QuickBooks to copy the memo you enter in the first line of a journal entry to every subsequent line of the entry.

- **Use account numbers**. If you follow a numbering standard for your accounts (page 53 shows a common one), turn on this checkbox so you can assign a number, in addition to a name, to each account you create.

TIP When you assign an account to a transaction—such as applying your rent check to the Rent expense account—you can locate the account in the Account drop-down list by typing either its number *or* the first few letters of its name.

- **Require accounts**. If remembering details isn't your strong suit, keeping this checkbox turned on forces you to assign an account to every item and transaction you create, which, in turn, creates a trail that you, your accountant, and the IRS can follow. With this checkbox turned on, when you click Record without an assigned account, QuickBooks informs you that you have to enter an account. To record the transaction, in the Warning message box, click OK, and then choose the account in the transaction's Account field. After that, when you click Record again, QuickBooks completes the transaction.

  If you turn this checkbox off and record transactions without assigned accounts, QuickBooks assigns the transaction amounts to either the Uncategorized Income or Uncategorized Expense account. For example, if you receive a payment from a customer and don't assign an account to the deposit, that income posts to the Uncategorized Income account.

WARNING If the IRS decides to audit your tax returns, you'll have to go back and move your uncategorized income and expenses into the right accounts to prove that you paid the right amount of taxes. And, if you happened to pay too little, the IRS will charge you penalties and interest.

- **Show lowest subaccount only**. If you use only top-level accounts in your chart of accounts, you have no need for this behavior. And if you don't use account numbers, this checkbox is grayed out. But if your chart of accounts is a hierarchy of accounts and subaccounts, as described in the box on page 60, turn on this checkbox so Account fields show only the subaccount's number and name instead of the full account path from the top-level account to the lowest subaccount. Figure 3-4 on page 60 shows examples of both behaviors.

- **Use class tracking for transactions**. If you want to track your business in more ways than accounts, items, customer types, and job types can offer, you can use classes (page 140) to add another type of categorization to your reports. For example, you can create classes to track business units' income and expenses, regardless of which types of customers they support or the type of work they do. To activate the class tracking feature, turn on this checkbox, which adds a Class field to every transaction window.

  — **Prompt to assign classes**. If you turn on class tracking, you should assign classes to *all* your class-related transactions; if you don't, reports organized by class won't accurately reflect your business performance. Turn on this checkbox so that QuickBooks reminds you when you forget to assign a class to a transaction.

- **Automatically assign general journal entry number**. Journal entries get their name from the traditional approach to accounting, in which accountants assign credits and debits to accounts in paper-based journals. There's no reason to turn this checkbox off. With it on, QuickBooks makes sure that each journal entry has a unique number, as shown in Figure 25-2. When you create a new journal entry, QuickBooks increments the previous journal entry number by one, which makes it easier for you and your accountant to refer to the correct journal entries.

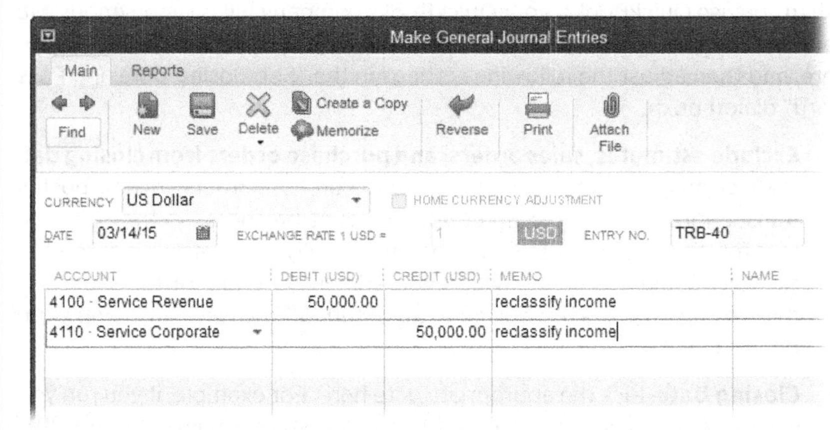

FIGURE 25-2

QuickBooks follows your lead in numbering journal entries. When you create your first journal entry, you can type a code in the Entry No. box, such as your initials and a sequence number (TRB-1, for example). As you create additional journal entries, QuickBooks increments the code to TRB-2, TRB-3, and so on.

NOTE If the previous journal entry's Entry No. box is blank, QuickBooks won't automatically assign a number to the next journal entry. So if you notice that QuickBooks has begun to shirk its automatic numbering duties, look for a journal entry with a blank Entry No. field and add numbers to any existing journal entries that don't have them. After that, when you add a new journal entry, QuickBooks will number it correctly.

- **Warn when posting a transaction to Retained Earnings**. QuickBooks automatically turns on this checkbox, and it's a good idea to leave it on. The program creates a Retained Earnings account to track past profits that you've retained in the company's coffers. For example, if your company earned $50,000 in 2015 and didn't distribute that money to the owners or as profit-sharing bonuses to employees, the money becomes Retained Earnings once your fiscal year 2016 begins. QuickBooks automatically updates the balance in the account at the beginning of a new fiscal year by transferring the previous year's net profit into it. With this preference turned on, QuickBooks warns you when you try to post a transfer directly to the Retained Earning account, which would create inaccurate records. (See the box on page 454 to learn how to differentiate your most recent year's retained earnings from earlier retained earnings.)
- **Date warnings**. If your books are up to date, then dates far in the past or future are usually mistakes. To receive warnings for dates like those, leave the "Warn if transactions are _ day(s) in the past" and "Warn if transactions are _ day(s) in the future" checkboxes turned on. The boxes are initially set to 90 for past dates and 30 for future dates, but you can change them.

- **Closing date**. After producing the financial reports for a fiscal year and paying corporate income taxes, most companies *close their books*, which means locking that fiscal year's transactions so no one can change anything. By closing the books, you ensure that your past transactions continue to match what you submitted to your accountant, reported to the IRS, and communicated to your shareholders.

  When you use QuickBooks, your QuickBooks company file is synonymous with your "books." Therefore, you close your books by clicking Set Date/Password here, and then adjust the following settings in the "Set Closing Date and Password" dialog box:

  - **Exclude estimates, sales orders, and purchase orders from closing date restrictions**. Estimates, sales orders, and purchase orders are non-posting transactions—they don't affect your account balances, so they don't affect the financial reports you generate. Initially, this setting is turned off so QuickBooks warns you when you edit those types of transactions if they're dated before the closing date. To turn off the warnings, simply turn *on* this checkbox.
  - **Closing Date**. Pick the appropriate date here. For example, if you run your company on a calendar year and just reported and paid taxes for 2015, type or choose *12/31/2015*.
  - **Password**. You can assign a password so that you can edit, delete, or create transactions that alter account balances in closed books. To do so, type the password in the Closing Date Password and Confirm Password boxes, and then click OK. That way, if you have to edit a transaction prior to the closing date, you'll first have to type the password to tell QuickBooks you mean it.

Bills

This category lets you specify how you want to handle bills that vendors send you. The My Preferences tab is empty, so these settings all appear on the Company Preferences tab:

- **Bills are due _ days after receipt**. Initially, QuickBooks sets this preference so that bills you enter show a due date 10 days after the date of the bill. (For instance, if you receive a bill dated June 15 and you enter that date in the Enter Bills window's Date field, QuickBooks automatically changes the Bill Due field to June 25.) This value is fine in most cases. If a bill arrives that's due in a different number of days, you can simply change its due date in the Enter Bills window's Bill Due field.

NOTE If you assign terms to your vendors (page 84), then when you choose a vendor in the Enter Bills window, the program calculates the bill's due date based on the bill's Date field and those terms rather than using the "Bills are due _ days after receipt" value.

- **Warn about duplicate bill numbers from same vendor**. Surely you don't want to pay the same bill twice, so be sure to leave this checkbox turned on so QuickBooks warns you that you're entering a bill with the same number as one you already entered from the same vendor.
- **Paying bills**. If you want QuickBooks to automatically apply to your bills any credits and discounts to which you're entitled, turn on the "Automatically use credits" and "Automatically use discounts" checkboxes. For example, if you've earned an early payment discount and also have a $100 credit, QuickBooks applies these adjustments to your bill before calculating the total. If you turn on the "Automatically use discounts" checkbox, then in the Default Discount Account drop-down list, choose the account to which you post the discounts you take, such as an expense account specifically for vendor discounts.

Calendar

QuickBooks' Calendar window (page 486) shows you when transactions and to-dos are due, so you can be sure to perform the tasks you're supposed to, such as paying bills and following up on open invoices. Calendar preferences are all on the My Preferences tab, so that each person who works in the company file can choose what he sees:

- **Calendar settings**. The preferences in this section control the calendar's appearance. You can see one day, one week, or one month at a time. If you choose "Remember last view" in the "Calendar view" drop-down list, QuickBooks opens the calendar to the last duration you selected. For the weekly view, you can specify whether you want to see Monday through Friday or the entire week. Initially, the Show preference is set to All Transactions, but you can change it to Transactions Due or To Do, or choose a specific type of transaction, such as Invoice, Received Payment, or Bill.
- **Upcoming & past due settings**. On the right side of the Calendar window is a pane that lists to-dos and transactions that are coming up or overdue. You can use the Display drop-down menu here to tell QuickBooks to show or hide this pane, or better yet, show the pane only if there are upcoming or past-due items. Initially, the Calendar window shows what's coming up in the next 7 days and what was due in the past 60 days. You can change the period in the future to up to 31 days, while the past-due period can shrink to as few as 14 days.

Checking

Checking preferences let you adjust company-wide settings to control the appearance of the checks your company prints through QuickBooks. On the My Preferences tab for this category (Figure 25-3), you can tell QuickBooks which accounts to select automatically for several types of financial transactions. This section explains your options.

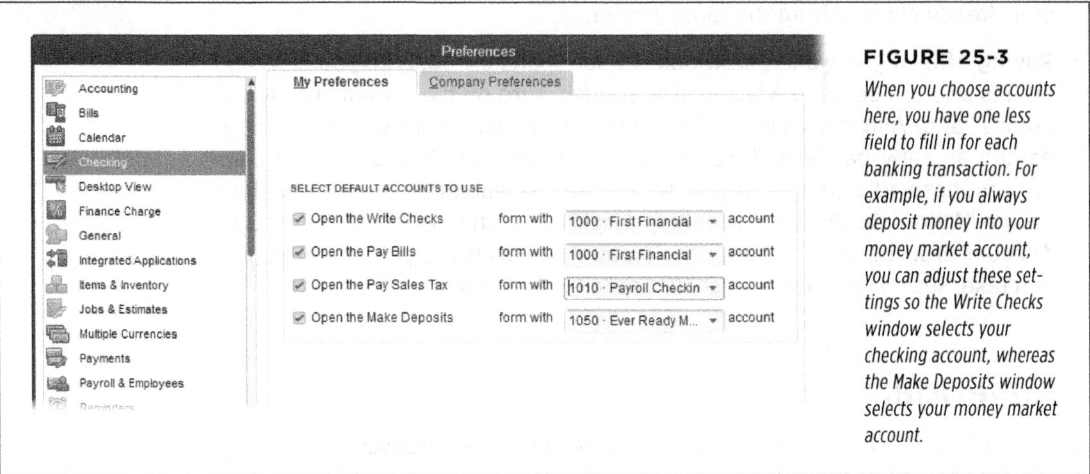

FIGURE 25-3

When you choose accounts here, you have one less field to fill in for each banking transaction. For example, if you always deposit money into your money market account, you can adjust these settings so the Write Checks window selects your checking account, whereas the Make Deposits window selects your money market account.

Choosing the Bank Accounts You Use

If you have only one bank account, you can ignore the preferences for default accounts and QuickBooks will automatically choose your bank account for writing checks, paying bills, paying sales tax, *and* making deposits. But suppose your company has stores in several states and each store has its own checking account. Because these options are on the My Preferences tab, each person who logs into QuickBooks can choose her store's bank accounts for financial transactions. For example, the person in Miami wants the Florida checking account to appear in the Write Checks window, but the person in New York wants to see the Manhattan checking account. To save some time (and to prevent folks from selecting the wrong account in a drop-down list), set your accounts according to the following guidelines:

- **Open the Write Checks form with _ account**. In this drop-down list, choose the account you typically use to write checks. That way, when you open the Write Checks window, QuickBooks automatically fills in the Bank Account field with the account you specify here.
- **Open the Pay Bills form with _ account**. For this preference, choose the account you typically use to pay bills, which is often the same checking account that you chose in the "Open the Write Checks form with" preference. When you open the Pay Bills window, QuickBooks automatically fills in the Account field at the bottom right of the window with the account you specify here.
- **Open the Pay Sales Tax form with _ account**. If you collect sales tax from your customers (see Chapter 21), you have to remit the taxes you collect to the appropriate tax authority, such as the state where your business is located. When it's time to send the taxes in, you open the Pay Sales Tax dialog box and

create a payment. This preference sets the account that QuickBooks uses in that dialog box's Pay From Account field.

- **Open the Make Deposits form with _ account**. Unlike the other options on the My Preferences tab, this preference sets up the account you typically use when you *deposit* money. For many small businesses, the deposit account and checking account are one and the same. But some businesses deposit money into an account that pays interest and then transfer money into a checking account only when it's time to pay bills. After you choose the account you use to deposit money, QuickBooks automatically puts it in the Make Deposits window's Deposit To field.

Settings for Company Checks

Although a company might have several checking accounts, QuickBooks assumes that company checks should look the same no matter who prints them. Most preferences on the Checking category's Company Preferences tab let you set the company standard for printing checks from QuickBooks. (If you use preprinted checks and write them out by hand, you can skip some of these options.) Here's what these preferences do:

- **Print account names on voucher**. If the checks you print include check stubs, you might as well turn on this checkbox so QuickBooks prints the name of the account you used to pay the check on the stub. If you use only one bank account, printing the account name might not seem all that useful. But with this preference turned on, QuickBooks also prints the Payroll item on the stub for payroll checks and, on checks used to purchase inventory, it prints the name of the inventory item you purchased—both of which can help you keep track of where your money is going.

NOTE Regardless of how you set the "Print account names on voucher" preference, QuickBooks always prints the payee, date, memo, amount, and total amount on check stubs.

- **Change check date when non-cleared check is printed**. When you turn on this checkbox, QuickBooks inserts the date that you *print* checks as the check date, which is just fine in most situations. You can then enter checks into QuickBooks over several days but date all the checks with the day you print them. Leave this checkbox turned off if you want to control the check dates—for example, to defer payments for a few days by post-dating checks with the date the payees receive them.
- **Start with payee field on check**. If you always write checks from the same account, or you use the "Open the Write Checks form with" preference to specify an account (page 640), pressing Tab in the Write Checks window to skip the Bank Account field for each check transaction gets old quickly. When you turn on this checkbox, you can save one pesky keystroke each time you write a check.

Turning on this preference also makes it so that the Enter Credit Card Charges window opens with the cursor in the Purchased From box.

- **Warn about duplicate check numbers**. Not surprisingly, when this checkbox is turned on, QuickBooks warns you if you're trying to record a check with the same number as one you already entered.
- **Autofill payee account number in check memo**. Just as you assign account numbers to your customers, the vendors you do business with assign your company an account number, too. Printing account numbers on the checks you write helps vendors credit your account, even if the check gets separated from its accompanying payment slip. If you enter your company's account number in each vendor record in QuickBooks (page 84), be sure to leave this checkbox on to print these account numbers on your checks.

Choosing Company-Wide Payroll Accounts

If you don't use QuickBooks' payroll features, don't bother with these preferences. If you *do* use Intuit Payroll Services (page 415), the two settings in the Select Default Accounts To Use section of the Company Preferences tab let you set the accounts you use for payroll. (These settings are on the Company Preferences tab because most companies centralize payroll no matter how regional other operations are.) Here are your options:

- **Open the Create Paychecks form with _ account**. In this drop-down list, choose the account you use to write payroll checks. If you use QuickBooks payroll, then when you open the Create Paychecks window, the program automatically fills in the Bank Account field with the account you specify here.
- **Open the Pay Payroll Liabilities form with _ account**. In this drop-down list, choose the account you use to pay payroll taxes.

TIP Using a separate bank account for payroll simplifies reconciling your regular checking account, particularly if your company has numerous employees and weekly paychecks. Otherwise, you'll have to reconcile dozens or even hundreds of paychecks each month in addition to the other checks you write.

Selecting a Bank Feeds Mode

QuickBooks lets you choose between two versions of the Bank Feeds Center: Express mode is more flexible and powerful than Classic mode, but you can switch between the two modes anytime by selecting an option in this section of the Checking category's Company Preferences tab. Page 613 explains the two modes in detail.

If you select the Express Mode option, you can tell QuickBooks to create renaming rules for the transactions you download. The "Create rules automatically" checkbox is turned on initially, which means that the program sets up a new renaming rule each time you edit a downloaded transaction's payee. That way, the next time you download a transaction from that payee, the program automatically fills in the edited name. If you turn this checkbox off, QuickBooks doesn't create renaming rules for you. The "Always ask before creating a rule" checkbox is also turned on initially, which means that, when you edit a downloaded transaction's payee name and approve the transaction, the Rule Creation dialog box opens. (To save the rule that QuickBooks created, click OK in the dialog box; to discard it, click Don't Create Any Rules.)

If you select the Classic Mode option, payee aliasing (which is similar, though not identical, to renaming rules) options appear. The On radio button is initially selected. Page 627 explains the differences between Express mode's renaming rules and Classic mode's payee aliasing. To turn off payee aliasing, select the Off radio button.

Desktop View

Each person can customize her own QuickBooks desktop with the settings on this category's My Preferences tab—these choices don't affect anybody else who logs into QuickBooks. On the other hand, the Company Preferences tab includes preferences that control what appears on the QuickBooks Home Page for *everyone* who uses this company file. This section explains your options.

Window Preferences

With the settings on the My Preferences tab, you can tell QuickBooks to keep your desktop neat with only one window at a time, or you can view multiple windows:

- **One Window**. If you're not good at multitasking or you prefer full-size windows, choose this option so that QuickBooks displays only one full-size window at a time. You can still *open* multiple windows, but QuickBooks stacks them on top of one another so you see only the top one. With this approach, you can switch windows by choosing them in the Open Window List (to display it, choose View→Open Window List or, in the left icon bar's middle section, choose Open Windows) or, on the program's main menu bar, choosing Window and then selecting the name of the window you want to display.
- **Multiple Windows**. If you like to view several windows at once or want to size windows based on how much information they display, as shown in Figure 25-4, choose this option. When you do, the Window menu includes items for arranging windows, such as Cascade and Tile Vertically.

NOTE You can also switch between one and multiple windows by choosing View→One Window or View→Multiple Windows.

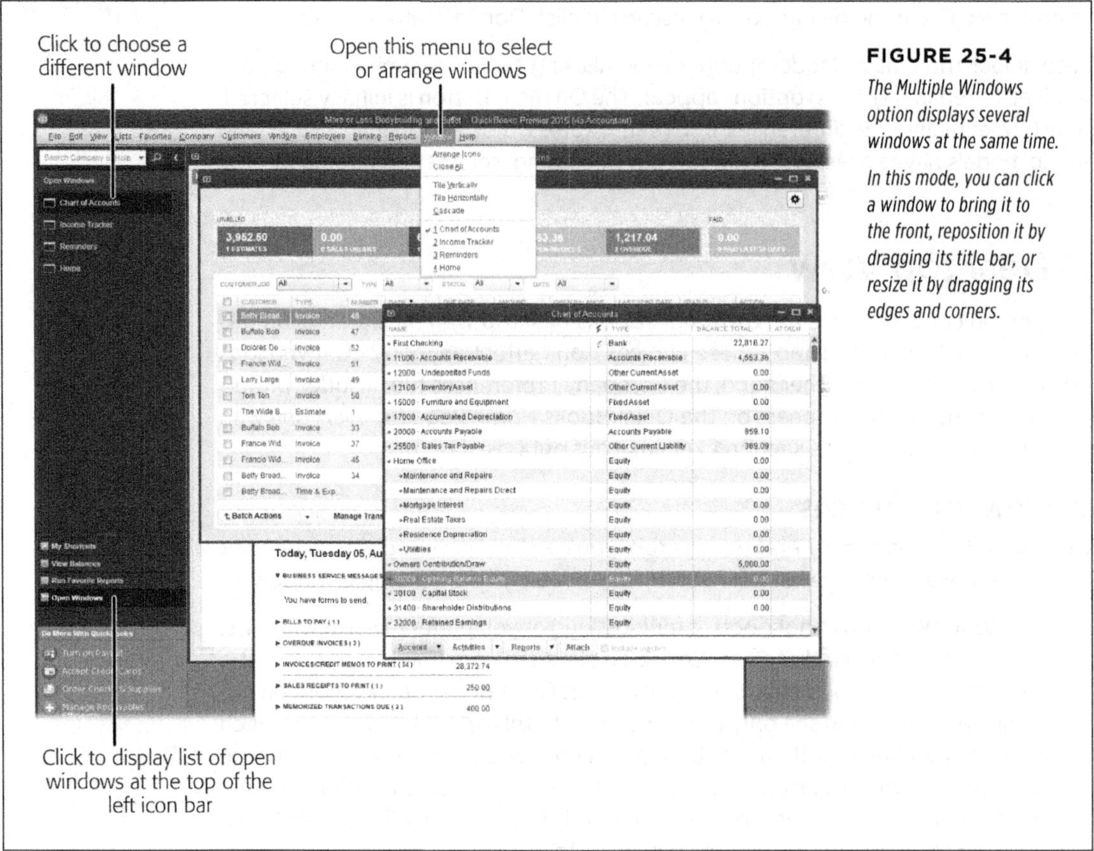
Click to choose a different window
Open this menu to select or arrange windows
Click to display list of open windows at the top of the left icon bar

FIGURE 25-4

The Multiple Windows option displays several windows at the same time.

In this mode, you can click a window to bring it to the front, reposition it by dragging its title bar, or resize it by dragging its edges and corners.

Preferences for Saving the Desktop

The My Preferences tab in the Desktop View category includes four choices for what QuickBooks does with the windows that are open when you exit the program. For example, if you have the windows arranged just the way you like, you can save your QuickBooks desktop so the windows open in exactly the same arrangement the next time you log in. You can also choose when to display the Home Page and whether to use colored or gray icons in the top icon bar. Here's the lowdown on the options in the My Preferences tab's Desktop section:

- **Save when closing company**. If you typically continue bookkeeping tasks from one QuickBooks session to the next, this option saves the open windows and their positions when you exit the program. The next time you log in, QuickBooks opens the same windows and puts them where they were last time so you can finish entering the remaining 300 checks you have to write.

- **Save current desktop**. If you have a favorite arrangement of windows that works well for the bulk of your efforts in QuickBooks, you can save that arrangement and display it every time you log in. To do so, first open the windows you want and position them. Next, open the Preferences dialog box, choose this option, and then click OK. From then on, the next time you open the Preferences dialog box, QuickBooks adds the "Keep previously saved desktop" option (explained below) to the My Preferences tab.
- **Don't save the desktop**. Choosing this option displays a desktop with only the menu bar, the icon bar, and the Home Page. This makes QuickBooks open faster, and the menu bar, icon bars, and Home Page give you fast access to the windows and dialog boxes you use regularly.
- **Keep previously saved desktop**. Once you've saved a desktop you like, this option appears on the My Preferences tab of the Desktop View category. In fact, once you choose "Save current desktop" and click OK to close the Preferences dialog box, QuickBooks *automatically* selects this option the next time you open the dialog box. With this option selected, QuickBooks opens with the desktop as it was when you selected "Save current desktop," regardless of which windows you've opened since then or how you've arranged them. If you want to save a *new* desktop arrangement, position your windows how you want them, select "Save current desktop," and then click OK.
- **Show Home page when opening a company file**. QuickBooks' Home Page shows the entire workflow of your accounting tasks, as well as links to oft-opened windows like the Chart of Accounts. Keep this checkbox turned on to see the Home Page each time you log in. If you turn this checkbox off, the Home Page appears only if it's open when you save your desktop or if you open it by choosing Company→Home Page.

TIP In QuickBooks 2015, the Home Page window sports two tabs: Home Page and Insights (page 44). Regardless of whether you tell QuickBooks to display the Home Page window or it appears automatically when you open your company file, you see the tab that was visible when you closed your previous session.

- **Switch to colored icons/light background on the Top Icon Bar**. If you use the top icon bar (page 30), its out-of-the-box color scheme is blue-and-gray icons on a dark-blue background. If you turn on this checkbox, that changes to blue, green, and yellow icons on a light-gray background, as shown in Figure 25-5 (if you're reading an electronic version of this book, that is; in the printed book, all the figures are black and white).

NOTE The Windows Settings section in the Desktop View category's My Preferences tab has two buttons: Display and Sounds. These buttons take you to the appropriate category of the Windows Control Panel to change your Windows settings, where any changes you make affect *every* program on your computer, not just QuickBooks.

- **Company File Color Scheme**. If you work on several different company files, you can assign a different color to each of them so you can tell them apart. In this drop-down list, pick a color (there are 15 to choose from) and QuickBooks changes the title bars of its main window and all open windows in QuickBooks, as shown in Figure 25-5. If you don't like the result, choose a different color.

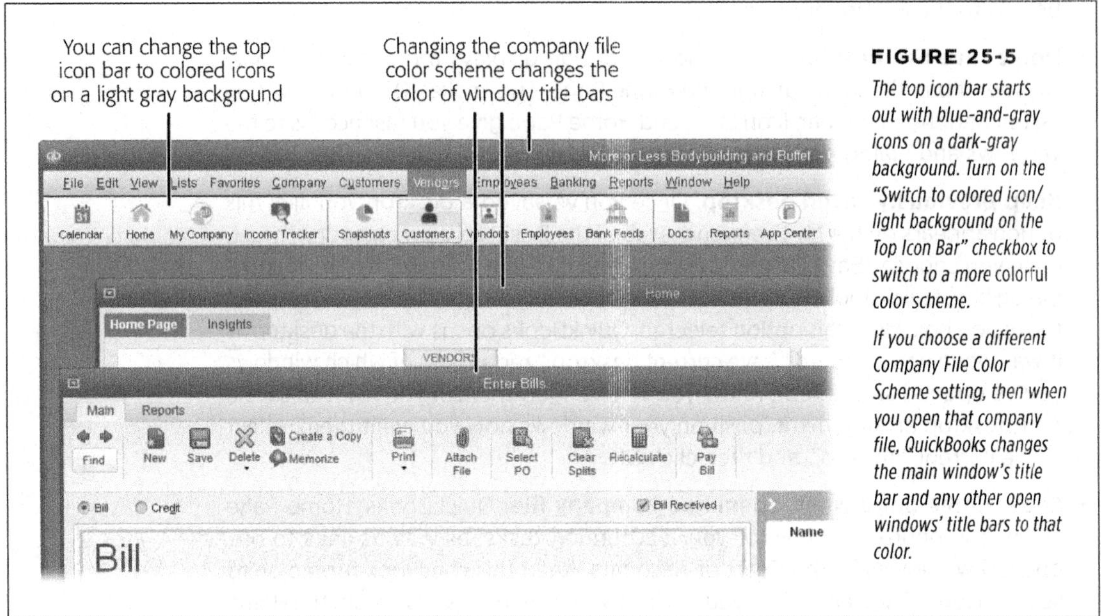
You can change the top icon bar to colored icons on a light gray background
Changing the company file color scheme changes the color of window title bars

FIGURE 25-5

The top icon bar starts out with blue-and-gray icons on a dark-gray background. Turn on the "Switch to colored icon/light background on the Top Icon Bar" checkbox to switch to a more colorful color scheme.

If you choose a different Company File Color Scheme setting, then when you open that company file, QuickBooks changes the main window's title bar and any other open windows' title bars to that color.

Customizing the Home Page

The Home Page has three horizontal panels for tasks related to vendors, customers, and employees, and additional panels for other accounting staples. The Company Preferences tab of the Desktop View category is where you can customize what appears there. See page 696 for the full story on customizing the Home Page.

Finance Charge

If you're lucky enough to have customers who always pay on time or if you run a nonprofit organization that graciously accepts donations, you can bypass this preference category. But if you want to add an incentive for customers to pay on time, these preferences determine your level of persuasion.

Because you probably want a consistent policy for charging customers for late payments, all the preferences in the Finance Charge category are on the Company Preferences tab. That means only someone logged into QuickBooks as an administrator can change these settings. (Page 359 explains how to add finance charges to the invoices you create.)

TIP If you plan to charge late fees, include the finance charge terms in your contracts. Your customers are less likely to complain if the added charges aren't a surprise.

Here are the finance charge preferences you can set and what they mean to your customers:

- **Annual Interest Rate (%)**. Type the interest rate that you charge per year for overdue payments. For example, if you charge 18 percent per year, type *18* in this box. QuickBooks adds the percent sign and calculates the finance charge due by prorating the annual interest date to the number of days that a payment is late.
- **Minimum Finance Charge**. If you charge a minimum finance charge no matter how inconsequential the overdue amount, type that value in this box. For example, to charge at least $20, type *20*. (If you work with more than one currency, you still specify your minimum finance charge in your home currency. QuickBooks then converts the amount to the customer's currency when you apply finance charges.)
- **Grace Period (days)**. Just like the grace period that you probably appreciate on your mortgage, the grace period in QuickBooks is the number of days that a payment can be late before finance charges kick in. In this box, type the number of days of grace you're willing to extend to your customers.
- **Finance Charge Account**. Choose the account you use to track finance charges you collect. Most companies create an Other Income account (page 57) to track these charges, which are interest income.
- **Assess finance charges on overdue finance charges**. If a customer goes AWOL and doesn't pay the bill *or* the finance charges, you could consider levying finance charges on the finance charges that the customer already owes. For example, if your customer owes $100 in finance charges and you assess an 18 percent finance charge, turning on this checkbox would result in an additional $18 the first year on the outstanding charges alone.

NOTE Most companies find it excessive to tack finance charges on overdue finance charges. Moreover, you should check the lending laws that apply to your location and business—some laws restrict your ability to charge interest on outstanding interest payments.

- **Calculate charges from**. You can calculate finance charges from two different dates, depending on how painful you want the finance-charge penalty to be. Choosing the "due date" option here is the more lenient approach; it tells QuickBooks to assess finance charges only on the days that an invoice is paid past its due date. For example, if the customer pays 10 days late, QuickBooks calculates the finance charges for 10 days. If you want to assess finance charges from the date on the invoice, choose the "invoice/billed date" option instead. In that case, if the customer pays 10 days late on a Net 30 invoice (meaning payment is due within 30 days after the invoice date), QuickBooks calculates finance charges based on 40 days—the 30 days until the invoice was due *and* the 10 days that the payment was late.

- **Mark finance charge invoices "To be printed**." If you want QuickBooks to remind you to print invoices with finance charges, turn on this checkbox. Invoices that you haven't printed yet then appear as alerts in the Reminders window. If you send statements to your customers, turn off this checkbox, because the finance charge invoices you generate will be included on the statements you create.

General

QuickBooks selects the General preferences category the very first time you open the Preferences dialog box. Most of the General preferences appear on the My Preferences tab, so you can make QuickBooks work the way you do, but a few preferences apply to everyone who works on the company file.

Tuning QuickBooks to Your Liking

The following settings on the My Preferences tab can help you fine-tune QuickBooks' behavior:

- **Pressing Enter moves between fields**. In the Windows world, pressing the Enter key usually activates the default button in a dialog box, while the Tab key advances the cursor to the next field. If you press Enter in QuickBooks and find that a dialog box or window closes unexpectedly, this checkbox can provide some relief. When you turn it on, pressing Enter moves the cursor between fields in a dialog box or window rather than closing it. However, because Enter no longer closes dialog boxes and windows, you have to press Ctrl+Enter or click a button—such as OK, Record, Save & Close, or Save & New (depending on the dialog box or window)—to do so.
- **Automatically open drop-down lists when typing**. This setting makes drop-down menus spring open as soon as you type a letter in a field. You can then click the entry you want or press Enter to select the highlighted menu item, as shown in Figure 25-6.
- **Beep when recording a transaction**. If you like auditory assurance that your software is working, leave this checkbox turned on to have QuickBooks beep when it records a transaction. (You'll hear the beep only if you haven't muted the audio on your computer.) If you prefer peace and quiet, simply turn off this setting.
- **Automatically place decimal point**. When you turn on this checkbox, QuickBooks places decimals so that the last two numbers you type represent cents. For example, typing *19995* automatically becomes 199.95. (If you want to enter a whole dollar, type a period at the end of the number.) Having QuickBooks place decimal points in numbers for you can be quite addictive once you get used to it, particularly if you haven't graduated to rapid-fire entry on your computer's

numeric keypad—or if you work on a laptop and haven't realized that your keyboard *has* a numeric keypad.

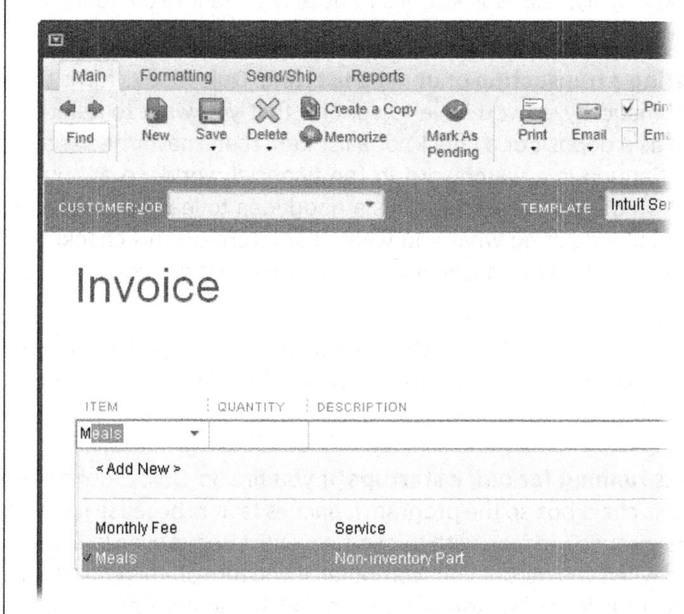

FIGURE 25-6

With the "Automatically open drop-down lists when typing" preference turned on, drop-down lists appear as soon as you begin typing an entry in a field, so you can simply keep typing, click an entry, or press Enter when QuickBooks highlights the entry you want. The list displays only choices that match what you've typed so far. The list shown here includes "Meals" and "Monthly Fee" after typing "M."

- **Warn when editing a transaction**. QuickBooks turns on this checkbox automatically, which means that the program displays a warning if you edit a transaction and attempt to leave it (for instance, by clicking another transaction) without explicitly saving the change. If you inadvertently modify a transaction, like a check or invoice, this warning gives you a chance to either save the changes or exit without saving.

  If you decide to turn off this feature, QuickBooks automatically records transactions that aren't linked to other transactions. However, if a transaction has links—such as a payment that links to a customer invoice—you need to save it after you change it regardless of how you've set this preference.

- **Bring back all one time messages**. One-time messages instruct beginners in the ways of QuickBooks, but for experienced folks, dismissing these messages simply consumes valuable time. If you were overly enthusiastic about hiding one-time messages and find yourself in need of QuickBooks' mentoring, turn this checkbox on.

- **Turn off pop-up messages for products and services**. Initially, QuickBooks displays pop-up messages about other products and services that Intuit offers. If you're content with what QuickBooks offers out of the box, turn this checkbox on.

- **Show ToolTips for clipped text**. Text in QuickBooks fields is often longer than what you can see onscreen. For example, if you see the text "Make sure you always" in a text box, you'll want to read the rest of the message. This checkbox, which is turned on initially, tells QuickBooks to display the entire contents of a field when you put your cursor over it.
- **Warn when deleting a transaction or unused list item**. QuickBooks turns this checkbox on automatically, so you have to confirm that you want to delete a transaction (such as a deposit or a check) or a list item that's never been used in a transaction. Caution is a watchword in the financial world, so although QuickBooks lets you delete transactions, it's a good idea to leave this setting on to make sure you're deleting what you want. If you turn off this checkbox, you can delete a transaction or unused list item without confirmation.

NOTE Regardless of how this preference is set, QuickBooks won't let you delete a list item, such as a customer type or shipping method, if it's been used in even one transaction. Page 119 explains how to delete or inactivate list items.

- **Keep QuickBooks running for quick startups**. If you fire up QuickBooks frequently, turn on this checkbox so the program launches faster (because it stays running in the background). In fact, with this setting, QuickBooks even launches in the background when you reboot your computer. If you turn off this checkbox, QuickBooks doesn't run in the background or use your computer's memory, so it takes longer to start up. That could be just what you want if your machine is short on memory and you want all your *other* programs to run more quickly.
- **Automatically remember account or transaction information**. Say you write checks each month to the same vendor, for the same amount, and post them to the same account. Out of the box, QuickBooks turns on the "Pre-fill accounts for vendor based on past entries" option in this section, which means that the program automatically fills in the accounts you use consistently for vendor transactions. But since you can set up pre-fill accounts for vendors with other QuickBooks features (page 85), the "Automatically recall last transaction for this name" option gives you more bang for the buck. With that option selected, when you type a name in a transaction, QuickBooks fills in the accounts and the rest of the values you used in the last transaction for that name.

  However, AutoRecall has a couple of limitations: It can't recall a transaction in one account if the previous transaction was in another account, and it can only recall transactions for bills, checks, and credit card charges. For other transactions—such as purchase orders, invoices, sales receipts, and credit memos—you have to fill in all the fields or use a memorized transaction.
- **Default date to use for new transactions**. In this section of the My Preferences tab, choose the "Use today's date as default" option if you want QuickBooks to put the current date in the Date field of every new transaction you create.

If you create invoices over the course of several days but want each one to reflect the first day of the month, for example, choose the "Use the last entered date as default" option instead. Then, in the first invoice you create, type the date you want for all your invoices. For subsequent invoices, QuickBooks fills in the Date field with the date you entered on the previous invoice. When you want to use a new date (after all the month's invoices are complete), simply type it in your next transaction.

TIP When the "Use the last entered date as default" option is selected, be sure to check the Date box in transaction windows (like Create Invoices) to make sure it's the one you want.

- **Keep custom item information when changing item in transactions**. This setting determines how QuickBooks responds when you change an item in a transaction after customizing its description. Say you add an item to an invoice, edit the description in the invoice, and *then* realize that you added the wrong item. When you choose a new item to replace it, if you've selected the Ask option for this setting, QuickBooks asks whether you want to use the edited description for the new item. The Always option automatically applies the edited description to the new item. And the Never option discards the edited description and uses the description from the new item's record.

Company-Wide General Preferences

The Company Preferences tab (Figure 25-7) includes four settings. (Remember, only a QuickBooks administrator can change these settings.) Here's what they do:

- **Time format**. You can *enter* hours as either decimal numbers that represent hours and fractions of hours, or as hours and minutes separated by a colon, as you can see in Figure 25-7. This preference tells QuickBooks which way to *display* time values.

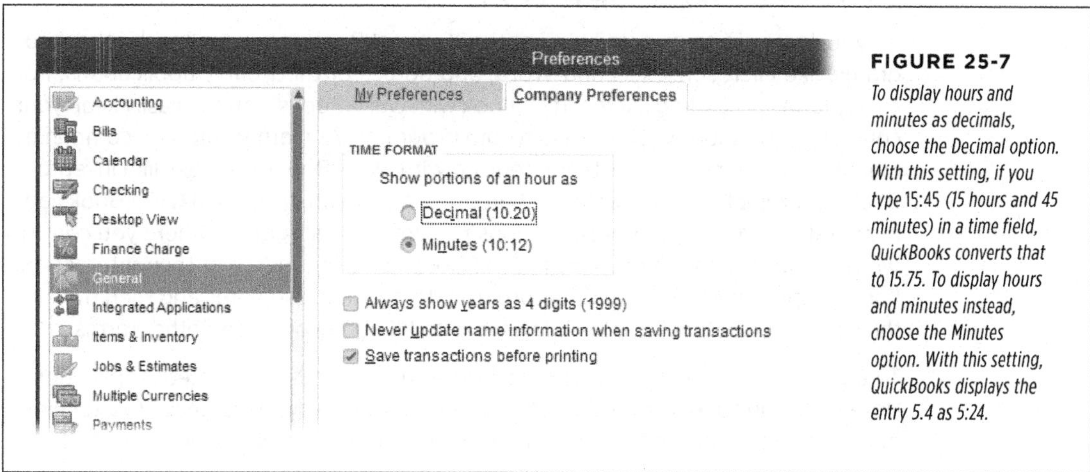

FIGURE 25-7

To display hours and minutes as decimals, choose the Decimal option. With this setting, if you type 15:45 (15 hours and 45 minutes) in a time field, QuickBooks converts that to 15.75. To display hours and minutes instead, choose the Minutes option. With this setting, QuickBooks displays the entry 5.4 as 5:24.

- **Always show years as 4 digits (1999)**. Turning on this setting tells QuickBooks to display all four digits of the year whether you type two digits or four. For example, if you type *15*, then QuickBooks displays 2015. Turning off this checkbox makes the program display years as two digits. When you type a two-digit number for a year, QuickBooks translates numbers from 00 through 43 as years 2000 through 2043; 44 through 99 become 1944 through 1999.

TIP If you turn off the "Always show years as 4 digits" checkbox, QuickBooks does as it's told and displays only two digits for the year. If a date field shows 40 and you want to see whether that stands for 1940 or 2040, in the date field, click the Calendar icon. The Calendar shows both the month and the full four-digit year.

- **Never update name information when saving transactions**. QuickBooks initially turns this checkbox off so that, when you edit the name of a customer or vendor, for example, the program asks if you want to replicate that change back in the original record—on the Customer:Job List or Vendor List. The only situation where you might want to change this behavior (by turning on this checkbox) is if you use generic names, such as Donor or Member. If you receive donations and your donors want receipts with their names and addresses filled in, you don't want the names and addresses you enter on sales receipts to alter your generic donor record.
- **Save transactions before printing**. QuickBooks turns this checkbox on initially, and it's a good idea to leave it that way. It tells the program to save transactions before you print them so that the transactions in QuickBooks are the same as the ones you print. If you turn this checkbox off, you could print the transaction with one set of data and then close the dialog box or window *without* saving that data, thus making your QuickBooks records different from your paper records.

Integrated Applications

As you'll learn in more detail in Chapter 26, QuickBooks plays well with other programs, like Microsoft Excel and Word, and oodles of third-party applications. For example, by integrating Microsoft Outlook with QuickBooks, you can easily keep your contact information synchronized in both programs. And other software companies create all sorts of programs that integrate with QuickBooks for tasks like inventory tracking, project tracking, creating barcodes, and so on. If you're a QuickBooks administrator, the Integrated Applications preferences category is where you control *which* programs can interact with QuickBooks and the *extent* of their interaction. For example, you can use another program to produce estimates and then transfer the completed estimates into QuickBooks to fill out invoices and other forms.

To access these preferences, choose Edit→Preferences→Integrated Applications. Here's a guide to adjusting the settings on the Company Preferences tab to allow or restrict other programs' access to your QuickBooks company file:

- **Don't allow any applications to access this company file**. The quickest way to prevent other programs from using a QuickBooks company file is to turn on this checkbox. When you do so, QuickBooks doesn't allow integrated programs to access the file and stops displaying screens requesting access. If you want QuickBooks to display access screens, leave this checkbox off.
- **Notify the user before running any application whose certificate has expired**. The most security conscious of administrators might turn on this checkbox to see a warning if a program trying to access the QuickBooks company file has an expired certificate. But an expired certificate doesn't mean that the program has changed or has morphed into malicious code—only that the certificate has expired. For most administrators, leaving this checkbox off is preferable.
- **Applications that have previously requested access to this company file**. When programs request access to a company file, QuickBooks displays an access screen to the QuickBooks administrator, who has to approve or deny access. Programs that have received approval to access your company file appear in this list. To deny access to one of these programs, click its checkmark in the Allow Access column, or select the program and then click Remove.

Items & Inventory

These preferences apply mainly to what QuickBooks does when you create purchase orders or invoices for inventory. The first setting on the Company Preferences tab is the most important: You tell QuickBooks that you want to track inventory by turning on the "Inventory and purchase orders are active" checkbox, which activates the program's inventory-related features (Chapter 20) and adds icons like Purchase Orders and Receive Inventory to the Home Page. (The box on page 654 describes the inventory preferences you can set if you use QuickBooks Premier or Enterprise.)

If you turn on inventory tracking, here are the other settings you may want to adjust:

- **Warn about duplicate purchase order numbers**. Leave this checkbox on if you want QuickBooks to alert you when you're creating a purchase order with the same number as one you already entered.
- **Warn if not enough inventory quantity on hand (QOH) to sell**. In QuickBooks Pro, you can turn this checkbox on so QuickBooks will warn you if you prepare an invoice to sell more doodads than you have in stock. Suppose you sell 500 quarts of mascarpone blackberry ice cream, but you have only 400 quarts in stock. When you attempt to save the invoice for the 500-quart order, QuickBooks displays a message box informing you of the shortage—but doesn't go any further than that. You can save the invoice, but it's up to you to order more inventory. Besides giving you a heads-up that inventory is low, this setting helps you keep your customers happy, since you can ask them if they want to wait for a backorder to be filled. The box on page 654 explains QuickBooks Premier's inventory-on-hand options.

POWER USERS' CLINIC

QuickBooks Premier's Inventory Settings

You can obtain a few additional inventory preferences by upgrading from QuickBooks Pro to QuickBooks Premier, which lets you adjust the following settings:

- **When calculating Quantity Available for my inventory, deduct**. QuickBooks Premier tracks two quantities for inventory items. Quantity On Hand is the actual number of items sitting in inventory. Quantity Available can equal Quantity On Hand, but you can also tell QuickBooks to remove the number of items on sales orders or used in pending builds (when you build products out of components) from the Quantity Available number. If you use sales orders (page 654) to track orders that haven't been invoiced, QuickBooks automatically turns on the "Quantity on Sales Order" checkbox here. With this setting selected, QuickBooks calculates the number of inventory items available by deducting the number of items on sales orders from the number of items on hand, which helps prevent you from accidentally selling out-of-stock items. If you turn this checkbox off, the Quantity Available reflects only the inventory that's been invoiced and shipped, so you won't know that your inventory is low until you start filling the sales orders you created.
- **Warn if not enough inventory to sell**. In QuickBooks Premier, you can specify whether you want the program to warn you when the quantity being sold is greater than the quantity on hand or the quantity available. Because quantity available is equal to or less than the quantity on hand, choosing that option is the safest route.
- **Unit of measure**. In QuickBooks Premier and Enterprise, you can specify units of measure for inventory items. To do this, in the Unit of Measure section, click the Enable button. You can then select Single U/M Per Item to define one unit of measure per inventory item. If you use QuickBooks Enterprise and some QuickBooks Premier editions (Accountant, Contractor, and Manufacturing & Wholesale), you can assign more than one unit of measure in case you sell wine by the bottle, by the case, and by the barrel, for example. To do that, select the Multiple U/M Per Item option.

You define units of measure in the Create Item or Edit Item window (page 106). To open the Unit of Measure dialog box to the "Select a Unit of Measure Type" screen in either of those windows, in the Unit of Measure box, click the down arrow, and then choose the measure you want. To add a new unit of measure, click <Add New> in the drop-down list.

NOTE Unless you use QuickBooks Enterprise, the Advanced Inventory Settings button (located on the Items & Inventory category's Company Preferences tab) is grayed out. To see whether these settings are worth the cost of upgrading, click the "Learn about serial #/lots, FIFO and multi-location inventory" link.

Jobs & Estimates

If you create estimates or document job progress in QuickBooks, head to the Jobs & Estimates preferences category to set up your progress terminology and estimating features.

QuickBooks includes five job-status settings, which are all listed on the Company Preferences tab in this category: Pending, Awarded, In progress, Closed, and Not awarded. Despite the fields' names, you can type any term you want in any of the five boxes. For example, you can type *Waiting* in the Pending box, *Whoopie!* in the Awarded box, and *Finally!* in the Closed box. Then, when you edit a job and display the Job Status drop-down list (page 82), you can choose from these custom terms.

Here are the other settings on the Company Preferences tab for this category:

- **Do you create estimates?** Choose the Yes option only if you want to create estimates *in QuickBooks*, as described on page 278, so the program adds the Estimates icon to the Home Page. If you create estimates in a program other than QuickBooks, choose the No option.
- **Do you do progress invoicing?** Also known as "partial billing," progress invoicing means that you invoice your customer for work as you go instead of billing for the entire job at the end. For example, if you're building a shopping mall, you don't want to carry the costs of construction until shoppers walk in the front door—you want to charge your client as you meet milestones. To create invoices for portions of your estimates, choose the Yes option. That way, you can invoice for part of an estimate and show how much you billed previously, as described on page 284.

NOTE If you choose the No option, you can still create progress invoices from your entire estimate. After you bring the whole estimate into your invoice, remove entries until the invoice includes only what you want to bill. The flaw in this approach is that you can't show previous billed totals or compare the billed and remaining amounts with your estimate.

- **Close estimates after converting to invoice**. This checkbox is grayed out if progress invoicing is turned on. If you don't do progress invoicing, turn on this checkbox to tell QuickBooks to make an estimate inactive after you've converted it to an invoice. That way, you won't accidentally create another invoice from an estimate you've already invoiced. You might decide to turn this checkbox off to keep estimates around in case you end up with a similar job in the future. However, a better way to create boilerplate estimates is to memorize the ones you want to reuse, as explained on page 321.
- **Warn about duplicate estimate numbers**. Leave this checkbox on if you want QuickBooks to alert you if you're creating an estimate with the same number as one you already entered.
- **Don't print items that have zero amount**. This checkbox is grayed out unless you select Yes in the "Do you do progress invoicing?" section. If you do use progress invoicing, you might not charge for every estimated item on every progress invoice. To keep your progress invoices tidy, suppress the items that you're not charging for by leaving this checkbox turned on.

Multiple Currencies

If you use only one currency, you can skip these preferences, because QuickBooks automatically selects the "No, I use only one currency" option. But if you have customers who pay you in other currencies (as shown in Figure 25-8) or vendors who want to be paid in their countries' currencies, you can turn on the multiple currency preference. Just know that once you turn this setting on, it's on for *good*. If you stop doing business with foreign-currency customers and vendors, you can simply skip the currency boxes in QuickBooks' windows and dialog boxes (the program automatically fills them in with your home currency).

To turn on multiple currencies, choose Edit→Preferences→Multiple Currencies, and then click the Company Preferences tab. Select the "Yes, I use more than one currency" option. QuickBooks initially sets the home currency to US Dollar, but you can change that in the "Select the home currency you use in transactions" drop-down list.

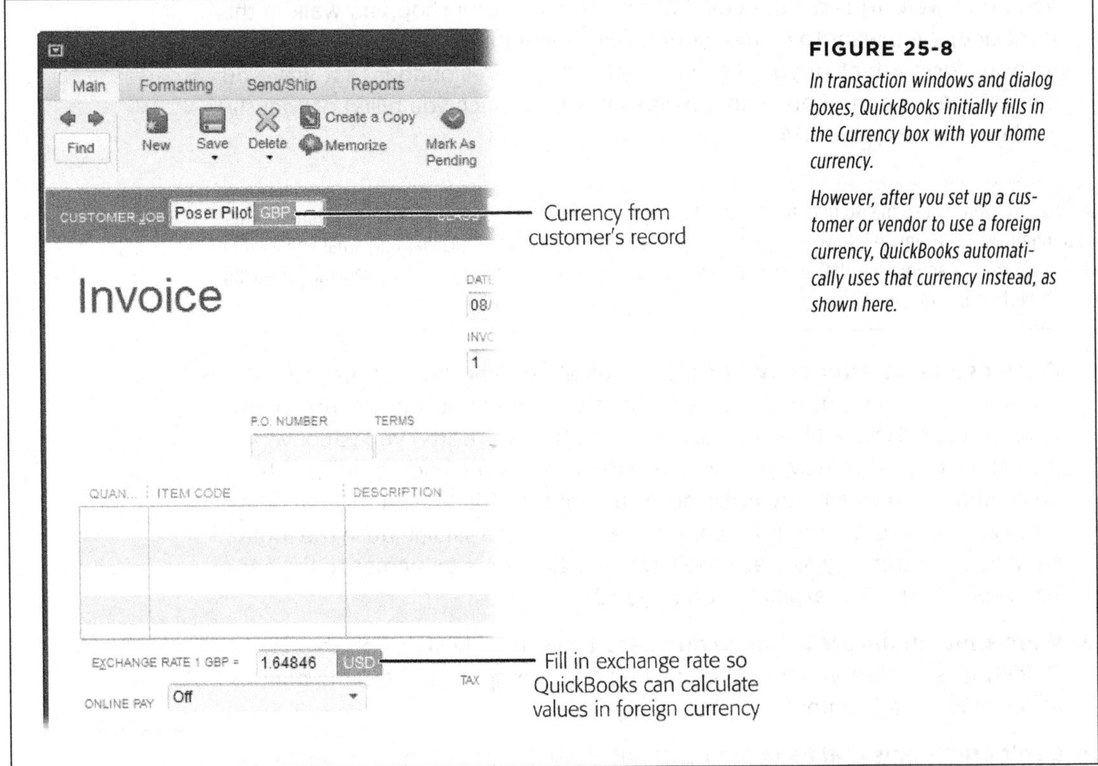

FIGURE 25-8

In transaction windows and dialog boxes, QuickBooks initially fills in the Currency box with your home currency.

However, after you set up a customer or vendor to use a foreign currency, QuickBooks automatically uses that currency instead, as shown here.

Payments

In this category, the Company Preferences tab lets you set the following options:

- **Automatically apply payments**. You'll probably want to turn this checkbox off so you can choose the customer invoices to which you want to apply payments you receive. With this checkbox on, QuickBooks applies customer payments to invoices *for* you. If a payment doesn't match any of the invoice amounts, QuickBooks applies the payment to the oldest invoices first, which could mask the fact that a payment wasn't received or that a customer's check was for the wrong amount.
- **Automatically calculate payments**. This preference, on the other hand, is one you'll want to keep turned on. When you receive a payment from a customer, in the Receive Payments window's Amount box, you typically type the amount that the customer sent. Then, as you choose the invoices to apply the payment to, QuickBooks calculates the payment for you. If the customer underpaid, QuickBooks asks if you want to keep the underpayment or write off the amount that the customer didn't pay. When this checkbox is off, as you choose invoices, you also have to enter the amount of the payment that you want to allocate to each invoice.
- **Use Undeposited Funds as a default deposit to account**. If you typically collect several payments before heading to the bank to deposit them, leave this checkbox turned on so QuickBooks automatically adds payments you receive to the Undeposited Funds account and doesn't display the "Deposit to" box in the Receive Payments window. If, on the other hand, you want a say in whether to deposit payments right away, turn this checkbox off. That way, in the Receive Payments window's Deposit To field, you can choose a bank account to deposit funds immediately, or you can choose Undeposited Funds to collect several payments before you make a deposit.

NOTE Intuit e-Invoicing is QuickBooks 2015's new and improved online payment subscription service. To learn about getting paid electronically, download Appendix E from this book's Missing CD page at *www.missingmanuals.com/cds*.

Payroll & Employees

Perhaps the most annoying thing about employees is their insistence on being paid. Sad to say, but using QuickBooks for payroll doesn't eliminate the need to pay your employees, and it can only simplify the task so much. If you choose one of the QuickBooks payroll service options, head to the Payroll & Employees preference category to configure your payroll service and how it operates. (Chapter 15 explains what Intuit's various payroll services offer. To learn how to sign up for one and use it to set up employee records, run payroll, and remit payroll taxes, download online Appendix D from this book's Missing CD page at *www.missing manuals.com/cds.*)

Payroll and employee preferences appear on the Company Preferences tab, so only QuickBooks administrators can set them. The tab's QuickBooks Payroll Features section gives you three options for choosing a payroll service. Here's some info that can help you determine which one to choose:

- **Full payroll**. This is the option you want if you use an Intuit payroll service to figure out payroll amounts or if you calculate payroll yourself and use QuickBooks' features to produce the necessary documents. With this option selected, you can produce documents such as paychecks; payroll reports; and payroll forms, including 940s (employer federal unemployment taxes), 941s (employer quarterly federal taxes), W-2s (employee wage and tax statements), and W-3s (transmittal of W-2s).
- **No payroll**. Choose this option if you don't run payroll in any way or you use a third-party payroll service. For example, if you're a sole proprietor and pay yourself by taking owner's draws, or if you use an outside payroll service such as Paychex or ADP and have no need to print payroll documents or assign payroll costs to jobs, choose this option. With this option selected, you don't see payroll-related features in the Employees menu or in the Employee Center.

NOTE If you have transactions from prior payrolls and then switch to using an outside payroll service, the past payroll data remains in your QuickBooks file.

- **Online Payroll**. If you use Intuit Online Payroll, choose this option. When you use this service, you can also run payroll without QuickBooks.

The Payroll & Employees preference category has plenty of additional settings that are intimately linked to payroll. For example, you can specify the deductions and Payroll items that affect every employee, and control the fields that appear on paychecks and paycheck stubs. Download online Appendix D from this book's Missing CD page at *www.missing manuals.com/cds* to learn how to set these preferences.

Whether you run payroll or not, here's the lowdown on the remaining preferences that *don't* relate to payroll:

- **Display employee list by**. If your company employs only a few people, you can choose the First Name option so that QuickBooks sorts the Employee List by first names. However, if you have hundreds of employees, choose the Last Name option. Regardless of which option you choose, QuickBooks prints paychecks with employee first names first and last names last.
- **Mark new employees as sales reps**. If only a few of your employees act as customer contacts and receive commissions, you can reserve the Sales Rep List for them by leaving this checkbox off and adding names to that list manually (page 147). But if you consider every employee a potential sales rep, turn on this

checkbox so that QuickBooks automatically adds every employee you create to the Sales Rep List, saving you a five-step process each time.

- **Display employee social security numbers in headers on reports**. QuickBooks automatically turns off this checkbox, which is preferable if you want to protect your employees' financial privacy.

Reminders

QuickBooks can remind you when it's time to perform tasks like printing checks, paying bills, and depositing money. You can even turn on reminders for to-dos so the program can remind you about tasks that you don't want to forget. Page 483 describes how reminders work and how to set preferences so you receive the reminders you want when you want them.

In the Reminders preference category, the My Preferences tab has only one setting: "Show Reminders List when opening a Company file." Turn this checkbox on to tell QuickBooks to display the Reminders window whenever you open your company file.

The Company Preferences tab contains settings for different types of reminders, which are available only if you've turned on the corresponding feature. For example, if you don't use QuickBooks inventory, the "Inventory to Reorder" reminder is grayed out. See page 484 to learn the difference between the Show Summary and Show List options for each reminder. Page 484 also describes how to specify the level of detail you want to see in the Reminders window and, in some cases, when you want QuickBooks to remind you.

> **TIP** Regardless of which Reminders settings you choose, the "View reminders" icon appears at the top right of the program's main window. The icon looks like an alarm clock, and the numbered label to its right shows how many reminders await you. To open the Reminders window, click this icon.

Reports and Graphs

Each person who logs into QuickBooks can specify a few preferences for the reports and graphs he generates. And QuickBooks administrators can modify settings that apply to *every* report and graph their company produces.

Preferences for the Reports You Generate

Here's a guide to the personal preferences shown in Figure 25-9:

- **Prompt me to modify report options before opening a report**. You usually need to tweak reports a little to make them show exactly what you want—a different date range, perhaps—so turning on this checkbox works for most people. With this checkbox turned on, QuickBooks automatically opens the Modify Report window when you generate a report so you can make any changes you want. (After you make your changes, click OK to view the results.) If you leave this checkbox turned off, then you can make changes by clicking Customize Report in a report window.

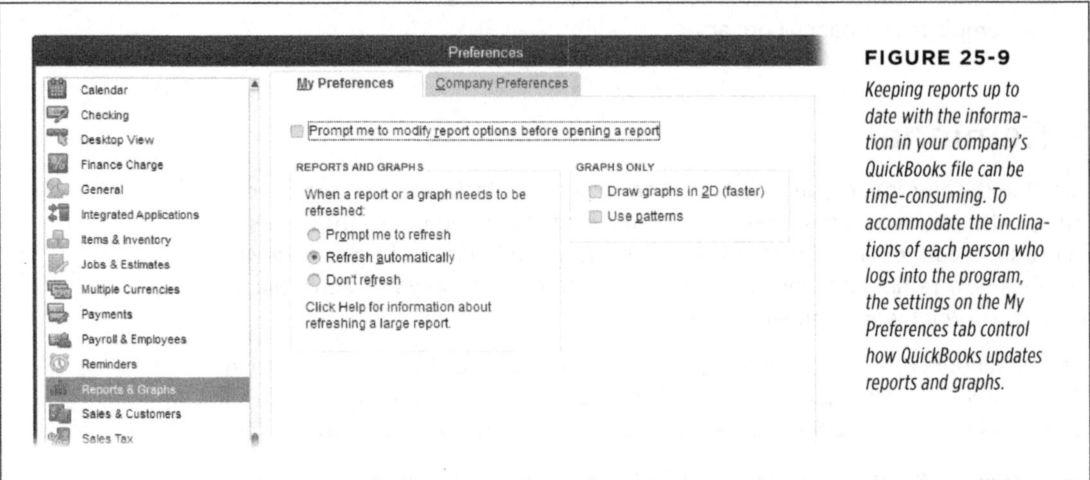

FIGURE 25-9

Keeping reports up to date with the information in your company's QuickBooks file can be time-consuming. To accommodate the inclinations of each person who logs into the program, the settings on the My Preferences tab control how QuickBooks updates reports and graphs.

- **Reports and Graphs**. This set of preferences lets you decide what QuickBooks should do when a report or graph needs to be refreshed because the data within it has changed. You can choose one of the following options (QuickBooks automatically selects the first option unless you change it):
  - **Prompt me to refresh**. If your QuickBooks file changes frequently and you don't want to wait while the program refreshes every report you have open, choose this option. When you do, QuickBooks reminds you to refresh reports when you've changed data that affects them. For example, suppose you generated a Profit & Loss report and then received a payment for a customer; with this setting selected, QuickBooks would prompt you to refresh the report. To refresh a report or graph, simply click Refresh in the report's window.
  - **Refresh automatically**. If numerous people are frantically changing data in the company file, as often happens as year-end approaches, this option can slow your work. However, if it's critical that your reports and graphs are always accurate, choose this option so QuickBooks automatically refreshes reports and graphs whenever the underlying data changes.
  - **Don't refresh**. If you find yourself distracted by refreshes or even prompts about refreshing, choose this option. That way, QuickBooks won't refresh your reports and graphs or remind you—no matter how significant the changes to the underlying data. When you've finished your report and graph customizations, click Refresh in the report's window to generate the report with the current data.

- **Draw graphs in 2D (faster)**. If you care about time more than fancy graphics, turn on this checkbox. QuickBooks then displays graphs in two dimensions, which is faster than drawing the 3-D graphs it generates if you leave this checkbox off.
- **Use patterns**. When you turn on this checkbox, QuickBooks uses black-and-white patterns instead of colors to differentiate areas on graphs. If you leave this checkbox off, QuickBooks displays colors on color monitors and shades of gray on black-and-white monitors.

Company-Wide Report Preferences

The Company Preferences tab has several preferences for the reports and graphs your company generates. If you're a QuickBooks administrator, use the following preferences to format reports and graphs:

- **Summary Reports Basis**. Nothing starts adrenaline flowing like financial reports that aren't what you expect, particularly when IRS auditors are dropping by to peruse your company's books. Be sure to choose the correct option here—Cash or Accrual (page xxii explains the difference)—so that the reports you generate accurately reflect your financial performance.
- **Aging Reports**. You can control how QuickBooks calculates age for invoices, statements, and bills. If you choose the "Age from due date" option, the program shows the number of days between the due date and the current date. If you choose "Age from transaction date" instead, QuickBooks shows the number of overdue days from the date of the transaction to the current date. For example, suppose an invoice is dated September 1 with a due date of October 1. On October 10, the "Age from due date" option shows the invoice's age as 10 days, whereas the "Age from transaction date" option shows the invoice's age as *40* days.
- **Reports – Show Items By**. Reports initially list items by name and description, but you can choose a different option here to show only the name or only the description.
- **Reports – Show Accounts By**. Reports typically list accounts by name. If you use especially short account names, you can use the account descriptions in reports instead. You can also show both names *and* descriptions.
- **Statement of Cash Flows**. Although QuickBooks does a great job of associating your accounts with the Operating, Investing, and Financing categories of the Statement of Cash Flows report, some companies are bound to require a customized cash flow report. In that case, click Classify Cash here to open the Classify Cash dialog box. (See page 454 to learn how to generate and customize a cash flow statement for your company.)
- **Default formatting for reports**. Turn on this checkbox if you want to use QuickBooks' default formatting for your reports. If you want to set the formatting for your reports, keep this checkbox turned off, and then click the Format button to open the Report Format Preferences dialog box. The settings in *this* dialog

box are the same ones that appear in the Modify Report dialog box's Header/Footer and Fonts & Numbers tabs (page 599). You can choose the information that you want to appear in headers and footers, and whether they're aligned to the left, right, or center of the page. You can also choose formatting for the report's text and numbers.

Sales & Customers

These preferences, shown in Figure 25-10, control how QuickBooks handles sales you make to your customers, including the shipping method you use and whether the program notifies you that you've created a duplicate invoice number.

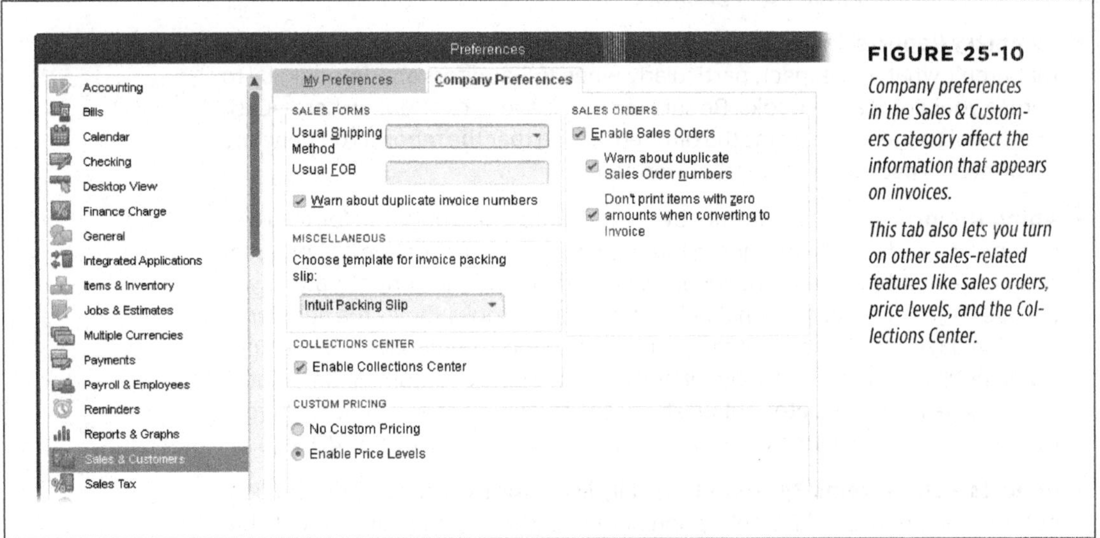

FIGURE 25-10

Company preferences in the Sales & Customers category affect the information that appears on invoices.

This tab also lets you turn on other sales-related features like sales orders, price levels, and the Collections Center.

The My Preferences tab has options that tell the program what to do about outstanding billable time and expenses. Here's what each one does:

- **Prompt for time/costs to add**. If you often bill for time and expenses, select this option. That way, the "Choose Billable Time and Costs" dialog box (shown in Figure 10-18 on page 255) opens automatically when you create an invoice for a customer who has outstanding billable time charges or expenses.
- **Don't add any**. Select this option if you rarely have time or expenses to invoice and don't want to see the "Choose Billable Time and Costs" dialog box or receive a reminder that outstanding time and expenses exist.
- **Ask what to do**. This option merely adds an additional step to what the "Prompt for time/costs to add" option does because you have to tell QuickBooks whether to open the "Choose Billable Time and Costs" dialog box. Selecting the "Prompt for time/costs to add" option instead is your best bet.

Here's a guide to the Sales & Customers preferences on the Company Preferences tab, all of which only QuickBooks administrators can change:

- **Usual Shipping Method**. If you negotiate a sweet deal with a shipping company and use it whenever possible, choose that company in this drop-down list. From then on, QuickBooks automatically selects this method in sales forms' Ship Via (or Via) fields. If the method you want to use isn't on the list, choose <Add New> to open the New Ship Method dialog box (page 152).
- **Usual FOB**. FOB stands for "free on board" and represents the location at which the customer becomes responsible for the products you ship. For example, suppose you ship products from your warehouse in Severance, Colorado, and you use Severance as your FOB location. As soon as your shipments leave Severance, the customer becomes the official owner of the products and is responsible for them if they get lost, damaged, or stolen in transit. Type a brief description of your FOB location in this box, and QuickBooks puts that info in the FOB field on invoices and other sales forms.
- **Warn about duplicate invoice numbers**. Turn on this checkbox if you want QuickBooks to alert you when you create an invoice with the same number as one you already entered.
- **Choose template for invoice packing slip**. If you ship products to customers, you can print a packing slip from QuickBooks to include in your shipments. To specify the packing slip you want to use, choose it in this drop-down list. From then on, when you create an invoice and choose Print→Packing Slip (page 317), QuickBooks automatically uses the template you selected. The program initially selects its built-in Intuit Packing Slip here, but you can create your own, as described on page 707.
- **Enable Collections Center**. If your customers always pay on time, you can turn this checkbox off. On the other hand, if you regularly get after customers to pay up, the Collections Center can help (see page 341). When you turn this checkbox on, you'll see the Collections Center icon in the Customer Center's toolbar. Income Tracker, introduced in QuickBooks 2014, provides another way to see the customer payments that are overdue.
- **Custom Pricing**. You can set multiple prices for the items you sell by using price levels. To do so, select the Enable Price Levels option here. Then refer to page 144 and page 146 to learn how to define and apply price levels, respectively.
- **Sales orders**. This preference is available only in QuickBooks Premier and Enterprise, which let you use sales orders to record customer orders before you create invoices. To do so, turn on the Enable Sales Orders checkbox. With it turned on, you can tell QuickBooks to warn you when you create a sales order with duplicate numbers, and to leave off any items with zero amounts when you convert a sales order into an invoice.

Sales Tax

Charging sales tax can be a complicated business, as the number of preferences on the Sales Tax category's Company Preferences tab indicates. If you don't charge sales tax, then in the "Do You Charge Sales Tax?" area, simply leave the No option selected and move on to more important endeavors. If you *do* charge sales tax, you can learn how to adjust the rest of these preferences as you set up Sales Tax items, charge sales tax, and pay sales tax to the appropriate authorities starting on page 547.

Search

The Search box (which is located at the top of the left icon bar or at the right end of the top icon bar) lets you search your company file to find customers, vendors, and other names; transactions like invoices and bills; amounts; dates; and text within memos, notes, and descriptions. If you use the top icon bar, on the My Preferences tab in this category, the "Show Search field in the Icon Bar" checkbox is turned on automatically, which makes the Search box easy to access at all times; if you turn this checkbox off, you can access the search feature by choosing Edit→Search. If you use the left icon bar or hide both icon bars, these preferences are grayed out because the Search box always appears at the top of the left icon bar.

Sometimes, you want to find things in your company file, like an invoice number or an inventory item. Other times, you want to search QuickBooks' help files to find out how to do something in the program. Out of the box, QuickBooks sets the "Choose where to search by default" setting to "Let me choose where I search each time." That way, when you type in the Search box in the top or left icon bar, you can choose "Search company file" or "Help" from the box's drop-down menu. However, if you're a whiz at QuickBooks, you can choose the "Search my company file" option instead so that QuickBooks automatically searches your company file for whatever you type in the Search box. If you usually need help using QuickBooks, select the "Search QuickBooks help" option instead.

NOTE QuickBooks always searches your company file when you choose Edit→Search.

The Company Preferences tab contains settings that control how often QuickBooks updates the data it uses to search. Because these updates make the program run a little slower, you have to compromise between performance and up-to-date information. QuickBooks initially turns on the "Update automatically" checkbox, and that's usually what you want. In the "Update every" drop-down list, choose a frequency for the automatic updates. In most cases, 30 or 60 minutes works well. If you want to update search info now, click Update Now. If you turn off the "Update automatically" checkbox, QuickBooks might run a little faster but you then have to click the Update Now button to be sure that you're searching up-to-date info in your company file.

Send Forms

As you've learned throughout this book, you can include a cover note when you send invoices, purchase orders, and other business forms via email. For example, if you email a purchase order, you can include details about the delivery in the note. Or you can include a cover note along with an invoice to add some personal interaction with your customer. When you email an invoice or other form, QuickBooks opens an Outlook email window—or, if you use a web-based email service, the dialog box corresponding to the form you're sending (Send Invoice, for example)—with your note filled in. The program attaches your invoice or other sales form to the email as a PDF file.

The settings in this preference category let you tell QuickBooks about your email program and email address, and set up templates for the messages you send.

Setting Your Send Preferences

On the My Preferences tab, QuickBooks automatically turns on the "Auto-check the 'Email Later' checkbox if customer's Preferred Delivery Method is e-mail" checkbox. That way, you don't have to remember whether customers prefer to receive paperwork by email or snail mail.

In the tab's Send E-mail Using section, select the Outlook option if you want to send QuickBooks email using Microsoft Outlook. (This option appears only if Outlook is installed on your computer.) If you use a web-based email service, select the Web Mail option, as shown in Figure 25-11, and then click Add at the bottom of the tab to tell QuickBooks about your email service. In the Add Email Info dialog box, fill in your email address and select your email provider (Gmail or Yahoo, for example), and QuickBooks fills in the Server Name and Port fields with the typical settings for that provider. If you use an email provider *other* than the ones on the list, choose Others as your provider, and then fill in the Server Name and Port fields manually. The third option in the tab's Send E-mail Using section, QuickBooks E-mail, is active only if you subscribe to services such as QuickBooks Payroll, Intuit Merchant Services, and QuickBooks Enterprise Full Service Plan.

Customizing Messages

QuickBooks includes standard messages for each type of form you send via email. If you want to customize the messages you send out, any QuickBooks administrator can change them. (You can create more than one template for a transaction type. However, you can choose the template you want to apply to a message only if you use Web Mail, not Outlook, to send messages from QuickBooks.) You can create standard notes for invoices, estimates, statements, sales orders, sales receipts, credit memos, purchase orders, reports, pay stubs, overdue invoices, almost-due invoices, and payment receipts. If your company has standard letters on file, you can simply copy and paste the contents of those letters from another program, such as Microsoft Word, into QuickBooks, as explained next.

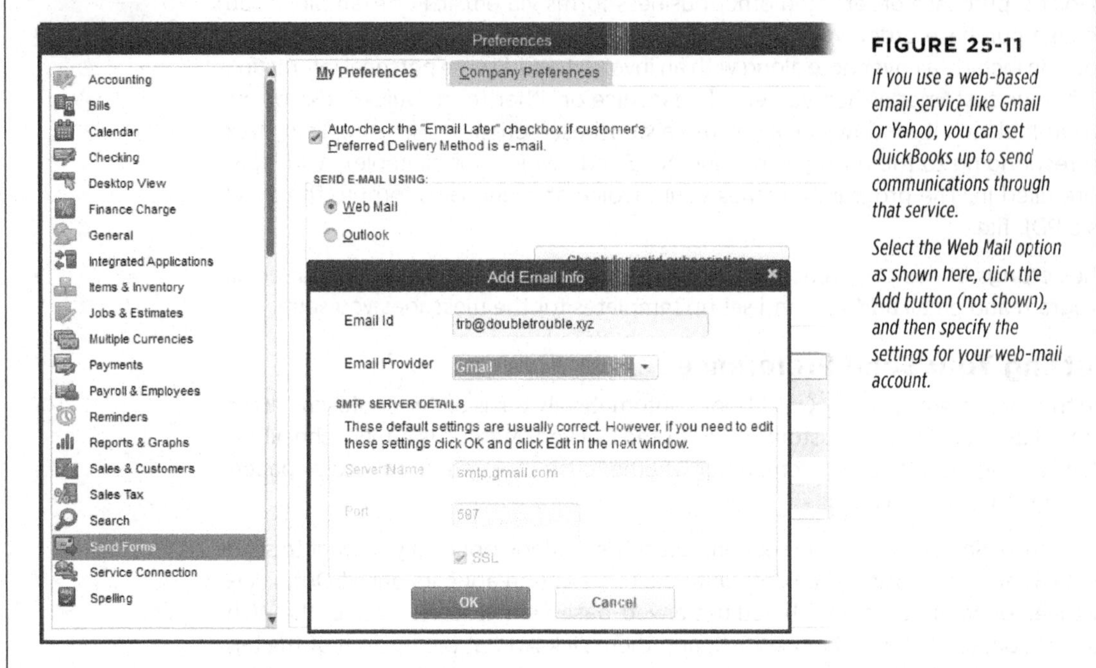

FIGURE 25-11

If you use a web-based email service like Gmail or Yahoo, you can set QuickBooks up to send communications through that service.

Select the Web Mail option as shown here, click the Add button (not shown), and then specify the settings for your web-mail account.

To configure a standard note for a particular type of form, in the Preferences dialog box, go to the Send Forms category, click the Company Preferences tab, and then follow these steps:

1. **In the Show drop-down list, choose the form you want to customize.**

   For example, to set up a cover letter for your invoices, choose Invoices.

2. **To create a new template, click Add Template. To edit an existing template, select it in the template table, and then click Edit.**

   Depending on which button you clicked, the Add Email Template or Edit Email Template dialog box opens. The former displays a sample message.

3. **If you're creating a new template, in the Template Name box, type the name of the template.**

   To tell QuickBooks to use this template automatically, turn on the Default checkbox.

4. **To insert a field in the subject or message, click to position your cursor in the text, and then click the Insert Field button and choose what you want to insert.**

For example, to tell QuickBooks to insert a name with the first name followed by the last name, choose Name-First-Last.

5. **Edit the content of the note using typical editing techniques.**

   For instance, click in the text to position the cursor where you want to add text, drag your cursor to select text you want to replace, or double-click a word to select it. To use a standard letter that's stored in another program, open the letter in that program and copy the text, and then paste it into QuickBooks by pressing Ctrl+V.

   To make sure everything is spelled correctly, click the Check Spelling button at the dialog box's bottom left, and QuickBooks alerts you to any suspect words in the subject line or body of your letter.

6. **To save your changes, click Save.**

   If you created a new template, it appears in the template table.

Service Connection

If your company uses QuickBooks' services, such as bank feeds, QuickBooks administrators can control how people log into those services by adjusting the settings in this preference category. (The easiest way to learn about or sign up for these services is to choose Help→Add QuickBooks Services, and then click the Learn More button or the link for the one you want.)

As explained in a moment, each person who uses QuickBooks services can control the behavior of online sessions, but security is a company-wide issue, so the options for whether to prompt for a password appear on the Company Preferences tab. Here are the service connection preferences that administrators can set and when you might want to use them:

- **Automatically connect without asking for a password**. Choosing this option automatically logs people into the QuickBooks Business Services network without a login name or password. This option is appropriate if you're the only person who accesses the network or you aren't concerned about security.
- **Always ask for a password before connecting**. Choose this option to make your employees provide a login name and password each time they access QuickBooks Business Services. This option is handy if several people access the services or if different people have different privileges with the services you use.
- **Allow background downloading of service messages**. If you want QuickBooks to check for messages and updates when your Internet connection isn't tied up with other work, leave this checkbox turned on. QuickBooks then checks the Intuit website periodically and downloads updates or messages. If you turn this checkbox off, you can check for updates at a convenient time by choosing Help→Update QuickBooks.

If you aren't a QuickBooks administrator, you can still make some choices about your connection to QuickBooks Business Services. On the My Preferences tab, the "Give me the option of saving a file whenever I download Web Connect data" checkbox lets you decide when to process downloaded transactions. If you want QuickBooks to ask you whether to process downloaded transactions immediately or save them to a file, leave this checkbox on. If you turn it off, QuickBooks processes downloaded transactions immediately.

You can launch QuickBooks by downloading WebConnect data or by double-clicking a QuickBooks file that contains WebConnect data you downloaded previously. When you open the program this way, you often want to continue working in QuickBooks after you process the downloaded transactions. To keep QuickBooks open after it processes transactions, leave the "If QuickBooks is run by my browser, don't close it after WebConnect is done" checkbox turned on.

Spelling

QuickBooks' spell checker helps you find common misspellings in most text fields. Spell checking is a personal preference: Each person who logs into a company file can choose whether to use spell checking by leaving the "Always check spelling before printing, saving, or sending supported forms" checkbox on or turning it off.

If you leave spell checking on, you can choose words that you want the spell checker to ignore. You can tell it to ignore Internet addresses, words that contain numbers, words that begin with a capital letter, words that are in all uppercase letters, and words with a mixture of upper- and lowercase letters.

When QuickBooks checks spelling in transactions you record, such as item descriptions in invoices, you can click Add to add custom words to the program's dictionary so that QuickBooks won't flag those unusual spellings in future transactions. You'll see the custom words you've added in the Word table on the My Preferences tab. To remove a custom word from the dictionary, in the table, click its "Delete?" cell to add a checkmark.

Tax: 1099

The Company Preferences tab in this category begins with the most important 1099 question: "Do you file 1099-MISC forms?" If you don't use 1099 vendors such as self-employed subcontractors, or you delegate 1099 generation to your accountant, simply choose the No option and ignore the rest of the preferences in this category. If you *do* file 1099-MISC forms, you can specify the accounts you use to track 1099 vendor payments and the minimum amount you have to report to the IRS. To learn how to map accounts to 1099 boxes and generate 1099s, flip to page 468.

Time & Expenses

In this category, the first setting on the Company Preferences tab tells QuickBooks whether you track time at all. If you do, select the Yes option. Then you can choose the first day of the workweek that appears if you use weekly timesheets in QuickBooks (page 167). The "Mark all time entries as billable" checkbox is initially turned on, but if you bill only some of your time, turn this checkbox off. That way, you can designate time as billable by turning on the Billable checkbox or cell in the Write Checks or Enter Bills windows or in a timesheet.

The Invoicing Options section has settings related to how you handle billable time and expenses on invoices:

- **Create invoices from a list of time and expenses**. This checkbox is available only in QuickBooks Premier and Enterprise. If you turn it on, the Customer menu includes the "Invoice for Time & Expenses" entry, which lets you view a list of all your unbilled time and expenses and select the customers you want to bill, as described on page 254.
- **Track reimbursed expenses as income**. Companies differ in their approach to reimbursed expenses, as explained on page 193. Some assign reimbursed expenses as income and then deduct the expenses as costs. The method you choose doesn't affect the profit you earn—the reason for tracking reimbursable expenses as income is to charge sales tax on those expenses. If you want to post reimbursed expenses to an income account, turn on this checkbox.
- **Mark all expenses as billable**. This checkbox is initially turned on, which means QuickBooks automatically marks all your expenses as billable. If only *some* of your expenses are billable to your customers, turn this checkbox off so you can turn on the Billable checkbox or cell in a timesheet or bill to designate specific expenses as billable to a customer or job.
- **Default Markup Percentage**. Suppose you're an interior decorator and you mark up the furniture and bric-a-brac you sell by a standard percentage. When you specify your markup percentage in this box and then create a new item (page 106), QuickBooks calculates the item's sales price based on its cost. For example, if you create an inventory part for a black leather sofa and enter its cost as $10,000, a 20 percent markup results in a sales price of $12,000. If you charge a different markup on only a few of the things you sell, then simply modify the sales prices that QuickBooks calculates.
- **Default Markup Account**. To assign the income from your markup percentage to a specific account, select it in this drop-down list. You can choose an account dedicated to markup income or simply assign markup to your product-related income account.

CHAPTER

26

Integrating QuickBooks with Other Programs

Most companies use other programs in *addition* to QuickBooks to keep their businesses running smoothly. For example, you can use QuickBooks data in other programs to study your company's financial ratios, calculate employee bonuses based on services sold, send special sales letters to customers on their birthdays, and so on. Similarly, other programs may contain data that would be useful to pull into QuickBooks. For example, if you use an estimating program that has all the products and services you sell in its database, there's no reason to manually enter that info in QuickBooks.

QuickBooks doesn't share its most intimate details with just any program. It reserves its data for a few select programs—or the ones you tell it to play nicely with. For example, you can set up letters in QuickBooks to send to customers, and the program automatically opens Microsoft Word with your customer data merged into form letters and envelopes. And if you manage contacts with Microsoft Outlook (not Outlook Express), keeping records up to date is easy. By synchronizing your QuickBooks company file and your contact database, you enter changes in one place and both programs automatically reflect the updates.

Programs that can read a QuickBooks company file still have to ask permission to grab QuickBooks data. The QuickBooks administrator (or other QuickBooks users whom the administrator anoints) can say whether another program can have access and how much. And for software that can't read a company file directly but *can* provide valuable assistance processing your financial data (such as Excel, whose spreadsheets can calculate financial ratios that QuickBooks can't), you can export and import data between programs as described starting on page 684.

This chapter describes how to integrate QuickBooks at whatever level of trust you prefer. It also tells you about add-on services that Intuit provides and how to find third-party programs that work with QuickBooks.

Mail Merge to a Word Document

Business communications are the perfect marriage of QuickBooks data and word processing. You can generate letters and envelopes in no time by combining QuickBooks' customer or vendor contact info and other data with Microsoft Word mail-merge documents. QuickBooks includes dozens of ready-to-mail Word documents that cover the most common business communications, from customer thank-you notes to less-friendly denials of requests for credit. And if nothing less than Pulitzer Prize quality will do for your business letters, you can modify the built-in letters and envelopes in Word or write your own.

When you want to prepare letters in QuickBooks, the best way to start is by choosing Company→"Prepare Letters with Envelopes," which displays a submenu with the following categories (each of which includes several letter templates):

- **Collection Letters** include the invoices or statements that are overdue, and remind customers to pay up. QuickBooks automatically pulls the overdue balance and overdue invoices from your company file.
- **Customer Letters** pull the customer's contact and address information from QuickBooks to address the letter and envelope. The rest of the letter is boilerplate for situations such as thanking customers for their business, apologizing for a mistake, or sending a contract.
- **Vendor Letters** include credit requests, disputed charges, payments on your account, and two blank templates for sending mail or a fax to a vendor.
- **Employee Letters** cover birthdays, sick time, vacations, and general communications.
- **Letters to Other Names** cover a hodgepodge of different recipients, so QuickBooks doesn't even try to guess what you need. The only template in this category is a blank letter with basic mail merge fields.
- **Customize Letter Templates** is a feature that helps you create a brand-new template, convert a Word document into a template, edit an existing template, or organize the templates you already have, as described in the box on page 673.

NOTE The first time you choose one of the items on the Company→"Prepare Letters with Envelopes" submenu, QuickBooks may tell you it can't find the preinstalled letter templates in your company file folder. In that case, it asks if you want to copy its built-in templates. Click Copy to create copies of the built-in templates in the folder with your company file. (If you store letter templates in another folder on your computer, click Browse to choose that folder.)

POWER USERS' CLINIC

Customizing Letter Templates

To create, edit, or otherwise manage custom letter templates, choose Company→"Prepare Letters with Envelopes"→ Customize Letter Templates. Then, in the "Letters and Envelopes" wizard's window, choose one of these options:

- **Create a New Letter Template From Scratch**. When you choose this option, you can specify the type of letter you want to create and the name of the template. QuickBooks then sends a blank letter template to Word and adds a special toolbar to Word (see Figure 26-1). In addition to writing the content of the letter, you can add fields from QuickBooks to automatically fill in your company and customer (or other recipient) info.
- **Convert an Existing Microsoft Word Document to a Letter Template**. This option lets you use an existing Word document as the basis for a new template. Once you specify the type of letter, you can then add more text or QuickBooks fields to the document as if you were creating a new template from scratch.
- **View or Edit Existing Letter Templates**. You can open and edit any existing template.
- **Organize Existing Letter Templates**. When you choose this option, you can navigate through each template category, choose a template, and then delete, duplicate, rename, or move it to a different category.

QuickBooks stores the Word documents for letter templates in a document folder. In Windows 7 and 8, the templates are in *C:\Users\Public\Public Documents\Intuit\QuickBooks\Company Files\QuickBooks Letter Templates*. There's a subfolder for each category of template (Collections Letters, Customer Letters, and so on).

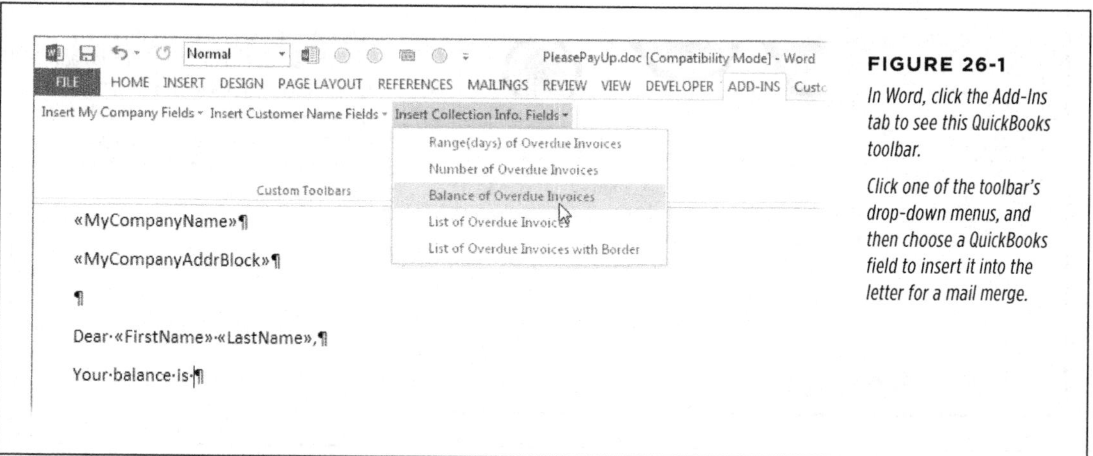

FIGURE 26-1

In Word, click the Add-Ins tab to see this QuickBooks toolbar.

Click one of the toolbar's drop-down menus, and then choose a QuickBooks field to insert it into the letter for a mail merge.

Creating Letters and Envelopes in QuickBooks

Preparing any kind of letter with QuickBooks' letter wizard takes no more than a few clicks, and the collection letter wizard has some extra smarts. For most letters, you can tell QuickBooks whether you want to include active and/or inactive names, and then select recipients. The collection letter wizard can also filter the Customer:Job List by how late payments are.

Here are the steps for creating letters and envelopes using a collection letter as an example:

1. **Choose Company→"Prepare Letters with Envelopes"→Collection Letters.**

   QuickBooks opens the "Letters and Envelopes" wizard and shows the recipient options for collection letters.

2. **Choose options to select who you want to send letters to (Figure 26-2).**

   QuickBooks remembers the options you choose and selects them automatically the next time you launch this wizard.

NOTE For non-collection letters, you still choose active or inactive customers (or both) and whether to send letters to each customer or each job, but those are your only choices. For a recall notice, for example, choose the Both option to send the letter to active and inactive customers alike. (The first screen you see for letters to vendors, employees, and people on the Other Names List combines the list of selected names and the options for filtering names.)

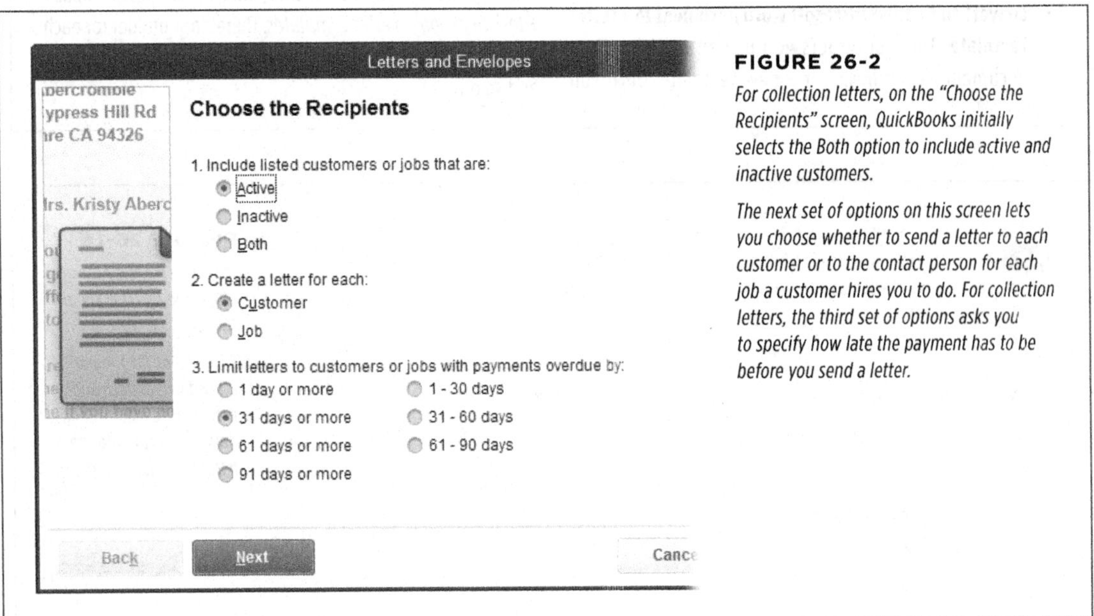

FIGURE 26-2

For collection letters, on the "Choose the Recipients" screen, QuickBooks initially selects the Both option to include active and inactive customers.

The next set of options on this screen lets you choose whether to send a letter to each customer or to the contact person for each job a customer hires you to do. For collection letters, the third set of options asks you to specify how late the payment has to be before you send a letter.

3. **Click Next to display the "Review and Edit Recipients" screen.**

   For collection letters, QuickBooks displays a message if any customers have unapplied credits or payments. Rather than embarrassing yourself by sending a collection letter to a customer whose payments are up to date, you're best off clicking OK to close the message box and then clicking Cancel to exit the wizard so you can apply credits and payments *before* preparing collection letters. (The box on page 677 explains how to check for customer credits and payments.)

If there aren't any unapplied credits or payments, QuickBooks automatically selects all the names that match the criteria you specified on the previous screen.

4. **If you've already talked to some customers and want to remove them from the list, click the checkmarks in front of their names to turn them off.**

   You can click Mark All or Unmark All to select or clear every name. If you want only a few names, it's faster to click Unmark All and then click each name you want. The list is initially sorted by name, but for collection letters you can also select the Amount option to sort by the amount that's overdue if you want to send letters only to customers whose balances are greater than, say, $100.

5. **When you've selected the customers you want to send letters to, click Next.**

   QuickBooks displays the Choose a Letter Template screen.

6. **Select the collection letter template you want to use, and then click Next.**

   QuickBooks includes three types of collection letters. The formal one is a straightforward request for payment, the friendly one assumes the customer simply forgot, and the harsh one includes the threat of turning the account over to a collection agency. The friendly and formal letters can't do any harm, but if you're considering sending harsh letters, you might want to create your own template for that communication.

   To use a different template entirely, select the "Create or Edit a letter template" option. When you click Next, you can choose one of the options described in the box on page 673 (create a new template, convert a Word document, or edit an existing template).

7. **In the "Enter a Name and Title" screen's Name box, type the name you want to include in the letter's signature block. In the Title box, type the signer's title.**

   When you click Next, QuickBooks sends the information to Microsoft Word, as shown in Figure 26-3. It also displays the "Print Letters and Envelopes" screen in the Letters and Envelopes wizard, but you aren't ready for that screen just yet. Depending on how many letters you're sending, you might have to wait a few minutes before Word launches with your letters.

NOTE QuickBooks warns you if there's any info missing, like a recipient's address. If there is, you can enter it in Word or close the Word document, add the missing info to QuickBooks, and then redo the steps in this section.

8. **After you print the letters from Word, go back to QuickBooks. On the "Print Letters and Envelopes" screen, click Next if you want to print envelopes that go with the letters you just printed in Word.**

   If you don't want to print envelopes, click Cancel. The wizard closes and you're done.

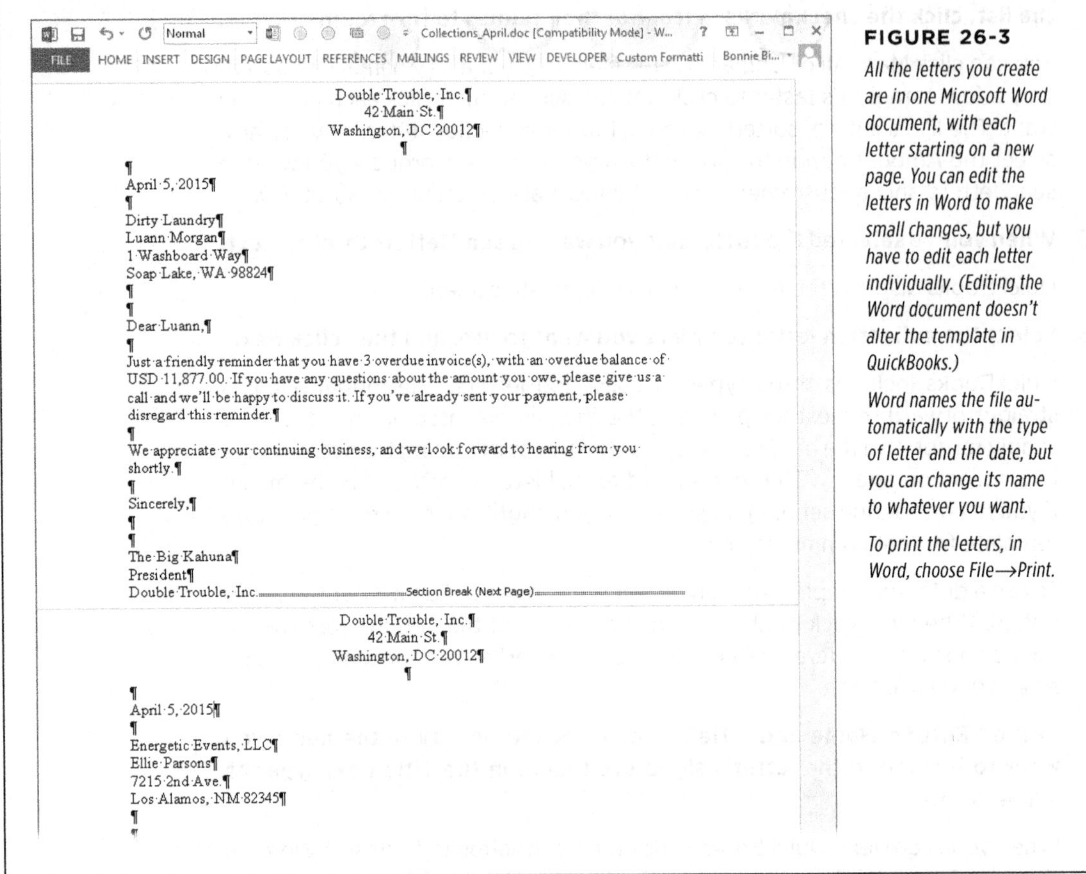

FIGURE 26-3

All the letters you create are in one Microsoft Word document, with each letter starting on a new page. You can edit the letters in Word to make small changes, but you have to edit each letter individually. (Editing the Word document doesn't alter the template in QuickBooks.)

Word names the file automatically with the type of letter and the date, but you can change its name to whatever you want.

To print the letters, in Word, choose File→Print.

9. **If you clicked Next to print envelopes, QuickBooks opens the Envelope Options dialog box. In the Envelope Size drop-down list, choose the type of envelope you use.**

   If your envelopes already include your return address, turn off the "Print return address" checkbox.

10. **In the Envelope Options dialog box, click OK.**

    You'll see a preview of the envelopes in Word and Word's Envelope Options dialog box.

11. **When you've got envelopes in your printer, in Word's Envelope Options dialog box, click OK.**

    Word starts printing your envelopes.

12. **Back in QuickBooks, in the "Letters and Envelopes" dialog box, click Finish.**

UP TO SPEED

Reviewing Customer Credits and Payments

The Open Invoices report shows unapplied credits and payments as well as open invoices, but you can modify this report to show only the payments and unapplied credits that are available. That way, you can apply those payments and credits to your customers' balances (as explained on page 345 and page 350, respectively) so that, when you create collection letters, QuickBooks selects only the customers with overdue balances.

Here's how to produce a report of payments and unapplied credits:

1. Choose Reports→Customers & Receivables→Open Invoices.
2. To see only unapplied credits and payments, in the report window's toolbar, click Customize Report, and then click the Filters tab. (If the Modify Report dialog box opens automatically, simply click its Filters tab.)
3. In the Filter list on the left, choose Transaction Type (you may have to scroll down to see this option).
4. In the Transaction Type drop-down list, choose Multiple Transaction Types.
5. In the Select Transaction Types dialog box, click Payment, and then click Credit Memo.
6. Click OK to close the Select Transaction Types dialog box, and then click OK in the Modify Report dialog box to update the report to show only unapplied credit memos and payments.

For a quick view of *one* customer's transactions, open the Customer Center (on the Home Page, click Customers) and select the customer on the Customers & Jobs tab. Then, at the top right of the Customer Information panel, click the QuickReport link.

Synchronizing Contacts

If you keep information about contacts in Microsoft Outlook (2007 through 2013)—*not* Outlook Express—you can use a tool called Contact Sync to synchronize those records with your QuickBooks contact data. In addition to saving time by not having to enter data twice, synchronizing your contact info also helps reduce errors. As long as you enter an update correctly in one program, you're sure to get the right info in your other contact database. Regardless of which program you update contact info in, you can transfer any changes to the other database.

NOTE The only time synchronizing doesn't apply is when you delete contacts. So if you delete contacts in Outlook, for example, QuickBooks *doesn't* delete the corresponding records in your company file. (If you really want those records gone, make them inactive, as described on page 90.) On the other hand, if you delete a contact in QuickBooks but don't delete it in Outlook, it'll reappear in QuickBooks unless you tell Contact Sync to ignore it (see step 11 on page 680).

Using QuickBooks Contact Sync for Outlook

If you use Outlook 2007 or later, QuickBooks' Contact Sync for Outlook tool can help you synchronize contact data. (Contact Sync works only with the 32-bit versions of Outlook 2010 and 2013.) Although the menu item for synchronizing appears in

QuickBooks' File→Utilities submenu automatically, you have to install Contact Sync before you can get started.

NOTE When this book was being written in the summer of 2014, Contact Sync for Outlook didn't work with Outlook 2013. The following instructions should work if you're using an earlier version of Outlook, and hopefully with Outlook 2013 by the time you read this. For updates, see this book's Missing CD page at *www.missingmanuals/cds*.

Here's how to download this tool and put it to work:

1. **Choose File→Utilities→Synchronize Contacts.**

   If Contact Sync isn't installed, a message box tells you that you have to download and install it. Click OK to do just that. QuickBooks opens a browser window to the QuickBooks Contact Sync for Outlook page (*http://support.quickbooks.intuit.com/support/tools/contact_sync*). Below the Download heading, type the email address you used when you registered QuickBooks (page 740), and then click Continue To Download. You can save the installation file (click Save) or run it immediately (click Run) to install the software.

   Installing is easy. Run the installation wizard as you do for other programs. Accept the license agreement, choose a destination folder, and then click Next, and the installation begins. You may have to restart your computer after the installation finishes.

2. **After you install Contact Sync, launch Outlook.**

   Contact Sync features appear on Outlook's Add-Ins tab.

3. **In QuickBooks, log in as the administrator and open the company file you want to synchronize.**

4. **In Outlook, click the Add-Ins tab, and then click Synchronize Contacts.**

   A Connecting To QuickBooks message box appears briefly while Outlook and QuickBooks talk to each other. Then the QuickBooks Contact Sync dialog box opens and selects the company file that's open in QuickBooks.

NOTE If you want to import contacts from a different company file, click Cancel and then, in QuickBooks, open the company file with the contacts you want to import.

5. **In the QuickBooks Contact Sync dialog box, click Setup to begin the setup in earnest.**

   The Select An Outlook Folder screen appears. If you're like most people, you have only one folder for contacts, named something like *\\Personal Folders\Contacts* or *\\Outlook\Contacts*, which the wizard selects automatically.

6. **If you want to synchronize to a different Outlook folder, choose it, and then click Next.**

   The Select QuickBooks List Types To Synchronize screen appears.

7. **To synchronize all contacts, turn on the Customer, Include Customer Jobs, and Vendor checkboxes, and then click Next.**

   For each checkbox you turn on, the Setup Assistant creates a subfolder in the Outlook Contacts folder.

8. **On the Exclude Contacts From Synchronization screen, turn on the checkboxes for the types of names you *don't* want to transfer back and forth, and then click Next.**

   When you turn on these checkboxes, names assigned to Outlook's Personal category or marked as Private won't transfer to QuickBooks.

9. **On the "Mapping Customer Fields (Part 1 of 2)" screen, change the mapping of any QuickBooks field that doesn't point to the right Outlook field, as shown in Figure 26-4. Click Next when the mappings are the way you want them.**

   The Mapping Customer Fields screen displays the QuickBooks contact fields on the left and its guesses about what Outlook fields they're equivalent to on the right.

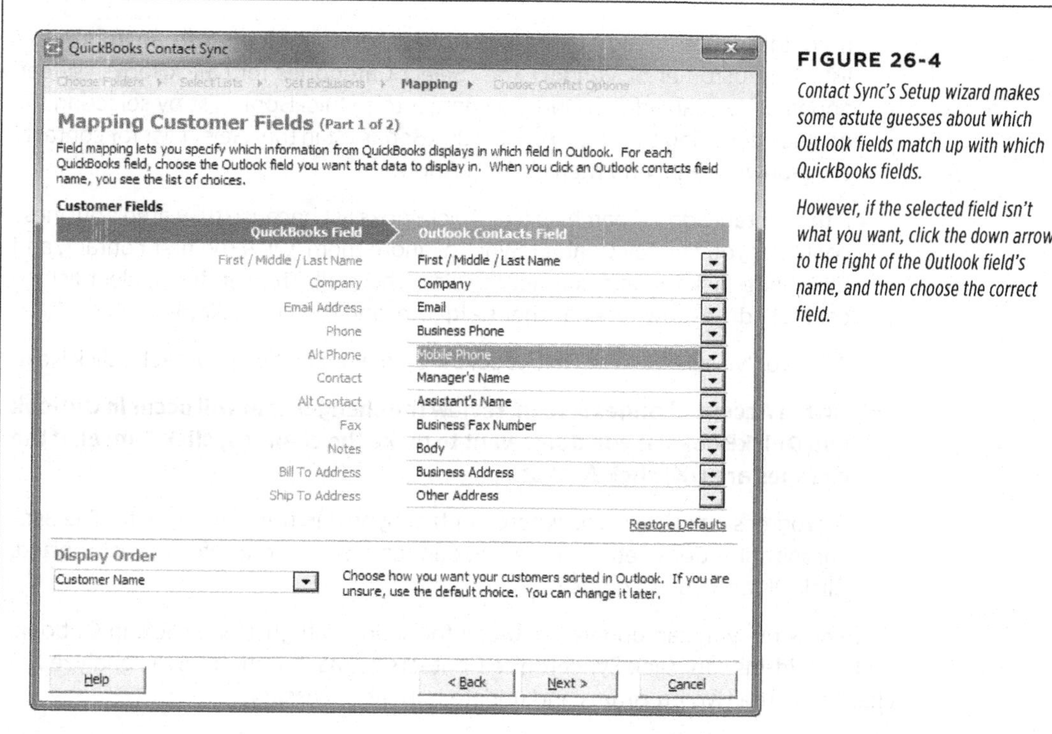

FIGURE 26-4

Contact Sync's Setup wizard makes some astute guesses about which Outlook fields match up with which QuickBooks fields.

However, if the selected field isn't what you want, click the down arrow to the right of the Outlook field's name, and then choose the correct field.

10. **If you turned on the checkboxes to import jobs and vendors, repeat step 9 to map job and vendor fields to the corresponding Outlook fields.**

    Chances are you'll make the same changes for jobs and vendors as you did for customer fields.

11. **On the Set Conflict Action screen, select how you want Contact Sync to resolve discrepancies between Outlook and QuickBooks, and then click Save.**

    Contact Sync automatically selects the "Let me decide each case" option, which means you get to tell QuickBooks what to do if the contact info in Outlook differs from the data in QuickBooks. If you usually update contacts in Outlook, select the Outlook Data Wins option. If you usually update contacts in QuickBooks, select the QuickBooks Data Wins option instead.

12. **On the "Change Settings or Synchronize Now" screen, if you want to change any settings, click Setup (you'll retrace your steps until you're back at this screen). If you're ready to synchronize, click Sync Now.**

    The Contact Sync screen keeps you updated on the progress it's making. When the synchronization is done, the Contact Overview Complete screen appears, showing you how many customers and vendors it found and either matched or added to Outlook.

13. **When you're done reviewing the Contact Overview Complete screen, click Next.**

    If contacts that already existed in Outlook don't match up to a QuickBooks list (like Customer or Vendor), the "Select Categories for QuickBooks" screen appears. You can add an Outlook contact to a QuickBooks list by selecting the contact, choosing the appropriate QuickBooks list in the "Select list for contact" drop-down menu, and then clicking Apply.

    If the contacts don't match up to a QuickBooks list because they aren't business contacts, you can tell Contact Sync to ignore them. Click the first contact, and then Shift-click the last contact to select them all. Then, in the "Select list for contact" drop-down menu, choose Ignore, and then click Apply.

    After you've selected the QuickBooks lists for your Outlook contacts, click Next.

14. **On the Accept Changes screen, review the changes that will occur in Outlook and QuickBooks. If you don't want to make the changes, click Cancel. If the changes are OK, click Accept.**

    A progress box shows you where Contact Sync is in transferring data. The Synchronization Complete message box appears when your info is synchronized. Click OK and you're done.

From now on, you can update contact information with just one click. In Outlook, on the Add-Ins tab, click Synchronize Contacts to make Contact Sync analyze the changes in the two programs and update both as necessary.

Working with Other Apps

Because QuickBooks is so popular, Intuit and plenty of other companies offer programs to fill the niches that QuickBooks doesn't handle—or doesn't handle the way you want. For example, QuickBooks Pro and Premier's inventory-tracking feature offers only average cost inventory (page 536), so many users turn to third-party inventory applications for LIFO (last in/first out) and FIFO (first in/first out) costing. Estimating is another example, and there are a gazillion more. Third-party software developers can build products that integrate with QuickBooks by using Intuit's software development kit (SDK). And Intuit offers quite a few add-ons of its own. This section describes how to find applications that meet your needs and how to set them up to play nicely with QuickBooks.

Finding Add-On Apps

Intuit and other companies offer scads of business services and add-on apps you can purchase. The price might be worthwhile when you take into account the cost of your employees' time or—far more valuable—you being able to relax on weekends instead of catching up on company paperwork. You can find many of these add-ons right within QuickBooks. If you don't find what you're looking for there, you might have more luck on the Intuit App Center website (*http://apps.intuit.com*) or Intuit Marketplace website (*http://marketplace.intuit.com*).

Here's some info about places you can look for add-on apps and services:

- **QuickBooks' windows** promote services that relate to the task you're performing. For example, click Receive Payments on the QuickBooks Home Page, and the Receive Payments window's Main tab displays an icon labeled Add Credit Card Processing. You can also access Intuit's offerings by choosing Help→Add QuickBooks Services.
- At the bottom of the left icon bar (page 30), the section labeled **Do More with QuickBooks** lists several Intuit services, including payroll, credit card processing, and ordering supplies.
- The **Intuit App Center** (*http://appcenter.intuit.com*) is a one-stop shop for apps that work with QuickBooks: Intuit and third-party apps, web-based apps, mobile apps, and more. You can get to it from within QuickBooks by going to the Home Page's Company panel and clicking the "Web and Mobile Apps" icon, or by choosing Help→"App Center: Find More Business Solutions."
- The **Intuit Marketplace** (*http://marketplace.intuit.com*) catalogs thousands of third-party desktop and web-based programs that work with QuickBooks data, most of which offer free trials that last from 30 to 90 days. Programs listed in the Marketplace share data with QuickBooks but target different industries or services. Sure, Intuit sells Premier editions of QuickBooks for a few industries (see page xix), but the Marketplace offers additional software for those industries, as well as customized accounting solutions for industries like agriculture, hotels and restaurants, transportation, and utilities. For example, the Construction/

Contractors section has programs that produce estimates and generate documents that conform to industry association standards—while still sharing data with your QuickBooks company file.

The Intuit Marketplace site lists third-party programs in two ways: by industry and by business function. For example, if you're looking for contact-management software, you don't have to navigate every industry link looking for programs. Below the Find Apps heading, click By Business Need and then, in the list that appears, choose Customer Management (CRM).

You can also refine your search for applications that are compatible with your edition of QuickBooks. After you select a category you're interested in on the main Marketplace page, click the down arrow to the right of the Check Product Compatibility box, and then choose the edition you use: Pro, Premier, Enterprise, Canada, and so on.

- If you use **Google** to search for basic terms like "QuickBooks third-party application," you'll get tons of results. Of course, if you focus your search (by adding "medical office," for example) you can narrow the results. And, if you use all of the 10 keywords that you can enter in a Google search to describe the QuickBooks add-ons you seek, you might get a few dozen links worth investigating.
- Try searching **websites like Download.com** (*www.download.com*) using "QuickBooks" as a keyword. Download.com has dozens of programs that work with QuickBooks, some of which aren't industry-based at all but are still incredibly valuable. For example, you can download an app that lets you transfer transaction data from Excel to your QuickBooks company file.

TIP Before you let a third-party program loose on your QuickBooks company file, you need to check it out. Does it work with your computer's operating system and your network? Does it have the features you need? Is it easy to use? Does it come with helpful documentation? If it meets all those criteria, you should still take a few safety measures before starting to use it: Back up your company file and any ancillary files. Store the backup on a CD, DVD, or thumb drive, so you can't overwrite it by mistake. Then make a copy of your company file specifically for your test. If the third-party program doesn't pass the test, you can uninstall it and go back to using your regular company file.

Setting Up an Integrated App

Integrated applications don't read data from exported text files; they actually access your company file to get info. To protect your data from programs that *shouldn't* read your company file, you have to tell QuickBooks which programs you *do* want digging into your financial data.

Letting programs access your data is something you set up with QuickBooks preferences. In QuickBooks, choose Edit→Preferences→Integrated Applications, and then click the Company Preferences tab (Figure 26-5). There you can turn on the "Don't allow any applications to access this company file" checkbox to keep *all* programs out. But if you're reading this section, you probably want at least one program to access your QuickBooks data, so leave that checkbox turned off. If you want QuickBooks to tell you when an application's certificate has expired turn on the—you guessed it—"Notify the user before running any application whose certificate has expired" checkbox. An expired certificate doesn't mean the application has changed, so you may choose to leave the checkbox turned off to bypass the warnings.

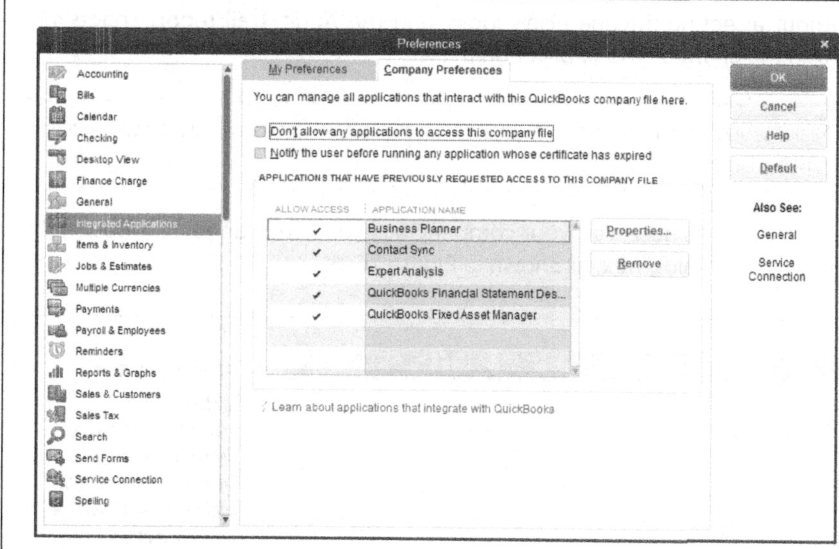

FIGURE 26-5

Only the QuickBooks administrator can give programs access rights.

To learn more about how integrated apps work with QuickBooks, click the "Learn about applications that integrate with QuickBooks" link shown here. When you do that, a browser window opens to a support page that describes Intuit Sync Manager, a feature that synchronizes your QuickBooks data with Intuit's online services and third-party apps you use.

As long as the "Don't allow any applications to access this company file" checkbox is turned off, when a program tries to access your company file, QuickBooks displays an Application Certificate dialog box. If you're the QuickBooks administrator or have permission to dole out file access, choose one of the dialog box's options to set the program's access to the company file. Obviously, choosing No keeps the program out. But if you want to let the program in, you have three options to choose from:

- **Yes, prompt each time**. When you're letting another program access your data, this is the safest option. The program can get in only when someone with the rights to approve access says so—a small obstacle that prevents someone from breaking in and running the program after hours. If no one who can approve access is available to say yes, the integrated application (or the person who's running it) is out of luck.
- **Yes, whenever this QuickBooks company file is open**. This option is a bit more trusting. As long as someone is working on the company file, the integrated application can access the file without asking permission.
- **Yes, always allow access even if QuickBooks is not running**. This is by far the most lenient choice. The integrated program can help itself to your financial data even if no one with a QuickBooks login is working on the file. This option

is exactly what you need if the integrated application is a resource hog that you run at night.

When you choose this option, you can specify that the application be a QuickBooks user and that it must log in. Rather than use one of your employee's logins, create a separate QuickBooks user (page 722) specifically for that integrated application. That way, you can control the type of data the program can access without affecting anyone else's login, and the Audit Trail report (page 437) shows the changes the application makes.

TIP Name the user after the third-party application. For example, call the user Fishbowl if you're setting it up for the Fishbowl inventory app.

After a program has accessed your company file, you can change its access rights in the Properties dialog box, as shown in Figure 26-6.

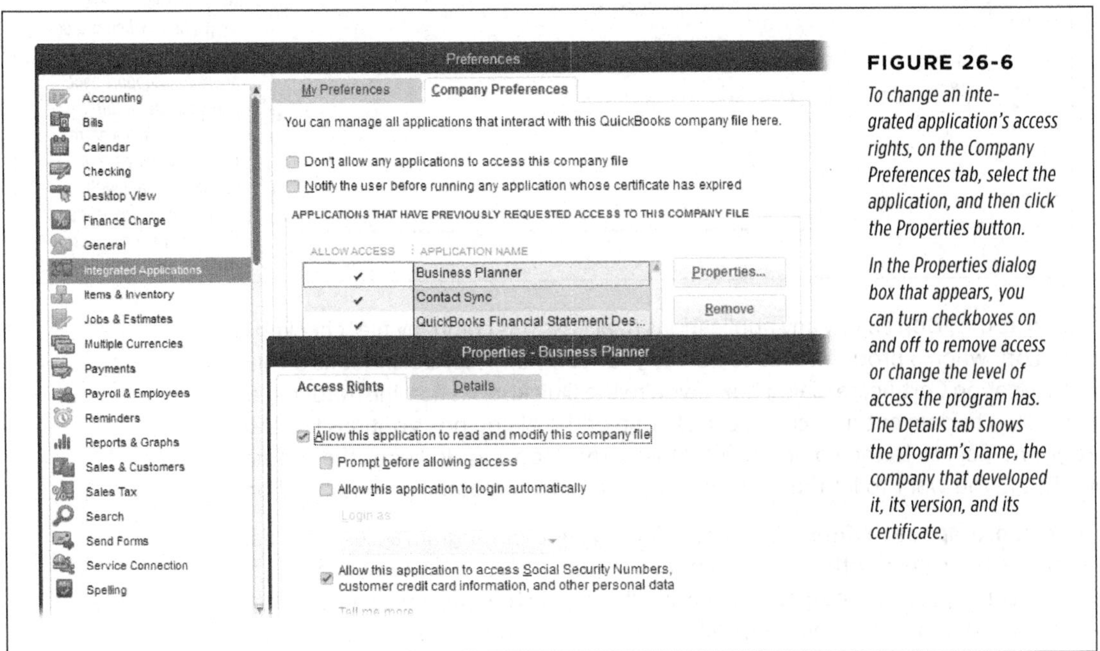

FIGURE 26-6

To change an integrated application's access rights, on the Company Preferences tab, select the application, and then click the Properties button.

In the Properties dialog box that appears, you can turn checkboxes on and off to remove access or change the level of access the program has. The Details tab shows the program's name, the company that developed it, its version, and its certificate.

Exporting QuickBooks Data

Programs that don't integrate with QuickBooks can still do things that QuickBooks can't. For example, you can export a report to Excel and take advantage of that program's wider range of calculations and formatting options. To get data out of your QuickBooks company file and into another program, you have three choices:

- **Export file**. You can create a *delimited text file* (a file that separates each field with a delimiter like a comma or a tab) that contains data from your QuickBooks file. For example, you can generate export files for QuickBooks lists, such as the Item List. For QuickBooks records with contact info, like your Customer:Job and Vendor lists, you can produce export files that contain *all* the contact info or only addresses.
- **Report file**. You can export any QuickBooks report to a file that you can use in another program. Compared with exporting a list in its entirety, this option gives you more control over how much information you export. If you want to export data from specific customers, specific data from several lists, from transactions, or from specific fields, exporting reports is your *only* choice. By creating a customized version of the Customer Contact List report or Vendor Contact List report (see page 690), for example, you can export the same set of records repeatedly, creating delimited files, spreadsheets, and so on. Chapter 23 covers QuickBooks' reports in detail.
- **Excel file**. This option is ideal if you're not sure what info you need and you'd rather delete and rearrange columns in a spreadsheet program. Throughout QuickBooks, you can get to the same Export dialog box that you see when you export reports. For example, at the bottom of the Item List window, click Excel→Export All Items. In the Customer Center's menu bar, click Excel, and then choose either Export Customer List or Export Transactions. (The Vendor Center and the Employee Center have similar features.) You can then edit the spreadsheet in Excel all you want and transfer the data to yet *another* program when you're done. The box on page 687 explains how to use Excel to view your QuickBooks data.

The following sections explain all your options.

Exporting Lists and Addresses

When you export QuickBooks lists as delimited text files, the export file (called an IIF file because of its .iif file extension, which stands for "Intuit interchange format") contains values from *all* the fields associated with those lists. Creating export files is easy—the only choice you have to make is which list(s) to export, and then QuickBooks creates an IIF file that contains every field for every list you chose.

EXPORTING LISTS TO A TEXT FILE

Exporting one or more lists to a delimited text file involves only a few quick steps:

1. **Choose File→Utilities→Export→Lists to IIF Files.**

   QuickBooks opens an Export dialog box that contains checkboxes for each list in QuickBooks, as shown in Figure 26-7.

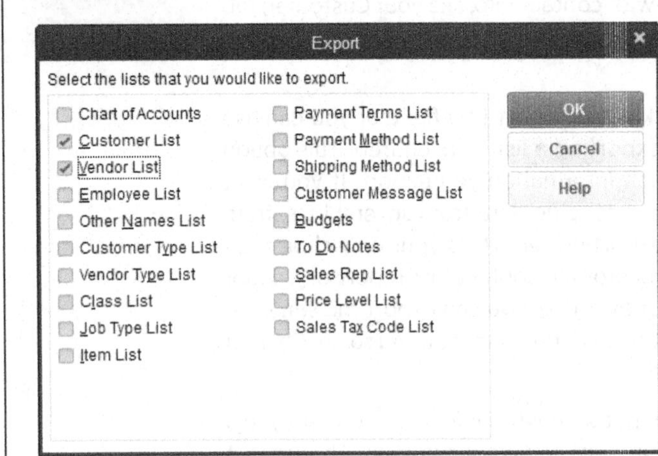

FIGURE 26-7

Turning on a checkbox tells QuickBooks that you want to export all the records in that list.

If you turn on more than one checkbox, the data for every list you choose ends up in a single export file.

2. **Turn on the checkbox for every list you want to export into the *same* file, and then click OK.**

   If you want to export lists into *separate* files, repeat these steps for each export file you want to create. For example, if you want to export your Customer:Job List and your Item List to two different files, repeat these steps twice through.

3. **In the second Export dialog box (which is basically a Save As dialog box), navigate to the folder where you want to save the export file and, in the "File name" box, type a name for the file.**

   Your export files are easier to find if you create a folder specifically for them. For example, you could create a subfolder called Export_Files within the folder that holds your company files.

4. **Click Save to create the file.**

   When the QuickBooks Information message box tells you that your data was exported successfully, click OK to close the message box. Now you're ready to import the file into Microsoft Excel or another program (page 687).

TIP Exporting QuickBooks data can help you learn the format you need to *import* data into your company file, as described on page 132. For example, the easiest way to create new budgets is to set them up in an Excel workbook (page 568).

EXPORTING ADDRESSES

Because QuickBooks has features that generate mail-merge letters, export contact list reports, and synchronize your company file with Outlook, you may not need the tab-delimited address files that QuickBooks produces. However, if you need a text file of names and addresses to import into another program, here's what you do:

1. **Choose File→Utilities→Export→Addresses to Text File.**

   The "Select Names for Export Addresses" dialog box opens.

2. **In the "Select Names to be exported to your Address data file" drop-down list, choose the category of names you want to export, and then click OK.**

   Initially, QuickBooks chooses "All names" to export all the names in your company file. You can also choose categories of names, like "All vendors." To select individual names, choose "Multiple names," and then pick the ones you want.

3. **In the Save Address Data File dialog box, select a folder where you want to save the exported file, type a filename in the "File name" box, and then click Save.**

   QuickBooks automatically assigns the file a .txt extension. You can now import it into any program that can handle tab-delimited addresses, such as Excel (see the box below).

POWER USERS' CLINIC

The Easy Way to View Data

Data is easier to examine when you view an export or import file with a spreadsheet program like Excel. Most programs can open or import delimited text files, but Excel is a master at reading the records stored in these text files and displaying them clearly.

When you export data to a delimited text file and then open it in Excel, the program puts the data into cells in a spreadsheet. Because records and fields appear in neat rows and columns, respectively, you can quickly identify, select, and edit the data you want. Furthermore, you can eliminate entire rows or columns with a few deft clicks or keystrokes.

Here's how to open a delimited text file with Excel:

1. In Excel, choose File→Open.
2. The delimited text files won't appear in the Open dialog box at first because they're not Excel files. Delimited text files come with a range of *file extensions* (the three characters that follow the last period in the filename), so choose All Files in the file-type drop-down list to make sure you'll see your delimited file listed.
3. To open the file, navigate to the folder where it's saved, and then double-click the file's name. The Text Import Wizard dialog box appears.
4. On the first screen, Excel automatically selects the Delimited option, which is what you want, so click Next. On the second screen, Excel turns on the Tab checkbox, which is also what you want if you're opening a QuickBooks IIF file, so click Next again.
5. On the third screen, click a column to select it, and then in the "Column data format" section at the top of the dialog box, select the type of data that column represents. Excel initially selects the General option, which works for most data. If a column contains text, select the Text option; for dates, select the Date option, and then choose the date format you want in the drop-down list to the option's right. To skip the column, select the "Do not import column (skip)" option instead.
6. The "Data preview" table at the bottom of the dialog box shows you what the data will look like after it's imported into Excel. When its interpretation of the data is correct, click Finish.

Now you can use Excel to rename column headings or delete the columns or rows you don't want to import.

Exporting Reports

As you learned in Chapter 23, you can customize reports so they contain exactly the information you want, presented just the way you want. When you want to export only *some* QuickBooks data or export it in a specific way, your best bet is to customize a report and then export it.

If the program you want to import the report data into is fussy about data formats, export the report to Excel, where it's easier to make changes than in a text-editing tool such as Windows Notepad. You can also export a report to a comma-delimited file if that's what another program needs. Exporting reports is an effective way to extract some QuickBooks lists like the Item List, Customer:Job List, Vendor List, and Employee List. Here are the different ways you can use this technique:

- **Running a report**. Start by running the report you want to export (page 580). Then, in the report window, click Excel→Create New Worksheet. The "Send Report to Excel" dialog box that appears lets you choose the file and options for the export, as shown in Figure 26-8.
- **From the Item List window**. Open the Item List window (on the Home Page, click the Items & Services icon) and then, at the bottom of the list window, click Excel→Export All Items. QuickBooks opens the Export dialog box, which has options similar to the ones you see when you export a report (Figure 26-8).

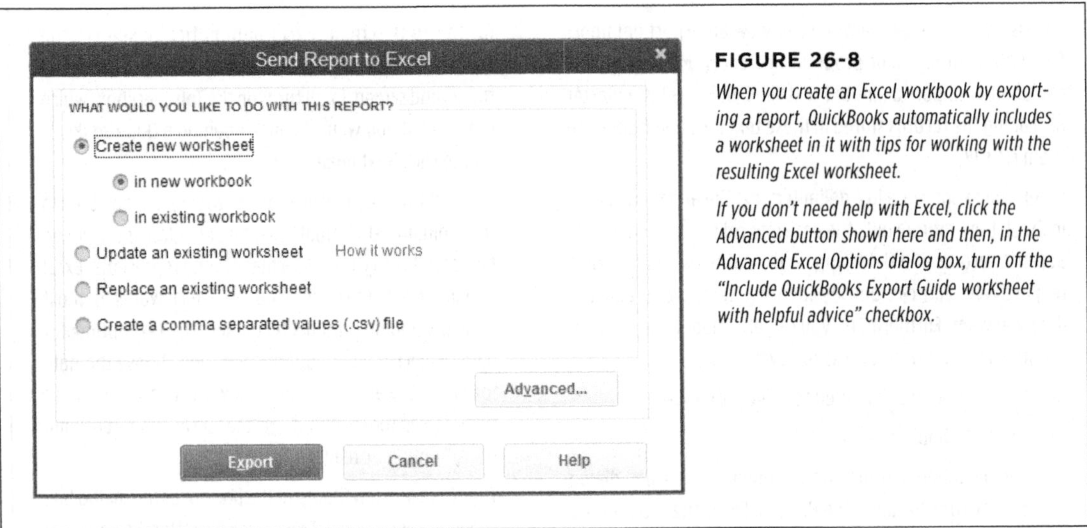

FIGURE 26-8

When you create an Excel workbook by exporting a report, QuickBooks automatically includes a worksheet in it with tips for working with the resulting Excel worksheet.

If you don't need help with Excel, click the Advanced button shown here and then, in the Advanced Excel Options dialog box, turn off the "Include QuickBooks Export Guide worksheet with helpful advice" checkbox.

- **From a QuickBooks center**. In the Customer Center's menu bar, click Excel, and then choose Export Customer List or Export Transactions. In the Vendor Center or Employee Center, choose Export Vendor List or Export Employee List, respectively.

Regardless of whether the Export dialog box or the "Send Report to Excel" dialog box opens, you can choose the same basic options for where you want to save the exported report:

- The **Create new worksheet** option creates a brand-new Excel worksheet for the report. If you choose Excel→Create New Worksheet in a report window, the "Create new worksheet" and "in new workbook" options are selected, which means QuickBooks will create a new Excel workbook with a worksheet for the exported data, as shown in Figure 26-9. If you export a list and the Export dialog box appears, selecting the "Create new worksheet" option also displays the "in new workbook" and "in existing workbook" options so you can create a new worksheet in an existing file or a brand-new one.

	Active Status	Type	Item	Description	Sales Tax Code	
2	Active	Service	Deposits and Retainers	Prepayments for services ordered	Non	220
3	Active	Service	OfficeAdmin	Support activities	Non	410
4	Active	Service	Overhead		Tax	823
5	Active	Service	Overhead:Accounting	Bookkeeping, accounts receivable, account	Non	823
6	Active	Service	Overhead:Administrative		Tax	823
7	Active	Service	Overhead:Customer Service		Non	823
8	Active	Service	Overhead:Other		Tax	604
9	Active	Service	Overhead:Sick Time		Tax	823
10	Active	Service	Overhead:Technical Support		Non	823
11	Active	Service	Overhead:Vacation/Holiday		Tax	823
12	Active	Service	Security services		Tax	410

FIGURE 26-9

When you export a report to Excel, the data in the report's columns and rows appear in columns and rows in the worksheet. If a report subtotals numbers, the workbook uses Excel's SUM function to add up the workbook cells that make up the subtotal.

If you choose the "Update an existing worksheet" option, QuickBooks can update values in an existing worksheet without overwriting most of the edits you've made.

- The **Update an existing worksheet** option exports the report to an existing worksheet in an existing file. This option is ideal if you're planning to calculate ratios and want to update that worksheet to include your most recent financial numbers. When you select this option, the "Select workbook" box appears so you can choose the file and worksheet you want to update. (If you choose Excel→Update Existing Worksheet in a report window, the "Send Report to Excel" dialog box opens with this option selected.)

- The **Replace an existing worksheet** option exports the report to an existing worksheet and *replaces* the contents of that worksheet. In the "Select workbook" box, choose the file and then specify the worksheet you want to replace.

- The **Create a comma separated values (.csv) file** option creates a comma-delimited file that you can use with programs that can read files formatted that way.

TIP The Advanced button in the Export and "Send Report to Excel" dialog boxes opens the Advanced Excel Options dialog box, which lets you set the formatting you want to transfer from QuickBooks to Excel, choose which Excel features you want the workbook to use (like AutoFit to size the columns to display all the data), and select where you want the report's header info displayed.

After you've selected the type of export file and other options, click Export. QuickBooks launches Excel and copies the data in the report to the Excel workbook you specified, placing the data from the report's columns into the worksheet's columns, as shown in Figure 26-9.

CUSTOMIZED EXPORTS USING CONTACT LIST REPORTS

Exporting the entire Customer:Job or Vendor list is overkill when all you want are the contacts' names and email addresses; that's where exporting a report shines. By modifying the settings in the Customer Contact List report or the Vendor Contact List report, you can export exactly the fields you want for specific customers or vendors. For example, storing email addresses in QuickBooks is perfect when you email invoices to customers, but you probably also want these addresses in your email program so you can communicate with customers about the work you're doing for them.

Out of the box, QuickBooks' Customer Contact List report includes Customer, Bill to, Primary Contact, Main Phone, Fax, and Balance Total columns. The Vendor Contact List report includes Vendor, Account No., Bill from, Primary Contact, Main Phone, Fax, and Balance Total columns. Here's how you transform these reports into an export tool, using the Customer Contact List as an example:

1. **Choose Reports→List→Customer Contact List.**

   The Customer Contact List report window opens. (For the Vendor Contact List, choose Reports→List→Vendor Contact List instead.)

2. **In the report window's toolbar, click Customize Report.**

   The Modify Report dialog box that appears lets you adjust the report to filter the data that you'll export. (See page 589 to learn about other ways of customizing reports.)

3. **Click the dialog box's Display tab (if you're not already on it) and, in the Columns section, choose the fields you want to export.**

   The Customer, Primary Contact, Main Phone, and Fax fields might be good ones to export. Then again, they might not. You can add or remove whichever fields you want by clicking a field's name in the Columns list to toggle that field on or off. If there's a checkmark in front of the field's name, the report will include a column for that field.

4. **To produce a report for only the customers you want, click the dialog box's Filters tab. In the Filter list on the left, choose Customer. In the Customer drop-down list that appears, choose "Multiple customers/jobs."**

QuickBooks displays the Select Customer:Job dialog box with the Manual option selected; that's what you want.

5. **In the list of customer names on the right side of the dialog box, click each customer you want to export, and then click OK. Then, in the Modify Report dialog box, click OK.**

   You see the report with the modifications you've made.

TIP Saving the modified report you just created reduces the number of steps you have to take the *next* time you export. Page 601 explains how to memorize a report.

6. **In the Customer Contact List report window's toolbar, click Excel→Create New Worksheet.**

   The "Send Report to Excel" dialog box opens. To create a new Excel workbook, keep the "Create new worksheet" option selected and click Export. Your computer launches Excel and displays the report in a workbook.

Importing Data from Other Programs

Importing data from other programs comes in handy mostly for generating lists in QuickBooks. However, you can also import data to generate your chart of accounts or to load different versions of your company budget. The biggest requirement for importing data is that the files have to be either Excel workbooks (.xls or .xlsx files) or delimited text files (which separate each piece of information with commas or tabs).

If you're familiar with importing Excel spreadsheets into other programs, importing them into QuickBooks is a snap. In fact, QuickBooks includes several Excel import templates that walk you through getting your Excel data for customers, vendors, and items into the format that QuickBooks requires.

If you're importing a Customer:Job List, Vendor List, or Item List, don't even *think* about importing it as a delimited file. It's much easier to open that kind of file in Excel and then use the QuickBooks' Excel import templates. Page 133 provides the full story on using these templates.

But if you want to import other kinds of lists or a budget, using a delimited file works just fine. The following section shows you how.

Importing a Delimited File

With a delimited file, QuickBooks needs to know the *kind* of data you're importing—and it learns that from special *keywords* for row and column headers. (Keywords are strings of characters in a delimited text file that identify QuickBooks' records and fields.)

Before you import data from another program into a QuickBooks list, you need to know the correct keywords for the fields you're importing. The easiest way to see the keywords for a list is to export that list from QuickBooks and examine the keywords at the beginning of the rows and at the tops of the columns.

Deciphering keywords requires a smattering of computerese. For example, when you see the column heading "Billing Address," you know instantly what kind of information you're looking at. But the only way *QuickBooks* recognizes the first line of a billing address is from the keyword BADDR1.

Figure 26-10 shows a delimited file in an Excel spreadsheet. (Even though the delimited file is a text file, viewing it in Excel makes the fields easier to read than they would be in a text editor like Notepad, as described in the box on page 687.) Here's the layout of a delimited file that QuickBooks can read:

- **QuickBooks list keyword**. In the first cell in the first row of a list, an exclamation point in front of the keyword tells QuickBooks that the data in the rows that follow is for that list. For example, !CUST (labeled 1 in Figure 26-10) represents data for the Customer:Job List.
- **Field names**. Keywords in the other cells of the same row specify QuickBooks field names, like cell B36 in Figure 26-10 (which is labeled 2). In that cell, the keyword NAME identifies the values in that column as the name of each customer. In cell F36, BADDR2 identifies the second part of the billing address.
- **Record keyword**. A keyword is the first text in the row. Each row that begins with CUST in the first cell (labeled 3 in Figure 26-10) represents a separate customer record.
- **Record values**. The other cells in a row contain the values that QuickBooks imports into the designated fields, as shown in the cell labeled 4 in Figure 26-10.

When you have an IIF file with the correct keywords, here's how to import it into QuickBooks:

1. **Choose File→Utilities→Import→IIF Files.**

   QuickBooks opens the Import dialog box with the "Files of type" box set to "IIF Files (*.IIF)."

2. **Navigate to the folder where the file you want to import is saved, and then double-click the file's name.**

   QuickBooks displays a message box telling you that it imported the data successfully. (If you didn't set up the keywords correctly or QuickBooks ran into other problems with the data in the file, it tells you that it *didn't* import the data successfully.)

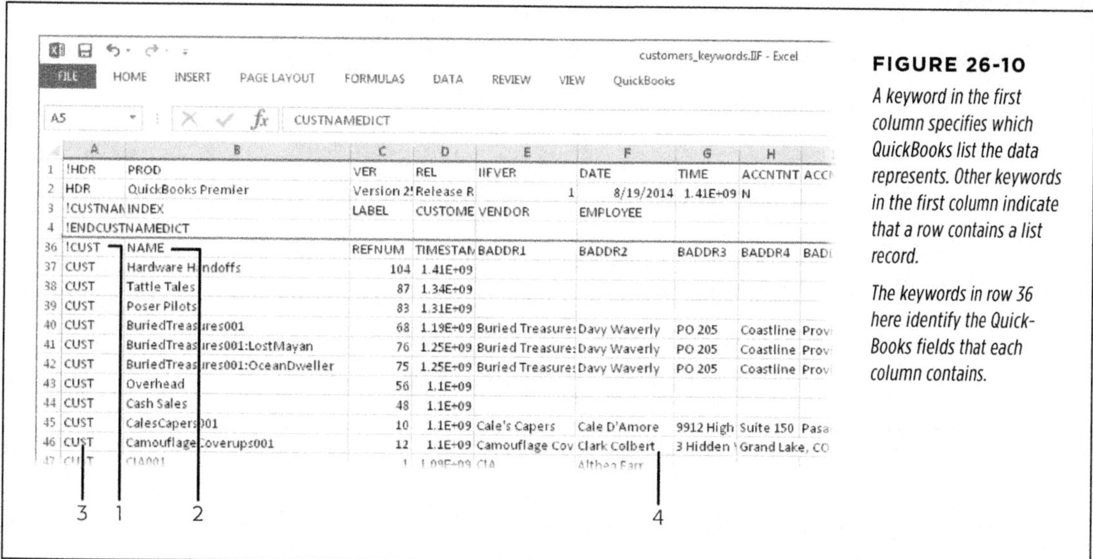

FIGURE 26-10

A keyword in the first column specifies which QuickBooks list the data represents. Other keywords in the first column indicate that a row contains a list record.

The keywords in row 36 here identify the QuickBooks fields that each column contains.

CHAPTER

27

Customizing QuickBooks

The QuickBooks Home Page is laid out like the workflow you follow when you're bookkeeping, so it acts like a roadmap to many of the accounting tasks you perform. Shortcuts to other helpful QuickBooks features are sprinkled throughout the program's icon bars and Vendor, Customer, and Employee centers.

But your business isn't like anyone else's. For example, if you run a strictly cash-sales business, you might not care about customer lists and invoices; making deposits, though, is a daily event. Fortunately, you don't have to accept QuickBooks' initial take on convenience. The Home Page and the icon bars come stocked with a set of popular shortcuts, but you can add, remove, rearrange, and otherwise edit which features appear on them. The box on page 697 describes several ways to customize the QuickBooks desktop. You can also add your favorite features, windows, and reports to the Favorites menu. This chapter covers all your options.

In addition to tweaking QuickBooks' layout, you can also customize the program's forms. QuickBooks helps you get up and running with built-in business form templates. They'll do if you have to blast out some invoices. But when you finally find a few spare minutes, you can create templates that show the information you want, formatted the way you want, and laid out to work with your letterhead. You can even create multiple versions of a form. For example, you can make one invoice template to print on your letterhead and another for creating electronic invoices to email that includes your logo, company name, and address. This chapter describes the most efficient ways to create forms: using QuickBooks' form designs or built-in templates as a basis for your own. In Appendix G (which is available from this book's Missing CD page at *www.missingmanuals.com/cds*), you can learn how to fine-tune forms with advanced customization techniques and even create templates from scratch.

Customizing the Home Page

The icons that QuickBooks initially displays on the Home Page are the result of the answers you gave during QuickBooks Setup: The program sets your companywide Desktop View preferences (page 643) based on your answers to things such as whether you track inventory, charge sales tax, or track time. But you can alter these settings if your business needs change. For example, if you want to start sending statements to customers, turn on the statement preference (see the Note on page 296), and the icons for statement-related tasks appear on the Home Page. And if you just hired your first employee and turn on payroll or time-tracking preferences, the Employees panel appears with payroll and time-tracking icons in it. This section describes how you change the icons that appear on your Home Page.

UP TO SPEED

Customizing the Desktop

Each person who uses QuickBooks can make the program's desktop look the way she wants by choosing Edit→Preferences→Desktop View and clicking the My Preferences tab. Page 643 gives the full scoop on how you set preferences to customize the desktop, but here are the different ways you can make the desktop your own:

- **One window or several**. You can focus on one window at a time with the One Window option. The Multiple Windows option lets you see—you guessed it—several windows at once.
- **Show Home page when opening a company file**. This setting makes QuickBooks display the Home Page when you open a company file.
- **Identify different company files by color**. If you work on several different company files, you can easily tell them apart by assigning a different color scheme to each one. When you assign a color scheme to a company file, QuickBooks changes the color of the main title bar and the title bars of every window you open while working on that file.
- **Change the top icon bar's color scheme**. If you use the top icon bar, you can choose between blue-and-gray icons on a dark-blue background or colored icons on a light-gray background.

Turning Customer and Vendor Icons On and Off

The Desktop View preference category controls some of the icons that appear in the Home Page's Vendors and Customers panels. To turn these icons on and off, choose Edit→Preferences→Desktop View, and then click the Company Preferences tab. (Because these settings apply to your whole company, they're on the Company Preferences tab, which means you have to be a QuickBooks admin to adjust them.) Then, in the Customers and Vendors sections, turn on a checkbox to display the corresponding icon, or turn it off to hide it. For example, if you want to create Sales Receipts, turn on the Sales Receipts checkbox, and the Create Sales Receipts icon appears in the Customers panel, as shown in Figure 27-1.

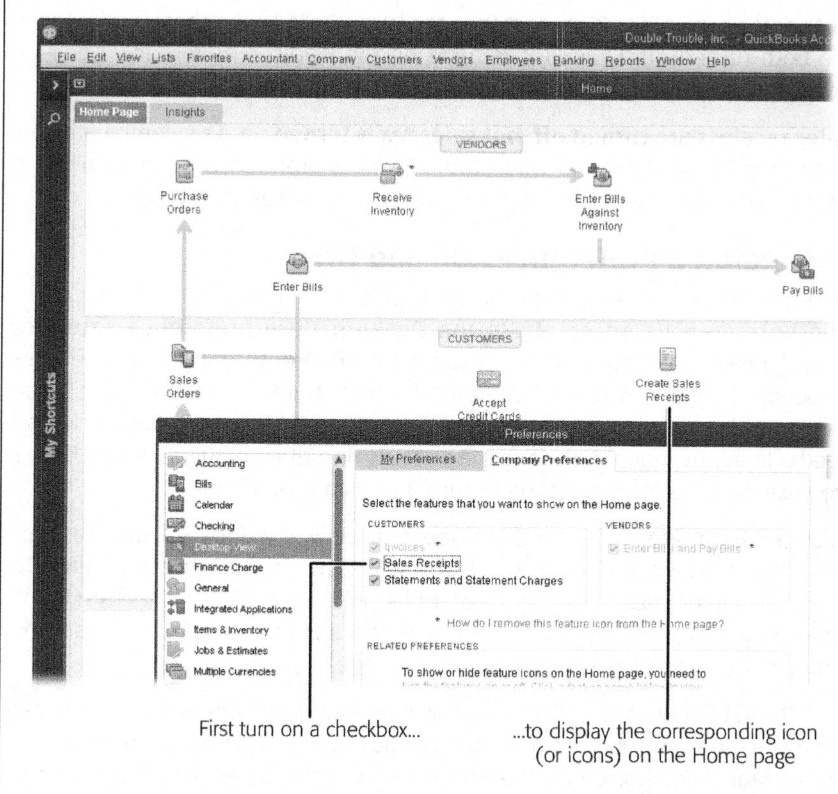
First turn on a checkbox...
...to display the corresponding icon (or icons) on the Home page

FIGURE 27-1

In the Desktop View preference category, the settings on the Company Preferences tab let you customize your Home Page. Display or hide icons on the Home Page by turning their checkboxes on or off here.

For example, if you want to create sales receipts, turn on the Sales Receipts checkbox. When you do that, QuickBooks displays the Create Sales Receipts icon on your Home Page.

The Invoices checkbox and the "Enter Bills and Pay Bills" checkbox have an additional trick up their sleeves. In some cases, they're active (meaning you can turn them on or off), just like the Sales Receipts checkbox in Figure 27-1. However, if they're dimmed (so you can't click them to toggle them on and off) and have an asterisk next to them, as shown in Figure 27-1, QuickBooks has turned them on automatically because of *other* preference selections you've made. For example, the "Enter Bills and Pay Bills" checkbox is turned on automatically if you turn on inventory. That makes sense if you think about it, because you have to enter bills to pay for inventory you purchase. (Click the "How do I remove this feature icon from the Home page?" link to read a Help topic that lists the settings you need to change.) The Invoices checkbox is turned on automatically in several situations:

- **Estimates are turned on**. QuickBooks turns on invoices when estimates are turned on because you can convert estimates into invoices (page 282).

- **Sales orders (available only in QuickBooks Premier and Enterprise) are turned on**. Because sales orders eventually lead to invoices, QuickBooks turns on the Invoices preference if you turn on this preference (page 663).
- **Both sales receipts and statements are turned off**. When these preferences are both turned off, QuickBooks turns on the Invoices preference, because invoices are the only other type of sales form available.
- **Sales receipts are turned off, but sales *tax* is turned on**. This combination of settings makes QuickBooks turn on the Invoices preference because invoices are the only other sales form besides sales receipts that handle sales tax.

Turning Related Preferences On and Off

Some Home Page icons appear or disappear when you turn their corresponding preferences on or off. In the Desktop View preference category (Edit→Preferences→Desktop View), the Company Preferences tab's Related Preferences section (visible in Figure 27-2) offers shortcuts to those preferences. (These links take you to the Company Preferences tabs in *other* preference categories, so you need admin privileges to change the settings described in this section.) Here's how you use the links in that section to turn these icons on or off:

- Click the **Estimates** link and QuickBooks displays the Jobs & Estimates category's Company Preferences tab. If you select the Yes radio button in the "Do You Create Estimates?" section, QuickBooks displays the Estimates icon in the Home Page's Customers panel. If you select the No radio button instead, the Estimates icon disappears from the Home Page.
- Click the **Sales Tax** link to jump to the Sales Tax category's Company Preferences tab. Select the Yes option next to the "Do you charge sales tax?" label to display the Manage Sales Tax icon in the Home Page's Vendors panel. If you select the No option instead, the Manage Sales Tax icon disappears from the Home Page.
- Clicking the **Inventory** link takes you to the Items & Inventory category's Company Preferences tab. If you need to track inventory, turn on the "Inventory and purchase orders are active" checkbox. When you do, the Purchase Orders, Receive Inventory, and Enter Bills Against Inventory icons appear on the Home Page. If you turn this checkbox off, these icons disappear.
- Click the **Payroll** link to display the Payroll & Employees category's Company Preferences tab. If you choose a payroll option in the QuickBooks Payroll Features section, such as Full Payroll, the Pay Employees and Pay Liabilities icons appear in the Employees panel of the Home Page. If you select No Payroll instead, those icons disappear.
- Click the **Time Tracking** link to jump to the Time & Expenses category's Company Preferences tab. If you click the Yes option next to the "Do you track time?" label, the program displays the Enter Time icon in the Home Page's Employees panel. If you select the No option instead, the Enter Time icon disappears from the Home Page.

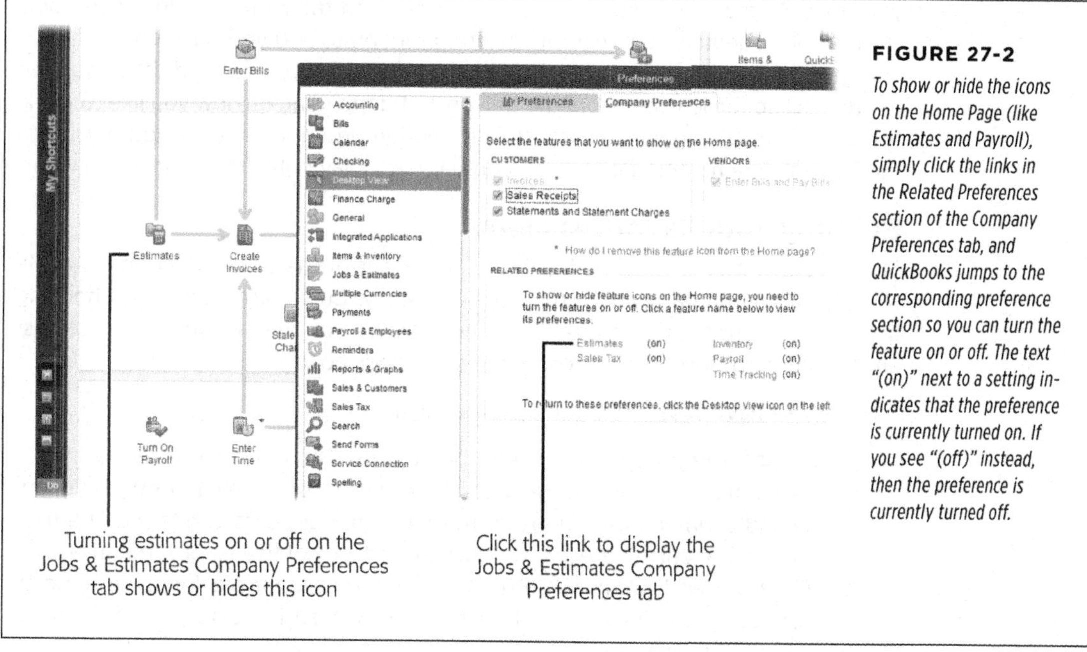

FIGURE 27-2

To show or hide the icons on the Home Page (like Estimates and Payroll), simply click the links in the Related Preferences section of the Company Preferences tab, and QuickBooks jumps to the corresponding preference section so you can turn the feature on or off. The text "(on)" next to a setting indicates that the preference is currently turned on. If you see "(off)" instead, then the preference is currently turned off.

TIP If you turn off both payroll *and* time tracking, the Employees panel disappears from the Home Page.

Account Balances

If you use the top icon bar, then at the Home Page's top right you'll see the Account Balances section, which displays your bank accounts and their balances. You can sort the account list by account name or balance.

If you use the left icon bar, the Account Balances section doesn't appear on the Home Page. Instead, you have to click View Balances in the left icon bar's middle section to display account balances in the icon bar's top section. When you display account balances in the left icon bar, you can choose the accounts you want to see in the list and the order in which they appear. To do that, click the "Customize view balances" link at the bottom of the View Balances section. The Customize Account Balances dialog box opens. To add an account to the list, select it in the Available Accounts list, and then click Add. To remove an account, select it in the Selected Accounts list, and then click Remove. To reposition an account, select it in the Selected Accounts list, and then click Move Up or Move Down until it's where you want it.

Fast Access to Favorite Features

In addition to the Home Page, QuickBooks gives you two other ways to access your favorite features fast: the Favorites menu and the icon bar. Out of the box, the Favorites menu is nearly empty, waiting for you to add your preferred features and reports. On the other hand, icons for QuickBooks' centers and other popular features fill up the icon bar from the get-go, but depending on how you like to work, those icons may languish unclicked. This section describes how to add entries to the Favorites menu and modify the icon bar to display only the features you want.

Building Your Favorites Menu

The Favorites menu, which is located to the right of the Lists menu on the main QuickBooks menu bar, initially has only one entry: Customize Favorites. Choosing this option opens the Customize Your Menus dialog box, where you can add almost any feature or report to the Favorites menu. Here's how:

1. **Choose Favorites→Customize Favorites.**

   The Customize Your Menus dialog box opens. The Available Menu Items list is a directory of *every* feature QuickBooks has to offer—every entry on every menu and submenu on the program's menu bar appears in this list. The top-level menu bar entries are aligned with the left side of the list box, menu entries are indented, and submenu entries are indented even more. Even the Reports section leaves nothing out—you can choose any built-in, custom, or memorized report in your company file.

2. **In the Available Menu Items list, select a feature you want to add to the Favorites menu, and then click Add.**

   The feature appears in the Chosen Menu Items list, as shown in Figure 27-3.

3. **To rearrange the entries, select one and then click Move Up or Move Down until it's in the position you want.**

   You can't indent entries or add any kind of separator to help you find the ones you want.

4. **Click OK to close the dialog box.**

Now when you click the Favorites menu, it displays all the features you added to it.

Customizing the Icon Bar

The QuickBooks icon bar initially includes icons that open some of the program's popular features, like the Home Page, the Report Center, and others, depending on which edition of the program you use. If the Home Page always seems to be hidden behind several open windows, you can use the icon bar instead to access your favorite features, memorized reports, or windows you open often. (When you display the icon bar by choosing either View→Left Icon Bar or View→Top Icon Bar, it remains on top of any open windows in the main QuickBooks window—including the Home Page.) You can customize the icon bar to include just the entries you want and change its appearance in several ways. (Any customizations you make apply to both the top *and* left icon bars.)

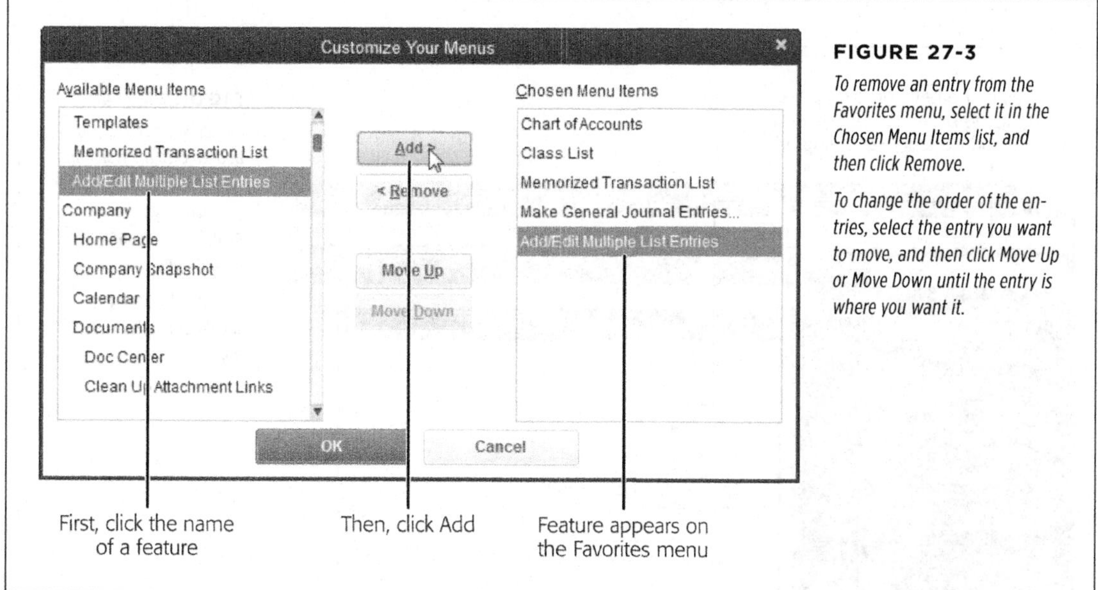

FIGURE 27-3

To remove an entry from the Favorites menu, select it in the Chosen Menu Items list, and then click Remove.

To change the order of the entries, select the entry you want to move, and then click Move Up or Move Down until the entry is where you want it.

NOTE The left icon bar makes features easy to find because you can see both their icons *and* their full text labels. It also offers several other handy features; for the full story, see page 30. If the left icon bar takes up too much screen real estate, click the left arrow at the icon bar's top right to collapse it. To expand it, click the right arrow at the top of the collapsed icon bar.

Here are the basic steps for customizing the icon bar:

1. **Choose View→Customize Icon Bar.**

   If you use the left icon bar and the My Shortcuts section is displayed at the top of it, you can also click the Customize Shortcuts link at the bottom of the My Shortcuts list (you may have to scroll down to see this link). If the top icon bar is visible, you can right-click it and choose Customize Icon Bar.

   Whatever route you use, QuickBooks opens the Customize Icon Bar dialog box.

NOTE The icon bar has to be visible before you can customize it. If you open the View menu when the icon bar is hidden, the Customize Icon Bar entry is dimmed. Simply choose View→Top Icon Bar or View→Left Icon Bar to turn the bar back on, and *then* choose View→Customize Icon Bar.

2. **In the Customize Icon Bar dialog box (Figure 27-4), add shortcuts to the icon bar, remove icons for features you don't want, and edit or change the order in which they appear, as described in the following sections.**

The top icon bar and the left icon bar's My Shortcuts section immediately reflect the changes you make in this dialog box.

3. **To save your changes, click OK.**

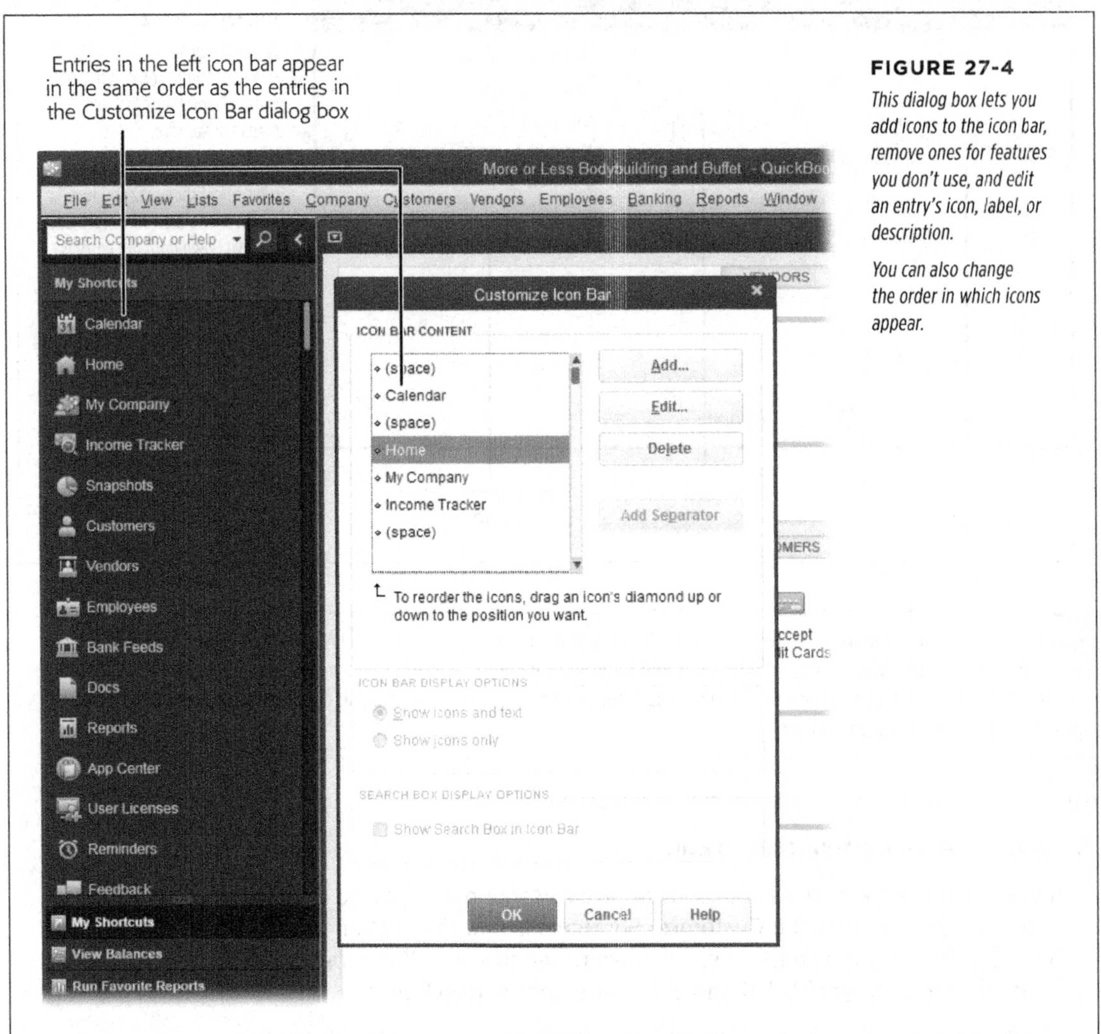

FIGURE 27-4

This dialog box lets you add icons to the icon bar, remove ones for features you don't use, and edit an entry's icon, label, or description.

You can also change the order in which icons appear.

ADDING AND REMOVING ICONS

If you know which icons you want and don't want, you can make those changes in one marathon session. Simply open the Customize Icon Bar dialog box by choosing View→Customize Icon Bar, and then do the following:

1. **In the Customize Icon Bar dialog box, select the entry that you want to be above or to the left of the new icon you're about to insert (depending on whether you use the left icon bar or the top icon bar).**

If you use the left icon bar, the icons appear in the same order as in the dialog box's Icon Bar Content list. The top icon bar, on the other hand, displays the top item in the list on its far left, and the other items to the right of that.

When you select an entry in the list and add an icon, QuickBooks inserts the new icon below the selected entry in the Icon Bar Content list, so it appears below the selected icon on the left icon bar or to the right of the selected icon on the top icon bar.

2. **Click Add.**

   The Add Icon Bar Item dialog box shown in Figure 27-5 opens.

3. **In the list on the Add Icon Bar Item dialog box's left, click the window or feature you want to add, like Create Invoices (which opens the Create Invoices window).**

   QuickBooks automatically selects an icon in the list of graphics and fills in the Label and Description boxes. If you like, click a different graphic and/or edit the text in these boxes to change the label that appears on the icon bar or the description that appears as a tooltip when you put your cursor over the icon.

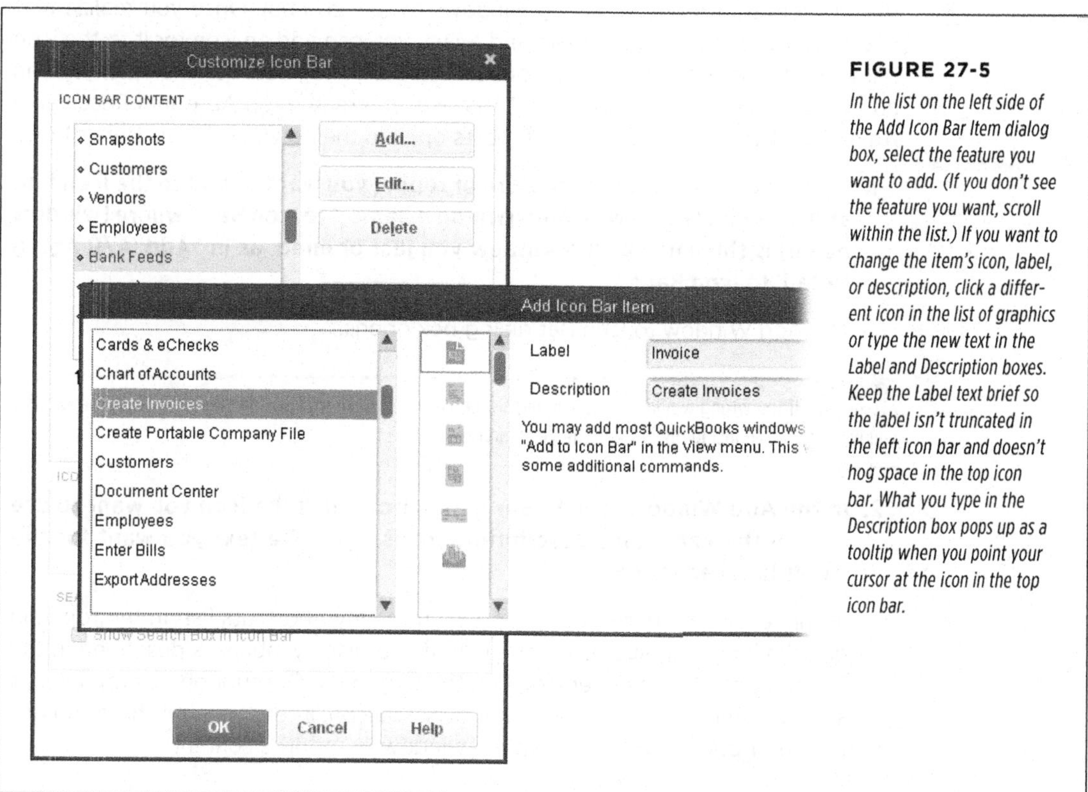

FIGURE 27-5

In the list on the left side of the Add Icon Bar Item dialog box, select the feature you want to add. (If you don't see the feature you want, scroll within the list.) If you want to change the item's icon, label, or description, click a different icon in the list of graphics or type the new text in the Label and Description boxes. Keep the Label text brief so the label isn't truncated in the left icon bar and doesn't hog space in the top icon bar. What you type in the Description box pops up as a tooltip when you point your cursor at the icon in the top icon bar.

TIP The section below explains how to add almost *any* QuickBooks window to the icon bar, even if it doesn't appear in the Add Icon Bar Item dialog box's list.

4. **Click OK to add the item to the icon bar.**

   You don't have to close the Customize Icon Bar dialog box to see your changes—QuickBooks makes them right away.

5. **Repeat steps 2–4 to add more icons to the bar.**

   Back in the Customize Icon Bar dialog box, you can rearrange or edit the entries as explained in the following pages.

6. **To remove an icon from the bar, simply select its entry in the Customize Icon Bar dialog box, and then click Delete.**

   When you're done customizing the icon bar, click OK to close the Customize Icon Bar dialog box.

ADDING WINDOWS OR REPORTS TO THE ICON BAR

The Add Icon Bar Item dialog box doesn't list every QuickBooks window, but that doesn't prevent you from adding windows to the icon bar. Once you realize that you open the same window again and again, you can add an icon for it to the icon bar without even opening the Customize Icon Bar dialog box. For example, you can add an icon for a memorized report that you've created (an Accounts Receivable Aging Detail report, say) because reports open in their own windows. Here's how:

1. **Open the window for the feature or report you want to add to the icon bar, and then choose View→"Add '[window name]' to Icon Bar," where [window name] is the name of the window you just opened, as in "Add 'A/R Aging Detail' to Icon Bar."**

   The Add Window to Icon Bar dialog box opens.

NOTE If the wrong window name appears in the View menu's Add entry, be sure to activate the window you want before choosing the entry in the View menu.

2. **In the Add Window to Icon Bar dialog box, click the icon you want to use and, in the Label and Description boxes, type the text you want for the icon's label and tooltip.**

   In the left icon bar, the label appears in the My Shortcuts list. In the top icon bar, the label appears below the icon *if* you display labels as described in the Tip on page 705. In either icon bar, the text in the Description box appears as a tooltip when you put your cursor over the icon. Keep the label short and use the description to elaborate on the window or report's contents.

3. **Click OK to add the window or report to the icon bar.**

   QuickBooks plunks the window or report's icon at the right end of the top icon bar or, if you're using the left icon bar, at the bottom of the My Shortcuts section. If you want the icon somewhere else, choose View→Customize Icon Bar, and then reposition it in the list (page 701).

CHANGING AN ICON'S APPEARANCE

To change an icon or its associated text, in the Customize Icon Bar dialog box, click the icon's entry and then click Edit. QuickBooks opens the Edit Icon Bar Item dialog box, which lets you change three features of each icon:

- **Icon**. In the icon list, select the graphic you want to appear on the icon bar. You can't design your own icons, and QuickBooks doesn't care whether you choose an icon that fits the feature you're adding. For instance, an icon with a checkbook register and pen might be good for Writing Checks, but you could choose the faucet with a drop of water if you prefer.
- **Label**. If you want to shorten the icon's label to condense the top icon bar (or to prevent the label from being truncated in the left icon bar), in the Label box, type the new text.
- **Description**. To change the text that appears as a tooltip for the icon, in the Description box, type your own.

TIP In the top icon bar, you can squeeze icons together and reduce the icon bar's height by removing icon labels. Simply open the Customize Icon Bar dialog box and select the "Show icons only" option. Without labels to tell you what the icons represent, you can see a hint by putting your cursor over the icon to display its tooltip description. If you change your mind and want to display labels again, select the "Show icons and text" option.

CHANGING THE ORDER OF ICONS

If you want to group related icons, you can change the order of the items in the icon bar as explained in Figure 27-6. Figure 27-6 also shows you how to add separators to make the groups stand out in the top icon bar. (The left icon bar doesn't display separators, so you can add them only when the top icon bar is displayed.) To make these changes, open the Customize Icon Bar dialog box.

Customizing the Company Snapshot

The Company Snapshot (page 43) displays key statistics about your business in one convenient window. You can choose from almost two dozen different views of financial status, like income and expense trends, account balances, customers who owe money, invoice payment status, receivables reports, and so on.

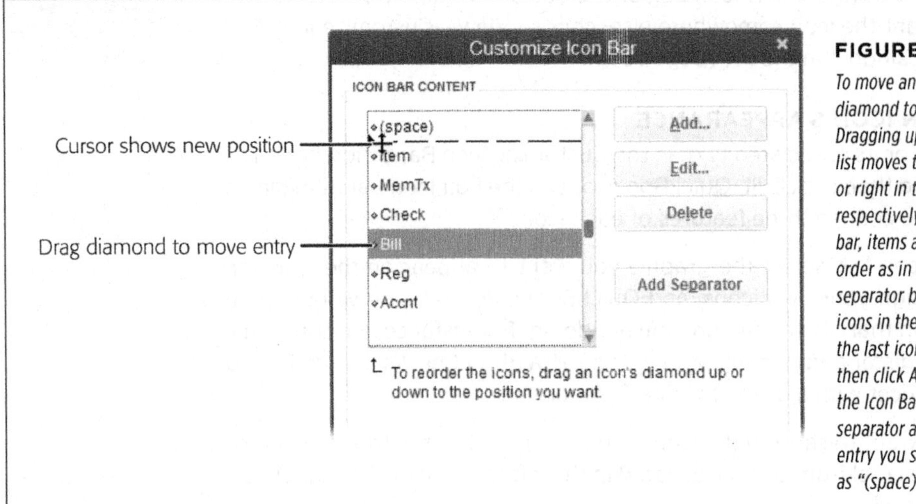

FIGURE 27-6

To move an icon, drag the diamond to the left of its name. Dragging up or down in this list moves the item to the left or right in the top icon bar, respectively. (In the left icon bar, items appear in the same order as in this list.) To add a separator between groups of icons in the top icon bar, select the last icon in the group, and then click Add Separator. In the Icon Bar Content list, the separator appears below the entry you selected and is listed as "(space)."

To change the views that appear in the Company Snapshot window, first open the window by choosing Company→Company Snapshot. Next, click the tab you want to customize (Company, Payments, or Customer), and then click Add Content near the top-left corner of the window. The "Add content to your [tab name] Snapshot" panel appears with the name and a thumbnail of each view you can choose, as shown in Figure 27-7. (You may need to resize or maximize the window to see everything shown in Figure 27-7.)

Here's how you customize the Company Snapshot:

- **Add a view**. In the Add Content panel, click the Add button to the right of the view you want, and QuickBooks adds it to the body of the Company Snapshot. After you add a view, its button's label changes to a green checkmark and the word "Added."
- **Remove a view**. In the lower part of the window, click the Close button (the X) at a view's top-right corner, and then click OK in the message box that appears. (If you change your mind about deleting the view, instead of clicking OK, click the X in the *message box's* top right instead.)
- **Reposition a view**. In the lower part of the window, put your cursor over the view's title and, when the cursor changes to a four-headed arrow, drag the view to its new location in the Company Snapshot window.

When the Company Snapshot shows what you want, click the down arrow to the right of the Add Content label to close the "Add content to your [tab name] Snapshot" panel. If you want to undo the changes you've made, click Restore Default near the top of the window.

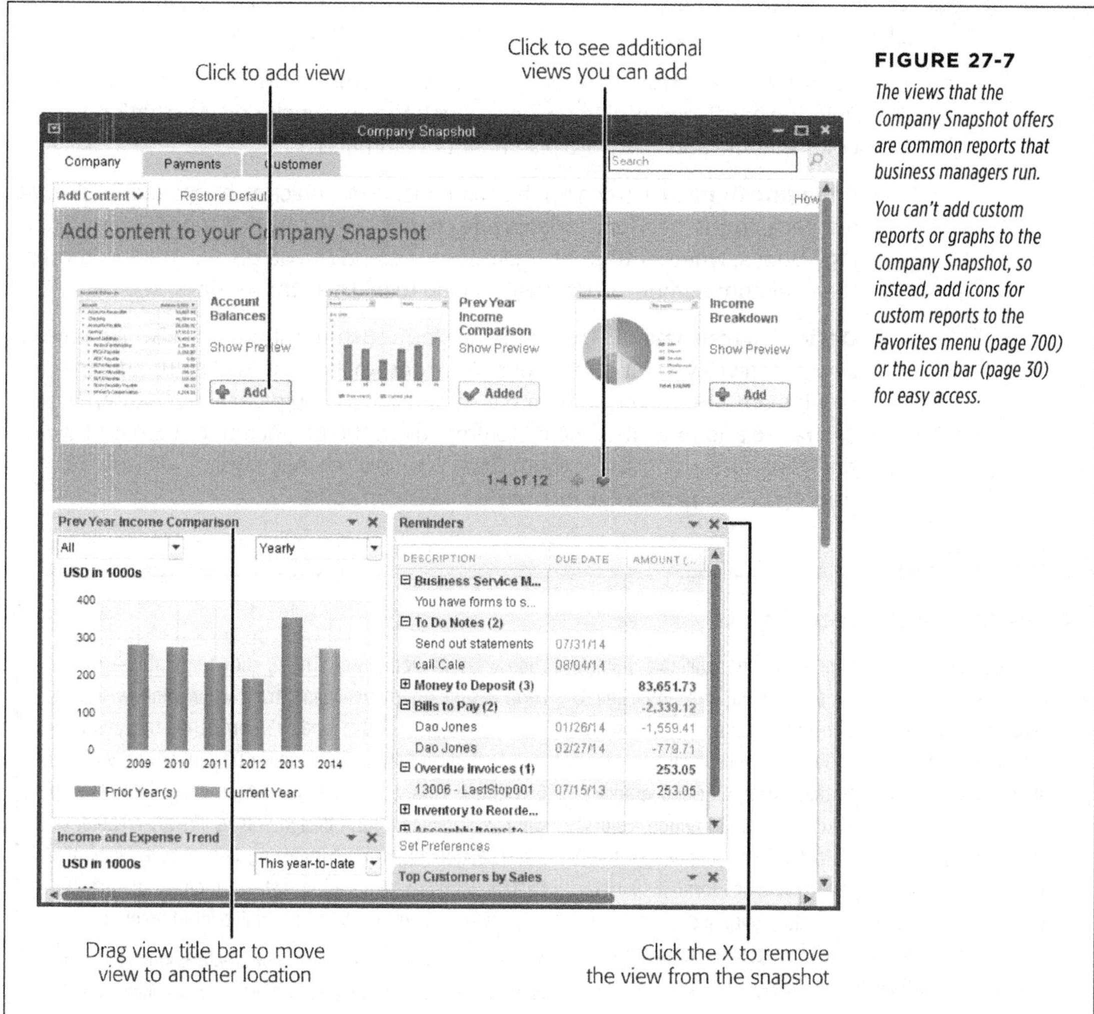

FIGURE 27-7

The views that the Company Snapshot offers are common reports that business managers run.

You can't add custom reports or graphs to the Company Snapshot, so instead, add icons for custom reports to the Favorites menu (page 700) or the icon bar (page 30) for easy access.

Customizing Forms

Everything you do says *something* about your business—even the forms you use. If you run a small company and don't have a spare second to customize forms, the built-in QuickBooks invoices and other form templates work just fine. But if you want business forms that convey your sense of style and attention to detail, customized form templates are the way to go. A *form template* controls the appearance of a specific type of form, such as a purchase order, invoice, or credit memo; you can specify what fields appear on the form, how the fields are formatted, and how they're laid out. (The box below describes another way to spiff up your QuickBooks forms.)

In QuickBooks, the customization you can apply to form templates comes in several shapes and sizes, described in detail in the sections that follow:

- **Basic customization**. You can add a logo to forms or turn company information fields on or off, depending on what your letterhead includes. Aesthetics like the color scheme and fonts are also at your command.
- **Changing fields**. To notch up the customization, you can choose the fields that appear in forms' headers, footers, and columns. You can also specify some printing options, whether to print trailing zeroes, and (if you display trailing zeroes) the minimum number of decimal places. To learn all these tricks, see page 714.
- **Designing form layout**. The ultimate in form customization, QuickBooks' Layout Designer gives you full control over form design. You can add fields and images, plunk them where you want, and format them as you please. For example, you can resize and reposition fields to emphasize the balance due. To learn how to fine-tune forms and build them from scratch, see Appendix G on this book's Missing CD page at *www.missingmanuals.com/cds*.

UP TO SPEED

A Design for All Your Forms

The QuickBooks Forms Customization tool (available online) helps you produce consistent, professional-looking business forms by creating a *form design* for your company file. Instead of a form *template*, the QuickBooks Form Customization tool helps you create a form *design* that specifies the appearance—including the background (like a watermark), logo, colors, fonts, and the format of the grid that holds your data—of *any* form. Because a form design applies to any form, it specifies only form *formatting*, not the fields contained in a form or where fields are located. (Don't expect miracles from form designs. The formatting you can choose is limited.)

Using this online tool is a step-by-step process that's easy to follow, and when you're done, you can save the design and apply it to *all* the forms in your QuickBooks company file in one fell swoop. From then on, you choose the forms you want to use as you would normally (page 230).

You can open a browser window to the QuickBooks Forms Customization tool from the Templates window. To do that, choose Lists→Templates. There, click Templates→Create Form Design. Alternatively, in a transaction window such as Create Invoices, click the window's Formatting tab, and then click Customize Design→Customize Design. Either way, the QuickBooks Forms Customization screen opens in a browser window. To apply a form design you've *already* created, on a transaction window's Formatting tab, choose Customize Design→Apply Saved Design instead; then, in the browser window that opens, log into your online Intuit account.

Although you can use the designs you create as long as you like, once you apply a design to a company file, you have only 30 days to edit your design, create new ones, and apply them to your forms. After that, you'll pay $4.99 to apply a new design to your forms or apply your original design to new forms. Each time you pay $4.99, you start a 60-day period during which you can edit your design and apply it to any form.

Starting with an Existing Template in QuickBooks

Whether you plan to make minor adjustments or major revisions, you don't have to start from scratch. One way to build your own forms is to start with a template that comes with QuickBooks or use another customized template that you've put together. (To learn how to customize a template while you're in the middle of a task like creating an invoice, see the box on page 710.)

Here's how to edit an existing template:

1. **Choose Lists→Templates.**

   QuickBooks opens the Templates window, which displays built-in templates and any that you've created. If you're looking for a specific type of form to start with, the Type column displays labels such as Invoice and Credit Memo.

2. **In the Name column, click the template you want to edit, and then press Ctrl+E to open the Basic Customization dialog box (shown in Figure 27-9 on page 711).**

   Alternatively, click the template's name, and then click Templates→Edit Template.

3. **In the Basic Customization dialog box, click Manage Templates.**

   The Manage Templates dialog box appears, and QuickBooks automatically selects the name of the template you're editing.

TIP If you ever want to rename a template, open the Manage Templates dialog box as described above, choose the template in the Select Template list and then, on the dialog box's right, type the new name in the Template Name box.

4. **In the Manage Templates dialog box, below the Select Template list, click Copy. Then, in the Template Name box on the dialog box's right, rename the copy you just created, and then click OK.**

   When you click Copy, QuickBooks automatically fills in the Template Name box on the right side of the dialog box with "Copy of: [template]." Type over this text to name the template something meaningful, and then click OK to return to the Basic Customization dialog box. By doing this, you can keep the edited template or go back to the original.

5. **Back in the Basic Customization dialog box, make the changes you want.**

   For basic customization instructions, see the next section. To learn how to change the fields on a template, see page 713. And, for full layout instructions, see Appendix G on this book's Missing CD page at *www.missingmanuals.com/cds*.

6. **When the template looks the way you want, in the Basic Customization dialog box, click OK.**

FREQUENTLY ASKED QUESTION

Editing a Template While You Work

I've created a transaction (specifically, an invoice), and the form preview doesn't look the way I want. Is there a way to change the form template without leaving the transaction window?

Happily, yes. If you're in the midst of creating a transaction and realize you need to modify the form's template, you can customize the template without interfering with the transaction-in-progress. In the transaction window (Create Invoices, for instance), make sure that the template you want to use (and modify) appears in the Template box. If it doesn't, click the down arrow on the right side of the box, and then choose the one you want.

To customize the template, click the transaction window's Formatting tab (Figure 27-8), and then click Manage Templates. In the Manage Templates window, click OK to open the Basic Customization dialog box (described below). From there, you can access the Additional Customization dialog box for middle-of-the-road changes (page 713) and the Layout Designer for advanced customization (see online Appendix G). The Formatting tab's Customize Design button opens a browser window to the QuickBooks Forms Customization tool, which is described in the box on page 708. (If you open this window inadvertently, simply close it, and then choose the feature you wanted on the Formatting tab.)

A word of warning: Working on a template and a transaction at the same time can overtax your brain or a computer that's low on system resources. To keep things straight and running smoothly, consider finishing the transaction first and *then* editing the template. After the template is the way you want it, you can reopen the transaction window, display the transaction you want, and then print or email it.

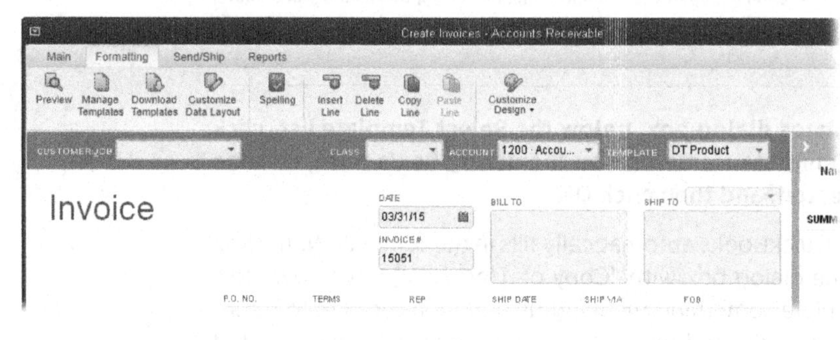

FIGURE 27-8

To preview a form before you print it, in the transaction window (like Create Invoices, shown here), click the Formatting tab, and then click Preview. If the form doesn't look the way you want, repeat the template customization steps to change it. When you're done, click the transaction window's Main tab, and then click the Print icon.

Basic Customization

QuickBooks' Basic Customization dialog box (Figure 27-9) lets you perform the most common types of form changes, while the fancier options stay hidden unless you ask for them. (The previous section explains how to open this dialog box and select a template.) The name of the template you're customizing appears at the top-left corner of the dialog box, just below the Selected Template label. (It's a good idea to verify that the template you're about to edit is the one you want.) This section walks you through your basic options.

NOTE The Basic Customization dialog box includes a Preview pane on its right side so you can see whether your template changes are what you want. To preview the *form* for a transaction like an invoice you're about to send, in the transaction's window, click the Formatting tab (shown in Figure 27-8), and then click Preview.

ADDING A LOGO

Adding a logo to a QuickBooks template can turn plain paper into a decent-looking document, and it's the *only* way to display your company logo on a form you send as a PDF file. Here's what you do:

1. **In the Basic Customization dialog box, turn on the "Use logo" checkbox.**

   The Select Image dialog box opens. QuickBooks sets the "Files of type" box to All Image Files, so you'll see any kind of graphic file in the selected folder. (Later on, if you want to change the image you chose, in the Basic Customization dialog box, click the Select Logo button.)

2. **In the Select Image dialog box, navigate to the folder that contains your logo file, and then double-click the filename. In the message box that appears telling you that QuickBooks will copy your image, click OK.**

   In the Basic Customization dialog box, the file's name and size appear to the right of the "Use logo" checkbox, as Figure 27-9 shows. In the dialog box's Preview pane, QuickBooks puts your logo in the form's top-left corner.

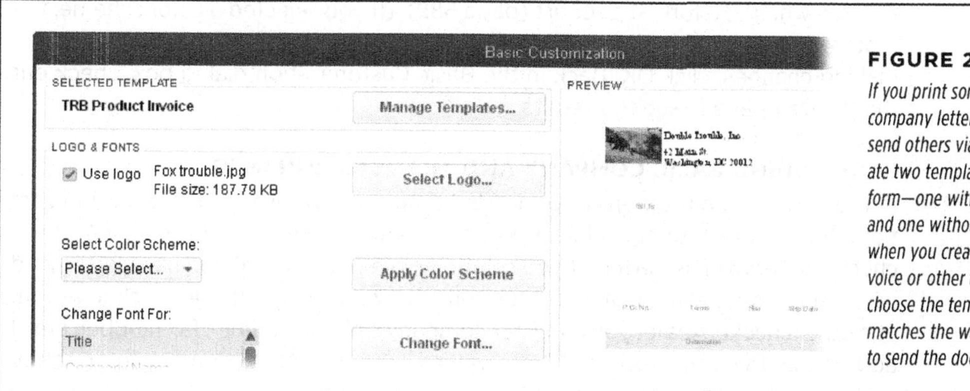

FIGURE 27-9

If you print some forms on company letterhead and send others via email, create two templates for the form—one with your logo and one without. Then, when you create the invoice or other transaction, choose the template that matches the way you plan to send the document.

NOTE QuickBooks copies the logo file into a subfolder within the folder that holds your company file. For instance, if your company file is named *DoubleTrouble.qbw* and resides in the folder *C:\QBCompanyFiles*, QuickBooks creates the folder *C:\QBCompanyFiles\DoubleTrouble - Images* and places the copy of the logo file there. If you decide to edit your original logo file, be sure to copy the edited file into this subfolder.

3. **If you want to reposition the logo, do so within the Layout Designer (see Appendix G, online).**

4. **When the logo looks good, proceed to another customization in the Basic Customization dialog box or click OK to close the dialog box.**

TIP If a logo that you added disappears from the template, don't panic—simply repeat the steps above to add the logo to the template again. If the logo *still* doesn't appear, exiting and restarting QuickBooks should solve the problem.

APPLYING A COLOR SCHEME

If you're eager to show off your new color printer, you can change the color of the lines and text on the form. In the Basic Customization dialog box's Select Color Scheme drop-down menu, choose the one you want, and then click the Apply Color Scheme button. The Preview pane shows the Technicolor results.

CHANGING FONTS

You can change a template's fonts to make them easier to read and/or more attractive. (You can also change the font for a single object in a form, as described in online Appendix G.) QuickBooks divides the text on forms into categories: Title, Company Name, Company Address, Labels, Data, Subtotals Label, and Total Label. The Labels category controls the font for all the field labels on the form; the Data category changes the font for the values, like item description and price.

To change the font for a text category, in the Basic Customization dialog box's Change Font For list, select the category, and then click the Change Font button. The dialog box that opens has all the usual font formatting options, just like the ones you see when you format a report (page 589). (If you selected a color scheme, the font is set to that scheme's color and you can't change it.) When you're finished making changes, click OK. Back in the Basic Customization dialog box, check out the Preview pane to see the results.

INCLUDING BASIC COMPANY AND TRANSACTION INFO

In the Basic Customization dialog box's Company & Transaction Information section, QuickBooks automatically turns on the Company Name and Company Address checkboxes, which is perfect if you print on plain paper. But if you have letterhead with your company name and address on it, be sure to turn these checkboxes off. The other checkboxes let you add your company's phone number, fax number, email address, and website address. These values come from the company information you entered; to edit them, choose Company→My Company and then, in the dialog box that appears, click the Edit button (its icon looks like a pencil).

NOTE If you're a QuickBooks administrator, you can modify your company info right from the Basic Customization dialog box. Simply click the Update Information button to open the Company Information dialog box.

Remember the status stamps that QuickBooks adds to forms, such as the word "PAID," which appears as a watermark on an invoice when you've received the payment? QuickBooks turns on the Print Status Stamp checkbox initially, so those watermarks appear when you print forms. If you don't want to print these status stamps, turn off this checkbox.

Additional Customization

At the bottom of the Basic Customization dialog box, clicking Additional Customization displays—you guessed it—the Additional Customization dialog box, which includes several tabs for picking the fields you want on the template and when they should appear. The tabs in this dialog box are the same for every type of form template, unless you create an invoice form and have the Progress Invoicing preference turned on (page 655). In that case, QuickBooks adds the Prog Cols tab, as shown in Figure 27-10, so you can pick the columns you want to add for progress billing.

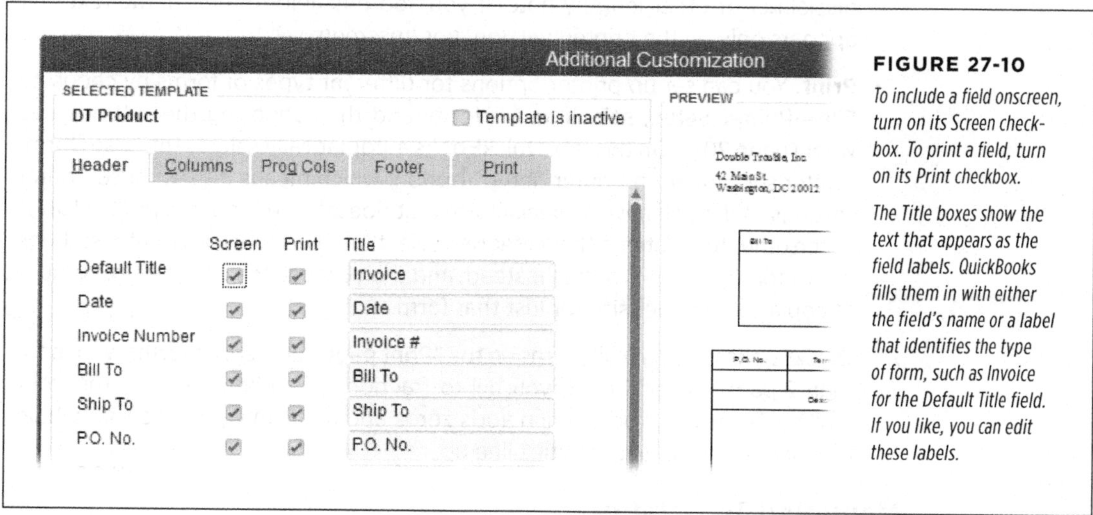

FIGURE 27-10

To include a field onscreen, turn on its Screen checkbox. To print a field, turn on its Print checkbox.

The Title boxes show the text that appears as the field labels. QuickBooks fills them in with either the field's name or a label that identifies the type of form, such as Invoice for the Default Title field. If you like, you can edit these labels.

NOTE If you try to customize one of Intuit's built-in form templates, you might see a warning that the template is designed for use with Intuit's preprinted forms. In that case, in the Locked Template message box, click Make a Copy so you can customize a *copy* of the template. That way, if you decide to use Intuit preprinted forms, you can still select the original template.

Each tab relates to a different area of the form. Setting up the fields on the tabs is straightforward, but a few of them have extra features:

- **Header**. The fields on this tab appear at the top of the form just above the table area. The more common fields for the type of form you're customizing (like Date, Bill To, P.O. No., and Terms for an invoice) are turned on automatically. At the bottom of the list, you can turn on the checkboxes for custom fields you've created to include them on your forms.

- **Columns**. These fields appear as columns in the form's table area, like the item description, quantity, rate, and amount for each line item in an invoice. In addition to specifying whether they appear onscreen and/or when printed, you can specify the *order* of the columns by filling in the Order boxes with numbers starting at 1 for the first field. If a field isn't included in the form, QuickBooks puts a zero in its Order box.

NOTE As mentioned on page 713, if you have progress invoicing turned on, you'll also see the Prog Cols tab.

- **Footer**. The fields that appear in the form's footer (the area below its table) include Message, Sales Tax, Total, and so on. For an invoice, if you want to include the *total* balance for a customer—including both the current balance and the previous balance—turn on the Customer Total Balance checkbox. The "Long text" box lets you add a substantial block of text to a form, like a legal disclaimer or other lengthy note. If you add this field to a form, the text in it appears only on the printed version, not onscreen.
- **Print**. You can set up printer options for different types of forms by choosing File→Printer Setup, selecting the form, and then choosing the settings you want (page 208). On this tab, QuickBooks automatically selects the "Use [form] printer settings from Printer Setup" option, which means it uses those printer settings. But if you have a special form that doesn't use the same print settings as the other templates in that category, select the "Use specified printer settings below for this [form]" option instead, and then choose the orientation, number of copies, and paper size for just that form.

  QuickBooks automatically turns on the "Print page numbers on forms with more than 2 pages" checkbox. If you bill to fractions of an hour, turn on the Print Trailing Zeros checkbox, which adds zeros and a decimal point so that whole number and decimal quantities line up.

Managing Templates

The Templates window (Lists→Templates) includes features for managing the templates you create. In that window's bottom left, click Templates and then choose an option from the menu. Besides obvious tasks like New, Edit Template, and Delete Template, this menu includes options for other helpful things you can do with templates. This section describes how to manage your templates, and the box on page 715 describes how to download premade templates. Templates are company specific, so you'll also learn how to export your custom templates from one company file to use in others.

TIP To preview templates before you choose one to work on, in the Templates window, select any template of the type you want (Invoices, Purchase Orders, and so on), and then press Ctrl+E. In the Basic Customization dialog box, click Manage Templates to see a list of *all* the templates of the same type as the one you selected in the Templates window. Simply click a template's name to see a preview of it in the Manage Templates dialog box's Preview pane.

POWER USERS' CLINIC

Templates Without Tedium

Say you find QuickBooks' built-in templates boring, but you don't have the time or design know-how to put together templates of your own. In that case, you can download spiffy templates from the QuickBooks website. For example, contractors can choose invoice templates with a drill or tape measure in the background.

In the Templates window (Lists→Templates), click Templates →Download Templates. The program opens a browser window to the Forms section of the QuickBooks Library. You can search for form templates and specify the type of form.

When you find a template you like, click its Download link to save the template's export file (which has a .des file extension) on your computer. Back in QuickBooks' Templates window, click Templates→Import. In the Select File to Import dialog box that appears, select the file you downloaded, and then click Open.

COPYING A TEMPLATE

Copying a template before you start editing it is always a good idea, in case your edits go awry and you want the original back. You can create a copy of a template in two ways:

- In the Basic Customization dialog box (page 709), click Manage Templates. In the Select Template list, click the template's name, and then click the Copy button below the list. QuickBooks adds the copy to the list and names it "Copy of: [template]." To rename the copy, on the right side of the Manage Templates window, type the new name in the Template Name box, and then click OK.
- In the Templates window, select the template you want to copy, and then click Templates→Duplicate. The Select Template Type dialog box appears, which lets you choose *any* type of template for the duplicate, regardless of what the original template type is. (For example, you can duplicate an invoice template but specify that the copy is a sales receipt instead.) When you click OK in the Select Template Type dialog box, QuickBooks adds the duplicate to the list with "Copy of:" in front of the original's name. To rename the copy, right-click it in the list and choose Edit Template. In the Basic Customization dialog box, click Manage Templates, type the new name in the Template Name box, and then click OK.

WARNING If you copy a template to use as a basis for a new one you want to create, be sure to edit the copy's name to identify what the form does, such as InvoiceNoLogo for the one you print on letterhead. If you copy a template as a backup in case you mangle the original, first check that the copy is what you want. (The words "Copy of:" that QuickBooks adds to the beginning of the template's name tell you that it's a backup.) After you've modified the original template and you're *completely* confident that the edited template is correct, you can delete the copy to keep your template list tidy.

DELETING OR HIDING A TEMPLATE

You can delete only the templates you create yourself, not ones that come with QuickBooks. To do so, click one in the Templates window, and then click Templates→Delete Template. If you try to delete a built-in QuickBooks template, the program tells you that you're out of luck.

However, you can *hide* built-in templates if you don't want them to appear in the Templates List. The process is just like making a customer, vendor, or invoice item inactive. To do so, in the Templates window, select the template, and then click Templates→Make Template Inactive. You can then reactivate it by first turning on the "Include inactive" checkbox at the bottom of the window to display all templates, and then clicking the X to the left of the template's name.

EXCHANGING TEMPLATES BETWEEN COMPANY FILES

If you want to trade form templates between company files, you can export them from one company file and import them into another. Here's how:

1. **To export a form template, in the Templates window (Lists→Templates), select the template you want to export (you can export only one at a time), and then click Templates→Export.**

   The "Specify Filename for Export" dialog box opens.

2. **Navigate to the folder where you want to save the file, and in the "File name" box, type a name for the file.**

   QuickBooks automatically sets the "Save as type" box to "Template Files (*.DES)," which is what you want.

3. **When everything looks good, click Save.**

After you've saved the template, simply open the other company file in QuickBooks, and then import the template file like so:

1. **In the Templates window, choose Templates→Import.**

   The "Select File to Import" dialog box opens.

2. **Double-click the template file you want to import, and you're done.**

CHAPTER

28

Keeping Your QuickBooks Data Secure

Your QuickBooks records are indispensable. They help you invoice customers and pay bills, and also provide the information you need to prepare your tax returns and plan for the future. A company file does *so* much, yet many companies don't take the time to keep their financial data safe and secure.

Losing data to a hard disk crash is a shock to your financial system as well as your computer's. But having someone embezzle money from your accounts could send years of hard work down the drain. Protecting your QuickBooks data takes so little time that there's no excuse for not doing it. (In addition to QuickBooks security, don't forget common-sense security like locking the door to your office.)

If you're the untrusting type or simply have no one else to do your bookkeeping, you can skip this chapter's discussion of creating users and setting up user permissions. The administrator login is all you need to work on your company file—and QuickBooks creates *that* automatically. But even if you don't intentionally let other people access your financial data, that doesn't mean that someone won't try to access it *without* your permission. Good computer security measures like firewalls, up-to-date antivirus software, and passwords that strangers can't guess go a long way toward preventing unauthorized fiddling with your finances.

When you have several people working on your company file, security is a bit trickier. Each person who accesses your financial data is a potential problem, whether intentional or inadvertent. By setting up users in QuickBooks and specifying which areas of the program they can access, you can delegate work to others without worrying about security quite so much. With the audit trail that QuickBooks keeps (page 437), every transaction that's modified or deleted is there for you to review.

Setting Up the Administrator

In QuickBooks, the administrator is all powerful. Only someone who logs in with administrator privileges can create new users, assign permissions and passwords to other users, and set company preferences. This section explains how to assign the administrator's user name and password, and turn on the feature for protecting your customers' credit card information (if you accept credit card payments).

NOTE Although QuickBooks doesn't ask you to set the administrator password, you *should* do that right away. If you don't, anyone who opens your company file is automatically logged in as the administrator, with full access to every feature of QuickBooks and every byte of your QuickBooks data.

Assigning the Administrator User Name and Password

When you create a company file, QuickBooks automatically creates the administrator user called Admin, but it doesn't require you to assign a password to that user. But because passwords are so important in helping keep your data secure, you can—and should—edit the administrator user to assign one (and change the administrator's user name, if you want).

TIP If you're the only person who acts as the QuickBooks administrator and you want to transfer those duties to someone else, create a new user and give that user access to all areas of QuickBooks (page 725). That way, the audit trail (page 437) can differentiate changes made by you from those made by the new administrator. In fact, it's a good idea to create a separate user with your name and use that login for most of the work you do, and reserve logging in as an administrator for tasks that only administrators can do.

You can use the following process to change the values for the administrator user anytime:

1. **Open the company file using your preferred method and, if necessary, log in as the administrator.**

   If you don't use QuickBooks Setup to create your company file, you can create, open, and close the company file without any sign of a login screen. But behind the scenes, QuickBooks automatically logs you in as the administrator without requiring a password.

   If the administrator is the only user and has a password assigned, the QuickBooks Login dialog box shows only the Password box. If this dialog box displays the User Name box, type the administrator's user name. If that user account has a password assigned, type that in the Password box. Otherwise, leave the Password box blank.

2. **Choose Company→Set Up Users and Passwords→Set Up Users.**

   If the QuickBooks Login dialog box appears, type the administrator password.

3. **In the User List window, click Edit User.**

   In the User List window, QuickBooks automatically selects whomever you're logged in as (which, in this case, is the administrator user). When you click Edit User, the "Change user password and access" dialog box (Figure 28-1) opens.

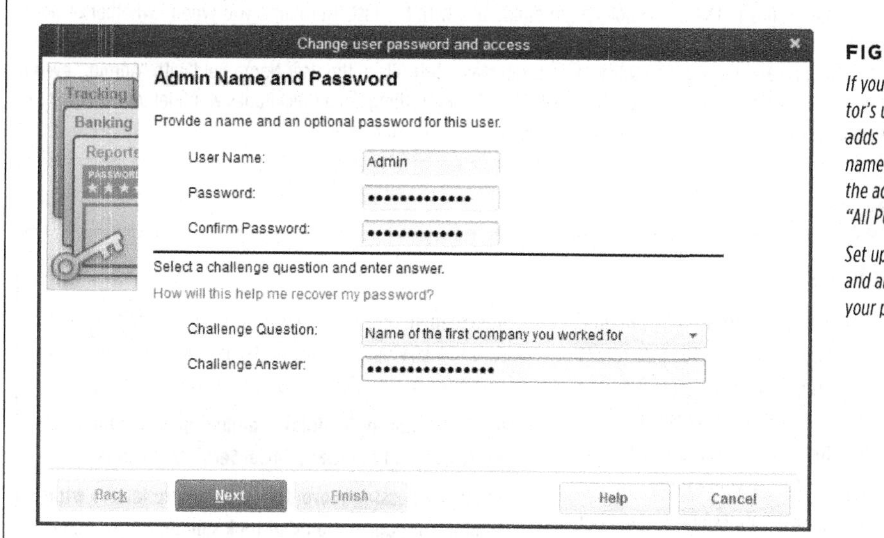

FIGURE 28-1

If you change the administrator's user name, the User List adds "(Admin)" after the user name to identify which user is the administrator, for example, "All Powerful (Admin)."

Set up a challenge question and answer so you can reset your password if you forget it.

4. **To change the administrator's name, type a new name in the User Name box.**

   You don't *have* to change the administrator's name, and it may be less confusing if you leave it as Admin. However, if you do change it, the User List identifies the administrator by adding "(Admin)" after the user name, so that it reads something like "QuickBooks Overlord (Admin)."

5. **In the Password box, type the password for the administrator user. In the Confirm Password box, type the password again.**

   See the box on page 720 for tips on creating good passwords. *Don't* copy and paste the password from the Password box into the Confirm Password box. If you copy a typo from one box to the other, you won't know what the administrator password is, and you won't be able to open your company file without jumping through several hoops.

6. **In the Challenge Question drop-down list, choose a question like "Favorite restaurant in college." In the Challenge Answer box, type the answer to the question.**

   The next section explains how to reset the administrator password with the help of this challenge question. (The box on page 721 tells you how to reset your administrator password if you don't know the password *and* don't know the answer to the challenge question.)

7. **Click Next.**

   The dialog box reminds you that the administrator has access to everything in QuickBooks. Click Finish to close the dialog box.

WARNING If you work on more than one QuickBooks company file, the program throws one user-related curve at you: It fills in the QuickBooks Login dialog box with the last user name you typed—whether or not it goes with the file you just opened. For example, say you open one company file using the user name Admin. When you open another file, the QuickBooks Login dialog box fills in the User Name field with "Admin," even if the administrator name for the second file is I_Can_Do_Everything. So if QuickBooks won't let you log in, make sure you're using the correct user name and password for that company file.

WORD TO THE WISE

Password Guidelines

Because the QuickBooks administrator can do *anything* in a company file, choosing a trustworthy person for that role is a good first step in preventing financial misfortune. But your efforts are in vain unless you secure the administrator's access with a good password. In fact, assigning passwords to *all* QuickBooks users is an important security measure.

Ideally, a password should be almost impossible to guess but easy for the rightful owner to remember. It's easy to meet the first criterion by using a random combination of upper- and lowercase letters, numbers, and punctuation, but that makes the password hard to remember. And if people have trouble recalling their passwords, they'll write them down somewhere, shooting holes in your security.

QuickBooks passwords are case-sensitive and can include up to 16 characters. Here are some tips for creating passwords that are both secure *and* easy to remember:

- **Make passwords at least seven characters long, and combine upper- and lowercase letters, numbers, and punctuation**. These are the same guidelines that the credit card industry uses as part of its standard for protecting customer information, as you can read on page 721.
- **Don't use family birthdays, names, phone numbers, addresses, and especially Social Security numbers**.
- **To make guessing more difficult, replace letters with numbers or punctuation that look similar**. For example, replace the letter "I" with the number 1 or an exclamation point (!). Or replace the letter S with the number 5, or the letter E with the number 3.
- **To make remembering easier, consider using names, birthdays, phone numbers, or addresses of people *not* obviously connected to you**. For example, if no one suspects that Daniel Craig is your favorite actor, Dan!elCra1g would be a good password (but not anymore).
- **To boost security, change your password every three to six months**.

Resetting the Administrator Password

If you can't remember your password and you selected a challenge question for the administrator user, you can answer that question to reset your password. Here's how to use this life-saving feature:

1. **In the QuickBooks Login dialog box, click the "I forgot my password" link.**

   The Reset QuickBooks Administrator Password dialog box opens.

2. **In the Reset QuickBooks Administrator Password dialog box, type the answer to the challenge question that appears, and then click OK.**

   A Password Removed message box tells you that your password, challenge question, and answer have been removed, which means your company file is no longer password-protected.

3. **Click Close.**

   QuickBooks nudges you to add a password by immediately opening the Change QuickBooks Password dialog box.

4. **Fill in the boxes as you would to edit the user (page 719), and then click OK.**

   A QuickBooks Information box tells you that your password has been changed.

5. **Click OK.**

   From now on, when you correctly fill in the boxes in the QuickBooks Login dialog box, the program opens your company file.

TROUBLESHOOTING MOMENT

What's the Administrator Password?

The time may come when QuickBooks asks you for a password you don't know. For instance, maybe the person with the administrator password left in a hurry, and you need it to open the company file. Or perhaps you're trying to open a QuickBooks file from a few years ago and the passwords you've tried don't work. If the challenge question doesn't help, try these solutions before you resort to Intuit's password-reset tool:

- **Check the Caps Lock and Num Lock keys.** They may not be set the way they were when you created your password, so try turning them on or off.
- **Test your keyboard.** Create a text document and then press each key to make sure it types the correct character.

If the password is still a mystery, you can reset it. In the QuickBooks Login dialog box, click the "I forgot my password" link. In the Reset QuickBooks Administrator Password dialog box, click the "I forgot my answer" link. When you do, the dialog box changes to include boxes for the information you used to register QuickBooks: your license number, name, email address, phone number, and Zip code. Fill in that info so Intuit can find your registration, and then click OK.

Intuit then verifies your info and sends you an email with a password-reset code. Paste that code into the Password Reset Code field in the Reset QuickBooks Administrator Password dialog box, and then click Next. When you do, the dialog box switches back to its original configuration so you can enter a new password, challenge question, and answer, as described on page 719.

Complying with Credit Card Security Regulations

If your company accepts credit cards, you probably already know that you have to comply with standards for protecting your customers' credit card information (known as the Payment Card Industry Data Security Standard). If you don't do so, not only is your customers' financial information at risk, but you also risk paying fines for your oversight.

Part of the standard requires that all users change their passwords every 90 days and use *complex passwords* (ones that are longer than seven characters and have a combination of numbers and upper- and lowercase letters). Fortunately, the steps you have to take in QuickBooks to comply with these requirements are simple, although you have to be a QuickBooks administrator to perform them:

1. **Choose Company→Customer Credit Card Protection.**

   The Customer Credit Card Protection dialog box opens and explains a little bit about the feature.

2. **Click Enable Protection.**

   The Sensitive Data Protection Setup dialog box opens. The fields are the same ones in the "Change user password and access" dialog box (page 719). The only difference is that the New Password and Confirm New Password boxes won't accept passwords that don't meet the secure-password criteria.

3. **In the Current Password box, type the current administrator password (which may not meet the criteria). Then fill in the New Password and Confirm New Password boxes with a complex password.**

   QuickBooks won't accept the password unless it's longer than seven characters and has at least one number and one uppercase letter, like "Kath3rine," for example.

4. **In the Challenge Question drop-down list, choose a question that you can answer in case you need to reset the password, like "Best friend's last or first name." Then type the answer in the Answer box.**

   Answers to QuickBooks' challenge questions aren't case-sensitive.

5. **Click OK.**

   After 90 days pass, QuickBooks asks you to set a new password.

NOTE After you enable credit card protection, every user that you've created in QuickBooks has to use a complex password and reset it every 90 days.

Creating QuickBooks Users

Setting up users in QuickBooks has the same advantages as setting up users in the Windows operating system or on your network: You can restrict people's access to just the data they need to see and keep track of what they're doing. Setting up user logins for the people who work on your company file helps you do several things:

- **Keep sensitive data confidential**. User names, passwords, and permissions (page 726) help protect both your and your customers' sensitive data from prying eyes.

- **Prevent financial hanky-panky**. By limiting each employee's access to job-relevant data and checking the audit trail for changes or deletions (page 437), you can prevent embezzlement—or catch the culprit early. These measures also help protect your data from unintentional errors by new or careless employees.
- **Let several people work in QuickBooks at the same time**. QuickBooks has no way of knowing whether several people share the same user name. If you want to protect your data and identify who's doing what in your financial records, each person who accesses your company file needs a unique user name and password. If more than one person works on your company file simultaneously, you have to switch it to multi-user mode, as the box below explains.

UP TO SPEED

Sharing Your Company File

Setting up multiple users for a company file doesn't mean more than one person can work on the file at the same time. If you want several people to work on your company file simultaneously, you have to buy a license for QuickBooks Pro, Premier, or Enterprise for *each* computer on which you want to run QuickBooks *and* switch the company file to multi-user mode.

Multi-user mode means that you access the data in your company files through a database server. Here's how it works: When someone performs a task in QuickBooks, his copy of the program asks the database server to send information or make changes. The database server makes the changes, retrieves information, and sends it back to him—and also makes sure that the changes don't conflict with changes someone else wants to make. (Don't worry—you won't be quizzed about this. You can concentrate on your business and let QuickBooks take care of the file sharing.) See page 489 to learn how to switch between multi- and single-user mode.

Adding New Users

Only the QuickBooks administrator can create additional users. After you log in as the administrator, here's how you create other users:

1. **Choose Company→Set Up Users and Passwords→Set Up Users.**

   If you've set up an administrator password, the QuickBooks Login dialog box opens, asking you for your password. This extra request for the administrator password prevents someone from walking up to your computer while you're away and creating an account for herself. After you enter your password, the program opens the User List dialog box shown in Figure 28-2.

2. **Click Add User.**

   QuickBooks opens the "Set up user password and access" dialog box.

3. **In the User Name box, type a user name for the person to use to access the company file. And in the Password box, type a password for the person.**

   In the Confirm Password box, retype the password.

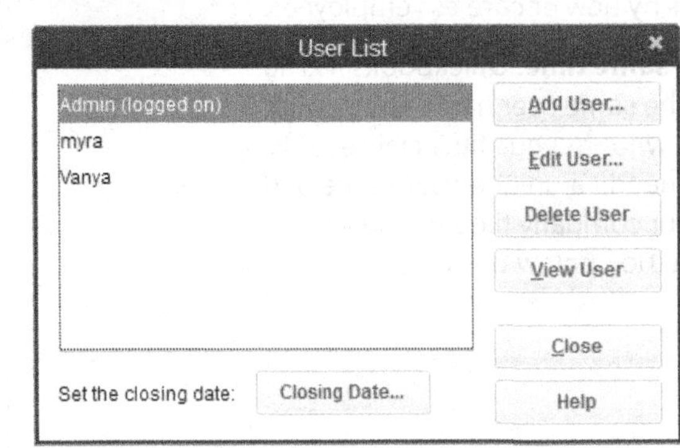

FIGURE 28-2

The text "(logged on)" after a user name indicates who you're logged in as.

If the administrator's user name is something other than Admin, the User List displays "(Admin)" after the name of the user who has administrator privileges.

4. **To allocate one of your licenses for QuickBooks to the user you're creating, turn on the "Add this user to my QuickBooks license" checkbox.**

   With this setting turned on, this user can open your company file at the same time as other users (as long as you have licenses for all of them). If people work on the company file one at a time, leave this checkbox turned off.

5. **Click Next to begin setting permissions.**

   In the list that appears, QuickBooks automatically selects the "Selected areas of QuickBooks" option, which lets you control exactly what the user can do in various parts of the program. See page 726 for details.

   Selecting the "All areas of QuickBooks" option instead gives this user access to *all* your financial data, as shown in Figure 28-3. That's why QuickBooks asks you to confirm that you want the person to have such broad access.

NOTE The external accountant user has access to all parts of your company file except sensitive customer information—perfect if you want to set up a QuickBooks user for your accountant or bookkeeper. To learn how to set up an external accountant user, see page 467.

Resetting a User Password

Users can change their own passwords, which makes your company data even more secure, since that way only users know their own passwords. That means users can't log in as someone else and perform transactions they shouldn't (like writing checks to themselves). To change their passwords, users simply choose Company→Set Up Users and Passwords→Change Your Password. They have to type their current password and then type the new one.

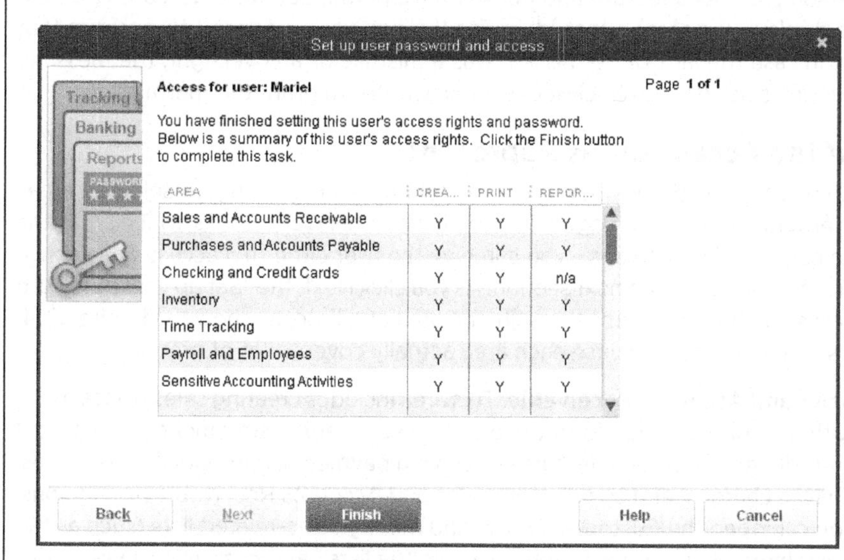

FIGURE 28-3

If you click Yes when QuickBooks asks you to confirm this user's full access, the "Set up user password and access" dialog box summarizes the person's access.

All you have to do is click Finish, and her user name appears in the User List dialog box, ready to log into QuickBooks.

The administrator can also change anyone's password. If you're logged in as the administrator, choose Company→Set Up Users and Passwords→Set Up Users. In the User List dialog box, select the user whose password you want to change, and then click Edit User. In the "Change user password and access" dialog box, fill in the Password and Confirm Password boxes with the new password, and then click Next. On the "Access for user:" screen, click Next. When the next screen appears, the Finish button becomes active. Click it to save the user with the new password.

NOTE If someone leaves your company, be sure to delete his QuickBooks user account so no one else can use it. Choose Company→Set Up Users and Passwords→Set Up Users. In the User List dialog box, select the user you want to delete, and then click Delete User. In the confirmation message box, click Yes, and that user account is history.

Restricting Access to Features and Data

When several people work on your company file, it's safer to limit what each person can do. For example, Trusty Ted has earned his nickname, so you could give him access to every QuickBooks feature, including sensitive financial reports and accounting activities. And Myra Meddler can't keep a secret, but there's no one faster at data entry, so you want to make sure that she gets no further than doing the checking, credit cards, and bill paying. The box on page 728 offers additional tips for keeping your data safe.

If a person chooses a feature and doesn't have permission for that feature, QuickBooks displays a message that identifies the permission needed to perform that action. In case the lack of permission was a mistake or an oversight, the message also suggests asking the QuickBooks administrator to grant that permission.

What the Access Areas Represent

When you tell QuickBooks that a user should have access only to selected areas of the program (step 5 on page 724), you have to tell QuickBooks *which* areas the person can use. For each area, you can give the user either full access or selective access, as explained in the next section. As you click Next, the "Set up user password and access" dialog box steps through one area at a time, as shown in Figure 28-4. There's some overlap, because each area actually covers a lot of ground:

- **Sales and Accounts Receivable**. This area includes creating sales transactions with any kind of sales form (invoices, sales receipts, statements, and so on) and with any additional features (receiving payments, reimbursable expenses, finance charges, and so on). With sales and Accounts Receivable permissions, you can open the Customer Center and modify sales-related lists (such as the Customer:Job, Customer Type, and Ship Via lists), and customize sales forms. Full access includes printing and creating sales-related reports.

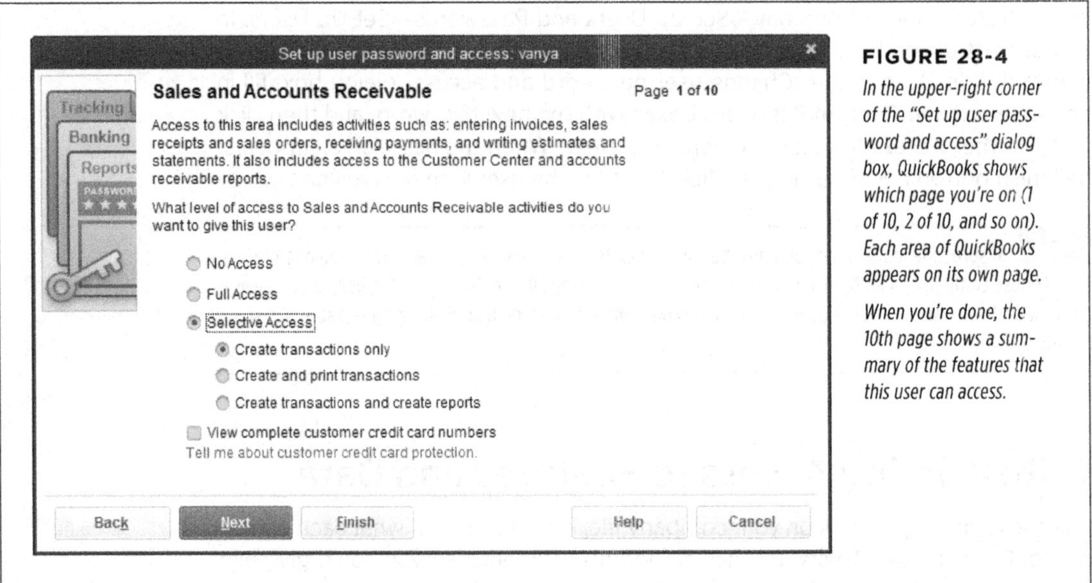

FIGURE 28-4

In the upper-right corner of the "Set up user password and access" dialog box, QuickBooks shows which page you're on (1 of 10, 2 of 10, and so on). Each area of QuickBooks appears on its own page.

When you're done, the 10th page shows a summary of the features that this user can access.

The "View complete customer credit card numbers" checkbox (visible in Figure 28-4) helps protect your customers' financial data. QuickBooks automatically turns this setting off to restrict who can see a customer's full credit card information. If you don't accept plastic, leave this setting as it is. Otherwise, turn the checkbox on for only the people you trust to work with customer credit card numbers.

- **Purchases and Accounts Payable**. These permissions include all aspects of dealing with bills and vendors: entering and paying bills, working with purchase orders, entering reimbursable expenses and credit card charges, and paying sales tax. You can grant people permission to open the Vendor Center and modify purchase lists—such as the Vendor and Vendor Type Lists—and to customize purchase forms. Full access includes printing 1099s and reports about vendors or purchases.
- **Checking and Credit Cards**. Permissions in this area let people write expense checks and refund checks (but not payroll checks), enter credit card charges, and make deposits.
- **Inventory**. If you've turned on QuickBooks' inventory features, this screen appears so you can give people permissions to maintain the inventory items on the Item List, receive products into inventory, adjust inventory quantities, work with purchase orders, and generate inventory reports.
- **Time Tracking**. These permissions include the ability to enter time transactions in the weekly and single-activity timesheets, import and export Timer data, and generate time reports.
- **Payroll and Employees**. Payroll permissions include opening the Employee Center and the Payroll Center, writing and printing paychecks, setting up and paying payroll liabilities, using your selected payroll service, maintaining the Employee and Payroll Items lists, and generating payroll forms and reports.
- **Sensitive Accounting Activities**. The features covered by these permissions don't belong to any one area of QuickBooks. Reserve these permissions for people who are not only trustworthy, but who also understand how your accounting system works. With these permissions, someone can maintain your chart of accounts, make journal entries, transfer funds, reconcile accounts, access accounts through online banking, work in balance sheet account registers, and create budgets. Other permissions include condensing data (which removes details of past transactions), using the Accountant's Review feature, and generating the payroll reports.
- **Sensitive Financial Reporting**. These permissions let someone print *every* report in QuickBooks, regardless of any reporting restrictions from the other access settings you choose.
- **Changing or Deleting Transactions**. As an extra precaution, you can give people permission to *create* transactions in an area, but not let them change or delete the transactions they've created. For example, for trainees just learning the ropes, you might remove their permission to edit transactions so they need to ask someone more experienced to make changes. An additional option lets people change transactions prior to the closing date for your books (page

472). Ideally, give this permission only to those who *really* know what they're doing—like your accountant.

UP TO SPEED

Commonsense Security Measures

Your QuickBooks company file isn't the only place you keep sensitive information. Be sure to set up your computers so that your QuickBooks data *and* all your other proprietary info are secure:

- **Back up regularly**. Back up your company file (page 491) and other data, and store the backups in a safe place. Make sure your backups save the files you want and that they restore without any problems.
- **Update your operating system with security updates**. If you use Windows, on the Start menu, choose All Programs→Windows Update.
- **Use antivirus software and keep it up to date**. These days, you need antivirus and anti-malware programs. Because the rogues who write viruses, worms, Trojans, and spyware don't look like they're going to stop anytime soon, be sure to regularly update your antivirus and anti-malware programs.
- **Install a firewall**. An Internet connection without a firewall is an invitation to nosy nerds and criminals alike. A firewall restricts access from the Internet to only the people or computers you specify.
- **Plan for problems**. Cross-train your employees so that more than one person knows how to do each procedure in your company, including working with QuickBooks. Store the QuickBooks administrator's password in the company safe deposit box or give it to a company officer for safekeeping.

Setting Access Rights

When you're setting up a new user in the "Set up user password and access" dialog box (page 723), choosing the "Selected areas of QuickBooks" option takes you on a journey of specifying access to areas of the program (listed above). As you click Next to set permissions for each area of the program, you can give someone no access at all, full access, or the right to perform some tasks in that area, as shown in Figure 28-4. Here's a guide to what each level of access lets people do:

- **No Access**. The person can't open any windows or dialog boxes for that area of QuickBooks, meaning he can't perform any actions in that area. QuickBooks automatically chooses this option; to give someone any access to an area, you have to choose either Full Access or Selective Access instead.
- **Full Access**. The person can perform *every* task in that area of QuickBooks except ones reserved for the administrator user.
- **Selective Access**. Selective Access separates tasks into creating transactions, creating and printing transactions, or creating transactions and generating associated reports.

The final screen of the "Set up user password and access" dialog box—shown in Figure 28-3 (page 725)—summarizes the access rights you chose for that person. The summary screen separates access into the same categories as the Selective Access level: Create, Print, and Reports. In most cases, giving someone full access means that "Y" appears in all three columns; giving her no access usually displays "N" in all three columns. When a permission isn't applicable to an area, QuickBooks displays "n/a"; for example, there aren't any reports associated with the right to change or delete transactions.

PART

5

Appendixes

APPENDIX A:

Installing QuickBooks

APPENDIX B:

Help, Support, and Other Resources

NOTE Appendixes C–G are available from this book's Missing CD page at *www.missingmanuals.com/cds*. (To learn about the Missing CD page, turn to page xxvii.)

APPENDIX C:

QuickBooks Keyboard Shortcuts

APPENDIX D:

Working with Intuit QuickBooks Payroll Services

APPENDIX E:

Using Intuit e-Invoicing

APPENDIX F:

Tracking Time with the Standalone QuickBooks Pro Timer

APPENDIX G:

Advanced Form Customization

Appendixes

APPENDIX

Installing QuickBooks

QuickBooks' installation process offers two basic options: Install the program from scratch or upgrade from a previous version. When you upgrade, you can run both the old *and* new versions on your computer at the same time, which is essential if you're an accountant or bookkeeper who works with company files from several different clients. Even if you use QuickBooks to run your own business, you might want to keep your old version around in case you decide that you don't like the new version. Be sure to back up your company file *before* you open it with the new version; once you open it in the new version of QuickBooks, it won't run in the earlier version (see the box on page 734).

This appendix walks you through both paths of the installation process. You'll also find out how to install QuickBooks 2015 on a company network, including where on a network you can store your company file—and which location to choose for best performance. (If several people need to access your company file at the same time, everyone has to run the same version of QuickBooks, so set aside time to install the program on all those machines.)

Before You Install

Intuit recommends a 2.4 GHz processor and 1 GB of RAM for a single user of QuickBooks Pro. Add another 1 GB of RAM for more than one concurrent user—but doubling the recommended RAM (at least 2 GB, as a rule of thumb) will probably bring you closer to acceptable number-crunching speeds. You also need about 2.5 GB of free disk space and a 4x CD/DVD drive to install the program if you bought it on CD rather than downloading it. QuickBooks 2015 can run on Windows Vista (Service

Pack 1 or later releases), Windows 7, Windows 8, Windows Server 2003 (Service Pack 2), Windows Server 2008 R2, and Windows Server 2012. QuickBooks can run on 32-bit and 64-bit editions of these operating systems.

NOTE Sometimes, you may have problems running QuickBooks if your computer has a Windows Home edition installed, particularly if you're working in a multi-user networked environment. The easiest solution (although it might cost you some money) is to install the Pro version of Windows Vista, Windows 7, or Windows 8 on your computer.

If you're planning to use QuickBooks' integration features, the versions of your other programs matter, too. For example, writing letters and exporting reports requires Microsoft Word and Excel 2007 or later (either the 32-bit or 64-bit edition), and synchronizing contacts requires Outlook 2007 or later. (QuickBooks Contact Sync integrates only with the 32-bit edition of Outlook 2010.)

If you have several QuickBooks users, plan on upgrading everyone's copy at the same time. Once you've upgraded everyone, you can update the company file to the new version of the program. Then have all your users make sure they can open the company file with the new version of QuickBooks. (If you update the company file *first*, your colleagues won't be able to work in it until they have the newest version of the program.)

TIP If you have a problem installing QuickBooks, you can look for an answer at *www.quickbooks.com/installation*.

POWER USERS' CLINIC

Installing Multiple Versions of QuickBooks

If you work with clients running different versions or editions of QuickBooks, don't panic: Different versions and editions of the program can run on the same computer *mostly* without squabbling with each other.

For example, you can run QuickBooks Pro 2013, QuickBooks Pro 2014, and QuickBooks Premier 2015 all on the same machine. As long as you access each company file with *only one version* or edition of the program, you'll be fine. However, there are two situations in which QuickBooks updates company files, which means you won't be able to use the files in the previous version or edition:

- **Opening a company file in a new version updates the file to work with the new version and prevents earlier versions from opening it.** So once you open your company file with QuickBooks 2015, your accountant won't be able to access your data if she's still running QuickBooks 2014.
- **Opening a company file in QuickBooks Enterprise edition optimizes the file for faster performance.** Once you open a company file in this edition, the file is off limits to QuickBooks Pro and QuickBooks Premier.

Installing QuickBooks

If you have a single-user license for QuickBooks, installing or upgrading the program on a computer running Windows 7 or Windows 8 is pretty simple. Even on a network with a multi-user license, installing QuickBooks is mostly common sense. (If you're installing it on a computer running Windows Vista, search the Intuit QuickBooks Support web page [page 752] for instructions.) This section describes the steps that work whether you're installing QuickBooks for the first time, installing a new version of the program on a computer that already has one or more older versions on it, or upgrading an existing version to QuickBooks 2015.

Installing QuickBooks for the First Time

If you don't have any other version of QuickBooks installed on your computer, installing QuickBooks 2015 is straightforward. Here's what you do:

1. **Log into Windows as a user with administrator rights.**

   Windows Server, Windows Vista, Windows 7, and Windows 8 require administrator rights to install QuickBooks. If you have trouble installing, try disabling your firewall, too. And shut down any running programs, including your virus-protection program (a good idea when you're installing any software).

2. **If you downloaded QuickBooks, double-click the file you downloaded. If you have a QuickBooks DVD, put the disc in your DVD drive.**

   You'll see the Intuit QuickBooks Installer screen and a "Welcome to QuickBooks!" greeting.

3. **When the Next button becomes active, click it.**

   The License Agreement screen appears.

4. **After you read the software agreement carefully, turn on the "I accept the terms of the license agreement" checkbox, and then click Next.**

   You should always read software license agreements so you know the legal terms you're accepting.

5. **On the "Choose your installation type" screen, select either "Express (recommended)" or "Custom and Network options," and then click Next.**

   Because you're installing QuickBooks for the first time, the Express option sets up QuickBooks for single-user access (page 489) and installs the program in *C:\Program Files\Intuit\QuickBooks 2015* on 32-bit computers (*C:\Program Files(x86)\Intuit\QuickBooks 2015* on 64-bit computers). If you choose this option, the installation jumps to a screen that asks for the license and product numbers; hop to step 7 of this list for details. (You can change the program's preferences to allow multiple users after QuickBooks is up and running; see page 489.)

The "Custom and Network options" setting lets you choose where to install QuickBooks on your computer, install the program and share a company file with others, or set up the computer only to share the company file (page 741). If you choose this option, continue with step 6 of this list.

6. **If you selected the "Custom and Network options" setting, choose a setting on the "Custom and Network Options" screen, and then click Next.**

   If you're the only person who uses QuickBooks, select "I'll be using QuickBooks on this computer." This option installs the program on your computer and sets it up for single-user access to your company file. (You can change this preference to allow multiple users once QuickBooks is up and running—see page 489.)

   If you're going to run QuickBooks and also want to store the company file on this computer to share with other QuickBooks jockeys, select "I'll be using QuickBooks on this computer, AND I'll be storing our company file here so it can be shared over our network."

   The third option, which begins with "I will NOT be using QuickBooks on this computer," is the one to choose when you're installing the program on a computer that acts as a file server; in other words, a computer that stores your company files but doesn't actually *run* QuickBooks (page 741). When you install the program using this option, you don't use up one of your QuickBooks licenses.

7. **On the "License and Product Numbers" screen, fill in the License Number and Product Number boxes, and then click Next.**

   These numbers are hard to miss—they're in the confirmation email you received if you downloaded the program, or printed somewhere on your QuickBooks DVD packaging if you bought a physical copy. As you finish typing the digits in one box, your insertion point automatically jumps to the next box. So if you're confident on the keyboard, you can keep your eyes on the email or yellow sticker and type all the digits for the license and product numbers without a break.

8. **If you chose "Custom and Network options" in step 5, then you see the Choose Installation Location screen, shown in Figure A-1 (if you chose the Express option, you won't see this screen, so skip to step 9); to change where QuickBooks will be installed, pick a new location, and then click Next.**

   Initially, the installation location is set to *C:\Program Files \Intuit\QuickBooks 2015* or *C:\Program Files (x86)\Intuit\QuickBooks 2015* depending on whether your computer is running a 32-bit or 64-bit version of Windows. To choose another spot, click Browse, select the new folder, and then click OK. If the folder you want to use doesn't exist, click the New Folder icon, which looks like a stylized folder with a starburst on its corner. To view the folders one level up, click the icon that looks like a folder containing an up arrow. To select a folder within the box, double-click it or select it and then click OK.

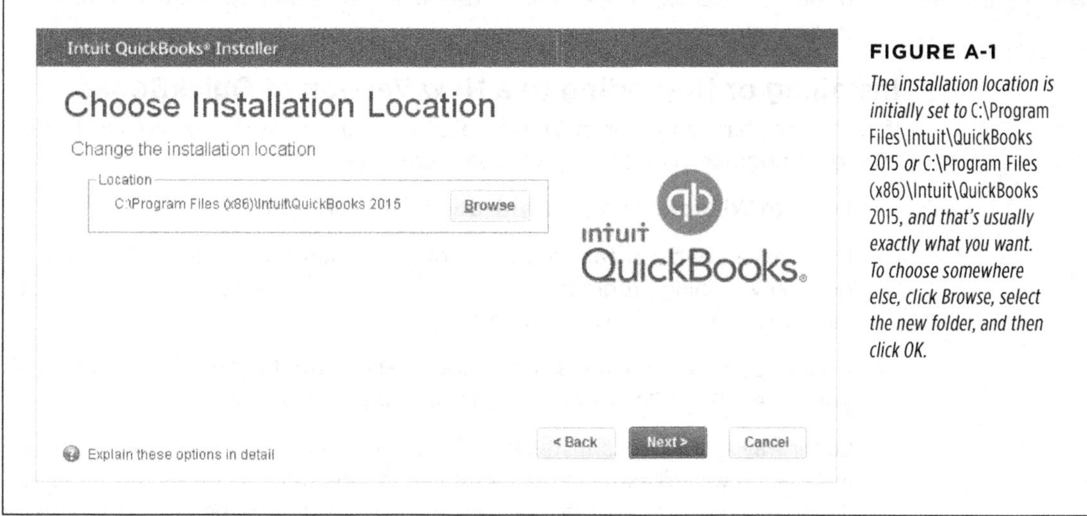

FIGURE A-1

The installation location is initially set to C:\Program Files\Intuit\QuickBooks 2015 *or* C:\Program Files (x86)\Intuit\QuickBooks 2015, *and that's usually exactly what you want. To choose somewhere else, click Browse, select the new folder, and then click OK.*

9. **If the settings on the "Ready to install" screen are the way you want, click Install.**

   This screen lists the program's version, its license and product numbers, and the folder where it will be installed. If you want to change, say, the folder you're installing to, click Back until you get to the appropriate screen, and then make your changes. Then click Next until you're back at the "Ready to Install" screen.

   When you click Install, your computer gets to work. The wizard shows the installation task it's performing, and progress bars indicate how far it's gotten.

   The installation wizard also displays a User ID text box so you can sign into QuickBooks. If you don't have an Intuit account yet or don't want to log into the account you have, click "Skip this" at the window's bottom right. If you *do* want to sign in to your Intuit account—for example, to register your copy of QuickBooks, type your email address in the User ID box, and then click Validate. If QuickBooks finds your account, the password box appears. Type your password in the box, and then click Log In at the dialog box's bottom right.

NOTE If you see the "Register your product and get started" message, hop to page 740 to get the full scoop on registering your copy of the program. If you want to skip registration for now, click the Remind Me Later link at the window's lower right.

10. **When the "Congratulations!" screen appears, click Open QuickBooks.**

    QuickBooks launches and you're ready to start working. Chapter 1 walks you through launching QuickBooks subsequent times and opening files for day-to-day work.

Installing or Upgrading to a New Version of QuickBooks

If you already have a version of QuickBooks installed, it's easy to install QuickBooks 2015 or to upgrade your existing version. Here's how:

1. **Log into Windows as a user with administrator rights.**

   If you have trouble installing QuickBooks, try disabling your firewall. And shut down any running programs, including your virus-protection program (a good idea when you're installing any software).

2. **If you downloaded QuickBooks, double-click the file you downloaded. If you have a QuickBooks CD, put the disc in your CD drive.**

   Either way, QuickBooks' installation dialog box appears on your screen and the installation wizard extracts the files it needs. This step can take a few minutes; you'll see progress bars that give you an idea of how long the process will take. (If you're installing from a CD and the dialog box *doesn't* appear, use Windows Explorer to open the CD; double-click *setup.exe*, and then follow the onscreen instructions.)

3. **When you see the Welcome screen in the QuickBooks installation dialog box, click Next.**

   The License Agreement screen appears.

4. **After you read the software agreement carefully, turn on the "I accept the terms of the license agreement" checkbox, and then click Next.**

   You should always read software license agreements so you know the legal terms you're accepting.

5. **On the "Choose your installation type" screen, select either "Express (recommended)" or "Custom and Network options," and then click Next.**

   The Express option sets up QuickBooks for single-user access (page 489) and installs the program in *C:\Program Files\Intuit\QuickBooks 2015* for computers running a 32-bit version of Windows or *C:\Program Files (x86)\Intuit\QuickBooks 2015* for computers running 64-bit Windows. If you choose this option, the installer jumps to a screen that asks for the license and product numbers—hop to step 7 of this list for details. (You can change the preference to allow multiple users after QuickBooks is up and running; see page 489.)

   The "Custom and Network options" setting lets you choose where to install QuickBooks on your computer, install the program and share a company file with others, or set up the computer only to share the company file (page 741). The next step explains your options.

6. **If you selected the "Custom and Network options" setting, choose a setting on the "Custom and Network Options" screen, and then click Next.**

   If you're the only person who uses QuickBooks, select "I'll be using QuickBooks on this computer." This option installs the program on your computer and sets it up for single-user access to your company file. (You can change this preference to allow multiple users once QuickBooks is up and running—see page 489.)

   If you're going to run QuickBooks and also want to store the company file on this computer to share with other QuickBooks jockeys, select "I'll be using QuickBooks on this computer, AND I'll be storing our company file here so it can be shared over our network."

   The third option, which begins with "I will NOT be using QuickBooks on this computer," is the one to choose when you're installing the program on a computer that acts as a file server; in other words, a computer that stores your company files but doesn't actually *run* QuickBooks (page 741). When you install the program using this option, you don't use up one of your QuickBooks licenses.

7. **On the "Enter your license and product numbers" screen, click the "Use your user ID instead" link below the Product Number boxes.**

   The "Install with your user ID" screen appears.

8. **Fill in the User ID and Password boxes with your Intuit account user ID and password, and then click Next.**

   QuickBooks obtains your license and product number from the registration info associated with your Intuit account.

   If you can't remember your account information, click the "Install with your product and license numbers instead" link to return to the "Enter your license and product numbers" screen, and then fill in the license number and product number from your confirmation email or CD.

9. **If you want to keep your current version of QuickBooks and install QuickBooks 2015 in *addition*, on the "Upgrade or Change Installation Location" screen, be sure to choose a different folder than the one where your current QuickBooks version is installed. Then jump to step 11.**

   Initially, the installation location is set to *C:\Program Files\Intuit\QuickBooks 2015* (for computers running a 32-bit version of Windows) or *C:\Program Files (x86)\Intuit\QuickBooks 2015* (for computers running 64-bit Windows).

   To change the installation location, click Browse, select the new folder, and then click OK. (You don't *have to* change this location. To continue the installation without changing the location, simply proceed to step 11.)

10. **If you want to *upgrade* an existing version of QuickBooks, on the "Upgrade or Change Installation Location" screen, select the "Replace the version selected below with the version I'm installing now" option and then, in the drop-down list, choose the version that you want to upgrade.**

    When you choose this option, the version you selected to replace will be uninstalled and QuickBooks 2015 will be installed.

11. **Click Next. Then, as long as the settings in the "Ready to install" screen are the way you want, click Install.**

    This screen includes a summary of the program's version, its license and product numbers, and the installation folder you chose. If you want to change, say, the folder you're installing to, click Back until you get to the appropriate screen, and then make your changes. Then click Next until you're back at the "Ready to Install" screen.

    When you click Install, your computer gets to work. The wizard shows the installation task it's performing, and progress bars indicate how far it's gotten.

NOTE If you see the "Register your product and get started" message, read the next section to learn how to register your copy of the program. Or you can skip registration for the time being by clicking the "I'll do this later" link at the window's lower right. But you have to register the program eventually, so go ahead and do it now.

12. **When the Congratulations screen appears, click Open QuickBooks.**

    QuickBooks launches and you're ready to start working. Chapter 1 walks you through launching QuickBooks subsequent times and opening files for day-to-day work.

Registering QuickBooks

At some point after you've installed QuickBooks, you'll see the Register QuickBooks dialog box. (You can also start the registration process by choosing Help→Register QuickBooks.) You don't have to register QuickBooks immediately, but you'll need to eventually—the program runs for only 60 days unless you register your copy. When you register, you'll also receive any updates that Intuit releases for this version of the program.

In the Register QuickBooks dialog box, click the Begin Registration button. A browser window opens to the QuickBooks Registration page and guides you through the steps. Be sure to keep a copy of the license number, product number, telephone number, and Zip code you use for registration. You'll need them if you have to reinstall QuickBooks or install it on a new hard drive.

Setting Up QuickBooks on a Network

For several people to work on the same company file from different computers, you have to perform two separate steps:

1. **Install the QuickBooks database server on the machine where you store your QuickBooks files.**

   When you run the QuickBooks installer on this machine, on the "Custom and Network Options" screen, choose the option that begins with "I will NOT be using QuickBooks on this computer" (see step 6 on page 736). This installs the database server software so that the computer acts as a file server and doesn't use up one of your QuickBooks licenses.

2. **Install QuickBooks 2015 on all the computers that you want to run QuickBooks, as explained earlier in this appendix.**

   You need a separate QuickBooks license for each computer on which you install the program. These computers need to be networked to the machine you use as the QuickBooks database server. They must all run the same version of QuickBooks (QuickBooks 2015, for example) and have permission to read, write, create, and delete in the folder where the company file resides. (A network administrator typically sets up these permissions for each user. If you're responsible for setting up users but you never wanted "network administrator" as your job title, in the Windows taskbar, choose Start→"Help and Support" and then, in the Search box, type *share files* to find instructions for sharing files using your operating system.)

TIP You can simplify access to the company-file folder by mapping a drive to that folder. In Windows' "Help and Support" window (which you get to from your computer's Start menu), search for "Map drive."

QuickBooks Pro and Premier can handle up to five people accessing a company file at the same time. (Intuit is happy to sell you more than five licenses for QuickBooks to install on other people's computers, but only five of the licensed users can work on the company file simultaneously.) QuickBooks Enterprise comes with 5-, 10-, or 15-user license packs and allows up to 30 simultaneous users.

Where to Store Your Company Files

QuickBooks 2015 has its own favorite spot for company files, but you can save them wherever makes the most sense for your company. For example, if several people work on your company files simultaneously, choose the storage location that gives you the quickest performance (you'll read about how to do that in a sec).

In Windows 7 and Windows 8, QuickBooks automatically stores company files to *C:\Users\Public\Public Documents\Intuit\QuickBooks\Company Files,* but you're free to choose a different folder. You can store company files anywhere you like, so you may as well keep them with the rest of your documents. It also makes sense to create a dedicated folder for your QuickBooks files since, in addition to company files, you'll probably create backup files, message templates, files that you export from QuickBooks, and files for importing into your company file. With a QuickBooks folder as a container, you can create subfolders for each type of file, as shown in Figure A-2.

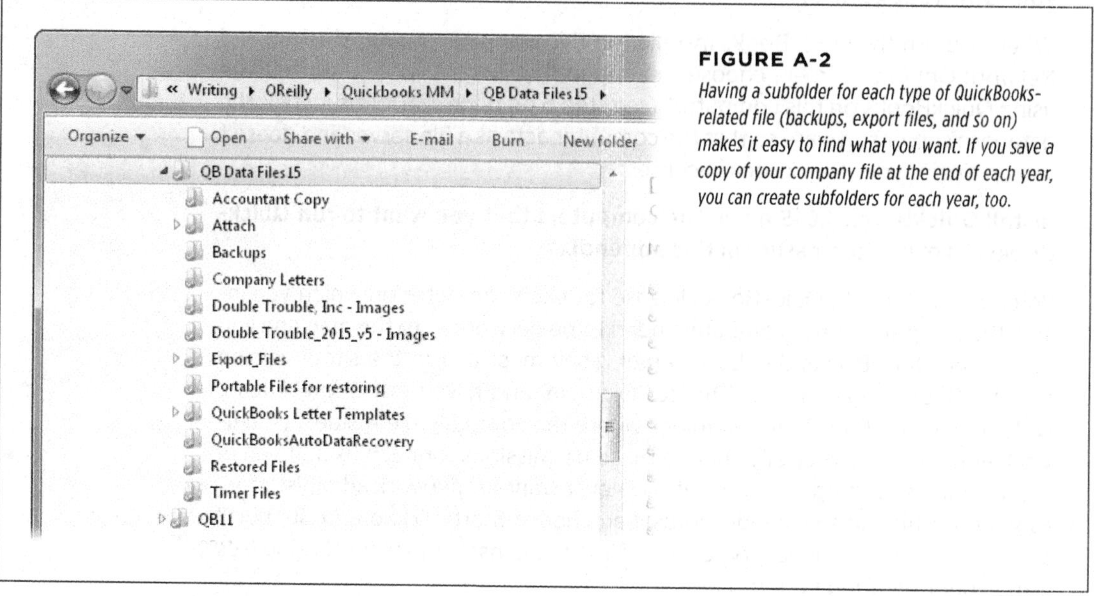

FIGURE A-2

Having a subfolder for each type of QuickBooks-related file (backups, export files, and so on) makes it easy to find what you want. If you save a copy of your company file at the end of each year, you can create subfolders for each year, too.

TIP If you aren't totally at ease working with files in your computer's operating system, *Windows 7: The Missing Manual*, *Windows 8: The Missing Manual*, or *Windows 8.1: The Missing Manual* will make you an expert in no time.

Storing Company Files on a Network

If several people work on your company files, where you store those files can determine whether those people get blisteringly fast responses or nod off waiting for processes to complete. For the best performance, put company files on the network computer with the most memory, the fastest processor, the most available disk space, and—ideally—the least amount of activity. The best location for your company file depends on the type of network you use:

- **Peer-to-peer networks** don't use dedicated file servers, so you can store your company file on any computer on the network. The computers running QuickBooks need to use Windows Server, Windows Vista, Windows 7, or Windows 8.

- On a **client-server network**, the company file typically resides on a *file server*, a dedicated computer for sharing files. Every computer on the network that has QuickBooks installed can access the company files, but one of the computers has to host multi-user access (page 489). Intuit recommends installing QuickBooks, QuickBooks Database Manager, and the company files on the server, which has to run Windows Server, Windows Vista, Windows 7, or Windows 8.

However, in some cases, you *can't* install QuickBooks on the computer that holds the company files (if you use a file server, for instance). You have to log into the computer that you want to use as the *host* and open company files in multi-user mode (page 489). When QuickBooks asks if you want this computer to host multi-user access, click Yes. This computer then plays traffic cop for several people working on the company files at the same time.

TIP When you perform resource-gobbling tasks, like running massive reports or reconciling accounts, performance is paramount. On a peer-to-peer network, when you need to perform these tough tasks, log into QuickBooks on the computer that holds the company files. On a client-server network, use the fastest computer on the network.

APPENDIX

B

Help, Support, and Other Resources

Between questions about how to do something in QuickBooks and how to handle something in accounting, you might need help occasionally. Happily, the QuickBooks Help system can actually help. When you open QuickBooks Help, it automatically shows links to topics relevant to what you're doing in the program. For example, if the Create Invoices window is open, QuickBooks Help tells you how to fill out or edit invoices, record payments toward invoices, customize your invoice form, and so on. You'll find topics with background info, troubleshooting tips, and even advice on why you should or shouldn't perform certain steps.

Another option is the Intuit Community. As its name suggests, this help comes from fellow QuickBooks wranglers. They use the program every day just like you and can help uncover solutions, not to mention lots of helpful tricks and tips. If you don't see a question and answer similar to the question you have, you can post your question. And if you're a QuickBooks veteran, you can answer someone else's plea for help.

In this appendix, you'll learn your way around QuickBooks Help. And, in case you want more help than you find there, you'll also learn about other resources that might do the trick.

QuickBooks Help

Wherever you are in the program, you can get help by pressing F1 or choosing Help→QuickBooks Help. The "Have a Question?" window opens and displays a list of how-to and troubleshooting topics related to the feature you're using, as shown in Figure B-1. (If the "Have a Question?" window is already open, the topics don't change as you click menu entries, display windows, and open dialog boxes.) When you click a topic link in the "Have a Question?" window, it displays that help topic (Figure B-2).

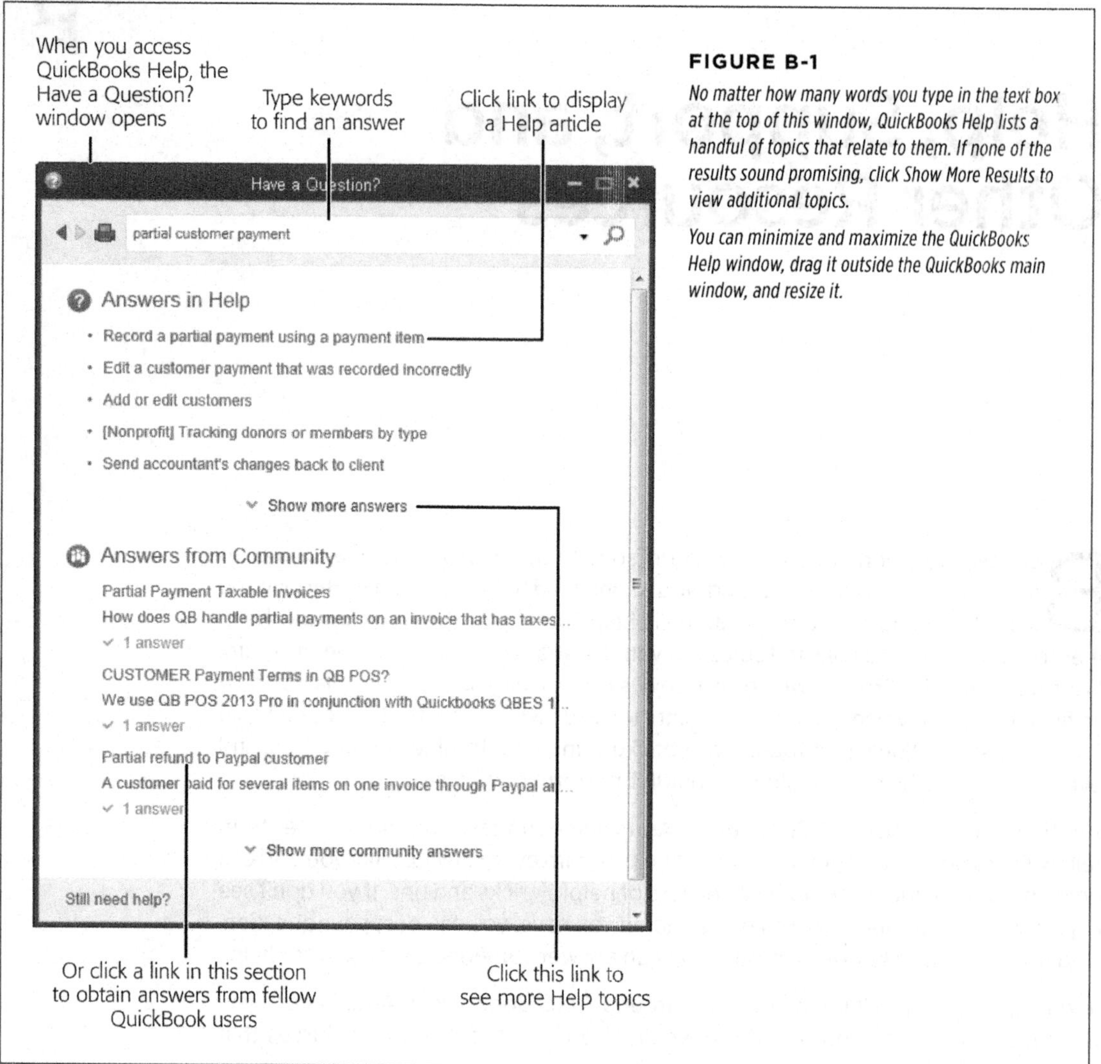
When you access QuickBooks Help, the Have a Question? window opens
Type keywords to find an answer
Click link to display a Help article
Have a Question?
partial customer payment
Answers in Help
Record a partial payment using a payment item
Edit a customer payment that was recorded incorrectly
Add or edit customers
[Nonprofit] Tracking donors or members by type
Send accountant's changes back to client
Show more answers
Answers from Community
Partial Payment Taxable Invoices
How does QB handle partial payments on an invoice that has taxes...
1 answer
CUSTOMER Payment Terms in QB POS?
We use QB POS 2013 Pro in conjunction with Quickbooks QBES 1...
1 answer
Partial refund to Paypal customer
A customer paid for several items on one invoice through Paypal a...
1 answer
Show more community answers
Still need help?
Or click a link in this section to obtain answers from fellow QuickBook users
Click this link to see more Help topics

FIGURE B-1

No matter how many words you type in the text box at the top of this window, QuickBooks Help lists a handful of topics that relate to them. If none of the results sound promising, click Show More Results to view additional topics.

You can minimize and maximize the QuickBooks Help window, drag it outside the QuickBooks main window, and resize it.

The other way to find a help topic is to type search terms into the text box at the top of the "Have a Question?" window, and then press Enter or click the Search button (it has a magnifying glass on it), as shown in Figure B-1. The "Answers in Help" section lists QuickBooks help articles. The "Answers from Community" section is described on page 748.

TIP If you use either icon bar, you can look for answers using the Search box, which is at the top of the left icon bar and at the right end of the top icon bar. (If you use the top icon bar and don't see the Search box, choose Edit→Preferences→Search and, on the My Preferences tab, turn on the "Show Search field in the Icon Bar" checkbox.) To search for help, type keywords or a question in the Search box, choose Help in the box's drop-down menu that appears, and then press Enter or click the Search button, which looks like a magnifying glass.

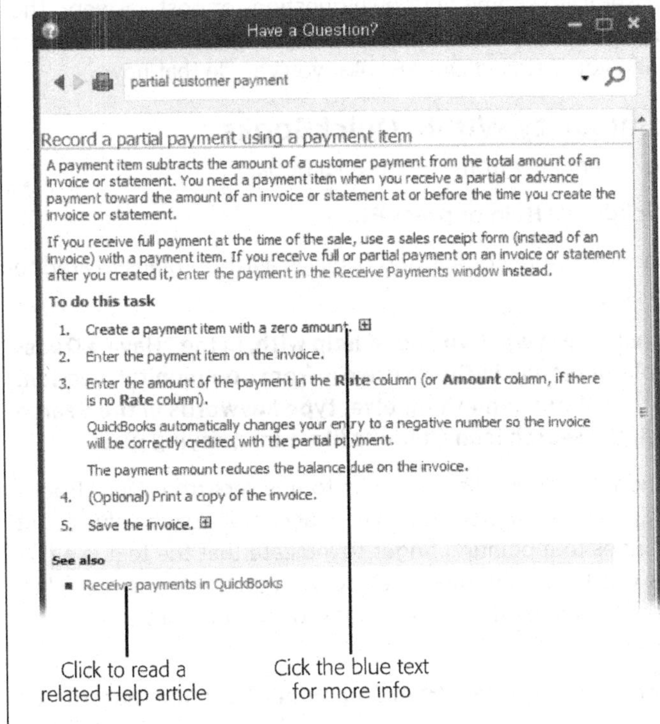

FIGURE B-2

When you click a topic in the "Have a Question?" window, it displays a Help article like the one shown here, with information, instructions, and additional links to related topics. If you click several links, you may quickly find yourself several topics from where you started. To navigate back to previous topics, click the left arrow (Back) at the top of the window.

TIP You can jump back to search terms you typed in previously by clicking the down arrow on the Search box's right side and then choosing the search you want.

Intuit Community

Intuit Community is the name of Intuit's QuickBooks community message boards. The system is simple to use: You ask a question, and the program checks whether it's already been answered by someone else who uses QuickBooks. (You can't control the answers that Intuit Community displays. You'll see different responses depending on how you phrase your question, so go ahead and try different wordings.) If none of the answers it finds are what you want, you can pose your question to the community. By the same token, you can post your solutions to questions that others have asked.

TIP If you want to scan existing questions and answers, see the Tip on page 750 to learn how to review the Intuit Community message boards without QuickBooks' help.

You can browse questions and answers in the community to your heart's content, but you need an Intuit User ID to submit your own questions or post answers. The first time you submit a post, Intuit Community asks you to sign in. If you didn't set up an Intuit account when you installed QuickBooks, you can do that now.

Accessing the Community Within QuickBooks

Here's how to use Intuit Community from within QuickBooks:

1. **Choose Help→QuickBooks Help or press F1.**

   The "Have a Question?" window opens and displays a list of topics related to the feature you're using.

2. **If the feature you're using is what you need help with, in the "Have a Question?" window, look for results in the "Answers from Community" section. If you have a question about something else, type keywords in the Search field, and then click the search icon (it looks like a magnifying glass).**

   The "Have a Question?" window displays links to answers from QuickBooks Help and the Intuit Community. When you point your cursor at some blue result text, the cursor changes to a pointing finger to indicate that the text is a link (the fact that the text is blue is another clue). To see additional answers, click "Show more answers" in the middle of the window or "Show more community answers" at the bottom.

3. **If you see a question in the "Answers from Community" section that sounds like yours, click it.**

   QuickBooks opens a browser window behind the "Have a Question? window. To get a clear view of the browser window (shown in Figure B-3), minimize the "Have a Question?" window.

4. **If you find your answer, click the X at the browser window's top right to close it and skip the remaining steps.**

5. **If this answer isn't what you're looking for, click links in the Similar Questions section at the bottom of the browser window.**

   The browser window displays that question and all its answers. Alternatively, you can type search terms in the Search box at the top of the browser window; enter a detailed question or description of your problem, and then press Enter or click the magnifying glass icon to the box's right. After you do that, the window lists results that match what you typed.

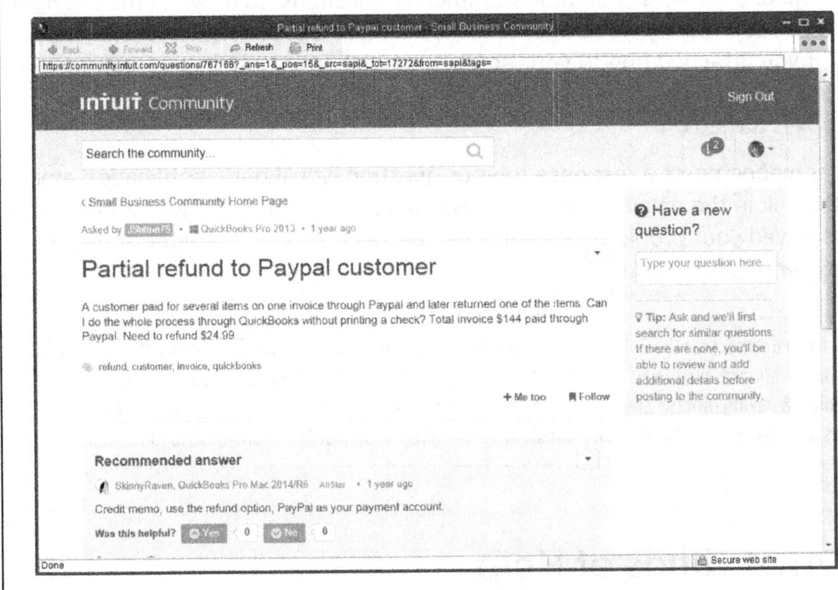

FIGURE B-3

If the first question you review isn't what you're looking for, you can review other similar questions by clicking links in the Similar Questions section (not visible here—you might have to scroll down the browser window to see it). And if none of the questions you see does the trick, type your question in the "Have a new question?" box shown here.

6. **To ask a question of your own, type it in the "Have a new question?" box on the window's right, and then click Ask.**

   Based on the words you used in your question, the window lists results that might answer your question. Click a blue question link to view the question and its answer.

7. **If none of the results is what you want, scroll to the bottom of the window and click the "Submit your question" link.**

   If you aren't signed into your Intuit account, the "Sign in or create an account" box appears. Click the "Sign in" button. On the "Sign in" page, fill in the Intuit user ID and password, and then click the Sign In button.

   On the screen that appears, in the "Your question" box, type a brief but meaningful title for your question to help people find it. Click the "Select your product" down arrow and choose the product your question applies to. In the "Select a topic" drop-down list, choose a topic category. In the "Add more details" box, provide a clear and complete question or description of your issue so you're likely to get a relevant answer. You can even attach an image file to your post by clicking the Attach button at the bottom of the page. When everything looks good, click Submit.

After that, you simply wait for someone to answer your question. But you don't have to constantly check the Intuit Community site to see if someone responds; when you're logged into your Intuit account, you can set things up so that you get emails when someone answers your Intuit Community questions. To do so, at the top right of the Intuit Community web page, click the icon that looks like a silhouette (or your photo, if you attached one to your account) and choose Notification Settings. On the screen that appears, make sure the "someone replies to a post you're following" checkbox is turned on.

When someone posts a response to your question, you'll get a notification email. Click the link in the email to see the response on the Intuit Community site. If the person solved your problem, you can click the Yes button to the right of the "Was this answer helpful?" label.

TIP If you'd rather scan the QuickBooks community message boards in your browser, go to *https://community.intuit.com/quickbooks*, where you'll see high-level topics like "Accounting, Banking & Taxes," Inventory, Canada, and "Vendors & Paying Others." Click one of the categories to see all the posts related to it. You can search existing questions and answers or post your own question using a process similar to the one described above.

Other Kinds of Help

Unsurprisingly, the first item on the Help menu is QuickBooks Help. However, items further down the menu may provide the assistance you want, depending on your level of experience and how you like to learn:

- **Learning Center Tutorials**. Choose this option to open the QuickBooks Learning Center window and watch video tutorials about popular tasks. For example, in the window's navigation bar, click the Tracking Money In icon to access tutorials for creating invoices, sales receipts, and payments. The tutorials are generally a few minutes long, so don't expect in-depth training. An audio track explains what's going on as you see the cursor move around the screen, buttons highlight, and windows or dialog boxes open and close.
- **Support**. This option opens a browser window to the Intuit QuickBooks Support web page. Below the "How can we help?" heading, you can click a link to view popular support topics, read answers from the Intuit Community, or find a local QuickBooks expert to help you. Or you can type something in the "Type your question, or error code" box, and then press Enter or click the Search button. (For example, if you receive an error message, type in the error number to find out what it means and what you can do about it.) The page that appears displays articles from a variety of sources, including the program's Troubleshooting and How To articles, the Intuit Community, YouTube, and so on. The box on page 752 tells you more about QuickBooks Support options.

- **Find A Local QuickBooks Expert**. If you're tired of figuring things out on your own, you can find plenty of accountants and bookkeepers who are QuickBooks experts—and you'll be glad you did. Clicking this option opens a web browser to the QuickBooks Find-a-ProAdvisor website so you can find someone in your area. (Alternatively, you can point your web browser to *http://accountants.intuit.com/accounting/proadvisor.*) ProAdvisors have passed Intuit's certification exams to prove their QuickBooks expertise. Finding one of these folks is free, but a ProAdvisor's services aren't, so when you find ProAdvisors near you, ask about their fees before hiring them.
- **Send Feedback Online**. This option won't provide instant gratification for your QuickBooks problems, although telling Intuit what you think may make you feel better. You can use this option to send suggestions for improvements to QuickBooks or QuickBooks Help and report any bugs you find.

Other Help Resources

If you don't find an answer to your questions in QuickBooks Help or the Intuit Community forums, you can use Google or another search engine to search online, or try an independent QuickBooks message board. QuickBooksUsers.com (*http://forums.quickbooksusers.com*) has forums for different editions of the program, including one each for QuickBooks overall, QuickBooks Pro, Premier Nonprofit, Premier Manufacturing and Wholesale, Enterprise, and QuickBooks for Mac. You can also find forums for the Australian, Canadian, and UK editions of the program. People post some gnarly problems on these message boards, but each question gets at least one reply. In some cases, you might receive several different solutions to the same problem.

TIP When you have a question or receive an error message in QuickBooks, typing the question, error message, or error number into a web search engine is a great way to find answers.

The QuickBooksUsers.com message boards are free. This site supports itself by selling data-recovery services and tech support. (Then again, a data-recovery service might be just what you need.) If you're looking for an add-on program or having problems with one, check out the site's QuickBooks 3rd Party Software Forum.

You might also consider joining a LinkedIn (*www.linkedin.com*) group related to QuickBooks. These groups have thousands of members, any of whom may chime in to help resolve your burning QuickBooks issues. The Expert QuickBooks Help group is run by Laura Madeira, a consultant, trainer and author on all things QuickBooks. Ruth Perryman, president of The QB Specialists—an Intuit Solutions Provider—runs the QuickBooks Tips & Tricks group. Laura and Ruth are both Advanced Certified QuickBooks ProAdvisors and members of Intuit's Trainer/Writer Network.

QuickBooks Training

Searching for QuickBooks training online yields more results than you could possibly want. You can narrow the list by including your city: "QuickBooks training Denver," for example. If you prefer to study on the Web, search for "QuickBooks training web-based" or "QuickBooks training online."

For example, you can take online courses by your humble author at *www.lynda.com*. Intuit's Endorsed Training Partner, Real World Training (*www.QuickBooksTraining.com*), offers regularly scheduled instructor-led classes in many cities around the country (or in your office), training on CD, and on-demand online classes. And QBalance.com (*www.qbalance.com*) offers QuickBooks training for folks at any level of experience; you can get one-on-one training with a QuickBooks expert, classroom-based training, or training on a CD. Also, the Accounting and Business School of the Rockies offers QuickBooks training in the classroom as well as self-paced online training and live online training. To contact the school, visit *www.absrschool.com* or call 1-800-772-6885.

UP TO SPEED

Getting Answers from Intuit

If you choose Help→Support, and then, in the horizontal navigation bar, click Contact Us, you'll see a web page with categories that you can click. But those simply display links to troubleshooting and how-to articles on the QuickBooks Support site (page 750). To get to an Intuit phone number, you have to perform a few more steps. For example, choose the "Download, install, register" category, click the View Support Option button on the screen's right, and then click the Contact Us button that appears. You'll see a telephone number you can call, although the screen warns you that charges may apply.

Here is the rundown of free versus for-a-fee support (although this can change at any time):

- Help is free for 12 months after you register your copy of QuickBooks 2013, 2014, and 2015—*if* the problem has to do with installing or upgrading QuickBooks, error messages that tell you to contact Intuit support (or that contain a 6xxx code), and some questions related to setting up a multi-user environment.
- Support plans come with monthly or yearly subscriptions. If you think you'll want to call support several times, a support plan is more cost-effective than paying for each call. One way to obtain a support plan is to buy QuickBooks Pro Plus and QuickBooks Premier Plus, which include one. For example, go to *http://quickbooks.intuit.com/pro* and click Pricing for the full story.
- If you're reinstalling QuickBooks and can't find your license number, in QuickBooks 2015, you can fill in your Intuit account info to grab your license number from your registration record (page 740). If that doesn't work, go to *http://support.quickbooks.intuit.com/support/LicenseNumber/Default.aspx*. There you can type in the business phone number you used to register QuickBooks or sign in using your Intuit account, and you'll see all the products associated with your account and the license and product number for each one.

Index

D

K

L

M

N

O

P

S

T

QuickBooks 2015

THE MISSING CD

There's no
CD with this book;
you just saved $5.00.

Instead, every single Web address, practice file, and piece of downloadable software mentioned in this book is available at *missingmanuals.com* (click the Missing CD icon). There you'll find a tidy list of links, organized by chapter.

CPSIA information can be obtained at www.ICGtesting.com
Printed in the USA
LVOW03s1529061114

412367LV00026B/138/P